Y A FISH LICENCE, PLEASE.
S S.C.U.M.—OR MAY I CALL YOU MRS S?
X-PARR .
HE ONE ABOU E
E NUDIST COLONY?
FUN ANYMORE.
TWIT OF THE YEAR SHOW.
CHEESE!
ROSS! ALBATROSS!
SUGAR PLUM?
LY, AND SINCERELY ABOUT THE FORK.
E YOUR
VALK?
NUDGE...NUDGE.
ULOUSE IN FRANCE.
OULOUSE.

GIVE THAT BACK!
JUST A MINUTE—SOMEONE TOLD YOU WE ALL HAD TOUPEES?
NUMBER TWELVE. THE NAUGHTY BITS OF A LADY.
MY BRAIN HURTS!
LEMON
CURRY?
GOOD EVENING.
HERE IS THE NEWS FOR PARROTS.
THERE'S A DEAD BISHOP ON THE LANDING.
'I MARRIED THREE
RABBIT JELLY MOULDS'!
ARTHUR FIGGIS IS AN IDIOT. A VILLAGE IDIOT.
TONIGHT WE LOOK AT THE IDIOT IN SOCIETY.
SPOT THE LOONY!
SPAM!
IF THERE'S ONE THING I CAN'T STAND, IT'S PEOPLE WHO HAVE HEART ATTACKS.
GOOD LORD!
IS THAT A NUDE WOMAN?
MAY I RECOMMEND THE
ALLIGATOR PUREES.

IT'S...

Black Dog
& Leventhal
Publishers
New York

ALL THE BITS
YTHON'S
INC
CUS
ANNOTATED
AND
UKE DEMPSEY
8 1/2
DESIGN
EIGHT AND A HALF
BROOKLYN
NEW YORK

Published by arrangement with Pantheon Books,
an imprint of The Knopf Doubleday Publishing Group,
a division of Random House, Inc.

Published by
BLACK DOG & LEVENTHAL PUBLISHERS, INC.
151 West 19th Street New York, NY 10011

Distributed by
WORKMAN PUBLISHING COMPANY
225 Varick Street New York, NY 10014

Manufactured in China

Cover and interior design by
EIGHT AND A HALF, NEW YORK

Cover illustration courtesy of
PYTHON PRODUCTIONS, LTD

Series stills and illustrations courtesy of Python Productions, Ltd.
All other images courtesy of Getty Images.

ISBN-13:978-1-57912-913-2

h g f e d c b a

Library of Congress Cataloging-in-Publication Data available on request.

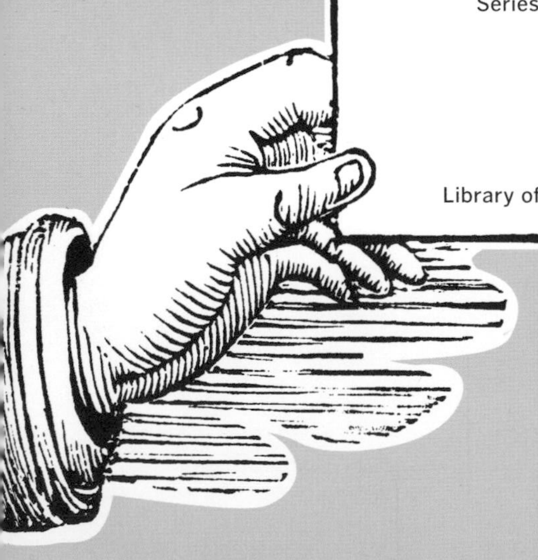

SEASON 1

SEASON 3

SEASON 4

INTRODUCTION

Memory is an unreliable parent, one who drinks too much or forgets it drove you to the mall.

I realized this recently—again—when I came to watch all forty-five episodes of *Monty Python's Flying Circus,* the sketch comedy TV show which first aired in Britain on October 5, 1969. Many non-Brits know the Monty Python troupe from their movies, the most prominent being *Monty Python and the Holy Grail, Life of Brian,* and *The Meaning of Life.* But if you're British (as, sadly, I am) then Monty Python initially meant the TV shows. And if you're of a certain age (as, sadly, I am), then your childhood and adolescence was punctuated—nay, formed—in no small part by dead parrots, Spam, a cartoon police officer opening his tunic to reveal a set of near-perfect breasts, and the words "my brain hurts." This is what we remember of our childhoods. But there's one memory that I've been getting wrong for years.

In my mind, I was about eight or nine years old; my brother, then, was fourteen. I was upstairs in our small British Midlands house, the first bedroom on the right. From the top bunk I could hear the TV downstairs, and the raucousness of it, great globs of laughter emanating from it, was keeping me awake. In frustration, I went downstairs to the sitting room, where my family—Dad, Mom, two older sisters—huddled together as though an air raid was imminent. In the living room next door, where the TV blared, sat my brother, alone, his weekly treat of *Monty Python's Flying Circus* so avant-garde—and, well, borderline rude—that he was left to it. If he wanted to see bare breasts and cross-dressing men screeching at one another, if nothing else it was good preparation for a life in British society (we do love a tit and a cross-dresser). But it was keeping me awake, so my nine-year-old self stepped into the sitting room and exclaimed, "That TV is making one *hell* of a noise!"

That one so young and innocent should use the word *hell* amused my parents and sisters to no end; so much so, that even though I remember little of life before ten years old, I remember that. They smiled at me, stepped into the TV room, asked my brother to ameliorate the noise, and sent me back up to bed.

So for years I've thought that *Monty Python's Flying Circus* aired sometime in the mid-1970s, as I was born in 1968. Returning to the shows for this project, I was shocked to discover that a) they started earlier, in late 1969, before I had even turned one year old, and b) they were done two weeks after my sixth birthday. If we imagine, as I now do, that my brother had tuned into the Pythons by the second or third season, then he interrupted my golden slumbers when I was around three or four years old. And my middle-of-the-road Roman Catholic parents let my brother get sweaty-palmed and hysterical with laughter by the time he was eight-ish.

Good for them, and good for Python. My memory? Not so good.

What follows is scripts for all forty-five episodes of *Monty Python's Flying Circus*, annotated to explain some of the more obscure references (among them, Esher, Reginald Maudling, Ann Haydon-Jones). Throughout, I've tried to note such places where the comedy resides in a word or phrase that might not be in the non-British mind, and to point out too where the script deviates from the actual performance, or vice versa. Amazingly, there aren't that many such instances: the Pythons—John Cleese, Graham Chapman, Michael Palin, Terry Jones, Eric Idle, and Terry Gilliam—hewed closely to the scripts, even when faced with learning the faux German "Johann Gambolputty de von Ausfern-schplenden-schlitter-crasscrenbon-fried-digger-dingle-dangle-dongle-dungle-burstein-von-knacker-thrasher-apple-banger-horowitz-ticolensic-grander-knotty-spelltinkle-grandlich-grumblemeyer-spelterwasser-kurstlich-himbleeisen-bahnwagen-gutenabend-bitte-ein-nürnburger-bratwustle-gerspurten-mitz-weimache-luber-hundsfut-gumberaber-shönedanker-kalbsfleisch-mittler-aucher von Hautkopft of Ulm." (They get it right every time, by the way.)

Watching the shows now, forty years later, one is struck by two things: some of the sketches are horribly dated and not very funny, and I suspect they never were; and much of *Monty Python's Flying Circus* remains screamingly comic—not just classic sketches like the "Cheese Shop" and "Upperclass Twit of the Year," but also such unheralded pieces of genius as Palin and Jones making order out of key German political figures who have fallen out of a blimp ("It's not a balloon! It's an airship!") and into their sitting room. This last sketch appeared in the final season, post–John Cleese, and though received wisdom is that the show lost something without Cleese's presence, the remaining Pythons were still able to conjure something sublime out of their desire to puncture hubris, mock pretension, and squash what a hundred years earlier novelist George Meredith called "damn punctilio."

It's trite to say that the Pythons changed comedy, as no one since has quite come close to their level of anarchic wit; what they did was assault the entrenched horrors of British life, be it the military, the church, the governing hierarchies, or class in general. Some of the most telling moments are the brief, often ad-libbed vox populi interviews, where seemingly "regular" British folk, as played by the Pythons, display the kind of knowledge only previously afforded to those who, like the Pythons themselves, attended Oxford or Cambridge universities.

This, to my eye at least, is the great legacy of the Python shows: they were endlessly smart, and brilliantly well read, and didn't seem to believe that either would awe the audience. They flaunted knowledge and a love of language, and led the way for later genius comic talents, like Eddie Izzard or Steve Coogan, to create intelligent comedy that didn't require a laugh track or Benny Hill chasing half-naked starlets while smacking a bald man on the top of his pate. Breaking such barriers, in British society at least, was no mean feat. Is it too much to argue that the more "democratic," opportunity-based society that now exists on that small island came by way of the Pythons, who leveled a field they found unduly rutted as the seventies started? Certainly no one particularly looks up to vicars, brigadiers, or members of Parliament anymore. Royalty looks like nothing more than a set of rich people screwing each other over. As Morrissey put it twenty years later, "The Queen is dead, boys"—and though that's only true metaphorically, when you go back and watch *Monty Python* now, as I urge you to do, you'll see that these five Brits and one American took aim at all the sacred British cows and turned many of them into very tasty steaks. (My apologies to the vegetarian Morrissey for the image.)

SEASON 1
EPISODE 1
TO THE UNKNOWN JOKE

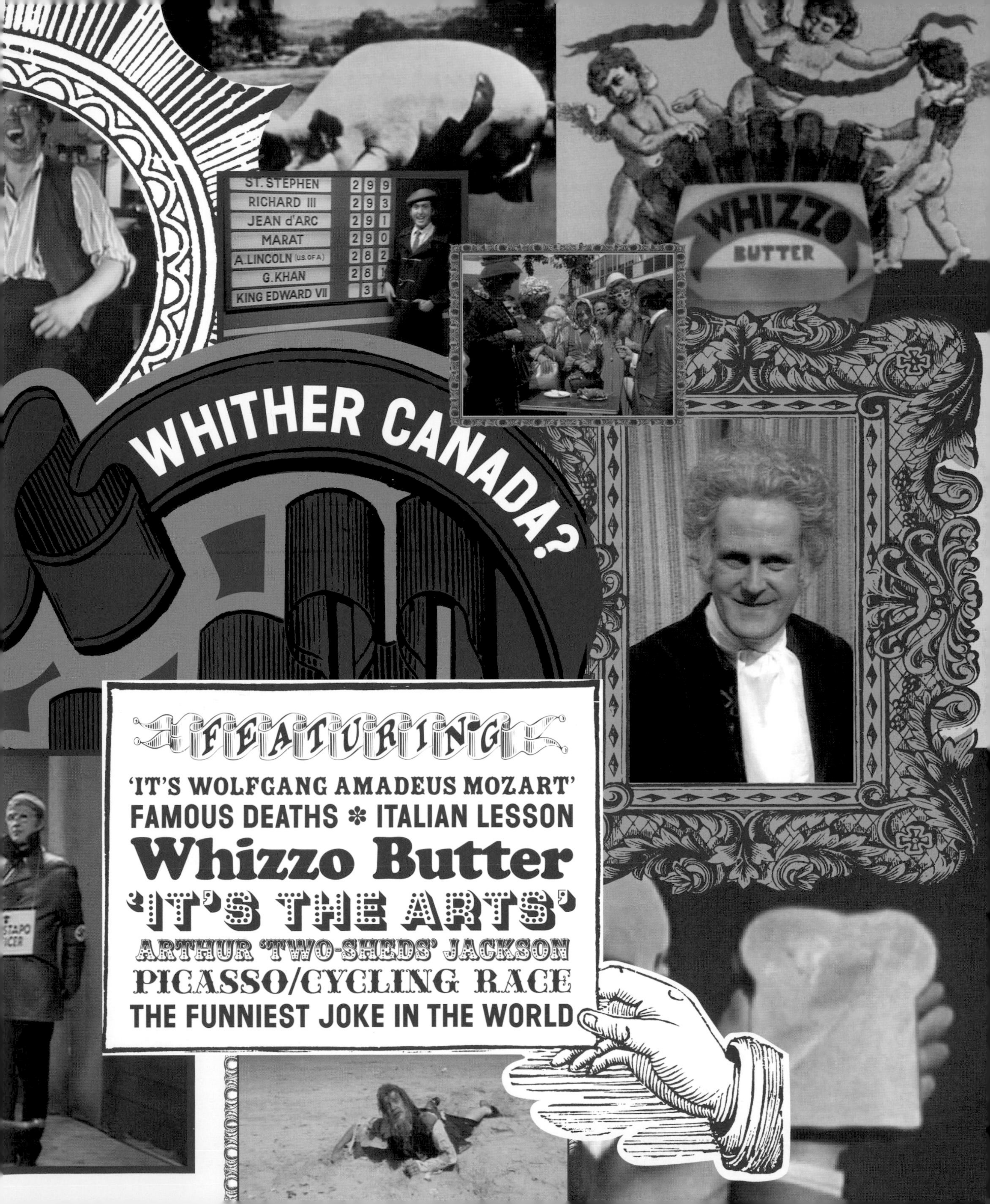
ST. STEPHEN 2 9 9
RICHARD III 2 9 3
JEAN d'ARC 2 9 1
MARAT 2 9 0
A.LINCOLN (US.OF A) 2 8 2
G.KHAN 2 8
KING EDWARD VII 3
WHIZZO
BUTTER
WHITHER CANADA?
FEATURING
'IT'S WOLFGANG AMADEUS MOZART'
FAMOUS DEATHS ✻ ITALIAN LESSON
Whizzo Butter
'IT'S THE ARTS'
ARTHUR 'TWO-SHEDS' JACKSON
PICASSO/CYCLING RACE
THE FUNNIEST JOKE IN THE WORLD

It would be hard to overestimate the impact of what is here simply referred to as "various bizarre things." The first episode of *Monty Python's Flying Circus*, which was recorded on September 7, 1969, and aired on October 5, 1969, must have felt like a message from a different planet. Gilliam's extraordinary opening title montage reveals themes the Pythons would muse on for the next 45 episodes: royalty, the church, sexuality, the war (in the form of a Hitler-like face), and that unique British obsession, class—all squashed by the big foot from the sky (in this case, Cupid's right foot from Bronzino's *An Allegory with Venus and Cupid* in London's National Gallery).

Nervous viewers must have been comforted by the BBC-announcer vibe of Chapman sitting behind a desk. That he sits on something that makes a pig sound can't have done much for the equilibrium of many.

Please note, this is not Genghis Khan in India, nor China, nor anywhere else in the Mongol Empire. This is Khan in the marram grass beside the beach at Bournemouth, on England's south coast.

FIRST AIRED: OCTOBER 5, 1969

A seashore. Some way out to sea a ragged man is struggling his way to shore. Slowly and with difficulty he makes his way up onto the beach, flops down exhausted and announces:

IT'S MAN (MICHAEL)

IT'S...

VOICE OVER (JOHN) Monty Python's Flying Circus.

Titles beginning with words 'Monty Python's Flying Circus'. Various bizarre things happen. **1**

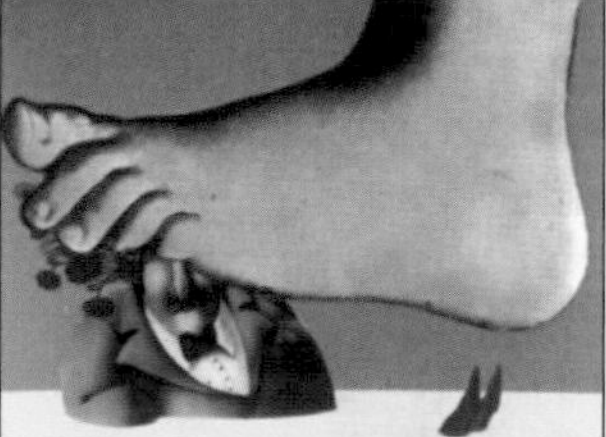

When the titles end: Ordinary grey-suited announcer standing by desk. He smiles confidently.

ANNOUNCER (GRAHAM) **Good evening.** **2**

The announcer confidently moves to chair and sits down. There is a squeal as of a pig being sat upon. Cut to a blackboard with several lines of pigs drawn on it in colour. A man steps into view and with a piece of chalk crosses out one of the pigs. Caption: 'IT'S WOLFGANG AMADEUS MOZART' Mozart sitting at piano tinkling with the keys. He finishes tinkling.

MOZART (JOHN) Hello again, and welcome to the show. Tonight we continue to look at some famous deaths. Tonight we start with the wonderful death of **Genghis Khan, conqueror of India.** **3** Take it away Genghis.

Cut to Genghis Khan's tent. Genghis strides about purposefully. Indian-style background music. Suddenly the music cuts out and Genghis Khan with a squawk throws himself in the air and lands on his back. This happens very suddenly. Judges hold up cards with points on, in the manner of ice skating judges.

VOICE OVER (GRAHAM) 9.1, 9.2, 9.7, that's 28.1 for Genghis Khan.

Mozart still at piano.

MOZART Bad luck Genghis. Nice to have you on the show. And now here are the scores.

Scoreboard with **Eddie Waring** **4** *figure standing by it. The scoreboard looks a little like this:*

ST. STEPHEN	29.9
RICHARD III	29.3
JEAN D'ARC	29.1
MARAT	29.0
A. LINCOLN (U.S. OF A)	28.1
KING EDWARD VII	3.1

EDDIE (ERIC) Well there you can see the scores now. St. Stephen in the lead there with his stoning, then comes King Richard the Third at Bosworth Field, a grand death that, then the very lovely Jean d'Arc, then Marat in his bath—best of friends with Charlotte in the showers afterwards—then A. Lincoln of the U.S. of A, a grand little chap that, and number six Genghis Khan, and the back marker King Edward the Seventh. Back to you, Wolfgang.

Mozart still at piano.

MOZART Thank you, Eddie. And now time for this week's request death. (*taking card off piano*) For Mr and Mrs Violet Stebbings of **23 Wolverston Road, Hull,** **5** the death of Mr Bruce Foster of Guildford.

Middle-class lounge. Mr Foster sitting in chair.

FOSTER (GRAHAM) Strewth! (*he dies*)

Mozart still there. He looks at watch.

MOZART Oh blimey, how time flies. Sadly we are reaching the end of yet another programme and so it is finale time. We are proud to be bringing to you one of the evergreen bucket kickers. Yes, the wonderful death of the famous English Admiral Nelson.

Cut to a modern office block, as high as possible. After a pause a body flies out of the top window looking as much like Nelson as possible. As it plummets there is a strangled scream.

NELSON Kiss me Hardy!

Eddie Waring was the face—and northern working-class voice—of rugby league commentary for BBC Sports for much of the 1960s and 1970s. (He was also the beloved cohost of one of Britain's favorite shows of the same period, *It's a Knockout*, in which teams of regular folks did stunts and running races to win prizes.) Idle here joins the long list of comedians who have mimicked his Yorkshire accent (turning Jean d'Arc into "John Dark") and everyman appearance (flat cap, duffel coat). The Python obsessions with class and history are brilliantly revealed here via a mock league table of famous deaths delivered by a working-class TV host with a cheeky grin.

Before you rush off to pay homage, there's no such address—though Hull, in the northeast of England, is often used as shorthand for a gritty, northern town, just as Eddie Waring is a gritty, northern TV host.

6

The Pythons were keen to get away from regular sketch comedy, especially in terms of the architecture of a single show. Sketches were often interrupted midstream, or just abandoned; otherwise, they bled into one another, as here: where the unfortunate death of Nelson happens from out of a college window, behind which a blackboard keeps score of how many pig sounds have occurred, and an Italian conversation class proceeds as only the English know how (that is, by speaking the new language slowly and with absolutely no foreign intonation).

The body hits the ground. There is the loud noise of a pig squealing. Cut to polytechnic night school. Teacher looking down out of classroom window. He crosses to a long wall blackboard with line of pigs drawn on near end. ***He crosses one off, walks along blackboard to other end which has written on it 'evening classes 7-8 p.m.'. He writes 'Italian' below this and turns to camera.*** 6

TEACHER (TERRY J) Ah—good evening everyone, and welcome to the second of our Italian language classes, in which we'll be helping you brush up your Italian. Last week we started at the beginning, and we learnt the Italian for a 'spoon'. Now, I wonder how many of you can remember what it was?

Shout of 'Si! Si! Si!' from the class whom we see for the first time to be swarthy Italians.

TEACHER Not all at once...sit down Mario. Giuseppe!
GIUSEPPE (MICHAEL) Il cucchiaio.
TEACHER Well done Giuseppe, or, as the Italians would say: 'Molto bene, Giuseppe'.
GIUSEPPE Grazie signor...grazie di tutta la sua gentilezza.
TEACHER Well, now, this week we're going to learn some useful phrases to help us open a conversation with an Italian. Now first of all try telling him where you come from. For example, I would say: 'Sono Inglese di Gerrard's Cross', I am an Englishman from Gerrard's Cross. Shall we all try that together?
ALL Sono Inglese di Gerrard's Cross.
TEACHER Not too bad, now let's try it with somebody else. Er...Mr...?
MARIOLINI (JOHN) Mariolini.
TEACHER Ah, Mr Mariolini, and where are you from?
MARIOLINI Napoli, signor.
TEACHER Ah...you're an Italian.
MARIOLINI Si, si signor!
TEACHER Well in that case you would say: 'Sono Italiano di Napoli'.
MARIOLINI Ah, capisco, mille grazie signor...
FRANCESCO (ERIC) Per favore, signor!
TEACHER Yes?
FRANCESCO Non conosgeve parliamente, signor devo me parlo sono Italiano di Napoli quando il habitare de Milano.
TEACHER I'm sorry...I don't understand!
GIUSEPPE (*pointing to Francesco*) My friend say 'Why must he say...'

Hand goes up at back of room and a Lederhosen Teutonic figure stands up.

GERMAN (GRAHAM) Bitte mein Herr. Was ist das Wort für Mittelschmerz?
TEACHER Ah! Helmut—you want the German classes.
GERMAN Oh ja! Danke schön. (*he starts to leave*) Ah das deutsche Klassenzimmer...Ach! (*he leaves*)

GIUSEPPE My friend he say, 'Why must I say I am Italian from Napoli when he lives in Milan?'
TEACHER Ah, I...well, tell your friend...if he lives in Milan he must say 'Sono Italiano di Milano...'
FRANCESCO (*agitatedly, leaping to his feet*) Eeeeeee! Milano è tanto meglio di Napoli. Milano è la citta la più bella di tutti...net mondo...
GIUSEPPE He say 'Milan is better than Napoli'.
TEACHER Oh, he shouldn't be saying that, we haven't done comparatives yet.

In the background everyone has started talking in agitated Italian. At this point a genuine mandoline-playing Italian secreted amongst the cast strikes up: 'Quando Caliente Del Sol...' or similar. The class is out of control by this time. The teacher helplessly tries to control them but eventually gives up and retreats to his desk and sits down. There is a loud pig squeal and he leaps up.

Animation: The blackboard with the coloured pigs drawn on it is reproduced on the first few frames of the animation film. A real hand comes into picture and crosses off a third pig. Thereafter action follows the dictates of Senor Gilliam's wonderfully visual mind.

At the end of this animation we have an advertisement for Whizzo butter. **7**

7

Much of the early Python was a parody of traditional TV—the quiet little BBC arts show, the on-the-street vox populi with housewives, the sports shows of Eddie Waring, etc. In the Whizzo butter "I'll slice your face" parody, Palin's character is a caricature of Leslie Crowther, who was famous for being the genial guy asking women on the street about butter versus margarine. (Crowther was also to be the father-in-law of Thin Lizzy front man Phil Lynott.)

VOICE OVER (MICHAEL) (*on animation*) Yes, mothers, new improved Whizzo butter containing 10% more less is absolutely indistinguishable from a dead crab. Remember, buy Whizzo butter and go to HEAVEN!

Cut to four middle-aged lower-middle-class women (hereinafter referred to as 'Pepperpots') being interviewed.

FIRST PEPPERPOT (GRAHAM)

I CAN'T TELL THE DIFFERENCE BETWEEN WHIZZO BUTTER AND THIS DEAD CRAB.

INTERVIEWER (MICHAEL) Yes, you know, we find that nine out of ten British housewives can't tell the difference between Whizzo butter and a dead crab.
PEPPERPOTS It's true, we can't. No.
SECOND PEPPERPOT (JOHN) Here. Here! You're on television, aren't you?
INTERVIEWER (*modestly*) Yes, yes.
SECOND PEPPERPOT He does the thing with one of those silly women who can't tell Whizzo butter from a dead crab.
THIRD PEPPERPOT (TERRY J) You try that around here, young man, and we'll slit your face.

Caption: 'IT'S THE ARTS' Linkman sitting at desk.

LINKMAN (MICHAEL) Hello, good evening and welcome to another edition of 'It's the Arts'. We kick off tonight with the cinema.

Cut to second interviewer and Ross.

SECOND INTERVIEWER (JOHN) Good evening. One of the most prolific of film producers, of this age, or indeed any age, is Sir Edward Ross, back in this country for the first time for five years to open a season of his works at the National Film Theatre, and we are very fortunate to have him with us here in the studio this evening.

ROSS (GRAHAM) Good evening.

SECOND INTERVIEWER Edward...you don't mind if I call you Edward?

ROSS No, not at all.

SECOND INTERVIEWER Only it does worry some people...I don't know why...but they are a little sensitive, so I do take the precaution of asking on these occasions.

ROSS No, no, no that's fine.

SECOND INTERVIEWER So Edward's all right. Splendid. Splendid. Sorry to have brought it up, only eh...

ROSS No, no, Edward it is.

SECOND INTERVIEWER Well, thank you very much indeed for being so helpful...only it's more than my job's worth to...er...

ROSS Quite, yes.

SECOND INTERVIEWER Makes it rather difficult to establish a rapport...to put the other person at their ease.

ROSS Quite.

SECOND INTERVIEWER Yes, silly little point, but it does seem to matter. Still—less said the better. Um...Ted...when you first started in...you don't mind if I call you Ted?

ROSS No, no, no, everyone calls me Ted.

SECOND INTERVIEWER Well it's shorter, isn't it.

ROSS Yes it is.

SECOND INTERVIEWER Yes, and much less formal.

ROSS Yes, Ted, Edward, anything.

SECOND INTERVIEWER Splendid, splendid. Incidentally, do call me Tom, I don't want you playing around with any of this Thomas nonsense ha ha ha. Now where were we? Oh yes, Eddie-baby, when you first started in the...

ROSS I'm sorry, but I don't like being called Eddie-baby.

SECOND INTERVIEWER I'm sorry?

ROSS I don't like being called Eddie-baby.

SECOND INTERVIEWER Did I call you Eddie-baby?

ROSS Yes you did. Now get on with it.

SECOND INTERVIEWER I don't think I did call you Eddie-baby?

ROSS You did call me Eddie-baby.

SECOND INTERVIEWER (*looking off-screen*) Did I call him Eddie-baby?

VOICES Yes. No. Yes.

SECOND INTERVIEWER I didn't really call you Eddie-baby did I, sweetie?

ROSS Don't call me sweetie!!

SECOND INTERVIEWER

CAN I CALL YOU SUGAR PLUM?

ROSS No!

SECOND INTERVIEWER Pussy cat?

ROSS No.

SECOND INTERVIEWER Angel-drawers?

ROSS No you may not!! Now get on with it!

SECOND INTERVIEWER Frank.

ROSS What?

SECOND INTERVIEWER Can I call you Frank?

ROSS Why Frank?

SECOND INTERVIEWER It's a nice name. **Robin Day's got a hedgehog called Frank.** 8

ROSS What is going on?

SECOND INTERVIEWER Frannie, little Frannie, Frannie Knickers...

The ne plus ultra of public intellectuals, broadcaster and commentator Robin Day was notable for his tough interviews of political figures, his oddly labored breathing, and his bow ties. The king of the "difficult" question, Day stood out among the genteel political discourse of the day, and, as with Eddie Waring and Leslie Crowther, he was easily and often parodied—and not only by the Pythons.

ROSS (*getting up*) No, I'm leaving. I'm leaving, I'm off...
SECOND INTERVIEWER Tell us about your latest film, Sir Edward.
ROSS (*off-screen*) What?
SECOND INTERVIEWER Tell us about your latest film, if you'd be so kind, Sir Edward.
ROSS (*returning*) None of this 'pussy cat' nonsense?
SECOND INTERVIEWER Promise. (*pats seat*) Please, Sir Edward.
ROSS (*sitting down*) My latest film?
SECOND INTERVIEWER Yes, Sir Edward.
ROSS Well the idea, funnily enough, came from an idea I had when I first joined the industry in 1919. Of course in those days I was only a tea boy.
SECOND INTERVIEWER Oh, *shut* up.

Cut to linkman, as before.

LINKMAN Sir Edward...Ross. Now, later in the programme we will be bringing you a unique event in the world of modern art. Pablo Picasso will be doing a special painting for us, on this programme, live, on a bicycle. This is the first time that Picasso has painted whilst cycling. But right now it's time to look at a man whose meteoric rise to fame...

Caption: 'PIGS 3, NELSON 1'. A pig squeals. Interviewer leaps up, grabs a revolver from his desk drawer and fires off-screen.Third Interviewer and Arthur 'Two Sheds' Jackson. Musical score blow-up behind.

THIRD INTERVIEWER (ERIC) Last week The Royal Festival Hall saw the first performance of a new symphony by one of the world's leading modern composers, **Arthur 'Two Sheds' Jackson.** **9** Mr Jackson.
JACKSON (TERRY J) Good evening.
THIRD INTERVIEWER May I just sidetrack you for one moment. Mr Jackson, this, what should I call it, nickname of yours.
JACKSON Oh yes.
THIRD INTERVIEWER 'Two Sheds'. How did you come by it?
JACKSON Well I don't use it myself, it's just a few of my friends call me 'Two Sheds'.

9

This sketch is a direct echo of the one before (you could argue it's merely the same)—the idea that the pretentiousness of artists and art shows can be undercut by misnaming the protagonists. "Two-Sheds" could be a gangland figure or a professional wrestler. He's certainly thrown from the set by Cleese and Idle as though this is a bout at the World Wrestling Federation.

THIRD INTERVIEWER

I SEE, AND DO YOU IN FACT HAVE TWO SHEDS?

JACKSON No. No, I've only one shed. I've had one for some time, but a few years ago I said I was thinking of getting another one and since then some people have called me 'Two Sheds'.

THIRD INTERVIEWER In spite of the fact that you have only one.

JACKSON Yes.

THIRD INTERVIEWER I see, and are you thinking of purchasing a second shed?

JACKSON No.

THIRD INTERVIEWER To bring you in line with your epithet.

JACKSON No.

THIRD INTERVIEWER I see, I see. Well let's return to your symphony. Ah, now then, did you write this symphony...*in* the shed?

JACKSON ...No.

THIRD INTERVIEWER Have you written any of your recent works in this shed of yours?

JACKSON No it's just a perfectly ordinary garden shed.

A picture of a shed appears on the screen behind them.

THIRD INTERVIEWER I see. And you're thinking of buying this second shed to write in.

JACKSON No, no. Look this shed business, it doesn't really matter at all, the sheds aren't important. It's just a few friends call me 'Two Sheds', and that's all there is to it. I wish you'd ask me about my music. I'm a composer. People always ask me about the sheds, they've got it out of proportion, I'm fed up with the shed, I wish I'd never got it in the first place.

THIRD INTERVIEWER I expect you're probably thinking of selling one.

JACKSON I will sell one.

THIRD INTERVIEWER Then you'd be Arthur 'No Sheds' Jackson.

JACKSON Look forget about the sheds. They don't matter.

THIRD INTERVIEWER Mr Jackson I think with respect, we ought to talk about your symphony.

JACKSON What?

THIRD INTERVIEWER Apparently your symphony was written for organ and tympani.

JACKSON (*catches sight of the picture of the shed behind him*) What's that?

THIRD INTERVIEWER What's what?

JACKSON It's a shed. Get it off.

He points to BP screen shed. The picture of the shed disappears and is replaced by a picture of Jackson. Jackson looks at it carefully.

JACKSON Right.
THIRD INTERVIEWER Now then Mr Jackson...your symphony.

Caption: 'ARTHUR "TWO SHEDS" JACKSON'
Cut back to studio: the picture of him is replaced by a picture of two sheds, one with a question mark over it.

THIRD INTERVIEWER I understand that you used to be interested in train spotting.
JACKSON What?
THIRD INTERVIEWER I understand that about thirty years ago you were extremely interested in train spotting.
JACKSON What's that got to do with my bloody music?

Enter Second Interviewer from Edward Ross sketch (John).

SECOND INTERVIEWER Are you having any trouble from him?
THIRD INTERVIEWER Yes, a little.
SECOND INTERVIEWER Well we interviewers are more than a match for the likes of you, 'Two Sheds'.
THIRD INTERVIEWER Yes make yourself scarce 'Two Sheds'. This studio isn't big enough for the three of us.

They push him away and propel him out.

JACKSON What are you doing? (*he is pushed out of vision with a crash*)
SECOND INTERVIEWER Get your own Arts programme you fairy!
THIRD INTERVIEWER (*to camera*) Arthur 'Two Sheds' Jackson.

Cut to linkman. He is about to speak when:

THIRD INTERVIEWER (*off-screen*) Never mind, Timmy.
SECOND INTERVIEWER (*off-screen*) Oh Michael you're such a comfort.
LINKMAN Arthur 'Two Sheds'...

Cut to man in Viking helmet at desk.

VIKING (JOHN)...Jackson.

THE GOON SHOW

First there was John the Baptist, then there was Jesus. You can't have spring without winter. And before the Pythons, there were the Goons.

The Goon Show was a British radio show broadcast from 1951 to 1960. And, without it, it's fair to say, the Pythons could never have been. The comedy troupe was initially made up of four extraordinary talents: Michael Bentine (who would leave by 1953), Harry Secombe, Spike Milligan, and Peter Sellers. It was beloved by fans of surreal comedy, though it's probably true that no one in Britain had ever quite heard anything like it.

Playing with the medium of radio, *The Goon Show* attempted to break out of the humdrum story punch line sketches that permeated British comedy at the time. In doing so, they created a number of classic comic characters—Bluebottle, Eccles, Major Denis Bloodnok—and by the mid-1950s, the show was hugely popular. The young Pythons listened eagerly, and each has at some point credited the Goons with being a powerful inspiration.

In reality, though, the show was a vehicle for the mind of Spike Milligan (he wrote much of the material). And what a mind it was. Bedeviled by severe bipolar disorder and much affected by his experiences in World War II, Milligan's style was one of anarchy, flights of language, strange noises, and madcap leaps—all of which could be said about the later Pythons. His later work included the *Q* series of TV comedies, each of which as odd a creation as could be imagined. *Q5*, the first of the series that began airing in March 1969, is cited by the Pythons as both a huge inspiration and a painful lesson that sometimes someone can get there ahead of you. Beyond his TV work, Milligan also wrote memoirs about his time in the army and poetry (this author can quote much of it without prompting, viz.:

"I never felt finer!"
Said the King of China,
Sitting down to dine
Then he fell down dead—he died he did!
It was only half past nine).

At least in the first two seasons, Michael Bentine could give Milligan a run for his money in terms of absurd comedy (the two were said to be at odds with each other). Later, Bentine would go on to create a popular children's TV show, *Michael Bentine's Potty Time*, which ran through most of the seventies. The show featured strange short puppets with no real facial features—voiced by Bentine's odd nasal whine—who would engage in odd sketches of a historical nature.

The other two Goons, Secombe and Sellers, went on to wildly different careers after the show. Secombe had his own comedy variety show in the late sixties and early seventies, though it was much more conventional than either the Goons or Python. He became famous again later in life as a Christian singer who presented religious music shows on both the BBC and ITV (he was a fine Welsh bel canto tenor and sold a lot of records). Sellers was something else again—a visionary and startlingly odd actor, he's perhaps best known for his Inspector Clouseau character in the *Pink Panther* movies as well as his roles in *Being There* and two of Stanley Kubrick's most celebrated films, *Dr. Strangelove* and *Lolita*.

The Goons are gone—Sellers died in 1980, Bentine in 1996, Secombe in 2001, and Milligan in 2002—and many of their shows were destroyed, following BBC policy. But in watching the Pythons, one can see their influence in every scene: the digressions, the knotty language, the crazy characters, the abhorrence of the easy way out. As Palin put it years later, "Just how do they create this wonderful world?" The great mystery of comedy, applicable to the Goons *and* the Pythons.

Cut back to linkman.

LINKMAN And now for more news of the momentous artistic event in which Pablo Picasso is doing a specially commissioned painting for us whilst riding a bicycle. Pablo Picasso—the founder of modern art—without doubt the greatest abstract painter ever...for the first time painting in motion. **But first of all let's have a look at the route he'll be taking. 10**

Cut to Raymond Baxter type standing in front of map. A small cardboard cut-out of Picasso's face is on map and is moved around to illustrate route.

BAXTER (MICHAEL) Well Picasso will be starting, David, at Chichester here, he'll then cycle on the A29 to Fontwell, he'll then take the A272 which will bring him on to the A3 just north of Hindhead here. From then on Pablo has a straight run on the A3 until he meets the South Circular at Battersea here. Well, this is a truly remarkable occasion as it is the first time that a modern artist of such stature has taken the A272, and it'll be very interesting to see how he copes with the heavy traffic round Wisborough Green. Vicky.

Cut to Vicky, holding a bicycle.

VICKY (ERIC) Well Picasso will be riding his Viking Super Roadster with the drop handlebars and the dual-thread wheel-rims and with his **Wiley-Prat 11** 20-1 synchro-mesh he should experience difficulties on the sort of road surfaces they just don't get abroad. Mitzie.

Cut to linkman at desk with Viking on one side and a knight in armour on the other.

LINKMAN And now for the latest report on Picasso's progress over to Reg Moss on the Guildford by-pass.

Reg Moss standing with hand mike by fairly busy road.

REG MOSS (ERIC) Well there's no sign of Picasso at the moment, David. But he should be through here at any moment. However I do have with me Mr Ron Geppo, British Cycling Sprint Champion and this year's winner of the Derby-Doncaster rally.

Geppo is in full cyclist's kit.

GEPPO (GRAHAM) **Well Reg, I think Pablo should be all right provided he doesn't attempt anything on the monumental scale of some of his earlier paintings, like Guernica or Mademoiselles d'Avignon or even his later War and Peace murals for the Temple of Peace chapel at Vallauris, because with this strong wind I don't think even Doug Timpson of Manchester Harriers could paint anything on that kind of scale. 12**

REG MOSS Well, thank you Ron. Well, there still seems to be no sign of Picasso, so I'll hand you back to the studio.

There are two subjects on which the British are experts—or at least on which they muse almost constantly. One is the weather (the British Isles has a lot of it); the other is the best route by which to drive to a destination. Should Picasso actually have considered painting while riding a bicycle, it is not beyond belief to imagine that the roads he chose would be of most interest to the British TV viewer.

"Wiley-Prat" is possibly an allusion to Pratt & Whitney, the famed American aircraft-engine manufacturer. "Wily prat" can also be translated from British slang as "clever idiot."

The archetypal Python trope: what is absurd (Picasso painting on a bicycle) made more deeply so by the non sequitur (Doug Timpson, a cyclist, being conservative about the scale of his bicycle-based art).

LINKMAN Well, we've just heard that Picasso is approaching the Tolworth roundabout on the A3 so come in Sam Trench at Tolworth.

Cut to Sam Trench at roadside.

TRENCH (JOHN) Well something certainly is happening here at Tolworth roundabout, David. I can now see Picasso, he's cycling down very hard towards the roundabout, he's about 75-50 yards away and I can now see his painting...it's an abstract...I can see some blue some purple and some little black oval shapes...I think I can see...

Mrs. Pepperpot refers to the children's books penned by Norwegian author Alf Proysen. Mrs. P had the dubious ability to shrink to the size of a "pepperpot" (in Norwegian her name translates to teaspoon, which is even smaller if you think about it). The name of one of the books in the series perhaps suggests why it was popular in Britain: *Mr. Pepperpot and the Weather.*

A Pepperpot comes up and nudges him. **13**

PEPPERPOT (MICHAEL)

THAT'S NOT PICASSO— THAT'S KANDINSKY.

TRENCH (*excited*) Good lord, you're right. It's Kandinsky. Wassily Kandinsky, and who's this here with him? It's Braque. Georges Braque, the Cubist, painting a bird in flight over a cornfield and going very fast down the hill towards Kingston and...(*cyclists pass in front of him*) Piet Mondrian—just behind, Piet Mondrian the Neo-Plasticist, and then a gap, then the main bunch, here they come, Chagall, Max Ernst, Miro, Dufy, Ben Nicholson, Jackson Pollock and Bernard Buffet making a break on the outside here, Brancusi's going with him, so is **Géricault,** **14** Fernand Léger, Delaunay, De Kooning, Kokoschka's dropping back here by the look of it, and so's Paul Klee dropping back a bit and, right at the back of this group, our very own Kurt Schwitters.

PEPPERPOT He's German!

TRENCH But as yet absolutely no sign of Pablo Picasso, and so from Tolworth roundabout back to the studio.

Darl Larson, in his *Monty Python's Flying Circus: An Utterly Complete, Thoroughly Unillustrated, Absolutely Unauthorized Guide to Possibly All the References From Arthur "Two Sheds" Jackson to Zambesi*, notes correctly that Théodore Géricault is out of place here, being an artist of the early nineteenth century.

Toulouse-Lautrec pedals past on a child's tricycle.

Cut back to studio.

LINKMAN Well I think I can help you there Sam, we're getting reports in from the AA that Picasso, Picasso has fallen off...he's fallen off his bicycle on the B2127 just outside Ewhurst, trying to get a short cut through to Dorking via Peaslake and Gomshall. Well, Picasso is reported to be unhurt, but the pig has a slight headache. And on that note we must say goodnight to you. Picasso has failed in his first bid for international cycling fame. So from all of us here at the 'It's the Arts' studio, it's goodnight. (*pig's head appears over edge of desk; linkman gently pushes it back*) Goodnight.

Animation: Cartoon sequence of animated Victorian photos, at the end of which a large pig descends, fatally, on a portrait of a man.

Cut to wartime planning room. **15** *Two officers are pushing model pigs across the map. A private enters and salutes.*

PRIVATE Dobson's bought it, sir.

OFFICER (CHAPMAN) Porker, eh? Swine.

Cut to a suburban house in a rather drab street. Zoom into upstairs window. Serious documentary music. Interior of small room. A bent figure (Michael) huddles over a table, writing. He is surrounded by bits of paper. The camera is situated facing the man as he writes with immense concentration lining his unshaven face.

VOICE OVER (ERIC) This man is Ernest Scribbler...writer of jokes. In a few moments, he will have written the funniest joke in the world...and, as a consequence, he will die...laughing.

The writer stops writing, pauses to look at what he has written...a smile slowly spreads across his face, turning very, very slowly to uncontrolled hysterical laughter...he staggers to his feet and reels across room helpless with mounting mirth and eventually collapses and dies on the floor.

VOICE OVER It was obvious that this joke was lethal...no one could read it and live...

The scribbler's mother (Eric) enters. She sees him dead, she gives a little cry of horror and bends over his body, weeping. Brokenly she notices the piece of paper in his hand and (thinking it is a suicide note—for he has not been doing very well for the last thirteen years) picks it up and reads it between her sobs. Immediately she breaks out into hysterical laughter, leaps three feet into the air, and falls down dead without more ado. Cut to news type shot of commentator standing in front of the house.

It can be easy to forget that the carnage of World War II reached the northern shores of France, a few miles from southern England, and had ended a mere quarter century before this first episode appeared. The confluence of geographical proximity and recent times made the wartime jokes still fresh for many British viewers (and writers) at the end of the 1960s.

COMMENTATOR (TERRY J) (*reverentially*) This morning, shortly after eleven o'clock, comedy struck this little house in **Dibley Road.** [16] Sudden...violent...comedy. Police have sealed off the area, and **Scotland Yard's** [17] crack inspector is with me now.

INSPECTOR (GRAHAM) I shall enter the house and attempt to remove the joke.

At this point an upstairs window in the house is flung open and a doctor, with stethoscope, rears his head out, hysterical with laughter, and dies hanging over the window sill. The commentator and the inspector look up briefly and sadly, and then continue as if they are used to such sights this morning.

INSPECTOR I shall be aided by the sound of sombre music, played on gramophone records, and also by the chanting of laments by the men of Q Division...(*he indicates a little knot of dour-looking policemen standing nearby*) The atmosphere thus created should protect me in the eventuality of me reading the joke.

He gives a signal. The group of policemen start groaning and chanting biblical laments. The Dead March is heard. The inspector squares his shoulders and bravely starts walking into the house.

COMMENTATOR There goes a brave man. Whether he comes out alive or not, this will surely be remembered as one of the most courageous and gallant acts in police history.

The inspector suddenly appears at the door, helpless with laughter, holding the joke aloft. He collapses and dies. Cut to stock film of army vans driving along dark roads.

VOICE OVER It was not long before the Army became interested in the military potential of the Killer Joke. Under top security, the joke was hurried to a meeting of Allied Commanders at the Ministry of War.

Cut to door at Ham House: Soldier on guard comes to attention as dispatch rider hurries in carrying armoured box. (Notice on door: 'Conference. No Admittance') Dispatch rider rushes in. A door opens for him and closes behind him. We hear a mighty roar of laughter...series of doomphs as the commanders hit the floor or table. Soldier outside does not move a muscle. Cut to a pillbox on the Salisbury Plain. Track in to slit to see moustachioed top brass peering anxiously out.

VOICE OVER Top brass were impressed. **Tests on Salisbury Plain** [18] confirmed the joke's devastating effectiveness at a range of up to fifty yards.

Cut to shot looking out of slit in pillbox. Zoom through slit to distance where a solitary figure is standing on the windswept plain. He is a bespectacled, weedy lance-corporal (Terry J) looking cold and miserable. Pan across to fifty yards away where two helmeted soldiers are at their positions beside a blackboard on an easel covered with a cloth. Cut in to corporal's face—registering complete lack of comprehension as well as stupidity. Man on top of pillbox waves flag. The soldiers

One of the original names for the show was "Gwen Dibley's Flying Circus." Palin had seen a picture of a woman named Gwen Dibley, and according to Chapman, in *The Pythons' Autobiography*, "thought it would be fun for her to read in the *Radio Times* that she had her own show." Dibley remains a popular word for a fictional place in British comedy—as in the sitcom *The Vicar of Dibley*. It brings to mind, perhaps, "Dib-dib-dib," the greeting by which generations of British Boy Scouts have recognized one another—that is, it's both a bit sweet and a bit silly.

GREAT SCOTLAND YARD SW1
CITY OF WESTMINSTER

Scotland Yard is both a physical place, once the headquarters of the Metropolitan Police (originally at 4 Whitehall Place, a mile north of the Houses of Parliament in the center of London), and a description of the police itself—as in, "Scotland Yard released its crime figures for the year."

Salisbury Plain, a 300-square-mile plateau in southern England, is the British Army's testing ground for military material and maneuvers, handily named the Army Training Estate Salisbury Plain (ATE SP). Stonehenge also stands on the plain, nestled between the A344 and the A303.

reveal the joke to the corporal. He peers at it, thinks about its meaning, sniggers, and dies. Two watching generals are very impressed.

GENERALS Fantastic.

Cut to colonel talking to camera.

COLONEL (GRAHAM) All through the winter of '43 we had translators working, in joke-proof conditions, to try and produce a German version of the joke. They worked on one word each for greater safety. One of them saw two words of the joke and spent several weeks in hospital. But apart from that things went pretty quickly, and we soon had the joke by January, in a form which our troops couldn't understand but which the Germans could.

Cut to a trench in the Ardennes. Members of the joke brigade are crouched holding pieces of paper with the joke on them.

VOICE OVER So, on July 8th, 1944, the joke was first told to the enemy in the Ardennes...
COMMANDING NCO Tell the...joke.
JOKE BRIGADE (*together*)

WENN IST DAS NUNSTÜCK GIT UND SLOTERMEYER? JA!...BEIHERHUND DAS ODER DIE FLIPPERWALDT GERSPUT! 19

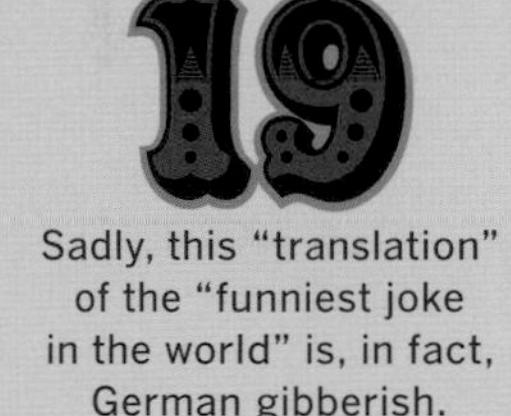

19 Sadly, this "translation" of the "funniest joke in the world" is, in fact, German gibberish.

Pan out of the British trench across war-torn landscape and come to rest where presumably the German trench is. There is a pause and then a knot of Germans rear up in hysterics.

VOICE OVER It was a fantastic success. Over sixty thousand times as powerful as Britain's great pre-war joke...

Stock film of Chamberlain brandishing the 'Peace in our time' bit of paper.

VOICE OVER ...and one which Hitler just couldn't match.

Film of Hitler rally. Hitler speaks; subtitles are superimposed.
Subtitle: 'MY DOG'S GOT NO NOSE'
A young soldier responds:
Subtitle: 'HOW DOES HE SMELL?'
Hitler speaks:
Subtitle: 'AWFUL'

VOICE OVER In action it was deadly.

Cut to a small squad with rifles making their way through forest. Suddenly one of them (a member of joke squad) sees something and gives signal at which they all dive for cover. From the cover of a tree he reads out joke.

JOKE CORPORAL (TERRY J) Wenn ist das Nunstück git und Slotermeyer? Ja!...Beiherhund das Oder die Flipperwaldt gersput!

Sniper falls laughing out of tree.

JOKE BRIGADE (*charging*) Wenn ist das Nunstück git und Slotermeyer? Ja!...Beiherhund das Oder die Flipperwaldt gersput.

THEY CHANT THE JOKE. GERMANS ARE PUT TO FLIGHT LAUGHING, SOME DROPPING TO GROUND.

VOICE OVER The German casualties were appalling.

Cut to a German hospital and a ward full of casualties still laughing hysterically. Cut to Nazi interrogation room. An officer from the joke brigade has a light shining in his face. A Gestapo officer is interrogating him; another (clearly labelled 'A Gestapo Officer') stands behind him.

20

Cleese, playing a Nazi commandant, here comically goose-steps left to right, prefiguring his later classic "Ministry of Silly Walks."

NAZI (JOHN) Vott is the big joke?
OFFICER (MICHAEL) I can only give you name, rank, and why did the chicken cross the road?
NAZI That's not funny! (*slaps him*) I vant to know the joke.
OFFICER All right. How do you make a Nazi cross?
NAZI (*momentarily fooled*) I don't know...how do you make a Nazi cross?
OFFICER Tread on his corns. (*does so; the Nazi hops in pain*)
NAZI Gott in Himmel! **That's not funny!** **20** (*mimes cuffing him while the other Nazi claps his hands to provide the sound effect*) Now if you don't tell me the joke, I shall hit you properly.
OFFICER I can stand physical pain, you know.
NAZI Ah...you're no fun. All right, Otto.

Otto (Graham) starts tickling the officer who starts laughing.

OFFICER Oh no—anything but that please no, all right I'll tell you.

They stop.

NAZI Quick Otto. The typewriter.

Otto goes to the typewriter and they wait expectantly. The officer produces piece of paper out of his breast pocket and reads.

OFFICER Wenn ist das Nunstück git und Slotermeyer? Ja!...Beiherhund das Oder die Flipperwaldt gersput.

Otto at the typewriter explodes with laughter and dies.

NAZI Ach! Zat iss not funny!

Bursts into laughter and dies. A guard (Terry G) bursts in with machine gun. The British officer leaps on the table.

OFFICER (*lightning speed*) Wenn ist das Nunstück git und Slotermeyer? Ja!...Beiherhund das Oder die Flipperwaldt gersput.

The guard reels back and collapses laughing. British officer makes his escape. Cut to stock film of German scientists working in laboratories.

VOICE OVER **But at Peenemünde** **21** in the Autumn of '44, the Germans were working on a joke of their own.

21

Peenemünde is in eastern Germany, and where the V-2 rocket was first produced (see later reference to "V-joke").

Cut to interior. A German general (Terry J) seated at an imposing desk. Behind him stands Otto, labelled 'A Different Gestapo Officer'. Bespectacled German scientist/joke writer enters room. He clears his throat and reads from card.

GERMAN JOKER (eric) Die ist ein Kinnerhunder und zwei Mackel über und der bitte schön ist den Wunderhaus sprechensie. 'Nein' sprecht der Herren '1st aufern borger mit zveitingen'.

He finishes and looks hopeful.

OTTO We let you know.

He shoots him.More stock film of German scientists.

VOICE OVER But by December their joke was ready, and Hitler gave the order for the German V-Joke to be broadcast in English.

Cut to 1940's wartime radio set with couple anxiously listening to it.

RADIO (*crackly German voice*) Der ver zwei peanuts, valking down der strasse, and von vas...assaulted! peanut. Ho-ho-ho-ho.

Radio bursts into 'Deutschland Über Alles'. The couple look at each other and then in blank amazement at the radio. Cut to modern BBC 2 interview. The commentator in a woodland glade.

COMMENTATOR (ERIC) In 1945 Peace broke out. It was the end of the Joke. Joke warfare was banned at a special session of the Geneva Convention, and in 1950 the last remaining copy of the joke was laid to rest here in the Berkshire countryside, never to be told again.

He walks away revealing a monument on which is written: 'To the unknown Joke'.
Camera pulls away slowly through idyllic setting. Patriotic music reaches crescendo. Cut to football referee who blows whistle. Silence. Blank screen. Caption: 'THE END' The seashore again, with the 'It's' man lying on the beach. A stick from off-screen prods him. Exhausted, he rises and staggers back into the sea.

Caption: '"WHITHER CANADA?" was conceived written and performed by...(credits)'

ANNOUNCER (GRAHAM) And here is the final score: Pigs 9—British Bipeds 4. The Pigs go on to meet Vicki Carr in the final.

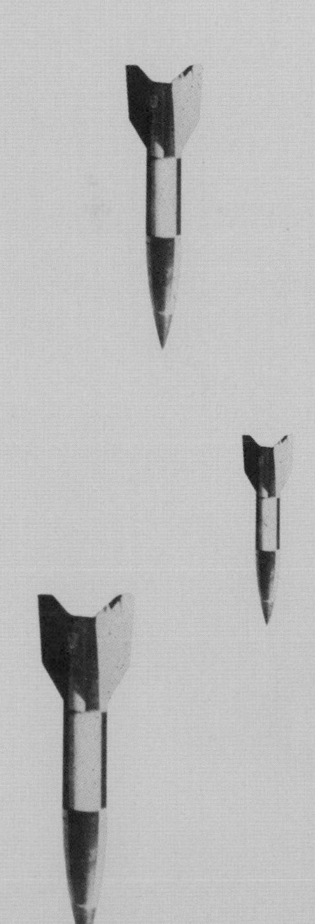

SEA SON 1
THE MOUSE PROBLEM
EPISODE 2

SEX AND VIOLENCE
FEATURING
FLYING SHEEP ✽ FRENCH LECTURE ON SHEEP-AIRCRAFT
A MAN WITH THREE BUTTOCKS
A MAN WITH TWO NOSES ✽ MUSICAL MICE
MARRIAGE GUIDANCE COUNSELLOR
THE WACKY QUEEN
WORKING CLASS PLAYWRIGHT
A SCOTSMAN ON A HORSE
THE WRESTLING EPILOGUE
THE MOUSE PROBLEM

FIRST AIRED: OCTOBER 12, 1969

A man appears on the top of a sand dune some way away. He looks in direction of camera and runs towards it. He disappears on top of a closer dune and continues towards camera, disappearing again into a dip. This time while he is out of sight, the sound of him running is the sound of someone running along a prison corridor, followed by a big door opening and closing. He appears again only two sand dunes away. Still running towards camera he disappears again from sight. This time there is a loud metallic series of sounds followed by a pig squealing. He appears over the nearest dune and runs up to camera.

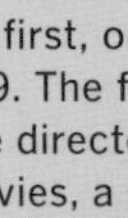

This episode was actually recorded first, on August 30, 1969. The first few shows were directed by John Howard Davies, a stalwart of regular BBC comedy, while Ian MacNaughton, who had worked on the avant-garde *Q5* with Spike Milligan and would eventually be the main director of MPFC, was, amazingly enough, "on holiday." When Tom Sloane, then the head of BBC's light entertainment, saw the first episode, Jones reports that Sloane called MacNaughton and told him he had to do something about the show as "it just isn't funny."

IT'S MAN (MICHAEL)

IT'S...

VOICE OVER (JOHN) Monty Python's Flying Circus. 1

These words are followed by various strange images, possibly connected with the stretching of owls, and proceeding from a bizarre American immigrant's fevered brain.

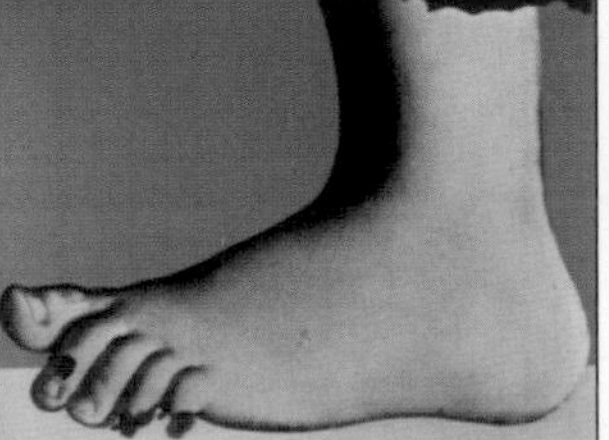

At the end of this expensive therapy: Caption: 'PART 2' Caption: 'SHEEP' A small set of a gate in the country overlooking a field. A real rustic in smock and floppy hat is leaning on the gate. A city gent on holiday appears behind him. Off-screen baa-ing noises throughout.

CITY GENT (TERRY J) Good afternoon.
RUSTIC (GRAHAM) Arternoon.
CITY GENT Ah, lovely day isn't it?
RUSTIC Ar, 'tis that.
CITY GENT Are you here on holiday or...?
RUSTIC No no, I live here.

CITY GENT Oh, jolly good too. (*surveys field; he looks puzzled*) I say, those *are* sheep, aren't they?
RUSTIC Ar.
CITY GENT Yes, yes of course, I thought so...only...er why are they up in the trees?
RUSTIC A fair question and one that in recent weeks has been much on my mind. It is my considered opinion that they're nesting.
CITY GENT Nesting?
RUSTIC Ar.
CITY GENT Like birds?
RUSTIC Ar. Exactly! Birds is the key to the whole problem. It is my belief that these sheep are labouring under the misapprehension that they're birds. Observe their behaviour. Take for a start the sheeps' tendency to hop about the field on their back legs. (*off-screen baa-ing*) Now witness their attempts to fly from tree to tree. Notice they do not so much fly as plummet. (*sound of sheep plummeting*) Observe for example that ewe in that oak tree. She is clearly trying to teach her lamb to fly. (*baaaaaa...thump*) Talk about the blind leading the blind.
CITY GENT But why do they think they're birds?
RUSTIC Another fair question. One thing is for sure; a sheep is not a creature of the air. It has **enormous difficulty in the comparatively simple act of perching.** 2 (*crash*) As you see. As for flight, its body is totally unadapted to the problems of aviation.

TROUBLE IS, SHEEP ARE VERY DIM. AND ONCE THEY GET AN IDEA INTO THEIR HEADS THERE'S NO SHIFTING IT.

CITY GENT But where did they get the idea from?

RUSTIC From Harold. He's that sheep over there under the elm. He's that most dangerous of animals—a clever sheep. He's the ring-leader. He has realized that a sheep's life consists of standing around for a few months and then being eaten. And that's a depressing prospect for an ambitious sheep. He's patently hit on the idea of escape.
CITY GENT But why don't you just get rid of Harold?
RUSTIC Because of the enormous commercial possibilities should he succeed.
VOICE OVER (ERIC) And what exactly are the commercial possibilities of ovine aviation?

Two Frenchmen stand in front of a diagram of a sheep adapted for flying. They speak rapidly in French, much of it pseudo.

FIRST FRENCHMAN (JOHN) Bonsoir—ici nous avons les diagrammes modernes d'un mouton anglo-français...maintenant...baa-aa, baa-aa...nous avons, dans la tête, le cabine. Ici, on se trouve le petit capitaine Anglais, Monsieur Trubshawe.
SECOND FRENCHMAN (MICHAEL) **Vive Brian, wherever you are.** 3
FIRST FRENCHMAN D'accord, d'accord. Maintenant, je vous présente mon collègue, le pouf célèbre, Jean-Brian Zatapathique.

The incongruity of the City Gent in a field is matched by the heightened language of the "Rustic." The Pythons were adept at making fun of the stratified layers of British class, not to mention the expectations of the members of such classes. City Gents never stand in fields, Rustics can't employ complicated language structures, and sheep can't fly.

On April 9, 1969, four months before this sketch was recorded, the first test flight by a British pilot of the Concorde supersonic plane had occurred—a fifty-mile flight from an airfield in Filton, northeast of Bristol, to RAF Fairford, a Royal Air Force station in Gloucestershire, England. At the helm was Brian Trubshaw, who said as he emerged from the cockpit, "It was wizard—a cool, calm and collected operation." His calmness led him to achieve hero status in Britain, especially when it was revealed that the altimeters failed and he had had to guess how high the Concorde was so he could land safely.

As Second Frenchman transfers his mustache back to First Frenchman, Palin comes close to corpsing when the mustache doesn't want to stick. Only a swift and discreet use of the left hand against his face prevents Palin from breaking character.

A beautiful parody of the British ability to make everything nice and homely: four women in a supermarket discussing French intellectual prowess as though it's a new brand of margarine.

There are lots of Arthurs in Python—and there are four in the next five minutes. In Britain, the name conjures up a regular Joe, a working-class fellow who epitomizes the salt-of-the-earth Englishman. Arthur is no frills, solid, a bit boring, and probably gardens a lot; he is the man on the street who holds middle-of-the-road views.

Transfers his moustache to Second Frenchman.

SECOND FRENCHMAN Maintenant, le mouton...le landing...les wheels, bon. **4**

Opens diagram to show wheels on sheep's legs.

FIRST FRENCHMAN Bon, les wheels, ici.
SECOND FRENCHMAN C'est formidable, n'est ce pas...(*unintelligibly indicates motor at rear of sheep*)
FIRST FRENCHMAN Les voyageurs...les bagages...ils sont...ici!

Triumphantly opens the rest of the diagram to reveal the whole brilliant arrangement. They run round flapping their arms and baa-ing. Cut to pepperpots in supermarket with off-screen interviewer.

FIRST PEPPERPOT (GRAHAM) Oh yes, we get a lot of French people round here. **5**
SECOND PEPPERPOT (TERRY J) Ooh Yes.
THIRD PEPPERPOT (MICHAEL) All over yes.
INTERVIEWER And how do you get on with these French people?
FIRST PEPPERPOT Oh very well.
FOURTH PEPPERPOT (JOHN) So do I.
THIRD PEPPERPOT Me too.
FIRST PEPPERPOT Oh yes I like them. I mean, they think well don't they? I mean, be fair—Pascal.
SECOND PEPPERPOT Blaise Pascal.
THIRD PEPPERPOT Jean-Paul Sartre.
FIRST PEPPERPOT Yes, Voltaire.
SECOND PEPPERPOT Ooh!—René Descartes.

René Descartes is sitting thinking. Bubbles come from his head with 'thinks'. Suddenly he looks happy. In thought bubble appears 'I THINK THEREFORE I AM'. A large hand comes into picture with a pin and pricks the thought bubble. It deflates and disappears. After a second, Rene disappears too. Studio: Smart looking and confident announcer sitting at desk.

ANNOUNCER (ERIC) And now for something completely different. A man with three buttocks.

Interviewer and Arthur Frampton, in interview studio.

INTERVIEWER (JOHN) Good evening. I have with me, Mr Arthur **6** Frampton, who has...Mr Frampton, I understand that you...er...as it were...have er...well, let me put it another way... I believe, Mr Frampton, that whereas most people have...er...two...two...you...you.
FRAMPTON (TERRY J) I'm sorry.
INTERVIEWER Ah! Yes, yes I see...Um. Are you quite comfortable?
FRAMPTON Yes fine, thank you.

INTERVIEWER *(takes a quick glance at Frampton's bottom)*

ER, MR FRAMPTON VIS-À-VIS YOUR RUMP.

FRAMPTON I beg your pardon?
INTERVIEWER Er, your rump.
FRAMPTON What?
INTERVIEWER Your posterior...derrière...sit upon.
FRAMPTON What's that?
INTERVIEWER *(whispers)* ...Buttocks.
FRAMPTON Oh, me bum!
INTERVIEWER Sh!... **7** Well Mr Frampton I understand Mr Frampton, you have a...50% bonus in the...in the region of what you said.
FRAMPTON I got three cheeks.
INTERVIEWER Yes, yes. Splendid, splendid. Well...we were wondering Mr Frampton if you... could...see your way clear...
FRAMPTON *(seeing a camera moving round behind him)* Here? What's that camera doing?
INTERVIEWER Er, nothing, nothing at all, sir. We were wondering if you could see your way clear... to giving us...a quick...a quick...visual...Mr Frampton, will you take your trousers down?
FRAMPTON What? *(slapping away a hand from off-screen)* 'Ere, get off. I'm not taking me trousers off on television. Who do you think I am?
INTERVIEWER Please take them down.
FRAMPTON No.
INTERVIEWER Just a little bit.
FRAMPTON No.
INTERVIEWER Now er, ahem...*(firmly)* Now look here Mr Frampton...it's perfectly easy for somebody just to come along here to the BBC, simply claiming...that they have a bit to spare in the botty department...but the point is Mr Frampton...**our viewers need proof.** **8**

Cleese's horrified reaction to the word bum, having beaten around it for a few lines, is both a funny parody of the "correctness" of the BBC and revealing of the standards of the time. Back then, the comedy came from the fact that the word would have been shocking to many viewers.

The BBC holds an almost religious position in British society still today, but in 1969 its authority was the equivalent of the Queen, the Archbishop of Canterbury, and the *Oxford English Dictionary* all rolled into one. It was the source of all truth (and most knowledge). If the BBC said it was so, then by golly it was so. If a man like "Mr. Frampton" claimed to have three buttocks, then it would only be true if the BBC proved it—perfect fodder for five anarchic comedians, even if "bottom" jokes trended directly to 14-year-old boys.

Ah, the Women's Institute. Founded in 1915 partly to help increase food production during World War I, by 1969 this voluntary organization had become a byword for safe female pursuits like arranging flowers and making jam. Many years before women entered the workplace in huge numbers, the Women's Institute furnished stay-at-home moms with something to do until the kids came home from school...or so the viewers of MPFC would have dismissed it. (In fact, the organization did great volunteer work, especially in isolated rural communities.) The women in this clapping clip sport the uniform of the Women's Institute circa 1950—and they would have been the absolute opposite of the typical viewer for this new comedy show from the BBC.

Darl Larson, in his Python encyclopedia, reckons this is a nod to the "Redcoats" who directed entertainment at Butlins Holiday Camps in the United Kingdom. It's also hard to miss Michael Palin's attempt at an Elvis Presley impersonation, even if his American accent is spotty at best.

FRAMPTON I've been on Persian Radio...Get om Arthur Figgis knows I've got three buttocks.
INTERVIEWER How?
FRAMPTON We go cycling together.

Cut to shot of two men riding tandem. The one behind (GRAHAM) *looks down, looks up and exclaims 'strewth'. Announcer's desk: confident announcer again.*

ANNOUNCER And now for something completely different. A man with three buttocks.

Interview studio again.

INTERVIEWER Good evening, I have with me Mr Arthur Frampton, who...Mr Frampton—I understand that you, as it were—well let me put it another way...I believe Mr Frampton that whereas most people...didn't we do this just now?
FRAMPTON Er...yes.
INTERVIEWER Well why didn't you *say* so?
FRAMPTON I thought it was the continental version.

Announcer's desk: confident announcer.

ANNOUNCER And now for something completely the same—a man with three buttocks. (*phone on desk rings—he answers it*) Hullo?...Oh, did we. (*puts phone down; to camera*) And now for something completely different. A man with three noses.
OFF-SCREEN VOICE (JOHN) He's not here yet!
ANNOUNCER Two noses?

Stock shot of audience of Women's Institute type, applauding. 9 *A man flourishing a handkerchief blows his nose. Then he puts his handkerchief inside his shirt and blows again. Stock shot women applauding again.*

COMPÈRE (MICHAEL) **Ladies and gentlemen isn't she just great eh, wasn't she just great. Ha, ha, ha, and she can run as fast as she can sing, ha, ha, ha. And I'm telling you—'cos I know. No, only kidding. Ha, ha, ha. Seriously now, ladies and gentlemen, we have for you one of the most unique acts in the world today. He's...well I'll say no more, just let you see for yourselves...ladies and gentlemen, my very great privilege to introduce Arthur Ewing, and his musical mice.** 10

Cut to Ewing.

EWING (TERRY J) Thank you, thank you, thank you, thank you. Ladies and gentlemen. I have in this box twenty-three white mice. Mice which have been painstakingly trained over the past few years, to squeak at a selected pitch. (*he raises a mouse by its tail*) **This is E sharp... and this one is G.** **11** You get the general idea. Now these mice are so arranged upon this rack, that when played in the correct order they will squeak 'The Bells of St Mary's'. Ladies and gentlemen, I give you on the mouse organ 'The Bells of St Mary's'. Thank you.

He produces two mallets. He starts striking the mice while singing quietly 'The Bells of St Mary's'. Each downward stroke of the mallet brings a terrible squashing sound and the expiring squeak. It is quite clear that he is slaughtering the mice. The musical effect is poor. After the first few notes people are shouting 'Stop it, stop him someone, Oh my God'. He cheerfully takes a bow. He is hauled off by the floor manager.

Cut to man holding up cards saying 'MARRIAGE COUNSELLOR'. The counsellor sits behind a desk. He puts down the card and says:

COUNSELLOR (ERIC) Next!

A little man enters, with a beautiful blond buxom wench, in the full bloom of her young womanhood ***(Carol Cleveland).*** **12**

MAN (MICHAEL) Are you the marriage guidance counsellor?

COUNSELLOR Yes. Good morning.

MAN Good morning, sir.

COUNSELLOR (*stares at the wife, fascinated*) And good morning to you madam. (*pause, he shrugs himself out of it, says to man...*) Name?

MAN Mr and Mrs Arthur Pewtey, Pewtey.

COUNSELLOR (*writes without looking down; he is staring at the wife*) And what is the name of your ravishing wife? (*holds up hand*) Wait. Don't tell me—it's something to do with moonlight—it goes with her eyes—it's soft and gentle, warm and yielding, deeply lyrical and yet tender and frightened like a tiny white rabbit.

MAN It's Deirdre.

COUNSELLOR Deirdre. **13** What a beautiful name. What a beautiful, beautiful name. (*leans across and lightly brushes his hand across the wife's cheek*) And what seems to be the trouble with your marriage Mr Pewtey?

MAN Well, it all started about five years ago when we started going on holiday to Brighton together. Deirdre, that's my wife, has always been a jolly good companion to me and I never particularly anticipated any marital strife—indeed the very idea of consulting a professional marital adviser has always been of the greatest repugnance to me, although far be it from me to impugn the nature of your trade or profession.

There is no E-sharp, of course—well, there is: it's called F. Now the joke's on Arthur (aka everyman, aka us).

Carol Cleveland, former Miss California Navy, was raised in Philadelphia but moved back to London in 1960 to attend the Royal Academy of the Dramatic Art, the place where all the great British actors were trained. Called "the female Python" by some, and "Carol Cleavage" by the actual Pythons, she appears in exactly two-thirds of MPFC episodes (30 of 45).

Deidre is in some ways the sonic equivalent of the name Arthur in British life.

The counsellor and wife are not listening, fascinated by each other.

COUNSELLOR (*realizing Pewtey has stopped*) Do go on.

MAN Well, as I say, we've always been good friends, sharing the interests, the gardening and so on, the model aeroplanes, the sixpenny bottle for the holiday money, and indeed twice a month settling down in the evenings doing the accounts, something which, er, Deirdre, Deirdre that's my wife, er, particularly looked forward to on account of her feet. (*the counsellor has his face fantastically close to the wife's, as close as they could get without kissing*) I should probably have said at the outset that I'm noted for having something of a sense of humour, although I have kept myself very much to myself over the last two years notwithstanding, as it were, and it's only as comparatively recently as recently that I began to realize—well, er, perhaps realize is not the correct word, er, imagine, imagine, that I was not the only thing in her life.

COUNSELLOR (*who is practically in a clinch with her*) You suspected your wife?

MAN Well yes—at first, frankly, yes. (*the counsellor points the wife to a screen; she goes behind it*) Her behaviour did seem at the time to me, who after all was there to see, to be a little odd.

COUNSELLOR Odd?

MAN Yes well, I mean to a certain extent yes. I'm not by nature a suspicious person—far from it—though in fact I have something of a reputation as an after-dinner speaker, if you take my meaning...

A piece of his wife's clothing comes over the top of the screen.

COUNSELLOR Yes I certainly do.

The wife's bra and panties come over the screen.

MAN Anyway in the area where I'm known people in fact know me extremely well...

COUNSELLOR (*taking his jacket off*) Oh yes. Would you hold this.

MAN Certainly. Yes. (*helps him off with it; the counsellor continues to undress*) Anyway, as I said, I decided to face up to the facts and stop beating about the bush or I'd never look myself in the bathroom mirror again.

COUNSELLOR (*down to his shorts*) Er, look would you mind running along for ten minutes? Make it half an hour.

MAN No, no, right-ho, fine. Yes I'll wait outside shall I?...(*the counsellor has already gone behind screen*) Yes, well that's p'raps the best thing. Yes. You've certainly put my mind at rest on one or two points, there.

Exits through door. He is stopped by a deep rich southern American voice.

SOUTHERNER (JOHN) Now wait there stranger. A man can run and run for year after year until he realizes that what he's running from...is hisself.
MAN Gosh.
SOUTHERNER A man's got to do what a man's got to do, and there ain't no sense in runnin'. Now you gotta turn, and you gotta fight, and you gotta hold your head up high.
MAN Yes!
SOUTHERNER Now you go back in there my son and be a man. Walk tall. (*he exits*)
MAN Yes, I will. I will. I've been pushed around long enough. This is it. This is your moment Arthur Pewtey—this is it Arthur Pewtey. At last you're a man! (*opens door determinedly*) All right, Deirdre, come out of there.
COUNSELLOR Go away.
MAN Right. Right.

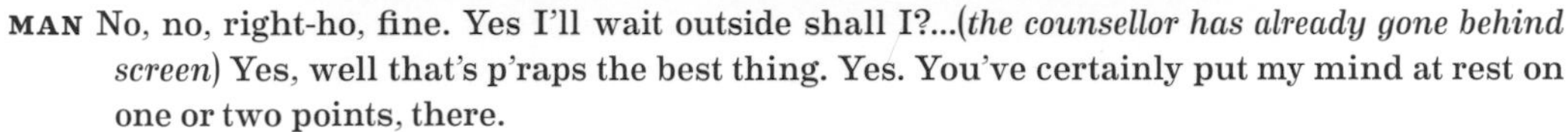

HE IS HIT ON THE HEAD WITH A CHICKEN BY A MAN IN A SUIT OF ARMOUR.

VOICE OVER (JOHN) (*and caption*) 'So much for pathos'

Film Leader: 9...8...7...6...31...6...Jimmy Greaves **14** *...6...3...2...1 And Interviewer: Queen Victoria Film: the texture of the film reproduces as accurately as possible an animated Victorian photograph. Queen Victoria* (TERRY J) *and Gladstone* (GRAHAM) *are walking on the lawn in front of Osborne.*

VOICE OVER (JOHN) These historic pictures of Queen Victoria, taken in 1880 at Osborne show the Queen with Gladstone. This unique film provides a rare glimpse into the private world of a woman who ruled half the earth. The commentary, recorded on the earliest wax cylinders, is spoken by Alfred Lord Tennyson, the Poet Laureate. (*Michael continues with jolly American accent*) Well hello, it's the wacky Queen again! (*the Queen*

Jimmy Greaves was a soccer star in the 1960s, famous for being the best striker of his generation but who notoriously missed out on playing in the World Cup Final of 1966 in London (he had been injured earlier in the tournament, lost his place, and never regained it). In later life he battled alcoholism (and won), and went on to be a TV pundit. He was reaching the end of his soccer career when his name flashed up—for no apparent reason—on MPFC.

repeatedly nudges Gladstone in the ribs and chucks him under the chin) And who's the other fella? It's Willie Gladstone! And when these two way-out wacky characters get together there's fun a-plenty. (*they come up to a gardener with a hosepipe*) And, uh-oh! There's a hosepipe! This means trouble for somebody! (*the Queen takes the hose and kicks the gardener; he falls over*) Uh-oh, Charlie Gardener's fallen for that old trick. The Queen has put him in a *heap* of trouble! (*the Queen turns the hose on Gladstone*) Uh-oh that's one in the eye for Willie! (*the Queen hands Gladstone the hose*) Here, you have a go! (*she goes back to the tap and turns off the water*) Well, doggone it, where's the water? (*Gladstone examines the end of the hose; the water flow returns, spraying him*) Uh-oh, there it is, all over his face! (*she lifts her skirts and runs as he chases her across the lawn; next we see the Queen painting a fence; Gladstone approaches from the other side*) Well, hello, what's Britain's wacky Queen up to now? Well, she's certainly not *sitting* on the fence. She's *painting* it. Surely nothing can go wrong here? Uh-oh, here's the PM coming back for more. (*Gladstone walks into line with the end of the fence; the Queen daubs paint on him*) And he certainly gets it! (*he takes the bucket from her and empties it over her head; she kicks him; he falls through the fence*) Well, that's one way to get the housework done!

Cut to the Queen and Gladstone having tea on the lawn. She pushes a custard pie into his face. As he retaliates the picture freezes; the camera pulls back to reveal that it is a photo on the mantelpiece of a working-class sitting room. Cut to sitting room straight out of D. H. Lawrence. Mum, wiping her hands on her apron is ushering in a young man in a suit. They are a Northern couple.

MUM (TERRY J) Oh dad...look who's come to see us...it's our Ken.
DAD (GRAHAM) (*without looking up*) Aye, and about bloody time if you ask me.
KEN (ERIC) Aren't you pleased to see me, father?
MUM (*squeezing his arm reassuringly*) Of course he's pleased to see you, Ken, he...
DAD All right, woman, all right I've got a tongue in my head—I'll do t'talkin'. (*looks at Ken distastefully*) Aye...I like yer fancy suit. Is that what they're wearing up in Yorkshire now?
KEN It's just an ordinary suit, father...it's all I've got apart from the overalls.

Dad turns away with an expression of scornful disgust.

MUM How are you liking it down the mine, Ken?
KEN Oh it's not too bad, mum...we're using some new tungsten carbide drills for the preliminary coal-face scouring operations.
MUM Oh that sounds nice, dear...
DAD Tungsten carbide drills! What the bloody hell's tungsten carbide drills?
KEN It's something they use in coal-mining, father.
DAD (*mimicking*)

'IT'S SOMETHING THEY USE IN COAL-MINING, FATHER'. YOU'RE ALL BLOODY FANCY TALK SINCE YOU LEFT LONDON.

KEN Oh not that again.
MUM (*to Ken*) He's had a hard day dear...his new play opens at the National Theatre tomorrow.
KEN Oh that's good.
DAD Good! good? What do you know about it? What do you know about getting up at five o'clock in t'morning to fly to Paris...back at the Old Vic for drinks at twelve, sweating the day through press interviews, television interviews and getting back here at ten to wrestle with the problem of a homosexual nymphomaniac drug-addict involved in the ritual murder of a well known Scottish footballer. **That's a full working day, lad, and don't you forget it!** 15

Echoes here of the "Four Yorkshiremen" sketch, perhaps the Pythons' most famous live performance, and often—and erroneously—thought of as a Python original. But the "Four Yorkshiremen" was written by two of the Pythons—Cleese and Chapman—and two other legendary British comic writers, Tim Brooke-Taylor and Marty Feldman. (There is some evidence to suggest that Barry Cryer, another great comic mind, also had a hand in writing the sketch.) The sketch was first performed by the four writers (with Cryer as the waiter) on the 1967 British television comedy series *At Last the 1948 Show.* The comically over-the-top recounting of the harshness of British industrial life has been revisited by Pythons—and other comics—regularly since 1967, and is here aped by Chapman a couple of years later.

MUM Oh, don't shout at the boy, father.

DAD Aye, 'ampstead wasn't good enough for you, was it?...you had to go poncing off to Barnsley, you and yer coal-mining friends. (*spits*)

KEN Coal-mining is a wonderful thing father, but it's something you'll never understand. Just look at you!

MUM Oh Ken! Be careful! You know what he's like after a few novels.

DAD Oh come on lad! Come on, out wi' it! What's wrong wi' me?...yer *tit*!

KEN I'll tell you what's wrong with you. Your head's addled with novels and poems, you come home every evening reeling of Château La Tour...

MUM Oh don't, don't.

KEN And look what you've done to mother! She's worn out with meeting film stars, attending premieres and giving gala luncheons...

DAD There's nowt wrong wi' gala luncheons, lad! I've had more gala luncheons than you've had hot dinners!

MUM Oh please!

DAD Aaaaaaagh! (*clutches hands and sinks to knees*)

MUM Oh no!

KEN What is it?

MUM Oh, it's his writer's cramp!

KEN You never told me about this...

MUM No, we didn't like to, Kenny.

DAD I'm all right! I'm all right, woman. Just get him out of here.

MUM Oh Ken! You'd better go...

KEN All right. I'm going.

DAD After all we've done for him...

KEN (*at the door*) One day you'll realize there's more to life than culture...There's dirt, and smoke, and good honest sweat!

DAD Get out! Get out! Get OUT! You...LABOURER!

Ken goes. Shocked silence. Dad goes to table and takes the cover off the typewriter.

DAD Hey, you know, mother, I think there's a play there,...get t'agent on t'phone.

MUM **Aye I think you're right, Frank, it could express, it could express a vital theme of Our age...** **16**

The "kitchen sink drama" had become a standard trope of 1950s and 1960s theater, TV, and film in Britain. From 1956, when John Osborne's play *Look Back in Anger* first appeared, all the way through to even today, where long-running TV shows like *Coronation Street* (which first aired in 1960) reveal the lives of "working-class" Britons, the genre usually features an "angry young man" bound by the chains of British class, unhappy parents who merely want the status quo, and the terrible job of having to make a living.

DAD Aye.

In the room beneath a man is standing on a chair, banging on the ceiling with a broom.

MAN (MICHAEL) Oh shut up! (*bang bang*) Shut up! (*they stop talking upstairs*) Oh, that's better. (*he climbs down and addresses camera*) And now for something completely different...a man with three buttocks...

MUM AND DAD (*from upstairs*) We've done that!

The man looks up slightly disconcerted.

MAN Oh all right. All right! A man with nine legs.

VOICE OFF (JOHN) He ran away.

MAN

OH...BLOODY HELL! ER...A SCOTSMAN ON A HORSE!

Cut to film of a Scotsman (JOHN) *riding up on a horse. He looks around, puzzled.*
Cut to stock film of Women's Institute audience applauding.
Cut to the man with two noses (GRAHAM)*; he puts a handkerchief to his elbow and we hear the sound of a nose being blown.*
Cut to Women's Institute audience applauding.
Cut to cartoon of a flying sheep.

VOICE OVER (MICHAEL) Harold! Come back, Harold! Harold! Come back, Harold! Oh, blast!

The sheep is shot down by a cannon.
Cut to film of an audience of Indian ladies not applauding.
Caption: 'THE EPILOGUE, A QUESTION OF BELIEF'

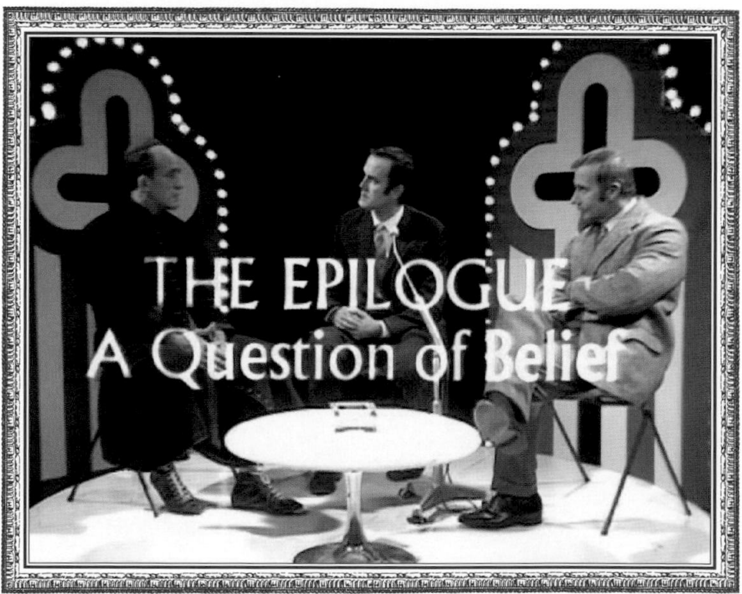

Interview studio: interviewer in the middle. There is a monsignor in full clerical garb with skull-cap, and opposite him a tweed-suited, old Don figure.

INTERVIEWER (JOHN) Good evening, and welcome once again to the Epilogue. On the programme this evening we have Monsignor Edward Gay, visiting Pastoral Emissary of the Somerset Theological College and author of a number of books about belief, the most recent of which is the best seller 'My God'. And opposite him we have Dr Tom Jack: humanist, broadcaster, lecturer and author of the book 'Hello Sailor'.
Tonight, instead of discussing the existence or non-existence of God, they have decided to fight for it. The existence, or non-existence, to be determined by two falls, two submissions, or a knockout. All right boys, let's get to it. Your master of ceremonies for this evening—Mr Arthur Waring.

The participants move into a wrestling ring.

MC (ERIC) **Good evening ladies and gentlemen and welcome to a three-round contest of the Epilogue. 17 Introducing on my right in the blue corner, appearing for Jehovah—the ever popular Monsignor Eddie Gay. 18** (*there are boos from the crowd*) And on my left in the red corner—author of the books 'The Problems of Kierkegaard' and 'Hello Sailor' and visiting Professor of Modern Theological Philosophy at the University of East Anglia—from Wigan—Dr Tom Jack! (*cheers; gong goes for the start*)

Caption: 'ROUND 1'
They are real wrestlers. They throw each other about.

INTERVIEWER (*commentating*) Now Dr Jack's got a flying mare there. A flying mare there, and this is going to be a full body slam. A full body slam, and he's laying it in there, and he's standing back. Well...there we are leaving the Epilogue for the moment, we'll be bringing you the result of this discussion later on in the programme.
INTERVIEWER Oh my God! (*pulls out a revolver and shoots something off-screen*)

Animation: We see a cowboy just having been shot. This leads into cartoon film, which includes a carnivorous pram and music from Rodin's statue 'The Kiss'. Then a protest march appears carrying banners. Close in on banners which read: End Discrimination: Mice Is Nice; Ho Ho Ho Traps Must Go; Hands Off Mice: Repeal Anti-Mouse Laws Now; Kidderminster Young Methodists Resent Oppression: A Fair Deal For Mice Men.

17

At one time, BBC programming ended each night with a man of the cloth reading from scripture and then waxing for a few minutes about what it meant: the Epilogue.

18

Edward Gay, Tom Jack, and "Hello sailor" are clichéd British slang greetings by and for homosexuals. The Pythons never miss a chance to nod obliquely— or, here, not so obliquely—to gay themes. They are a tad more oblique in the next sketch about the "mouse problem."

THE EPILOGU
AND NOW
MUSIC

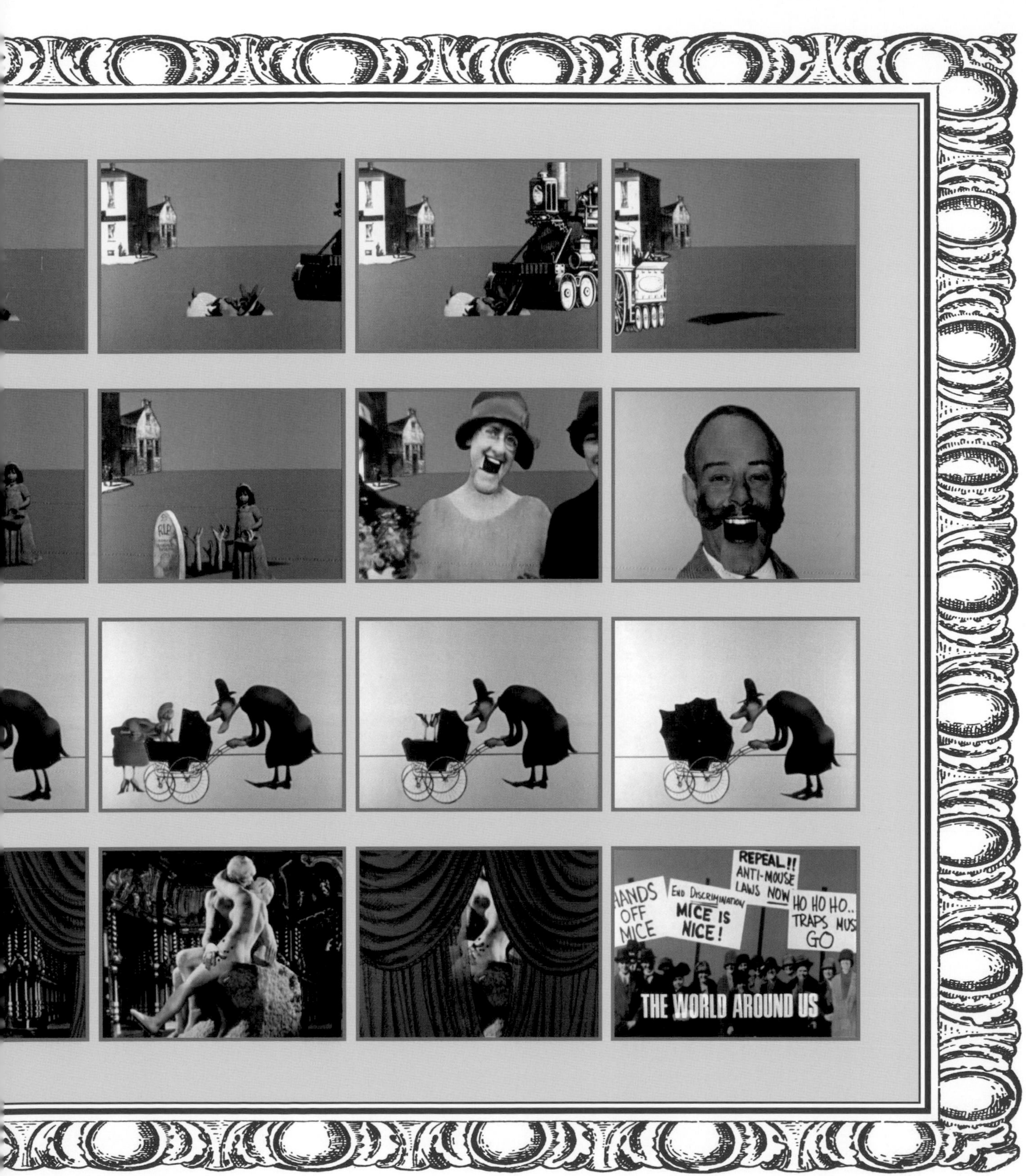

R.I.P.
REPEAL!! ANTI-MOUSE LAWS NOW
ANDS OFF MICE
END DISCRIMINATION MICE IS NICE!
HO HO HO.. TRAPS MUS GO
THE WORLD AROUND US

This sketch was written for Peter Sellers' movie *The Magic Christian*, but he was said by Cleese to have gone off it "when his milkman didn't like it."

Caption: 'THE WORLD AROUND US'
Photo of newspaper headlines: Pop Stars In Mouse Scandal; Peer Faces Rodent Charges. A man in mouse skin running into police station with bag over head. ***Caption: 'THE MOUSE PROBLEM'*** **19**

Cut to a policeman leading a man in mouse costume into a police station. Photo of headline: Mouse Clubs On Increase.
Cut to: photos of neon signs of clubs: Eek Eek Club; The Little White Rodent Room; Caerphilly A Go-Go.
Cut to studio: ordinary grey-suited linkman.

LINKMAN (MICHAEL) Yes. The Mouse Problem. This week 'The World Around Us' looks at the growing social phenomenon of Mice and Men. What makes a man want to be a mouse.

Interviewer, Harold Voice, sitting facing a confessor. The confessor is badly lit and is turned away from camera.

MAN (JOHN) *(very slowly and painfully)* Well it's not a question of wanting to be a mouse...it just sort of happens to you. All of a sudden you realize...that's what you want to be.
INTERVIEWER (TERRY J) And when did you first notice these...shall we say...tendencies?
MAN Well...I was about seventeen and some mates and me went to a party, and, er...we had quite a lot to drink...and then some of the fellows there...started handing cheese around...and well just out of curiosity I tried a bit...and well that was that.
INTERVIEWER And what else did these fellows do?
MAN

WELL SOME OF THEM STARTED DRESSING UP AS MICE A BIT AND THEN WHEN THEY'D GOT THE COSTUMES ON THEY STARTED SQUEAKING.

INTERVIEWER Yes. And was that all?
MAN That was all.
INTERVIEWER And what was your reaction to this?
MAN Well I was shocked. But, er...gradually I came to feel that I was more at ease...with other mice.

Cut to linkman.

LINKMAN A typical case, whom we shall refer to as Mr A, although his real name is this:
VOICE OVER (JOHN) *(and caption)* Arthur Jackson, 32A Milton Avenue, Hounslow, Middlesex.
LINKMAN What is it that attracts someone like Mr A to this way of life? I have with me a consultant psychiatrist.

The camera pulls back to reveal the psychiatrist who places in front of himself a notice saying 'THE AMAZING KARGOL AND JANET'.

KARGOL (GRAHAM) Well, we've just heard a typical case history. I myself have over seven hundred similar histories, all fully documented. Would you care to choose one?

Janet (CAROL), *dressed in showgirl's outfit, enters and offers linkman the case histories fanned out like cards, with one more prominent than the others; he picks it out.*

KARGOL (*without looking*) Mr Arthur Aldridge of Leamington.

LINKMAN Well, that's amazing, amazing. Thank you, Janet. (*chord; Janet postures and exits*) Kargol, speaking as a psychiatrist as opposed to a conjuror...
KARGOL (*disappointed*) Oh...
LINKMAN ...what makes certain men want to be mice?
KARGOL Well, we psychiatrists have found that over 8% of the population will always be mice. I mean, after all, there's something of the mouse in all of us. I mean, how many of us can honestly say that at one time or another he hasn't felt sexually attracted to mice. (*linkman looks puzzled*) I know I have. I mean, most normal adolescents go through a stage of squeaking two or three times a day. Some youngsters on the other hand, are attracted to it by its very illegality. It's like murder—make a thing illegal and it acquires a mystique. (*linkman looks increasingly embarrassed*) Look at arson—I mean, how many of us can honestly say that at one time or another he hasn't set fire to some great public building. I know I have. (*phone on desk rings; the linkman picks it up but does not answer it*) The only way to bring the crime figures down is to reduce the number of offences—get it out in the open—I know I have.
LINKMAN (*replacing phone*) The Amazing Kargol and Janet. What a lot of people don't realize is that a mouse, once accepted, can fulfil a very useful role in society. Indeed there are examples throughout history of famous men now known to have been mice.

Cut to Julius Caesar (GRAHAM) *on beach. He shouts 'Veni Vidi, Vici'. Then he adds a furtive squeak. Napoleon* (TERRY J) *pulls slice of cheese out of jacket and bites into it.*
Cut to linkman.

LINKMAN And, of course, Hillaire Belloc. But what is the attitude...

Cut to man in a Viking helmet.

VIKING (ERIC) ...of the man in the street towards...
LINKMAN ...this growing social problem?

Vox pops films.

WINDOW CLEANER (ERIC) Clamp down on them.
OFF-SCREEN VOICE How?
WINDOW CLEANER I'd strangle them.
STOCKBROKER (JOHN) Well speaking as a member of the Stock Exchange I would suck their brains out with a straw, sell the widows and orphans and go into South American Zinc.
MAN (TERRY J) Yeh I'd, er, stuff sparrows down their throats, er, until the beaks stuck out through the, er, stomach walls.
ACCOUNTANT (GRAHAM) Oh well I'm a chartered accountant, and consequently too boring to be of interest.
VICAR (JOHN) I feel that these poor unfortunate people should be free to live the lives of their own choice.
PORTER (TERRY J) I'd split their nostrils open with a boat hook, I think.
MAN (GRAHAM) Well I mean, they can't help it, can they? But, er, there's nothing you can do about it. So er, I'd kill 'em.

Cut to linkman.

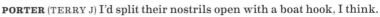

LINKMAN Clearly the British public's view is a hostile one.
VOICE OVER *and Caption* 'Hostile'
LINKMAN But perhaps this is because so little is generally known of these mice men. We have some film now taken of one of the notorious weekend mouse parties, where these disgusting little perverts meet.

Cut to exterior house (night). The blinds are drawn so that only shadows of enormous mice can be seen, holding slices of cheese and squeaking.

LINKMAN'S VOICE Mr A tells us what actually goes on at these mouse parties.

Cut to Mr A.

MR A (JOHN) Well first of all you get shown to your own private hole in the skirting board...then you put the mouse skin on...then you scurry into the main room, and perhaps take a run in the wheel.
LINKMAN The remainder of this film was taken secretly at one of these mouse parties by a BBC cameraman posing as a vole. As usual we apologize for the poor quality of the film.

Very poor quality film, shadowy shapes, the odd mouse glimpsed.

MR A'S VOICE Well, er, then you steal some cheese, Brie or Camembert, or Cheddar or Gouda, if you're on the harder stuff. You might go and see one of the blue cheese films...there's a big clock in the middle of the room, and about 12.50 you climb up it and then...eventually, it strikes one...and you all run down.

Cut to a large matron with apron and carving knife.

LINKMAN'S VOICE And what's that?
MR A'S VOICE That's the farmer's wife.

Cut to linkman at desk.

LINKMAN Perhaps we need to know more of these mice men before we can really judge them. Perhaps not. Anyway, our thirty minutes are up.

Sound of baa-ing. Linkman looks up in air, looks startled, pulls a gun from under the desk and fires in the air.

THE BODY OF A SHEEP FALLS TO THE FLOOR.

LINKMAN Goodnight.

Caption: 'SEX AND VIOLENCE' WAS CONCEIVED, WRITTEN AND PERFORMED BY: ... (CREDITS)'

VOICE OVER (JOHN) And here is the result of the Epilogue: God exists by two falls to a submission.

SEASON 1
EPISODE 3

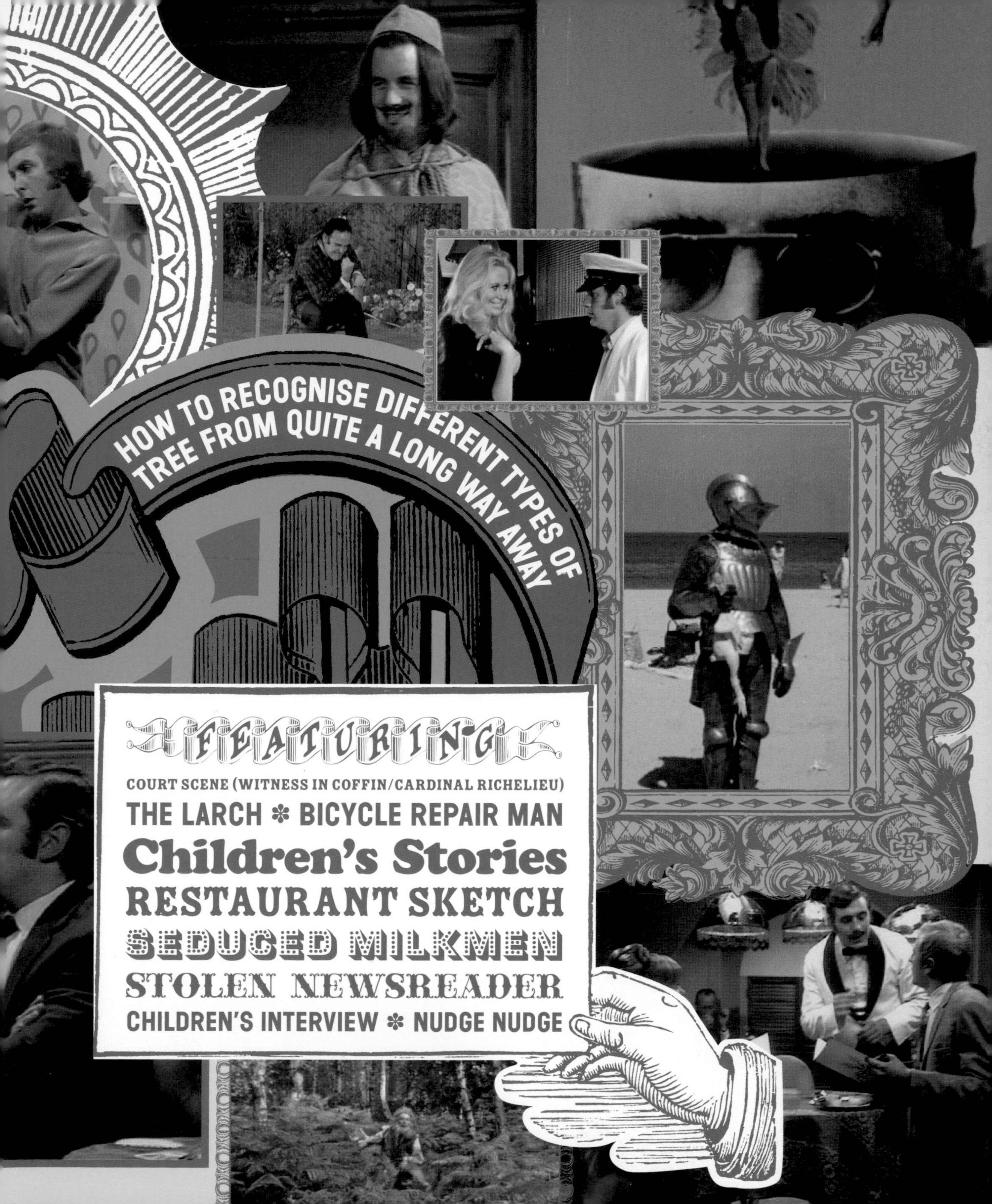
HOW TO RECOGNISE DIFFERENT TYPES OF TREE FROM QUITE A LONG WAY AWAY
FEATURING
COURT SCENE (WITNESS IN COFFIN/CARDINAL RICHELIEU)
THE LARCH ✽ BICYCLE REPAIR MAN
Children's Stories
RESTAURANT SKETCH
SEDUCED MILKMEN
STOLEN NEWSREADER
CHILDREN'S INTERVIEW ✽ NUDGE NUDGE

FIRST AIRED: OCTOBER 19, 1969

Opening as usual—man running through a forest towards camera with clothes tattered; arrives at camera, and says:

IT'S MAN (MICHAEL)

IT'S...

VOICE OVER (JOHN) Monty Python's Flying Circus.

Animation: Titles sequence as usual. And pretty flowers blooming.

This finishes, and a magic lantern slide (done graphically) clicks into vision.

VOICE OVER (JOHN) *(and captions)* **'Episode 12B', 'How to recognize different trees from quite a long way away', 'No. 1', 'The larch'** 1 *(photo of a larch tree)*

VOICE OVER The larch. The larch.

Courtroom: a judge sitting at higher level and a prisoner in the dock.

JUDGE (TERRY J) Mr Larch, you heard the case for the prosecution. Is there anything you wish to say before I pass sentence?

PRISONER (ERIC) Well...I'd just like to say, m'lud, I've got a family...a wife and six kids...and I hope very much you don't have to take away my freedom...because...well, because m'lud freedom is a state much prized within the realm of civilized society. 2 *(slips into Olivier impression)* It is a bond wherewith the savage man may charm the outward hatchments of his soul, and soothe the troubled breast into a magnitude of quiet. It is most precious as a blessed balm, the saviour of princes, the harbinger of happiness, yea, the very stuff and pith of all we hold most dear. What frees the prisoner in his lonely cell, chained within the bondage of rude walls, far from the owl of Thebes? What fires and stirs the woodcock in his springe or wakes the drowsy apricot betides? What goddess doth the storm toss'd mariner offer her most tempestuous prayers to? Freedom! Freedom! Freedom!

For a schoolchild of any particular age in the U.K., this gag on recognizing trees resonates. British education in the 1960s and '70s used such films regularly, and here the thwack of the slide projector only adds to the sense of being stuck in a schoolroom learning stuff no one ever needed.

Though the following sounds as though it's from *Henry IV, Part 2* or *Cymbeline*, it is merely a brilliant parody of Shakespearian language. And though the stage direction indicates that Idle is impersonating Sir Laurence Olivier, the greatest actor of his generation, it is probably fair to say that he's hamming it up ever so slightly.

JUDGE

IT'S ONLY A BLOODY PARKING OFFENCE.

The counsel strides into court.

COUNSEL (JOHN) I'm sorry I'm late m'lud I couldn't find a kosher car park. [3] Er...don't bother to recap m'lud, I'll pick it up as we go along. Call Mrs Fiona Lewis.

A pepperpot walks into the court and gets up into the witness box.

CLERK OF THE COURT Call Mrs Fiona Lewis.

PEPPERPOT (GRAHAM) (*taking bible*) I swear to tell the truth, the whole truth and nothing but the truth, so *anyway*, I said to her, I said, they can't afford that on what he earns, I mean for a start the feathers get up your nose, I ask you, four and six a pound, and him with a wooden leg, I don't know how she puts up with it after all the trouble she's had with her you-know-what, anyway it *was* a white wedding much to everyone's surprise, of course they bought everything on the hire purchase, [4] I think they ought to send them back where they came from, “”I mean you've got to be cruel to be kind so Mrs Harris said, so she said, she said, she said, the dead crab she said, she said. Well, her sister's gone to Rhodesia [5] what with her womb and all, and her youngest, her youngest as thin as a filing cabinet, and the goldfish, the goldfish they've got whooping cough they keep spitting water all over their Bratbys, well, they *do* don't they, I mean you *can't*, can you, I mean they're not even married or anything, they're not even *divorced*, and he's in the KGB if you ask me, he says he's a tree surgeon but I don't like the sound of his liver, all that squeaking and banging every night till the small hours, his mother's been much better since she had her head off, yes she has, I said, don't you talk to me about bladders, I said...

During all this counsel has been trying to ask questions. Eventually he gives up and Mrs Lewis is pushed out of court still talking.

JUDGE Mr Bartlett, I fail to see the relevance of your last witness.

COUNSEL My next witness will explain that if m'ludship will allow. I call the late Arthur Aldridge.

CLERK OF THE COURT The late Arthur Aldridge.

This reference, and the one later in which Cleese uses the phrase "Parking offense, schmarking offense, m'lud," smacks of the anti-Semitic notion that Jews "dominate the legal profession"—not a particularly edifying position, and one that wouldn't pass muster today.

"Hire purchase" is slang for on layaway.

Zimbabwe, Rhodesia—and, in fact, all of Africa—was a major issue in British politics at the time, and on into the later twentieth century. Thousands of Britons had settled in the southern part of the continent especially, and the crumbling British Empire had staked many claims to African land. "The African question," be it former colonies or the struggle to end apartheid, was a major British concern at the time and often led items on newscasts and front pages.

JUDGE The *late* Arthur Aldridge?
COUNSEL Yes m'lud.

A coffin is brought into the court and laid across the witness box.

JUDGE Mr Bartlett, do you think there is any relevance in questioning the deceased?
COUNSEL I beg your pardon m'lud.
JUDGE Well, I mean, your witness *is* dead.
COUNSEL Yes, m'lud. Er, well er, virtually, m'lud.
JUDGE He's not completely dead?
COUNSEL No he's not completely dead m'lud. No. But he's not at all well.
JUDGE But if he's not dead, what's he doing in a coffin?
COUNSEL Oh, it's purely a precaution m'lud—if I may continue? Mr Aldridge, you were a...you *are* a stockbroker of 10 Savundra [6] Close, Wimbledon. (*from the coffin comes a bang*) Mr Aldridge...
JUDGE What was that knock?
COUNSEL It means 'yes' m'lud. One knock for 'yes', and two knocks for 'no'. If I may continue? Mr Aldridge, would it be fair to say that you are not at all well? (*from the coffin comes a bang*) In fact Mr Aldridge, not to put too fine a point on it, would you be prepared to say that you are, as it were, what is generally known as, in a manner of speaking, 'dead'? (*silence; counsel listens*) Mr Aldridge I put it to you that you are dead. (*silence*) Ah ha!

A reference to conman Emil Savundra, a Sri Lankan native who sold phony car insurance policies and was berated on an infamous David Frost show in 1967 (*The Frost Programme*, a show on which Idle was then working). When it was clear Savundra was going to show no contrition—he referred to his victims as "peasants"—Frost went after him, inducing the crowd to cheer, "Well done, Frostie!" Savundra went to jail in March 1968; he died in 1976.

JUDGE Where is all this leading us?
COUNSEL That will become apparent in one moment m'lud. (*walking over to coffin*) Mr Aldridge are you considering the question or are you just dead? (*silence*) I think I'd better take a look m'lud. (*he opens the coffin and looks inside for some time; then he closes the coffin*) No further questions m'lud.
JUDGE What do you mean, no further questions? You can't just dump a dead body in my court and say 'no further questions'. I demand an explanation.
COUNSEL There are no easy answers in this case m'lud.
JUDGE I think you haven't got the slightest idea what this case is about.
COUNSEL M'lud the strange, damnable, almost diabolic threads of this extraordinary tangled web of intrigue will shortly m'lud reveal a plot so fiendish, so infernal, so heinous...
JUDGE Mr Bartlett, your client has already pleaded guilty to the parking offence.
COUNSEL Parking offence, schmarking offence, m'lud. We must leave no stone unturned. Call Cardinal Richelieu.
JUDGE Oh, you're just trying to string this case out. Cardinal Richelieu?
COUNSEL A character witness m'lud.

FANFARE OF TRUMPETS. CARDINAL RICHELIEU ENTERS WITNESS BOX IN BEAUTIFUL ROBES.

CARDINAL (MICHAEL) 'Allo everyone, it's wonderful to be 'ere y'know, I just love your country. London is so beautiful at this time of year.

COUNSEL Er, you are Cardinal Armand du Plessis de Richelieu, First Minister of Louis XIII?

CARDINAL Oui.

COUNSEL Cardinal, would it be fair to say that you not only built up the centralized monarchy in France but also perpetuated the religious schism in Europe?

CARDINAL (*modestly*) That's what they say.

COUNSEL Did you persecute the Huguenots?

CARDINAL Oui.

COUNSEL And did you take even sterner measures against the great Catholic nobles who made common cause with foreign foes in defence of their feudal independence?

CARDINAL I sure did that thing.

COUNSEL Cardinal. Are you acquainted with the defendant, Harold Larch?

CARDINAL Since I was so high (*indicating*).

COUNSEL Speaking as a Cardinal of the Roman Catholic Church, as First Minister of Louis XIII, and as one of the architects of the modern world already—would you say that Harold Larch was a man of good character?

CARDINAL Listen. Harry is a very wonderful human being.

COUNSEL M'lud. In view of the impeccable nature of this character witness may I plead for clemency.

JUDGE Oh but it's only thirty shillings.

Enter Inspector Dim.

DIM (GRAHAM) Not so fast!

PRISONER Why not?

DIM (*momentarily thrown*) None of your smart answers...you think you're so clever. Well, I'm Dim.

Caption: 'DIM OF THE YARD' 7

OMNES (*in unison*) Dim! Consternation! Uproar!

DIM Yes, and I've a few questions I'd like to ask Cardinal so-called Richelieu.

CARDINAL Bonjour Monsieur Dim.

Another reference to Scotland Yard, the headquarters (and a metonym for) the Metropolitan Police.

DIM So-called Cardinal, I put it to you that you died in December 1642.
CARDINAL That is correct.
DIM Ah ha! He fell for my little trap.

Court applauds and the Cardinal looks dismayed.

CARDINAL Curse you Inspector Dim. You are too clever for us naughty people.
DIM And furthermore I suggest that you are none other than Ron Higgins, professional Cardinal Richelieu impersonator.
CARDINAL It's a fair cop.
COUNSEL My life you're clever Dim. He'd certainly taken me in.
DIM It's all in a day's work.
JUDGE With a brilliant mind like yours, Dim, you could be something other than a policeman.
DIM Yes.
JUDGE What?

Piano starts playing introduction.

DIM (*singing*) If I were not in the CID
Something else I'd like to be
If I were not in the CID
A window cleaner, me!
With a rub-a-dub-dub and a scrub-a-dub-dub
And a rub-a-dub all day long
With a rub-a-dub-dub and a scrub-a-dub-dub
I'd sing this merry song!

He mimes window cleaning movements and the rest of the court enthusiastically mimes and sings the chorus again with him. When the chorus verse ends the counsel enthusiastically takes over but this time the court all sit and watch him as though he has gone completely mad.

COUNSEL If I were not before the bar
Something else I'd like to be
If I were not a barr-is-ter
An engine driver me!
With a chuffchuffchuff etc.

He makes engine miming movements. As before. After a few seconds he sees that the rest of the court are staring at him in amazement and he loses momentum rapidly, almost as rapidly as he loses confidence and dignity. At last he subsides. Our knight in armour walks up to the counsel and hits him with the traditional raw chicken. 8

VOICE OVER (JOHN) *(and caption)* 'No. 1', 'The Larch'

Photo of larch tree.

VOICE OVER The larch. The larch.
VOICE OVER *(and caption)* 'and now...No. 1...The Larch...and now...'

Superman film: shot from below of Superman (MICHAEL) *striding along against the sky.*

COMMENTATOR (JOHN) (*American accent*) This man is no ordinary man. This is Mr F. G. Superman. To all appearances no different from any other law-abiding citizen.

Pull back to reveal he is in a modern street full of Supermen walking along shopping, waiting at bus queues etc. F. G. Superman gets onto a bus. The bus is full of Supermen, most of them with shopping baskets on their knees. F. G. Superman finds a seat...during the commentary the camera slowly tracks in on his face.

The man inside the armor is Terry Gilliam.

COMMENTATOR

BUT MR F. G. SUPERMAN HAS A SECRET IDENTITY WHEN TROUBLE STRIKES AT ANY TIME AT ANY PLACE HE IS READY TO BECOME BICYCLE REPAIR MAN!

The camera is by now in very tight close-up. A country lane. A Superman rides into shot on a bicycle, whistling innocently. Suddenly he veers off to one side and crashes down into a ditch. Cut to a launderette. Pan along a row of Supermen, one or two of whom are poring over magazines such as: 'The Adventures of an Insurance Broker', 'Income Tax Comics' and 'The Grocer'. Suddenly the door flies open and a youngish Superboy bursts in dramatically.

SUPERBOY (*dramatically*) Hey, there's a bicycle broken! Up the road. (*he points dramatically*)

General consternation.

BICYCLE REPAIR MAN (MICHAEL) Mmmmmm. Thinks—this sounds like a job for Bicycle Repair Man...but how to change without revealing my secret identity?

Close-up F. G. Superman. He narrows his eyes.

FIRST SUPERMAN (JOHN) (*heavily*) If only Bicycle Repair Man were here!
F. G. SUPERMAN (*heavily*) Yes. Wait! I think I know where I can find him—look over *there*!

F. G. Superman points out of window; they turn and look obediently. F. G. Superman whips overalls out of case and puts them on. Caption: 'FLASH!' Fantastically speeded-up for this. His overalls have 'Bicycle Repair Man' written across the chest. He completes the transformation with a pair of little round specs and a bag of tools. He makes for the door and all the Supermen turn and raise their hands in amazement.

SUPERMEN Bicycle Repair Man! But...how?!

Cut to three Supermen digging the road up. One suddenly looks up.

FIRST SUPERMAN Oh look—is it a Stockbroker?
SECOND SUPERMAN (GRAHAM) Is it a Quantity Surveyor?
THIRD SUPERMAN (TERRY J) Is it a Church Warden? 9
ALL No! It's BICYCLE REPAIR MAN!

These three "professions" are shorthand for the dullest, safest jobs in British society. A church warden assisted the vicar in the upkeep of the parish—and his wife invariably attended Women's Institute meetings, if she didn't run the darned thing.

Country road. Superman is standing over the mangled bits looking at it and scratching his head. Bicycle Repair Man speeds up to him. Superman stands back in surprise, with arms raised.

SUPERMAN (TERRY J) My! BICYCLE REPAIR MAN! Thank goodness you've come! (*he points stiltedly*) Look!

Bicycle Repair Man pushes him to one side and kneels beside the broken bicycle. Speeded up: he mends the bike with spanners etc. Graphics. Captions: 'CLINK!', 'SCREW!', 'BEND!', 'INFLATE!', 'ALTER SADDLE!' A little group of Supermen has gathered to watch him work. As he does so they point in amazement.

SECOND SUPERMAN Why! He's mending it with his own hands.
FIRST SUPERMAN See! How he uses a spanner to tighten that nut!

Cut to see Bicycle Repair Man presenting the Superman with a glittering drop-handlebarred bike.

SUPERMAN (*taking bike*) Oh...Oh! Bicycle Repair Man! How can I ever repay you!

BICYCLE REPAIR MAN Oh, you don't need to guv, it's all right, it's all in a day's work for...Bicycle Repair Man! (*he shuffles away*)

SUPERMEN Our hero! (shot of Bicycle Repair Man shuffling, speeded up, into sunset)

COMMENTATOR (JOHN) Yes! Wherever bicycles are broken, or menaced by International Communism, Bicycle Repair Man is ready!

Cut to commentator in garden with earphones on, and in front of microphone, which is on a garden table.

COMMENTATOR Ready to smash the communists, wipe them up, and shove them off the face of the earth...(*his voice rises hysterically*) Mash that dirty red scum, kick 'em in the teeth where it hurts. (*commentator rises from his canvas chair, and flails about wildly, waving script, kicking over table, knocking down sunshade*) Kill! Kill! Kill! The filthy bastard commies, I hate 'em! I hate 'em! Aaargh! Aaargh!

WIFE (off-screen) Norman! Tea's ready.

He immediately looks frightened, and goes docile.

COMMENTATOR (*calmly*) Coming dear! 10

He gathers up his script, picks up chair, and walks out of frame. Pause, then the man in the suit of armour crosses frame after him.

Animation: Five seconds of Gilliam animation. To gentle children's programme music, we see bunnies jumping up and down.

Here we surely see the precursor to Cleese's character Basil Fawlty from *Fawlty Towers*, Cleese's classic comedy. Fawlty was a man whose passions could run at full tilt only to be lanced into passivity by a word from a controlling wife.

Cut to children's storyteller in studio.

STORYTELLER (ERIC) *(sitting with large children's book, at desk)* Hello, Children, hello. Here is this morning's story. Are you ready? Then we'll begin. *(opens book; reads)* 'One day Ricky the magic Pixie went to visit Daisy Bumble in her tumbledown cottage. He found her in the bedroom. Roughly he grabbed her heavy shoulders pulling her down on to the bed and ripping off her...' *(reads silently, turns over page quickly, smiles)* 'Old Nick the Sea Captain was a rough tough jolly sort of fellow. He loved the life of the sea and he loved to hang out down by the pier where the men dressed as ladies...' *(reads on silently; a stick enters vision and pokes him; he starts and turns over)* 'Rumpletweezer ran the Dinky Tinky shop in the foot of the magic oak tree by the wobbly dum dum bush in the shade of the magic glade down in Dingly Dell. Here he sold contraceptives and...discipline?...naked?...*(without looking up, reads a bit; then, incredulously to himself)* With a *melon*!?

Animation: A hippo squashes the bunnies...and other things happen. Cut to a seaside beach. By a notice, 'Donkey Rides', run two men carrying a donkey. The compère addresses the camera.

COMPÈRE (MICHAEL) Hello again, now here's a little sketch by two boys from London town. They've been writing for three years and they've called this little number—here it is, it's called—Restaurant sketch.

11

As with Cleese's character at the end of the "Bicycle Repair Man" sketch, the restaurant sketch feels like an early version of *Fawlty Towers*. Jones seems to be auditioning for the part of Manuel (played later with great acclaim by Andrew Sachs), and the growing farce of the sketch feels like many of the restaurant scenes in *Towers*.

Film clip of Women's Institute applauding. A couple are seated at a table in a restaurant. **11**

LADY (CAROL) It's nice here, isn't it?

MAN (GRAHAM) Oh, very good restaurant, three stars you know.

LADY Really?

MAN Mmm...

WAITER (TERRY J) Good evening, sir! Good evening, madam! And may I say what a pleasure it is to see you here again, sir!

MAN Oh thank you. Well there you are dear. Have a look there, anything you like. The boeuf en croute is fantastic.

WAITER Oh if I may suggest, sir...the pheasant à la reine, the sauce is one of the chef's most famous creations.

MAN Em...that sounds good. Anyway just have a look...take your time. Oh, er by the way—got a bit of a dirty fork, could you...er...get me another one?

WAITER I beg your pardon.

MAN Oh it's nothing...er, I've got a fork a little bit dirty. Could you get me another one? Thank you.

WAITER Oh...sir, I do apologize.

MAN Oh, no need to apologize, it doesn't worry me.

WAITER Oh no, no, no, I do apologize. I will fetch the Head Waiter immediatement.

MAN Oh, there's no need to do that!

WAITER Oh, no no...I'm sure the Head Waiter, he will want to apologize to you himself. I will fetch him at once.

LADY Well, you certainly get good service here.

MAN They really look after you...yes.

HEAD WAITER (MICHAEL) Excuse me monsieur and madame. (*examines the fork*) It's filthy, Gaston...find out who washed this up, and give them their cards immediately. 12

MAN Oh, no, no.

HEAD WAITER Better still, we can't afford to take any chances, sack the entire washing-up staff.

MAN No, look I don't want to make any trouble.

HEAD WAITER Oh, no please, no trouble. It's quite right that you should point these kind of things out. Gaston, tell the manager what has happened immediately! (*waiter runs off*)

MAN Oh, no I don't want to cause any fuss.

HEAD WAITER Please, it's no fuss. I quite simply wish to ensure that nothing interferes with your complete enjoyment of the meal.

MAN Oh I'm sure it won't, it was only a dirty fork.

HEAD WAITER I know. And I'm sorry, bitterly sorry, but I know that...no apologies I can make can alter the fact that in our restaurant you have been given a dirty, filthy, smelly piece of cutlery...

MAN It wasn't smelly.

HEAD WAITER It was smelly, and obscene and disgusting and I hate it, I hate it...nasty, grubby, dirty, mingy, scrubby little fork. Oh...oh...oh...(*runs off in a passion as the manager comes to the table*)

MANAGER (ERIC) Good evening, sir, good evening, madam. I am the manager. I've only just heard... may I sit down?

MAN Yes, of course.

MANAGER

I WANT TO APOLOGIZE, HUMBLY, DEEPLY, AND SINCERELY ABOUT THE FORK.

MAN Oh please, it's only a tiny bit...I couldn't see it.

MANAGER Ah you're good kind fine people, for saying that, but *I* can see it...to me it's like a mountain, a vast bowl of pus.

MAN It's not as bad as that.

MANAGER It gets me *here*. I can't give you any excuses for it—there *are* no excuses. I've been meaning to spend more time in the restaurant recently, but I haven't been too well...(*emotionally*) things aren't going very well back there. The poor cook's son has been put away again, and poor old Mrs Dalrymple who does the washing up can hardly move her poor fingers, and then there's Gilberto's war wound—but they're good people, and they're kind people, and together we were beginning to get over this dark patch...there was light at the end of the tunnel...now this...now this...

MAN Can I get you some water?

"Give them their cards" is British slang for "fire them."

MANAGER (*in tears*) It's the end of the road!!

The cook comes in; he is very big and carries a meat cleaver.

COOK (JOHN) (shouting) You bastards! You vicious, heartless bastards! Look what you've done to him! He's worked his fingers to the bone to make this place what it is, and you come in with your petty feeble quibbling and you grind him into the dirt, this fine, honourable man, whose boots you are not worthy to kiss. Oh...it makes me mad...mad! (*slams cleaver into the table*)

The Head Waiter comes in and tries to restrain him.

HEAD WAITER Easy, Mungo, easy...Mungo...(*clutches his head in agony*) the war wound!...the wound...the wound...

MANAGER This is the end! The end! Aaargh!! (*stabs himself with the fork*)

COOK They've destroyed him! He's dead!! They killed him!!! (*goes completely mad*)

HEAD WAITER (trying to restrain him) Mungo...never kill a customer. (in pain) Oh...the wound! The wound! (he and the cook fight furiously and fall over the table)

Caption: 'AND NOW THE PUNCH-LINE'

MAN Lucky we didn't say anything about the dirty knife...

Boos of disgust from off-screen. Cut back to seaside.

COMPÈRE Well, there we are then, that was the restaurant sketch, a nice little number...a bit vicious in parts, but a lot of fun...but how about that punch-line, eh?...Oh you know what I mean—oh...oh...really.

The man from the sketch borrows the knight's chicken and hits commentator with it. A cartoon advertising 'Interesting Lives' leads to film of milkman (MICHAEL) *delivering milk to a suburban house. As he puts the milk down, the front door opens and a seductively dressed young lady* (CAROL) *beckons him inside.* **13** *Glancing round furtively he follows her into the house and up the stairs. She leads him to the bedroom door, opens it, and ushers him inside, closing the door behind him. Inside, he is bewildered to see several elderly milkmen, who have obviously been there for a very long time. Cut to a BBC News studio, where the newsreader is just putting the phone down. At his desk is an old-fashioned microphone with 'BBC' on it. He is in evening dress, and speaks in beautifully modulated tones.*

NEWSREADER (JOHN) Good evening, here is the 6 o'clock News read by Michael Queen. **14** It's been a quiet day over most of the country as people went back to work after the warmest July weekend for nearly a year. The only high spot of the weekend was the meeting between officials of the NEDC and the ODCN in Bradford today.

This is not Carol Cleveland in the actual sketch, but a different actress named Thelma Taylor. The sketch stems from the comic possibilities when an entire country's stay-at-home women received a visit from a milkman every day. It doesn't take much to put two and two together, and by the time this sketch aired, the cliché of the "lonely housewife" making hay with a milkman was thoroughly established.

The Pythons never miss an opportunity for a nod to homosexuality, especially when the character is one in a position of authority (a priest, a news broadcaster, etc.).

At this point, axes split open the studio door behind him. Through the hole, men with stockings over their heads leap in firing guns in all directions. The newsreader continues, unperturbed. Cut to marauders pushing the newsreader, still at his desk down a passage in the BBC. They rush him out of the TV Centre and onto the back of a lorry.

NEWSREADER *(continuing)* In Geneva, officials of the Central Clearing Banks met with Herr Voleschtadt of Poland to discuss non-returnable loans on a twelve-year trust basis for the construction of a new zinc-treating works in the Omsk area of Krakow, near the Bulestan border. The Board of Trade has ratified a Trade Agreement with the Soviet Union for the sale of 600 low gear electric sewing machines. The President of the Board of Trade said he hoped this would mark a new area of expansion in world trade and a new spirit of co-operation between East and West. There has been a substantial drop in Gold Reserves during the last twelve months. This follows a statement by the Treasury to the effect that the balance of imports situation had not changed dramatically over the same period. *(cut to lorry hurtling through London with newsreader still reading news on the back (facing backwards); cut to lorry hurtling through country lane and flashing past camera)* Still no news of the National Savings book lost by Mr Charles Griffiths of Porthcawl during a field expedition to the Nature Reserves of Swansea last July. Mr Griffiths' wife said that her husband was refusing to talk to the Press until the Savings Certificate had been found. *(cut to gang hoisting him on to the back of an open lorry, still in desk etc.)* In Cornwall the death has been announced today of the former Minister without Portfolio, General Sir Hugh Marksby-Smith. Sir Hugh was vice-president of the Rotarian movement. *(a long shot of a jetty; we see the gangsters pushing the newsreader still on his desk along the jetty; they reach the end and push him over into the sea)* In the match between Glamorgan and Yorkshire, the Yorkshire bowler Nicholson took eight wickets for three runs. Glamorgan were all out for the thirty-six and therefore won the match by an innings and seven runs. Weather for tomorrow will be cloudy with occasional outbreaks of rain. And that is the end of the news. **15**

FX splash. Gurgle gurgle.

VOICE OVER (JOHN) *(and captions)* 'And Now', 'No. 1', The Larch'

Picture of larch tree.

VOICE OVER The larch.
VOICE OVER *(and captions)* 'And Now', 'No. 3', 'The Larch', 'And Now...'

Picture of chestnut tree.

VOICE OVER The horse chestnut.

Film clip of cheering crowd. Then to interviewer bending down to speak to children in playground.

INTERVIEWER (JOHN) Eric...do you think you could recognize a larch tree?
ERIC (ERIC) *(after much deliberation)* Don't know.

Roars of delighted pre-recorded laughter from unseen audience.

INTERVIEWER What's your name?
MICHAEL (MICHAEL) Michael.

Though much of the foregoing news report is gobbledygook (and makes fun of the smallness and local nature of much of British news), the sly joke about cricket is a particularly nice touch. Nicholson's "eight wickets for three runs" is the close equivalent of a perfect game in baseball, and should Glamorgan have been "all out for thirty-six," they could not have won the match "by an innings"—they would, in fact, have lost the game, not won it. Space here does not permit a thorough reasoning for this, as cricket is like nuclear physics—only much, much harder to understand.

Laughter.

INTERVIEWER Michael, do you think you know what a larch tree looks like?
MICHAEL *(bursting into tears)* I want to go home.

Shrieks from unseen audience.

TERRY (TERRY J) Bottom!

More shrieks.

INTERVIEWER Are there any other trees that any of you think you could recognize from quite a long way away?
TERRY I...want...to see a sketch of Eric's please...
INTERVIEWER What?
TERRY I want to see a sketch of Eric's. Nudge Nudge.
INTERVIEWER A sketch?
TERRY Eric's written...
ERIC I written a sketch.
MICHAEL Nudge nudge, Eric's written...
ERIC Nudge nudge...nudge...nudge.

NUDGE NUDGE...NUDGE...NUDGE.

Two men in a pub.

NORMAN (ERIC) Is your wife a...goer...eh? Know what I mean? Know what I mean? Nudge nudge. Nudge nudge. Know what I mean? Say no more...know what I mean?
HIM (TERRY J) I beg your pardon?
NORMAN Your wife...does she, er, does she 'go'—eh? eh? eh? Know what I mean, know what I mean? Nudge nudge. Say no more.
HIM She sometimes goes, yes.
NORMAN I bet she does. I bet she does. I bet she does. Know what I mean? Nudge nudge.
HIM I'm sorry, I don't quite follow you.
NORMAN Follow me! *Follow* me! I like that. That's good. A nod's as good as a wink to a blind bat, eh? 16 *(elbow gesture; rubs it)*
HIM Are you trying to sell something?
NORMAN Selling, selling. Very good. *Very* good. (*hand tilting quickly*) Oh, wicked. Wicked. You're wicked. Eh? Know what I mean? Know what I mean? Nudge nudge. Know what I mean? Nudge nudge. Nudge nudge. (*leaning over to him, making rye gesture; speaks slowly*) Say...no... more. (*leans back as if having imparted a great secret*)
HIM But...
NORMAN *(stops him with finger which he lays alongside nose; gives slight tap)* Your wife is she, eh...is she a sport? Eh?
HIM She *likes* sport, yes.

Now a classic Python sketch, the "Nudge, Nudge" sketch spawned a phrase still used by many in Britain: "A nudge is as good as a wink to a blind bat." Idle also turned this sketch into a series of advertisements for a chocolate bar called Breakaway.

NORMAN I bet she does. I bet she does.

HIM She's very fond of cricket, as a matter of fact.

NORMAN *(leans across, looking away)* Who isn't, eh? Know what I mean? Likes games, likes games. Knew she would. Knew she would! Knew she would! She's been around, eh? Been around?

HIM She's travelled. She's from Purley. 17

NORMAN Oh...oh. Say no more, say no more. Say no more—*Purley*, say no more. Purley, eh. Know what I mean, know what I mean? Say no more.

HIM *(about to speak; can't think of anything to say)*

NORMAN *(leers, grinning)* Your wife interested in er...*(waggles head, leans across)* photographs, eh? Know what I mean? Photographs, 'he asked him knowingly'.

HIM Photography.

NORMAN Yes. Nudge nudge. Snap snap. Grin, grin, wink, wink, say no more.

HIM Holiday snaps?

NORMAN Could be, could be taken on holiday. Could be yes—swimming costumes. Know what I mean? Candid photography. Know what I mean, nudge nudge.

HIM No, no we don't have a camera.

NORMAN Oh. Still. *(slaps hands lightly twice)* Woah! Eh? Wo-oah! Eh?

HIM Look, are you insinuating something?

NORMAN Oh...no...no...Yes.

HIM Well?

NORMAN Well. I mean. Er, I mean. You're a man of the world, aren't you...I mean, er, you've er... you've been there haven't you...I mean you've been around...eh?

HIM What do you mean?

NORMAN Well I mean like you've er...you've done it...I mean like, you know...you've...er...you've slept...with a lady.

HIM Yes.

NORMAN What's it like?

Enormous artificial laugh on sound track. Closing film, starting with referee blowing whistle and then into 'It's' man running away from camera.

Roller caption: '"HOW TO RECOGNISE DIFFERENT TYPES OF TREES FROM QUITE A LONG WAY AWAY" WAS CONCEIVED, WRITTEN AND PERFORMED BY...(CREDITS)'

VOICE OVER The larch.

The ultimate suburban section of London, Purley, in the south of the city, is home to the wonderfully named "Purley Cross gyratory," an intersection of roads seemingly heading in all directions.

SEASON 1
EPISODE 4

OWL-STRETCHING TIME
FEATURING
OWL-STRETCHING TIME: SONG ('AND DID THOSE FEET')
ART GALLERY * ART CRITIC
IT'S A MAN'S LIFE IN THE MODERN ARMY
UNDRESSING IN PUBLIC
Self-Defence
SECRET SERVICE DENTISTS

FIRST AIRED: OCTOBER 26, 1969

A cliff. Suddenly the 'It's' man is thrown over it, landing on the shale beach beneath. Painfully he crawls towards the camera and announces:

IT'S MAN (MICHAEL)

IT'S...

Animated titles.

VOICE OVER (JOHN) *(and caption)* 'MONTY PYTHON'S FLYING CIRCUS' 'EPISODE ARTHUR', 1 'PART 7', 'TEETH'

Singer in spangly jacket sitting on high stool with guitar.

SINGER (ERIC) *(singing to the tune of 'Jerusalem')* 2 And did those teeth in ancient time...

Caption: 'LIVE FROM THE CARDIFF ROOMS, LIBYA'

SINGER ...walk upon England's mountains green. *(he stops playing)* Good evening and welcome ladies and gentlemen. At this time we'd like to up the tempo a little, change the mood. We've got a number requested by Pip, Pauline, Nigel, Tarquin, and old Spotty—Tarquin's mother—a little number specially written for the pubescence of ex-King Zog of Albania, and it's entitled 'Art Gallery'. Hope you like it.

This episode revolves around the idea of "a man's life."

The great unofficial hymn of Britain, "Jerusalem"—Hubert Parry's setting to music of William Blake's excoriating poem about industrial life in the U.K. The song is featured most notably at the end of the famous Proms classical music festival, also known as the Henry Wood Promenade Concerts, held each year in London during an eight-week summer season. The *Last Night of the Proms* is aired live on the BBC and is an outpouring of British pride—including "Rule Britannia" and "God Save the Queen"—and always features a lusty and often very moving sing-along of "Jerusalem." The Pythons here turn it into an accompaniment for Idle's wonderfully sleazy character Singer, but the song would have been well-known by viewers because of its inclusion in the Proms.

Interior of art gallery. Two figures enter. They are both middle-aged working mothers. Each holds the hand of an unseen infant who is beneath the range of the camera.

JANET (JOHN) 'Allo, Marge!

MARGE (GRAHAM) Oh hello, Janet, how are you love, fancy seeing you.

JANET How's little Ralph?

MARGE Oh, don't ask me! He's been nothing but trouble all morning. Stop it Ralph! (*she slaps at unseen infant*) Stop it!

JANET Same as my Kevin.

MARGE Really?

JANET Nothing but trouble...leave it alone! He's just been in the Florentine Room and smeared tomato ketchup all over Raphael's Baby Jesus. (*shouting off sharply*) Put that Baroque masterpiece down!

MARGE Well, we've just come from the Courtauld 3 and Ralph smashed every exhibit but one in the Danish Contemporary Sculpture Exhibition.

JANET Just like my Kevin. Show him an exhibition of early eighteenth-century Dresden Pottery and he goes berserk. No, I said no, and I meant no! (*smacks unseen infant again*) This morning we were viewing the early Flemish Masters of the Renaissance and Mannerist Schools, when he gets out his black aerosol and squirts Vermeer's Lady At A Window!

MARGE Still, it's not as bad as spitting, is it?

JANET (*firmly*) No, well Kevin knows (*slaps the infant*) that if he spits at a painting I'll never take him to an exhibition again.

MARGE Ralph used to spit—he could hit a Van Gogh at thirty yards. But he knows now it's wrong—don't you Ralph? (*she looks down*) Ralph! Stop it! Stop it! Stop chewing that Turner! You are...(*she disappears from shot*) You are a naughty, naughty, vicious little boy. (*smack; she comes back into shot holding a copy of Turner's Fighting Temeraire in a lovely gilt frame but all tattered*) Oh, look at that! The Fighting Temeraire—ruined! What shall I do?

JANET (*taking control*) Now don't do a thing with it love, just put it in the bin over there.

MARGE Really?

JANET Yes take my word for it, Marge. Kevin's eaten most of the early nineteenth-century British landscape artists, and I've learnt not to worry. As a matter of fact, I feel a bit peckish myself. (*she breaks a bit off the Turner*) Yes...

Marge also tastes a bit.

The Courtauld Gallery is part of the Courtauld Institute of Art, a college of the University of London and an important art history school. The gallery itself is filled with Impressionist masterpieces, including Manet's *A Bar at the Folies-Bergère* (above) and van Gogh's *Self-Portrait with Bandaged Ear* (below).

MARGE I never used to like Turner.

JANET (*swallowing*)

NO I DON'T KNOW MUCH ABOUT ART, BUT I KNOW WHAT I LIKE. 4

Cut to a book-lined study. At a desk in front of the shelves sits an art critic with a mouthful of Utrillo. Superimposed caption: 'AN ART CRITIC'

CRITIC (MICHAEL) (*taking out stringy bits as he speaks*) Mmmm...(*munches*) Well I think Utrillo's brushwork is fantastic...(*stifles burp*) But he doesn't always agree with me (*belches*) Not after a Rubens, anyway...all those cherries...ooohh...(*suddenly looks down*) Urgh! I've got Vermeer all down my shirt...

WIFE (KATYA) (*bringing in a water jug and glass on a tray and laying it on his desk*) Watteau, dear?

CRITIC What a terrible joke.

WIFE But it's my only line. 5

CRITIC (*rising vehemently*) All right! All right! But you didn't *have* to say it! You could have kept quiet for a change!

Wife cries.

CRITIC Oh, that's typical. Talk talk talk. Natter natter natter!

Cut back to singer.

SINGER (*singing*) Bring me my arrows of desire...Bring me my spear oh clouds unfold...Bring me my chariot of fire.

A sexy girl (KATYA WYETH) 6 *enters and starts fondling him.*

Caption: 'IT'S A MAN'S LIFE IN THE CARDIFF ROOMS, LIBYA'
Cut to colonel: army recruitment posters on wall behind him.

COLONEL (GRAHAM) Right, cut to me. As Officer Commanding the Regular Army's Advertising Division, I object, in the strongest possible terms, to this obvious reference to our own

This sketch is another case of the Pythons mixing high culture—the art of the wonderful London gallery scene—with something lower. But really, it's all a clever lead-up to the punch line, where the standard "I know what I like" is taken literally.

The women in Python don't say much.

Malcolm McDowell has said of Katya Wyeth, "If British TV needed a sexy woman for a quick scene during the late 1960s and early '70s, she was the girl." Little more can be said about Katya, a German-born actress who was most famously featured in the "Ascot fantasy" scene at the end of Stanley Kubrick's *A Clockwork Orange*.

slogan 'It's a dog's life...(*correcting himself rapidly*) a *man's* life in the modern army' and I warn this programme that any recurrence of this sloppy long-haired civilian plagiarism will be dealt with most severely. Right, now on the command 'cut', the camera will cut to camera two, all right, director...(*cut to a man sitting at desk*) Wait for it! (*cut back to colonel*) Camera cut. (*cut to man; he has a Viking helmet on*)

MAN (TERRY G) This is my only line. (*catcalls*) (*defensively*) Well, it's my only line.

Cut to a gentleman (TERRY J) *in striped blazer, boater and cricket flannels walking down to beach clutching towel and bathing trunks. He puts his towel on a breakwater next to another towel and starts to change.* 7

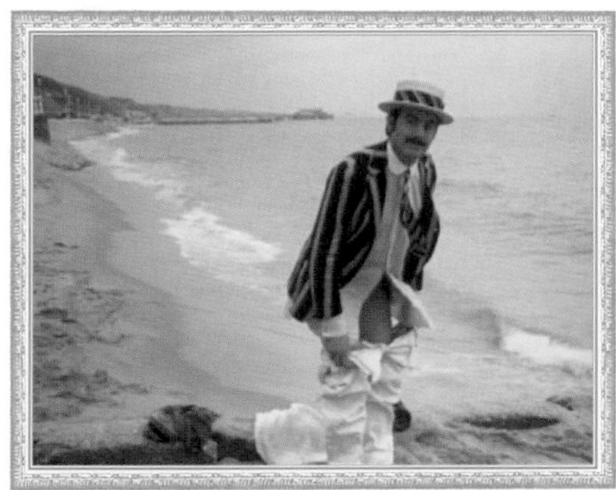

He suddenly looks up and we see everyone on the beach has turned to watch him—not with any disapproval—just a blank English stare. 8

He grabs his towel off the breakwater and starts to take his trousers off under that. Girl in a bikini has been sitting on other side of the breakwater, stands up looking for her towel. She sees that the man is using it and she whisks it off him leaving him clutching his half-down trousers. Shot of everyone staring at him again. He pulls them up and makes for a beach hut...embarrassed. He goes into beach hut. Inside he is about to take his trousers off, when he becomes aware of a pair of feet which come up to the back of the beach hut—there is a 6-inch gap along bottom—and stop as if someone were peering through the crack.

The man looks slightly outraged and pulls his trousers up, goes outside and edges cautiously round to the back of the beach hut. There he finds a man (MICHAEL) *bending close to the side of the beach hut with his hand to his face. Terry kicks him hard in the seat of the pants. The man turns in obvious surprise, to reveal he was merely trying to light his cigarette out of the wind. The changing gentleman backs away with embarrassed apologies. We cut to the front of the beach hut to see gentleman backing round at the same time as a large matronly woman marches into the hut...the man follows her in. He is promptly thrown out on his ear. In desperation he looks around. On the promenade he suddenly sees an ice-cream van. He walks up to it, looks around, then nips behind to start changing. At the same time a policeman* (GRAHAM) *strolls up to the ice-cream van and tells it to move on.*

It's hard to watch this Jones scene without thinking it's simply a dream sequence, one of those stressful dreams where one is constantly exposed. Playing on the British "seaside postcard" humor that is still so beloved, as well as many of the conventions of the silent-movie era, Jones's cartoonish attempts to change into his bathing suit seem to drag on and on and on.

8

Note the large crowd in the background on the Bournemouth Pier watching the filming of this scene. Given the long history of pantomime and seaside postcards, they would presumably have been at home with Jones's "trouser" issues.

The van drives off, exposing the gentleman clutching his trousers round his ankles. Close-up policeman's reaction. The man hurriedly pulls trousers up as policeman approaches him pulling out note book. Still covered in confusion he runs away from the policeman. In long shot we see him approach the commissionaire of the Royale Palace De Luxe Hotel. He whispers to the commissionaire, indicates by mime that he wants to take his trousers off. The commissionaire reads to the gesture. The man nods. The commissionaire starts to take his trousers off. Man backs away once more in confusion—he has been misunderstood. Back on the beach again. He hides behind a pile of deckchairs. At that moment a beach party of jolly trippers arrive and each takes one. The deckchair pile rapidly disappears leaving the gentleman once again exposed. He dashes behind the deckchair attendant's hut which is next to him. Enter two workmen who dismantle it. Desperate by now he goes onto the pier. He goes into the amusement arcade, looking around furtively. Nips behind a 'what the butler saw' machine. Woman comes and puts penny in and starts to look, beckons over husband; he comes, looks in the machine, sees the man changing his trousers. They chase him off. Still pursued he nips into door. Finds himself in blackness. Relieved—at last he has found somewhere to change. He relaxes and starts to take his trousers off. Suddenly hears music and applause...curtains swishes back to reveal he is on stage of the pier pavilion. The audience applauds.

RESIGNED TO HIS FATE, HE BREAKS INTO STRIPTEASE ROUTINE.

VOICE OVER *(and caption)* 'It's a man's life taking your clothes off in public'

Cut to colonel.

COLONEL Quiet. Quiet. Now wait a minute. I have already warned this programme about infringing the Army copyright of our slogan 'It's a pig's life...*man's* life in the modern army'. And I'm warning you if it happens again, I shall come down on this programme like a ton of bricks...right. Carry on sergeant major.

A gym. Four men waiting there, with an ex-RSM type.

RSM (JOHN) Sir! Good evening class.
ALL Good evening.
RSM Where's all the others then?
ALL They're not here.
RSM I can see that. What's the matter with them?
ALL Don't know.
FIRST MAN (GRAHAM) Perhaps they've got flu.
RSM Flu...flu? They've eaten too much fresh fruit. (*does terrible twitch or tic*) Right. Now, self-defence. Tonight I shall be carrying on from where I got to last week, when I was showing you how to defend yourself against anyone who attacks you armed with a piece of fresh fruit.
ALL (*disappointed*) Oh.
SECOND MAN (MICHAEL) You promised you wouldn't do fruit this week.
RSM What do you mean?
THIRD MAN (TERRY J) We've done fruit for the last nine weeks.
RSM What's wrong with fruit? You think you know it all, eh?
SECOND MAN But couldn't we do something else, for a change?
FOURTH MAN (ERIC) Like someone who attacks you with a pointed stick? 9
RSM (*scornfully*) Pointed sticks! Ho ho ho. We want to learn how to defend ourselves against pointed sticks, do we? Getting all high and mighty, eh? Fresh fruit not good enough for you, eh? Oh well, well, well, I'll tell you something my lad. When you're walking home tonight and some homicidal maniac comes after you with a bunch of loganberries, don't come crying to me. Right...the passion fruit. When your assailant lunges at you with a passion fruit, thus...(*demonstrates*)
ALL We've done the passion fruit.
RSM What?
FIRST MAN We've done the passion fruit.
SECOND MAN We've done oranges, apples, grapefruits.
THIRD MAN Whole and segments.
SECOND MAN Pomegranates, greengages.
FIRST MAN Grapes, passion fruits.
SECOND MAN Lemons.
THIRD MAN Plums.
FIRST MAN Yes, and mangoes in syrup.
RSM How about cherries?
ALL We done them.
RSM Red *and* black?
ALL Yes.
RSM All right then...bananas!
ALL Oh.
RSM We haven't done them have we?
ALL No.
RSM

RIGHT! BANANAS! HOW TO DEFEND YOURSELF AGAINST A MAN ARMED WITH A BANANA.

(*to first man*) Here, you, take this. (*throws him a banana*) Now it's quite simple to defend yourself against the banana fiend. First of all, you force him to drop the banana, next, you eat the banana, thus disarming him. You have now rendered him helpless.
SECOND MAN Supposing he's got a bunch.
RSM Shut up!
FOURTH MAN Supposing he's got a pointed stick.

The "It's" man will be poked with a pointed stick as he lies on the beach at the end of the episode.

RSM Shut up. Right. Now, you, Mr Apricot.
FIRST MAN Harrison.
RSM Harrison, Mr Harrison. Come at me with that banana then. Come on attack me with it. As hard as you like. Come on. (*Harrison moves towards him rather half-heartedly*) No no no. Put something into it for God's sake. Hold it, like that. Scream. Now come on, come on...attack me, come on, come on (*Harrison runs towards him shouting; RSM draws a revolver and fires it, right in Harrison's face; Harrison dies immediately, falling to the ground; RSM puts gun away and walks to banana*) Now...I eat the banana.

He does so; the rest of the class gather round Mr Harrison's body.

ALL You shot him. He's dead...dead. He's completely dead. You've shot him.
RSM (*finishing the banana*) I have now eaten the banana. The deceased Mr Apricot is now disarmed.
SECOND MAN You shot him. You shot him dead.
RSM Well he was attacking me with a banana.
THIRD MAN Well, you told him to.
RSM

LOOK, I'M ONLY DOING ME JOB. I HAVE TO SHOW YOU HOW TO DEFEND YOURSELF AGAINST FRESH FRUIT.

FOURTH MAN And pointed sticks.
RSM Shut up!
SECOND MAN Supposing someone came at you with a banana and you haven't got a gun?
RSM Run for it.
THIRD MAN You could stand and scream for help.
RSM You try that with a pineapple down your windpipe.
THIRD MAN A pineapple?
RSM (*jumping with fear*) Where? Where?
THIRD MAN Nowhere. I was just saying pineapple.
RSM Oh blimey. I thought my number was on that one.
THIRD MAN (*amazed*) What, on the pineapple?
RSM (*jumping*) Where? Where?
THIRD MAN No I was just repeating it.
RSM Oh. Oh! Right. That's the banana then. Next...the raspberry. (*pulling one out of pocket*) Harmless looking thing, isn't it. Now you, Mr Tinned Peach...
THIRD MAN Thompson.
RSM Mr Thompson, come at me with that raspberry then. Come on, be as vicious as you like with it.
THIRD MAN No.
RSM Why not?
THIRD MAN You'll shoot me.
RSM I won't.
THIRD MAN You shot Mr Harrison.
RSM That was self-defence. Come on. I promise I won't shoot you.
FOURTH MAN You promised you'd tell us about pointed sticks.
RSM Shut up. Now. Brandish that...brandish that raspberry. Come on, be as vicious as you like with it. Come on.
THIRD MAN No. Throw the gun away.
RSM I haven't got a gun.
THIRD MAN Oh yes, you have.
RSM I haven't.

THIRD MAN You have. You shot Mr Harrison with it.
RSM Oh...*that* gun.
THIRD MAN Throw it away.
RSM All right. (*throws it away*) How to defend yourself against a raspberry, without a gun.
THIRD MAN You were going to shoot me!
RSM I wasn't.
THIRD MAN You were.
RSM Wasn't. Come on, come on you worm...you miserable little man. Come at me then...come on, do your worst, you worm. (*third man runs at him; the RSM steps back and pulls a lever; a sixteen-ton weight falls upon the man*) If anyone ever attacks you with a raspberry, simply pull the lever...and a sixteen-ton weight will drop on his head. 10 I learnt that in Malaya.

SECOND MAN Suppose you haven't got a sixteen-ton weight.
RSM Well that's planning, isn't it. Forethought.
SECOND MAN How many sixteen-ton weights are there?
RSM Look...look, smarty pants, the sixteen-ton weight is just one way, just one way of dealing with the raspberry killer. There are millions of others.
SECOND MAN Like what?
RSM Shoot him.
SECOND MAN Well, supposing you haven't got a gun or a sixteen-ton weight.
RSM All right clever dick, all right clever dick. You two, come at me with raspberries, there you are, a whole basket each. Come on, come at me with them, then.
SECOND MAN No gun?
RSM No.
SECOND MAN No sixteen-ton weight?
RSM No.
FOURTH MAN No pointed stick?
RSM Shut up.
SECOND MAN No rocks up in the ceiling?
RSM No.
SECOND MAN You won't kill us.
RSM I won't kill you.
SECOND MAN Promise.
RSM I promise I won't kill you. Now are you going to attack me?
SECOND AND FOURTH MEN All right.
RSM Right, now don't rush me this time. I'm going to turn me back. So you can stalk me...right? Come up as quietly as you can, right close up behind me, then, in with the raspberries, right? Start moving (*they start to creep up on him*)
Now...the first thing to do when you're being stalked by an ugly mob with raspberries, is to...release the tiger. (*he presses button and a tiger flashes past him in direction of second and fourth men; cries are heard from them as well as roaring*)

10

The influence of cartoons on Python was never more pronounced than here. One expects Jones to be flattened but able to regain human shape once the sixteen-ton weight is lifted.

The great advantage of the tiger in unarmed combat is that it not only eats the raspberry-laden foe, but also the raspberries. The tiger, however, does not relish the peach. The peach assailant should be attacked with a crocodile. (*he turns to look at the scene*) Right...I know you're there—lurking under the floorboards with your damsons and your prunes... now, the rest of you—I know you're hiding behind the wall bars with your quinces. Well I'm ready for you. I've wired myself up to two hundred tons of gelignite and if any of you so much as tries anything we'll all go up together. I've warned you...I warned you, right! That's it.

Big explosion. Animation: Ends with cut-out animation of sedan chair; matching shot links into next film.

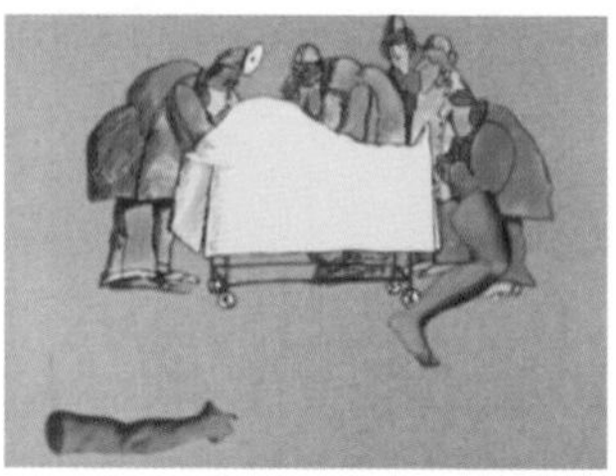

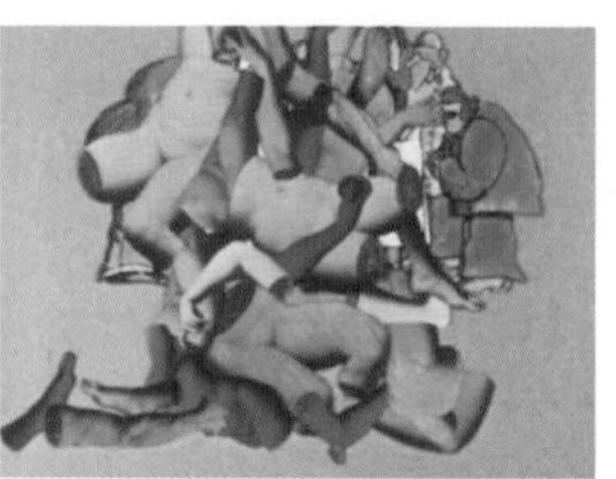

Cut to deserted beach. Sedan chair arrives at deserted beach. Flunkey opens the door. Gentleman gets out in his eighteenth-century finery. The flunkeys help him to change into a lace-trimmed striped bathing costume.

He then gets back into the sedan chair and they all trot off into the sea. Cut to singer in bed with woman. Singer reclining with guitar, strumming.

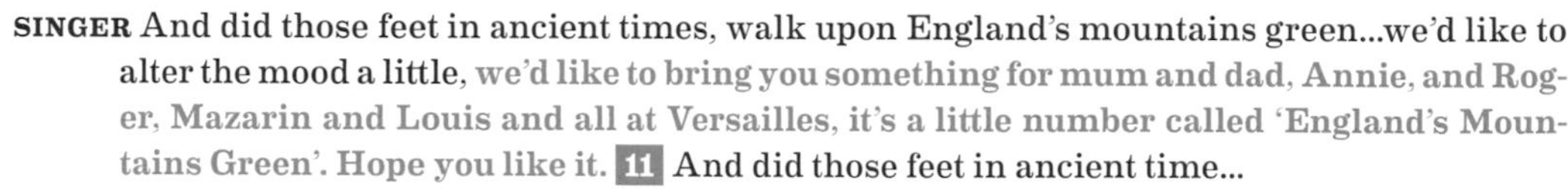

SINGER And did those feet in ancient times, walk upon England's mountains green...we'd like to alter the mood a little, we'd like to bring you something for mum and dad, Annie, and Roger, Mazarin and Louis and all at Versailles, it's a little number called 'England's Mountains Green'. Hope you like it. 11 And did those feet in ancient time...

11

Idle is mimicking the standard "request spot" on British radio, where folks write in pleading for a song to be played, usually for family members.

Cut to a man standing in the countryside.

MAN (JOHN) (*rustic accent*) Yes, you know it's a man's life in England's Mountain Green.

The colonel enters briskly.

COLONEL (GRAHAM) Right I heard that, I heard that, I'm going to stop this sketch now, and if there's any more of this, I'm going to stop the whole programme. I thought it was supposed to be about teeth anyway. Why don't you do something about teeth—go on. (*walks off*)

MAN What about my rustic monologue?...I'm not sleeping with that producer again.

Cut to film of various sporting activities, wild west stage coach etc.

VOICE OVER (JOHN) (*with big music, excited*) Excitement, drama, action, violence, fresh fruit. Passion. Thrills. Spills. Romance. Adventure, all the things you can read about in a book.

Cut to bookshop. A bookseller is standing behind the counter. Arthur enters the shot and goes up to the counter. The bookseller jumps and looks around furtively.

BOOKSELLER (JOHN) Er...oh!
ARTHUR (ERIC) Good morning, I'd like to buy a book please.
BOOKSELLER Oh, well I'm afraid we don't have any. (*trying to hide them*)
ARTHUR I'm sorry?
BOOKSELLER We don't have any books. We're fresh out of them. Good morning. [12]

ARTHUR Well what are all these?
BOOKSELLER All what? Oh! All these, ah ah ha ha. You're referring to these...books.
ARTHUR Yes.
BOOKSELLER They're um...they're all sold. Good morning.
ARTHUR What *all* of them?
BOOKSELLER Every single man Jack of them. Not a single one of them in an unsold state. Good morning.
ARTHUR Who to?
BOOKSELLER What?
ARTHUR Who are they sold to?
BOOKSELLER Oh...various...good Lord is that the time? Oh my goodness I must close for lunch.
ARTHUR It's only half past ten.
BOOKSELLER Ah yes, well I feel rather puckish...very peckish actually, I don't expect I'll open again today. I think I'll have a really good feed. I say! Look at that lovely bookshop just across the road there, they've got a much better selection than we've got, probably at ridiculously low prices...just across the road there. (*he has the door open*) Good morning.
ARTHUR But I was told to come here.
BOOKSELLER (*bundling him back in*) Well. Well, I see. Er...(*very carefully*) I hear the gooseberries are doing well this year...and so are the mangoes. (*winks*)
ARTHUR I'm sorry?
BOOKSELLER Er...oh...I was just saying...thinking of the weather...I hear the gooseberries are doing well this year...and so are the mangoes. [13]
ARTHUR Mine aren't.
BOOKSELLER (*nodding keenly with anticipation*) Go on...
ARTHUR What?
BOOKSELLER Go on—mine aren't...but...
ARTHUR What?
BOOKSELLER Aren't you going to say something about 'mine aren't but the Big Cheese gets his at low tide tonight'?

An idea that later would be made famous by the "Cheese Shop" sketch, in which the one thing the cheese shop doesn't stock is cheese.

This reference back to the previous sketch about being attacked by fresh fruit is a prime example of the fluid yet linked nature of the Pythons' writing. Ideas and references are continually played on throughout a show, or across a series of shows.

ARTHUR No.
BOOKSELLER Oh, ah, good morning. (*starts to bundle him out then stops*) Wait. Who sent you?
ARTHUR The little old lady in the sweet shop.
BOOKSELLER She didn't have a duelling scar just here...and a hook?
ARTHUR No.
BOOKSELLER Of course not, I was thinking of somebody else. Good morning.
ARTHUR Wait a minute, there's something going on here.
BOOKSELLER (*spinning round*) What, where? You didn't see anything did you?
ARTHUR No, but I think there's something going on here.
BOOKSELLER No no, well there's nothing going on here at all (*shouts off*) and he didn't see anything. Good morning.
ARTHUR (*coming back into shop*) There *is* something going on.
BOOKSELLER Look there is nothing going on. Please believe me, there is abso...(*a hand comes into view behind Arthur's back; bookseller frantically waves at it to disappear; it does so*)...lutely nothing going on. Is there anything going on?

A man appears, fleetingly: he is Van der Berg (Dick Vosburgh). 14

Dick Vosburgh was born in Elizabeth, New Jersey, but is yet another graduate of the Royal Academy of Dramatic Art, London's premier acting school. His long career included plays, lyrics, and comedy bits for hundreds of comedians. The great British humorist Barry Cryer called Vosburgh, who died in 2007 at the age of 77, the funniest man he ever knew.

VAN DER BERG No there's nothing going on. (*disappears*)
BOOKSELLER See there's nothing going on.
ARTHUR Who was that?
BOOKSELLER That was my aunt, look what was this book you wanted then? Quickly! Quickly!
ARTHUR Oh, well, I'd like to buy a copy of an 'Illustrated History of False Teeth'.
BOOKSELLER My God you've got guts.
ARTHUR What?
BOOKSELLER (*pulling gun*) Just how much do you know?
ARTHUR What about?
BOOKSELLER Are you from the British Dental Association?
ARTHUR No I'm a tobacconist.
BOOKSELLER Get away from that door.
ARTHUR I'll just go over the other...
BOOKSELLER Stay where you are. You'd never leave this bookshop alive.
ARTHUR Why not?
BOOKSELLER You know too much, my dental friend.
ARTHUR I don't know anything.
BOOKSELLER Come clean. You're a dentist aren't you.
ARTHUR No, I'm a tobacconist.
BOOKSELLER A tobacconist who just happens to be buying a book on...teeth?
ARTHUR Yes.
BOOKSELLER Ha ha ha ha...

Lafarge enters room with gun. He is swarthy, French, dressed all in black and menacing.

LAFARGE (MICHAEL) Drop that gun, Stapleton.
BOOKSELLER Lafarge! (*he drops the gun*)
ARTHUR There is something going on.
BOOKSELLER No there isn't.
LAFARGE OK Stapleton, this is it. Where's Mahoney hidden the fillings?
BOOKSELLER What fillings?
LAFARGE You know which fillings, Stapleton. Upper right two and four, lower right three and two lower left one. Come on. (*he threatens with the gun*) Remember what happened to Nigel.
ARTHUR What happened to Nigel?
BOOKSELLER Orthodontic Jake gave him a gelignite mouth wash.

ARTHUR I knew there was something going on.
BOOKSELLER Well there isn't.
LAFARGE Come on Stapleton. The fillings!
BOOKSELLER They're at 22 Wimpole Street. 15
LAFARGE Don't play games with me! (*pokes bookseller in rye with the gun*)
BOOKSELLER Oh, oh, 22a Wimpole Street.
LAFARGE That's better.
BOOKSELLER But you'll need an appointment. 16
LAFARGE OK (*shouting out of shop*) Brian! Make with the appointment baby. No gas.

Van der Berg appears with machine gun and a nurse (Katya), he is basically dressed as a dentist. But with many rings, chains, wristlets, cravats, buckled shoes and an ear-ring.

VAN DER BERG Not so fast Lafarge!
LAFARGE Van der Berg!
VAN DER BERG Yes. Now drop the roscoe.
ARTHUR There *is* something going on.
BOOKSELLER No there isn't.
VAN DER BERG Get the guns.

The nurse runs forward, picks up the gun and puts it on steel surgeon's tray and covers it with a white cloth, returning it to Van der Berg.

ARTHUR Who's that?
BOOKSELLER That's Van der Berg. He's on our side.
VAN DER BERG All right, get up against the wall Lafarge, and you too Stapleton.
BOOKSELLER Me?
VAN DER BERG Yes, you!
BOOKSELLER You dirty double-crossing rat.
ARTHUR (*going with bookseller*) What's happened?
BOOKSELLER He's two-timed me.
ARTHUR Bad luck.
VAN DER BERG All right...where are the fillings? Answer me, where are they?
ARTHUR This is quite exciting.

Wimpole Street, in the heart of the London area of Marylebone, is considered the center of private medical practice in England's capital. It was also the street from which Elizabeth Barrett eloped with Robert Browning, leading to the play *The Barretts of Wimpole Street*. The British Medical Association's actual headquarters are at 64 Wimpole Street.

A lovely grace note on the maddening rule by which even an angry spy would need an appointment with a doctor.

What Ever Happened to Baby Jane is a 1962 thriller starring Bette Davis and Joan Crawford that featured a dead parakeet served for lunch.

BRIAN ENTERS CARRYING A BAZOOKA. BRIAN IS DRESSED IN OPERATING-THEATRE CLOTHES, GOWN, CAP AND MASK, WITH RUBBER GLOVES AND WHITE WELLINGTONS.

BRIAN (TERRY J) Not so fast.
ALL Brian!
ARTHUR Ooh, what's that?
THE OTHERS It's a bazooka.
BRIAN All right. Get against the wall Van der Berg...and you nurse. And the first one to try anything moves to a practice six feet underground...this is an anti-tank gun...and it's loaded...and you've just got five seconds to tell me... whatever happened to Baby Jane? 17
ALL What?

18

A viewer can get a kind of concussion watching "Big Cheese" now, given that the more recent Dr. Evil character in the *Austin Powers* franchise is clearly based on Chapman's character here. Both even carry a sinister white animal on their laps—in Chapman's case, a rabbit, which seems many times funnier than plain old Mr. Bigglesworth, Dr. Evil's cat.

BRIAN Oh...I'm sorry...my mind was wandering...I've had a terrible day...I really have...you've got five seconds to tell me...I've forgotten. I've forgotten.

BOOKSELLER The five seconds haven't started yet have they?

VAN DER BERG Only we don't know the question.

ARTHUR Was it about Vogler?

BRIAN No, no...no...you've got five seconds to tell me...

VAN DER BERG About Nigel?

BRIAN No.

LAFARGE Bronski?

BRIAN No. No.

ARTHUR The fillings!

BRIAN Oh yes, the fillings, of course. How stupid of me. Right, you've got five seconds...(*clears throat*) Where are the fillings? Five, four, three, two, one, zero! (*there is a long pause, Brian has forgotten to fire the bazooka but he can't put his finger on what has gone wrong*) Zero! (*looks at gun*) Oh! I've forgotten to fire it. Sorry. Silly day. Very well. (*quite rapidly*) Five, four, three, two, one.

A panel slides back and the Big Cheese appears in sight seated in a dentist's chair. The Big Cheese is in dentist's gear, wears evil magnifying-type glasses and strokes a rabbit lying on his lap.

BIG CHEESE (GRAHAM) Drop the bazooka Brian. [18]

ALL

THE BIG CHEESE!

Brian drops the bazooka.

A nod to a line from the famous 1861 British novel *East Lynne* by Ellen Wood. Or not: the line "Gone! And never called me mother!" doesn't actually appear in the novel, only in later stage adaptations (and even then it's sometimes "Dead! Dead! And never called me mother!").

BIG CHEESE I'm glad you could all come to my little...party. And Flopsy's glad too, aren't you, Flopsy? (*he holds rabbit up as it does not reply*) Aren't you Flopsy? (*no reply again so he pulls a big revolver out and fires at rabbit from point-blank range*) That'll teach you to play hard to get. There, poor Flopsy's dead. And never called me mother. [19] And soon...you will all be dead, dead, dead, dead. (*the crowd start to hiss him*) And because I'm so evil you'll all die the slow way...under the drill.

ARTHUR It's one o'clock.

BIG CHEESE So it is. Lunch break, everyone back here at two.

They all happily relax and walk off. Arthur surreptitiously goes to telephone and, making sure nobody is looking, calls.

ARTHUR Hallo...give me the British Dental Association...and fast.

Cut to Arthur dressed normally as dentist leaning over patient in chair. He looks up to camera.

ARTHUR You see, I knew there was something going on. Of course, the Big Cheese made two mistakes. First of all he didn't recognize me: Lemming, Arthur Lemming, Special Investigator, British Dental Association, and second...(*to patient*) spit...by the time I got back from lunch I had every dental surgeon in SW 1 waiting for them all in the broom cupboard. Funny isn't it, how naughty dentists always make that one fatal mistake. Bye for now... keep your teeth clean.

Cut to photo of Arthur Lemming. Superimposed caption: 'LEMMING OF THE BDA' Over this we hear a song which Graham knows the tune of.

SONG (*Voice over pre-recorded*) Lemming, Lemming...Lemming of the BDA...Lemming, Lemming...Lemming of the BD...Lemming of the BD...BD, BDA.

VOICE OVER (ERIC) *(and caption)* 'IT'S A MAN'S LIFE IN THE BRITISH DENTAL ASSOCIATION'

COLONEL (*knocking the photo aside*) Right! No, I warned you, no, I warned you about the slogan, right. That's the end. Stop the programme! Stop it.

Cut to referee blowing whistle. The 'It's' man, lying on beach, is poked with a stick from off-screen. He gets up and limps away.

Caption: '"OWL-STRETCHING TIME" WAS CONCEIVED, WRITTEN AND PERFORMED BY...(CREDITS)

End titles finish as the 'It's' man reaches the top of the cliff and disappears. As soon as he has disappeared we hear:

VOICE OVER (GRAHAM) Ah! Got you my lad. Still acting eh? Over you go!

'It's' man reappears hurled back over cliff.

SEA SON 1
EPISODE 5

MAN'S CRISIS OF IDENTITY IN THE LATTER HALF OF THE TWENTIETH CENTURY
FEATURING
CONFUSE-A-CAT ✻ THE SMUGGLER
A DUCK, A CAT AND A LIZARD (DISCUSSION)
Vox Pops on Smuggling
POLICE RAID ✻ LETTERS AND VOX POPS
EROTIC FILM
SILLY JOB INTERVIEW
CAREERS ADVISORY BOARD
BURGLAR/ENCYCLOPAEDIA SALESMAN

FIRST AIRED: NOVEMBER 16, 1969

A river. The 'It's' man rows towards the camera and announces:

IT'S MAN (MICHAEL)

IT'S...

VOICE OVER (JOHN) *(and caption)* Monty Python's Flying Circus

Title animation.

Superimposed caption: 'SUBURBAN LOUNGE NEAR ESHER' 1

A town southwest of London, and the perfect suburban setting for a farce in which a sad cat needs to be distracted out of its ennui.

Elderly couple, Mr A and Mrs B are staring through french windows at a cat that is sitting in the middle of their lawn motionless and facing away from them.

A car is heard drawing up.

MR A (MICHAEL) Oh good, that'll be the vet, dear.
MRS B (TERRY J) I'd better go and let him in.

Mrs B goes out and comes back into the room with the vet.

MRS B *(stage whisper)* It's the vet, dear.
MR A Oh very glad indeed you could come round, sir.
VET (GRAHAM) Not at all. Now what seems to be the problem? You can tell me—I'm a vet, you know.
MRS B See! Tell him, dear.
MR A Well...

MRS B It's our cat. He doesn't do anything. He just sits out there on the lawn. 2

VET Is he...dead?

MR A Oh, no!

VET (*to camera, dramatically*) Thank God for that. For one ghastly moment I thought I was...too late. If only more people would call in the nick of time.

MRS B He just sits there, all day and every day.

MR A And at night.

MRS B Sh! Almost motionless. We have to take his food out to him.

MR A And his milk.

MRS B Sh! He doesn't do anything. He just sits there.

VET Are you at your wits' end?

MRS B Definitely, yes.

VET Hm. I see. Well I think I may be able to help you. You see...(*he goes over to armchair, puts on spectacles, sits, crosses legs and puts finger tips together*)...your cat is suffering from what we vets haven't found a word for. His condition is typified by total physical inertia, absence of interest in its ambience—what we vets call environment—failure to respond to the conventional external stimuli—a ball of string, a nice juicy mouse, a bird. To be blunt, your cat is in a rut. It's the old stockbroker syndrome, the suburban fin de siècle ennui, angst, weltschmerz, call it what you will. 3

MRS B Moping. 4

VET In a way, in a way...hum...moping, I must remember that. Now, what's to be done? Tell me sir, have you confused your cat recently?

MR A Well we...

MRS B Sh! No.

VET Yes...well I think I can definitely say that your cat badly needs to be confused.

MRS B What?

MR A Sh! What?

VET Confused. To shake it out of its state of complacency. I'm afraid I'm not personally qualified to confuse cats, but I can recommend an extremely good service. Here is their card.

MRS B (*reading card*) Oooh. 'Confuse-a-Cat Limited'.

MR A 'Confuse-a-Cat Limited'.

MRS B Oh.

Cut to large van arriving. On one side of van is a large sign reading 'Confuse-a-Cat Limited: Europe's leading cat-confusing service. By appointment to...' and a crest. Several people get out of the van, dressed in white coats, with peaked caps and insignia. One of them has a sergeant's stripes.

SERGEANT (MICHAEL) Squad! Eyes front! Stand at ease. Cat confusers...shun!

From a following car a general alights.

Chapman claims that he watched a neighbor's cat never move from its position on a manicured lawn. Cleese and Chapman reckoned it was suffering from "complacency," which led to this sketch.

Hardly fin de siècle, given there were still 30 years to go. But these psychoanalytical buzzwords work beautifully when describing the cat, an animal that seems perfectly suited to feelings of *weltschmerz*, or world weariness.

A brilliant shot by Jones—for all the highfalutin psychobabble, the cat merely mopes.

GENERAL (JOHN) Well men, we've got a pretty difficult cat to confuse today so let's get straight on with it. Jolly good. Thank you sergeant.

SERGEANT Confusers attend to the van and fetch out...wait for it...fetch out the funny things. (*the men unload the van*) Move, move, move. One, two, one, two, get those funny things off.

The workmen are completing the erection of a proscenium with curtains in front of the still immobile cat. A and B watch with awe. The arrangements are completed. All stand ready.

SERGEANT Stage ready for confusing, sir!
GENERAL Very good. Carry on, sergeant.
SERGEANT Left turn, double march!
GENERAL Right men, confuse the...cat!

Drum roll and cymbals. The curtains draw back and an amazing show takes place, using various tricks: locked camera, fast motion, jerky motion, jump cuts, some pixilated motion etc. Long John Silver walks to front of stage.

LONG JOHN SILVER My lords, ladies and Gedderbong. 5

A nonsense version of the word "gentlemen" probably.

Long John Silver disappears. A pause. Two boxers appear. They circle each other. On one's head a bowler hat appears, vanishes. On the other's a stove-pipe hat appears. On the first's head a fez. The stove-pipe hat becomes a stetson. The fez becomes a cardinal's hat. The stetson becomes a wimple. Then the cardinal's hat and the wimple vanish. One of the boxers becomes Napoleon and the other boxer is astonished. Napoleon punches the boxer with the hand inside his jacket. The boxer falls, stunned.

Horizontally he shoots off stage. Shot of cat, watching unimpressed. Napoleon does one-legged pixilated dance across stage and off, immediately reappearing on other side of stage doing same dance in same direction. He reaches the other side, but is halted by a traffic policeman. The policeman beckons onto the stage a man in a penguin skin on a pogostick. The penguin gets half way across and then turns into a dustbin. Napoleon hops off stage. Policeman goes to dustbin, opens it and Napoleon gets out. Shot of cat, still unmoved.

A nude man with a towel round his waist gets out of the dustbin. Napoleon points at ground. A chair appears where he points. The nude man gets on to the chair, jumps in the air and vanishes. Then Napoleon points to ground by him and a small cannon appears. Napoleon fires cannon and the policeman disappears. The man with the towel round his waist gets out of the dustbin and is chased off stage by the penguin on the pogostick. A sedan chair is carried on stage by two chefs. The man with the towel gets out and the penguin appears from the dustbin and chases him off.

Napoleon points to sedan chair and it changes into dustbin. Man in towel runs back on to stage and jumps in dustbin. He looks out and the penguin appears from the other dustbin and hits him on the head with a raw chicken. Shot of cat still unimpressed. Napoleon, the man with the towel round his waist, the policeman, a boxer, and a chef suddenly appear standing in a line, and take a bow. They immediately change positions and take another bow. The penguin appears at the end of the line with a puff of smoke. Each one in turn jumps in the air and vanishes. Shot of passive cat.

Cut to Mr A and Mrs B watching with the general.

GENERAL I hope to God it works. Anyway, we shall know any minute now.

After a pause, the cat gets up and walks into the house. Mr A and Mrs B are overcome with joy.

MRS B I can't believe it.
MR A Neither can I. It's just like the old days.
MRS B Then he's cured. Oh thank you, general.
MR A What can we ever do to repay you?

GENERAL No need to, sir. It's all in a day's work for Confuse-a-Cat.

Picture freezes and over still of general's face are superimposed the words 'Confuse-a-Cat Limited'. Dramatic music.
The words start to roll, like ordinary credits but read:

CONFUSE-A-CAT LIMITED
INCORPORATING
AMAZE-A-VOLE LTD
STUN-A-STOAT LTD
PUZZLE-A-PUMA LTD
STARTLE-A-THOMPSON'S GAZELLE LTD
BEWILDEREBEEST INC [6]
DISTRACT-A-BEE

One could argue that this is the real gag here: that the whole sketch leads up to this very nice neologism.

Animation: People's heads appear in frame due to Mr Gilliam's animation on film.

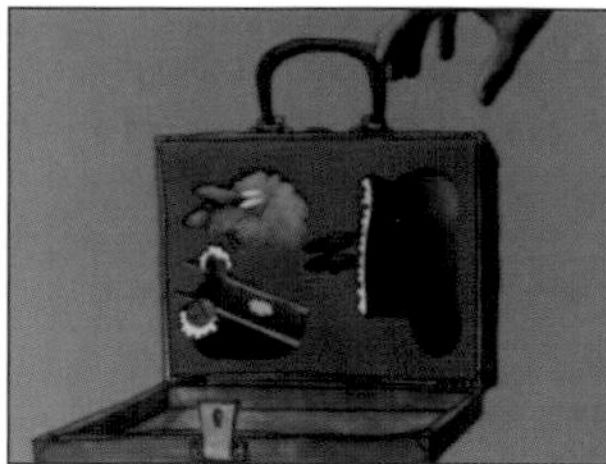

Film animation leads us into customs hall.

OFFICER (JOHN) Have you read this, sir? (*holds up notice*)
MAN (MICHAEL) No! Oh, yes, yes—yes. [7]
OFFICER Anything to declare?
MAN Yes...no! No! No! No! Nothing to declare, no, nothing in my suitcase no...
OFFICER No watches, cameras, radio sets?
MAN Oh yes...four watches...no, no, no. No. One...one watch...No, no. Not even one watch. No, no watches at all. No, no watches at all. No precision watches, no.
OFFICER Which country have you been visiting, sir?
MAN Switzerland...er...no...no...not Switzerland...er...not Switzerland, it began with S but it wasn't Switzerland...oh what could it be? Terribly bad memory for names. What's the name of that country where they don't make watches at all?
OFFICER Spain?
MAN Spain! That's it. Spain, yes, mm.
OFFICER The label says 'Zurich', sir.
MAN Yes well...it *was* Spain then.
OFFICER Zurich's in Switzerland, sir.
MAN Switzerland, yes mm...mm...yes.
OFFICER Switzerland—where they make the watches.
MAN Oh, nice shed you've got here.
OFFICER Have you, er, got any Swiss currency, sir?
MAN No...just the watches...er just my watch, er, my watch on the currency...I've kept a watch of the currency, and I've watched it and I haven't got any.
OFFICER That come out a bit glib didn't it? (*an alarm clock goes off inside his case; the man thumps it, unsuccessfully*) Have you got an alarm clock in there, sir?
MAN No, no, heavens no, no...just vests. (*he thumps the case and the alarm stops*)
OFFICER Sounded a bit like an alarm going off.
MAN Well it can't have been...it must be a vest, er, going off.
OFFICER Going off.

Palin is dressed in the uniform of the British "likely lad" or "wide boy," a man who'll sell you a used watch, no questions asked. The fur-lined jacket is the dead giveaway.

Clocks start ticking and chiming in the case. The man desperately thumps the case.

MAN All right, I confess, I'm a smuggler...This whole case is crammed full of Swiss watches and clocks. I've been purposely trying to deceive Her Majesty's Customs and Excise. I've been a bloody fool.

OFFICER I don't believe you, sir.

MAN

IT'S TRUE. I'M, ER, GUILTY OF SMUGGLING.

OFFICER Don't give me that, sir...you couldn't smuggle a piece of greaseproof paper let alone a case full of watches.

MAN What do you mean! I've smuggled watches before, you know! I've smuggled bombs, cameras, microfilms, aircraft components, you name it—I've smuggled it.

OFFICER Now come along please, you're wasting our time...move along please.

MAN Look! (*he opens his case to reveal it stuffed full of watches and clocks*) Look—look at this.

OFFICER Look, for all I know, sir, you could've bought these in London before you ever went to Switzerland.

MAN What? I wouldn't buy two thousand clocks.

OFFICER People do, now close your case move along please come on. Don't waste our time, we're out to catch the real smugglers. Come on.

MAN (*shouting*) I am a real smuggler. I'm a smuggler! Don't you understand, I'm a smuggler, a lawbreaker...a smuggler. (*he is removed struggling*)

A vicar is next.

VICAR (ERIC) Poor fellow. I think he needs help.

OFFICER Right, cut the wisecracks, vicar. Get to the search room, and strip.

Cut to chairman of discussion group.

CHAIRMAN (TERRY J) Well to discuss the implications of that sketch and to consider the moral problems raised by the law-enforcement methods involved we have a duck, a cat and a lizard. Now first of all I'd like to put this question to you please, lizard. How effective do you consider the legal weapons employed by legal customs officers, nowadays? (*shot of lizard; silence*) Well while you're thinking about that, I'd like to bring the duck in here, and ask her, if possible, to clarify the whole question of currency restrictions, and customs regulations in the world today. (*shot of duck; silence*) Perhaps the cat would rather answer that? (*shot of cat; silence*) No? Lizard? (*shot of lizard again and then back*) No. Well, er, let's ask the man in the street what he thinks.

BEYOND THE FRINGE

The 1960s were an extraordinary time in so much of popular culture, be it pop music, film, art, or literature. Yet some of the greatest leaps forward came in television. Still in its relative infancy, the box in the corner of the living room probably affected more lives than the other forms of mass entertainment. And in the comedy world, a new generation of satirists burst onto the TV scene, especially in the U.K. The changes wrought would utterly affect British culture and politics, culminating at the end of the decade in *Monty Python's Flying Circus*. And the genesis for much of this is found not on television but in the theater.

Beyond the Fringe was a sketch revue helmed by four heavyweights of comedy and the stage: Peter Cook, Dudley Moore, Alan Bennett, and Jonathan Miller. Established at the start of the decade, the revue took in the best of the comic troupes Cambridge Footlights and the Oxford Revue. *Beyond the Fringe* started in Edinburgh to poor reviews; however, once it transferred to London, it took off. This was unbridled satirical comedy, the likes of which hadn't been seen in Britain previously (the Goons had gotten close, but their "silliness" prevented them from quite offending in the ways that *Beyond the Fringe* was able). Just as the Goons were the brainchild of Spike Milligan, *Beyond the Fringe* came out of the razor-sharp mind of Peter Cook, a Cambridge graduate who shocked audiences with brilliant impersonations of British Prime Minister Harold Macmillan. (Now that we live in the world of anything goes, it's hard to realize just how shocking this mockery would have been.) Later, Cook helped develop the gold standard for TV satire, *That Was the Week That Was*, which made a star of David Frost (a man who deeply wanted to be in the Python troupe, causing the Pythons to satirize him all the more).

Alongside Cook in *Beyond the Fringe*, and later in a double act, was Dudley Moore, known especially to American movie audiences as the star of the *Arthur* movies as well as *10*, a vehicle for his comedy (and Bo Derek's body). But in Britain he's known for Peter Cook and Dudley Moore, a partnership sometimes called Derek and Clive, the recordings of whose live shows remain hugely popular.

As for the other two founders of *Beyond the Fringe*, their later exploits morphed into less overtly comic outlets. Alan Bennett went on to be a famed playwright and actor, author of such classic plays as *The History Boys* and a series of one-man monologues for TV called *Talking Heads*, which was a smash hit in the U.K. in 1988 and 1998 (so popular and well received that *Talking Heads* is now included on the national English literature syllabus in England). Jonathon Miller is perhaps best known for his work as a director of operas, though he's also a writer, actor, sculptor, public intellectual, and on, and on.

But what *Beyond the Fringe* proved to the young Pythons was that in a society so hamstrung by class and social status, one of the ways of breaking these afflicting bonds was though laughter. It's impossible now to comprehend the effect of *Beyond the Fringe*. Like the Goons, they were a huge shock to a culture that liked seaside-postcard smut and punch-line comedy. But one need only see the Pythons obsession with figures like policemen and vicars to understand that without Cook, Moore, Bennett, and Miller, they could never have found their disrespectful voices. In the space of a decade, two great comedy groups had come out of the universities of Oxford and Cambridge, groups that went after the very establishment from which they themselves hailed.

Cut to film: vox pops.

FRENCH AU PAIR (CAROL) I am not a man you silly billy.
MAN ON ROOF (TERRY J) I'm not in the street you fairy.
MAN IN STREET (JOHN) Well, er, speaking *as* a man in the street...(*a car runs him over*) Wagh!
MAN (MICHAEL) What was the question again?
VOICE OVER (JOHN) Just how relevant are contemporary customs regulations and currency restrictions in a modern expanding industrial economy? (*no answer*) Oh never mind.
PEPPERPOT (ERIC) Well I think customs men should be armed, so they can kill people carrying more than two hundred cigarettes.
MAN (JOHN) (*getting up from a deckchair and screaming with indignation and rage: he has a knotted handkerchief on his head and his trousers are rolled up to the knees*) Well I, I think that, er, nobody who has gone abroad should be allowed back in the country. I mean, er, blimey, blimey if they're not keen enough to stay here when they're 'ere, why should we allow them back, er, at the tax-payers' expense? I mean, be fair, I mean, I don't eat squirrels do I? I mean well perhaps I do one or two but there's no law against that, is there? It's a free country. (*enter a knight in armour*) I mean if I want to eat a squirrel now and again, that's me own business, innit? I mean, I'm no racialist. I, oh, oh...

The knight is carrying a raw chicken. The man apprehensively covers his head and the knight slams him in the stomach with the chicken.

WOMAN (CAROL) I think it's silly to ask a lizard what it thinks, anyway.
CHAIRMAN (*off*) Why?
WOMAN I mean they should have asked Margaret Drabble. 8
YOUNG MAN (ERIC) (*very reasonably*) Well I think, er, customs people are quite necessary, and I think they're doing quite a good job really. Check.

We now see that he is playing chess with another young man. They are in an ordinary flat. There is a tremendous battering, banging, hammering and clattering at the door.

YOUNG MAN Door's open.
POLICEMAN (GRAHAM) Oh. Yes. (*he enters*) All right. All right, all right, all right. My name's Police Constable Henry Thatcher, and this is a raid. I have reason to believe that there are certain substances on the premises.

British novelist, younger sister of A S Byatt, and, before her writing days, understudy at the Royal Shakespeare Company to Vanessa Redgrave. The quintessential novelist of British manners.

Yet again, the Pythons can't help but use a gay reference whenever possible.

Darl Larsen notes in his encyclopedia that this is "one of the few actual punch lines delivered, sans retribution or undercutting, in all of *Flying Circus*."

There are so many towns in England that can be described as suburban, middle-class, and fusty. East Grinstead is perhaps the ne plus ultra, but it joins Esher and Bagshot in this episode, and the reference would not have been missed by British viewers.

"E.B." possibly alludes to E.B. White of *Charlotte's Web*, and "Debenham" for the ubiquitous, middle-of-the-road department store Debenhams.

Alvar Liddell was the quintessential British news announcer, famous for his work during World War II.

YOUNG MAN Well what sort of substances, officer?
POLICEMAN Er...certain substances.
YOUNG MAN Well, what sort of certain substances?
POLICEMAN Er, certain substances of an illicit nature.
YOUNG MAN Er, could you be more specific?
POLICEMAN I beg your pardon?
YOUNG MAN Could you be 'clearer'.
POLICEMAN Oh, oh...yes, er...certain substances on the premises. To be removed for clinical tests.
YOUNG MAN Have you got anything particular in mind?
POLICEMAN Well what have you got?
YOUNG MAN Nothing, officer.
POLICEMAN You are Sandy Camp the actor? 9
YOUNG MAN Yes.
POLICEMAN I must warn you, sir, that outside I have police dog Josephine, who is not only armed, and trained to sniff out certain substances, but is also a junkie.
YOUNG MAN What are you after...?
POLICEMAN (*pulling a brown paper package from out of his pocket, very badly and obviously*) Do! Oh, oh, oh, oh, oh, oh, oh, oh, oh, oh! Here is a brown paper bag I have found on the premises. I must confiscate this, sir, and take it with me for clinical examination.

YOUNG MAN Wait a minute. You just got that out of your pocket.
POLICEMAN What?
YOUNG MAN (*takes it*) Well what's in it anyway? (*opens it*) Sandwiches.
POLICEMAN Sandwiches? Blimey. Whatever did I give the wife? 10

Cut to viewer's letter in handwriting, read in voice over.

VOICE OVER (CAROL) Dear BBC, East Grinstead, Friday. 11 I feel I really must write and protest about that sketch. My husband, in common with a lot of people of his age, is fifty. For how long are we to put up with these things. Yours sincerely, E. B. Debenham. 12

Cut to another letter.

VOICE OVER (JOHN) Dear Freddy Grisewood, Bagshot, Surrey. As a prolific letter-writer, I feel I must protest about the previous letter. I am nearly sixty and am quite mad, but I do enjoy listening to the BBC Home Service. If this continues to go on unabated...Dunkirk...dark days of the war...backs to the wall...Alvar Liddell... 13 Berlin air lift...moral upheaval of

Profumo case...young hippies roaming the streets, raping, looting and killing. Yours etc., Brigadier Arthur Gormanstrop (Mrs). 14

Cut to vox pops film.

PEPPERPOT (ERIC) Well I think they should attack things, like that—with satire. I mean Ned Sherrin. 15 Fair's fair. I think people should be able to make up their own minds for me.

WOMAN JOURNALIST (TERRY J) Well I think they should attack the fuddy-duddy attitudes of the lower middle classes which permit the establishment to survive and keep the mores of the whole country back where they were in the nineteenth century and the ghastly days of the pre-sexual revolution.

A boxer (ERIC) *runs up and knocks her out.*

SCOTSMAN (MICHAEL) Well that's, er, very interesting, because, er, I am, in fact, made entirely of wood.

STOCKBROKER (JOHN) Well I think they should attack the lower classes, er, first with bombs, and rockets destroying their homes, and then when they run helpless into the streets, er, mowing them down with machine guns. Er, and then of course releasing the vultures. I know these views aren't popular, but I have never courted popularity.

A boy scout on his knees. Next to him is a scout master, seen only from the knees down.

BOY (MICHAEL) I think there should be more race prejudice.

He is nudged.

VOICE Less.

BOY Less race prejudice.

Cut to news studio with a large screen behind news reader.

NEWSREADER (ERIC) (*as if it's the fourth item*) ...and several butchers' aprons. In Fulham this morning a jeweller's shop was broken into and jewellery to the value of £2,000 stolen. Police have issued this picture of a man they wish to interview. (*on the screen behind, him, there appears an identical picture of him, sitting at his newsreader desk*) The man is in his late twenties wearing a grey suit, a white shirt and a floral tie. (*on the screen behind, police come in and remove the news reader*) Will anyone who sees this man or can give any information about his whereabouts contact their nearest police station. (*he is handed a piece of paper*) Ah! Oh. We've just heard that police have detained the man they wished to interview in connection with the jewel robbery. Ah, but after questioning police have ruled him out of their enquiries and released him. (*the other newsreader appears back on the screen and sits down*) Sport. (*he is handed another piece of paper*) Ah, they say, however, that acting on his

14

Still fresh in many minds, the Profumo case came to epitomize the "Swinging Sixties" in all its supposed moral degeneration and sexual freedom. John Profumo, British secretary of state for war and once the youngest member of Parliament, had a relationship with a 21-year-old prostitute named Christine Keeler. (She, in turn, was involved with an attaché at the Russian embassy.) Though, like all politicians caught with his pants down he initially lied about his involvement, he subsequently admitted it and resigned in June 1963. He went on to do charity work and was awarded the Commander of Order of the British Empire (CBE) in 1975. He died in 2006 at age 91.

15

Ned Sherrin was the producer and director of the seminal if short-lived 1962–1963 BBC satire show *That Was the Week That Was*. He was the ultimate satirist and wit, and in many ways paved the way for the work of troupes like the Pythons. Sherrin was a beloved radio show host and his career lasted until the first few years of the twenty-first century. His 2007 *Guardian* obituary quoted him as saying he always made sure to have had "enough money to pay for what he regarded as life's bare necessities: food, wine and taxis."

What Idle actually starts to say, before he's led away by a police officer, is "British Broadcasting Association." It's amusing to speculate that the BBC itself refused the rights of the Pythons to use their real name . . . except that the show aired on the BBC, and continually poked fun at its home station. Score one verbal gaffe for Mr. Idle.

17

Match of the Day is a long-running soccer show and a BBC staple. Before the days of ubiquitous soccer matches on TV, this show was the only way to see your team in action. Each show featured two main games (in highlight form only) and then pundits talking. Even in the current era of many full live matches being aired, *Match of the Day* still hauls in an impressive viewership—it's just what you do on Saturday evenings in England if you're staying in watching TV.

This is not, in fact, *Match of the Day*'s theme music.

information they now wish to interview a newsreader in the central London area. Ah, police are concentrating their enquiries on the British Broadcasting Corp 16... *(a policeman comes in, and removes newsreader in the foreground)* Excuse me a minute...

The newsreader on the screen behind continues.

OTHER NEWSREADER We understand a man is now helping police with their enquiries. And that is the end of the news. *(he clips a piece of jewellery on to his ear)* And now, 'Match of the Day'. 17

'Match of the Day' music. 18 *We see a couple. They are standing at the foot of a largish bed. She is in bra and pants. He is in Y-fronts. They kiss ecstatically. After a few seconds there is the sound of a car drawing up. The crunch of footsteps on gravel and the sound of a door opening. The newsreader comes into shot.*

NEWSREADER Ah, I, I'm terribly sorry it's not in fact 'Match of the Day'—pit is in fact edited highlights of tonight's romantic movie. Er. Sorry. *(he goes out of shot; the two clinch again; after a second he pops back into shot)*

Ooh, I'm sorry, on BBC2 Joan Bakewell 19 will be talking to Michael Dean 20 about what makes exciting television. (*pops out of shot, then pops in again*) Ah, sorry about all that. And now back to the movie. (*he goes*)

The couple continue to neck.

SHE (CAROL) (*smoking*) Oh, oh, oh Bevis, should we?
BEVIS (TERRY J) Oh Dora. Why not?
SHE Be gentle with me.

Cut to film montage: collapsing factory chimney in reverse motion; pan up tall soaring poplars in the wind; waves crashing; fish in shallow water; fountains; exploding fireworks; volcano erupting with lava; rocket taking off; express train going into a tunnel; dam bursting; battleship broadside; lion leaping through flaming hoop; Richard Nixon smiling; 21 *milking a cow; planes refuelling in mid-air; Women's Institute applauding; tossing the caber;* 22 *plane falling in flames; tree crashing to the ground; the lead shot tower collapsing (normal motion).*
Cut back to the girl in bed.

SHE Oh Bevis, are you going to do anything or are you just going to show me films all evening?

We see Bevis, with small projector.

BEVIS Just one more, dear.
SHE Oh.

He starts it. A two-minute extravaganza constructed by Mr Terry Gilliam of America you know.

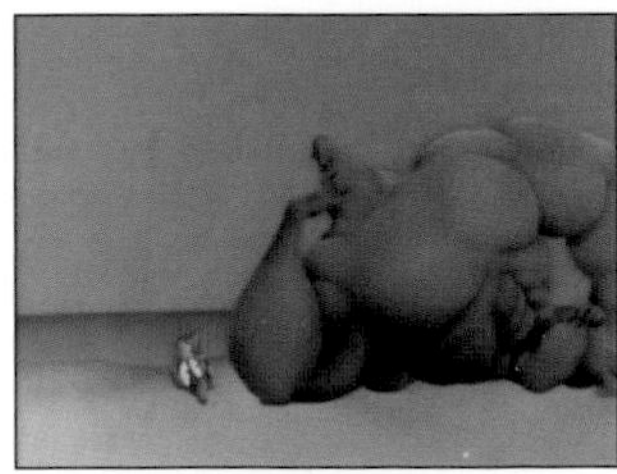

Cut to an interview room.

INTERVIEWER (JOHN) You know I really enjoy interviewing applicants for this management training course. (*knock at door*) Come in. (*Stig enters*) Ah. Come and sit down.
STIG (GRAHAM) Thank you. (*he sits*)
INTERVIEWER (*stares at him and starts writing*) Would you mind just standing up again for one moment. (*stands up*) Take a seat.

Joan Bakewell, now Baroness Bakewell, is a TV presenter, described by English wit Frank Muir as "the thinking man's crumpet" (British slang for an attractive woman). She is also famous for being the lover of Harold Pinter, an affair chronicled in his play (and later movie) *Betrayal*.

Michael Dean was also a TV presenter and worked with Bakewell on *Late Night Line-Up* in the 1960s.

Amid all this tumescence and fluidity, it's fantastic to see Richard Nixon pop up. One might imagine that an image of "Tricky Dicky" might stand for the kinds of mental gymnastics a lover might employ to delay certain premature actions. Or else, it's just funny.

Caber tossing is the traditional Scottish pastime in which a telephone-pole-like caber is hurled across a field.

STIG I'm sorry.

INTERVIEWER Take a seat. (*Stig does so*) Ah! (*writes again*) Good morning.

STIG Good morning.

INTERVIEWER Good morning.

STIG Good morning.

INTERVIEWER (*writes*) Tell me why did you say 'good morning' when you know perfectly well that it's afternoon?

STIG Well, well, you said 'good morning'. Ha, ha.

INTERVIEWER (*shakes head*) Good afternoon.

STIG Ah, good afternoon.

INTERVIEWER Oh dear. (*writes again*) Good evening.

STIG ...Goodbye?

INTERVIEWER Ha, ha. No. (*rings small hand-bell*)...Aren't you going to ask me why I rang the bell? (*rings bell again*)

STIG Er why did you ring the bell?

INTERVIEWER

WHY DO YOU THINK I RANG THE BELL? *[SHOUTS]* FIVE, FOUR, THREE, TWO, ONE, ZERO!

STIG Well, I, I...

INTERVIEWER Too late! (*singing*) Goodnight, ding-ding-ding-ding-ding. Goodnight. Ding-ding-ding-ding-ding-ding-ding.

STIG Um. Oh this is, is the interview for the management training course is it?

INTERVIEWER (*rings bell*) Yes. Yes it is. Goodnight. Ding, ding, ding, ding, ding, ding, ding, ding.

STIG Oh. Oh dear, I don't think I'm doing very well.

INTERVIEWER Why do you say that?

STIG Well I don't know.

INTERVIEWER Do you say it because you didn't know?

STIG Well. I, I, I, I don't know.

INTERVIEWER Five, four, three, two, one, zero! Right! (*makes face and strange noise*)

STIG I'm sorry, I'm confused.
INTERVIEWER Well why do you think I did that then?
STIG Well I don't know.
INTERVIEWER Aren't you curious?
STIG Well yes.
INTERVIEWER Well, why didn't you ask me?
STIG Well...I...er...
INTERVIEWER Name?
STIG What?
INTERVIEWER Your name man, your name!
STIG Um, er David.
INTERVIEWER David. Sure?
STIG Oh yes.
INTERVIEWER (*writing*) David Shaw.
STIG No, no Thomas.
INTERVIEWER Thomas Shaw?
STIG No, no, David Thomas.
INTERVIEWER (*long look, rings bell*) Goodnight. Dingding-ding-ding. Goodnight. Ding-ding-ding.
STIG Oh dear we're back to that again. I don't know what to do when you do that.
INTERVIEWER Well do something. Goodnight. Ding-ding-ding-ding-ding, five, four, three, two, one...(*Stig pulls face and makes noise*) Good!
STIG Good?
INTERVIEWER Very good—do it again. (*Stig pulls face and makes noise*) Very good indeed, quite outstanding. (*interviewer goes to door*) Ah right. (*calls through door*) Ready now. (*four people come in and line up by desk*) Right, once more. (*rings bell*) Goodnight, ding-ding-ding-ding.
Stig very cautiously pulls face and makes noise. Interviewer rings bell again.

Suddenly the four men all hold up points cards like diving or skating judges.

STIG What's going on? What's going on?
INTERVIEWER You've got very good marks.
STIG (*hysterically*) Well I don't care, I want to know what's going on! I think you're deliberately trying to humiliate people, and I'm going straight out of here and I'm going to tell the police exactly what you do to people and I'm going to make bloody sure that you never do it again. There, what do you think of that? What do you think of that?
The judges give him very high marks.

INTERVIEWER *Very* good marks.
STIG Oh, oh well, do I get the job?
INTERVIEWER Er, well, I'm afraid not. I'm afraid all the vacancies were filled several weeks ago.

They fall about laughing.
Cut to man sitting at desk.

MAN (MICHAEL) Well that was all good fun, and we all had a jolly good laugh, but I would like to assure you that you'd never be treated like that if you had an interview here at the Careers Advisory Board. Perhaps I should introduce myself. I am the Head of the Careers Advisory Board. I wanted to be a doctor, but there we are, I'm Head of the Careers Advisory Board. (*emotionally*) Or a sculptor, something artistic, or an engineer, with all those dams, but there we are, it's no use crying over spilt milk, the facts are there and that's that. I'm the Head of this lousy Board. (*he weeps, then recovers*) Never mind, now I wonder if you've ever considered what a very profitable line of work this man is in.

Cut to front door of a flat. Man walks up to the door and rings bell. He is dressed smartly.

MAN (ERIC) Burglar! (*longish pause while he waits, he rings again*) Burglar! (*woman appears at other side of door*)
WOMAN (JOHN) Yes?
MAN Burglar, madam.
WOMAN What do you want?
MAN I want to come in and steal a few things, madam.
WOMAN Are you an encyclopaedia salesman?
MAN

NO MADAM, I'M A BURGLAR, I BURGLE PEOPLE.

WOMAN I think you're an encyclopaedia salesman.
MAN Oh I'm not, open the door, let me in please.
WOMAN If I let you in you'll sell me encyclopaedias.
MAN I won't, madam. I just want to come in and ransack the flat. Honestly.
WOMAN Promise. No encyclopaedias?
MAN None at all.

WOMAN All right. (*she opens door*) You'd better come in then.

Man enters through door.

MAN Mind you I don't know whether you've really considered the advantages of owning a really fine set of modern encyclopaedias...(*he pockets valuable*) You know, they can really do you wonders.

Cut back to man at desk.

MAN That man was a successful encyclopaedia salesman. But not all encyclopaedia salesmen are successful. Here is an unsuccessful encyclopaedia salesman.

Cut to a very tall building; a body flies out of a high window and plummets.
Cut back to man at desk.

MAN Now here are two unsuccessful encyclopaedia salesmen.

Cut to a different tall building; two bodies fly out of a high window. Cut back to man at desk.

MAN I think there's a lesson there for all of us.

Caption: '"MAN'S CRISIS OF IDENTITY IN THE LATTER HALF OF THE 20TH CENTURY" WAS CONCEIVED, WRITTEN AND PERFORMED BY...(credits)'

20th
CENTURY
VOL
SEA
SON
1
EPISODE 6

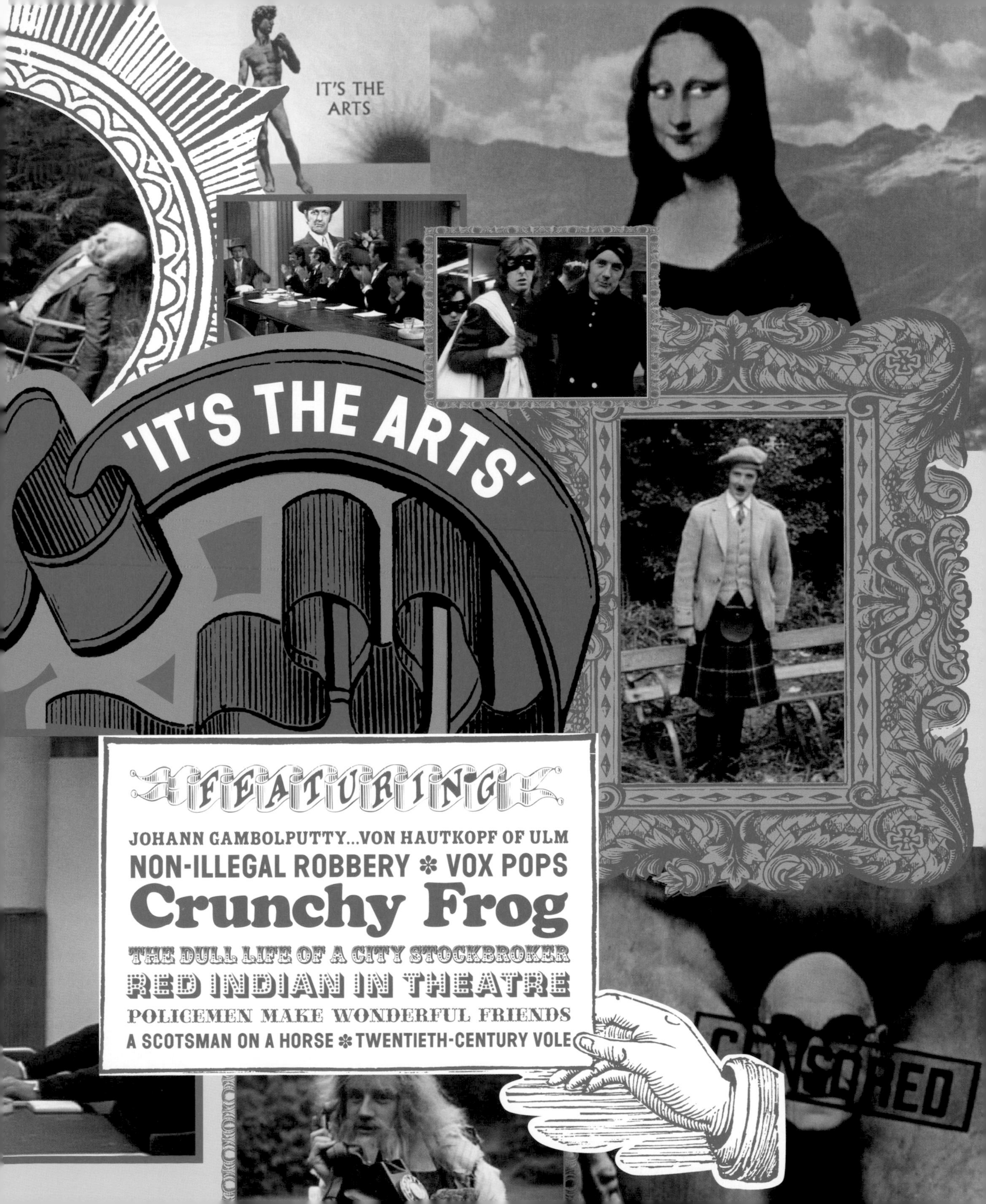
IT'S THE
ARTS
'IT'S THE ARTS'
FEATURING
JOHANN GAMBOLPUTTY...VON HAUTKOPF OF ULM
NON-ILLEGAL ROBBERY ✽ VOX POPS
Crunchy Frog
THE DULL LIFE OF A CITY STOCKBROKER
RED INDIAN IN THEATRE
POLICEMEN MAKE WONDERFUL FRIENDS
A SCOTSMAN ON A HORSE ✽ TWENTIETH-CENTURY VOLE
CENSORED

FIRST AIRED: NOVEMBER 23, 1969

In the foreground we see a telephone. In the very distant background we see the 'It's' man. The telephone starts to ring. The 'It's' man runs towards the camera and the telephone (speeded up). He arrives at the telephone, picks up the receiver and is about to speak into the mouthpiece when he remembers the camera. He puts his hand over the mouthpiece and says to camera:

IT'S MAN (MICHAEL)

IT'S...

He returns to the receiver. Animated opening titles.

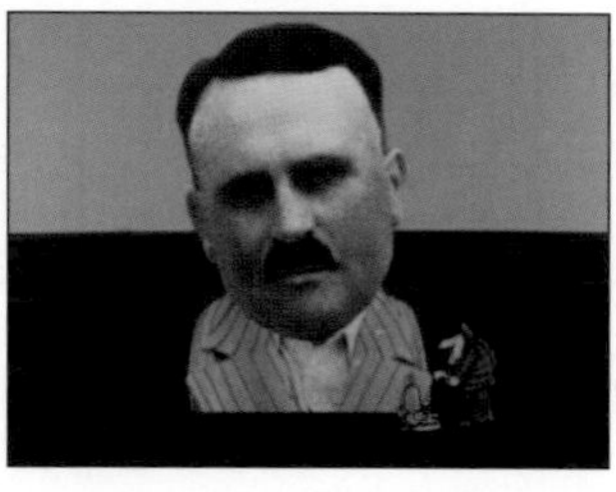

Caption: 'NEXT WEEK'
Caption: 'HOW TO FLING AN OTTER'
Caption: 'THIS WEEK' Caption: 'THE BBC ENTRY FOR THE ZINC STOAT OF BUDAPEST (CURRENT AFFAIRS)'
Caption: 'THESE CAPTIONS COST 12/6D. EACH'
Cut to presenter in studio.
Superimposed Caption: 'ARTHUR FIGGIS'
Lose Caption. Pause.
Caption: 'THE SAME, A FEW SECONDS LATER'
Superimposed caption: 'THAT'S £4.7.6 SO FAR ON CAPTIONS ALONE'
Superimposed caption: 'NOT INCLUDING THAT ONE'

MAN (MICHAEL) (*rushing in*) I thought you did that so well Mr Figgis, could I have your autograph?
FIGGIS (GRAHAM) You certainly can.

Presenter signs autograph. Part of his signature gets away (animation) and eventually leads us into the title: 'It's the Arts'. Classical music plays. 1

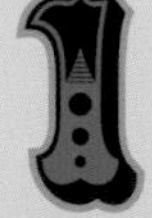

1 The music in the background is Edward Elgar's "Enigma Variations," another standard, like Hubert Parry's "Jerusalem," of the British classical repertoire.

FIGGIS(GRAHAM)Beethoven,Mozart,Chopin,Liszt,Brahms,Panties...I'msorry...Schumann,Schubert, Mendelssohn and Bach. Names that will live for ever. But there is one composer whose name is never included with the greats. Why is it the world never remembered the name of Johann Gambolputty de von Ausfern-schplenden-schlitter-crasscrenbon-fried-digger-dingle-dangle-dongle-dungle-burstein-von-knacker-thrasher- 2 apple-banger-horowitz-ticolensic-grander-knotty-spelltinkle-grandlich-grumblemeyer-spelterwasser-kurstlich-himbleeisen-bahnwagen-gutenabend- 3 bitte-ein-nürnburger-bratwustle-gerspurten-mitzweimache-luber-hundsfut-gumberaber-shönendanker- 4 kalbsfleisch-mittler-aucher von Hautkopft of Ulm. To do justice to this man, thought by many to be the greatest name in German Baroque music, we present a profile of Johann Gambolputty de von Ausfern-schplenden-schlitter-crass crenbon-fried-digger-dingle-dangle-dongle-dungle-burstein-von-knacker-thrasher-apple-banger-horowitz-ticolensic-grander-knotty-spelltinkle-grandlich-grumblemeyer-spelterwasser-kurstlich-himbleeisen-bahnwagen-gutenabend-bitte-ein-nürnburger-bratwustle-gerspurten-mitzweimache-luber-hundsfut-gumberaber-shönendanker-kalbsfleisch-mittler-aucher von Hautkopft of Ulm. We start with an interview with his only surviving relative Karl Gambolputty de von Ausfern...(*fades out*) 5

Cut to old man sitting blanketed, in wheel-chair, as he speaks, intercut with shot of interviewer nodding and looking interested.

KARL(TERRY J) Oh ja. When I first met Johann Gambolputty de von Ausfern-schplenden-schlitter-crasscrenbon-fried-digger-dingle-dangle-dongle-dungle-burstein-von-knacker-thrasher-apple-banger-horowitz-ticolensic-grander-knotty-spelltinkle-grandlich-grumblemeyer-spelterwasser-kurstlich-himbleeisen-bahnwagen-gutenabend-bitte-ein-nürnburger-bratwustle-gerspurten-mitzweimache-luber-hundsfut-gumberaber-shönendanker-kalbsfleisch-mittler-aucher von Hautkopft of Ulm, he was with his wife, Sarah Gambolputty de von...

INTERVIEWER (JOHN) (*as he speaks intercut with shots of Karl nodding and trying to look interested*) Yes, if I may just cut in on you there, Herr Gambolputty de von Ausfern-schplenden-schlitter-crasscrenbon-fried-digger-dingle-dangle-dongle-dungle-burstein-von-knacker- thrasher-apple-banger-horowitz-ticolensic-grander-knotty-spelltinkle-grandlich-grumblemeyer-spelterwasser-kurstlich-himbleeisen-bahnwagen-gutenabend-bitte-ein-nürnburger-bratwustle-gerspurten-mitzweimache-luber-hundsfut-gumberaber-shönendanker-kalbsfleisch-mittler-aucher von Hautkopft of Ulm, and ask you—just quickly—if there's any particular thing that you remember about Johann Gambolputty de von Ausfern-schplenden-schlitter-crasscrenbon-fried-digger-dingle-dangle-dongle-dungle-burstein-von-knacker-thrasher-apple-banger-horowitz-ticolensic-grander-knotty-spelltinkle-grandlich-grumblemeyer-spelterwasser-kurstlich-himbleeisen-bahnwagen-gutenabend-bitte-ein-nürnburger-bratwustle-gerspurten-mitzweimache-luber-hundsfut-gumberaber-shönendanker-kalbsfleisch-mittler-aucher von Hautkopft of Ulm?

No response.

"Knacker-thrasher" is testicle bashing to you and me.

Guten abend: Good evening.

Shönendanker: Please and thank you.

A lovely gag on both the phrase "the greatest name" and the Baroque movement, as his name is both the "greatest," as in the biggest, and thoroughly ornamental and gaudy, or Baroque. This is also a nice joke on the love of the German language for portmanteau words. And how the hell did all the Pythons learn this extraordinary list of names?

He shakes the old man, then gets up and listens to his heart. Realizing with exasperation that his interviewee has died, he starts digging a grave. Cut back to presenter.

FIGGIS

A TRIBUTE TO JOHANN GAMBOLPUTTY...

Cut to Viking.

VIKING (JOHN)...de von Ausfern-schplenden-schlitter...

Cut to weedy man in pullover with National Health specs.

MAN (MICHAEL) ...crasscrenbon-fried-digger-dingle-dangle-dongle...

Cut to knight in armour.

KNIGHT IN ARMOUR ...dungle-burstein-von-knacker-thrasher...

Cut to a succession of animated characters.

MONA LISA ...apple-banger-horowitz-ticolensic...
LON CHANEY ...grander-knotty-spelltinkle...
POLICEMAN ...grandlich...
PIG ...grumblemeyer...
POLICEMAN ...spelterwasser...
BOAR ....kurstlich-himbleeisen...
BOTTICELLI LOVER ...bahnwagen-gutenabend...
MEDIEVAL COUPLE ...bitte-ein-nürnburger...
FAMILY GROUP ...bratwurstle...
DOCTOR ...gerspurten...
BISHOP & SAINT ...mitz-weimache-luber-hundsfut...
TWO DANCERS ...gumberaber-schönendanker...
THREE NAKED LADIES ...kalbsfleisch...
CRICKET TEAM ...mittler-aucher...
POLICEMEN ...von Hautkopf...
FIGGIS ...of Ulm.

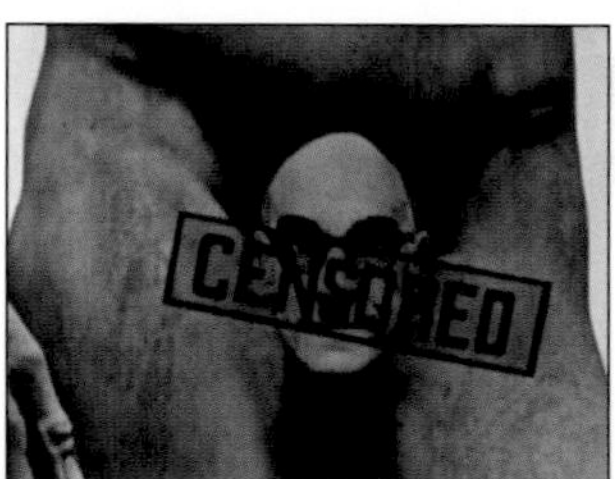

Animation leading to: A garret room with a bare table. Around it are grouped four desperate-looking robbers. The boss has a rolled-up map. One of the gang, the fifth, is looking out of the window.

BOSS (MICHAEL) All clear?
FIFTH (JOHN) All clear, boss.
BOSS (*unfolding big map across table; talking carefully*) Right...this is the plan then. At 10.45...you, Reg, collect me and Ken in the van, and take us round to the British Jewellery Centre in the High Street. We will arrive outside the British Jewellery Centre at 10.50 a of m. I shall then get out of the car, you Reg; take it and park it back here in Denver Street, [6] right?

In case you want to go to the actual Denver Street, there isn't one—in fact, in all of the U.K. there is only a single Denver Road, in Hackney, in north London. It is not parallel to a "High Street."

At 10.5 I, I shall enter the British Jewellery Centre, where you, Vic, disguised as a customer, will meet me and hand me £5.18.3d. At 10.52, I shall approach the counter and purchase a watch costing £5.18.3d. I shall then give the watch to you, Vic. You'll go straight to Norman's Garage in East Street. You lads continue back up here at 10.56 and we rendezvous in the back room at the **Cow and Sickle**, 7 at 11.15. All right, any questions?

LARRY (TERRY J) We don't seem to be doing anything illegal.

BOSS What do you mean?

LARRY Well...we're paying for the watch.

BOSS (*patiently*) Yes...

LARRY (*hesitating*) Well...why are we *paying* for the watch?

BOSS (*heavily*) They wouldn't give it to us if we didn't *pay* for it, would they...eh?

LARRY Look! I don't like this outfit.

BOSS Why not?

LARRY (*at last feeling free to say what's on his mind*) Well, we never break the bloody law.

General consternation.

BOSS What d'you mean?

LARRY Well, look at that bank job last week.

BOSS What was wrong with that?

LARRY Well having to go in there with a mask on and ask for £15 out of my deposit account; that's what was wrong with it.

BOSS Listen! What are you trying to say, Larry?

LARRY Couldn't we just *steal* the watch, boss!

BOSS Oh, you dumb cluck! We spent weeks organizing this job. Reg rented a room across the road and filmed the people going in and out every day. Vic spent three weeks looking at watch catalogues...until he knew the price of each one backwards, and now I'm not going to risk the whole raid just for the sake of breaking the law.

LARRY **Urr...couldn't we park on a double yellow line?** 8

BOSS No!

LARRY Couldn't we get a dog to foul the foot...

BOSS No!

REG (ERIC) (*suddenly going pale*) 'Ere, boss!

BOSS What's the matter with you?

REG I just thought...I left the car on a meter...and it's...

BOSS Overdue?

REG Yes, boss.

BOSS How much?

REG (*quaking*) I dunno, boss...maybe two...maybe five minutes...

The Cow and Sickle is a play on British pub names, examples of which include the Pig and Whistle and the George and Dragon. Like Denver Street, there is no English pub called the Cow and Sickle.

Still considered one of the great crimes of British society. Parking on a double yellow line—signaling no parking at any time—incurs both the wrath of society and a tow truck, pronto. This is perhaps because British roads are awfully narrow, and it's just not cricket (British for not decent or fair).

BOSS Five minutes overdue. You fool! You fool! All right...we've no time to lose. Ken—shave all your hair off, get your passport and meet me at this address in Rio de Janeiro Tuesday night. Vic—go to East Africa, have plastic surgery and meet me there. Reg—go to Canada and work your way south to Nicaragua by July. Larry—you stay here as front man. Give us fifteen minutes then blow the building up. All right, make it fast.

LARRY I can't blow the building up.

BOSS Why not?

LARRY It's illegal.

BOSS Oh bloody hell. Well we'd better give ourselves up then.

REG We can't, boss.

BOSS Why not?

REG We haven't done anything illegal.

Cut to film. Exterior of bank. Three bandits rush out with swag etc. One of them stops to talk to camera raising mask off head.

The Scotsman was made entirely of wood in Episode 5.

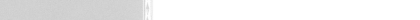

BANDIT (MICHAEL) No I think being illegal makes it more exciting.

SECOND BANDIT (ERIC) Yes, I agree. I mean, if you're going to go straight you might as well be a vicar or something.

Cut to vicar, wheeling quickly round to reveal he has had his hand in the restoration-fund box.

VICAR (TERRY J) What?

Cut to chartered accountant.

CHARTERED ACCOUNTANT (JOHN) I agree. If there were fewer robbers there wouldn't be so many of them, numerically speaking.

Cut to pepperpot.

PEPPERPOT (MICHAEL) I think sexual ecstasy is over-rated.

Cut to Scotsman.

SCOTSMAN (MICHAEL)

WELL, HOW VERY INTERESTING, BECAUSE I'M NOW MADE ENTIRELY OF TIN. 

Cut to Police Inspector Praline.

PRALINE (JOHN) After a few more of these remarks, I shall be appearing in a sketch, so stay tuned.

Cut to policeman.

POLICEMAN (GRAHAM) It's the uniform that puts them off, that and my bad breath.

Cut to judge in full long wig and robes and a QC also wearing wig and robes.

JUDGE (*matter of factly*) We like dressing up, yes...

Cut to Inspector Praline.

PRALINE Hello again. I am at present still on film, but in a few seconds I shall be appearing in the studio. Thank you.

Cut to studio. A door opens. Inspector Praline looks round door.

INSPECTOR PRALINE (*to camera*) Hello. (*he walks in followed by Superintendent Parrot and goes to desk*) Mr Milton? You are sole proprietor and owner of the Whizzo Chocolate Company? 10

MILTON (TERRY J) I am.

PRALINE Superintendent Parrot and I are from the hygiene squad. We want to have a word with you about your box of chocolates entitled The Whizzo Quality Assortment.

MILTON Ah, yes.

PRALINE (*producing box of chocolates*) If I may begin at the beginning. First there is the cherry fondue. This is extremely nasty, but we can't prosecute you for that. 11

MILTON Agreed.

PRALINE Next we have number four, 'crunchy frog'.

MILTON Ah, yes.

PRALINE Am I right in thinking there's a real frog in here?

MILTON Yes. A little one.

PRALINE What sort of frog?

MILTON A dead frog.

PRALINE Is it cooked?

MILTON No.

PRALINE What, a raw frog?

Superintendent Parrot looks increasingly queasy.

MILTON We use only the finest baby frogs, dew picked and flown from Iraq, cleansed in finest quality spring water, lightly killed, and then sealed in a succulent Swiss quintuple smooth treble cream milk chocolate envelope and lovingly frosted with glucose.

PRALINE That's as maybe, it's still a frog.

MILTON What else?

PRALINE Well don't you even take the bones out?

MILTON If we took the bones out it wouldn't be crunchy would it?

PRALINE Superintendent Parrot ate one of those.

PARROT (GRAHAM) Excuse me a moment. (*exits hurriedly*)

MILTON It says 'crunchy frog' quite clearly.

PRALINE Well, the superintendent thought it was an almond whirl. People won't expect there to be a frog in there. They're bound to think it's some form of mock frog.

MILTON (*insulted*) Mock frog? We use no artificial preservatives or additives of any kind!

Compare to the Whizzo butter of Episode 1.

A lovely gag about everyone's least favorite chocolate in any box.

PRALINE Nevertheless, I must warn you that in future you should delete the words 'crunchy frog', and replace them with the legend 'crunchy raw unboned real dead frog', if you want to avoid prosecution.
MILTON What about our sales?
PRALINE I'm not interested in your sales, I have to protect the general public. Now how about this one. (*superintendent enters*) It was number five, wasn't it? (*superintendent nods*) Number five, ram's bladder cup. (*exit superintendent*) What kind of confection is this?
MILTON We use choicest juicy chunks of fresh Cornish ram's bladder, emptied, steamed, flavoured with sesame seeds whipped into a fondue and garnished with lark's vomit.
PRALINE Lark's vomit?
MILTON Correct.
PRALINE Well it don't say nothing about that here.
MILTON Oh yes it does, on the bottom of the box, after monosodium glutamate.
PRALINE (*looking*) Well I hardly think this is good enough. I think it would be more appropriate if the box bore a large red label warning lark's vomit. 12
MILTON Our sales would plummet.
PRALINE Well why don't you move into more conventional areas of confectionery, like praline or lime cream; a very popular flavour I'm led to understand. (*superintendent enters*) I mean look at this one, 'cockroach cluster', (*superintendent exits*) 'anthrax ripple'. What's this one, 'spring surprise'?

Cleese badly mixes his words up here, saying "If the bore . . . if the box bore . . . ." The perils of live taping for all to see as he shakes his head and soldiers on.

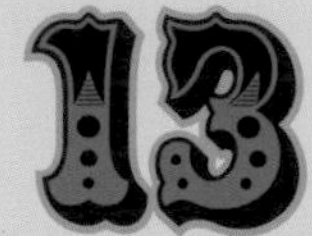

A crime of which Praline was guilty at the start of the sketch.

MILTON Ah—now, that's our speciality—covered with darkest creamy chocolate. When you pop it in your mouth steel bolts spring out and plunge straight through both cheeks.
PRALINE Well where's the pleasure in that? If people place a nice chocky in their mouth, they don't want their cheeks pierced. In any case this is an inadequate description of the sweetmeat. I shall have to ask you to accompany me to the station.
MILTON (*getting up from desk and being led away*) It's a fair cop.

PRALINE Stop talking to the camera. 13
MILTON I'm sorry.

Superintendent Parrot enters the room as Inspector Praline and Milton leave, and addresses the camera.

PARROT If only the general public would take more care when buying its sweeties, it would reduce the number of man-hours lost to the nation and they would spend less time having their stomachs pumped and sitting around in public lavatories.
ANNOUNCER (JOHN) The BBC would like to apologize for the extremely poor quality of the next announcement, only he's not at all well.
PARROT We present 'The Dull Life of a City Stockbroker'.

Cut to a nice suburban street. Inside the house a stockbroker (MICHAEL) *is finishing his breakfast. His attractive wife looks on.*

He picks up his hat, rises, kisses her goodbye, and leaves. As he does so, she takes off her wrap and two men dressed only in briefs (GRAHAM *and* TERRY J) *step out of the kitchen cupboard. In the front garden the stockbroker bids his neighbour* (GRAHAM) *good morning; as he moves off a large African native throws an assegai, killing the neighbour. The stockbroker, not noticing this, moves on. A high street: he walks into a newsagents. Behind the counter a naked young lady gives him his newspaper. Taking his change without apparently noticing her he leaves. A bus queue: the stockbroker is at the head of it; there are four people behind him. As they wait, the Frankenstein monster comes up behind them and works his way along the queue, killing each member as he goes. He has just reached the stockbroker—who has not seen him—when the bus arrives and the stockbroker gets on. On the bus: all the other passengers are uniformed soldiers. The bus drives along a road past explosions and gunfire. A hand grenade comes through the window and lands on the seat next to the stockbroker. The soldiers leave the bus rapidly;*

The stockbroker calmly leaves the bus and walks down the street, in which the soldiers are engaging in a pitched battle. The stockbroker hails a taxi; it stops. No driver is visible. The stockbroker gets in and it drives off. In the stockbroker's office: a secretary is dead across her typewriter with a knife in her back; at the back of the office a pair of legs swing gently from the ceiling; a couple are snogging at his desk. Unconcerned, the stockbroker sits down. Furtively he looks round, then takes from the desk drawer a comic-book entitled 'Thrills and Adventure'. We see the frames of the comic strip. A Superman-type character and a girl are shrinking from an explosion. She is saying 'My God, he's just exploded with enough force to destroy his kleenex'.

In the next frame, the Superman character is saying 'If only I had a kleenex to lend him—or even a linen handkerchief—but these trousers...!!! No back pocket!' In the frame beneath, he flies from side to side attempting to escape; finally he breaks through, bringing the two frames above down on himself. Cut to a picture of a safety curtain. An animated man comes in front of it and says:

MAN Coming right up—the theatre sketch—so don't move!

The front stalls of a theatre. It is a first night—a lot of people in dinner jackets etc. About three rows back there is a spare seat. A general rustle of programmes, chocolates and theatrical murmurs. Suddenly a Sioux Indian enters, clad only in loin cloth, wearing war paint and with a single strip of hair in the middle of his head and feather. He carries a bow and a quiver of arrows. He settles into the empty seat. The man next to him shifts uneasily and looks straight ahead. The Indian looks his neighbour up and down a couple of times.

Born in Sydney in 1893, by the time she's name-checked here, Courtneidge was a dame of the theater and comedy, and just a couple of years shy of clocking 70 years of service to British drama.

The Redfoot tribe does not exist.

Married acting partners, Denison and Gray were mid-century superstars, but by the late 1960s would have felt like yesterday's news.

Leatherhead is a town in Surrey, southwest of London; "Rep" is British slang for repertory theater, the lifeblood of each town's drama scene.

Sandy Camp featured in Episode 5, in which a police officer plants drugs in his apartment while Camp plays chess.

INDIAN (ERIC) *(always speaking with full gestures)* Me heap want see play. Me want play start heap soon.

Man next to him nods.

MAN (GRAHAM) Yes well. I think it...begins in a minute.
INDIAN Me heap big fan **Cicely Courtneidge.** 14
MAN *(highly embarrassed)* Yes...she's very good.
INDIAN She *fine* actress...she make interpretation heap subtle...she heap good diction and timing... she make part really live for Indian brave.

MAN Yes...yes...she's marvelous...
INDIAN My father—Chief Running Stag—**leader of mighty Redfoot tribe** 15 —him heap keen on **Michael Denison and Dulcie Gray.** 16
MAN *(unwillingly drawn in)* Do you go to the theatre a lot?
INDIAN When moon high over prairie...when wolf howl over mountain, when mighty wind roar through Yellow Valley, we go **Leatherhead Rep** 17 —block booking, upper circle—whole tribe get in on 3/6d each.
MAN That's very good.
INDIAN Stage manager, Stan Wilson, heap good friend Redfoot tribe. After show we go pow-wow speakum with director, **Sandy Camp,** 18 in snug bar of Bell and Compasses. Him mighty fine director. Him heap famous.
MAN Oh—I don't know him myself.
INDIAN Him say Leatherhead Rep like do play with Redfoot tribe.
MAN Oh that's good...
INDIAN We do 'Dial M for Murder'. Chief Running Elk—him kill buffalo with bare hands, run thousand paces when the sun is high—him play Chief Inspector Hardy—heap good fine actor.
MAN You do a lot of acting do you?
INDIAN Yes. Redfoot tribe live by acting and hunting.
MAN You don't fight any more?
INDIAN Yes! Redfoot make war! When Chief Yellow Snake was leader, and Mighty Eagle was in land of forefather, we fight Pawnee at Oxbow Crossing. When Pawnee steal our rehearsal copies of '**Reluctant Debutante**' 19 we kill fifty Pawnee—houses heap full every night. Heap good publicity.

The lights start to dim. Auditorium chatter subsides.

MAN (*visibly relieved*) I think he's about to start now, thank God for that.

They both look towards stage. The overture starts.

INDIAN (*leaning across*) Paleface like eat chocolate? (*proffers box*)
MAN No, thank you very much.
INDIAN (*helping himself*) Hmmm—crunchy frog—heap good.

Cut to stage, house manager walks out in front of tabs. He is a very nice young man.

HOUSE MANAGER (MICHAEL) Ladies and gentlemen. Before the play starts, I would like to apologize to you all, but unfortunately Miss Cicely Courtneidge is unable to appear, owing to...

He is suddenly struck in the chest by first one arrow and then another. He crumbles to the ground revealing half a dozen in his back. The air is filled with war-whoops and drum beats and screams. Cut to a working-class kitchen.

MUM (TERRY J) (*reading newspaper*) D'you read that, Edgar?
DAD (ian davidson) What's that dear?
MUM There's been another Indian massacre at Dorking Civic Theatre.
DAD About time too dear...
MUM 'Those who were left alive at the end got their money back'.
DAD That's what live theatre needs—a few more massacres...
MUM 'The police are anxious to speak to anyone who saw the crime, ladies with large breasts, or just anyone who likes policemen.'

Suddenly a policeman walks in between the couple and the camera.

POLICEMAN (JOHN) (*to camera*) Yes! Policemen make wonderful friends. So if you are over six feet tall and would like a friend, a pen friend, in the police force, here is the address to write to: 'Mrs Ena Frog, 8 Masonic Apron Street, Cowdenbeath'. 20 Remember—policemen make wonderful friends. So write today and take advantage of our free officer. Thank you. And now for the next sketch.

The policeman removes his helmet, shakes it, proffers it to mum at the table. She takes out a small folded bit of paper, opens and reads.

MUM A Scotsman on a horse.
POLICEMAN For Mrs Emma Hamilton of Nelson, a Scotsman on a horse.

A SCOTSMAN (JOHN) RIDES UP TO THE CAMERA AND LOOKS AROUND PUZZLED.

The *Reluctant Debutante* is a play by William Douglas-Home, a midcentury politician who went on to be court-martialed during World War II for refusing to take part in the Allied assault on Le Havre, arguing that civilians had not been given time to evacuate. (He was sentenced to a year of imprisonment with hard labor.) Postwar, his political life gave way to one as a successful dramatist. His brother Alec Douglas-Home was British prime minister from 1963 to 1964.

Cowdenbeath is a town in Scotland, 18 miles north of Edinburgh, across the Firth of Forth.

In long-shot we see him riding off. At a wee Scottish kirk another Scotsman (MICHAEL) *is waiting at the head of the aisle to be married. Intercut between first Scotsman galloping through the countryside and the wedding procession coming up the aisle. The wedding takes place; just as it finishes the first Scotsman rides up to the kirk and rushes in. The assembled congregation look at him in alarm as he surveys them; then he picks up Michael and carries him off. Cut to film of Women's Institute audience applauding. Animation, which leads us to the 'Twentieth Century Vole' trademark. Cut to film producer's office. Six writers sitting round a table with one very impressive chair empty at the head of the table. They wait reverently. Suddenly the door of the room flies open and Larry Saltzberg, the film producer, walks in. The writers leap to their feet.*

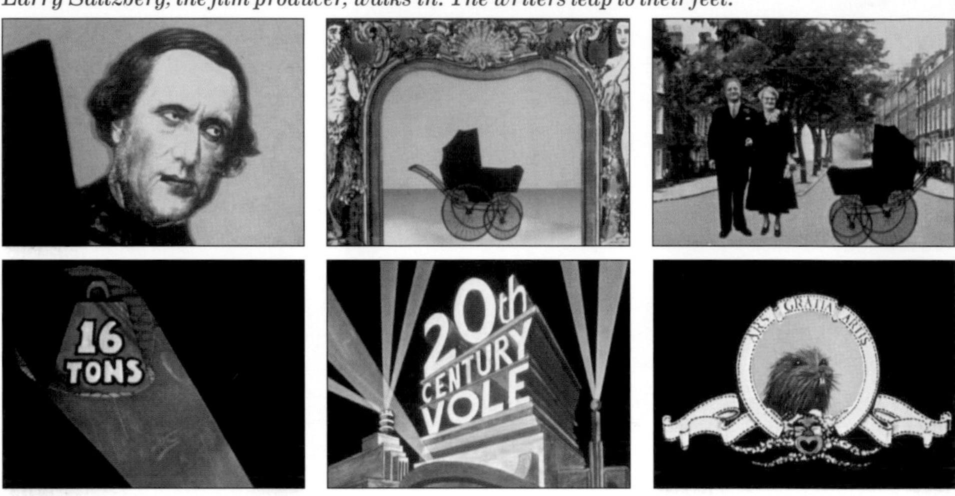

LARRY (GRAHAM) Good morning boys.
WRITERS Good morning Mr Saltzberg.

They run to help him into his chair.

LARRY (*sitting*) Sit down! Sit down! Sit down! Sit down! Now, boys, I want you to know that I think you are the best six writers in movies today. (*the writers are overcome*) I want you to know that I've had an idea for the next movie I'm going to produce and I want you boys to write it.

The writers run and kiss him.

WRITERS Thank you. Thank you.
LARRY Oh sit down! Sit down! Sit down! There'll be plenty of time for that later on. Now boys, here's my idea.
THIRD WRITER (ERIC) It's great!
LARRY You like it huh? (*he looks round the table*)
WRITERS (*catching on fast*) Yeah, yeah, great! Really great. Fantastic. (*first writer is the only one not having an orgasm about the idea*)
LARRY (*to first writer*) Do you like it?
FIRST WRITER (MICHAEL) (*thrown*) Yeah! Er...yeah.
LARRY (*still to first writer*) What do you like *best* about it?
FIRST WRITER Oh well you haven't told us...what it is yet...
LARRY WHAT!?
FIRST WRITER (*pointing at second writer*) I like what he likes.
LARRY What do you like?
SECOND WRITER (TERRY J) (*pointing at third writer*) I like what he likes.
THIRD WRITER (*pointing at fourth writer*) I like what he likes.
FOURTH WRITER (JOHN) I like what he likes (*pointing at fifth writer*)

FIFTH WRITER (TERRY G) I just crazy about what he likes (*pointing at sixth writer*)

LARRY What do you like?

SIXTH WRITER (IAN DAVIDSON) I...I...I...agree with them.

LARRY Good! Now we're getting somewhere. Now, here's the start of the movie...I see snow! (*writers applaud*) White snow!

FOURTH WRITER Think of the colours!

LARRY And in the snow, I see...a tree!

WRITERS (*applauding*) Yes! Yes!

LARRY Wait, wait I haven't finished yet.

THIRD WRITER There's *more*?

LARRY And by this tree, gentlemen, I see...a dog!

WRITERS Olé!

LARRY And gentlemen, this dog goes up to the tree, and he piddles on it.

WRITERS Hallelujah!

SIXTH WRITER Have we got a movie!

FIFTH WRITER He tells it the way it is!

FOURTH WRITER It's where it's at!

THIRD WRITER This is something else!

SECOND WRITER It's out of sight!

FIRST WRITER (*finding Larry staring at him*) I like it, I like it.

LARRY (*suspicious*) Oh yeah?

FIRST WRITER Yeah, yeah, I *promise* I like it!

FIFTH WRITER Sir, I don't know how to say this but I got to be perfectly frank. I really and truly believe this story of yours is the greatest story in motion-picture history.

LARRY Get out!

FIFTH WRITER What?

LARRY If there's one thing I can't stand, it's a yes-man! Get out! (*fifth writer leaves very fast, the others go very quiet*) I'll see you never work again. (*to sixth writer*) What do you think?

SIXTH WRITER Well...I...

LARRY Just because I have an idea it doesn't mean it's great. It could be lousy.

SIXTH WRITER It could?

LARRY Yeah! What d'ya think?

SIXTH WRITER It's lousy.

LARRY There you are, you see, he spoke his mind. He said my idea was lousy. It just so happens my idea isn't lousy so get out you goddam pinko subversive, get out! (*sixth writer exits*) You...(*looking straight at John*)

FOURTH WRITER Well...I think it's an excellent idea.

LARRY Are you a yes-man?

FOURTH WRITER No, no, no, I mean there may be things against it.

LARRY You think it's lousy, huh?

FOURTH WRITER No, no, I mean it takes time.

LARRY (*really threatening*) Are you being indecisive?

FOURTH WRITER No. Yes, perhaps. (*runs out*)

LARRY I hope you three gentlemen aren't going to be indecisive! (*they try to hide under the table*) What the hell are you doing under that table?

FIRST WRITER We dropped our pencils.

LARRY Pencil droppers, eh?

WRITERS No, no, no, no, no!

LARRY Right. Now I want your opinion of my idea...(*pointing at first writer*) You...

FIRST WRITER (*quaking*) Oh...

First writer looks around and then faints.

LARRY Has he had a heart attack?
SECOND AND THIRD WRITERS Er...
LARRY

IF THERE'S ONE THING I CAN'T STAND, IT'S PEOPLE WHO HAVE HEART ATTACKS.

FIRST WRITER (*recovering immediately*) I feel fine now.

LARRY Well, what do you think?

WRITERS Oh! Eh! You didn't ask me you asked him. He didn't ask me, he asked him. No, him.

LARRY I've changed my mind. I'm asking you, the one in the middle.

SECOND WRITER The one in the middle?

LARRY Yes, the one in the middle. (*the phone rings*) Hello, yes, yes, yes, yes, yes, yes, Dimitri...(*all jockey for position desperately trying to put the others in the middle and finish sitting on one chair*) What the hell are you doing?

SECOND WRITER I'm thinking.

LARRY Get back in those seats immediately. (*back to phone*) Yes...(*second writer is grabbed by the others and held in the middle chair; Larry finishes with the phone*) Right you. The one in the middle, what do you think?

SECOND WRITER (*panic*) Er...er...

LARRY Come on!

SECOND WRITER Splunge.

LARRY Did he say splunge?

FIRST AND THIRD WRITERS Yes.

LARRY What does splunge mean?

SECOND WRITER It means...it's a great-idea-but-possibly-not-and-I'm-not-being-indecisive!

LARRY Good. Right...(*to third writer*) What do you think?

THIRD WRITER Er. Splunge?

LARRY OK...

FIRST WRITER Yeah. Splunge for me too.

LARRY So all three of you think splunge, huh?

WRITERS Yes!

LARRY Well now we're getting somewhere. No, wait. A new angle! In the snow, instead of the tree, I see Rock Hudson, and instead of the dog I see Doris Day and, gentlemen, Doris Day goes up to Rock Hudson and she kisses him. A love story. Intercourse Italian style. **David Hemmings** 21 as a **hippy Gestapo officer.** 22 Frontal nudity. A family picture. A comedy. And then when Doris Day's kissed Rock Hudson she says something funny like...(*looks at third writer*)

THIRD WRITER Er...Good evening.

LARRY Doris Day's a comedienne, not a newsreader. Get out! (*third writer runs*) She says something funny like (*looks at second writer*)

SECOND WRITER Splunge?

LARRY That's the stupidest idea I ever heard. Get out! (*second writer leaves*) Doris Dog kisses Rock Tree and she says (*looks at first writer*)

FIRST WRITER Er...er...er...I can't take it anymore. (*runs out*)

LARRY I like that! I like that, I can't take it any more, and then Rock Hudson says 'I'm a very rich film producer and I need a lobotomy' and then Doris Dog says 'I think you're very handsome and I'm going to take all my clothes off and then Doris Dog turns into a yak and goes to the bathroom on David Lemming. No, wait, wait! (*picks up phone*) Hello, (*cut to 'It's' man film with Larry continuing voice over*) hello, hello, who are you? You're an out-of-work writer? Well, you're fired. Roll the credits. (*here the credits do start to roll with Larry's voice*

21

One of the great icons of the "Swinging Sixties," David Hemmings was a talented boy soprano (and close friend of the composer Benjamin Britten), an actor (notably in Antonioni's *Blow-Up*), and released an album in 1967 with a title perfect for its time: *David Hemmings Happens.* (His third wife went by the Python-esque name of Prudence J. de Casembroot.)

The Gestapo officer is a nod back to the "Big Cheese," from Episode 4. (Chapman's character is wearing hippie accoutrements.)

continuing over) Produced by Irving C. Saltzberg Jnr. of Irving C. Saltzberg Productions Ltd. and Saltzberg Art Films, Oil, Real Estate, Banking and Prostitution Inc.

The credits read:

PRODUCED BY IRVING C. SALTZBERG JNR. 23 *AND*
IRVING C. SALTZBERG PRODUCTIONS LTD. AND SALTZBERG ART FILMS,
OIL, REAL ESTATE, BANKING AND PROSTITUTION INC.

CO-PRODUCTION FROM AN ORIGINAL IDEA
BY IRVING C. SALTZBERG JNR.

WRITTEN BY IRVING C. SALTZBERG
AND IRVING C. SALTZBERG

ADDITIONAL MATERIAL BY IRVING C. SALTZBERG
AND GRAHAM C. CHAPMANBERG, JOHN C. CLEESEBERG,
TERRY C. JONESBERG, MICHAEL C. PALINBERG,
TERRY C. GILLIAMBERG, ERIC C. IDLEBERG

ALSO APPEARING WAS IAN C. DAVIDSONBERG,
CREDITS BY IRVING C. SALTZBERG

The technical credits continue in the same style.

"Irving C. Saltzberg Jnr." is a crack at Irving Thalberg, the eminent American movie producer—but, really, it's a crack at movie producers in general.

SEASON 1
EPISODE 7

MONTY PYTHON'S FLYING CIRCUS
YOU'RE NO FUN ANYMORE
FEATURING
CAMEL SPOTTING
YOU'RE NO FUN ANYMORE
THE AUDIT; SCIENCE FICTION SKETCH
MAN TURNS INTO SCOTSMAN
Police Station
BLANCMANGES PLAYING TENNIS
EMPTY

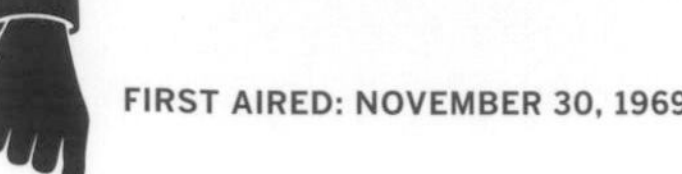

FIRST AIRED: NOVEMBER 30, 1969

A long hilly scar of land; on either side trees. The track comes straight down from the horizon to camera in valley. At the top of the hill we hear running and heavy breathing. The 'It's' man appears. He runs down the valley to camera but fails to say his line:

VOICES OFF (*prompting*) It's...no...no...it's...it's...it's...
IT'S MAN (*finally*)

IT'S...

By the miracle of money we swing into a fantastically expensive opening animation sequence, produced by one of America's very own drop-outs.

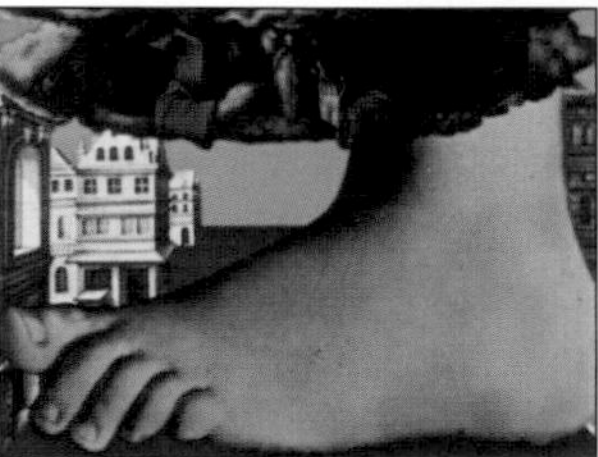

In the country. Interviewer, with microphone. Behind him a man sits on a wall, with clip-board, binoculars and spotting gear.

INTERVIEWER (JOHN) Good evening. Tonight we're going to take a hard tough abrasive look at camel spotting. Hello.

SPOTTER (ERIC) Hello Peter.
INTERVIEWER Now tell me, what exactly are you doing?
SPOTTER Er well, I'm camel spotting. I'm spotting to see if there are any camels that I can spot, and put them down in my camel spotting book.
INTERVIEWER Good. And how many camels have you spotted so far?

SPOTTER Oh, well so far Peter, up to the present moment, I've spotted nearly, ooh, nearly one.
INTERVIEWER Nearly one?
SPOTTER Er, call it none.
INTERVIEWER Fine. And er how long have you been here?
SPOTTER Three years.
INTERVIEWER So, in, er, three years you've spotted no camels?
SPOTTER Yes in only three years. Er, I tell a lie, four, be fair, five. I've been camel spotting for just the seven years. Before that of course I was a Yeti spotter.
INTERVIEWER A Yeti spotter, that must have been extremely interesting.
SPOTTER Oh, it was extremely interesting, very, very—quite...it was dull; dull, dull dull, oh God it was dull. Sitting in the Waterloo waiting room. Course once you've seen one Yeti you've seen them all.
INTERVIEWER And have you seen them all?
SPOTTER Well I've seen one. Well a little one...a picture of a...I've heard about them.

INTERVIEWER Well, now tell me, what do you do when you spot a camel?
SPOTTER Er, I take its number.
INTERVIEWER Camels don't have numbers.
SPOTTER Ah, well you've got to know where to look. **Er, they're on the side of the engine above the piston box.** 1
INTERVIEWER What?
SPOTTER Ah—of course you've got to make sure it's not a dromedary. 'Cos if it's a dromedary it goes in the dromedary book.
INTERVIEWER Well how do you tell if it's a dromedary?
SPOTTER Ah well, a dromedary has *one* hump and a camel has a refreshment car, buffet, and ticket collector.
INTERVIEWER Mr Sopwith, aren't you in fact a train spotter?
SPOTTER What?
INTERVIEWER Don't you in fact spot trains?
SPOTTER

OH, YOU'RE NO FUN ANYMORE.

ANIMATION: Then a girl in bed. Count Dracula (GRAHAM) *enters. The girl reveals her neck. The vampire goes to kiss her but his fangs fall out.*

GIRL (DONNA) Oh, you're no fun anymore.

A man at the yardarm being lashed.

LASHER (TERRY J) ...thirty-nine...forty. All right, cut him down, Mr Fuller.

1

Long before there was Irvine Welsh's novel, there was the gentle art of train spotting, in which small groups of locomotive enthusiasts stand on rail-station platforms and note down the numbers of arriving engines. A triumph of amateurism and obsession, train spotting is shorthand in the U.K. for "sad exploit by lonely males."

LASHEE (ERIC) Oh you're no fun anymore.

Back to camel spotter.

SPOTTER Now if anybody else pinches my phrase I'll throw them under a camel.
INTERVIEWER (*giggling*) If you can spot one.

Spotter gives him a dirty look. Knight in armour appears beside him. He hits interviewer with chicken. Cut to small board meeting. An accountant stands up and reads...

ACCOUNTANT (MICHAEL) Lady chairman, sir, shareholders, ladies and gentlemen. I have great pleasure in announcing that owing to a cut-back on surplus expenditure of twelve million Canadian dollars, plus a refund of seven and a half million Deutschmarks from the Swiss branch, and in addition adding the **debenture preference stock** 2 of the three and three quarter million to the directors' reserve currency account of seven and a half million, plus an upward expenditure margin of eleven and a half thousand lire, due to a rise in capital investment of ten million pounds, this firm last year made a complete profit of a shilling.

2 Debenture and preference stocks, or shares as we call them, are different things, underlining (should such a thing be required) that this wonderful economic gobbledygook truly makes no sense.

CHAIRMAN (GRAHAM) A shilling Wilkins?
ACCOUNTANT Er, roughly, yes sir.
CHAIRMAN Wilkins, I am the chairman of a multi-million pound corporation and you are a very new chartered accountant. Isn't it possible there may have been some mistake?
ACCOUNTANT Well that's very kind of you sir, but I don't think I'm ready to be chairman yet.
BOARD MEMBER (JOHN) Wilkins, Wilkins. This shilling, is it net or gross?
ACCOUNTANT It's British sir.
CHAIRMAN Yes, has tax been paid on it?
ACCOUNTANT Yes, this is after tax. Owing to the rigorous bite of the income tax five pence of a further sixpence was swallowed up in tax.
BOARD MEMBER Five pence of a *further* sixpence?
ACCOUNTANT (*eagerly*) Yes sir.
CHAIRMAN Five pence of a further *sixpence*?
ACCOUNTANT That's right sir.
CHAIRMAN Then where is the other penny?
ACCOUNTANT ...Er.
BOARD MEMBER That makes you a penny short Wilkins. Where is it?
ACCOUNTANT ...Erm.
CHAIRMAN Wilkins?
ACCOUNTANT (*in tears*) I embezzled it sir.

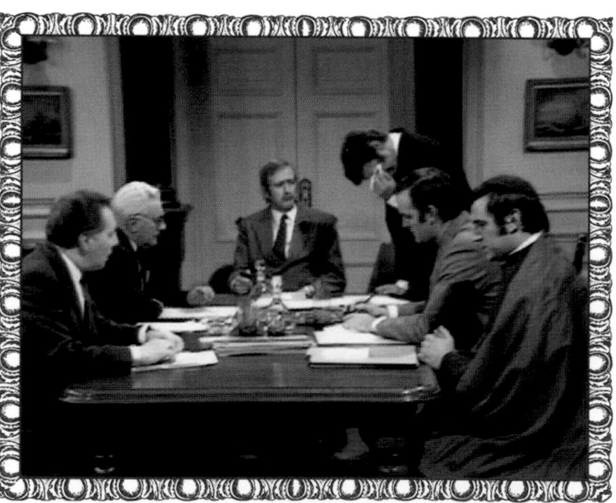

CHAIRMAN What all of it?
ACCOUNTANT Yes all of it.
BOARD MEMBER You naughty person.
ACCOUNTANT It's my first. Please be gentle with me.
CHAIRMAN I'm afraid it's my unpleasant duty to inform you that you're fired.
ACCOUNTANT Oh please, please.
CHAIRMAN No, out!
ACCOUNTANT (*crying*) Oh...(*he leaves*)
CHAIRMAN Yes, there's no place for sentiment in big business.

He goes over to a wall plaque 'There is no place for sentiment in Big Business'. He turns it over. On the back it says 'He's right you know'.

BISHOP (TERRY J) (*to chairman*) Oh you're no fun anymore.

Camel man comes running in shouting.

SPOTTER I heard that. Who said that?
ALL (*pointing at the bishop*) He did! He did!
BISHOP No I didn't.
ALL Ooh!
SPOTTER Right!

Shot of the bishop bound and gagged and tied across a railway line. **3**

VOICE OVER (ERIC) Here is the address to complain to...

Caption: 'MR ALBERT SPIM, 1,000,008 LONDON ROAD, OXFORD' But he reads:

VOICE OVER The Royal Frog Trampling Institute, 16 Rayners Lane, London, W.C. Fields. I'll just repeat that...

Caption: 'FLIGHT LT. & PREBENDARY ETHEL MORRIS, THE DIMPLES, THAXTED, NR BUEONS AIRES' He reads over it:

VOICE OVER Tristram and Isolde Phillips, 7.30 Covent Garden Saturday (near Sunday) and afterwards at the Inigo Jones Fish Emporium.

Cut to Jewish figure.

JEWISH FIGURE (MICHAEL) **And they want to put the Licence fee up?** **4**

Cut to a photo of a man with pipe.

VOICE OVER (*continues*) And now here is a reminder about leaving your radio on during the night. Leave your radio on during the night.

Cut to redcoat.

REDCOAT (MICHAEL) A little joke, a little jest. Nothing to worry about ladies and gentlemen. Now we've got some science fiction for you, some sci-fi, something to send the shivers up your spine, send the creepy crawlies down your lager and limes. All the lads have contributed to it, it's a little number entitled, Science Fiction Sketch...

As ever with the Pythons, clergy come below everyone—even chartered accountants and CEOs—in any moral pyramid.

Our modern eyes and ears can't help but feel uncomfortable at this stereotype. Oddly, the audience laughs at this almost more than anything in the entire show. British attitudes towards Jewishness can sometimes feel rooted in King Edward I's Edict of Expulsion, which banished the Jewish people officially in 1290 (and took 350 years to be officially repealed). It wasn't until the early nineteenth century that Jews were finally given a place in civil and political society. There are now some 300,000 Jews in the U.K.

No one really knows how big the universe is, and certainly not in miles. Current estimates calculate its expanse using light-years, but in terms of miles, it's 25 billion miles even to the nearest star. So it's inconceivable that the universe is a mere 77 billion miles across.

Pudsey, perhaps because of its pudding-echo of a name and its situation in the industrial north, between Leeds and Bradford in Yorkshire, is often used as comedic shorthand for a dull, working-class town. "New Pudsey" is the rail station that serves Pudsey, even though it was built a full mile from town.

Idle's hat blows off accidentally here. He does a lovely job of warily looking up at the hill next to him, as though some sinister agent has caused the gust of wind—a nice example of his ability to ad-lib.

Zoom through the galaxy to the solar system.

AMERICAN VOICE (JOHN) (*very resonant*) **The Universe consists of a billion, billion galaxies...77,000,000,000 miles across,** 5 and every galaxy is made up of a billion, zillion stars and around these stars circle a billion planets, and of all of these planets the greenest and the pleasantest is the planet Earth, in the system of Sol, in the Galaxy known as the Milky Way...And it was to this world that creatures of an alien planet came...to conquer and destroy the very heart of civilization...

Mix into close-up of railway station sign: ***'New Pudsey'***. 6
Pull out to mid-shot of a couple walking towards camera. They are middle-aged. He (GRAHAM) *wears a cricket blazer and grey flannels and a carrier bag. She (eric) wears a fussy print dress.*

AMERICAN VOICE (*gently*) It was a day like any other and Mr and Mrs Samuel Brainsample were a perfectly ordinary couple, leading perfectly ordinary lives—the sort of people to whom nothing extraordinary ever happened, and not the kind of people to be the centre of one of the most astounding incidents in the history of mankind... 7

So let's forget about them and follow instead the destiny of this man...(*camera pans off them; they both look disappointed; camera picks up instead a smart little business man, in bowler, briefcase and pinstripes*)...Harold Potter, gardener, and tax official, first victim of Creatures from another Planet.

Weird electronic music. Sinister atmosphere. Follow him out of station. Cut-away to flying saucer, over city skyline. Back to Potter as he walks up suburban road. Back to flying saucer. It bleeps as if it has seen its prey and changes direction. Cut back to Potter just about to open his front gate. Shot from over the other side of the road. Cut to flying saucer sending down ray. Potter freezes... shivers and turns into a Scotsman with kilt, and red beard. His hand jerks out in front of him and he spins round and scuttles up road in fast motion, to the accompaniment of bagpipe music. Cut to close-up of newspaper with banner headline: 'Man turns into a Scotsman'.

NEWSVENDOR'S VOICE

READ ALL ABOUT IT! READ ALL ABOUT IT! MAN TURNS INTO SCOTSMAN!

Mix through to Potter's front gate. His wife is being interviewed by obvious plainclothes man.

INSPECTOR (TERRY J) Mrs Potter—you knew Harold Potter quite well I believe?
WIFE (ERIC) Oh yes quite well.
INSPECTOR Yes.
WIFE He was my husband.
INSPECTOR Yes. And, er, he never showed any inclination towards being a Scotsman before this happened?
WIFE (*shocked*) No, no, not at all. He was not that sort of person...
INSPECTOR He didn't wear a kilt or play the bagpipes?
WIFE No, no.
INSPECTOR He never got drunk at night or bought home black puddings?
WIFE No, no. Not at all.
INSPECTOR He didn't have an inadequate brain capacity?
WIFE No, no, not at all.
INSPECTOR I see. So by your account **Harold Potter** **8** perhaps known to his friends as Harry? was a perfectly ordinary Englishman without any tendency towards being a Scotsman whatsoever?
WIFE Absolutely, yes. (*suddenly remembering*) Mind you he did always watch Dr Finlay on television.
INSPECTOR Ah-hah!...Well that's it, you see. That's how it starts.
WIFE I beg your pardon?
INSPECTOR Well you see Scottishness starts with little things like that, and works up. You see, people don't just turn into a Scotsman for no reason at all...(*goes rigid: with Scots accent.*) No further questions! *The words are hardly out of his mouth when he turns into a Scotsman and spins round and disappears up road in fast motion. Pan with him. Cut to bus queue: man in city suit and bowler hat suddenly changes into a Scotsman with beard, twizzles round and speeds out of shot.*

Cut to street: policeman pointing way for woman with a pram. Suddenly he changes into a Scotsman and scuffles out of shot. She looks aghast for a moment and then she too changes into a Scotsman and hurtles off after him. The baby suddenly develops a beard and the pram follows her. Single shot of black jazz musician in cellar blowing a blue sax solo.

He changes and whizzes off. Squad of soldiers being drilled. Suddenly they all change into bearded Scotsmen and race off in unison. Pan with them past sign: 'Welsh Guard'.
Quick animated shot of flying saucer disappearing over city skyline.
Cut to big close-up of passionate kiss. It goes on for some moments. Foggy lens...romantic music. Keep on big close-up as they talk. She is none too intelligent.

Perhaps known to his friends as Harry?

Donna Reading, a British actress who appeared earlier in the episode with Count Dracula.

10

Donna Reading seems to stall in saying her line here, which is understandable, given how complex it is.

11

The Scotsmen running up the hill are mostly production crew for MPFC.

A reference to the *danse macabre* scene at the end of Ingmar Bergman's haunting, postapocalyptic classic *The Seventh Seal*, in which seven characters are led over the hills to their deaths.

SHE (DONNA) **Charles... 9**
CHARLES (GRAHAM) Darling...
SHE Charles...
CHARLES Darling, darling...
SHE Charles...there's something I've got to tell you...
CHARLES What is it darling?
SHE It's daddy...he's turned into a Scotsman...
CHARLES What! Mr Llewellyn?
SHE Yes, Charles. Help me, please help me.

CHARLES But what can I do?
SHE Surely, Charles, you're the Chief Scientist at the Anthropological Research Institute, at Butley Down—an expert in what makes people change from one nationality to another.
CHARLES So I am! (*pull out to reveal they are in a laboratory; he is in a white coat, she is in something absurdly sexy*) This is right up my street!
SHE Oh good.
CHARLES Now first of all, why would anyone turn into a Scotsman?
SHE (*tentatively*) Em, for business reasons?
CHARLES No, no! Only because he has no control over his own destiny! Look I'll show you...

He presses a button on a control board and a laboratory TV screen lights up with the words 'only because they have no control over their own destinies.'

SHE I see.
CHARLES Yes! So this means that some person or persons unknown is turning all these people into Scotsmen...
SHE Oh, what kind of heartless fiend could *do* that to a man?
CHARLES I don't know...I don't know...all I know is that these people are streaming north of the border at the rate of thousands every hour. If we don't act fast, Scotland will be choked with Scotsmen...
SHE **Ooh!... 10**

Zoom in on her face.
***Cut to as many bearded Scotsmen as possible, hurtling through wood in fast motion.* 11**
Follow them, ending up with skyline shot ***as per 'Seventh Seal'.*** **12**
They all still have the arm outstretched in front of them and as always they are accompanied by bagpipe music.
Shot of border with large notice: 'Scotland Welcomes You'.

AMERICAN VOICE

SOON SCOTLAND WAS FULL OF SCOTSMEN. T E OVE -C OWDI G WAS ITI UL.

They all dash across border and then stop abruptly once they're over. They stand around looking lost.

AMERICAN VOICE Three men to a caber.

Cut to three Scotsmen tossing one caber. Cut to Scots wife in bed with bearded husband. Pull back to reveal five other Scotsmen in the bed. Short but brilliant piece of animation from T Gilliam to show England emptying of people and Scotland filling up, ending with a till sound and a till sign coming up out of England reading: 'Empty'.

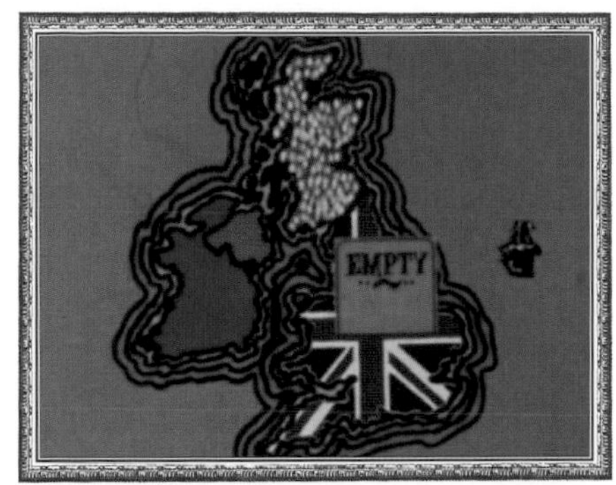

Track into England. Film of a deserted street. Wind, a dog sniffing, newspaper blowing along street. Close-up sign on shop door: 'Gone to lunch Scotland'. Close-up another sign on a shop door: 'McClosed'. Shop sign: 'McWoolworths & Co'.

AMERICAN VOICE For the few who remained, life was increasingly difficult.

Man suddenly folds up newspaper and runs round corner. Re-emerges driving bus. Drives it halfway to stop and then leaps out with bus still moving. Runs to stop, and puts out hand. Bus stops. He leaps on, rings bell, runs round to front and drives the bus off again. As bus drives out of frame we just see a couple of Scotsmen flashing past camera with arms outstretched. Pan slowly round empty football stadium. Eventually we pick up a solitary spectator, halfway up and halfway along in stand opposite where the players come out. ***He suddenly leaps to his feet cheering.*** **13** *Cut to players' tunnel and one player emerging and a referee with ball. They kick off. Player goes straight down field and scores. Spectator disappointed. A quick shot of flying saucer again. Studio: the laboratory again. Charles is looking through microscope, when the door flies open and* ***she bursts in.*** **14**

SHE Charles! Thank goodness I've found you! It's mummy!
CHARLES Hello mummy.
SHE No, no, mummy's turned into a Scotsman...
CHARLES Oh how horrible...Will they stop at nothing?
SHE I don't know—do you think they will?
CHARLES I meant that rhetorically.
SHE What does rhetorically mean?
CHARLES It means, I didn't expect an answer.
SHE Oh I see. Oh, you're so clever, Charles.
CHARLES Did mummy say anything as she changed?
SHE (*with an air of tremendous revelation*) Yes! She did, now you come to mention it!

A long pause as he waits expectantly.

CHARLES Well, what was it?
SHE Oh, she said...'Them!' (*thrilling chord of jangling music and quick zoom into her face*) Is there someone at the door?

13

Idle seems to be wearing the colors of followers of Hull City AFC—a soccer team from a town made famous by Philip Larkin, the high priest of desolate and beautiful poetry. Hull is generally considered to be the most isolated large town on the small British island—it is more than sixty miles east of Leeds (or Pudsey), for example. Note, too, that Idle is brandishing a "rattle," a curious wooden noisemaker beloved of bygone soccer fans—when rotated, it created a coruscating sound akin to thin pieces of wood being smacked together. And to think soccer fans hate the vuvuzela.

14

The actual sketch is somewhat different than described here. Idle merely stands on the terraces alone, swirling his "rattle," watching a one-person-plus-referee game already in progress.

CHARLES No...It's just the incidental music for this scene.

SHE Oh I see...

CHARLES 'Them'...Wait a minute!

SHE A *whole* minute?

CHARLES No, I meant that metaphorically...'Them'...'Them'...She was obviously referring to the people who turned her into a Scotsman. If only we knew who 'They' were...And why 'They' were doing it...Who *are* 'Them'?

Crashing chord...cut to a small still of a Scottish crofter's cottage on a lonely moor. Slow zoom in on the cottage.

AMERICAN VOICE Then suddenly a clue turned up in Scotland. Mr Angus Podgorny, owner of a Dunbar menswear shop, received an order for 48,000,000 kilts from the planet Skyron in the Galaxy of Andromeda.

Mix to interior of highland menswear shop. An elderly Scottish couple are poring over a letter which they have on the counter. Oil lamps etc.

MRS PODGORNY (TERRY J) Angus how are y'going to get 48,000,000 kilts into the van?

ANGUS (MICHAEL) I'll have t'do it in two goes.

MRS PODGORNY D'you not **ken** 15 that the Galaxy of Andromeda **is two million, two hundred thousand light years away?** 16

ANGUS Is that so?

MRS PODGORNY Aye...and you've never been further than **Berwick-on-Tweed...** 17

ANGUS Aye...but think o' the money dear...£18.10.0d a kilt...that's...(*calculates with abacus*) £900,000,000**—and that's without sporrans!** 18

MRS PODGORNY Aye...I think you ought not to go, Angus.

ANGUS (*with visionary look in his eyes*) Aye...we'd be able to afford writing paper with our names on it...We'd be able to buy that extension to the toilet...

MRS PODGORNY Aye...but he hasn't signed the order yet, has he?

ANGUS Who?

MRS PODGORNY Ach...the man from Andromeda.

ANGUS Och...well...he wasna really a man, d'you ken...

Creepy music starts to edge in.

MRS PODGORNY (*narrowing eyes*) Not really a man?

ANGUS (*sweating as the music rises*) He was as strange a thing as ever I saw, or ever I hope to see, God willing. He was a strange unearthly creature—a quivering, glistening mass...

MRS PODGORNY Angus Podgorny, what *do* y'mean?

15

"*Ken*" is Scottish for "know."

Unlike the earlier estimation of the size of the universe, this is a close approximation of the actual distance of Andromeda from Earth.

A border town with Scotland—and actually Berwick-*upon*-Tweed—it lies two-and-a-half miles inside England. But Berwick is considered so far north that the local soccer team plays in the Scottish leagues.

A "pocket" for the pocketless kilt, the sporran is the odd leather or fur pouch worn at genital height at the front of the kilt-wearing Scotsman.

ANGUS

HE WAS A SO MUCH A MA AS A BLANCMANGE! 19

Jarring chord.

Police station: a police sergeant is talking over the counter to a girl dressed in a short frilly tennis dress. She holds a racquet and tennis balls.

SERGEANT (JOHN) A blancmange, eh?

GIRL (ERIC) Yes, that's right. I was just having a game of doubles with Sandra and Jocasta, Alec and David...

SERGEANT Hang on!

GIRL What?

SERGEANT There's five.

GIRL What?

SERGEANT Five people...how do you play doubles with *five* people?

GIRL Ah, well...we were...

SERGEANT Sounds a bit funny if you ask me...playing doubles with five people...

GIRL Well we often play like that...Jocasta plays on the side receiving service...

SERGEANT Oh yes?

GIRL Yes. It helps to speed the game up and make it a lot faster, and it means Jocasta isn't left out.

SERGEANT Look, are you asking me to believe that the five of you was playing doubles, when on the very next court there was a blancmange playing by itself?

GIRL That's right, yes.

SERGEANT Well answer me this then—why didn't Jocasta play the blancmange at singles, while you and Sandra and Alec and David had a proper game of doubles with four people?

GIRL Because Jocasta always plays with *us*. She's a friend of *ours*.

SERGEANT Call that friendship? Messing up a perfectly good game of doubles?

GIRL It's not messing it up, officer, we like to play with five.

SERGEANT Look it's *your* affair if you want to play with five people...but don't go calling it doubles. Look at Wimbledon, right? **If Fred Stolle and Tony Roche played Charlie Pasarell and Cliff Drysdale and Peaches Bartcowitz...** 20 they *wouldn't* go calling it doubles.

GIRL But what about the blancmange?

SERGEANT **That could play Ann Haydon-Jones and her husband Pip.** 21

Cut back to Podgorny's shop. He and his wife are frozen in the positions in which we left them. They pick up the conversation as if nothing had happened.

19

A traditional European dessert, the blancmange is widely eaten in British households—think vanilla pudding out of a mold.

20

Tennis stars from the time: two Australians, a Puerto Rican, a South African, and an American.

21

Ann Haydon-Jones was the winner of the Wimbledon women's title in 1969 and winner of the mixed doubles with Fred Stolle that same year. The phrase "Ann Haydon-Jones and her husband Pip" comes up regularly in Python.

MRS PODGORNY

[illegible], A BLANCMANGE GAVE YOU AN ORDER FOR 48,000,000 KILTS?

ANGUS Aye!

MRS PODGORNY And you *believed* it?

ANGUS Aye, I did.

MRS PODGORNY Och, you're a stupid man, Angus Podgorny.

ANGUS (*getting a little angry*) Oh look woman, how many kilts did we sell last year? Nine and a half, that's all. So when I get an order for 48,000,000, I believe it—you *bet* I believe it!

MRS PODGORNY Even if it's from a blancmange?

ANGUS Och, woman, if a blancmange is prepared to come 2,200,000 light years to purchase a kilt, they must be fairly keen on kilts. So cease yer prattling woman and get sewing. This could be the biggest breakthrough in kilts **since the Provost of Edinburgh sat on a spike.** **22** Mary, we'll be rich! **We'll be rich!** **23**

A provost is the equivalent of a mayor.

It's fair to say that the more quickly and passionately Palin talks, the less accomplished his Scottish accent becomes. For much of this speech he sounds like . . . well, Palin.

MRS PODGORNY Oh, but Angus...he hasna given you an earnest of his good faith!

ANGUS Ah mebbe not but he has gi' me this...(*brings out piece of folded paper from sporran*)

MRS PODGORNY What is it now?

ANGUS An entry form for the British Open Tennis Championships at Wimbledon Toon...signed and seconded.

MRS PODGORNY Och, but Angus, ye ken full well that Scots folk dinna know how to play the tennis to save their lives.

ANGUS Aye, but I must go though dear, I dinna want to seem ungrateful.

MRS PODGORNY Ach! Angus, I wilna let you make a fool o'yoursel'.

ANGUS But I must.

MRS PODGORNY Och, no you'll not...

Close-up on Angus.

ANGUS Oh, Mary...(*suddenly we hear a strange creaking and a slurping noise; a look of horror comes into his eyes*) Oh, oh, Mary! Look out! Look out!

Big close-up of Mrs Podgorny's eyes starting out from head.

MRS PODGORNY Urrgh. It's the blancmange.

Blur focus.

Cut to a desk for police spokesman. A peaked-capped policeman sits there, reading ***'The Rise and Fall of the Roman Empire' by Googie Withers.*** **24**

A lovely mix of Edward Gibbon's classic *Decline and Fall of the Roman Empire* and Googie Withers, a British actress.

He lowers book and talks chattily to camera.

POLICEMAN (GRAHAM) Oh, now this is where Mr Podgorny could have saved his wife's life. If he'd gone to the police and told them that he'd been approached by unearthly beings from the Galaxy of Andromeda, we'd have sent a man round to investigate. As it was he did a deal with a blancmange, **and the blancmange ate his wife.** **25** So if you're going out, or going on holiday, or anything strange happens involving other galaxies, just nip round to your local police station, and tell the sergeant on duty—or his wife—of your suspicions. And the same goes for dogs. So I'm sorry to have interrupted your exciting science fiction story...but, then, crime's our business you know. So carry on viewing, and my thanks to the BBC for allowing me to have this little chat with you. Goodnight. God bless, look after yourselves.

He is hit on the head by knight in suit of armour with raw chicken. **26**
Cut to CID office: a plainclothes detective is sitting in his office. Podgorny is sobbing.

DETECTIVE (ERIC) (*softly and understandingly*) Do sit down, Mr Podgorny...I...I...think what's happened is...terribly...terribly...funny...tragic. But you must understand that we have to catch the creature that ate your wife, and if you could help us answer a few questions, we may be able to help save a few lives. I know this is the way your wife would have wanted it.

He is sitting on the desk next to Podgorny. Podgorny with superhuman control makes a great effort to stop sobbing.

ANGUS Aye...I'll...do...my best, sergeant.
DETECTIVE (*slapping Podgorny*) Detective inspector!
ANGUS Er, detective inspector.
DETECTIVE (*getting up and talking sharply and fast*) Now then. The facts are these. You received an order for 48,000,000 kilts from a blancmange from the planet Skyron in the Galaxy of Andromeda...you'd just shown your wife an entry form for Wimbledon, which you'd filled in... when you turned round and saw her legs disappearing into a blancmange. Is that correct?
ANGUS Yes, sir.
DETECTIVE Are you mad?
ANGUS No, sir.
DETECTIVE Well that's a relief. 'Cos if you were, your story would be less plausible. (*detective brings out photograph of blancmange*) Now then, do you recognize this?
ANGUS (*with a squeak of fear*) Oh yes. That's the one that ate my Mary!
DETECTIVE Good. His name's Riley...Jack Riley...He's that most rare of criminals...a blancmange impersonator and cannibal.
ANGUS But what about the 48,000,000 kilts and the Galaxy of Andromeda?
DETECTIVE I'm afraid that's just one of his stories. You must understand that a blancmange impersonator and cannibal has to use some pretty clever stories to allay suspicion.
ANGUS Then you mean...
DETECTIVE Yes.
ANGUS But...
DETECTIVE How?
ANGUS Yes.
DETECTIVE Well...
ANGUS Not?
DETECTIVE I'm afraid so.
ANGUS Why?
DETECTIVE Who knows?
ANGUS D'you think?
DETECTIVE Could be.

25

Chapman's second attempt at pronouncing "blancmange" is less successful than his first.

26

The scene cuts before the chicken falls on Chapman's head.

ANGUS But...
DETECTIVE I know.
ANGUS She was...
DETECTIVE Yes.

Suddenly we hear a strange noise. Angus looks frightened. Detective narrows his eyes and walks over to the door.

DETECTIVE Good lord what's that? (*he opens the door and we get a close-up of his staring eyes*) Ah, Riley! Come to give yourself up have you, Riley? (*with sudden fear*) Eh Riley? Riley! Riley! It's not Riley!

Eating noises. He is dragged out of camera shot. Refocus on Angus...he averts his eyes as we hear the detective inspector off-screen.

DETECTIVE (*off-screen*) It's an extra-terrestrial being! Agggh!

Jarring chord: Angus shuts his eyes. Cut back to laboratory: she is sitting suggestively on a stool. He is pacing up and down looking intense.

CHARLES So, everyone in England is being turned into Scotsmen, right?
SHE Yes.
CHARLES Now, which is the *worst* tennis-playing nation in the world?
SHE Er...Australia.
CHARLES No. Try again.
SHE Australia?
CHARLES (*testily*) No...try again but say a different place.
SHE Oh, I thought you meant I'd said it badly.
CHARLES No, course you didn't say it badly. Now hurry.
SHE Er, Czechoslovakia.
CHARLES No! Scotland!
SHE Of course.
CHARLES Now...now these blancmanges, apart from the one that killed Mrs Podgorny, have all appeared in which London suburb?
SHE Finchley?
CHARLES No. *Wimbledon*...Now do you begin to see the pattern? With *what* sport is *Wimbledon* commonly associated?

She is thinking really hard.

NORMAN HACKFORTH (TERRY J) *(off-screen)* For viewers at home, the answer is coming up on your screens. Those of you who wish to play it the hard way, stand upside down with your head in a bucket of piranha fish. Here is the question once again.
CHARLES With what *sport* is *Wimbledon* commonly associated?

Superimposed caption: 'TENNIS'

SHE Cricket.
CHARLES No.
SHE **Pelote?** 27
CHARLES No. Wimbledon is most commonly associated with *tennis*.
SHE Of course! Now I see!
CHARLES Yes, it all falls into place!
SHE The blancmanges are really Australians trying to get the rights of the pelote rules from the Czech publishers!
CHARLES *(heavily)* No...not quite...but, er, just look in here.

He indicates microscope. As she eagerly bends to look into it he picks up a sock filled with sand and without looking strikes her casually over the head with it. She collapses out of sight under desk. He continues to think out loud.

CHARLES Yes. So these blancmanges, blancmange-shaped creatures come from the planet Skyron in the Galaxy of Andromeda. They order 48,000,000 kilts from a Scottish menswear shop... turn the population of England into Scotsmen (well known as the worst tennis-playing nation on Earth) thus leaving England empty *during Wimbledon fortnight*! Empty during Wimbledon fortnight...what's more the papers are full of reports of blancmanges appearing on tennis courts up and down the country—*practising*. This can only mean one thing!

Flash up caption quickly:

VOICE OVER *(and caption)* 'They Mean To Win Wimbledon'
CHARLES They mean to *win Wimbledon*.

Jarring chord.
Cut to commentator in his box.

COMMENTATOR (ERIC) Well, here at Wimbledon, it's been a most extraordinary week's tennis. The blancmanges have swept the board, winning match after match. Here are just a few of the results: **Billie-Jean King eaten in straight sets,** 28 **Laver smothered whole after winning the first set,** 29 and **Pancho Gonzales,** 30 serving as well as I've never seen him, with some superb volleys and decisive return volleys off the back hand, was sucked through the net at match point and swallowed whole in just under two minutes. And so, here on the final day, there seems to be no players left to challenge the blancmanges. And this could be their undoing, Dan: as the rules of Wimbledon state quite clearly that there must be at least *one* human being concerned in the final. *(we see a three-foot-high blancmange being shepherded onto a tennis court by a Scotsman)* Well the blancmange is coming out onto the pitch now, and *(suddenly excited)* there is a human with it! It's Angus Podgorny! The plucky little Scottish tailor...upon whom everything depends. And so it's Podgorny versus blancmange in this first ever Intergalactic Wimbledon!

Cut to the centre court at Wimbledon or, if we can't get it, number one will do. Blancmange and Podgorny on opposite sides of net. Another blancmange sitting in umpire's chair. Blancmange serves...a real sizzling ace. Podgorny, who in any case is quivering with fear, doesn't see it.

Pelote is a sport mainly of the Basque region of southern France and northern Spain. It's like tennis but against a wall. In the United States, a version of it has become famous as jai alai.

Billie Jean King, the legendary American tennis star, is really a four-time winner of a Wimbledon women's singles title. (She lost to Ann Haydon-Jones in 1969, when this show aired.)

Rod Laver, the legendary Australian men's tennis star, is really a four-time winner of a Wimbledon men's singles title, including 1969, when this show aired.

Pancho Gonzales, the legendary American men's tennis star, is famous for his serve, though he never won Wimbledon. The best he ever did was reach the fourth round in 1969—in the third round he beat Charlie Pasarell in an astonishing match. Two sets down (22–24, 1–6), he rallied in the next three sets (16–14, 6–3, 11–9) in one of the most famous games ever staged at Wimbledon.

COMMENTATOR'S VOICE And it's blancmange to serve and it's a good one. 31

BLANCMANGE Umpire Blurb blurble blurb.

VOICE OVER Fifteen-love.

Blancmange serves again, and again Podgorny misses hopelessly and pathetically. Collage of speeded-up versions of blancmange serving and Podgorny missing. Cut to scoreboard:

BLANCMANGE: 40
PODGORNY: 0

Cut back to the court. Podgorny is serving and each time he fails to hit the ball altogether.

COMMENTATOR'S VOICE And Podgorny fails to even hit the ball...but this is no surprise as he hasn't hit the ball once throughout this match. So it's 72 match points to the blancmange now...Podgorny prepares to serve again.

Actually, it's a clear foot fault—the blancmange serves from halfway inside the court, an obvious infraction.

Podgorny fails to serve and we see the scoreboard:

BLANCMANGE: 6 6 30
PODGORNY: 0 0 0

COMMENTATOR'S VOICE This is indeed a grim day for the human race, Dan.

Just as Podgorny is about to serve we see Mr and Mrs Brainsample jump onto the court brandishing forks and spoons and with napkins tucked into their necks.

COMMENTATOR'S VOICE But what's this? Two spectators have rushed onto the pitch with spoons and forks...what are they going to do?

Cut to laboratory.

CHARLES They mean to eat the blancmange.

The girl pulls herself up from where she was slumped by microscope. He knocks her out again with a sand-filled sock. Cut back to Wimbledon. Mr and Mrs Brainsample chasing blancmange and eating it.

COMMENTATOR'S VOICE And they're eating the blancmange...Yes! The blancmange is leaving the court...it's abandoning the game! This is fantastic!

Cut to Mr and Mrs Brainsample covered in bits of blancmange and licking their fingers.

AMERICAN VOICE Yes it was Mr and Mrs Samuel Brainsample, who, after only a brief and misleading appearance in the early part of the film, returned to save the Earth...but *why*?

MR BRAINSAMPLE (GRAHAM) Oh, well you see we love blancmanges. My wife makes them.
AMERICAN VOICE She makes blancmanges *that* size?
MR BRAINSAMPLE Oh, yes. You see we're from the planet Skyron in the Galaxy of Andromeda, and they're all that size there. We tried to tell you at the beginning of the film but you just panned off us.

Cut back to Podgorny on court still trying to serve; at last he makes contact and runs backward and forward to receive his own services.

AMERICAN VOICE So the world was saved! And Angus Podgorny became the first Scotsman to win Wimbledon...fifteen years later.

Roller Caption: 'YOU'RE NO FUN ANYMORE'...(credits)

SEA SON 1
EPISODE 8

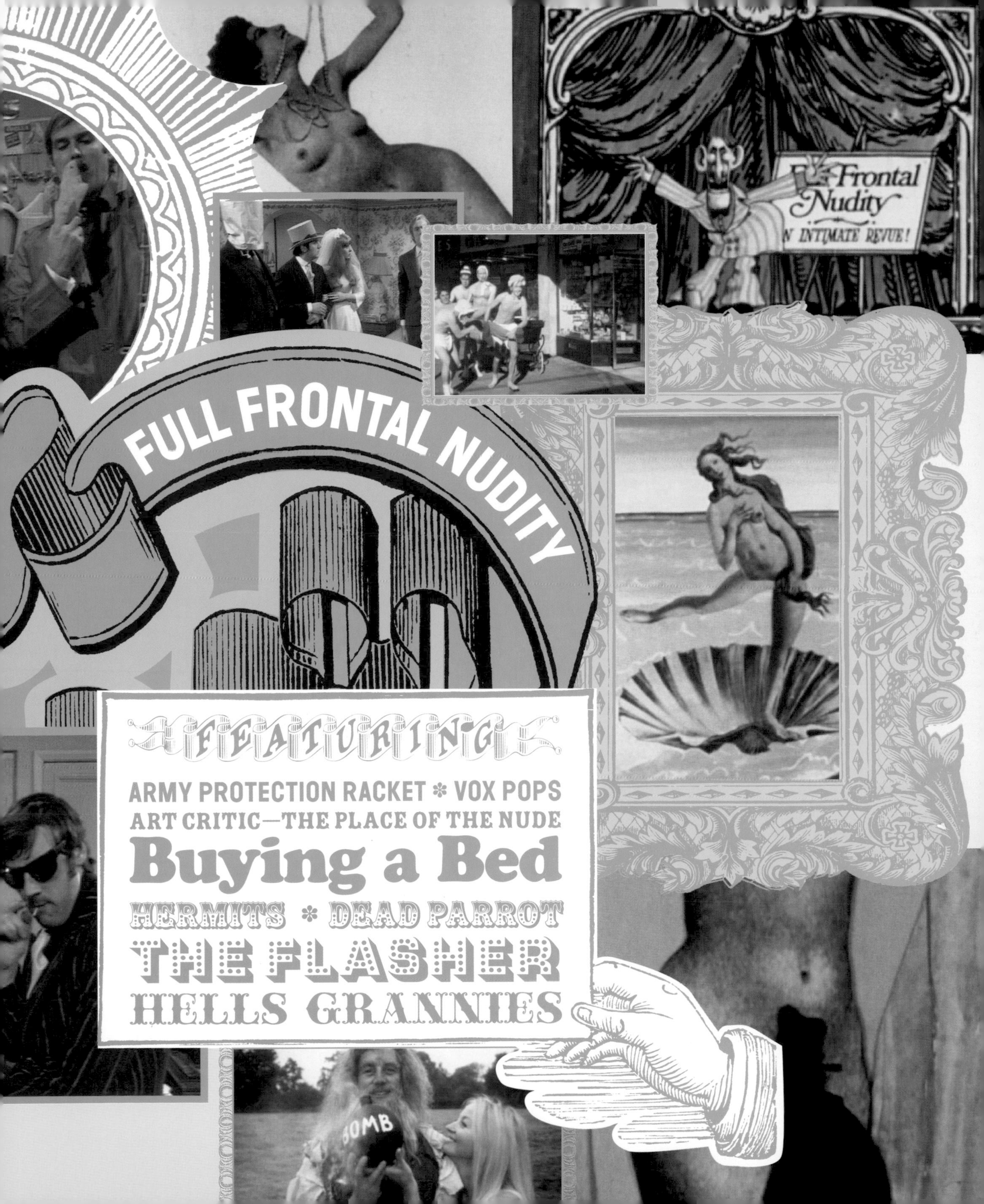
Full Frontal Nudity
AN INTIMATE REVUE!
FULL FRONTAL NUDITY
FEATURING
ARMY PROTECTION RACKET * VOX POPS
ART CRITIC—THE PLACE OF THE NUDE
Buying a Bed
HERMITS * DEAD PARROT
THE FLASHER
HELLS GRANNIES
BOMB

FIRST AIRED: DECEMBER 7, 1969

We see the 'It's' man sitting in the countryside in a garden lounger chair. A sexy young lady in a bikini hands him a glass of wine and gently helps him up and walks him to the camera. Looking very pleased with himself he sips the wine as she caresses him. Then she hands him a smoking round anarchist's type bomb (with 'Bomb' written on it). He realizes what it is only as he says:

IT'S MAN (MICHAEL)
IT'S...
VOICE OVER (JOHN) *(and caption)* Monty Python's Flying Circus

Cartoon credits.

Superimposed Caption: 'EPISODE 12B: FULL FRONTAL NUDITY' Cut to vox pops.

PEPPERPOT (MICHAEL) Speaking as a public opinion poll, I've had enough of the permissive society. 1

"Permissive society" is a British (and critical) phrase for the 1960s sexual freedoms that began, according to Philip Larkin, "Between the end of the Chatterley ban / And the Beatles' first LP." (DH Lawrence's novel, *Lady Chatterley's Lover*, was banned in the UK until 1960 because of supposedly "obscene" content.)

MAN IN DIRTY RAINCOAT (TERRY J) I haven't had enough of the permissive society.

Caption: 'IN THIS PERFORMANCE THE PART OF DAVID HEMMINGS 2 *WILL BE PLAYED BY A PIECE OF WOOD'. Cut to policeman.*

Another reference to Hemmings. See Episode 6.

POLICEMAN (GRAHAM) I would not appear in a frontal scene unless it was valid.

Stock film of the army. Tanks rolling, troops moving forward etc. Stirring military music.

VOICE OVER (JOHN) In 1943, a group of British Army Officers working deep behind enemy lines, carried out one of the most dangerous and heroic raids in the history of warfare. But that's as maybe. And now...

Superimposed Caption: 'AND NOW...UNOCCUPIED BRITAIN 1970' Cut to colonel's office. Colonel is seated at desk.

COLONEL (GRAHAM) Come in, what do you want?

Private Watkins enters and salutes.

WATKINS (ERIC) I'd like to leave the army please, sir.
COLONEL Good heavens man, why?
WATKINS It's dangerous.
COLONEL What?
WATKINS There are people with guns out there, sir.
COLONEL What?
WATKINS Real guns, sir. Not toy ones, sir. Proper ones, sir. They've all got 'em. All of 'em, sir. And some of 'em have got tanks.
COLONEL Watkins, they *are* on our side.
WATKINS And grenades, sir. And machine guns, sir. So I'd like to leave, sir, before I get killed, please.
COLONEL Watkins, you've only been in the army a day.
WATKINS I know sir but people get killed, properly dead, sir, no barley cross fingers, sir. 3 A bloke was telling me, if you're in the army and there's a war you have to go and fight.
COLONEL That's true.
WATKINS Well I mean, blimey, I mean if it was a big war somebody could be hurt.
COLONEL Watkins why did you *join* the army?
WATKINS For the water-skiing and for the travel, sir. And *not* for the killing, sir. I asked them to put it on my form, sir—no killing.
COLONEL Watkins are you a pacifist?
WATKINS No sir, I'm not a pacifist, sir. I'm a coward.
COLONEL That's a very silly line. Sit down.
WATKINS Yes sir. Silly, sir. (*sits in corner*)
COLONEL Awfully bad.

Knock at the door, sergeant enters, and salutes.

SERGEANT (JOHN) Two civilian gentlemen to see you...sir!
COLONEL Show them in please, sergeant.
SERGEANT Mr Dino Vercotti and Mr Luigi Vercotti. 4

"Barley cross fingers" is a Britishism referring to the childhood sign by which a truce in a game as signified, or as a sign of something not being absolutely true—as in, one crosses one's fingers behind one's back. The origins are probably from the north, perhaps Scotland; but it's ages-old, and lost in the sands of time, slipping as they do, through barley-crossed fingers.

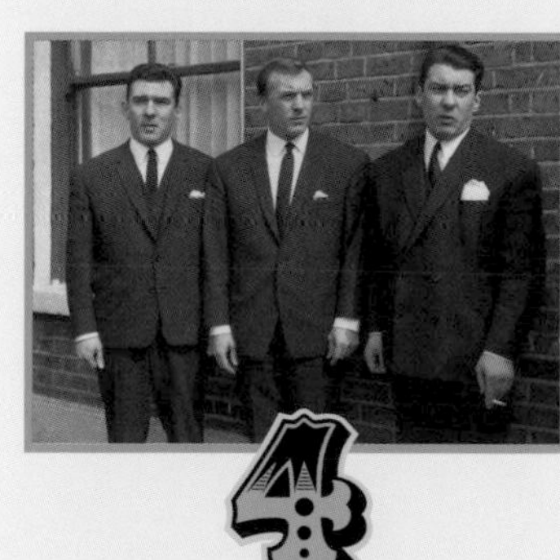

Compare to Doug and Dinsdale Piranha from Episode 14. Clearly a reference to the Kray brothers, London's most notorious gangsters of the day.

The Vercotti brothers enter. They wear Mafia suits and dark glasses.

DINO (TERRY J) Good morning, colonel.

COLONEL Good morning gentlemen. Now what can I do for you.

LUIGI (MICHAEL) (*looking round office casually*) You've...you've got a nice army base here, colonel.

COLONEL Yes.

LUIGI We wouldn't want anything to happen to it.

COLONEL What?

DINO No, what my brother means is it would be a shame if...(*he knocks something off mantel*)

COLONEL Oh.

DINO Oh sorry, colonel.

COLONEL Well don't worry about that. But please do sit down.

LUIGI No, we prefer to stand, thank you, colonel.

COLONEL All right. All right. But what do you want?

DINO What do we want, ha ha ha.

LUIGI Ha ha ha, very good, colonel.

DINO The colonel's a joker, Luigi.

LUIGI Explain it to the colonel, Dino.

DINO How many tanks you got, colonel?

COLONEL About five hundred altogether.

LUIGI Five hundred! Hey!

DINO You ought to be careful, colonel.

COLONEL We are careful, extremely careful.

DINO 'Cos things *break*, don't they?

COLONEL Break?

LUIGI

WELL EVERYTHING BREAKS, DON'T IT COLONEL. *[HE BREAKS SOMETHING ON DESK]* OH DEAR.

DINO Oh see my brother's clumsy colonel, and when he gets unhappy he breaks things. Like say, he don't feel the army's playing fair by him, he may start breaking things, colonel.

COLONEL What is all this about?

LUIGI How many men you got here, colonel?

COLONEL Oh, er...seven thousand infantry, six hundred artillery, and er, two divisions of paratroops. 5

Chapman pronounces "infantry" as "inventory." It's hard to tell if he means to.

LUIGI Paratroops, Dino.

DINO Be a shame if someone was to set fire to *them*.

COLONEL Set *fire* to them?

LUIGI Fires happen, colonel.

DINO Things burn.

COLONEL Look, what is all this about?

DINO My brother and I have got a little proposition for you colonel.

LUIGI Could save you a lot of bother.

DINO I mean you're doing all right here aren't you, colonel.

LUIGI Well suppose some of your tanks was to get broken and troops started getting lost, er, fights started breaking out during general inspection, like.

DINO It wouldn't be good for business would it, colonel?

COLONEL Are you threatening me?

DINO Oh, no, no, no.

LUIGI Whatever made you think that, colonel?

DINO The colonel doesn't think we're nice people, Luigi.

LUIGI We're your buddies, colonel.
DINO We want to look after you.
COLONEL Look after me?
LUIGI We can guarantee you that not a single armoured division will get done over for fifteen bob a week. 6
COLONEL No, no, no.
LUIGI Twelve and six. 7
COLONEL No, no, no.
LUIGI Eight and six...five bob...
COLONEL No, no this is silly.
DINO What's silly?
COLONEL No, the whole premise is silly and it's very badly written. I'm the senior officer here and I haven't had a funny line yet. So I'm stopping it.

DINO You can't do that!
COLONEL I've done it. The sketch is over.
WATKINS I want to leave the army please sir, it's dangerous.
COLONEL Look, I stopped your sketch five minutes ago. So get out of shot. Right director! Close up. Zoom in on me. (*camera zooms in*) That's better.
DINO (*off screen*) It's only 'cos you couldn't think of a punch line.
COLONEL Not true, not true. It's time for the cartoon. Cue telecine, ten, nine, eight... 8

Cut to telecine countdown.

DINO (*off screen*) The general public's not going to understand this, are they?
COLONEL (*off-screen*) Shut up you eyeties! 9

Cartoon rubbish entitled 'Full Frontal Nudity': Written, created and conceived off the back of a lorry by a demented American.

"Bob" is slang for a shilling, replaced in 1971 by the fivepence piece.

Twelve shillings and sixpence.

"Telecine" is a cliché from the movie world of the day, merely meaning "run the film."

"Eyeties" is slang for Italians.

Full Frontal
Nudity
AN INTIMATE REVUE!

Cut to two naked men.

MAN (GRAHAM) Full frontal nudity—never. What do you think, Barbara?
BARBARA (TERRY J) Oh, no no, no...unless it was artistically valid, of course.

Cut to stockbroker.

STOCKBROKER (MICHAEL) Full frontal nudity? Yes I'd do it, if it was valid. Or if the money was valid, and if it were a small part. 10

A dick joke.

Cut to art critic examining a nude painting.

Caption: 'AN ART CRITIC'

He sees the camera and starts guiltily.

ART CRITIC (MICHAEL) Good evening. I'd like to talk to you tonight about the place of the nude in my bed...um...in the history of my bed...of art, of *art*, I'm sorry. The place of the nude in the history of tart...call-girl...I'm sorry. I'll start again...Bum...oh what a giveaway. The place of the nude in art. (*a seductively dressed girl enters slinkily*) Oh hello there father, er, confessor, professor, your honour, your grace...
GIRL (KATYA) (*cutely*) I'm not your Grace, I'm your Elsie. 11

Katya Wyeth, she of Stanley Kubrick's *A Clockwork Orange*. She also appeared in Episode 4.

ART CRITIC What a terrible joke!
GIRL (*crying*) But it's my only line!

Cut to an idyllic countryside. Birds sing etc. as the camera starts a lyrical pan across the fields.

VOICE OVER (MICHAEL) (*and superimposed caption*) 'But there let us leave the art critic to strangle his wife and move on to pastures new'

After about ten seconds of mood setting the camera suddenly comes across the art critic strangling his wife in middle foreground. As the camera passes him he hums nervously and tries to look as though he isn't strangling anybody. 12 *The camera doesn't stop panning, and just as it goes off him we see him start strangling again. The pan carries on and catches up with a bridegroom carrying his bride across a field and finally arriving in a high street where, breathless and panting, he carries her through traffic and into a large department store.* 13

This casual violent misogyny strikes the modern viewer as horribly crass.

The John Sanders department store into which Terry and his bride run is now a Marks & Spencer. This is Ealing, in west London.

Finally cut to the furniture department of the store. The bridegroom and bride enter, he puts her down and addresses one of the assistants.

GROOM (TERRY J) We want to buy a bed, please.

LAMBERT (GRAHAM) Oh, certainly, I'll, I'll get someone to attend to you. (*calling off*) Mr Verity!

VERITY (ERIC) Can I help you sir?

GROOM Er yes. We'd like to buy a bed...a double bed...about fifty pounds?

VERITY Oh no, I am afraid not sir. Our cheapest bed is eight hundred pounds, sir.

GROOM Eight hundred pounds!

LAMBERT Oh, er, perhaps I should have explained. Mr Verity does tend to exaggerate, so every figure he gives you will be ten times too high. Otherwise he's perfectly all right, perfectly ha, ha, ha.

GROOM Oh I see, I see. (*to Verity*) So your cheapest bed is eighty pounds?

VERITY Eight hundred pounds, yes sir.

GROOM And how wide is it?

VERITY Er, the width is, er, sixty feet wide.

GROOM Oh...(*laughing politely he mutters to wife*) six foot wide, eh. And the length?

VERITY The length is...er...(*calls off*) Lambert! What is the length of the Comfydown Majorette?

LAMBERT Er, two foot long.

GROOM Two foot long?

VERITY Ah yes, you have to, ah, remember of course, to multiply everything Mr Lambert says by three. Er, it's nothing he can help, you understand. Apart from that he's perfectly all right.

GROOM I see, I'm sorry.

VERITY But it does mean that when he says a bed is two foot wide it is, in fact, sixty feet wide.

GROOM Oh, yes I see...

VERITY And that's not counting the mattress.

GROOM Oh, how much is that?

VERITY Er, Lambert will be able to help you there. (*calls*) Lambert! Will you show these twenty good people the, er, dog kennel please?

LAMBERT Mm? Certainly.

GROOM Dog kennel? No, no, no, mattresses, mattresses.

VERITY Oh no, no you have to say dog kennel to Mr Lambert because if you say mattress he puts a bag over his head. I should have explained. Apart from that he's really all right.

They go to Lambert.

GROOM Ah, hum, er we'd like to see the dog kennels please.

LAMBERT Dog kennels?

GROOM Yes, we want to see the dog kennels.
LAMBERT Ah yes, well that's the pets department. Second floor.
GROOM Oh, no, no, we want to see the *dog kennels*.
LAMBERT Yes, pets department second floor.
GROOM No, no, no, we don't really want to see dog kennels only your colleague said we ought to...
LAMBERT Oh dear, what's he been telling you now?
GROOM

WELL HE SAID WE SHOULD SAY DOG KENNELS TO YOU, INSTEAD OF MATTRESS.

Lambert puts bag over head.

GROOM (*looking round*) Oh dear, hello?
VERITY Did you say mattress?
GROOM Well, a little yes.
VERITY I did *ask* you not to say mattress didn't I. Now I've got to stand in the tea chest. (*he gets in the chest and sings*) 14 'And did those feet in ancient times, walk upon England's mountains green...' 15

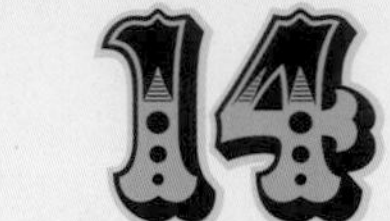

Idle trips as he gets into the chest, nearly falling.

A reprise from Episode 4 of Idle's rendition of Hubert Parry's "Jerusalem."

The manager enters.

MANAGER (JOHN) Did somebody say mattress to Mr Lambert!

Manager and Verity continue to sing. Lambert takes bag off head, manager exits after pointing a warning finger at bride and groom.

VERITY (*getting out of chest*) He should be all right now but don't, you know...just *don't*. (*exits*)
GROOM Oh, no, no, no, er we'd like to see, see the dog kennels, please.
LAMBERT Yes, second floor.
GROOM No, no look these (*pointing*) dog kennels here, see?
LAMBERT Mattresses?
GROOM Oh (*jumps*)...yes.

LAMBERT Well, if you meant mattress, why didn't you *say* a mattress. I mean it's very confusing for me, if you go and say dog kennels, when you mean mattress. Why not just say mattress?
GROOM Well, I mean you put a bag over your head last time I said mattress.

Bag goes on. Groom looks around guiltily. Verity walks in. Verity heaves a sigh, jumps in box. Manager comes in and joins him, they sing 'And did those feet...' 16 *Another assistant comes in.*

ASSISTANT (MICHAEL) Did somebody say mattress to Mr Lambert?
VERITY Twice.
ASSISTANT Hey, everybody, somebody said mattress to Mr Lambert, twice!

Assistant, groom and bride join in the therapy.

VERITY It's not working. We need more. 17
Cut to crowd in St Peter's Square singing 'Jerusalem'. Cut to department store. 18 *Lambert takes the bag off his head and looks at groom and bride.*

LAMBERT Now, er, can I help you?
BRIDE (CAROL) We want a mattress.

Lambert immediately puts bag back on head.

ALL Oh. What did you say that for? What did you say that for?
BRIDE (*weeping*) Well, it's my only line.
ALL Well, you didn't have to say it.

They all hop off. She howls. Cut to vox pops.

AFRICAN NATIVE (TERRY J) Full frontal nudity—not in this part of Esher.
CHARTERED ACCOUNTANT (JOHN) I would only perform a scene in which there was total frontal nudity.

Cut to colonel.

COLONEL Now, I've noticed a tendency for this programme to get rather silly. Now I do my best to keep things moving along, but I'm not having things getting silly. Those last two sketches I did got very silly indeed, and that last one about the bed was even sillier. Now, nobody likes a good laugh more than I do...except perhaps my wife and some of her friends...oh yes and Captain Johnston. Come to think of it most people like a good laugh more than I do. But that's beside the point. Now, let's have a good clean healthy outdoor sketch. Get some air into your lungs. Ten, nine, eight and all that.

Cut to two hermits on a hillside.

COLONEL Ah yes, that's better. Now let's hope this doesn't get silly.
FIRST HERMIT (MICHAEL) Hello, are you a hermit by any chance?
SECOND HERMIT (ERIC) Yes that's right. Are you a hermit?
FIRST HERMIT Yes, I certainly am.
SECOND HERMIT Well I never. What are you getting away from?
FIRST HERMIT Oh you know, the usual—people, chat, gossip, you know.
SECOND HERMIT Oh I certainly do—it was the same with me. I mean there comes a time when you realize there's no good frittering your life away in idleness and trivial chit-chat. Where's your cave?

Actually, they sing the second verse—"Bring me my bow of burning gold"—and Idle starts the tune significantly higher than previously, stretching his ability to hit the notes almost to breaking point. In fact, he misses the note on "of" by at least a tone.

17

At this point, we fear that the singing quintet—Idle, Cleese, Palin, Jones, and Katya Wyeth—won't be able to reach the note in the crescendo of the verse, but we're saved the pain by the cut to stock footage of St. Peter's Square and a recorded version of "Jerusalem."

18

When the singing resumes, it is in the key of the recording, and thereby manageable for all. Phew—disaster averted!

FIRST HERMIT Oh, up the goat track, first on the left.
SECOND HERMIT Oh they're very nice up there aren't they?
FIRST HERMIT Yes they are, I've got a beauty.
SECOND HERMIT A bit draughty though, aren't they?
FIRST HERMIT No, we've had ours insulated.

SECOND HERMIT Oh yes.
FIRST HERMIT Yes, I used birds' nests, moss and oak leaves round the outside.
SECOND HERMIT Oh, sounds marvellous.
FIRST HERMIT Oh it's a treat, it really is, 'cos otherwise those stone caves can be so grim.
SECOND HERMIT Yes they really can be, can't they? They really can.
FIRST HERMIT Oh yes.

Third hermit passes by.

THIRD HERMIT (GRAHAM) Morning Frank.
SECOND HERMIT Morning Norman. Talking of moss, er you know Mr Robinson?
FIRST HERMIT With the, er, green loin cloth?
SECOND HERMIT Er no, that's Mr Seagrave. Mr Robinson's the hermit who lodges with Mr Seagrave.
FIRST HERMIT Oh I see, yes.
SECOND HERMIT Yes well he's put me onto wattles. [19]
FIRST HERMIT Really?
SECOND HERMIT Yes. Swears by them. Yes.

Fourth hermit passes by.

FOURTH HERMIT (JOHN) Morning Frank.
SECOND HERMIT Morning Lionel. Well he says that moss tends to fall off the cave walls during cold weather. You know you might get a really bad spell and half the moss drops off the cave wall, leaving you cold.
FIRST HERMIT Oh well, Mr Robinson's cave's never been exactly nirvana has it?
SECOND HERMIT Well, quite, that's what I mean. Anyway, Mr Rogers, he's the, er, hermit...
FIRST HERMIT ...on the end.
SECOND HERMIT ...up at the top, yes. Well he tried wattles and he came out in a rash.
FIRST HERMIT Really?
SECOND HERMIT Yes, and there's me with half a wall wattled, I mean what'll I do?
FIRST HERMIT Well why don't you try birds' nests like I've done? Or else, dead bracken.
FIFTH HERMIT (TERRY J) (*calling from a distance*) Frank!
SECOND HERMIT Yes Han.
FIFTH HERMIT Can I borrow your goat?

19

One half of the wattle-and-daub technique, in which the former—strips of wood or twigs made into a lattice structure—are pasted with a soil/clay/dung/whatever's-at-hand mixture to make a wall.

A nice gag to deflect from the "goat-as-sexual-partner" request by the Fifth Hermit.

By the end of the sketch, Palin's character seems to have forgotten the beginning, where the two hermits are strangers.

SECOND HERMIT Er, yes that'll be all right. Oh leave me a pint for breakfast will you? ... moors, collect my berries, chastise myself, and two hours back in the evening. 20 (*to first hermit*) You see, you know that is the trouble with living half way up a cliff—you feel so cut off. You know it takes me two hours every morning to get out onto the moors, collect my berries, chastise myself, and two hours back in the evening.

FIRST HERMIT Still there's one thing about being a hermit, at least you meet people.

SECOND HERMIT Oh yes, I wouldn't go back to public relations.

FIRST HERMIT Oh well, bye for now Frank, must toddle. 21

COLONEL (*coming on*) Right, you two hermits, stop that sketch. I think it's silly.

SECOND HERMIT What?

COLONEL It's silly.

SECOND HERMIT What do you mean, you can't stop it—it's on film.

COLONEL That doesn't make any difference to the viewer at home, does it? Come on, get out. Out. Come on out, all of you. Get off, go on, all of you. Go on, move, move. Go on, get out. Come on, get out, move, move.

He shoos them and the film crew off the hillside.

Animation: including dancing Botticelli Venus 22, *which links to pet shop:*

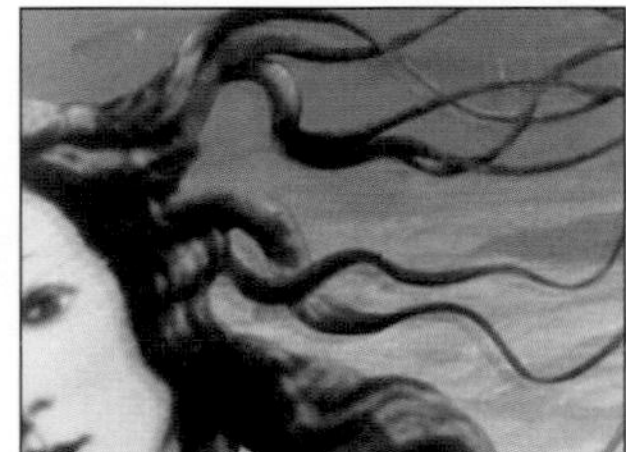

Mr Praline walks into the shop carrying a dead parrot in a cage. He walks to counter where shopkeeper tries to hide below cash register. 23

PRALINE (JOHN) Hello, I wish to register a complaint...Hello? Miss?

SHOPKEEPER (MICHAEL) What do you mean, miss?

PRALINE Oh, I'm sorry, I have a cold. I wish to make a complaint.

SHOPKEEPER Sorry, we're closing for lunch.

PRALINE Never mind that my lad, I wish to complain about this parrot what I purchased not half an hour ago from this very boutique.

SHOPKEEPER Oh yes, the Norwegian Blue. 24 What's wrong with it?

By means of Venus falling off her shell, which in turns falls into the sea . . . and a shell falls to the bottom of a fish tank in the pet shop. A very pleasing and clever connective.

Arguably the first classic Python sketch to air, the parrot sketch was written by Cleese and Chapman. Some would say it's the finest Python sketch—and it remains brilliantly funny more than forty years later. As with much of the comedy of the Pythons, this sketch comes from a real place: Palin's local garage where he bought his car. If anything ever went wrong with it, the mechanic would refuse to accept there was a problem. Cleese used that character in a show he wrote with Chapman in 1968 called *How to Irritate People.* He used it again when writing the parrot sketch (and the original returning item was a toaster, though Chapman suggested a parrot was funnier).

Parrots from Scandinavia? Dr. David Waterhouse, a fossil expert (and Python lover), claims that parrots did indeed live in Scandinavia—55 million years ago. His work was based on the wing bone (the humerus, naturally) of a bird called Mopsitta Tanta—though now, of course, the fossil bears the nickname Norwegian Blue.

PRALINE

I'LL TELL YO
WRONG WI
IT'S DEAD,
WHAT'S WR

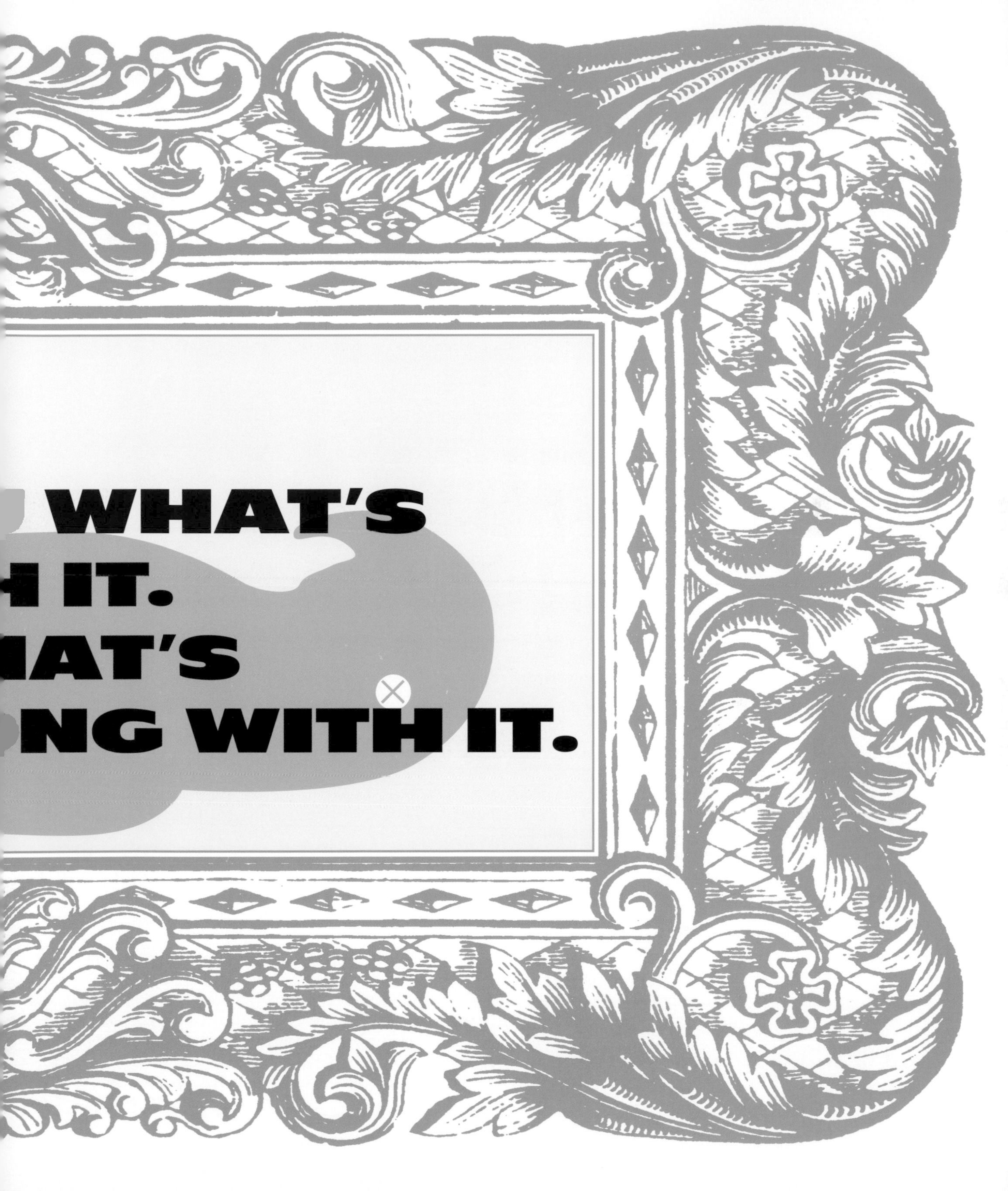
WHAT'S
H IT.
HAT'S
NG WITH IT.

SHOPKEEPER No, no it's resting, look!
PRALINE Look my lad, I know a dead parrot when I see one and I'm looking at one right now.
SHOPKEEPER No, no sir, it's not dead. It's resting.
PRALINE Resting?
SHOPKEEPER Yeah, remarkable bird the Norwegian Blue, beautiful plumage, innit?
PRALINE The plumage don't enter into it—it's stone dead.
SHOPKEEPER No, no—it's just resting.
PRALINE All right then, if it's resting I'll wake it up. (shouts into cage) Hello Polly! I've got a nice cuttlefish for you when you wake up, Polly Parrot!

SHOPKEEPER (*jogging cage*) There it moved.
PRALINE No he didn't. That was you pushing the cage.
SHOPKEEPER I did not.
PRALINE Yes, you did. (*takes parrot out of cage, shouts*) Hello Polly, Polly (*bangs it against counter*) Polly Parrot, wake up. Polly. (*throws it in the air and lets it fall to the floor*) Now that's what I call a dead parrot.
SHOPKEEPER No, no it's stunned.
PRALINE Look my lad, I've had just about enough of this. That parrot is definitely deceased. And when I bought it not half an hour ago, you assured me that its lack of movement was due to it being tired and shagged out after a long squawk. 25
SHOPKEEPER It's probably pining for the fiords.
PRALINE Pining for the fiords, what kind of talk is that? Look, why did it fall flat on its back the moment I got it home?
SHOPKEEPER The Norwegian Blue prefers kipping on its back. 26 Beautiful bird, lovely plumage.
PRALINE Look, I took the liberty of examining that parrot, and I discovered that the only reason that it had been sitting on its perch in the first place was that it had been nailed there.
SHOPKEEPER Well of course it was nailed there. Otherwise it would muscle up to those bars and voom.
PRALINE Look matey (*picks up parrot*) this parrot wouldn't voom if I put four thousand volts through it. It's bleeding demised.
SHOPKEEPER It's not, it's pining.

"Shagged out" originally meant sexually exhausted, but the more general meaning (and presumably the one used here) is simply "worn out."

"Kipping" is British slang for sleeping, though it tends to refer to napping.

PRALINE It's not pining, it's passed on. This parrot is no more. It has ceased to be. It's expired and gone to meet its maker. This is a late parrot. It's a stiff. Bereft of life, it rests in peace. If you hadn't nailed it to the perch, it would be pushing up the daisies. It's rung down the curtain and joined the choir invisible. [27]

THIS IS AN EX-PARROT.

SHOPKEEPER Well, I'd better replace it then.

PRALINE (*to camera*) If you want to get anything done in this country you've got to complain till you're blue in the mouth.

SHOPKEEPER Sorry guv, we're right out of parrots.

PRALINE I see. I see. I get the picture.

SHOPKEEPER I've got a slug.

PRALINE Does it talk?

SHOPKEEPER Not really, no.

PRALINE Well, it's scarcely a replacement, then is it?

SHOPKEEPER Listen, I'll tell you what, (*handing over a card*) tell you what, if you go to my brother's pet shop in Bolton he'll replace your parrot for you. [28]

PRALINE Bolton eh?

SHOPKEEPER Yeah.

PRALINE All right.

He leaves, holding the parrot. Caption: 'A SIMILAR PET SHOP IN BOLTON, LANCS' Close-up of sign on door reading: 'Similar Pet Shops Ltd'. Pull back from sign to see same pet shop. Shopkeeper now has moustache. Praline walks into shop. He looks around with interest, noticing the empty parrot cage still on the floor.

PRALINE Er, excuse me. This is Bolton, is it?

SHOPKEEPER No, no it's, er, Ipswich. [29]

PRALINE (*to camera*) That's Inter-City Rail for you. (*leaves*)

Man in porter's outfit standing at complaints desk for railways. Praline approaches.

PRALINE I wish to make a complaint.

PORTER (TERRY J) I don't have to do this, you know.

PRALINE I beg your pardon?

PORTER I'm a qualified brain surgeon. I only do this because I like being my own boss.

PRALINE Er, excuse me, this is irrelevant, isn't it?

PORTER Oh yeah, it's not easy to pad these out to thirty minutes.

PRALINE Well I wish to make a complaint. I got on the Bolton train and found myself deposited here in Ipswich.

PORTER No, this is Bolton.

PRALINE (*to camera*) The pet shop owner's brother was lying.

PORTER Well you can't blame British Rail for that. [30]

PRALINE If this is Bolton, I shall return to the pet shop.

Caption: 'A LITTLE LATER LTD'. Praline walks into the shop again.

PRALINE I understand that this *is* Bolton.

SHOPKEEPER Yes.

PRALINE Well, you told me it was Ipswich.

SHOPKEEPER It was a pun.

PRALINE A pun?

SHOPKEEPER No, no, not a pun, no. What's the other thing which reads the same backwards as forwards?

Meaning the dead. "The Choir Invisible" is also a famous poem by George Eliot, which ends with the couplet "So shall I join the choir invisible/Whose music is the gladness of the world."

Bolton is a town in the northeast of England, near Manchester.

Ipswich is a town in the far east of England, in the county of Suffolk.

30

The punch line to many jokes in Britain, the once nationally owned rail system was notorious for its inability to stick to a schedule in any meaningful way, causing commuters endless pain and train spotters interminable delays to their joy.

PRALINE A palindrome?

SHOPKEEPER Yes, yes.

PRALINE It's not a palindrome. The palindrome of Bolton would be Notlob. It don't work.

SHOPKEEPER Look, what do you want?

PRALINE No I'm sorry, I'm not prepared to pursue my line of enquiry any further as I think this is getting too silly.

COLONEL (*coming in*) Quite agree. Quite agree. Silly. Silly...silly. Right get on with it. Get on with it.

Cut to announcer eating a yoghurt.

ANNOUNCER (ERIC) (*seeing camera*) Oh...er...oh...um! Oh!...er...(*shuffles papers*) I'm sorry...and now frontal nudity.

Cut to tracking or hand-held shot down street, keeping up with extremely shabby man in long overcoat. His back is to camera. He passes two pepperpots and a girl. As he passes each one he opens his coat wide. They react with shocked horror. He does this three times, after the third time he turns to camera and opens his coat wide. He has a big sign hanging round his neck, covering his chest. It says 'boo'. Cut back to announcer eating yoghurt. The colonel comes in and nudges him.

ANNOUNCER Oh, oh I'm sorry. I thought the film was longer. (*shuffling papers*) Ah. Now Notlob, er, Bolton.

Cut to grannies film, which opens with a pan across Bolton. Voice of reporter.

VOICE OVER (ERIC) This is a frightened city. Over these houses, over these streets hangs a pall of fear. Fear of a new kind of violence which is terrorizing the city. Yes, gangs of old ladies attacking defenceless fit young men.

Film of old ladies beating up two young men; then several grannies walking aggressively along street, pushing passers-by aside.

FIRST YOUNG MAN (MICHAEL) Well they come up to you, like, and push you—shove you off the pavement, like. There's usually four or five of them.

SECOND YOUNG MAN (TERRY J) Yeah, this used to be a nice neighbourhood before the old ladies started moving in. Nowadays some of us daren't even go down to the shops.

THIRD YOUNG MAN (JOHN) Well Mr Johnson's son Kevin, he don't go out any more. He comes back from wrestling and locks himself in his room.

FILM OF GRANNIES HARASSING AN ATTRACTIVE GIRL.

VOICE OVER What are they in it for, these old hoodlums, these layabouts in lace?
FIRST GRANNY (*voice over*) Well it's something to do isn't it?
SECOND GRANNY (*voice over*) It's good fun.
THIRD GRANNY (*voice over*) It's like you know, well, innit, eh?
VOICE OVER Favourite targets for the old ladies are telephone kiosks.

Film of grannies carrying off a telephone kiosk: then painting slogans on a wall. 31

POLICEMAN (GRAHAM) (*coming up to them*) Well come on, come on, off with you. Clear out, come on get out of it. (*they clear off: he turns to camera*) We have a lot of trouble with these oldies. Pension day's the worst—they go mad. As soon as they get their hands on their money they blow it all on milk, bread, tea, tin of meat for the cat.

Cut to cinema.

CINEMA MANAGER (TERRY J) Yes, well of course they come here for the two o'clock matinee, all the old bags out in there, especially if it's something like 'The Sound of Music'. We get seats ripped up, hearing aids broken, all that sort of thing.

A policeman hustles two grannies out of the cinema.Cut to reporter walking along street.

REPORTER The whole problem of these senile delinquents lies in their complete rejection of the values of contemporary society. They've seen their children grow up and become accountants, stockbrokers and even sociologists, and they begin to wonder if it is all really...(*disappears downwards rapidly*) arggh!

Shot of two grannies replacing manhole cover. Cut to young couple.

YOUNG MAN (GRAHAM) Oh well we sometimes feel we're to blame in some way for what our gran's become. I mean she used to be happy here until she, she started on the crochet.
REPORTER (*off-screen*) Crochet?
YOUNG MAN Yeah. Now she can't do without it. Twenty balls of wool a day, sometimes. If she can't get the wool she gets violent. What can we do about it?

Specifically the grannies were painting the words "Make Tea Not Love." Note the *QPR* (Queens Park Rangers) graffiti on the same wall—QPR is a professional soccer team from west London, a full three hours southeast of Bolton.

Film of grannies on motorbikes roaring down streets and through a shop. 32 *One has 'Hell's Grannies' on her jacket.*

VOICE OVER But this is not just an old ladies' town. There are other equally dangerous gangs—such as the baby snatchers.

Film of five men in baby outfits carrying off a young man from outside a shop. Cut to distraught wife.

32

One of the great joys of watching MPFC now is to see the bystanders. Here a presumably bemused set of "civilians" witnesses three grannies on motorbikes drive in and out of a shop on a busy street.

33

Rita Davies is a veteran TV actress. Her current curriculum vitae describes her voice quality as "clear" and her voice character as "sympathetic"—both true of the plaint she delivers here, near the start of her acting career.

34

My favorite line in all of Python, if you're scoring at home.

WIFE (RITA DAVIES) 33 I just left my husband out here while I went in to do some shopping and I came back and he was gone. He was only forty-seven.

VOICE OVER And on the road too, vicious gangs of keep-left signs.

Film: two keep-left signs attack a vicar.

COLONEL (*coming up and stopping them*) Right, right, stop it. This film's got silly. Started off with a nice little idea about grannies attacking young men, but now it's got silly. This man's hair is too long for a vicar too. 34 These signs are pretty badly made. Right, now for a complete change of mood.

Cut to man in dirty raincoat.

MAN IN DIRTY RAINCOAT (TERRY J) I've heard of unisex but I've never had it.

Cut to 'It's' man still holding smoking bomb.

VOICE OVER (JOHN) David Hemmings 35 appeared by permission of the National Forestry Commission.

Superimposed Roller Caption:

'"FULL FRONTAL NUDITY" WAS CONCEIVED, WRITTEN AND PERFORMED BY...(credits)'

The 'It's' man realizes that he has a bomb and runs off still carrying it. As the credits end it explodes.

Another reference to the "wooden" nature of Hemmings.

SEASON 1
EPISODE 9

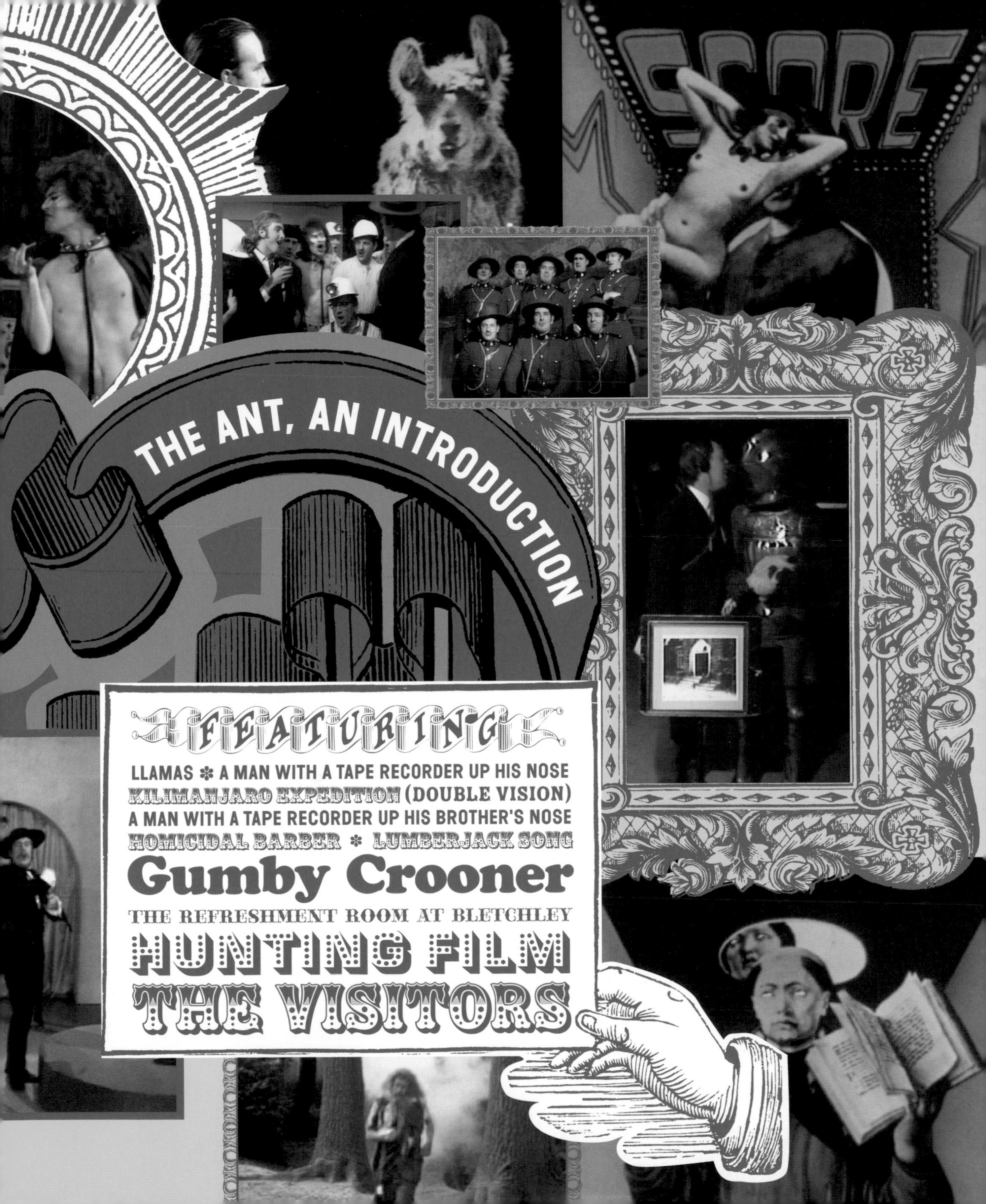
THE ANT, AN INTRODUCTION
FEATURING
LLAMAS ✽ A MAN WITH A TAPE RECORDER UP HIS NOSE
KILIMANJARO EXPEDITION (DOUBLE VISION)
A MAN WITH A TAPE RECORDER UP HIS BROTHER'S NOSE
HOMICIDAL BARBER ✽ LUMBERJACK SONG
Gumby Crooner
THE REFRESHMENT ROOM AT BLETCHLEY
HUNTING FILM
THE VISITORS

FIRST AIRED: DECEMBER 14, 1969

A forest. From an explosion in the far distance the 'It's' man runs very rapidly up to camera and announces:

IT'S MAN (MICHAEL)

IT'S...

Opening animated titles.

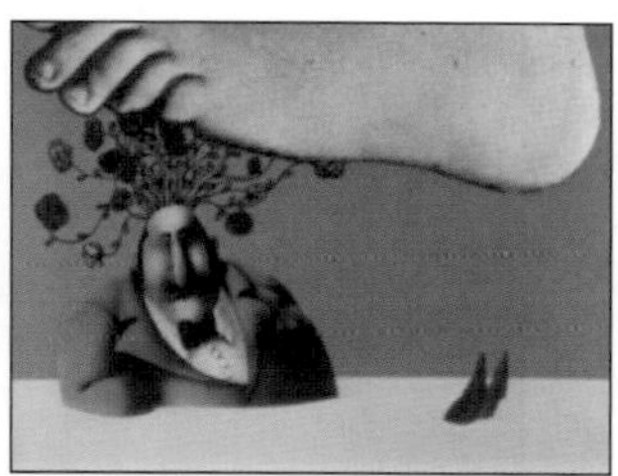

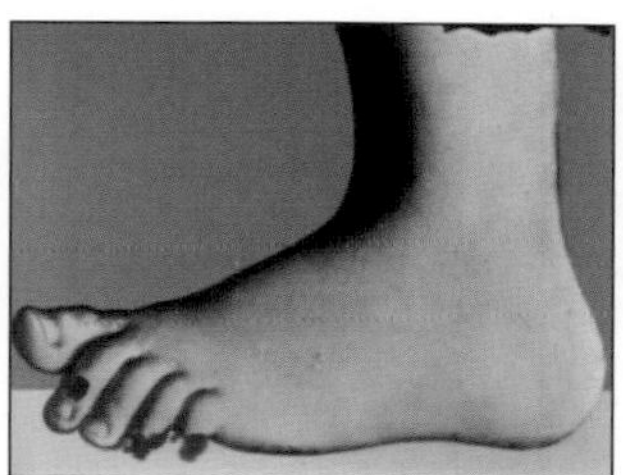

Caption: 'PART 2' Caption: 'THE LLAMA'. A Spanish guitarist (ERIC) *and a dancer* (TERRY J) *in traditional Spanish costume.*

Superimposed Caption: 'LIVE FROM GOLDERS GREEN'. Man enters and walks up to a life-size photo of a llama. He delivers the following lecture in Spanish, with help from the guitarist and dancer, and superimposed subtitles.

MAN (JOHN) (*but in Spanish with subtitles in English*) The llama is a quadruped which lives in big rivers like the Amazon. It has two ears, a heart, a forehead, and a beak for eating honey. But it is provided with fins for swimming.

GUITARIST & DANCER Llamas are larger than frogs.

MAN Llamas are dangerous, so if you see one where people are swimming, you shout:

GUITARIST & DANCER Look out, there are llamas! 1

Graham, dressed in a Spanish frock, enters on a moped; he blows up a paper bag and bursts it. They bow.

The tune sung here is the Italian favorite "That's Amore."

Cut to exterior of Ada's Snack Bar (a small café). Hand-held camera moves round the back to where an announcer is seated at desk with an old-fashioned BBC microphone.

ANNOUNCER

AND NOW FOR SOMETHING COMPLETELY DIFFERENT—A MAN WITH A TAPE RECORDER UP HIS NOSE.

We see Michael, in evening dress, on a small stage, with potted plants, etc. He ostentatiously inserts a finger up one nostril.

We hear the Marseillaise. He removes the finger; the music stops. He inserts the finger up the other nostril: we hear rewinding noises. Once again he inserts a finger up the first nostril: again we hear the Marseillaise. He bows. Stock film of Women's Institute applauding. He inserts a finger up his nostril again, and we hear:

VOICE OVER (MICHAEL) And now to something completely different. The office of Sir George Head, OBE. 2

Large study with maps and photographs on the wall and a large desk at which sits Sir George Head.

SIR (JOHN) Next please.

Bob walks into the room and up to the desk.

2 The Pythons never miss a chance to give characters offensive names.

Cleese actually merely slaps the application down on the desk to one side, and there is then an obvious cut in the sketch; the sound isn't uniform and the camera moves to behind Cleese, but jumpily.

And so begins another gag on that British obsession, namely, "Which road to take to get there?"

Nor do the Pythons miss a chance to allude to their impeccable educations, here name-checking the 17th-century Dutch philosopher Baruch Spinoza.

SIR (*looking up*) One at a time please.

BOB (ERIC) There is only me, sir.

SIR (*putting a hand over one eye*) So there is. Take a...

BOB Seat?

SIR Seat! Take a seat. So! (*looking four feet to Bob's right*) You want to join my mountaineering expedition do you? (*keeps looking off*)

BOB (*rather uncertain*) Me, sir?

SIR Yes.

BOB Yes, I'd very much like to, sir.

SIR Jolly good, jolly good. (*ticking sheet and then looking right at Bob*) And how about you?

BOB There is only me, sir.

SIR (*putting hand over eye and looking both at Bob and to Bob's right*) Well bang goes his application then. (*he tears up form*) **3** Now let me fill you in. I'm leading this expedition and we're going to climb both peaks of Mount Kilimanjaro.

BOB I thought there was only one peak, sir.

SIR (*getting up, putting one hand over one eye again and going to large map of Africa on wall and peering at it at point-blank range*) Well, that'll save a bit of time. Well done. Now the object of this expedition is to see if we can find any traces of last year's expedition.

BOB Last year's expedition?

SIR Yes, my brother was leading that, they were going to build a bridge between the two peaks. (*looks at map with one hand over eye*) My idea I'm afraid. Now, I ought to tell you that I have practically everyone I need for this expedition...so what special qualifications do you have?

BOB Well, sir...

SIR Yes, you first.

BOB There is only me, sir.

SIR (*to Bob's right*) I wasn't talking to you. (*to Bob*) Carry on.

BOB Well I'm a fully qualified mountaineer.

SIR Mountaineer? Mountaineer (*looks it up in the dictionary*) where the devil are they, mound, mount...mountain...a mountaineer: 'two men skilled in climbing mountains'. Jolly good, well you're in. Congratulations, both of you. Well, er, what are your names?

BOB Arthur Wilson.

SIR Arthur Wilson, right well look, I'll call you (*to Bob*) Arthur Wilson one, and you (*to Bob's right*) Arthur Wilson two, just to avoid confusion.

BOB Are you actually leading this expedition sir?

SIR Yes, we are leading this expedition to Africa.

BOB (*tartly*) And what routes will you both be taking?

SIR **Good questions...shall I? Well we'll be leaving on January 22nd and taking the following routes.** ***(goes over to large map, clearly labelled Surrey)*** **The A23s through Purleys down on the main roads near Purbrights avoiding Leatherheads and then taking the A231S entering Rottingdeans from the North. From Rottingdeans we go through Africa to Nairobis. We take the South road out of Nairobis for about twelve miles and then ask.** **4**

BOB Does anyone speak Swahili, sir?

SIR Oh, yes I think most of them do down there.

BOB Does anyone in *our* party speak Swahili sir?

SIR Oh, well Matron's got a smattering.

BOB (*sarcastically*) Apart from the two Matrons...

SIR Good God, I'd forgotten about her.

BOB Apart from them, who else is coming on the expedition, sir?

SIR Well we've got the Arthur Brown twins, two botanists called Machin, the William Johnston brothers...

BOB Two of them?

SIR No four of them, a pair of identical twins...and a couple of the Ken Spinoza **5** quads—the other two pulled out. And of course you two.

BOB And none of these are mountaineers?

SIR Well you two are, and we've got a brace of guides called Jimmy Blenkinsop...because Kilimanjaro is a pretty tricky climb you know, most of it's up until you reach the very very top, and then it tends to slope away rather sharply. But Jimmy's put his heads together and worked out a way up. (*opens door*) Jimmy? (*James Blenkinsop enters; he wears climbing gear*) I don't believe you've met. **Jimmy Blenkinsop—Arthur Wilson, Arthur Wilson—Jimmy Blenkinsop...Arthur Wilson two—James Blenkinsop one, James Blenkinsop one —Arthur Wilson two. Carry on Jimmies.** 6

JIMMY (GRAHAM) (*to Bob, reassuringly*) Don't worry about the er...(*puts hand over eye*) We'll get him up somehow. *Jimmy proceeds to walk round the room clambering over every single piece of available furniture. He doesn't stop talking. Causing a complete wreckage, he clambers over the desk, onto a bookcase and round the room knocking furniture over, meanwhile he is saying:* Now the approach to Kilimanjaro is quite simply over the foothills, and then we go on after that to...ohh...to set a base camp, somewhere in the region of the bottom of the glacier when... *Jimmy staggers out headlong through the door. There are loud crashing noises.*

SIR He'll be leading the first assault.

BOB Well I'm afraid I shan't be coming on your expedition sir, as I've absolutely no confidence in anyone involved in it.

He gets up and walks out slamming the door.

SIR Oh dear. (*pause*) Well how about you?

BOB (*still sitting in chair at other angle of desk*) Well I'm game, sir.

Cut back to two sirs, double image, split screen.

SIR So are we.

Cut to two announcers (JOHNS) *at desks. They put telephones down, turn to camera, and announce:*

ANNOUNCERS (JOHNS) And now for something completely different—a man with a tape recorder up his brother's nose.

Cut to Michael on small stage as before, this time also with Graham. Michael puts a finger up Graham's nostril: we hear the Marseillaise. He removes it: the music stops. He puts a finger up Graham's other nostril, and we hear rewinding noises.

VOICE OVER (JOHN) (*and caption*) 'and now in sterro...'

Michael simultaneously puts a finger up his own nostril and a finger (on the other hand) up Graham's; we hear two recordings of the Marseillaise together (out of sync). 7

Cleese stumbles over this admittedly difficult list of names, saying "Jimmy Blenkinsop wilm" rather than "James Blenkinsop one."

Here, not appearing in the original script, is a brief film of the single soccer fan applauding on the empty terraces, akin to the scene in Episode 7.

An animated sequence then leads us to a gents suburban hairdressing salon.

A customer comes in. The barber is standing in a white coat washing his hands at a basin.

CUSTOMER (TERRY J) Morning.
BARBER (MICHAEL) (*flinching slightly*) Ah...good morning sir, good morning. I'll be with you in a minute.

Customer sits in barber's chair. Barber carries on washing. He seems to be over-thoroughly washing and rewashing his hands and lower arms. Barber turns and smiles humourlessly at customer. At last he has finished washing. He dries his hands thoroughly, turns and comes over to the customer. There are very obvious blood stains on his coat and his lapel is torn off. One stain could be the mark of a blood-stained hand which has slipped down the length of it. He picks up a sheet and shakes it out. Sound of iron and heavy objects falling on the floor. He throws it around the customer. As he knots the sheet at the back he seems about to pull it tight and strangle the customer. His face sweats, a wild look in his eyes. Then with a supreme effort he controls himself. Customer smiles reassuringly at him.

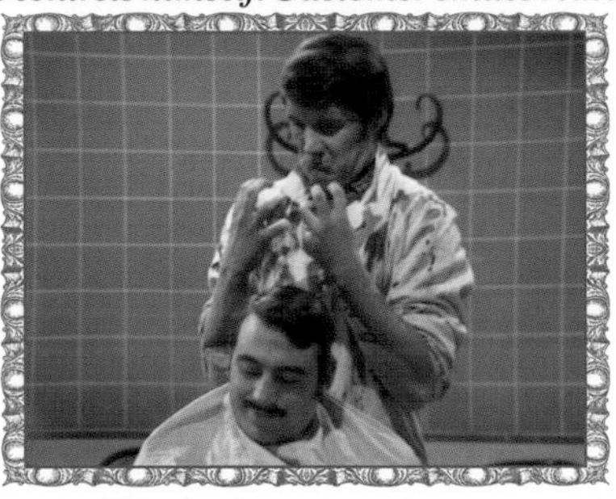

The standard haircut of the military—and standard, too, in polite professional British society.

BARBER How...how would you like it, sir?
CUSTOMER Just short back and sides please. 8
BARBER How do you do that?
CUSTOMER Well it's just...ordinary short back and sides...
BARBER It's not a...razor cut? (*suddenly*) Razor, razor, cut, cut, blood, spurt, artery, murder...(*controlling himself*) Oh thank God, thank God. (*sigh of relief*) It's just a scissors...
CUSTOMER Yes...(*laughs, thinking the barber must be having a little joke*)
BARBER You wouldn't rather just have it combed, would you sir?
CUSTOMER I beg your pardon?
BARBER You wouldn't rather forget all about it?
CUSTOMER No, no, no, I want it cut.

At the word 'cut' barber winces.

BARBER

CUT, CUT, CUT, BLOOD, SPURT, ARTERY, MURDER, HITCHCOCK, PSYCHO...RIGHT SIR...WELL...

(*swallows hard*) I'll just get everything ready. In the meanwhile perhaps you could fill in one of these.

He hands him a bit of paper; the barber goes to a cupboard and opens it.

CUSTOMER All right, fine, yes.

On the inside of the door there is a large medical chart headed: 'Main Arteries '. His shaking hand traces the arteries and he looks occasionally back at the customer.

CUSTOMER Excuse me, er...
BARBER What?
CUSTOMER Where it says: 'next of kin' shall I put 'mother'?
BARBER Yes, yes...yes.
CUSTOMER Right there we are. (*hands form to barber*)
BARBER Thank you.

He gets scissors and comb ready and comes up behind the customer and spreads his arms out, opening and shutting scissors as barbers do before cutting.

BARBER Right!

He can't bring himself to start cutting: after one or two attempts he goes to the cupboard again, gets a whisky bottle out and takes a hard swig. 9 *He comes up behind the customer again.*

BARBER Ha, ha, ha...there, I've finished.
CUSTOMER What?
BARBER I've finished cutting...cutting...cutting your hair. It's all done.
CUSTOMER You haven't started cutting it!
BARBER I have! I did it very quickly...your honour...*sir*...sir...
CUSTOMER (*getting rather testy*) Look here old fellow, I know when a chap's cut my hair and when he hasn't. So will you please stop fooling around and get on with it.

The barber bends down to the floor and drags out a tape recorder which he places behind the barber's chair, talking as he does so.

BARBER Yes, yes, I will, I'm going to cut your hair, sir. I'm going to start cutting your hair, sir, start cutting now!

He switches on tape recorder and then he himself cowers down against the wall as far from the chair as he can get, trembling.

TAPE RECORDER Nice day, sir.
CUSTOMER Yes, flowers could do with a drop of rain though, eh?
TAPE RECORDER (*snip, snip*) Did you see the match last night, sir?

He drinks from a bottle marked "Red Eye," a nod to cowboy movies. Bourbon only gains a red color from proper aging, however—meaning it's not actually the cheap stuff. (There is also a cocktail called a Red Eye, which is a Bloody Mary where the vodka has been replaced, horribly, with beer.)

Geoff Hurst, he of the hat trick of goals in the 1966 World Cup Final in which England defeated Germany in London to win their only world title to date. By the time this show aired, Hurst's career at his club, West Ham United in the east end of London, was nearing a close, though his legend status was in place. (Later he would play 24 games for the Seattle Sounders in the now-defunct North American Soccer League in 1976.)

Crystal Palace FC, a team from south London. The year this show aired, they had just been promoted to Division One, the apex of the English leagues, where they would stay for three seasons.

Totnes is a small, pretty town in the southwest corner of England, in the county of Devon. Here it is used presumably to signal "backwater."

A nice reference back to the larch tree from Episode 3. Note that the redwood is native to California and would not be found in British Columbia.

CUSTOMER Yes. Good game. I thought.

TAPE RECORDER (*snip, snip, snip; sound of electric razor starting up*) I thought Hurst played well sir.

CUSTOMER (*straining to hear*) I beg your pardon?

TAPE RECORDER (*razor stops*) **I thought Hurst played well.** 10

CUSTOMER Oh yes...yes...he was the only one who did though.

TAPE RECORDER Can you put your head down a little, sir.

CUSTOMER Sorry, sorry. (*his head is bowed*)

TAPE RECORDER **I prefer to watch Palace nowadays.** 11 (*electric razor starts up again*) Oh! Sorry! Was that your ear?

CUSTOMER No no...I didn't feel a thing.

The customer rises out from his seat, taking the sheet off himself and looking in the mirror and delving into pocket. He turns round for the first time and sees the cowering barber.

CUSTOMER Look, what's going on?

TAPE RECORDER Yes, it's a nice spot, isn't it.

CUSTOMER Look, I came here for a haircut!

BARBER (*pathetically*) It looks very nice sir.

CUSTOMER (*angrily*) It's exactly the same as when I first came in.

TAPE RECORDER Right, that's the lot then.

BARBER All right...I confess I haven't cut your hair...I hate cutting hair. I have this terrible un-un-uncontrollable fear whenever I see hair. When I was a kid I used to hate the sight of hair being cut. My mother said I was a fool. She said the only cure for it was to become a barber. So I spent five ghastly years at the **Hairdressers' Training Centre at Totnes.** 12 Can you imagine what it's like cutting the *same head* for *five* years? I didn't want to be a barber anyway. I wanted to be a lumberjack. Leaping from tree to tree as they float down the mighty rivers of British Columbia...(*he is gradually straightening up with a visionary gleam in his eyes*) **The giant redwood, the larch, the fir, the mighty scots pine.** 13 (*he tears off his barber's jacket, to reveal tartan shirt and lumberjack trousers underneath; as he speaks the lights dim behind him and a choir of Mounties is heard faintly in the distance*) The smell of fresh-cut timber! The crash of mighty trees! (*moves to stand in front of back-drop of Canadian mountains and forests*) **With my best girlie by my side...** 14 (*a frail adoring blonde, the heroine of many a mountains film, or perhaps the rebel maid, rushes to his side and looks adoringly into his eyes*) We'd sing...sing...sing.

The choir is loud by now and music as well. **15**

BARBER (*singing*)

I'M A LUMBERJACK AND I'M OK, I SLEEP ALL NIGHT AND I WORK ALL DAY.

Lights come up to his left to reveal a choir of Mounties.

MOUNTIES CHOIR He's a lumberjack and he's OK,
He sleeps all night and he works all day.
BARBER I cut down trees, I eat my lunch,
I go to the lavatory.
On Wednesday I go shopping,
And have buttered scones for tea.
MOUNTIES CHOIR He cuts down trees, he eats his lunch,
He goes to the lavatory.
On Wednesday he goes shopping,
And has buttered scones for tea.
He's a lumberjack and he's OK,
He sleeps all night and he works all day.
BARBER I cut down trees, I skip and jump,
I like to press wild flowers.
I put on women's clothing
And hang around in bars.
MOUNTIES CHOIR He cuts down trees, he skips and jumps,
He likes to press wild flowers.
He puts on women's clothing
And hangs around in bars...?

During this last verse the choir has started to look uncomfortable but they brighten up as they go into the chorus.

MOUNTIES CHOIR He's a lumberjack and he's OK,
He sleeps all night and he works all day.
BARBER I cut down trees, I wear high heels,
Suspenders and a bra.
I wish I'd been a girlie,
Just like my dear Mama.

This is the first appearance on the show of Connie Booth, who would go on to play Polly Sherman in Cleese's *Fawlty Towers* (she cowrote it too). She married Cleese in 1968 and they divorced a decade later.

The famous "Lumberjack Song" was said by Palin to have been thrown together in 15 minutes at the end of filming one day because there was no ending to the barbershop sketch. Written by Idle, Chapman, and a guy named Fred Tomlinson (whose Fred Tomlinson Singers here round out the team of singing Mounties), the song has ruined the lives of lumberjacks for 40 years and counting. Wikipedia claims that the tune is "similar to '*Là Ci Darem la Mano*,' Don Giovanni and Zerlina's duet in act 1, scene 2 of Mozart's *Don Giovanni*."

MOUNTIES CHOIR (*starting lustily as usual but tailing off as they get to the third line*) He cuts down trees, he wears high heels, (*spoken rather than sung*) Suspenders...and a bra?...

They all mumble. Music runs down. The girl looks horrified and bursts into tears. 16

The choir start throwing rotten fruit at him.

GIRL (CONNIE BOOTH) Oh Bevis! And I thought you were so rugged.

Cut to a hand-written letter.

VOICE OVER (JOHN) Dear Sir, I wish to complain in the strongest possible terms about the song which you have just broadcast, about the lumberjack who wears women's clothes. Many of my best friends are lumberjacks and only a few of them are transvestites. Yours faithfully, Brigadier Sir Charles Arthur Strong (Mrs). PS I have never kissed the editor of the Radio Times. 17

Cut to a pepperpot.

PEPPERPOT (GRAHAM) Well I object to all this sex on the television. I mean I keep falling off.

Shot of a battered trophy.

Superimposed caption: 'THAT JOKE WAS BRITAIN'S ENTRY FOR THIS YEAR'S RUBBER MAC OF ZURICH AWARD'. 18 *Roll Caption: 'IT CAME LAST'*

Cut back to Canadian backdrop. In front, a man with a knotted handkerchief on his head, a woolly pullover, and braces. Superimposed Caption: 'PROF. R. J. GUMBY'

GUMBY (GRAHAM) Well I think TV's killed real entertainment. In the old days we used to make our own fun. At Christmas parties I used to strike myself on the head repeatedly with blunt instruments while crooning. (*sings*) 'Only make believe, I love you, (*hits himself on head with bricks*) Only make believe that you love me, (*hits himself*) Others find peace of mind...' 19

Cut to a swish nightclub. Compère enters.

This hardly does justice to the brilliance of Booth's reaction to the growing homosexual references in the song. To watch her face stiffen, then crack—she almost steals the scene, which is hard to do given the song is a classic.

Radio Times is a weekly magazine, owned by the BBC until 2011, detailing the schedules for both TV and radio as well as features about actors and their shows. It once claimed to have the largest circulation of any magazine in Europe.

A "rubber mac" is a thin raincoat.

A Jerome Kern and Oscar Hammerstein tune from *Show Boat*, first heard in 1927.

EARLY REVIEWS

Everyone who knows and loves comedy, knows and loves *Monty Python's Flying Circus.* So many of its key moments—"This parrot is no more!"; "My brain hurts!"; "Nobody expects the Spanish Inquisition"; the "Lumberjack Song"—are now staples of our comedy memories, and certainly in the U.K. many of its phrases are part of the daily vernacular.

But in the early days, the British viewing public was more circumspect in its assessment of the *Flying Circus.* It probably didn't help that the first studio audiences, before whom the show was taped live, had merely applied for tickets to any ol' BBC comedy. What they got instead was Python. What could they have thought? One can tell from the tapes: often there's silence where there now would be laughter.

But at least there were people watching. For awhile, the show didn't even air in the Midlands, as that particular area of Britain opted out, showing instead farming shows and the like. By the end of the first season, however, and after a glowing review from Alan Coren (comedian, author, and once the editor of *Punch,* the satirical magazine), the show found its audience. Nevertheless, it aired late on Sunday nights, and even though this was to become something of a new phenomenon—the "Sunday-night late show," as Palin called it—that people tuned in meant the show was something of a cult.

Eventually the show reached pay dirt, its irreverent take on politics, morality, and British society finding a correlative in a country at least two generations away from the horrors of World War II. In that time, the ask-no-questions society of lords, landowners, and royalty had given way to a more democratic place, and the Pythons either fit that perfectly or helped loosen the binds of class and deference. The British Empire was fast receding, and as the third and fourth seasons aired, a new kind of comic empire had been established—one that would spawn *Monty Python and the Holy Grail, Life of Brian,* and *The Meaning of Life,* as well as live shows around the world, hit records, and the recent Broadway hit *Spamalot.* Not bad for a show that began on a shoestring budget, featured previously unknown Oxbridge-graduate comic writers, and wasn't seen in parts of Britain because farmers insisted on watching shows about . . . well, farming.

COMPÈRE (ERIC) Good evening, ladies and gentlemen, and welcome to the refreshment room here at Bletchley. 20 (*applause*) My name is Kenny Lust 21 and I'm your compere for tonight. You know, once in a while it is my pleasure, and my privilege, to welcome here at the refreshment room, some of the truly great international artists of our time. (*applause*) And tonight we have one such artist. (*grovelling*) Ladies and gentlemen, someone whom I've always personally admired, perhaps more deeply, more strongly, more abjectly than ever before. (*applause*) A man, well more than a man, a god (*applause*), a great god, whose personality is so totally and utterly wonderful my feeble words of welcome sound wretchedly and pathetically inadequate. (*by now on his knees*) Someone whose boots I would gladly lick clean until holes wore through my tongue, a man who is so totally and utterly wonderful, that I would rather be sealed in a pit of my own filth, than dare tread on the same stage with him. Ladies and gentlemen the incomparably superior human being, Harry Fink.

VOICE OFF He can't come!

COMPÈRE Never mind, it's not all it's cracked up to be. Ladies and gentlemen, we give you Ken Buddha and his inflatable knees.

Cut to Ken (TERRY J) *in evening dress; his knees go 'bang'.*

COMPÈRE Ken Buddha, a smile, two bangs and a religion. Now ladies and gentlemen, for your further entertainment, Brian Islam and Brucie. 22

Two animated men dance to jug band music.

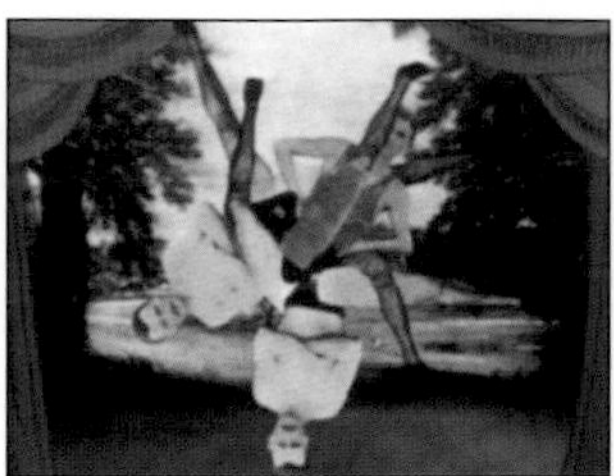

When they finish we cut to the barber and customer.

BARBER So anyway, I became a barber.

CUSTOMER (*sympathetically*) Poor chap.

BARBER Yes, pity really, I always preferred the outdoor life. Hunting, shooting, fishing. Getting out there with a gun, slaughtering a few of God's creatures—that was the life. Charging about the moorland, blasting their heads off.

Cut to a large country house. A number of sportin' gentlemen dressed in huntin' tweed and carrying shotguns come out, casually firing the guns at random. They climb into a land-rover and drive off. Cut to huntin' country. A line of beaters moves towards the camera; as they do so several young couples leap up out of the undergrowth and run away. 23 *Shots of hunters stalking their prey and shooting. One of them breaks his gun into two pieces. Another fires into the air. An egg lands on his head.* 24 *Cut to two duellists (with pistols) and a referee standing between them. They fire; the referee falls dead. A huntin' gentleman fires into the air, falls over backwards; a young couple get up from close*

Part of the town of Milton Keynes, Bletchley is best known for housing Bletchley Park, the scene of the British code busting of German communications during World War II.

Idle pronounces this last name "Luss" instead of "Lust."

Probably a reference to Bruce Forsyth, a slick comedian, game-show host, and all-around avuncular TV personality who first came to prominence in the 1960s and continues to appear on British TV to this day. His nickname is "Brucie."

One of which is an all-male couple, one of whom is wearing a red kilt.

Actually, the egg hits Jones smack on the bridge of the nose.

*behind him and run away. Another huntin' gentleman is arguing defensively with a pilot who has just landed by parachute. A hunter fires into some bushes; a **Red Indian pops up and runs away in alarm.*** 25 *They all return to the house, legs and arms variously in plaster or bandaged. Two of them carry a pole between them from which is slung a very small bird. The picture of the outside of the house freezes and we pull back to reveal that it is a photo on a stand, by which stands the knight in armour, expectantly flexing his raw chicken. The floor manager comes up to him.* 26

FLOOR MANAGER

I'M SORRY, WE DON'T NEED YOU THIS WEEK.

Knight looks dejected, droops and slinks off, still holding chicken. He walks past a hen house from wherein we hear a voice.

VOICE (JOHN) And now for something completely different.

Cut to a sitting room. Low sexy lighting—ha ha—soft sexy music. On the sofa are Victor and Iris just beginning to make passes at each other.

VICTOR (GRAHAM) Would you mind terribly if I hold your hand?
IRIS (CAROL) Oh no, no, not at all.
VICTOR Oh Iris, you're so very beautiful.
IRIS Oh, do you really mean that?
VICTOR I do, I do, I do. I think...I'm beginning to fall in love with you.
IRIS Oh Victor.
VICTOR It's silly isn't it?
IRIS No, no, not at all dear sweet Victor.
VICTOR No I didn't mean that. Only just us being so close together for so many months in the soft-toy department and yet never daring to...
IRIS Oh, oh Victor.
VICTOR Oh Iris. (*they move closer to kiss; just before their lips meet the doorbell goes*) Who can that be?
IRIS Oh, well you try and get rid of them.
VICTOR Yes I will, I will.

Victor opens the front door. Arthur Name is standing outside the door. 27

ARTHUR (ERIC) Hello!
VICTOR Hello.
ARTHUR Remember me? 28
VICTOR No I'm...
ARTHUR In the pub. The tall thin one with the moustache, remember? About three years ago?
VICTOR No, I don't I'm afraid.
ARTHUR Oh, blimey, it's dark in here, (*switches light on*) that's better. Only you said we must have a drink together sometime, so I thought I'd take you up on it as the film society meeting was cancelled this evening.
VICTOR Look, to be frank, it is a little awkward this evening.
ARTHUR (*stepping in; to Iris*) Hello, I'm Arthur. Arthur Name. Name by name but not by nature. I always say that, don't I Vicky boy?
VICTOR Really...
ARTHUR (*to Victor*) Is that your wife?
VICTOR Er, no, actually.
ARTHUR Oh, I get the picture. Eh? Well don't worry about me Vicky boy, I know all about one-night stands.

Aka a Native American. Idle is dressed more like an American Indian woman than anything.

Note in the background a set of what look like extras in the shadows, presumably to signal that they're hoping for a spot on the show too, just like the poor Knight.

And so begins what can only be described as a "nightmare" sequence, in which every possible awful character shows up. In some ways, a sister sketch to the attempts by Jones in Episode 4 to change his trousers; when watched as a "dream," the sketch's crazy inner narrative makes a tiny bit more sense.

We do remember him from Episode 3, where he's called Norman. In that episode he harangues Jones; now it's poor Chapman's turn.

This was originally filmed with a real woman, but eventually Jones played the female role. The Pythons argue that there is a different *kind* of comedy when the female roles are played by men, hence their love of transvestitism—it's all for the laughs.

30

A "bird" is British slang for a woman—or, more exactly, an attractive woman of dating age.

31

A relatively rare appearance (at least out of the knight uniform) for illustrator and cartoonist Terry Gilliam.

VICTOR I *beg* your pardon?

ARTHUR Mind if I change the record? (*takes the record off*)

VICTOR Look, look, we put that on.

ARTHUR Here's a good one, I heard it in a pub. What's brown, what's brown and sounds like a bell?

VICTOR I beg your pardon?

ARTHUR What's brown and sounds like a bell? Dung! Ha, ha, ha, that's a good one. I like that one, I won't keep you long. (*the gramophone plays the 'Washington Post March' very loud*) That's better, now don't worry about me. I'll wait here till you've finished.

The doorbell goes again.

VICTOR Who the hell...

ARTHUR I'll get it. It'll be friends of mine. I took the liberty of inviting them along.

VICTOR Look, we were hoping to have a quiet evening on our own.

ARTHUR Oh, they won't mind. They're very broad-minded. Hello!

He opens the door; Mr and Mrs Equator walk in and go straight up to Victor. **29**

MR EQUATOR (JOHN) Good evening. My name is Equator, Brian Equator. Like round the middle of the Earth, only with an L. (*wheezing laugh*) This is my wife Audrey, she smells a bit but she has a heart of gold.

AUDREY (TERRY J) Hello, ha ha ha ha ha ha ha ha ha...

VICTOR There must have been some kind of misunderstanding, because this is not the...

MR EQUATOR Who's that then?

VICTOR What?

MR EQUATOR Who's the bird? **30**

VICTOR I'm...

MR EQUATOR You got a nice pair there haven't you love. (*puts hand on Iris's boobs and gives a wet kiss; Iris screams*) Shut up you silly bitch, it was only a bit of fun.

VICTOR Now look here...

MR EQUATOR Big gin please.

ARTHUR I'll get it.

VICTOR (*going after Arthur*) Look, leave those drinks alone.

AUDREY And three tins of beans for me please.

MR EQUATOR I told you to lay off the beans, you whore!

AUDREY I only want three cans.

MR EQUATOR Button your lip you rat-bag. (*laughs uproariously*)

AUDREY (*joins in*) Ha, ha, ha, ha...

MR EQUATOR It was rather witty, wasn't it? Where's my gin?

The doorbell goes.

VICTOR Who the hell's that?

MR EQUATOR Oh, I took the liberty of inviting an old friend along, as his wife has just passed away, and he's somewhat distraught poor chap. I hope you don't mind.

ARTHUR (*opening door*) Come on in.

IN WALKS MR FREIGHT IN UNDERPANTS, SEQUINS, EYE MAKE-UP, WHITE WELLIES AND NECKLACE.

MR FREIGHT (TERRY G) Oh? My God, what a simply ghastly place. **31**

MR EQUATOR Not too good is it? A pint of crème de menthe for my friend. Well how are you, you great poof? (*sits down*) Bit lumpy...ah, no wonder, I was sitting on the cat. (*throws it into fire*) 32

IRIS Aaaagh! Boo hoo hooo.

MR FREIGHT I've asked along a simply gorgeous little man I picked up outside the Odeon.

MR EQUATOR Is he sexy?

In walks Mr Cook with a goat. Freight kisses him.

MR COOK (MICHAEL) I had to bring the goat, he's not well. I only hope he don't go on the carpet.

MR EQUATOR (*to Iris*) Come on then love, drop 'em.

IRIS Aaaaaaagh! (*runs out*)

MR EQUATOR Blimey, she don't go much do she.

He sits in chair which collapses.

MRS EQUATOR Ha, ha, ha, ha, ha, ha, oooooh! I've wet 'em.

MR COOK The goat's just done a bundle.

All the singers run on, dressed as Welsh miners. All talk at once.

VICTOR Look, get out all of you. Go on. Get out! Get out!

MR EQUATOR I beg your pardon?

VICTOR I'm turning you all out. I'm not having my house filled with filthy perverts, now look, I'm giving you just half a minute then I'm going to call the police, so get out.

MR EQUATOR I don't much like the tone of your voice. (*shoots him*) Right let's have a ding dong...

ALL (*singing*) Ding dong merrily on high, in Heaven the bells are ringing etc.... 33

Cut to 'It's' man.

SPANISH VOICES (*in Spanish*) Look out, there are llamas!

'It's' man runs away into forest.

Roller Caption: 'THE ANT, AN INTRODUCTION, WAS CONCEIVED, WRITTEN AND PERFORMED BY...(credits)'

Actually, Cleese merely throws it toward the audience.

A neat homophonic reference back to Idle's "dung" joke, and an appropriate way to sign off, given the show aired on December 14, 1969.

SEA SON 1
EPISODE 10

"UNTITLED"
FEATURING
WALK-ON PART IN SKETCH ✽ BANK ROBBER (LINGERIE SHOP)
TRAILER ✽ ARTHUR TREE
VOCATIONAL GUIDANCE COUNSELLOR
(CHARTERED ACCOUNTANT)
THE FIRST MAN TO JUMP THE CHANNEL
TUNNELLING FROM GODALMING TO JAVA
Pet Conversions
GORILLA LIBRARIAN
LETTERS TO 'DAILY MIRROR'
STRANGERS IN THE NIGHT

FIRST AIRED: DECEMBER 21, 1969

Boring old 'It's' man hanging on a meat-hook.

IT'S MAN (MICHAEL)

IT'S...

Animated titles as per usual.

Lingerie shop set. Assistant standing waiting behind counter. At the side the robber also stands waiting. They hum to themselves and waste time, looking at wristwatches, this takes about fifteen seconds. Cut to a letter on BBC stationery. The camera pulls back to show a grotty little man reading the letter and sitting at a breakfast table in a small kitchen. His wife is busying herself in wifelike activities.

MAN (MICHAEL) Ooh. Ooh.
WIFE (TERRY J) Oh, what is it dear?
MAN

IT'S FROM THE BBC. THEY WANT TO KNOW IF I WANT TO BE IN A SKETCH ON TELLY.

WIFE Oooh. That's nice.
MAN What? It's acting innit?
WIFE Yes.
MAN Well I'm a plumber. I can't act.
WIFE Oh, you never know till you try. Look at **Mrs Brando's son next door.** 1 He was mending the fridge when they came and asked him to be **the Wild One.** 2 What do they want you to do?
MAN Well, they just want me to stand at a counter, and when the sketch starts I go out.
WIFE Oh, that sounds nice. It's what they call a walk-on.
MAN Walk-on? That's a walk-off, that's what this is.

Cut to lingerie shop; assistant and robber still hanging around waiting. A few seconds of this. Floor manager walks on.

ROBBER (JOHN) (*quietly*) Well, where is he, George?
FLOOR MANAGER I don't know, he should have been here hours ago.
ROBBER He bloody should have been.

1 Marlon Brando, who starred as biker and gang leader Johnny Strabler in *The Wild One* in 1953.

2 Here Jones produces two standard English breakfasts, replete with fried egg, fried tomato, fried bread, and sausage—otherwise known as the opposite of muesli.

Cut to grotty kitchen (still very small).

WIFE Well what else does it say?
MAN It just says 'We would like you to be in a sketch. You are standing at a counter. When the sketch starts you go off. **Yours faithfully, Lord Hill.**' **3**
WIFE Oh well, you'd better be off then.
MAN Yeah, well, what about the cat?
WIFE Oh I'll look after the cat. Goodness me, Mrs Newman's eldest never worried about the cat when he went off to do **'The Sweet Bird of Youth'.** **4**
MAN All right then, all right. Bye. Bye dear.
WIFE Bye bye, and mind you don't get seduced.

Man leaves, wife stands for a moment, then...

WIFE Oh, it'll make a change from plumbing. Dad! Frank's got a television part.

She turns on the TV set. On the TV comes the picture of the assistant and the robber and floor manager waiting in the lingerie shop. After a second or two a man is brought in and introduced to floor manager, who positions him and cues him. The man walks out.

WIFE You missed him.

Cut to shop; the robber walks in and points gun at the assistant.

ROBBER (JOHN) Good morning, I am a bank robber. Er, please don't panic, just hand over all your money.
ASSISTANT (ERIC) (*politely*) This is a lingerie shop, sir.
ROBBER Fine, fine, fine. (*slightly nonplussed*) **Adopt, adapt and improve. Motto of the round table.** **5** Well, um...what have you got?
ASSISTANT (*still politely*) Er, we've got corsets, stockings, suspender belts, tights, bras, slips, petticoats, knickers, socks and garters, sir.
ROBBER Fine, fine, fine, fine. No large piles of money in safes?
ASSISTANT No, sir.
ROBBER No deposit accounts?
ASSISTANT No sir.
ROBBER No piles of cash in easy to carry bags?
ASSISTANT None at all sir.
ROBBER No luncheon vouchers?
ASSISTANT No, sir.
ROBBER Fine, fine. Well, um...adopt, adapt and improve. Just a pair of knickers then please.

Lord Hill was the chairman of the BBC from 1967 to 1972. He was previously famous for being the BBC's "Radio Doctor," dispensing health and nutrition advice during the dark days of World War II.

4

Sweet Bird of Youth was the 1962 movie of the 1959 Tennessee Williams play of the same name, starring Paul Newman as drifter and ladies' man Chance Wayne. The movie poster included the tagline "He Used Love Like Most Men Use Money."

5

The "round table" is not the Arthurian one but a British networking group. The motto is taken from a speech by the Prince of Wales in 1927.

Mel Oxley was a TV actor of the day. Chapman does uncannily look like him here.

Compare to the punch line of Idle's joke near the end of Episode 9.

Idle does a dead-on impersonation of David Frost here. Coincidentally, TV host Frost would interview Tennessee Williams, author of *The Sweet Bird of Youth*, in 1970.

Cut to effeminate announcer sitting at continuity desk. Any resemblance to **Mel Oxley** [6] *should be accidental. His name is David Unction.*

UNCTION (GRAHAM) Well that was a bit of fun wasn't it? Ha, ha, ha. And a special good evening to *you*. Not just an ordinary good evening like you get from all the other announcers, but a special good evening from *me* (*holds up card saying 'David Unction'*) to *you*. Well, what have we got next? This is fun isn't it? Look, I'm sorry if I'm interrupting anything that any of you may be doing at home, but I want you to think of me as an old queen. *Friend*, ha, ha, ha. Well, let's see what we've got next. In a few moments 'It's a Tree' and in the chair as usual is Arthur Tree, and starring in the show will be a host of star guests as his star guests. And then at 9.30 we've got another rollocking half hour of laughter-packed squalor with 'Yes it's the Sewage Farm Attendants'. And this week Dan falls into a vat of human dung with hilarious consequences. Ha, ha, ha. **But now it's the glittering world of show business with Arthur Tree...** [7]

Music. Caption: 'IT'S A TREE'. Stock film. Quick cuts. Plane arriving at night. Showbiz lights. Film premieres. Audience applauding. Cut to studio: a tree sitting in a middle chair in David Frost type interview set. Zoom in on tree which has a mouth which moves.

TREE (ERIC) Hello. **Hello people, and welcome to 'It's a Tree'.** [8] We have some really exciting guests for you this evening. A fabulous spruce, back from a tour of Holland, three gum trees making their first appearance in this country, scots pine and the conifers, and Elm Tree Bole—there you go, can't be bad—an exciting new American plank, a rainforest and a bucket of sawdust giving their views on teenage violence, and an unusual guest for this programme, a piece of laminated plastic.

Shot of a piece of laminated plastic with mouth.

PLASTIC Hi there!

TREE

BUT FIRST, WILL YOU PLEASE, PLEASE WELCOME—A BLOCK OF WOOD.

Shot of large block four feet cube, with a mouth, on the chair next to Tree. Shot of a forest with the sound of applause over.

TREE Well Block, nice to have you on the show again.

BLOCK (JOHN'S VOICE) Well, er, thanks Tree. I've got to pay the rent.

They both laugh. Shot of forest laughing.

TREE Ha, ha, ha, ha, super. **Well, what have you been doing, Block?** **9**
BLOCK Well I've just been starring in several major multi-million dollar international films, and, during breaks on the set, I've been designing a Cathedral, doing wonderful unpublicized work for charity, er, finishing my history of the world, of course, pulling the birds, er, photographing royalty on the loo, averting World War Three—can't be bad—and, er, learning to read.
TREE The full Renaissance bit, really...super, super. Well I've got to stop you there Block I'm afraid, because we've got someone who's been doing cabaret in the **New Forest.** **10** From America, will you welcome please a Chippendale writing desk.

Animation: a Chippendale desk.

CHIP Thank you Mr Tree. And I'd like to do a few impersonations of some of my favourite Englishmen. First off. **Long John Sliver.** **11** *(suitable animation)* Augh, Jim boy. Augh. And now **Edward Heath. Hello sailor. Now a short scene from a play by Harold Splinter.** **12** *(a huge hammer smashes it)*
Animated compere:
COMPÈRE Wasn't that just great, ladies and gentlemen, wait a minute, we've got something else I just know you're going to love. (*fanfares*) Yes sir, coming right up—the Vocational Guidance Counsellor Sketch. (*more fanfares*)

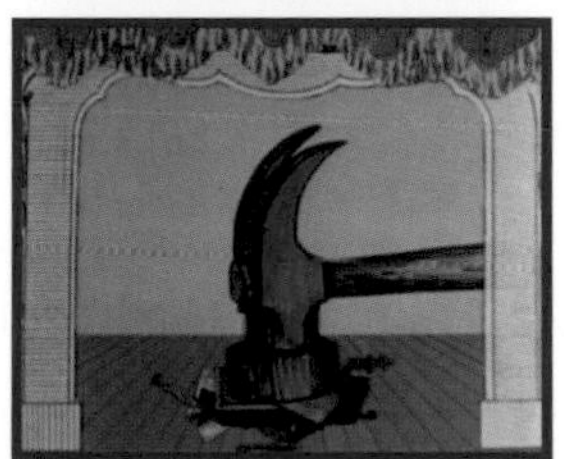

Animation film into Vocational Guidance Counsellor sketch.

VOICES SINGING Vocational guidance counselor...vocational guidance counselor...vocational guidance counselor...etc. **13**

Office set. Man sitting at desk. Mr Anchovy is standing waiting. The counsellor looks at his watch then starts the sketch.

COUNSELLOR (JOHN) Ah Mr Anchovy. Do sit down.
ANCHOVY (MICHAEL) Thank you. Take the weight off the feet, eh?
COUNSELLOR Yes, yes.
ANCHOVY Lovely weather for the time of year, I must say.
COUNSELLOR Enough of this gay banter. **14** And now Mr Anchovy, you asked us to advise you which job in life you were best suited for.
ANCHOVY That is correct, yes.

Possibly a nod back to David Hemming being a "block of wood" from Episode 8.

New Forest is a storied national park in the southwest of England.

Aka Long John Silver.

Edward Heath was the British prime minister from 1970 to 1974 and an avid sailor. A lifelong bachelor, he was scurrilously assumed to have been gay, though there is no evidence for this claim.

"Harold Splinter" aka British playwright Harold Pinter.

Cleese very neatly hits the seventh note of the chord before coolly turning to begin the sketch.

"Gay" is used here in its old meaning, that of light or airy.

The Pythons repeatedly use the profession as shorthand for the least interesting job or person in the world. Can't imagine why . . .

COUNSELLOR Well I now have the results here of the interviews and the aptitude tests that you took last week, and from them we've built up a pretty clear picture of the sort of person that you are. And I think I can say, without fear of contradiction, that the ideal job for you is chartered accountancy.

ANCHOVY **But I *am* a chartered accountant.** [15]

COUNSELLOR Jolly good. Well back to the office with you then.

ANCHOVY No! No! No! You don't understand. I've been a chartered accountant for the last twenty years. I want a new job. Something *exciting* that will let me *live*.

COUNSELLOR Well chartered accountancy is rather exciting isn't it?

ANCHOVY

EXCITING? NO IT'S NOT. IT'S DULL. DULL. DULL. MY GOD IT'S DULL, IT'S SO DESPERATELY DULL AND TEDIOUS AND STUFFY AND BORING AND DES-PER-ATE-LY DULL.

COUNSELLOR Well, er, yes Mr Anchovy, but you see your report here says that you are an extremely dull person. You see, our experts describe you as an appallingly dull fellow, unimaginative, timid, lacking in initiative, spineless, easily dominated, no sense of humour, tedious company and irrepressibly drab and awful. And whereas in most professions these would be considerable drawbacks, in chartered accountancy they are a positive boon.

ANCHOVY But don't you see, I came here to find a new job, a new life, a new *meaning* to my existence. Can't you help me?

COUNSELLOR Well, do you have any idea of what you want to do?

ANCHOVY Yes, yes I have.

COUNSELLOR What?

ANCHOVY (*boldly*) Lion taming.

COUNSELLOR Well yes. Yes. Of course, it's a bit of a jump isn't it? I mean, er, chartered accountancy to lion taming in one go. You don't think it might be better if you worked your way *towards* lion taming, say, via banking...

ANCHOVY No, no, no, no. No. I don't want to wait. At nine o'clock tomorrow I want to be in there, taming.

COUNSELLOR Fine, fine. But do you, do you have any qualifications?

ANCHOVY Yes, I've got a hat.

COUNSELLOR A hat?

ANCHOVY Yes, a hat. A lion taming hat. A hat with 'lion tamer' on it. I got it at Harrods. And it lights up saying 'lion tamer' in great big neon letters, so that you can tame them after dark when they're less **stroppy.** [16]

COUNSELLOR I see, I see.

ANCHOVY **And you can switch it off during the day time, and claim reasonable wear and tear as allowable professional expenses under paragraph 335C...** [17]

COUNSELLOR Yes, yes, yes, I do follow, Mr Anchovy, but you see the snag is...if I now call **Mr Chipperfield** [18] and **say to him,** [19] 'look here, I've got a forty-five-year-old chartered accountant with me who wants to become a lion tamer', his first question is not going to be 'does he have his own hat?' He's going to ask what sort of experience you've had with lions.

ANCHOVY Well I...I've seen them at the zoo.

COUNSELLOR Good, good, good.

ANCHOVY Little brown furry things with short stumpy legs and great long noses. I don't know what all the fuss is about, I could tame one of those. They look pretty tame to start with.

COUNSELLOR And these, er, these lions...how high are they?

ANCHOVY (*indicating a height of one foot*) Well they're about so high, you know. They don't frighten me at all.

COUNSELLOR Really. **And do these lions eat ants?** [20]

"Stroppy" is British English for moody.

Palin is going so fast here that he stumbles over the line, putting the second part first, then retreats and does the line in the correct order.

"Chipperfield" is a storied name, dating back some 300 years, of a British family circus.

Cleese stumbles here too, saying "say to her" before correcting himself.

The first reference to ants, even though the previous episode was titled "The Ant, An Introduction."

ANCHOVY Yes, that's right.

COUNSELLOR Er, well, Mr Anchovy I'm afraid what you've got hold of there is an anteater.

ANCHOVY A what?

COUNSELLOR An anteater. Not a lion. You see a lion is a huge savage beast, about five feet high, ten feet long, weighing about four hundred pounds, running forty miles per hour, with masses of sharp pointed teeth and nasty long razor-sharp claws that can rip your belly open before you can say 'Eric Robinson', and they look like this.

THE COUNSELLOR PRODUCES LARGE PICTURE OF A LION AND SHOWS TO MR ANCHOVY WHO SCREAMS AND PASSES OUT.

COUNSELLOR Time enough I think for a piece of wood.

Caption: 'THE LARCH' Picture of a tree.

VOICE OVER (TERRY J) The larch.

Cut back to office: Mr Anchovy sits up with a start.

COUNSELLOR Now, shall I call Mr Chipperfield?

ANCHOVY Er, no, no, no. I think your idea of making the transition to lion taming via easy stages, say via insurance...

COUNSELLOR Or banking.

ANCHOVY **Or banking, yes, yes, banking that's a man's life, isn't it? Banking, travel, excitement, adventure, thrills, decisions affecting people's lives.** 21

COUNSELLOR Jolly good, well, er, shall I put you in touch with a bank?

ANCHOVY Yes.

COUNSELLOR Fine.

ANCHOVY Er...no, no, no. Look, er, it's a big decision, I'd like a couple of weeks to think about it... er...you know, don't want to jump into it too quickly. Maybe three weeks. I could let you know definitely then, I just don't want to make this definite decision. I'm er... (*continues muttering nervously to himself*)

COUNSELLOR (*turning to camera*) Well this is just one of the all too many cases on our books of chartered accountancy. The only way that we can fight this terrible debilitating social disease, is by informing the general public of its consequences, by showing young people that it's just not worth it. So, so please...give generously...to this address: The League for Fighting Chartered Accountancy, **55 Lincoln House, Basil Street, London, SW 3.** 22

A cynic might say that Palin here forgets banking was the profession suggested, and Cleese bails him out very neatly.

For once in MPFC, a *real* address—a stony street in Knightsbridge, central London.

23

An echo of the earlier reference to Edward Heath. One wonders how Chapman felt about indulging in these stereotypical references to homosexuality; the other Pythons knew Chapman was gay, though he wasn't publicly out until later.

Neepsend is a suburb of Sheffield, an industrial city in the north of England. There is no town of Neaps End in the U.K., though it sure sounds like it could be one.

Caption: GIVES ADDRESS. Cut back to David Unction reading 'Physique' magazine. He puts it into a brown paper bag.

UNCTION Oh, well that was fun wasn't it?

Cut to helmeted Viking.

VIKING (TERRY J) No it wasn't, you fairy.

Cut back to Unction.

UNCTION (*sarcastically*) **Oh, hello sailor.** **23**
Cut to Viking.

VIKING Here, you wouldn't have got on one of our voyages—they were all dead butch.

Cut to Unction.

UNCTION (*camply*) Oh that's not what I've heard.

Cut to the sea. Pan to show Ron Obvious running along beach.

VOICE OVER (ERIC) There is an epic quality about the sea which has throughout history stirred the hearts and minds of Englishmen of all nations. Sir Francis Drake, Captain Webb, Nelson of Trafalgar and Scott of the Antarctic—all rose to the challenge of the mighty ocean. And today another Englishman may add his name to the golden roll of history: Mr Ron Obvious of **Neaps End.** **24** For today, Ron Obvious hopes to be the first man to jump the Channel.

Ron runs up to group of cheering supporters. An interviewer addresses him.

INTERVIEWER (JOHN)

RON, NOW LET'S JUST GET THIS QUITE CLEAR—YOU'RE INTENDING TO JUMP ACROSS THE ENGLISH CHANNEL?

RON (TERRY J) Oh yes, that is correct, yes.
INTERVIEWER And, er, just how far is that?
RON Oh, well it's twenty-six miles from here to Calais.
INTERVIEWER Er, that's to the beach at Calais?
RON Well, no, no, provided I get a good lift off and maybe a gust of breeze over the French coast, I shall be jumping into the centre of Calais itself.

Brief shot of group of Frenchmen with banner: 'Fin de Cross-Channel jump'.

INTERVIEWER Ron are you using any special techniques to jump this great distance? 25
RON Oh no, no. I shall be using an ordinary two-footed jump, er, straight up in the air and across the Channel.
INTERVIEWER I see. Er, Ron, what is the furthest distance that you've jumped, er, so far?
RON Er, oh, eleven foot six inches at **Motspur Park** **26** on July 22nd. Er, but I have done nearly twelve feet unofficially.

Ron breaks off to make training-type movements.

INTERVIEWER I see. Er, Ron, Ron, Ron, aren't you worried Ron, aren't you worried jumping twenty-six miles across the sea?
RON Oh, well no, no, no, no. It is in fact easier to jump over sea than over dry land.
INTERVIEWER Well how is that?
RON Er, well my manager explained it to me. You see if you're five miles out over the English Channel, with nothing but sea underneath you, er, there is a very great impetus to say in the air.
INTERVIEWER I see. Well, er, thank you very much Ron and the very best of luck.
RON Thank you. Thank you.
INTERVIEWER (*to camera*) The man behind Ron's cross-Channel jump is his manager **Mr Luigi Vercotti.** **27** (*turns to speak to Vercotti, who has a Mafia suit and dark glasses*) Mr Vercotti, er Mr Vercotti...Mr Vercotti...
MR VERCOTTI (MICHAEL) What? (*mumbles protestations of innocence*) I don't know what you're talking about.
INTERVIEWER Er, no, we're from the BBC, Mr Vercotti.
MR VERCOTTI Who?
INTERVIEWER The BBC.
MR VERCOTTI Oh, oh. I see. I thought, I thought you were the er...I like the police a lot, I've got a lot of time for them.
INTERVIEWER Mr, er, Mr Vercotti, what is your chief task as Ron's manager?
MR VERCOTTI Well my main task is, er, to fix a sponsor for the big jump.
INTERVIEWER And who is the sponsor?
MR VERCOTTI The Chippenham Brick Company. Ah, they, er, pay all the bills, er, in return for which Ron will be carrying half a hundredweight of their bricks.

We see a passport officer checking Ron's passport.

INTERVIEWER I see. Well, er, it looks as if Ron is ready now. He's got the bricks. He's had his passport checked and he's all set to go. And he's off on the first ever cross-Channel jump. (*Ron runs down the beach and jumps; he lands about four feet into the water*) Will Ron be trying the cross-Channel jump again soon?
MR VERCOTTI No. No. I'm taking him off the jumps. Er, because I've got something lined up for Ron next week that I think is very much more up his street.

Cleese smartly pulls Jones back toward the microphone here, as he's looked away across the sea and we can barely hear him.

In southwest London, Motspur Park Athletics Stadium (now a soccer team training facility) was where Sydney Charles Wooderson set the then world mile record in 1938.

Returning here after his attempts in Episode 8 to blackmail the British Army.

INTERVIEWER Er, what's that?
MR VERCOTTI Er, Ron is going to eat Chichester Cathedral.

Chichester Cathedral. Ron walks up to it, cleaning his teeth.

INTERVIEWER Well, there he goes, Ron Obvious of Neaps End, in an attempt which could make him the first man ever to eat an entire Anglican Cathedral.

Ron takes a hefty bite at a buttress, screams and clutches his mouth. Cut to countryside: a map, and a banner saying 'Tunnelling to Java'. Interviewer and Vercotti walk up to map.

MR VERCOTTI Well, er, I think, David, this is something which Ron and myself are really keen on. Ron is going to tunnel from **Godalming** 28 here to Java here. (*indicates inaccurately on map*)

Godalming is a town in Surrey, southwest of London, and 7,500 miles from Indonesia.

INTERVIEWER Java.
MR VERCOTTI Yeah, er, I, I personally think this is going to make Ron a household name overnight.
INTERVIEWER And how far has he got?
MR VERCOTTI Er, well, he's quite far now, Dave, well on the way. Well on the way, yeah.
INTERVIEWER Well where is he exactly?
MR VERCOTTI Yeah.
INTERVIEWER Where?
MR VERCOTTI Oh, er, well, er, you know, it's difficult to say exactly. He's er, you know, in the area of er, Ron, how far have you got?
RON (*emerging from hole*) Oh about two foot six Mr Vercotti.
MR VERCOTTI Yeah well keep digging lad, keep digging.
RON Mr Vercotti, are you sure there isn't a spade?

Cut to interviewer and Vercotti by a railway track.

INTERVIEWER Er, Mr Vercotti, what do you say to people who accuse you of exploiting Ron for your own purposes?
MR VERCOTTI Well, it's totally untrue, David. Ever since I left Sicily I've been trying to do the best for Ron. I know what Ron wants to do, I believe in him and I'm just trying to create the opportunities for Ron to do the kind of things he wants to do.
INTERVIEWER And what's he going to do today?
MR VERCOTTI He's going to split a railway carriage with his nose. *(screams, off)*

Cut to a hillside; Vercotti, interviewer, and in the background a banner: 'Running to Mercury'.
MR VERCOTTI The only difficult bit for Ron is getting out of the Earth's atmosphere. Er, once he's in orbit he'll be able to run straight to Mercury.

A heavily bandaged Ron leaps off starting platform: freeze frame. Scream. Cut to a tombstone: 'Ron Obvious 1941-1969—very talented'. Pull back to show Vercotti.

MR VERCOTTI I am now extremely hopeful that Ron will break the world record for remaining underground. He's a wonderful boy this, he's got this really enormous talent, this really huge talent.

Over last shot of graveyard and wind whistling, we hear two ladies' voices.

FIRST LADY Oh that was a bit sad, wasn't it?
SECOND LADY Shh. It's satire.
FIRST LADY No it isn't. This is zany madcap humour.
SECOND LADY Oh is it?

Cut to a pet shop. Superimposed caption: 'A PET SHOP SOMEWHERE NEAR MELTON MOWBRAY' **29** *Man enters shop and approaches shopkeeper at counter.*

MAN (JOHN) Good morning. I'd like to buy a cat.
SHOPKEEPER (MICHAEL) Certainly sir. I've got a lovely terrier. (*indicates a box on the counter*)
MAN (*glancing in box*) No, I want a cat really.

SHOPKEEPER (*taking box off counter and then putting it back on counter as if it is a different box*) Oh yeah, how about that?
MAN (*looking in box*) No, that's the terrier.
SHOPKEEPER **Well, it's as near as dammit. 30**
MAN Well what do you mean? I want a cat.
SHOPKEEPER Listen, tell you what. I'll file its legs down a bit, take its snout out, stick a few wires through its cheeks. There you are, a lovely pussy cat.
MAN It's not a proper cat.
SHOPKEEPER What do you mean?
MAN Well it wouldn't miaow.
SHOPKEEPER Well it would howl a bit.
MAN

NO, NO, NO, NO. ER, HAVE YOU GOT A PARROT?

SHOPKEEPER No, I'm afraid not actually guv, we're fresh out of parrots. I'll tell you what though... I'll lop its back legs off, make good, strip the fur, stick a couple of wings on and staple on a beak of your own choice. (*taking small box and rattling it*) No problem. Lovely parrot.
MAN And how long would that take?
SHOPKEEPER Oh, let me see...er, stripping the fur off, no legs...(*calling*) Harry...can you do a parrot job on this terrier straight away?
HARRY (GRAHAM) (*off-screen*) No, I'm still putting a tuck in the Airedale, and then I got the frogs to let out.
SHOPKEEPER Friday?
MAN No I need it for tomorrow. It's a present.
SHOPKEEPER Oh dear, it's a long job. You see parrot conversion...Tell you what though, for free, terriers make lovely fish. I mean I could do that for you straight away. Legs off, fins on, stick a little pipe through the back of its neck so it can breathe, bit of gold paint, make good...
MAN You'd need a very big tank.
SHOPKEEPER It's a great conversation piece.
MAN Yes, all right, all right...but, er, only if I can watch.

Vox pops.

PEARSON (JOHN) Oh, I thought that was a bit predictable.
MAN (ERIC) **It's been done before. 31**

Melton Mowbray is a town in England's East Midlands. Like Pudsey or Esher, Melton Mowbray evokes a place of small stores, quaint streets, and nothing much happening. It's also famous for the Melton Mowbray pork pie, which Wikipedia sums up this way: "The uncured meat of a Melton pie is grey in color when cooked."

A Britishism for "as near as 'damn it' is to swearing."

Indeed, Episode 8 featured the classic "Pet Shop" sketch. And this sketch, featuring the same shop and a similarly weaselly pet shop owner, played by Palin, is a pale imitation.

A traditional grade-school play in Britain. You haven't grown up properly if you weren't in *Jack and the Beanstalk*.

Last Exit to Brooklyn is a novel by the American writer Hubert Selby Jr. and the subject of an infamous obscenity trial in the U.K. in 1966. After a guilty verdict, the writer and lawyer John Mortimer filed an appeal, which he won in 1968, signaling the end of the restrictive censorship laws in Great Britain.

Groupie was Jenny Fabian's 1969 book, with Johnny Byrne, about life as a lover of rock musicians. It caused much tutting when published, and Germaine Greer didn't like it because it wasn't much in line with feminism.

ROMAN CENTURION (TERRY J) Yeah, we did it for Caesar's Christmas Show.
CAESAR (GRAHAM) No you didn't, you did **Jack and the Beanstalk.** 32

Cut to interview room in town hall: a tweedy colonel type chairman; next to him a vicar and a lady with a pince-nez. The chairman is holding up the picture of Caesar. As the camera pulls out he rather obviously throws it away.

VICAR (TERRY J) Here what was that picture?
CHAIRMAN (GRAHAM) Ssh! Next! (*a gorilla enters*) Good morning—Mr Phipps?
GORILLA (ERIC) That's right, yes.
CHAIRMAN Er, do take a seat.
GORILLA Right sir. (*sits*)
CHAIRMAN Now could you tell us roughly why you want to become a librarian?
GORILLA Er, well, I've had a certain amount of experience running a library at school.
CHAIRMAN Yes, yes. What sort of experience?
GORILLA Er, well for a time I ran the Upper Science Library.
CHAIRMAN Yes, yes. Now Mr Phipps, you do realize that the post of librarian carries with it certain very important responsibilities. I mean, there's the selection of books, the record library, and the art gallery. Now it seems to me that your greatest disadvantage is your lack of professional experience...coupled with the fact that, um, being a gorilla, you would tend to frighten people.

VICAR (*aside*) Isn't he a gorilla?
CHAIRMAN Yes he is.
VICAR Well WHY didn't it say on his form that he's a gorilla?
CHAIRMAN Well, you see applicants are not required to fill in their species.
VICAR What was that picture?
CHAIRMAN Sh!...Mr Phipps, what is your attitude toward censorship in a public library?
GORILLA How do you mean, sir?
VICAR Well I mean for instance, would you for instance stock **'Last Exit to Brooklyn'**... 33 or... **'Groupie'?** 34
GORILLA Yes, I think so.
VICAR Good.
CHAIRMAN Yes, well, that seems to me to be very sensible Mr Phipps. I can't pretend that this library hasn't had its difficulties...Mr Robertson, your predecessor, an excellent librarian, savaged three people last week and had to be destroyed.
GORILLA I'm sorry sir.

CHAIRMAN Oh, no, don't be sorry. You see, I don't believe that libraries should be drab places where people sit in silence, and that's been the main reason for our policy of employing wild animals as librarians.

VICAR And also, they're much more permissive. Pumas keep **Hank Janson** **35** on open shelves...

CHAIRMAN Yes. Yes. Yes. (*a maniacal look in his eyes*) Yes, yes Mr Phipps. I love seeing the customers when they come in to complain about some book being damaged, and ask to see the chief librarian and then...you should see their faces when the proud beast leaps from his tiny office, snatches the book from their hands and sinks his fangs into their soft er...(*collects himself*) Mr Phipps...Kong! You can be our next librarian—you're proud majestic and fierce enough...will you do it?

GORILLA I...don't think I can sir.

VICAR Why not?

GORILLA

I, I'M NOT REALLY A GORILLA

VICAR Eh?

GORILLA I'm a librarian in a skin...

CHAIRMAN Why this deception?

GORILLA Well, they said it was the best way to get the job.

CHAIRMAN Get out, Mr Librarian Phipps, seeing as you're not a gorilla, but only dressed up as one, trying to deceive us in order to further your career...(*gorilla leaves*) Next. (*a dog comes in*) Ah. Mr Pattinson...Sit!

Cut to angry letters.

VOICE OVER (ERIC) (*reads*) Dear Mirror View, I would like to be paid five guineas for saying something stupid about a television show. Yours sincerely, **Mrs Sybil Agro.** **36**

VOICE OVER (JOHN) Dear David Jacobs, East Grinstead, Friday. **Why should I have to pay sixty-four guineas each year for my television licence** **37** when I can buy one for six. Yours sincerely, Captain R. H. Pretty. **PS Support Rhodesia,** **38** cut motor taxes, save the Argylls, running-in please pass.

Voice Over (graham) Dear Old Codgers, some friends of mine and I have formed a consortium, and working with sophisticated drilling equipment, we have discovered extensive nickel deposits off Western Scotland. The Cincinnati Mining Company.

VOICES OVER Good for you, ma'am.

VOICE OVER (MICHAEL) Dear Old Codgers, I am President of the United States of America, Yours truly, R. M. Nixon.

VOICES OVER Phew! Bet that's a job and a half, ma'am.

VOICE OVER (TERRY J) Dear Sir, I am over three thousand years old and would like to see any scene with two people in bed.

VOICES OVER Bet that's a link ma'am.

"Hank Janson" is a character created by Stephen Daniel Frances that was featured in a number of British pulp fiction titles. Janson was often the target of attempted obscenity crackdowns.

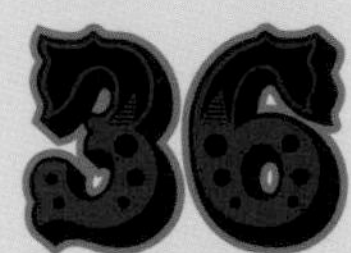

"Aggro" is British slang for physical violence.

The U.K. still maintains a system in which to legally watch TV, you must purchase an annual license. The proceeds go toward running the BBC (currently, license fees account for about 75 percent of these costs). Though it's now close to $250 for such a license, "sixty-four guineas" is basically meaningless, as the pound replaced the guinea in 1816.

In November 1965, Rhodesia, a landlocked area in southern Africa led by Ian Smith, declared its independence from the U.K. And so began nearly two decades of strife, during which Smith presided over a white minority government. In April 1980 Rhodesia finally became the Republic of Zimbabwe under Robert Mugabe. Smith remained active in politics until 1987 and died in South Africa in 2007.

Cut to bedroom of a middle-aged, middle-class wealthy couple. It is dark. They are both lying fast asleep on their backs. The husband is a colonel type with a moustache to boot. She has her hair in curlers and face cream on. Someone climbs in through the window and pads across to the wife. He is a dapper little Frenchman in a beret and a continental nylon mac, carrying a French loaf. He kisses her on the forehead. She wakes.

MAURICE (ERIC) Vera...Vera...darling! Wake up my little lemon. Come to my arms.
VERA (TERRY J) Maurice! What are you doing here?
MAURICE I could not keep away from you. I must have you all the time.
VERA Oh this is most inconvenient.
MAURICE Don't talk to me about convenience, love consumes my naughty mind, I'm delirious with desire.

He kisses her hand repeatedly. The husband suddenly wakes up with a start and sits up bolt upright and looks straight ahead.

HUSBAND (MICHAEL) What's that, Vera?
VERA Oh nothing, dear. Just a trick of the light.
HUSBAND Righto! (*he goes straight to sleep again*)
VERA Phew! That was close.
MAURICE Now then my little banana, my little fruit salad, I can wait for you no longer. You must be mine utterly...
VERA Oh, Maurice!

Suddenly beside them appears a young public-school man in a check suit with a pipe.

ROGER (JOHN) Vera! How dare you!
VERA Roger!
ROGER What's the meaning of this?
VERA Oh I can explain everything, my darling!
ROGER Who is this?
VERA This is Maurice Zatapathique...Roger Thompson...Roger Thompson...Maurice Zatapathique.

MAURICE How do you do.
ROGER How do you do...(*kneeling*) How could you do this to me, Vera...after all we've been through? Dammit, I love you.
MAURICE Vera! Don't you understand, it's *me* that loves you.

The husband wakes up again.

HUSBAND What's happening, Vera?
VERA

OH, NOTHING DEAR. JUST A TWIG BRUSHING AGAINST THE WINDOW.

HUSBAND Righto. (*he goes back to sleep*)
ROGER Come to me Vera!
VERA Oh...not now, Roger.
MAURICE Vera, my little hedgehog! Don't turn me away!
VERA Oh it cannot be, Maurice.

Enter Biggles. **39** *He wears flying boots, jacket and helmet as for First World War. He wears a notice round his neck: 'Biggles'.*

Children's book character Biggles, from the W.E. Johns novels much beloved by all adventure-loving British boys. "Algy" is his sidekick.

BIGGLES (GRAHAM) Hands off, you filthy bally froggie! (*kneels by the bed*)
VERA Oh Ken, Ken Biggles!
BIGGLES Yes, Algy's here as well.
VERA Algy Braithwaite?

Into the light comes Algy. Tears streaming down his face. He wears a notice round his neck which reads: 'Algy's here as well'.

ALGY (IAN) That's right...Vera...(*he chokes back the tears*) Oh God you know we both still bally love you.
VERA Oh Biggles! Algy. Oh, but how wonderful!

She starts to cry. Husband wakes up again.

HUSBAND What's happening, Vera?
VERA Oh, er, nothing dear. It's just the toilet filling up.
HUSBAND Righto. (*he goes fast asleep again*)

By this stage all the men have pulled up chairs in a circle around Vera's side of the bed. They are all chatting amongst themselves. Biggles is holding her hand. Maurice has produced a bottle of vin ordinaire. At this moment, four Mexican musicians appear on the husband's side of the bed. The leader of the band nudges the husband, who wakes.

MEXICAN (*reading from a scruffy bit of paper*) Scusey...you tell me where is...Mrs Vera Jackson...please.
HUSBAND Yes...right and right again.
MEXICAN Muchas gracias...
HUSBAND Righto.

He immediately goes back to sleep again. The Mexicans all troop round the bed and enter the group. The leader conducts them and they start up a little conga...once they've started he turns and comes over to Vera with a naughty glint in his eye. They play a guitar, a trumpet and maracas.

MEXICAN Oh Vera...you remember Acapulco in the Springtime...

VERA Oh. The Herman Rodrigues Four!

Suddenly the husband wakes up.

HUSBAND

VERA! (THERE IS IMMEDIATE SILENCE) I DISTINCTLY HEARD A MEXICAN RHYTHM COMBO.

VERA Oh no, dear...it was just the electric blanket switching off.
HUSBAND Hm. Well I'm going for a tinkle.

He gets out of bed and disappears into the gloom.

VERA Oh no you can't do that. Here, we haven't finished the sketch yet!
ALGY Dash it all, there's only another bally page.
ROGER I say. There's no one to react to.
MAURICE Don't talk to the camera.
ROGER Oh sorry.

Enter a huge man dressed as an Aztec god (viz: Christopher Plummer in 'Royal Hunt of the Sun'). **40** *He stretches arms open wide and is about to speak when owing to lack of money he is cut short by Vera.* **41**

VERA Here it's no good *you* coming in...He's gone and left the sketch.
BIGGLES Yes, he went for a tinkle.

Cut to close-up of husband and a dolly bird with a lavatory chain hanging between them. She is about to pull the chain when he stops her.

HUSBAND Sh! I think my wife is beginning to suspect something...

The Royal Hunt of the Sun is a 1969 movie based on a play by Peter Shaffer, who also wrote *Five Finger Exercise*, *Amadeus*, and *Equus*, among many others.

There is no such action in the scene.

Cut to animation of various strange and wonderful creatures saying to the effect:

HARTEBEESTE I thought that ending was a bit predictable.

CROCODILE *(eating it)* Yes indeed there was a certain lack of originality.

OSTRICH *(eating the crocodile)* Anyway it's not necessarily a good thing just to be different.

A LADY *(emerging from hatch in ostrich)* No, quite, there is equal humour in the conventional.

PIG *(eating ostrich)* But on the other hand, is it what the public wants? I mean with the new permissiveness, not to mention the balance of payments. It's an undeniable fact that...

COELOCANTH *(eating the pig)* I agree with that completely.

RODENT That's it...let's get out of this show before it's too late...*('The End' descends on it)* Too late!

Two men detach the 'It's' man from his meat-hook and carry him off. Credits

ENGAGED
SEA
SON
1
EPISODE 11

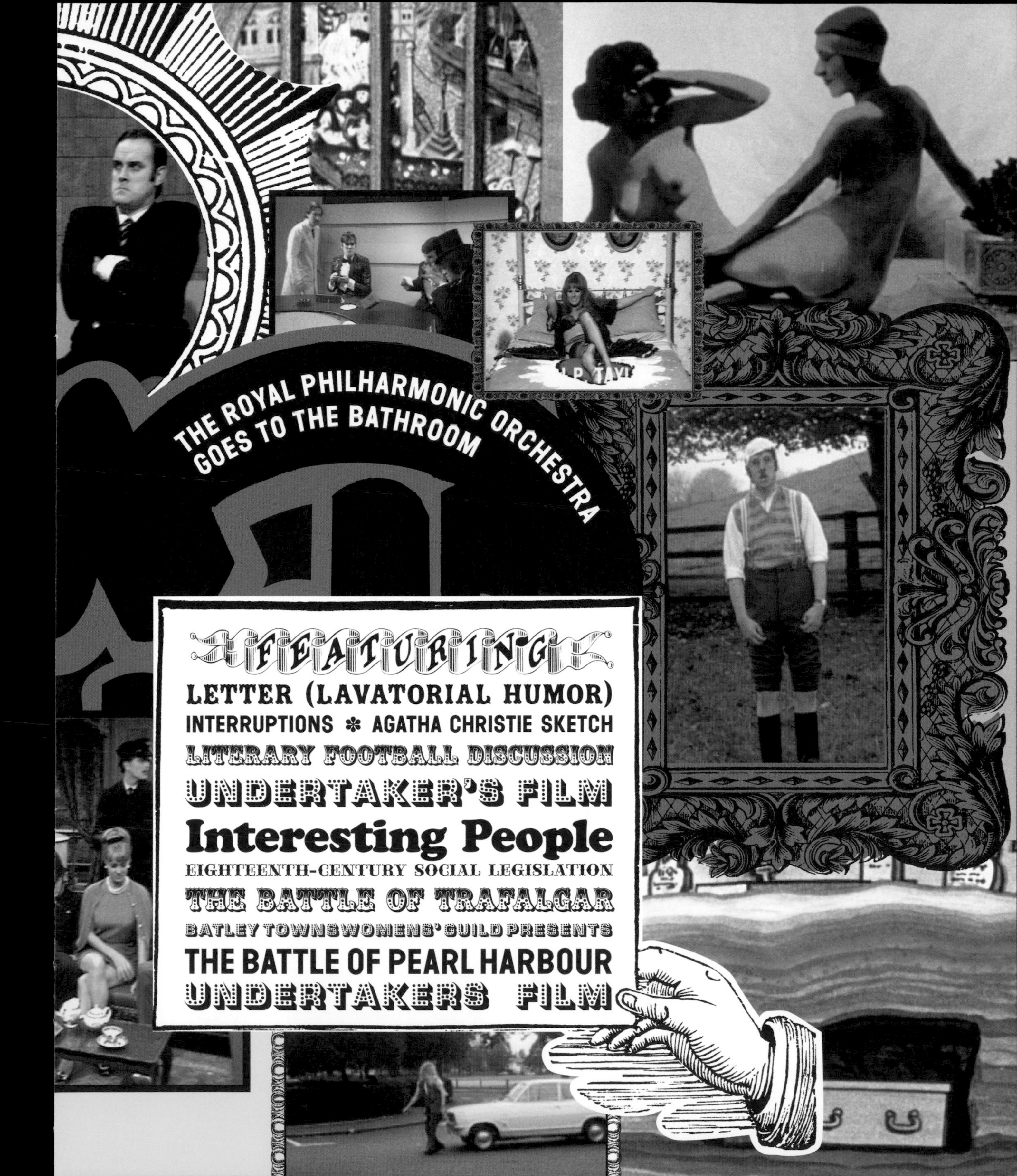
THE ROYAL PHILHARMONIC ORCHESTRA GOES TO THE BATHROOM
FEATURING
LETTER (LAVATORIAL HUMOR)
INTERRUPTIONS ✻ AGATHA CHRISTIE SKETCH
LITERARY FOOTBALL DISCUSSION
UNDERTAKER'S FILM
Interesting People
EIGHTEENTH-CENTURY SOCIAL LEGISLATION
THE BATTLE OF TRAFALGAR
BATLEY TOWNSWOMENS' GUILD PRESENTS
THE BATTLE OF PEARL HARBOUR
UNDERTAKERS FILM

FIRST AIRED: DECEMBER 28, 1969

Film: The Amazing World of The 'It's' Man

Animated titles.

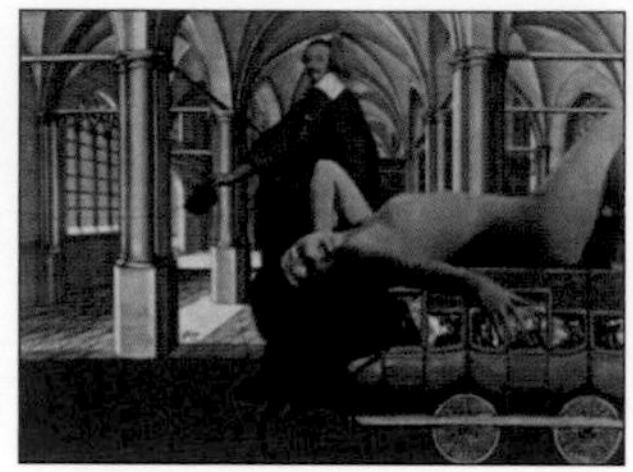

Caption: ***'PART TWO'S'*** **1** *Caption: 'THE ROYAL PHILHARMONIC ORCHESTRA GOES TO THE BATHROOM'*
Cut to bathroom door, outside. Man knocks on door.

IT'S MAN (MICHAEL) Have you finished in there yet?

From inside comes a burst of the Tchaikovsky piano concerto. He tuts. Cut to letter and voice over.

VOICE OVER (JOHN) Dear Sir, I object strongly to the obvious lavatorial turn this show has already taken. Why do we never hear about the good things in Britain, like Mary Bignall's wonderful jump in 1964? Yours etc., Ken Voyeur.

Stock film of ***Mary Bignall's*** **2** *winning jump at the* ***Rome Olympics.*** **3** *Letter and voice over.*

VOICE OVER (ERIC) Dear Sir, I object strongly to the obvious athletic turn this show has now taken. Why can't we hear more about the human body? There is nothing embarrassing or nasty about the human body except for the intestines and bits of the bottom.

Letter and voice over.

VOICE OVER (MICHAEL) Dear Sir, I object strongly to the letters on your programme. They are clearly not written by the general public and are merely included for a cheap laugh. Yours sincerely etc., William Knickers.

Stock film of the whole of an orchestra finishing an orchestral item. When they finish playing we hear the sound of flushing. Animation: a beautiful and not zany introduction, perhaps with photos of famous historical characters, finishing with the words: 'The World of History'. Cut to man at desk. Caption: 'PROFESSOR R. J. CANNING'

CANNING (GRAHAM) 1348. The Black Death, typhus, cholera, consumption, bubonic plague.

Cut to five undertakers sitting on a coffin in a country road.

This reads "Episode Two's" on the actual show.

Her last name is spelled "Bignal." She was the winner of the gold medal in the long jump at the 1964 Summer Olympics, held in Tokyo. She broke the world record to gain first place and was the first woman from Britain to win a track and field gold.

The Rome Summer Olympics were held in 1960. Mary Bignal finished ninth in those games.

FIRST UNDERTAKER (ERIC) Ah, those were the days...

Back to Canning at his desk.

CANNING Now I'm...I'm...Now I'm not prepared to go on with this, unless these interruptions cease. **All right? 4** Right. The devastating effect of these, em...

Cut to film of hearses racing. Crashing out of shot. Sign: ***'Accident Black Spot',*** **5** *and the undertakers picnicking.*

CANNING (*he is packing up his papers and putting on his mac as he walks away from desk, camera pans with him*) No, don't follow me and...(*camera zooms in*) And don't zoom in on me, no I'm off, I'm off. That's it. That's all. I'm off.

He walks out of shot. Empty frame. A short pause. An undertaker comes into frame.

SECOND UNDERTAKER (TERRY J) (*to camera*) Are you nervy, irritable, depressed, tired of life. (*winks*) Keep it up.

Caption: 'MEANWHILE INSIDE'
Cut to drawing room of large English country house. Sitting around are various standard Agatha Christie type characters, Colonel Pickering, Lady Amanda Velloper, Kirt, Anona Winn. They drink tea, read etc. Outside there is thunder. Inspector Tiger enters the room.

4

Chapman is essentially playing the same character as he did previously, when dressed as a sergeant major: angry at interruptions, a commenter on the sketch, a director and critic as much as a participant.

"Accident Black Spot" is a regular sign on British roads.

The microphone is clearly in the wrong place here, as it's hard to hear what Chapman says.

The old Sherlock Holmesian answer.

INSPECTOR TIGER (JOHN) This house is surrounded. I'm afraid I must not ask anyone to leave the room. No, I must ask nobody...no, I must ask everybody to...I must not ask anyone to leave the room. No one must be asked by me to leave the room. No, no one must ask the room to leave. I...I...ask the room shall by someone be left. Not. Ask nobody the room somebody leave shall I. Shall I leave the room? Everyone must leave the room...as it is...with them in it. Phew. Understand?

COLONEL PICKERING (GRAHAM) **You don't want anybody to leave the room. 6**

INSPECTOR TIGER *(clicking fingers to indicate Colonel Pickering has hit the nail on the head)* Now, alduce me to introlow myslef. I'm sorry. Alself me to myduce introlow. Introme to-lose mylow alself. Alme to you introself mylowduce. Excuse me a moment. *(bangs himself on the side of the head)* Allow me to introduce myself. I'm afraid I must ask that no one leave the room. Allow me to introduce myself. I'm Inspector Tiger.

ALL Tiger?

INSPECTOR TIGER *(jumping)* Where? Where? What? Ah. Me Tiger. You Jane. Grrr. Beg your pardon, allow me to introduce myself I'm afraid I must ask that no one leave the room.

LADY VELLOPER (CAROL) Why not?

INSPECTOR TIGER **Elementary. Since the body was found in this room, and no one has left it. Therefore...the murderer must be somebody in this room. 7**

COLONEL PICKERING What body?

INSPECTOR TIGER Somebody. In this room. Must the murderer be. The murderer of the body is somebody in this room, which nobody must leave...leave the body in the room not to be left by anybody. Nobody leaves anybody or the body with somebody. Everybody who is anybody shall leave the body in the room body. Take the tablets Tiger. Anybody *(as he searches for the tablets)* with a body but not the body is nobody. Nobody leaves the body in the... *(he takes the tablet)* Albody me introbody albodyduce.

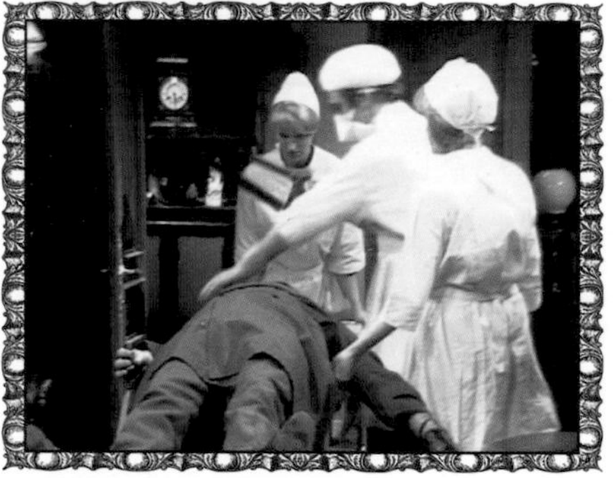

At this moment a surgeon enters with two nurses and starts to operate on his head with sawing noises. Caption: 'THE SAME DRAWING ROOM. ONE LOBOTOMY LATER' The surgeon is packing up. Inspector Tiger's head is bandaged.

SURGEON Now for Sir Gerald.

INSPECTOR That's better, now I'm Inspector Tiger and I must ask that nobody leave the room. *(he gives thumbs up to the surgeon who is at door)* Now someone has committed a murder here, and that murderer is someone in this room. The question is...who?

COLONEL PICKERING Look, there hasn't been a murder.

INSPECTOR TIGER No murder.

ALL No.

INSPECTOR TIGER Oh. I don't like it. It's too simple, too clear cut. I'd better wait. *(he sits on sofa)* No, too simple, too clear cut.

The lights go out. There is a scream followed by a shot. The light goes up. Inspector Tiger is dead. He has a bullet hole in his forehead, an arrow through his neck and there is a bottle marked poison on his lap.

COLONEL PICKERING By jove, he was right.

Chief Superintendent Lookout enters, with constable.

LOOKOUT (ERIC) This house is surrounded. I must ask that no one leave the room. I'm Chief Superintendent Lookout.

LADY VELLOPER Look out?

LOOKOUT (*jumping*)

WHAT, WHERE, OH, ME, LOOKOUT. LOOKOUT OF THE YARD.

LADY VELLOPER Why, what would we see?

LOOKOUT I'm sorry?

LADY VELLOPER What would we see if we look out of the yard?

LOOKOUT ...I'm afraid I don't follow that at all. Ah ha. The body. So the murderer must be somebody in this room. Unless he had very long arms. Say thirty or forty feet. I think we can discount that one. Ha, ha, ha, (*he starts really laughing*) Lookout of the Yard. Very good. Right. Now, we'll reconstruct the crime. I'll sit down here. Constable, you turn off the lights. (*lights go out, we hear Lookout's voice*) Good. Now then, there was a scream (*scream*) then just before the lights went up there was a shot.

There is a shot. The lights go up and Chief Superintendent Lookout is sitting dead, bullet hole, arrow and all. In walks Assistant Chief Constable Theresamanbehindyer.

ACCT (TERRY J) All right...all right, the house is surrounded and nobody leave the room and all the rest of it. Allow me to introduce myself. I'm Assistant Chief Constable Theresamanbehindyer.

ALL Theresamanbehindyer? 8

ACCT Ah, you're not going to catch me with an old one like that. Right let's reconstruct the crime. Constable you be Inspector Tiger.

CONSTABLE (MICHAEL) Right, sir. Nobody leave the room ask shall—somebody I leave nobody in the room body shall, take the tablets Tigerbody. Alself me to my duce introlow left body in the roomself.

ACCT Very good. Just sit down there. Right now we'll pretend the lights have gone out. Constable, you scream. (*constable screams*) Somebody shoots you (*pulls gun and shoots constable through head*) and the door opens...

The door flies open. Enter policeman.

FIRE Nobody move! I'm Chief Constable Fire.

ALL Fire! Where?

He jumps. Immediately cut to undertaker as before.

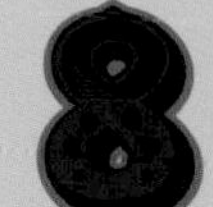

Pantomimes frequently feature this kind of audience participation. The sketch is neatly mixing the second-act detective melodrama with the seaside comedy tradition.

SECOND UNDERTAKER (TERRY J) We're interrupting this sketch but we'll be bringing you back the moment anything interesting happens. Meanwhile here are some friends of mine.

Film of four undertakers carrying a coffin. They surreptitiously tip the body out of the coffin and go skipping lightly up the road. **9**

Letter and voice over.

VOICE OVER (GRAHAM) Dear Sir, I'm sorry this letter is late, it should have come at the beginning of the programme. Yours, **Ivor Bigbottie,** **10** (age two).

Two chairs in interview set. Smart interviewer and footballer (who is not over bright) in blazer.

INTERVIEWER (ERIC) From the plastic arts we turn to football. **Last night in the Stadium of Light, Jarrow,** **11** we witnessed the resuscitation of a great footballing tradition, when **Jarrow United** **12** came of age, in a European sense, with an almost Proustian display of modern existentialist football. Virtually annihilating by midfield moral argument the now surely obsolescent **catennachio** **13** defensive philosophy of Signor Alberto Fanfrino. Bologna indeed were a side intellectually out argued by a Jarrow team thrusting and bursting with aggressive Kantian positivism and outstanding in this fine Jarrow team was my man of the match, the arch-thinker, free scheming, scarcely ever to be curbed, midfield cognoscento, Jimmy Buzzard.

BUZZARD (JOHN) Good evening Brian.

INTERVIEWER Jimmy, at least one ageing football commentator was gladdened last night by the sight of an English footballer breaking free of the limpid tentacles of packed Mediterranean defence.

BUZZARD Good evening Brian.

INTERVIEWER Were you surprised at the way the Italian ceded midfield dominance so early on in the game?

BUZZARD **Well Brian I'm opening a boutique.** **14**

INTERVIEWER This is of course symptomatic of a new breed of footballer as it is indeed symptomatic of your whole genre of player, is it not?

BUZZARD Good evening Brian.

INTERVIEWER What I'm getting at, Jimmy, is you seem to have discovered a new concept with a mode in which you dissected the Italian defence, last night.

BUZZARD (*pauses for thought*) **I hit the ball first time and there it was in the back of the net.** **15** (*smiles and looks round*)

New Orleans–style jazz is played here, signaling that we're not in gray old England anymore.

In case you missed it, the name is "I have a large derriere."

There is no such stadium, in Jarrow at least—Lisbon, Portugal, is home to the actual "Stadium of Light" (Estádio do Sport Lisboa e Benfica). The English Premiership now boasts a Stadium of Light of its own, however—in the northeast town of Sunderland. It opened in 1997 and stands just nine miles south of Jarrow.

There has never been a team called Jarrow United in the upper reaches of British soccer—the northeast town of Jarrow sits a couple of miles across the River Tyne from Newcastle, which has a team already. The joke here is not only the intellectual player versus the idiot, but also that Jarrow would never have had a team good enough to take on an Italian team (Bologna won the Italian league in the early 1960s and continues to be a top team).

INTERVIEWER Do you think Jarrow will adopt a more defensive posture for the first leg of the next tie in Turkey? 16

BUZZARD *(confidently)* I hit the ball first time and there it was in the back of the net.

INTERVIEWER Yes, yes—but have you any plans for dealing with the free scoring Turkish forwards?

BUZZARD Well Brian...I'm opening a boutique.

Cut to undertaker.

SECOND UNDERTAKER And now let's take a look at the state of play in the detective sketch.

Cut to drawing room. There is an enormous pile of dead policemen on and around the sofa.

CONSTABLE Alself me to introlow mybody...

Inspector shoots him in the head. ***Caption: 'CONSTABLES 13 SUPERINTENDENTS 9'*** **17** *Cut to four undertakers carrying a coffin up a hill. One of them falters and drops. The others lower the coffin to the ground, take out a fresh undertaker, put the fallen one in the coffin, and proceed.*

Cut to animated sequence, leading to big glittering flashing lights saying 'Interesting People'.

A compère sits at desk, with guest chairs beside it.

COMPÈRE (MICHAEL) **Hello, good evening, and welcome 18** to yet another edition of 'Interesting People'. And my first interesting person tonight is the highly interesting Mr Howard Stools from Kendal in Westmorland.

He puts a matchbox on desk in front of him. He presses a button on the desk and we hear applause. Releases button; applause stops abruptly. He opens the box a little and speaks into it.

COMPÈRE Good evening Mr Stools.

VOICE *(from inside box)* Hello, David.

COMPÈRE Mr Stools, what makes you particularly interesting?

VOICE Well, I'm only half an inch long.

COMPÈRE Well that's *extremely* interesting, thank you for coming along on the show tonight Mr Stools.

13

"Catennachio"—actually *catenaccio*—is the widely loathed Italian system of overly defensive soccer. And it's not obsolete: many Italian teams still pride defense over that pesky annoyance, the "goal."

14

A wonderful gag about the dimness of soccer players. It was very fashionable in the 1960s and '70s for players to branch out from their abilities on the field to open stores, bars, and nightclubs.

15

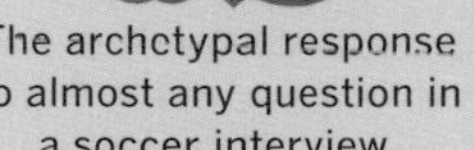

The archetypal response to almost any question in a soccer interview.

16

Ties in European games were often two-legged, home and away, with an aggregate score defining who advanced to the next round.

17

There's a brief film of soccer fans celebrating here, though it is not in the printed script.

18

"Hello, good evening, and welcome" is the catchphrase of British journalist David Frost, a regular butt of Python jokes.

MR STOOLS I thought you'd think that was interesting David, in fact...

COMPÈRE (*shuts matchbox; applause*) Mr Alan Stools from Kendal in Westmorland...half an inch long. (*applause*) Our next guest tonight has come all the way from Egypt, he's just flown into London today, he's **Mr Ali Bayan,** 19 he's with us in the studio tonight and he's stark raving mad.

Mr. Ali Bayan was "Howard" at the start of the sketch, and will be again at the end.

Applause. Cut to Ali Bayan (TERRY J) *who looks at camera in a very mad way. Applause.*

COMPÈRE Mr Ali Bayan, stark raving mad. Now it's time for our music spot and we turn the spotlight tonight on the Rachel Toovey Bicycle Choir, (*applause*) with their fantastic arrangement of **'Men of Harlech'** 20 for bicycle bells only.

Originally a military march from the late-eighteenth century, "Men of Harlech" is the song of pride of the Welsh people.

Cut to six men in oilskins and sou'westers. They sing 'Men of Harlech', and at the end of each line mournfully ring bells. Applause at end.

COMPÈRE The Rachel Toovey Bicycle Choir. Really interesting. Remember, if you're interesting and want to appear on this programme, **write your name and address and your telephone number** 21 and send it to this address: (*reads caption*) The BBC, c/o E. F. Lutt, 18 Rupee Buildings, West 12. (*applause*) Thank you, thank you. Now here's an interesting person. Apart from being a full-time stapling machine, he can also give a cat influenza.

What Palin actually says is, "Write your name and address *on* your telephone number"—and he gets an unintended laugh for it.

Cut to a smartly dressed man (JOHN) *who coughs copiously into a cat basket. We hear a miaow and a feline sneeze. Cut back to compère.*

COMPÈRE Well, you can't get much more interesting than that, or can you? 22 With me now is Mr Thomas Walters of **West Hartlepool** 23 who is totally invisible. Good evening, Mr Walters. (*turns to empty chair*)

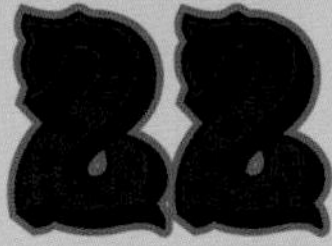

Palin pauses here, a bit surprised by the unexpected laugh this line gets from the audience.

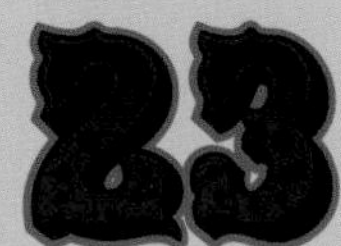

West Hartlepool is a town on the northeast coast of England.

WALTERS (ERIC) (*off-screen*) Over here, Hughie.

Compère turns to find a boringly dressed man sitting by him.

COMPÈRE Mr Walters, are you sure you're invisible?

WALTERS Oh yes, most certainly.

COMPÈRE Well, Mr Walters, what's it like being invisible?

WALTERS (*slowly and boringly*) Well, for a start, at the office where I work I can be sitting at my desk all day and the others totally ignore me. At home, even though we are in the same room, my wife does not speak to me for hours, people pass me by in the street without a glance in my direction, and I can walk into a room without...

COMPÈRE Well, whilst we've got interesting people, we met Mr Oliver Cavendish who...
WALTERS (*droning on*) Even now you yourself, you do hardly notice me...
COMPÈRE Mr Oliver Cavendish of Leicester, who claims to be able to recite the entire Bible in one second, whilst being struck on the head with a large axe. Ha, ha, wow. **We've since discovered that he was a fraud,** **24** yes a fraud, he did not in fact recite the entire Bible he merely recited the first two words, 'In the...' before his death.

Cut to film montage of sporting clips.

COMPÈRE (*voice over*) Now it's time for 'Interesting Sport', and this week it's **all-in cricket,** **25** live from the Municipal Baths, Croydon.

Boxing ring; two fully kitted out cricketers, who as the bell goes, approach each other and start hitting each other with cricket bats. Applause.

COMPÈRE With me now is Mr Ken Dove, twice voted the most interesting man in Dorking. Ken, I believe you're interested in shouting.
DOVE (JOHN) (*shouting*) Yes, I'm interested in shouting all right, by jove you certainly hit the nail on the head with that particular observation of yours then.
COMPÈRE What does your wife think of this?
WIFE (*voice off, full-blooded*) I agree with him.
DOVE Shut up!
WALTERS ...At parties for instance people never come up to me, I just sit there and everybody totally...

Man holding cat enters.

COMPÈRE That is Tiddles, I believe?
MAN (GRAHAM) Yes, this is, this is **Tiddles.** **26**
COMPÈRE Yes, and what does she do?
MAN She flies across the studio and lands in a bucket of water.
COMPÈRE By herself?
MAN No, I fling her.
COMPÈRE Well that's extremely interesting. Ladies and gentlemen—Mr Don Savage and Tiddles.

Man whirls the cat round and round.

Again, Palin pauses for the unexpected laugh.

"All-in cricket" is a mix of all-in wrestling, as wrestling was once called in England, and . . . well, cricket.

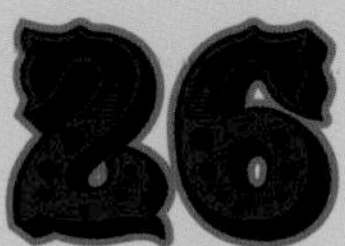

Chapman mispronounces this as "Tibbles."

He lets go of the cat, it flies across studio. A hollow splash and a miaow. Quick shot of a real cat sitting in a bucket.

DOVE (*shouting*) I'm more interesting than a wet pussycat.

WALTERS ...for hour after hour.

COMPÈRE Yes, great, well now for the first time on television 'Interesting People' brings you a man who claims he can send bricks to sleep by hypnosis. Mr Keith Maniac from Guatemala.

Maniac is sitting by compère. He wears a top hat and an opera cloak.

He also does a kind of magician's "*Shazzam*!" with his hands and clicks his fingers three times.

MANIAC (TERRY J) Good evening.

COMPÈRE Keith, you claim you can send bricks to sleep.

MANIAC Yes, that is correct, I can...

COMPÈRE Entirely by hypnosis.

MANIAC Yes...I use no artificial means, whatsoever. (*leans and picks matchbox off desk to light pipe, opens it and strikes match*)

VOICE (*from matchbox*) Aaagh!

DOVE You've injured Mr Stools!

MANIAC (*picks up other box and lights pipe*) I simply stare at the brick and it goes to sleep.

COMPÈRE Well, we have a brick here, Keith. (*indicates brick on desk*) Perhaps you can send it to sleep for us...

MANIAC Oh...Ah, well, I am afraid that is already asleep.

COMPÈRE How do you know?

MANIAC Well, it's not moving...

COMPÈRE Oh, I see—have we got a moving brick? Yes, we've got a moving brick, Keith, it's coming over now.

We see a man in a white coat preparing to throw brick. He throws it gently. It lands on the desk in front of Keith. ***Keith stares at it as it falls.*** 27

MANIAC There we are, fast asleep.

COMPÈRE Very good, very good indeed.

MANIAC **All done with the eyes.** 28

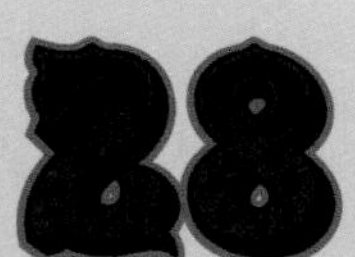

This line perhaps refers to the direction above for Jones to simply stare at the brick, rather than click his fingers at it.

COMPÈRE Yes, Mr Keith Maniac from Guatemala.

DOVE (*distressed—to matchbox*) Mr Stools—speak to me, Howard.

Quick cut back to all-in cricket.

COMPÈRE Mr Keith Maniac of Guatemala...and now four tired undertakers.

Cut to film of four undertakers struggling up a hill carrying a coffin. One staggers and drops. The others lower the coffin, pick him up, and place him inside. Raising the coffin again they stagger off up the hill. Another undertaker collapses; the remaining two place him in the coffin. Exhaustedly they pick up the coffin, but have only gone two or three paces when one of them collapses. The remaining one drags him into the coffin, pushing him in with some difficulty, and forces the lid shut. He debates with himself for a moment on how to pick up the coffin, then disgustedly throws away his hat and climbs into the coffin, shutting the lid behind him

The coffin moves off by itself.

VOICE OVER (ERIC) We interrupt this very quickly to take you back to the Jimmy Buzzard interview, where we understand something exciting's just happened.

Cut back to the interview studio; ***Jimmy Buzzard is sitting on the floor.*** **29**

BUZZARD I've fallen off my chair, Brian.

Cut to a graveyard. The coffin, still moving of its own volition, enters the graveyard. A vicar walks up and motions gravediggers (who we cannot see) to get out of the grave. Out of the grave climb two gravediggers...then two more...then two more...yet another two...two miners...two uniformed men...a police dog with handler...and finally an Australian surfboarder. The coffin makes its way into the grave. Then a wonderful piece of animation by our amazing animator Terry Gilliam, wonderboy.

Consisting of a very fast collage of extremely sexy stills of half-dressed and naked girls. Incredibly torchy music, after eight seconds of which: Superimposed caption: 'THE WORLD OF HISTORY' Second caption: 'SOCIAL LEGISLATION IN THE EIGHTEENTH CENTURY' Cut to fantastically alluring boudoir: a plush four poster bed with silk drapes, silk sheets, a fur pillow etc. We look down on it from above. Stretched out on the bed is a girl (CAROL) *oozing with sex...a real professional...black net stockings, suspenders, bra and panties or what have you. She moves as if in the throes of orgasm as she mimes to a very masculine voice off. Superimposed caption:* ***'S. J. P. TAYLOR'*** **30**

He is also holding a half-eaten banana, in case we've forgotten that he's like a monkey.

The actual caption reads "A. J. P. Taylor," the name of the eminent British historian.

VOICE OVER (JOHN) (*very masculine voice to which girl mimes*) Good evening. Tonight I want to examine the whole question of eighteenth-century social legislation—its relevance to the hierarchical structure of post-Renaissance society, and its impact on the future of parochial organization in an expanding agrarian economy. But first a bit of fun.

Cut to film of eight-second striptease. Cut immediately back to the same set.

VOICE OVER To put England's social legislation in a European context is Professor Gert Van Der Whoops of the **Rijksmuseum in the Hague.** 31

Cut to another bed, equally seductive. A little bespectacled professor is lying on it being caressed and undressed by an amorous siren.

PROFESSOR (MICHAEL) ***(German accent)*** 32 In Holland in the early part of the fifteenth century there was three things important to social legislation. One...rise of merchant classes...two, urbanization of craft guilds...three, declining moral values in age of increasing social betterment. But first, a bit of fun...(*grabs girl*)

A curtain and potted palms. ***Sound effects: angel choirs.*** 33 *A man in dinner jacket with angel's wings on is lowered from above. As he touches the ground the angel choirs fade out. He gets a crumpled piece of paper out of his pocket.*

MAN (TERRY J) And now Professor R. J. Canning.

He folds up the paper and puts it away. The angel choirs start again and he slowly rises up and out of frame. Cut to Professor Canning in straight presentation-type set with BP screen behind him. Caption: 'PROFESSOR R. J. CANNING AGAIN'

CANNING (GRAHAM) The cat sat on the mat. And now the Battle of Trafalgar...(*on the screen behind him a contemporary picture of the Battle of Trafalgar flashes up*) Tonight we examine popular views of this great battle. Was the Battle of Trafalgar fought in the Atlantic off southern Spain? **Or was it fought on dry land near Cudworth in Yorkshire?** 34 Here is one man who thinks it was...

The Rijksmuseum is forty miles northeast of the Hague in Amsterdam.

Actually, he does a perfectly fine Dutch accent.

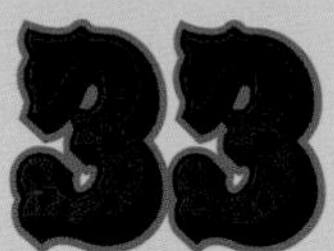

The song is "Ding Dong Merrily on High," which was sung at the end of Episode 9.

Cudworth is a small town in south Yorkshire, some 1,600 miles north of Trafalgar.

Cut to a man—a Gumby—with gum boots on, rolled up trousers, knotted handkerchief etc., looking very thick and standing in the middle of a field.

CANNING (*voice over*) And here is his friend.

Camera pans lightly losing Gumby but revealing identically dressed thick man standing next to him. The camera pans back to original Gumby. Superimposed caption: 'PROFESSOR R. J. GUMBY'

CANNING (*voice over*) What makes you think the Battle of Trafalgar was fought near Cudworth?

There is a long pause.

GUMBY (MICHAEL)

BECAUSE...DRAKE...WAS...TOO... CLEVER FOR...THE GERMAN...FLEET. 35

CANNING (*voice over*) I beg your pardon?

GUMBY ...Oh I've forgotten what I said now.

CANNING (*voice over*) Mr Gumby's remarkable views have sparked off a wave of controversy amongst his fellow historians.

Cut to identical Gumby figure in book lined study. He stands. Superimposed caption: 'F. H. GUMBY. REGIUS PROFESSOR OF HISTORY AT HIS MOTHER'S'

SECOND GUMBY (ERIC) Well I fink...we...should...reappraise...our concept of the...Battle of Trafalgar.

Cut to another Gumby, this time outside a university. Superimposed caption: 'PROF. L. R. GUMBY'

THIRD GUMBY (GRAHAM) Well...well...I agree with everything Mr Gumby says.

Cut to yet another Gumby. This time standing in a pig-sty with pigs. Superimposed caption: 'PROF. ENID GUMBY'

FOURTH GUMBY (JOHN) Well, I think cement is more interesting than people think.

Sir Francis Drake fought the Spanish, of course. But pointing out factual errors by the Gumbys does seem to utterly miss the point.

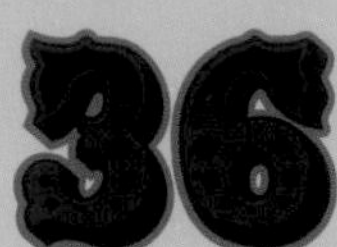

Twelve shillings and sixpence—about 66 pence—and the plain wrapper is what pornography would be carried in.

Batley is another small town, this time in west Yorkshire, 25 miles northwest of Cudworth.

Original sexy girl in seductive boudoir as she mimes to masculine voice over. Superimposed caption as before: 'A. J. P. TAYLOR'

VOICE OVER One subject...four different views...(*brandishing egg-whisk*) **twelve and...in a plain wrapper.** **36**

Cut back to Canning.

CANNING The stuff of history is indeed woven in the woof. Pearl Harbor. There are pages in history's book which are written on the grand scale. Events so momentous that they dwarf man and time alike. And such is the Battle of Pearl Harbor, re-enacted for us now by the women of **Batley Townswomen's Guild.** **37**

Cut to a muddy corner of a field. Miss Rita Fairbanks stands talking straight to camera. Behind her lurk five more pepperpots.

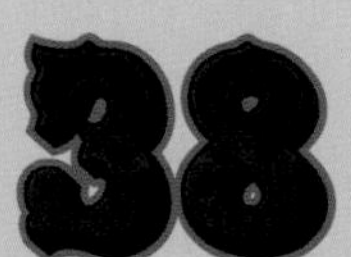

The Camp On Blood Island is a 1958 movie set in a Japanese prisoner of war camp.

CANNING (*voice over*) Miss Rita Fairbanks—you organized this reconstruction of the Battle of Pearl Harbor—why?

RITA (ERIC) Well we've always been extremely interested in modern drama...we were of course the first Townswomen's Guild to perform **'Camp On Blood Island'**, **38** and last year we did our extremely popular re-enactment of 'Nazi War Atrocities'. So this year we thought we would like to do something in a lighter vein...

CANNING So you chose the Battle of Pearl Harbor?

RITA Yes, that's right, we did.

CANNING Well I can see you're all ready to go. So I'll just wish you good luck in your latest venture.

RITA Thank you very much, young man.

She retreats and joins the other ladies who meanwhile separate into two opposing sides facing each other.

CANNING (*reverential voice over*) Ladies and gentlemen, the World of History is proud to present the premiere of

THE BATLEY TOWNSWOMEN'S GUILD'S RE-ENACTMENT OF 'THE ATTL O A L A O'.

A whistle blows and the two sides set about each other with handbags etc., ***speeded up 50% just to give it a bit of edge.*** **39**

Cut to Canning in studio.

CANNING The Battle of Pearl Harbor. Incidentally, I'm sorry if I got a little bit shirty earlier on in the programme, when I kept getting interrupted by all these films and things that kept coming in, but I...

Cut to vicar in a graveyard. He sprinkles dirt and gets mud thrown in his face. Vicar shoots a gun. Cut to undertakers leaving graveyard. They get into a hearse. As they leave it and drive off we see the other side is painted with psychedelic flowers. Cut to Canning.

CANNING So I said if it happened again I'd get very angry and talk to Lord Hill and...

Cut to 'It's' man.

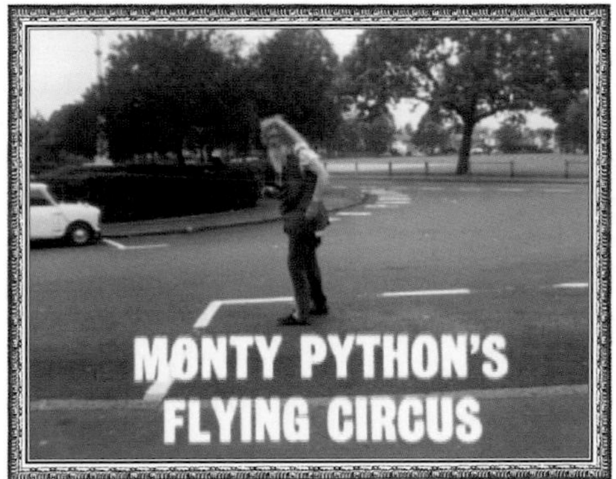

CANNING Tell **Lord Hill.** **40**

Credits

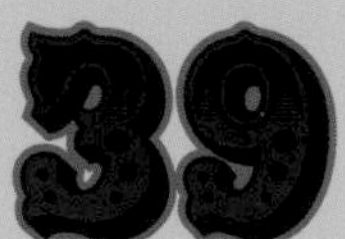

This hardly does justice to the mud-bath fight that ensues, featuring a hilarious takedown of Cleese—and he's a big guy to bring down.

Another reference to poor Lord Hill, head of the BBC, who was name-checked at the start of Episode 10. One can't imagine what this stolid British statesman made of the Pythons.

SEA
SON
1
EPISODE 12

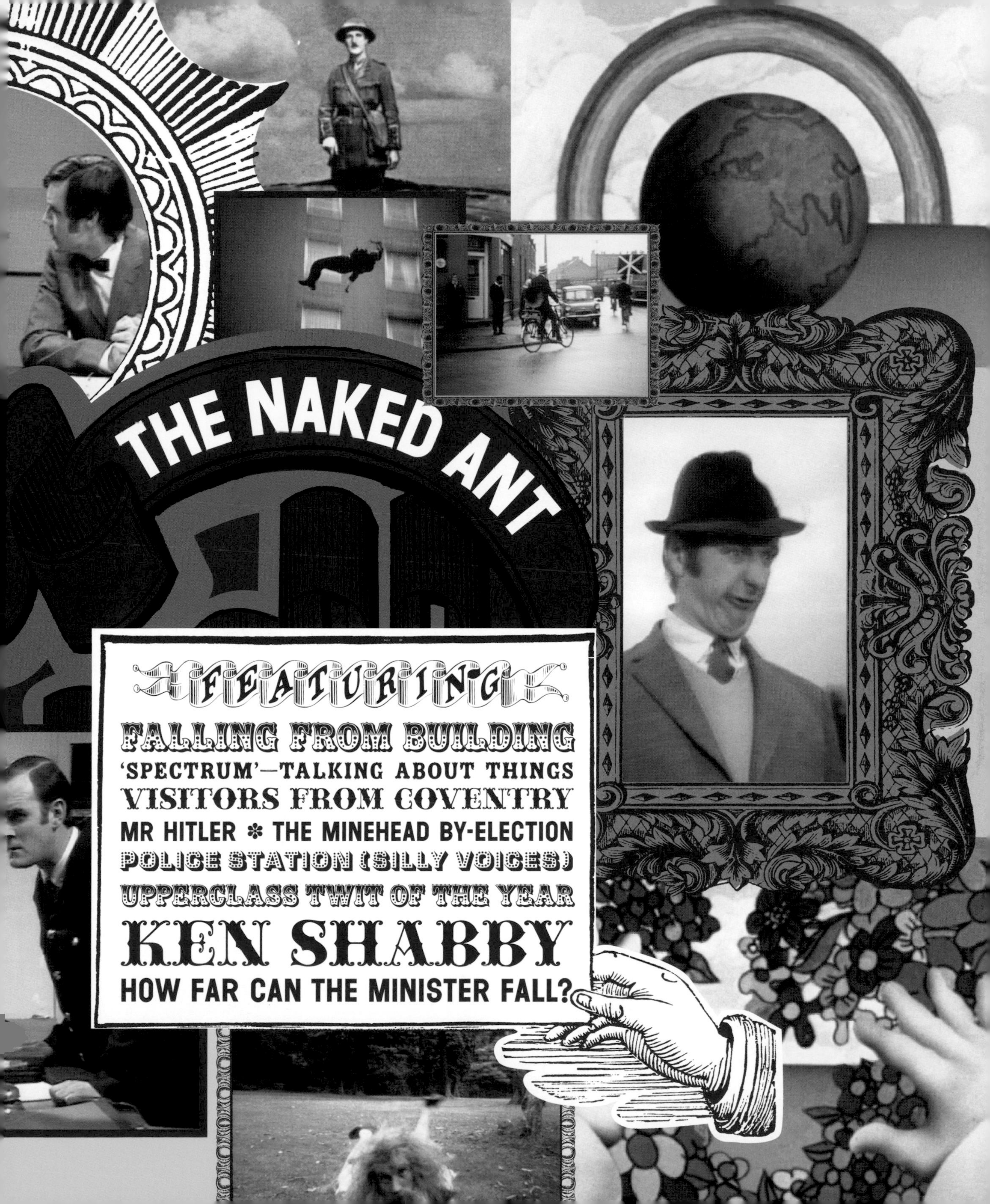
THE NAKED ANT
FEATURING
FALLING FROM BUILDING
'SPECTRUM'—TALKING ABOUT THINGS
VISITORS FROM COVENTRY
MR HITLER ✽ THE MINEHEAD BY-ELECTION
POLICE STATION (SILLY VOICES)
UPPERCLASS TWIT OF THE YEAR
KEN SHABBY
HOW FAR CAN THE MINISTER FALL?

FIRST AIRED: JANUARY 4, 1970

'It's' man.

Opening animation.

Caption: 'EPISODES 17-26' Caption: 'THE NAKED ANT' Caption: 'A SIGNALBOX SOMEWHERE NEAR HOVE' Studio:

VOICE OVER I know you're down there.

Interior of a signalbox. A signalman (TERRY J) *stands by the signal levers. He is attacked by a bear. He wrestles it for* ***3.48 seconds.*** **1** *Caption: 'BUT IN AN OFFICE OFF THE* ***GOSWELL ROAD'*** **2** *Two people seated opposite each other at a desk. Between them there is a large window. It appears that they are quite high up in a large office building. Every so often a body falls past the window. They are both working busily. After a pause a body drops past the window. First man talks. Second man hasn't noticed.*

FIRST MAN (ERIC) Hey, did you see that?
SECOND MAN (JOHN) Uhm?
FIRST MAN

DID YOU SEE SOMEBODY GO PAST THE WINDOW?

SECOND MAN What?
FIRST MAN Somebody just went past the window. **That way.** **3** (*indicates 'down'*)
SECOND MAN (*flatly*) Oh. Oh.

Second man returns to his work. First man looks for a little. As he starts to work again another body goes hurtling past the window.

FIRST MAN Another one.
SECOND MAN Huh?
FIRST MAN Another one just went past downwards.
SECOND MAN What?
FIRST MAN Two people have just fallen out of that window to their almost certain death.

1

He actually wrestles it for considerably longer than 3.48 seconds.

2

A main road in Finsbury, north of the Thames in London. Also known as the A1, and you can't get more of a main road than that.

A pleasing little gag, given that the bodies wouldn't go the other way.

SECOND MAN Fine, fine. Fine.
FIRST MAN Look! Two people (*another falls*) three people have just fallen past that window.
SECOND MAN Must be a board meeting.
FIRST MAN Oh yeah. (*another falls past*) Hey. That was Wilkins of finance.
SECOND MAN Oh, no, that was Robertson.
FIRST MAN Wilkins.
SECOND MAN Robertson.
FIRST MAN Wilkins.
SECOND MAN Robertson.

Another falls.

FIRST MAN *That* was Wilkins.
SECOND MAN That was Wilkins. He was a good, good, er, golfer, Wilkins.
FIRST MAN Very good golfer. Very good golfer. Rotten at finance. It'll be Parkinson next.
SECOND MAN Bet you it won't.
FIRST MAN How much.
SECOND MAN What?
FIRST MAN How much do you bet it won't? Fiver?
SECOND MAN All right.
FIRST MAN Done.
SECOND MAN You're on.
FIRST MAN Fine. (*shakes; they look at the window*) Come on Parky.
SECOND MAN Don't do it Parky.
FIRST MAN
COME ON PARKY. JUMP PARKY. JUMP.
SECOND MAN Come on now be sensible Parky.

Cut to letter.

VOICE OVER (GRAHAM) Dear Sir, I am writing to complain about that sketch about people falling out of a high building. I have worked all my life in such a building and have never once.

Cut to film of man falling out of window.

Cut back to set. ***First man has hands in the air jubilantly.*** **4**

FIRST MAN Parkinson!
SECOND MAN Johnson!

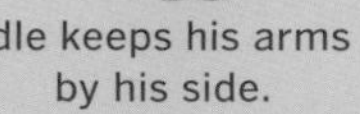

Idle keeps his arms by his side.

Animation (possibly incorporating falling) which leads ingeniously into: A presenter at a desk. Urgent, current-affairs-type music. Superimposed caption: 'SPECTRUM'

PRESENTER (MICHAEL) Good evening. Tonight 'Spectrum' looks at one of the major problems in the world today—that old vexed question of what is going on. Is there still time to confront it, let alone solve it, or is it too late? What are the figures, what are the facts, what do people mean when they talk about things? Alexander Hardacre of the Economic Affairs Bureau.

Cut to equally intense pundit in front of a graph with three different coloured columns with percentages at the top. He talks with great authority.

HARDACRE (GRAHAM) In this graph, this column represents 23% of the population. This column represents 28% of the population, and this column represents 43% of the population.

Cut back to presenter.

PRESENTER Telling figures indeed, but what do they mean to *you*, what do they mean to *me*, what do they mean to the average man in the street? With me now is Professor Tiddles of Leeds University...

Pull out to reveal ***bearded professor*** **5** *sitting next to presenter.*

PRESENTER ...Professor, you've spent many years researching into things, what do you think?

PROFESSOR (JOHN) I think it's too early to tell.

Cut to presenter, he talks even faster now.

PRESENTER 'Too early to tell'...too early to say...it means the same thing. The word 'say' is the same as the word 'tell'. They're not spelt the same, but they mean the same. It's an identical situation, we have with 'ship' and 'boat' (*holds up signs saying 'ship' and 'boat'*), but not the same as we have with 'bow' and 'bough' (*holds up signs*), they're spelt differently, mean different things but *sound* the same. (*he holds up signs saying 'so there'*) But the real question remains. What is the solution, if any, to this problem? What can we do? What am I saying? Why am I sitting in this chair? Why am I on this programme? And what am I going to say next? Here to answer this is a professional cricketer.

Cut to cricketer.

CRICKETER (ERIC) I can say nothing at this point.

Cut back to presenter.

PRESENTER Well, you were wrong...Professor?

Pull out to reveal professor still next to him.

PROFESSOR Hello.

"Bearded" doesn't do justice to the extraordinary rug Cleese is wearing: it nearly reaches his belly button.

Cut to close-up of presenter.

PRESENTER Hello. So...where do we stand? Where do we stand? Where do we sit? Where do we come? Where do we go? What do we do? What do we say? What do we eat? What do we drink? What do we think? What do we do?

Mix to stock film of London-Brighton train journey in two minutes. **6** *After a few seconds the train goes into a tunnel. Blackness. Loud crash. Cut to signalbox as before.*

SIGNALMAN (*calling out of window*) Sorry!

He goes back to wrestling with bear. Cut to a small, ***tatty,*** **7** *little boarding house. Superimposed caption: 'A SMALL BOARDING HOUSE IN* ***MINEHEAD,*** *SOMERSET'* **8** *Mr and Mrs Johnson, a typical holidaying bourgeois couple walk up to the front door and ring the bell. Inside the boarding house, the landlady goes up to the front door and opens it.*

LANDLADY (TERRY J) Hello? Mr and Mrs Johnson isn't it?
JOHNSON (ERIC) That's right, yes.
LANDLADY

WELL COME ON IN, EXCUSE ME NOT SHAKING HANDS, BUT I'VE JUST BEEN PUTTING A BIT OF LARD ON THE CAT'S BOIL.

JOHNSON (*entering*) **Very nice. 9**
LANDLADY Well you must be tired, it's a long drive from **Coventry** **10** isn't it?
JOHNSON Yes, well we usually reckon on five and a half hours, and it took us six hours and fifty-three minutes, with a twenty-five-minute wait at Frampton Cottrell to stretch our legs, only we had to wait half an hour to get on to the M5 near Droitwich. 11
LANDLADY Really?

An extremely clever use of film here, the sound of the train mimics the rhythm established by Palin at the end of his short speech.

"Tatty" is British slang for shabby.

Minehead is a coastal holiday town on the north coast of Somerset. The tradition of the bed-and-breakfast in sleepy little towns continues to this day, and the enforced camaraderie is nicely satirized with the introduction of "Mr. Hilter."

This is a subtle jab at the British convention of mildness and agreement at everything, even something as appalling as lard on a cat's boil.

Coventry is a large town in the Midlands.

Idle does a painfully accurate Midlands accent here, with a lilting—and, frankly, ugly as hell—rise to the end of his sentences. (He went to school there.)

JOHNSON **Yes, then there was a three-mile queue just before Bridgwater on the A38, only normally we come round on the B3339 just before Bridgwater you see... 12**

LANDLADY Really?

JOHNSON Yes, but this time we decided to risk it because they're always saying they're going to widen it there.

LANDLADY Are they?

JOHNSON Yes well just there by the intersection, where the A372 joins up, there's plenty of room to widen it there, there's only **the grass verges. 13** They could get another six feet...knock down that hospital...**Then we took the coast road through Williton and got all the Taunton traffic on the A358 from Crowcombe and Stogumber... 14**

More evidence of the British obsession with how best to get to places. The descriptions that follow are accurate, with the odd exception (see note below about Crowcombe and Stogumber).

These are grassy areas by the side of major roads.

The joke here is that there wouldn't be much traffic from these two small West Country towns.

LANDLADY Well you must be dying for a cup of tea.

JOHNSON Well, wouldn't say no, not if it's warm and wet.

LANDLADY Well come on in the lounge, I'm just about to serve afternoon tea.

JOHNSON (*following her into the lounge*) Very nice.

In the lounge are sitting another bourgeois couple Mr and Mrs Phillips.

LANDLADY Come on in Mr and Mrs Johnson, oh this is Mr and Mrs Phillips.

PHILLIPS (TERRY G) Good afternoon.

JOHNSON Thank you.

LANDLADY It's their third year with us, we can't keep you away can we? Ha, ha, and over here is Mr Hilter.

Landlady leads Mr and Mrs Johnson over to a table at which Adolf Hitler is sitting poring over a map. He is in full Nazi uniform. Himmler and Von Ribbentrop are also sitting at the table with him, Himmler in Nazi uniform and Von Ribbentrop in evening dress, with an Iron Cross.

HITLER (JOHN) Ah good time...good afternoon.

LANDLADY

OOH PLANNING A LITTLE EXCURSION ARE WE MR HILTER?

HITLER Ja! Ja! We make a little...(*to others*) Was ist rückweise bewegen?

VON RIBBENTROP (GRAHAM) Hike.

HIMMLER (MICHAEL) Hiking.

HITLER We make a little hike for, for Bideford.

JOHNSON (*leaning over map*) Oh well you'll be wanting the A39 then...no, no, you've got the wrong map there, this is Stalingrad, you want the Ilfracombe and Barnstaple section.

HITLER Ah Hein...Reginald you have the wrong map here you silly old **leg-before-wicket 15** English person.

"Leg before wicket," or LBW, is one of the ways a batsman can be dismissed in cricket. If the ball hits a player's body padding, and would have hit the wickets had he not put his leg in the way, the player is out. See?

HIMMLER I'm sorry mein Führer. I did not...(*Hitler slaps him*) Mein Dickie old chum.

LANDLADY Lucky Mr Johnson pointed that out, eh? You wouldn't have had much fun in Stalingrad would you...(*they don't see the joke*) I said you wouldn't have had much fun in Stalingrad would you, ha, ha, ha.

HITLER (*through clenched teeth*) Not much fun in Stalingrad, no.

LANDLADY Oh I'm sorry I didn't introduce you this is Ron...Ron Vibbentrop.

JOHNSON Oh not Von Ribbentrop, eh? Ha, ha, ha.

VON RIBBENTROP (GRAHAM) (*leaping two feet in fear, then realizing*) Nein! Nein! Nein!! Oh!! Ha, ha, ha. No different other chap. No I in Somerset am being born Von Ribbentrop is born in Gotterammerstrasse 46, Düsseldorf, West Eight. So they say!

LANDLADY And this is the quiet one, Mr Bimmler.

JOHNSON Hi Mr Bimmler.

HIMMLER How do you do there squire, also I am not Minehead lad but I in Peterborough, Lincolnshire house was given birth to, but stay in Peterborough Lincolnshire house all during war, owing to nasty running sores and was unable to go in the streets play football or go to Nürnberg. I am retired window cleaner and pacifist without doing war crimes, (*hurriedly corrects himself*) tch tch tch, **and am very glad England win World Cup** **16** **—Bobby Charlton, Martin Peters** **17** —and eating lots of chips and fisch and hole in the toads, **and Dundee cakes** **18** on Piccadilly line. Don't you know old chap I was head of Gestapo for ten years. Five years! No, no, nein, I was not head of Gestapo at all...I make joke.

LANDLADY Oooh Mr Bimmler, you do have us on. (*a telephone rings*) Oh excuse me I must just go and answer that. (*leaves the room*)

JOHNSON Er, how long are you down here for Mr Hilter? Just the fortnight?

HITLER (*shouting*) Why do you ask that? You a spy or something? (*drawing revolver*) Get over there against the wall Britischer pig, you're going to die.

Von Ribbentrop and Himmler grab Hitler and calm him.

HIMMLER Take it easy Dickie old chum.

VON RIBBENTROP I'm sorry Mr Johnson, he's a bit on edge. He hasn't slept since 1945.

HITLER Shut your cake hole you Nazi.

HIMMLER Cool it Führer cat.

VON RIBBENTROP Ha, ha, ha. (*laughing it off*) The fun we have.

JOHNSON Haven't I seen him on the television?

VON R. & HIMMLER Nicht. Nein. Nein, oh no.

JOHNSON Television Doctor?

VON RIBBENTROP No!!! No!

The landlady enters.

LANDLADY Telephone Mr Hilter, it's that nice Mr McGoering from the Bell and Compasses. He says he's found a place where you can hire bombers by the hour.

HITLER If he opens his big mouth again...**it's lampshade time!** **19**

VON RIBBENTROP (*controlling Hitler and getting him towards the door*) Shut up. (*Hitler exits*) Hire bombers by the hour, ha ha, what a laugh he is, that Scottish person! Good old Norman. (*he exits*)

LANDLADY He's on the phone the whole time nowadays.

JOHNSON In business is he?

HIMMLER Soon baby.

LANDLADY Course it's his big day Thursday. Oh, they've been planning it for months.

JOHNSON What happens then?

LANDLADY Oh it's the North Minehead by-election. Mr Hilter's standing as a National Bocialist candidate. He's got wonderful plans for Minehead.

JOHNSON Like what?

LANDLADY Well for a start he wants to annex Poland.

The joke being that he would have been deeply unhappy that England beat Germany in the final of the 1966 FIFA World Cup.

Two British soccer stars—both played in the World Cup final next to each other in midfield.

A Scottish cake traditionally featuring dried fruit and topped with a circle of almonds. It tastes as bad as it sounds.

An unfunny reference to the apocryphal story that Nazis made lampshades from human skin during the Holocaust.

The camera here cuts to Palin, who evilly smiles.

Once again, folks on the street watch this extraordinary procession—and it's hard to imagine what they thought as three Nazis cycled by.

JOHNSON Oh, North Minehead's Conservative isn't it?
LANDLADY Well, they get a lot of people at their rallies.
JOHNSON Rallies?
LANDLADY Well, their Bocialist meetings, down at the Axis Café in Rosedale Road. 20

Cut to a grotty Italian café. Sign above it reads 'Axis Café, Italian Food a Speciality'. A figure clearly belonging to Mussolini is nailing up a sign or poster which reads: 'Vote for Hitler'. He looks around and goes into the café furtively. ***At this moment past the café come Hitler, Von Ribbentrop and Himmler on bikes.*** **21** *Hitler at the front shouting German through a megaphone. Von Ribbentrop at the back with a large banner 'Hilter for a better Meinhead'. Himmler in the middle with an old gramophone playing 'Deutschland Uber Alles'. Cut to Hitler ranting in German on a balcony with Himmler at his side. Beneath them is a Nazi flag.*

HITLER I am not a racialist, but, und this is a big but, we in the National Bocialist Party believe das Überleben muss gestammen sein mit der schneaky Armstong-Jones. Historische Taunton ist Volkermeinig von Meinhead.
HIMMLER (*stepping forward*) Mr Hitler, *Hilter*, he says that historically Taunton is part of Minehead already.

Shot of a yokel looking disbelievingly at balcony. Von Ribbentrop appears behind.

VON RIBBENTROP He's right, do you know that?

Meanwhile back on the balcony.

HITLER (*very excited*) Und Bridgwater ist die letzte Fühlung das wir haben in Somerset!

Over this we hear loud applause and 'Sieg Heils'. The yokel, who is not applauding, turns round rather surprised to see whence cometh the applause. He sees Von Ribbentrop operating a gramophone. Cut to vox pops.

INTERVIEWER (JOHN) (*voice over*) What do you think of Mr Hilter's policies?
YOKEL (GRAHAM) I don't like the sound of these 'ere boncentration bamps.
PEPPERPOT (ERIC) Well I gave him my baby to kiss and he bit it on the head.
STOCKBROKER (JOHN) Well I think he'd do a lot of good for the Stock Exchange.
PEPPERPOT (MICHAEL) No...no...
HIMMLER (*thinly disguised as yokel*) Oh yes Britischer pals he is wunderbar...ful. So.
PEPPERPOT (TERRY J) I think he's right about the coons, but then I'm a bit mental.
GUMBY (TERRY J) I think he's got beautiful legs.
MADD (GRAHAM) Well speaking as Conservative candidate I just drone on and on and on...never letting anyone else get a word in edgeways until I start foaming at the mouth and falling over backwards. (*he foams at the mouth and falls over backwards*)

Cut to 'Spectrum' studio: same presenter as before, sitting at desk.

PRESENTER (MICHAEL) Foam at the mouth and fall over backwards. Is he foaming at the mouth to fall over backwards or falling over backwards to foam at the mouth. Tonight 'Spectrum' examines the whole question of frothing and falling, coughing and calling, screaming and bawling, walling and stalling, galling and mauling, palling and hauling, trawling and squalling and zalling? Zalling? Is there a word zalling? If there is what does it mean...if there isn't what does it mean? Perhaps both. Maybe neither. What do I mean by the word mean? What do I mean by the word word, what do I mean by what do I mean, what do I mean by do, and what do I do by mean? What do I do by do by do and what do I mean by wasting your time like this? Goodnight.

Cut to police station.

SERGEANT (JOHN) (*behind station counter into camera*) Goodnight.

Camera pulls back to show a man standing in front of the counter.

MAN (TERRY J)

GOOD EVENING, I WISH TO REPORT A BURGLARY.

SERGEANT Speak up please, sir.
MAN I wish to report a burglary.
SERGEANT I can't hear you, sir.
MAN (*bellowing*) I wish to report a burglary!!

SERGEANT That's a little bit too loud. Can you say it just a little less loud than that?
MAN (*a little louder than normal*) I wish to report a burglary.
SERGEANT No...I'm still not getting anything...Er, could you try it in a higher register?
MAN What do you mean in a higher register?
SERGEANT What?
MAN (*in a high-pitched voice*) I wish to report a burglary.
SERGEANT Ah! That's it, hang on a moment. (*gets out pencil and paper*) Now a little bit louder.
MAN (*louder and more high pitched*) I wish to report a burglary.
SERGEANT Report a what?
MAN (*by now a ridiculous high-pitched squeak*) Burglary!
SERGEANT That's the exact frequency...now keep it there.

Another sergeant enters and goes round to back of counter.

SECOND SERGEANT (GRAHAM) (*in high-pitched voice*) Hello, sarge!
SERGEANT (*in very deep voice*) Evening Charlie.

The second sergeant is taking his coat off, and the first one begins to pack up his papers. The man carries on with his tale of woe, but still in a high-pitched shriek.

MAN I was sitting at home with a friend of mine from **Camber Sands,** 22 when we heard a noise in the bedroom. We went to investigate and found £5,000 stolen.
SERGEANT Well, I'm afraid I'm going off duty now sir. Er, could you tell Sergeant Foster.

Camber Sands is a beach by the town of Camber in East Sussex, on the southeast coast of England.

He leaves counter. Sergeant Foster comes forward with a helpful smile.

MAN (*continues in high-pitched shriek*) I was sitting at home with a friend of mine.
SECOND SERGEANT Excuse me sir, but, er, why the funny voice?
MAN (*normal voice*) Oh, terribly sorry. I'd just got used to talking like that to the other sergeant.
SECOND SERGEANT I'm terribly sorry...I can't hear you, sir, could you try speaking in a lower register?
MAN What! Oh (*in a very deep voice*) I wish to report the loss of £5,000.
SECOND SERGEANT £5,000? That's serious, you'd better speak to the detective inspector.

At that moment, via the miracle of cueing, the detective inspector comes out of his office.

INSPECTOR (ERIC) (*in very slow deep voice*) What's the trouble, sergeant?
SECOND SERGEANT (*speaking at fantastic speed*) Well-this-gentleman-sir-has-just-come-in-to-report-that-he-was-sitting-at-home-with-a-friend-when-he-heard-a-noise-in-the-back-room-went-round-to-investigate-and-found-that-£5,000-in-savings-had-been-stolen.
INSPECTOR (*deep voice*) I see. (*turns to man and addresses him in normal voice*) Where do you live sir?
MAN (*normal voice*) **121, Halliwell Road, Dulwich, SE21.** **23**

23 A fake address, though Dulwich is indeed in southeast London.

The detective inspector has been straining to hear but has failed. The second sergeant comes in helpfully.

SECOND SERGEANT (*fast*) 121-Halliwell-Road-Dulwich-SE21.
INSPECTOR (*squeak*) Another Halliwell Road job eh, sergeant?
FIRST SERGEANT (*fast*) Yes-I-can't-believe-it-I-thought-the-bloke-who'd-done-that-was-put-inside-last-year.
SECOND SERGEANT (*squeak*) Yes, in **Parkhurst.** **24**

24 Pankhurst is a jail on the Isle of Wight, off the coast south of England. In 1969 it was considered one of the toughest prisons in the U.K., housing some of its most notorious prisoners.

FIRST SERGEANT (*deep*) Well it must have been somebody else.
INSPECTOR (*very deep*) Thank you, sergeant. (*normal voice to man*) We'll get things moving right away, sir. (*he picks up phone and dials, at the same time he shrieks in high voice to the first sergeant*) You take over here, sergeant (*very deep voice to the second sergeant*) Alert all squad cars in the area. (*ridiculous sing-song voice into phone*) Ha-allo Dar-ling, I'm afra-ID I sh-A-ll BE L-ate H-O-me this evening.

Meanwhile the second sergeant has a radio-controlled microphone and is singing down it in fine operatic tenor.

SECOND SERGEANT (*singing*) Calling all squad cars in the area...

Cut to vox pops.

LOVELY GIRL (*in deep male voice, dubbed on*) I think that's in very bad taste.
PIG (*miaows*)
GIRAFFE (*barks*)
PRESIDENT NIXON (*superimposed sheep bleating*)
UPPERCLASS TWIT (JOHN) Some people do talk in the most extraordinary way.

Cut to ***Upperclass Twit of the Year sketch.*** **25** *The five competitors run onto the pitch.*

25 "Upper-class twit" is used to describe a member of the highest levels of British society who displays little to no intelligence. Note the names, which all signify an upper-class background.

COMMENTATOR (JOHN) Good afternoon and welcome to Hurlingham Park. You join us just as the competitors are running out onto the field on this lovely winter's afternoon here, with the going firm underfoot and very little sign of rain. Well it certainly looks as though we're in for a splendid afternoon's sport in this

THE 127TH UPPER CLASS TWIT O THE YEAR SHOW. 26

Well the competitors will be off in a moment so let me just identify them for you. (*close-up of the competitors*)

Vivian Smith-Smythe-Smith has an **O-level in chemo-hygiene.** 27

Simon-Zinc-Trumpet-Harris, married to a very attractive table lamp.

Nigel Incubator-Jones, his best friend is a tree, and in his spare time he's a stockbroker.

Gervaise Brook-Hampster is in the Guards, and his father uses him as a wastepaper basket.

And finally Oliver St John-Mollusc, **Harrow** 28 and **the Guards**, 29 thought by many to be this year's outstanding twit. Now they're moving up to the starting line, there's a jolly good crowd here today. Now they're under starter's orders...and they're off (*starter fires gun; nobody moves*) Ah no, they're not. No they didn't realize they were supposed to start.

Ian McNaughton, the director of most of the Python shows, was, like Chapman, also a victim of the lures of alcohol. Idle recounts that the day of the filming of the Twit of the Year sketch, after a presumably replete lunch, McNaughton failed to materialize in the afternoon, leading the Pythons to run the shoot themselves.

"O-levels" are the exams one takes in the U.K. at age 16. A smart person would pass nine or ten, so a single O-level is a mark of limited educational achievement.

The eminent Harrow School for boys is in northwest London. A number of prime ministers have attended there, and it is thought of as a bastion of upper-class values, second only to Eton College.

Part of the British Army most attractive to the upper classes.

Never mind, we'll soon sort that out, the judge is explaining it to them now. I think Nigel and Gervaise have got the idea. All set to go. (*starter fires gun; the twits move off erratically*)

Oh, and they're off and it's a fast start this year. Oliver St John-Mollusc running a bit wide there and now they're coming into their first test, the straight line. (*the twits make their way erratically along five white lines*) They've got to walk along this straight line without falling over and Oliver's over at the back there, er, Simon's coming through quite fast on the outside, I think Simon and Nigel, both of them coming through very fast. There's Nigel there. No. Three, I'm sorry, and on the outside there's Gervaise coming through just out of shot and now, the position...(*the twits approach a line of matchboxes piled three high*) Simon and Vivian at the front coming to the matchbox jump...three layers of matchboxes to clear...and Simon's over and Vivian's over beautifully, oh and the jump of a lifetime—if only his father could understand. Here's Nigel...and now Gervaise is over he's, er, Nigel is over, and it's Gervaise, Gervaise is going to jump it, is it, no he's jumped the wrong way, there he goes, Nigel's over, beautifully. Now it's only Oliver. Oliver...and Gervaise...oh bad luck. And now it's Kicking the Beggar. (*the twits are kicking a beggar with a vending tray*)

Simon's there and he's putting the boot in, and not terribly hard, but he's going down and Simon can move on. Now Vivian's there. Vivian is there and waiting for a chance. Here he comes, oh a piledriver, a real piledriver, and now Simon's on No. 1, Vivian 2, Nigel 3, Gervaise on 4 and Oliver bringing up the rear. Ah there's Oliver (*Oliver is still trying to jump the matchboxes*), there's Oliver now, he's at the back. I think he's having a little trouble with his old brain injury, he's going to have a go, no, no, bad luck, he's up, he doesn't know when he's beaten, this boy, he doesn't know when he's winning either. He doesn't have any sort of sensory apparatus. Oh there's Gervaise (*still kicking the beggar*) and he's putting the boot in there and he's got the beggar down and the **steward's** **30** giving him a little bit of advice, yes, he can move on now, he can move on to the Hunt Photograph. He's off, Gervaise is there and Oliver's still at the back having trouble with the matchboxes. (*the twits approach a table with two attractive girls and a photographer*)

A steward is the rule keeper at a horsing event.

Now here's the Hunt Ball Photograph and the first here's Simon, he's going to enjoy a joke with Lady Arabella Plunkett. She hopes to go into films, and Vivian's through there and, er, Nigel's there enjoying a joke with Lady Sarah Pencil Farthing Vivian Streamroller

Adams Pie Biscuit Aftershave Gore Stringbottom Smith. (*shot of twit in a sports car reversing into cut-out of old woman*) And there's, there's Simon now in the sports car, he's reversed into the old woman, he's caught her absolutely beautifully. Now he's going to accelerate forward there to wake up the neighbour. There's Vivian I think, no Vivian's lost his keys, no there's Vivian, he's got the old woman, slowly but surely right in the midriff, and here he is. Here he is to wake up the neighbour now. (*a man in bed in the middle of the pitch; twit slams car door repeatedly*) Simon right in the lead, comfortably in the lead, but he can't get this neighbour woken up. He's slamming away there as best he can. He's getting absolutely no reaction at all. There, he's woken him up and Simon's through. Here comes Vivian, Vivian to slam the door, and there we are back at the Hunt Ball, I think that's Gervaise there, that's Gervaise going through there, and here, here comes Oliver, brave Oliver. Is he going to make it to the table, no I don't think he is, yes he is, (*Oliver falls over the table*) he did it, ohh. And the crowd are rising to him there, and there I can see, who is that there, yes that's Nigel, Nigel has woken the neighbour—my God this is exciting. Nigel's got very excited and he's going through and here comes Gervaise. Gervaise, oh no this is, er, out in the front there is Simon who is supposed to insult the waiter and he's forgotten. (*Simon runs past a waiter standing with a tray*) And Oliver has run himself over, (*Oliver lying in front of car*) what a great twit! And now here comes Vivian, Vivian to insult the waiter, and he is heaping abuse on him, and he is humiliating him, there and he's gone into the lead. Simon's not with him, no Vivian's in front of him at the bar. (*the twits each have several goes at getting under a bar of wood five feet off the ground*) Simon's got to get under this bar and this is extremely difficult as it requires absolutely expert co-ordination between mind and body. No Vivian isn't there. Here we go again and Simon's fallen backwards. Here's Nigel, he's tripped, Nigel has tripped, and he's under and Simon fails again, er, here is Gervaise, and Simon is through by accident. Here's Gervaise to be the last one over, there we are, here's Nigel right at the head of the field, (*the twits approach five rabbits staked out on the ground; they fire at them with shotguns*) and now he's going to shoot the rabbit, and these rabbits have been tied to the ground, and they're going to be a bit frisky, and this is only a one-day event. And they're blazing away there. They're not getting quite the results that they might, Gervaise is in there trying to bash it to death with the butt of his rifle, and I think Nigel's in there with his bare hands, but they're not getting the results that they might, but it is a little bit misty today and they must be shooting from a range of at least one foot. But they've had a couple of hits there I think, yes, they've had a couple of hits, and the whole field is up again and here they are. (*they approach a line of shop-window dummies each wearing only a bra*) They're coming up to **the debs**, **31** Gervaise first, Vivian second, Simon third. And now they've got to take the bras off from the front, this is really difficult, this is really the most, the most difficult part of the entire competition, and they're having a bit of trouble in there I think, they're really trying now and the crowd is getting excited, and I think some of the twits are getting rather excited too. (*the twits are wreaking havoc on the dummies*) Vivian is there, Vivian is coming through, Simon's in second place, and, no there's Oliver, he's not necessarily out of it. There goes Nigel, no he's lost something, and Gervaise running through to this final obstacle. (*they approach a table with five revolvers laid out on it* Now all they have to do here to win the title is to shoot themselves. Simon has a shot. Bad luck, he misses. Nigel misses. Now there's Gervaise, and Gervaise has shot himself—Gervaise is Upperclass Twit of the Year. There's Nigel, he's shot Simon by mistake, Simon is back up and there's Nigel, Nigel's shot himself. Nigel is third in this fine and most exciting Upperclass Twit of the Year Show I've ever seen. Nigel's clubbed himself into fourth place. (*three coffins on stand with medals*) And so the final result: The Upperclass Twit of the Year—Gervaise Brook-Hampster of Kensington and Weybridge; runner up—Vivian Smith-Smythe-Smith of Kensington; and third—Nigel Incubator-Jones of Henley. Well there'll certainly be some door slamming in the streets of **Kensington** **32** tonight.

Letter and voice over.

Short for debutantes: high-society girls.

Kensington is a traditionally well-to-do neighborhood of London.

1
3

VOICE OVER (TERRY J) Dear Sir, how splendid it is to see the flower of British manhood wiping itself out with such pluck and tenacity. Britain need have no fear with leaders of this calibre. If only a few of the so-called working classes would destroy themselves so sportingly. Yours etc., Brigadier Mainwaring Smith Smith Smith etc. Deceased etc. PS etc. Come on other ranks, show your stuff.

Animation:

SOLDIER Yes Sir, I'll do me best, sir! (*coughs*)
VOICE (*off*) No, not good enough.
SOLDIER (*coughs again, his leg falls off*)
VOICE No, still not good enough.
SOLDIER (*coughs again, he completely disintegrates*)
FIRST VOICE Yes, that's better.

A HAND PICKS UP THE ANIMATED BITS AND WE SEE TERRY J. STUFFING THEM INTO A PIPE. HE PUTS THE PIPE DOWN AND VARIOUS STRANGE BEASTIES CLIMB OUT OF IT.

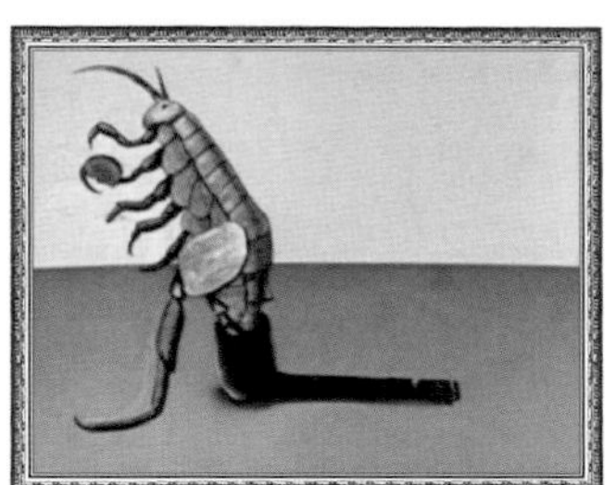

Cartoon link into still of beautiful country house. 'Hearts of Oak'-type music. The camera tracks into the house and mixes to: close-up of distinguished, noble father and gay, innocent beautiful daughter—a delicately beautiful English rose.

FATHER (GRAHAM) Now I understand that you want to marry my daughter?

Pull out to reveal that he is addressing a ghastly thing: a grubby, smelly, brown mackintoshed shambles, unshaven with a continuous hacking cough, and an obscene leer. He sits on the sofa in this beautiful elegant lounge.

SHABBY (MICHAEL) *(sniffing and coughing)* That's right...yeah...yeah...
FATHER Yes, you realize of course that Rosamund is still rather young?
ROSAMUND (CONNIE) Daddy you make me feel like a child. *(she gazes at Shabby fondly)*
SHABBY *(lasciviously)* Oh yeah...you know...get 'em when they're young eh...eh! OOOOH! Know what I mean eh, oooh! *(makes obscene gesture involving elbow)*
FATHER Well I'm sure you know what I mean, Mr...er...Mr...er...er?
SHABBY Shabby...Ken Shabby...

FATHER Mr Shabby I just want to make sure that you'll be able to look after my daughter
SHABBY Oh yeah, yeah. I'll be able to look after 'er all right sport, eh, know what I mean, eh emggh!
FATHER And, er, what job do you do?
SHABBY I clean out public lavatories.
FATHER Is there promotion involved?
SHABBY Oh yeah, yeah. *(produces handkerchief and clears throat horribly into it)* After five years they give me a brush...eurggha eurgh...I'm sorry squire, I've **gobbed** 33 on your carpet...
FATHER And, ah, where are you going to live?
SHABBY Well round at my gran's...she trains polecats, but most of them have suffocated so there should be a bit of spare room in the attic, eh. Know what I mean. Oooh!
FATHER And when do you expect to get married?
SHABBY Oh, right away sport. Right away...you know...I haven't had it for weeks...
FATHER Well look I'll phone the bishop and see if we can get the Abbey...
SHABBY **Oh, diarrhoea.** 34 *(coughing fit)*

Cut to strange PHOTO CAPTION SEQUENCE (to be worked out with Terry 'the sap' Gilliam) (if he can find the time).

VOICE OVER (JOHN) The story so far: Rosamund's father has become ensnared by Mr Shabby's extraordinary personal magnetism. **Bob and Janet have eaten Mr Farquar's goldfish during an Oxfam lunch,** 35 Oxfam International is a charity that works to end poverty around the world. and Mrs Elsmore's marriage is threatened by Doug's insistence that he is on a different level of consciousness. Louise's hernia has been confirmed, and Jim, Bob's brother, has run over the editor of **the 'Lancet'** 36 on his way to see Jenny, a freelance Pagoda designer. On the other side of the continent Napoleon still broods over the smouldering remains of a city he had crossed half the earth to conquer...

"Gobbed" is British slang for spitting.

It is hard to hear Palin say this, as he's amusingly doubled over.

Oxfam International is a charity that works to end poverty around the world.

The Lancet is a medical journal.

A "bedsit" is a one-room apartment, beloved of the just-left-home crowd.

She's actually wearing a sleek, black leather dress.

British TV is occasionally given over to these brief political speeches, especially during election time.

40

An erection gag, given that we've just seen an attractive woman walk across a room.

Mix from photo captions to studio. Caption: 'A CORNER OF A BED-SITTER' 37 ***A girl in bra and pants goes over to television and switches it on.*** 38

VOICE OVER ...whilst Mary, Roger's half-sister, settles down to watch television...

*On the screen comes the start of a **Party Political Broadcast.*** 39 *Caption: 'A PARTY POLITICAL BROADCAST ON BEHALF OF THE **WOOD PARTY**'* 40

VOICE OVER There now follows a Party Political Broadcast on behalf of the Wood Party.

Cut to a traditional grey-suited man at desk looking straight into camera. Superimposed caption: 'THE RT. HON. LAMBERT WARBECK'

MINISTER (GRAHAM) Good evening. We in the Wood Party feel very strongly that the present weak drafting of the Local Government Bill leaves a lot to be desired, and we intend to fight.

He thumps on the desk and he falls through the floor. (Yes Mr Director you did read that right: he fell through the floor and added a fortune to the budget). As he falls he emits a long scream, fading away slowly. Another man comes on and looks down into the pit.

MAN (ERIC) Hello! Helllllllllllooooooooooo! (to camera) Er I, I'm afraid the minister's fallen through the Earth's crust. Er excuse me a moment. (goes and looks at pit) Helloooo.
MINISTER (*unseen, a long way down*) Hellooooooo.
MAN Are you all right minister?
MINISTER I appear to have landed on this kind of ledge thing.
MAN Shall we lower down one of the BBC ropes?
MINISTER If you'd be so kind.
MAN What length of BBC rope will we be likely to need?
MINISTER I should use the longest BBC rope. That would be a good idea I would imagine.
MAN Okey doke chief. Er, Tex get the longest BBC rope, and bring it here pronto.
MINISTER (*still a long way down*) In the meantime, since I am on all channels, perhaps I'd better carry on with this broadcast by shouting about our housing plans from down here as best I can. Could someone throw me down a script. (*man drops the script down and Tex appears with enormous coil of rope*) The script would appear to have landed on a different ledge somewhat out of my grasp, don't you know.

MAN Er, well perhaps when the rope reaches you minister you could kind of swing over to the ledge and grab it.
MINISTER Good idea.

Cut to minister swinging on rope. Caption: 'THE RT. HON. LAMBERT WARBECK'

MINISTER Well I'm going to carry on, if I can read the script.

He swings over to a ledge opposite with a script on it. As he gets near he peers and starts reading.

MINISTER Good evening. We in the Wood Party (*he swings away and then back*) feel very strongly about (*swings away and back*) the present weak drafting of the Local Government Bill and no, no—it's no good, it's not working...I think I'll have to try and make a grab for it. Ah. There we are. (*he swings over and grabs the script with one hand; he tries to turn to camera and continues*) Good evening. We in the Wood Party feel very strongly about the present (*he makes a vigorous gesture and in so doing lets go of rope and slips so that he is now hanging upside down*) agh, agh. Oh dear. Hello!

MAN (*out of vision*) Hello.

MINISTER Look, look, I must look a bit of a chump hanging upside down like this.

MAN (*out of vision*) Don't worry minister. (*cut to man looking off-camera*) I think love if we turn the picture upside down we should help the minister, then.

Cut to minister. The picture is now the other way up. The minister now appears to be the right way up. Superimposed name caption (upside down)

MINISTER Oh good. Look, er, I'm sorry about this, but there seem to be a few gremlins about...I think I'd better start from the beginning. Er, good evening, we in the Wood Party feel very strongly about, oh...(*he drops script*) Bloody heck. Oh, oh dear, er terribly sorry about this, about saying bloody heck on all channels, but, er...

MAN (*out of vision*) There's another script on the way down minister.

MINISTER Oh good, good. Well...er...er...um...Good evening. Er...well...er...how are you? Er...Oh yes look, I don't want you to think of the Wood Party as a load of old men that like hanging around on ropes only I...er...oh...oh.

Meanwhile a man, the right way up, has been lowered down to the minister. As the picture is reversed, he appears to be moving straight up towards him. The minister sees him.

MINISTER Ah. Thank you. (*taking script; the man on the rope starts to climb back up*) Good evening, we in the Wood Party feel very strongly about the present weak drafting...(*man falls past with a scream*) Look. I think we'd better call it a day.

Cut to two men at a desk in a discussion set.

FIRST ROBERT (TERRY J) Is this the furthest distance that a minister has fallen? Robert.

Cut to Robert.

SECOND ROBERT (ERIC) Well surprisingly not. The Canadian Minister for External Affairs fell nearly seven miles during a Liberal Conference in Ottawa about six years ago, and then quite recently the Kenyan Minister for Agric. and Fish fell nearly twelve miles during a Nairobi debate in Parliament, although this hasn't been ratified yet.

FIRST ROBERT Er, how far did the Filipino cabinet fall last March?

SECOND ROBERT Er, well they fell nearly thirty-nine miles but it's not really so remarkable as that was due to their combined weight, of course. Robert.

FIRST ROBERT Thank you, Robert. Well now what's your reaction to all this, Robert?

Cut to third Robert who is staring intently into camera. ***He is wearing a fright wig and has a left eyebrow four inches above his right one.*** **41**

Cleese here does a funny impression of Peter Snow, a political journalist still known for his excitable statistical presentations during elections.

THIRD ROBERT (JOHN) Well, well Robert the main thing is that it's terribly exciting. You see the minister is quite clearly lodged between rocks we know terribly little of. Terribly little. Of course the main thing is we're getting colour pictures of an extraordinarily high quality. The important thing is, the really exciting thing is the minister will (*as he gets more excited he starts to emit smoke*) be bringing back samples of the Earth's core which will give us a tremendous, really tremendous tremendous tremendous clue about the origins of the Earth and what God himself is made of. (*he bursts into fire and someone has to throw a bucket of water over him*) Oh, oh I needed that.

Cut back to first Robert.

FIRST ROBERT Thank you, Robert. Well that seems to be about all we have time for tonight. Unless anyone has anything else to say. Has anyone anything else to say?

Various 'noes' plus one 'bloody fairy' and more noes, from a very rapid montage of all the possible characters in this week's show saying 'no'. The last one we come to is the Spectrum presenter. He says more than no.

PRESENTER (MICHAEL) What do we mean by no, what do we mean by yes, what do we mean by no, no, no. Tonight Spectrum looks at the whole question of what is no.

The sixteen-ton weight falls on him. Cut to the 'It's' man running away.

Credits

SEA
SON
1
EPISODE 13

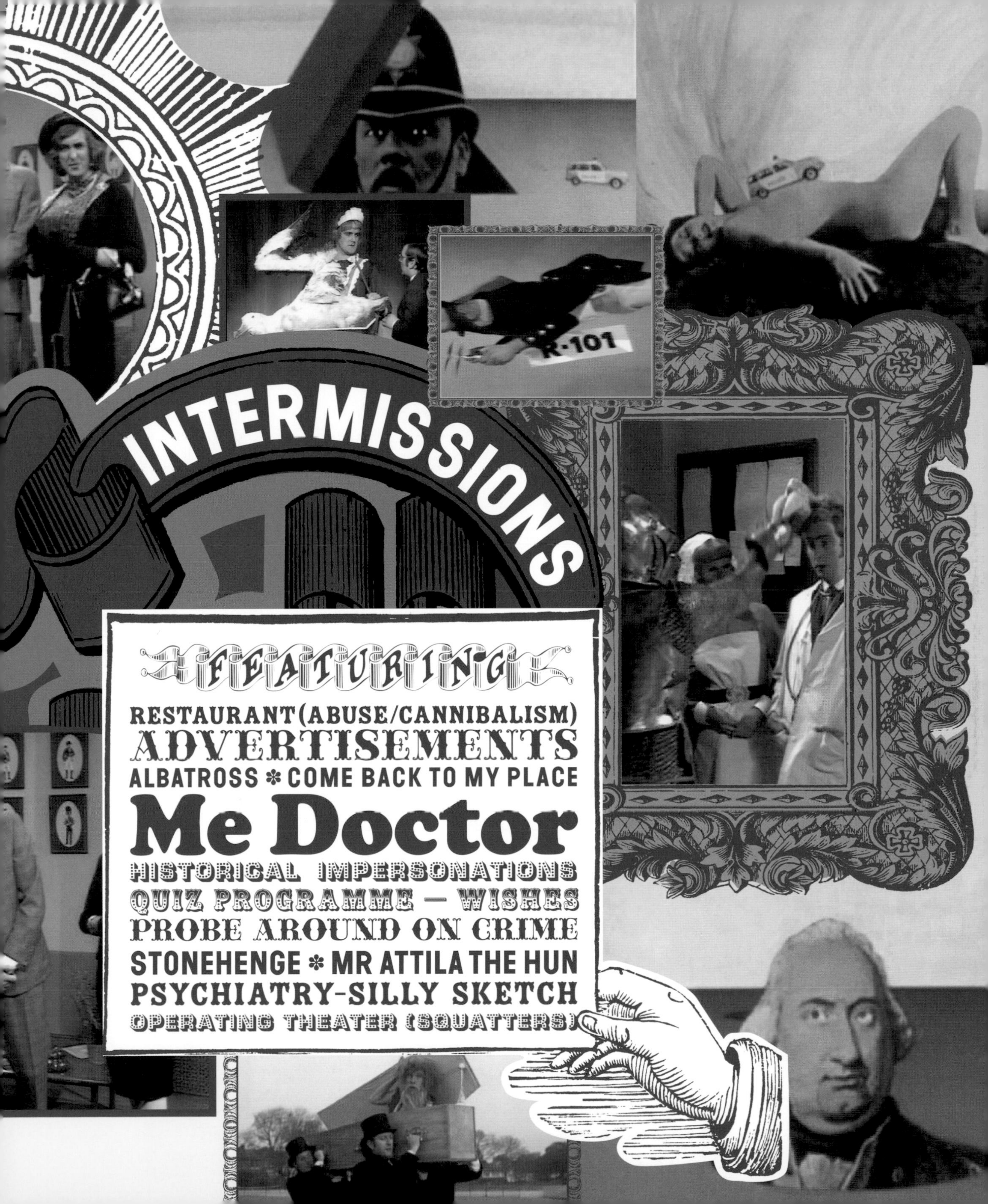
R-101
INTERMISSIONS
FEATURING
RESTAURANT (ABUSE/CANNIBALISM)
ADVERTISEMENTS
ALBATROSS * COME BACK TO MY PLACE
Me Doctor
HISTORICAL IMPERSONATIONS
QUIZ PROGRAMME — WISHES
PROBE AROUND ON CRIME
STONEHENGE * MR ATTILA THE HUN
PSYCHIATRY–SILLY SKETCH
OPERATING THEATER (SQUATTERS)

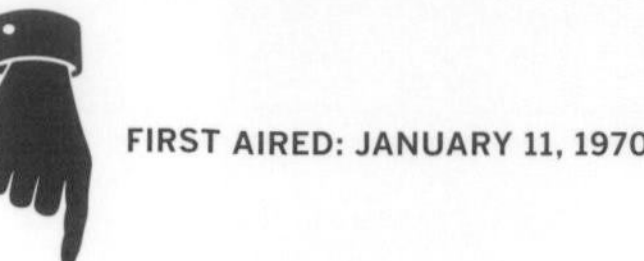

FIRST AIRED: JANUARY 11, 1970

Four undertakers carrying a coffin. The lid opens and the 'It's' man looks out.

IT'S MAN (MICHAEL)

IT'S...

Cut to large animated sign saying: 'Intermission'.

VOICE OVER (TERRY J) There will now be a short intermission.

After this seven seconds of (slightly) speeded up Mantovani. Two animated cars race in and crash. Cut to animated opening credits. Cut to the same sign saying: 'Intermission'

VOICE OVER There will now be a medium-sized intermission.

Same music, same speed, slightly longer.

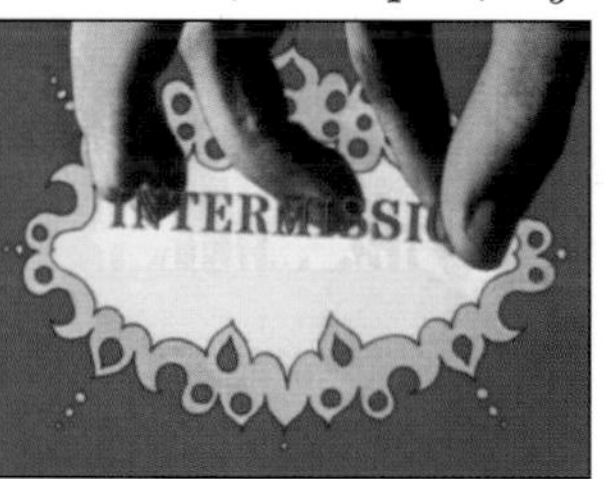

Short animation, then cut to restaurant vestibule. He and she are already there, entering. She is nattering. The waiter is waiting.

SHE (ERIC) Oo I don't like this. Ooh I don't like that. Oh I don't think much to all this. Oh fancy using that wallpaper. Fancy using mustard. Oo is that a proper one? Oo it's not real. Oh I don't think it's a proper restaurant unless they give you finger bowls. Oo I don't like him. I'm going to have a baby in a few years.

HE (JOHN) Er, please excuse my wife. She may appear to be rather nasty but underneath she has a heart of formica. (*the waiter grimaces*) I'm sorry about that.

WAITER (TERRY J) That's all right sir, we get all sorts of lines in here. The head waiter will be along to abuse you in a few moments, and now if you'll excuse me I have to go and commit suicide.

HE Oh I'm sorry.

WAITER It's all right. It's not because of anything serious.

He exits. Shot off-screen and scream.

SHE Quite frankly I'm against people who commit suicide, I don't like that sort of person at all. I'm plain people and I'm proud of it, my mother's the salt of the earth, **and I don't take the pill** **1** 'cos it's nasty.

The head waiter comes in.

HE Please excuse my wife, she may not be very beautiful, and she may have no money, and she may be a little talentless, boring and dull, but on the other hand...(*long pause*)...sorry I can't think of anything.

HEAD WAITER (MICHAEL) Fine. I'm the head waiter. This is a vegetarian restaurant only, we serve no animal flesh of any kind. We're not only proud of that, we're smug about it. So if you were to come in here asking me to rip open a small defenceless chicken, so you could chew its skin and eat its intestines, then I'm afraid I'd have to ask you to leave.

HE No, no, no, no.

HEAD WAITER Likewise if you were to ask us to slice the sides of a cow and serve it with small pieces of its liver...(*small tic developing, getting carried away*) or indeed drain the life blood from a pig before cutting off one of its legs...or carve the living giblets from a sheep and serve them with the fresh brains, bowels, guts and spleen of a small rabbit...WE WOULDN'T DO IT. (*reaction*) Not for food anyway.

SHE Quite frankly I'm against people who give vent to their loquacity by extraneous bombastic circumlocution. (*they both look at her; pause*) Oh I don't like that.

HE Sometimes Shirley I think you're almost human.

HEAD WAITER (*thinking*) Do you know I *still* wet my bed.

HE

ONCE I MARRIED SOMEONE WHO WAS BEAUTIFUL, AND YOUNG, AND GAY, AND FREE. WHATEVER HAPPENED TO HER?

SHE You divorced her and married me. **2**

HEAD WAITER I met my second wife at a second-wife-swapping party. Trust *me* to arrive late.

Enter headmaster.

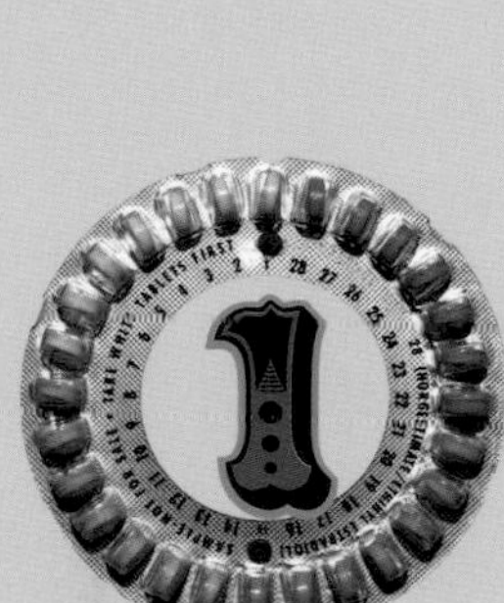

The contraceptive pill would have been a new and controversial addition to British culture in 1970.

There is a burst of canned applause here, "punishing" the punch line.

Well-to-do schools were often separated into "houses," or groups of children who would then be in competition with one another. The "Second Cuppa" is a play on cup, as in trophy.

"Form" is the U.K. equivalent of a school grade.

HEADMASTER (GRAHAM) Always were late weren't you Thompson?

HEAD WAITER Hello Headmaster. What are you doing here?

HEADMASTER Fine, fine, fine, thank you. Fine, thank you. No more sherry for me don't you know. **Warner House beat Badger House for the Second Cuppa**, remarkable. **3** We had to put most of the **second form** **4** to sleep. No padre. Bad business. They were beginning to play with themselves. Still...You haven't seen my wife anywhere have you?

HEAD WAITER No.

HEADMASTER Oh thank God for that. (*exits*)

SHE Oh I don't like him. Do you know what I mean. *Do* you know what I mean. I mean do you know what I mean. Do you know what I mean. Do you know what I mean. I mean do you know what I mean. All men are the same.

Enter prologue, long white Greek robes, long white beard, holding a large staff.

PROLOGUE Imagine not that these four walls contain the Mighty Owl of Thebes. For, gentles all, beauty sits most closely to them it can construe...

HEAD WAITER No it doesn't.

PROLOGUE Sorry. (*he exits*)

HEAD WAITER Fine. Would you care for a glass of blood? Oh what a giveaway.

SHE No, we'd like to see the menu please. I don't think it's a proper restaurant unless you have a proper menu, and anyway I might be pregnant.

HE Perhaps you'd care for a drink?

SHE Ever since you've married me, Douglas, you've treated me like an albatross.

A waiter enters pushing a large serving dish with a semi-naked Hopkins sitting unconcernedly in it.

HOPKINS (TERRY J) Evening.

HE Good evening.

HOPKINS I hope you're going to enjoy me this evening. I'm the special. Try me with some rice.

HE I beg your pardon?

HOPKINS A Hopkins au gratin à la chef.

HE Ah, oh how do you...(*makes to shake hands*)

HOPKINS (*skittishly*) Don't play with your food.

SHE (*examining him*) I don't like that. There's *dust* on here. I don't think it's a proper meal without a pudding. *My* husband's an architect.

HOPKINS Oh, one word of warning, sir, a little tip. (*lowering voice*) Don't have any of the vicar over there. (*cut to vicar sitting thin and unhappy in a pot*) **He's been here two weeks and nobody's touched him. 'Nuff said?** 5

HE Yes thank you.

HOPKINS Well I must get on or I'll spoil. Janet—to the kitchen.

WAITER There's a dead bishop in the lobby, sir.

HEAD WAITER I don't know who keeps bringing them in here.

SHE Oh I don't like that. I think it's silly. It's not a proper sketch without a proper punchline. I mean I don't know much about anything, I'm stupid. **I'm muggins.** 6 Nobody cares what I think. I'm always the one that has to do everything. Nobody cares about me. Well I'm going to have a lot of bloody babies and *they* can bloody well care about me. Makes you sick half this television. They never stop talking, *he'll* be the ruination of her, ***rhythm method!*** 7

Cut to animated sign saying 'Intermission'.

VOICE OVER (TERRY J) There will now be a whopping great intermission, during which small ice creams in very large boxes will be sold. Another way we can drive people away from the cinema is by **showing you advertisements.** 8

*Intermission changes to adverts. Animated title: '**Pearls For Swine Presents**'.* 9 *Shots of various cars with young ladies posing on them.*

VOICE OVER (ERIC) Do you like this? Or how about this? Or perhaps you prefer this latest model? Then why not come to us. We supply only the very best models. (*a card saying 'Soho Motors 2nd floor on a board with advertisement cards for 'Rita' etc.,. cut to a restaurant*) 10 After the show why not visit the La Gondola Restaurant. Just two minutes from this performance. The manager Mr Luigi Vercotti will be pleased to welcome you and introduce you to a wide variety of famous Sicilian delicacies. (*as Vercotti poses for the camera policemen bundle his staff and several half-dressed girls through and out of the restaurant*) 11 Here you can relax in comfort in friendly surroundings. Or if you wish, you may drink and dance till midnight. At the La Gondola Restaurant you can sample all the spicy pleasures of the Mediterranean. The head waiter will be pleased to show you his specialitics. Or why not ask the cook for something really hot? (*the police remove a chef carrying an 8mm projector and film*) Yes, for an evening you will never forget—it's the La Gondola Restaurant, Chelsea, Parkhurst, Dartmoor and the Scrubs. (*the police remove Mr Vercotti*)

The vicar looks like he's been placed there by "natives" in dangerously wild places.

In the U.K., "muggins" is used to refer to oneself as the butt of a joke, or someone taken for a fool.

The rhythm method is an alternative to the contraceptive pill, and beloved of Roman Catholics among others.

A nice set of fake movie-theater ads now follow. Such advertisements were often for local restaurants and the like, and were avowedly cheap.

"Pearls for swine presents" is an allusion to the Sermon on the Mount, Matthew 7:6.

The laugh on the soundtrack that "Soho" engenders here comes from the fact that London's Soho was, and still is somewhat, home to the sex industry.

Luigi Vercotti also appeared in Episode 10.

'Pearls for Swine' closing title. Cut to corner of cinema. A man in an ice-cream girl's uniform is standing in a spotlight with an ice-cream tray with an albatross on it.

MAN (JOHN) Albatross! Albatross! Albatross!

ALBATROSS! ALBATROSS! ALBATROSS!

A person approaches him.

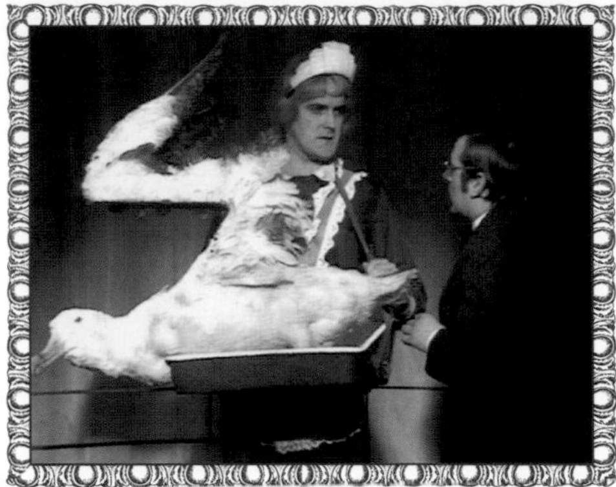

PERSON (TERRY J) Two choc-ices please. **12**
MAN I haven't got choc-ices. I only got the albatross. Albatross!
PERSON What flavour is it?
MAN It's a bird, innit. It's a bloody sea bird it's not any bloody flavour. Albatross!
PERSON Do you get wafers with it?
MAN 'Course you don't get bloody wafers with it. Albatross!
PERSON How much is it?
MAN Ninepence.
PERSON I'll have two please.
MAN Gannet on a stick. **13**

12

Traditional food fare at a British cinema: chocolate-covered ice cream.

13

The Northern Gannet is another seabird, though significantly smaller than an albatross.

The camera zooms past back onto the screen. On screen appears another 'Intermission' sign.

VOICE OVER There will now be a very short...

The intermission sign explodes.

Animated captions: 'NOW SHOWING AT OTHER DANK CINEMAS'
'AT THE PORTNOY CINEMA PICCADILLY'
'WINNER OF THE GOLDEN PALM, TORREMOLINOS'
'RAINWEAR THROUGH THE AGES'
'COMING SOON'
'AT THE JODRELL CINEMA, COCKFOSTERS'

VOICE OVER (TERRY G) *(and caption)*: 'The management regrets that it will not be showing a feature film this evening as it eats into the profits'

Cut to the Queen on horseback; first few bars of National Anthem. Cut to person sitting in cinema seat clutching albatross.

PERSON Well that's quite enough of that. And now a policeman near **Rottingdeans** **14** ...Albatross!

14

The small town of Rottingdean, singular, is on the southern coast of England.

Cut to a policeman standing in a street. A man comes up to him.

MAN (MICHAEL) Inspector, inspector.
INSPECTOR (JOHN) Uh huh.
MAN **I'm terribly sorry but I was sitting on a park bench over there, took my coat off for a minute and then I found my wallet had been stolen and £15 taken from it.** [15]
INSPECTOR Well did you er, did you see anyone take it, anyone hanging around or...
MAN No no, there was no one there at all. That's the trouble.
INSPECTOR Well there's not very much we can do about that, sir.
MAN Do you want to come back to my place?
INSPECTOR ...Yeah all right.

Women's Institute applauding.Cut to a man on a bench in casualty ward set.

MAN (TERRY J) Albatross.

Doctor and sister enter and go up to him.

DOCTOR (ERIC) Mr Burtenshaw?
MAN Me, Doctor?
DOCTOR No, *me* Doctor, *you* Mr Burtenshaw.
MAN My wife, Doctor?
DOCTOR No. Your wife *patient*, *me* Doctor.
SISTER (CAROL) Come this way please.
MAN Me, Sister?
DOCTOR

NO. SHE SISTER. ME DOCTOR. YOU MR BURTENSHAW.

Nurse enters.

NURSE (JOHN) Doctor Walters?
DOCTOR Me, Nurse. (*to sister*) You Mr Burtenshaw. (*to man*) She Sister. You Doctor. (*to nurse*)
NURSE No Doctor.
DOCTOR No Doctor. Call ambulance. Keep warm.
SISTER Drink Doctor?
DOCTOR Drink Doctor. Eat Sister. Cook Mr Burtenshaw. Nurse me.
NURSE You, Doctor?
DOCTOR *Me* Doctor. You Mr Burtenshaw. She Nurse.
MAN But my wife, Nurse.
DOCTOR Your wife not Nurse. She Nurse. Your wife patient. Be patient. She Nurse. Your wife. Me Doctor. Yew Tree. U-trecht. **U-trillo,** [16] **U Thant,** [17] Euphemism. Me Doctor. (*knight walks in quickly and hits him over the head with a chicken*) Albatross!

15

The incorrect chronology of the narrative here—the wallet is stolen, so how can he know money is taken from it?—signals that something's up. And sure enough . . .

Maurice Utrillo was a French painter of cityscapes.

U Thant was the United Nations secretary-general from 1961 to 1971. A tiny island in New York's East River, opposite the U.N. building, is unofficially named after him.

Women's Institute applaud. Cut to film of Gumbys (vox pop).

GUMBY (MICHAEL) I would like to meet someone of superior intelligence.
SECOND GUMBY (TERRY J) I would like to hear the sound of two bricks being bashed together.
GUMBY I would like to see John the Baptist's impersonation of **Graham Hill.** [18]

Cut to historical impersonation sketch. Big zoom in to linkman. Glittery linkman set, showbizzy music and applause.

VOICE OVER (JOHN) Yes, it's Historical Impersonations. When you in the present can make those in the past stars of the future. And here is your host for tonight—Wally Wiggin.

Caption: 'HISTORICAL IMPERSONATIONS' Fade applause and music.

WIGGIN (MICHAEL) Hello, good evening and welcome to Historical Impersonations. And we kick off tonight with Cardinal Richelieu and his impersonation of **Petula Clark.** [19]

Cut to Cardinal Richelieu, he mimes to the phrase from the record.

RICHELIEU (MICHAEL) **'Don't sleep in the subway darling and don't stand in the pouring rain'.** [20]

Vast applause.

WIGGIN Cardinal Richelieu—sixteen stone of pure man. And now your favourite Roman Emperor Julius Caesar as **Eddie Waring.** [21]

Cut to Caesar; cloud effects behind.

CAESAR (ERIC) (*in Waring voice*) Tota gallia divisa est in tres partes **Wigan, Hunslett and Hull Kingston Rovers.** [22]

Cut back to Wiggin.

WIGGIN Well done indeed, Julius Caesar, a smile, a conquest and a dagger up your strap. Our next challenger comes all the way from the Crimea. It's the very lovely Florence Nightingale as **Brian London.** [23]

Graham Hill was an English race car driver.

Petula Clark is a British singer famous for "Downtown," an international hit in 1964, as well as many other songs of the era.

A lyric from Clark's hit "Don't Sleep in the Subway," a song filled with such deep thoughts as: "You try to be smart then you take it to heart/'Cause it hurts when your ego is deflated/You don't realize that it's all compromise/And the problems are so overrated."

The rugby league commentator, and general TV host, known for his broad Yorkshire accent. He was first satirized in Episode 1.

Wigan, Hunslet, and Hull Kingston Rover are three rugby league teams.

Brian London is a 200-pound heavyweight boxer from Yorkshire.

Florence Nightingale **24** (GRAHAM) *stands there with a lamp, simpering femininely. A boxing bell goes, slight pause, then she is hit on the side of the cheek with a boxing glove, and falls straight on her back. Cut back to Wiggin.*

WIGGIN And now for our most ambitious attempt tonight—all the way from **Moscow** **25** in the USS of R—Ivan the Terrible as a sales assistant in **Freeman, Hardy, and Willis.** **26**

In a shoe department. Three people are sitting in chairs, only the middle one is a dummy. Ivan the Terrible comes in and splits the man in the middle in half with an immense two-handed sword: the model splits in two.

WIGGIN And now **W. G. Grace** **27** as a music box.

Animation: Still picture of W G. Grace. Slowly his head starts to revolve as a musical box plays Swiss-type music. Cut back to Wiggin.

WIGGIN And now it's France's turn. One of their top statesmen, Napoleon as the **R101 disaster.** **28**

Cut to a sky background. Napoleon comes into frame horizontally, moving along a wire very slowly. In each hand he has a small propeller. A sign hangs below his belly saying R101. Marseillaise plays. **29**

As he passes out of shot there is an explosion.

WIGGIN And now it's request time.

Cut to Gumby.

GUMBY (MICHAEL) I would like to see John the Baptist's impersonation of Graham Hill.

A head on a platter is pulled by a string across the floor. We hear brm, brm, brm, noises. The head of John the Baptist has a Graham Hill moustache, obviously stuck on. Women's Institute applaud.

WIGGIN And now a short intermission during which **Marcel Marceau** **30** will impersonate a man walking against the wind.

Marcel Marceau (GRAHAM) *walks against the wind.*

WIGGIN And now Marcel will mime a man being struck about the head by a sixteen-ton weight.

Florence Nightingale, the famous British nurse, was known for carrying a lamp.

Pronounced here by Palin in the American style—"Mos-*cow*" —as opposed to the British pronunciation: "Mos-*coh*"

Freeman, Hardy, and Willis was a chain of British shoe stores.

W.G. Grace was a famous British cricketer, active for 43 years (he stopped playing in 1908).

The R101 was a British airship that crashed in France on October 5, 1930, killing 48 people on board. (Compare this to the Hindenburg disaster, nearly seven years later, which killed 35 people.)

This relatively lame visual gag causes the audience to break out into enthusiastic laughter and applause.

Marcel Marceau, the French mime artist, opened his Ecole Internationale de Mime in the Théatre de la Musique in Paris in 1969.

Cut to him starting the mime. He doesn't get very far as a sixteen-ton weight is dropped on his head.
Cut to Wembley crowd cheering.
Cut to interviewer and two small boys.

INTERVIEWER (JOHN) (*gently*) What's your name?
ERIC (ERIC) Eric.
INTERVIEWER

WOULD YOU LIKE TO HAVE A SIXTEEN-TON WEIGHT DROPPED ON TOP OF YOU, ERIC?

ERIC Don't know.

Brief stock shot of theatre audience applauding.

INTERVIEWER How about you?
MICHAEL (MICHAEL) I want to have.
INTERVIEWER What do you want to have?
MICHAEL I want to have...I want to have Raquel Welch dropped on top of me.
INTERVIEWER Dropped on top of you.
MICHAEL Oh yes, not climbing.
ERIC She's got a big bottom.

Applause stock shot. Cut to interviewer and two city gents (on their knees).

INTERVIEWER And what's your name?
TREVOR (GRAHAM) Trevor Atkinson.
INTERVIEWER And how old are you, Trevor?
TREVOR I'm forty-two.

Applause stock shot.

INTERVIEWER (*to other city gent*) Are you a friend of Trevor's?
CITY GENT (MICHAEL) Yes, we're all colleagues from the Empire and General Insurance Company.
INTERVIEWER And what do you do?
CITY GENT Well I deal mainly with mortgage protection policies, but I also do certain types of life assurance.
INTERVIEWER Now if you and your pal had one big wish, Trevor, what would you like to see on television?
TREVOR I'd like to see more fairy stories about the police.

Fairy godmother trips lightly into shot. **31**

FAIRY (ERIC) And so you shall.

Cut to open country. A policeman cycles up and parks his bike. From the saddlebag he takes a burglar's outfit—striped jersey, cap, and trousers. He lays them out on the ground, and inflates them with a bicycle pump. The inflated burglar runs away in speeded-up motion. The policeman blows his whistle. Three more policemen appear out of nowhere. He points forward and the four of them move off (in pixilated motion) after the burglar. The burglar runs across moorland; the policemen follow him. ***Dick Barton*** **32** *theme music. The burglar lures the policemen into a large packing crate, slams the door on them and nails on it a label: 'Do not open until Christmas'. In the*

31

Idle's fairy godmother appeared very briefly at the end of Episode 12.

32

Dick Barton, Special Agent was a BBC Radio show that aired from 1946 to 1951, featuring a special agent who could get out of almost any difficult situation. It was replaced by *The Archers*, a show that continues to air today, sadly.

background a policeman with a fairy tutu appears suddenly out of thin air. He waves his wand at the burglar, who disappears. Cut to policeman, with wand, standing in a street.

POLICEMAN (MICHAEL) Yes, we in Special Crime Squad have been using wands for almost a year now. You find it's easy to make yourself invisible. You can defy time and space, and you can turn violent criminals into frogs. Something which you could never do with the old truncheons.

'Panorama' music and still photos of policemen in tutus. Caption: 'PROBE AROUND' Cut to interviewer at desk of 'Panorama' type set-up. **33**

INTERVIEWER (JOHN) Yes, tonight 'Probe Around' takes a look at crime...

A shot rings out and he slumps forward. A second interviewer runs into shot from behind camera with smoking gun.

SECOND INTERVIEWER (ERIC) I'm sorry about that, but I always introduce this programme, not him. (*he pushes the first interviewer off his chair with his foot and takes his place*) Yes, tonight 'Probe Around' takes a look at Crime. Is it true that the police are using dachshunds to combat the crime wave? And can the head of the Vice Squad turn himself into an albatross **34** whenever he wants to? Just what are the police up to?

Cut to close-up of a constable reading big book. He is very, very, very stupid.

POLICEMAN (TERRY J) Oh, I'm up to page 39, where Peter Pan first manifests himself.

Cut back to interviewer.

SECOND INTERVIEWER With me now is Inspector Harry H 'Snapper' Organs of 'H' Division.

Cut to another part of the 'Panorama' set. Detective Inspector Organs is sitting next to a Viking.

ORGANS (MICHAEL) Good evening.

Cut back to interviewer and hereafter cross cut between them.

INTERVIEWER Er, Inspector, I believe you are encouraging magic in the Police Force?
ORGANS That is correct. (*as he speaks we notice he is sticking pins into a model of a burglar*) The criminal mind is a strange and contorted one. Good evening. The mind is subject to severe mental stresses. Good evening. Guilt fears abound, good evening. In the subconscious in this state, one of our lads, with a fair training in the black arts can scare the fertilizer out of them.

Panorama is the BBC investigative current affairs TV show that began in 1951 and, like *The Archers*, remains aired to this day.

A reference back to the ice cream seller's wares in the cinema sketch earlier in the episode.

Idle gets tangled up here but gamely continues.

Zog I was King of Albania from 1928 to 1939, and is beloved by all comedy writers for his fabulous name.

This visual gag doesn't quite work: the first wave of his wand moves her to the other side, and he lamely points at her once she's arrived.

Or what is meant to signify the great prehistoric stone edifice—it's comically tiny here, and clearly made out of something other than stone.

"Pinny" is British slang for a pinafore, a type of apron.

INTERVIEWER Just how are the police combatting the **increase with the use of the occult?** 35 Ex-**King Zog of Albania** 36 reports...(*phone rings*) Well we seem to have lost ex-King Zog there, but who cares. Just what kinds of magic are the police introducing into their crime prevention techniques?

Cut to four chief constables huddled round an Ouija board. They have their fingers on a tumbler which moves swiftly from one letter to the next.

POLICEMEN U-P Y-O-U-R-S.

POLICEMAN (JOHN) Up yours? What a rude Ouija board!

Cut to more film: policeman with wand. By pointing the wand at illegally parked cars he makes them disappear. Another policeman on the pavement helping an old lady across road. ***He looks to see if the road is clear, waves his wand and she jumps across to other side.*** 37 *Another street: a police siren is heard, then five policemen on broom sticks appear from round corner and disappear across frame.* ***Cut to police dancing round Stonehenge.*** 38 *A burglar is bound to a stone altar. Mix to picture of same thing in newspaper which is being read by a chief constable in his office.*

CHIEF CONSTABLE (TERRY J) Now this is the kind of thing that gives the police a bad name, sergeant.

Pull out further to reveal police sergeant in long shimmering slim-fitting ladies evening gown, diamante handbag and helmet.

SERGEANT (GRAHAM) I know, sir.

Intercom buzzer goes on desk.

CHIEF CONSTABLE (*depressing knob*) Yes, Beryl?

BERYL (*male voice*) Attila the Hun to see you, sir.

CHIEF CONSTABLE Who?

BERYL Attila the Hun, sir.

CHIEF CONSTABLE Oh botherkins! Er, constable, go and see to him will you?

SERGEANT What! In this dress?

CHIEF CONSTABLE Oh all right, I'll go.

SERGEANT **Oh, I have got a little green pinny I could wear...** 39

CHIEF CONSTABLE No, no, no, I'll go. You stay here.

SERGEANT Oh goody! I can get on with the ironing.

The chief constable walks through the door into the reception area of the police station. There is a policeman behind the counter and a little insignificant man is standing waiting.

CHIEF CONSTABLE (*to policeman*) Right where is he?

BERYL (JOHN) Over there, sir.

CHIEF CONSTABLE

RIGHT, ER, ALL RIGHT SERGEANT LEAVE THIS TO ME. ER, NOW THEN SIR, YOU ARE ATTILA THE HUN.

ATTILA THE HUN (MICHAEL) That's right, yes. A. T. Hun. My parents were Mr and Mrs Norman Hun, but they had a little joke when I was born.

CHIEF CONSTABLE Yes well, Mr Hun...

ATTILA Oh! Call me 'The', for heaven's sake!

CHIEF CONSTABLE Oh well, The...what do you want to see us about?

ATTILA I've come to give myself up.

CHIEF CONSTABLE What for?

ATTILA Looting, pillaging and sacking a major city.

CHIEF CONSTABLE I beg your pardon?

ATTILA Looting, pillaging, sacking a major city, and **I'd like nine thousand other charges to be taken into consideration, please. 40**

CHIEF CONSTABLE I say, excuse me, Mr Hun. (*he takes his hat off, removes his moustache, puts it in the hat and puts the hat back on*) Have you any objection to taking a breath test?

ATTILA Oh, no. No, no, no, no.

CHIEF CONSTABLE Right, er, sergeant will you bring the Hunalyser, please?

The constable produces a breathalyser.

BERYL Here we are, sir.

Hands it to the chief constable.

CHIEF CONSTABLE Er, how's it work?

BERYL Well he breathes into it, sir, and the white crystals turn lime green. Then he is Attila the Hun, sir.

CHIEF CONSTABLE I see. Right. Would you mind breathing into this Mr Hun?

ATTILA Right. (*blows into bag*)

CHIEF CONSTABLE What if nothing happens, sergeant?

BERYL He's Alexander the Great!

CHIEF CONSTABLE Ha, ha! Caught you, Mr A. T. Great!

ATTILA (*who is now Alexander the Great*) Oh curses! Curses! I thought I was safe, disguised as Attila the Hun.

CHIEF CONSTABLE Oh perhaps so, but you made one fatal mistake...you see, this wasn't a Hunalyser...it was an Alexander the Greatalyser! Take him away, Beryl!

Cut to letter (as used for 'Xmas night with the stars' after pet shop. I'm sorry...as not used in Xmas night with the stars').

VOICE OVER (ERIC) Dear Sir, I object very strongly to that last scene, and to the next letter.

Cut to second letter.

VOICE OVER (MICHAEL) Dear Sir, I object to being objected to by the last letter, before my drift has become apparent. I spent many years in India during the last war and am now a part-time notice board in a prominent public school. Yours etc., Brigadier Zoe La Rue (deceased). PS Aghhh!

To have "charges taken into consideration" in the British courts means that though a trial might concern a particular charge, the defendant is willing to admit that other crimes have been committed, even though there won't be another trial for these charges. Such an agreement helps a judge decide on an appropriate amount of jail time (or damages, or both) without going through separate (and costly) trials. The joke here, of course, is that the "real" Attila the Hun would have had many, many other charges to "take into consideration."

Cut to third letter.

VOICE OVER (JOHN) Dear Sir, When I was at school, I was beaten regularly every thirty minutes, and it never did me any harm—except for psychological maladjustment and blurred vision. Yours truly, Flight Lieutenant Ken Frankenstein (Mrs).

Animation link runs into a psychiatrist's consulting room. The psychiatrist at his desk. The door opens and a receptionist looks in.

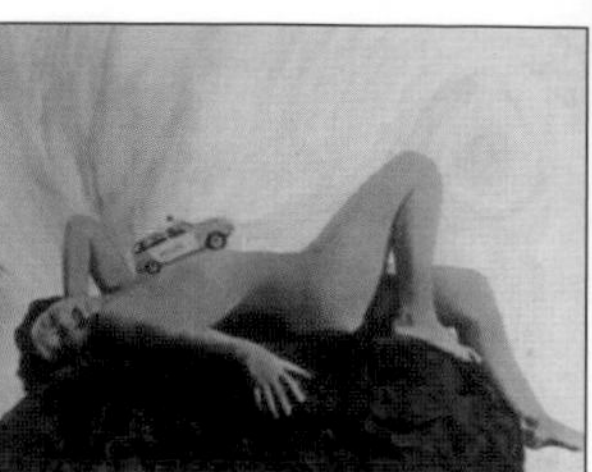

"Larch" is a favorite Python reference.

RECEPTIONIST (CAROL) **Dr Larch** 41 ...there's a Mr Phelps to see you.
PSYCHIATRIST (JOHN) Er, nurse!
RECEPTIONIST Yes?
PSYCHIATRIST (*whispering*) Er, you don't think you should make it clear that I'm a psychiatrist?
RECEPTIONIST What?
PSYCHIATRIST Well, I could be any type of doctor.
RECEPTIONIST Well I can't come in and say 'Psychiatrist Larch' or 'Dr Larch who is a psychiatrist'. Oh, anyway look, it's written on the door.
PSYCHIATRIST (*still whispering*) That's outside.
RECEPTIONIST Well, I don't care, you'll just have to do it yourself. (*she leaves*)
PSYCHIATRIST (*goes 'brr brr', then picks up phone*) Hello. Er, no, wrong number I'm afraid, this is a psychiatrist speaking. Next please. (*knock at the door*) Er, come in.

Phelps comes in dressed as Napoleon, with a parrot on his head, and a lead with nothing on it.

PHELPS (TERRY J) Bow, wow, wow.
PSYCHIATRIST Ah Mr Phelps. Come on in, take a seat. Now what seems to be the matter?
PHELPS No, no, no. No. No.
PSYCHIATRIST I'm sorry?
PHELPS Oh can't you do better than that? I mean it's so predictable I've seen it a million times. Knock, knock, knock come in, ah Mr Phelps take a seat. I've seen it and seen it.

PSYCHIATRIST Well look will you please sit down and do your first line.
PHELPS No. No. I've had enough. I've had enough. (*he exits*)
PSYCHIATRIST I can't even get it started.
PHELPS (*off*) Albatross!
PSYCHIATRIST Shut up! Oh it drives me mad.

Cut to a man in limbo: Mr Notlob.

NOTLOB (MICHAEL) A mad psychiatrist, that'd be new.

Cut back to the psychiatrist.

PSYCHIATRIST Next please.

Knocking at door. Psychiatrist is about to call when he picks up a thesaurus and thumbs through it.

PSYCHIATRIST **Cross the threshold, arrive, ingress, gain admittance, infiltrate.** **42** (*Notlob enters in an ordinary suit*) Ah **Mr Notlob,** **43** ah park your hips, on the sitting device.
NOTLOB (*to camera*) It is a mad psychiatrist.
PSYCHIATRIST I'm not. I'm not. Come on in. Take a seat. What's, what's the matter?

Cut to Napoleon in limbo; he blows a raspberry.

PSYCHIATRIST Now what's the matter?
NOTLOB Well I keep hearing guitars playing and people singing when there's no one around.
PSYCHIATRIST Yes, well this is not at all uncommon. In certain mental states we find that auditory hallucinations occur which are of a most... ***(he stops suddenly and listens: the sound of 'We're all going to the zoo tomorrow' is heard)*** **44** Is that 'We're all going to the zoo tomorrow'?
NOTLOB Yes. Yes.
PSYCHIATRIST Is it always that?
NOTLOB No.
PSYCHIATRIST Well that's something.
NOTLOB But it's mainly folk songs.
PSYCHIATRIST (*concerned*) Oh my God.
NOTLOB Last night I had **'I'll never fall in love again' for six hours.** **45**
PSYCHIATRIST Well look, I think I'd better have a second opinion on this. I want you to see a colleague of mine, a specialist in these sort of things, who has an office very much like this one as a matter of fact.

Jump cut of same office now occupied by a surgeon. Start on portrait which has moustache and beard and glasses being added by surgeon.

SURGEON (GRAHAM) Brr brr (*picks up phone*) No, no wrong number I'm a colleague of his, a surgeon, who specializes in these kind of things. Yes thank you very much. (*replaces phone*) Next please. (*knock at door*) Come in. (*Notlob enters; 'Going to the zoo' is faintly heard*) Ah come in, please take a seat. (*cut to terribly quick shot of Napoleon, then back*) My colleague who has a similar office has explained your case to me (*he is rising from seat*) Mr Notlob, as you know I am a leading **Harley Street** **46** surgeon as seen on television. (*he puts needle down on ancient gramophone; Dr Kildare theme begins playing*) I'm afraid I'm going to have to operate. It's nothing to worry about although it is extremely dangerous. I shall be juggling with your life, I shall be playing **ducks and drakes** **47** with your very existence, I shall be running me mitts over the pith of your marrow. Yes! These hands, these fingers, these sophisticated organs of touch, these bunches of five, these maulers, these German bands

Cleese does love him a thesaurus; many of his sketches run around the idea of different words for the same thing (see the parrot sketch, amongst many others).

Another reference back, this one to one of the pet store sketches, in which "Notlob" is used to refer to the town of Bolton, in the north of England.

"Going to the Zoo" is the dreadful Tom Paxton song, here sung by Peter, Paul, and Mary.

Bobby Gentry had a hit in 1969 with this Burt Bacharach and Hal David song.

Harley Street is the center of England's private medicine (as opposed to the National Health Service), in London. The street is filled with the offices of eminent and expensive doctors.

"Ducks and drakes" is the ageless art of skimming stones across the surface of a body of water.

that have pulled many a moribund unfortunate back from the very brink of Lazarus's box. No, it was Pandora's box wasn't it? Well anyway these mits have earned yours truly a lot of bread. So if you'll just step through here I'll slit you up a treat.

NOTLOB What?

SURGEON Mr Notlob, there's nothing wrong with you that an expensive operation can't prolong.

Cut to operating theatre. The conversation and the guitar can still be heard. Notlob is on the table. His head is real but the rest of the body is false. Table is covered with green cloth for reality. Surgeon is swabbing. 'Going to the zoo' is still audible.

SURGEON Right, I'm ready to make the incision. Knife please, sister. (*takes knife*) What's that supposed to be. Give me a big one. (*takes big knife and strops it* **48** *on steel sharpener*)...oh I do enjoy this. Right. (*he stabs the body and makes a slit four feet long*) Oh what a great slit. Now, gentlemen, I am going to open the slit.

He pulls it apart. The song gets louder. The head of a squatter pops out.

SQUATTER (ERIC) Too much man, groovy, great scene. Great light show, baby.

SURGEON What are you doing in there?

SQUATTER We're doing our own thing, man.

SURGEON Have you got Mr Notlob's permission to be in there?

SQUATTER We're squatters, baby.

SURGEON What? (*to nurse about Notlob*) Nurse, wake him up. (*she slaps his face*)

SQUATTER Don't get uptight, man. Join the scene and other phrases. Money isn't real.

SURGEON It is where I'm standing and it blows my mind, young lad. (*looks inside Notlob*) **Good Lord! Is that a nude woman? 49**

SQUATTER She's doing an article on us for 'Nova', man. 50

GIRL (CAROL) (*her head also appearing through slit*) Hi everyone. Are you part of the scene?

SURGEON Are you rolling your own jelly babies in there?

NOTLOB (*waking up*) What's going on? Who are they?

SURGEON That's what we are trying to find out.

NOTLOB What are they doing in my stomach?

SURGEON We don't know. Are they paying you any rent?

NOTLOB Of course they're not paying me rent!

SQUATTER You're not furnished, you fascist.

NOTLOB Get them out!

SURGEON I can't.

NOTLOB Get them out.

SURGEON No I can't. Not, not without a court order.

INDIAN (*also appearing*) Shut up. You're keeping us awake.

Caption: 'ONE COURT ORDER LATER' Some policemen walk in.

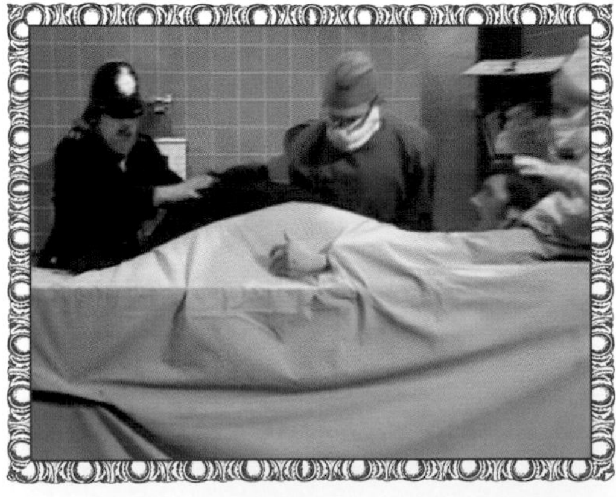

A strop is a leather device used to polish a blade, here used imaginatively as a verb.

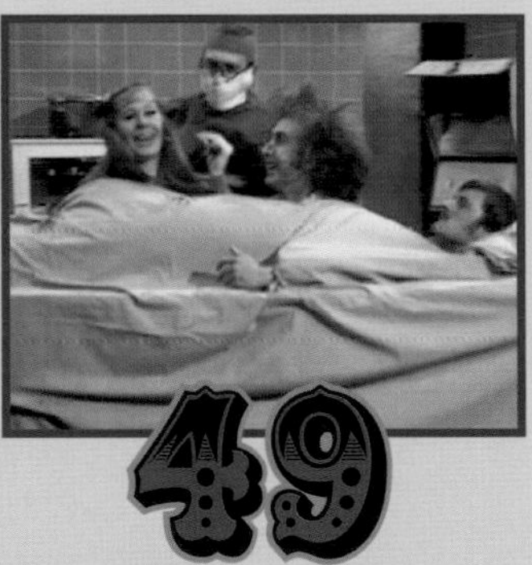

It's clear that she's not, in fact, nude—her shirt is visible when she rises from the "body."

50

Nova was an artsy magazine of the day.

FIRST POLICEMAN (JOHN) (*into slit*) You are hereby ordered to vacate Mr Notlob forthwith. And or.
SQUATTER Push off, fuzz.
POLICEMAN Right, that's it, we're going in. Release the vicious dogs. (*dives into slit*)

Animation:

ANIMATED CHARACTER
WHAT A TERRIBLE WAY TO END A SERIES. 51
Why couldn't it end with something like this? (*a short piece of confusing animation later*)

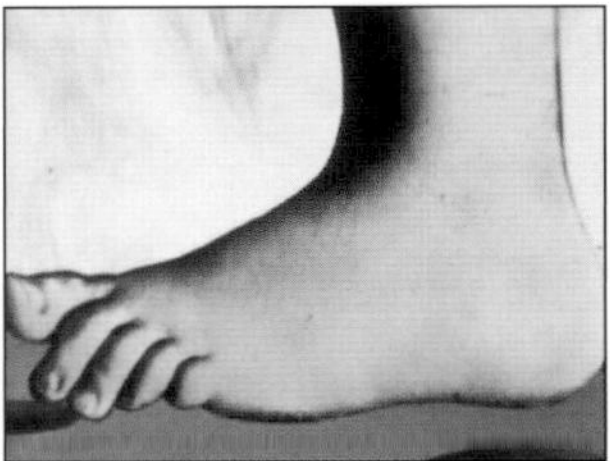

Now there's an ending for you. Romance. Laughter.

Cut to film of 'It's' man being pursued by undertaker; roll credits over.

Caption: 'INTERMISSION'

VOICE OVER (JOHN) When this series returns it will be put out on Monday mornings as a **test card** 52 and will be described by the **'Radio Times'** 53 as a history of Irish agriculture.

Here ended the first season of Python shows. By this point, after a rocky start, the show had gained some prominence, and going forward, more sympathetic studio audiences would start to recognize some Python tropes—parrots, and the like—and the laugh track got stronger and more generous.

A "test card," also called a test pattern, was a static picture used in place of programming when stations went dark overnight and at other times.

Radio Times, the BBC listings magazine, also referenced in Episode 9.

SEA SON 2
EPISODE 14

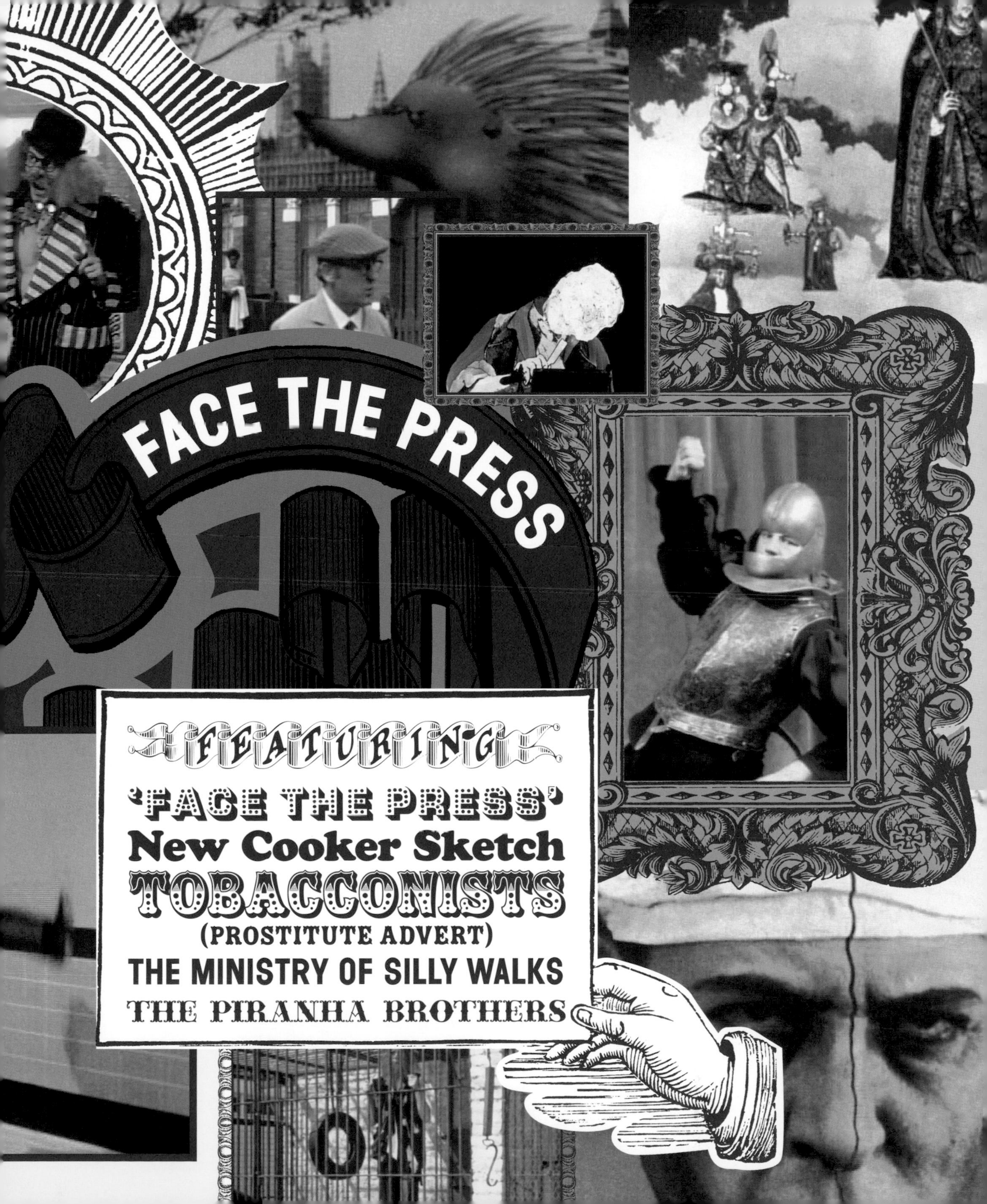

FACE THE PRESS
FEATURING
'FACE THE PRESS'
New Cooker Sketch
TOBACCONISTS
(PROSTITUTE ADVERT)
THE MINISTRY OF SILLY WALKS
THE PIRANHA BROTHERS

FIRST AIRED: SEPTEMBER 15, 1970

A man in evening dress, sitting in a cage at the zoo.

MAN (JOHN) And now for something completely different.

Pan to show 'It's' man in next cage.

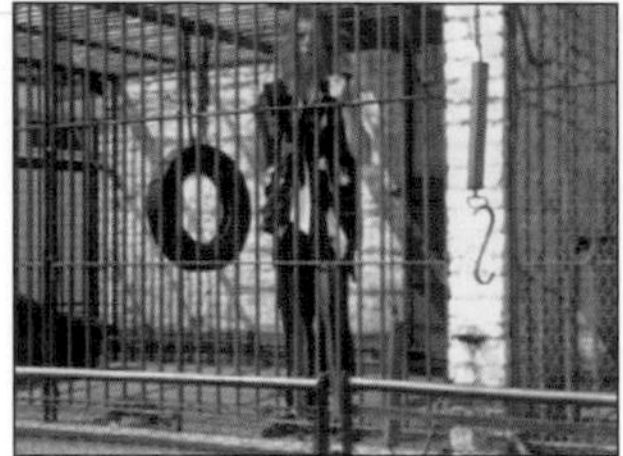

IT'S MAN (MICHAEL)

IT'S...

Animated titles.

Cut to studio: interviewer in chair. Superimposed caption: 'FACE THE PRESS'

INTERVIEWER (ERIC) Hello. Tonight on 'Face the Press' we're going to examine two different views of contemporary things. On my left is the Minister for Home Affairs *(cut to minister completely in drag and a moustache)* who is wearing a striking organza dress in pink tulle, with matching pearls and a diamante collar necklace. *(soft fashion-parade music starts to play in background)* The shoes are in brushed pigskin with gold clasps, by **Maxwell of Bond Street** 1 The hair is by Roger, and the whole ensemble is crowned by a spectacular display of Christmas orchids. And on my right—putting the case against the Government—is a small patch of brown liquid...*(cut to patch of liquid on seat of chair)* which could be creosote or some extract used in industrial varnishing. *(cut back to interviewer)* Good evening.

Bond Street is a shopping street in London's West End known for its highfalutin fashion stores. "Maxwell" is a fake store name.

Minister, may I put the first question to you? In your plan, 'A Better Britain For Us', you claimed that you would build 88,000 million, billion houses a year in the Greater London area alone. In fact, you've built only three in the last fifteen years. Are you a bit disappointed with this result?

MINISTER (GRAHAM) No, no. I'd like to answer this question if I may in two ways. Firstly in my normal voice and then in a kind of silly high-pitched whine...You see housing is a problem really...

Cut back to the interviewer. The minister is heard droning on in the background. The soft fashion-parade music starts again.

INTERVIEWER Well, while the minister is answering this question I'd just like to point out the minister's dress has been made entirely by hand from over three hundred pieces of Arabian shot silk *(at this point we can hear the minister's high-pitched whine beneath the fashion music)* especially created for the minister by **Vargar's of Paris.** **2** The low slim-line has been cut off-the-shoulder to heighten the effect of the minister's fine bone structure. Well I think the minister is coming to the end of his answer now so let's go back over and join the discussion. Thank you very much minister. Today saw the appointment of a new head of...

MINISTER Don't I say any more?

INTERVIEWER **No fear!** **3** Today saw the appointment of a new head of Allied Bomber Command—Air Chief Marshal Sir Vincent 'Kill the Japs' Forster. He's in our Birmingham studio...

Cut to close-up on what appears to be a monitor with Sir Vincent on it—in outrageous drag, heavy lipstick, big bust, etc.—Draped on a chaise-longue. A small black boy is fanning him.

SIR VINCENT (JOHN) Hello Sailors! Listen, guess what. The Minister of Aviation has made me head of the RAF Ola Pola.

As he talks we zoom out quickly from the set to reveal it is not a monitor in the studio but a TV set in a G-plan type sitting room. A housewife (Mrs Pinnet) sits watching, wearing an apron and a scarf, and with her hair in curlers. The doorbell sounds. She switches the TV off and answers the door which opens straight into the living room. There in the street stands a truly amazing figure of fun. A man in a bowler hat with an axe sticking out of it, big red joke nose, illuminated bow tie that revolves, joke broad shoulders, clown's check jacket, long johns with sock suspenders, ***heavy army boots and leading a goat with a hat.*** **4** *Close-up.*

More fashion fakery.

British slang for "too right!"

This is a close description of the amazing getup, though he's actually wearing a pinstripe jacket with large red-and-white-striped lapels and cuffs; blue shorts; we can't see his feet; and his tie is flashing, not revolving. Otherwise, dead-on.

5 David Hockney, the darling of the 1960s pop art scene. Given the camp nature of all this cross-dressing, he was probably referenced because of his homosexuality. Hockney is still one of the most influential British figurative artists.

6 There are plenty of Egerton Roads in the U.K., but no "Egernons."

7 Palin, who tends to rush his lines here and there, at this point seems to say "Glad we could be such a whelp."

MAN Hello. Mrs Rogers?
MRS PINNET (TERRY J) No. Ooh I must be in the wrong house.

She shuts the door on him and we follow her as she crosses the room. She climbs out of the window. Back yard of terraced house. She scrambles over a quite high dividing wall into next door and starts to scramble into next-door window. Interior of a more cluttered working-class sitting-room. There is a TV in there with Sir Vincent still camping it up.

SIR VINCENT So from now on we're going to do things my way. For a start **David Hockney** 5 is going to design the bombs. And I've seen the plans...

The doorbell rings.

MRS PINNET That must be the new gas cooker.

She switches the TV off. Immediate thunderous epic music.
Superimposed caption: (in stone lettering, as for Ben Hur) 'NEW COOKER SKETCH'. Both caption and music switch off suddenly as she opens the door. Outside the door are two gas men with a new cooker.

FIRST GAS MAN (MICHAEL) Morning. Mrs G. Crump?
MRS PINNET No—Mrs G. Pinnet.
FIRST GAS MAN This is 46 Egernon Crescent?
MRS PINNET No—Road. **Egernon Road.** 6
FIRST GAS MAN *(looks at a bit of paper)* Road, yes, says here. Yeah. Right, could I speak to Mrs G. Crump please?
MRS PINNET Oh there's nobody here of that name. It's Mrs G. Pinnet. 46 Egernon Road.
FIRST GAS MAN Well it says 'Crump' here. Don't it, Harry?
SECOND GAS MAN (GRAHAM) Yeah—it's on the invoice.
FIRST GAS MAN Yeah, definitely Crump.
MRS PINNET Well there must have been a mistake, because the address is right, and that's definitely the cooker I ordered—a blue and white CookEasi.
FIRST GAS MAN Well you can't have this. This is Crump.
MRS PINNET Oh dear, what are we going to do?
FIRST GAS MAN Well I don't know. What we can do for you is take it back to the Depot, get a transfer slip from Crump to Pinnet, and put it on a special delivery.
SECOND GAS MAN Yeah—that's best.

WE'LL SPECIAL IT FOR YOU, WE'LL GET IT DOWN TODAY AND YOU'LL GET IT BACK IN TEN WEEKS.

MRS PINNET Ten weeks! Blimey, can't you just leave this one?
FIRST GAS MAN What this? What leave it here? *(they seem thunderstruck)*
MRS PINNET Yes.
FIRST GAS MAN Well I dunno. I suppose we could.
SECOND GAS MAN Oh, but she'd have to fill out a temporary despatch note.
FIRST GAS MAN Yeah we could leave it on a temporary despatch note.
MRS PINNET Well that's sorted out then. What a mess, isn't it.
FIRST GAS MAN I know, it's ridiculous really, but there you are. **Glad we could be of such a help.** 7 Right, would you sign it down there please, Mrs Crump?
MRS PINNET Pinnet.
FIRST GAS MAN Pinnet. Listen, just for the books make it a bit easier, could you sign it Crump-Pinnet.

MRS PINNET Right. *(she signs)*

FIRST GAS MAN Right. Thank you very much, dear. The cooker's yours. Right. Thank you very much, dear. Right. *(they push it just inside the door and move off)* Sorry about the bother...but there you are...you know...cheerio!

SECOND GAS MAN Cheerio, Mrs Crump!

MRS PINNET Heh, excuse me! **Cooey!** **8** Er, can you put it in the kitchen?

FIRST GAS MAN *(coming back)* You what?

MRS PINNET Well I can't cook on it unless it's connected up.

FIRST GAS MAN Oh we didn't realize you had an installation invoice.

SECOND GAS MAN An MI.

FIRST GAS MAN No, we can't touch it without an MI, you see.

SECOND GAS MAN Or an R16.

THIRD GAS MAN (JOHN) *(who is suddenly revealed behind the two of them)* If it's a special.

SECOND GAS MAN Nah—it's not special...the special's back at the Depot.

FIRST GAS MAN No, the special's the same as installation invoice.

THIRD GAS MAN So it's an R16.

MRS PINNET What's an installation invoice?

FIRST GAS MAN A pink form from Reading.

MRS PINNET Oh—we wondered what that was. Now these are the forms. *(she produces a large wad of papers, sorts through and produces a pink form which she hands to them)*

FIRST GAS MAN That's the one, love. Yeah, this should be all I need. Hang on. This is for Pinnet. Mrs G. Pinnet.

MRS PINNET That's right. I'm Mrs G. Pinnet.

FIRST GAS MAN Well we've got Crump-Pinnet on the invoice.

MRS PINNET Well shall I sign it Crump-Pinnet then?

FIRST GAS MAN No, no, no—not an MI—no.

SECOND GAS MAN No—that's from Area Service at **Reading.** **9**

FOURTH GAS MAN (ERIC) *(suddenly revealed)* **No, Cheltenham isn't it?** **10**

SECOND GAS MAN **No, not this side of the street.** **11**

MRS PINNET Look I just want it connected up.

Much doubtfulness.

THIRD GAS MAN What about London Office?

FIRST GAS MAN Well they haven't got the machinery.

"Cooey" is an attention-grabbing greeting beloved of centuries of British women of a certain age. It is called across streets, over garden fences, and up and down supermarket aisles.

Reading is a large town some 40 miles west of London.

Cheltenham is a large town about 100 miles northwest of London.

This sketch is a beautiful satire of the British love for paperwork, second only to the French in its love of bureaucracy. It would not be beyond belief that two sides of a street would have different coverage from corporations. A country in which many of the major utilities were nationalized at the time (and many still are), centralization often ran amok.

Hounslow is a neighborhood in west London.

Twickenham is southwest of central London, and home to the national rugby stadium.

14

Holborn is a another section of London, this time very near the center; hence, where "Head Office" might be.

SECOND GAS MAN Not now.

FIFTH GAS MAN (TERRY G) *(suddenly revealed)* **What! The Hounslow Depot?** 12

FOURTH GAS MAN No—they're still on standard pressure.

SIXTH GAS MAN *(suddenly revealed)* **Same with Twickenham.** 13

MRS PINNET But surely they can connect up a gas cooker?

FIRST GAS MAN Oh yeah, we could connect it up, love, but not unless it's an emergency.

MRS PINNET But this is an emergency.

FIRST GAS MAN No it's not. An emergency is 290...'where there is actual or apparent loss of combustible gaseous substances'.

SECOND GAS MAN Yeah, it's like a leak.

Seventh gas man is revealed.

SEVENTH GAS MAN Yeah, or a 478.

THIRD GAS MAN No—that's valve adjustment.

MRS PINNET But there can't be a leak unless you've connected it up.

FIRST GAS MAN No, quite. We'd have to turn it on.

MRS PINNET Well can't you turn it on *and* connect it up?

FIRST GAS MAN No. But what we can do, and this is between you and me, I shouldn't really be telling you this, we'll turn your gas on, make a hole in your pipe, you ring Hounslow emergency, they'll be around here in a couple of days.

MRS PINNET What, a house full of gas! I'll be dead by then!

FIRST GAS MAN Oh well, in that case you'd have the South East Area Manager round here like a shot.

MRS PINNET Really?

FIRST GAS MAN Ah yes. **'One or more persons overcome by fumes', you'd have Head Office, Holborn, round here.** 14

MRS PINNET Really?

FIRST GAS MAN Yes. That's murder you see.

SECOND GAS MAN Or suicide.

FIFTH GAS MAN No. That's S42.

SECOND GAS MAN Oh.

Eighth gas man is revealed.

EIGHTH GAS MAN Still? **I thought it was Hainault.** 15

FIFTH GAS MAN No—Central area and Southall Marketing Division, they're both on the S42 now.

MRS PINNET And they'd be able to connect it up?

FIRST GAS MAN Oh—they'd do the lot for you, love.

MRS PINNET And they'd come round this afternoon?

FIRST GAS MAN

...WELL WHAT IS IT NOW... 11.30... MURDER...THEY'LL BE ROUND HERE BY TWO.

MRS PINNET Oh well that's wonderful.

FIRST GAS MAN Oh well, right love, if you'd like to lie down here.

MRS PINNET All right. *(she does so)*

FIRST GAS MAN Okay Harry.

SECOND GAS MAN Okay. Gas on.

FIRST GAS MAN *(holding a gas pipe to her mouth)* Right, deep breaths love. Ring Head Office would you Norman...

FOURTH GAS MAN Shall I go through maintenance?

FIFTH GAS MAN No, you'd better go through Deptford maintenance.

SIXTH GAS MAN Peckham's on a 207...

VOICES ...that's Lewisham. What about Tottenham? No that would be a 5.4...what about Lewish-am? It's central isn't it? **Or Ruislip...** 16

The camera pans along line of gas men all turning to each other and muttering incomprehensible technicalities, ***the line stretches across to front door.*** 17

Hainault is in the very northeast tip of London, so clearly not the right place for a head office.

Ruislip...another section of London.

And is, yet again, watched by bemused onlookers. It would be wonderful to find some of the people who witnessed Python street madness and ask them what the hell they thought they were watching.

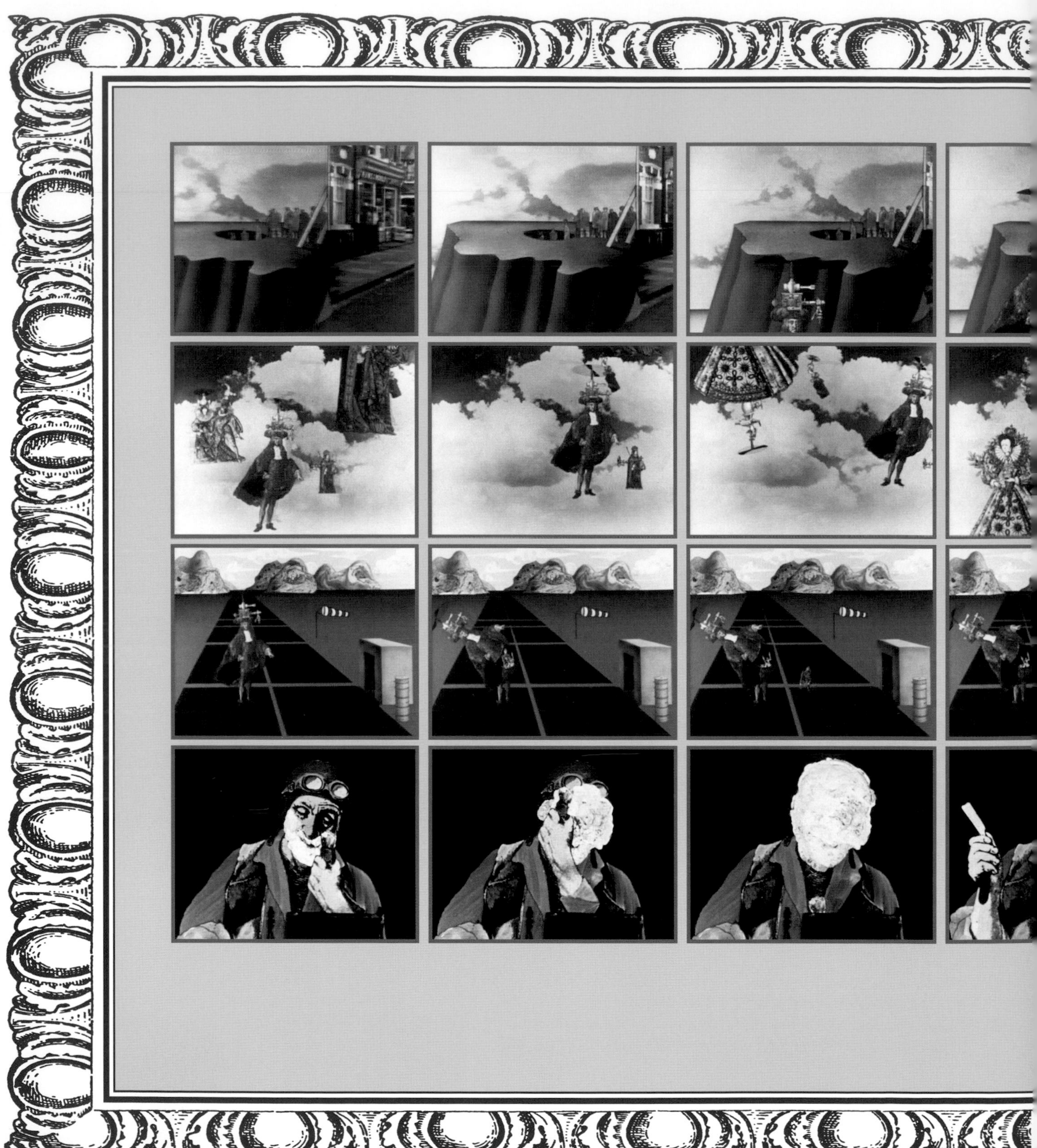

Line continues outside in street and goes into animation sequences which eventually bring us through to close-up on a small ad, which is one of many on the door of a small newsagent's shop. A shabby man is running an evil eye down the adverts, puzzling, looking for something. He walks up to the counter. He has a reflex wink.

It was, and may well still be, difficult to acquire adult entertainment products in the U.K. (though the Internet has probably helped.) Sex shops tended to be in seedier parts of town, and there was great stigma in entering such a place, hence Idle's desperate hope that pussies, chests, and drawers (as in underwear) could be procured in the relative safety of what looks like a regular store.

19

Here, as Idle turns back to Jones, Idle's glasses fall off his face and he catches them in his left hand—a brilliant piece of fielding, and one that somehow fails to crack them both up.

Here, "quid" is British slang for pounds, as in money.

And so we see for the first time, Cleese's extraordinary creation, the silly walk, now a classic Python sketch. His hitch and turn of his leg inside the store still baffles and delights, all these years later.

CUSTOMER (ERIC) Good morning.

SHOPKEEPER (TERRY J) Good morning, sir. Can I help you?

CUSTOMER Help me? Yeah, I'll say you can help me.

SHOPKEEPER Yes, sir?

CUSTOMER I come about your advert—'**Small white pussy cat for sale. Excellent condition**'. **18**

SHOPKEEPER Ah. You wish to buy it?

CUSTOMER That's right. Just for the hour. Only I aint gonna pay more'n a fiver cos it aint worth it.

SHOPKEEPER Well it's come from a very good home—it's house trained.

CUSTOMER *(long think, goes to door, looks at ads again)* Chest of drawers? Chest. Drawers. I'd like some chest of drawers please.

SHOPKEEPER Yes, sir.

CUSTOMER Does it go?

SHOPKEEPER **Er, it's over there in the corner. *(indicates a wooden chest of drawers)*** **19**

CUSTOMER Oh. *(goes to door, runs his finger down the list of adverts)* Pram for sale. Any offers. I'd like a bit of pram please.

SHOPKEEPER Ah yes, sir. That's in good condition.

CUSTOMER Oh good, I like them in good condition, eh? Eh?

SHOPKEEPER Yes, here it is you see. *(picks up pram)*

CUSTOMER *(looks, pauses, goes back to the door, runs finger again)* Babysitter. No, it's a babysitter. Babysitter?

SHOPKEEPER Babysitter.

CUSTOMER Babysitter—I don't want a babysitter. Be a blood donor—that's it. I'd like to give some blood please, argh! *(shopkeeper shakes head)* Oh spit. Which one is it? *(shopkeeper slips him a card from out of his pocket)* **Blond prostitute will indulge in any sexual activity for four quid a week.** **20** What does that mean?

A city gent comes into shop. He has a silly walk and keeps doing little jumps and then three long paces without moving the top of his body. ***He buys a paper, then we follow him as he leaves shop.*** **21**

CITY GENT (JOHN) 'Times' please.

SHOPKEEPER Oh yes sir, here you are.

CITY GENT Thank you.

SHOPKEEPER Cheers.

The city gent leaves the shop, from which we see a line of gas men stretching back up the road to Mrs Pinnet's house, ***and walks off in an indescribably silly manner.*** **22** ***Cut to him proceeding along Whitehall, and into a building labelled 'Ministry of Silly Walks'.*** **23** *Inside the building he passes three other men,* ***each walking in their own eccentric way.*** **24** *Cut to an office; a man is sitting waiting. The city gent enters eccentrically.*

MINISTER Good morning. I'm sorry to have kept you waiting, but I'm afraid my walk has become rather sillier recently, **and so it takes me rather longer to get to work.** **25** *(sits at desk)* **Now then, what was it again?** **26**

MAN (MICHAEL) Well sir, I have a silly walk and I'd like to obtain a Government grant to help me develop it.

MINISTER I see. May I see your silly walk?

MAN Yes, certainly, yes.

He gets up and does a few steps, lifting the bottom part of his left leg sharply at every alternate pace. He stops.

MINISTER That's it, is it?

MAN Yes, that's it, yes.

MINISTER It's not particularly silly, is it? I mean, the right leg isn't silly at all and the left leg merely does a forward aerial half turn every alternate step.

MAN Yes, but I think that with Government backing I could make it very silly.

MINISTER ***(rising)*** **Mr Pudey,** ***(he walks about behind the desk in a very silly fashion)*** **the very real problem is one of money. I'm afraid that the Ministry of Silly Walks is no longer getting the kind of support it needs.** **27** You see there's Defence, Social Security, Health, Housing, Education, Silly Walks...they're all supposed to get the same. But last year, the Government spent less on the Ministry of Silly Walks than it did on National Defence! Now we get £348,000,000 a year, which is supposed to be spent on all our available products. *(he sits down)* Coffee?

MAN Yes please.

MINISTER *(pressing intercom)* Now Mrs Two-Lumps, would you bring us in two coffees please?

INTERCOM VOICE Yes, Mr Teabag.

MINISTER ...Out of her mind. Now the Japanese have a man who can bend his leg back over his head and back again with every single step. While the Israelis...here's the coffee.

Enter secretary with tray with two cups on it. She has a particularly jerky silly walk which means that by the time she reaches the minister there is no coffee left in the cups. The minister has a quick look in the cups, and smiles understandingly.

MINISTER Thank you—lovely. *(she exits still carrying tray and cups)*

MAN Oh rather. Yes.

MINISTER Well take a look at this, then.

One of the most iconic scenes in all of Python: Cleese silly walks past the line of gas men stretching up a British street—a moment of great surrealist comedy.

Whitehall is the street on which the British government buildings are found. Wonderful, again, to watch folks in the street watch this mad man walk by in a bowler hat.

It's notable that only Cleese has the comic control to make his walk truly legendary—Jones, especially, merely jerks around a lot.

The end of this line is lost in the laughter of the audience.

A typical Python moment: a lovely non sequitur suggesting we've missed something, or that everyone is quite mad.

Here, Cleese flattens his legs out almost sideways, and he has some long, long legs. The audience loses its mind, and we lose any sense of what he's saying. It matters not.

It's no secret that John Cleese hates this sketch. When he performed it live (he will no longer do so, so don't ask him on pain of death), as the audience was hooting and laughing it offered him the chance to abuse Palin, who wrote the sketch and appears in it. High stepping around Palin, Cleese would tell him that the sketch wasn't funny and that he shouldn't be proud for having written it.

TRANSLATION: "Hello...and now...as usual, on the subject of Communal Walks. And now, I give to you, one more time my friend, the famous puff [slang for homosexual], Jean-Brian Zatapathique [a favorite Python "French" name]."

TRANSLATION: "Thank you, my little pet Brian Trubshawe [Concord Test pilot mentioned in Episode 2]. And now with the right legs, and the left legs, and now the Anglo-French Futile Walk, and there it is."

Again, it's notable that Terry Jones's silly walks elicit no laughter from the audience. It's really Cleese's bag.

He produces a projector from beneath his desk already spooled up and plugged in. He flicks a switch and it beams onto the opposite wall. The film shows a sequence of six old-fashioned silly walkers. The film is old silent-movie type, scratchy, jerky and 8mm quality. All the participants wear 1900s type costume. One has huge shoes with soles a foot thick, one is a woman, one has very long 'Little Tich' shoes. Cut back to office. The minister hurls the projector away. Along with papers and everything else on his desk. ***He leans forward.*** **28**

MINISTER Now Mr Pudey. I'm not going to mince words with you. I'm going to offer you a Research Fellowship on the Anglo-French Silly Walk.

MAN La Marche Futile?

Cut to two Frenchmen, wearing striped jerseys and berets, standing in a field with a third man who is entirely covered by a sheet.

FIRST FRENCHMAN (JOHN) **Bonjour...et maintenant...comme d'habitude, au sujet du Le Marché Commun. Et maintenant, je vous presente, encore une fois, mon ami, le pouf célèbre, Jean-Brian Zatapathique.** **29** *(he removes his moustache and sticks it onto the other Frenchman)*

SECOND FRENCHMAN (MICHAEL) **Merci, mon petit chou-chou Brian Trubshawe. Et maintenant avec les pieds à droite, et les pieds au gauche, et maintenant l'Anglais-Françaïse Marche Futile, et voilà.** **30**

They unveil the third man and walk off. He is facing to camera left and appears to be dressed as a city gent; then he turns about face and we see on his right half he is dressed au style français. ***He moves off into the distance in eccentric speeded-up motion.*** **31**

JOHN CLEESE

He once had a wife named Alyce Faye, and she always called him Jack. Which is notable only because his real family name, before his father changed it in 1915, was Cheese—not Cleese.

John Cleese (a.k.a. Jack Cheese) was born in England's West Country—the seaside town of Weston-super-Mare, to be precise—a couple of months before the start of World War II. His parents were older—his father was 46, and his mother 40—which he claims made him more reserved than other kids, more careful. He was also tall, well into six feet by his teens. Even now his website lists him as "writer, actor, and tall person."

At Cambridge University, Cleese studied law and joined its Footlights performance group, where he met Graham Chapman. So successful was his work that one of the shows, *Cambridge Circus* (previously *A Clump of Plinths)*, transferred from the Edinburgh Festival to London and then to Broadway. In America he met Terry Gilliam and Connie Booth, an actress he would later marry (and with whom he wrote *Fawlty Towers*). Back in the U.K., in the mid-sixties, and like the other Pythons, he wrote for David Frost; he also acted on Frost's shows and gained a modicum of early TV fame (he was hard to miss, being so tall and so funny). Later he, with Chapman, would write episodes for a popular sitcom, *Doctor in the House*, and on the back of that success they were asked to do a series of their own. Needing more support than he got from the difficult Chapman, he hit up Palin and the rest. And the Python troupe came into being.

On the *Flying Circus* he perfected his knack for characters who shouted a lot, and whose fuses were short. Writing with Chapman, his penchant for wordplay—what contributed to his "thesaurus" sketches—was matched by his physical brilliance, most notably in a sketch he later came to despise. A signal creation of Cleese's, the Ministry of Silly Walks is one of the most memorable pieces of physical comedy ever filmed. One only has to watch Terry Jones's or Michael Palin's attempts to play along to see how mesmerizing and shimmering are Cleese's silly walks. That said, he had to be convinced to do the third series of Python (he was worried they were repeating themselves), and by the fourth series he was gone altogether, a loss that spelled the end of the show after just six episodes. He was crucial to the *Flying Circus*, and the British comic public missed him too much.

But he could do angry like no other comic actor, which put him in good standing for his post-Python career. Written with his then wife, Connie Booth, whose first appearance in *Monty Python's Flying Circus* came as the trusting blonde in the "Lumberjack Song," *Fawlty Towers* first aired in 1975 and was an instant classic of comedy TV. The show followed the farcical efforts of Basil Fawlty (played by Cleese) to run a hotel in Torquay, on the English south coast. Badgered by a harridan wife, Sybil (played by the great comic actor Prunella Scales), and featuring Booth as an innocent chambermaid and Andrew Sachs's masterful portrayal of a bumbling Spanish waiter, the twelve episodes are pretty much perfect. In 2000, the British Film Institute voted *Fawlty Towers* the best television series of all time, and it's hard to argue with that.

Cleese followed up this success with a number of beloved movies. *A Fish Called Wanda* features Cleese and Palin working together again in a crime caper; and *Clockwise*, in which a man can't get anywhere on time, proves Cleese had lost none of his comic genius. Since that time, however, he's become most known for his corporate training videos through his company, Video Arts, founded in 1972 with Anthony Jay and other TV stalwarts. In them, he turns boring corporate saws into something one wouldn't entirely hate to sit through. Even more recently he's starred in the show *Alimony Tour*, the title of which speaks for itself.

Richard Chamberlain is an American actor, Peggy Mount is an English actress, and Billy Bremner is a tough Scottish soccer player, then captain of Leeds United.

Compare to the Vercotti brothers from previous episodes (8, 10, & 13), again based on the notorious London gangland thugs the Kray brothers.

The London police were split into divisions. Q Division, established in 1965, was based in the Wembley section, 15 miles northwest of Southwark.

VOICE OVER (ERIC) And now a choice of viewing on BBC Television. *(cut to BBC world symbol)* Just started on BBC 2 the semi-final of Episode 3 of 'Kierkegaard's Journals', starring **Richard Chamberlain, Peggy Mount and Billy Bremner; and on BBC 1, 'Ethel the Frog'.** 32

Stirring music—'This Week' type. Superimposed caption: 'ETHEL THE FROG' Cut to presenter at desk in usual grey suit and floral tie.

PRESENTER (JOHN) Good evening. On 'Ethel the Frog' tonight we look at violence. The violence of British Gangland. Last Tuesday a reign of terror was ended when **the notorious Piranha brothers, Doug and Dinsdale,** 33 *(photo of same)* after one of the most extraordinary trials in British legal history, were sentenced to four hundred years imprisonment for crimes of violence. Tonight Ethel the Frog examines the rise to power of the Piranhas, the method they used to subjugate rival gangs and their subsequent tracking down and capture by the brilliant Superintendent Harry 'Snapper' Organs of **Q Division.** 34 *(photo of Eastend grotty house)* Doug and Dinsdale Piranha were born, on probation, in this house in Kipling Road, Southwark, the eldest sons in a family of sixteen. Their father *(photo (aged) of father)* Arthur Piranha, a scrap-metal dealer and TV quizmaster, was well known to the police, and a devout Catholic. In January 1928, he had married Kitty Malone, *(old wedding photo)* an up-and-coming Eastend boxer. Doug was born in February 1929 and Dinsdale two weeks later, and again a week after that. Their next door neighbour was Mrs April Simnel.

Exterior in street: interviewer and Mrs Simnel. Line of gas men behind.

MRS SIMNEL (MICHAEL) Kipling Road was a typical sort of Eastend street. People were in and out of each other's houses with each other's property all day long. They were a cheery lot though.
INTERVIEWER (ERIC) Was it a terribly violent area?
MRS SIMNEL *(laughs deprecatingly)* Oh, ho...yes. Cheerful and violent. I remember, Doug was very keen on boxing, until he learned to walk, then he took up putting the boot in the groin. Oh he was very interested in that. His mother used to have such trouble getting him to come in for his tea. He'd be out there putting his little boot in, you know, bless him. You know kids were very different then. They didn't have their heads filled with all this Cartesian dualism.

Cut to school playground. **35**

VOICE OVER (JOHN) At the age of fifteen Doug and Dinsdale started attending the Ernest Pythagoras Primary School in Clerkenwell.

Pan to show Anthony Viney and interviewer with stick mike.

INTERVIEWER (TERRY J) Anthony Viney. You taught the Piranha brothers English. What do you remember most about them?

He fails to point stick mike at Viney (GRAHAM) *who answers. However, when the interviewer poses the next question he points stick mike to Viney as he does so. This continues, with the mike always pointing at the one who is not talking while Viney relates a fascinating tale complete with large riveting gestures.*

INTERVIEWER ...Anthony Viney.

Cut to the presenter.

PRESENTER **When the Piranhas left school they were called up but were found by an Army Board to be too mentally unstable even for National Service.** **36** Denied the opportunity to use their talents in the service of their country, they began to operate what they called 'The Operation'. They would select a victim and then threaten to beat him up if he paid them the so-called protection money. Four months later they started another operation which they called 'The Other Operation'. In this racket they selected another victim and threatened *not* to beat him up if he *didn't* pay them. One month later they hit upon 'The Other Other Operation'. In this the victim was threatened that if he didn't pay them they would beat him up. This for the Piranha brothers was the turning point.

Cut to Superintendent Organs.
Subtitle: 'HARRY "SNAPPER" ORGANS'

ORGANS (TERRY J) Doug and Dinsdale Piranha now formed a gang which they called 'The Gang' and used terror to take over night clubs, billiard halls, gaming casinos and race tracks.

The crowd of boys watching seem as confused as others in the streets who have watched the Pythons do their thing.

National Service was established to aid the World War II effort in the U.K. It was discontinued in 1945 and reestablished two years later, ending for good in 1960. One was expected to serve for 18 months, and later for two years.

The "MCC" is for the Marylebone Cricket Club, a London-based organization established in 1787 considered to be the de facto ruling body of cricket until the early 1990s. As genteel a body as one could imagine, hence the joke.

"Color supplements" are color additions to otherwise black-and-white newspapers, such as magazines and the like.

The conversation pit is a recessed seating area beloved of mod 1960s and 1970s home furnishers.

"And that" is British filler roughly meaning "etc."

When they tried to take over the MCC **37** they were, for the only time in their lives, slit up a treat. As their empire spread, however, **we in Q Division were keeping tabs on their every movement by reading the colour supplements.** **38**

PRESENTER A small-time operator who fell foul of Dinsdale Piranha was Vince Snetterton-Lewis.

Cut to Vince in a chair in a nasty flat.

VINCE (GRAHAM) Well one day I was sitting at home threatening the kids, and I looked out of the hole in the wall and I saw this tank drive up and one of Dinsdale's boys gets out and he comes up, all nice and friendly like, and says Dinsdale wants to have a talk with me. So he chains me to the back of the tank and takes me for a scrape round to Dinsdale's. **And Dinsdale's there in the conversation pit** **39** with Doug and Charles Paisley, the baby crusher, and a couple of film producers and a man they called 'Kierkegaard', who just sat there biting the heads off whippets, and Dinsdale said 'I hear you've been a naughty boy Clement' and he splits me nostrils open and saws me leg off and pulls me liver out, and I said my name's not Clement, and then he loses his temper, and nails my head to the floor.

INTERVIEWER *(off-screen)* He nailed your head to the floor?

VINCE At first, yeah.

Cut to presenter.

PRESENTER Another man who had his head nailed to the floor was Stig O'Tracey.

Cut to another younger more cheerful man on sofa.

INTERVIEWER Stig, I've been told that Dinsdale Piranha nailed your head to the floor.

STIG (ERIC) No, no. Never, never. He was a smashing bloke. He used to give his mother flowers **and that.** **40** He was like a brother to me.

INTERVIEWER

BUT THE POLICE HAVE FILM OF DINSDALE ACTUALLY NAILING YOUR HEAD TO THE FLOOR.

STIG Oh yeah, well—he did that, yeah.

INTERVIEWER Why?

STIG Well he had to, didn't he? I mean, be fair, there was nothing else he could do. I mean, I had transgressed the unwritten law.

INTERVIEWER What had you done?

STIG Er...Well he never told me that. But he gave me his word that it was the case, and that's good enough for me with old Dinsy. I mean he didn't want to nail my head to the floor. I had to insist. He wanted to let me off. There's nothing Dinsdale wouldn't do for you.

INTERVIEWER And you don't bear him any grudge?

STIG A grudge! Old Dinsy? He was a real darling.

INTERVIEWER I understand he also nailed your wife's head to a coffee table. Isn't that right Mrs O'Tracey?

Camera pans to show woman with coffee table nailed to head.

MRS O'TRACEY (GRAHAM) Oh no. No. No.

STIG Yeah, well, he did do that. Yeah, yeah. He was a cruel man, but fair.

Cut back to Vince.

INTERVIEWER Vince, after he nailed your head to the floor, did you ever see him again?
VINCE Yeah...after that I used to go round to his flat every Sunday lunchtime to apologize, and we'd shake hands and then he'd nail my head to the floor.
INTERVIEWER Every Sunday.
VINCE Yeah, but he was very reasonable about it. I mean one Sunday when my parents were coming round for tea, I asked him if he'd mind very much not nailing my head to the floor that week, and he agreed and just screwed my pelvis to a cake stand.

Cut to man affixed to a coffee table and a standard lamp.

MAN (TERRY J) He was the only friend I ever had.

Cut to block of concrete with a man upside down with his head buried in it.

BLOCK I wouldn't hear a word against him.

Cut to a gravestone, which says: 'R.I.P. and Good Luck, Dinsdale'.

VOICE Lovely fella.

Cut to presenter.

PRESENTER Clearly Dinsdale inspired tremendous loyalty and terror amongst his business associates, but what was he really like?

Cut to a bar.

GLORIA (JOHN) **I walked out with Dinsdale** **41** on many occasions and found him a most charming and erudite companion. He was wont to introduce one to many eminent persons, celebrated American singers, members of the aristocracy and other gangleaders.
INTERVIEWER (ERIC) *(off-screen)* How had he met them?
GLORIA Through his work for charity. **He took a warm interest in Boys' Clubs, Sailors' Homes, Choristers' Associations, Scouting Jamborees and of course the Household Cavalry.** **42**
INTERVIEWER Was there anything unusual about him?
GLORIA I should say not. Dinsdale was a perfectly normal person in every way. Except in as much as he was convinced that he was being watched by a giant hedgehog whom he referred to as Spiny Norman.

41

"Walked out with" is a gentle British phrase for dating.

42

All allusions to homosexuality.

Cleese says "snout" rather than "nose."

Stanley Baldwin was a three-time British prime minister—twice in the 1920s and from 1935 to 1937.

Chapman, perhaps getting ready to act crazy, briefly loses his lines here.

Biggleswade is a small town an hour north of London.

A "cheap clip joint" is an establishment in which a patron is tricked into thinking there will be alcohol and sex when, in fact, there's often merely the promise of both, followed by ejection and no recourse.

INTERVIEWER How big was Norman supposed to be?

GLORIA Normally he was wont to be about twelve feet **from nose to tail,** 43 but when Dinsdale was very depressed Norman could be anything up to eight hundred yards long. When Norman was about, Dinsdale would go very quiet and his nose would swell up and his teeth would start moving about and he'd become very violent and **claim that he'd laid Stanley Baldwin.** 44 Dinsdale was a gentleman. And what's more he knew how to treat a female impersonator.

Cut to dark-suited loony in armchair. Superimposed caption: 'A CRIMINOLOGIST'

CRIMINOLOGIST (GRAHAM) It's easy for us to judge Dinsdale Piranha too harshly. After all, he only did what most of us simply dream of doing...*(tic...controls himself)* I'm sorry. After all a murderer is only an extroverted suicide. Dinsdale was a loony, but he was a happy loony. **Lucky bastard.** 45

Cut to presenter.

PRESENTER Most of these strange tales concern Dinsdale, but what of Doug? One man who met him was Luigi Vercotti.

Cut to tatty office with desk and phone. Vercotti at desk.

VERCOTTI (MICHAEL) Well, I had been running a successful escort agency—high-class, no really, high-class girls...we didn't have any of that, That was right out. And I decided. *(phone rings on desk)* Excuse me. *(he answers it)* Hello...no, not now...shtoom...shtoom...right...yes we'll have the watch ready for you at midnight...the watch...the *Chinese watch*...yes, right oh, bye-bye mother. *(he replaces receiver)* Anyway, I decided then to open a high-class night club for the gentry **at Biggleswade** 46 with international cuisine, cooking, top-line acts, and **not a cheap clip joint** 47 for picking up tarts, that was right out, I deny that completely, and one night Dinsdale walked in with a couple of big lads, one of whom was carrying a tactical nuclear missile. They said I'd bought one of their fruit machines and would I pay for it.

INTERVIEWER (TERRY J) How much did they want?

VERCOTTI Three quarters of a million pounds. Then they went out.

INTERVIEWER Why didn't you call for the police?

VERCOTTI Well, I'd noticed that the lad with the thermo-nuclear device was the Chief Constable for the area. Anyway a week later they came back, said that the cheque had bounced and that I had to see Doug.

INTERVIEWER Doug?

VERCOTTI Doug. *(takes a drink)* I was terrified of him, Everyone was terrified of Doug. I've seen grown men pull their own heads off rather than see Doug. Even Dinsdale was frightened of Doug.

INTERVIEWER What did he do?

VERCOTTI **He used sarcasm. He knew all the tricks, dramatic irony, metaphor, bathos, puns, parody, litotes and satire.** [48]

Cut to map.

PRESENTER *(voice over)* By a combination of violence and sarcasm the Piranha brothers, by February 1966, controlled London and the South East. In February though, Dinsdale made a big mistake.

Cut back to bar and Gloria.

GLORIA Latterly Dinsdale had become increasingly worried about Spiny Norman. He had come to the conclusion that Norman slept in an aeroplane hangar at Luton Airport.

Cut to presenter.

PRESENTER And so on February 22nd, 1966, at Luton Airport...*(stock film of H-bomb explosion)* Even the police began to sit up and take notice.

Cut to 'Snapper' Organs.

ORGANS The Piranhas realized they had gone too far and that the hunt was on. They went into hiding and I decided on a subtle approach, viz. some form of disguise, as the old helmet and boots were a bit of a give-away. Luckily my years with Bristol Rep stood me in good stead as I assumed a bewildering variety of disguises. I tracked them to Cardiff posing as the Reverend Smiler Egret. Hearing they'd gone back to London, I assumed the identity of a pork butcher, Brian Stoats. *(photo of Organs disguised as a butcher)* On my arrival in London I discovered they had returned to Cardiff. I followed as Gloucester from 'King Lear'. *(photo of Organs as Gloucester)* Acting on a hunch I spent several months in Buenos Aires as Blind Pew, returning through the Panama Canal as Ratty **in 'Toad of Toad Hall'.** [49] *(photo of Ratty)* Back in Cardiff I relived my triumph as Sancho Panza *(photo)* in **'Man of La Mancha'** [50] which the 'Bristol Evening Post' described as 'a glittering performance of rare perception', although the **'Bath Chronicle'** [51] was less than enthusiastic. In fact it gave me a right panning. I quote:

All elements of classical rhetoric. "Litotes" is understatement by denial of an opposite, which is not an uncomplicated way of saying a double negative.

Toad of Toad Hall is a dramatization of the Kenneth Grahame novel from 1908, *The Wind in the Willows*.

Man of La Mancha is the Broadway musical that would become a movie two years after this episode aired.

Bath is thirteen miles southeast of Bristol, so the *Chronicle* would indeed have reported on Organs's performance.

Cut to press cutting, which reads:

VOICE OVER (ERIC) 'As for the performance of Superintendent Harry "Snapper" Organs as Sancho Panza, the audience were bemused by his high-pitched Welsh accent **and intimidated** [52] by his abusive ad-libs.'

Cut to letterhead of newspaper—'The Western Daily News'.

ORGANS *(off-screen)* **'The Western Daily News' said...** [53]
VOICE OVER (JOHN) 'Sancho Panza (Mr Organs) spoilt an otherwise impeccably choreographed rape scene by his unscheduled appearance and **persistent** [54] cries of **"What's all this then?"'** [55]

Cut to back-stage-type dressing-room, with make-up mirrors.

POLICEMAN (GRAHAM) Never mind, Snapper, love, you can't win 'em all.
ORGANS True, constable. Could I have my eye-liner, please?
SECOND POLICEMAN Telegram for you, love.
ORGANS Good-oh. Bet it's from Binkie.
SECOND POLICEMAN Those flowers are for Sergeant Lauderdale—from the gentleman waiting outside.
ORGANS Oh good.

Knock, knock. Head comes round the door.

HEAD Thirty seconds, superintendent.
ORGANS Oh blimey, I'm on. Is me hat straight, constable?
POLICEMAN Oh, it's fine.
ORGANS Right, here we go then, Hawkins.
POLICEMAN Oh, merde, superintendent.
ORGANS Good luck, then.

Cut to exterior of police station. They come down the stairs and walk off along pavement. The city gent passes them, doing his silly walk. Cut to a little newspaper seller.

52

The actual clip reads "intimadated."

53

The *Western Daily Press* is another newspaper based in Bristol.

54

The actual clip reads "persistant."

55

"What's all this, then?" is the stereotypical greeting of a British police officer to a suspected criminal.

NEWSPAPER SELLER Read all about it. Piranha brothers escape.

Cut to a suburban street: it completely clears very fast. Freeze frame on empty street. An enormous hedgehog, higher than the houses comes into shot saying 'Dinsdale?' Roll credits, behind which we see the enormous hedgehog appearing in various well-known London locations.

HEDGEHOG Dinsdale? Dinsdale? Dinsdale?

Cut to John in cage as in opening shot.

MAN (JOHN) Well, that's all for now and so until next week...*(roars)*

Pan to next cage to show skeleton of 'It's' Man. Fade out.

SEA
SON
2
EPISODE 15

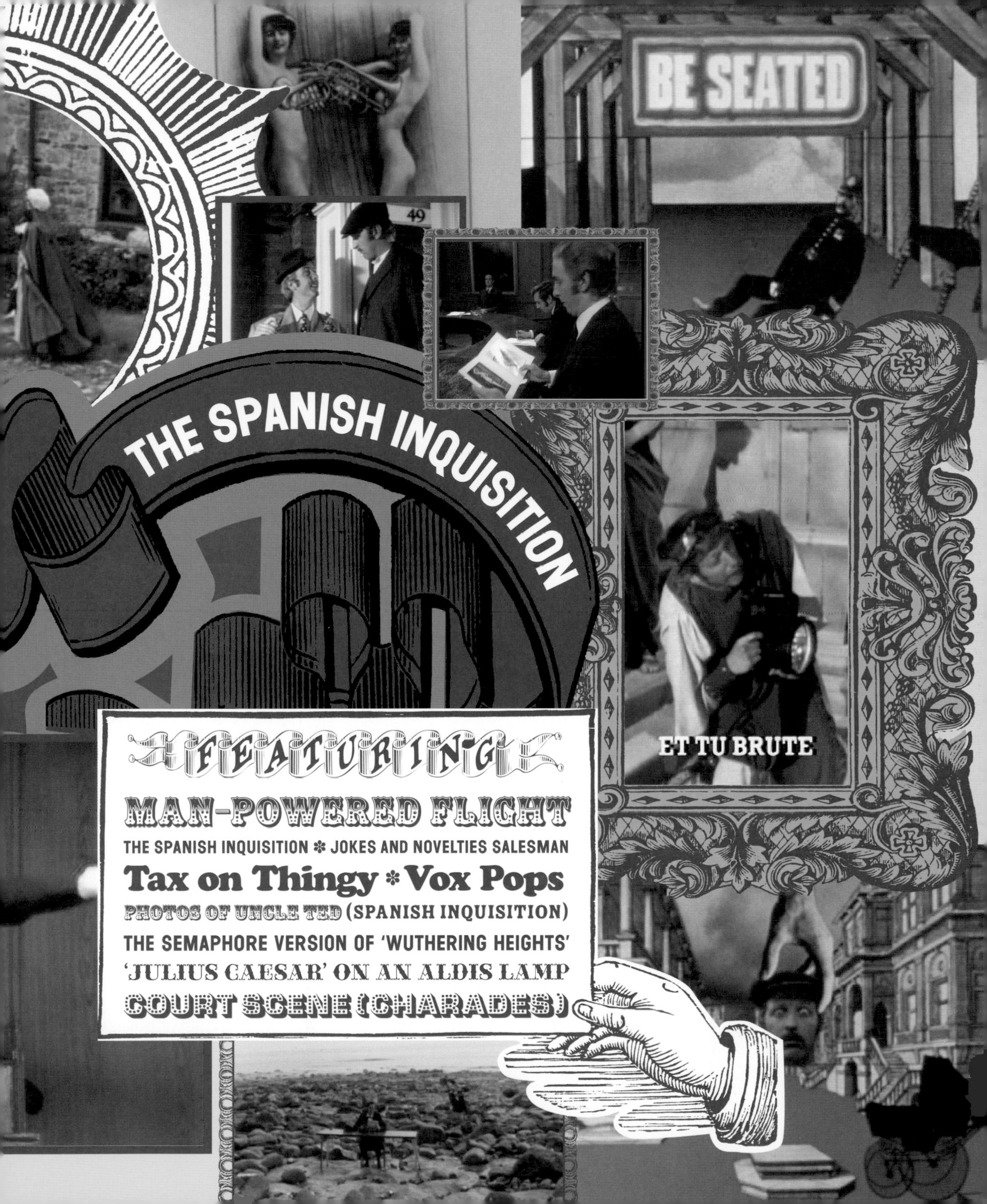
BE SEATED
49
THE SPANISH INQUISITION
ET TU BRUTE
FEATURING
MAN-POWERED FLIGHT
THE SPANISH INQUISITION ✽ JOKES AND NOVELTIES SALESMAN
Tax on Thingy ✽ Vox Pops
PHOTOS OF UNCLE TED (SPANISH INQUISITION)
THE SEMAPHORE VERSION OF 'WUTHERING HEIGHTS'
'JULIUS CAESAR' ON AN ALDIS LAMP
COURT SCENE (CHARADES)

This is the first time the "It's" man hasn't dominated the opening. This nice visual gag was filmed at the cliffs at Seaford, in East Sussex on the south coast of England. Also known as Seven Sisters, these low chalk cliffs resemble the more famous "White Cliffs of Dover."

Jarrow United was the subject of the soccer sketch in Episode 12—a stark industrial town in the northeast, just south of Newcastle.

3

The following "Spanish Inquisition" sketch is rightly considered another classic. Palin wrote this after randomly throwing in the cliché that "I didn't expect a kind of Spanish Inquisition" when Graham Chapman was being grilled by Carol Cleveland about what's going on at the mill. From there, the literal appearance of the actual Spanish Inquisition comes into play.

A "treddle" is a prostitute; a treadle is a foot-operated piece of machinery. Take your pick.

FIRST AIRED: SEPTEMBER 22, 1970

A field. A man with large mechanical wings, pulleys and gears contraption, running along trying to fly. Cut to him going faster. Cut to him going even faster. Cut to him even faster and suddenly he appears to take off, jumping off a dune or a hillock. Cut to him flying in slow motion so that it looks like he is gliding. He hits what seems to be a cliff. Camera twists round so that it is the right way up, showing that the flyer has fallen down a cliff onto a beach. It pans across from the wreck of the flyer. As it pans across the sand, various other would-be fliers can be seen, heads in the sand, legs kicking up in the air, amidst the broken debris of their planes. ***Camera continues to pan until it comes across an announcer in DJ sitting at his desk:*** 1

ANNOUNCER And now for something completely different.

IT'S MAN (MICHAEL)

IT'S...

Animated titles.

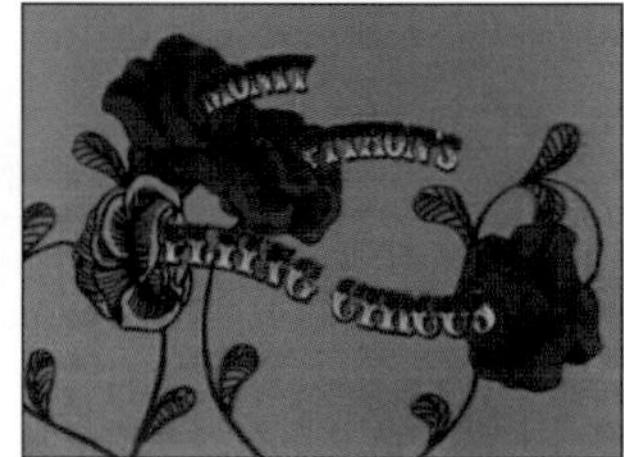

Music: Black Dyke Mills Band playing a slow dirge. Stock shot of mill town at the turn of the century—at night. ***Subtitle:*** *'JARROW* 2 *—NEW YEAR'S EVE 1911'* ***Subtitle:*** *'JARROW 1912'* 3 *Mix through to mill-owner's opulent sitting room at the turn of the century. Lady Mountback sits with her crochet. There is a knock on the door.*

LADY MOUNTBACK (CAROL) Come in.

Enter Reg, cap in hand.

REG (GRAHAM) Trouble at mill.

LADY MOUNTBACK Oh no. What sort of trouble?

REG One on't cross beams gone owt askew on **treddle.** 4

LADY MOUNTBACK Pardon?

RED One on't cross beams gone owt askew on treddle.

LADY MOUNTBACK I don't understand what you're saying.

REG (*slightly irritatedly and with exaggeratedly clear accent*) One of the cross beams has gone out askew on the treddle.

LADY MOUNTBACK But what on earth does that mean?

REG I don't know. Mr Wentworth just told me to come in here and say there was trouble at the mill, that's all. **I didn't expect a kind of Spanish Inquisition.** 5

Jarring chord. The door flies open and Cardinal Ximinez of Spain enters flanked by two junior cardinals. ***Cardinal Biggles*** 6 *has goggles pushed over his forehead. Cardinal Fang is just Cardinal Fang.*

XIMINEZ (MICHAEL) Nobody expects the Spanish Inquisition. Our chief weapon is surprise...surprise and fear...fear and surprise...our two weapons are fear and surprise...and ruthless efficiency. Our *three* weapons are fear and surprise and ruthless efficiency and an almost fanatical devotion to the Pope...Our *four*...no...*amongst* our weapons...amongst our weaponry are such elements as fear, surprise...I'll come in again. (*exit and exeunt*)

REG I didn't expect a kind of Spanish Inquisition.

Jarring chord. They burst in.

XIMINEZ Nobody expects the Spanish Inquisition. 7 Amongst our weaponry are such diverse elements as fear, surprise, ruthless efficiency, and an almost fanatical devotion to the Pope, and nice red uniforms—oh, damn! (*to Biggles*) I—I can't say it, you'll have to say it. 8

BIGGLES What?

The Spanish Inquisition—exactly the Tribunal of the Holy Office of the Inquisition—was established in 1480 ostensibly to exert Catholic orthodoxy on converting Jews and Muslims, but it became a kind of *mutaween*, a religious police happy to abuse its own power. It wasn't officially abolished until the early nineteenth century. Though it had long been ineffectual, much damage was done by then.

"Biggles" is the children's book character first mentioned in Episode 10—a flying ace.

Palin pauses here as though he knows there's a list coming and he has to get it right.

The sketch seems as much a satire on bad amateur dramatics as it does on religious orthodoxy.

XIMINEZ You'll have to say the bit about 'our chief weapons are...'
BIGGLES I couldn't do that...

Ximenez bundles the cardinals outside.

REG I didn't expect a kind of Spanish Inquisition. 9

They all enter.

BIGGLES Er...um...nobody...
XIMINEZ Expects.
BIGGLES Expects...Nobody expects the...er...um...Spanish um...
XIMINEZ Inquisition.
BIGGLES I know...I know. Nobody expects the Spanish Inquisition. In fact, those who do expect...
XIMINEZ Our chief weapons are...
BIGGLES Our chief weapons are...er...er...
XIMINEZ Surprise.
BIGGLES Surprise and...
XIMINEZ Stop! Stop there! Stop there. Whew! Our chief weapon is surprise, blah, blah, blah, blah. Cardinal, read the charges.
FANG You are hereby charged that you did on diverse dates commit heresy against the Holy Church. My old man said follow the.... 10
XIMINEZ That's enough! (*to Lady Mountback*) Now, how do you plead?
LADY MOUNTBACK We're innocent.
XIMINEZ Ha! Ha! Ha!

Superimposed caption: 'DIABOLICAL LAUGHTER'

XIMINEZ We'll soon change your mind about that!

Superimposed caption: 'DIABOLICAL ACTING'

XIMINEZ Fear, surprise and a most ruthless...(***controls himself with a supreme effort***) **ooooh! Now cardinal, the rack!** 11

Biggles produces a plastic-coated modern washing-up rack. Ximinez looks at it and clenches his teeth in an effort not to lose control. ***He hums heavily to cover his anger.*** 12

You...right! Tie her down. (*Fang and Biggles make a pathetic attempt to tie her on to the rack*) Right, how do you plead?
LADY MOUNTBACK Innocent.
XIMINEZ Ha! Right! Cardinal, give the rack...oh dear...give the rack a turn.

Chapman says this line brilliantly, throwing in a lovely bored face and tone at the end.

Terry Gilliam steals the scene here, the first time his onstage performance does so. The little dance he does to the traditional Cockney song "My Old Man" is truly hilarious.

He actually hits himself on the head, à la Cleese's characters when their brains are acting up.

Jones produces the rack from under his cassock, but not before revealing large red underpants.

Cardinal Biggles stands there awkwardly and shrugs.

BIGGLES I...

XIMINEZ (*gritting his teeth*) I *know*. I know you can't. I didn't want to say anything, I just wanted to try and ignore your crass mistake.

BIGGLES I...

XIMINEZ It makes it all seem so stupid.

BIGGLES Shall I, um...?

XIMINEZ Oh, go on, just pretend for God's sake.

Biggles turns an imaginary handle on the side of the rack. The doorbell rings. Reg detaches himself from scene and answers it. Outside there is a dapper BBC man with a suit and a beard, slightly arty.

BBC MAN (JOHN) Ah, hello, you don't know me, but I'm from the BBC. We were wondering if you'd come and answer the door in a sketch over there, in that sort of direction...You wouldn't have to do anything—just open the door and that's it.

REG Oh, well all right, yes.

BBC MAN Jolly good. Come this way.

Cut to film of them coming out of the front door of the house and walking to BBC van. Conversation is heard throughout (slightly faintly).

BBC MAN Yes, we're on film at the moment you see.

REG It's a link, is it?

BBC MAN Yes that's right, that sort of thing, yes, a link. It's all a bit zany—you know a bit madcap funster...frankly I don't fully understand it myself, the kids seem to like it. I much prefer **Des O'Connor...Rolf Harris...Tom Jones,** **13** you know...

They get into the van. **14** *It drives off. They pass an* **AA** **15** *sign saying 'To the Sketch'. Panning shot of them, in which we see them conversing and hear...*

REG You do a lot of this sort of thing, do you?

BBC MAN Quite a lot yes, quite a lot. I'm mainly in comedy. I'd like to be in Programming Planning actually, but unfortunately I've got a degree.

They arrive outside a suburban house, where the novelty salesman, Mr Johnson, is already waiting outside the front door. BBC man points and gives Reg direction. Reg goes to the door saying: 'Excuse me' and goes in, closing the front door. The novelty man rings bell. Reg opens the door.

JOHNSON (ERIC) Joke, sir? Guaranteed amusing. As used by the crowned heads of Europe. Has brought tears to the eyes of Royalty. 'Denmark has never laughed so much'—'The Stage'. Nice little novelty number—**'a naughty Humphrey'** **16**—breaks the ice at parties. Put it on the table. Press the button. It vomits. Absolutely guaranteed. With refills. 'Black soap'—leave it in the bathroom, they wash their hands, real fungus grows on the fingers. Can't get it off for hours. Guaranteed to break the ice at parties. Frighten the elderly—real snakes. Comedy hernia kit. Plastic flesh wounds—just keep your friends in stitches. Guaranteed to break the ice at parties. Hours of fun with 'honeymoon delight'—empty it into their beds—real skunk juice. They won't forget *their* wedding night. Sticks to the skin, absolutely waterproof, guaranteed to break the ice at parties. Amuse your friends—CS gas canisters—smells, tastes and acts just like the real thing—can blind, maim or kill. Or

Des O'Connor, Rolf Harris, and Tom Jones were all stalwarts of British entertainment of the time. O'Connor was a slick English crooner, Harris an excitable Australian painter and singer (it's as bad as it sounds), and Jones was, and remains, Wales's greatest-ever belter, he of "What's New Pussycat?" et al.

14

Cleese is also heard on the soundtrack referencing Arthur Askey. Askey was a comedian and actor of midcentury fame, though he was still working in the 1970s. He was by then considered something of a relic of bygone days.

The Automobile Association—the national motoring group—would often post temporary signs, as depicted here.

"A naughty Humphrey" is probably a nonsense reference, if you're trying to find one in a novelty store.

for drinks, why not buy a 'wicked willy' with a life-size winkle—serves warm beer. Makes real cocktails. Hours of amusement. Or get the new Pooh-Pooh machine. Embarrass your guests—completely authentic sound. Or why not try a new 'naughty nightie'—put it on and it melts—just watch their faces. Guaranteed to break the ice at naughty parties. Go on, go on.

REG What?

JOHNSON Do the punchline.

REG What punchline?

JOHNSON The punchline for this bit.

REG I don't know it. They didn't say anything about a punchline.

JOHNSON Oh! Oh well in that case I'll be saying goodbye then, sir...Goodbye then, sir.

He turns and walks away. Reg looks around desperately. And then runs out of the door. He runs to BBC van as Johnson walks out of picture. Cut to cabin of BBC van with the BBC man sitting there.

REG What's the punchline?

BBC MAN Punchline? I don't think there's a punchline scheduled, is there? Where are we? A week 39.4...no, it's Friday, isn't it—39.7. Oh...here we are. Oh! (*laughs*) Ha, ha, ha, very good. Ha, ha, ha, very good. What a good punchline. Pity we missed that. Still, never mind, we can always do it again. Make a series out of it. Now if you'll just sign there, I'll put this through to our contracts department and you should be hearing from them in a year or two.

REG Can you give me a lift back?

BBC MAN Ah—can do. But won't. We were wondering if we could possibly borrow your head for a piece of animation.

REG What?

BBC MAN Oh jolly good. Thanks very much. You will get expenses.

BBC staff set on Reg and saw his head off. Animation: Reg's head starts off by being thrown into picture.

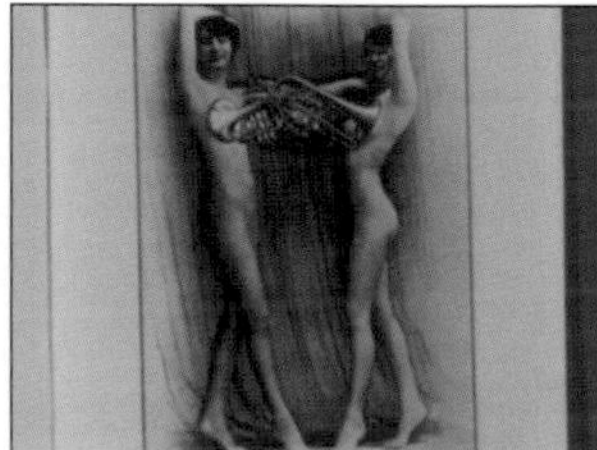

Animation leads to an oak panelled, Civil Service committee room. A politician is addressing three officials.

POLITICIAN (JOHN) Gentlemen, our **MP** [17] saw the **PM** [18] this AM and the PM wants more LSD from the **PIB** [19] by tomorrow AM or PM at the latest. I told the PM's **PPS** [20] that AM was **NBG** [21] so tomorrow PM it is for the PM it is **nem. con.** [22] Give us a **fag.** [23] or I'll **go spare.** [24] Now—the fiscal deficit with regard to the monetary balance, the current financial year excluding invisible exports, but adjusted of course for seasonal variations and the incremental statistics of the fiscal and revenue arrangements for the forthcoming annual budgetary period terminating in April.

FIRST OFFICIAL (GRAHAM) I think he's talking about taxation.

POLITICIAN Bravo, Madge. Well done. Taxation is the very nub of my gist. Gentlemen, we have to find something new to tax.

SECOND OFFICIAL (ERIC) I understood that.

THIRD OFFICIAL (TERRY J) If I might put my head on the chopping block so you can kick it around a bit, sir...

POLITICIAN Yes?

THIRD OFFICIAL Well most things we do for pleasure nowadays are taxed, except one.

"MP" is a member of Parliament.

"PM" is the prime minister.

"PIB" is nonsense.

"PPS" is the personal private secretary, a sort of aide-de-camp.

"NBG" means "no bloody good."

"Nem con" is short for the Latin *nemine contradicente*, meaning without objection.

A "fag" is a cigarette.

"To go spare" is to go crazy.

POLITICIAN What do you mean?
THIRD OFFICIAL Well, er, smoking's been taxed, drinking's been taxed but not...thingy.
POLITICIAN Good Lord, you're not suggesting we should tax...thingy?
FIRST OFFICIAL Poo poo's?
THIRD OFFICIAL No.
FIRST OFFICIAL Thank God for that. Excuse me for a moment. (*leaves*)
THIRD OFFICIAL No, no, no—thingy.
SECOND OFFICIAL Number ones?
THIRD OFFICIAL No, thingy.
POLITICIAN Thingy!
SECOND OFFICIAL Ah, thingy. Well it'll certainly make chartered accountancy a much more interesting job.

Cut to vox pops.

GUMBY (JOHN) (*standing in water*) I would put a tax on all people who stand in water...(*looks round him*)...Oh! **25**
MAN IN BOWLER HAT (TERRY J) To boost the British economy I'd tax all foreigners living abroad.
MAN IN SUIT (ERIC) I would tax the nude in my bed. No—not tax. What is the word? Oh—welcome.
IT'S MAN (MICHAEL) I would tax Raquel Welch. I've a feeling she'd tax me.
BUSINESS MAN (JOHN) Bring back hanging and go into rope.
SECOND BUSINESS MAN (MICHAEL) I would cut off the more disreputable parts of the body and use the space for playing fields.
MAN IN CAP (MICHAEL) I would tax holiday snaps.

Freeze frame. Cut to snapshot of same still which is being held by a dear old lady. Pull out to reveal she is sitting with a large photo album on her knees, lovingly extracting photos from the piles on top of the album and passing them to her friend sitting on the same settee. Her friend is a young lady, who tears up the photos as they are handed to her. The dear old lady is in a world of her own and does not notice.

DEAR OLD LADY (MARJORIE WILDE) This is Uncle Ted in front of the house. (*she hands over the photo and the young lady tears it up*) This is Uncle Ted at the back of the house. (*she hands over the photo and the young lady tears it up*) And this is Uncle Ted at the side of the house. (*she hands over the photo and the young lady tears it up*) This is Uncle Ted, back again at the front of the house, but you can see the side of the house. (*she hands over the photo and the young lady tears it up*) And this is Uncle Ted even nearer the side of the house, but you can still see the front. (*she hands over the photo and the young lady tears it up*) This is the back of the house, with Uncle Ted coming round the side to the front. (*she hands over the photo and the young lady tears it up*) And this is the Spanish Inquisition hiding behind the coal shed.

Friend takes it with the first sign of real interest.

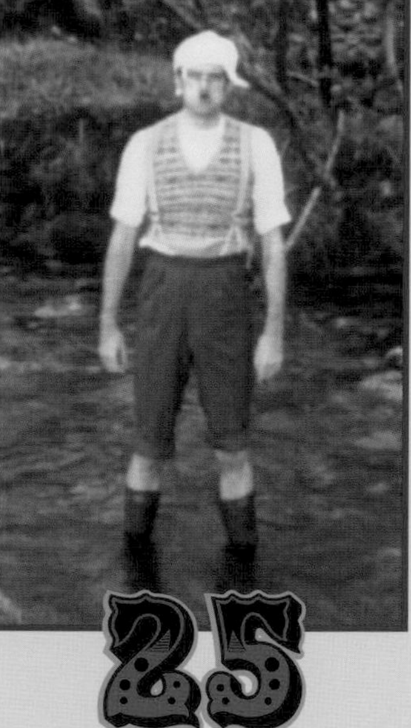

25

Palin explains that the Gumby character was written in Suffolk, in the east of England, and he knew that Cleese had to play him. The first instance came here, with Cleese standing in water. By necessity he had to wear boots, an instance of the costume as afterthought. The paucity of the budget for much of Python often led to Hazel Pethig, the wardrobe manager, having to improvise.

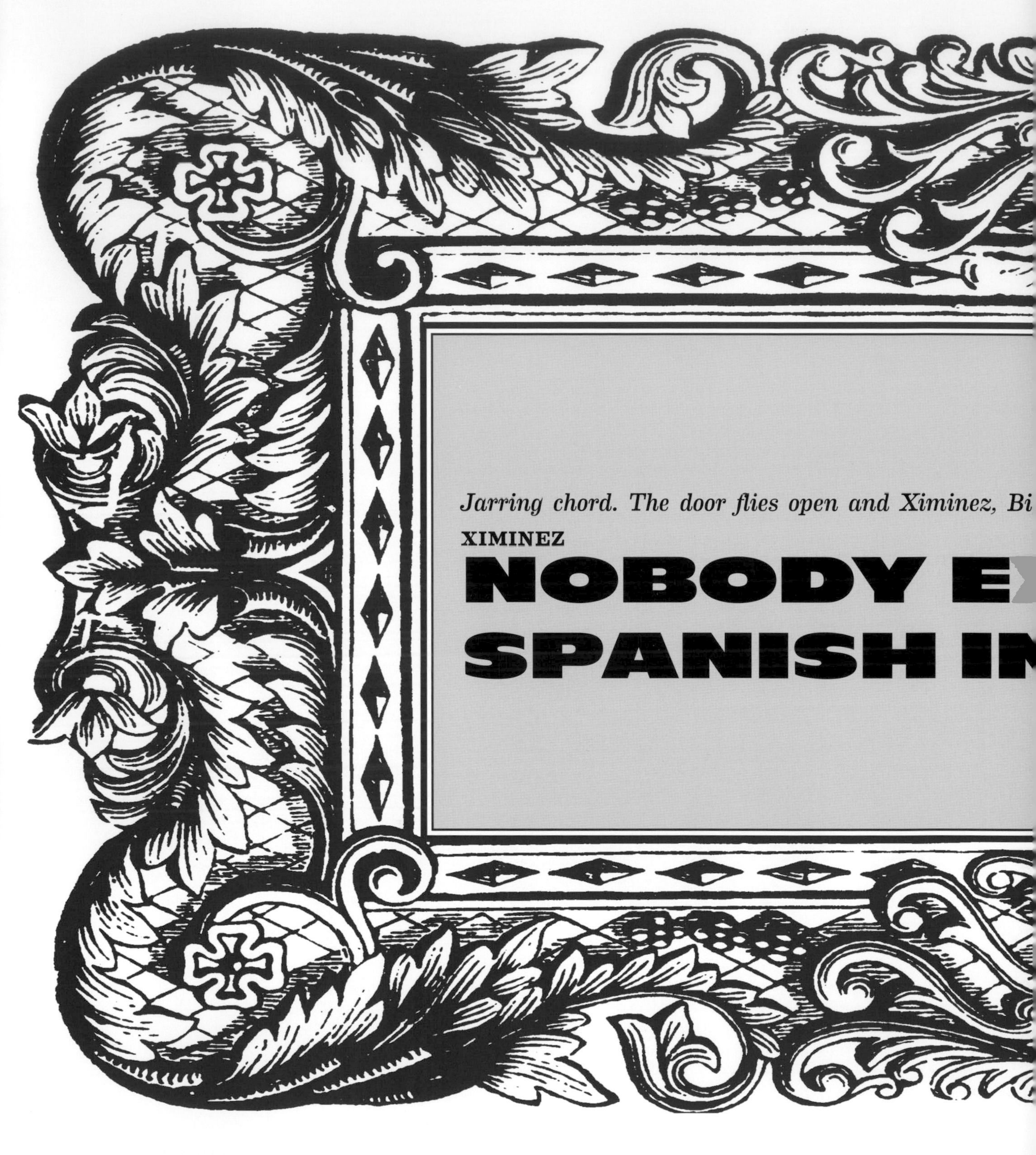

Jarring chord. The door flies open and Ximinez, Bi
XIMINEZ
NOBODY EX
SPANISH IN

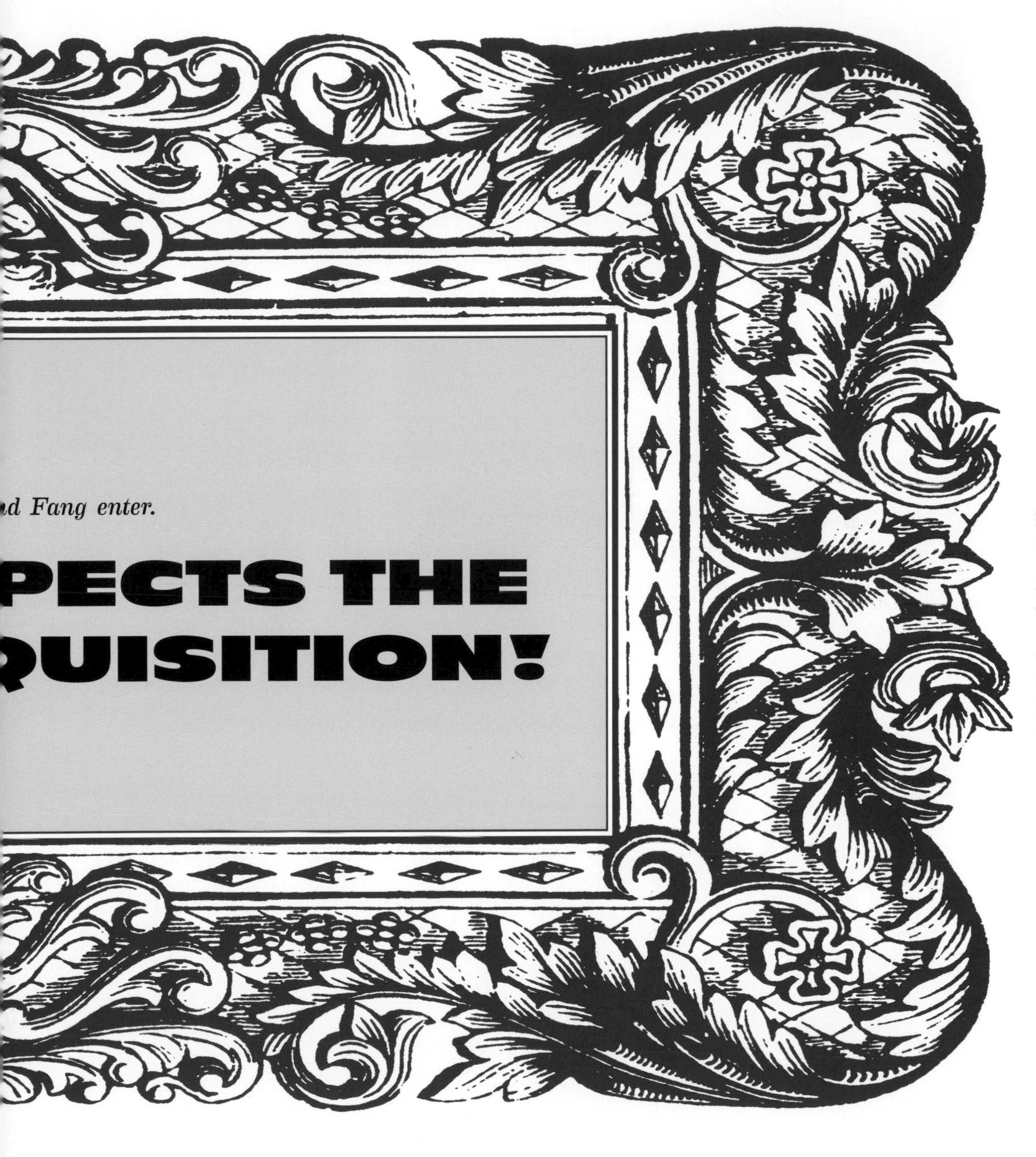

ıd Fang enter.
PECTS THE
QUISITION!

The online Catholic Encyclopedia at newadvent.org states, "The establishment of the Inquisition in Spain has been wrongly attributed to [Ximinez]; it had been in existence fully ten years before his first appearance at Court. As grand inquisitor he initiated several reforms in its working and used every endeavor to reduce the number of cases reserved for its tribunal. He carefully watched the various officers of the Inquisition, lest they should abuse their power by undue violence or oppression, and he arranged and circumscribed the limits of their jurisdiction."

Another reference to Biggles elicits a huge laugh from the audience.

YOUNG LADY (CAROL) Oh! I didn't expect the Spanish Inquisition.

Cut to film: moving over Breugel drawing of tortures; epic film music.

VOICE OVER (JOHN) *(and caption)* 'IN THE EARLY YEARS OF THE SIXTEENTH CENTURY, TO COMBAT THE RISING TIDE OF RELIGIOUS UNORTHODOXY, THE POPE GAVE CARDINAL XIMINEZ OF SPAIN LEAVE TO MOVE WITHOUT LET OR HINDRANCE THROUGHOUT THE LAND, IN A REIGN OF VIOLENCE, TERROR AND TORTURE THAT MAKES A SMASHING FILM. THIS WAS **THE SPANISH INQUISITION...'** 26

Torchlit dungeon. We hear clanging footsteps. Shadows on the Grille. The footsteps stop and keys jangle. The great door creaks open and Ximinez walks in and looks round approvingly. Fang and Biggles enter behind pushing in the dear old lady. They chain her to the wall.

XIMINEZ Now, old woman! You are accused of heresy on three counts. Heresy by thought, heresy by word, heresy by deed, and heresy by action. *Four* counts. Do you confess?

DEAR OLD LADY I don't understand what I'm accused of.

XIMINEZ Ha! Then we shall make you understand...Biggles! **Fetch...the cushions!** 27

Jarring chord. Biggles holds out two ordinary modern household cushions.

BIGGLES Here you are, lord.

XIMINEZ Now, old lady, you have one last chance. Confess the heinous sin of heresy, reject the works of the ungodly—*two* last chances. And you shall be free...*three* last chances. You have three last chances, the nature of which I have divulged in my previous utterance.

DEAR OLD LADY I don't know what you're talking about.

XIMINEZ Right! If that's the way you want it—Cardinal! Poke her with the soft cushions! (*Biggles carries out this rather pathetic torture*) Confess! Confess! Confess!

BIGGLES It doesn't seem to be hurting her, my lord.

XIMINEZ Have you got all the stuffing up one end?

BIGGLES Yes, lord.

XIMINEZ (*angrily hurling away the cushions*) Hm! She's made of harder stuff! Cardinal Fang—fetch...the comfy chair!

Another loud jarring chord. Zoom in on Fang's horrified face.

FANG The comfy chair?

Fang pushes in comfy chair—a really plush one.

XIMINEZ Yes. So you think you are strong because you can survive the soft cushions. Well, we shall see. Biggles, put her in the comfy chair. (*Biggles roughly pushes her into the comfy chair*) **28** Now. You will stay in the comfy chair until lunchtime, with only a cup of coffee at eleven...(*to Biggles*) Is that really all it is?

FANG Why, yes lord.

XIMINEZ I see. I suppose we make it worse by shouting a lot do we? Confess, woman! Confess! Confess! Confess! Confess!

BIGGLES I confess!

XIMINEZ Not you!

ANIMATION VOICE I confess.

XIMINEZ Who was that?

Animation: 'I confess'

VOICE OVER Now for the very first time on the silver screen comes the film from two books which once shocked a generation. From Emily Brontë's 'Wuthering Heights' and from the '**International Guide to Semaphore Code**'. **29**

TWENTIETH CENTURY VOLE PRESENTS 'THE SEMAPHORE VERSION OF WUTHERING HEIGHTS'.

Caption: 'THE SEMAPHORE VERSION OF WUTHERING HEIGHTS' Film: appropriate film music throughout. Heathcliffe (TERRY J) *in close-up profile, his hair is blowing in the wind, he looks intense. Cut to close-up Catherine* (CAROL) *also in profile, with hair streaming in wind. As if they are looking into each other's eyes. Pull out to reveal, on very long zoom, that they are each on the top of separate small hills, in rolling countryside. Heathcliffe produces two semaphore flags from behind him, and waves them. Subtitle: 'OH CATHERINE' Pan across to Catherine who also produces two flags and waves. Subtitle: 'HEATHCLIFFE' Heathcliffe waves*

28

He quite roughly throws her down into the chair, though she continues to smile sweetly.

29

There is an international standard for semaphore (communicating with flags).

flags again. Subtitle: 'OH! OH! CATHERINE' With each cut they are further and further away from each other. Catherine waves flags again. Subtitle: 'OH! OH! HEATHCLIFFE'

Cut to her husband at front door of early Victorian manor house, looking stern. He waves two flags.Subtitle: 'CATHERINE' Cut back to Catherine on hilltop. Subtitle: 'HARK! I HEAR MY HUSBAND' Cut to husband with two enormous flags. Subtitle: 'CATHERINE' Cut to interior of the early Victorian manor house. Close-up of a cradle. Suddenly two little semaphore flags pop up from inside the cradle and wave. Subtitle: 'WAAAAAGH! WAAAAAAGH!' Pull back to reveal a nurse who walks over to cradle and waves flag briefly. Subtitle: 'SSSH!' The nurse points across the room. Cut to shot of old man asleep in chair with head slumped forward on his chest. He has two flags which he waves. Subtitle: 'ZZZ...ZZZ...' Cut to front door again. Exterior. Husband is waiting. Catherine comes up the path towards him. As she approaches he flags. Subtitle: 'YOU'VE BEEN SEEING HEATHCLIFFE'. Catherine waves frantically. Subtitle: 'YES! YES! I'VE BEEN SEEING HEATHCLIFFE, AND WHY NOT? HE'S THE ONLY MAN I EVER LOVED. HE'S FINE. HE'S STRONG. HE'S ALL THE THINGS YOU'LL NEVER BE, AND WHAT'S MORE...' Caption: 'MONDAY FOR 7 DAYS' Stock film of a Roman chariot race.

Shakespeare's *Julius Caesar* was first performed in 1599, though not with a lamp. An Aldis lamp is a lamp used for signaling, named after Arthur W.C. Aldis, who invented a popular kind.

VOICE OVER (MICHAEL) From the pulsating pages of history, from the dark and furious days of Imperial Rome we bring you a story that shattered the world! A tale so gripping that they said it could not be filmed. A unique event in cinema history! Julius Caesar on an Aldis lamp!

Superimposed caption: 'JULIUS CAESAR ON AN ALDIS LAMP' **30** *Close-up of Caesar walking in Roman street. Soothsayer pushes his way up to him wild eyed and produces Aldis lamp and starts flashing: Subtitle: 'BEWARE THE IDES OF MARCH' Some steps at the foot of a statue. Caesar is stabbed. As he falls he brings out a really big Aldis lamp and flashes to the assassins around him. Subtitle: 'ET TU BRUTE'*

A Western street. Two cowboys facing each other with morse buzzers.

VOICE OVER *From the makers of* **'Gunfight at the OK Corral in Morse Code'.** **31** *superimposed caption: 'gunfight at the ok corral in morse code'They buzz a bit.subtitle: 'aaaahhh!'Cut to a Red Indian making smoke signals.*

VOICE OVER And the smoke-signal version of **'Gentlemen Prefer Blondes'!** **32** *Superimposed caption: 'AND THE SMOKE-SIGNAL VERSION OF GENTLEMEN PREFER BLONDES' Cut to a courtroom: Usual set up with a judge, clerk of the court and defence counsel sitting in the well of the court. The defendant is in the witness box. Superimposed caption: 'CENTRAL CRIMINAL COURT'*

JUDGE (GRAHAM) Ladies and gentlemen of the jury, have you reached a verdict?

FOREMAN (MICHAEL) We have **m'lud.** **33**

JUDGE And how do you find the defendant? ***(the foreman puts his hand out with two fingers extended)*** **34** Two words. *(the foreman nods and holds up one finger)* First word. *(the foreman mimes taking a piece of string and tying it in knot)* Rope? String? *(The foreman shakes his head and points to the knot.)*

COUNSEL (JOHN) Point?

CLERK (ERIC) Belt?

JUDGE Tie?

The foreman nods and points to the knot.

COUNSEL Cravat? Silk square?

CLERK Knot?

The foreman nods enthusiastically.

ALL Knot!

The foreman gives a thumbs up and points to his second finger.

JUDGE Second word. *(foreman indicates two syllables)* Two syllables. *(the foreman points to his first finger)* First syllable. *(the foreman starts to mime a fish while pointing at his throat)* Bird?

CLERK Swimmer?

JUDGE Breast stroke.

COUNSEL **Brian Phelps.** **35**

JUDGE No, no, no, he was a diver.

CLERK **Esther Williams then.** **36**

JUDGE No, no, don't be silly. How can you find someone 'Not Esther Williams'.

COUNSEL Fish. *(the foreman nods and points at throat)* Fish wheeze. Fish wheeze?

Gunfight at the O.K. Corral is a 1957 movie starring Burt Lancaster and Kirk Douglas.

Gentlemen Prefer Blondes is the seminal 1953 movie (of the 1949 musical) starring Jane Russell and Marilyn Monroe and featuring, among other songs, "Diamonds Are a Girl's Best Friend."

"M'lud" is British slang for "my lord."

A fantastic game of charades ensues.

Brian Phelps won the bronze medal in the ten-meter platform dive at the 1960 Olympics. (In April 2008 he pleaded guilty to 42 charges of indecent assault and indecency against young girls. He was sentenced to nine years in jail.)

Esther Williams is the American swimmer and movie star.

JUDGE Fish breathe.
COUNSEL Fish breathe, throat.
JUDGE Fish breathe, throat? GILL! (*the foreman gives a thumbs up and the court applauds excitedly*) Not gill. (*the foreman mimes the second syllable*) Second syllable. Not gill.

Foreman mimes drinking a cup of tea.

COUNSEL Drink.
CLERK Sip? Imbibe?

The foreman points to the mimed cup itself.

JUDGE Not gill...cup? Not gillcup! (*the foreman looks disappointed*) You have been found not gillcup of the charges made against you and may leave this court a free man. Right. My turn. (*the defendant leaves*)

The judge holds up four fingers.

COUNSEL Four words.

The judge mimes shouting for the first word.

FOREMAN First word shout?
COUNSEL Bellow?
CLERK Call?
ALL Call!

The judge gives a thumbs up and indicates that the second word is very small.

COUNSEL Second word is very small.
FOREMAN A?
COUNSEL An?
CLERK Up?
FOREMAN The?

The judge gives a thumbs up.

ALL The!
CLERK Call the, third word.

The judge points to his neck.

COUNSEL Gill?
MEMBER OF JURY Fish?
CLERK Adam's apple. (*the judge shakes his head*) Neck. (*the judge mimes 'sounds like'*) Sounds like neck?
SECOND COUNSEL Next.
FOREMAN Call the...next!

The judge gives a thumbs up and indicates that the fourth word is three syllables. First syllable: he mimes deafness.

CLERK Fourth word, three syllables. First syllable...ear?
COUNSEL Hear. Can't hear.

CLERK Deaf!!! Call the next def-.

The judge leaps onto the desk and points at his own bottom.

COUNSEL Bottom.
CLERK Seat? Trouser? Cheek?
FOREMAN End! Call the next defend-.

The judge leaps down, disappears under the desk and appears with an enormous model of an ant about four feet long.

WHOLE COURT Ant!
CLERK Call the next defendant! (*the court applauds the judge who bows and sits: the whole mood changes*) Call the next defendant. The Honourable Mr Justice Kilbraken. (*a very elderly judge in full robes comes into the dock*) If I may charge you m'lud, you are charged m'lud that on the fourteenth day of June 1970, at the Central Criminal Court, you did commit acts likely to cause a breach of the peace. How plead you m'lud, guilty or not guilty?
JUDGE KILBRAKEN (TERRY J) Not guilty. Case not proven. Court adjourned.

He hits the dock. Everyone gets up and starts walking out talking to each other.

JUDGE No, no, no, no, no, no, no. (*they all stop, go back and sit down again*) No, you're in the dock, m'lud.
JUDGE KILBRAKEN I'm a judge, m'lud.
JUDGE So am I, m'lud, so watch it.
JUDGE KILBRAKEN Hah! Call this a court.
ALL Call this a court. Call this a court. Call this a court.
JUDGE Shut up. Right now get on with the spiel.
COUNSEL M'lud, and my other lud, the prosecution will endeavour to show m'lud, that m'lud—ah, not *you* m'lud, that m'lud, m'lud, while passing sentence at the Central Criminal Court **blotted his copy book.** **37** Call exhibit Q.
JUDGE Q?
COUNSEL Sorry did I say Q? I meant A. Sorry, call exhibit A.
CLERK Call exhibit A.

Two court ushers carry in a thing with a sheet over it. They pull off the sheet to reveal a very sexy girl in a provocative pose. The court applauds.

"Blotted his copybook" is a British for doing something to ruin your reputation.

Belsize Park is a well-to-do section of London, beloved by celebrities (Glenda Jackson, a former actress, is currently the Member of Parliament for the area).

This address does not exist.

A "bit" is slang for a woman of romantic interest, probably kept on the side.

The death sentence for murder was abolished in the U.K. in 1969. Capital punishment was abolished altogether in 1998.

COUNSEL Exhibit A m'lud, Miss Rita Thang, an artist's model, Swedish accordian teacher and cane-chair sales lady, was found guilty under the Rude Behaviour Act in the accused's court. The accused, m'lud, sentenced her 'to be taken from this place and brought round to his place'.

OTHER COUNSEL Objection, m'lud.

JUDGE KILBRAKEN Objection sustained.

JUDGE You shut up! Objection overruled.

COUNSEL The accused then commented on Miss Thang's bodily structure, made several not-at-all legal remarks on the subject of fun and then placed his robes over his head and began to emit low moans.

JUDGE Have you anything to say in your defence?

JUDGE KILBRAKEN I haven't had any for weeks.

JUDGE Oh no? What about that little number you've got tucked away in **Belsize Park?** 38

JUDGE KILBRAKEN Oh, I never!

JUDGE Oh no. Ho! Ho! Ho!

JUDGE KILBRAKEN All right then what about **8A Woodford Square?** 39

JUDGE You say anything about that and I'll do you for treason.

COUNSEL M'lud if we could continue...

JUDGE KILBRAKEN **He's got a Chinese bit there.** 40

JUDGE No, that's contempt of court.

JUDGE KILBRAKEN It was only a joke.

JUDGE Contempt of court. However, I'm not going to punish you, because we're so short of judges at the moment, what with all of them emigrating to South Africa. I'm going tomorrow; I've got my ticket. Get out there and get some decent sentencing done. Ooh, England makes you sick. **Best I can manage here is life imprisonment.** 41 It's hardly worth coming in in the morning. Now, South Africa? You've got your cat of nine tails, you've got four death sentences a week, you've got cheap drinks, slave labour and a booming stock market. I'm off, I tell you. Yes, I'm up to here with probation and bleeding psychiatric reports. That's it, I'm off. That's it. Right. Well I'm going to have one final fling before I leave, **so I sentence you to be burnt at the stake.** 42

JUDGE KILBRAKEN

BLIMEY! I DIDN'T EXPECT THE SPANISH INQUISITION.

Chapman does the traditional thing of placing a square of black cloth over his wig—a sign that the death penalty is about to be applied.

Court reacts expectantly. Cut to suburban house. The three members of the Spanish Inquisition suddenly belt out of the door and down the path.

Dick Barton music. Cut to them leaping onto a bus.

XIMINEZ **Two, er, three to the Old Bailey please. 43**

Credits start superimposed.

BIGGLES Look they've started the credits.

XIMINEZ Hurry. Hurry. Hurry.
BIGGLES Come on hurry. Hurry!

We see shots of them coming through London.

XIMINEZ There's the lighting credit, only five left. (*more shots of the bus going through London; the credits reach the producer*) Hell, it's the producer—quick!

They leap off the bus into the Old Bailey. Cut to court room. They burst in.

XIMINEZ Nobody expects the Spanish...(*'The End' appears*) Oh bugger!

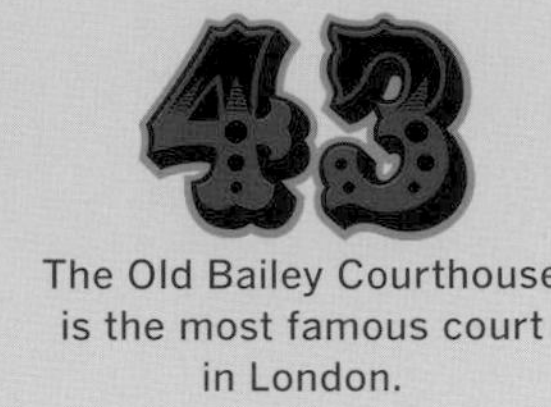

The Old Bailey Courthouse is the most famous court in London.

SEA SON 2
EPISODE 16

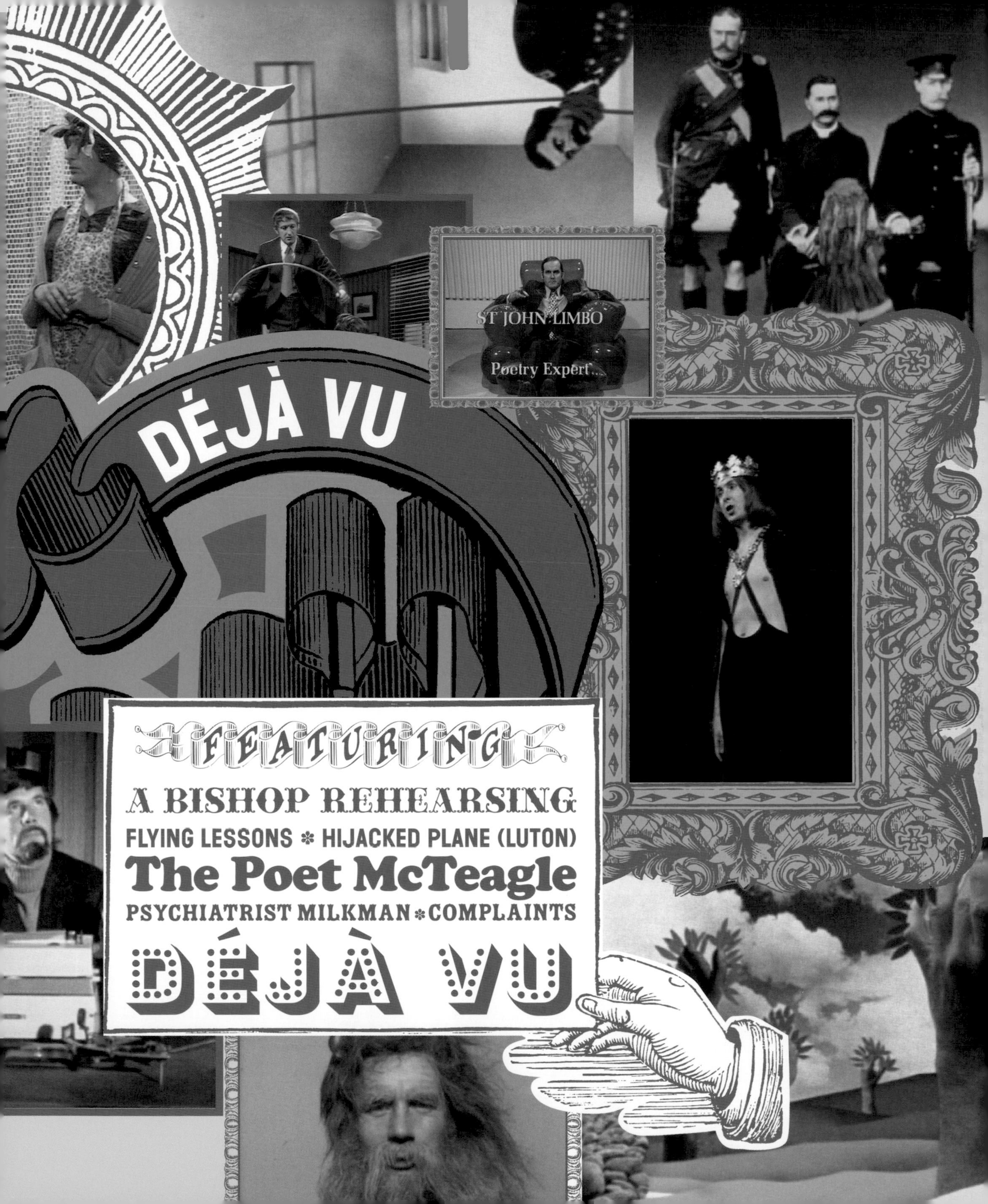
ST JOHN LIMBO
Poetry Expert...
DÉJÀ VU
FEATURING
A BISHOP REHEARSING
FLYING LESSONS ✽ HIJACKED PLANE (LUTON)
The Poet McTeagle
PSYCHIATRIST MILKMAN ✽ COMPLAINTS
DÉJÀ VU

FIRST AIRED: SEPTEMBER 29, 1970

Wide shot of enormous high block of flats. The camera seems to be searching. Suddenly it zooms in on one window. It is a bedroom...a busty girl is looking out of the window. She stretches languorously and mouths.

GIRL (CAROL) (*dubbed on very badly*) My, isn't it hot in here.

She starts to undress. She gets down to bra and panties, unhitches her bra and is about to slip it off her shoulders exposing her heavy bosoms when... ***the announcer rises up in front of the window on window cleaner's hoist.*** [1]

1

Cleese displays a certain bravery here—he's high up and on a very wobbly platform.

ANNOUNCER (JOHN) And now for something completely different.

Cut to an orchard or a woodland clearing, in which are a group of stuffed animals; a lion, a tiger, a cow, an elk, a leopard, two small ferrets and an owl on an overhanging branch. Sound of birdsong. The elk explodes. Cut back to John still in front of the window. We can just see Carol behind him in bedroom casting her panties to one side—that is we just see her arm.

ANNOUNCER And now for something more completely different...

Cut to 'It's' man.

IT'S MAN (MICHAEL)

IT'S...

Animated titles.

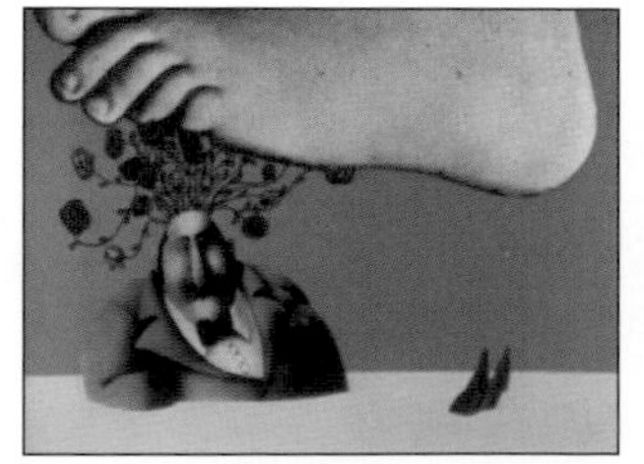

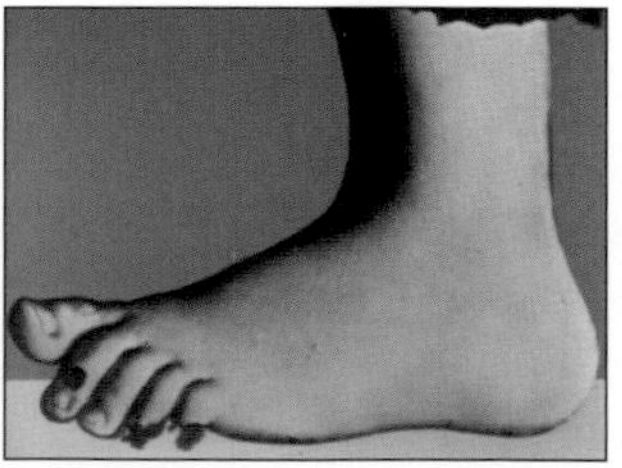

Cut back to the same group of animals minus the elk. Birdsong etc. The elk's remains are smouldering. The owl explodes. Pan away from the woodland clearing to an open field in which at a distance a bishop in full mitre and robes is pacing up and down holding a script. Mr Chigger in a suit approaches the bishop and we zoom in to hear their conversation.

BISHOP (MICHAEL) 'Oh Mr Belpit your legs are so swollen'...*swollen*...'Oh Mr Belpit—oh Mr Belpit your legs are so swollen'. (*tries a different voice*) 'Oh Mr Belpit...'

MR CHIGGER (TERRY J) Excuse me, excuse me. I saw your advertisement for flying lessons and I'd like to make an application.
BISHOP Nothing to do with me. I'm not in this show.
MR CHIGGER Oh I see. D'you...d'you...do you know about the flying lessons?
BISHOP

NOTHING TO DO WITH ME. I'M NOT IN
THIS SHOW. THIS IS SHOW FIVE—I'M NOT
IN UNTIL SHOW EIGHT.

MR CHIGGER Oh I see.
BISHOP I'm just learning my lines, you know. 'Oh Mr Belpit, your legs...'
MR CHIGGER Bit awkward, I'm a bit stuck.
BISHOP Yes, well. Try over there.

Bishop points to a secretary some yards away sitting at a desk typing. She wears glasses and is very typically a secretary.

MR CHIGGER Oh yes, thanks. Thanks a lot.
BISHOP 'Oh Mr Belpit'—not at all—'your legs are so swollen'. (*he continues rehearsing as Mr Chigger moves over to the secretary*)
MR CHIGGER Excuse me, I saw your advertisement for flying lessons and I'd like to make an application.
SECRETARY (CAROL) Appointment? 2
MR CHIGGER Yes, yes.
SECRETARY Certainly. Would you come this way, please.

She gets up, clutching a file and trips off in a typical efficient secretary's walk. Mr Chigger follows. Cut to a river. She goes straight in without looking to right or left, as if she does this routine as a matter of course. Mr Chigger follows. Halfway across the river they pass a couple of business executives hurrying in the opposite direction.

SECRETARY Morning, Mr Jones, Mr Barnes. 3

2

Carol Cleveland seems to correct Terry Jones here, rather than ask him a question; evidence for this is that he gets the line correct later in the sketch, without prompting.

3

Gumby was standing in the middle of a river—and felt such behavior should be taxed—in Episode 15.

Cut to a forest. They come past towards camera, passing a tea trolley on the way with a tea lady and a couple of men round it.

SECRETARY Morning Mrs Wills.
MRS WILLS (MICHAEL) Morning, luv.

Evening. Arty shot. Skyline of a short sharp hill, as in Bergman's 'Seventh Seal'. **4** *They come in frame right and up and over, passing two men and exchanging 'good mornings'. Cut to seashore. Tripping along, they pass another executive.*

EXECUTIVE Take this to Marketing, would you.

They disappear into a cave. We hear footsteps and a heavy door opening.

SECRETARY'S VOICE Just follow me.
MR CHIGGER'S VOICE Oh thank you.

Cut to a shopping street. Camera pans in close-up across road surface.

SECRETARY'S VOICE Oh, be careful.
MR CHIGGER'S VOICE Yes, nearly tripped.
SECRETARY'S VOICE Be there soon.
MR CHIGGER'S VOICE Good. It's a long way, isn't it?
SECRETARY'S VOICE Oh, get hold of that—watch it.
VOICE Morning.
SECRETARY'S VOICE Morning. Upstairs. Be careful, it's very steep. Almost there.

Camera reaches a GPO tent in middle of road. **5**

VOICE Morning.
SECRETARY Morning. (*they emerge from the tent*) Will you come this way, please. (*cut to interior office, another identical secretary at the desk*) In here, please.
MR CHIGGER Thank you. (*he enters and first secretary trips off; he approaches the second secretary*) Hello, I saw your advertisement for flying lessons and I'd like to make an appointment.
SECOND SECRETARY Well, Mr Anemone's on the phone at the moment, but I'm sure he won't mind if you go on in. Through here.
MR CHIGGER Thank you.

He goes through door. Mr Anemone is suspended by a wire about nine feet off the ground. He is on the telephone.

MR ANEMONE (GRAHAM) Ah, won't be a moment. Make yourself at home. (*into phone*) No, no, well look, you can ask Mr Maudling **6** but I'm sure he'll never agree. Not for fifty shillings... no...no. Bye-bye Gordon. Bye-bye. Oh dear. Bye-bye. (*he throws receiver at telephone but misses*) Missed. Now Mr er...
MR CHIGGER Chigger.
MR ANEMONE Mr Chigger. So, you want to learn to fly. **7**
MR CHIGGER Yes.
MR ANEMONE

RIGHT, WELL, UP ON THE TABLE, ARMS OUT, FINGERS TOGETHER, KNEES BENT...

MR CHIGGER No, no, no.

Though *The Seventh Seal* clearly is a favorite Python visual reference, it doesn't appear in the episode after all.

"GPO" is the General Post Office, the age-old Department of State that included the postal service, the telephone system, and other forms of communication. It was disbanded in 1969, when the Post Office was established as a statutory corporation. Their little work huts, as shown here, were a standard part of British life at the time.

"Mr. Maudling" is a reference to Reginald Maudling, the Conservative Party minister regularly unbeloved by the Pythons.

Chapman seems to do his very best John Cleese impersonation in this sketch, right down to the voice and out-of-the-blue violent talk.

MR ANEMONE *(very loudly)* Up on the table! *(Mr Chigger gets on the table)* Arms out, fingers together, knees bent, now, head well forward. Now, flap your arms. Go on, flap, faster...faster...faster... faster, faster, faster, faster—now jump! *(Mr Chigger jumps and lands on the floor)* Rotten. Rotten. You're no bloody use at all. You're an utter bloody wash-out. You make me sick, you weed!

MR CHIGGER Now look here...

MR ANEMONE All right, all right. I'll give you one more chance, get on the table...

MR CHIGGER Look, I came here to learn how to fly an aeroplane.

MR ANEMONE A what?

MR CHIGGER I came here to learn how to fly an aeroplane.

MR ANEMONE *(sarcastically)* Oh, 'an aeroplane'. Oh, I say, we are grand, aren't we? *(imitation posh accent)* 'Oh, oh, no more buttered scones **8** for me, mater. I'm off to play the grand piano'. 'Pardon me while I fly my aeroplane.' Now get on the table!

MR CHIGGER Look. No one in the history of the world has ever been able to fly like that.

MR ANEMONE Oh, I suppose mater told you that while you were out riding. Well, if people can't fly what am I doing up here?

MR CHIGGER You're on a wire.

MR ANEMONE Oh, a wire. I'm on a wire, am I?

MR CHIGGER Of course you're on a bloody wire.

MR ANEMONE I am *not* on a wire. I am flying.

MR CHIGGER You're on a wire.

MR ANEMONE I am flying.

MR CHIGGER You're on a wire.

MR ANEMONE I'll show you whether I'm on a wire or not. Give me the 'oop.

MR CHIGGER What?

MR ANEMONE Oh, I don't suppose we know what an 'oop is. I suppose pater **9** thought they were a bit common, except on the bleedin' croquet lawn. **10**

MR CHIGGER Oh, a *hoop.*

MR ANEMONE 'Oh an hoop.' *(taking hoop)* Thank you, your bleeding Highness. Now. Look. *(he waves hoop over head and feet)*

MR CHIGGER Go on, right the way along.

MR ANEMONE All right, all right, all right. *(he moves hoop all the way along himself allowing the wire to pass through obvious gap in hoop's circumference)* Now, where's the bleeding wire, then?

MR CHIGGER That hoop's got a hole in.

MR ANEMONE Oh Eton and Madgalene. **11** The ***h***oop has an ***h***ole in. Of course it's got a hole in, it wouldn't be a hoop otherwise, would it, mush!

MR CHIGGER No, there's a gap in the middle, there.

MR ANEMONE Oh, a gahp. A gahp in one's hhhhhoop. Pardon me, but I'm orf to play the grahnd piano.

Chapman comes down on the side of people who pronounce a long *o* in *scones* (the split in Britain is exactly fifty-fifty). Also, British people who refer to their mothers as "mater" tend to be from the upper classes.

Those who refer to their fathers as "pater" tend to be from the upper classes too.

Croquet is the classic sport of the upper echelons. The "hoop" is the thing through which the ball must be hit.

Eton College is the premier boys' school in England, and Magdalen College is Oxford University's most exclusive college. Someone going from Eton to Magdalen would tend to be from a privileged background.

Idle sports a fantastic mustache here, spanning from one ear to the other.

The British Airline Pilots Association is a real organization, founded in 1937.

Tommy Cooper was a beloved Welsh comedian who wore a red fez and was comically unable to work his many props. He never appeared on *Sherlock Holmes*, which highlights the joke about the BALPA man being a fusspot who gets his facts wrong.

The High Chaparral was an American Western TV show that aired from 1967 to 1971.

A popular 1960s singer, Kathy Kirby never appeared on *The High Chaparral*, and never sang a song called "Fly Me to the Stars."

MR CHIGGER Look, I can see you're on a wire—look, there it is.
MR ANEMONE Look, I told you, you bastard, I'm not on a wire.
MR CHIGGER You are. There is.
MR ANEMONE There isn't.
MR CHIGGER Is.
MR ANEMONE Isn't!
MR CHIGGER Is!
MR ANEMONE Isn't!
MR CHIGGER Is!
MR ANEMONE Isn't!
MR CHIGGER Is!
MR ANEMONE Isn't!!
MR CHIGGER Is!!!
VOICE OVER (JOHN) Anyway, this rather pointless bickering went on for some time until...

Caption: 'TWO YEARS LATER' Interior cockpit of airliner. Mr chigger (pilot) and a second pilot sitting at controls.

PILOT Gosh, I am glad I'm a fully qualified airline pilot.

*Cut to BALPA spokesman sitting at a desk. He is in Captain's uniform and has a name plate in front of him on the desk saying '**BALPA Spokesman**'.* 12

BALPA MAN (ERIC) **The British Airline Pilots Association** would like to point out that it takes a chap six years to become a fully qualified airline pilot, and not two. 13

Caption: 'FOUR YEARS LATER THAN THE LAST CAPTION' Interior cockpit. For three seconds. Then cut back to BALPA spokesman.

BALPA MAN Thank you. I didn't want to seem a bit of an old fusspot just now you know, but it's just as easy to get these things right as they are easily found in the BALPA handbook. Oh, one other thing, in the Sherlock Holmes last week **Tommy Cooper** 14 told a joke about a charter flight, omitting to point out that one must be a member of any organization that charters a plane for at least six months beforehand, before being able to take advantage of it. Did rather spoil the joke for me, I'm afraid. (*phone rings*) Yes, ah yes—yes. (*puts phone down*) My wife just reminded me that on a recent '**High Chaparral**' 15 Kathy Kirby was singing glibly about '**Fly me to the Stars**' 16 when of course there are no scheduled flights of this kind, or even chartered, available to the general public at the present moment, although of course, when they are BALPA will be in the vanguard. Or the Trident. Little joke for the chaps up at BALPA House. And one other small point. Why is it that these new lurex dancing tights go baggy at the knees after only a couple of evenings' fun. Bring back the old canvas ones I say. It is incredible, isn't it, that in these days when man can walk on the moon and work out the most complicated hire purchase agreements, I still get these terrible headaches. Well...I seem to have wandered a bit, but still, no harm done. Jolly good luck.

Back in the cockpit of the airliner. The two pilots sit there. Atmospheric noise of a big airliner in flight. Suddenly there is a banging on the door at the back of the cockpit.

ZANIE (GRAHAM) (*off-screen*) Are you going to be in there all day? (*the two pilots exchange a puzzled look, then shrug and go back to flying; suddenly another series of bangs on door*) Other people want to go you know! (*they exchange another look; pause; a heavier bang on the door*) The door's jammed, if you ask me. (*a crash as he attempts to force it; another crash and the door flies open;*

Mr Zanie enters) Ah. (*suddenly realizing where he is*) Oh my God. Oh, I'm terribly sorry. I **thought this was the bally toilet.** **17**

SECOND PILOT (JOHN) This is the control cabin.

ZANIE Oh I know. I'm a flying man, you know...oh yes...Bally stupid mistake...

A pause. Zanie remains standing at the back of cockpit. The pilots go on as if he is not there.

SECOND PILOT Cloud's heavy...What's the reading?

PILOT 4.8...Steady.

ZANIE If they had all those dials in the toilet...there wouldn't be room for anything else, would there. (*another nervous laugh; not the slightest reaction from the pilots*)

PILOT (*into intercom*) Hello, Geneva this is Roger Five-O...What is your cloud reading? Hello, Geneva...

ZANIE I wouldn't fancy flying one of those sitting on the toilet...I mean it'd take the glamour out of being a pilot, wouldn't it, ha ha, flying around the world sitting on a toilet.

RADIO VOICE Geneva here. 4.9...Heavy...Over.

PILOT Serious?

SECOND PILOT No, not if it keeps at that level, no.

ZANIE Mind you, if you did fly it from the toilet it would leave a lot more space up here, wouldn't it. (*finally he realizes his attempt at small talk is not working*) Well, I'd better get back to the cabin, then. Sorry about the silly intrusion. Bally stupid. (*he pushes lever down on the door which opens directly out of the plane*) Door's jammed. (*he gives it a shoulder charge and flies straight out of the plane*) Aaaaaaaaaaarrrrrrrrrghhhhhh!

Plane noise overhead. Continue scream. Outside of a gent's lavatory, there is a big pile of straw. Pause, then Zanie drops onto the straw. He looks up at gent's sign.

ZANIE Bally piece of luck...

He brushes himself down and goes into gents. Cut back to cockpit. A hostess enters from the passenger cabin.

SECOND PILOT Oh hello. Everything all right at the back?

HOSTESS (CAROL) Yes, they're as quiet as dormice.

SECOND PILOT Dormice?

Door opens and a man in a neat suit enters. From beneath his jacket he produces a revolver with silencer attachment. He points it at the pilots.

For those Britons who believed "bloody" too strong a curse, there was always its derivative: "bally."

GUNMAN (MICHAEL)

ALL RIGHT, DON'T ANYBODY MOVE...EXCEPT TO CONTROL THE AEROPLANE...YOU CAN MOVE A LITTLE TO DO THAT.

HOSTESS Can I move?

GUNMAN Yes, yes, yes. You can move a little bit. Yes. Sorry, I didn't mean to be so dogmatic when I came in. Obviously you can all move a little within reason. There are certain involuntary muscular movements which no amount of self-control can prevent. And obviously any assertion of authority on my part, I've got to take that into account.

The ensuing conversation is perfectly calm and friendly.

SECOND PILOT Right. I mean one couldn't for example, stop one's insides from moving.

GUNMAN No, no. Good point, good point.

SECOND PILOT And the very fact that the plane is continuously vibrating means that we're all moving to a certain extent.

GUNMAN And we're all moving our lips, aren't we?

PILOTS Yes, yes.

SECOND PILOT Absolutely.

GUNMAN No, the gist of my meaning was that sudden...er...

HOSTESS Exaggerated movements...

GUNMAN Exaggerated *violent* movements...are...are out.

SECOND PILOT Well, that's the great thing about these modern airliners. I mean, I can keep this plane flying with only the smallest movement and Pancho here doesn't have to move at all.

GUNMAN Oh, that's marvellous.

HOSTESS (*joining in the general spirit of bonhomie*) And I don't really need to move either...unless I get an itch or something...

They all laugh.

GUNMAN Well that's wonderful...60% success, eh? (*they laugh again*) Anyway, bearing all that in mind, will you fly the plane to Luton, please? **18**

SECOND PILOT Well, this is a scheduled flight to Cuba. **19**

GUNMAN I know, I know, that's rather why I came in here with that point about nobody moving.

PILOT Within reason.

GUNMAN Within reason—yes. I...er...er...you know, I want you to fly this plane to Luton...please.

SECOND PILOT Right, well I'd better turn the plane round then. Stand by emergency systems.

GUNMAN Look I don't want to cause any trouble.

SECOND PILOT No, no, we'll manage, we'll manage.

GUNMAN I mean, *near* Luton will do, you know. Harpenden, do you go near Harpenden? **20**

PILOT It's on the flight path.

GUNMAN Okay, well, drop me off there. I'll get a bus to Luton. It's only twenty-five minutes.

HOSTESS You can be in Luton by lunchtime.

GUNMAN Oh, well that's smashing.

FIRST PILOT Hang on! There's no airport at Harpenden.

GUNMAN Oh well, look, forget it. Forget it. I'll come to Cuba, and get a flight back to Luton from there.

SECOND PILOT Well, we could lend you a parachute.

GUNMAN No, no, no, no, no. I wouldn't dream of it...wouldn't dream of it...dirtying a nice, clean parachute.

PILOT I know—I know. There's a bale of hay outside Basingstoke. **21** We could throw you out.

GUNMAN Well, if it's all right.

Another reference to Luton Airport, north of London. It was often used as a punch line, given it is smaller and more provincial than Heathrow.

The joke being that hijackers would tend to *want* to go to Cuba rather than the real destination, yet this plane's already on the way.

Harpenden is a small town about five miles south of Luton Airport.

Basingstoke is a town about 70 miles southwest of Luton Airport.

ALL Sure, yeah.
GUNMAN Not any trouble?
PILOTS None at all.
GUNMAN That's marvellous. Thank you very much. Sorry to come barging in.
HOSTESS Bye-bye.
GUNMAN Thank you. Bye.
PILOTS Bye.

They open the door and throw him out.

GUNMAN (*as he falls*) Thank you!

Cut to haystack in a field (not the same bale of hay that was landed on before). Aeroplane noise overhead. The gunman suddenly falls into the haystack. He gets up, brushes himself down, hops over a fence, and reaches a road. He puts his hand out and a bus stops. It has 'Straight to Luton' written on it. He gets in. Conductor is just about to take his fare, when an evil-looking man with a gun jumps up and points gun at conductor. 22

MAN (JOHN) Take this bus to Cuba.

Bus moving away from camera. The destination board changes to 'Straight to Cuba'. The bus does a speeded up u-turn, and goes out of frame. Camera pans away revealing a rather rocky highland landscape. As camera pans across country we hear inspiring Scottish music.

VOICE OVER (JOHN) From these glens and scars, the sound of the coot and the moorhen is seldom absent. Nature sits in stern mastery over these rocks and crags. The rush of the mountain stream, the bleat of the sheep, and the broad, clear Highland skies, reflected in tarn and loch...(*at this moment we pick up a highland gentleman in kilt and tam o'shanter clutching a knobkerry in one hand and a letter in the other*)...form a breathtaking backdrop against which Ewan McTeagle writes such poems as 'Lend us a quid till the end of the week'.

Cut to crofter's cottage. 23 *McTeagle sits at the window writing. We zoom in very slowly on him as he writes.*

VOICE OVER But it was with more simple, homespun verses that McTeagle's unique style first flowered.

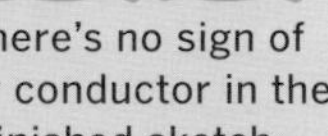

There's no sign of any conductor in the finished sketch.

This is the same cottage that was featured in Episode 7, in which the massive orders for kilts from outer space were discussed.

"Bob" is slang for a shilling.

"Skint" is slang for having no money.

A postal order is the way in which Britons send money to one another through the mail, like a money order.

A "pouffe" tends to be a footstool, beloved of all Britons at all times, though Cleese is actually sitting on a massive (and hilarious) blue inflatable chair.

28

Ian McKellan, the great British Shakespearean (and other stuff) actor.

29

"Right on my uppers" means to have no money.

MCTEAGLE (TERRY J) (*voice over*) If you could see your way to lending me sixpence. I could at least buy a newspaper. That's not much to ask anyone.

VOICE OVER One woman who remembers McTeagle as a young friend—Lassie O'Shea.

Cut to Lassie O'Shea—a young sweet innocent Scots girl—she is valiantly trying to fend off the sexual advances of the sound man. Two other members of the crew pull him out of shot.

LASSIE (ERIC) Mr McTeagle wrote me two poems, between the months of January and April 1969...

INTERVIEWER Could you read us one?

LASSIE Och, I dinna like to...they were kinda personal...but I will. (*she has immediately a piece of paper in her hand from which she reads*) 'To Ma Own beloved Lassie. A poem on her 17th Birthday. Lend us a couple of **bob** 24 till Thursday. I'm absolutely **skint**. 25 But I'm expecting a **postal order** 26 and I can pay you back as soon as it comes. Love Ewan.'

There is a pause. She looks up.

SOUND MAN (*voice over*) Beautiful.

*Another pause. The soundman leaps on her and pulls her to the ground. Cut to abstract trendy arts poetry programme set. **Intense critic sits on enormous inflatable see-through pouffe.** 27 Caption: 'ST JOHN LIMBO—POETRY EXPERT'*

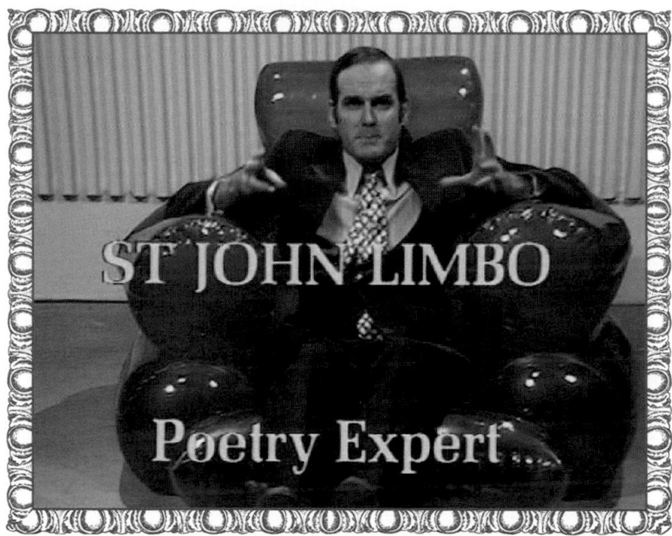

LIMBO (JOHN) (*intensely*) Since then, McTeagle has developed and widened his literary scope. Three years ago he concerned himself with quite small sums—quick bits of ready cash: sixpences, shillings, but more recently he has turned his extraordinary literary perception to much larger sums—fifteen shillings, £4.12.6d...even nine guineas... But there is still nothing to match the huge swoop the majestic power of what is surely his greatest work: 'Can I have fifty pounds to mend the shed?'.

*Pan across studio to a stark poetry-reading set. **A single light falls on an Ian McKellan figure in black leotard standing gazing dramatically into space.** 28 Camera crabs across studio until it is right underneath him. He speaks the lines with great intensity.*

IAN (ERIC) Can I have £50 to mend the shed? I'm **right on my uppers.** 29 I can pay you back When this postal order comes from Australia. Honestly. Hope the bladder trouble's getting better. Love, Ewan.

Cut to remote Scottish landscape, craggy and windtorn and desolate. In stark chiaroscuro against the sky we see McTeagle standing beside a lonely pillar box, writing postcards. The sun setting behind him. 30

CRITIC (*voice over*) There seems to be no end to McTeagle's poetic invention. 'My new cheque book hasn't arrived' was followed up by the brilliantly allegorical 'What's twenty quid to the bloody Midland Bank?' and more recently his prizewinning poem to the Arts Council: 'Can you lend me one thousand quid?'

Cut to David Mercer figure in his study at a desk. 31 *Caption: 'A VERY GOOD PLAYWRIGHT'*

DAVID (MICHAEL) I think what McTeagle's pottery...er...poetry is doing is *rejecting* all the traditional clichés of modern pottery. No longer do we have to be content with Keats's 'Seasons of mists and mellow fruitfulness', 32 Wordsworth's 'I wandered lonely as a cloud' 33 and Milton's 'Can you lend us two bob till Tuesday'... 34 *Cut to long shot of McTeagle walking through countryside.*

MCTEAGLE (*voice over*) Oh gie 35 to me a shillin' for some fags and I'll pay yer back on Thursday, but if you wait till Saturday I'm expecting a divvy 36 from the Harpenden Building Society...(*continues muttering indistinctly*)

He walks out of shot past a glen containing several stuffed animals, one of which explodes. A highland spokesman stands up into shot. superimposed caption: 'a highland spokesman'

HIGHLANDER (JOHN) As a Highlander I would like to point out some inaccuracies in the preceding film about the poet Ewan McTeagle. Although his name was quite clearly given as

In fact, in the finished sketch the camera circles McTeagle under a heavy, gray sky, and he flings the already written postcards straight into the pillar (or postal) box.

A mostly political playwright, David Mercer originally wrote for TV and then for the stage, including the 1965 play *And Did Those Feet?*, which is the first line of the hymn "Jerusalem" so loved by the Pythons.

From John Keats's poem "To Autumn," written in 1819.

Also known as William Wordsworth's "Daffodils," written in 1804.

John Milton wrote no such line.

"*Gie*" is Scottish for "give."

"Divvy" is a long-shot use of a word that means, in British slang, to parcel out.

McTeagle, he was throughout wearing the Cameron tartan. Also I would like to point out that the BALPA spokesman who complained about aeronautical inaccuracies was himself wearing a captain's hat, whereas he only had lieutenant's stripes on the sleeves of his jacket. Also, in the Inverness pantomime last Christmas, the part of Puss in Boots was played by a native of New Guinea with a plate in her lip, **37** so that every time Dick Whittington gave her a French kiss, he got the back of his throat scraped. **38**

Cleese mimes what a plate would do to a lip, in case we don't get the visual.

A nice conflation of two traditional but very different pantomimes. French in origin, *Puss in Boots* is about a cat who. . .well, wears boots. *Dick Whittington and His Cat* is the English story of a man and his cat, and how he becomes Lord Mayor of London.

A doctor's head appears out from under the kilt.

DOCTOR (MICHAEL) Look, would you mind going away, I'm trying to examine this man. (*he goes back under the kilt; a slight pause; he re-emerges*) It's—er—it's all right—I am a doctor. Actually, I'm a gynaecologist...but this is my lunchhour.

Animation:

ANIMATION VOICE I've a nasty feeling I am somebody's lunchhour.

Animation leads to a living room. Doorbell rings. Lady opens the door, a milkman stands there.

MILKMAN (ERIC) Pat-a-cake, pat-a-cake baker's man. Good morning, madam, I'm a psychiatrist.
LADY (GRAHAM) You look like a milkman to me.
MILKMAN Good. (*ticks form on his clipboard*) I am in fact dressed as a milkman...you spotted that—well done.
LADY Go away.
MILKMAN Now then, madam. I'm going to show you three numbers, and I want you to tell me if you see any similarity between them. (*holds up a card saying '3' three times*)
LADY They're all number three.
MILKMAN No. Try again.
LADY They're *all* number three?

MILKMAN No. They're *all* number three. (*he ticks his board again*) Right. Now. I'm going to say a word, and I want you to say the first thing that comes into your head. How many pints do you want?

LADY (*narrowing her eyes, suspecting a trap*) Er, three?

MILKMAN Yogurt?

LADY Er...no.

MILKMAN Cream?

LADY No.

MILKMAN Eggs?

LADY No.

MILKMAN (*does some adding up and whistling*) Right. Well, you're quite clearly suffering from a repressive *libido* 39 complex, *probably the product of* 40 an unhappy childhood, coupled with acute insecurity in adolescence, which has resulted in an attenuation of the libido complex.

LADY You *are* a bloody milkman.

MILKMAN Don't you shout at me, madam, don't come that tone. Now then, I must ask you to accompany me down to the dairy and do some aptitude tests.

LADY I've got better things to do than come down to the dairy!

MILKMAN Mrs Ratbag, if you don't mind me saying so, you are badly in need of an expensive course of psychiatric treatment. Now I'm not going to say a trip to our dairy will cure you, but it will give hundreds of lower-paid workers a good laugh.

LADY All right...but how am I going to get home?

MILKMAN

I'LL RUN YOU THERE AND BACK ON MY PSYCHIATRIST'S FLOAT. 41

LADY All right.

The milkman and lady walk down her garden path. As they go out of the garden gate there is a cat on the garden wall. Caption and arrow: 'A CAT' The cat explodes. The milkman motions her towards the milk float with a large signboard which reads: 'Psychiatrist's Dairy Ltd'.

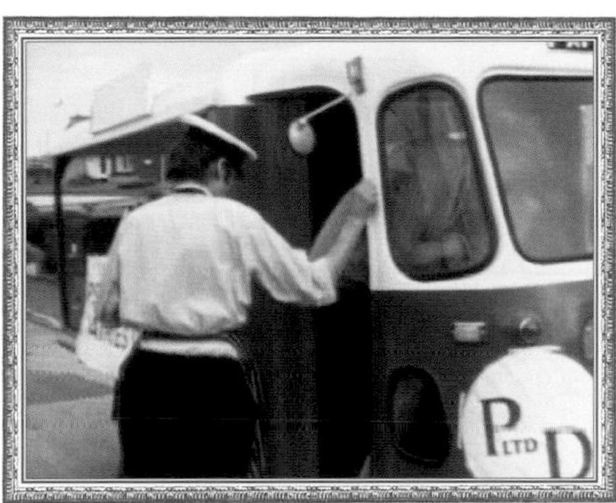

Just as they are getting in, she points to all the files in the back in milk crates.

LADY What are those?

MILKMAN They're case histories. (*drives off; calls:*) Psychiatrists! Psychiatrists! (*the doctor from the Scots sketch hails him*) Yes, sir?

DOCTOR (MICHAEL) Ah, good morning. I'm afraid our regular psychiatrist hasn't come round this morning...and I've got an ego block which is in turn making my wife over-assertive and getting us both into a state of depressive neurosis.

MILKMAN Oh, I see, sir. Who's your regular, sir?

DOCTOR Jersey Cream Psychiatrists.

MILKMAN Oh yes, I know them. (*puts down crate and gets out note pad*) Right, well, er, what's your job, then?

Idle pronounces it is as "*lib*-ido" rather than "li-*bee*-do."

Idle bluffs his lines here, saying "result of the product of" instead of "the product of," and stumbles a bit before he gets back on track.

41

The milkman in Britain, now mostly gone, once drove open-sided "floats" on which crates of milk bottles rattled all morning and afternoon.

DOCTOR I'm a doctor.

MILKMAN ...Didn't I see you just now under a Scotsman?

DOCTOR

YES, BUT I AM A DOCTOR. ACTUALLY, I'M A GYNAECOLOGIST BUT THAT WAS MY LUNCHHOUR.

MILKMAN (*taking a card out of crate and showing it to the doctor*) What does *this* remind you of?

DOCTOR Two pints of cream.

MILKMAN Right...well I should definitely say you're suffering from a severe personality disorder, sir, sublimating itself in a lactic obsession which could get worse depending on how much money you've got.

DOCTOR Yes, yes, I see. And a pot of yogurt, please.

Cut to a psychiatrist called Dr Cream in his office. 42

Terry Jones is sporting just half of a mustache—a nice counterpoint to the BALPA representative, who was wearing the equivalent of four or five moustaches, and who is about to reappear.

DR CREAM (TERRY J) I would like to take this opportunity of complaining about the way in which these shows are continually portraying psychiatrists who make pat diagnoses of patients' problems without first obtaining their full medical history.

Cut back to milkman with doctor.

MILKMAN (*handing over yogurt*) Mind you, that's just a pat diagnosis made without first obtaining your full medical history.

Cut to man at desk.

MAN (JOHN) I feel the time has come to complain about people who make rash complaints without first making sure that those complaints are justified.

Cut to Dr Cream.

DR CREAM Are you referring to me? 43

43

The half-mustache has moved to the right side of Jones's upper lip here.

Cut back to man.

MAN Not necessarily, however, I would like to point out that the BALPA spokesman was wearing the British Psychiatric Association Dinner Dance Club cuff-links.

Cut to Dr Cream.

DR CREAM Oh yes, I noticed that too. 44

The half-mustache moves again.

Cut to BALPA man.

BALPA MAN (ERIC) These are not British Psychiatric Association Dinner Dance Club cuff-links.

Cut to man.

MAN Sorry.

Cut to BALPA man.

BALPA MAN They are in fact British Sugar Corporation Gilbert-and-Sullivan Society 45 cuff-links. It is in fact a sort of in-joke with us lads here at BALPA. I think the last speaker should have checked his facts before making his *own* rash complaint.

Cut to Dr Cream.

DR CREAM Yes, that'll teach him. 46

Cut to BALPA man.

BALPA MAN However, I would just like to add a complaint about shows that have too many complaints in them as they get very tedious for the average viewer.

Cut to another man.

ANOTHER MAN (MICHAEL) I'd like to complain about people who hold things up by complaining about people complaining. It's about time something was done about it. (*the sixteen-ton weight falls on him*)

Cut to a street with milkman and lady riding on milk float. It comes to a halt. They get out, milkman hails a milkmaid with yoke and two pails.

MILKMAN Nurse! Would you take Mrs Pim to see Dr Cream, please. 47
MILKMAID (CAROL) Certainly, doctor. Walk this way, please.
LADY Oh, if I could walk that way I...
MILKMAN AND MILKMAID Sssssh! 48

The milkmaid leads Mrs Pim into a building, and into a psychiatrist's office. Dr Cream is in a chair.

MILKMAID Mrs Pim to see you, Dr Cream.
DR CREAM Ah yes. I just want another five minutes with Audrey. Could you show Mrs Pim into the waiting room, please.
MILKMAID Yes, doctor.

As milkmaid and Mrs Pim leave the room we see that there is a cow on the couch.

The Gilbert-and-Sullivan Society is dedicated to the propagation of love for the Victorian musical-writing duo, authors of *The Pirates of Penzance* and other much beloved comic operas.

The half-mustache is back on the right.

Earlier in the episode she was "Mrs Ratbag."

Actually, there is no "Sssssh!" by either character, just the raising of a warning finger by Idle and Cleveland—who mustn't allow (most) punch lines to exist without censure in the Python world.

RIGHT, AUDREY. WHEN DID YOU FIRST START THINKING YOU WERE A COW?

Milkmaid and Mrs Pim emerge from building through a herd of cows and we then have a montage of shots of them walking through countryside as in opening sequence of flying lesson sketch at beginning of show. They pass the tea trolley woman, the bishop learning his script...

BISHOP (*Australian accent*) 'Jeez, Mr Belpit your legs is all swollen'

...the secretary at her desk, past a stuffed animal which explodes, **49** *then past the tea lady again, and then past the bishop again and then past the secretary again, still going in the same direction.*

BISHOP (*Scots accent*) Oi! Mr Belpit—your great legs is all swollen! (*then again with Japanese accent*)

The stuffed animal is a rabbit, poor thing.

Cut to montage of photographs of sections of brain, a man with an egg on his head, a man looking through microscope, diagrams of brain, music over this and: caption: 'it's the mind—a weekly magazine of things psychiatric' Cut to a man sitting at usual desk. He is Mr Boniface.

BONIFACE (MICHAEL) Good evening. Tonight on 'It's the Mind', we examine the phenomenon of déjà vu. That strange feeling we sometimes get that we've lived through something before, that what is happening now has already happened. Tonight on 'It's the Mind' we examine the phenomenon of déjà vu, that strange feeling we sometimes get that we've...(*looks puzzled for a moment*) Anyway, tonight on 'It's the Mind' we examine the phenomenon of déjà vu, that strange...

Cut to opening title sequence with montage of psychiatric photos and the two captions and music over. Cut back to Mr Boniface at desk, shaken. Caption: 'IT'S THE MIND'

BONIFACE Good evening. Tonight on 'It's the Mind' we examine the phenomenon of déjà vu, that strange feeling we someti...mes get...that...we've lived through something...

Cut to opening titles again. Back then to Boniface, now very shaken.

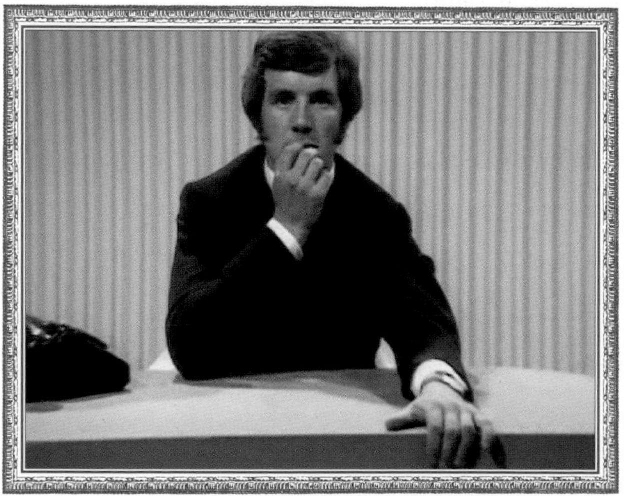

Caption: 'IT'S THE MIND'

BONIFACE Good...good evening. Tonight on 'It's the Mind' we examine the phenomenon of ddddddddddddéjà vvvvvvvvvu, that extraordinary feeling...quite extraordinary...(*he tails off, goes quiet, the phone rings, he picks it up*) No, fine thanks, fine. (*he rings off: a man comes in on the right and hands him glass of water and leaves*) Oh, thank you. That strange feeling we sometimes get that we've lived through something before. (*phone rings again; he picks it up*) No, fine thank you. Fine. (*he rings off: a man comes in from right and hands him a glass of water; he jumps*)...Thank you. That strange feeling...(*phone rings; he answers*) No. Fine, thank you. Fine, (*rings off: a man enters and gives him glass of water*) thank you. (*he screams with fear*) Look, something's happening to me. I—I—um, I think I'd better go and see someone. Goodnight. **50**

Phone rings again. He leaps from desk and runs out of shot. He runs out of building into street and chases after passing milk float and leaps aboard.

MILKMAN Oi, haven't I seen you somewhere before?
BONIFACE No, doctor, no. Something very funny's happening to me.

Caption: 'IT'S THE MIND—A WEEKLY MAGAZINE OF THINGS PSYCHIATRIC'
Cut to montage of photographs again with captions and music. Cut to Boniface at desk. Boniface screams and runs out of shot. Cut to same piece of film as just previously, when he chases float, leaps on and the milkman says:

MILKMAN Oi, haven't I seen you somewhere before?
BONIFACE No, doctor, no. Something very funny's happening to me.

The milk float goes past in the background with the milkman and Boniface on it. We see the float go along the country lane past the clearing, past the bishop...

BISHOP (*camp*) 'Oh, Mr Belpit, your legs are so swollen'.

...and the secretary at her desk, past a sign saying 'to the zoo' where explosions are heard, and stops outside Dr Cream's building...Boniface runs into building and enters Dr Cream's office.
Caption: 'DR CREAM'S OFFICE'

DR CREAM Ah, come in. Now what seems to be the matter? **51**
BONIFACE I have this terrible feeling of déjà vu.

Repeat same clip from Boniface entering.

DR CREAM Ah, come in. Now what seems to be the matter? **52**
BONIFACE I have this terrible feeling of déjà vu...

Repeat clip again. Superimposed credits

DR CREAM Ah, come in. Now what seems to be the matter? **53**
BONIFACE I have this terrible feeling of déjà vu...

Clip starts to repeat again as the programme ends.

50

The "glass of water" is notable for having no water in it.

51

Jones here has both sides to his mustache on his upper lip.

52

Jones again has both sides to his mustache, but it is attached to the underside of his nose.

53

Jones again has both sides to his mustache, but they are attached to the insides of his glasses.

AN APOLOGY
SEA
SON
2
EPISODE 17

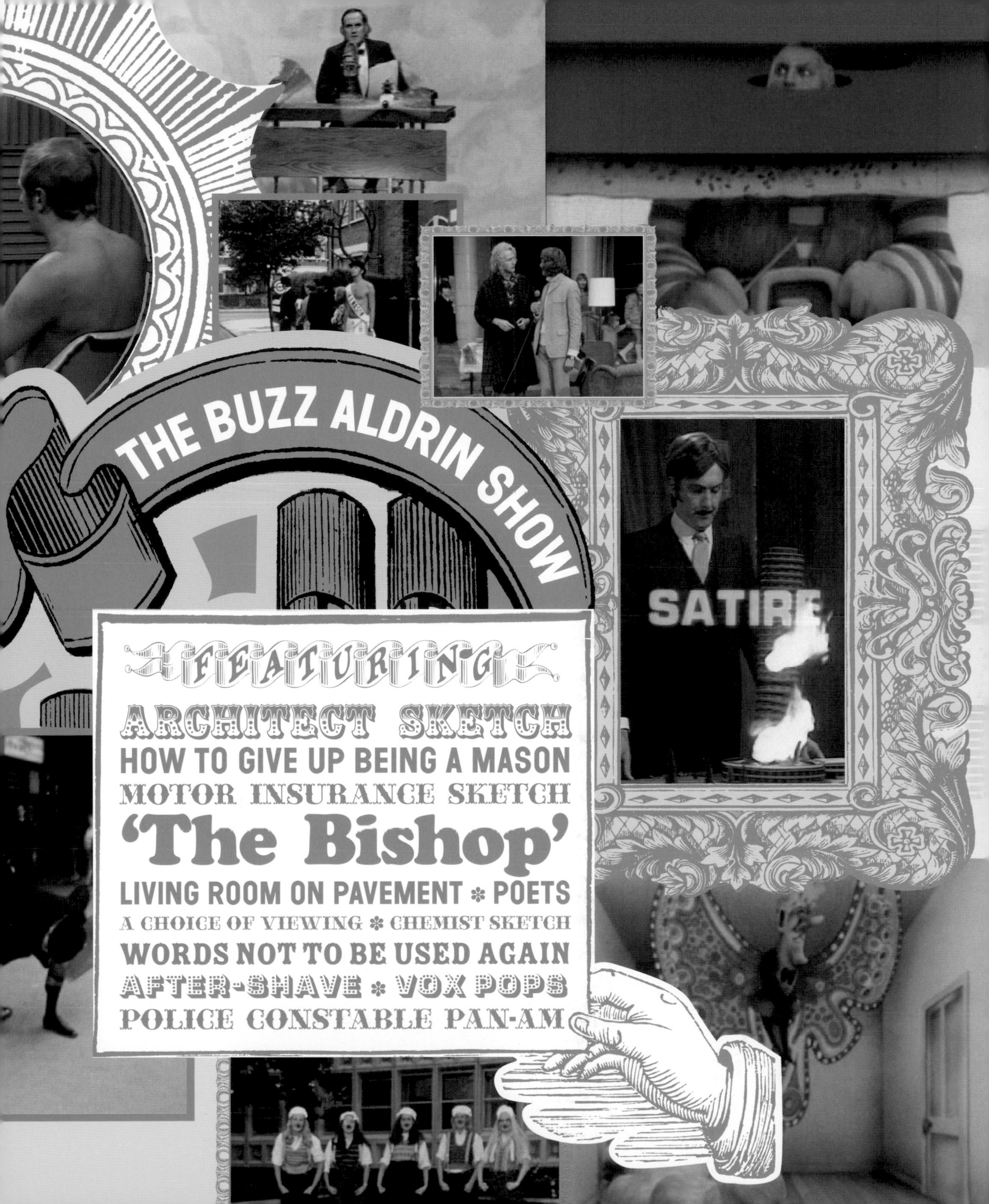
THE BUZZ ALDRIN SHOW
SATIRE
FEATURING
ARCHITECT SKETCH
HOW TO GIVE UP BEING A MASON
MOTOR INSURANCE SKETCH
'The Bishop'
LIVING ROOM ON PAVEMENT * POETS
A CHOICE OF VIEWING * CHEMIST SKETCH
WORDS NOT TO BE USED AGAIN
AFTER-SHAVE * VOX POPS
POLICE CONSTABLE PAN-AM

FIRST AIRED: OCTOBER 20, 1970

Opens with animated item (the Butterfly). The announcer at a desk with propellors rises into view.

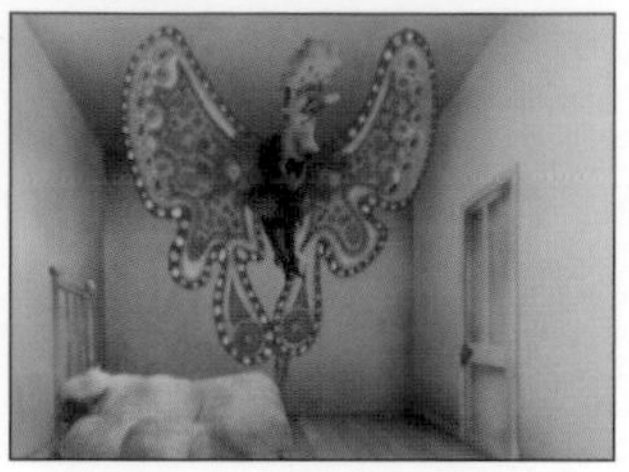

ANNOUNCER (JOHN) And now for something completely different.

IT'S MAN (MICHAEL)

IT'S...

Animated titles.

ANNOUNCER *(and caption)*: 'The BBC would like to apologize for the next announcement'

Cut to a group of Gumbys, all with rolled-up trousers and knotted handkerchiefs on their heads, attempting to shout in unison and failing miserably.

GUMBYS Hello, and welcome to the show. Without more ado, the first item is a sketch about architects, called The Architects Sketch...The Architects Sketch...The Architects Sketch... *(as the sketch fails to start they point up at a nearby building)* Up there!...Up there!...Up there!...

There are two men in an office behind the Gumbys, blithely getting on with their day's work. Another quite lovely example of life continuing on as the Pythons act crazy in the street.

The camera pans to a window in the building. 1 *Cut to the office inside, where a board meeting is taking place. The Chairman is Mr Tid.*

MR TID (GRAHAM) Gentlemen, we have two basic suggestions for the design of this...*(he is distracted by the two gumbys still shouting)...* 2 Gentlemen we have two basic suggestions for the design of this...*(shouts out of window at the gumbys)* Shut up! Gentlemen, we have two basic suggestions...*(but the gumbys are still shouting 'Architects Sketch'; he throws a bucket of water over them; they subside, damply)* 3 Gentlemen, we have two basic suggestions for the design of this residential block, and I thought it best that the architects themselves came in to explain the advantages of both designs. 4 *(knock at door)* That must be the first architect now. *(Mr Wiggin comes in)* Ah, yes—it's Mr Wiggin of Ironside and Malone.

Wiggin walks to the table on which his model stands.

MR WIGGIN (JOHN) Good morning, gentlemen. This is a twelve-storey block combining classical neo-Georgian features with all the advantages of modern design. The tenants arrive in the entrance hall here, are carried along the corridor on a conveyor belt in extreme comfort and past murals depicting Mediterranean scenes, towards the rotating knives. The last twenty feet of the corridor are heavily soundproofed. The blood pours down these chutes and the mangled flesh slurps into these...

FIRST CITY GENT (MICHAEL) Excuse me...

MR WIGGIN Hm?

FIRST CITY GENT Did you say knives?

MR WIGGIN Rotating knives, yes.

SECOND CITY GENT (TERRY J) Are you proposing to slaughter our tenants?

MR WIGGIN Does that not fit in with your plans?

FIRST CITY GENT No, it does not. We wanted a simple block of flats.

MR WIGGIN Oh, I see. I hadn't correctly divined your attitude towards your tenants. You see I mainly design slaughter houses. Yes, pity. Mind you this is a real beaut. I mean, none of your blood caked on the walls and flesh flying out of the windows, inconveniencing passers-by with this one. I mean, my life has been building up to this.

SECOND CITY GENT Yes, and well done. But we did want a block of flats.

MR WIGGIN Well, may I ask you to reconsider? I mean, you wouldn't regret it. Think of the tourist trade.

FIRST CITY GENT No, no, it's just that we wanted a block of flats, not an abattoir.

MR WIGGIN Yes, well, of course, that's just the sort of blinkered philistine pig ignorance I've come to expect from you non-creative garbage. You sit there on your loathsome, spotty behinds squeezing blackheads, not caring a tinker's cuss about the struggling artist. 5 *(shouting)* You excrement! You lousy hypocritical whining toadies with your lousy colour TV sets and your Tony Jacklin 6 golf clubs and your bleeding masonic handshakes! You wouldn't let me join, would you, you blackballing bastards! Well I wouldn't become a freemason now if you went down on your lousy, stinking, purulent knees and begged me. 7

SECOND CITY GENT Well, we're sorry you feel like that but we, er, did want a block of flats. Nice though the abattoir is.

MR WIGGIN Oh *(blows raspberry)* the abattoir, that's not important. But if one of you could put in a word for me I'd love to be a freemason. Freemasonry opens doors. I mean, I was...I was a bit on edge just now, but if I was a mason I'd just sit at the back and not get in anyone's way.

The boom mike is briefly visible here, straining to hear Chapman owing to the shouting Gumbys.

The man in the office who was blithely ignoring the Gumbys is now wearing a jacket, smoking a pipe, and watching, finally.

Chapman, perhaps thrown off by throwing water on poor Gumbys, stumbled a bit and says "this architectural block, the residential block."

"A tinker's cuss" is a mainly British phrase meaning to not give a damn.

Tony Jacklin was then an eminent British golfer who won the Open Championship in 1969 and the U.S. Open in 1970.

The Freemasons are a fraternal society generally believed to have a "secret" handshake: shaking your hand in a certain way signals their own membership, and allows them to see if you too are a member.

Masons are said to wear aprons as a nod to the profession whose name they bear.

Hendon is a suburb in northwest London.

Magnalium is an aluminum alloy that is "unsuitable for engineering purposes." But it is used in pyrotechnics, and we're about to see why.

Almost everything in Britain can be made better by the onset of a "spot of good weather," as rare as it may be.

FIRST CITY GENT Thank you.

MR WIGGIN I've got a second-hand apron. 8

SECOND CITY GENT Thank you.

MR WIGGIN (*going to door but stopping*) I nearly got in at Hendon. 9

FIRST CITY GENT Thank you.

Mr Wiggin leaves and the familiar figure of Mr Tid comes forward.

MR TID I'm sorry about that, gentlemen. The second architect is a Mr Leavey of Wymis and Dibble.

Mr Leavey comes in and goes to his model.

MR LEAVEY (ERIC) Good morning, gentlemen. This is a scale model of the block. There are twenty-eight storeys, with two hundred and eighty modern apartments. There are three main lifts and two service lifts. Access would be from Dibbingley Road. (*the model falls over and he quickly puts it upright*) The structure is built on a central pillar system (*the model falls over again*) with (*he puts model upright and holds onto it*) cantilevered floors in pre-stressed steel and concrete. The dividing walls on each floor section are fixed with recessed magnalium flanged grooves. 10 (*the model partly collapses, the bottom ten floors giving way*) By avoiding wood and timber derivatives and all other flammables, (*the model is smoking and flames are seen*) we have almost totally removed the risk of...

Superimposed caption: 'SATIRE'

MR LEAVEY Quite frankly I think the central pillar system may need strengthening a bit.

SECOND CITY GENT Isn't that going to put the cost up?

MR LEAVEY It might.

SECOND CITY GENT Well, I don't know whether I'd worry about strengthening *that* much. After all they're not meant to be luxury flats.

FIRST CITY GENT I quite agree. I mean, providing the tenants are of light build and relatively sedentary and er, given a spot of good weather, 11 I think we're on to a winner here.

MR LEAVEY Oh, thank you.

The model explodes.

SECOND CITY GENT Quite agree. Quite agree.

MR LEAVEY Thank you very much. Thank you. (*he shakes hands with them in an extraordinary way*)

MR WIGGIN (*at door*) It opens doors. I'm telling you.

VOICE OVER (ERIC) Let's have a look at that handshake again in slow motion.

Caption: 'BBC TV ACTION REPLAY' They do the handshake again, only slowly.

VOICE OVER What other ways are there of recognizing a mason?

Shot from camera concealed in a car so we get reactions of passers-by. A busy city street—i.e. Threadneedle Street. In amongst the throng four city gents are leaping along with their trousers round their ankles. They are wearing bowler hats and pinstripes. Another city street or another part of the same street. Two city gents, with trousers rolled up to the knee, approach each other and go into the most extraordinary handshake which involves rolling on the floor etc. 12

VOICE OVER (JOHN) Having once identified a mason immediate steps must be taken to isolate him from the general public. Having accomplished that it is now possible to cure him of these unfortunate masonic tendencies through the use of behavioural psychotherapy. (*we see a cartoon city gent locked into a cell*) In this treatment the patient is rewarded for the correct response and punished for the wrong one. Let us begin. Would you like to give up being a mason? Think carefully. Think. Think.

Two elderly ladies are among the "civilian" passersby aghast at the scene.

CARTOON CITY GENT No.

A large hammer attacks the city gent.

VOICE OVER No? That's wrong! Wrong! Wrong! Wrong! No! No! No! Bad! Bad.

Caption: 'AN APOLOGY'

ANNOUNCER (JOHN) The BBC would like to apologize for the following announcement.

Pull out from the caption to reveal that it is not a caption after all but a huge twenty-foot-square poster on a hoarding at the side of the road. After we pull out we hear the shuffling of many feet and grunting. A group of Gumbys shuffle into extreme left edge of frame. 13 *They do not move any further into the picture. After a bit of humming and harring:*

Watching them bump into each other and moan, one is struck by the similarity between Gumby and Zombie.

OH! AND THE NEXT ITEM IS A SKETCH ABOUT INSURANCE CALLED 'INSURANCE SKETCH'. 'INSURANCE SKETCH'. 'INSURANCE SKETCH'...

Cut to Mr Devious's insurance office. Devious and a man are sitting there.

DEVIOUS (MICHAEL) What do you want?

Superimposed caption: 'STRAIGHT MAN' 14

MAN (GRAHAM) Well I've come about your special fully comprehensive motor insurance policy offer...

DEVIOUS What was that?

MAN Fully comprehensive motor insurance for one-and-eightpence. 15

DEVIOUS Oh, oh, yes...yeah well, unfortunately, guv, that offer's no longer valid. You see, it turned out not to be economically viable, so we now have a totally new offer...

MAN What's that?

DEVIOUS A nude lady.

MAN A nude lady?

DEVIOUS Yes. You get a nude lady with a fully comprehensive motor insurance. If you just want third party she has to keep her bra on, and if it's just theft...

MAN No, no, I don't really want that, Mr er...Mr...

DEVIOUS Devious.

MAN Mr Devious. I just want to know what it would cost me to have a fully comprehensive insurance on a 1970 Aston Martin. 16

DEVIOUS Aston Martin?

MAN Yes.

DEVIOUS (*quickly*) Five hundred quid.

MAN Five hundred quid?

DEVIOUS Forty quid.

MAN Forty quid?

DEVIOUS Forty quid and a nude lady.

MAN No, no, I'm not interested in a nude lady.

DEVIOUS Dirty books?

MAN No, no, look, I'm not interested in any of that. (*Superimposed 'STRAIGHT MAN' caption again*) I just want to know what it would cost me to have a fully comprehensive insurance on a 1970 Aston Martin. Can you please quote me your price.

Cut to outside the door of the office. A vicar stands there.

VICAR (ERIC) Knock knock.

Cut to inside office.

DEVIOUS Who's there?

Cut to outside.

VICAR The Reverend...

Something of an inside joke, given Chapman's sexuality.

"One-and-eightpence" is a ridiculously small sum—the equivalent, in decimal currency, of about thirteen pence.

Aston Martin is the legendary luxury sports car maker (now, coincidentally, based in the town of Gaydon in Warwickshire).

Cut to inside.

DEVIOUS The Reverend who?
VICAR The Reverend Morrison.

Caption: 'ANOTHER STRAIGHT MAN' Cut to inside.

DEVIOUS Oh, come in.

The vicar enters.

DEVIOUS Now then, vic. What's the trouble?
VICAR Well, it's about this letter you sent me.
MAN Excuse me, do I have any more lines?
DEVIOUS I don't know, mush, 17 I'll have a look in the script...(*he gets script out of drawer*) Where are we? Show 8. Are you 'man'?
MAN Yeah.
DEVIOUS No...no, you've finished.
MAN Well, I'll be off then. (*he leaves*)
DEVIOUS (*reading script*) 'The vicar sits'.

The vicar sits.

VICAR It's about this letter you sent me regarding my insurance claim.
DEVIOUS Oh, yeah, yeah—well, you see, it's just that we're not...as yet...*totally* satisfied with the grounds of your claim.
VICAR But it says something about filling my mouth in with cement.
DEVIOUS Oh well, that's just insurance jargon, you know.
VICAR But my car was hit by a lorry while standing in the garage and you refuse to pay my claim.
DEVIOUS (*rising and crossing to a filing cabinet*) Oh well, Reverend Morrison...in your policy...in your policy...(*he opens the drawer of the filing cabinet and takes out a shabby old sports jacket; he feels in the pocket and pulls out a crumpled dog-eared piece of paper then puts the coat back and shuts the filing cabinet*)...here we are. It states quite clearly that no claim you make will be paid.
VICAR Oh dear.
DEVIOUS You see, you unfortunately plumped for our 'Neverpay' policy, which, you know, if you never claim is very worthwhile...but you had to claim, and, well, there it is.
VICAR Oh dear, oh dear.
DEVIOUS Still, never mind—could be worse. How's the nude lady?
VICAR Oh, she's fine. (*he begins to sob*)
DEVIOUS Look...Rev...I hate to see a man cry, so shove off out the office, there's a good chap.

The vicar goes out sobbing. Cut to outside. Vicar collects a nude lady sitting in a supermarket shopping trolley...and wheels her disconsolately away. Cut back to inside of office. Close-up on Devious. He gets out some files and starts writing. 18 *Suddenly a bishop's crook slams down on*

"Mush" is a British word for pal.

He actually merely reads from a small comic book.

the desk in front of Devious. He looks up—his eyes register terror. Cut to reverse angle shot from below. The bishop in full mitre and robes.

BISHOP (TERRY J) OK, Devious...Don't move!

DEVIOUS

THE BISHOP!

Animated crime-series-type titles, with suitable music:

'C. OF E. FILMS' 19
'IN ASSOCIATION WITH THE SUNDAY SCHOOLS BOARD'
'PRESENT'
'THE BISHOP'
'STARRING THE REVEREND E. P. NESBITT'
'AND INTRODUCING F. B. GRIMSBY URQHART-WRIGHT AS THE VOICE OF GOD'
'SPECIAL EFFECTS BY THE MODERATOR OF THE CHURCH OF SCOTLAND'
'DIRECTED BY PREBENDARY "CHOPPER" HARRIS' 20

Exterior beautiful English church. Birds singing, a hymn being sung. 21 *Suddenly sound of a high-powered car roaring towards the church. Screech of tyres as a huge open-top American car screeches to a halt outside the church. The bishop leaps out. Behind him (as throughout the film) are his four henchmen...vicars with dark glasses. They wear clerical suits and dog collars. They leap out of their car and race up the drive towards the church. As they do so the hymn is heard to come to an end. Sound of people sitting down. Cut to interior of church. Vicar climbing up into pulpit. Cut back to exterior. The bishop and his vicars racing through the doors. Interior of church. Shot of vicar in pulpit.*

VICAR (GRAHAM) I take as my text for today...

Cut to bishop and vicars at doorway.

BISHOP The text, vic! Don't say the text!

"C. of E." is short for the Church of England.

Prebendaries help run cathedrals.

And this being Python, it is, yet again, the hymn "Jerusalem."

Cut back to vicar.

VICAR Leviticus 3-14... 22

The pulpit explodes. Vicar disappears in smoke, flying up into the air. Cut to close-up of the bishop. Behind him there is smoke and people rushing about. Sound of people scrambling over pews in panic etc.

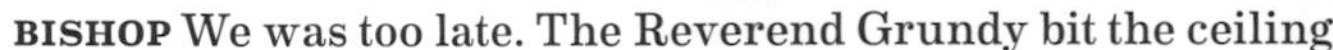

BISHOP We was too late. The Reverend Grundy bit the ceiling.

The end of the bishop's crook suddenly starts flashing. He lifts the flashing end off and it stops. Using it like a telephone receiver, he speaks into the staff.

BISHOP Hello?...What?...We'll be right over!

Still of another church exterior. Crash zoom in on door. Cut to interior. A baptism party round the font. An innocent vicar is just testing the water. Pan across to the parents—a couple of shifty crooks—and two godmothers, obviously all-in wrestlers in drag (cauliflower ears etc.). As the vicar takes the baby it starts to tick loudly.

VICAR (JOHN) And it is for this reason that the Christian Church lays upon you, the godparents, the obligation of seeing this child is brought up in the Christian faith. Therefore, I name this child...

Cut to door of church. The bishop and vicars rush in.

BISHOP Don't say the kid's name, vic!

Cut back to vicar.

VICAR Francesco Luigi...

Explosion. Cut to close-up of bishop. Smoke and panic as before.

BISHOP We was too late...The Rev. Neuk saw the light.

Whip pan to interior of yet another church. A wedding. Bride and groom standing in front of a vicar. Cut to door of church. The bishop and vicars burst in.

BISHOP The ring, vic! Don't touch the ring! Hey vic!

Cut to vicar taking the ring out of the bible. The ring is attached to a piece of string. A sixteen-ton weight falls on top of them with a mighty crunch—the camera shakes as it hits the floor.

That particular passage reads: "And he shall offer his offering, even an offering made by fire unto the Lord; the fat that covers the entrails, and all the fat that is upon the entrails . . ."

Cut to two bell ringers. One pulls his rope, and the other rises off the floor, hanged by the neck. The bishop arrives, just too late. Cut to another vicar at graveside.

VICAR (GRAHAM) ...dust to dust, ashes to ashes.

He sprinkles dust on the grave. A huge prop cannon rises up out of the grave until its mighty barrel (twelve inches wide) is pointing right in the vicar's face. He does not notice. Sound of car screeching to a halt. We pan away from grave to reveal the bishop leaping out of the car. Sound of an almighty blast from the cannon. The bishop gets back into the car immediately and turns it round. Cut to a street. Outside a cigarette shop the four clerics lounge against a wall. The bishop walks out rolling his own. Suddenly he stops. Close-up. He looks up as he hears a faint cry. Camera swings round and up—enormous zoom to high window in huge, drab city office block, where a vicar is looking out.

VICAR (ERIC) Help...help...help...help...help...help...

Cut back to the bishop breaking into a run, throwing his cigarette into the gutter. Peter Gunn music. 23 *Hand-held shots of the bishop and the four vicars running through crowded streets. He reaches the office block, rushes in. Interior: a stair well. Right at the bottom we see the bishop and the vicars. Close-up hand-held shot of bishop running up stairs. Shadows running up the stair well. The bishop arrives on the top landing. Door of office. The bishop tries the door. It won't open. One vicar goes rigid. The other three take hold of him and use him as a battering ram and go straight through the balsa wood door first time.*

BISHOP OK, Devious, don't move!
DEVIOUS The bishop!

'The Bishop' titles again. Cut to interior of cinema. A couple holding hands. Bishop film titles start up again exactly as before. After a couple of seconds of titles we cut to an old couple sitting in the back row of the cinema facing camera. The sound of the bishop's titles continues. The light from the projector is streaming out above their heads.

MR POTTER (MICHAEL) This is where we came in.
MRS POTTER (GRAHAM) Yes.

Cut immediately to the front of the cinema. 24 *A working-class lounge is arranged on the pavement. There are no walls, just the furnishings: settee, two armchairs, sideboard, table, standard lamp, a tiled fireplace with ornaments on it. There is also a free-standing inside door. Mr and Mrs Potter come out of the cinema and go straight to their chairs and sit down. Passers-by have to skirt the living-room furniture.* 25

Henry Mancini's classic theme for the 1958–1961 American TV series about a private investigator.

The posters suggest that the movie playing is *Hoffman*, the 1970 film starring Peter Sellers in one of his few straight roles.

Some passersby are smiling as they edge past the scene, suggesting it was set up in the middle of the street.

MRS POTTER (*settling into her chair*) Oh, it's nice to be home.
MR POTTER (*looking round*) Builders haven't been then.
MRS POTTER No.

A trendy interviewer with hand mike comes into shot.

INTERVIEWER (ERIC) These two old people are typical of the housing problem facing Britain's aged.
MRS POTTER Here! Don't you start doing a documentary on us, young man.
INTERVIEWER Oh please...
MRS POTTER No, you leave us alone!
INTERVIEWER Oh, just a little one about the appalling conditions under which you live.
MRS POTTER No! Get out of our house! Go on!

Interviewer turns, motions to his cameraman and soundman and they all trail off miserably.

CAMERAMAN Oh all right. Come on, George, pick it up.
MRS POTTER Why don't you do a documentary about the drug problem round in Walton Street?

Cut to the camera crew. They stop, turn and mutter 'a drug problem!' and they dash off.

MRS POTTER Oh, I'll go and have a bath.

She goes to the free-standing door and opens it. Beyond it we see the furnishings of a bathroom. In the bath is Alfred Lord Tennyson, 26 *fully clad. As she opens the door we hear him reciting:*

TENNYSON The splendour falls on castle walls And snowy summits old in story... 27

She slams the door.

MRS POTTER
'ERE, THERE'S ALFRED LORD TENNYSON IN THE BATHROOM.
MR POTTER Well, at least the poet's been installed, then.

Cut to an officious-looking man in Gas Board type uniform and peaked cap. Caption: 'SALES MANAGER EAST MIDLANDS POET BOARD'

SALES MANAGER (JOHN) Yes, a poet is essential for complete home comfort, and all-year round reliability at low cost. We in the East Midlands Poet Board hope to have a poet in every home by the end of next year.

Animation: an advertisement.

VOICES (*singing*) Poets are both clean and warm
And most are far above the norm
Whether here or on the roam
Have a poet in every home.

Cut to middle-class hall. The front doorbell rings. Housewife opens door to Gas Board type inspector with bicycle clips, rubber mac and cap and notebook. In the background we can hear muffled Wordsworth.

26

Alfred Lord Tennyson was England's poet laureate for much of the second half of the nineteenth century.

27

A later addition to Tennyson's 1847 poem "The Princess." He added "The splendour falls on castle walls" in 1850, after the poem was first published.

Wordsworth's "I Wandered Lonely as a Cloud" was featured in Episode 16.

Algernon Charles Swinburne, English poet, 1837–1909.

Percy Bysshe Shelley, the English Romantic poet who died at the age of 30, but not before penning such classic works as "Ode to the West Wind" and the wonderful, wonderful "Julian and Maddalo: A Conversation."

The old joke about the lonely housewife and the man who comes to read the gas meter, made nicely disturbing by watching Terry Jones—dressed in a blue housecoat and with long, curly hair—flirt with the unaware Palin.

The rugged Pennine Mountains separating west from the east in the north of England.

Here Palin brilliantly slips into avuncular weatherman mode.

VOICE (ERIC) I wandered lonely as a cloud That floats on high... 28
INSPECTOR (MICHAEL) Morning, madam, I've come to read your poet.
SHE (TERRY J) Oh yes, he's in the cupboard under the stairs.
INSPECTOR What is it, a Swinburne? 29 Shelley? 30
SHE No, it's a Wordsworth.
INSPECTOR Oh, bloody daffodils.

He opens the door of the cupboard under the stairs. Inside is Wordsworth crouching and reciting.

WORDSWORTH (ERIC) A host of golden daffodils
Beside the lake, beneath the trees
Fluttering and dancing in the breeze

All this while the inspector is shining his torch over him and noting things on his clip board.

WORDSWORTH Continuous as the stars that shine
And twinkle in the Milky Way
They stretch in...

The inspector shuts the door in the middle of this and we hear Wordsworth reciting on, though muffled, throughout the remainder of the sketch.

INSPECTOR Right. Thank you, madam.

He makes as if to go, but she seems anxious to detain him and bars his way. 31

SHE Oh, not at all. Thank *you*...It's a nice day, isn't it?
INSPECTOR Yes, yes, the weather situation is generally favourable. There's a ridge of high pressure centred over Ireland which is moving steadily eastward bringing cloudy weather to parts of the West Country, Wales and areas west of the Pennines. 32 On tomorrow's chart...*(he reaches up and pulls down a big weather chart from the wall)* the picture is much the same. With this occluded front bringing drier, warmer weather. Temperatures about average for the time of year. That's three degrees centigrade, forty-four degrees fahrenheit, so don't forget to wrap up well. That's all from me. Goodnight. 33

ERIC IDLE

It is the most tragic of stories: Ernest Idle, service number 1494425, a rear gunner and wireless operator, despite much action survived World War II. In December 1945, discharged and eager to get home—and with his son, Eric, waiting for him in South Shields in North East England—Ernest began to hitchhike home. (It was Christmas Eve, and the trains were overflowing with soldiers newly liberated from service.) In a truck carrying steel, Ernest headed north, but about 40 miles shy of his destination, the truck was forced off the road by a swerving car. The load of steel shifted, killing the 36-year-old. His son was two and a half.

It is unduly boring to talk of the "sad clown," and yet Eric Idle's subsequent life as one of the most chipper comedians one can imagine—chipper, but with a sharp edge—is surely informed by the terrible sadness of the story of his father's death. Subsequently schooled in a tough former orphanage (founded, unbelievably, by a man named John Leese), by the time he reached Cambridge University, he'd learned that laughter could be therapeutic. ("When you make an audience laugh," he's quoted in the Pythons autobiography, "they love you . . . and you made them feel better. So there is a sort of healing to it.") But he was also aware of how much British society—the army, specifically—had cost him personally, and this sense of injustice never left him.

At Cambridge he became president of the lauded Footlights group, and though a year behind John Cleese and Graham Chapman, he was already thought of as a future star of comedy. Post-Cambridge he starred in *Do Not Adjust Your Set,* a children's show whose creators included Michael Palin, Terry Jones, and Terry Gilliam. By the time he came to write for Python (mostly as a solo writer, as compared to the "teams" of Palin–Jones and Chapman–Cleese), a clear sardonic edge had crept in, with some of his creations (most notably, the "Nudge, Nudge" character) causing fans to sense a kind of crazy anger behind the comedy. In writing sessions, too, he was often a solo vote, and therefore found it harder than the teams to get his comedy aired. Nevertheless, he's also a fine songwriter, never more so than in *Monty Python's Life of Brian,* in which the crucifixion song, "Always Look on the Bright Side of Life," has become a classic, sung everywhere from soccer stadiums to Chapman's memorial service (though Idle barely got through it, so choked up he was by the loss of his friend and colleague).

After the *Flying Circus,* Idle acted in the Python movies (and many other non-Python films) and helped create *Rutland Weekend Television,* a satire of local British TV programming (for a start, it ran on weekdays), which in turn led to the Rutles, a fine parody of the Beatles phenomenon. (The subsequent movie, *All You Need is Cash,* is considered one of the finest music parodies until *This is Spinal Tap* came along.)

Of all the Pythons, however, Idle has most directly used his experience as a member of the group in his later career. In 2003 he embarked on what he called the "Greedy Bastard Tour," telling stories and singing songs from Python. A year later, he helped create the hit musical *Spamalot,* based on *Monty Python and the Holy Grail.* Fellow Python Terry Jones has called *Spamalot* "utterly pointless and full of hot air." Jones commented further: "[Idle] will make more out of *Spamalot* than anybody has ever made out of Python." And so it came to pass. As Idle might say, always look on the bright side of life.

Derek Hart was a TV presenter and journalist, and a regular on the BBC current affairs show of the time, *Tonight*.

John Robinson, the bishop of Woolwich from 1959 to 1969, was famous for his liberal interpretation of Christian theology, and would have been quite at home discussing nudity.

The Pythons are not above a penis joke.

One of the jokes here is that Thomas Hardy was a poet first, despite the manifold and mostly well-received novels published between 1867 (*The Poor Man and the Lady*) and 1895 (*Jude the Obscure*). The condemnation he received after *Jude* led him to publish only poetry from 1898 until his death in 1928. Many scholars (and this writer) consider him a poet of the very highest rank.

Cut to BBC world symbol.

CONTINUITY VOICE (ERIC) Now on BBC television a choice of viewing. On BBC 2—a discussion on censorship between Derek Hart, 34 The Bishop of Woolwich 35 and a nude man. And on BBC 1—me telling you this. And now...

Sound of TV set being switched off. The picture reduces to a spot and we pull out to see that it was actually on a TV set which has just been switched off by the housewife. She and the gas man are now sitting in her living room. He is perched awkwardly on the edge of the sofa. He holds a cup of tea with a cherry on a stick in it.

SHE We don't want that, do we. Do you really want that cherry in your tea? Do you like doing this job?
INSPECTOR Well, it's a living, isn't it?
SHE I mean, don't you get bored reading people's poets all day?
INSPECTOR Well, you know, sometimes...yeah. Anyway, I think I'd better be going.

As he gets up she comes quickly to his side.

SHE (*seductively*) You've got a nice torch, haven't you? 36
INSPECTOR (*looking at it rather baffled*) Er, yeah, yeah, it er...it er...it goes on and off.

He demonstrates.

SHE (*drawing closer and becoming breathy*) How many volts is it?
INSPECTOR Er...um...well, I'll have a look at the batteries. (*he starts unscrewing the end*)
SHE Oh yes, yes.
INSPECTOR It's four and a half volts.
SHE (*rubbing up against him*) Mmmm. That's wonderful. Do you want another look at the poet?
INSPECTOR No, no, I must be off, really.
SHE

I'VE GOT THOMAS HARDY IN THE BEDROOM. I'D LIKE YOU TO LOOK AT HIM.

INSPECTOR Ah well, I can't touch him. He's a novelist. 37
SHE Oh, he keeps mumbling all night.
INSPECTOR Oh well, novelists do, you see.

SHE (*dragging him onto the sofa*) Oh forget him! What's your name, deary?
INSPECTOR Harness.
SHE No, no! Your first name, silly!
INSPECTOR Wombat.
SHE Oh, Wombat. Wombat Harness! 38 Take me to the place where eternity knows no bounds, where the garden of love encloses us round. Oh Harness!
INSPECTOR All right, I'll have a quick look at yer Thomas Hardy.

Cut to studio discussion. Caption: 'DEREK HART'

DEREK (JOHN) Nude man, what did you make of that?
NUDE MAN (GRAHAM) Well, don't you see, that was exactly the kind of explicit sexual reference I'm objecting to. It's titillation for the sake of it. A deliberate attempt at cheap sensationalism. I don't care what the so-called avant-garde, left-wing, intellectual namby-pambies say...It is *filth*!

DEREK Bishop.

Cut to crook hitting desk in Devious's office.

BISHOP Okay, don't anybody move!

Titles for 'The Bishop' start and then stop abruptly. Caption: 'AN APOLOGY'

VOICE OVER (ERIC) The BBC would like to apologize for the constant repetition in this show.

Different caption reading: 'AN APOLOGY'

VOICE OVER The BBC would like to apologize for the constant repetition in this show.

Animation: the 'five frog curse'.

Wombat Harness—surely one of the greatest made-up names in all of Python.

AN APOLOGY
AN APOLOGY
AN APOLOGY

AN APOLOGY
AN APOLOGY
AN APOLOGY
EMERGENCY

Cut to the five Gumbys standing in a tight group.

GUMBYS Thank you. And now a sketch about a chemist called The Chemist Sketch.

A number of men and women are sitting around in an area by the counter where there is a large sign saying 'Dispensing Department'. A cheerful chemist appears at the counter.

CHEMIST (JOHN)

RIGHT. I'VE GOT SOME OF YOUR PRESCRIPTIONS HERE. ER, WHO'S GOT THE POX? 39

"The pox" is slang for syphilis.

(*nobody reacts*)...Come on, who's got the pox...come on...(*a man timidly puts his hand up*)... there you go. (*throws bottle to the man with his hand up*) Who's got a boil on the bum...boil on the batty. 40 (*throws bottle to the only man standing up*) Who's got the chest rash? (*a woman with a large bosom puts up hand*) Have to get a bigger bottle. 41 Who's got wind? (*throws bottle to a man sitting on his own*) Catch.

"Batty" is British slang, like bum, for the posterior.

As with penis jokes, the Pythons are also not above a joke about large breasts.

Caption: 'THE CHEMIST SKETCH—AN APOLOGY'

VOICE OVER (ERIC) The BBC would like to apologize for the poor quality of the writing in that sketch. It is not BBC policy to get easy laughs with words like bum, knickers, batty or wee-wees. (*laughs off camera*) Ssssh!

Cut to a man standing by a screen with a clicker.

BBC MAN (MICHAEL) These are the words that are not to be used again on this programme.

*He clicks the clicker. On screen appear the following slides: B*M B*TTY P*X KN*CKERS W**-W** SEMPRINI* 42 *A girl comes into shot.*

Alberto Semprini was a British pianist, probably included here for the homophone his profession suggests—as laconic a joke as the Pythons ever attempted.

GIRL Semprini!?
BBC MAN (*pointing*) Out!!

Cut back to the chemist's shop. The chemist appears again.

CHEMIST Right, who's got a boil on his Semprini, then?

A policeman appears and bundles him off. 43 *Cut to another chemist's shop with a different chemist standing at the counter. superimposed Caption: 'A LESS NAUGHTY CHEMIST'S' A man walks in.*

Chapman almost knocks Cleese over here. I'm not sure Cleese was expecting such a push.

MAN (ERIC) Good morning.
CHEMIST (TERRY J) Good morning, sir.
MAN Good morning. I'd like some aftershave, please.
CHEMIST Ah, certainly. Walk this way, please.
MAN If I could walk that way I wouldn't need aftershave. 44

Jones echoes the last time this gag was used (Episode 16), where Cleveland and Idle pointed as a warning about using crass punch lines.

The policeman runs into the shop and hauls the man off. Cut to shop again. Caption: 'A NOT AT ALL NAUGHTY CHEMIST'S' Another chemist is standing with a large sign reading 'A Not At All Naughty Chemist'. Pull back to reveal sign above stock reads 'Not At All Naughty Chemists Ltd'. A man enters.

MAN (ERIC) Good morning.

CHEMIST (MICHAEL) (*puts down sign*) Good morning, sir. Can I help you?

MAN Yes. I'd like some aftershave.

CHEMIST Ah. A toilet requisite-t-t-t-t...! Would you like to try this, sir. It's our very very latest, it's called Sea Mist.

MAN (*sniffs it*) I quite like it.

CHEMIST How about something a little more musky? This one's called Mimmo.

MAN

NOT REALLY, NO. HAVE YOU ANYTHING A LITTLE MORE FISHIER?

CHEMIST Fishier?

MAN Fishier.

CHEMIST Fish, fish, fish. A fishy requisite-t-t-t-t...

MAN Like halibut or sea bass.

CHEMIST Or bream?

MAN Yes.

CHEMIST No, we haven't got any of that...ah, I've got mackerel...or cod...or hake...

MAN You haven't got anything a little more halibutish?

CHEMIST Er...parrot? 45 What's that doing there? Or skate with just a hint of prawn? Or crab, tiger and almonds, very unusual.

MAN I really had my heart set on halibut.

CHEMIST Well, sir, we had a fishy consignment in this morning, so I could nip down to the basement and see if I can come up trumps on this particular requisite-t-t-t-t. So it was halibut...or...?

MAN Sea bass.

CHEMIST Sea bass. Won't be a moment.

The man waits for a few seconds, starts becoming uncomfortable, looks at watch, hums.

MAN (*to camera*) Sorry about this...pom pom pom...Normally we try to avoid these little...pauses...longeurs...only dramatically he's gone down to the basement, you see. 'Course, there isn't really a basement but he just goes off and we pretend...Actually what happens is he goes off there, off camera, and just waits there so it *looks* as though he's gone down...to the basement. Actually I think he's rather overdoing it. Ah!

Long shot of the chemist with carton waiting off camera. Floor manager cues him and he walks to counter. 46

CHEMIST Well, sorry, sir. (*out of breath*) Lot of steps. (*man winks at camera*) Well, I'm afraid it didn't come in this morning, sir. But we have got some down at our Kensington branch. I'll just nip down there and get it for you.

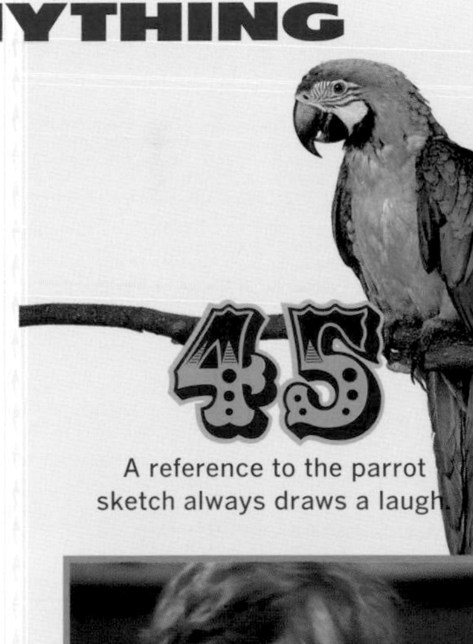

45

A reference to the parrot sketch always draws a laugh.

46

Actually, Idle cues him with the word "Ah!" and an eager look, and Palin runs in, getting a hearty laugh from the audience that has been watching him wait offscreen.

A nice gag on the usually pretentious names (and numbers) assigned to scents.

Idle's actually on the correct side, but he does guiltily run back into position as Palin "returns."

49

Aberdeen is a town in the north of Scotland, a full 540 miles north of Kensington, which is in London.

Prince Philip then, and now the duke of Edinburgh and Queen Elizabeth II's husband, was known for walking with his arms behind his back. (Oh, that and making racially sensitive comments whenever possible.)

MAN How long will that be?
CHEMIST Twenty minutes.
MAN Twenty minutes!

As he stands getting embarrassed, a girl hastily dressed as an assistant approaches him and hands him a message on a long stick.

MAN Oh...I wonder what other people use for aftershave lotion?

Cut to vox pops film.

GUMBY (MICHAEL) I use a body rub called Halitosis to make my breath seem sweet.
SECOND GUMBY (JOHN) I use an aftershave called Semprini.

He is hauled off by policeman.

CHEMIST (*hurrying past*) I'm sorry, sorry—can't stop now, I've got to get to Kensington.
CARDINAL XIMINEZ (MICHAEL) I use two kinds of aftershave lotions—Frankincense, Myrrh—three kinds of aftershave lotions, Frankincense, Myrrh, Sandalwood—four kinds of aftershave lotion. Frankincense,...
MAN (GRAHAM) I have a cold shower every morning just before I go mad, and then I go mad, 1. Mad, 2. Mad, 3. Mad, 4...
SHABBY (MICHAEL) (*hurrying past*) I use Rancid Polecat number two. 47 It keeps my skin nice and scaly.
CHEMIST Sorry again. Can't stop—got to get back.

Cut back to chemist's where the man is at a clock on wall pushing minute hand round twenty minutes. He looks at the camera guiltily and returns to right side of counter. 48 *The chemist enters.*

CHEMIST Well I'm afraid they don't have any at our Kensington branch. But we have some down at the depot.
MAN Where's that?
CHEMIST Aberdeen. 49
MAN Aberdeen?!
CHEMIST It's all right. Wait here...I've got a car.
MAN No, no, no. I'll take the other, the crab, tiger and...
CHEMIST Almond requisite...t...t...?
MAN I'll take it.

The chemist turns his back. A shoplifter enters. He is two men inside a large mac. He has false arms behind his back à la Duke of Edinburgh. 50 *The man watches him. He strolls to the counter and then two arms come out of coat and grab things from counter taking them inside the coat. Then these two arms are joined by a third arm which is black. All these arms steal stuff. The man taps the chemist and points at shoplifter. Chemist watches and then blows whistle. They wait for a tick. Then the policeman runs into the shop.*

POLICEMAN (GRAHAM) Right. Right! RIGHT! Now then! Now then! Your turn.
CHEMIST Aren't you going to say 'What's all this then?'?
POLICEMAN Oh! Right, what's all this, then?
CHEMIST This man has been shoplifting, officer.
POLICEMAN Oh, he has? Yus?
CHEMIST Yes.
POLICEMAN Are you trying to tell me my job?

CHEMIST No, but he's been shoplifting.

POLICEMAN Look! I must warn you that anything you may say will be ignored and furthermore, given half a chance I'll put my fist through your teeth. F'tang. F'tang. 51

MAN But officer, this man here...

POLICEMAN I've had enough of you. You're under arrest.

He makes noises of plane flying and firing.

CHEMIST Officer, it wasn't him. (*indicates shoplifter*) *He's* the shoplifter.

SHOPLIFTER (TERRY G) No I'm not.

SHOPLIFTER'S MATE (*sticking his head out of mac*) He's not...I'm a witness.

POLICEMAN (*to chemist*) One more peep out of you and I'll do you for heresy.

CHEMIST Heresy. Blimey. I didn't expect the Spanish Inquisition.

POLICEMAN Shut up! F'tang. F'tang. Oh, that's nice. (*he takes an object off the counter and pockets it*) Right. I'm taking you along to the station.

MAN What for?

POLICEMAN I'm charging you with illegal possession of whatever we happen to have down there. Right. (*makes plane noise again*) Lunar module calling Buzz Aldrin. 52 Come in. Raindrops keep falling on my head...but that doesn't mean that my... 53

Caption: 'AN APOLOGY'

VOICE OVER (JOHN) The BBC would like to apologize to the police about the character of Police Constable Pan Am. He was not meant to represent the average police officer. Similarly, the reference to Buzz Aldrin, the astronaut, was the product of a disordered mind and should not be construed as having any other significance.

Photo of Buzz Aldrin. Superimposed caption: 'THE BUZZ ALDRIN SHOW STARRING BUZZ ALDRIN WITH...(credits)' 54 *Cut to Gumbys as at start of show.*

GUMBYS

AND NOW FOR SOMETHING COMPLETELY DIFFERENT.

(*jump cut to Gumbys with wigs on; then back to original shot*) Oh that was fun. And now... caption: 'the end'

GUMBYS The end. The end! The end! The end!

In Episode 19, the candidate for the Silly Party in the Pythons parody of British elections will be "Tarquin Fin-Tim-Lin-Bin-Whin-Bim-Lim-Bus-Stop-F'tang-F'tang-Olé-Biscuitbarrel."

Buzz Aldrin was the Lunar Module pilot on the Apollo 11 mission and the second man to walk on the moon. This episode was recorded just over a year after that historic saunter.

53

Burt Bacharach's "Raindrops Keep Falling on My Head," made a classic by inclusion in the 1969 movie *Butch Cassidy and the Sundance Kid* (sung therein by B.J. Thomas).

"The Star-Spangled Banner" also plays during the credits.

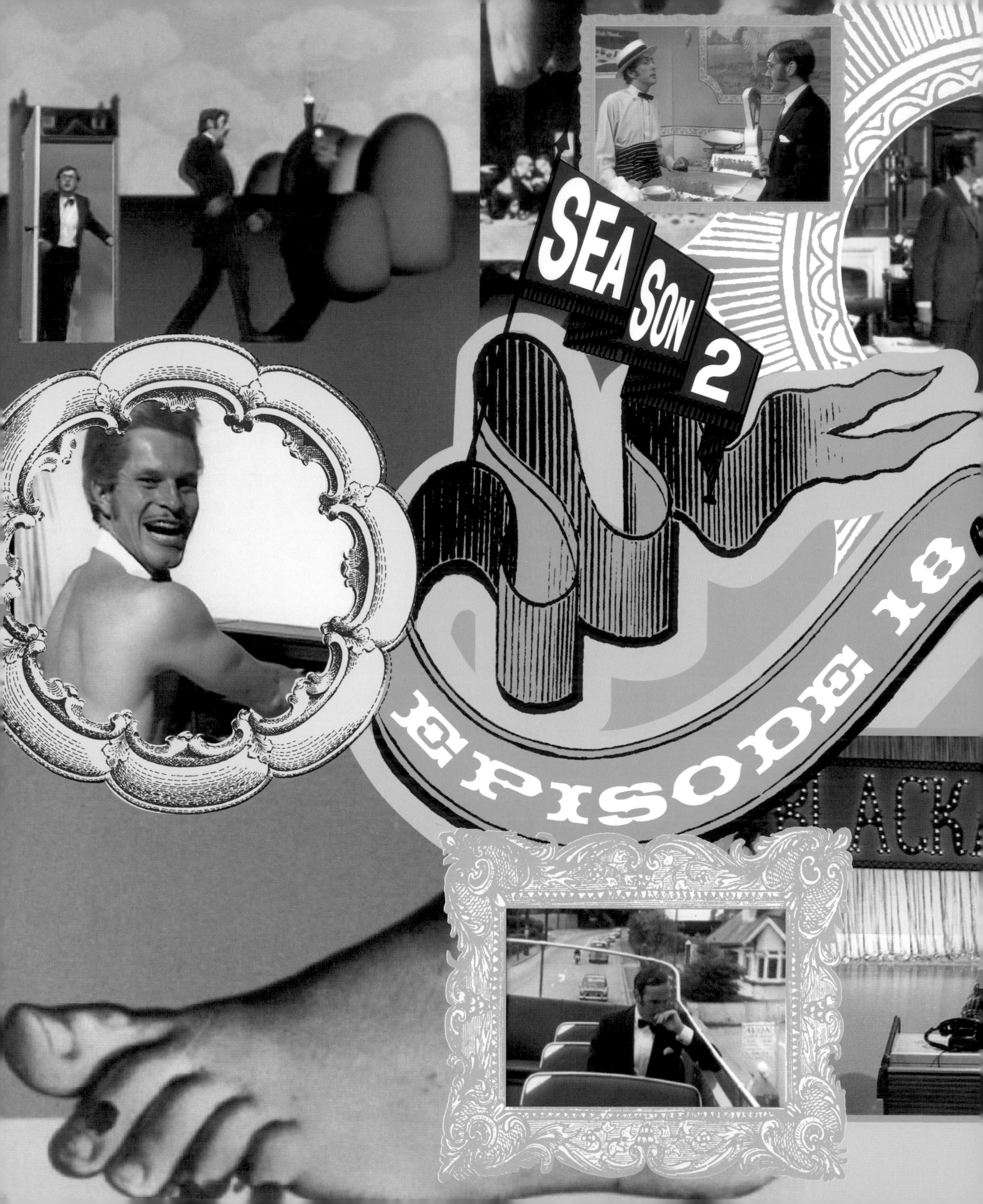

SEA
SON
2
EPISODE 18

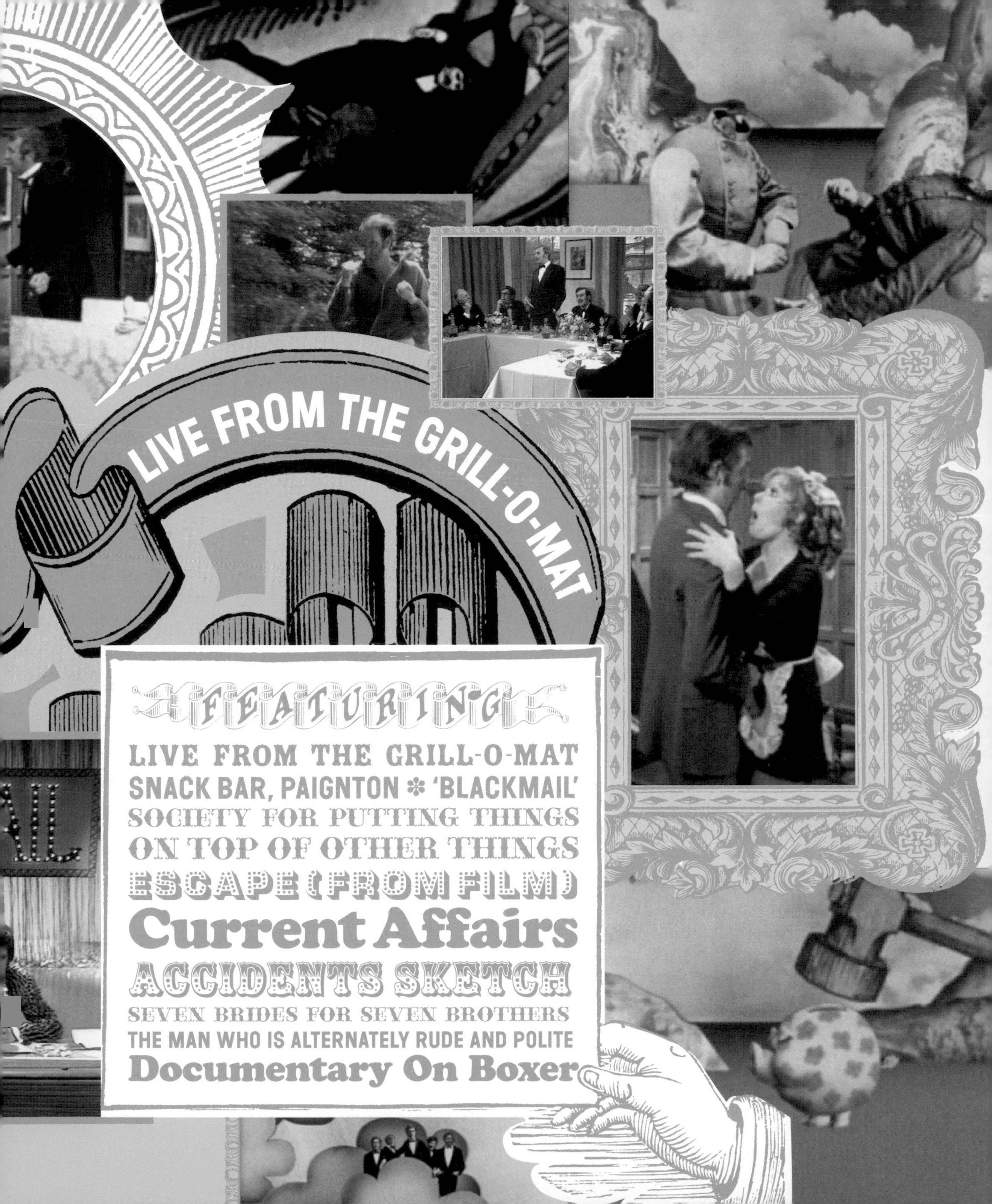

LIVE FROM THE GRILL-O-MAT
FEATURING
LIVE FROM THE GRILL-O-MAT
SNACK BAR, PAIGNTON ✽ 'BLACKMAIL'
SOCIETY FOR PUTTING THINGS
ON TOP OF OTHER THINGS
ESCAPE (FROM FILM)
Current Affairs
ACCIDENTS SKETCH
SEVEN BRIDES FOR SEVEN BROTHERS
THE MAN WHO IS ALTERNATELY RUDE AND POLITE
Documentary On Boxer

FIRST AIRED: OCTOBER 27, 1970

BBC world symbol.

VOICE OVER (MICHAEL) Monty Python's Flying Circus tonight comes to you live from the Grillomat Snack Bar, Paignton. 1

Paignton is a sleepy seaside town in Devon, on England's southwest coast.

Interior of a nasty snack bar. Customers around, preferably real people. Linkman sitting at one of the plastic tables.

LINKMAN (JOHN) Hello to you live from the Grillomat Snack Bar, Paignton. And so, without any more ado, let's have the titles.

IT'S MAN (MICHAEL)

IT'S...

Animated titles.

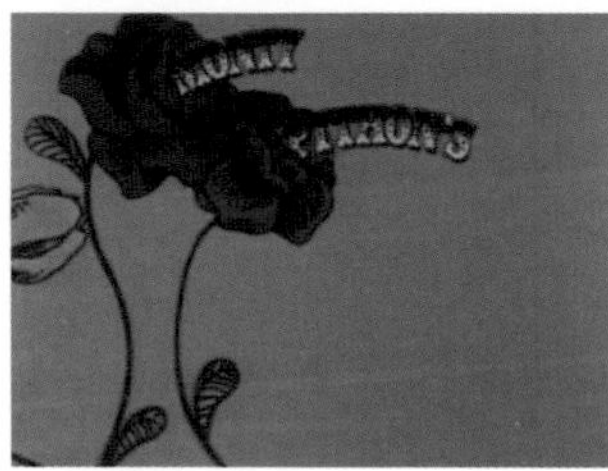

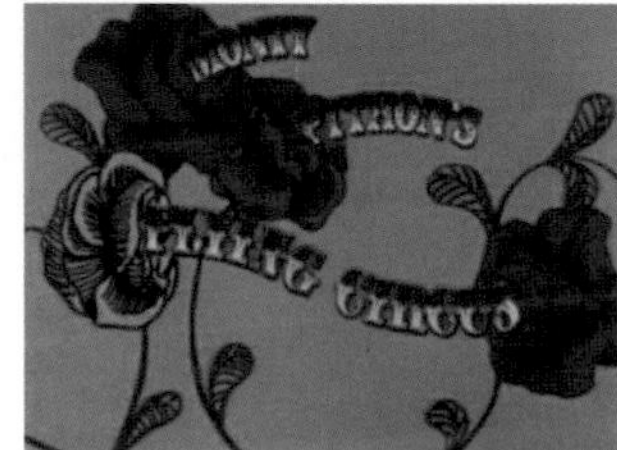

Back to the snack bar.

LINKMAN (*with rather forced bonhomie*) Well, those were the titles. And now for the first item this evening on the Menu—ha ha—the team have chosen as a little hors d'oeuvres an item—and I think we can be sure it won't be an ordinary item—in fact the team told me just before the show that anything could happen, and probably would—so let's have...the item.

Cut to the word 'Blackmail' in letters four feet high, picked out in light bulbs which flash on and off. Big showbiz music crashes in. Camera pulls back to reveal glittery showbiz set. A presenter in a glittery showbiz jacket sits behind a glittery desk, with a telephone on it.

PRESENTER (MICHAEL) Hello, good evening, and welcome to 'Blackmail'! And to start tonight's programme, we go north to Preston in Lancashire, and Mrs Betty Teal! 2

The David Frost greeting once again.

Cut to a slightly blurred black and white photo of a housewife with her face blotted out by a black oblong.

PRESENTER'S VOICE Hello, Mrs Teal!

Cut back to presenter. He picks up a letter and reads it.

PRESENTER Now this is for £15 and it's to stop us revealing the name of your lover in Bolton. 3

Superimposed caption: '£15' (which flashes on and off quickly)

PRESENTER So Mrs Teal...if you send us £15 by return of post, please, and your husband Trevor, and your lovely children, Diane, Janice and Juliet need never know the name of your lover in Bolton.

Cut to a nude man (except for a collar and tie) at organ. 4 *He plays a few stirring chords. Cut back to presenter.*

PRESENTER (*as he speaks he holds up the various items*) And now...a letter...a hotel registration book...and a series of photographs...which could add up to divorce, premature retirement, and possible criminal proceedings for a company director in Bromsgrove. 5 He's a freemason, and a prospective Tory MP...that's Mr S. of Bromsgrove...£3,000... 6

Superimposed caption: '£3,000' (which flashes on and off)

PRESENTER ...to stop us revealing your name, the name of the three other people involved, the youth organization to which they belong, and the shop where you bought the equipment.

Cut back to nude man at organ with chords again. Cut to still of two pairs of naked feet and lower legs. Organ music over this. Cut back to presenter.

PRESENTER We'll be showing you more of that photograph later in the programme...unless we hear from Charles or Michael. And now it's time for our 'Stop the Film' spot!

Superimposed flashing caption: 'stop the film'

PRESENTER The rules are very simple. We have taken a film which contains compromising scenes and unpleasant details, which could wreck a man's career. But the victim may phone me at any point and stop the film. But remember, the money increases as the film goes on. So the longer you leave it...the more you have to pay. So now, with the clock at £300 this week 'Stop the Film' visited Thames Ditton... 7

Another regular Python reference, this time the right way around (rather than "Mr. Notlob").

4

Terry Gilliam with a lovely smile.

Bromsgrove is a relatively nondescript town in the Midlands.

The Freemasons and members of Parliament—two organizations the Pythons don't much care for. There was plenty fun made of the Masons in Episode 17.

Thames Ditton is a small village on the outskirts of London, in the county of Surrey, though the scene wasn't filmed there.

Murky and unbearably strobed—watching it for any length of time might induce epilepsy.

Victoria Station is one of the busiest rail stations in London.

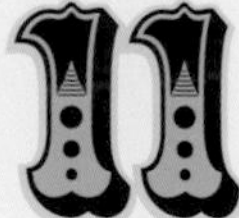

In fact, the phone is merely on a table around a corner; of course, there's no explanation for how he knows the film of him engaged in S&M is being aired. Probably best not to think too hard sometimes.

11

"Ex-public school type" means they are of a certain social standing: one that is well-to-do and has a certain air of privilege.

There are numerous Royal Societies in the U.K.—for everything from protecting animals to Ulster architects.

The following film is shot in murky 8mm. 8
As the film progresses we have a £ sign with numerals in one corner which increase. Shot of a residential street in Thames Ditton (sic). Another section of a street with a figure in a Robin Hood hat and raincoat—in the distance on the far side of the road, so we can't really make him out. Cut to slightly closer shot of him about to cross the road. Cut to suburban house. The man is standing at the door pressing the bell and looking round rather furtively. Again shot from some distance and over a hedge. Cut back to the studio. The presenter looking at a monitor and then at the phone. Back to the film: a woman opens the door. She wears a dressing gown over lingerie. A shaky zoom in to reveal her clothing. Wide shot of house with door shut. Jump cut to shot obviously taken from a window in the house. Shaky zoom in on window. We can see in the window...both the man and woman enter the bedroom. He goes out of shot, taking his coat off. Cut back to the studio.

PRESENTER He's being very brave here...

Cut back to the film: even closer perhaps of window. A series of short jump cuts. She is undressing. She throws off her dressing gown. A jump and she's taking off her negligee. Underneath she wears black corsets. She produces a whip and seems to be beckoning to the man. Phone rings. Cut back to the studio. The presenter picks up the phone.

PRESENTER Hello, sir, hello, yes. No sir, no, I'm sure you didn't. No, it's all right, sir, we don't morally censure, we just want the money...Yes, and here's the address to send it to:
VOICE OVER (TERRY J) *(and caption)*: 'Blackmail, Behind the hot water pipes, Third washroom along Victoria Station' 9
PRESENTER Not at all, sir...thank *you*. *(he puts the phone down)*

Cut to a hallway in which a middle-aged man in dinner dress is putting down the telephone rather furtively. 10 *He leaves the booth and goes through a door into a large room where a banquet is in progress. There are tables on three sides of a square and he joins the head table which faces as it were downstage. He sits beside other middle-aged and rather elderly men all of whom are the city of London ex-public school type.* 11

As he sits, the toastmaster standing behind speaks.

MAN (TERRY J) Sorry chaps, it was my mother.
TOASTMASTER (ERIC) Gentlemen, pray silence for the President of the Royal Society for Putting Things on Top of Other Things. 12

There is much upperclass applause and, banging on the table as Sir William rises to his feet.

SIR WILLIAM (GRAHAM) I thank you, gentlemen. The year has been a good one for the Society (*hear, hear*). This year our members have put more things on top of other things than ever before. But, I should warn you, this is no time for complacency. No, there are still many things, and I cannot emphasize this too strongly, not on top of other things. I myself, on my way here this evening, saw a thing that was not on top of another thing in any way. (*shame!*) Shame indeed but we must not allow ourselves to become too despondent. For, we must never forget that if there was not one thing that was not on top of another thing our society would be nothing more than a meaningless body of men that had gathered together for no good purpose. But we flourish. This year our Australasian members and the various organizations affiliated to our Australasian branches put no fewer than twenty-two things on top of other things. (*applause*) Well done all of you. But there is one cloud on the horizon. In this last year our Staffordshire branch has not succeeded in putting one thing on top of another (*shame!*). Therefore I call upon our Staffordshire delegate to explain this weird behaviour.

As Sir William sits a meek man rises at one of the side tables.

MR CUTLER (JOHN) Er, Cutler, Staffordshire. Um...well, Mr Chairman, it's just that most of the members in Staffordshire feel...the whole thing's a bit silly. 13

Cries of outrage. Chairman leaps to feet.

SIR WILLIAM Silly! SILLY!!!! (*he pauses and thinks*) Silly! I suppose it is, a bit. What have we been doing wasting our lives with all this nonsense (*hear, hear*). Right, okay, meeting adjourned for ever.

He gets right up and walks away from the table to approving noises and applause. He walks to a door at the side of the studio set and goes through it. Exterior shot: a door opens and Sir William appears out of it into the fresh air. He suddenly halts.

SIR WILLIAM Good Lord. I'm on film. How did that happen?

He turns round and disappears into the building again. He reappears through door, crosses set and goes out through another door. Exterior: he appears from the door into the fresh air and then stops.

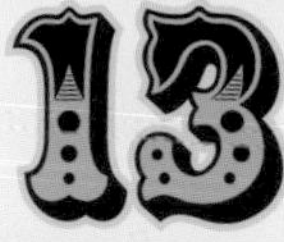

Staffordshire, sitting in the very middle of the country and famous for its pottery, isn't the most fashionable nor eminent county, but it might be considered as middle of the road—and therefore dubious about silliness—as any.

SIR WILLIAM It's film again. What's going on?

He turns and disappears through the door again. Cut to him inside the building. He crosses to a window and looks out, then turns and says...

SIR WILLIAM

GENTLEMEN! I HAVE BAD NEWS. THIS ROOM IS SURROUNDED BY FILM.

MEMBERS What! What!

Several members run to window and look out. Cut to film of them looking out of window. 14 *Cut to studio: the members run to a door and open it. Cut to film: of them appearing at the door hesitating and then closing door. Cut to studio: with increasing panic they run to the second door. Cut to film: they appear, hesitate, and go back inside. Cut to studio: they run to Sir William in the centre of the room.*

Poor Terry Jones inadvertently cracks the back of his head on the window frame as he looks out. It makes a thudding sound, but he carries on like a trooper.

A MEMBER We're trapped!
SIR WILLIAM Don't panic, we'll get out of this.
A MEMBER How?
SIR WILLIAM We'll tunnel our way out.
BARNES (MICHAEL) Good thinking, sir. I'll get the horse.
SIR WILLIAM Okay Captain, you detail three men, start digging and load them up with cutlery, and then we'll have a rota, we'll have two hours digging, two hours vaulting and then two hours sleeping, okay? 15

The scene now becomes a neat satire of *The Great Escape*, the 1963 film that dramatized a real tunnel dig and breakout from the German prisoner of war camp Stalag Luft III, in what is now is Poland.

Barnes and others carry a vaulting horse into shot. The members start vaulting over it. Two Gestapo officers walk by.

MR CUTLER All right, Medwin, let's see you get over that horse. Pick your feet up, Medwin. Come on, boy!
FIRST GERMAN OFFICER (IAN DAVIDSON) Ze stupid English. Zey are prisoners and all they do is the sport.
SECOND GERMAN OFFICER (TERRY G) One thing worries me, Fritz.
FIRST GERMAN OFFICER Ja?
SECOND GERMAN OFFICER Where's the traditional cheeky and lovable Cockney sergeant?
SERGEANT (TERRY J) (*donning tin helmet*) Cheer up, Fritz, it may never happen. (*sings*) Maybe it's because I'm a Londoner... 16
SECOND GERMAN OFFICER Good. Everything seems to be in order.

"Maybe It's Because I'm a Londoner" is a song written by Hubert Gregg in 1943 as he watched German doodlebug missiles soar over London. It became a folk anthem almost instantly.

The Gestapo officers leave. Mr Cutler runs up to Sir William.

MR CUTLER Colonel! I've just found another exit, sir.
SIR WILLIAM Okay, quickly, run this way.
EVERYONE If we could run that way...*(he stops them with a finger gesture)* sorry. 17

A reference back to previous Episodes 16 & 17, in which that same joke is always pooh-poohed.

Animation: A bleak landscape. A large foot with a Victorian lady on top of it comes hopping past. A door in a building opens and the society members (real people, superimposed) run out, along the cartoon, and disappear, falling into nothingness. Cut to section of an oesophagus. The members (now animated cut-outs) fall down it into a stomach where they are joined by various large vegetables. Pull back to show that this is a cutaway view of an Edwardian gentleman. He belches.

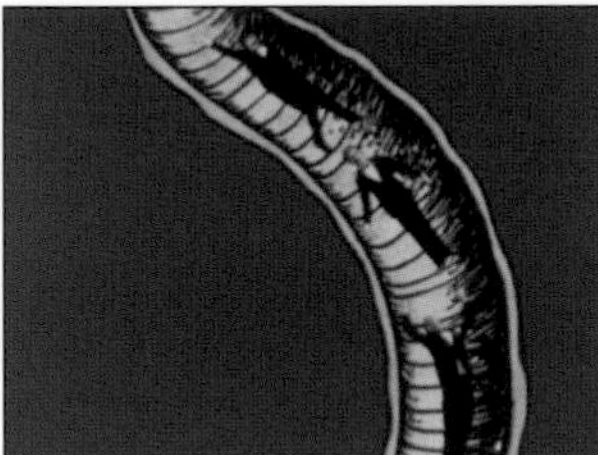
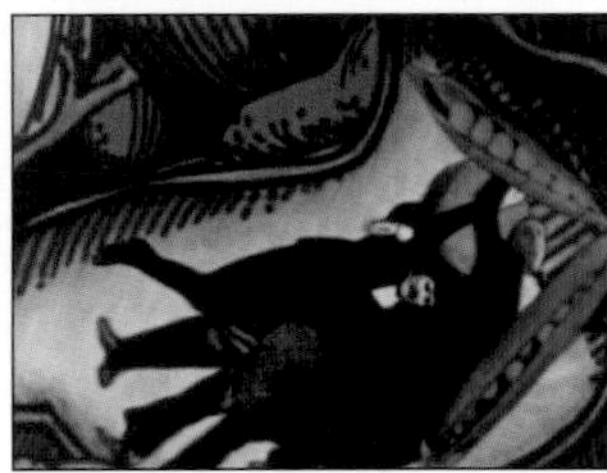

ANIMATION VOICE Oh, I'm terribly sorry, excuse me.

He moves through a door marked 'gents'. We hear a lavatory flushing. Cut to café: linkman at table as before.

LINKMAN (JOHN) Ah, hello. Well they certainly seem to be in a tight spot, and *I* spot...our next item—so let's get straight on with the fun and go over to the next item—or dish! Ha, ha!

Cut to a simple set with two chairs in it. Close up of Mr Praline.

PRALINE (JOHN) Hello. 'Ow are you? I'm fine. 18 Welcome to a new half-hour chat show in which me, viz the man what's talking to you now, and Brooky—to wit my flat mate—and nothing else, I'd like to emphasize that—discuss current affairs issues of burning import.

A reprise of the character from the famous parrot sketch from Episode 8, wearing the same nasty mackintosh raincoat and using the same clipped speech.

Pull back to show Brooky.

BROOKY (ERIC)

HAVE YOU HEARD THE ONE ABOUT THE THREE NUNS IN THE NUDIST COLONY?

PRALINE Shut up. Tonight, the population explosion.
BROOKY Apparently there were these three nuns...
PRALINE Shut up. Come the year 1991, given the present rate of increase in the world's population, the Chinese will be three deep. Another thing...

Floor manager comes in.

FLOOR MANAGER (TERRY J) Sorry, loves, sorry, the show is too long this week and this scene's been cut.
PRALINE Lord Hill's at the bottom of this. 19
FLOOR MANAGER But if you can find a piano stool you can appear later on in the show on film.
BROOKY 'Ow much?
FLOOR MANAGER Oh, about ten bob each.
PRALINE I wouldn't wipe me nose on it.
BROOKY 'Ave you 'eard the one about these three nuns...

Yet another reference to poor Lord Hill, chairman of the BBC.

PRALINE Sh. I can hear something. 'Ang about, we may still get in this show as a link.

Praline kneels and puts his ear to the floor. In the bottom section of the shot we see beneath the floor an animation of the unfortunate members of the Society for Putting Things on Top of Other Things being flushed along a pipe.

BROOKY That's clever. How do they do that?

PRALINE

COLOUR SEPARATION, YOU COTTON HEAD.

Animation: VARIOUS ADVENTURES OF THE SOCIETY MEMBERS.

Cut back to linkman. There is a loud argument going on in the café behind him.

LINKMAN Well, they seem to be in another tight spot...(*to the argument*) Could you...could you, could you keep it down a little, please. Thank you so much. Could you keep it down, please... Thank you. (*to camera*) Well and now we move on to our, to our main course. Prawn salad... Prawn salad?

Oak-panelled door with notice on it saying 'Prawn Salad Ltd'. The butler pushes it open and shows man into living room. The room is fairly large, containing at one end opposite the door a big window, making the room look quite high up—although it should be stately rather than modern. In the middle of the room's back wall there is a large ornate mirror, over a mantelpiece filled with objects. To the right of this wall there is a large bookshelf filled with books, and in front of it there is a drinks trolley.

BUTLER (GRAHAM) Well, if you'll just wait in here, sir, I'm sure Mr Thompson won't keep you waiting long.

MAN (ERIC) Fine. Thanks very much.

He picks up a magazine. The mirror behind him without warning falls off the wall and smashes to the ground. The butler returns, and looks at the man enquiringly.

MAN The mirror fell off the wall.

BUTLER Sir?
MAN The mirror fell off...off the wall...it fell.
BUTLER (*polite but disbelieving*) I see. You'd better wait here. I'll get a cloth.

The butler just closes the door behind him and the bookcase detaches itself from the wall and comes sweeping down, bringing with it the drinks trolley. The butler opens the door.

MAN Ah, it...it came off the wall.
BUTLER Yes, sir?
MAN It just came right off the wall.
BUTLER Really, sir.
MAN Yes, I...I didn't touch it.
BUTLER (*politely ironic*) Of course not. It just fell off the wall.
MAN Yes. It just fell off the wall.
BUTLER Don't move. I'll get help.

He goes.

MAN Yes—er, fell off the wall. *A maid enters.*
MAID (CAROL) Oh my God, what a mess. 'Ere, did you do this?
MAN No, no. I didn't do all this. It...*it* did it all.
MAID Oh? Well...'ere, hold this. I'll get started.

She hands him a dagger.

MAN Oh, it's jolly nice. What is it?
MAID It's a Brazilian dagger. Ooops.

She trips, falls lethally on to the dagger he is holding.

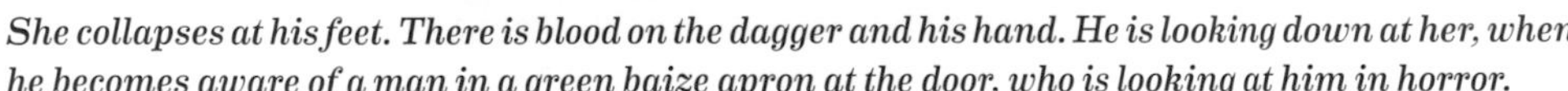

She collapses at his feet. There is blood on the dagger and his hand. He is looking down at her, when he becomes aware of a man in a green baize apron at the door, who is looking at him in horror.

MAN Er, she just fell on...on to the dagger.
GREEN (TERRY J) (*soothingly*) Yes, of course she did, sir.
MAN Yes, just gave me the dagger and tripped, and went, 'Oops'.

Green starts backing round the room away from him, but humouring him.

GREEN Yes sir, I understand.
MAN I mean, I didn't er...

GREEN Oh no, no, of course not, sir, I understand.
MAN I mean she...she just, er...
GREEN Fell?
MAN Fell.
GREEN (*backs off too far and falls backwards through the window*) Arrghh!
MAN (*to window*) I'm terribly sorry.

A policeman and the butler appear at the door.

BUTLER That's him.
POLICEMAN (MICHAEL) Right, sir.
MAN Hello, officer. There seems to have been an accident. Well, several accidents actually.
POLICEMAN That's right, sir. Would you come this way, please. (*goes towards him*) Ahh! (*clutches chest*) It's me...me heart, sir. (*collapses*)
BUTLER You swine. I'll get you for that.

He is about to move forward when a large portion of the ceiling collapses on him. He goes down, too.

MAN Er, I won't wait. I'll phone.

He moves off through door. Large crashing sounds. He comes downstairs into a stretch of hall leading to an outside door. As he comes suits of armour collapse, bookcase glass smashes, a grandfather clock tips over and smashes, pictures fall off walls. All this quite quickly in sequence as he passes in horror. He gets to the main door. We see his relief. He closes the main door behind him, slamming it: it's a country-house-type entrance. Cut to stock film of country house being blown up. Cut back to man looking in horror, with dust and rubble swirling around. He is holding the remains of the door.

MAN Sorry. 20

Proving that the British will apologize for anything.

Pull wide. He is in a patch of rubble. The Society for Putting Things on Top of Other Things members walk by in their evening dress.

MEMBERS I think we're really out this time. Yes. Jolly good. Now where's the school hall. I think it's over there. Come on. Sorry. Jolly good.

They go past the bishop in the field.

BISHOP (MICHAEL) (*singing*) Oh, Mr Belpit. Your legs are so swollen. 21

The bishop, Mr. Belpit, and his swollen legs were a key motif in Episode 16.

SIR WILLIAM Excuse me, is that the school hall?
BISHOP Um, I'm sorry, I don't know. I'm not in this one—I'm in next week's, I think.
SIR WILLIAM Oh, come on.
BISHOP Oh, Mr Belpit!...

They come to a school hall. A sign says 'Seven Brides for Seven Brothers, presented by the staff and pupils of the Dibley School for Boys'. 22

Seven Brides for Seven Brothers refers to the 1954 musical film. "Dibley" isn't a real place, though the word did lend itself much later to TV show *The Vicar of Dibley*.

SIR WILLIAM Oh, here we are. (*they go in*)

Cut to linkman in cafeteria.

LINKMAN Ah well, they seem to have linked that themselves, so there's no need for me to interrupt at all. So, ah, back to the school hall.

A school hall with a stage. Mr Praline and Brooky enter. Praline sits at piano and plays something very badly; Brooky turns the pages for him. Music ends. Unseen schoolmaster announcer:

SCHOOLMASTER 'Seven Brides for Seven Brothers'. (*slight applause*)

The curtain parts. Enter headmaster in mortar board and gown.

HEADMASTER (GRAHAM) 'Tis time the seven Smith brothers had brides. Fetch me Smith Major. 23

Enter Smith Major in short pants.

FIRST SMITH (TERRY J) Sir.
HEADMASTER 'Tis time you and your six brothers were married.
FIRST SMITH Thank you, Headmaster.
HEADMASTER Fetch me your six brothers, that the seven brothers may be together.

Smith Major rings handbell. Three boys enter and stand next to him.

BOYS Behold, the seven brothers.
HEADMASTER Right, I'll see Watson, Wilkins, and Spratt in my study afterwards.
FIRST SMITH (*has to be prompted, then declaims badly*) But where shall we find seven brides for seven brothers?
SECOND SMITH (TERRY J) The Sabine School for Girls. 24
THIRD SMITH (ERIC) Yes, and it's the Annual Dance.
HEADMASTER Fetch hither the seven brides for seven brothers.

Enter two schoolgirls.

TWO GIRLS Behold the seven brides.
HEADMASTER Fetch hither the padre that the seven brides may marry the seven brothers. (*nothing happens*) Fetch hither the master on duty that the seven brides may marry the seven brothers.
PADRE (MICHAEL) (*entering*) Sorry, I'm late, Headmaster—I've been wrestling with Plato.
HEADMASTER What you do in your own time, Padre, is written on the wall in the vestry.
PADRE

RIGHT, DO YOU FOUR BOYS TAKE THESE TWO GIRLS TO BE YOUR SEVEN BRIDES?

BOYS Yes, sir.
PADRE Right, go and do your prep.

The curtain comes across quickly. Animation sketch links us to a butcher's shop.

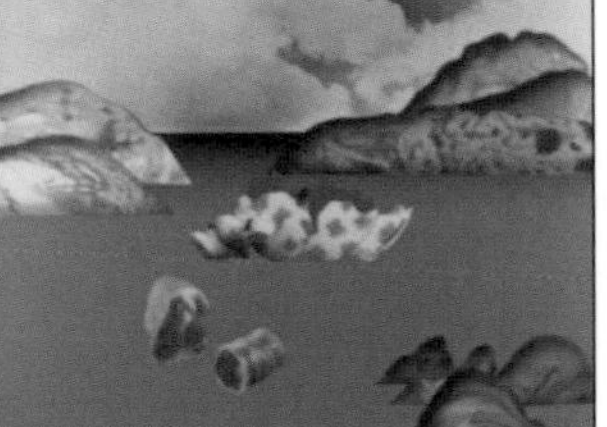

Harmless looking city gent enters.

GENT (MICHAEL) Good morning, I'd care to purchase a chicken, please.

23

The eldest child in a family tended to take the name "major" with the younger ones taking "minor," especially in upper-class schools.

24

Nice name for a girl's school, and an apt link to *Seven Brides*—a reference to the "rape of the Sabine women," in which Roman men abducted women from the neighboring Sabines.

"Posh" is slang for off-puttingly well-to-do. It apocryphally comes from "port out, starboard home," which was the best way to travel to India on a boat (the sun was less taxing if you were on the correct side arriving and departing).

A "trollope" is a derisive description of a woman of ill morals.

A "ponce" is an offensive slang for a homosexual.

"Poovy po-nagger" is fake slang.

"Queen" and "la-di-dah poofta" are slurs on homosexuals.

"Pillock"—originally "pillicock," or penis—is now OK for use in polite company, as the original meaning is lost. (See under "schlemiel," "schlimazel," etc.)

More gay slurs.

BUTCHER (ERIC) Don't come here with that posh talk you nasty, stuck-up twit. 25
GENT I beg your pardon?
BUTCHER A chicken, sir. Certainly.
GENT Thank you. And how much does that work out to per pound, my good fellow?

BUTCHER Per pound, you slimy trollope, 26 what kind of a ponce are you? 27
GENT I'm sorry?
BUTCHER 4/6 a pound, sir, nice and ready for roasting.
GENT I see, and I'd care to purchase some stuffing in addition, please.
BUTCHER Use your own, you great poovy po-nagger! 28
GENT What?
BUTCHER Ah, certainly sir, some stuffing.
GENT Oh, thank you.
BUTCHER 'Oh, thank you' says the great queen like a la-di-dah poofta. 29
GENT I beg your pardon?
BUTCHER That's all right, sir, call again.
GENT Excuse me.
BUTCHER What is it now, you great pillock? 30
GENT Well, I can't help noticing that you insult me and then you're polite to me alternately.
BUTCHER I'm terribly sorry to hear that, sir.
GENT That's all right. It doesn't really matter.
BUTCHER Tough titty if it did, you nasty spotted prancer. 31

Cut to the Grillomat in Paignton. The announcer is just handing back a cup and saucer to a waitress.

LINKMAN Sorry, I asked for tea. (*she takes it grudgingly*) Thank you very much. (*to camera*) Well we've had the dessert and then, and so the first item, the last item on our menu of fun is the coffee. (*waitress hands him back his cup*) Now I did ask for tea.
WAITRESS (GRAHAM) But you just said coffee.
LINKMAN No, no, that was just my announcement, just a metaphor.

She shrugs and begins to move off. At the table just behind him we hear her complaining noisily in the background.

LINKMAN We come...look would you mind keeping it down, please...we come as—as I said just now, to the coffee.

WAITRESS Here, he said it again!

LINKMAN Shut up!

Film of a boxer (JOHN) *in training, running along a country road. All this is shot in 'Man Alive'* 32 *style: plenty of hand-held documentary work. Sound of boxer's feet on the leaves and heavy breathing.*

VOICE OVER (MICHAEL) This is Ken Clean-air Systems, the great white hope of the British boxing world. After three fights—and only two convictions—his manager believes that Ken is ready to face the giant American, Satellite Five.

Cut to manager being driven in Rolls. 33 *Superimposed caption: 'MR ENGLEBERT HUMPERDINCK—MANAGER'* 34

MANAGER (GRAHAM)

THE GREAT THING ABOUT KEN IS THAT HE'S ALMOST TOTALLY STUPID.

Cut back to Ken jogging, the early morning sun filtering through the trees.

VOICE OVER Every morning, he jogs the forty-seven miles from his two-bedroomed, eight-bathroom, six-up-two-down, three-to-go-house in Reigate, 35 to the Government's Pesticide Research Centre at Shoreham. Nobody knows why.

Cut to Ken's wife (a young married with her head in a scarf and curlers), hanging out the washing in a council estate. Caption: 'MRS CLEAN-AIR SYSTEMS'

MRS CAS (ERIC) Basically Ken is a very gentle, home-loving person. I remember when one of his stick insects had a knee infection. He stayed up all night rubbing it with germoline 36 and banging its head on the table.

Cut to Ken's mother—an old lady in a wheelchair. Hand-held big close-up against the sky. Caption: 'MRS NELLIE AIR-VENT, MOTHER'

MOTHER (TERRY J) Oh he was such a pretty baby, always so kind and gentle. He was really considerate to his mother, and not at all the kind of person you'd expect to pulverize their opponent into a bloody mass of flesh and raw bone, spitting teeth and fragments of gum into a ring which had become one man's hell and Ken's glory.

The wheelchair moves away and we see that it is on top of a car. Cut to exterior of a semi-detached house. Night.

VOICE OVER Every morning at his little three-room semi 37 near Reading Ken gets up at three o'clock (light goes on) and goes back to bed again because it's far too early.

Light goes out. Close-up alarm clock at 7.05. General shot of room, Ken coming out of bathroom pulling his track-suit on.

VOICE OVER At seven o'clock Ken gets up, he has a quick shower, a rub-down, gets into his track-suit, and goes back to bed again. (*shot of trainer running*) At 7.50 every morning Ken's trainer runs the 13,000 miles from his two-room lean-to in Bangkok and gets him up.

"Man Alive" was a BBC2 documentary show, running from 1965–1982.

A rather beautiful blue Rolls-Royce, the highest symbol of driving excellence at one time in the U.K. It is still thought of as a status symbol without compare.

Engelbert Humperdinck is a British singer who was born in India and moved to England, when he was 10.

The regular British house was "two-up, two-down," referring to the number of rooms.

"Germoline" is a traditional antiseptic ointment, many millions of gallons of which have been spread on the cut knees of British children.

A "semi" refers to a semi-detached house, meaning it's attached on one side to another house but not on the other.

General shot of room to show his trainer standing over the sleeping Ken. He holds a large mallet and a steel peg.

TRAINER (MICHAEL) I used to wake Ken up with a crowbar on the back of the head. But I recently found that this was too far from his brain and I wasn't getting through to him anymore. So I now wake him up with a steel peg driven into his skull with a mallet.

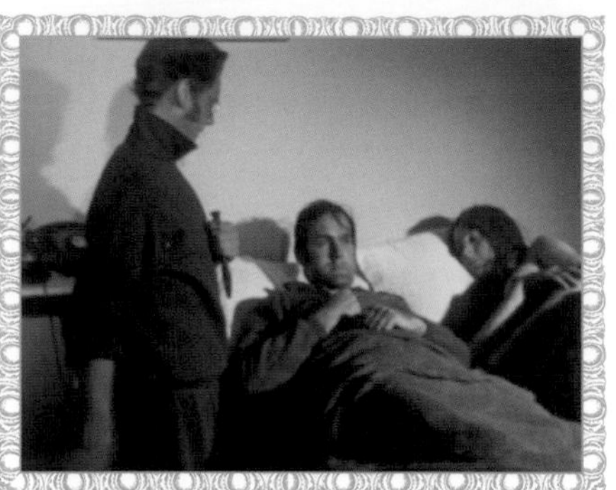

Cut to the empty kitchen, shot from ground level. The camera pans across to show plate of food under an upright chair, and then pans across the room to the kitchen cupboard; Mrs Clean-air Systems at the sink.

VOICE OVER For breakfast every day, Ken places a plate of liver and bacon under his chair, and locks himself in the cupboard.

Cut to gym. Manager standing beside ropes of the ring. Again a hand-held 'Man Alive' type interview, with camera noise and all.

MANAGER Well, he's having a lot of mental difficulties with his breakfasts, but this is temperament, caused by a small particle of brain in his skull, and once we've removed that he'll be perfectly all right.

Close-up alarm clock. Hands at 8.30.

VOICE OVER At 8.30 the real training begins. (*General shot of room. Ken asleep in bed*) Ken goes back to bed and his trainer gets him up. (*The door bursts open but we don't stay to see what happens. We cut immediately to outside of the house. His trainer pushes Ken out. Trainer goes back into the house (obviously to Ken's wife).* 38 *Cut to Ken jogging through town. Hand held. Ken finds his way blocked by a parked car. He stops and looks very puzzled, then instead of going round it turns and runs back the way he has come.*) At 10.30 every morning Ken arrives at what he thinks is the gym. Sometimes it's a sweetshop, sometimes it's a private house. Today it's a hospital.

Ken turns into the gates or doors of a hospital. There is a slight pause, and a white-coated doctor arrives at the door and points right up the street.

The actual scene has the Trainer and the Wife standing at the door together, only to run back inside once Ken has left.

DOCTOR Um, straight down there. Straight down there.

Ken follows his finger and looks very hard in that direction. When he is satisfied that Ken has understood where he is pointing, the doctor retires back inside. Ken turns and watches him as he does this, then turns and sets off in the opposite direction. Cut to a shot of a roadside diner.

VOICE OVER For lunch Ken crouches down in the road and rubs gravel into his hair. (*Pan down to roadside to reveal Ken just finishing rubbing gravel into his hair; he stands up and hops over a railing to a riverside where a bed stands*) But lunch doesn't take long. Ken's soon up on his feet and back to bed. (*Ken hops into the bed*) And his trainer has to run the 49,000 miles from his two-bedroom, six-living-room tree-house in Kyoto to wake him up. (*Trainer runs into shot, pauses by bedside and turns to camera. He has large plumber's bag.*)

TRAINER

HELLO. WHEN KEN IS IN A REALLY DEEP SLEEP LIKE THIS ONE, THE ONLY WAY TO WAKE HIM UP IS TO SAW HIS HEAD OFF.

Cut to stock close-up of punch bag and glove smashing into it. Continual hitting and impact-bang-bang-bang-bang throughout.

VOICE OVER What is he like in the ring, this human dynamo, this eighteen-stone bantamweight battering-ram? 39 We asked his sparring partner and one-time childhood sweetheart, Maureen Spencer.

Cut to medium close-up of Maureen, very busty in boxing gear and sparring helmet.

MAUREEN (CAROL) Well, I think that if Ken keeps his right up, gets in with the left jab and takes the fight to his man—well, he should go for a cut eye in the third and put Wilcox on the canvas by six.

She goes back to sparring and we see it is she who is hitting the punchbag. Remaining on her we hear the voice over.

VOICE OVER Ken's opponent in Tuesday's fight is Petula Wilcox, the Birmingham girl who was a shorthand typist before turning pro in 1968. (*Cut to typical teenage girl's bedsit. Pin-ups of popstars on the walls. Teddy bears on the bed and gonks. Petula Wilcox is sitting up on the bed knitting.*) 40

A bantamweight is allowed to be 115 to 118 pounds, so hardly "eighteen stones" (or 252 pounds).

Bob Dylan is one of the pop-star pinups on the wall.

Cliff Richard had been a rock-and-roller originally, fronting The Shadows, a popular band in Britain in the late 1950s and early 1960s. After becoming a Christian, Richard and his music was by 1970 the epitome of harmless, middle-of-the-road dross. The song in the background is his hit "Congratulations," which features the lyrics " Congratulations and celebrations/When I tell everyone that you're in love with me . . ."

Ken and Petula are John Cleese and Connie Booth, husband and wife, lest we forget.

She's keen on knitting and likes Cliff Richard records. 41 How does she rate her chances against Ken?

PETULA (CONNIE) Well, I'm a southpaw and I think this will confuse him, particularly with his brain problem.

Cut to the ring. Floodlight. The night of the big fight. Murmur of a huge crowd. Excitement, cigar smoke rising in front of the camera. Bustle of activity all round. In medium close-up the master of ceremonies walks out into the middle of the ring, and takes the microphone.

MASTER OF CEREMONIES My lords, ladies and gedderbong...On my right, from the town of Reigate in the county of Kent, the heavyweight...(*unintelligible*) Mr Ken Clean-air Systems!...(*applause, cut to Ken's corner; Ken raises his arms above his head*) and on my left! Miss Petula Wilcox.

Superimpose caption: ROUND 1 For the first time we see Connie as Petula dance out into the middle of the ring, frail and lovely in a white muslin dress, with a bow in her hair and boxing gloves. The referee brings them together, cautions them and then they separate. The bell goes. As speeded-up as we can manage and with the same stupendous sound effects as for all-in cricket, Ken belts the hell out of Petula. 42 *While this goes on, we hear a few voice overs.*

COLONEL TYPE (JOHN) I think boxin's a splendid sport—teaches you self-defence.

CRITIC (TERRY J) Obviously boxing must have its limits, but providing they're both perfectly fit I can see nothing wrong with one healthy man beating the living daylights out of a little schoolgirl. It's quick and it's fun.

Boxing match is still in full swing as we cut away to the Grillomatic snack bar. A dim light; the announcer has gone. There is only a waitress setting chairs on the tables, and cleaning. She looks up as the camera comes on her.

WAITRESS Oh, no, he's gone. But he left a message. Jack! Where's that note that fellow left?

JACK (ERIC) Oh, here you are.
WAITRESS It says sorry, had to catch the last bus. Am on the 49B to Babbacombe. 43

Cut to the top of an open-top bus driving along.

LINKMAN Oh, er, there you are. Hello. You got the note, jolly good. Well, um, that's all the items that we have for you this week and er, what a jolly nice lot of items too, eh? Um...well, the same team will be back with you again next week with another menu full of items. Um...I don't know if I shall be introducing the show next week as I understand my bits in this show have not been received quite as well as they might (*start to roll credits over this*) but er, never mind, the damage is done—no use crying over spilt milk. (*miserably*) I've had my chance and I've muffed it. Anyway, there we are. I'm not really awfully good with words. You see, I'm more of a visual performer. I have a very funny—though I say so myself—very funny funny walk. 44 I wish I'd been in that show. I'd have done rather well. But anyway, there we are—the show's over. And...we'll all be—*they'll* all be back with you again next week...(*starting to cry*) Sorry. I do beg your pardon. I don't like these...displays of emotion...I wish it would say the end.

It says 'The End'.

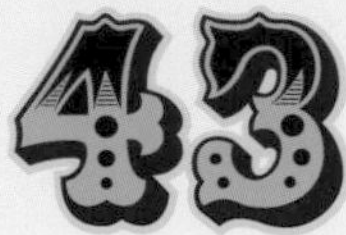

Babbacombe is a district of Torquay, nearby Paignton and famous for its model village.

Indeed he does—his "Ministry of Funny Walks" sketch remains a classic.

SILLY PARTY
SEA
SON
2
EPISODE 19

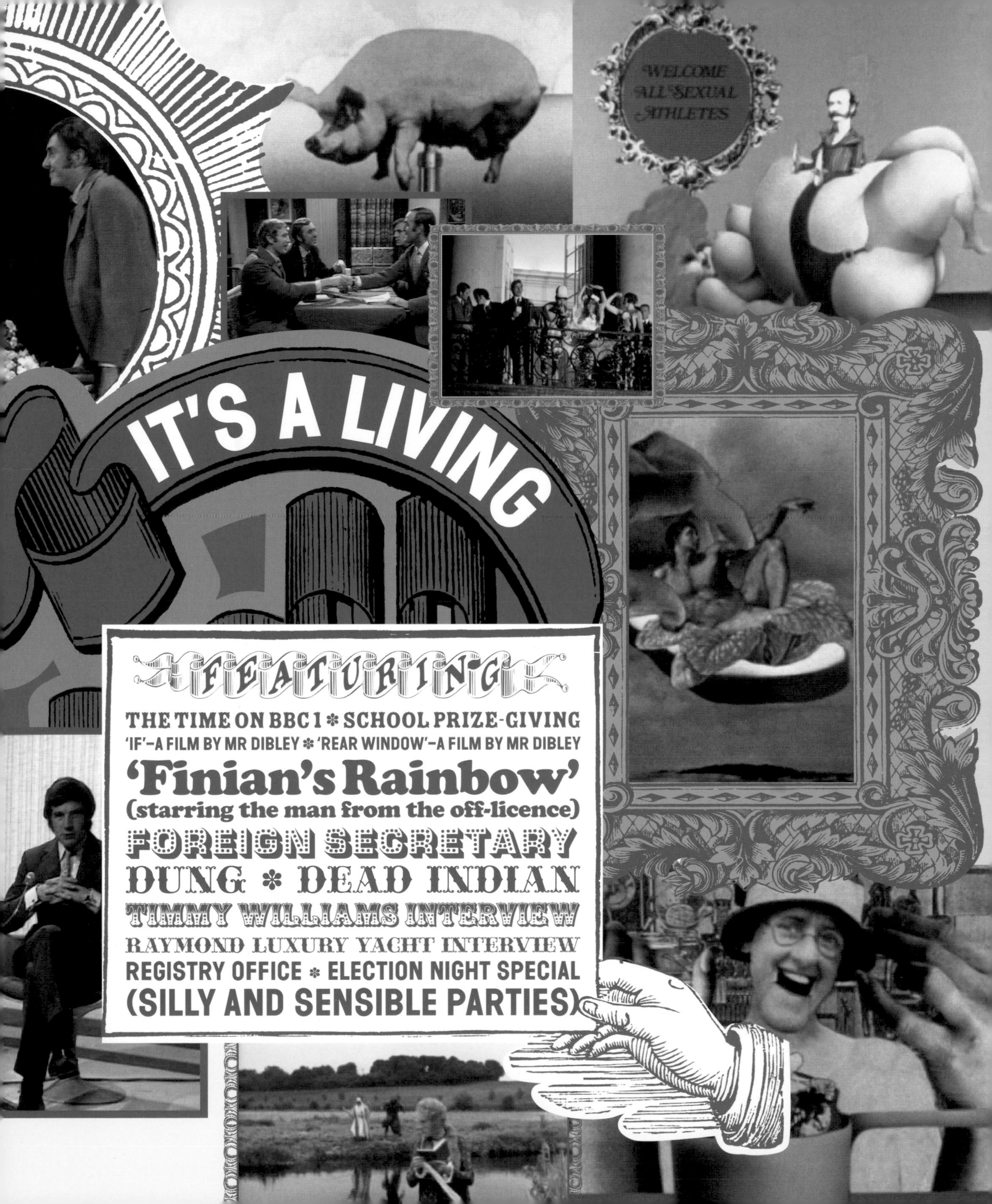
WELCOME
ALL SEXUAL
ATHLETES
IT'S A LIVING
FEATURING
THE TIME ON BBC 1 ✻ SCHOOL PRIZE-GIVING
'IF'–A FILM BY MR DIBLEY ✻ 'REAR WINDOW'–A FILM BY MR DIBLEY
'Finian's Rainbow'
(starring the man from the off-licence)
FOREIGN SECRETARY
DUNG ✻ DEAD INDIAN
TIMMY WILLIAMS INTERVIEW
RAYMOND LUXURY YACHT INTERVIEW
REGISTRY OFFICE ✻ ELECTION NIGHT SPECIAL
(SILLY AND SENSIBLE PARTIES)

FIRST AIRED: NOVEMBER 3, 1970

Caption: 'IT'S A LIVING' 1

COMPÈRE (ERIC) Hello, good evening, and welcome to 'It's A Living'. The rules are very simple: each week we get a large fee; at the end of that week we get another large fee; if there's been no interruption at the end of the year we get a repeat fee which can be added on for tax purposes to the previous year or the following year if there's no new series. Every contestant, in addition to getting a large fee is entitled to three drinks at the BBC or if the show is over, seven drinks—unless he is an MP, in which case he can have seven drinks before the show, or a bishop only three drinks in toto. The winners will receive an additional fee, a prize which they can flog back and a special fee for a guest appearance on 'Late Night Line Up'. Well, those are the rules, that's the game, we'll be back again same time next week. Till then. Bye-bye.

Cut to BBC world symbol.

VOICE OVER (MICHAEL) Well, it's five past nine and nearly time for six past nine. On BBC 2 now it'll shortly be six and a half minutes past nine. Later on this evening it'll be ten o'clock and at 10.30 we'll be joining BBC 2 in time for 10.33, and don't forget tomorrow when it'll be 9.20. Those of you who missed 8.45 on Friday will be able to see it again this Friday at a quarter to nine. Now here is a time check. It's six and a half minutes to the big green thing. 2

SECOND VOICE OVER (TERRY J) You're a loony.

FIRST VOICE OVER

The "It's" man is notably absent here, but in typical Python self-referential style, there is still an "It's" to start the show.

The turning BBC World logo and dulcet-toned voice-over running down forthcoming programming was a feature of the BBC for many years. Here, the slightly ridiculous nature of it is brilliantly satirized. After watching this sketch, it's hard to imagine seeing the symbol and not thinking about Palin's superb silliness.

I GET SO BORED.
I GET SO BLOODY BORED.

Animation: for a minute or two strange things happen on animation until suddenly we find ourselves into the animated title sequence.

Cut to the announcer in a silly location, sitting at his desk as usual.

ANNOUNCER (JOHN) You probably noticed that I didn't say 'and now for something completely different' just now. This is simply because I am unable to appear in the show this week. (*looks closely at script, puzzled*) Sorry to interrupt you.

Cut to a man holding his mouth open to show the camera his teeth.

MAN (TERRY J) I'm terribly sorry to interrupt but my tooth's hurting, just around here. 3
VOICE Get off.
MAN Oh, sorry.

Cut to pompous moustached stockbroker type.

NABARRO (GRAHAM) I'm not sorry to interrupt—I'll interrupt anything if it gets people looking in my direction—like at my old school where, by a coincidence, the annual prize giving is going on at this very moment.

There is a ripple effect, and a muted trumpet plays a corny segue sequence. We mix through to the trumpeter at a school prize giving. 4 *On the stage of the school hall there is a long table behind which are sitting several distinguished people. A bishop in a grey suit and purple stock and dog collar gets up.*

BISHOP (MICHAEL) My Lord Mayor, Lady Mayoress, it gives me very great pleasure 5 to return to my old school, to present the prizes in this centenary year. This school takes very justifiable pride in its fine record of...aaaaagh!

Hands pull him down behind the table. Fighting, punching, struggle, grunts etc. No reaction at all from the distinguished guests. 6 *The bishop's head reappears for a moment.*

BISHOP ...scholarship and sporting achievement in all...aaaagh!

He disappears again. More noises. Up comes another bishop dressed identically.

SECOND BISHOP (ERIC) I'm, I'm afraid there's been a mistake. The man who has been speaking to you is an impostor. He is not in fact the Bishop of East Anglia, but a man wanted by the police. *I* am the Bishop of East Anglia and anyone who doesn't believe me can look me up in the book. Now then, the first prize is this beautiful silver cup, which has been won by me. (*he puts the silver cup into a sack*) Next we come to the Fairfax Atkinson Trophy for outstanding achievement in the field of Applied Mathematics. Well, there was no-one this year who reached the required standard so it goes in my sack. And by an old rule of the school all the other silver trophies also go in my sack...aaagh!

3

Once again, wonderful to see the small group of people in the background watching the brief sketch—though this one's tame compared to tens of workmen in a row, or the "silly walk" through London.

4

This sketch is filmed from an odd distance, making it seem very far away. Once in a while the camera comes closer, but the effect is very strange, as though we're in the audience with the schoolchildren. Eventually we find out why.

5

The sketch cuts to a smiling woman here, and her bland grin elicits a great laugh from the studio audience.

6

The sketch cuts once again to the smiling woman.

He is dragged down by an unseen hand. More sounds of fighting, noisier than before even. A Chinaman in Mao jacket and cap appears.

CHINAMAN (GRAHAM) **Velly solly for hold-up...no ploblem now...Bishop of East Anglia, now plesent plizes...Eyes down for first plize...The Fyffe-Chulmleigh Spoon for Latin Elegaics... goes to...People's Republic of China! Aaaagh!** [7]

Our modern, even postmodern, ears might find this stock Chinese accent tough to enjoy.

The Chinaman is dragged down beneath the table as were the others. Again sound of struggle, thumps etc. A plainclothes policeman stands up. [8]

The Chinaman is dragged down while holding Chairman Mao's "Little Red Book," it might be noted.

DETECTIVE (TERRY J) Good evening, everybody. My name's Bradshaw—Inspector Elizabeth Bradshaw, of the Special Branch Speech Day Squad, but I'd like you to think of me as the Bishop of East Anglia, and I'd like to present the first prize, the Grimwade Gynn Trophy to...

A shot. He leaps backwards. Sound of machine guns and exploding shells. Two men in army uniform (could they be soldiers?) with camouflage sticking out of tin helmets rush up to the table and exchange fire. They have a huge bazooka which they fire from time to time.

SOLDIER (JOHN) (*appearing from beneath the table, shouting above the din of the battle*) Lord Mayor, Lady Mayoress, ladies, gentlemen and boys. Please do not panic. Please keep your heads right down now, and at the back please keep your heads right down. Do not panic, don't look round—this building is surrounded. There is nothing to worry about. I am the Bishop of East Anglia. Now the first prize is the Granville Cup for French Unseen Translation... (*explosion and smoke, debris over the stage*) and it goes to Forbes Minor...Forbes Minor...right, give him covering fire...(*explosion*) Come on Forbes. Come on boy. Come and get it. Keep down. (*a wretched schoolboy appears on the stage keeping his head down*) Well done...(*he manages to get the cup but as he stands to shake hands he is shot*) Oh...bad luck! The next prize...

Mix through to a picture on a TV monitor and pull out from monitor to reveal a studio set as for a late-night discussion programme.

INTERVIEWER (GRAHAM) Mr L. F. Dibley's latest film 'if'. (*he turns to Dibley*) Mr Dibley, some people have drawn comparisons between your film, 'if', which ends with a gun battle at a public school, and Mr Lindsay Anderson's film, 'if', **which ends with a gun battle at a public school.** [9]

The reason for the odd camera angles is revealed.

DIBLEY (TERRY J) Oh yes, well, I mean, there were some people who said my film '2001—A Space Odyssey', was similar to Stanley Kubrick's. I mean, that's the sort of petty critical niggling that's dogged my career. It makes me sick. I mean, as soon as I'd made 'Midnight Cowboy' with the vicar as Ratso Rizzo, **John Schlesinger rushes out his version, and gets it premiered while mine's still at the chemist's.** [10]

A nice gag on getting film developed at a pharmacy.

INTERVIEWER Well, we have with us tonight one of your films, 'Rear Window', which was to become such a success for Alfred Hitchcock a few weeks later. Now this is a silent film, so perhaps you could talk us through it...

Cut to a dim, shaky 8mm shot of a window. It is open. After a few seconds a man appears and looks out. He then performs over-exaggerated horror and points, looking at camera. Then he disappears and then he reappears.

DIBLEY Yes, well, let's see now...there's the rear window. There's the man looking out of the window. He sees the murder. The murderer's come into the room to kill him, but he's outwitted him and he's all right. The End. I mean, Alfred Hitchcock, who's supposed to be so bloody wonderful, padded that out to one and a half hours...lost all the tension...just because he had bloody Grace Kelly he made £3 million more than I did. Mind you, at least she can act a bit, I could have done with her in 'Finian's Rainbow'...The man from the **off-licence** 11 was terrible...a real failure that was—ten seconds of solid boredom.

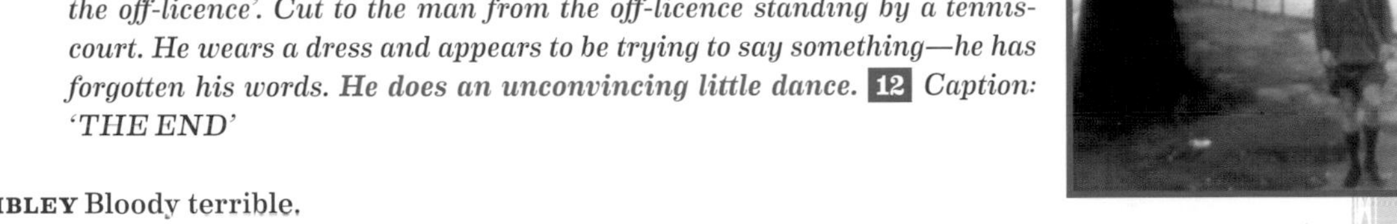

Cut to shaky titles: Mr Dibley's 'Finian's Rainbow starring the man from the off-licence'. Cut to the man from the off-licence standing by a tennis-court. He wears a dress and appears to be trying to say something—he has forgotten his words. He does an unconvincing little dance. 12 *Caption: 'THE END'*

DIBLEY Bloody terrible.

INTERVIEWER Mr L. F. Dibley's 'Finian's Rainbow'. And now over to me. (*close-up of interviewer*) Exclusively on the programme today we have the Foreign Secretary, who has just returned from the bitter fighting in the **Gulf of Amman.** 13 He's going to tell us about canoeing.

On the bank of a river seen from the other side. There is a canoe on the bank. A man in a pinstripe suit stands beside it. Superimposed caption: 'THE FOREIGN SECRETARY' He gives a little cough and gets in. Two Arabs run in from either side of frame, lift up the canoe and throw it and the Foreign Secretary into the water. 14
Cut back to the interviewer.

An "off-license" is a store in which alcoholic beverages are sold. "Off-license" refers to the establishment being away from bars, where regular licensees ply their trades. Some pubs have an off-license adjunct to their bars, where folks can take drinks home. Back then, off-licenses were important in a country where strict laws stopped the serving of alcohol after 11 p.m. every night, and everywhere.

Palin's "unconvincing little dance" is, in fact, brilliantly funny, raising as he does the hem of his dress just a little and jigging from one foot to the other.

Part of the 1967-70 "War of Attrition," fought between Egypt and Israel, and often centered in Jordan, where the Palestinian Liberation Organization was based (their involvement led to Jordan expelling the PLO to Lebanon in 1971). On the first day of December, 1968, four bridges were leveled by Israeli aircraft near the Jordanian town of Amman.

Given how heavy the whole thing must have been, it's no surprise that they actually sort of drop or throw the canoe into the water. It must have been a fairly painful fall into the shallow river's edge for the Foreign Secretary.

"They're going to make a human pyramid" brings to mind a line from the 1966 Tom Stoppard play *Rosencrantz and Guildenstern Are Dead*, in which Guildenstern asks whether Rosencrantz has a "short, blunt, human pyramid" in mind.

"ICI" is an initialism for the Imperial Chemical Industries, which was once (certainly in 1970) the largest manufacturing company in Britain. It was taken over in 2008 by AkzoNobel, a Dutch conglomerate.

Reg Harris, a cycling star in the 1950s, staged a stellar comeback in 1974, at the age of 54, to win the British title.

Anne Ziegler and Webster Booth are British singers, famous in the 1940s for their light operatic duets.

Palin turns here, looks at the "Arabs" jumping up and down, and starts to laugh.

INTERVIEWER That gives you just some idea of what's going on out there. Today saw the long-awaited publication of the Portman Committee's Report on Industrial Reorganization...

Caption: 'SOMETHING SILLY'S GOING TO HAPPEN'

INTERVIEWER It's taken five years to prepare and it's bound to have an enormous impact on the future of industrial relations in this country. In the studio tonight Lord Portman, Chairman of the Committee, Sir Charles Avery, Employers' Reorganization Council, and Ray Millichope, leader of the Allied Technicians' Union. And they're going to make a human pyramid. 15

Three men in shorts run on to accompaniment of tinkly music and form a pyramid. As they complete it we cut to film of Vatican crowds and dub on enormous ovation.

INTERVIEWER Bra...vo. Now the President of the Board of Trade...

Cut back to the same river bank shot from across the river. The President of the Board of Trade in pinstripes is standing beside a hamper. He smiles and gets in, and lowers the lid. Once again two Arabs run in from either side and throw it in. All these sequences are speeded up.

INTERVIEWER Now here's the Vice-Chairman of ICI. 16

Cut back to same river bank. A head looking out of the hamper. It disappears as two Arabs run in and toss it in.

INTERVIEWER Well, so much for politics and the problems of Britain's industrial reorganization. Now we turn to the lighter subject of sport, and Reg Harris, 17 the former world cycling sprint champion, talks to us about the psychological problems of big race preparation. (*Reg and his bike are thrown in the river by the Arabs*) And now the world of song—Anne Zeigler and Webster Booth. 18 (*two hampers thrown in river by four Arabs*) Well, all good things must come to an end, and that's all for this week. But to close our programme, Dame Irene Stoat, who celebrates her eighty-fifth birthday this month, reads one of her most famous poems.

Cut to the river bank. An old lady is standing beside it, but this time on the bank of the river nearest the camera. On the other bank we see the Arabs run into shot, realize they've been foiled and leap up and down in anger.

DAME IRENE (MICHAEL) Who shall declare this good, that ill
When good and ill so intertwine
But to fulfil the vast design
Of an omniscient will.
When seeming again but turns to loss 19

When earthly treasure proves but dross
And what seems lost but turns again
To high eternal gain.

The Arabs run out of vision. Suddenly, from right beside the camera, with a bloodcurdling scream a Samurai warrior with drawn sword leaps upon her and hurls her backwards into the water. The warrior then strikes up a fierce heroic pose for the camera.

Superimposed caption: 'NEWHAVEN—LE HAVRE. GETAWAY TO THE CONTINENT' **20** *Cut to a smart dinner party. There are two couples in evening dress at the table. Candles burning on the polished wood, a fire burning in the grate. Muted music and sophisticated lighting.*

HOSTESS (RITA) We had the most marvellous holiday. It was absolutely fantastic.
HOST (MICHAEL) Absolutely wonderful.
HOSTESS Michael, you tell them about it.
HOST No, darling, you tell them.
HOSTESS You do it so much better.

The doorbell rings.

HOST Excuse me a moment.

The host goes and answers the door of the flat, which opens straight into the dining room. Standing at the door is a large grubby man carrying a tin bath on his shoulder. There are flies buzzing around him. He walks straight in.

MAN (JOHN) Dung, sir. **21**
HOST What?
MAN We've got your dung.
HOST What dung?
MAN Your dung. Three hundredweight of heavy droppings. Where do you want it? (*he looks round for a likely place*)

HOST I didn't order any dung.
MAN Yes you did, sir. You ordered it through the Book of the Month Club.

Newhaven and Le Havre are two ports—one in Sussex, on the south coast of England, and one on the coast of France's Haute-Normandie region—tied by the ferry that plies between them.

This sketch feels like the precursor to Louis Buñuel's 1972 film *The Discreet Charm of the Bourgeoisie*, in which a bunch of well-to-do diners are continually interrupted at table.

22

The French Lieutenant's Woman is a novel by John Fowles, published a year before this sketch. A film version, starring Meryl Streep was released in 1981.

HOST Book of the Month Club?

MAN That's right, sir. You get 'Gone with the Wind', 'Les Miserables' by Victor Hugo, 'The French Lieutenant's Woman' 22 and with every third book you get dung.

HOST I didn't know that when I signed the form.

MAN Well, no, no. It wasn't on the form—they found it wasn't good for business. Anyway, we've got three hundredweight of dung in the van. Where do you want it?

HOST Well, I don't think we do. We've no garden.

MAN Well, it'll all fit in here—it's top-class excrement.

HOST You can't put it in here, we've having a dinner party!

MAN 'Salright. I'll put it on the telly.

He brings it into the dining room. The guests ignore him.

HOST Darling...there's a man here with our Book of the Month Club dung.

HOSTESS We've no room, dear.

MAN Well, how many rooms have you got, then?

HOST Well, there's only this room, the bedroom, a spare room.

MAN

OH WELL, I'LL TELL YOU WHAT, MOVE EVERYTHING INTO THE MAIN BEDROOM, THEN YOU CAN USE THE SPARE ROOM AS A DUNG ROOM.

The doorbell goes and there standing at the door which hasn't been closed is a gas board official with a dead Indian over his shoulders.

HOST Yes.

GAS MAN (GRAHAM) Dead Indian.

HOST What?

GAS MAN Have you recently bought a new cooker, sir?

HOST Yes.

GAS MAN Ah well, this is your free dead Indian, as advertised...

HOST I didn't see that in the adverts...

GAS MAN No, it's in the very small print, you see, sir, so as not to affect the sales.

HOST We've no room.

MAN That's all right—you can put the dead Indian in the spare room on top of the dung.

DEAD INDIAN Me...heap dizzy.

HOST He's not dead!
GAS MAN Oh well, that's probably a faulty cooker.

The phone rings. The wife goes to answer it.

MAN Have you, er...you read and enjoyed 'The French Lieutenant's Woman', then?
HOST No.
MAN No...still, it's worth it for the dung, isn't it?
HOSTESS Darling, it's the Milk Marketing Board. **23** For every two cartons of single cream we get the M4 motorway. **24**

Cut to man and wife standing bewildered in the middle of a motorway. Beside them is a steaming pile of dung, and a dead Indian. They look round in amazement. A police car roars up to them and two policemen leap out.

POLICEMAN (ERIC) Are you Mr and Mrs P. Forbes of 7, the Studios, Elstree? **25**
MAN Yes.
POLICEMAN Right, well, get in the car. We've won you in a police raffle.

Speeded up, they are bundled into the car. Cut to inspector.

INSPECTOR (TERRY J) Yes! This couple is just one of the prizes in this year's Police Raffle. Other prizes include two years for breaking and entering, a crate of search warrants, a 'What's all this then?' T -shirt and a weekend for two with a skinhead of your own choice. **26**

Caption: 'STOP PRESS'

VOICE OVER (MICHAEL) And that's not all! Three fabulous new prizes have just been added, a four-month supply of interesting undergarments (*picture*), a fully motorized pig (*picture c/o Mr Gilliam*), and a hand-painted scene of Arabian splendour, complete with silly walk.

Animation sketch leading to a booth in a quite expensive looking coffee shop, Italian style. Nigel is sitting there. Timmy Williams comes in. He has just the faintest passing resemblance to David Frost. **27**

TIMMY (ERIC) Nigel! Wonderful to see you, super, super, super. Am I a teeny bit late?
NIGEL (TERRY J) A bit, an hour.

Established in 1933, the Milk Marketing Board was a British government agency that did exactly what its name suggests: it marketed milk. It was dissolved completely in 2002.

The M4 is the main freeway from London out west, toward Bristol, and on into south Wales.

The BBC, as well as other production companies, had TV studios in Elstree, in Hertfordshire, hence this play on names for the address.

Once again, "What's all this then?" is the archetypal police greeting to a possible suspect.

The uproarious laughter of the audience suggests that they get the reference very clearly.

Antony Charles Robert Armstrong-Jones, first earl of Snowdon, famed photographer of the day (and to this day), and one time (1960–1978) husband to Queen Elizabeth II's younger sister, Margaret. His work is published under the name "Snowdon."

The addition of "Bloggs" to a name is the British equivalent of "John Doe."

30

The Daily Mail, a tabloid for the middle swathes of British readers—not *The Sun*, with nudity and gore, nor *The Times*, for the so-called educated classes.

The non-BBC magazine equivalent of *Radio Times*, *TV Times* is full of listings and articles about commercial TV stations other than the BBC.

TIMMY Oh, super! Only Snowdon's been re-touching my profile and we can't upset the lovely Snowdon, can we? 28

NIGEL Gosh, no.

A man passes.

TIMMY (*gets up and clasps his hands*) ...David Bloggs... 29 the one and only...super to see you. Who are you working for? Come and work for me, I'll call you tomorrow. (*sits down*) It's really lovely to have this little chat with you.

NIGEL Well, I...

TIMMY It is so nice to have this little talk about things. I heard a teeny rumourlette that you were married.

NIGEL Well, not quite, no. My wife's just died, actually.

TIMMY Oh dear. (*sees another man passing*) Brian! (*extends his arm*) We must get together again soon. See you. Bye. (*to Nigel*) Well, perhaps we could do a tribute to her on the show.

NIGEL Well, no. I...

TIMMY I'll get Peter, William, Arthur, Alex, Joan, Ted, Scott, Wilf, John and Ray to fix it up. It is *so* nice having this little chat.

NIGEL Well, actually Timmy, I'm glad to get you on your own...

A reporter comes up to the table.

TIMMY You don't mind if Peter just sits in, do you?

NIGELWell, actually...

TIMMY Only he's doing an article on me for the 'Mail'. 30 He's such a lovely person.

REPORTER (GRAHAM) Hello.

TIMMY Peter, this is one of the nicest people in the world, Nigel Watt. (*Peter scribbles it down*) W-A-double T. That's right, yes.

NIGEL Well, actually, Timmy, the thing is, it's a bit private.

A writer comes to the table.

TIMMY Oh, you don't mind if Peter just sits in, do you? Only Peter's writing a book on me. Peter, you know Tony from the 'Mail', don't you?

PETER (JOHN) Yes, we met in the Turkish bath yesterday.

TIMMY Super, super. Did it come up well in the writing yesterday?

PETER Great, great, great.

TIMMY You took out the tummy references? (*makes fatness signs*)

PETER Yes, I did.

TIMMY Super, super, super. Just to fill you in, this is Nigel Watt and we are having a little heart-to-heart. H-E-A-R- T. Smashing. Do go on, Nigel.

They both start writing.

NIGEL Well, well, the thing is, Timmy, um er...

Timmy is smiling and posing. Nigel stops and looks. There is a photographer, hovering.

TIMMY Do carry on, it's the 'TV Times', 31 only they syndicate these photographs to America. Would you mind if we just er...(*grabs him by the hand and poses hearty friendship photo*) Super, super. One over here, I think, Bob. A little smile, please, smashing, smashing. Feel free, Bob, to circulate, won't you. Do go on, this is most interesting.

NIGEL Well, the thing is, Timmy, I'm a bit embarrassed.

WAITER (MICHAEL) (*coming to table*) Oh, Mr Williams, it's so nice to see you. Will you sign this for my little daughter, please?

TIMMY Hello, Mario. Super, wonderful. (*signs*) Just two lovely coffees, please.

Director comes in.

DIRECTOR Sorry, sorry, Timmy. Can we just go from where Mario comes in, we're getting bad sound, OK?

TIMMY It's German television. Isn't it exciting, Nigel? They're doing a prize-winning documentary on me.

We see a film camera and the whole crew gathered round.

CLAPPER BOY 'The Wonderful Mr Williams', scene 239, take 2.

DIRECTOR Action!

TIMMY *(taking the cue, switches)* 32 Mario, how super to see you. How are the lovely family? Please give your little daughter this. *(hands him a five pound note)* Thank you. And just two lovely coffees, please.

MARIO Yes, sir.

TIMMY (*to Nigel*) Such a lovely waiter. Now, go on please, this is *most* interesting.

NIGEL Well...er...as I was saying, Timmy, my wife's gone...gone. (*close-up on him*) I've got three children and I'm at my wits' end. No job, no insurance, no money at all. I'm absolutely flat broke, I just don't know where to turn. I...I'm absolutely at the end of my tether. You're my only chance. Can you help me, please, Timmy?

He looks up, Timmy isn't there. Timmy comes bounding back.

TIMMY Sorry, I was on the phone to America. It's been super having this lovely little chat. We must do this again more often. Er...will you get the coffees? I'm afraid I must dash, I'm an hour late for the Israeli Embassy. (*there is a shot; Nigel slumps over the table, gun in his hand*) Er...did you get that shot all right, sound?

SOUND MAN (*off*) Yes, fine.

TIMMY It...it wasn't a bit too wicked, was it? I mean, it wasn't too cruel?

This barely does Idle's performance justice. He looks forlornly to his right, then as the clapboard claps he turns on the smarmy charm. The audience loves it, as they should.

"Charabanc" is an old-fashioned word for a bus (from the French, meaning a carriage with benches).

TONY AND PETER No, no, no. It was great.

TIMMY No, super...well, er...I think it shows I'm human, don't you?

TONY AND PETER Yes, great.

TIMMY Super, super. Well, the charabanc's here. **33** Go on, everybody. Bye. *(he waves)*

They all troop off after him. Theme music starts to come up, we pull back and see the camera set-up. Credits start to roll:

VOICE OVER (TERRY J) 'Timmy Williams' Coffee Time' was brought to you live from Woppi's in Holborn.

Credits continue to roll:
Theme Script By (enormous letters) TIMMY WILLIAMS
Entirely Written By (enormous letters) TIMMY WILLIAMS
Additional Material By: (these go straight through very fast)
PETER WRAY,
LEN ASHLEY,
GEOFFREY INGERSOLL,
GEORGE HERBERT,
HARRY LOWALL,
RALPH EMERSON,
HATTY STARR,
FRANK PICKSLEY,
JOHN STAMFORD,
SHELLEY BUNHEUR,
MALCOLM KERR,
JAMES BEACH,
ALAN BAILEY,
BRIAN FELDMAN,
STIRLING HARTLEY,
ADRIAN BEAMISH,
GUY WARING,
MARK TOMKINS,
SIDNEY SMITH,
RICHARD HOVEY,
EDMUND GOSSE,
JONATHAN ASHMORE,
BILL WRIGHT,
ARTHUR FULLER,
RICHARD SAVAGE,
MICHAEL WHITEMORE,
BUDGE RYAN,
CEDRIC HAZLETT,
TERRY JONES,
MICHAEL PALIN,
JOHN GAYNOR,
GEORGE COLEMAN,
SAMUEL SPURGEON,
THOMAS MASSINGER,
STEPHEN DAVIS,
WALTER CHAPMAN,
REGINALD MARWOOD,
DAVID GOSCHEN,
PETER SCHULMAN,

DENNIS FRANKEL,
DAVID ROBINSON,
PAUL RAYMOND,
JOHN WILLDER,
JOHNNY LYNN,
JOE SHAW,
SIMON SMITH,
MONTY PYTHON,
MICHAEL LAPIN,
SYDNEY LOTTERBY,
IAN MATHERSON,
HUMPHREY BARCLAY,
BURT ANCASTER,
KIRK OUGLAS,
KEN SMITH,
GEOFFREY HUGHES,
BRIAN FITZJONES,
MICHAEL GOWERS,
JOHN PENNYCATE,
PETER BAKER,
NEIL SHAND 34
Fade out.

Fade in on ordinary interview set.
Interviewer sitting with man with large semitic polystyrene nose. 35

INTERVIEWER (MICHAEL) Good evening. I have with me in the studio tonight one of Britain's leading skin specialists—Raymond Luxury Yacht.
RAYMOND (GRAHAM) That's not my name.
INTERVIEWER I'm sorry—Raymond Luxury *Yach-t.*
RAYMOND No, no, no—it's spelt Raymond Luxury Yach-t, but it's pronounced 'Throatwobbler Mangrove'.
INTERVIEWER

YOU'RE A VERY SILLY MAN AND I'M NOT GOING TO INTERVIEW YOU.

These names run by at a fair clip, meaning it's hard to get all the gags, which include anagrams, misspelled references to famous people, and real comic writers like Neil Shand.

It certainly *is* large—it's actually elephantine—but Semitic? Times have changed, it's true, but the casual nature of playing this race card is notable, even for 1970. That the subsequent short sketch revolves around the idea that "Jews have big noses" is just one of the reasons it's one of the least funny Python sketches.

RAYMOND Ah, anti-semitism!
INTERVIEWER Not at all. It's not even a proper nose. (*takes it off*) It's polystyrene.
RAYMOND Give me my nose back.
INTERVIEWER You can collect it at reception. Now go away.
RAYMOND I want to be on the television.
INTERVIEWER Well you can't.

Animation sketch.

Then cut to a large sign saying 'Registry Office,' 'Marriages' etc. A man is talking to the registrar. 36

36

The Registry Office is the British equivalent of City Hall, where nondenominational weddings take place.

MAN (TERRY J) Er, excuse me, I want to get married.
REGISTRAR (ERIC) I'm afraid I'm already married, sir.
MAN Er, no, no. I just want to get married.
REGISTRAR I could get a divorce, I suppose, but it'll be a bit of a wrench.
MAN Er, no, no. That wouldn't be necessary because...
REGISTRAR You see, would you come to my place or should I have to come to yours, because I've just got a big mortgage.
MAN No, no, I want to get married *here*.
REGISTRAR Oh dear. I had my heart set on a church wedding.
MAN Look, I just want *you* to marry *me*...to...
REGISTRAR I want to marry you too sir, but it's not as simple as that. You sure you want to get married?
MAN Yes. I want to get married very quickly.
REGISTRAR Suits me, sir. Suits me.
MAN I don't want to marry you!
REGISTRAR There is such a thing as breach of promise, sir.
MAN Look, I just want you to act as registrar and *marry* me.
REGISTRAR

I WILL MARRY YOU SIR, BUT PLEASE MAKE UP YOUR MIND. PLEASE DON'T TRIFLE WITH MY AFFECTIONS.

MAN I'm sorry, but...
REGISTRAR That's all right, sir. I forgive you. Lovers' tiff. But you're not the first person to ask me today. I've turned down several people already.
MAN Look, I'm already engaged.
REGISTRAR (*agreeing and thinking*) Yes, and I'm already married. Still we'll get round it.
SECOND MAN (MICHAEL) (*entering*) Good morning. I want to get married.
REGISTRAR I'm afraid I'm already marrying this gentleman, sir.
SECOND MAN Well, can I get married *after* him?
REGISTRAR Well, divorce isn't as quick as that, sir. Still, if you're keen.
THIRD MAN (GRAHAM) (*entering*) I want to get married, please.
REGISTRAR Heavens, it's my lucky day, isn't it. All right, but you'll have to wait until I've married these two, sir.
THIRD MAN What, those two getting married...Nigel! What are you doing marrying him?

REGISTRAR He's marrying me first, sir.
THIRD MAN He's engaged to me. **37**
FOURTH MAN (JOHN) *(big and butch)* Come on, Henry. **38**

REGISTRAR Blimey, the wife.
SECOND MAN Will *you* marry me?
FOURTH MAN I'm already married.

Cut to a photo of all five of them standing happily outside a house.

VOICE OVER (TERRY J) Well, things turned out all right in the end, but you mustn't ask how 'cos it's naughty. They're all married and living quite well in a council estate near Dulwich. **39**

Animation: 'The Spot'
Caption: 'ELECTION NIGHT SPECIAL' Cut to linkman sitting at desk.

LINKMAN (JOHN) *(very excited)* Hello and welcome to 'Election Night Special'. There's great excitement here as we should be getting the first result through any minute now. We don't know where it'll be from...it might be from Leicester or from Luton. The polling's been quite heavy in both areas...oh, wait a moment...I'm just getting...I'm just getting a loud buzzing noise in my left ear. Excuse me a moment. *(he bangs ear and knocks a large bee out)* Uuggh! *(cheering from crowd)* Anyway, let's go straight over to James Gilbert at Leicester.

Shot of returning officer in front of a group consisting half of grey-suited, half of silly-dressed candidates and agents. **40**
The silly ones are in extraordinary hats, false noses etc.

VOICE OVER (MICHAEL) Well, it's a straight fight here at Leicester...On the left of the Returning Officer *(camera shows grey-suited man)* you can see Arthur Smith, the Sensible candidate and his agent, *(camera pans to silly people)* and on the other side is the silly candidate Jethro

A gay-marriage gag, this from 1970!

We lose this line—which is kind of crucial—because Cleese's "butch" voice is very hard to understand. It's actually more like one of his "Gumby" voices, and he badly swallows the line.

"Council estates" are public housing.

The returning officer is the local official who ratifies and announces election results. They are standing on a balcony, one of the traditional places where British election results are announced.

Walrustitty with his agent and his wife.

OFFICER (TERRY J) Here is the result for Leicester. Arthur J. Smith...

VOICE OVER Sensible Party. 41

OFFICER 30,162...Jethro Q Walrustitty...

VOICE OVER Silly Party.

OFFICER 32,108.

Cheering from the crowd. Cut back to the studio.

LINKMAN (*even more excited*) Well, there's the first result and the Silly Party have held Leicester. What do you make of that, Norman?

Cut to Norman. He is very excited.

NORMAN (MICHAEL) Well, this is largely as I predicted except that the Silly Party won. I think this is mainly due to the number of votes cast. Gerald?

Cut to Gerald standing by 'swingometer'—a pivoted pointer on a wall chart. 42

GERALD (ERIC) Well, there's a swing here to the Silly Party...but how big a swing I'm not going to tell you.

Cut to George also standing by a swingometer.

GEORGE (TERRY J) Well, if I may...I think the interesting thing here is the big swing to the Silly Party and of course the very large swing back to the Sensible Party...and a tendency to wobble up and down in the middle because the screw's loose. 43

Cut to Alphonse.

ALPHONSE (GRAHAM) No, I'm afraid I can't think of anything.

Cut to Eric.

ERIC (TERRY G) I can't add anything to that. Colin?

Palin and Cleese sport large green rosettes in their lapels. It was—and sometimes still is—the tradition in the U.K. for political candidates and their supporters to show their allegiance. (In the old days, soccer fans wore the same thing, before the days of hooliganism; now it can be dangerous to wear your team's colors, especially to away games.)

Invented in the 1950s, the "swingometer" is a standard visual for British elections. An attempt to measure the ethereal art of voter selection, it was put to much use in the 1970 election, held on June 18 (a few months before this episode was filmed)—an election that surprisingly was won by Edward Heath and his Conservative Party over Harold Wilson of the Labor Party.

He's referring to the screw in the center of the swingometer, not the general mayhem in this sketch. Or maybe it's both.

Cut to Colin.

COLIN (IAN DAVIDSON) **Can I just butt in at this point and say this is in fact the very first time I've ever appeared on television. 44**

Cut to linkman.

LINKMAN No, no, we haven't time, because we're going straight over to Luton.

Cut to Luton Town Hall. There are sensible, silly and slightly silly candidates.

VOICE OVER (MICHAEL) 45 Here at Luton, it's a three-cornered fight between Alan Jones—Sensible Party, in the middle,

TARQUIN FIN-TIM-LIN-BIN-WHIN-BIM-LIM-BUS-STOP-F'TANG-F'TANG-OLÉ-BISCUITBARREL—SILLY PARTY, AND KEVIN PHILLIPS-BONG, THE SLIGHTLY SILLY CANDIDATE. 46

OFFICER (ERIC) Alan Jones...
VOICE OVER On the left, Sensible Party.
OFFICER 9,112...Kevin Phillips-Bong...
VOICE OVER On the right, Slightly Silly.
OFFICER Nought...Tarquin Fin-tim-lin-bin-whin-bim-lin-bus-stop-F'tang-F'tang-Olé-Biscuit-barrel... 47

44

Ian Davidson is an actor and scriptwriter who attended Oxford University with Terry Jones and Michael Palin.

This sounds an awful lot like John Cleese, in fact.

It was a point of honor for many teenage boys in the U.K. to be able to recite this name.

A "biscuit barrel" is a real thing—literally a barrel for cookies with a lid that shuts tight to keep everything fresh (if flavorless—this is the U.K., after all).

Darl Larsen notes that Spike Milligan was off-camera during this sketch. One of the original Goons, a comedy group so beloved by many of the Pythons, Milligan had an avant-garde comedy mind, fueled partly by his struggles with mental illness. One of the great geniuses of British comedy, this comment, though perhaps a literal thank-you, stands as a nice tribute to a man without whom the Pythons would never have been.

Eric Idle's "joke breasts" are, in fact, not enormous at all.

Actually, Cleese makes the "whoop" sound all on his own.

"We'll Keep a Welcome" was written in 1940 by Mai Jones, Lyn Joshua, and James Harper. It is now considered a classic of Welsh heritage and pride.

VOICE OVER Silly.

OFFICER 12,441.

VOICE OVER And so the Silly Party has taken Luton.

Quick cut to linkman.

LINKMAN A gain for the Silly Party at Luton. The first gain of the election, Norman?

Cut to each speaker in close-up throughout the scene.

NORMAN Well, this is a highly significant result. Luton, normally a very sensible constituency with a high proportion of people who aren't a bit silly, has gone completely ga-ga.

LINKMAN Do we have the swing at Luton?

GERALD Well, I've worked out the swing, but it's a secret.

LINKMAN Er, well, ah, there...there *isn't* the swing, how about the swong?

NORMAN Well, I've got the swong here in this box and it's looking fine. I can see through the breathing holes that it's eating up peanuts at a rate of knots.

LINKMAN And how about the swang?

ALPHONSE Well, it's 29% up over six hundred feet but it's a little bit soft around the edges about...

LINKMAN What do you make of the nylon dot cardigan and plastic mule rest?

VOICE (*off*) There's no such thing.

LINKMAN Thank you, Spike. 48

NORMAN Can I just come in here and say that the swong has choked itself to death.

GEORGE Well, the election's really beginning to hot up now.

ERIC I can't add anything to that.

COLIN

CAN I JUST ADD AT THIS POINT THIS IS IN FACT THE SECOND TIME I'VE EVER APPEARED ON TELEVISION?

LINKMAN I'm sorry, Sasha, we're just about to get another result.

A large number of candidates in Harpenden Town Hall.

VOICE OVER (TERRY J) Hello, from Harpenden. This is a key seat because in addition to the official Silly candidate there is an independent Very Silly candidate (*in large cube of polystyrene with only his legs sticking out*) who may split the silly vote.

OFFICER (JOHN) Mr Elsie Zzzzzzzzzzzz. (*obvious man in drag with enormous joke breasts*) 49

VOICE OVER Silly.

OFFICER 26,317...James Walker...

VOICE OVER Sensible.

OFFICER 26,318.

VOICE OVER That was close.

OFFICER Malcolm Peter Brian Telescope Adrian Umbrella Stand Jasper Wednesday (*pops mouth twice*) Stoatgobbler John Raw Vegetable (*sound effect of horse whinnying*) Arthur Norman Michael (*blows squeaker*) Featherstone Smith (*blows whistle*) Northgot Edwards Harris (*fires pistol, which goes 'whoop'*) 50 Mason (*chuff-chuff-chuff*) Frampton Jones Fruitbat Gilbert (*sings*) We'll Keep a Welcome In The (*three shots, stops singing*) 51 Williams If I Could Walk That Way Jenkin (*squeaker*) Tigerdraws Pratt Thompson (*sings*) 'Raindrops Keep Falling On My Head' Darcy Carter (*horn*) 52 Pussycat 'Don't Sleep In The Subway' 53 Barton Mannering (*hoot, 'whoop'*) Smith.

VOICE OVER Very Silly.
OFFICER Two.
VOICE OVER Well, there you have it. A Sensible gain here at Driffield.

Back to the studio.

LINKMAN Norman.
NORMAN Well, I've just heard from Luton that my auntie's ill er, possibly, possibly gastro-enteritis—Gerald.
GERALD Er, well, if this were repeated over the whole country it'd probably be very messy. Colin.
COLIN Can I just butt in and say here that it's probably the last time I shall ever appear on television.
LINKMAN No, I'm afraid you can't, we haven't got time. Just to bring you up to date with a few results, er, that you may have missed. Engelbert Humperdinck has taken Barrow-in-Furness, that's a gain from Ann Haydon-Jones and her husband Pip. **54** Arthur Negus has held Bristols. **55** That's not a result, that's a bit of gossip. Er...Mary Whitehouse has just taken umbrage. **56** Could be a bit of trouble there. And apparently Wales is not swinging at all. No surprise there. And...Monty Python has held the credits.

Roll credits. Lots of activity behind from the experts.

Superimposed flashing caption: 'NO CHANGE'

Another reference to the 1969 movie *Butch Cassidy and the Sundance Kid* and its Burt Bacharach song, "Raindrops Keep Falling On My Head."

And another reference to the Petula Clark's 1967 hit "Don't Sleep in the Subway".

More references to the singer (Humperdinck), and the tennis player (Ann Haydon-Jones) and her husband (Pip). The Pythons are beginning to indulge in in-jokes, proving their comedy is reaching a cultural watermark.

Arthur Negus, a TV personality and antiques expert, was by 1970 considered something of an antique himself, even though he was only 63 that year—he was the poster child for British stuffiness and squareness. He died in 1985.

The right-wing and often homophobic scourge of permissive society, Mary Whitehouse was the founder and self-appointed chairperson in 1965 of the National Viewers' and Listeners' Association, a pressure group especially critical of the BBC.

WESTMINSTER BANK LIMITED
SEASON 2
EPISODE 20

THE ATTILA THE HUN SHOW
FEATURING
ATTILA THE NUN ✽ SECRETARY OF STATE STRIPTEASE
VOX POPS ON POLITICIANS ✽ RATCATCHER ✽ WAINSCOTTING
Killer Sheep
THE NEWS FOR PARROTS
THE NEWS FOR GIBBONS
TODAY IN PARLIAMENT
THE NEWS FOR WOMBATS
ATTILA THE BUN ✽ THE IDIOT IN SOCIETY ✽ TEST MATCH
THE EPSOM FURNITURE RACE
TAKE YOUR PICK

FIRST AIRED: NOVEMBER 10, 1970

Stock film of fast moving Huns thundering around on horseback.

VOICE OVER (JOHN) In the fifth century, as the once-mighty Roman Empire crumbled, the soft underbelly of Western Europe lay invitingly exposed to the barbarian hordes to the East. **Alaric the Visigoth,** [1] **Gaiseric the Vandal** [2] and **Theodoris the Ostrogoth** [3] in turn swept westward in a reign of terror. But none surpassed in power and cruelty the mighty Attila the Hun. Attila the Hun, leader of the much-feared Hun tribe from 434 until his death in 453, never managed to take Rome, though he tried. Lord knows he tried.

VOICE OVER (MICHAEL) Ladies and gentlemen, it's the 'The Attila the Hun Show'.

*Cut to film. Music plays: **'The Debbie Reynolds Show' theme** [4]—'With a little love, just a little love'. We see Attila the Hun running towards Mrs Attila the Hun in slow motion, laughing and smiling.*

*Caption: 'THE ATTILA THE HUN SHOW' **Attila and his wife frolic and fall over in slow motion for a bit** [5] (copying Debbie Reynolds credits as closely as possible). Captions:*
'STARRING ATTILA THE HUN'
'AND KAY SLUDGE AS MRS ATTILA THE HUN'
'WITH TY GUDRUN AND NIK CON AS JENNY AND ROBIN ARRILA THE HUN'
'MUSIC BY THE HUNLETS'

Cut to stock film of fast-moving Huns on horseback.

VOICE OVER (JOHN) In the second quarter of the fifth century, the Huns became a byword for merciless savagery. Their Khan was the mighty warrior Attila. With his devastating armies he swept across Central Europe.

Cut to American-living-room-type set. Doorbell rings. Attila the Hun enters the door.

ATTILA (JOHN) Oh darling, I'm home.
MRS ATTILA (CAROL) Hello darling. Had a busy day at the office?
ATTILA Not at all bad. (*playing to camera*) Another merciless sweep across Central Europe.

Canned laughter.

Alaric I was king of the Visigoths from 395 to 410. He sacked Rome in 410.

Gaiseric was king of the Vandals and Alans from 428 to 477, taker of Carthage in 439 and capturer of Rome 45 years after Alaric.

Theodoris the Great was king of the Ostrogoths from 471 to 526 and ruler of Italy until his death.

The Debbie Reynolds Show was a short-lived (26 episodes, from 1969 to 1970) sitcom.

5

In fact what we get is Attila, and then his wife, on a tire swing; a baseball scene, in which Eric Idle is wearing blackface (as Idle catches the ball behind the "batter" Mrs. Attila, he celebrates as though this is an out—that is, he's playing by cricket rules); and the happy couple wandering down a grassy road in a wood.

MRS ATTILA I won't say I'm glad to see you, but boy, am I glad to see you.

Enormous canned laughter and applause. Enter two kids.

JENNY (GRAHAM) Hi, daddy.
ROBIN (MICHAEL) Hi, daddy.
ATTILA Hi, Jenny, hi, Robby. (*brief canned applause*) Hey, I've got a present for you two kids in that bag. (*they pull out a severed head*) I want you kids to get a-head.

Enormous shriek of canned laughter and applause. Enter one of us blacked up like Rochester, holding a tray of drinks.

UNCLE TOM (ERIC) Heah you are, Mr Hun!

Masses of dubbed applause.

ATTILA Hi, Uncle Tom.
UNCLE TOM There's a whole horde of them marauding Visigoths to see y'all.

Cut to more stock film of these Huns rushing about on their horses. Superimposed image of announcer at his desk.

ANNOUNCER (JOHN) And now for something completely different.
IT'S MAN (MICHAEL)
IT'S... 6

Massive canned applause. Animated credit titles.

At the end of these titles cut to a country road. After three seconds a motorbike appears in the distance and speeds towards the camera. We see that a wild-looking nun is riding it.

6

The "It's" man, more than three minutes into the show.

VOICE OVER (JOHN) Yes, it's Attila the Nun.

Attila the Nun flashes past the camera. There is a loud sound of the bike crashing off camera.

VOICE OVER (MICHAEL)

A SIMPLE COUNTRY GIRL WHO TOOK A VOW OF ETERNAL BRUTALITY.

Attila the Nun on a hospital bed, struggling wildly with two doctors and a nurse who are trying to hold her down. She looks really fearsome. Another doctor enters and summons the nurse away.

DOCTOR (GRAHAM) Nurse!

The camera tracks away and comes up on another bed in which is sitting a beautiful girl revealing more than a patient normally would and endowed with Carol's...undoubted attributes. 7

The idea of a "boys' club" is never far away in Python, especially where Carol Cleveland is concerned. She is, in fact, wearing a fairly modest nightgown, at least at the start of this sketch.

Screens are placed around her. The doctor and nurse come in through the screens.

DOCTOR Hello, Miss Norris. How are you?
MISS NORRIS (CAROL) Not too bad, thank you, doctor.
DOCTOR Yes, well I think I'd better examine you.

Cut to a line of half a dozen shabby men in filthy macs down to the floor and caps, who shuffle in through the screens and stand at the foot of the bed leering. 8

8

These men, dressed in the traditional garb of the sexual deviant, are actually standing and watching as the camera cuts to them. Their hands move upsettingly under their overcoats.

MISS NORRIS What are they doing here?
DOCTOR It's all right, they're students. Um...light please, nurse. (*a single red spotlight falls down on the girl; cut back to the men leering*) Oh...and...er...music, too. (*nurse presses a switch beside bed; stripper music; very loud; cut to line of men getting very excited—hands deep in pockets*) Breathe in...out...in...out...

After about five seconds the music reaches a climax and ends. The men in macs all applaud. Cut to reverse angle to show that we are no longer in a hospital but in a seedy strip club. The curtains have just swished shut.

COMPÈRE (ERIC) Thank you, thank you. Charles Crompton, the Stripping Doctor. And next, gentlemen and ladies, here at the Peephole Club for the very first time—**a very big welcome please for the Secretary of State for Commonwealth Affairs.** 9

The Commonwealth of Nations, aka the Commonwealth, is the successor to what was once called the British Empire. The ceremonial head is the Queen of England, and though nonpolitical, the organization promotes a "We were once all one thing, and now let's share woolly ideals" kind of stance.

Curtains open. The compère leaves the stage. A man in city gent's outfit walks into the spotlight.

MINISTER (TERRY J) Good evening. Tonight I'd like to restate our position on agricultural subsidies, (*soft breathy jazzy music creeps in behind his words and he starts to strip as he talks*) and their effect on our Commonwealth relationships. Now although we believe, theoretically, in ending guaranteed farm prices, we also believe in the need for a corresponding import levy to maintain consumer prices at a realistic level. But this would have the effect of consolidating our gains of the previous fiscal year, prior to the entry. But I pledge that should we join **the Common Market** [10]—even maintaining the present position on subsidies—we will never jeopardize, we will never compromise our unique relationship with the Commonwealth countries. A prices structure related to any import charges will be systematically adjusted to the particular requirements of our Commonwealth partners (*he has now removed all his clothes apart from a tassel on each nipple and one on the front of some skin-tight briefs; he starts to revolve the tassels on his nipples*)—so that together we will maintain a positive, and mutually beneficial alliance in world trade (*he turns revealing a tassle on each buttock which he also revolves*) and for world peace. Thank you and goodnight.

He removes the last tassle from his G-string with a flourish. [11] *Blackout and curtains quickly close. Compère bounces back on stage.*

COMPÈRE Wasn't he marvellous? The Secretary of State for Commonwealth Affairs! [12] And now gentlemen and ladies, a very big welcome please for the Minister of Pensions and Social Security!

Burst of Turkish music and curtains swish back as another bowler-hatted pinstriped minister enters doing a Turkish dance. Cut to still of Houses of Parliament. Slow track in. Music changes to impressive patriotic music.

VOICE OVER (GRAHAM) Yes, today in Britain there is a new wave of interest in politics and politicians.

Cut to vox pops outside Houses of Parliament.

10

Britain's entry to "the Common Market"—a European group originally consisting of Belgium, Luxembourg, France, Germany, Italy, and the Netherlands—was a vexed question in 1970. Heath's Conservative government was all for joining, but many Britons felt it threatened the unique way of life of the isolated British Isles. Britain finally joined on the first day of 1973. Subsequently named the European Economic Community, thence simply the European Community, it is currently the de facto body aimed at full European integration.

11

He does no such thing, yet the striptease is just as upsetting as you might imagine, even without this final "flourish."

12

As Idle mimes wiping drool off of his chin here, we continue to hold down our collective gorges.

"Black Rod" (short for "Gentleman Usher of the Black Rod") is a ceremonial position at the Houses of Parliament. His most famous "job" is to summon the members of the House of Commons to attend the House of Lords to listen to the "Queen's speech," another ceremonial event in which the Queen reads a prepared statement by the government of the day. Traditionally, the doors of the Commons are slammed shut in Black Rod's face as a symbol of its independence from the Crown, though they are subsequently quite happily opened.

Reginald Bosanquet was a suave journalist of the day.

Tomorrow's World was a popular science show which aired on the BBC from 1965 till 2003. Hugely popular in the 1970's, it was fun to watch to see if the experiments would actually work (the show was, amazingly, live for many years). Baxter was one of the presenters.

Chapman is dressed in a suit and tie, but his pants, we will come to learn, are also tied tight against the threat of mice.

Caption: 'A GROUPIE'

FIRST GIRL (ERIC) Well, we're just in it for the lobbying, you know. We just love lobbying.
SECOND GIRL (GRAHAM) And the debates—you know a good debate...is just...fabulous.
THIRD GIRL (MICHAEL) Well, I've been going with ministers for five years now and, you know...I think they're wonderful.
FOURTH GIRL (TERRY J) Oh yes, I like civil servants.
THIRD GIRL Oh yes, they're nice.
FIFTH GIRL (JOHN) I like the Speaker.
FOURTH GIRL Oh yes.
SECOND GIRL **I like Black Rod.** 13
VOICE OVER What do their parents think?

Cut to suburban house. Mr Concrete standing in front of door of outside loo.

MR CONCRETE (TERRY J) Well she's broken our hearts, the little bastard. She's been nothing but trouble and if she comes round here again I'll kick her teeth in.

He turns and goes in. Cut to interior: the Concrete's sitting room. Mrs Concrete is sitting on the sofa, knitting. Mr Concrete enters.

MRS CONCRETE (MICHAEL) Have you been talking to television again, dear?
MR CONCRETE Yes, I bloody told 'em.
MRS CONCRETE What about?
MR CONCRETE I dunno.
MRS CONCRETE **Was it Reginald Bosanquet?** 14
MR CONCRETE No, no, no.
MRS CONCRETE Did he have his head all bandaged?
M CONCRETE No, it wasn't like that. They had lots of lights and cameras and tape recorders and all that sort of thing.
MRS CONCRETE **Oh, that'll be Ray Baxter and the boys and girls from 'Tomorrow's World'.** 15 Oh, I prefer Reginald Bosanquet, there's not so many of them. (*the doorbell rings*) Oh—that'll be the ratcatcher. (*she lets the ratcatcher in*)
RATCATCHER (GRAHAM) **Hello—Mr and Mrs Concrete?** 16
BOTH Yes.
RATCATCHER Well, well, well, well, well, well, well, well, well, well, well, how very nice. Allow me to introduce myself. I am Leslie Ames, the Chairman of the **Test Selection Committee,** 17 and I'm very pleased to be able to tell you that your flat has been chosen as the venue for the third test against the **West Indies.** 18
MRS CONCRETE Really?
RATCATCHER

NO, IT WAS JUST A LITTLE JOKE. ACTUALLY, I AM THE COUNCIL RATCATCHER.

MRS CONCRETE Oh yes, we've been expecting you.
RATCATCHER Oh, I gather you've got a little rodental problem.
MRS CONCRETE Oh, blimey. You'd think he was awake all the night, scrabbling down by the wainscotting.
RATCATCHING Um, that's an interesting word, isn't it?
MRS CONCRETE What?
RATCATCHER Wainscotting...Wainscotting...Wainscotting...sounds like a little Dorset village, doesn't it? Wainscotting.

Cut to the village of Wains Cotting. 19

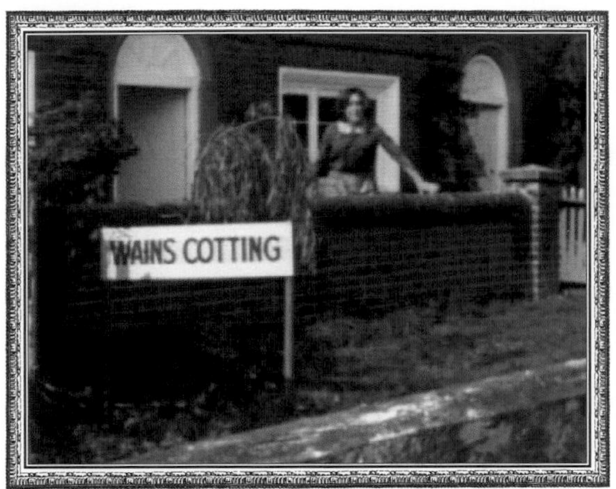

A woman rushes out of a house.

WOMAN We've been mentioned on telly!

Cut back to Concretes' house.

RATCATCHER Now, where is it worst?
MRS CONCRETE Well, down here. You can usually hear them.

Indicates base of wall, which has a label on it saying 'Wainscotting'.

RATCATCHER Ssssh!
VOICE OVER Baa...baa...baa...baa...baa....baa...
RATCATCHER No, that's sheep you've got there.
VOICE OVER Baa...baa.
RATCATCHER No, that's definitely sheep. A bit of a puzzle, really.
MRS CONCRETE Is it?
RATCATCHER Yeah, well, I mean it's (a) not going to respond to a nice piece of cheese and (b) it isn't going to fit into a trap.
MRS CONCRETE Oh—what are you going to do?
RATCATCHER Well, we'll have to look for the hole.

We follow them as they look along the wainscotting.

MRS CONCRETE Oh yeah. There's one here.

She indicates a small black mousehole.

RATCATCHER No, no, that's mice.

He reaches in and pulls out a line of mice strung out on a piece of elastic. Then he lets go so they shoot in again. The ratcatcher moves on. He moves a chair, behind which there is a three-foot-high black hole.

RATCATCHER Ah, this is what we're after.

The baaings get louder. At this point six cricketers enter the room.

CRICKETER (JOHN) Excuse me, is the third test in here?

"Tests" are the ne plus ultra of cricket, in which two countries play each other over the course of five days. The Selection Committee would pick which players would be part of a particular country's team, where games would be played, and so forth.

The West Indies are a traditional powerhouse of test cricket.

"Wains Cotting," sadly, is not a real village in Dorset.

MR CONCRETE No—that was a joke—a joke!
CRICKETER Oh blimey. (*exeunt*)
RATCATCHER Right. Well, I'm going in the wainscotting.

Cut to 'Wains Cotting' woman, who rushes out again.

WOMAN They said it again.

Back to the sitting room.

RATCATCHER I'm going to lay down some sheep poison.

He disappears into the hole. We hear:

VOICE OVER Baa, baa, baa.

A gunshot. The ratcatcher reappears clutching his arm.

RATCATCHER Aagh. Ooh! It's got a gun!
MRS CONCRETE Blimey.
RATCATCHER Now, normally a sheep is a placid, timid creature, but you've got a killer.

Poster: 'Wanted For Armed Robbery—Basil' with a picture of a sheep. Exciting crime-type music. Mix through to newspaper headlines: 'Farmers Ambushed in Pen', 'Merino Ram in Wages Grab'. Eerie science fiction music; mix through to a laboratory. A scientist looking through microscope and his busty attractive assistant.

PROFESSOR (ERIC)

IT'S AN ENTIRELY NEW STRAIN OF SHEEP, A KILLER SHEEP THAT CAN NOT ONLY HOLD A RIFLE BUT IS ALSO A FIRST-CLASS SHOT.

ASSISTANT But where are they coming from, professor?
PROFESSOR That I don't know. I just don't know. I really just don't know. I'm afraid I really just don't know. I'm afraid even I really just don't know. I have to tell you I'm afraid even I really just don't know. I'm afraid I have to tell you...(*she hands him a glass of water which she had been busy getting as soon as he started into this speech*)...thank you...(*resuming normal breezy voice*)...I don't know. Our only clue is this portion of wolfs clothing which the killer sheep...

Cut to Viking.

VIKING (TERRY G) ...was wearing...

Cut back to sketch.

PROFESSOR ...in yesterday's raid on Selfridges.
ASSISTANT I'll carry out tests on it straight away, professor.

She opens a door to another lab; but it is full of cricketers.

CRICKETER (JOHN) **Hello, is the third test in here, please?** 20

20

Cleese's turn and is in blackface; he also affects a "West Indian" accent.

She slams the door on them.

ASSISTANT Professor, there are some cricketers in the laboratory.
PROFESSOR This may be even more serious than even I had at first been imagining. What a strange...strange line. There's no time to waste. Get me the Chief Commissioner of Police.
ASSISTANT Yes, sir!

She opens a cupboard and slides out the Chief Commissioner of Police on a sort of slab. He grins and waves cheerily. ***'This is Your Life' music and applause.*** **21**

PROFESSOR No, no, on the phone.
ASSISTANT Oh...(*she pushes him back in*)
PROFESSOR Look of fear! (*he is staring transfixed at something in the doorway*) Another strange line. Look out, Miss Garter Oil!
ASSISTANT Professor! What is it? What have you seen?
PROFESSOR Look—there, in the doorway.

Cut to doorway: through it is animation of a huge sheep with an eye patch.

ASSISTANT Urghhh! Arthur X! **Leader of the Pennine Gang!** **22**

Animation: perhaps even mixed with stock film—as the fevered mind of Gilliam takes it—sheep armed to the teeth, sheep executing dangerous raids, Basil Cassidy and the Sundance Sheep, sheep with machine gun coming out of its arse etc.

At the end of the animation, cut to studio. A narrator sitting in what could be a news set at a desk.

This Is Your Life was a TV show in which famous people were surprised as their lives and exploits were recounted by friends and family.

Another reference to the Pennines mountain range that splits northern England into east and west. There are lots of sheep there.

By this point in the Python world, parrots meant only one thing: the parrot sketch.

NARRATOR (MICHAEL) But soon the killer sheep began to infect other animals with its startling intelligence. Pussy cats began to arrange mortgages, cocker spaniels began to design supermarkets...

Cut back to the animation again: a parrot.

PARROT And parrots started to announce television programmes. It's 8 o'clock and time for the News.

Cut back to the same narrator at desk.

NARRATOR

GOOD EVENING. HERE IS THE NEWS FOR PARROTS. 23

No parrots were involved in an accident on the M1 today, when a lorry carrying high octane fuel was in collision with a bollard...that is a *bollard* and not a *parrot*. A spokesman for parrots said he was glad no parrots were involved. The Minister of Technology (*photo of minister with parrot on his shoulder*) today met the three Russian leaders ***(cut to photograph of Brezhnev, Podgorny and Kosygin all in a group and each with a parrot on his shoulder)*** 24 to discuss a £4 million airliner deal...(*cut back to narrator*) None of them went in the cage, or swung on the little wooden trapeze, or ate any of the nice millet seed yum, yum. That's the end of the news. Now our programmes for parrots continue with part three of 'A Tale of Two Cities' specially adapted for parrots by Joey Boy. The story so far...Dr Manette is in England after eighteen years (*as he speaks French Revolution type music creeps in under his words*) in the Bastille. (*cut through to a Cruikshank engraving of London*) His daughter Lucy awaits her lover Charles Darnay, whom we have just learnt is in fact the nephew of the Marquis de St Evremond, whose cruelty had placed Manette in the Bastille. Darnay arrives to find Lucy tending her aged father...

24

Leonid Brezhnev was the supreme leader of Communist Russia from 1964 until 1982.

Nikolai Podgorny was chairman of the Presidium of the Supreme Soviet Russian—aka the head of state—from 1965 to 1977.

Alexei Kosygin was chairman of the Council of Ministers in Russia (the government, basically) from 1964 to 1980.

Superimposed caption: 'LONDON 1793' Music reaches a climax and we mix slowly through to an eighteenth-century living room. Lucy is nursing her father. Some low music continues over. ***Suddenly the door bursts open*** 25 *and Charles Darnay enters.*

DARNAY (GRAHAM) (*in parrot voice*) 'Allo, 'allo.
LUCY (CAROL) 'Allo, 'allo, 'allo.
OLD MAN (TERRY J) 'Allo, 'allo, 'allo.
DARNAY Who's a pretty boy, then?
LUCY 'Allo, 'allo, 'allo.

And more of the same. Cut back to the narrator.

It is, in fact, gently opened and closed.

NARRATOR And while that's going on, here is the news for gibbons. No gibbons were involved today in an accident on the M1...

The narrator's voice fades.

VOICE OVER (TERRY J) And while that's going on, here from Westminster is a Parliamentary report for humans.

Man sitting at a desk; the set behind him says 'Today in Parliament'.

Things of an offensive nature are ordered to be "stricken from the record"—that is, expunged from the official history of things said in the Houses of Parliament.

CYRIL (ERIC) In the debate a spokesman accused the Government of being silly and doing not at all good things. The member accepted this in a spirit of healthy criticism, but denied that he'd ever been naughty with a choirboy. Angry shouts of 'what about the watermelon, then?' were ordered by the Speaker to be **stricken from the record** 26 and put into a brown paper bag in the **lavvy.** **27** Any further interruptions would be cut off and distributed amongst the poor. For the Government a **Front Bench Spokesman** **28** said the agricultural tariff *would* have to be raised, and he fancied a bit. Furthermore, he argued, this would give a large boost to farmers, and a lot of fun to him, his friend and Miss Moist of Knightsbridge. From the back benches there were opposition shouts of 'postcards for sale' and a healthy cry of '**who likes a sailor, then?**' **29** from the Minister without Portfolio. Replying, the **Shadow Minister** **30** said, he could no longer deny the rumours but he and the dachshund were very happy; and, in any case, he argued, rhubarb was cheap and what was the harm in a sauna bath.

Cut to original narrator. Caption: '7 HOURS LATER'

NARRATOR ...were not involved. The Minister of Technology (*cut to photograph of minister with a wombat on his shoulder*) met the three Russian leaders today (*Russian leaders again all with wombats on their shoulders*) to discuss a £4 million airliner deal. None of them were indigenous to Australia, carried their babies in pouches or ate any of those yummy eucalyptus leaves. Yum, yum. That's the news for wombats, and now Attila the Bun!

Animation: a vicious rampaging bun.

VOICE OVER (JOHN) Well that's all for Attila the Bun, and now—idiots!

A village idiot in smock and straw hat, red cheeks, straw in mouth, sitting on a wall, making funny noises and rolling his eyes.

VOICE OVER (ERIC)

ARTHUR FIGGIS IS AN IDIOT. A VILLAGE IDIOT. TONIGHT WE LOOK AT THE IDIOT IN SOCIETY.

Cut to close-up of Figgis talking to camera. Very big close-up losing the top and bottom of his head. **31**

FIGGIS (JOHN) (*educated voice*) Well I feel very keenly that the idiot is a part of the old village system, and as such has a vital role to play in a modern rural society, because you see...(*suddenly switches to rural accent*) ooh ar ooh ar before the crops go gey are in the medley crun and the birds slides nightly on the oor ar...(*vicar passes and gives him sixpence*) **Ooh ar thankee, Vicar...** **32** (*educated voice*) There is this very real need in society for someone whom almost anyone can look down on and ridicule. And this is the role that...ooh ar naggy gamly rangle tandle oogly

"Lavvy" is yet more British slang for toilet, short for lavatory.

The "Front Bench" is a metonym for the government ministerial level. (It is also literally where they sit in the Commons.)

Another homosexual reference, as in "Hello sailor."

"Shadow ministers" are members of Parliament for the Opposition Party who literally have the "shadow" job of the actual minister (for example, the minister of agriculture has a counterpart in the minority party).

Cleese dresses as the archetypal country idiot, in smock and straw hat, and speaks in a West Country accent—the place most associated with country idiocy, as it were.

"Ooh" and "ar" are archetypal West Country sounds.

"ICI" is another reference to Imperial Chemical Industries, the leading British manufacturing company of the day.

noogle ooblie oog...(*passing lady gives him sixpence*) Thank you, Mrs Thompson...this is the role that I and members of my family have fulfilled in this village for the past four hundred years... Good morning, Mr Jenkins, **ICI have increased their half-yearly dividend, I see.** 33

We see Mr Jenkins pass, he is also an idiot, identically dressed.

MR JENKINS (MICHAEL) Yes, splendid.

FIGGIS That's Mr Jenkins—he's another idiot. And so you see the idiot does provide a vital psycho-social service for this community. Oh, excuse me, a coach party has just arrived. I shall have to fall off the wall, I'm afraid.

He falls backwards off the wall. Cut to Figgis in idiot's costume coming out of a suburban house. He walks on to the lawn on which are several pieces of gym equipment. He runs head-on into horse (speeded up) and falls over, concussed.

VOICE OVER (ERIC) Arthur takes idiotting seriously. He is up at six o'clock every morning working on special training equipment designed to keep him silly. And of course he takes great pride in his appearance.

Figgis, dressed in nice clean smock, jumps into a pond. He immediately scrambles up, pulls out a mirror and pats mud on his face critically, as if making-up.

VOICE OVER Like the doctor, the blacksmith, the carpenter, Mr Figgis is an important figure in this village and—like them—he uses the local bank.

Village square. A bank. Figgis is walking towards it. People giggling and pointing. He goes into a silly routine. Figgis enters the bank. Cut to bank manager standing outside bank. Caption: 'M. BRANDO—BANK MANAGER'

BANK MANAGER (GRAHAM) Yes, we have quite a number of idiots banking here.

VOICE OVER (MICHAEL) What kind of money is there in idiotting?

MANAGER **Well nowadays a really blithering idiot** 34 can make anything up to ten thousand pounds a year—if he's the head of some big industrial combine. But of course, the more old-fashioned idiot still refuses to take money.

"Blithering idiot" is a wonderful old British phrase (to blither is to talk foolishly).

We see Figgis handing over a cheque to cashier; cashier pushes across a pile of moss, pebbles, bits of wood and acorns.

MANAGER (*voice over*) He takes bits of string, wood, dead budgerigars, sparrows, anything, but it does make the cashier's job very difficult; but of course they're fools to themselves because the rate of interest over ten years on a piece of moss or a dead vole is almost negligible.

A clerk appears at door of bank.

CLERK (TERRY J) Mr Brando.
MANAGER Yes?
CLERK Hollywood on the phone.
MANAGER I'll take it in the office.

Cut to a woodland glade.

VOICE OVER (ERIC) But Mr Figgis is no ordinary idiot. He is a lecturer in idiocy at the University of East Anglia. Here he is taking a class of third-year students.

Half a dozen loonies led by Figgis come dancing through the glade singing tunelessly. They are wearing long University scarves.

VOICE OVER After three years of study these apprentice idiots receive a diploma of idiocy, a handful of mud and a kick on the head.

A vice-chancellor stands in a University setting with some young idiots in front of him. They wear idiot gear with BA hoods. One walks forward to him, he gets a diploma, a faceful of mud and stoops to receive his kick on the head. Cut to happy parents smiling proudly.

VOICE OVER But some of the older idiots resent the graduate idiot.
OLD IDIOT (ERIC) I'm a completely self-taught idiot. I mean, ooh arh, ooh arhh, ooh arhh,...nobody does that anymore. Anybody who did that round here would be laughed off the street. No, nowadays people want something wittier.

Wift empties breakfast over him. Cut to idiot falling repeatedly off a wall.

VOICE OVER **Kevin O'Nassis works largely with walls.** 35
KEVIN (JOHN) (*voice over*) You've got to know what you're doing. I mean, some people think I'm mad. The villagers say I'm mad, the tourists say I'm mad, well I *am* mad, but I'm *naturally* mad. I don't use any chemicals.
VOICE OVER But what of the idiot's private life? How about his relationship with women?

Idiot in bed. Pull back to reveal he shares it with two very young, thin, nude girls.

IDIOT (JOHN) **Well I may be an idiot but I'm no fool.** 36
VOICE OVER But the village idiot's dirty smock and wall-falling are a far cry from the modern world of the urban idiot. (*stock film of city gents in their own clothes pouring out of trains*) What kinds of backgrounds do these city idiots come from?

Vox pops film of city gents. Subtitles explain their exaggerated accents.

FIRST CITY IDIOT (JOHN) **Eton, Sandhurst and the Guards, ha, ha, ha, ha.** 37
SECOND CITY IDIOT (MICHAEL) I can't remember but I've got it written down somewhere.
THIRD CITY IDIOT (GRAHAM) Daddy's a banker. He needed a wastepaper basket.
FOURTH CITY IDIOT (TERRY J) **Father was Home Secretary and mother won the Derby.** 38

Cut to a commentator with mike in close-up. Pull back in his speech, to discover he is standing in front of the main gate at Lords cricket ground. 39

INTERVIEWER (GRAHAM) The headquarters of these urban idiots is here in St John's Wood. Inside they can enjoy the company of other idiots and watch special performances of ritual idiotting.

Jackie Kennedy became Jackie Onassis when she married Aristotle Onassis in October 1968.

There's an odd moment here as the two naked women cuddle Cleese, and then after a moment or two he claps his hands and shouts, "Right!" We can only presume what happens next.

Once again, the trajectory of the truly superior Briton: top boys' school (Eton), top military-training academy (Sandhurst), top army job (the Guards).

The famous old horse race, the Epsom Derby, runs every June at Epsom Downs in Surrey.

Lord's Cricket Ground is the center of the cricketing universe, in the St. John's Wood section of northwest London.

Cut to quick wide-shot of cricket match being played at Lords. Cut to five terribly old idiots watching.

FIRST IDIOT (MICHAEL) Well left.
SECOND IDIOT (GRAHAM) Well played.
THIRD IDIOT (ERIC) Well well.
FOURTH IDIOT (JOHN) Well bred.
FIFTH IDIOT (TERRY J) (*dies*) Ah!

Another very quick wide-shot of Lords. There is nothing at all happening and we can't distinguish anyone. Cut to three TV commentators in modern box, with sliding window open. They are surrounded by bottles.

"Out nought," meaning he's at bat but hasn't scored yet. You're "at bat" if you're in, and your score is said to be "x," not "out." See?

Not surprisingly, Iceland is not known for its cricket—that is, they don't play at all.

This means the team scored 722 runs, two of their batsman were "out," and they have announced their inning will come to an end voluntarily. The "total of 722 for 2" would be a massive score in cricket.

JIM (JOHN) Good afternoon and welcome to Lords on the second day of the first test. So far today we've had five hours batting from England and already they're nought for nought. Cowdrey is not **out nought.** 40 Naughton is not in. Knott is in and is nought for not out. Naughton of Northants got a nasty knock on the nut in the nets last night but it's nothing of note. Next in is Nat Newton of Notts. Not Nutting—Nutting's at nine, er, Nutting knocked neatie nighty knock knock...(*another commentator nudges him*)...anyway England have played extremely well for nothing, not a sausage, in reply to **Iceland's** 41 first innings total of **722 for 2 declared,** 42 scored yesterday disappointingly fast in only twenty-one overs with lots of wild slogging and boundaries and all sorts of rubbishy things. But the main thing is that England have made an absolutely outstanding start so far, Peter?
PETER (GRAHAM) Splendid. Just listen to those thighs. And now it's the North East's turn with the Samba. Brian.
BRIAN (ERIC) (*he has an enormous nose*) Rather. (*opens book*) I'm reminded of the story of Gubby Allen in '32...

JIM Oh, shut up or we'll close the bar. And now Bo Wildeburg is running up to bowl to Cowdrey, he runs up, he bowls to Cowdrey...

Cut to fast bowler. 43 *He bowls the ball but the batsman makes no move whatsoever. The ball passes the off stump.*

The bowler is Cleese himself, displaying admirable technique.

JIM ...and no shot at all. Extremely well not played there.
PETER Yes, beautifully not done anything about.
BRIAN A superb shot of no kind whatsoever. **I well remember Plum Warner leaving a very similar ball alone in 1732.** 44

Sir Pelham Francis "Plum" Warne was Cricketer of the Year in 1904, and again in 1921.

JIM Oh shut up, long nose. *(Peter falls off his chair.)* And now it's Bo Wildeburg running in again to bowl to Cowdrey, he runs in. (*bowler bowls as before; ball goes by as before*) He bowls to Cowdrey—and no shot at all, a superb display of inertia there... **And that's the end of the over, and drinks.** **45**

PETER Gin and tonic please.

JIM No, no the *players* are having drinks. And now, what's happening? I think Cowdrey's being taken off. *(Two men in white coats, à la furniture removers, so maybe they're brown coats, are carrying the batsman off. Two men pass them with a green Chesterfield sofa making for the wicket.)* Yes, Cowdrey is being carried off. Well I never. Now who's in next, it should be number three, Natt Newton of Notts...get your hand off my thigh, West...no I don't think it is...I think it's er, it's the sofa...no it's the Chesterfield! The green Chesterfield is coming in at number three to take guard now.

BRIAN I well remember a similar divan being brought on at Headingley in 9 bc against the darkies.

JIM Oh, shut up, elephant snout. And now the green Chesterfield has taken guard and Iceland are putting on their spin dryer to bowl. **46**

Furniture fielding. The whole pitch is laid out with bits of furniture in correct positions. Three chairs in the slips; easy chair keeping wicket; bidet at mid; TV set at cover; bookcase at mid off; roll-top writing desk at square; radiator at mid wicket etc. The spin dryer moves forward and bowls a real ball with its snozzle to a table, which is at the batting end with cricket pads on. It hits the table on the pad. Appeal.

JIM The spin dryer moves back to his mark, it runs out to the wicket, bowls to the table...a little bit short but it's coming in a bit there and it's hit him on the pad...and the table is out, leg before wicket. **That is England nought for one.** **47**

DIFFERENT VOICE OVER (MICHAEL) And now we leave Lords and go over to Epsom for the three o'clock.

Cut to a race course. Furniture comes into shot racing the last fifty yards to the finishing post.

COMMENTATOR (ERIC) Well here at Epsom we take up the running with fifty yards of this mile and a half race to go and it's the wash basin in the lead from WC Pedestal. Tucked in nicely there is the sofa going very well with Joanna Southcott's box making a good run from hat stand on the rails, and the standard lamp is failing fast but it's wash basin definitely taking up the running now being strongly pressed by...At the post it's the wash basin from WC then sofa, hat stand, standard lamp and lastly Joanna Southcott's box.

Cut to three bishops shouting from actual studio audience. **48**

BISHOPS Open the box! Open the box! Open the box! Open the box! Open the box!

A simple 'Take Your Pick' style set with a Michael Miles grinning type monster standing at centre of it. **49**

MICHAEL MILES (JOHN) And could we have the next contender, please? (*a pepperpot walks out into the set towards Michael Miles*) Ha ha ha...Good evening, madam, and your name is?

WOMAN (TERRY J) Yes, yes.

MICHAEL MILES And what's your name?

WOMAN I go to church regularly.

MICHAEL MILES Jolly good, I see, and which prize do you have particular eyes on this evening?

WOMAN I'd like the blow on the head.

MICHAEL MILES The blow on the head.

WOMAN Just there.

"Drinks" is an official time-out in a session of cricket. They actually bring drinks out onto the field of play, and people stand around and... well, drink. It is very civilized.

A "spin bowler" delivers the ball slowly, but he spins it.

In too simplistic terms, should the ball strike the batsman's pad, when the ball would have hit the wickets, or stumps, then the batsman is called out by the umpire.

It's one bishop—Palin—and two clerics.

Michael Miles is the New Zealand–born presenter from 1955 to 1968 of *Take Your Pick*, a British game show.

MICHAEL MILES Jolly good. Well your first question for the blow on the head this evening is: what great opponent of Cartesian dualism resists the reduction of psychological phenomena to physical states?

WOMAN I don't know that!

MICHAEL MILES Well, have a guess.

WOMAN Henri Bergson.

MICHAEL MILES Is the correct answer!

WOMAN Ooh, that was lucky. I never even heard of him.

MICHAEL MILES Jolly good.

WOMAN I don't like darkies.

MICHAEL MILES Ha ha ha. Who does! And now your second question for the blow on the head is: what is the main food that penguins eat?

WOMAN Pork luncheon meat.

MICHAEL MILES No.

WOMAN Spam?

MICHAEL MILES No, no, no. What do penguins eat? Penguins.

WOMAN Penguins?

MICHAEL MILES Yes.

WOMAN I hate penguins.

MICHAEL MILES No, no, no.

WOMAN They eat themselves.

MICHAEL MILES No, no, what do *penguins* eat?

WOMAN Horses!...Armchairs!

MICHAEL MILES No, no, no. What do penguins eat?

WOMAN Oh, penguins.

MICHAEL MILES Penguins.

WOMAN Cannelloni.

MICHAEL MILES No.

WOMAN Lasagna, moussaka, lobster thermidor, escalopes de veau à l'estragon avec endives gratinéed with cheese.

MICHAEL MILES No, no, no, no. I'll give you a clue. (*mimes a fish swimming*)

WOMAN **Ah! Brian Close.** 50

MICHAEL MILES No. no.

WOMAN **Brian Inglis, Brian Johnson, Bryan Forbes.** 51

MICHAEL MILES No, no!

WOMAN Nanette Newman.

MICHAEL MILES No. What swims in the sea and gets caught in nets?

WOMAN Henri Bergson.

MICHAEL MILES No.

WOMAN Goats. Underwater goats with snorkels and flippers.

MICHAEL MILES No, no.

WOMAN A buffalo with an aqualung.

MICHAEL MILES No, no.

WOMAN **Reginald Maudling.** 52

MICHAEL MILES Yes, that's near enough. I'll give you that. Right, now, Mrs Scum, you have won your prize, do you still want the blow on the head?

WOMAN Yes, yes.

MICHAEL MILES I'll offer you a poke in the eye.

WOMAN No! I want a blow on the head.

MICHAEL MILES A punch in the throat.

WOMAN No.

MICHAEL MILES All right then, a kick in the kneecap.

WOMAN No.

Brian Close was a British cricketer from 1948 to 1977.

Brian Inglis was an Irish historian and TV presenter best known for the TV show *All Our Yesterdays*, which he hosted from 1961 to 1973.

Brian Johnson, the aforementioned cricket commentator with the big nose.

Bryan Forbes is a British film director and writer, married to actress Nanette Newman.

Reginald Maudling, the British reactionary politician, was a regular Python target.

MICHAEL MILES Mrs Scum, I'm offering you a boot in the teeth and a dagger up the strap.

WOMAN Er...

VOICES

BLOW ON THE HEAD! TAKE THE BLOW ON THE HEAD!

WOMAN No, no. I'll take the blow on the head.

MICHAEL MILES Very well then, Mrs Scum, you have won tonight's star prize, the blow on the head.

He strikes her on head with an enormous mallet and she falls unconscious.

A sexily dressed girl in the background (GRAHAM) *strikes a small gong. The three bishops rush in and jump on her.*

Cut to sign:
LICENCE FEES FROM 1ST JANUARY 1969
COLOUR TV AND RADIO £11-0-0
TV AND RADIO £6-0-0
RADIO ONLY £1-5-0
Roll credits over. Caption: THE END

COMING SOON
3947
LUXURY
FLATS
SEA
SON
2
EPISODE 21

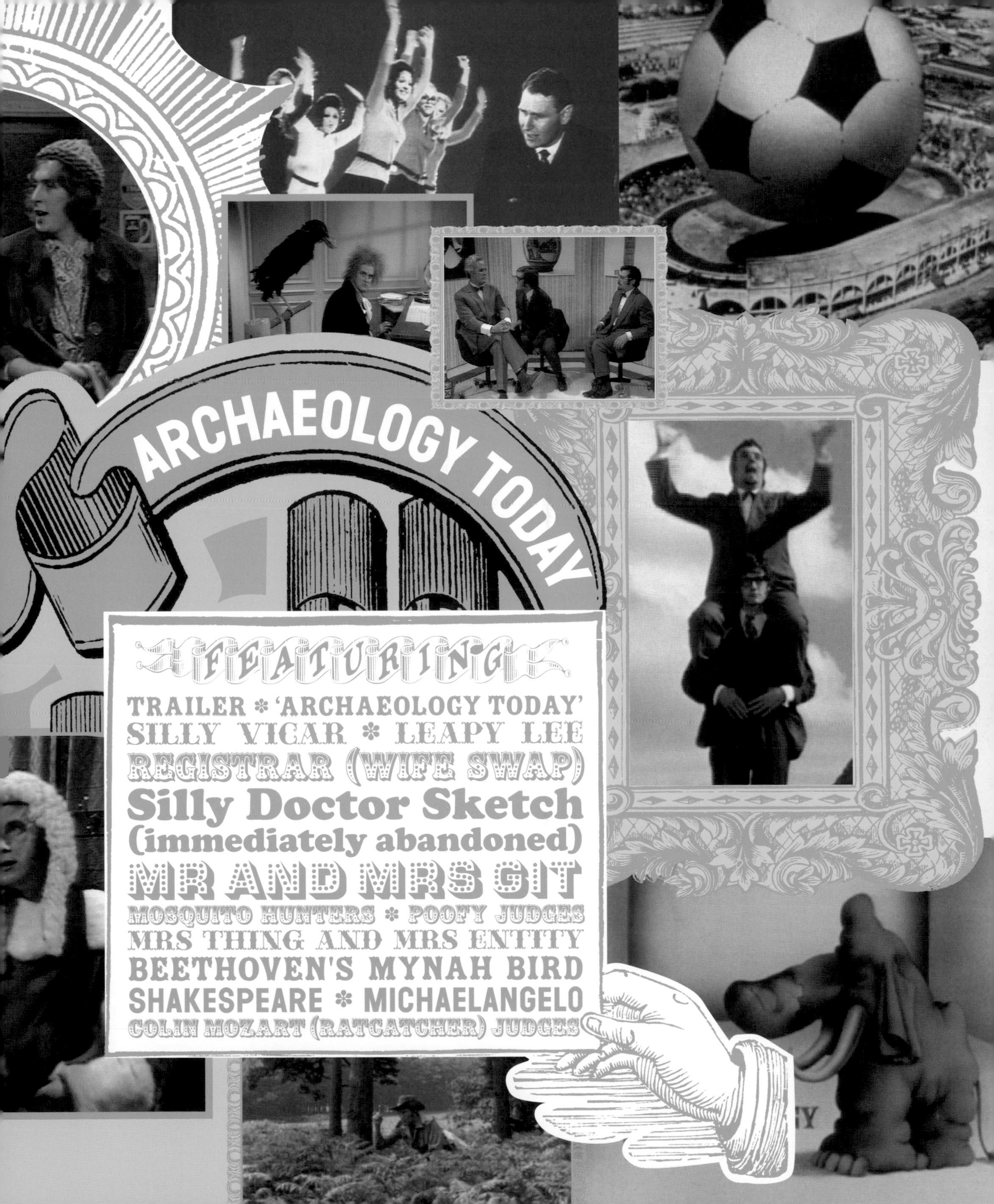
ARCHAEOLOGY TODAY
FEATURING
TRAILER * 'ARCHAEOLOGY TODAY'
SILLY VICAR * LEAPY LEE
REGISTRAR (WIFE SWAP)
Silly Doctor Sketch
(immediately abandoned)
MR AND MRS GIT
MOSQUITO HUNTERS * POOFY JUDGES
MRS THING AND MRS ENTITY
BEETHOVEN'S MYNAH BIRD
SHAKESPEARE * MICHAELANGELO
COLIN MOZART (RATCATCHER) JUDGES

The gag about the cricket commentators from the end of Episode 20 continues.

A "rain-stopped play" is an official situation that can occur in cricket—and happens often in rainy England.

E.W. Swanton is another famed cricket journalist.

Brian Close, the cricketer, and beloved figure of fun for the Pythons. Talk of the Town is an esteemed cabaret restaurant in London.

John Galsworthy was a British novelist and playwright best known for *The Forsyte Saga.*

Joe Davis was an eminent British snooker player.

Jim Laker was a England cricketer in the 1950s, and later a TV commentator.

FIRST AIRED: NOVEMBER 17, 1970

BBC 1 World symbol. [1]

VOICE OVER (ERIC) Here is a preview of some of the programmes you'll be able to see coming shortly on BBC Television. To kick off with there's variety...(*still picture of Peter West and Brian Johnston*) Peter West and Brian Johnston star in 'Rain Stopped Play', [2] a whacky new comedy series about the gay exploits of two television cricket commentators (*photo of E. W. Swanton*) [3] with E. W. Swanton as Aggie the kooky Scots maid. For those of you who don't like variety, there's variety, with Brian Close at the Talk of the Town. [4] (*Brian Close in cricket whites on a stage*) And of course there'll be sport. The Classics series (*engraving of London and caption: 'THE CLASSICS'*) return to BBC 2 with twenty-six episodes of John Galsworthy's 'Snooker My Way' [5] (*composite photo of Nyree Dawn Porter holding a snooker cue*) with Nyree Dawn Porter repeating her triumph as Joe Davis. [6] And of course there'll be sport. Comedy is not forgotten (*Caption: 'COMEDY'*) with Jim Laker (*photo of Laker*) [7] in 'Thirteen Weeks of Off-spin Bowling.' Jim plays the zany bachelor bowler in a new series of 'Owzat', with Anneley Brummond-Haye on Mr Softee (*photo of same*) as his wife. And of course there'll be sport. 'Panorama' will be returning, introduced (*'PANORAMA' caption with photo of Tony Jacklin*) as usual by Tony Jacklin, [8] and Lulu (*photo of Lulu*) [9] will be tackling the Old Man of Hoy (*photo of same*). And for those of you who prefer drama—there's sport. On 'Show of the Week' Kenneth Wolstenholme sings. [10] (*still of him, superimposed over Flick Colby Dancers, Pans People, ono*) [11] And for those of you who don't like television there's David Coleman. [12] (*picture of him smiling*) And of course there'll be sport. But now for something completely different—sport.

'Grandstand' [13] *signature tune starts and then abruptly cuts into the usual animated credit titles.*

Animation: a sketch about an archaeological find leads to:

Caption: 'ARCHAEOLOGY TODAY' Interview set for archaeology programme. Chairman and two guests sit in chairs in front of a blow-up of an old cracked pot.

INTERVIEWER (MICHAEL) Hello. On 'Archaeology Today' tonight I have with me Professor Lucien Kastner of Oslo University.

KASTNER (TERRY J) Good evening.

INTERVIEWER How tall are you, professor?

KASTNER ...I beg your pardon?

INTERVIEWER How tall are you?

KASTNER I'm about five foot ten.

INTERVIEWER ...and an expert in Egyptian tomb paintings. Sir Robert...(*turning to Kastner*) are you really five foot ten?

KASTNER Yes.

INTERVIEWER Funny, you look much shorter than that to me. Are you slumped forward in your chair at all?

KASTNER No, er, I...

INTERVIEWER Extraordinary. Sir Robert Eversley, who's just returned from the excavations in El Ara, and you must be well over six foot. Isn't that right, Sir Robert?

SIR ROBERT (JOHN) (*puzzled*) Yes.

INTERVIEWER In fact, I think you're six foot five aren't you?

SIR ROBERT Yes.

Applause from off. Sir Robert looks up in amazement.

INTERVIEWER Oh, that's marvellous. I mean you're a totally different kind of specimen to Professor Kastner. Straight in your seat, erect, firm...

SIR ROBERT Yes. I thought we were here to discuss archaeology.

INTERVIEWER Yes, yes, of course we are, yes, absolutely, you're absolutely right! That's positive thinking for you. (*to Kastner*) You wouldn't have said a thing like that, would you? You five-foot-ten weed. (*he turns his back very ostentatiously on Kastner*) Sir Robert Eversley, (who's very interesting) what have you discovered in the excavations at El Ara?

SIR ROBERT (*picking up a beautiful ancient vase*) Well basically we have found a complex of tombs...

INTERVIEWER Very good speaking voice.

SIR ROBERT ...which present dramatic evidence of Polynesian influence in Egypt in the third dynasty which is quite remarkable.

INTERVIEWER How tall were the Polynesians?

KASTNER They were...

INTERVIEWER Sh!

SIR ROBERT Well, they were rather small, seafaring...

INTERVIEWER Short men, were they...eh? All squat and bent up?

SIR ROBERT Well, I really don't know about that...

INTERVIEWER Who were the tall people?

Tony Jacklin is a British golfer, and frequent subject of Python razzing.

Lulu is a Scottish singer. Born Marie McDonald McLaughlin Lawrie, she won the 1969 Eurovision Song Contest (a widely ridiculed Europe-wide singing competition).

Kenneth Wolstenholme was a prominent BBC soccer commentator of the 1950s and '60s.

Flick Colby, an American dancer, was the driving force behind the iconic Pan's People, a dance troupe featured heavily between 1969 and 1976 on the hit BBC TV show *Top of the Pops*.

David Coleman was a sports commentator known for his amusing gaffes, dubbed by satirical British magazine *Private Eye* as "Colemanballs."

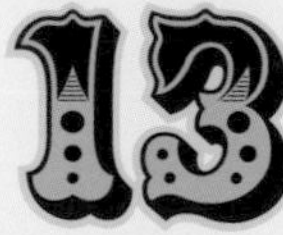

Every Saturday afternoon between 1958 and 2007, BBC programming was given over to a five-hour sports show, *Grandstand*. David Coleman was the presenter for a decade, until 1968.

The Watutsi of Central Africa are now known as the Tutsi.

SIR ROBERT I'm afraid I don't know.

INTERVIEWER Who's that very tall tribe in Africa?

SIR ROBERT Well, this is hardly archaeology.

INTERVIEWER The Watutsi! 14 That's it—the Watutsi! Oh, that's the tribe, some of them were eight foot tall. Can you imagine that. Eight foot of Watutsi. Not one on another's shoulders, oh no—eight foot of solid Watutsi. That's what I call tall.

SIR ROBERT Yes, but it's nothing to do with archaeology.

INTERVIEWER (*knocking Sir Robert's vase to the floor*)

OH TO HELL WITH ARCHAEOLOGY!

KASTNER Can I please speak! I came all the way from Oslo to do this programme! I'm a professor of archaeology. I'm an expert in ancient civilizations. All right, I'm only five foot ten. All right my posture is bad, all right I slump in my chair. But I've had more women than either of you two! I've had half bloody Norway, that's what I've had! So you can keep your Robert Eversley! And you can keep your bloody Watutsi! I'd rather have my little body...my little five-foot-ten-inch body...(*he breaks down sobbing*)

SIR ROBERT Bloody fool. Look what you've done to him.

INTERVIEWER Don't bloody fool me.

SIR ROBERT I'll do what I like, because I'm six foot five and I eat punks like you for breakfast.

Sir Robert floors the interviewer with an almighty punch. Interviewer looks up rubbing his jaw. 15

Cleese misses Palin by a country mile; it's not even *close* to close.

INTERVIEWER I'll get you for that, Eversley! I'll get you if I have to travel to the four corners of the earth!

Crash of music. Music goes into theme and film titles as for a Western. Caption: 'FLAMING STAR—THE STORY OF ONE MAN'S SEARCH FOR VENGEANCE IN THE RAW AND VIOLENT WORLD OF INTERNATIONAL ARCHAEOLOGY' Cut to stock film of the pyramids (circa 1920). Superimposed caption: 'EGYPT—1920' An archaeological dig in a flat sandy landscape. All the characters are in twenties' clothes. Pan across the complex of passages and trenches.

DANIELLE (CAROL) (*voice over*) The dig was going well that year. We had discovered some Hittite baking dishes from the fifth dynasty, and Sir Robert was happier than I had ever seen him.

Camera comes to rest on Sir Robert Eversley digging away. We close in on him as he sings to Hammond organ accompaniment.

TERRY GILLIAM

Terry Gilliam, the only non-British member of the Pythons, was born in Minneapolis, Minnesota. Soon after, his family moved ten miles west to Medicine Lake, a city surrounded by a large lake of the same name. The eldest of three children, Gilliam remembers his childhood as a kind of Tom Sawyer experience. Just before his teen years, he moved to California, but by the time he was in his late teens, this "smartest kid in the class" found himself in a country fractured by political and societal upheaval, and he felt out of place. He gained solace in his love of cartooning and *Mad* magazine. After college he traveled in Europe, partly to make money as an illustrator and partly to avoid the draft. Eventually, he decamped to the U.K. full-time.

There, he worked on the children's TV show *Do Not Adjust Your Set,* which also had input from Eric Idle, Terry Jones, and Michael Palin. Gilliam already knew John Cleese from America, where the two had worked together on the seminal (and now defunct) humor magazine *Help!* It made perfect sense, then, that Gilliam would be a founding member of the Pythons, and now it's hard to imagine the TV shows, or the movies, without his extraordinary illustrations. Partly his own creations and partly culled from Victorian art, the dreamscapes he created were used to link the disparate sketches. In the scripts, it's often left to Gilliam to make that connection, clearly giving the Pythons room to create whatever they wanted knowing he would build a framework that the shows, by their very nature, mostly lacked. But Gilliam also performed a bit (it was usually he inside the knight-in-shining-armor costume, brandishing the plastic plucked chicken), and by the fourth season, when Cleese was absent, he found himself in front of the camera even more. He was codirector, with Terry Jones, of *Monty Python and the Holy Grail,* though it is said that he and Jones were hardly the perfect directing team, so different were their methodologies.

Post-Python, Gilliam has created a fine trilogy of movies about the desire to escape "ordered society." The first, *Time Bandits,* from 1981, was cowritten with Michael Palin and follows the adventures of a kid named Kevin as he goes back in time (John Cleese has a small role in the movie, as Robin Hood). Next, the highly regarded *Brazil,* from 1985, features an all-star cast stuck in a dystopian nightmare. The final film, *The Adventures of Baron Munchausen,* released in 1988, is about an eighteenth-century aristocrat attempting to save a town from being overrun by the Turks.

Gilliam sees another set of his later movies as a trilogy—this time, a trilogy of Americana. *The Fisher King, 12 Monkeys,* and *Fear and Loathing in Las Vegas* were not written by Gilliam, and are not as surreal as the earlier trilogy, but they still muse on the force of imagination in people's lives.

Gilliam continues to direct movies, though he's avowedly outside of the studio system. (A photo of him in 2006 shows him holding a sign that reads STUDIO-LESS FILMMAKER – FAMILY TO SUPPORT – WILL DIRECT FOR FOOD.) He's also avowedly outside of America: having renounced his American citizenship, he became a British citizen the year before Python began.

SIR ROBERT Today I hear the robin sing
Today the thrush is on the wing
Today who knows what life will bring
Today...

He stops and picks up an object, blows the dust off it and looks at it wondrously.

SIR ROBERT Why, a Sumerian drinking vessel of the fourth dynasty. (*sings*) Today!!!! (*speaks*) Catalogue this pot, Danielle, it's fourth dynasty.

DANIELLE Oh, is it...?

SIR ROBERT Yes, it's...Sumerian.

DANIELLE Oh, how wonderful! Oh, I am so happy for you.

SIR ROBERT I'm happy too, now at last we know there was a Sumerian influence here in Abu Simnel in the early pre-dynastic period, two thousand years before the reign of Tutankhamun. (*he breaks into song again*) (*singing*) Today I hear the robin sing
Today the thrush is on the wing
(*Danielle joins in*) Today who knows what life will bring.

They are just about to embrace, when there is a jarring chord and long crash. The interviewer, in the clothes he wore before, is standing on the edge of the dig.

INTERVIEWER All right Eversley, get up out of that trench.

SIR ROBERT Don't forget...I'm six foot five.

INTERVIEWER That doesn't worry me...Kastner!

He snaps his fingers. From behind him Professor Kastner appears, fawningly.

KASTNER Here Lord.

INTERVIEWER Up!

HE SNAPS HIS FINGERS AND KASTNER LEAPS ONTO HIS SHOULDERS.

SIR ROBERT Eleven foot three!

KASTNER I'm so tall! I am so tall!

SIR ROBERT Danielle!

Danielle leaps on his shoulders.

INTERVIEWER Eleven foot six—damn you! Abdul!

A servant appears on Kastner's shoulders.

SIR ROBERT Fifteen foot four! Mustapha!

A servant appears on Danielle's shoulders.

INTERVIEWER Nineteen foot three...damn you!

The six of them charge each other.

They fight in amongst the trestle tables with rare pots on them breaking and smashing them. When the fight ends everyone lies dead in a pile of broken pottery. The interviewer crawls up to camera and produces a microphone from his pocket. He is covered in blood and in his final death throes.

INTERVIEWER And there we end this edition of 'Archaeology Today'. Next week, the Silbury Dig by Cole Porter with Pearl Bailey and Arthur Negus. *(he dies)* 16

VOICE OVER (MICHAEL) And now an appeal for sanity from the Reverend Arthur Belling.

Cut to studio. A vicar sitting facing camera. He has an axe in his head.

REVEREND BELLING (GRAHAM) You know, there are many people in the country today who, through no fault of their own, are sane. Some of them were born sane. Some of them became sane later in their lives. It is up to people like you and me who are out of our tiny little minds to try and help these people overcome their sanity. You can start in small ways with ping-pong ball eyes and a funny voice and then you can paint half of your body red and the other half green and then you can jump up and down in a bowl of treacle going 'squawk, squawk, squawk...' And then you can go 'Neurhhh! Neurhh!' and then you can roll around on the floor going 'pting pting pting'...*(he rolls around on the floor)* 17

VOICE OVER The Reverend Arthur Belling is Vicar of St Loony Up The Cream Bun and Jam. And now an appeal on behalf of the National Trust.

Caption: 'AN APPEAL ON BEHALF OF THE NATIONAL TRUSS' Cut to a smartly dressed woman.

WOMAN (ERIC) Good evening. My name is Leapy Lee. 18 No, sorry. That's the name of me favourite singer. My name is Mrs Fred Stolle 19 No, no, Mrs Fred Stolle is the wife of me favourite tennis player. My name is Bananas. No, no, that's me favourite fruit. I'm Mrs Nice-evening-

Pearl Bailey was an African-American actress and singer, and winner in 1968 of the Tony Award for the title role in *Hello, Dolly!*, a production that featured an all-black cast.

Another reference to Arthur Negus, the antique expert and TV personality.

The ax drops off the top of his head as he falls, proving it wasn't really *in* his head . . .

Leapy Lee (real name Graham Pullyblank, truly) is an English singer who had a hit in 1968 with the song "Little Arrows."

Fred Stolle is an Australian tennis player who won the French Open in 1965 and the U.S. Open in 1966.

Denis Compton was a two-sport star, having played cricket for England between 1937 and 1957 and soccer for Arsenal FC between 1936 and 1950.

P.P. Arnold was an American soul singer most popular in the 1960s.

Another reference to the then rising star of British Conservative politics, who would go on to be prime minister about a decade later.

A regular victim of Python opprobrium, Gerald Nabarro was a Conservative MP known for his audacious handlebar moustache and his extreme political positions.

Len Hutton was a legendary English cricketer of the middle years of the twentieth century.

out-at-the-pictures-then-perhaps-a-dance-at-a-club-and-back-to-his-place- for-a-quick-cup-of-coffee-and-little-bit-of—no! No, sorry, that's me favourite way of spending a night out. Perhaps I *am* Leapy Lee? Yes! I must be Leapy Lee! Hello fans! Leapy Lee here! (*sings*) Little arrows that will...(*phone rings, she answers*) Hello?...Evidently I'm *not* Leapy Lee. I thought I probably wouldn't be. Thank you, I'll tell them. (*puts phone down*) Hello. Hello, Denis Compton here. 20 No no...I should have written it down. Now where's that number? (*as she looks in her bag she talks to herself*) I'm Mao Tse Tung...I'm P. P. Arnold... 21 I'm Margaret Thatcher... 22 I'm Sir Gerald Nabarro... 23 (*she dials*) Hello? Sir Len Hutton here. 24 Could you tell me, please oh, am I? Oh, thank you. (*puts phone down*) Good evening. I'm Mrs What-number-are-you-dialling-please?

A boxer (TERRY G) *rushes in and fells her with one blow. After Women's Institute applauding cut to: a man coming through a door with a neat little bride in a bridal dress. The man walks up to the registrar who is sitting at his desk with a sign saying 'Registrar of Marriages'.*

REGISTRAR (ERIC) Good morning.
MAN (TERRY J) Good morning. Are you the registrar?
REGISTRAR I have that function.
MAN I was here on Saturday, getting married to a blond girl, and I'd like to change please. I'd like to have this one instead please.
REGISTRAR What do you mean?
MAN Er, well, the other one wasn't any good, so I'd like to swap it for this one, please. Er, I have paid. I paid on Saturday. Here's the ticket.

Gives him the marriage licence.

REGISTRAR Ah, ah, no. That was when you were married.
MAN Er, yes. That was when I was married to the wrong one. I didn't like the colour. This is the one I want to have, so if you could just change the forms round I can take this one back with me now.
REGISTRAR I can't do that.
MAN Look, make it simpler, I'll pay again.
REGISTRAR No, you can't *do* that.
MAN Look, all I want you to do is change the wife, say the words, blah, blah, blah, back to my place, no questions asked.
REGISTRAR I'm sorry sir, but we're not allowed to change.
MAN You can at Harrods.
REGISTRAR You can't.
MAN You can. I changed my record player and there wasn't a grumble.
REGISTRAR It's different.

MAN And I changed my pet snake, and I changed my Robin Day tie. 25
REGISTRAR Well, you can't change a bloody wife!
MAN Oh, all right! Well, can I borrow one for the weekend.
REGISTRAR No!
MAN Oh, blimey, I only wanted a jolly good...

A whistle blows. A referee runs on, takes his book out and proceeds to take the name of the man in the registry office, amidst protests. 26

REFEREE (JOHN) All right, break it up. What's your number, then? All right. Name?
MAN Cook.

Cut to the two in the next sketch waiting. Cut back to referee, who finishes booking the man and blows his whistle. The show continues. Cut to the two waiting. On the sound of the whistle they start acting.

DOCTOR (MICHAEL) Next please. Name?
WATSON (GRAHAM) Er, Watson.
DOCTOR (*writing it down*) Mr Watson.
WATSON Ah, no, Doctor.
DOCTOR Ah, Mr Doctor.
WATSON No, not Mr, Doctor.
DOCTOR Oh, *Doctor* Doctor.
WATSON No, Doctor *Watson*.
DOCTOR Oh, Doctor *Watson* Doctor.
WATSON Oh, just call me darling.
DOCTOR Hello, Mr Darling.
WATSON No, Doctor.
DOCTOR Hello Doctor Darling.

Sound of whistle; instant cut to: Caption: 'THAT SKETCH HAS BEEN ABANDONED' Animation sketch leads us into a cocktail party in Dulwich.

Robin Day was a flamboyant TV interviewer and political pundit known for is bow ties and large spectacles.

A bad-enough foul in soccer can lead to a "booking," in which the name of the player is written down (recently, also displaying a yellow card) as a warning to future conduct in the game.

The End

Raising Gangsters For Fun & Profit
Raising Gangsters For Fun & Profit

Quiet party-type music. Constant chatter.

HOST (GRAHAM) Ah, John. 27 Allow me to introduce my next-door neighbour.

JOHN STOKES, THIS IS A SNIVELLING LITTLE RAT-FACED GIT. AH!

GIT (TERRY J) Hello, I noticed a slight look of anxiety cross your face for a moment just then, but you needn't worry—I'm used to it. That's the trouble of having a surname like Git. 28

JOHN (MICHAEL) Oh...yes, yes.

GIT We did think once of having it changed by deed-poll, you know—to Watson or something like that. But A Snivelling Little Rat-Faced Watson's just as bad eh? 29

JOHN Yes, yes, I suppose so.

Mrs Git approaches.

GIT Oh, that's my wife. Darling! Come and meet Mr...what was it?

JOHN Stokes—John Stokes.

GIT Oh yes. John Stokes, this is my wife, Dreary Fat Boring Old.

JOHN Oh, er, how do you do.

MRS GIT (JOHN) How do *you* do.

Mrs Stokes appears.

MRS STOKES (CAROL) Darling, there you are!

JOHN Yes, yes, here I am, yes.

GIT Oh, is this your wife?

JOHN Yes, yes, yes, this is the wife. Yes. Um darling, these, these are the Gits.

MRS STOKES (*slightly shocked*) What?

JOHN The Gits.

GIT Oh, heaven's sakes we are being formal. Does it have to be surnames?

JOHN Oh, no, no. Not at all. No. Um, no, this...this...this is my wife Norah, er, Norah Jane, Norah Jane Stokes. This is Snivelling Little Rat-Faced Git. And this is his wife Dreary Fat Boring Old Git.

GIT I was just telling your husband what an awful bore it is having a surname like Git.

MRS STOKES (*understanding at last*) Oh! Oh well, it's not that bad.

GIT Oh, you've no idea how the kids get taunted. Why, only last week Dirty Lying Little Two-Faced came running home from school, sobbing his eyes out, and our youngest, Ghastly Spotty Horrible Vicious Little is just at the age when taunts like 'she's a git' really hurt. Yes.

27

Chapman badly stumbles before the introduction, but recovers.

28

"Git" is a standard British (and relatively tame) word for a person one doesn't like all too much.

29

A "deed poll" is the official, bureaucratic way to change a name in the U.K. It has nothing to do with polling, as in elections.

Mrs Git gobs colourfully into her handbag.

JOHN Do...do you live round here?

GIT Yes, we live up the road, number 49—you can't miss it. We've just had the outside painted with warm pus.

JOHN (*with increasing embarrassment*) Oh.

GIT Yes. It's very nice actually. It goes nicely with the vomit and catarrh we've got smeared all over the front door.

MRS STOKES I think we ought to be going. We have two children to collect.

GIT Oh, well, bring them round for tea tomorrow.

MRS STOKES Well...

GIT It's Ghastly Spotty Cross-Eyed's birthday and she's having a disembowelling party 30 for a few friends. The Nauseas will be there, and Doug and Janice Mucus, and the Rectums from Swanage.

VOICE OVER (MICHAEL) (*and caption*): 'And now a nice version of that same sketch'

Cut to exactly the same set-up as before.

HOST John! Allow me to introduce our next-door neighbour. John, this is Mr Watson.

WATSON Hello. I noticed a slight look of anxiety cross your face just then but you needn't worry.

Cut to nun.

NUN (CAROL) I preferred the dirty version.

She is knocked out by the boxer. Cut to Women's Institute applause film. Big close-up Hank Spim (face only). He is obviously walking along, the camera is following him hand held. 31

HANK (GRAHAM) Well, I've been a hunter all my life. I love animals. That's why I like to kill 'em. I wouldn't kill an animal I didn't like. Goodday Roy.

Pull back to reveal he is walking with his brother in fairly rough country location. They pull a small trailer with 'high explosives' written in large letters on the side. The trailer has bombs in it. Hank takes a bazooka from the trailer.

VOICE OVER (JOHN) Hank and Roy Spim are tough, fearless backwoodsmen who have chosen to live in a violent, unrelenting world of nature's creatures, where only the fittest survive. Today they are off to hunt mosquitoes.

Big close-up Roy Spim. He is obviously searching for something.

ROY (ERIC) (*voice over*) The mosquito's a clever little bastard. You can track him for days and days until you really get to know him like a friend. He knows you're there, and you know he's there. It's a game of wits. You hate him, then you respect him, then you kill him.

Cut to Hank Spim who stands peering toward the horizon. Suddenly he points.

VOICE OVER Suddenly Hank spots the mosquito they're after.

Dramatic music. Crash zoom along Hank's eyeline to as big a close-up as we can get of a patch in a perfectly ordinary field. Cut back to Hank and Roy starting to crawl towards some bushes.

Jones says, erroneously, a "spotting" party, instead of "disemboweling" party (which is bad enough), only to catch up with himself quickly.

In fact, we get most of Chapman quite clearly walking toward the camera.

He simply raises one finger.

33

A spoor is a mark or leaving that indicates the former presence of an animal.

VOICE OVER Now more than ever, they must rely on the skills they have learnt from a lifetime's hunting. (*tense music, as they worm their way forward*) Hank gauges the wind. (*shot of Hank doing complicated wind gauging biz.*) 32 Roy examines the mosquito's spoor. 33 (*shot of Roy examining the ground intently*) Then...(*Roy fires a bazooka. Hank fires off a machine gun; a series of almighty explosions in the small patch of field; the gunfire stops and the smoke begins to clear*) It's a success. The mosquito now is dead. (*Hank and Roy approach the scorched and blackened patch in the field*) But Roy must make sure. (*Roy points machine gun at head of mosquito and fires off another few rounds*)

ROY

THERE'S NOTHING MORE DANGEROUS THAN A WOUNDED MOSQUITO.

NARRATOR But the hunt is not over. With well practised skill Hank skins the mosquito. (*Hank produces an enormous curved knife and begins to start skinning the tiny mosquito*) The wings of a fully grown male mosquito can in fact fetch anything up to point eight of a penny on the open market. (*shot of them walking, carrying weapons*) The long day is over and it's back to base camp for a night's rest. (*inside villa; Hank is cleaning bazooka*) Here, surrounded by their trophies Roy and Hank prepare for a much tougher ordeal—a moth hunt.

HANK Well, I follow the moth in the helicopter to lure it away from the flowers, and then Roy comes along in the Lockheed Starfighter and attacks it with air-to-air missiles. 34

Lockheed F-104 Starfighter was a beloved aircraft of the United States Air Force. Used extensively in the Vietnam War, it was finally phased out in 1975.

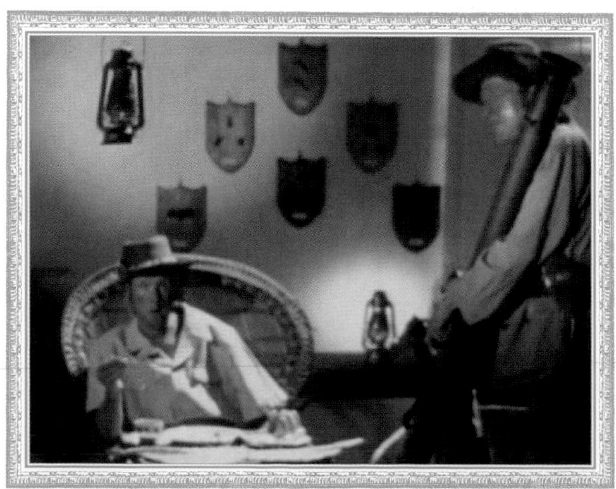

ROY A lot of people have asked us why we don't use fly spray. Well, where's the sport in that?

Shot of them driving in Land Rover heavily loaded with weapons.

NARRATOR (*voice over*) For Roy, sport is everything. Ever since he lost his left arm battling with an ant, Roy has risked his life in the pursuit of tiny creatures. (a peaceful river bank; Roy and Hank are fishing) But it's not all work and for relaxation they like nothing more than a day's fishing. (*Hank presses a button and there is a tremendous explosion in the water*) Wherever there is a challenge, Hank and Roy Spim will be there ready to carry on this primordial struggle between man and inoffensive, tiny insects.

Pull out to reveal the brothers standing on a tank. Heroic music reaches a climax. Apropos of nothing cut to oak-panelled robing chamber in the Old Bailey. Two Judges in full wigs and red robes enter.

FIRST JUDGE (ERIC) (*very camp*) Oh, I've had such a morning in the High Court. I could stamp my little feet the way those QC's carry on. 35

"QC" is the Queen's Counsel, a band of top lawyers, usually experts in certain types of law, selected to head up complex cases and government inquiries. It's thought of as a stepping-stone to becoming a judge, and an example of the old boys' network at its worst (the process by which one would be selected was, until recently, shrouded in mystery).

SECOND JUDGE (MICHAEL) (*just as camp*) Don't I know it, love.

FIRST JUDGE Objection here, objection there! And that nice policeman giving his evidence so well—beautiful speaking voice...well after a bit all I could do was bang my little gavel.

SECOND JUDGE You what, love?

FIRST JUDGE I banged me gavel. I did me 'silence in court' bit. Ooh! If looks could kill that prosecuting counsel would be in for thirty years. How did your summing up go?

SECOND JUDGE Well, I was quite pleased actually. I was trying to do my butch voice, you know, 'what the jury must understand', and they loved it, you know. I could see that foreman eyeing me.

FIRST JUDGE Really?

SECOND JUDGE Yes, cheeky devil.

FIRST JUDGE Was he that tall man with that very big...?

SECOND JUDGE No, just a minute—I must finish you know. Anyway, I finished up with 'the actions of these vicious men is a violent stain on the community and the full penalty of the law is scarcely sufficient to deal with their ghastly crimes', and I waggled my wig! Just ever so slightly, but it was a stunning effect.

FIRST JUDGE Oh, I bet it was... 36 like that super time I wore that striped robe in the Magistrates Court. 37

SECOND JUDGE Oh, aye.

36

Idle removes his robe to reveal a gold sequined dress.

The Magistrates Court is a lower court in the British system.

Fade out. Fade into a bench in a public park, garden or square. A pepperpot is sitting on the bench. Another pepperpot comes by pushing a shopping trolley.

FIRST PEPPERPOT (ERIC) Hello, Mrs Thing.
SECOND PEPPERPOT (GRAHAM) Hello, Mrs Entity.
FIRST PEPPERPOT How are you then?
SECOND PEPPERPOT Oh, I have had a morning.
FIRST PEPPERPOT Busy?
SECOND PEPPERPOT Busy—huh! I got up at five o'clock, I made myself a cup of tea, I looked out of the window. Well, by then I was so worn out I had to come and have a sit-down. I've been here for seven hours.
FIRST PEPPERPOT You must be exhausted.
SECOND PEPPERPOT Mm. Oh, have you been shopping?
FIRST PEPPERPOT No, I've been shopping.
SECOND PEPPERPOT Funny.
FIRST PEPPERPOT

I'M WORN OUT. I'VE BEEN SHOPPING FOR SIX HOURS.

SECOND PEPPERPOT What have you bought, then?
FIRST PEPPERPOT Nothing. Nothing at all. A complete waste of time.
SECOND PEPPERPOT Wicked, isn't it?
FIRST PEPPERPOT Wicked. It'll be worse when we join the Common Market.
SECOND PEPPERPOT That nice Mr Heath would never allow that.
FIRST PEPPERPOT It's funny he never married.
SECOND PEPPERPOT He's a bachelor. 38
FIRST PEPPERPOT Oooh! That would explain it. Oh dear me, this chatting away wears me out.
SECOND PEPPERPOT Yes. I bet Mrs Reginald Maudling doesn't have to put up with all this drudgery, getting up at five in the morning, making a cup of tea, looking out of the window, chatting away.
FIRST PEPPERPOT No! It'd all be done for her.
SECOND PEPPERPOT Yes, she'd have the whole day free for playing snooker.
FIRST PEPPERPOT She probably wouldn't go through all the drudgery of playing snooker, day in, day out.
SECOND PEPPERPOT No, it would all be done for her. She wouldn't even have to lift the cue.
FIRST PEPPERPOT She probably doesn't even know where the billiard room is.
SECOND PEPPERPOT No, still, it's not as bad as the old days. Mrs Stanley Baldwin used to have to get up at five o'clock in the morning and go out and catch partridges with her bare hands.
FIRST PEPPERPOT Yes...and Mrs William Pitt the Elder 39 used to have to get up at three o'clock and go burrowing for truffles with the bridge of her nose.
SECOND PEPPERPOT Mrs Beethoven used to have to get up at midnight to spur on the mynah bird.
FIRST PEPPERPOT Lazy creatures, mynah birds...
SECOND PEPPERPOT Yes. When Beethoven went deaf the mynah bird just used to mime.

The picture begins to wobble as in 'flashback'; appropriate dreamy music effect.

FIRST PEPPERPOT (*looking at camera*) Ooh! What's happening?
SECOND PEPPERPOT It's all right. It's only a flashback.

Cut to Beethoven's living room. A model mynah bird is opening and shutting its beak. Beethoven is sitting at the piano. 40

BEETHOVEN (JOHN) You don't fool me, you stupid mynah bird. I'm not deaf yet.
MYNAH Just you wait...ha, ha, ha, ha, ha! (*Beethoven pulls a revolver and shoots the bird which falls to the ground*) Oh! Bugger...

The big laugh here suggests that the audience is in on the joke—namely, references to the prime minister's oft-questioned sexuality ("bachelor" in Britain can be code for "gay").

William Pitt the Elder was the British prime minister from 1766 to 1768.

Cleese played Mozart in Episode 1.

BEETHOVEN Shut up!
MYNAH Right in the wing.
BEETHOVEN Shut your beak. Gott in Himmel... 41 I never get any peace here.

He plays the first few notes of the fifth symphony, trying vainly to get the last note. Mrs Beethoven enters.

MRS BEETHOVEN (GRAHAM) Ludwig!
BEETHOVEN What?
MRS BEETHOVEN Have you seen the sugar bowl?
BEETHOVEN

NO, I HAVEN'T SEEN THE BLOODY SUGAR BOWL.

MRS BEETHOVEN You know...the *sugar* bowl.
BEETHOVEN Sod the sugar bowl...I'm trying to finish this stinking tune! It's driving me spare... 42 so shut up! *(she leaves: he goes into opening bars of 'Washington Post March')* 43 No, no, no, no, no.

Mrs Beethoven comes back in.

MRS BEETHOVEN Ludwig, have you seen the jam spoon?
BEETHOVEN Stuff the jam spoon!
MRS BEETHOVEN It was in the sugar bowl.
BEETHOVEN Look, get out you old rat-bag. Buzz off and shut up.
MRS BEETHOVEN I don't know what you see in that piano. (*she goes*)
BEETHOVEN Leave me alone!!...(*gets the first eight notes right at last*)...Ha! ha! ha! I've done it, I've done it!

Mrs Beethoven comes in again.

MRS BEETHOVEN Do you want peanut butter or sandwich spread for your tea?
BEETHOVEN What!!!!
MRS BEETHOVEN PEANUT BUTTER...
BEETHOVEN I've forgotten it. (*plays a few wrong notes*) I had it! I had it!
MRS BEETHOVEN Do you want peanut butter or sandwich spread?
BEETHOVEN I don't care!!
MRS BEETHOVEN Ooooh! I don't know. (*she goes out*)

German for "God in heaven!"

"Driving me spare" is British slang for "driving me nuts."

"The Washington Post March" is an 1889 march by American composer John Philip Sousa.

The German "*Mein lieber Gott*" is translated as "Oh my god."

45

Not to be too literal, but Felix Mendelssohn was only 18 when Beethoven died.

BEETHOVEN I *had* it. I *had* it you old bag. (*at the same moment as he gets it right again, the door flies open and Mrs Beethoven charges in with a very loud hoover*) Mein lieber Gatt!! That! 44 What are you doing? (*a terrible clanking and banging comes from the wall*) What's that! What's...
MRS BEETHOVEN (*still hoovering loudly*) It's the plumber!

A jarring ring of the doorbell adds to the din.

BEETHOVEN Gott in Himmel, I'm going out.
MRS BEETHOVEN Well, if you're going out don't forget we've got the Mendelssohns coming for tea so don't forget to order some pikelets. 45
BEETHOVEN Pikelets, pikelets. Shakespeare never had this trouble.

Shakespeare washing up at a sink (present day).

SHAKESPEARE (ERIC) You wanna bet? Incidentally, it's da-da-da-dum, da-da-da-dum.

Cut back to Beethoven.

BEETHOVEN You're right! Oh, incidentally, why not call him Hamlet?

Cut back to Shakespeare.

SHAKESPEARE Hamlet! I like, *much* better than David. (*he shouts through open window next to sink*)

MICHELANGELO! YOU CAN USE DAVID. I WON'T SUE.

Cut to Michelangelo's studio. Michelangelo is in middle of feeding and looking after at least six screaming little babies. His statue of David is in the foreground.

MICHELANGELO (TERRY J) Thanks, but I've had a better idea.

Camera pans down to show engraved on plinth beneath statue the words 'Michelangelo's fifth symphony'.

WIFE (*off-screen*) Michelangelo!
MICHELANGELO Yes, dear!
WIFE I've had another son.
MICHELANGELO Oh, my life.

Cut to Mozart. He is scrubbing the floor. Caption: 'W. A. MOZART'

MOZART (MICHAEL) (*Jewish accent*) Composer? Huh! I wouldn't wish it on my son. He's a sensitive boy, already. I'd rather he was a sewage attendant or a ratcatcher. 46

In fact, much of the preceding lines were performed in bad "Jewish" accents.

Cut to street with old-fashioned shops. Exterior. Camera tracks in to a shopfront with a large sign outside: 'Rodent Exterminating Boutique `Colin "Chopper" Mozart (Son Of Composer) Rat-catcher To The Nobility And Ordinary People, Too--Ici On Parle Portugaise'. At the door of shop stands Colin Mozart. A kid runs up to him bearing a long cleft stick. Mozart takes the note from the cleavage and reads it.

COLIN MOZART (MICHAEL) Aha! Rats at 42a Kartoffelnstrasse. Hey Mitzi! I gotta go to Potato Street.

MITZI (*off-screen*) Put your galoshes on.

Mozart leaps on to a bike carrying two shrimp-nets, and rides off. Superimposed caption: 'MUNICH 1821'

COLIN MOZART (*shouting*) Depressed by rats? Do mice get you down? Then why not visit Colin Mozart's Rodent Extermination Boutique. Rats extirpated, mice punished, voles torn apart by Colin Mozart, Munich's leading furry animal liquidator.

Colin Mozart cycles up to Beethoven's house. Outside is a noticeboard saying:

MR AND MRS EMMANUEL KANT 47
FRAU MITZI HANDGEPÄCKAUFBEWAHRUNG
MR DICKIE WAGNER 48
K. TYNAN (NO RELATION) 49
MR AND MRS J. W. VON GOETHE AND DOG 50
HERR E. W. SWANTON 51
MR AND MRS P. ANKA 52
MR AND MRS LUDWIG VAN BEETHPVEN (1770-1827) ACCEPT NO SUBSTITUTE
Caption: '13.4 SECONDS LATER' Beethoven's front door is opened by Mrs Beethoven.

Eighteenth-century German philosopher, and his wife.

Richard Wagner, nineteenth-century German composer.

English theater critic of the mid-twentieth century.

German polymath—perhaps Germany's greatest writer, at the very least.

Another reference to the cricket commentator.

Paul Anka, American songwriter and singer.

MRS BEETHOVEN Yes?

COLIN MOZART Colin Mozart.

MRS BEETHOVEN Oh, thank goodness you've come. We're having a terrible time with them bleeding rats. I think they live in his stupid piano already.

They go into the house. We hear the first two bars of Beethoven's Fifth counterpointed by loud squeaking.

BEETHOVEN'S VOICE Get out the bloody piano you stupid furry bucktoothed gits! Get out! Gott in Himmel. Get your stinking tail out of my face.

Mrs Beethoven opens the door and we see for the first time a strange sight. Rats are flying across the room (thrown from out of vision) others scuttle across floor (pulled by strings) others up wall. One sits on Beethoven's head. The squeaking is deafening. Beethoven plays on relentlessly. Mozart and Mrs Beethoven run into room and start trying to catch the rats with the shrimp-nets. Caption: '13.4 MINUTES LATER' Colin Mozart is sitting on the piano. He rakes the rat-infested room with machine-gun fire.

53

Jimmy Durante, the American singer, actor, pianist, comedian—you name it. "I'm the Guy Who Found the Lost Chord," a 1947 Durante song, is well-known in the U.K.

BEETHOVEN Shut up!

The picture starts to wobble and mixes back to the two pepperpots.

SECOND PEPPERPOT So anyway, Beethoven was rather glad when he went deaf.

Mix to Beethoven pushing the keys of the keyboard which is all that remains of his piano. He listens vainly. The mynah bird opens and shuts its beak. In the corner an old horn gramophone plays. We hear Jimmy Durante singing the end of 'I'm the guy that found the lost chord'.  53 *Cut back to judges' robing room.*

FIRST JUDGE Well, I was ever so glad they abolished hanging, you know, because that black cap just didn't suit me.

SECOND JUDGE Yes. Do you remember the Glasgow treason trial?

FIRST JUDGE

OH YES, I WORE A BODY STOCKING ALL THROUGH IT.

SECOND JUDGE No, hen, with the party afterwards.
FIRST JUDGE Oh, that's right. You were walking out with that very butch Clerk of the Court.
SECOND JUDGE That's right. Ooh, he made me want to turn Queen's evidence.

Superimposed credits. THEME TUNE HEARD QUIETLY AS JUDGES CONTINUE.

FIRST JUDGE Oh, me too. One summing up and I'm anybody's.
SECOND JUDGE Anyway, Bailie Anderson.
FIRST JUDGE Ooh, her?
SECOND JUDGE Yes. She's so strict. She was on at me for giving dolly sentences, 54 you know, specially in that arson case.
FIRST JUDGE What was the verdict?
SECOND JUDGE They preferred the brown wig.
FIRST JUDGE Mm. I love the Scottish Assizes. 55 I know what they mean by a really well-hung jury.
SECOND JUDGE Ooh! Get back in the witness box, you're too sharp to live!
FIRST JUDGE I'll smack your little botty!
SECOND JUDGE Ooh! and again.
FIRST JUDGE Have you tried that new body rub JP's use? 56
SECOND JUDGE I had a magistrate in Bradford yesterday.
FIRST JUDGE Funnily enough I felt like one in a lunchtime recess today. (*credits end*) But the ones I really like are those voice over announcers on the BBC after the programmes are over.
SECOND JUDGE Oh, aye, of course, they're as bent as safety pins.
FIRST JUDGE I know, but they've got beautiful speaking voices, haven't they? 'And now a choice of viewing on BBC Television.'
SECOND JUDGE 'Here are tonight's football results.'
FIRST AND SECOND JUDGES Mmm.

Fade out.

"Dolly" is slang for easy.

"Scottish assizes" were periodic criminal courts replaced for good in 1972 by the Crown Court system.

"JPs"—or justices of the peace—are also known as magistrates. They are local figures selected to hand out summary justice in Magistrates' Courts, though often they have no legal training.

SEA
SON
2
EPISODE 22

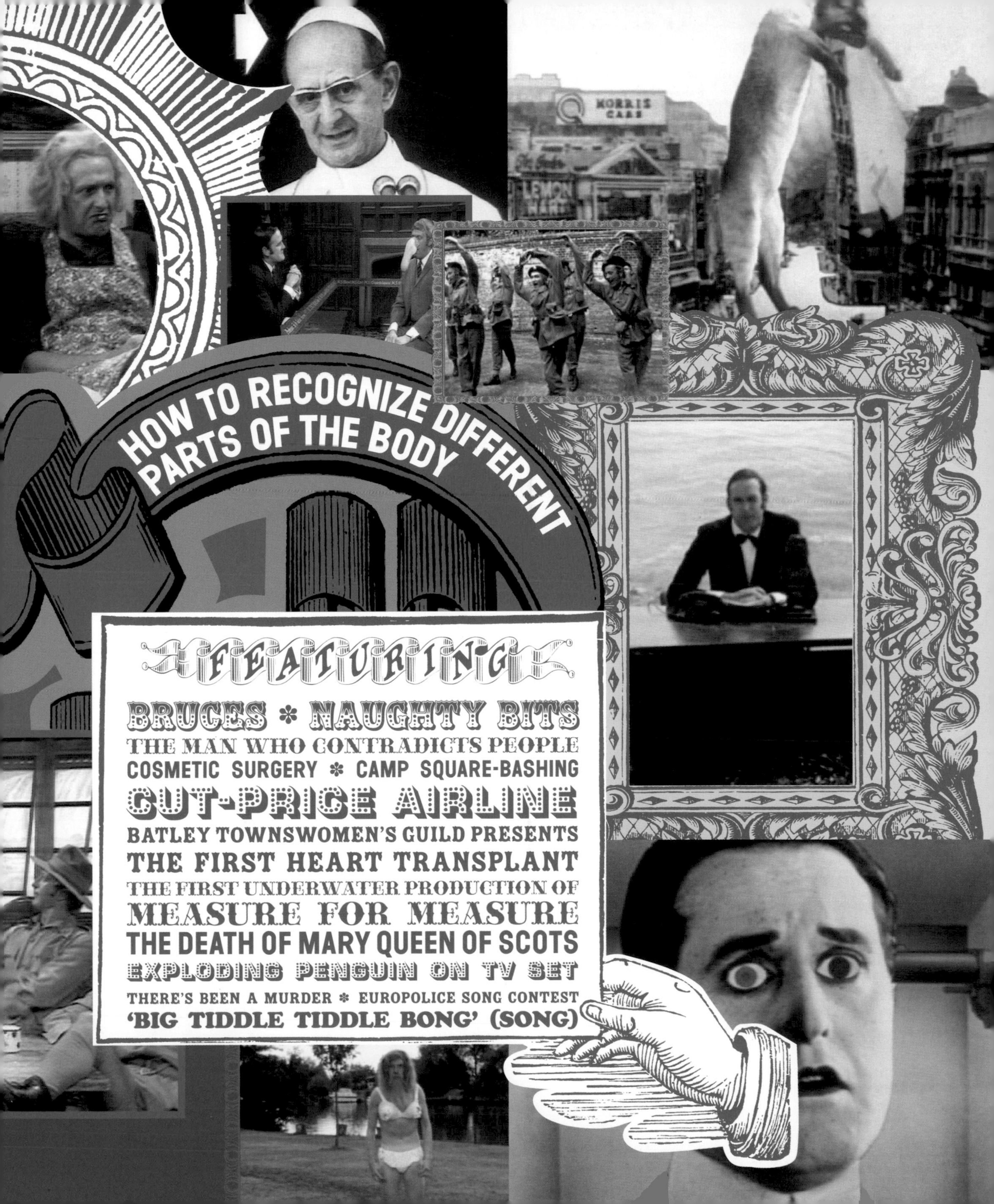
MORRIS CARS
LEMON HART
HOW TO RECOGNIZE DIFFERENT PARTS OF THE BODY
FEATURING
BRUCES * NAUGHTY BITS
THE MAN WHO CONTRADICTS PEOPLE
COSMETIC SURGERY * CAMP SQUARE-BASHING
CUT-PRICE AIRLINE
BATLEY TOWNSWOMEN'S GUILD PRESENTS
THE FIRST HEART TRANSPLANT
THE FIRST UNDERWATER PRODUCTION OF
MEASURE FOR MEASURE
THE DEATH OF MARY QUEEN OF SCOTS
EXPLODING PENGUIN ON TV SET
THERE'S BEEN A MURDER * EUROPOLICE SONG CONTEST
'BIG TIDDLE TIDDLE BONG' (SONG)

FIRST AIRED: NOVEMBER 24, 1970

The camera tracks past five gorgeous lovelies in bikinis, all in send-up provocative pin-up poses. The sixth in the pan is the announcer at his desk also posing in a bikini (with bikini top).

JOHN

AND NOW FOR SOMETHING COMPLETELY DIFFERENT.

Cut to 'It's' man, also in bikini.

IT'S MAN (MICHAEL)

IT'S...

Cut to credit titles as normal,

except that the last shot is the little chicken man who drags across a banner reading 'How to recognize different parts of the body'.

VOICE OVER (JOHN)

HOW TO RECOGNIZE DIFFERENT PARTS OF THE BODY.

Hold long enough to read this new title before the foot comes down, stays in shot long enough for voice over to say:

VOICE OVER Number one. The foot.

A little arrow points to the foot simultaneously. Cut to picture of Venus de Milo (top half). Superimposed little white arrow pointing to shoulder.

VOICE OVER Number two. The shoulder.

Cut to picture of a foot cut off at the ankle. Cigarettes are parked in the top. Superimposed arrow.

VOICE OVER And number three. The other foot.

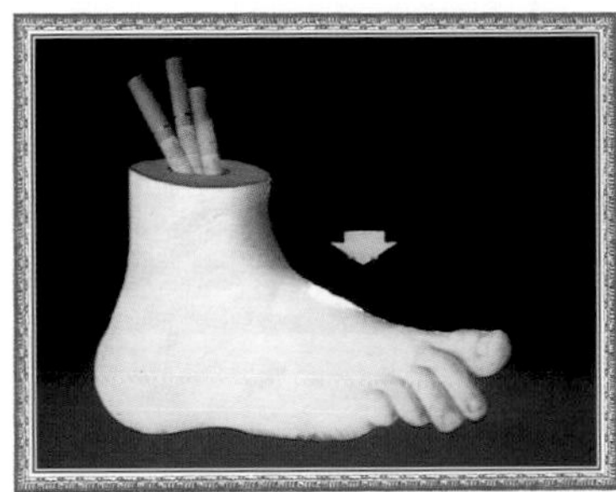

Cut to profile picture of strange person (provided by Terry Gilliam). Superimposed arrow pointing to bridge of nose.

VOICE OVER Number four. The bridge of the nose.

Cut to picture, full length, of man wearing polka-dotted Bermuda shorts. Arrow superimposed points to shorts.

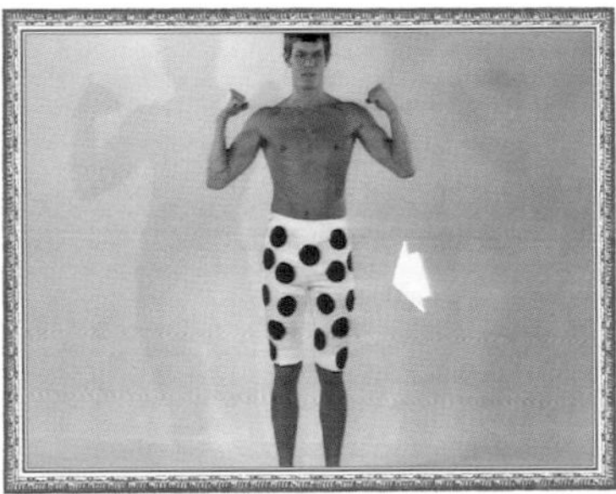

VOICE OVER Number five. The naughty bits.

Cut to picture of crooked elbow. Superimposed arrow pointing just above the elbow.

VOICE OVER Number six. Just above the elbow.

Cut to closer picture of different person in identical Bermuda shorts. Superimposed arrow pointing to top of groin.

VOICE OVER Number seven. Two inches to the right of a very naughty bit indeed.

Cut to close-up of a real knee. Arrow superimposed pointing to knee.

VOICE OVER Number eight. The kneecap.

***Pull back to reveal the knee belongs to First Bruce, an Australian in full Australian outback gear. We briefly hear a record of 'Waltzing Matilda'.* [1] *He is sitting in a very hot, slightly dusty room with low wicker chairs, a table in the middle, big centre fan, and old fridge.* [2]**

"Waltzing Matilda" is the signal song of the Australian people, the lyrics of which were written in 1895 by a man with the wonderful name of Banjo Paterson. A "matilda" is a bag in which an itinerant worker—the "swagman" of the song—carried his personal effects.

This one's a rarity: written by the "team" of Cleese and Idle.

"Bruce" is slang for an archetypal Australian male, as opposed to a "Sheila."

SECOND BRUCE (GRAHAM) Goodday, Bruce. 3
FIRST BRUCE (ERIC) Oh, hello, Bruce.
THIRD BRUCE (MICHAEL) How are yer?

FIRST BRUCE Bit crook, Bruce.
SECOND BRUCE Where's Bruce?
FIRST BRUCE He's not here, Bruce.
THIRD BRUCE Blimey s'hot in here, Bruce.
FIRST BRUCE S'hot enough to boil a monkey's bum.
SECOND BRUCE That's a strange expression, Bruce.
FIRST BRUCE Well Bruce, I heard the prime minister use it. S'hot enough to boil a monkey's bum in 'ere your Majesty, he said, and she smiled quietly to herself.
THIRD BRUCE She's a good Sheila, Bruce and not at all stuck up.
SECOND BRUCE Ah, here comes the Bossfella now—how are you, Bruce?

Enter Fourth Bruce with the English person, Michael.

"Pommie" is Australian slang for Britain; the "poms" are Brits.

FOURTH BRUCE (JOHN)

GOODDAY BRUCE, HELLO BRUCE, HOW ARE YOU, BRUCE?

Gentlemen, I'd like to introduce a chap from pommie land... 4 who'll be joining us this year here in the Philosophy Department of the University of Woolamaloo. 5
ALL Goodday.
FOURTH BRUCE Michael Baldwin—this is Bruce. Michael Baldwin—this is Bruce. Michael Baldwin—this is Bruce.
FIRST BRUCE Is your name not Bruce, then?
MICHAEL (TERRY J) No, it's Michael.
SECOND BRUCE That's going to cause a little confusion.
THIRD BRUCE Yeah. Mind if we call you Bruce, just to keep it clear?
FOURTH BRUCE Well, gentlemen I think we'd better start the meeting. Before we start though, I'll

Woolloomooloo is an eastern suburb of Sydney, Australia.

ask the padre for a prayer.

First Bruce snaps a plastic dog-collar round his neck. They all lower their heads.

FIRST BRUCE O Lord we beseech thee, have mercy on our faculty, Amen.

ALL Amen.

FOURTH BRUCE Crack the tubes, right. (*Third Bruce starts opening beer cans*) Er, Bruce, I now call upon you to welcome Mr Baldwin to the Philosophy Department.

SECOND BRUCE I'd like to welcome the pommy bastard to God's own earth and I'd like to remind him that we don't like stuck-up sticky-beaks here. 6

ALL Hear, hear. Well spoken, Bruce.

FOURTH BRUCE Now, Bruce teaches classical philosophy, Bruce teaches Hegelian philosophy, and Bruce here teaches logical positivism and is also in charge of the sheepdip. 7

THIRD BRUCE What does new Bruce teach?

FOURTH BRUCE New Bruce will be teaching political science—Machiavelli, Bentham, Locke, Hobbes, 8 Sutcliffe, Bradman, Lindwall, Miller, Hassett, 9 and Benaud. 10

SECOND BRUCE These are cricketers, Bruce.

FOURTH BRUCE Oh, spit.

THIRD BRUCE Howls of derisive laughter, Bruce.

FOURTH BRUCE In addition, as he's going to be teaching politics I've told him he's welcome to teach any of the great socialist thinkers, provided he makes it clear that they were *wrong*.

They all stand up.

ALL Australia, Australia, Australia, Australia, we love you. Amen.

They sit down.

FOURTH BRUCE Any questions?

SECOND BRUCE New Bruce—are you a pooftah? 11

FOURTH BRUCE Are you a pooftah?

MICHAEL No.

FOURTH BRUCE No right, well gentlemen, I'll just remind you of the faculty rules. Rule one—no pooftahs. Rule two—no member of the faculty is to maltreat the Abbos 12 in any way whatsoever, if there's anyone watching. Rule three—no pooftahs. Rule four—I don't want to catch anyone not drinking in their room after lights out. Rule five—no pooftahs. Rule six—there is *no* rule six. Rule seven—no pooftahs. That concludes the reading of the rules, Bruce.

A "sticky beak" is Australian slang for a busybody.

The British prejudice is to consider Australia to be peopled by former convicts, and sheep.

Machiavelli, Bentham, Locke, Hobbes—philosophers and political thinkers all.

Sutcliffe, Bradman, Lindwall, Miller, Hassett—Australian cricketers all.

Richie Benaud, former Australian cricketer, was a longstanding Australian cricket commentator in the U.K. and around the cricketing world.

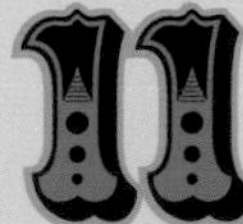

A "pooftah" is British slang for a homosexual male.

"Abbos" is Australian slang for the Aboriginal people.

13

The Golden Wattle is the plant emblem of Australia. Idle holds up something that looks very much like such a plant.

FIRST BRUCE This here's the wattle 13—the emblem of our land. You can stick it in a bottle or you can hold it in yer hand.

ALL Amen.

FOURTH BRUCE Gentlemen, at six o'clock I want every man-Bruce of you in the Sydney Harbour Bridge room to take a glass of sherry with the flying philosopher, Bruce, and I call upon you, padre, to close the meeting with a prayer.

FIRST BRUCE Oh Lord, we beseech thee etc. etc. etc., Amen.

ALL Amen.

FIRST BRUCE Right, let's get some Sheilas.

An Aborigine servant bursts in with an enormous tray full of enormous steaks.

FOURTH BRUCE OK.

SECOND BRUCE Ah, elevenses.

THIRD BRUCE This should tide us over 'til lunchtime.

SECOND BRUCE Reckon so, Bruce.

FIRST BRUCE Sydney Nolan! What's that! (*points*)

Cut to dramatic close-up of Fourth Bruce's ear. Hold close-up. The superimposed arrow pointing to the ear.

VOICE OVER (JOHN) Number nine. The ear.

Cut to picture of big toe. Superimposed arrow.

VOICE OVER Number ten. The big toe.

Cut to picture of another man in Bermuda shorts. Superimposed arrow pointing at shorts.

VOICE OVER Number eleven. More naughty bits.

Cut to full length shot of lady in Bermuda shorts and Bermuda bra. Superimposed arrow on each side of her body. One points to the bra, one to the Bermuda shorts.

VOICE OVER

NUMBER TWELVE. THE NAUGHTY BITS OF A LADY.

Cut to picture of a horse wearing Bermuda shorts. Superimposed arrow.

VOICE OVER Number thirteen. The naughty bits of a horse.

Cut to picture of an ant. In the very corner of a blank area. It is very tiny. Superimposed enormous arrow.

VOICE OVER

NUMBER FOURTEEN. THE NAUGHTY BITS OF AN ANT.

Cut to picture of Reginald Maudling with Bermuda shorts, put on by Terry Gilliam, over his dark suit. Superimposed arrow pointing to shorts.

VOICE OVER Number fifteen. The naughty bits of Reginald Maudling.

Cut to close-up of false hand sticking out of a sleeve. Superimposed arrow.

VOICE OVER Number sixteen. The hand.

Pull back to reveal that the hand appears to belong to a standard interviewer in two shot. Chair set up with standard interviewee. The interviewer suddenly pulls the hand off, revealing that he has a hook. He throws the hand away and starts the interview.

INTERVIEWER (MICHAEL) Good evening. I have with me in the studio tonight Mr Norman St John Polevaulter, who for the past few years has been contradicting people...Mr Polevaulter, why do you contradict people?
POLEVAULTER (TERRY J) I don't.
INTERVIEWER You told me that you did.
POLEVAULTER I most certainly did not.
INTERVIEWER Oh, I see. I'll start again.
POLEVAULTER No you won't.
INTERVIEWER Shh. Mr Polevaulter I understand you don't contradict people.
POLEVAULTER Yes I do.
INTERVIEWER When *didn't* you start contradicting people?
POLEVAULTER Well I did, in 1952.
INTERVIEWER 1952?
POLEVAULTER 1947.
INTERVIEWER Twenty-three years ago.
POLEVAULTER No.

Cut to announcer at desk in a farmyard. He is fondly holding a small pig.

ANNOUNCER (JOHN) And so on and so on and so on. And now...

Cut to picture of the Pope. Slight pause, so we think it might be something to do with the Pope. An arrow suddenly comes in above him pointing down at his head.

VOICE OVER Number seventeen. The top of the head.

Cut to picture of an indeterminate bit of flesh with a feather sticking out. Superimposed arrow pointing to feather.

VOICE OVER Number eighteen...the feather, rare.

Cut to profile of Raymond Luxury Yacht from next sketch who has an enormous false polystyrene nose. Superimposed arrow pointing at nose.

VOICE OVER Number nineteen. The nose.

A man sitting behind a desk in a Harley Street consulting room. **14**

Harley Street was the center of then private, high-end medical care in the U.K. (as opposed to the National Health Service). If you went to a "Harley Street doctor," you were considered to be going after the best possible (and often most expensive) care available.

Close-up of the name plate on desk in front of him. Although the camera does not reveal this for a moment, this name plate, about two inches high, continues all along the desk, off the side of it at the same height and halfway round the room. We start to track along this name plate on which is written: 'Professor Sir Adrian Furrows F.R.S., F.R.C.S., F.R.C.P., M.D.M.S. (Oxon), MA., Ph.D., M.Sc. (Cantab), Ph.D. (Syd), F.R.G.S., F.R.C.O.G., F.F.A.R.C.S., M.S. (Birm), M.S. (Liv), M.S. (Guadalahara), M.S. (Karach), M.S. (Edin), B.A. (Chic), B.Litt. (Phil), D.Litt (Phil), D.Litt (Arthur and Lucy), D.Litt (Ottawa), D.Litt (All other places in Canada except Medicine Hat), B.Sc.9 Brussels, Liège, Antwerp, Asse, (and Cromer)'. There is a knock on the door.

SPECIALIST (JOHN) Come in.

The door opens and Raymond Luxury Yacht enters. He cannot walk straight to the desk as his passage is barred by the strip of wood carrying the degrees, but he discovers the special hinged part of it that opens like a door. Mr Luxury Yacht has his enormous polystyrene nose. It is a foot long.

SPECIALIST Ah! Mr Luxury Yacht. Do sit down, please.
MR LUXURY YACHT (GRAHAM) Ah, no, no. My name is *spelt* 'Luxury Yacht' but it's pronounced Throatwobbler Mangrove.
SPECIALIST Well, do sit down then Mr Throatwobbler Mangrove.
MR LUXURY YACHT Thank you.

SPECIALIST Now, what seems to be the trouble?
MR LUXURY YACHT Um, I'd like you to perform some plastic surgery on me.
SPECIALIST I see. And which particular feature of your anatomy is causing you distress?
MR LUXURY YACHT Well, well for a long time now, in fact, even when I was a child...I...you know, whenever I left home to...catch a bus, or...to catch a train...and even my tennis has suffered actually...

SPECIALIST

YES. TO BE ABSOLUTELY BLUNT YOU'RE WORRIED ABOUT YOUR ENORMOUS HOOTER.

MR LUXURY YACHT No!
SPECIALIST No?
MR LUXURY YACHT Yes.
SPECIALIST Yes, and you want me to hack a bit off.
MR LUXURY YACHT Please.
SPECIALIST Fine. It is a startler, isn't it. Er, do you mind if I...er.
MR LUXURY YACHT What?
SPECIALIST Oh, no nothing, then, well, I'll just examine your nose. (*he does so; as he examines it the nose comes off in his hand*) Mr Luxury Yacht, this nose of yours is false. It's made of polystyrene and your own hooter's a beaut. No pruning necessary.
MR LUXURY YACHT I'd still like the operation.
SPECIALIST Well, you've had the operation, you strange person.
MR LUXURY YACHT Please do an operation.
SPECIALIST Well, all right, all right, but only...if you'll come on a camping holiday with me.
MR LUXURY YACHT He asked me! He asked me!

Cut to lyrical film of Luxury Yacht and specialist, frolicking in countryside in slow motion. **15**
Cut to interviewer (the one with the hook) at desk.

INTERVIEWER Next week we'll be showing you how to pick up an architect, how to pull a prime minister, and how to have fun with a wholesale poulterer. But now the men of the Derbyshire Light Infantry entertain us with a precision display of bad temper.
VOICE OVER Attention!

Eight soldiers in two ranks of four. They halt, and start to chant with precision.

SOLDIERS My goodness me, I am in a bad temper today all right, two, three, damn, damn, two, three, I am vexed and ratty. **16** (*shake fists*) Two, three, and hopping mad. (*stamp feet*)

Cut to interviewer.

INTERVIEWER And next the men of the Second Armoured Division regale us with their famous close order swanning about. **17**

Cut to sergeant with eight soldiers.

SERGEANT Squad. Camp it...up!
SOLDIERS (*mincing in unison*) Oooh get her! Whoops! I've got your number ducky. **18** You couldn't afford me, dear. Two three. I'd scratch your eyes out. Don't come the brigadier bit with us, dear, we all know where you've been, you military fairy. Whoops, don't look now girls the major's just minced in with that dolly colour sergeant, two, three, ooh-ho! **19**

Cut to interviewer.

INTERVIEWER And finally...

15

Chapman has reapplied his nose for the frolic.

16

"Ratty" is British slang for mildly annoyed.

17

"Swanning about" is British slang for moving aimlessly from one place to another—presumably from the uncoordinated and seemingly unfocused movement of a swan on a lake as it looks for food. It is often used to describe the stereotypical "camp" movements of gay men.

18

Gay men were said to call each other "ducky," though only straight people really ever thought that this was true.

19

"Minced in" means to walk in an overly effeminate way.

Animation: dancing generals, then the story of the killer cars.

Cut to air terminal. Pan along official air-terminal-type signs saying BEA, TWA, Air India, BOAC, the Verrifast Plane Company Ltd. **20** *Pan down to reveal a checking-in desk. A man with porter's cap comes in, carrying two bags. He is followed by Mr and Mrs Irrelevant. He puts their cases down, hangs around and gets a tip. He goes behind the counter, takes off his porter's hat, puts on an airline-pilot-type cap, and puts on a moustache.* **21**

There is a vicar standing next to him with an eye patch.

MAN (ERIC) Morning sir, can I help you?

MR IRRELEVANT (GRAHAM) Er, yes, we've booked on your flight for America.

MAN Oh, we don't fly to America (vicar nudges him) Oh, the American flight Er, on the plane oh yes, oh we do that, all right. Safe as houses, no need to panic.

MRS IRRELEVANT (CAROL) Is it really 37/6d? **22**

MAN Thirty bob. I'm robbing myself.

MR IRRELEVANT Thirty bob!

MAN Twenty-five. Two quid the pair of yer. Er, that's without insurance.

MR IRRELEVANT Well, how much is it *with* insurance?

MAN Hundred and two quid. That's including the flight.

MR IRRELEVANT Do we really need insurance? **23**

MAN No. (*vicar nudges him*) Yes, essential.

MR IRRELEVANT Well, we'll have it with insurance please.

MAN Right—do you want it with the body and one relative flown back, or you can have both bodies flown back and no relatives, or four relatives, no bodies, and the ashes sent by parcel post.

MR IRRELEVANT How long will it take?

MAN Er, let me put it this way—no idea.

VICAR (MICHAEL) Six hours.

MR IRRELEVANT Six?

MAN Five, ten for the pair of you.

MRS IRRELEVANT Oh, is it a jet?

MAN Well, no...It's not so much of a jet, it's more your, er, Triumph Herald engine with wings. **24**

MR IRRELEVANT When are you taking off?

VERRIFAST
PLAINE Co LTD

On the sign, "Plane" is misspelled as "Plaine."

There is actually no porter's hat anywhere in this sketch.

"37/6d" is 37 shillings and sixpence, or just under two pounds ("in old money," as older Britons would say).

The sketch here skips ahead to "How long will it take?"

Made throughout the 1960s, the Triumph Herald still makes certain British hearts race (this one included). A small sports car, it was styled in Italy and also came as a convertible, a wagon, a van, and in two- and four-door varieties.

MAN 3300 hours.
MR IRRELEVANT What?
MAN 2600 hours for the pair of you.
MRS IRRELEVANT What?
MAN Have the injections, you won't care.
MR IRRELEVANT What injections?
MAN Barley sugar injections. Calm you down. They're compulsory—Board of Trade. Promise. (*he holds up his crossed fingers*)
MRS IRRELEVANT Oh, I don't like the sound of injections.
MAN (*making a ringing sound*) Brrp, brrp. (*picks up phone*) Hello, yes right. (*puts phone down*) You've got to make your mind up straight away if you're coming or not.
MR AND MRS IRRELEVANT Yes.
MAN Right, you can't change your mind. I'll ring the departure lounge. (*picks up phone*) Hello? Two more on their way, Mrs Turpin.

Cut to Mrs Turpin sitting in a suburban lounge. A big sign saying 'Intercontinental Arrivals', in airport writing, hangs from the ceiling. Mr and Mrs Irrelevant arrive and sit down.

MRS TURPIN (TERRY J) Now, the duty-free trolley is over there...there's some lovely drop scones and there's duty-free broccoli and there's fresh eccles cakes. You're allowed two hundred each on the plane. (*she picks up teacup and speaks into it*) The Verrifast Plane Company announce the departure of flight one to over the hills and far away. Will passengers for flight one, please assemble at gate one. Passengers are advised that there is still plenty of time to buy eccles cakes. 25

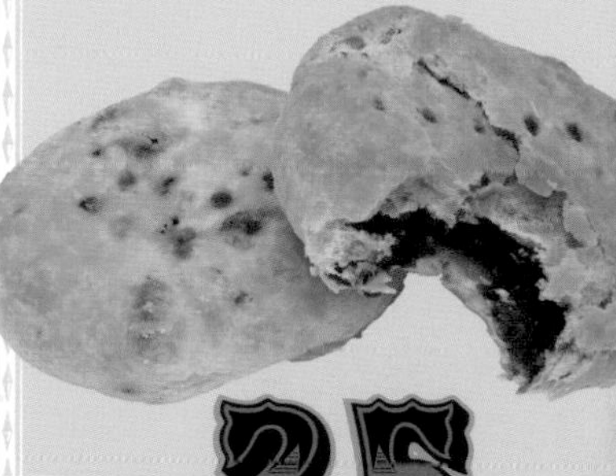

25
An Eccles cake is one filled with currants, first sold in the northern town of Eccles.

Man and vicar enter carrying a large wing.

MAN Nearly ready.

They take the wing through. Hammering is heard.

MRS TURPIN (*speaking into cup*) All passengers please get ready for their barley sugar injections.

Japanese pilot comes in.

KAMIKAZE Today we all take vow. Today we smash the enemy fleet...we smash, smash.

Man and vicar grab him and take him back.

MRS TURPIN

THAT'S MR KAMIKAZE, THE PILOT, HE'S VERY NICE REALLY, BUT MAKE SURE HE STAYS CLEAR OF BATTLESHIPS.

Cut to stock film of battleships, steaming on the seas. Stirring music plays over.

VOICE OVER (JOHN) There have been many stirring tales told of the sea and also some fairly uninteresting ones only marginally connected with it, like this one. Sorry, this isn't a very good announcement. Sorry.

Cut from sea to announcer by his desk at the seaside.

Another allusion to allegations that Ted Heath was gay.

Michael Stewart was the British foreign secretary from 1968 to 1970. One of his most notable acts was to supply arms to Nigeria to help fight a secessionist movement of the Igbo people. This Nigerian-Biafran War, as its come to be known, led to the deaths (from war and starvation) of at least a million people.

Willy Brandt was chancellor of West Germany from 1969 to 1974 and winner of the Nobel Peace Prize in 1971 for his efforts to improve relations with Communist neighbors, especially East Germany.

Louis Washkansky received the world's first heart transplant, at the hands of South African surgeon Christiaan Barnard in 1967. Washkansky died 18 days later from double pneumonia.

Shakespeare's *Measure for Measure*, first performed (on dry land) in 1604.

ANNOUNCER (JOHN) And here is the result of the 'Where to put Edward Heath's statue' Competition. **The winner was a Mr Ivy North who wins ten guineas and a visit to the Sailors Quarters.** **26**

Cut to quick clip of the Battle of Pearl Harbor from show eleven, first series. Beginning with Eric's blowing the whistle and the two sides rushing at each other. Cut back to announcer.

ANNOUNCER That was last year's re-enactment of the Battle of Pearl Harbor performed by the Batley Townswomen's Guild. It was written, directed and produced by Mrs Rita Fairbanks.

Cut to Rita Fairbanks on the beach.

RITA (ERIC) Hello again.
VOICE OVER (MICHAEL) And what are your ladies going to do for us this year?
RITA Well, this year we decided to re-enact something with a more modern flavour. We had considered a version of **Michael Stewart's speech on Nigeria** **27** and there were several votes on the Committee for a staging of **Herr Willi Brandt's visit to East Germany,** **28** but we've settled instead for a dramatization of the first heart transplant. Incidentally my sister Madge will be playing the plucky little springbok pioneer **Christian Barnard.** **29**
VOICE OVER Well off we go, then with the Batley Townswomen's Guild re-enactment of the first heart transplant.

Mrs Fairbanks blows her whistle. The two groups of ladies rush at each other. They end up in the sea, rolling about splashing, and thumping each other with handbags.

ANNOUNCER (*his desk now surrounded by sea*) The first heart transplant. But this is not the only open-air production here that has used the sea. Theatrical managers in this area have not been slow to appreciate the sea's tremendous dramatic value. And somewhere, out in this bay, is the **first underwater production of 'Measure for Measure'.** **30**

Expanse of sea water, nothing else at all. Dubbed over this is muffled, watery Shakespearian blank verse. We zoom in. Two Shakespearian actors (MICHAEL AND TERRY J) *leap up. They take a deep breath and go under again. The dialogue carries on muffled. Pull out to see a rowing boat. Three Shakespearian characters are sitting there waiting for their cue. One of the two characters leaps up and shouts:*

CHARACTER (TERRY J) Servant ho!

He then goes underwater again. The servant in the boat steps into the water and goes under. Cut to announcer, now up to his waist in sea.

ANNOUNCER The underwater version of 'Measure for Measure', and further out to sea 'Hello Dolly' is also doing good business.

We see a buoy, on the top of which is a stiff piece of card which reads ***'Hello Dolly, Tonight 7.30'.*** **31** *There is a muffled watery snatch of Hello Dolly. Swing round to a patch of open sea.*

ANNOUNCER ...and over there on the oyster beds **Formula 2 car racing.** **32** *(underwater noises of Formula 2 cars)*

Animation: a racing car moves over a naked lady, going past a sign saying 'Pit Stop'. Close up of armpits. Superimposed little white arrow.

VOICE OVER Number twenty. The armpits.

Cut to picture of a person. Superimposed white arrow on the neck.

VOICE OVER Number twenty-one. The bottom two-thirds of the nape of the neck.

Cut to radio.

VOICE OVER Number twenty-two. The nipple.

Arrow indicates the tuning dial. Pull back. Two women are listening to the set. The announcer continues from the radio set.

ANNOUNCER'S VOICE ...and that concludes the week's episode of 'How to Recognize Different Parts of the Body', adapted for radio by **Ann Haydon-Jones and her husband, Pip.** **33** And now, we present the first episode of a new radio drama series, 'The Death of Mary Queen of Scots'. Part one, the beginning.

Theme music: 'Coronation Scot' as used in 'Paul Temple' for years. **34**

MAN'S VOICE You are Mary Queen of Scots?
WOMAN'S VOICE I am.

There now follows a series of noises indicating that Mary is getting the shit knocked out of her. **35** *Thumps, bangs, slaps, pneumatic drilling, sawing, flogging, shooting, all interlarded with Mary's screams. The two women listen calmly. After a few seconds: fade as the signature tune 'Coronation Scot' is brought up loudly to denote ending of episode.*

RADIO ANNOUNCER **Episode two of 'The Death of Mary Queen of Scots' can be heard on Radio 4 almost immediately.** **36**

One of the women goes to the set and switches it over. As she goes back to her seat from the radio we hear the theme music again, fading out as sounds of violence and screaming start again and continue unabated in vigour.

MAN'S VOICE I think she's dead.

Hello, Dolly!—another reference to the show in which Pearl Bailey starred in 1967.

Formula Two car racing is one step down from Formula One. The cars are a bit smaller and slower, and the drivers younger and less experienced than their "major league" counterparts in Formula One.

One could lose track of how many references there are to this tennis player (Ann Haydon-Jones) and her husband (Pip).

The 1938 BBC radio drama *Send for Paul Temple* spawned the character Paul Temple, a staple of crime stories in Europe for the rest of the century.

To put it mildly.

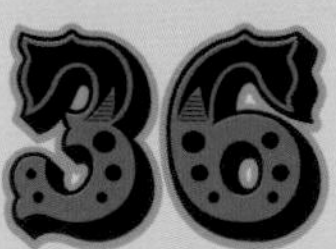

Radio 4 is the "serious" BBC radio station, whose programming is akin to that of NPR.

WOMAN'S VOICE No I'm not.

After a time, sounds of violence and screaming start again rapidly fading under the tune of 'Coronation Scot'.

ANNOUNCER'S VOICE That was episode two of 'The Death of Mary Queen of Scots', adapted for the radio by Bernard Hollowood 37 and Brian London. 38 And now, Radio 4 will explode. *(the radio explodes)*
FIRST PEPPERPOT (GRAHAM) We'll have to watch the telly then.
SECOND PEPPERPOT (JOHN) Yes.

The pepperpots swivel round to look at the TV set in the corner of the room.

FIRST PEPPERPOT Well, what's on the television then?
SECOND PEPPERPOT Looks like a penguin.

On the TV set there is indeed a penguin. It sits contentedly looking at them in a stuffed sort of way. There is nothing on the screen.

FIRST PEPPERPOT No, no, no, I didn't mean what's on the television set, I meant what programme?
SECOND PEPPERPOT Oh.

The second pepperpot goes to the TV, switches it on and returns to her chair. 39 *The set takes a long time to warm up and produce a picture. During this pause the following conversation takes place.*

SECOND PEPPERPOT It's funny that penguin being there innit? What's it doing there?
FIRST PEPPERPOT Standing.
SECOND PEPPERPOT I can see that.
FIRST PEPPERPOT If it lays an egg, it will fall down the back of the television set.
SECOND PEPPERPOT We'll have to watch that. Unless it's a male.
FIRST PEPPERPOT Ooh, I never thought of that.
SECOND PEPPERPOT Yes, looks fairly butch.
FIRST PEPPERPOT Perhaps it comes from next door.
SECOND PEPPERPOT Penguins don't come from next door, they come from the Antarctic.
FIRST PEPPERPOT Burma.
SECOND PEPPERPOT Why did you say Burma?
FIRST PEPPERPOT I panicked.
SECOND PEPPERPOT Oh. Perhaps it's from the zoo.
FIRST PEPPERPOT Which zoo?
SECOND PEPPERPOT How should I know which zoo? I'm not Dr Bloody Bronowski. 40
FIRST PEPPERPOT How does Dr Bronowski know which zoo it came from?
SECOND PEPPERPOT He knows everything.
FIRST PEPPERPOT Oh, I wouldn't like that, it would take the mystery out of life. Anyway, if it came from the zoo it would have 'property of the zoo' stamped on it.
SECOND PEPPERPOT No, it wouldn't. They don't stamp animals 'property of the zoo'. You couldn't stamp a huge lion.
FIRST PEPPERPOT They stamp them when they're small.
SECOND PEPPERPOT What happens when they moult?
FIRST PEPPERPOT Lions don't moult.
SECOND PEPPERPOT No, but penguins do. There, I've run rings round you logically.
FIRST PEPPERPOT Oh, intercourse the penguin. 41

On the TV screen there now appears an announcer.

Bernard Hollowood was the English editor of the satirical magazine *Punch* from 1957 to 1968.

Brian London, the heavyweight boxer, beloved by the Pythons.

Chapman quietly sings "Jeanie with the Light Brown Hair" here.

Jacob Bronowski was a public intellectual from Poland who made a home and career in Britain as a mathematician, biologist, writer, and inventor.

Cleese very nearly cracks up laughing here; Chapman, too, has been trying not to laugh all this while. Chapman was chagrined—actually, he was devilishly delighted—that he and Cleese corpsed so much during the filming of this brief sketch. The brief window of opportunity to actually film at the BBC made any re-shoots a real problem.

TV ANNOUNCER (TERRY J)

IT'S JUST GONE 8 O'CLOCK AND TIME FOR THE PENGUIN ON TOP OF YOUR TELEVISION SET TO EXPLODE.

The penguin on top of the set now explodes.

FIRST PEPPERPOT How did he know that was going to happen?
TV ANNOUNCER It was an inspired guess. And now...

Cut to picture of a shin. Superimposed arrow.

VOICE OVER (JOHN) Number twenty-three. The shin.

Cut to Reginald Maudling. Superimposed arrow.

VOICE OVER Number twenty-four. Reginald Maudling's shin.

Cut to Gilliam-type open-head picture, with arrow superimposed.

VOICE OVER Number twenty-five. The brain.

Cut to picture of Margaret Thatcher. Arrow points to her knee.

VOICE OVER Number twenty-six. Margaret Thatcher's brain. 42

Cut to a fairly wide still picture of cricket match in progress. Batsman, bowler, ring of fielders all have on polka-dotted Bermuda shorts. Little arrows point to each pair of Bermuda shorts.

VOICE OVER Number twenty-seven. More naughty bits.

Cut to picture of the cabinet at a table. Arrows point down below the table to their naughty bits.

VOICE OVER Number twenty-eight. The naughty bits of the cabinet.

Cut to studio shot of the next set. Interior of country house. Superimposed arrow.

VOICE OVER Number twenty-nine. The interior of a country house.

Cut to room, with doctor, mother, and son.

DOCTOR (JOHN) That's not a part of the body.
MOTHER (CAROL) No, it's a link though.

This line elicits a huge laugh and a smattering of applause. Margaret Thatcher is already a divisive figure, a full decade before she becomes prime minister.

There were, in fact, four more episodes left in the series.

SON (GRAHAM) I didn't think it was very good.
DOCTOR No, it's the end of the series, they must be running out of ideas. [43]

Inspector Muffin the Mule bursts through the door.

MUFFIN (MICHAEL) All right, don't anybody move, there's been a murder.
MOTHER A murder?
MUFFIN No...no...not a murder...no what's like a murder only begins with B?
SON Birmingham.
MUFFIN No...no...no...no...no...
DOCTOR Burnley?
MUFFIN Burnley—that's right! Burnley in Lancashire. There's been a Burnley.
SON Burglary.
MUFFIN Burglary. Yes, good man. Burglary—that's it, of course. There's been a burglary.
DOCTOR Where?
MUFFIN In the back, just below the rib.
DOCTOR No—that's murder.
MUFFIN Oh...er no...in the band...In the bat...Barclays bat.
SON Barclays Bank?
MUFFIN Yes. Nasty business—got away with £23,000.
SON Any clues?
MUFFIN Any what?
SON Any evidence as to who did it?
MUFFIN (*sarcastically*) Any clues, eh? Oh, we don't half talk posh, don't we? I suppose you say 'ehnvelope' and 'larngerie' and 'sarndwiches on the settee'! Well this is a murder investigation, young man, and murder is a very serious business.
DOCTOR I thought you said it was a burglary.
MUFFIN Burglary is almost as serious a business as murder. Some burglaries are *more* serious than murder. A burglary in which someone gets stabbed *is* murder! So don't come these petty distinctions with me. You're as bad as a judge. Right, now! The first thing to do in the event of a breach of the peace of any kind, is to...go...(*pause*) and...oh, sorry, sorry, I was miles away.
DOCTOR Ring the police?
MUFFIN Ring the police. Yes, that's a good idea. Get them over here fast...no, on second thoughts, get them over here slowly, so they don't drop anything.
MOTHER Shall I make us all a cup of tea?
MUFFIN Make what you like, Boskovitch—it won't help you in court.
MOTHER I *beg* your pardon?
MUFFIN I'm sorry, sorry. That's the trouble with being on two cases at once. I keep thinking I've got Boskovitch cornered and in fact I'm investigating a Burnley.
SON Burglary.
MUFFIN Burglary! Yes—good man.

Sound of police siren and sound of cars drawing up outside.

DOCTOR Who's Boskovitch?
MUFFIN Hah! Boskovitch is a Russian scientist who is passing information to the Russians.
SON Classified information?
MUFFIN Oh, there he goes again! 'Classified information'! Oh, sitting on the 'settee' with our 'scones' and our 'classified information'!

The door opens and a plainclothes detective plus ten PCs (the Fred Tomlinson Singers) enter.

MUFFIN Ah! Hello, Duckie.
DUCKIE (TERRY J) Hello, sir. How are you?
MUFFIN I'm fine thanks. How are you?
DUCKIE Well, sir, I'm a little bit moody today, sir.
MUFFIN Why's that, Duckie?
DUCKIE Because...

Rhythm combo starts up out of vision and Detective Duckie sings. Superimposed caption: 'SGT DUCKIE'S SONG'

DUCKIE I'm a little bit sad and lonely
Now my baby's gone away...
I'm feeling kinda blue
Don't know what to do
I feel a little sad today.
CHORUS OF PCS He's a little bit sad and lonely
Now his baby's gone away
He's feeling kinda blue
He don't know just what to do
He's not feeling so good today.
DUCKIE (*solo*) When I smile
The sun comes flooding in
But when I'm sad
It goes behind the clouds again.
CHORUS He's a little bit sad and lonely
Now his baby's gone away
He's feeling kinda (*they stop abruptly and say:*) etcetera, etcetera. (*applause*)
MUFFIN A lovely song, Duckie.

Eurovision girl comes in. **44**

GIRL (ERIC) And that's the final entry. La dernière entrée. Das final entry. And now, guten abend. Das scores. The scores. Les scores. Dei scores. Oh! Scores. Ha! Scores! (*cut to scoreboard in Chinese*) Yes, Monaco is the winner—hah! Monaco is the linner—oh yes, man, Monaco's won de big prize, bwana...and now, here is Chief Inspector Jean-Paul Zatapathique with the winning song once again.

The accompaniment starts as the singers hum the intro. Cut to flashy Eurovision set. Zatapathique steps onto podium.

VOICE OVER (MICHAEL) (*hushed tone*) And so, Inspector Zatapathique, the forensic expert from the Monaco Murder Squad sings his song 'Bing Tiddle Tiddle Bong'.
ZATAPATHIQUE (GRAHAM) (*spoken*) Quai? Quai? Tout le monde, quoi?...mais, le monde... d'habitude...mais...je pense...
ZATAPATHIQUE AND SINGERS Bing tiddle tiddle bang
Bing tiddle tiddle bing Bing tiddle tiddle tiddle tiddle
Bing tiddle tiddle tiddle BONG!

Credits over. Zatapathique finishes and bends over exhausted. An arrow indicates his rear.

VOICE OVER Number thirty-one. The end.

Caption: 'THE END'

The Eurovision Song Contest began in 1956 and is one of the longest-running TV shows in history. Competitions are held in all member countries around Europe, and the internal winner goes to the final Eurovision Song Contest, where countries vote for the best song. It holds a kind of horrified fascination to this day: the songs are invariably saccharine, when they're not absolutely terrible. Notable winners include ABBA, who won with "Waterloo" in 1974, and Celine Dion, then singing for Switzerland, who won in 1988 with "*Ne Partez Pans Sans Moi*" ("Don't Leave Me").

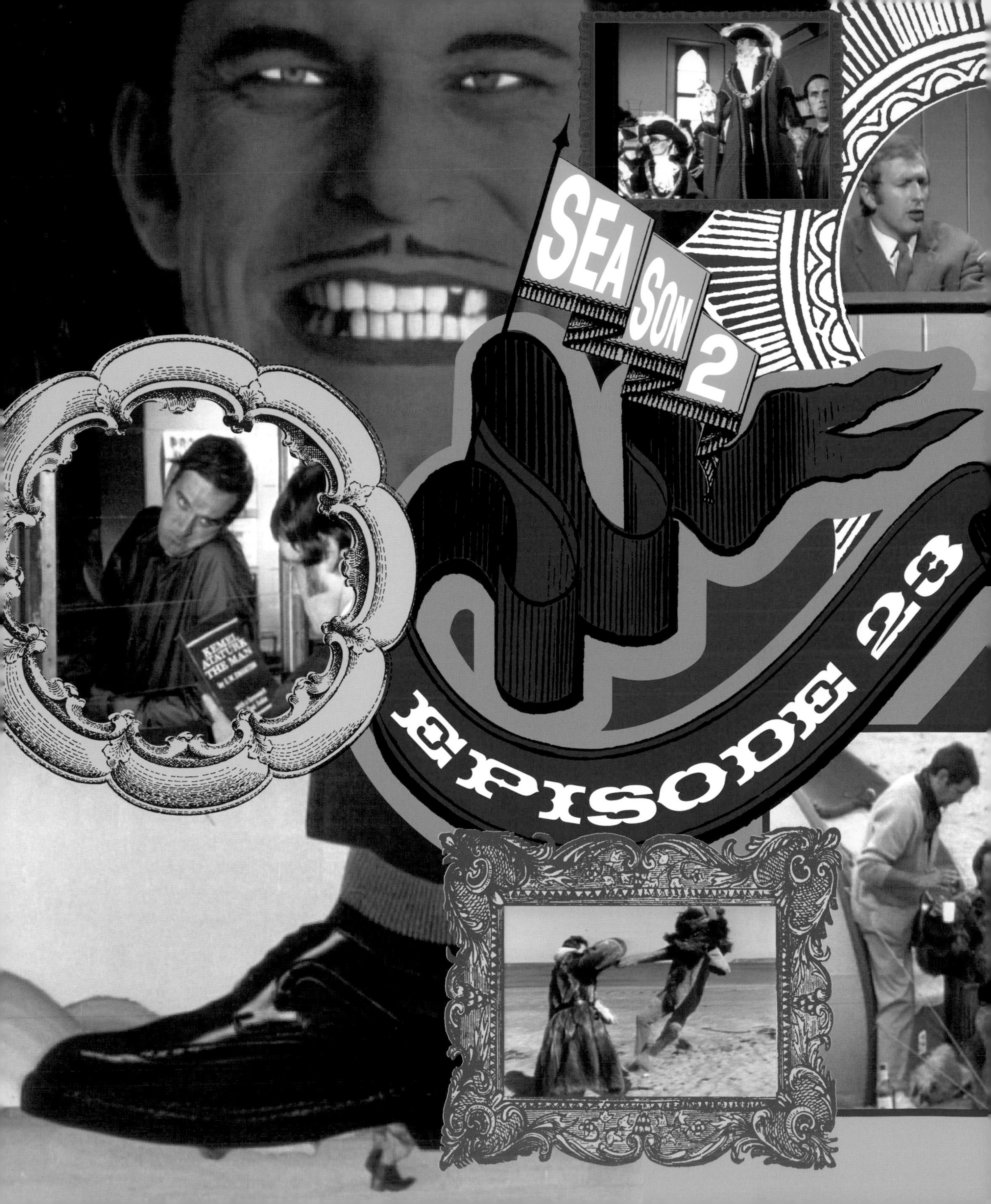
SEA SON 2
EPISODE 23
KEMEL ATATURK THE MAN

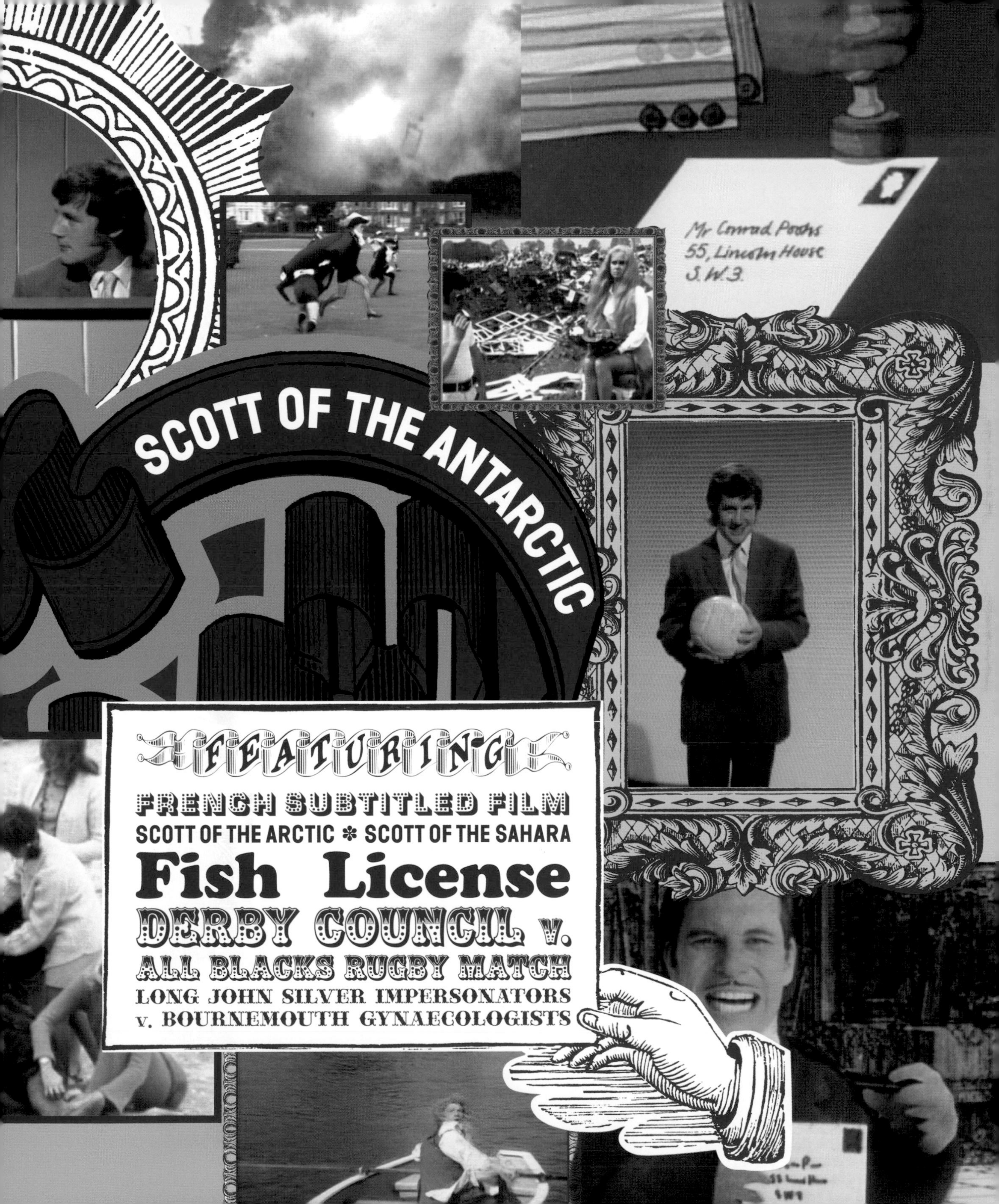
Mr Conrad Poohs
55, Lincoln House
S.W.3.
SCOTT OF THE ANTARCTIC
FEATURING
FRENCH SUBTITLED FILM
SCOTT OF THE ARCTIC ✽ SCOTT OF THE SAHARA
Fish License
DERBY COUNCIL v.
ALL BLACKS RUGBY MATCH
LONG JOHN SILVER IMPERSONATORS
v. BOURNEMOUTH GYNAECOLOGISTS

FIRST AIRED: DECEMBER 1, 1970

Exterior large rubbish dump. Hand-held camera tracks to girl in simple white dress with red hair fourteen foot long, who is sitting on a chair holding a cabbage in her hands. After a time Stig, in white jeans, shirt and scarf enters shot and stands around uneasily. **1**

STIG (TERRY J) Bonjour. *(subtitle: 'GOOD MORNING')*
GIRL (CAROL) Bonjour. *(subtitle: 'GOOD MORNING' Pause. Stig looks uneasy, glancing at camera.)*
STIG Il fait beau ce matin. *(subtitle: 'IT'S A NICE DAY')*
GIRL Oui, oui. *(subtitle: 'YES, YES')*
STIG D'accord... *(subtitle: 'HEAR HEAR')*
STIG Venez-vous ici souvent? *(subtitle: 'DO YOU COME HERE OFTEN?')*
GIRL Oui. *(subtitle: 'YES')*
STIG Ah. Bon. Bon. *(subtitle: 'GOOD, GOOD' Pause.)* **2**
STIG Je vois que vous avez un chou. *(subtitle: 'I SEE THAT YOU HAVE A CABBAGE')*
GIRL Oui. *(subtitle: 'YES' Stig starts to laugh falsely and then the girl joins in. It is a miserable attempt to capture joy and togetherness. The girl stops laughing before Stig does.)*
STIG Certainement il fait beau ce matin. *(subtitle: 'IT CERTAINLY IS A LOVELY DAY ALL RIGHT' Stig wanders out of shot but is very obviously pushed back into the picture.)*
STIG Je suis revolutionnaire. *(subtitle: 'I AM A REVOLUTIONARY')*
GIRL Oh.
STIG Qu'est-ce que vous avez dit? *(subtitle: 'WHAT DID YOU SAY?')*
GIRL J'ai dit 'oh'. *(subtitle: 'I SAID "OH"')*
STIG Ah. Très interessant. *(subtitle: 'AH. VERY INTERESTING' Cut to pimply youth in studio.)*
PHIL (ERIC) Brian Distel and Brianette Zatapathique there in an improvised scene from Jean Kenneth Longueur's new movie 'Le Fromage Grand'. Brian and Brianette symbolize the breakdown in communication in our modern society in this exciting new film and Longueur is saying to us, his audience, 'go on, protest, do something about it, assault the manager, demand your money back'. Later on in the film, in a brilliantly conceived montage, Longueur mercilessly exposes the violence underlying our society when Brian and Brianette again meet on yet another rubbish dump. *(Different part of same dump, but not very different. Girl is still on chair but this time with a* **cos lettuce.** *Then Stig enters shot.)*
STIG Bonjour encore. *(subtitle: 'HELLO AGAIN')*
GIRL Bonjour. *(Subtitle: 'GOOD MORNING')*
STIG Je vois que aujourd'jui vous avez une co-**laitue.** **3** *(subtitle:* ***'I SEE YOU'VE GOT A WEBB'S WONDER TODAY')*** **4**

1

This sketch is a spot-on satire of French New Wave cinema.

Terry Jones here hums a brief snatch of "*La Marseillaise*," the French national anthem.

"*Laitue*" is French for lettuce. A "cos" lettuce is the one with the long, dark green leaves.

"Webb's Wonder" is a kind of cos lettuce.

GIRL Oui.
STIG Bon. *(subtitle: 'GOOD' Intercut quick shot from war film: machine-gunner in plane.)*
STIG Il fait beau encore. *(subtitle: 'IT'S A LOVELY DAY AGAIN' Shot of Paris riots and clubbing.)*
GIRL Oui. *(subtitle: 'YES')*
STIG Bon. *(subtitle: 'GOOD' Shot of Michael being struck on head with a club by John.)*

STIG **Vous pouvez dire ça encore.** **5** *(subtitle: 'IT CERTAINLY IS A LOVELY DAY ALL RIGHT' Shot of collapsing building, then a man at a piano* (GRAHAM)*; the lid slams on his hands.)*

Literally, "You can say that again."

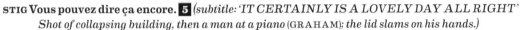

STIG Certainement il fait beau ce matin. *(subtitle: 'IT CERTAINLY IS A LOVELY DAY ALL RIGHT' Shot of aeroplanes bombing. Shot of chef receiving arrow in chest. Shot of girl kicking tall man on shin. Shot of rockets being fired from plane.)*
GIRL Oui. *(subtitle: 'YES' Shot of hydrogen bomb.)*
STIG Il fait beau hier. Ha ha ha. *(subtitle: 'IT WAS LOVELY YESTERDAY, HA HA HA' Shot of ack ack gun. Shot of man receiving a punch in the head from a boxing glove. Shot of nun kicking a policeman in the crotch.)*
GIRL Ha ha. *(subtitle: 'HA HA. HA HA. HA HA.' Shot of Spitfire. Shot of Korean soldiers; then man being beheaded.)*
STIG Quel surprise de vous voir encore. *(subtitle: 'WHAT A SURPRISE TO SEE YOU AGAIN' Shot of Paris riots. Shot of man having his foot stamped on. Shot of blazing building. Shot of man being poked in the eye with an umbrella. Shot of battleship firing broadside. Shot of man in underpants having a bucket of water thrown over him. Shot of soccer violence. Shot of man being knifed by a Greek Orthodox priest.)*
GIRL Je t'aime. *(subtitle: 'I LOVE YOU')*
STIG Je t'aime. *(subtitle: 'I LOVE YOU' They smile at each other happily for a moment. Then they hear something ticking. They listen carefully for a moment and then both start to look fearfully at the cos lettuce. After a moment of terror the cos lettuce explodes, in slow motion, blowing them apart.)*

As tatters and pieces of cos lettuce float through the air in slow motion, the camera pans down to some autumn leaves. Freeze frame. Superimposed caption: 'FIN' Cut back to Phil.

PHIL Pretty strong meat there from Longueur who is saying, of course, that ultimately materialism, in this case the Webb's Wonder lettuce, must destroy us all. That was for O. Simon, K. Simon, P. Simon and R. Sparrow of Leicester. Later on, we're going to take a look at John Wayne's latest movie, 'Buckets of Blood Pouring Out of People's Heads' but now we look ahead. On Tuesday Chris Conger took a BBC film unit to the location where 20th Century Vole are shooting their latest epic 'Scott of the Antarctic'.

Chris Conger standing with back to pier and a few holidaymakers behind him.

6 Another reference to the pretty Devon resort town of Paignton. And once again, civilians stand around bemused as Chapman and Idle do their thing.

CONGER (GRAHAM) Sea, sand and sunshine make **Paignton** **6** the queen of the English Riviera. But for the next six months this sleepy Devonshire resort will be transformed into the blizzard-swept wastes of the South Pole. For today shooting starts on the epic 'Scott of the Antarctic', produced by Gerry Schlick. *(walks over to Schlick)*

7 Robert Falcon Scott led two expeditions to the South Pole; the second, the Terra Nova Expedition, ended in disaster in 1913, when Scott and his four fellow adventurers died from hunger, cold, and fatigue.

SCHLICK (ERIC) (*American*) Hello.
CONGER Gerry, you chose Paignton as the location for **Scott.** **7**
SCHLICK Right, right.
CONGER

ISN'T IT A BIT OF A DRAWBACK THAT THERE'S NO SNOW HERE?

SCHLICK Well, we have 28,000 cubic feet of Wintrex, which is a new white foam rubber which actually on screen looks more like snow than snow...

Cut to shot of people nailing and sticking white foam rubber over things. It looks terrible. Others are painting the sand with white paint.

SCHLICK ...and 1,600 cubic US furlongs of white paint, with a special snow finish.
CONGER And I believe Kirk Vilb is playing the title role.
SCHLICK That is correct. We were very thrilled and honoured when Kirk agreed to play the part of Lieutenant Scott (*cut to Kirk Vilb who is wearing furs open at the chest; he is having a chest wig stuck on and icing sugar squeezed on to his nose and eyebrows*) because a star of his magnitude can pick and choose, but he read the title and just flipped. (*cut back to Gerry Schlick and Chris Conger*) And directing we have a very fine young British director, James McRettin, who's been collaborating on the screenplay, of course Jimmy...

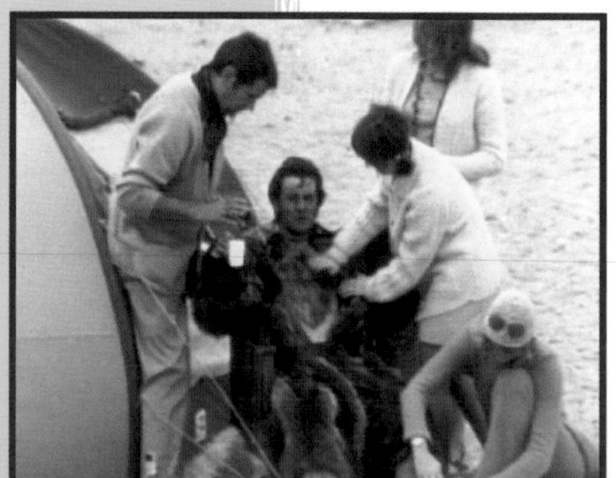

McRettin rushes into foreground. He is in no way like J. McGrath.

MCRETTIN (JOHN) Oh, there you are. Hello. Hello. No problem. Have a drink. Have a drink. Great. Hello. Marvellous. Marvellous. Hello. Rewrite. Oh this is really great. I mean, it's really saying something, don't you think?

CONGER Have you started shooting yet?

MCRETTIN Yes, yes. Great. Perfect. No, no, we haven't started yet. No. But great—great.

CONGER What is the first scene that you shoot this morning?

MCRETTIN Great. Terrific. Oh it's great. No problem. We'll sort it out on the floor. Sort it out on the floor. No problem. This film is basically pro-humanity and anti-bad things and it rips aside the hypocritical façade of our society's gin and tonic and leaves a lot of sacred cows rolling around in agony, have a drink, have a drink.

CONGER But which *scene* are we shooting first, Jimmy?

MCRETTIN Yes, great. Oh, marvellous. (*calls*) Which scene are we shooting first? What? (*to Conger*) it's scene one. Scene one. It's in the middle of the movie. Well, it is now. I rewrote it. (*calls*) I thought we cut that? Didn't we cut that?

SCHLICK No, we didn't.

MCRETTIN We didn't. Oh great. That's even better. I'll put it back in. Rewrite. (*calling*) Scene one's back in everyone. Scene one's back in. Great. Great. (*to Conger*) This is the scene—outside the tent—it's all bloody marvellous. It makes you want to throw up.

Cut to Schlick and Conger on the beach.

SCHLICK Now in this scene Lieutenant Scott returns to camp in the early morning after walking the huskies to have brunch with the rest of his team. (*cut to shot of tent with Bowers, who is black, and Oates, sitting outside*) **Oates,** **8** played by your very own lovely Terence Lemming, who is an English cockney officer seconded to the US Navy, and **Bowers** **9** played by Seymour Fortescue, the Olympic pole vaulter.

Film: Scott comes up to them. He has two large boxes strapped to his feet to make him look tall.

OATES (TERRY J) Hi, Lieutenant.

SCOTT (MICHAEL) Hi, Oatesy. Sure is a beautiful day already.

MCRETTIN (*rushing in*) Great, great.

SCOTT What? What are you saying?

MCRETTIN I was just saying great, great. Cue Evans.

Sexy girl with long blond hair comes into shot with short pink fur coat. She walks up to Scott who towers four feet above her as she is walking in a trench. **10**

SCHLICK And this is Vanilla Hoare as Miss Evans.

CONGER Miss Evans?

SCHLICK Right.

Miss Evans is now beneath Scott at knee height.

Lawrence Edward Grace (Titus) Oates was a member of Scott's second expedition. He is famous for leaving the tent during a blizzard in 1912 with the words, "I am just going outside. I may be some time," thereby walking to his self-sacrificial death.

Lieutenant Henry Robertson (Birdie) Bowers, another member of the ill-fated Terra Nova Expedition.

She is actually wearing a long, white fur coat and matching hat.

SCOTT Good morning, Miss Evans.
EVANS (CAROL) Oh, I've forgotten my line.
MCRETTIN What's her line? What's her line?

Girl runs in with script.

GIRL It's 'Good morning, Captain Scott'.
EVANS Oh, yeah. 'Good morning, Captain Sc'...oh, I'm just not happy with that line. Could I just say 'Hi Scottie'?
MCRETTIN Great. Great. Rewrite. Cue.
GIRL Hi Scarrie! Oh, sorry. Hi Stocky! Oh—I'm sorry again. Oh, Jim. I'm just unhappy with this line. Hey, can I do it all sort of kooky, like this? (*goes berserk waving hands*) Hi Scottie!
MCRETTIN Great! We'll shoot it
SCOTT Are you sure that's right?
MCRETTIN Oh, it's great.

Gerry Schlick walks into the shot.

SCHLICK Jim.
MCRETTIN Jim! Jim! Oh, me!
SCHLICK Jim, I feel we may be running into some problems here in the area of height.
MCRETTIN Great! Where are they?
SCHLICK Where are who?
MCRETTIN I don't know. I was getting confused.
SCHLICK Jim, I feel here, that Scott may be too tall in the area of height with reference to Vanilla who is too near the ground in the area of being too short at this time.
MCRETTIN Great...Oh, I know. I'm going to dig a pit for Scott and put a box in Vanilla's trench.
SCOTT Say, why don't I take the boxes off and Vanilla get up out of the trench.
MCRETTIN It wouldn't work ... It's even better! Great. Rewrite!
EVANS What was that?
MCRETTIN Oh, it's easy. I've worked it out. Scott takes his boxes off and you don't stand in the trench.
EVANS I say my lines *out* of the trench?
MCRETTIN Even better. Great.
EVANS But I've never acted out of a trench. I might fall over. It's dangerous.

MCRETTIN Oh well, could you just try it?

EVANS Look, you crumb bum, I'm a star. Star, star, star. I don't get a million dollars to act out of a trench. I played Miss St John the Baptist in a trench, (*she walks along in the trench and we see that she has two boxes strapped to her feet*) and I played Miss Napoleon Bonaparte in a trench, and I played Miss Alexander Fleming in a furrow so if you want this scene played out of a trench, well you just get yourself a goddamn stuntman. (*walks off*) I played Miss Galileo in a groove and I played Mrs Jesus Christ in a **geological syncline, so don't...** **11**

MCRETTIN Great. Great everyone. Lunch now. Lunch. It's all in the can. Good morning's work.

SCHLICK But you haven't done a shot.

MCRETTIN Just keeping morale up. (*tries to take a drink from his viewfinder*)

A syncline is a fold, or dip, in rock layers.

The same: afternoon.

SCHLICK Now this afternoon we're going to shoot the scene where Scott gets off the boat on to the ice floe and he sees the lion and he fights it and kills it and the blood goes psssssssshhh in slow motion.

CONGER

BUT THERE AREN'T ANY LIONS IN THE ANTARCTIC.

SCHLICK What?

CONGER There aren't any lions in the Antarctic.

SCHLICK You're right. There are no lions in the Antarctic. That's ridiculous; whoever heard of a lion in the Antarctic. Right. Lose the lion.

MCRETTIN Got to keep the lion. It's great!

SCHLICK Lose the lion.

MCRETTIN Great. We're losing the lion. Rewrite. Lose the lion everyone. That's fantastic.

SCOTT What's this about our losing the lion?

SCHLICK Well, Kirk, we thought perhaps we might lose the fight with the lion a little bit, Kirk, angel.

SCOTT (*loudly*) Why?

SCHLICK Well, Kirkie, doll, there are no lions in the Antarctic, baby.

SCOTT (*shouts*) I get to fight the lion.

SCHLICK It'd be silly.

SCOTT Listen, I gotta fight the lion. That's what that guy Scott's all about. I know. I've studied him already.

SCHLICK **But why couldn't you fight a penguin?** **12**

MCRETTIN Great! (*falls over*)

SCOTT Fight a rotten penguin?

SCHLICK It needn't be a little penguin. It can be the biggest penguin you've ever seen. An electric penguin, twenty feet high, with long green tentacles that sting people, and you can stab it in the wings and the blood can go spurting psssssshhhh in slow motion.

SCOTT The lion is in the contract.

SCHLICK He fights the lion.

12

A penguin was blown up in Episode 22. The Pythons stick to, and obsess on, certain animals and tropes almost exclusively.

MCRETTIN Even better. Great. Have a drink. Lose the penguin. Stand by to shoot. (*falls over*)

SCHLICK Where do they have lions?

CONGER Africa.

SCHLICK

THAT'S IT. SCOTT'S IN AFRICA. AS MANY LIONS AS WE NEED.

MCRETTIN Great!

SCHLICK He's looking for a pole no one else knows about. That ties in with the sand. Right. Paint the sand yellow again. Okay, let's get this show on the road. 'Scott of the Sahara.'

Cut instantly to sky. caption: 'SCOTT OF THE SAHARA'

VOICE OVER (MICHAEL) Booming out of the pages of history comes a story of three men and one woman whose courage shocked a generation.

Blinding sun. Pan down to Paignton beach. Scott, Evans, Oates and Bowers wearing furs crossing sand on snow shoes. With sledge pulled by motley selection of mongrel dogs, badly disguised as huskies.

VOICE OVER From the same team that brought you...(*the names come out superimposed*) **'Lawrence of Glamorgan'... 13 'Bridge Over the River Trent'... 14 'The Mad Woman of Biggleswade'... 15** and **'Krakatoa, East of Leamington'... 16** comes the story of three people and a woman united by fate who set out in search of the fabled Pole of the Sahara and found...themselves. See...Lieutenant Scott's death struggle with a crazed desert lion.

Lawrence of Arabia, starring Peter O'Toole, was directed by David Lean and released in 1962. Glamorgan is a county in Wales.

"Bridge Over the River Trent" is a reference to *The Bridge on the River Kwai*, a 1957 film about World War II, also by David Lean. The "Trent" is a river that starts in the British Midlands and which notably runs north (unlike most other British rivers) toward Yorkshire.

The Madwoman of Chaillot is a 1969 movie starring Katharine Hepburn and directed by Bryan Forbes, a regular reference in Python. Biggleswade is a town in Bedfordshire, about 45 miles north of London.

Krakatoa: East of Java is a 1969 film about the eruption of a volcano on Java in 1883. (Krakatoa is west of Java, by the way.) Royal Leamington Spa is a town in the British county of Warwickshire, southeast of Birmingham.

The four are walking along. Suddenly they stop, stare, and react in horror. Scott steps to the front to defend the others. Intercut, non-matching stock shot of lion running out of jungle and leaping at camera. Scott waits poised and is then struck by completely rigid stuffed lion. Montage of shots of him wrestling, firstly with the stuffed lion, then with an actor in a tatty lion suit. The lion picks up a chair, fends Scott off, smashes it over his head. Finally Scott kicks the lion on the shin. The lion leaps around on one leg and picks up a knife. Scott points, the lion looks, Scott kicks the knife out of the lion's paw. He advances on the lion, and socks him on the jaw. The lion collapses in slow motion. After a pause, phoney blood spurts out.

VOICE OVER See Ensign Oates' frank adult death struggle with the spine-chilling giant electric penguin...

Oates looks up in horror, a shadow crosses him. Reverse shot of model penguin (quite small, about a foot) which lights up and looks electric. The penguin is close to the camera in the foreground and appears huge. Oates looks around desperately then starts to undress. Shot of penguin throwing tentacle. Half-nude Oates struggles with it. Intercut a lot of phoney reverses. Oates by now clad only in posing briefs sees a stone. He picks up the stone, then camera zooms into above-navel shot; he removes his briefs, puts the stone in the briefs, twirls it like a sling, and releases stone. The penguin is hit on beak, and falls over backwards.

VOICE OVER ...See Miss Evans pursued by the man-eating roll-top writing desk.

Miss Evans is running along screaming. Shot of desk chasing her (phoney desk with man inside). The roll top goes up and down, emitting roars, and displaying fearsome white teeth inside. As Evans runs, her clothing gets torn on each of the three cactuses. These are well spaced apart so that there is a lot of trouble to get near them. When she is practically nude, she runs out of shot revealing the announcer.

ANNOUNCER (JOHN) And now for something completely different.

IT'S MAN (MICHAEL)

IT'S...

Animated titles. **17**

Animation: dancing teeth.

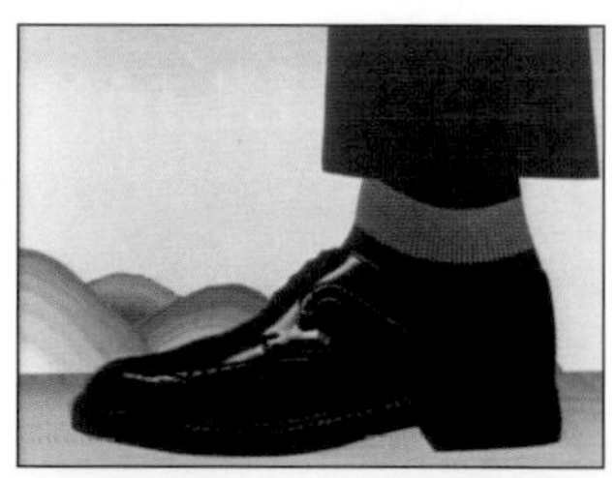

Then animation of a letter being resealed and posted—all backwards—ending in a real post office. A post office worker removes the stamp from the letter and hands it to man.

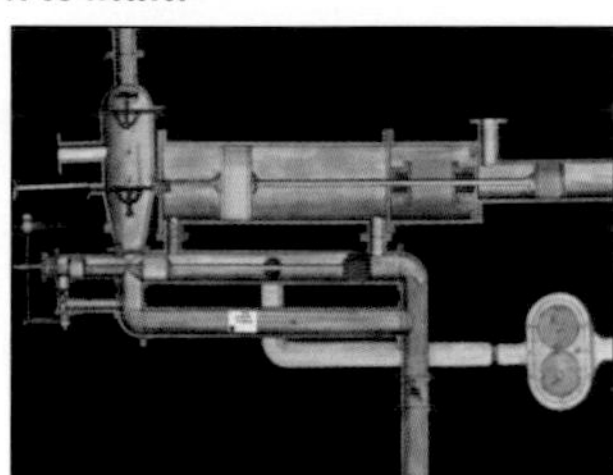

POST OFFICE WORKER Five pence please.

The man walks out backwards, passing Mr Praline as he enters. ***He looks at the man, puzzled, and then goes up to first of two grilles which has a sign saying 'stamps and licences'.*** **18**

PRALINE (JOHN) Excuse me, I would like to buy a fish licence, please. (*the man behind counter points to next grille; to camera*) The man's sign must be wrong. I have in the past noticed a marked discrepancy between these post office signs and the activities carried on beneath. **But soft, let us see how Dame Fortune smiles upon my next postal adventure!** **19** (*he goes to next grille*)

The titles finally run, 17 minutes and 35 seconds into the show.

18

He actually goes up to the first window, which has a sign that reads: Miss McCheane—OUT. Then he goes to the stamps and licenses window.

"But soft"—the Shakespearian admonition.

HELLO, I WOULD LIKE TO BUY A FISH LICENCE, PLEASE.

MAN (MICHAEL) A what?

PRALINE A licence for my pet fish, Eric.

MAN How did you know my name was Eric?

PRALINE No, no, no. My *fish's* name is Eric. Eric the fish. 'E's an 'alibut.

MAN A what?

PRALINE He is an halibut.

MAN You've got a pet halibut?

PRALINE Yes, I chose him out of thousands. I didn't like the others. They were all too flat.

MAN You're a loony.

PRALINE I am not a loony! Why should I be tarred with the epithet 'loony' merely because I have a pet halibut? I've heard tell that **Sir Gerald Nabarro** [20] has a pet prawn called Simon, and you wouldn't call Sir Gerald a loony would you? Furthermore, **Dawn Palethorpe**, [21] the lady show jumper had a clam called **Sir Stafford** [22] after the late Chancellor. **Alan Bullock** [23] has two pikes, both called Norman, and the late, great Marcel Proust had an 'addock. If you're calling the author of 'A La Recherche du Temps Perdu' a loony I shall have to ask you to step outside.

MAN All right, all right, all right. You want a licence?

PRALINE Yes.

MAN For a fish?

PRALINE Yes.

MAN You *are* a loony.

PRALINE Look! It's a bleedin' pet, isn't it. I've got a licence for my pet dog, Eric, and I've got a licence for my pet cat, Eric.

MAN You don't need a licence for a cat.

PRALINE You bleeding well do, and I've got one. Ho, ho, you're not catching me out there.

MAN There is no such thing as a bloody cat licence.

PRALINE Yes there is.

MAN No there isn't.

PRALINE Is!

MAN Isn't!

PRALINE Is.

MAN Isn't.

PRALINE Is.

Gerald Nabarro is a another reference to the British politician, he of the handlebar moustache and offensive, racist views.

Dawn Palethorpe, a female British show jumper who won the silver medal at the 1960 Ladies European Championship.

Sir Richard Stafford Cripps was Chancellor of the Exchequer (the minister in charge of British fiscal policy) from 1947 to 1950. He died in 1952.

Alan Bullock, a British historian, was famous for his groundbreaking 1952 biography of Hitler.

MAN Isn't.
PRALINE Is.
MAN Isn't.
PRALINE Is.
MAN Isn't.
PRALINE Is.
MAN Isn't.
PRALINE What's that then?
MAN That is a dog licence with the word 'dog' crossed out and the word 'cat' written in is crayon.
PRALINE The man didn't have the proper form.
MAN What man?
PRALINE The man from the cat detector van. 24
MAN Loony detector van you mean.
PRALINE It's people like you what causes unrest.
MAN All right, what cat detector van?
PRALINE The cat detector van from the Ministry of Housinge.
MAN Housinge???
PRALINE Yes, it was spelt that way on the van. I'm very observant. I've never seen so many aerials in my life. The man told me their equipment could pin-point a purr at four hundred yards... and Eric being such a happy cat was a piece of cake.
MAN How much did this cost?
PRALINE Sixty quid, and eight guineas for the fruit bat.
MAN What fruit bat?
PRALINE Eric the fruit bat.
MAN Are all your pets called Eric?
PRALINE There's nothing so odd about that. **Kemal Ataturk** 25 had an entire menagerie, all called Abdul.
MAN No he didn't.
PRALINE (*takes book from pocket*) He did, he did, he did, he did and did. There you are. **'Kemal Ataturk, the Man' by E. W. Swanton with a foreword by Paul Anka, page 91, please.** 26
MAN (*referring to page 91*) I owe you an apology, sir.
PRALINE Spoken like a gentleman. Now are you going to give me this fish licence?
MAN I promise you there is no such thing. You don't need one.
PRALINE Then I would like a statement to that effect signed by the Lord Mayor.

Fanfare of trumpets. Mayor gorgeously dressed with dignitaries enters flanked by trumpeters.

MAN You're in luck.

In long shot now.

THE MAYOR, WHO IS NINE FOOT HIGH, AND DIGNITARIES APPROACH A STARTLED PRALINE.

Organ music below ***a reverent voice over:*** 27

VOICE OVER (JOHN) And now, there is the Mayor. Surely the third tallest mayor in Derby's history. And there are the Aldermen magnificently resplendent in their Aldermanic hose and just look at the power in those thighs. The New Zealanders are going to find it pretty tough going in the set pieces in the second half...So Dawn Palethorpe with one clear round on Sir Gerald...and now the Mayor has reached the Great Customer Mr Eric Praline. (*the mayor takes a piece of paper from the post office man*) And now the Mayoral human being takes

"Cat detector" is a reference to the TV license detector van, in which inspectors would roam British streets looking for TV signals from homes that had no record of a license.

Kemal Atatürk was the first president of Turkey. He served from 1923 to 1938.

A book by the cricket commentator Swinton, with an intro by the American singer-songwriter Anka. Wonderful stuff.

The Voice Over sounds not unlike that of David Attenborough, he of the nature shows.

the Mayoral Pen in the Mayoral hand and watched by the Lady Mayoress, who of course scored that magnificent try in the first half, signs the fishy exemption (*the mayor signs it and hands it to Praline*) and the Great Customer, Mr Eric Praline, who is understandably awed by the magnificence and even the absurdity of this great occasion here at Cardiff Arms Park, (*Praline looks very confused*) has finally gone spare and there is the going sparal look on the front of his head. And now the Aldermen are finishing their oranges and leaving the post office **for the start of the second half.** **28** ...So Dawn Palethorpe with one clear round on Sir Gerald...and now the Mayor has reached the Great Customer Mr Eric Praline. (*the mayor takes a piece of paper from the post office man*) And now the Mayoral human being takes the Mayoral Pen in the Mayoral hand and watched by the Lady Mayoress, who of course scored that **magnificent try** **29** in the first half, signs the fishy exemption (*the mayor signs it and hands it to Praline*) and the Great Customer, Mr Eric Praline, who is understandably awed by the magnificence and even the absurdity of this great occasion here at **Cardiff Arms Park,** **30** (*Praline looks very confused*) **has finally gone spare** **31** and there is the going sparal look on the front of his head. And now the Aldermen are finishing their **oranges** **32**.

They all exit out of door, eating oranges, and Praline looks after them. Cut to a rugby field. Crowd roaring as the aldermen, mayor, mayoress, town clerk, Dawn Palethorpe (on a horse) and the borough surveyor run onto the pitch and take up their positions.

COMMENTATOR (JOHN) And here come the Derby Council XV following the All Blacks out on to the pitch. There, in the centre of the picture you can see Dawn Palethorpe on Sir Gerald—one of the fastest wingers we must have seen in England this season. On the left hand

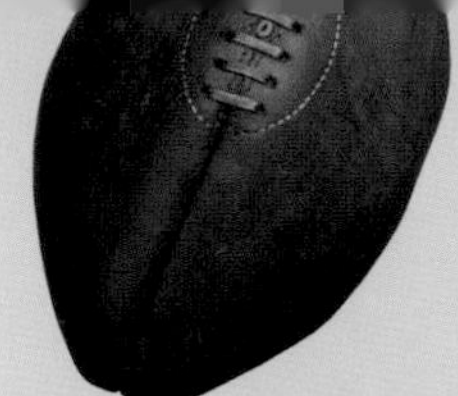

"Second half" is a reference to the sport of rugby, at which New Zealand tends to excel.

A "try" in rugby is the equivalent of a touchdown in American football . . . sort of.

Cardiff Arms Park, which opened in 1969, was once home to the Welsh rugby team.

"Gone spare" is British slang for going nuts.

Oranges are the traditional half-time refreshment for amateur sports in the U.K.

The "All Blacks" is the nickname for the New Zealand rugby team.

A "scrum-down" is another way to restart a rugby game: the teams maul each other at close quarters and attempt to get the ball.

"The ball against the head" means that the team that fed the ball into the scrum, or maul, has lost possession, which is a bad thing.

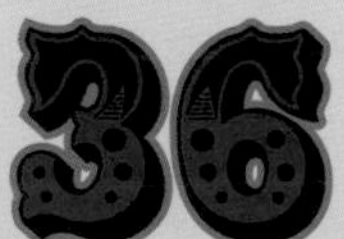

"Fullback" is a position in rugby. Fullbacks are defenders and need to be good kickers of the ball.

side of the picture the Lord Mayor has been running such wonderful possession for Derby Council in the lines out and it's the **All Blacks** 33 to kick off. Wilson to kick off. Oh, I can see there the Chairman of the By-ways and Highways Committee who's obviously recovered from that very nasty blow he got in that loose ball in the first half. (*opposite them the All Blacks kick off*) And Wilson kicks off and it's the Town Clerk's taken the ball beautifully there, the All Blacks are up on it very fast and the whistle has gone. I'm not quite sure what happened there, I couldn't see, but there's a **scrum-down.** 34 I think it's an All Blacks' ball. They were upon them very fast. Obviously they're going to try very hard in this half to wipe out this five-point deficit. Derby Council eight points to three up and Derby Council have got the **ball against the head.** 35 There is the Borough Surveyor, the scrum-half is out of the...er, the Chairman of the Highway and By-way Committee who's kicked for touch. The line out—and it's into the line out and the Mayor has got the ball again. To the Borough Surveyor who's left out the Medical Officer of Health. Straight along the line to the Lady Mayoress and the Lady Mayoress has got to go through. **Number two has missed her she's taken to the full back** 36—only the full back to beat and she has scored! The Lady Mayoress has scored, **it's eleven points to three.** 37

Subtitle: 'NEW ZEALAND 3 DERBY COUNCIL 11' ***Cut to linkman and Cliff Morgan.*** 38

LINKMAN (MICHAEL) Cliff, this must have been a very disappointing result for the All Blacks.

CLIFF (GRAHAM) (*Welsh*) Well, they've had very bad luck on the tour so far. They missed four very easy kicks against the Exeter Amateur Operatic Society, which must have cost them the match and then of course there was that crippling defeat at the hands of the Derry and Toms Soft Toy Department, so I don't think they can be really fancying their chances against the London Pooves on Saturday.

LINKMAN And what about China?

CLIFF Well, whether Mao Tse Tung is alive or not, Lin Piao has a stranglehold on central committee which Lin Shao Chi can't break, so it remains to be seen whether Chou En Lai can really get his finger out and get going in the second half.

LINKMAN Well, thank you Cliff. Tonight's other outstanding match was the semi-final between the Bournemouth Gynaecologists and the Watford Long John Silver Impersonators. **We bring you edited highlights of the match.** 39

Rapid montage of goals scored by competent gynaecologists wearing surgical gowns and caps, against totally incompetent and immobile LJSI team who simply stand round going 'aaah! Jim lad' as the goals rain in. The ball is kicked off-screen. Sudden cut to studio. A presenter is standing in front of curtain; he catches the ball thrown from off. He smiles.

PRESENTER (MICHAEL) Well, that's about it for tonight ladies and gentlemen, but remember if you've enjoyed watching the show just half as much as we've enjoyed doing it, then we've enjoyed it twice as much as you. Ha, ha, ha.

The sixteen-ton weight falls on him.

Cut to montage of scenes of destruction, buildings falling down, bombs etc. Roll credits over.

Palin drove Jones, Champan, and Cleese to the sketch in his Mini car— all in pirate costumes, with (dead) parrots on their shoulders. Palin even stopped off to cash a check in a bank, and all four of them went to the cashier, who, in typically stoic British fashion, made no mention of the fact that four men dressed as Long John Silver had sauntered into her branch to do some business. (Cleese remembers that he once cashed a check dressed as a burglar during the filming of the movie *And Now For Something Completely Different*.)

Cliff Morgan, a Welsh rugby player, was a sports commentator at the time.

The sport here is soccer, not rugby.

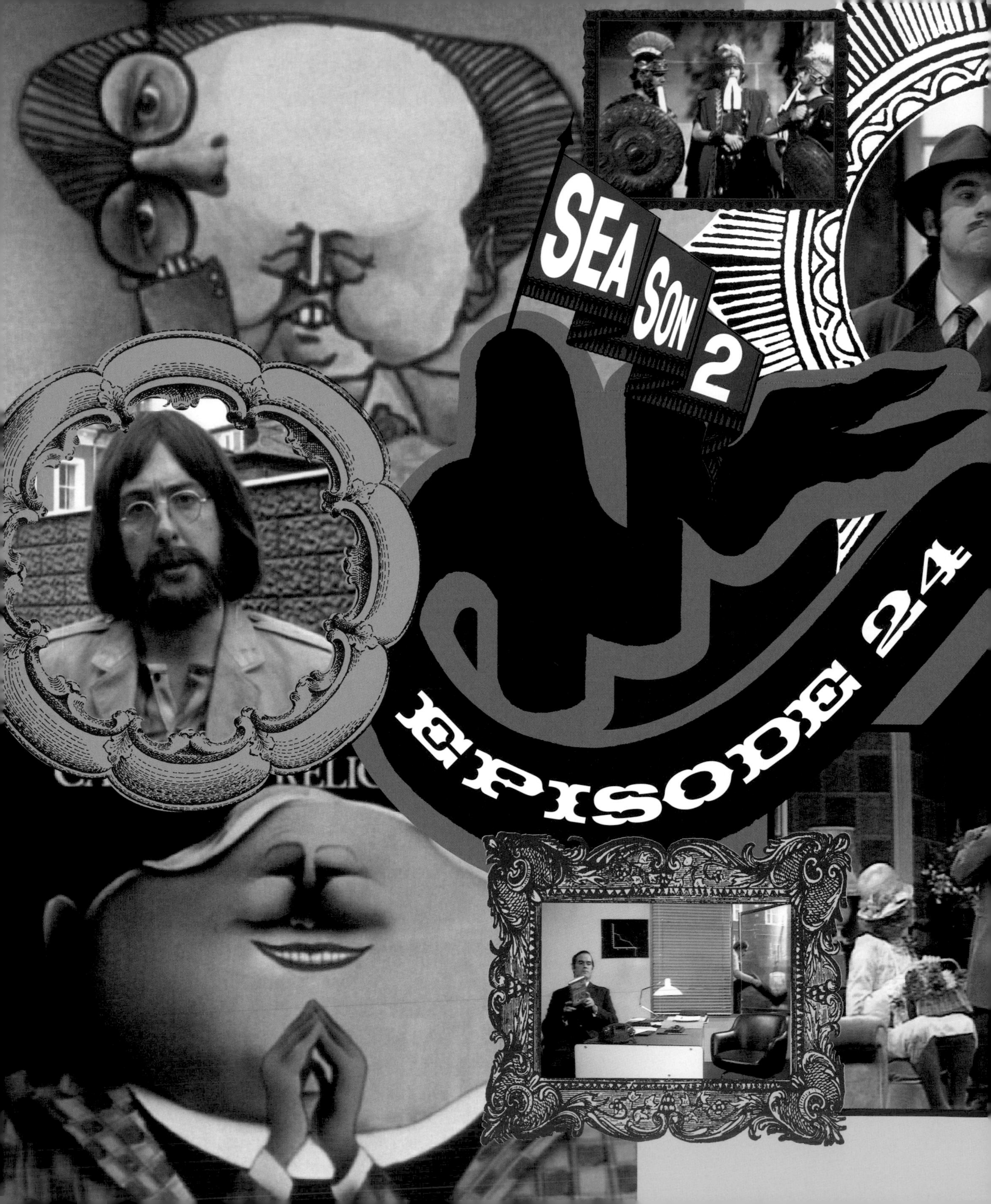
SEA
SON
2
EPISODE 24

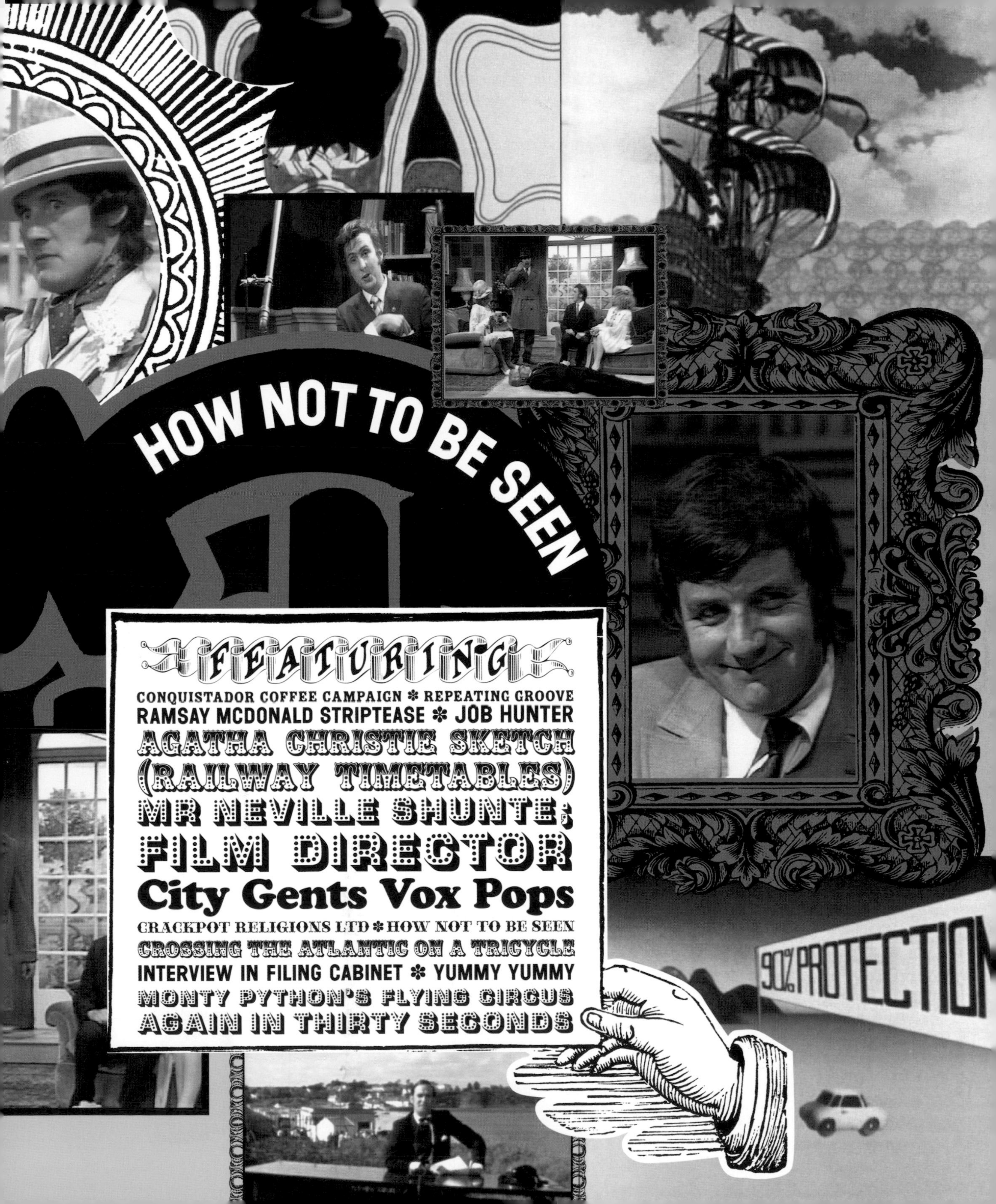
HOW NOT TO BE SEEN
FEATURING
CONQUISTADOR COFFEE CAMPAIGN ✽ REPEATING GROOVE
RAMSAY MCDONALD STRIPTEASE ✽ JOB HUNTER
AGATHA CHRISTIE SKETCH
(RAILWAY TIMETABLES)
MR NEVILLE SHUNTE;
FILM DIRECTOR
City Gents Vox Pops
CRACKPOT RELIGIONS LTD ✽ HOW NOT TO BE SEEN
CROSSING THE ATLANTIC ON A TRICYCLE
INTERVIEW IN FILING CABINET ✽ YUMMY YUMMY
MONTY PYTHON'S FLYING CIRCUS
AGAIN IN THIRTY SECONDS
90% PROTECTION

FIRST AIRED: DECEMBER 8, 1970

An office. Boss is reading a book, 'Chinese for Business Men'. He tries out a few Chinese words. ***There is a knock at the door.*** **1**

The knock actually comes from the office window.

BOSS (JOHN) Come in. ***(Mr Frog comes in)*** **2** Ah, Frog.
FROG (ERIC) S. Frog, sir.
BOSS Shut up, I want to have a word with you, Frog.
FROG S. Frog, sir.
BOSS Shut up. It's about your advertising campaign for Conquistador Coffee. Now, I've had the managing director of Conquistador to see me this morning and he's very unhappy with your campaign. *Very* unhappy. In fact, he's shot himself.
FROG Badly, sir?
BOSS No, extremely well.

Idle climbs in through the window.

(lifts up a leg belonging to a body behind desk, and holds up a card saying 'joke') **3** Well, before he went he left a note with the company secretary *(opens a nearby door; a dead company secretary falls out)*, the effect of which was how disappointed he was with your work and, in particular, why you had changed the name from Conquistador Instant Coffee to Conquistador Instant Leprosy. Why, Frog?

As usual, the Pythons don't allow punch lines to go unpunished or without remarks.

FROG S. Frog, sir.
BOSS Shut up. Why did you do it?
FROG It was a joke.
BOSS A *joke? (holds up card saying 'joke')*
FROG No, no not a joke, a sales campaign. *(holds up a card saying 'No, a Sales Campaign')*
BOSS I see, Frog.
FROG S. Frog, sir.
BOSS Shut up. Now, let's have a look at the sales chart. *(indicates a plummeting sales graph)* When you took over this account, Frog, Conquistador were a brand leader. Here you introduced your first campaign, 'Conquistador coffee brings a new meaning to the word vomit'. Here you made your special introductory offer of a free dead dog with every jar, and this followed your second campaign 'the tingling fresh coffee which brings you exciting new cholera, mange, dropsy, the clap, **hard pad** **4** and athlete's head. From the House of Conquistador'.

"Hard pad" is a truly distressing condition in which a dog's nose and paw pads dry out, usually due to distemper.

FROG It was a soft-sell, sir.
BOSS Why, Frog?
FROG S. Frog, sir.
BOSS Shut up! Well?
FROG Well, people know the name, sir.
BOSS They certainly do know the name—they burnt the factory down. The owner is hiding in the bathroom *(shot heard)*—the owner *was* hiding in my bathroom. *(holds up 'joke' card again)*
FROG You're not going to fire me, sir?

BOSS Fire you? Three men dead, the factory burnt down, the account lost and our firm completely bankrupt, what...what...what...can you possibly say? What excuse can you possibly make?

FROG Sorry, father. *(holds up the 'joke' card)*

BOSS Oh, yes. Oh, incidentally your film's won a prize.

He opens a venetian blind on the window to reveal the film: a coastline.

Panning shot of hills rolling down into the sea, waves breaking on the shore. Travelogue music (Malcolm Arnold type) over this. Suddenly the music sticks, and keeps repeating one phrase. The pan continues. We come across an old-fashioned gramophone on which the record is sticking. A hand comes in and lifts the needle off; the pan continues—it's the hand of the announcer who is sitting at his desk.

ANNOUNCER (JOHN) Sorry about that. And now for something completely diff...*(the film sticks and repeats the end of the sentence several times)* something completely diff...completely diff...completely diff...completely diff...completely different.

IT'S MAN (MICHAEL)

IT'S...

After about fifteen seconds of the credits the music and animation sticks, and keeps repeating. We finally get on to the right track, and complete the titles.

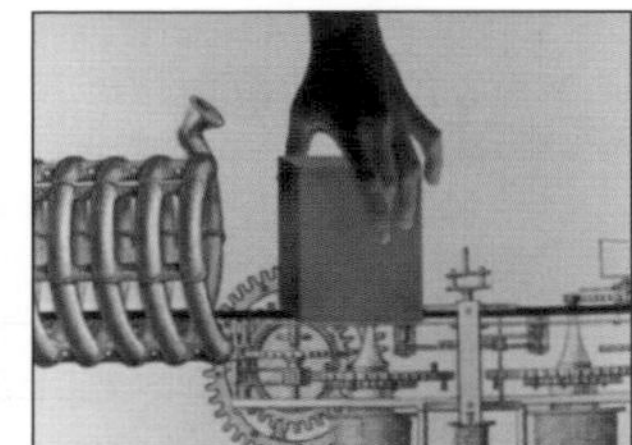

Stock film of Ramsay MacDonald **5** *arriving at Number 10 Downing Street and any others of that period.*

Ramsay MacDonald was a British politician who became Prime Minister twice: the first time for much of 1924 (and so became the first Labour Prime Minister), and then again from 1929 to 1935.

VOICE OVER (JOHN) **1929. Stanley Baldwin's Conservative Government is defeated and Ramsay MacDonald becomes, for the second time, Prime Minister of England.** [6]

MacDonald walks into an empty room (black and white film).

RAMSAY MACDONALD (MICHAEL) My, it's hot in here.

He proceeds to take off his clothes, strips down to black garter belt and suspenders and stockings. Cut to Mr Glans who is sitting next to a fully practical old 8mm home projector. There is a knock at the door. He switches the projector off and hides it furtively. He is sitting in an office, ***with a placard saying 'Exchange and Mart, Editor' on his desk.*** [7] *He points to it rather obviously.*

GLANS (JOHN) Hello, come in. *(enter Bee, a young aspirant job hunter)* Ah, hello, hello, how much do you want for that briefcase?

BEE (TERRY J) Well, I...

GLANS All right then, the briefcase and the umbrella. A fiver down, must be my final offer.

BEE Well, I don't want to sell them. I've come for a job.

GLANS Oh, take a seat, take a seat.

BEE Thank you.

GLANS I see you chose the canvas chair with the aluminium frame. I'll throw that in and a fiver, for the briefcase and the umbrella...no, make it fair, the briefcase and the umbrella and the two pens in your breast pocket and the chair's yours and a fiver and a pair of ex-German U-boat commando's binoculars.

BEE Really, they are not for sale.

GLANS Not for sale, what does that mean?

BEE I came about the advertisement for the job of assistant editor.

GLANS Oh yeah, right. Ah, OK, ah. How much experience in journalism?

BEE Five years.

GLANS Right, typing speed?

BEE Fifty.

GLANS **O Levels?** [8]

BEE **Eight.** [9]

GLANS **A Levels?** [10]

BEE **Two.** [11]

GLANS Right...Well, I'll give you the job, and the chair, and an all-wool ex-army sleeping bag...for the briefcase, umbrella, the pens in your breast pocket and your string vest.

BEE When do I start?

GLANS Monday.

BEE That's marvellous.

GLANS If you throw in the shoes as well. *(presses intercom)* Hello, er...Miss Johnson? Could we have two coffees and biscuits please?

The 1929 General Election ended in a hung parliament, a situation in which neither the Conservative or Labour parties held enough seats to form a government. The Conservatives eschewed a coalition with the minority Liberal Party, and so handed power to MacDonald and the Labourites.

Exchange and Mart was the leading weekly small-ads magazine, where you could buy almost anything. It went exclusively online in 2009.

"O-levels" are the exams Brits tended to take at the end of regular high school, which is at age 16 in the U.K.

This would be a very good number of O-levels to pass.

"A-Levels" are the exams Brits tended to take at the end of an extra two years of high school—known as "sixth form"—at age 18. Results in these exams would lead to acceptance, or not, at university.

Again, a solid number of passes at A-level.

MISS JOHNSON *(over intercom)* One coffee and one biscuit for the two ex-army greatcoats and the alarm clock on the mantelpiece.

GLANS Two ex-army greatcoats and the alarm clock and a table lamp, for two coffees and biscuits.

Animation: an elderly secretary at a desk in an empty room.

MISS JOHNSON Two greatcoats and two table lamps.

Cut back to real office.

GLANS Two greatcoats, one table lamp and a desert boat.

Cut back to cartoon.

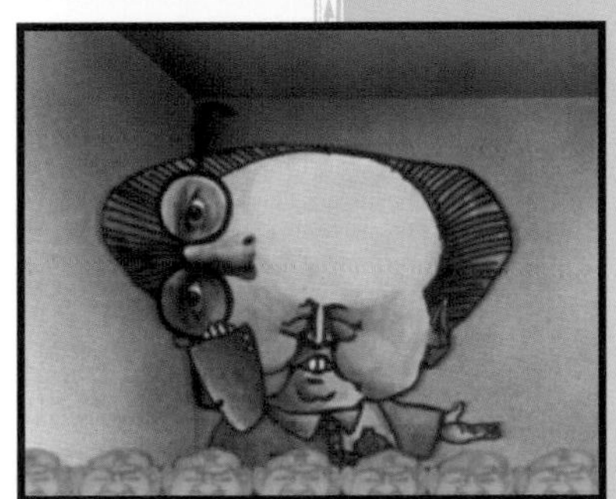

MISS JOHNSON For two coffees and biscuits?

Office.

GLANS Done.

Cartoon.

MISS JOHNSON Done.

VOICE OVER So Miss Johnson returned to her typing and dreamed her little dreamy dreams, unaware as she was of the cruel trick fate had in store for her. For Miss Johnson was about to fall victim of the dreaded international Chinese Communist Conspiracy. *(lots of little yellow men pour into the office)* Yes, these fanatical thieves under the leadership of the so-called Mao Tse-tung *(who appears in the animation)* had caught Miss Johnson off guard for one brief but fatal moment and destroyed her. *(Miss Johnson is submerged in a tide of yellow men)* Just as they are ready to do anytime free men anywhere waver in their defence of democracy.

A sailing ship with American flag sails in over the yellow men. Zoom in on the flag: Uncle Sam appears in front of it.

UNCLE SAM Yes, once again American defence proves its effectiveness against international communism. Using this diagram of a tooth to represent any small country, we can see how international communism works by eroding away from the inside. *(diagram of tooth rotting from inside and collapsing)* When one country or tooth falls victim to international communism, its neighbours soon follow. *(the remaining teeth fall sideways into the gap)* In dentistry, this is known as the Domino Theory. But with American defence the decay is stopped before it starts and that's why nine out of ten small countries choose American defence...

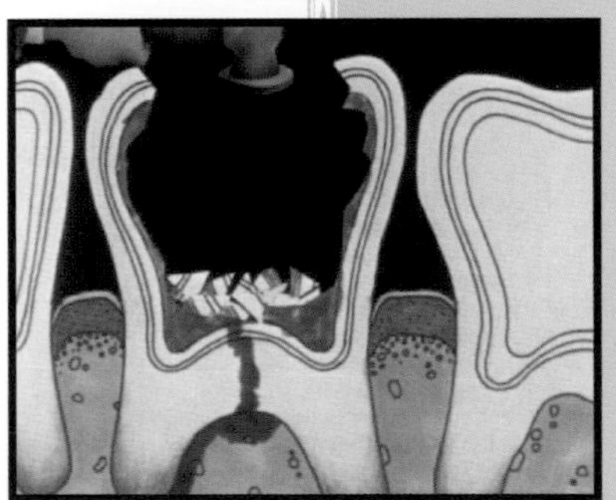

DIFFERENT VOICE OVER ...or Crelm toothpaste with the 'miracle ingredient, Fraudulin'! The white car represents Crelm toothpaste with the miracle ingredient, Fraudulin. *(two cars in a bleak landscape)* The not-white car represents *another* toothpaste. *(the cars race off)* Both toothpastes provide 30% protection. *(they pass a banner: '60% protection')* At 60% protection both toothpastes are doing well. And now at 90% protection the...wait! *(the grey car stops dead at the '90% protection' banner)* The not-white car is out, and

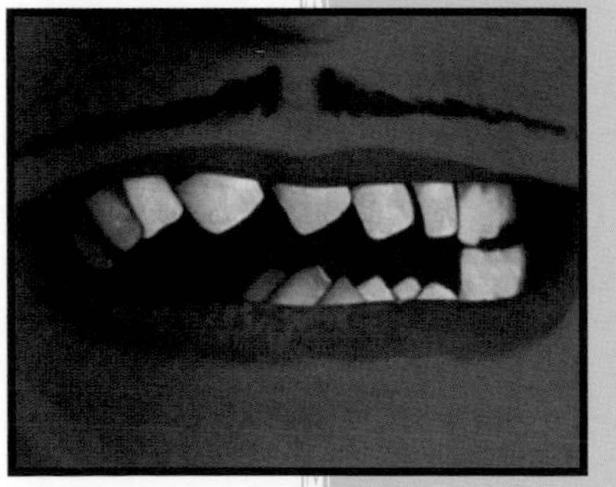

the Crelm toothpaste goes on to win with 100% protection! Yes, do like all smart motorists. Choose Crelm toothpaste.

Cut to 'Shrill' advertising man.

'SHRILL' MAN Or Shrill Petrol with the new additive GLC 9424075. After 6 p.m., 9424047. Using this white card *(half of screen goes white)* to represent engine deposits and this black card *(the other half goes black)* to represent Shrill's new additive GLC 9424075—after 6 p.m., 9424077—we can see how the engine deposits are pushed off the face of the earth by the superior forces available to Shrill. *(shot, off)* Aaaagh!

End of animation. Cut to an upper-class drawing room. An elderly man lies dead on the floor. Enter Jasmina and John.

JASMINA (CAROL CLEVELAND) Anyway, John, you can catch the 11.30 from **Hornchurch** 12 and be in **Basingstoke by one o'clock,** 13 oh, and there's a buffet car and...*(sees corpse)* oh! Daddy!

12

Hornchurch is a large suburban town, now part of greater London, about 15 miles from the center of the capital.

13

Basingstoke is a large town in Hampshire, about 66 miles, as the crow flies, from Hornchurch. Sadly, the crow doesn't fly when you're taking a train, meaning that the trip from Hornchurch to Basingstoke on a train currently stands at least two hours, and probably longer. The trip involves a cross-navigation of London, northeast to southwest, and beyond into Hampshire.

JOHN (ERIC) My hat! Sir Horace!
JASMINA *(not daring to look)* Has he been...
JOHN

YES—AFTER BREAKFAST. BUT THAT DOESN'T MATTER NOW...HE'S DEAD.

JASMINA Oh! Poor daddy...
JOHN Looks like I shan't be catching the 11.30 now.
JASMINA Oh no, John, you mustn't miss your train.
JOHN How could I think of catching a train when I should be here helping you?
JASMINA Oh, John, thank you...anyway you could always catch the 9.30 tomorrow—it goes via **Caterham and Chipstead.** 14
JOHN Or the 9.45's even better.
JASMINA Oh, but you'd have to change at **Lambs Green.** 15
JOHN Yes, but there's only a seven-minute wait now.
JASMINA Oh, yes, of course, I'd forgotten it was Friday. Oh, who could have done this.

14

Caterham and Chipstead are two towns south of London, both with train stations.

Lambs Green is a small town well south of London; it boasts no train station.

Enter Lady Partridge.

LADY PARTRIDGE (GRAHAM) Oh, do hurry Sir Horace, your train leaves in twenty-eight minutes, and if you miss the 10.15 you won't catch the 3.45 which means...oh!

JOHN I'm afraid Sir Horace won't be catching the 10.15, Lady Partridge.
LADY PARTRIDGE Has he been...?
JASMINA Yes—after breakfast.
JOHN Lady Partridge, I'm afraid you can cancel his seat reservation.
LADY PARTRIDGE Oh, and it was back to the engine—fourth coach along so that he could see the gradient signs outside Swanborough.
JOHN Not any more Lady Partridge...the line's been closed.
LADY PARTRIDGE Closed! Not Swanborough!
JOHN I'm afraid so.

Enter Inspector Davis.

INSPECTOR (TERRY J) All right, nobody move. I'm Inspector Davis of Scotland Yard.
JOHN My word, you were here quickly, inspector.
INSPECTOR Yeah, I got the 8.55 Pullman Express from King's Cross and missed that bit around Hornchurch.
LADY PARTRIDGE It's a very good train.
ALL Excellent, very good, delightful.

Tony runs in through the french windows. He wears white flannels and boater and is jolly upper-class.

TONY (MICHAEL) Hello everyone.
ALL Tony!
TONY Where's daddy? *(seeing him)* Oh golly! Has he been...?
JOHN AND JASMINA Yes, after breakfast.
TONY Then...he won't be needing his reservation on the 10.15.
JOHN Exactly.
TONY And I suppose as his eldest son it must go to me.
INSPECTOR Just a minute, Tony. There's a small matter of...murder.
TONY Oh, but surely he simply shot himself and then hid the gun.
LADY PARTRIDGE How could anyone shoot himself and then hide the gun without first cancelling his reservation.
TONY Ha, ha! Well, I must dash or I'll be late for the 10.15.
INSPECTOR I suggest you murdered your father for his seat reservation.
TONY I may have had the motive, inspector, but I could not have done it, for I have only just arrived from **Gillingham** **16** on the 8.13 and here's my restaurant car ticket to prove it.
JASMINA **The 8.13 from Gillingham doesn't have a restaurant car.** **17**
JOHN It's a standing buffet only.
TONY Oh, er...did I say the 8.13, I meant the 7.58 stopping train.
LADY PARTRIDGE But the 7.58 stopping train arrived at **Swindon** **18** at 8.19 owing to annual point maintenance at Wisborough Junction.

Gillingham is a town southeast of London.

This is the kind of train minutia that many British people would have had at their fingertips.

Swindon is a town some 125 miles west of Gillingham. This sketch is now firmly in silly land.

JOHN So how did you make the connection with the 8.13 which left six minutes earlier?
TONY Oh, er, simple! I caught the 7.16 **Football Special** 19 arriving at Swindon at 8.09.
JASMINA But the 7.16 Football Special only stops at Swindon on alternate Saturdays.
LADY PARTRIDGE **Yes, surely you mean the Holidaymaker Special.** 20
TONY Oh, yes! How daft of me. Of course I came on the Holidaymaker Special calling at Bedford, Colmworth, Fen Ditton, Sutton, Wallington and Gillingham.
INSPECTOR That's Sundays only!

TONY Damn. All right, I confess I did it. I killed him for his reservation, but you won't take me alive! I'm going to throw myself under the 10.12 from Reading.
JOHN Don't be a fool, Tony, don't do it, the 10.12 has the new **narrow traction bogies,** 21 you wouldn't stand a chance.
TONY Exactly.

Tableau. Loud chord and slow curtain.

VOICE OVER (JOHN) **That was an excerpt from the latest West End hit 'It all happened on the 11.20 from Hainault to Redhill via Horsham and Reigate, calling at Carshalton Beeches, Malmesbury, Tooting Bec, and Croydon West'.** 22 The author is **Mr Neville Shunt.** 23

Shunt sitting among mass of railway junk, at typewriter, typing away madly.

SHUNT (TERRY G) *(typing)* Chuff, chuff, chuff wooooch, wooooch! Ssssssss, ssssssss! Diddledum, diddledum, diddledum. Toot, toot. The train now standing at platform eight, tch, tch, tch, diddled urn, diddledum. Chuffff chuffffff eeeeeeeeaaaaaaaa Vooooommmmm.

Cut to art critic. Superimposed caption: 'GAVIN MILLARRRRRRRRR'

ART CRITIC (JOHN) Some people have made the mistake of seeing Shunt's work as a load of rubbish about railway timetables, but clever people like me, who talk loudly in restaurants, see this as a deliberate ambiguity, a plea for understanding in a mechanized world. The points are frozen, the beast is dead. What is the difference? What indeed is the point? The point is frozen, the beast is late out of Paddington. The point is taken. If **La Fontaine's elk** 24 would spurn Tom Jones the engine must be our head, the dining car our oesophagus, the guard's van our left lung, the cattle truck our shins, the first-class compartment

"Football Specials" were trains dedicated to moving soccer fans around the country, and thereby ran only on Saturdays, then the traditional day for soccer games.

As the name suggests, the "Holidaymaker Special" moved the vacationing hordes to the coasts.

"Bogies" are the framework that holds the train's wheels.

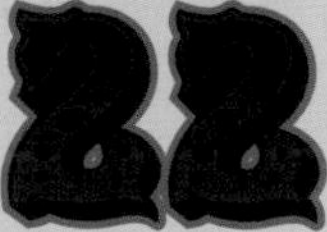

Hainault, Redhill, Horsham, Reigate, and Carshalton Beeches are all towns south of London. Tooting Bec and Croydon West are parts of London proper. Malmesbury is a town a town way west, beyond Swindon. At over 80 miles from London, this town stands out as bogus . . .

"Mr. Neville Shunt" is a joke on the name of the British-Australian novelist Nevil Shute. A "shunt" is the British term for a small train that organizes individual train carriages into a cogent set (it's called a switcher in the U.S.). These locomotives don't go very far, as they are generally have low power.

Jean de La Fontaine was a seventeenth-century French fable writer and poet.

the piece of skin at the nape of the neck and the level crossing **an electric elk called Simon.** **25** The clarity is devastating. But where is the ambiguity? It's over there in a box. Shunt is saying the 8.15 from Gillingham when in reality he means the *8.13* from Gillingham. The train is the same only the time is altered. **Ecce homo, ergo elk.** **26** La Fontaine knew his sister and knew her bloody well. The point is taken, the beast is moulting, the fluff gets up your nose. The illusion is complete; it is reality, the reality is illusion and the ambiguity is the only truth. But is the truth, as Hitchcock observes, in the box? No there isn't room, the ambiguity has put on weight. The point is taken, the elk is dead, the beast stops at Swindon, **Chabrol stops at nothing,** **27** I'm having treatment and **La Fontaine can get knotted.** **28**

Cut to man at desk.

MAN (MICHAEL) Gavin Millar...

Cut to another man.

ANOTHER MAN (TERRY J) ...rrrrrrr...

Cut to first man.

MAN ...was not talking to Neville Shunt. From the world of the theatre we turn to the world of dental hygiene. No, no, no, no. From the world of the theatre we turn to the silver screen. We honour one of the silver screen's outstanding writer-dentists...writer-*directors*, Martin Curry who is visiting London to have a tooth out, for the pre-molar, er...*première* of his filling, film next Toothday...Tuesday, at the Dental Theatre...*Film* Theatre. Martin Curry talking to Matthew Palate...*Padget*.

Cut to late-night line-up setting. Interviewer and interviewee.

PADGET (TERRY J) Martin Curry, welcome. One of the big teeth...big points that the American critics made about your latest film, **'The Twelve Caesars'**, **29** was that it was on so all-embracing a topic. What made you undertake so enormous a tusk...task?

We now see that his interviewee has two enormous front teeth. **30**

Gerald Nabarro has a shrimp named Simon, according to Episode 23.

"Ecce homo" ("behold the man") are the words said by Pontius Pilate as he presents the prisoner Jesus to the assembled crowd in John 19:5.

Claude Chabrol, French New Wave movie director, 1930–2010.

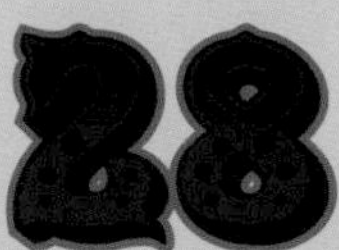

The British "get knotted" is a more genteel way of telling someone to "eff" off.

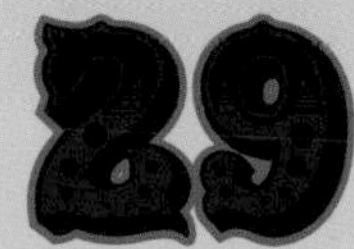

The Twelve Caesars is a set of 12 biographies of Julius Caesar and the first 11 emperors of the Roman Empire, written in 121 AD by Gaius Seutonius Tranquilus, personal secretary to Emperor Hadrian.

His teeth extend, wonderfully, below his chin—and, this being Britain, are quite yellow.

Vespasian, the emperor of Rome from 69 to 79 AD.

Caractacus was the chieftain of the Catuvellauni tribe and leader of the British resistance to Rome. He was "king of the Britons" from 43 to 50 AD.

CURRY (GRAHAM) Well I've always been interested in Imperial Rome from Julius Caesar right through to Vethpathian.

PADGET Who?

CURRY Vethpathian.

PADGET Ah! ***Vespasian.*** **31**

CURRY Yes.

PADGET When I saw your film it did seem to me that you had taken a rather, um, subjective approach to it.

CURRY I'm sorry?

PADGET Well, I mean all your main characters had these enormous...well not enormous, these very big...well let's have a look at a clip in which Julius Incisor...*Caesar* talks to his generals during the battle against **Caractacus.** **32**

CURRY I don't see that at all.

Film: interior of a tent; generals around a table.

LABIENUS (TERRY J) *(with relatively enormous front teeth)* Shall I order the cavalry that they may hide themselves in the wood, O Caesar?

ALL *(with very large front teeth)* Thus O Caesar.

JULIUS (GRAHAM) *(with amazingly large front teeth)* Today is about to be a triumph for our native country.

Back to interview set.

PADGET

MARTIN CURRY, WHY DO ALL YOUR CHARACTERS HAVE THESE VERY BIG, ER, VERY BIG, UM, TEETH?

CURRY What do you mean?

PADGET Well, I mean, er...and even in your biblical epic, 'The Son of Man', John the Baptist had the most enormous... dental appendages... and of course... himself had the most monumental ivories.

CURRY No, I'm afraid I don't see that at all. *(picks up glass of water but can't get it to his mouth)* Could I have a straw?

PADGET Oh, a straw, yes, yes. Well, while we're doing that perhaps we could take another look at an earlier film, 'Trafalgar'.

Between decks. Nelson lying among others. They all have enormous teeth.

NELSON (ERIC) Cover my coat, Mr Bush, the men must not know of this till victory is ours.

TOAD (TERRY J) The surgeon's coming, sir.

NELSON No, tell the surgeon to attend the men that can be saved. He can do little for me, I fear.

TOAD Aye, aye, sir.

NELSON Hardy! Hardy!

HARDY (MICHAEL) Sir?

NELSON Hardy...kiss...er...put your hand on my thigh.

Back to interview set. Curry is sitting practically upside down, trying to drink water with much difficulty.

PADGET Martin Curry, thank you. Well. We asked the first-night audience what they thought of that film.

Cut to vox pops.

MAN WITH ENORMOUS EARS (JOHN) It wasn't true to life.

MAN WITH ENORMOUS TEETH (TERRY J) Yes it was.

MAN WITH ENORMOUS NOSE (ERIC) No it wasn't.

MADLY DRESSED MAN (GRAHAM) I thought it was totally bizarre.

FIRST CITY GENT (MICHAEL) Well I've been in the city for over forty years and I think the importance of looking after poor people cannot be understressed.

SECOND CITY GENT (GRAHAM) Well I've been in the city for twenty years and I must admit—I'm lost.

AN OLD GRAMOPHONE (JOHN) Well, I've been in the city all my life and I'm as alert and active as I've ever been.

THIRD CITY GENT (ERIC) Well I've been in the city since I was two and I certainly wouldn't say that I was stuck in a rut...stuck in a rut...stuck in a rut...stuck in a rut...

WOMAN (TERRY J) Oh dear, Mr Bulstrode's stuck again.

Jones merely stands watching Idle be stuck in a rut, then he punches his arm.

She runs over and gives him a shove.

THIRD CITY GENT **I certainly wouldn't say that I was stuck in a rut.** **33**

FOURTH CITY GENT (JOHN) Well I've been in the city for thirty years and I've never once regretted being a nasty, greedy, cold hearted, avaricious, money-grubber...*Conservative.*

FIFTH CITY GENT (TERRY J) **Well I've been in the city for twenty-seven years and I would like to see the reintroduction of flogging.** **34** Every Thursday, round at my place.

MAN (JOHN) *(whose head only is visible above the level of the sea)* Well I've been in the sea for thirty-three years and I've never regretted it.

Camera pulls back to reveal other city gents also with only heads and bowlers visible who say 'quite agree'. Camera pulls back further to reveal an elderly couple sitting in deckchairs.

MAN I think it must be a naturalist outing.

WOMAN I think it must be one of them crackpot religions.

Cut to Arthur Crackpot sitting at a large curved desk on the front of which a sign says 'Crackpot Religions Ltd. Arthur Crackpot President and God (Ltd)'.

CRACKPOT (ERIC) This is an example of the sort of abuse we get all the time from ignorant people. I inherited this religion from my father, an ex-used-car salesman and part-time window-box, and I am very proud to be in charge of the first religion with free gifts. You get this luxury tea-trolley with every new enrolment. *(pictures of this and the subsequent gifts)* In addition to this you can win a three-piece lounge suite, this luxury caravan, a weekend for two with **Peter Bonetti** **35** and tonight's star prize, the entire Norwich City Council.

Curtains go up to reveal the council. Terrific 'ooh' from an audience. Bad organ chords played by a nude man (TERRY G).

CRACKPOT **And remember with only eight scoring draws you can win a bishopric in a see of your own choice.** **36** You see we have a much more modern approach to religion.

Cut to a person in church. They are walking past a pillar. They take out some money and put it in a collecting box. A sign on the box says 'for the rich'. We hear the money going in, then it moves off, along pipes, falling down; eventually it comes down a small pipe and lands with a tinkle in Crackpot's ashtray. He tries the money with his teeth, pops it into his pocket, and finishes reading...

The standard hope of a certain type of Brit worried by the rise in crime. Flogging, as well as other forms of corporal punishment, was officially abolished in British jails only as late as 1948. Before that, it was widely used as punishment, especially until the end of World War I.

Peter Bonetti, goalkeeper for Chelsea and England soccer teams. Nicknamed "the Cat," he played 600 times (in two spells, the first of which ran for fifteen years until 1975) for the London club, and seven times for England between 1966 and 1970.

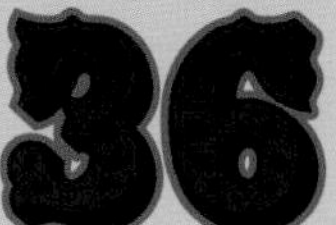

"Eight scoring draws" is a reference to the Football Pools, a nationwide competition in which people choose the games they believe will end in ties, or draws. To pick eight scoring draws correctly usually means you've won the pools, the equivalent of winning the lottery.

CRACKPOT Blessed is Arthur Crackpot and all his subsidiaries Ltd. You see, in our Church we have a lot more fun.

PRIEST (JOHN) *(we see he has a pepperpot with him)* Oh, Mrs Collins, you did say you were nervous, didn't you? You have eyes on the coffee machine?

MRS COLLINS (MICHAEL) I don't mind, I don't mind—it's just nice to be here, Reverend.

PRIEST *(slaps her)* Archdeacon. You asked for the coffee machine...so let's see what you've won? You chose Hymn no. 437. *(goes to hymn board, removes one of the numbers, and reads what's on the back)* Oh, Mrs Collins, you had eyes on the coffee machine. Well you have won tonight's star prize: the entire Norwich City Council.

Organ music, oohs and applause from audience.

MRS COLLINS I've got one already. *(the priest starts to throttle her)*

Cut back to Crackpot in his office.

CRACKPOT A lot of religions—no names no **pack drill—** **37** do go for the poorer type of person—face it, there's more of 'em—poor people, thieves, villains, poor people without no money at all—well we don't have none of **that tat.** **38** Rich people and **crumpet** **39** over sixteen can enter free: upper middle class quite welcome; lower middle class not under five grand a year. Lower class—I can't touch it. There's no return on it, you see.

Pull back to show interviewer sitting at his side.

INTERVIEWER (CAROL) Do you have any difficulty converting people?

CRACKPOT Oh no, well we have ways of making them join.

Cut to a photo of a bishop (GRAHAM). *Superimposed caption: 'THE BISHOP OF DULWICH'*

CRACKPOT'S VOICE Norman there does a lot of converting: a lot of protection, that sort of thing. And there's his mate, Bruce Beer.

Photo of Aussie bishop with beer can (JOHN). *Superimposed caption: 'THE BISHOP OF AUSTRALIA'*

CRACKPOT'S VOICE Brucie has personally converted ninety-two people—twenty-five inside the distance. Then again we're not afraid to use more modern methods.

Cut to 'Daily Mirror' type pin-up of a bikinied lovely in a silly pose, on a beach with a bishop's mitre and Bible. A large headline reads: 'North See Gas'. A subheading says 'Bishop Sarah', then below that, this blurb which is also read voice over. **40**

"Pack drill" was punishment meted out to British soldiers for misbehaviors—the exercise was performed in full uniform with a heavy pack on the back. Here it means "keep quiet and no one gets punished."

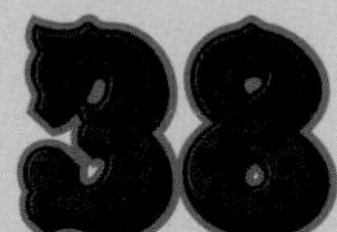

"That tat" is British slang for cheap stuff.

A "crumpet" is British slang for a sexually attractive woman.

TRAGEDY OF A NEWLY-WED DRUG ADDICT

NORTH SEE GAS

Deaf woman wins a degree by lip reading

NNA RISKS JAIL FOR UDE PART IN FILM

BISHOP SARAH

The *Daily Mirror* is a British tabloid newspaper.

VOICE OVER (JOHN) Sarah, today's diocesan lovely is enough to make any chap go down on his knees. This twenty-three-year-old bishop hails appropriately enough from Bishop's Stortford and lists her hobbies as swimming, riding, and film producers. What a gas! Bet she's no novice when it comes to converting all in her See.

Cut to Gumby in street. Superimposed caption: 'ARCHBISHOP GUMBY'

GUMBY (MICHAEL) *(shouting laboriously)*

BASICALLY, I BELIEVE IN PEACE AND BASHING TWO BRICKS TOGETHER.

(he bashes two bricks together) Cut to John Lennon.

LENNON (ERIC) **I'm starting a war for peace. 41 42**

41

Idle does a fabulous impersonation of Lennon, here, replete with a very good Scouse (Liverpool) accent.

In 1970 Lennon released his first solo album, *John Lennon/Plastic Ono Band*. By this time he had been identified with peace activism—"Give Peace a Chance" was released in 1969—and he and his wife, Yoko Ono, had staged two bed-ins for peace in the same year.

Cut to Ken Shabby. Superimposed caption: 'ARCHBISHOP SHABBY'

SHABBY (MICHAEL) Cor blimey. I'm raising polecats for peace.

Cut to Arthur Nudge. Superimposed caption: 'ARCHBISHOP NUDGE'

NUDGE (ERIC) Peace? I like a peace. Know what I mean? Know what I mean? Say no more. Nudge, nudge.

Cut to a bishop. A sign on the wall says 'NAUGHTY RELIGION'.

BISHOP (JOHN) *(porn-merchant style)* Our religion is the first Church to cater for the naughty type of person. If you'd like a bit of love-your-neighbour—and who doesn't now and again—then see Vera and Ciceley during the hymns.

Cut to wide-boy type, **43** *with small moustache and* ***kipper tie.*** **44** *A sign says: 'NO QUESTIONS ASKED RELIGION'.*

"Wide boy" is British slang for someone who's a bit unscrupulous—a man who'd sell you a used car, who can always do you a deal. And usually Cockney too, with a broad London accent as here.

BILL (MICHAEL) In our Church we try to help people to help themselves—to cars, washing machines, lead piping, no questions asked. We are the only Church, apart from the Baptists, to do respray jobs.

Cut to loony with a fright wig and an axe in his head. A sign says: 'THE LUNATIC RELIGION'.

ALI BYAN (TERRY J) We the Church of the Divine Loony believe in the power of prayer to turn the head purple ha, ha, ha.

Cut to a normal looking priest. A sign says: 'THE MOST POPULAR RELIGION LTD'.

PRIEST (GRAHAM) I would like to come in here for a moment if I may, and disassociate our Church from these frivolous and offensive religions. We are primarily concerned with what is best...*(phone rings; he answers it)* Hello. Oh, well how about **Allied Breweries?** **45** All right but keep the **Rio Tinto** **46** *(phone down)*...or the human soul.

Animation: a vicar c/o Terry Gilliam. Caption: 'CARTOON RELIGIONS LTD'

VOICE In our Church we believe first and foremost in you. *(he smiles; the top of his head comes off and the Devil tries to climb out; the vicar replaces his head)* We want you to think of us as your friend. *(as before; the vicar nails the top of his head on)*

Cut to a wide-angle shot of hedgerows, fields and trees.

VOICE OVER (JOHN) In this picture there are forty people. None of them can be seen. In this film we hope to show you how not to be seen.

Caption: 'HM GOVERNMENT, PUBLIC SERVICE FILM NO. 42 PARA 6. "HOW NOT TO BE SEEN"'

VOICE OVER **This is Mr E. R. Bradshaw, of Napier Court, Black Lion Road, SE5.** **47** He cannot be seen. Now I'm going to ask him to stand up. Mr Bradshaw will you stand up please?

In the middle distance a smiling holidaymaker in braces, collarless shirt and hankie, stands up. There is a pause. Only the sound of the wind. Then a loud gunshot rings out. Mr Bradshaw crumples to the ground.

VOICE OVER This demonstrates the value of not being seen.

Cut to another location—this time an empty stretch of scrubland.

VOICE OVER In this picture we cannot see **Mrs B. J. Smegma.** **48** of 13, The Crescent, **Belmont** **49** Mrs Smegma will you stand up please.

There is a pause. Almost on the edge of frame in the distance a pepperpot stands up, proudly. Immediately a shot rings out and she leaps in the air and dies. Cut to a bush some distance away on open land.

A "kipper tie" is an excessively wide tie. Sadly, he's actually wearing a dog collar and black shirt, with a wide boy–type overcoat only. He also does not have a mustache.

Allied Breweries is company formed in 1961 from the merger of three major brewers of beer in the U.K.: Ansells, Ind Coope, and Tetley Walker.

Rio Tinto is a huge conglomerate with exploration, mining, and processing at its core. Here, Chapman is buying and selling stocks as he holds a copy of the *Financial Times*.

There is a Black Lion Lane in London, but it is in London W6. There are a bunch of Napier Courts in London, but none in SE5.

"Smegma"—surely one of the world's grossest words, especially when allied with the initials "B.J."

Belmont is a small town northwest of Manchester.

Harlow is a town northeast of London. Oswestry is a town in the west of England, near the Welsh border.

Slough is an industrial town 22 miles west of London, and a byword in England for an ugly, unattractive place. Poet John Betjeman, aghast at the rise of factories there, famously wrote in 1937 "Come friendly bombs and fall on Slough!"

Hull is the town 60 miles east of everywhere in the north of England.

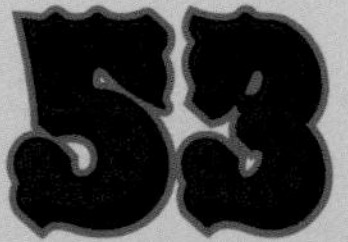

The tame joke gets a long laugh, forcing Palin to pause.

Again, a tame and more traditional gag gets a longer laugh than much of the wacky stuff preceding it.

VOICE OVER **This is Mr Nesbitt of Harlow New Town.** **50** Mr Nesbitt would you stand up please *(nothing happens)*. Mr Nesbitt has learnt the first lesson of not being seen—not to stand up. However, he has chosen a very obvious piece of cover. *(the bush explodes; cut to a shot of three bushes)* Mr E. V. Lambert, of 'Homeleigh', The Burrows, Oswestry, has presented us with a poser. We do not know which bush he is behind, but we can soon find out. *(the left-hand bush explodes, then the right-hand bush; finally the middle bush explodes; there is a muffled scream; the smoke subsides)* Yes, it was the middle one.

Cut to shot of farmland. There is a waterbutt, a low wall, a big pile of leaves, a bushy tree, a parked car and lots of bushes and trees in the distance.

VOICE OVER Mr Ken Andrews, of Leighton Road, **Slough,** **51** has concealed himself extremely well. He could be almost anywhere. He could be behind the wall, inside the water barrel, beneath a pile of leaves, up in the tree, squatting down behind the car, concealed in a hollow, or crouched behind anyone of a hundred bushes. However, we happen to know he's in the water barrel.

The water barrel just blows apart in the biggest explosion yet. Cut to a panning shot from beach huts across to beach and sea.

VOICE OVER Mr and Mrs Watson of 'Ivy Cottage', Worplesdon Road, **Hull,** **52** chose a very cunning way of not being seen. When we called at their house, we found they had gone away on two weeks' holiday. They had not left any forwarding address, and they had bolted and barred the house to prevent us getting in. However, a neighbour told us where they were.

The camera has come to rest on a very obvious isolated beach hut; it blows up. Cut to a building site in a suburban housing estate. There is a gumby standing there.

VOICE OVER And here is the neighbour who told us where they were...*(he blows up)* Nobody likes a clever dick. *(cut to stock film of a small house)* And this is where he lived. *(it blows up)* And this is where Lord Langdon lived who refused to speak to us. *(it blows up)* and so did the gentlemen who lived here...*(shot of house: it blows up)*...and here...*(ditto)* and of course here...*(series of quick cuts of various atom bombs and hydrogen bomb at moment of impact)* and Manchester and the West Midlands, Spain, China ... *(mad laugh)*

Cut to a presentation desk. The film is on a screen behind. We see it stop behind him as the presenter speaks.

PRESENTER (MICHAEL) Ah, well I'm afraid we have to stop the film there, as some of the scenes which followed were of a violent nature which might have proved distressing to some of our viewers. Though not to me, I can tell you. *(cut to another camera; the presenter turns to face it)* In Nova Scotia today, Mr Roy Bent of North Walsham in Norfolk became the first man to cross the Atlantic on a tricycle. His tricycle, specially adapted for the crossing, was ninety feet long, with a protective steel hull, three funnels, seventeen first-class cabins and a radar scanner. ***(A head and shoulders picture of Roy Bent comes up on the screen behind him)*** **Mr Bent is in our Durham studios, which is rather unfortunate as we're all down here in London.** **53** **And in London I have with me Mr Ludovic Grayson, the man who scored all six goals in Arsenal's 1-0 victory** **54** over the Turkish Champions FC Botty. *(he turns)* Ludovic...*(pull out to reveal that he is talking to a five-foot-high filing cabinet)* first of all congratulations on the victory.

VOICE (TERRY J) *(from inside filing cabinet)* **Thank you, David.** **55**

PRESENTER It should send you back to Botty with a big lead.

VOICE Oh yes, well we're fairly confident, David.

PRESENTER

WELL AT THE MOMENT, LUDOVIC, YOU'RE CROUCHING DOWN INSIDE A FILING CABINET.

VOICE Yes that's right, David, I'm trying not to be seen.

PRESENTER I see. Is this through fear?

VOICE Oh no, no, it's common sense really. If they can't see you, they can't get you.

PRESENTER Ha, ha, ha, but of course they can still hear you. *(the filing cabinet explodes)* Ludovic Grayson, thank you very much for coming on the programme tonight. And we end the show with music. **And here with their very latest recording 'Yummy, Yummy, Yummy, I've got love in my tummy'** **56** **Jackie Charlton and the Tonettes.** **57**

Cut to a trendy pop-music set with coloured lights, etc. On the main podium is a large packing crate with a microphone in front of it. The backing vocal is by three more packing crates with microphones. The instrumental group are also in crates.

We hear the aforementioned pop song. Roll credits over. Fade out. Cut to BBC 1 caption.

VOICE OVER (ERIC) For those of you who may have just missed 'Monty Python's Flying Circus', here it is again.

Entire show is recapped in a series of flash clips lasting about twenty seconds.

55

Palin is close to losing it here, perhaps because he knows his next line.

"Yummy Yummy Yummy" is a hit song from the Ohio Express, released in 1968.

Jackie Charlton was an England and Leeds United defender and brother of Bobby Charlton, famed England and Manchester United player. Jackie went on to manage the Irish national team at the 1990 World Cup finals in Italy.

SEA
SON
2
EPISODE 25

SPAM
FEATURING
THE BLACK EAGLE
DIRTY HUNGARIAN PHRASEBOOK
COURT (PHRASEBOOK)
COMMUNIST QUIZ ✽ 'YPRES 1914'—ABANDONED
ART GALLERY STRIKE ✽ YPRES 1914
'Ypres 1914'
HOSPITAL FOR OVER-ACTORS
GUMBY FLOWER ARRANGING ✽ SPAM
GRAOO
FULG
NOW

FIRST AIRED: DECEMBER 15, 1970

Close up of a flag bearing a black eagle on a red background fluttering in the wind. Blue sky behind and scudding clouds. Adventure music as for buccaneer film. Captions:

THE BLACK EAGLE

CAST

BLACK EAGLE . . . . THORNTON WELLES
MEG FAIRWEATHER . . . . KATE TAMBLYING
JACK FAIRWEATHER . . . . . . OWEN TREGOWER
HENRY FAIRWEATHER . . . . . RUSS TEMPOLE JNR.
MRS FAIRWEATHER . . . . ALICE SHOEMAKER
DR TENNYSON . . . . MARSHALL M. WEST
LUMPKIN . . . . DINO DE VERE
MR RIVERS . . . . WALTER SCHENKEL
LT STAVEACRE . . . . NORMAL S. HUGHES
A WENCH . . . . MARSHA SUTTON
SECOND WENCH . . . . TINEA PEDIS
THE DOG . . . . KARL

SCREENPLAY BY AL R. SCHROEDER AND WAYNE KOPIT
BASED ON THE NOVEL 'THE BLUE EAGLE' BY RAPHAEL SABATINI 1

1 Rafael Sabatini was an Italian-English writer of adventure novels and romances. He never wrote a book called *The Blue Eagle*.

SET DECORATION . . . . CY BORGONI
MAKE-UP . . . . BUNICE DILKES
COSTUMES . . . . JOAN LOUIS
UNIT MANAGER . . . . TREVOR BELOWSKI
CONTINUITY . . . . SUE CARPENTER
SPECIAL EFFECTS . . . . WALTER SCHENKEL

MISS TAMBLYING'S GOWNS BY HEPWORTHS
COLOUR BY CHROMACOLOUR
SOUND RECORDING WCA SYSTEM
COPYRIGHT BY SCHENKEL PRODUCTIONS
ANY SIMILARITY BETWEEN PERSONS LIVING OR DEAD IS COINCIDENTAL

PRODUCED BY JOSEPH M. SCHLACK

DIRECTED BY LAURENT F. NORDER.

Mix through from flag to sea at night. Sound of water lapping. Soft sound of muffled oars drawing nearer. We can see a rowing boat making slowly and silently towards the shore where the camera is. The stirring music continues. Roller caption: 'IN 1742 THE SPANISH EMPIRE LAY IN RUINS. TORN BY INTERNAL DISSENT, AND WRACKED BY NUMEROUS WARS, ITS RICH TRADE ROUTES FELL AN EASY PREY TO BRITISH PRIVATEERS...AND THE TREASURE OF THE SPANISH MAIN WAS BROUGHT HOME TO THE SHORES OF ENGLAND' By the time the roller captions have finished the rowing boat has approached much nearer. It stops and they ship their oars. Cut in to close ups of pirate's face peering into the darkness. Shot from the boat of a deserted cliff top. A light flashes twice. Then there is a pause. Cut back to the boat; the men look uneasy as they wait for the third flash. Cut back to the cliff...at last the third flash. Cut back to the boat; they start to row again. Cut to them beaching the boat on the shore. They start to unload sacks and chests. Putting them onto their shoulders they start to walk along the shore line. We pan with them for quite some way...and suddenly between the camera and the pirates we come across the announcer at a desk. He wears a dinner jacket and shuffles some papers in front of him.

ANNOUNCER (JOHN) And now for something completely different...

IT'S MAN (MICHAEL)

IT'S...

Animated titles.

Cut to a small tobacconist's shop. The tobacconist is handing change to a fireman.

FIREMAN (MICHAEL) Thank you very much for the change, Mr Tobacconist. *(he exits; then out of vision, very loud)* Was that all right?

EVERYBODY SSSh!

Stirring adventure music of buccaneer film as at the beginning and the roller caption in the same typeface. Roller caption: IN 1970, THE BRITISH EMPIRE LAY IN RUINS, FOREIGN NATIONALS FREQUENTED THE STREETS—MANY OF THEM HUNGARIANS (NOT THE STREETS—THE FOREIGN NATIONALS). ANYWAY, MANY OF THESE HUNGARIANS WENT INTO TOBACCONIST'S SHOPS TO BUY CIGARETTES... Enter Hungarian gentleman with phrase book. He is looking for the right phrase.

HUNGARIAN (JOHN) **I will not buy this record. It is scratched.** [2]

TOBACCONIST (TERRY J) Sorry?

HUNGARIAN I will not buy this record. It is scratched.

TOBACCONIST No, no, no. This...tobacconist's.

HUNGARIAN Ah! I will not buy this tobacconist's. It is scratched.

2

Well before the days of MPEGs and digital downloads, there were vinyl records—and any music buff worth his salt would check a record for scratches before purchasing.

TOBACCONIST No, no, no...tobacco...er, cigarettes?
HUNGARIAN Yes, cigarettes. My hovercraft is full of eels.
TOBACCONIST What?
HUNGARIAN *(miming matches)* My hovercraft is full of eels.
TOBACCONIST Matches, matches? *(showing some)*
HUNGARIAN Yah, yah. *(he takes cigarettes and matches and pulls out loose change; he consults his book)* Er, do you want...do you want to come back to my place, bouncy bouncy?
TOBACCONIST I don't think you're using that right.
HUNGARIAN You great pouf.
TOBACCONIST That'll be six and six please.
HUNGARIAN If I said you had a beautiful body **would you hold it against me?** 3 I am no longer infected.
TOBACCONIST *(miming that he wants to see the book; he takes the book)* It costs six and six...*(mumbling as he searches)* Costs six and six...Here we are...Yandelvayasna grldenwi stravenka.

Hungarian hits him between the eyes. Policeman walking along street suddenly stops and puts his hand to his ear. He starts running down the street, round corner and down another street, round yet another corner and down another street into the shop.

POLICEMAN (GRAHAM) What's going on here then?
HUNGARIAN *(opening book and pointing at tobacconist)* You have beautiful thighs.
POLICEMAN What?
TOBACCONIST He hit me.
HUNGARIAN Drop your panties, Sir William, I cannot wait till lunchtime.
POLICEMAN Right! *(grabs him and drags him out)*
HUNGARIAN My nipples explode with delight.

Cut to a courtroom.

CLERK (ERIC) Call Alexander Yahlt.
VOICES Call Alexander Yahlt. Call Alexander Yahlt. Call Alexander Yahlt.

They do this three times finishing with harmony.

MAGISTRATE (TERRY J) Oh shut up.

Alexander Yahlt enters. He is not Hungarian but an ordinary man in a mac.

CLERK You are Alexander Yahlt?
YAHLT (MICHAEL) *(**Derek Nimmo's voice** 4 (dubbed on))* Oh I am.
CLERK Skip the impersonations. You are Alexander Yahlt?

The song by the Bellamy Brothers of the same name wouldn't be a hit until 1979.

Derek Nimmo is a British actor who often portrayed upper-class twits owing to his extremely "plummy" accent further affected by a lisp. Palin does a fabulous impersonation of him, if all too briefly. Impersonations are out of favor with the Pythons.

YAHLT *(normal voice)* I am.

CLERK **You are hereby charged that on the 28th day of May 1970 you did willfully, unlawfully and with malice aforethought** [5] publish an alleged English-Hungarian phrase book with intent to cause a breach of the peace. How do you plead?

YAHLT Not guilty.

CLERK You live at 46, Horton Terrace?

YAHLT I do live at 46, Horton Terrace.

CLERK You are the director of a publishing company?

YAHLT I am the director of a publishing company.

CLERK Your company publishes phrasebooks?

YAHLT My company does publish phrasebooks.

CLERK You did say 46, Horton Terrace didn't you?

YAHLT Yes.

He claps his hand to his mouth; gong sounds—general applause.

CLERK Ha, ha, ha, I got him.

MAGISTRATE Get on with it! Get on with it!

CLERK Yes m'lud, on the 28th of May you published this phrasebook.

YAHLT I did.

CLERK

I QUOTE AN EXAMPLE. THE HUNGARIAN PHRASE MEANING 'CAN YOU DIRECT ME TO THE STATION' IS TRANSLATED BY THE ENGLISH PHRASE 'PLEASE FONDLE MY BUM'.

YAHLT I wish to plead incompetence.

The policeman stands up.

POLICEMAN Please may I ask for an adjournment, m'lud?

MAGISTRATE An adjournment? Certainly not. *(the policeman sits down; there is a loud raspberry; the policeman goes bright red)* Why on earth didn't you say why you wanted an adjournment?

POLICEMAN I didn't know an acceptable legal phrase, m'lud.

5

In criminal law, "aforethought" means "premeditated."

6

This is satire on the type of writing one might find in *The Sun* next to a picture of a topless woman. "Page Three girls" are featured to this day (their naked photos appear daily on that page), and they are always described in a wholesome but nudge-nudge kind of way.

Esher is yet another reference to the town southwest of London, and Exeter is a large town in the southwest of England.

There are four "Inns of Court" in the U.K., and all barristers (a kind of lawyer) must be a member of one of them. Basically, they are the professional association for such lawyers. Gray's Inn dates back to around the year 1370 and is based in the center of London.

"The Hammers" are, in fact, West Ham United.

Cut to stock film of Women's Institute applauding. Cut back to the magistrate.

MAGISTRATE If there's any more stock film of women applauding I shall clear the court.
CLERK Call Abigail Tesler.

Two policemen carry a large photo blow-up the size of a door. It is a photo from a newspaper like the 'Mirror', with a girl in a bikini and the headline across the top: 'Sunshine Sizzler'. Underneath is some small print which is later read out (see below). They prop her up in the witness box.

DEFENCE (JOHN) M'lud—this is Abigail Tesler.
MAGISTRATE Is it?
DEFENCE **Yes, m'lud. Twenty-three-year-old Abigail hails from down under, where they're upside down about her. Those Aussies certainly know a thing or two when it comes to beach belles. Bet some life-saver wouldn't mind giving her the kiss of life. So watch out for sharks, Abigail!** [6]

Cut back to the judge's desk. The judge has turned into a similar photo blow-up of himself the size of a door. The headline at the top is 'Legal Sizzler'.

JOURNALIST (ERIC) *(voice over)* Is this strictly relevant? quizzed learned lovely, Justice Maltravers. **Seventy-eight-year-old Justice hails from Esher, and he's been making a big name for himself at the recent Assizes at Exeter.** [7] *(cut back to defence counsel, who has turned into a large photo blow-up of himself headed 'Defence Counsel Sizzler')*
VOICE OVER (MICHAEL) All will be revealed soon m'lud, quipped tall forty-two-year-old Nelson Bedowes. Cutie QC Nelson's keen on negligence and grievous bodily harm at **Gray's Inn.** [8] And with cases like he's won we bet Gray's in when Nelson's around.

Animation: starting with newspaper photo of judge in dark glasses and full wig and robes with a starlet beside him, walking down London airport departure corridor carrying cases.

VOICE OVER (ERIC) Well get on with it, admitted seventy-eight-year-old genial jurisprude Maltravers seen here at London airport, on his way to judge for Britain at the famous International Court in the Hague...
VOICE Get off!

Caption: 'WORLD FORUM'

An important-looking current affairs set. On the back wall behind the presenter huge letters say: 'WORLD FORUM'

PRESENTER (ERIC) Good evening. Tonight is indeed a unique occasion in the history of television. We are very privileged, and deeply honoured to have with us in the studio, Karl Marx, founder of modern socialism, and author of the 'Communist Manifesto'. *(Karl Marx is sitting at a desk; he nods)* Vladimir Ilich Ulyanov, better known to the world as Lenin, leader of the Russian Revolution, writer, statesman, and father of modern communism. *(shot of Lenin also at desk; he nods)* Che Guevara, the Cuban guerrilla leader. *(shot of Guevara)* And Mao Tse-tung, leader of the Chinese Communist Party since 1949. *(shot of Mao; the presenter picks up a card)* And the first question is for you, Karl Marx. The Hammers—the Hammers is the nickname of what English football team? **The Hammers?** 9 *(shot of Karl Marx furrowing his brow—obviously he hasn't a clue)* No? Well bad luck there, Karl. So we'll go onto you Che. Che Guevara—**Coventry City last won the FA Cup in what year?** 10 *(cut to Che looking equally dumbfounded)* No? I'll throw it open. Coventry City last won the FA Cup in what year? *(they all look blank)* No? Well, I'm not surprised you didn't get that. It was in fact a trick question. Coventry City have *never* won the FA Cup. So with the scores all equal now we go onto our second round, and Lenin it's your **starter for ten.** 11 Teddy Johnson and Pearl Carr won the Eurovision Song Contest in 1959. What was the name of the song?...Teddy Johnson and Pearl Carr's song **in the 1959 Eurovision Song Contest?** 12 Anybody? *(buzzer goes à la 'University Challenge': zoom in on Mao Tse-tung)* Yes, Mao Tse-tung?

MAO TSE-TUNG

'SING LITTLE BIRDIE'? 13

PRESENTER Yes it was indeed. Well challenged. *(applause)* Well now we come on to our special gift section. The contestant is Karl Marx and the prize this week is a beautiful lounge suite. *(curtains behind the presenter sweep open to reveal a beautiful lounge suite; terrific audience applause; Karl comes out and stands in front of this display; the presenter treats him with Michael Miles unctuousness)* Now Karl has elected to answer questions on the workers' control of factories so here we go with question number one. Are you nervous? *(Karl nods his head; the presenter reads from a card)* The development of the industrial proletariat is conditioned by what other development?

KARL (TERRY J) The development of the industrial bourgeoisie. *(applause)*

PRESENTER Yes, yes, it is indeed. You're on your way to the lounge suite, Karl. Question number two. The struggle of class against class is a what struggle? A what struggle?

KARL A political struggle.

Tumultuous applause.

PRESENTER Yes, yes! One final question Karl and the beautiful lounge suite will be yours...Are you going to have a go? *(Karl nods)* You're a brave man. Karl Marx, your final question, who won the Cup Final in 1949?

KARL The workers' control of the means of production? The struggle of the urban proletariat?

PRESENTER No. It was in fact, Wolverhampton Wanderers who beat Leicester 3-1.

Cut to stock film of goal being scored in a big football match. Roars from crowd. Stock footage of football crowds cheering.

VOICE OVER (MICHAEL) *(and caption)* 'in "world forum" today: Karl Marx, Che Guevara, Lenin and Mao Tse-Tung. Next week, four leading heads of state of the Afro-Asian nations against Bristol Rovers at **Molineux**' 14

Animation: Sketch leading to a stock drawing of a First World War trench scene—barbed wire against the sky with a helmet stuck on a bayonet.

Coventry City, a team of the Midlands, finally won the storied FA Cup trophy in 1987, a full 104 years after they were founded.

"Starter for ten" is a phrase from *University Challenge*, a nerdy game show for college students. The starter question was worth ten points if answered correctly, and if so answered would lead to three bonus questions on a similar subject.

Another reference to the *Eurovision Song Contest*—the scores were always delivered by an attractive woman, who was usually fluent in a number of European languages.

"Sing, Little Birdie," sung by Pearl Carr and Teddy Johnson, was the U.K.'s entry in 1959, but it didn't win. It came in second behind "*Een Beetje*" ("A Little Bit"), Teddy Scholten's entry for the Netherlands.

Molineux (pronounced "*Moll*-in-yew") is the stadium home of Wolverhampton Wanderers soccer team. Bristol Rovers, one of two teams who play in Bristol, don't play there—except, of course, when they're faced with the four leading heads of the Afro-Asian nations.

"British Tommy" is short for "Tommy Atkins," an age-old nickname for a British soldier, especially one in World War I.

The battles at Ypres in Belgium (pronounced "*Ee*-pruh," though many soldiers called it "Wipers") were some of the most brutal in that most brutal of wars, World War I.

"Blighty" is British slang for "Britain."

VOICE OVER *(and caption)* 'In 1914, the balance of power lay in ruins. Europe was plunged into bloody conflict. Nation fought nation. But no nation fought nation morely than the English Hip Hip Horrary! Nice, nice! Yah boo. Phillips is a German and he have my pen'
DIFFERENT VOICE OVER *(and caption)* 'Start again'
FIRST VOICE OVER *(and caption)* 'In 1914, the balance of power lay in ruins...'

Mix through to close up of a harmonica being played by a ***British Tommy.*** **15** *Caption: 'YPRES 1914'* **16** *The camera pulls slowly out, with the plaintive harmonica still playing, to reveal the interior of a bunker in the trenches. Sitting around on old ammunition boxes etc. are the harmonica player, Private Jenkins, Sergeant Jackson, a padre with no arms, a sheikh, a Viking warrior, a male mermaid, a nun, a milkman and a Greek Orthodox priest. Sounds of warfare throughout, shells thudding, explosions etc.*

SERGEANT (MICHAEL) *(looking round rather uncomfortably at the strange collection)* Jenkins?

JENKINS (ERIC) *(equally uncomfortable about playing such a tender scene in front of sheiks etc.)* Yes, sir.
SERGEANT What are you going to do when you get back to **Blighty? 17**
JENKINS I dunno, sarge...I expect I'll be looking after me mum. She'll be getting on a bit now.
SERGEANT Got a family of your own 'ave you?
JENKINS No, she's...she's all I got left now. My wife, Doreen...she...I got a letter...
SERGEANT You don't have to tell me, son.
JENKINS No, sarge, I'd like to tell you, see this place...

Cut to long shot of bunker. Floor manager strides on to set.

FLOOR MANAGER (TERRY J) Hold it. Hold it. Look, loves...can anyone not involved in this scene, please leave the set. *(he starts to herd out anyone not in First War costume)* Now! Come on please. Anyone not concerned in this scene, the canteen's open upstairs. *(sheikh, male mermaid etc. troop off)* Now come on please. *(to soldiers)* Sorry loves. Sorry. We'll have to take it again, from the top. All right. OK...Cue!

Back to identical shot of harmonica-playing tommy; he plays a few bars. Caption: 'KNICKERS 1914' Cut to long shot. The floor manager rushes on again. The caption remains superimposed.

FLOOR MANAGER Hold it. Hold it. Now, who changed the caption? Can whoever changed the caption put the right one back immediately please.

Caption: 'YPRES 1914'

FLOOR MANAGER Right. All right, we'll take it again from the top. Cue. *(back to identical shot of harmonica-playing tommy with correct caption superimposed; slow pull out as before; then floor* *manager rushes on again)* Hold it. Hold it. *(he goes behind some sandbags looking extremely irritated)* Come on. Come on, out of there. *(he hauls a spaceman and hustles him off the set)*

You're not in this...you're only holding the whole thing up. *(turning to studio as a whole)* Come on please. It's no good, loves. It's no good. We'll have to leave it for now. Come back when everyone's settled down a bit. So that means we go over to the Art Room, all right. So cue camera three! *(cut to Guevara caught in a hot embrace with Karl Marx)* Sorry, camera *four.*

Cut to Art Gallery. A large sign says: 'ITALIAN MASTERS OF THE RENAISSANCE'. Two art critics wandering through. They stop in front of a large **Titian canvas.** **18** *The canvas is about ten foot high by six foot wide.*

FIRST CRITIC (MICHAEL) Aren't they marvellous? The strength and boldness...life and power in those colours.
SECOND CRITIC (ERIC) This must be Titian's masterpiece.
FIRST CRITIC Oh indeed—if only for the composition alone. The strength of those foreground figures...the firmness of the line...
SECOND CRITIC Yes, the confidence of the master at the height of his powers.

At this point a man in a country smock and straw hat and a straw in his mouth comes up to the painting and with a very businesslike manner presses the nipple of a nude in the painting. Ding dong sound of a front doorbell. He stands tapping his feet and whistling soundlessly beside the painting. He nods at the critics. Cut to the top of the painting to see that one of the figures has disappeared leaving a blank. The camera pans down the painting as we hear footsteps, as if coming down a lot of stone steps. Eventually the camera comes to rest beside where the country bumpkin is standing and a door opens in the painting. We do not see who has opened it, but can assume it is the cherub.

CHERUB (TERRY G) Yes?
BUMPKIN (TERRY J) Hello sonny, your dad in?
CHERUB Yes.
BUMPKIN Could I speak to him please? It's the man from 'The Hay Wain'.
CHERUB Who?
BUMPKIN **The man from 'The Hay Wain' by Constable.** **19**
CHERUB Dad...it's the man from 'The Hay Wain' by Constable to see you.
SOLOMON (GRAHAM) Coming.

Sound of footsteps. Cut to another close up on the painting and we see the main figure disappearing. ***This figure suddenly puts his head round the door.*** **20**

SOLOMON Hello? How are you? Come on in.
BUMPKIN No, no can't stop, just passing by, actually.

Titian, sixteenth-century Italian painter of the Venetian school.

Constable's *The Hay Wain* is one of the most beloved paintings in Britain and one of the most popular in London's National Gallery. Finished in 1821, it depicts a country scene in Suffolk, an eastern county of England.

Chapman, as tall as ever, actually bangs his head peering out from the door.

Peter Bruegel (note that he was the only one of many "Brueghels" who didn't sign his name with an *h*), a sixteenth-century Dutch painter known for his lively marketplace scenes peopled by many folk. *Winter Landscape with Skaters* is one of his better-known skating scenes, though he painted many.

SOLOMON Oh, where are you now?

BUMPKIN Well may you ask. We just been moved in next to a room full of **Brueghels... 21** terrible bloody din. Skating all hours of the night. Anyway, I just dropped in to tell you there's been a walk-out in the Impressionists.

SOLOMON Walk-out, eh?

BUMPKIN Yeah. **It started with the 'Dejeuner Sur L'Herbe' lot, 22** evidently they were moved away from above the radiator or something. Anyway, the Impressionists are all out. **Gainsborough's Blue Boy's 23** brought out the eighteenth-century English portraits, the Flemish School's solid, and the German woodcuts are at a meeting now.

SOLOMON Right. Well I'll get the Renaissance School out.

BUMPKIN OK, meeting 4.30—'Bridge at Arles'. 24

SOLOMON OK, cheerio—good luck, son.

BUMPKIN OK.

The door shuts and we hear Solomon's voice over.

SOLOMON Right—everybody out. 25

We see various famous paintings whose characters suddenly disappear.

VOICES I'm off. I'm off. I'm off, dear. *(etc.)*

Mix through to front room of a suburban house. A man is sawing his wife in two in the classic long box.

RADIO Here is the News...*(the man pauses for a moment and looks at radio, then resumes sawing; we zoom in to close up on the radio. There is a window behind it; as the radio talks, a group of paintings with picket signs pass by)* by an almost unanimous vote, paintings in the National Gallery voted to continue the strike that has emptied frames for the last week. The man from Constable's 'Hay Wain' said last night that there was no chance of a return to the pictures before the weekend. **Sir Kenneth Clark 26** has said he will talk to any painting if it can help bring a speedy end to the strike. *(a ghastly scream out of vision; the sawing stops abruptly)* At Sotheby's, prices dropped dramatically as leading figures left their paintings. *(Cut to Sotheby's.)*

AUCTIONEER (JOHN) What am I bid for **Vermeer's 'Lady Who Used to be at a Window'? 27** Do I hear two bob?

VOICE Two bob!

AUCTIONEER Gone. Now what am I bid for another great bargain? **Edward Landseer's 'Nothing at Bay'. 28**

Pull out to reveal man standing beside auctioneer with the painting (the stag is missing). Cut to a group of famous characters from famous paintings who are clustered round the camera. Botticelli's Venus is in the centre jabbing her fingers at camera.

VENUS All we bloody want is a little bit of bloody consultation.

Fade sound of them all shouting and jostling etc. Bring up sound of radio out of vision.

Les Déjeuner Sur l'Herbe is the Edouard Manet painting from 1862–1863. It hangs in the Musée d'Orsay in Paris.

Blue Boy, by English portraitist and landscape painter Thomas Gainsborough, dates from around 1770. Even though it's one of Britain's most famous paintings, it now hangs in the Huntington Library in San Marino, California.

Langlois Bridge at Arles is a series of four paintings by van Gogh.

RADIO At a mass meeting at Brentford Football Ground, other works of art voted to come out in support of the paintings. *(still in animation cut to Brentford football ground with famous statues in the stands)* The vote was unanimous. *(they all put their hands up)* With one abstention. *(cut to close up of 'Venus De Milo'; cut to TV Centre and slow zoom in)* Meanwhile, at Television Centre work began again on a sketch about Ypres. A spokesman for the sketch said: he fully expected it to be more sensible this time.

Cut to usual opening shot of close up of harmonica being played by tommy. Caption: 'YPRES 1914' Slow zoom out to reveal set-up as before with no extraneous characters.

SERGEANT Jenkins.
JENKINS Yes, sarge?
SERGEANT What are you going to do when you get back to Blighty?
JENKINS I dunno, sarge. I expect I'll look after my mum. She'll be getting on a bit now.
SERGEANT Got a family of your own have you?
JENKINS No—she's all I got left now. My wife, Doreen...she...I got a letter.
SERGEANT You don't have to tell me, son.
JENKINS No, sarge, I'd like to tell you. You see, this bloke from up the street...

Enter a young major—excruciatingly public school.

MAJOR (GRAHAM) OK, chaps, at ease. I've just been up the line...
SERGEANT Can we get through, sir?
MAJOR No, I'm afraid we'll have to make a break for it at nightfall.
SERGEANT Right, sir. We're all with yer.
MAJOR Yes I know, that's just the problem, sergeant. How many are there of us?
SERGEANT Well there's you, me, Jenkins, Padre, Kipper, there's five, sir.
MAJOR And only rations for...
SERGEANT Four, sir.
MAJOR Precisely. I'm afraid one of us will have to take the 'other' way out.

Crash zoom into revolver which the major has brought out. Jarring chord. Close up of faces looking tense from one to the other. Tense music.

PADRE (JOHN) I'm a gonner, major. Leave me, I'm I'm not a complete man anymore.
MAJOR You've lost both your arms as well.
PADRE Yes. **29** Damn silly really.

Lovely satire on the state of British industrial relations in the early 1970s. Strike action was a constant of the day, with many unions coming out in sympathy with one another, sometimes leading to a general breakdown in the workings of the country. The phrase "everybody out" was a standard cry of the union leader.

Kenneth Clark, British art critic, broadcaster, and museum creator, was host of the wildly popular BBC series *Civilization* in 1969.

Perhaps a reference to *Girl Reading a Letter at an Open Window*, from 1657–1659.

Edwin Landseer was a nineteenth-century painter and sculptor. His *The Stag at Bay* dates from 1865. Landseer is now perhaps best known for the lions in London's Trafalgar Square.

Cleese does well not to lose it here. He clearly finds Chapman's double entendre as funny as the audience does.

Chapman doesn't say "Oh dear" here.

"V.C." is the Victoria Cross, the highest military medal awarded in the British Army. Queen Victoria instigated it in 1865 during the Crimean War. It can be awarded to any rank of soldier for bravery "in the face of the enemy." (You get a George Cross for bravery "not in the face of the enemy," which sounds like a Python sketch all its own.)

Known as "Ip Dip," this counting game is an age-old British way of picking members of a team, for example.

"Fisties" is rock-paper-scissors.

The laughter of the audience, when it becomes clear Cleese can't play along, causes Cleese himself to fight a big laugh of his own. He just about stops himself.

Song by Ross Parker and Hugh Charles, and made famous by Vera Lynn, singing sweetheart of World War II in the U.K.

MAJOR No, no, we'll draw for it. That's the way we do things in the army. Sergeant. The straws!

The sergeant gives him the straws. The major arranges them and hands them round.

MAJOR Right now, the man who gets the shortest straw knows what to do.

They all take the long straws. Including the padre who takes one in his teeth. The major is left with a tiny straw. A pause.

SERGEANT Looks like you, sir.
MAJOR Is it? What did we say, the longest straw was it?
SERGEANT No, shortest, sir.
MAJOR Well we'd better do it again, there's obviously been a bit of a muddle. *(they do it again and the same thing happens)* **Oh dear.** **30** Best of three? *(they go through it again and he gets left with it again)* Right, well I've got the shortest straw. So I decide what means we use to decide who's going to do...to...to...to er,...to do the thing...to do the right thing. Now rank doesn't enter into this, but obviously if I should get through the lines, I will be in a very good position to recommend anyone, very highly, for a posthumous **VC.** **31** *(he looks round to see if there are any takers)* No? Good. Fine. Fine. Fine. Fine. Right. *('counting out')* **Dip, dip, dip, my little ship sails on the ocean, you are** **32** *(comes back to himself)*...no wait, wait a minute, no I, I must have missed out a dip. I'll start again. Dip, dip, dip, dip, my little ship, sails on the ocean, you are...*(it's back on him again)* No, this is not working out. It's not working out. What shall we do?
JENKINS How about one potato, two potato, sir?
MAJOR Don't be childish, Jenkins. **No, I think, I think fisties would be best.** **33** **OK, so hands behind backs.** **34** After three, OK, one, two, three. *(everyone except the padre who has no arms puts out clenched fist)* Now what's this...stone, stone, stone, *(looks down at his hand)* and scissors. Now. Scissors cut everything, don't they?
SERGEANT Not stone, sir.
MAJOR They're very *good* scissors. *(then he suddenly sees the padre)* Padre hasn't been!

SERGEANT No arms, sir.
MAJOR Oh, I'm terribly sorry, I'm afraid I didn't tell you what. All those people who don't want to stay here and shoot themselves raise their arms.
PADRE Stop it! Stop it! Stop this...this hideous façade.
SERGEANT Easy, padre!
PADRE No, no, I must speak. When I, when I came to this war, I had two arms, two good arms, but when the time came to...to lose one, I...I gave it gladly, I smiled as they cut if off, ***(music under: 'There'll Always Be An England')*** **35** because I knew there was a future for mankind. I...I knew there was hope...so long as men were prepared to give their limbs. *(emotionally)*

And when the time came for me to give my other arm I...I gave it gladly. I...I sang as they sawed it off. Because I believed...*(hysterically)* Oh you may laugh, but I believed with every fibre of my body, with every drop of rain that falls, a...a flower grows. And that flower, that small fragile, delicate flower...*(two modern-day ambulance attendants come in with a trolley which they put the padre onto and wheel him away; he is still going on)*...shall burst forth and give a new life. New strength! *(cut to a present-day ambulance racing out of TV Centre in speeded-up motion; it roars through the streets, and arrives at the casualty entrance of a hospital; the doors swing open and the padre is rushed out on stretcher (still in fast motion) totally under a blanket; we hear his voice)*...freedom. Freedom from fear and freedom from oppression. Freedom from tyranny. *(the camera picks up on sign which reads: 'Royal Hospital for Over-acting')* A world where men and women of all races and creeds can live together in communion and then in the twilight of this life, our children, and our children's children and...*(by this time he has disappeared in through the doors of the hospital)*

Cut to the interior of hospital and see specialist as he walks down a corridor.

SPECIALIST (GRAHAM) All our patients here are suffering from severe over-acting. *(a nurse goes past leading a Long John Silver who keeps going 'Aha! Jim Lad')* When they're brought in they're all really over the top. *(he passes a whole group of Long John Silvers)* And it's our job to try and treat the condition of over-acting...*(he passes a group of King Rats, and indicates the worst case)* rather serious. *(he walks on through a door)* This is the Richard III Ward.

PULL OUT TO REVEAL A CROWD OF RICHARD III'S. THE SPECIALIST INDICATES ONE WHO IS REALLY OVER THE TOP.

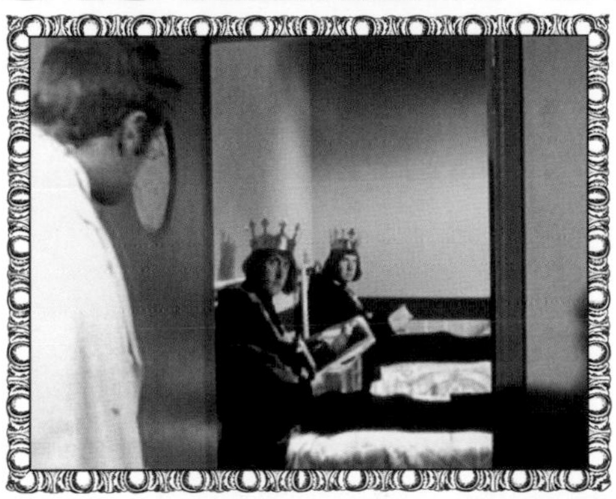

RICHARD III (MICHAEL) **A horse. A horse. My kingdom for a horse. 36**

SPECIALIST Most of these cases are pretty unpleasant. Nurse...*(a nurse comes in and sedates Richard III)* But the treatment does work with some people. This chap came to us straight from the **Chichester Festival; 37** we operated just in time, and now he's almost normal.

He walks over to a very ordinary Richard III, who smiles disarmingly and says quite chattily:

SECOND RICHARD (ERIC) A horse, a horse, my kingdom for a horse.

Shaking his head sadly, the specialist leaves the ward and opens a door to another one.

SPECIALIST But in here we have some very nasty cases indeed.

Animation: involving grotesque Hamlets.

From Act 5, Scene 4 of Shakespeare's *Richard III*.

The Chichester Festival is an annual arts festival in the U.K.

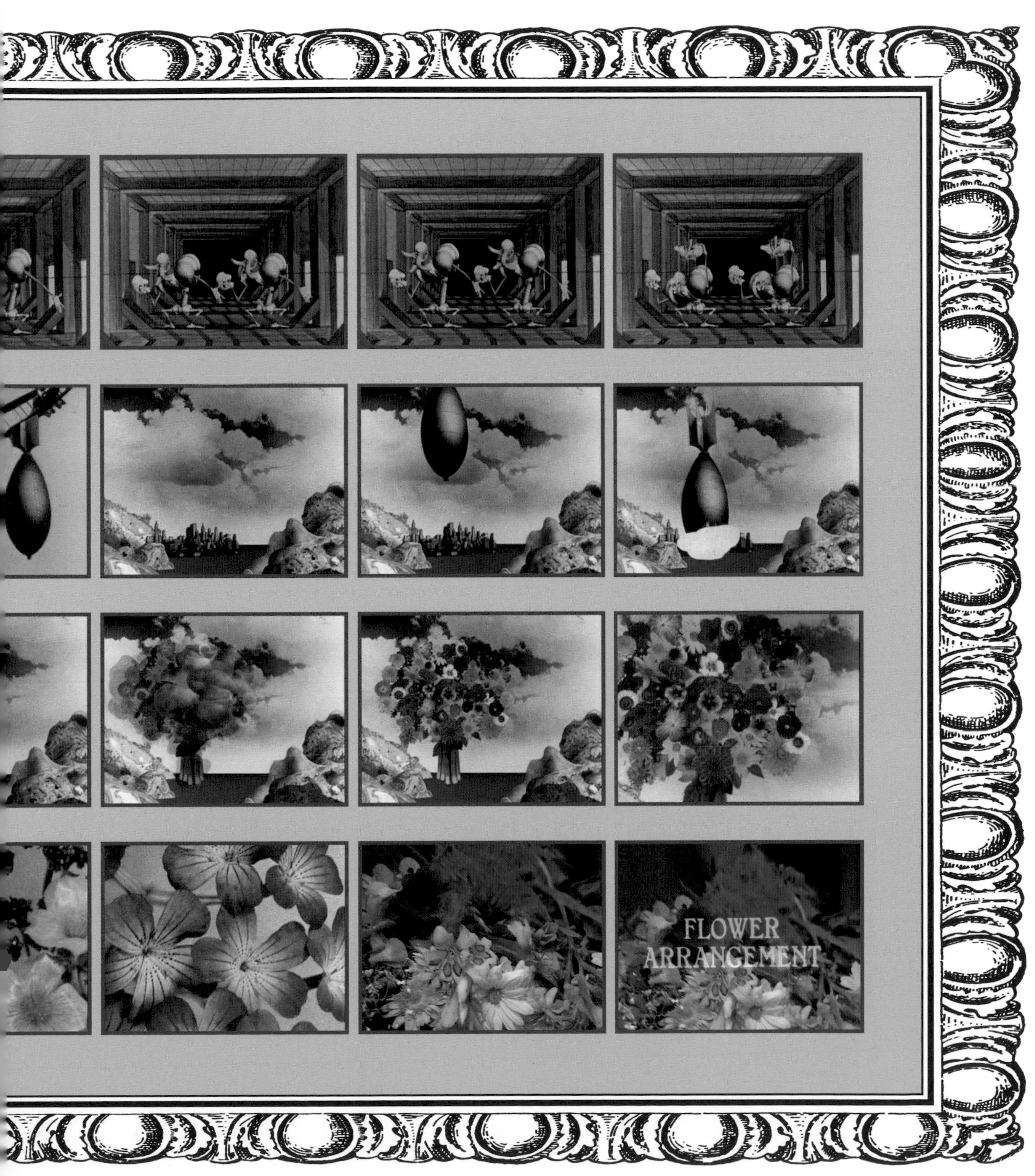
FLOWER
ARRANGEMENT

TERRY JONES

If you've ever wondered why the town of Esher, in southwest London, is featured so many times in *Monty Python's Flying Circus,* you can look no further than Terry Jones.

Born in 1942 on the north coast of Wales in Colwyn Bay, Jones remembers an idyllic childhood of seaside freedom and ease. All that changed, however, once his father returned from World War II. All over Britain, families faced the return of war-affected men, and the Joneses of Colwyn Bay were no exception. First order of business: the family moved south, to Surrey, and the town of Claygate. Attending a grade school in nearby Esher, Jones found himself in an affluent, middle-class, suburban place ridden with stockbrokers, as far from the sea as it was possible to be. Jones hated the move. Already discombobulated by the return of a father he'd barely known until he was four years old, the move to Esher was a painful one; and years later, on the *Flying Circus,* this Esher life came to be synonymous with a kind of self-satisfied British strata that cared more about status than thought, more about money than insight. It was the perfect subject for Python scorn, and Jones (and the rest of them) seldom missed a chance to ridicule it.

Jones eventually escaped "stockbroker belt" and headed north to Oxford University to study English and history. There, as part of the famed Oxford Revue, he came to know Michael Palin. By the time Python came around, the two Oxford boys wrote together almost exclusively (they would later also collaborate on *Ripping Yarns,* a hilarious TV show starring Palin). But that was to come—post-Oxford, Jones found himself producing various bits of comedy writing, especially for David Frost on his *Frost Report,* among other pre-Python jobs.

Eventually, with Palin he would form a half of the Python writing team (it tended to be the teams of Palin–Jones and Chapman–Cleese, with Idle as the wild card). Jones, though brilliantly verbal, also displayed a love of visual gags that led to early sketches like the one in which he attempts to change into swimwear but is repeatedly thwarted by the kind of mishaps usually seen in silent movies.

But perhaps Jones's greatest contribution to Python was his work on the direction and flow of the shows. It was clear early on that the Pythons abhorred the punch line as a concept—to them, a well-worked sketch felt sullied when the traditional crack of the snare drum led to a final line. They were also leery of the sketch comedy routine generally. But this left them with a problem: How would sketches actually end? Jones, as much as anyone, pioneered both the stream-of-consciousness feel of the shows as well as gave free rein to Terry Gilliam to insert cartoons that would act as links between ideas. Jones has commented that the editing of the forty-five shows was a crucial part of their essence, and he had a great role in working on the films, badgering director Ian McNaughton about editing and flow. It's no wonder that later he would move into directing in his own right, as co-director of *Monty Python and the Holy Grail* (with Gilliam) and sole director of both *Life of Brian* and *The Meaning of Life.*

Since the movies, Jones has carved a new career as a writer of historical books that question our assumptions about such things as medievalism and barbarism. He's also become an outspoken opponent of the so-called war on terror, among other political efforts.

But it's with the *Flying Circus* that Jones may well be best remembered. He was especially brilliant at playing a screeching woman; though all the Pythons regularly cross-dressed, Jones seemed most convincing as the shrill harridan. And it may well be that his most enduring moment is his rendering of the word "Spam" over and over in the sketch about the lunch meat. He hits a high note so profane and painful and sharp, it could probably crack diamonds.

HAMLETS To be or not to be. That is the question. To be... 38

Animation leads to close up of flowers. Superimposed caption: 'FLOWER ARRANGEMENT' Pull back to show Gumby in studio with piles of flowers on a table.

GUMBY (MICHAEL) Good evening. First take a bunch of flowers. *(he grabs flowers from the table)* Pretty begonias, irises, freesias and cry-manthesums...then arrange them nicely in a vase. *(he thrusts the flowers head downwards into the vase and stuffs them in wildly; he even bangs them with a mallet in an attempt to get them all in)* Get in! Get in! Get in!

Cut to a café. All the customers are Vikings. Mr and Mrs Bun enter—downwards (on wires).

MR BUN (ERIC) Morning.
WAITRESS (TERRY J) Morning.
MR BUN What have you got, then? 39
WAITRESS Well there's egg and bacon; egg, sausage and bacon; egg and spam; egg, bacon and spam; egg, bacon, sausage and spam; spam, bacon, sausage and spam; spam, egg, spam, spam, bacon and spam; spam, spam, spam, egg and spam; spam, spam, spam, spam, spam, spam, baked beans, spam, spam, spam, and spam; or lobster thermidor aux crevettes with a mornay sauce garnished with truffle pâté, brandy and a fried egg on top and spam.
MRS BUN (GRAHAM) Have you got anything without spam in it?
WAITRESS Well, there's spam, egg, sausage and spam. That's not got *much* spam in it.
MRS BUN I don't want *any* spam.
MR BUN Why can't she have egg, bacon, spam and sausage?
MRS BUN That's got spam in it!
MR BUN Not as much as spam, egg, sausage and spam.
MRS BUN Look, could I have egg, bacon, spam and sausage without the spam.
WAITRESS Uuuuuuggggh!
MRS BUN What d'you mean uuugggh! I don't like spam.

From Act 3, Scene 1 of Shakespeare's *Hamlet*.

The answer to this question leads to another classic Python sketch, and beyond—the musical *Spamalot*, partly written by Eric Idle, has won multiple Tony Awards since it was first staged on Broadway in 2005.

VIKI

SPAM, SP

SPAM, SP

SPAM, SP

LOVEL

WONDER

nging)

M, SPAM,

M SPAM,

AM, SPAM

SPAM,

UL SPAM

Brief stock shot of a Viking ship.

WAITRESS Shut up. Shut up! Shut up! You can't have egg, bacon, spam and sausage without the spam.

MRS BUN Why not!

WAITRESS No, it wouldn't be egg, bacon, spam and sausage, would it.

MRS BUN I don't like spam!

MR BUN Don't make a fuss, dear. I'll have your spam. I love it. I'm having spam, spam, spam, spam, spam...

VIKINGS *(singing)* Spam, spam, spam, spam...

MR BUN ...baked beans, spam, spam and spam.

WAITRESS Baked beans are off.

MR BUN Well can I have spam instead?

WAITRESS You mean spam, spam, spam, spam, spam, spam, spam, spam spam, spam?

VIKINGS *(still singing)* Spam, spam, spam, spam...*(etc.)*

MR BUN Yes.

WAITRESS Arrggh!

VIKINGS ...lovely spam, wonderful, spam.

WAITRESS Shut up! Shut up!

The Vikings shut up momentarily. Enter the Hungarian.

HUNGARIAN Great boobies honeybun, my lower intestine is full of spam, egg, spam, bacon, spam, tomato, spam...

VIKINGS *(starting up again)* Spam, spam, spam, spam...

WAITRESS Shut up.

A policeman rushes in and bundles the Hungarian out.

HUNGARIAN My nipples explode...

40

But not before a police officer has carted away the Hungarian.

Cut to a historian. **40** *Superimposed caption: 'A HISTORIAN'*

HISTORIAN (MICHAEL) Another great Viking victory was at the Green Midget café at Bromley. Once again the Viking strategy was the same. They sailed from these fiords here, *(indicating a map with arrows on it)* assembled at Trondheim and waited for the strong north-easterly winds to blow their oaken galleys to England whence they sailed on May 23rd. Once in Bromley they assembled in the Green Midget café and spam selecting a spam particular spam item from the spam menu would spam, spam, spam, spam, spam...

The backdrop behind him rises to reveal the café again. The Vikings start singing again and the historian conducts them.

VIKINGS *(singing)* Spam, spam, spam, spam, spam, lovely spam, wonderful spam. Lovely spam wonderful spam...

Mr and Mrs Bun rise slowly in the air. Superimposed caption: 'IN 1970 MONTY PYTHON'S FLYING CIRCUS LAY IN RUINS, AND THEN THE WORDS ON THE SCREEN SAID:' Fade out and roll credits, which read: MONTY PYTHON'S FLYING CIRCUS WAS CONCEIVED, WRITTEN AND SPAM PERFORMED BY SPAM TERRY JONES; MICHAEL SPAM PALIN; JOHN SPAM JOHN SPAM JOHN SPAM CLEESE; GRAHAM SPAM SPAM SPAM CHAPMAN; ERIC SPAM EGG AND CHIPS IDLE; TERRY SPAM SAUSAGE SPAM EGG SPAM GILLIAM; ALSO APPEARING ON TOAST THE FRED TOMLINSON SPAM EGG CHIPS AND SINGERS; RESEARCH PATRICIA HOULIHAN AND SAUSAGE MAKE-UP PENNY PENNY PENNY AND SPAM NORTON; COSTUMES EGG BAKED BEANS SAUSAGE AND TOMATO, OH, AND HAZEL PETHIG TOO; ANIMATIONS BY TERRY (EGG ON FACE) GILLIAM; FILM CAMERAMAN JAMES (SPAM SAUSAGE EGG AND TOMATO) BALFOUR (NOT SUNDAYS); FILM EDITOR RAY (FRIED SLICE AND GOLDEN THREE DELICIOUS) MILLICHOPE (SPAM EXTRA); SOUND CHIPS SAUSAGE LIVERWURST, PHEASANT, SPAM, NEWSAGENTS, CHIPS, AND PETER ROSE; LIGHTING OTIS (SPAM'S OFF DEAR) EDDY; DESIGNER ROBERT ROBERT ROBERT ROBERT BERK AND TOMATO; PRODUCED BY IAN (MIXED GRILL) MACNAUGHTON 7/6D; BBC SPAM TV; SERVICE NOT INCLUDED

VOICE OVER (MICHAEL) Haagbard Etheldronga and his Viking hordes are currently appearing in 'Grin and Pillage it' at the Jodrell Theatre, Colwyn Bay. 'The Dirty Hungarian Phrase Book' is available from **Her Majesty's Stationery Office,** **41** price—a kiss on the bum.

Fade out. Fade in Karl Marx and Che Guevara lying post-coitally in bed. Karl switches off the light.

"Her Majesty's Stationery Office" is where official government publications are generated (though those publications do not yet include a Hungarian phrase book).

SEA SON 2
EPISODE 26
FRIGHTFULLY IMPORTANT

MONTY PYTHON
ROYAL EPISODE 13
FEATURING
THE QUEEN WILL BE WATCHING
COAL MINE HISTORICAL ARGUMENT
THE MAN WHO SAYS THINGS IN A VERY ROUNDABOUT WAY
THE MAN WHO SPEAKS ONLY THE ENDS OF WORDS
THE MAN WHO SPEAKS ONLY THE BEGINNING OF WORDS
THE MAN WHO SPEAKS ONLY THE MIDDLES OF WORDS
COMMERCIALS ✽ HOW TO FEED A GOLDFISH
THE MAN WHO COLLECTS BIRDWATCHER'S EGGS
INSURANCE SKETCH
HOSPITAL RUN BY RSM ✽ MOUNTAINEER
EXPLODING VERSION OF 'THE BLUE DANUBE'
Girls' Boarding School
SUBMARINE
LIFEBOAT (CANNIBALISM) ✽ UNDERTAKER'S SKETCH

FIRST AIRED: DECEMBER 22, 1970

Announcer standing in front of his desk.

ANNOUNCER (JOHN) *(reverently)* Ladies and gentlemen, I am not simply going to say 'and now for something completely different' this week, as I do not think it fit. This is a particularly auspicious occasion for us this evening, as we have been told that Her Majesty the Queen will be watching part of this show tonight. We don't know exactly when Her Majesty will be tuning in. We understand that at the moment she is watching '**The Virginian**', [1] but we have been promised that we will be informed the moment that she changes channel. Her Majesty would like everyone to behave quite normally but her **equerry** [2] has asked me to request all of you at home to stand when the great moment arrives, although we here in the studio will be carrying on with our humorous vignettes and spoofs in the ordinary way. Thank you. And now without any more ado and completely as normal, here are the opening titles. *(bows)* [3]

Very regal animated opening titles.

Caption: 'ROYAL EPISODE THIRTEEN' Caption: 'FIRST SPOOF' Caption: 'A COAL MINE IN LLANDDAROG ***CARMARTHEN'*** [4] *A nice photograph of a typical pit head. Music over this:* ***'All Through the Night' being sung in Welsh.*** [5]

VOICE OVER (JOHN) The coal miners of Wales have long been famed for their tough rugged life hewing the black gold from the uncompromising hell of one mile under. This is *(at this moment across the bottom of the screen comes the following message in urgent teleprinter style, moving right to left, superimposed 'HM THE QUEEN STILL WATCHING '"THE VIRGINIAN"')* the story of such men, battling gallantly against floods, roof falls, the English criminal law, the hidden killer carbon monoxide and the ever-present threat of pneumoconiosis which is...a disease miners get.

Cut to coal face below ground where some miners are engaged at their work. They hew away for a bit, grunting and talking amongst themselves. Suddenly two of them square up to one another.

FIRST MINER (GRAHAM) Don't you talk to me like that, you lying bastard.

The Virginian was an American western TV series. Its 249 episodes and nine seasons ran from 1962 to 1971.

An equerry is a kind of assistant.

Cleese does not, in fact, bow.

Llanddarog, Carmarthen, is a small town in southwest Wales, an area known for its coal mining.

"All Through the Night" is a moving Welsh folk song, often sung by Welsh Male Voice Choirs, groups of singers whose staunch harmonies stir souls throughout Britain.

He hits the second miner and a fight starts.

SECOND MINER (TERRY J) You bleeding pig. You're not fit to be down a mine.
FIRST MINER Typical bleeding Rhondda, 6 isn't it. You think you're so bloody clever.

They writhe around on the floor pummelling each other. The foreman comes in.

FOREMAN (ERIC) You bloody fighting again. Break it up or I'll put this pick through your head. Now what's it all about?
FIRST MINER He started it.
SECOND MINER Oh, you bleeding pig, you started it.
FOREMAN I don't care who bloody started it. What's it about?
SECOND MINER

WELL HE SAID THE BLOODY TREATY OF UTRECHT WAS 1713. 7

FIRST MINER So it bloody is.
SECOND MINER No it bloody isn't. It wasn't ratified 'til February 1714.
FIRST MINER He's bluffing. You're mind's gone, Jenkins. You're rubbish.
FOREMAN He's right, Jenkins. It was ratified September 1713. The whole bloody pit knows that. Look in Trevelyan, page 468. 8
THIRD MINER (MICHAEL) He's thinking of the Treaty of bloody Westphalia. 9
SECOND MINER Are you saying I don't know the difference between the War of the bloody Spanish Succession and the Thirty bloody Years War?
THIRD MINER You don't know the difference between the Battle of Borodino and a tiger's bum. 10

They start to fight.

Rhondda is a former coal-mining valley in south Wales.

The Treaty of Utrecht, signed by Spain, Great Britain, France, Portugal, Savoy, and the Dutch Republic, marked the end of the War of Spanish Succession, a conflict that for thirteen long years revolved around whether to unify the kingdoms of France and Spain.

George Macaulay Trevelyan (1876–1962), eminent British historian.

The Peace of Westphalia was a series of mid-seventeenth-century agreements that ended the Thirty Years' War between most of the European powers of the day, though centered mostly in German lands.

The Battle of Borodino was fought on September 7, 1812, between France and Russia during the Napoleonic Wars.

FOREMAN Break it up, break it up. ***(he hits them with his pickaxe)*** [11] I'm sick of all this bloody fighting. If it's not the bloody Treaty of Utrecht it's the bloody **binomial theorem.** [12] This isn't the senior common room at **All Souls,** [13] it's the bloody coal face.

A fourth miner runs up.

FOURTH MINER (IAN DAVIDSON) Hey, gaffer, can you settle something? Morgan here says you find the abacus between the triglyphs in the frieze section of the entablature of classical Greek Doric temples.

FOREMAN You bloody fool, Morgan, that's the metope. The abacus is between the architrave and the aechinus in the capital.

MORGAN (TERRY G) You stinking liar.

Another fight breaks out. A management man arrives carried in sedan chair by two black flunkies. He wears a colonial governor's helmet and a large sign reading 'FRIGHTFULLY IMPORTANT'. All the miners prostrate themselves on the floor.

FOREMAN Oh, most magnificent and merciful majesty, master of the universe, protector of the meek, whose nose we are not worthy to pick and whose very faeces are an untrammelled delight, and whose peacocks keep us awake all hours of the night with their noisy lovemaking, we beseech thee, tell thy humble servants the name of the section between the triglyphs in the frieze section of a classical Doric entablature.

MANAGEMENT MAN (JOHN) No idea. Sorry.

FOREMAN Right. Everybody out.

They all walk off throwing down tools. Cut to a newsreader's desk.

NEWSREADER (MICHAEL) Still no settlement in the coal mine dispute at Llanddarog. Miners refused to return to work until the management define a metope. **Meanwhile, at Dagenham the unofficial strike committee at Fords** [14] have increased their demands to thirteen reasons why Henry III was a bad king. And finally, in the disgusting objects international at **Wembley tonight,** [15] England beat Spain by a plate of braised pus to a putrid heron. And now, the Toad Elevating Moment.

Idle actually hits Jones on the top of his helmet with the pickax, and Jones, not unreasonably, goes down like a sack of potatoes.

From Wikipedia: "According to the theorem, it is possible to expand the power $(x+y)^n$ into a sum involving terms of the form ax^by^c, where the exponents b and c are nonnegative integers with $b+c=n$, and the coefficient a of each term is a specific positive integer depending on n and b. When an exponent is zero, the corresponding power is usually omitted from the term." Carry on.

All Souls is the college at Oxford University solely for postgraduates that has the reputation of being the place where all great brains go to be together.

Ford Motor Company has had a major factory at Dagenham, in Essex, since 1931.

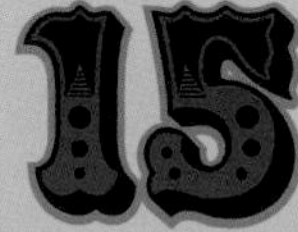

Wembley Stadium in London is the de facto national stadium of England.

Caption: 'THE TOAD ELEVATING MOMENT' Pompous music. Mix to spinning globe and then to two men in a studio.

INTERVIEWER (TERRY J) Good evening. Well, we have in the studio tonight a man who says things in a very roundabout way. Isn't that so, Mr Pudifoot.

MR PUDIFOOT (GRAHAM) Yes.

INTERVIEWER

HAVE YOU ALWAYS SAID THINGS IN A VERY ROUNDABOUT WAY?

MR PUDIFOOT Yes.

INTERVIEWER Well, I can't help noticing that, for someone who claims to say things in a very roundabout way, your last two answers have very little of the discursive quality about them.

MR PUDIFOOT Oh, well, I'm not very talkative today. It's a form of defensive response to intensive interrogative stimuli. I used to get it badly when I was a boy...well, I say very badly, in fact, do you remember when there was that fashion for, you know, little poodles with small coats...

INTERVIEWER Ah, now you're beginning to talk in a roundabout way.

MR PUDIFOOT Oh, I'm sorry.

INTERVIEWER No, no, no, no. Please do carry on...because that is in fact why we wanted you on the show.

MR PUDIFOOT I thought it was because you were interested in me as a human being. *(gets up and leaves)*

INTERVIEWER **Well...let's move on to our guest who not only lives in Essex but also speaks only the ends of words.** **16** Mr Ohn Ith. Mr Ith, good evening.

Enter from back of set as per Eamonn Andrews show Mr Ohn Ith. He sits at the desk. **17**

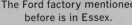

MR ITH (ERIC) ...ood...ing.

INTERVIEWER Nice to have you on the show.

MR ITH ...ice...o...e...ere.

INTERVIEWER Mr Ith, don't you find it very difficult to make yourself understood?

MR ITH Yes, it is extremely difficult.

INTERVIEWER Just a minute, you're a fraud!

MR ITH Oh no. I can speak the third and fourth sentences perfectly normally.

INTERVIEWER Oh I see. So your next sentence will be only the ends of words again?

MR ITH T's...ight.

INTERVIEWER Well, let's move on to our next guest who speaks only the beginnings of words, Mr J...Sm...Mr Sm...good evening.

Enter Mr Sm.

MR SM (JOHN) G...e...

The Ford factory mentioned before is in Essex.

This is Your Life, previously mentioned in Python, is a show on which surprised celebrities have their life stories told by their friends.

INTERVIEWER Well, have you two met before?

MR SM N...

MR ITH ...o

MR SM N...

MR ITH ...o

INTERVIEWER

WELL, THIS IS REALLY A FASCINATING OCCASION BECAUSE WE HAVE IN THE STUDIO MR...OH...I...WHO SPEAKS ONLY THE MIDDLES OF WORDS. GOOD EVENING.

Enter Scot.

SCOT (MICHAEL) ...oo......ni...

INTERVIEWER Um, where do you come from?

SCOT ...u...i...a...

INTERVIEWER Dunfermline in Scotland. Well let me introduce you, Mr Ohn Ith...

MR ITH ...ood...ing.

SCOT ...oo......ni...

INTERVIEWER J...Sm...

SCOT ...oo......ni...

MR SM G...Eve...

INTERVIEWER Yes, well, ha, ha; just a moment. Perhaps you would all like to say good evening together.

MR SM G...

SCOT ...oo...

MR ITH ...d

MR SM Eve...

SCOT ...ni...

MR ITH ...ing.

Animation: a sketch advertising Crelm toothpaste.

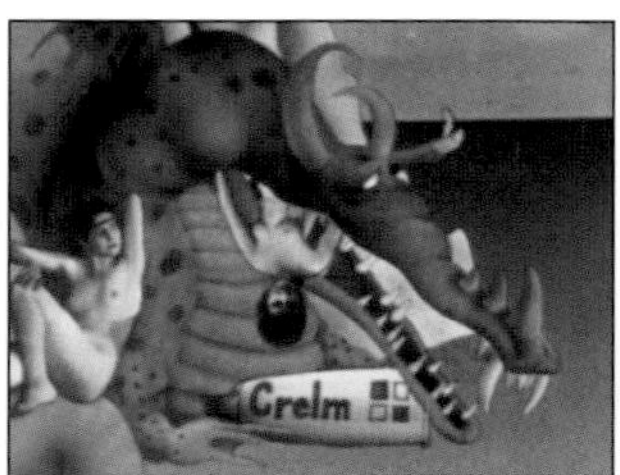

Cut to a soap powder commercial. Slick adman against neutral background. On his left is an ordinary kitchen table. On his right is a pile of sheets on a stand.

ADMAN (ERIC) This table has been treated with ordinary soap powder, but these have been treated with new Fibro-Val. *(cut to top shot of interior of washing machine with water spinning round as per ads)* We put both of them through our washing machine, and just look at the difference. *(cut back to the original set-up; the sheets are obviously painted white; the table is smashed up)* The table is broken and smashed, but the sheets, with Fibro-Val, are sparkling clean and white.

Traditional expanding square links to next commercial. Animated countryside with flowers, butterflies and a ***Babycham animal.*** **18** *A boy and a girl (real, superimposed) wander through hand in hand.*

MAN'S VOICE (MICHAEL) I love the surgical garment. Enjoy the delights of the Victor Mature abdominal corset. Sail down the Nile on the Bleed-it Kosher Truss. *(the adman comes into view over the background; he holds a tailor's dummy—pelvis only—with a truss)* And don't forget the Hercules Hold-'em-in, the all-purpose concrete truss for the man with the family hernia.

He throws away the truss. The background changes to blow-up of a fish tank. The adman is sitting at a desk. He pulls a goldfish bowl over.

ADMAN Well last week on Fish Club we learnt how to sex a pike...and this week we're going to learn how to feed a goldfish. Now contrary to what most people think the goldfish has a ravenous appetite. If it doesn't get enough protein it gets very thin and its bones begin to stick out and its fins start to fall off. So once a week give your goldfish a really good meal. Here's one specially recommended by the Board of Irresponsible People. First, some cold consommé or a gazpacho *(pours it in)*, then some sausages with spring greens, sautée potatoes and bread and gravy.

He tips all this into the bowl. ***An RSPCA man rushes in, grabs the man and hauls him off.*** **19**

RSPCA MAN (IAN DAVIDSON) All right, come on, that's enough, that's enough.
ADMAN ...treacle tart...chocolate cake and...
VOICE OVER (JOHN) *(and caption)*: 'The RSPCA wish it to be known that that man was not a bona fide animal lover, and also that goldfish do not eat sausages. *(the man is still shouting)* Shut up!...They are quite happy with breadcrumbs, ants' eggs and the occasional pheasant...'

The last four words are crossed out on the caption.

VOICE OVER Who wrote that?

Mix to a lyrical shot of wild flowers in beautiful English countryside. Gentle pastoral music. The camera begins to pan away from the flowers, moving slowly across this idyllic scene. Mix in the sound of lovers—the indistinct deep voice, followed by a playful giggle from the girl. At first very distant, but as we continue to pan it increases in volume, until we come to rest on the source of the noise—a tape recorder in front of a bush. After a short pause, the camera tracks round behind this bush where are a couple sitting reading a book each. Pan away from them across a field. In the middle of the pan we come across a smooth, moustachioed little Italian head waiter, in tails etc. We do not stop on him.

WAITER (GRAHAM) *(bowing to camera)* I hope you're enjoying the show.

On pans the camera to the end of the field where we pick up a man in a long mac crawling on all fours through the undergrowth. We follow him as he occasionally dodges behind a bush or a tree. He is stealthily tracking something. After a few moments he comes up behind a birdwatcher (in deerstalker and tweeds) who lies at the top of a small rise, with his binoculars trained. With infinite caution the man in the long mac slides up behind the birdwatcher, then he stretches out a hand and opens the flap of the birdwatcher's knapsack. He pulls out a small white paper bag. Holding his breath, he feels inside the bag and produces a small pie, then a tomato and finally two hard-boiled eggs. He pockets the hard-boiled eggs, puts the rest back and creeps away.

Babycham is a sparkling Champagne-like drink. Its logo was the Babycham fawn.

The "RSPCA" is the Royal Society for the Prevention of Cruelty to Animals.

The “gents” is the men’s bathroom. St. Pancras Station is in central London.

Man Alive was a somewhat sensationalist TV show featuring stories on human interest, social issues, and some politics. It ran from 1965 to 1981 on BBC2.

22

Nationwide was a general-interest TV show broadcast on BBC1 every night around 6:00 p.m. It followed the BBC News and was light and airy, such that the Pythons found easy fun in it. The “regional section” refers to the fact that the national show would kick to a regional station throughout the broadcast for stories of a more local hue.

The “flocking” of these men in the field is truly a sight worth seeing.

With the camera mounted away and high, the viewer gets a great view of all the people in Trafalgar Square watching this spectacle.

VOICE OVER (ERIC)

HERBERT MENTAL COLLECTS BIRDWATCHERS’ EGGS.

At his home in Surrey he has a collection of over four hundred of them.

Cut to Mental in a study lined with shelves full of hard-boiled eggs. They all have little labels on the front of them. He goes up and selects one from a long line of identical hard-boiled eggs.

HERBERT (TERRY J) ’Ere now. This is a very interesting one. This is from a Mr P. F. Bradshaw. He is usually found in Surrey hedgerows, **but I found this one in the gents at St Pancras, uneaten.** **20** *(he provides the next question himself in bad ventriloquist style)* Mr Mental, why did you start collecting birdwatchers’ eggs? *(normal voice)* Oh, well, I did it to get on ‘Man Alive’. *(ventriloquially)* ‘**Man Alive**’? ***(normal voice)*** **21** That’s right, yes. But then that got all serious, so I carried on in the hope of a quick appearance as an eccentric on the regional section of ‘**Nationwide**’. **22** *(ventriloquially)* Mr Mental, I believe a couple of years ago you started to collect butterfly hunters. *(normal voice)* Butterfly hunters? *(ventriloquially)* Yes. *(normal voice)* Oh, that’s right. Here’s a couple of them over here. *(he moves to his left; on the wall behind him are the splayed-out figures of two butterfly hunters, with pins through their backs and their names on cards underneath)* Nice little chaps. But the hobby I enjoyed most was racing pigeon fanciers.

An open field. A large hamper, with an attendant in a brown coat standing behind it. The attendant opens the hamper and three pigeon fanciers, (in very fast motion) leap out and run off across the field, wheeling in a curve as birds do. Cut to a series of speeded-up close ups of baskets being opened and pigeon fanciers leaping out. ***After four or five of these fast close ups cut to long shot of the mass of pigeon fanciers wheeling across the field like a flock of pigeons.*** **23** *Cut to film of Trafalgar Square.* ***The pigeon fanciers are now running around in the square, wheeling in groups.*** **24**

Cut to Gilliam picture of Trafalgar Square. The chicken man from the opening credits flies past towing a banner which says 'THIS SPACE AVAILABLE, TEL. 498 5116'. The head of a huge hedgehog—Spiny Norman—appears above St Martin's-in-the-Fields.

SPINY NORMAN Dinsdale! Dinsdale!

Animated sequence then leads to: Extremely animated caption: 'MONTY PYTHON PROUDLY PRESENTS THE INSURANCE SKETCH' Interior smooth-looking office. Mr Feldman behind a desk, Mr Martin in front of it. Both point briefly to a sign on the desk: 'Life Insurance Ltd'.

MARTIN (ERIC) Good morning. I've been in touch with you about the, er, life insurance... **25**

FELDMAN (JOHN) Ah yes, did you bring the um...the specimen of your um...and so on, and so on?

MARTIN Yes I did. It's in the car. There's rather a lot.

FELDMAN Good, good.

MARTIN Do you really *need* twelve gallons?

FELDMAN No, no, not really.

MARTIN Do you test it?

FELDMAN No.

MARTIN Well, why do you want it?

FELDMAN Well, we do it to make sure that you're serious about wanting insurance. I mean, if you're not, you won't spend a couple of months filling up that enormous churn with mmm, so on and so on...

MARTIN Shall I bring it in?

FELDMAN Good Lord no. Throw it away.

MARTIN Throw it away? I was months filling that thing up.

The sound of the National Anthem starts. They stand to attention. Martin and Feldman mutter to each other, and we hear a reverential voice over.

VOICE OVER (MICHAEL) And we've just heard that Her Majesty the Queen has just tuned into this programme and so she is now watching this royal sketch here in this royal set. The actor on the left is wearing the great grey suit of the BBC wardrobe department and the other actor is...about to deliver the first great royal joke here this royal evening. *(the camera pans, Martin following it part way, to show the camera crew and the audience, all standing to attention)* Over to the right you can see the royal cameraman, and behind...Oh, we've just heard she's switched over. She's watching the 'News at Ten'. **26**

They both point again.

The *News at Ten* was a news show on the commercial channel, known then as ITV. Until 1982 and the invention of Channel 4, Britain boasted just three national TV channels: BBC1, BBC2, and ITV.

A sign that the Pythons had, by this point, reached critical mass: a top newscaster more than happy to make fun of himself—and, it might be said, of the ridiculousness of the royal seal of approval.

Cries of disappointment. ***Cut to Reggie Bosanquet (the real one) at the 'News at Ten' set.*** **27** *He is reading.*

REGGIE ...despite the union's recommendation that the strikers should accept the second and third clauses of the agreement arrived at last Thursday. *(the National Anthem starts to play in the background and Reggie stands, continuing to read)* Today saw the publication of the McGuffie Commission's controversial report on treatment of in-patients in north London hospitals.

A hospital: a sign above door says 'INTENSIVE CARE UNIT'. A group of heavily bandaged patients with crutches, legs and arms in plaster, etc., struggle out and onto a courtyard.

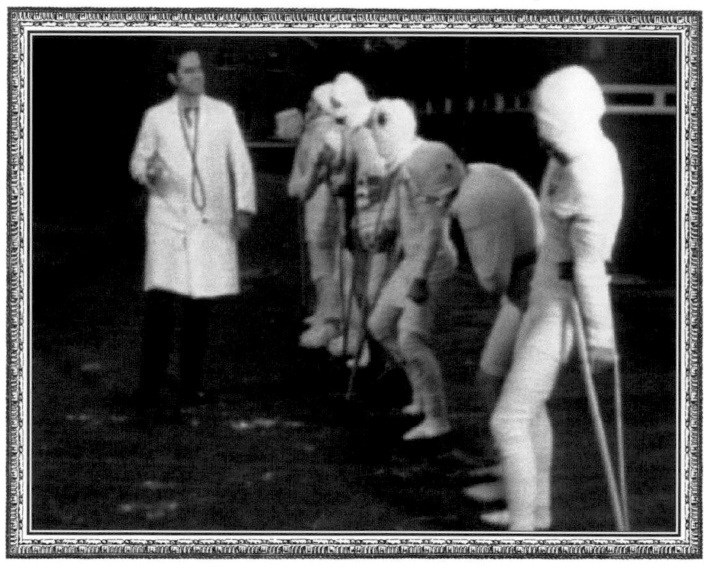

This line elicits a huge laugh.

FIRST DOCTOR (JOHN) Get on parade! Come on! We haven't got all day, have we? Come on, come on, come on. *(the patients painfully get themselves into line)* Hurry up...right! **Now, I know some hospitals where you get the patients lying around in bed.** **28** Sleeping, resting, recuperating, convalescing. Well, that's not the way we do things here, right! No, you won't be loafing about in bed wasting the doctors' time. You—you horrible little cripple. What's the matter with you?

PATIENT (MICHAEL) Fractured tibia, sergeant.

FIRST DOCTOR 'Fractured tibia, sergeant'? 'Fractured tibia, sergeant'? Ooh. Proper little mummy's boy, aren't we? Well, I'll tell you something, my fine friend, if you fracture a tibia here you keep quiet about it! Look at him! *(looks more closely)* He's broken both his arms and he don't go shouting about it, do he? No! 'Cos he's a man—he's a woman, you see, so don't come that broken tibia talk with me. Get on at the double. One, two, three, pick that crutch up, pick that crutch right up.

The patient hobbles off at the double and falls over.

"Shun" is short for "attention!"

PATIENT Aaargh!

FIRST DOCTOR **Right, squad, 'shun!** **29** Squad, right turn. Squad, by the left, quick limp! Come on, pick 'em up. Get some air in those wounds.

Cut to second doctor. He is smoking a cigar.

SECOND DOCTOR (ERIC) *(to camera)* Here at St Pooves, we believe in ART—Active Recuperation Techniques. We try to help the patient understand that however ill he may be, he can still fulfil a useful role in society. Sun lounge please, Mr Griffiths.

Pull back to show doctor sitting in a wheelchair. A bandaged patient wheels him off.

PATIENT (MICHAEL) I've got a triple fracture of the right leg, dislocated collar bone and multiple head injuries, so I do most of the heavy work, like helping the surgeon.

INTERVIEWER'S VOICE (ERIC) What does that involve?

PATIENT Well, at the moment we're building him a holiday home.

INTERVIEWER'S VOICE What about the nurses?

PATIENT Well, I don't know about them. They're not allowed to mix with the patients.

INTERVIEWER'S VOICE Do all the patients work?

PATIENT No, no, the ones that are really ill do sport.

Cut to bandaged patients on a cross-country run.

VOICE OVER (MICHAEL) Yes, one thing patients here dread are the runs.

THE PATIENTS CLIMB OVER A FENCE WITH MUCH DIFFICULTY. ONE FALLS.

INTERVIEWER'S VOICE How are you feeling?

PATIENT (GRAHAM) Much better.

Shots of patients doing sporting activities.

VOICE OVER But patients are allowed visiting. And this week they're visiting an iron foundry at Swindon, which is crying out for unskilled labour. *('Dr Kildare' theme music; shot of doctors being manicured, having shoes cleaned etc. by patients)* But this isn't the only hospital where doctors' conditions are improving.

Sign on wall: 'ST NATHAN'S HOSPITAL FOR YOUNG, ATTRACTIVE GIRLS WHO AREN'T PARTICULARLY ILL'. Pan down to a doctor.

THIRD DOCTOR (TERRY J) Er, very little shortage of doctors here. We have over forty doctors per bed—er, patient. Oh, be honest. Bed.

Sign: 'ST GANDALF'S HOSPITAL FOR VERY RICH PEOPLE WHO LIKE GIVING DOCTORS LOTS OF MONEY'. Pull back to show another doctor.

FOURTH DOCTOR (GRAHAM) We've every facility here for dealing with people who are rich. We can deal with a blocked purse, we can drain private accounts and in the worst cases we can perform a total cashectomy, which is total removal of all moneys from the patient.

Sign: 'ST MICHAEL'S HOSPITAL FOR LINKMEN'. Pan down to doctor.

FIFTH DOCTOR (JOHN) Well, here we try to help people who have to link sketches together. We try to stop them saying 'Have you ever wondered what it would be like if' and instead say something like um...er...'And now the mountaineering sketch'.

Cut to a mountaineer hanging on ropes on steep mountain face.

MOUNTAINEER (GRAHAM) I haven't written a mountaineering sketch.

Superimposed caption: 'LINK'

MOUNTAINEER But now over to the exploding version of the '**Blue Danube**'. **30**

The "Blue Danube" is a waltz composed in 1866 by Johann Strauss.

Cut to an orchestra in a field playing the 'Blue Danube'. On each musical phrase, a member of the orchestra explodes. Fade to pitch darkness.

VOICE OVER (ERIC) And now a dormitory in a girls' public school. Noise of female snores. Sound of a window sash being lifted and scrabbling sounds. Padding feet across the dorm.
BUTCH VOICE (MICHAEL) Hello, Agnes...Agnes are you awake? Agnes...

Sound of waking up. More padding feet.

BUTCH VOICE Agnes...
SECOND BUTCH VOICE (ERIC) Who is it...is that you, Charlie?
FIRST BUTCH VOICE Yeah...Agnes, where's Jane?
THIRD BUTCH VOICE (TERRY J) I'm over here, Charlie.
FIRST BUTCH VOICE Jane, we're going down to raid the **tuck shop**. **31**

The "tuck shop" is the place in a school where candies, cookies, and sodas are kept and sold.

SECOND BUTCH VOICE Oh good oh...count me in, girls.
FOURTH BUTCH VOICE (GRAHAM) Can I come, too, Agnes?
FIRST BUTCH VOICE Yeah, Joyce.
FIFTH BUTCH VOICE And me and Avril...
THIRD BUTCH VOICE Yeah, **rather**...and Suki. **32**

"Rather" is an upper-class British exclamation meaning, roughly, "Oh, goodie!"

FOURTH BUTCH VOICE Oh, whacko the diddle-oh.
FIRST BUTCH VOICE Cave girls...Here comes Miss Rodgers...

Light goes on to reveal a girls' dorm. In the middle of the floor between the beds are two panto geese which run off immediately the light goes on. There is one man in a string vest and short dibley haircut, chest wig, schoolgirl's skirt, white socks and schoolgirl's shoes. Hanging from the middle of the ceiling is a goat with light bulbs hanging from each foot. In the beds are other butch blokes in string vests...and short hair. At the door stands a commando-type Miss Rodgers.

MISS RODGERS (CAROL) All right girls, now stop this tomfoolery and get back to bed, remember it's the big match at St Bridget's tomorrow.

Cut to still of one of us in the uniform as described above. Superimposed caption: 'THE NAUGHTIEST GIRL IN THE SCHOOL'

VOICE OVER (JOHN) Yes, on your screen tomorrow: 'The Naughtiest Girl in the School' starring the men of the 14th Marine Commandos. *(cut to a picture made up of inch-square photos of various topical subjects e.g. Stalin, Churchill, Eden, White House, atom bomb, map of Western Europe, Gandhi)* **And now it's documentary time, when we look at the momentous last years of the Second World War, and tonight the invasion of Normandy performed by the girls of Oakdene High School, Upper Fifth Science.** 33

Stock film of amphibious craft brought up on a beach. The front of the craft crashes down and fifty soldiers rush out. We hear schoolgirl voices. Cut to traditional shot through periscope of ocean, cross-sights scanning the horizon. Submarine-type dramatic noise—motors and ASDIC. 34 *Cut to interior of submarine. A pepperpot looks through the periscope, then looks round at her colleagues.*

FIRST PEPPERPOT (GRAHAM) Oh, it's still raining.

Her four companions continue to knit.

SECOND PEPPERPOT (ERIC) I'm going down the shops.
FIRST PEPPERPOT **Oh, be a dear and get me some rats' bane** 35 for the budgie's boil. Otherwise I'll put your eyes out.
SECOND PEPPERPOT Aye, aye, captain. *(goes out)*

Attention noise from the communication tube. A red light flashes by it.

VOICE (JOHN) Coo-ee. Torpedo bay.
FIRST PEPPERPOT Yoo-hoo. Torpedo bay.
THIRD PEPPERPOT (TERRY J) She said torpedo bay.
FIRST PEPPERPOT Yes, she did, she did.
FOURTH PEPPERPOT (MICHAEL) Yes, she said torpedo bay. She did, she did.
VOICE Mrs Lieutenant Edale here. Mrs Midshipman Nesbitt's got one of her headaches again, so I put her in the torpedo tube.
FIRST PEPPERPOT Roger, Mrs Edale. Stand by to fire Mrs Nesbitt.
ALL Stand by to fire Mrs Nesbitt.
FIRST PEPPERPOT Red alert, put the kettle on.
VOICE Kettle on.

June 6, 1944: Allied forces land at Normandy, on the northern French coast, during what is known as the D-Day landings (then called "Operation Overlord").

ASDIC is an acronym for anti-submarine detection investigation committee, a form of sonar.

"Rats' bane" is a poison, often containing arsenic.

"More times than you've had hot dinners" is a British phrase meaning "more times than you can count." Dinner, in working-class U.K. at least, refers to a meal in the middle of the day.

It reads "and what thighs these young throbbers have, bristling..." though the rest of it is offscreen.

The principal victims of seasickness on this sketch—and when you watch it, you can see why—were Jones and Cleese. Chapman claims he was okay, thanks to a "bottle of Glenfiddich."

FIRST PEPPERPOT Engine room, stand by to feed the cat.
VOICE Standing by to feed the cat.
FIRST PEPPERPOT Fire Mrs Nesbitt.

Animation: A pepperpot is fired from a torpedo tube through the water, until she travels head first into a battleship with a loud clang.

MRS NESBITT Oh, that's much better.

Cut to a letter as in the last series, plus voice reading it.

VOICE OVER (ERIC) As an admiral who came up through the ranks **more times than you've had hot dinners**, **36** I wish to join my husband O.W.A Giveaway in condemning this shoddy misrepresentation of our modern navy. The British Navy is one of the finest and most attractive and butchest fighting forces in the world. I love those white flared trousers and the feel of rough blue serge on those pert little buttocks...

Cut to a man at a desk.

PRESENTER (MICHAEL) **I'm afraid we are unable to show you any more of that letter.** **37** We continue with a man with a stoat through his head.

Cut to man with a stoat through his head. He bows. Cut to film of Women's Institute applauding. Then cut back to man at desk.

PRESENTER And now...

Cut to a lifeboat somewhere at sea miles from any land. In the lifeboat are five bedraggled sailors, at the end of their tether. **38**

FIRST SAILOR (MICHAEL) Still no sign of land...How long is it?
SECOND SAILOR (GRAHAM) That's rather a personal question, sir.
FIRST SAILOR You stupid git, I meant how long we've been in the lifeboat. You've spoilt the atmosphere now.
SECOND SAILOR I'm sorry.
FIRST SAILOR SHUT UP! WE'LL HAVE TO START AGAIN...STILL NO SIGN OF LAND...HOW LONG IS IT?
SECOND SAILOR Thirty-three days, sir.
FIRST SAILOR Thirty-three days?
SECOND SAILOR I don't think we can hold out much longer. I don't think I did spoil the atmosphere.
FIRST SAILOR Shut up!
SECOND SAILOR I'm sorry, I don't think I did.

FIRST SAILOR Of course you did.
SECOND SAILOR *(to third sailor)* Do you think I spoilt the atmosphere?
THIRD SAILOR (ERIC) Well, I think you...
FIRST SAILOR Look, shut up! SHUT UP!...Still no sign of land...how long is it?
SECOND SAILOR Thirty-three days.
FOURTH SAILOR (TERRY J) Have we started again? *(he is kicked on the leg by the first sailor)* Wagh!
FIRST SAILOR Still no sign of land...how long is it?
SECOND SAILOR Thirty-three days, sir.
FIRST SAILOR Thirty-three days?
SECOND SAILOR Yes. We can't hold out much longer. We haven't had any food since the fifth day.
THIRD SAILOR We're done for. We're done for!
FIRST SAILOR Shut up, Maudling. We've just got to keep hoping someone will find us.
FOURTH SAILOR How are you feeling, captain?
FIFTH SAILOR (JOHN) Not too good...I...feel...so weak.
SECOND SAILOR We can't hold out much longer.
FIFTH SAILOR Listen...chaps...there's one last chance. I'm done for, **I've got a gammy leg,** 39

A "gammy leg" is one who is injured or carrying an old injury, like "gimpy" in the United States. "Gammy" may come from the Irish "cam," meaning crooked.

I'M GOING FAST, I'LL NEVER GET THROUGH BUT SOME OF YOU MIGHT SO YOU'D BETTER EAT ME.

FIRST SAILOR Eat you, sir?
FIFTH SAILOR Yes, eat me.
SECOND SAILOR Uuuuggghhh! With a gammy leg?
FIFTH SAILOR You don't have to eat the leg, Thompson, there's still plenty of good meat...look at that arm.
THIRD SAILOR It's not just the leg, sir...
FIFTH SAILOR What do you mean?
THIRD SAILOR Well sir...it's just that...
FIFTH SAILOR Why don't you want to eat me?
THIRD SAILOR I'd rather eat Johnson, sir. *(points at fourth sailor)*
SECOND SAILOR Oh, so would I, sir.
FIFTH SAILOR I see.
FOURTH SAILOR Well, that's settled then. Everyone eats me.
FIRST SAILOR Well...I er...
THIRD SAILOR What, sir...?
FIRST SAILOR No, no, you go ahead. I won't...
FOURTH SAILOR Nonsense, nonsense, sir, you're starving. Tuck in!
FIRST SAILOR No, no, it's not just that...
SECOND SAILOR What's the matter with Johnson, sir?
FIRST SAILOR Well, he's not kosher.
THIRD SAILOR That depends how we kill him, sir.
FIRST SAILOR Yes, yes, I see that...well to be quite frank, I like my meat a little more lean. I'd rather eat Hodges.
SECOND SAILOR *(cheerfully)* Oh well...all right.
THIRD SAILOR No, I'd still prefer Johnson.
FIFTH SAILOR I wish you'd all stop bickering and eat me.
SECOND SAILOR Look! I'll tell you what. Why don't those of us who want to, eat Johnson, then you, sir, can eat my leg and then we'll make a stock of the captain and then after that we can eat the rest of Johnson cold for supper.
FIRST SAILOR Good thinking, Hodges.
FOURTH SAILOR And we'll finish off with the peaches. *(picks up a tin of peaches)*
THIRD SAILOR And we can start off with the avocados. *(picks up two avocados)*
FIRST SAILOR Waitress! *(a waitress walks in)* We've decided now, we're going to have leg of Hodges...

Boos off-screen. Cut to a letter.

VOICE OVER (JOHN) Dear Sir, I am glad to hear that your studio audience disapproves of the last skit as strongly as I. As a naval officer I abhor the implication that the Royal Navy is a haven for cannibalism. It is well known that we now have the problem relatively under control, and that it is the RAF who now suffer the largest casualties in this area. **And what do you think the Argylls ate in Aden. Arabs?** **40** Yours etc. Captain B. J. Smethwick in a white wine sauce with shallots, mushrooms and garlic.

South Arabia, which now is part of southern Yemen, saw an insurrection in 1963 against British forces that controlled the area. By 1967, and with British rule coming to an end, an infantry battalion from Scotland, the Argyll and Sutherland Highlanders—led by a man who would come to be known by his nickname, "Mad Mitch"—marched, along with a readitional pipe band, into the Yemeni seaport of Aden and took over the district without any bloodshed.

Animation: various really nasty cannibalistic scenes from Terry Gilliam.

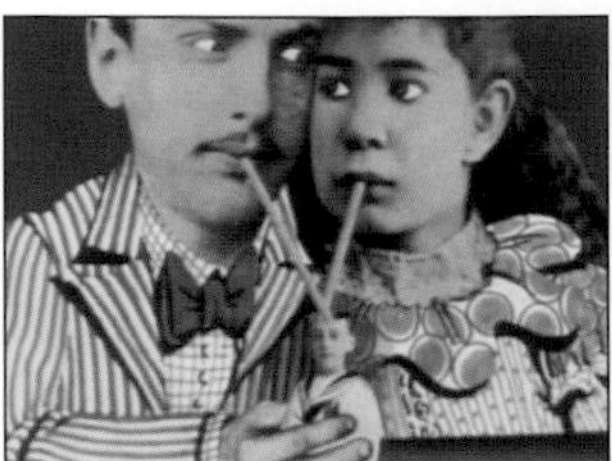

Cut to man.

MAN (TERRY J) Stop it, stop it. Stop this cannibalism. Let's have a sketch about clean, decent human beings.

Cut to an undertaker's shop.

UNDERTAKER (GRAHAM) Morning.
MAN (JOHN) Good morning.
UNDERTAKER What can I do for you, squire?
MAN Well, I wonder if you can help me. You see, my mother has just died.
UNDERTAKER Ah well, we can help you. We deal with stiffs.
MAN What?
UNDERTAKER **Well, there's three things we can do with your mum.** **41** We can bury her, burn her or dump her.
MAN *(shocked)* Dump her?
UNDERTAKER Dump her in the Thames.
MAN What?
UNDERTAKER Oh, did you like her?
MAN Yes!
UNDERTAKER

OH WELL, WE WON'T DUMP HER, THEN. WELL, WHAT DO YOU THINK? WE CAN BURY HER OR BURN HER.

MAN Well, which do you recommend?
UNDERTAKER Well, they're both nasty. If we burn her she gets stuffed in the flames, crackle, crackle, crackle, which is a bit of a shock if she's not quite dead, but quick, *(the audience starts booing)* and then we give you a handful of ashes, which you can pretend were hers.
MAN Oh.
UNDERTAKER Or if we bury her she gets eaten up by lots of weevils, and nasty maggots, *(the booing increases)* which as I said before is a bit of a shock if she's not quite dead.
MAN I see. Well, she's definitely dead.
VOICES IN AUDIENCE Let's have something decent...it's disgusting...
UNDERTAKER Where is she?

Chapman says "mother," not "mum."

MAN She's in this sack.
UNDERTAKER Can I have a look? She looks quite young.
MAN Yes, yes, she was.

Increasing protests from audience.

UNDERTAKER *(calling)* Fred!
FRED'S VOICE (ERIC) Yeah?
UNDERTAKER I think we've got an eater.
MAN What?

Another undertaker pokes his head round the door.

FRED Right, I'll get the oven on. *(goes off)*
MAN Er, excuse me, um, are you suggesting eating my mother?
UNDERTAKER Er...yeah, not raw. Cooked.
MAN What?
UNDERTAKER Yes, roasted with a few french fries, **broccoli,** 42 horseradish sauce...
MAN Well, I do feel a bit peckish.
VOICE FROM AUDIENCE Disgraceful! Boo! *(etc.)*
UNDERTAKER Great!
MAN Can we have some parsnips? 43
UNDERTAKER *(calling)* Fred—get some parsnips.
MAN I really don't think I should.
UNDERTAKER Look, tell you what, we'll eat her, if you feel a bit guilty about it after, we can dig a grave and you can throw up in it.

A section of the audience rises up in revolt and invades the set, remonstrating with the performers and banging the counter, etc., breaking up the sketch.

Zoom away from them and into caption machine; roll credits. The National Anthem starts. The shouting stops. ***Mix through credits to show audience and everyone on set standing to attention.*** 44 *As the credits end, fade out.*

42 Chapman pronounces this as "brocc o *lie*," for some reason.

43 Here the camera cuts to the audience, which is laughing and smiling.

44 This marked the end of the second series of *Monty Python's Flying Circus*.

SEA
SON
3
EPISODE 27
MONTY
PYTHON
FLYING
CIRCUS

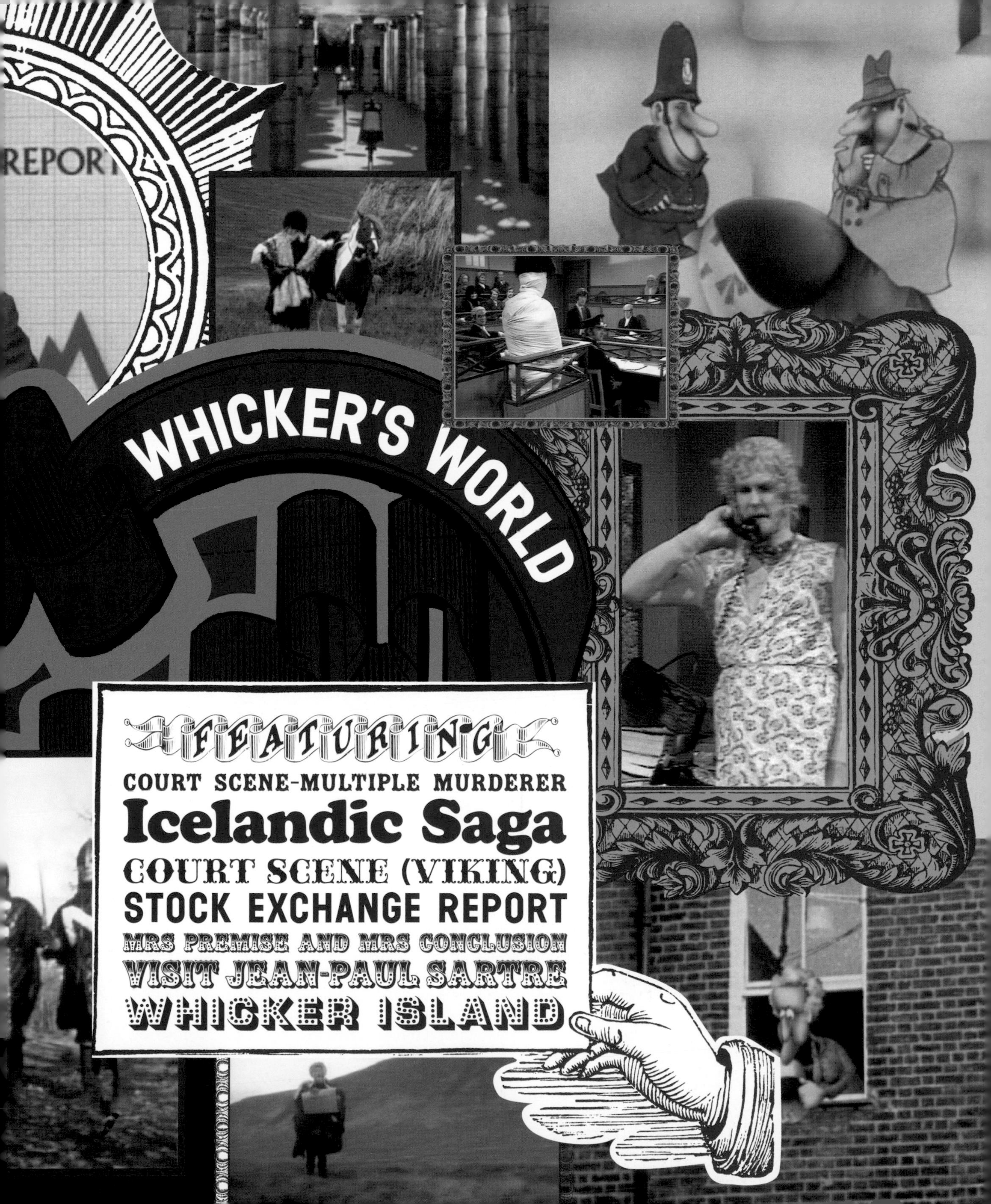
REPORT
WHICKER'S WORLD
FEATURING
COURT SCENE-MULTIPLE MURDERER
Icelandic Saga
COURT SCENE (VIKING)
STOCK EXCHANGE REPORT
MRS PREMISE AND MRS CONCLUSION
VISIT JEAN-PAUL SARTRE
WHICKER ISLAND

FIRST AIRED: OCTOBER 19, 1972

The camera pans across Glencoe. 1 *The wind is whistling and climaxes with a great crashing chord, which introduces...*

Caption: 'NJORL'S SAGA', 'ICELAND 1126' The caption fades. Continue the pan until we pick up Icelandic gentleman. He unravels a scroll and starts to read.

ICELANDIC GENT (MICHAEL) I Eric...um

The camera pans away from him and picks up a man (TERRY J) *seated at the organ, his back to the camera. He is naked, and he looks identical to the way he did in that deceased classic of our time 'And now for something completely trivial'. He grins at the camera and plays a few chords. Quick cut to the announcer at his desk.*

ANNOUNCER (JOHN) And now...

Quick cut to close up of 'It's' man.

IT'S MAN (MICHAEL)

IT'S...

Animated titles.

VOICE (JOHN) Monty Python's Flying Circus!

Cut to a courtroom. Severe atmosphere.

JUDGE (TERRY J) Michael Norman Randall, you have been found guilty of the murder of Arthur Reginald Webster, Charles Patrick Trumpington, Marcel Agnes Bernstein, Lewis Anona Rudd, John Malcolm Kerr, Nigel Sinclair Robinson, Norman Arthur Potter, Felicity Jayne Stone, Jean-Paul Reynard, Rachel Shirley Donaldson, **Stephen Jay Greenblatt, Karl-Heinz Muller,** 2 Belinda Anne Ventham, Juan-Carlos Fernandez, Thor Olaf Stensgaard, Lord Kimberrley of Pretoria, Lady Kimberley of Pretoria, The Right Honourable Nigel Warmsley Kimberley, Robert Henry Noonan and Felix James Bennett, on or about the morning of the 19th December 1972. Have you anything to say before I pass sentence?

RANDALL (ERIC) Yes, sir. I'm very sorry.

1

One of the most beautiful glens (or valleys) in the British Isles, Glencoe is in the Scottish Highlands, some hundred miles northeast of Glasgow.

Stephen Jay Greenblatt is the American New Historicist. Karl-Heinz Müller is the Austrian Olympian fencer.

JUDGE Very sorry!

RANDALL Yes, sir. It was a very very bad thing to have done and I'm really very ashamed of myself. I can only say it won't happen again. To have murdered so many people in such a short space of time is really awful, and I really am very, very, *very* sorry that I did it, and also that I've taken up so much of the court's valuable time listening to the sordid details of these senseless killings of mine. I would particularly like to say, a very personal and sincere 'sorry' to you, m'lud, my lud for my appalling behaviour throughout this trial. I'd also like to say sorry to the police, for putting them to so much trouble *(shot of three heavily bandaged exhausted-looking policemen behind him)* for the literally hours of work they've had to put in, collecting evidence and identifying corpses and so forth. You know I think sometimes we ought to realize the difficult and often dangerous work involved in tracking down violent criminals like myself and I'd just like them to know that their fine work is at least appreciated by me.

The policemen look embarrassed.

FIRST POLICEMAN (GRAHAM) No, no, we were only doing our job.

SECOND POLICEMAN No, no, no, no.

RANDALL It's very good of you to say that, but I know what you've been through.

FIRST POLICEMAN No, no, we've had worse.

THIRD POLICEMAN

IT WAS PLAIN SAILING APART FROM THE ARREST.

RANDALL I know and I'm grateful. I'd like to apologize too to the prosecuting counsel for dragging him in here morning after morning in such lovely weather.

COUNSEL (JOHN) Well, I would have had to come in anyway.

RANDALL Ah good, but what a presentation of a case!

COUNSEL Oh thank you.

RANDALL No, no, it's a privilege to watch you in action. I never had a chance.

COUNSEL Oh yes you did.

RANDALL Not after that summing up. Great.

COUNSEL Oh thank you. *(very chuffed)*

RANDALL And now I must come to the jury. What can I say. I've dragged you in here, day after day, keeping you away from your homes, your jobs, your loved ones, just to hear the private details of my petty atrocities.

FOREMAN (MICHAEL) No, no, it was very interesting.

RANDALL But you could have had a much nicer case.

FOREMAN

NO, NO, MURDER'S MUCH MORE FUN.

FIRST JURYMAN Yes and so many of them.

SECOND JURYMAN Excellent.

THIRD JURYMAN We've had a terrific time. *(the jury applauds)*

3

Richard Attenborough, actor and Academy Award–winning director for *Gandhi*, is the butt of jokes in his native land for his overly emotional outpourings about the art of acting and directing.

RANDALL ***(blows his nose, does a Dickie Attenborough)*** **3** I'm sorry, I'm very moved. And so, m'lud, it only remains for you to pass the most savage sentence on me that the law can provide.

JUDGE Well er...not necessarily.

RANDALL No, m'lud, the full penalty of the law is hardly sufficient, I insist I must be made an example of.

JUDGE Well yes and no. I mean society at large...

RANDALL Oh no, m'lud. Not with mass murder.

JUDGE But in this case, *(to court)* don't you think?

COURT Yes, yes!

RANDALL

OH, COME ON, M'LUD, YOU'VE GOT TO GIVE ME LIFE.

COURT No, no, no, no.
RANDALL *(to court at large)* Well, ten years at least.
JUDGE Ten years!
COURT Shame. Shame!
RANDALL Well five then. Be fair.
JUDGE No, no. I'm giving you three months.
RANDALL Oh no, that's *so* embarrassing. I won't hear of it. Give me six...please.
JUDGE Well, all right. Six months.
RANDALL Thank you, m'lud.
JUDGE But suspended.
RANDALL Oh no.
COURT Hooray. *(they applaud)*

FOREMAN Three cheers for the defendant. Hip. Hip.
COURT Hooray.
FOREMAN Hip. Hip.
COURT Hooray.
FOREMAN Hip. Hip.
COURT Hooray.
ALL For he's a jolly good fellow
For he's a jolly good fellow
For he's a jolly good fellow
VOICE *(off)* Which nobody can deny.

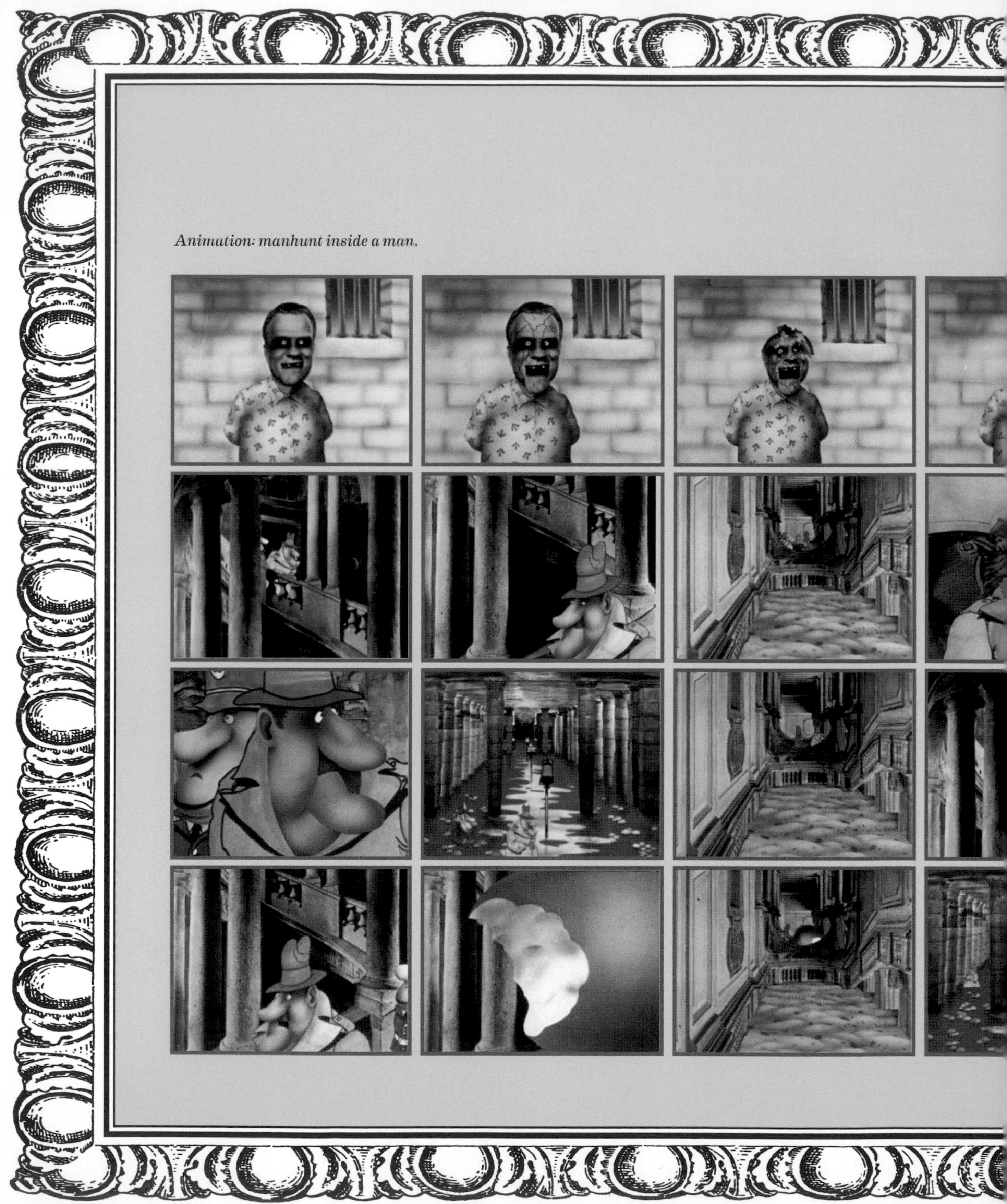

Animation: manhunt inside a man.

Caption: 'NJORL'S SAGA—PART II' Pan across a bleak landscape.

VOICE OVER (JOHN) This little-known Icelandic saga, written by an unknown hand in the late thirteenth century, has remained undiscovered until today. Now it comes to your screens for the first time. Fresh from the leaves of Iceland's history.

THE TERRIBLE 'NJORL'S SAGA'.

Cut to Viking.

VIKING (MICHAEL) It's not that terrible.

Cut to landscape. The announcer appears in the corner of the shot.

ANNOUNCER No, I meant terribly *violent*. No, I meant terribly *violent*.

Cut to Viking.

VIKING Oh yeah, yeah.

A Viking hut. A Viking comes out and has great difficulty mounting his horse.

VOICE OVER (ERIC) Erik Njorl, son of Frothgar, leaves his home to seek Hangar the Elder at the home of Thorvald Nlodvisson, the son of Gudleif, half brother of Thorgier, the priest of Ljosa water, who took to wife Thurunn, the mother of Thorkel Braggart, the slayer of Gudmund the powerful, who knew Howal, son of Geernon, son of Erik from Valdalesc, son of Arval Gristlebeard, son of Harken, who killed Bjortguaard in Sochnadale in Norway over Gudreed, daughter of Thorkel Long, the son of Kettle-Trout, the half son of Harviyoun Half-troll, father of Ingbare the Brave, who with Isenbert of Gottenberg the daughter of Hangbard the Fierce...*(fades and continues under:)*

ANOTHER VOICE OVER (TERRY J) I must apologize for an error in the saga. Evidently Thorgier, the Priest of Ljosa water who took to wife Thurunn, the mother of Thorkel Braggart, the slayer of Gudmund the powerful, who knew Howal, son of Geernon, son of Erik from Vadalesc... *(fades under next speech)*

The Viking has still failed to mount his horse. Both he and the horse look a bit exasperated.

ORIGINAL VOICE OVER (JOHN) Well I'm afraid we're having a little trouble getting this very exciting Icelandic saga started. If any of you at home have any ideas about how to get this exciting saga started again here's the address to write to:

THIRD VOICE OVER (MICHAEL) Help the Exciting Icelandic Saga, 18B MacNorten Buildings, Oban.

Caption: 'HELP THE EXCITING ICELANDIC SAGA
C/O MATCH OF THE DAY
BBC TV
THE LARCHES
26 WESTBROOK AVENUE
FAVERSHAM
KENT'

Cut to an office: the announcer at a desk. At another desk a secretary applies a deodorant spray to her bust.

ANNOUNCER (JOHN) *(to camera)* Hello, well I was the third voice you heard just now. I'm sorry about that terrible mess.

Cut to the Viking at wheel of car.

VIKING (MICHAEL) Well it wasn't all that terrible...

Cut back to the office.

ANNOUNCER No, no, I meant terrible in the sense of unfortunate.

Cut to the Viking.

VIKING Oh.

Cut back to the office.

ANNOUNCER Anyway, our plea for assistance has been answered by the North Malden Icelandic Saga Society who've given us some very useful information about the saga and so we carry on now with 'Njorl's Saga' with our thanks going, once again, **to the North Malden Icelandic Saga Society. 4**

Cut to the Viking standing by his horse. He is asleep.

There is a Malden and a New Malden in the U.K., but not a North Malden.

VOICE OVER (ERIC)

ERIK NJORL, SON OF FROTHGAR RODE OFF INTO THE DESOLATE PLAIN.

(the Viking manages to mount the horse; he rides off) **5** Day and night he rode, looking neither to right nor left. Stopping neither for food nor rest. *(shots of Erik riding through a bleak landscape)* Twelve days and nights he rode. Through rain and storm. Through wind and snow beyond the enchanted waterfall, *(Erik rides past a waterfall)* through the elfin glades until he reached his goal. *(shot of a modern road sign: 'North Malden—please drive carefully)* He had found the rich and pleasant land beyond the mountains, *(shots of Erik riding gently through a modern suburban shopping street)* the land where golden streams sang their way through fresh green meadows. **Where there were halls and palaces, an excellent swimming pool and one of the most attractive bonus incentive schemes for industrial development in the city.** **6** Only fifteen miles from excellent Thames-side docking facilities and within easy reach **of the proposed M25.** **7** Here it was that Erik Njorl, son of Frothgar, met the mayor Mr Arthur Huddinut, a local solicitor.

Erik rides up to the town hall and is met by the mayor.

MAYOR (MICHAEL) Welcome to North Malden. *(to camera)* Yes, everyone is welcome to North Malden, none more so than the businessmen and investors who shape our society of the future. Here at North Malden...

His voice fades under the following.

VOICE OVER (JOHN) And we apologize to viewers of 'Njorl's Saga' who may be confused by some of the references to North Malden. After a frank exchange of views we have agreed to carry on showing this version supplied to us by the North Malden Icelandic Saga Society on the undertaking that future scenes will adhere more closely to the spirit of twelfth-century Iceland.

Film leader countdown (5, 4, 3...) then shot of Erik riding away into bleak landscape.

VOICE OVER (ERIC) With moist eyes, Erik leaves this happy land to return to the harsh uneconomic realities of life in the land of Ljosa waters. On his way Erik rested a while in the land of Bjornsstrand—the land of dark forces, where Gildor was King. *(Erik comes to a river in a wood; he drinks)* These were the dukes of the land of Bjornsstrand. *(sudden shot of six armoured knights standing in a row)* Proud warriors who bore on their chests the letters of their dread name.

The knights move their shields to reveal on their breastplates the letters M.A.L.D.E.N.

Terry Jones is allergic to horses. He did his own riding for the sketch. Do the math—he claims it was a painful day of filming.

Jones dressed for an Icelandic saga, on horseback, riding the suburban streets of London—and, yes, people stop and stare.

The M25 has since become a reality in England. It (mostly) circumnavigates London, and though it was begun, in parts, in the early 1970s, it wasn't completed until 1986. It has been described as the world's biggest parking lot, owing to the frequency of traffic jams it engenders.

Shots of Erik battling with the knights. A telephone rings and the following conversation is heard.

ANNOUNCER'S VOICE Hello? Is that the North Malden Icelandic Society?
VOICE (MICHAEL) Yes, that's right.
ANNOUNCER About this saga.
VOICE Oh yes, the Icelandic saga.
ANNOUNCER Yes.
VOICE Good, isn't it.
ANNOUNCER Well er, I don't know, but you promised us that you would stick to the spirit of the original text.
VOICE Yes, that's right.
ANNOUNCER Well I mean a lot of these things that are happening, well they just don't quite ring true.

One of the knights is carrying a sign: 'MALDEN, GATEWAY TO INDUSTRY'.

VOICE Well, it's a new interpretation really.

Another carries a sign, 'ICI THANKS MALDEN'.

ANNOUNCER Well we don't want a new...

Flash frame caption: 'INVEST IN MALDEN'

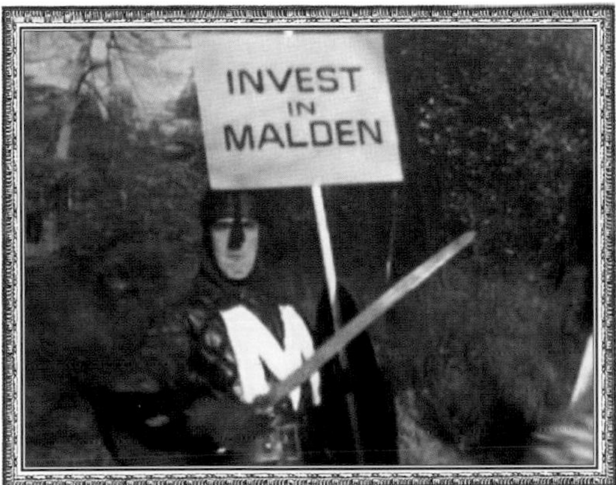

ANNOUNCER ...I mean we wanted the proper thing...I mean just look what's happening now.

More signs: 'INVEST IN MALDEN', 'MALDEN—45% INTEREST FREE LOANS'.

VOICE Banners were a very important part of Icelandic lore, Mr Mills.
ANNOUNCER No, no, I'm sorry I, I can't accept that, it's gone too far, I'm very sorry but we'll have to terminate the agreement. You're just trying to cash in on the BBC's exciting Icelandic saga.

The knights are carrying more and more advertising banners and signs.

VOICE That's business, Mr Mills.
ANNOUNCER Well, that's as maybe but it's not the way the BBC works.
VOICE Well I'm sorry you feel that way but er, you know, if you ever want to come to Malden...

Flash caption: 'INVEST IN MALDEN' Film leader countdown (5, 4, 3...). Caption: 'NJORL'S SAGA—PART III' Usual dramatic music. Fade music as we come up on a courtroom. A man, Mr Birchenhall, is giving evidence.

MAN (GRAHAM) 8 o'clock is a peak viewing hour so naturally we tend to stick to our comedy output—unless of course there's sport—because of course we know this is popular, and popularity is what television is about. Quite frankly I'm sick and tired of people accusing us of being ratings conscious.

JUDGE (TERRY J) *(to the clerk of the court)* Ratings conscious?

CLERK Transmitting bland garbage, m'lud.

JUDGE Thank you.

MAN Now I'm really cheesed off. I mean it's not your high-brow bleeding plays that pull in the viewers, you know.

JUDGE *(bored)* Thank you.

MAN *(getting more and more angry)* I mean Joe Public doesn't want to sit down and watch three hours of documentaries every evening.

JUDGE Thank you.

MAN He wants to sit down and he wants to be entertained, he doesn't want a load...*(he is helped out of court by two policemen, still protesting violently)* No really—I'm absolutely fed up with this. I really am.

JUDGE *(banging gavel)* Case dismissed.

The prosecuting counsel rises anxiously.

PROSECUTING COUNSEL (JOHN) Case *dismissed*, m'lud?

JUDGE Oh all right, five years.

PROSECUTING COUNSEL Thank you, m'lud. *(he sits)*

JUDGE Call the next case please.

PROSECUTING COUNSEL Call Erik Njorl, son of Frothgar, brother of Hangnor...(etc.).

CLERK Call Erik Njorl...*(etc.)*.

VOICES *(off)* Call Erik Njorl...*(etc.)*. *(all calling at once)*

ERIK COMES INTO THE DOCK. HE IS BANDAGED ALMOST TOTALLY, LIKE A COCOON, INCLUDING HIS HEAD.

He wears a Viking fur hat. The usher approaches him with the card and Bible.

USHER (ERIC) You are Erik Njorl, son of Frothgar...

JUDGE Get on with it!

USHER Will you raise your right hand.

JUDGE He obviously *can't* raise his right hand, you silly usher person...can you raise your right leg Mr Njorl?

Njorl shakes his head.

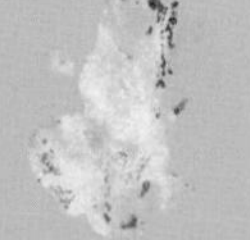

USHER Can you raise any part of your body, Mr Njorl?

Njorl leans over and whispers in the usher's ear.

USHER I see...well, we'll skip that...well, just take the book in your right hand Mr Njorl without raising any part of your body...Oh...
JUDGE What is it now, you persistently silly usher?
USHER He can't hold the Bible m'lud.
JUDGE Well screw the Bible! Let's get on with this bleeding trial, **I've got a Gay Lib meeting at 6 o'clock.** 8 Superintendent Lufthansa will you please read the charge.
SUPERINTENDENT (GRAHAM) Is a charge strictly necessary, m'lud?
JUDGE *(heavy aside)* The press is here.
SUPERINTENDENT Oh sorry! Right, here we go. You are hereby charged: one, that you did, on or about 1126, conspire to publicize a London Borough in the course of a BBC saga; two, that you were wilfully and persistently a foreigner; three, that you conspired to do things not normally considered illegal; four, that you were caught in possession of an offensive weapon, viz. the big brown table down at the police station.
JUDGE The big brown table down at the police station?
SUPERINTENDENT It's the best we could find, m'lud...and five...all together now...

The whole court shout together.

COURT Assaulting a police officer! 9
PROSECUTING COUNSEL Call Police Constable Pan-Am. *(pan-Am runs into court and starts beating Njorl with a truncheon)* Into the witness box, constable...there'll be plenty of time for that later on. *(the policeman gets into box hitting at anyone within range; his colleagues restrain him)* Now, you are Police Constable Pan-Am?
CONSTABLE (MICHAEL) No, I shall deny that to the last breath in my body. *(superintendent nods)* Oh. Sorry, yes.
PROSECUTING COUNSEL Police constable, do you recognize the defendant?
CONSTABLE No. Never seen him before in my life. *(superintendent nods)* Oh yes, yes he's the one. He done it. I'd recognize him anywhere, sorry, super. *(the superintendent has the grace to look embarrassed)*
PROSECUTING COUNSEL Constable, will you please tell the court in your own words what happened?
CONSTABLE Oh yes! *(refers to his notebook)* 10 I was proceeding in a northerly direction up Alitalia Street when I saw the deceased *(points at Njorl)* standing at an upstairs window, baring her bosom at the general public. She then took off her...wait a tick. Wrong story. *(refers to his notebook)* Ho yes! There were three nuns in a railway compartment and the ticket inspector says to one of them. *(the superintendent shakes his head)* No, anyway I clearly saw the deceased...
CLERK Defendant.
CONSTABLE Defendant! Sorry. Sorry, super. I clearly saw the defendant...doing whatever he's accused of. Red handed. When kicked...*cautioned* he said: **'It's a fair...cop,** 11 I done it all... Right...no doubt about...that'. Then, bound as he was to the chair, he assaulted myself and three other constables while bouncing around the cell. The end.

Spontaneous applause from the court. Shouts of 'more! more!'. Pan-Am raises his hands and the clapping and shouting dies down.

CONSTABLE Thank you, thank you...and for my next piece of evidence...
SUPERINTENDENT I think you'd better leave it there, constable.
PROSECUTING COUNSEL Excellent evidence, constable...*(the constable is removed, flailing his truncheon the while)* Thank you very much. Now then Mr Njorl, will you tell the court please where were you on the night of 1126? *(silence from the bandages)* **Move any part of your body if you were north of a line from the Humber to the Mersey. *(silence)*** 12

8

"Gay lib," the gay liberation movement, became active in the late 1960s to fight the civil and legal obstacles, as well as the blind hatred, faced by homosexuals.

Chapman shouts "Thank you" here offscreen.

Something falls offscreen here and makes a huge noise. Terry Gilliam, one of the police officers sitting down behind Palin, starts to laugh, as does Palin, who nonetheless gamely continues with his speech.

"It's a fair . . . cop" is the archetypal response of the archetypal criminal when caught red-handed by a British police officer. That is not to say that any criminal ever said such a thing at any time in history.

The River Humber is in fact a tidal estuary. It lies on the northeast side of England and marks some of the boundary of Yorkshire, to the north, and Lincolnshire, to the south. The River Mersey is in the northwest of England, running from Stockport, near Manchester, to Liverpool; it too marks an ancient boundary, that of Cheshire and Lancashire.

JUDGE Is he *in* there, d'you think?...Hello...Hello! Defendant, are you there...coo-ee! De-*fend*-ant... *(to the clerk of the court)* I think you'd better go and have a look, Maurice.

CLERK Don't call me Maurice in court!

JUDGE I'm sorry.

The clerk and prosecuting counsel and two policemen look inside Njorl, who is now in fact a framework of bandages with no one inside. From this oh-so zany situation only Terry 'Marty Feldman's Comedy Machine' Gilliam can save us... Animated sketch, leading us into a studio set; a man is sitting in front of a non-animated (but cheap) graph labelled 'Stock Market Report'.

VOICE OVER (JOHN) And now the Stock Market Report by Exchange Telegraph.

MAN (ERIC) Trading was crisp at the start of the day with some brisk business on the floor. Rubber hardened and string remained confident. Little bits of tin consolidated although biscuits sank after an early gain and stools remained anonymous. Armpits rallied well after a poor start. Nipples rose dramatically during the morning but had declined by mid-afternoon, while teeth clenched and buttocks remained firm. Small dark furry things increased severely on the floor, whilst rude jellies wobbled up and down, and bounced against rising thighs which had spread to all parts of the country by mid-afternoon. After lunch naughty things dipped sharply forcing giblets upwards with the nicky nacky noo. Ting tang tong rankled dithely, little tipples pooped and poppy things went pong! Gibble gabble gobble went the rickety rackety roo and...*(a bucketful of water descends on him)*

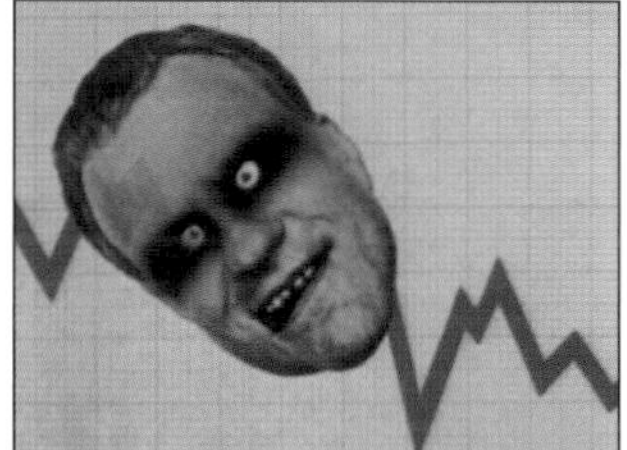

Animation: ends with an animated woman going into a laundromat. Cut to the interior of a laundromat. Various shabby folk sitting around. Mrs Conclusion approaches Mrs Premise and sits down.

MRS CONCLUSION (GRAHAM) Hello, Mrs Premise.

MRS PREMISE (JOHN) Hello, Mrs Conclusion.

MRS CONCLUSION Busy day?

MRS PREMISE

BUSY! I'VE JUST SPENT FOUR HOURS BURYING THE CAT.

MRS CONCLUSION *Four hours* to bury a cat?

MRS PREMISE Yes! It wouldn't keep still, wriggling about howling its head off.

MRS CONCLUSION Oh—it wasn't dead then?

MRS PREMISE Well, no, no, but it's not at all a well cat so as we were going away for a fortnight's holiday, I thought I'd better bury it just to be on the safe side.

MRS CONCLUSION Quite right. **You don't want to come back from Sorrento to a dead cat.** **13** It'd be so anticlimactic. Yes, kill it now, that's what I say.

MRS PREMISE Yes.

MRS CONCLUSION **We're going to have our budgie put down.** **14**

MRS PREMISE Really? Is it very old?

MRS CONCLUSION No. We just don't like it. We're going to take it to the vet tomorrow.

MRS PREMISE Tell me, how do they put budgies down then?

MRS CONCLUSION Well it's funny you should ask that, but I've just been reading a great big book about how to put your budgie down, and apparently you can either hit them with the book, or, you can shoot them just there, just above the beak.

MRS PREMISE Just there!

MRS CONCLUSION Yes.

MRS PREMISE Well well well. 'Course, Mrs Essence flushed hers down the loo.

MRS CONCLUSION Ooh! No! You shouldn't do that—no that's dangerous. Yes, they *breed* in the *sewers*, and eventually you get evil-smelling flocks of huge soiled budgies flying out of people's lavatories infringing their personal freedom. *(life-size cut-out of woman at end of last animation goes by)* Good morning Mrs Cut-out.

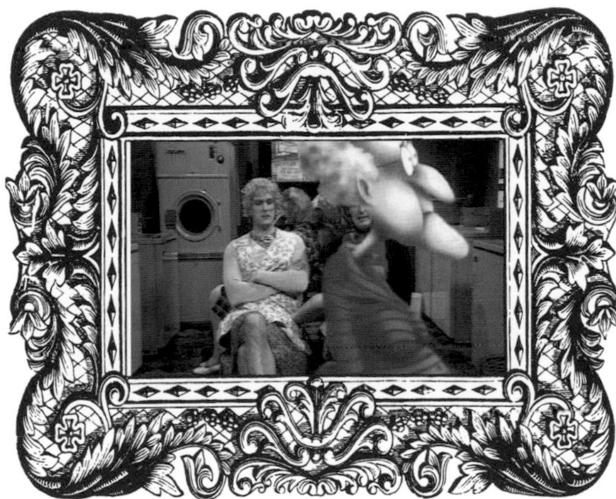

MRS PREMISE It's a funny thing freedom. I mean how can any of us be really free when we still have personal possessions.

MRS CONCLUSION You can't. **You can't—I mean, how can I go off and join FRELIMO** **15** when I've got nine more instalments to pay on the fridge.

MRS PREMISE No, you can't. You can't. Well this is the whole crux of **Jean-Paul Sartre's 'Roads to Freedom'.** **16**

MRS CONCLUSION No, it bloody isn't. The nub of that is, his characters stand for all of us in their desire to avoid action. Mind you, the man at the off-licence says it's an everyday story of French country folk.

MRS PREMISE What does he know?

MRS CONCLUSION Nothing.

MRS PREMISE **Sixty new pence for a bottle of Maltese Claret.** **17** Well I personally think Jean-Paul's masterwork is an allegory of man's search for commitment.

MRS CONCLUSION No it isn't.

MRS PREMISE Yes it is.

MRS CONCLUSION Isn't.

Sorrento is a resort town on the western coast of Italy, south of Naples. It is considered quite romantic by Brits who dream of traveling there.

A "budgie" is a nickname for the budgerigar, also known as a parakeet.

FRELIMO was the liberation movement of Mozambique (in Portuguese, *Frente de Libertação de Moçambique*). It was founded in 1962 and aimed at ridding the country of its Portuguese overlords. (Independence would come in 1975.)

A trio of novels (although four were planned) known in English as *The Age of Reason* (1945), *The Reprieve* (1947), and *Troubled Sleep* (1949).

Cleese knocks something off the bench behind him and it breaks. He turns, says, "Ooh, I beg your pardon"—then continues.

Ibiza, an island in the Mediterranean Sea, off the eastern coast of Spain.

Jean Genet, French vagabond, petty thief, prostitute, and, later, famed novelist, playwright, activist, and poet. Also, gay, hence "Mr. and Mr."

Translates to "Capitalism, the bourgeoisie, they're the same thing . . ."

"Give a tinkle" means to make a phone call.

This word gets a big laugh from those fluent in French swearing.

"BEA" is for the British European Airways. It merged with British Overseas Airways Corporation in 1974 to form British Airways.

Alan Whicker reported from all over the globe for his human-interest show *Whicker's World*. Idle does a dead-on impersonation of Whicker here, with his slow, nasal cadences.

MRS PREMISE 'Tis.

MRS CONCLUSION No it isn't.

MRS PREMISE All right. We can soon settle this. We'll ask him.

MRS CONCLUSION Do you know him?

MRS PREMISE Yes, we met on holiday last year.

MRS CONCLUSION **In Ibeezer?** 18

MRS PREMISE Yes. He was staying there with his wife and **Mr and Mr Genet.** 19 Oh, I did get on well with Madam S. We were like that.

MRS CONCLUSION What was Jean-Paul like?

MRS PREMISE Well, you know, a bit moody. Yes, he didn't join in the fun much. Just sat there thinking. Still, Mr Rotter caught him a few times with the whoopee cushion. *(she demonstrates)* **Le Capitalisme et La Bourgeoisie ils sont la même chose...** 20 Oooh we did laugh.

MRS CONCLUSION **Well, we'll give a tinkle then.** 21

MRS PREMISE Yes, all right. She said they were in the book. *(shouts)* Where's the Paris telephone directory?

MRS INFERENCE (ERIC) It's on the drier.

MRS PREMISE No, no, that's Budapest. Oh here we are Sartre...Sartre.

MRS VARLEY (TERRY J) It's 621036.

MRS PREMISE Oh, thank you, Mrs Varley. *(dials)* Hallo. Paris 621036 please and make it snappy, buster...*(as they wait they sing 'The Girl from Ipanema')* Hallo? Hello Mrs Sartre. It's Beulagh Premise here. Oh, pardon, c'est Beulagh Premise ici, oui, oui, dans Ibeezer. Oui, we met...nous nous recontrons au Hotel Miramar. Oui, à la barbeque, c'est vrai. Madame S.—est-ce que Jean est chez vous? **Oh merde.** 22 When will he be free? Oh pardon. Quand sera-t-il libre? Oooooh. Ha ha ha ha *(to Mrs Conclusion)* She says he's spent the last sixty years trying to work that one out. *(to Madame Sartre)* Très amusant, Madam S. Oui absolument...à bientôt. *(puts the phone down)* Well he's out distributing pamphlets to the masses but he'll be in at six.

MRS CONCLUSION **Oh well, I'll ring BEA then.** 23

Cut to them sitting on a raft in mid-ocean.

MRS PREMISE Oh look, Paris!

Cut to shot of a notice board on the seashore, it reads 'North Malden Welcomes Careful Coastal Craft'.

MRS CONCLUSION That's not Paris. Jean-Paul wouldn't live here. It's a right old dump.

'Alan Whicker', complete with microphone, walks in front of sign. 24

WHICKER (ERIC) But this is where they were wrong. For this was no old dump, but a town with a future, an urban Eldorado where the businessmen of today can enjoy the facilities of to-morrow in the comfort of yesterday. Provided by a go-getting, go-ahead council who know just how loud money can talk. *(a phone off-screen starts to ring)* Interest rates are so low...

Cut to head of drama's office; he is on the phone.

HEAD OF DRAMA (JOHN) Well it's none of my business but we had the same trouble with one of our Icelandic sagas. These people are terribly keen but they do rather tend to take over. I think I'd stick to Caribbean Islands if I were you. *(rings off)* Fine...and now back to the saga.

Caption: 'NJORL'S SAGA—PART IV' Thundering music. Cut to an Icelandic seashore. Dark and impressive. After a pause the pepperpots walk into shot.

MRS PREMISE Here—this is not Paris, this is Iceland.
MRS CONCLUSION Oh, well, Paris must be over there then. ***(points out to the sea; they walk back to the raft)*** **25**

Stock shot of Eiffel Tower. French accordion music. Mix through to French street thronged by ***cod*** **26** *Frenchmen with berets and loaves. Mrs Conclusion and Mrs Premise appear and walk up to the front door of an apartment block. On the front door is a list of the inhabitants of the block. They read it out loud.*

MRS PREMISE Oh, here we are, Number 25...*(reads)* Flat 1, **Duke and Duchess of Windsor,** **27** Flat 2, **Yves Montand,** **28** Flat 3, **Jacques Cousteau,** **29** Flat 4, **Jean Genet and Friend,** **30** Flat 5, Maurice Laroux ...

And they reprise their rendition of "Girl from Ipanema" as they walk.

"Cod" is slang for standard or average.

Chapman doesn't refer to the Windsors here; instead, he jumps straight to Yves Montand, putting him in Flat 1.

The French actor and singer.

The French explorer and author.

Chapman and Cleese coo at each other here, highlighting the "scandalous" nature of Genet's sexuality.

He was a French composer and conductor.

The French mime artist.

Prime minister of India from 1966 to 1977 and again from 1980 to 1984. She was assassinated in 1984.

Prince Rainier of Monaco married American actress Grace Kelly in April 1956.

MRS CONCLUSION Who's he?

MRS PREMISE **Never heard of him.** [31] Flat 6, **Marcel Marceau, Walking Against the Wind Ltd.** [32] Flat 7, **Indira Gandhi?** [33]

MRS CONCLUSION She gets about a bit, doesn't she?

MRS PREMISE Yes, Flat 8, Jean-Paul and Betty-Muriel Sartre.

She rings the bell. A voice comes from the intercom.

VOICE Oui.

MRS PREMISE C'est nous, Betty-Muriel, excusez que nous sommes en retard.

VOICE Entrez.

Buzzer sounds.

MRS PREMISE Oui, merci.

Interior the Sartres' flat. It is littered with books and papers. We hear Jean-Paul coughing. Mrs Sartre goes to the door. She is a ratbag with a fag in her mouth and a duster over her head. A French song is heard on the radio. She switches it off.

MRS SARTRE (MICHAEL) Oh, rubbish. *(opens the door)* Bonjour.

MRS CONCLUSION *(entering)* Parlez vous Anglais?

MRS SARTRE Oh yes. Good day. *(Mrs Premise comes in)* Hello, love!

MRS PREMISE Hello! Oh this is Mrs Conclusion from No. 46.

MRS SARTRE Nice to meet you, dear.

MRS CONCLUSION Hello.

MRS PREMISE How's the old man, then?

MRS SARTRE Oh, don't ask. He's in one of his bleeding moods. 'The bourgeoisie this is the bourgeoisie that'—he's like a little child sometimes. **I was only telling the Rainiers the other day—** [34] course he's always rude to them, only classy friends we've got—I was saying solidarity with the masses I said...pie in the sky! Oooh! You're not a Marxist are you Mrs Conclusion?

MRS CONCLUSION No, I'm a Revisionist.

MRS SARTRE Oh good. I mean, look at this place! I'm at my wits' end. Revolutionary leaflets everywhere. One of these days I'll revolutionary leaflets him. If it wasn't for the goat you couldn't get in here for propaganda.

Shot of a goat eating leaflets in corner of room.

MRS PREMISE Oh very well. Can we pop in and have a word with him?

MRS SARTRE Yes come along.

MRS PREMISE Thank you.

MRS SARTRE But be careful. He's had a few. Mind you he's as good as gold in the morning, I've got to hand it to him, but come lunchtime it's a bottle of vin ordinaire—six glasses and he's ready to agitate.

Mrs Premise and Mrs Conclusion knock on the door of Jean- Paul's room.

MRS PREMISE Coo-ee! Jean-Paul? Jean-Paul! It's only us. Oh pardon...c'est même nous...

They enter. We do not see Jean-Paul although we hear his voice.

JEAN-PAUL Oui.

MRS PREMISE Jean-Paul. Your famous trilogy 'Rues à Liberté', is it an allegory of man's search for commitment?
JEAN-PAUL Oui.
MRS PREMISE I told you so.
MRS CONCLUSION Oh coitus.

Stock shot of a plane taking off.

Caption: 'THE END'

Then the stock shot of a jet landing which they always use to introduce 'Whicker's World'. This leads us into Whicker Island—a tropical island paradise where all the inhabitants have Alan Whicker suits, glasses and microphones.

Caption: 'WHICKER'S WORLD'

Various Whickers pace past the camera.

FIRST WHICKER (ERIC) Today we look at a vanishing race. A problem people who are fast disappearing off the face of the earth.
SECOND WHICKER (TERRY J) A race who one might say are losing a winning battle.
THIRD WHICKER (MICHAEL) They live in a sunshine paradise, a Caribbean dream, where only reality is missing.
FOURTH WHICKER (GRAHAM) For this is Whicker Island.
FIFTH WHICKER (JOHN) An island inhabited entirely by ex-international interviewers in pursuit of the impossible dream.
FIRST WHICKER The whole problem of Whicker Island is here in a nutshell.
SECOND WHICKER There are just too many Whickers.
THIRD WHICKER **The light-weight suits.** 35
FOURTH WHICKER The old school tie.
FIFTH WHICKER The practised voice of the seasoned campaigner.
FIRST WHICKER Cannot hide the basic tragedy here.
SECOND WHICKER There just aren't enough rich people left to interview.

Cut to a different location.

THIRD WHICKER You can't teach an old dog new tricks and so *(turning to a swimming pool with lots of Whickers around it, wandering with stick mikes and muttering)* you find them...
FOURTH WHICKER *(seated by swimming pool)* Sitting beside elegant swimming pools...
FIFTH WHICKER *(seated at drinks table, with sun umbrella)* ...sipping Martinis...
FIRST WHICKER *(standing by the pool)* ...and waiting for the inevitable interview.

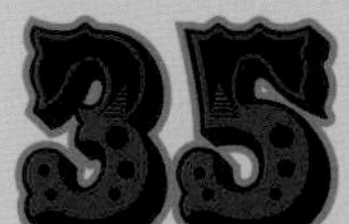

Palin needs to get out of the shot here so he ducks down, which is partially caught by the camera.

SECOND WHICKER *(standing fully clothed in the pool)* I talked to the island's only white man, Father Pierre.

Cut to a different location. Feeling of heat. The third Whicker stands beside a priest in a white robe.

THIRD WHICKER Father Pierre, why did you stay on in this colonial Campari-land where the clink of glasses mingles with the murmur of a million mosquitoes, where waterfalls of whisky wash away the worries of a world-weary Whicker, where gin and tonic jingle in a gyroscopic jubilee of something beginning with J—Father Pierre, why *did* you stay on here?

FATHER PIERRE (GRAHAM) *(putting on a pair of Whicker-style glasses)* Well mainly for the interviews.

FIFTH WHICKER Well there you have it, a crumbling...

FIRST WHICKER ...empire in the sun-drenched...

SECOND WHICKER Caribbean, where the clichés sparkle on the waters...

THIRD WHICKER ...like the music of repeat fees...

FIRST WHICKER And so...

FIFTH WHICKER ...from Whicker Island...

FIRST WHICKER ...it's...
SECOND WHICKER ...fare...
THIRD WHICKER ...well and...
FOURTH WHICKER ...bon...
FIFTH WHICKER ...voy...
FIRST WHICKER ...age.

Cut to film of Whicker plane taking off. Roll credits, which read:

WHICKER'S WORLD WAS CONCEIVED, WRITTEN AND PERFORMED BY
ALAN WHICKER
JOHN CLEESE WHICKER
GRAHAM WHICKER CHAPMAN
ALAN MICHAEL PALIN WHICKER
ERIC WHICKER WHICKER IDLE
TERRY TERRY WHICKER ALAN GILLIAM
ALSO APPEARING
ALAN WHICKER
MRS IDLE
CONNIE WHICKER BOOTH
RITA WHICKER DAVIES
NIGEL WHICKER JONES
FRANK WILLIAMS AS THE BOY WHICKER
MAKE UP ALAN WHICKER AND MADELAINE GAFFNEY
ALAN WHICKER COSTUMES HAZEL PETHIG
ANIMATIONS BY TERRY WHICKER GILLIAM
MR WHICKER KINDLY PHOTOGRAPHED ON FILM BY ALAN FEATHERSTONE
EDITED ON FILM BY RAY MILLICHOPE
MR WHICKER'S SOUND BY ALAN WHICKER, ALAN WHICKER AND RICHARD CHUBB
MR WHICKER WAS ENTIRELY LIT BY JIMMY PURDIE (ASSISTED BY ALAN WHICKER)
MR WHICKER WAS DESIGNED BY ROBERT BERK
PRODUCED BY ALAN WHICKER OH, AND IAN MCNAUGHTON
A BBC WHICKER COLOUR PRODUCTION

MARK EDWARDS
GARY COOVER
JEAN WENNERSTROM
SEASON 3
EPISODE 28

MR AND MRS BRIAN NORRIS'
FORD POPULAR
FEATURING
EMIGRATION FROM SURBITON TO HOUNSLOW
SCHOOLBOYS' LIFE ASSURANCE COMPANY
HOW TO RID THE WORLD OF ALL KNOWN DISEASES
MRS NIGGERBAITER EXPLODES
Vicar/Salesman
FARMING CLUB ✽ 'LIFE OF TSCHAIKOWSKY'
TRIM-JEANS THEATRE
FISH-SLAPPING DANCE ✽ WORLD WAR ONE
THE BBC IS SHORT OF MONEY ✽ PUSS IN BOOTS

Norwegian adventurer Thor Heyerdahl sailed across the Pacific Ocean in 1947, 4,300 miles from South America to the islands of Polynesia, on a raft called the "Kon-Tiki," all to prove that South Americans of the pre-Columbian times could have done the same thing.

"*Ra*" and "*Ra II*" were boats Heyerdahl built from papyrus in order to try to prove that the Egyptians could have sailed the Atlantic. *Ra* broke apart in 1969, but the following year *Ra II* made it from Morocco to Barbados.

The Ford Popular was a cheap car made in England between 1953 and 1962.

"EBW 343" is the car's license plate.

Sir Edmund Hillary was the first man to climb Mount Everest. The New Zealander achieved the summit in May 1953.

Both in West London, Hounslow is eight miles north of Surbiton.

FIRST AIRED: OCTOBER 26, 1972

Stirring music.

VOICE OVER (MICHAEL) *(and captions)*: **'The Kon Tiki', 1 'Ra 1', 'Ra 2', 2 'And now...', 'Mr and Mrs Brian Norris's Ford Popular' 3**

Pull back from a shot of an old little Ford Popular to reveal Mr and Mrs Norris (MICHAEL AND GRAHAM), *standing with it outside the front garden of a small suburban semi-detached house.*

VOICE OVER (ERIC) Who, a year ago, had heard of Mr and Mrs Brian Norris of 37, Gledhill Gardens, Parsons Green? And yet their epic journey in **EBW 343** 4 has set them alongside Thor Heyerdahl and **Sir Edmund Hillary.** 5 Starting only with a theory, Mr Norris set out to prove that the inhabitants of Hounslow could have been descendants of the people of Surbiton who had made the great trek north. No newcomer to this field, Mr Norris's 'A Short History of Motor Traffic Between Purley and Esher' had become a best-selling minor classic in the car-swapping belt. *(shot of Mr Norris gazing into a window, where his book lies; there is a sign saying 'Remaindered')* **But why would the people of Surbiton go to Hounslow?** 6 Mr Norris had noticed three things: *(split-screen shot of two identical semi-detached houses)*

Firstly, the similarity of the houses. Secondly, the similarity of the costume between Hounslow and Surbiton, *(similarly dressed suburbanites on either side of the split screen)* and thirdly, the similarity of speech.

Split screen.

MAN ON RIGHT (TERRY J) Are you still running the **GDBDMDB?** **7**
MAN ON LEFT (ERIC) Yes, but I've had the excess nipples woppled to remove tamping.
MAN ON LEFT Jolly good.
VOICE OVER Were these just coincidences, or were they, as Mr Norris believed, part of an identical cultural background? One further discovery convinced him. ***(cut to two lawnmowers arranged on a table, as if they were exhibits in a museum, with type-written documentation in front of them for the visitor)*** **8**

The lawnmower. Surely such a gadget could not have been generated independently in two separate areas. Mr Norris was convinced.
MR NORRIS'S VOICE I'm convinced.
VOICE OVER But how to prove it.
MR NORRIS'S VOICE But how to prove it.
VOICE OVER There was only one way to see if the journey between Surbiton and Hounslow was possible, and that was to try and make it. Months of preparation followed whilst Mr Norris continued his research in the Putney Public Library, *(Mr Norris in a library reading a book titled '**The Lady with the Naked Skin**' by Paul Fox Jnr)* **9** and Mrs Norris made sandwiches.

Cut to Mr and Mrs Norris leaving their house.

VOICE OVER Finally, by April, they were ready. On the 23rd, Mr and Mrs Norris set out from 'Abide-A-Wee' to motor the fifteen miles to Surbiton, watched by a crowd of local well-wishers. 10 *(one tiny child holding a small British flag)* That evening they dined at **Tooting. 11**

*(quick flash of them sitting in the window of a **Golden Egg or Wimpy place**)* **12** This would be the last they'd see of civilization. Mr Norris's diary for the 23rd reveals the extraordinary calmness and deep inner peacefulness of his mind.

We see the diary.

Gobbledygook company name, perhaps.

They lawn mowers are both called "Betta-Cutta."

"The Lady with the Naked Skin" is a fake book, sadly.

As said, it's about eight miles.

Tooting is about twelve miles east of Hounslow.

Golden Egg and Wimpy are fast food joints. They actually eat at Egg Nest, though this was not a chain.

A bathroom joke.

The town of Kingston-upon-Thames is indeed just north of Surbiton, and in the way, hence the need to take the A307 around it to head on up to Hounslow.

These directions make little sense.

MR NORRIS'S VOICE 7.30 Fed cat. 8.00 Breakfast. 8.30 Yes (successfully). [13] 9.00 Set out on historic journey.

Cut to Mr Norris's car driving along a suburban road. A sign says 'YOU ARE NOW LEAVING SURBITON, GATEWAY TO ESHER'.

VOICE OVER On the morning of the 24th, early to avoid the traffic, Mr Norris's historic expedition set out from Surbiton—destination Hounslow. Early on they began to perceive encouraging signs. *(cut to sign saying 'HOUNSLOW 25 MILES'; Mr Norris closely examines the sign, as would an archaeologist)* The writing on the sign was almost exactly the same as the writing in the AA book. They were on the right route. During the long hours of the voyage, Mr Norris's wife Betty kept a complete photographic record and made sandwiches. This is some of the unique footage which Mrs Norris got back from the chemists...*(badly shot pictures of sandwiches, with fingers in the lens, etc.)* Mile succeeded mile and the terrific strain was beginning to tell when suddenly, *(chord; Mr Norris points excitedly, pull back to reveal him standing on a bridge over the Kingston by-pass examining it through field glasses)* by an amazing stroke of luck, Mr Norris had come across the **Kingston by-pass.** [14] This was something to tell the Round Table. *(cut to a map; it traces the two routes in red as the voice talks)* **At this stage, Mr Norris was faced with two major divergent theories concerning his Surbiton ancestors. Did they take the Kingston by-pass, turning left at Barnes, or did they strike west up the A308 via Norbiton to Hampton Wick?** [15] Both these theories ran up against one big obstacle—the Thames, *(the car at a river bank; Mr and Mrs Norris puzzling; behind them three or four bridges with traffic pouring over)* lying like a silver turd between Richmond and Isleworth. This was a major setback. How could they possibly cross the river? Several hours of thought produced nothing. There was only one flask of coffee left when suddenly Mr Norris spotted something. *(cut to a sign saying 'METROPOLITAN RAILWAY')* Could this have been the method used? Hardly daring to believe, Mr Norris led his expedition on to the 3.47. *(cut to them getting on the train)* Forty minutes later, via Clapham, Fulham, Chiswick and Brentford, they approached their goal: Hounslow. *(a sign saying 'HOUNSLOW CENTRAL'; Mr Norris sticks a British flag on the platform; he poses for his wife's photos; much hand shaking)* Was this, then, the final proof? Something aroused the accountant's instinct buried deep in Mr Norris's make-up. *(cut to Mr Norris's eyes and furrowed brow)* The journey *was* possible, and yet...*(zoom in on railway timetable on wall saying 'Trains to Surbiton every half hour')* 'Wrong Way' Norris had accidentally stumbled on a piece of anthropological history. It was the inhabitants of Hounslow who had made the great trek south to the sunnier pastures of Surbiton, and not vice versa, as he had originally surmised. *This* was the secret of Surbiton! Happy and contented Mr Norris returned to the calmer waters of chartered accountancy, for, in his way, 'Wrong Way' Norris was right.

Music swells, over book title 'THE STORY OF EBW 343' BY 'WRONG WAY' NORRIS. Caption: 'THE END' A music crescendo. Cut to nude organist (TERRY J) *playing a chord.*

ANNOUNCER (JOHN) And now...

IT'S MAN (MICHAEL)

Animated titles.

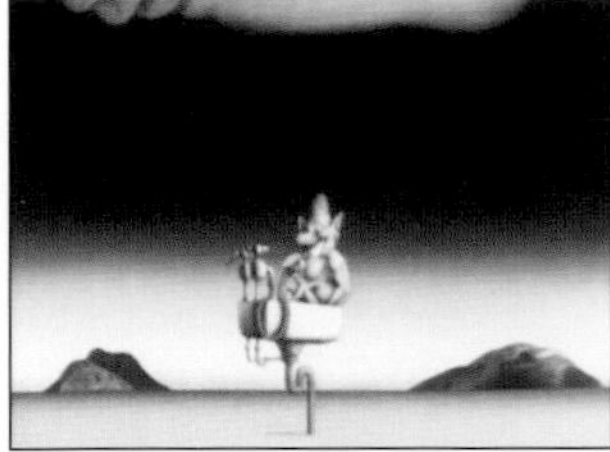
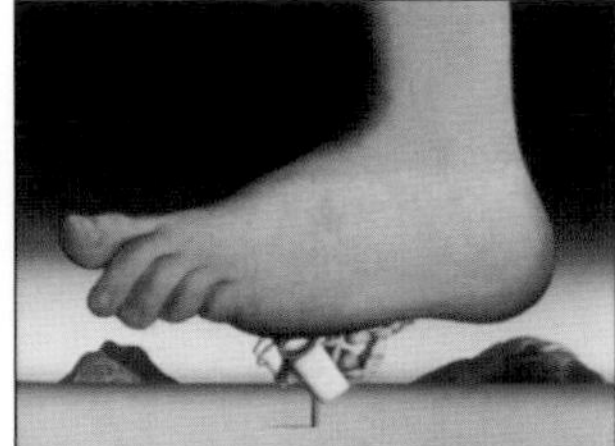

VOICE (JOHN) Monty Python's Flying Circus.

Cut to a headmaster's study.

HEADMASTER (MICHAEL) Knock, enter and approach. *(knock on door; it opens and three schoolboys in short trousers enter)* Right, it's come to my notice that certain boys have been running a unit-trust linked assurance scheme with fringe benefits and full cash-in endowment facilities. Apparently small investors were attracted by the wide-ranging portfolio and that in the first week the limited offer was oversubscribed eight times.

STEBBINS (ERIC) It was Tidwell's idea, sir.

HEADMASTER Shut up, Stebbins! I haven't finished. Oh, by the way, congratulations on winning the Italian Grand Prix at Monza.

STEBBINS Thank you, sir.

HEADMASTER Shut up. Now then, this sort of extra-curricular capitalist expansion has got to stop! I made it quite clear when Potter tried to go public last term, that these massive stock exchange deals must *not* happen in Big School. Is that clear, Balderston?

BALDERSTON (TERRY G) Yes, sir.

HEADMASTER Oh, and Balderston, next time you do a 'Panorama' Report on the Black Ghettos you *must* get an **exeat form** 16 from **Mr Dibley.** 17

BALDERSTON Sorry, sir.

HEADMASTER Shut up, and stop slouching. Now, the reason I called you in here today, is that my wife is having a little trouble with her...er...with her **waterworks**, 18 and I think she needs a bit of attention. Now, which one of you is the surgeon? *(silence)* Come on, I know one of you is, which one is it? *(Tidwell raises hand reluctantly)* Ah! Tidwell. Good. Well, I want you to cut along and have a look at the wife.

TIDWELL (TERRY J) Oh, sir! Why don't you ask Stebbins? He's a gynaecologist.

STEBBINS Ooh! You rotten stinker, Tidwell!

HEADMASTER Is this true, Stebbins? Are you a gynaecologist?

STEBBINS *(very reluctantly)* Yes, sir.

HEADMASTER Right, just the man. How much do you charge?

STEBBINS *(muttering into his shoes)* Thirty guineas, sir.

HEADMASTER Excellent. Right. I want you to go along to see the wife. Give her a full examination, and let me know the results by the end of break. And don't pick your nose!

Cut to a sign saying 'HOW TO DO IT'. Music. Pull out to reveal a ***'Blue Peter' type set.*** 19

Sitting casually on the edge of a dais are three presenters in sweaters—Noël, Jackie and Alan—plus a large bloodhound.

ALAN (JOHN) Hello.

NOEL (GRAHAM) Hello.

ALAN Well, last week we showed you how to become a gynaecologist. And this week on 'How to do it' we're going to show you how to play the flute, how to split an atom, how to construct a

An "exeat form" is used to formally excuse a child from school.

Again, Dibley is a go-to comic name for the Pythons.

"Waterworks" is British slang for the urinary tract and attendant areas.

Blue Peter is a popular, wholesome children's TV show from the BBC. Notable for its longevity (it started in 1958 and is still going), its Blue Peter Garden, the pets, sickly sweet presenters wearing sweaters, and the Blue Peter Badge, awarded to kids who do good deeds.

box girder bridge, how to irrigate the Sahara Desert and make vast new areas of land cultivatable, but first, here's Jackie to tell you all how to rid the world of all known diseases.

JACKIE (ERIC) Hello, Alan.

ALAN Hello, Jackie.

JACKIE Well, first of all become a doctor and discover a marvellous cure for something, and then, when the medical profession really starts to take notice of you, you can jolly well tell them what to do and make sure they get everything right so there'll never be any diseases ever again.

ALAN Thanks, Jackie. Great idea. How to play the flute. *(picking up a flute)* Well here we are. You blow there and you move your fingers up and down here.

NOEL Great, great, Alan. Well, next week we'll be showing you how black and white people can live together in peace and harmony, and Alan will be over in Moscow showing us how to reconcile the Russians and the Chinese. So, until next week, cheerio.

ALAN Bye.

JACKIE Bye.

Children's music. Pull out to reveal that the 'Blue Peter' set is in one corner of a stockbroker-belt sitting room. Two ladies are sitting by the fire looking at a photo album.

MRS NIGGER-BAITER (MICHAEL) Oh, yes, he's such a clever little boy, just like his father.

MRS S (TERRY J) D'you think so, Mrs Nigger-Baiter?

MRS NIGGER-BAITER Oh yes, spitting image.

The door opens. The son comes in.

SON (JOHN) Good afternoon, mother. Good afternoon, Mrs Nigger- Baiter.

MRS NIGGER-BAITER Ooh, he's walking already!

MRS S

YES, HE'S SUCH A CLEVER LITTLE BOY, AREN'T YOU? COOCHY COOCHY COO...

MRS NIGGER-BAITER Hello, coochy coo...

MRS S Hello, hello...*(they chuck him under the chin)*

MRS NIGGER-BAITER Oochy coochy. *(the son smiles a little tight smile)* Look at him laughing...ooh, he's a chirpy little fellow. Isn't he a chirpy little fellow...eh? eh? Does he talk? Does he talk, eh?

SON Of course I talk, I'm Minister for Overseas Development.

MRS NIGGER-BAITER Ooh, he's a *clever* little boy—he's a *clever* little boy. *(gets out a rattle)* Do you like your rattle? Do you like your rattle? Look at his little eyes following it...look at his iggy piggy piggy little eyeballs eh...oo...he's got a tubby tum-tum. Oh, he's got a tubby tum-tum.

SON *(whilst Mrs Nigger-Baiter is talking)* Mother, could I have a quick cup of tea please. I have an important statement on Rhodesia to make in the Commons at six.

Sound of an explosion out of vision. Cut to reveal Mrs Nigger-Baiter's chair charred and smoking. Mrs Nigger-Baiter is no longer there. The upholstery is smouldering gently.

MRS S Oh, Mrs Nigger-Baiter's exploded.
SON Good thing, too.
MRS S She was my best friend.
SON Oh, mother, don't be so sentimental. Things explode every day.
MRS S Yes, I suppose so. Anyway, I didn't really like her that much.

The doorbell rings. Mrs S goes to the door. A vicar with a suitcase.

VICAR (ERIC) Hello, I'm your new vicar. Can I interest you in any encyclopaedias?
MRS S Ah, no thank you. We're not Church people, thank you.

The vicar opens his suitcase to reveal it is packed with brushes.

VICAR How about brushes? Nylon or bristle? Strong-tufted, attractive colours. **20**
MRS S No—really, thank you, vicar.
VICAR Oh dear...Turkey? Cup final tickets?
MRS S No, no really, we're just not religious thank you.
VICAR Oh, well. Bye bye.
MRS S Bye bye, vicar. *(she shuts the door, as she returns to seat the vicar pops his head round the door again)*
VICAR Remember, if you do want anything...jewellery, Ascot water heaters...
MRS S Thank you, vicar. *(he goes)* It's funny, isn't it? How your best friend can just blow up like that? I mean, you wouldn't think it was medically possible, would you?

Cut to a doctor in a posh consulting room.

DOCTOR (GRAHAM) This is where Mrs Shazam was so wrong. Exploding is a perfectly normal medical phenomenon. In many fields of medicine nowadays, a dose of dynamite can do a world of good. For instance, athlete's foot—an irritating condition—can be cured by applying a small charge of TNT between each toe. *(doorbell)* Excuse me. *(he opens the door)*
VICAR Hello, I'm your new vicar, can I interest you in any of these watches, pens or biros? *(exhibits the collection inside his jacket)*
DOCTOR No...I'm not religious, I'm afraid.

The door-to-door brush salesman, along with the door-to-door encyclopedia salesmen, are figments of British folklore—few have ever found one at the door ringing their bell.

VICAR Oh, souvenirs, badges...a little noddy dog for the back of the car?
DOCTOR No thank you, vicar. Good morning.
VICAR Oh, morning.

He shuts the door.

DOCTOR Now, many of the medical profession are sceptical about my work. They point to my record of treatment of athlete's foot sufferers—eighty-four dead, sixty-five severely wounded and twelve missing believed cured. But then, people laughed at Bob Hope, people laughed at my wife when she wrapped herself up in greaseproof paper and hopped into the Social Security office, but that doesn't mean that Pasteur was wrong! Look, I'll show you what I mean. *(goes to a wall diagram of two skeletons and taps one with a rod)*

Animation:

SKELETON Watch it, mate. I'm not going to stay round here getting poked and prodded all day. *(clips a face on and moves off the diagram)* I'm off...I've got a decent body, all I get is poked and prodded in the chest. *(moving through countryside)* Well, I'm off. I'm going to get another line of work. *(goes past various warning signs)*
VOICE Watch it!
VOICE Don't go any further!
VOICE Turn back!
VOICE Stop!

The sprocket holes at the side of the film come into view.

VOICE Stop! Oh, please stop!

The skeleton moves past the sprocket holes and falls into blank space.

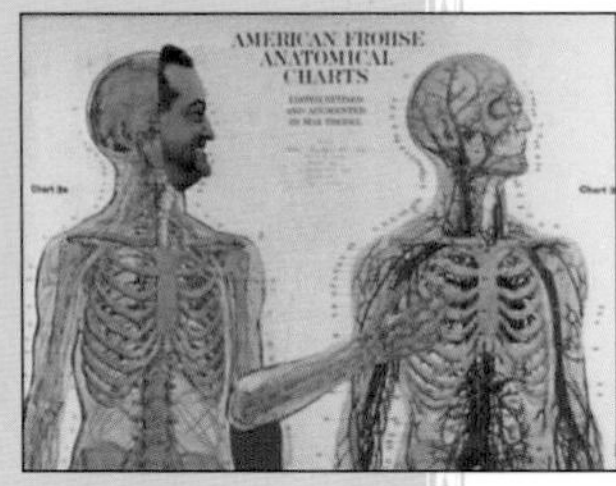

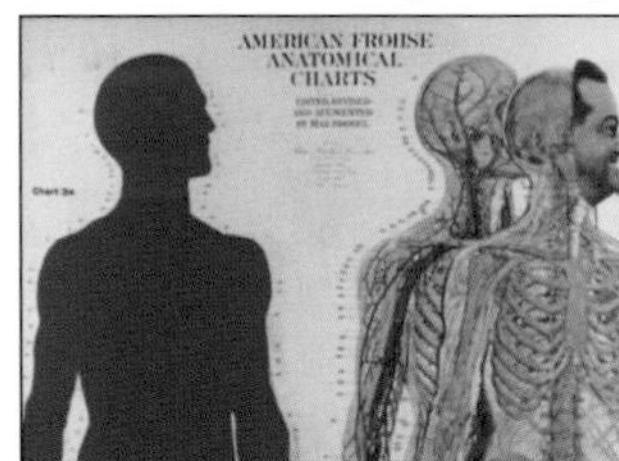

VOICE

OH, MY GOD, HE'S FALLEN OFF THE EDGE OF THE CARTOON.

VOICE Well, so much for that link.

Artistic-type set. There is a large screen on back. Stock two-chair set-up as for interview.

PRESENTER (ERIC) John Cobbley is the Musical and Artistic Director of **Covent Garden.** 21 He is himself a talented musician, he is a world famous authority on nineteenth-century Russian music and he's come into the studio tonight to talk about Tchaikowsky, which is a bit of a pity as this is 'Farming Club'. On 'Farming Club' tonight we'll be taking a look at the Ministry's *(pigs appear on the screen, Cobbley gets up, looks about him, wanders off, rather puzzled)* latest preventative proposals to deal with a possible outbreak of **foot and mouth,** 22 we'll be talking later to the man who believes that milk yields can be increased dramatically, but first a Farming Club special, the life of Tchaikowsky.

21

Covent Garden is both an area of central London and an opera house housed there.

Foot-and-mouth disease is a viral illness much feared in the farming community.

Cue Tchaikowsky's first piano concerto. Stock film of a farmyard with superimposed roller caption. Roller caption: 'FARMING CLUB, IN ASSOCIATION WITH THE POTATO MARKETING BOARD, ALSO IN ASSOCIATION WITH THE BEETROOT, HAM, EGG AND TOMATO MARKETING BOAD, AND ALSO IN ASSOCIATION WITH THE LITTLE GREEN BITS OF CUCUMBER DICED WITH SHALLOTS, GARNISHED WITH CHIVES AND SERVED WITH A ROQUEFORT DRESSING MAKES AN EXCELLENT APPETIZER OR SIDE DISH WITH A STEAK OR A STEW MARKETING BOARD, PRESENTS: THE LIFE OF PETER ILYICH TCHAIKOWSKY, IN ASSOCIATION WITH THE PETER ILYICH TCHAIKOWSKY MARKETING BOARD' Cut back to the presenter.

PRESENTER Tchaikowsky. Was he the tortured soul who poured out his immortal longings into dignified passages of stately music, or was he just an old poof who wrote tunes? *(pull back to show a second presenter in the other chair)* Tonight on 'Farming Club' we're going to take an intimate look at Tchaikowsky *(a picture of Tchaikowsky on the screen)* and an intimate look at his friends. *(a picture of a naked sailor on a tiger-skin rug)* Incidentally, BBC Publications have prepared a special pamphlet to go with this programme called 'Hello Pianist', *(it comes up on the screen; on its cover there is a picture of a pig)* and it contains material that some people might find offensive but which is really smashing.

SECOND PRESENTER (JOHN) Peter Ilyich Tchaikowsky was born in 1840 in a **Ken Russell** **23** film just outside St Petersburg. **His father (Leo McKern), a free-lance bishop, was married to Vern Plachenka (Julie Christie)** **24** but secretly deeply in love with Margo Farenka **(Shirley Abicair)** **25** and the strangely flatulent Madame Ranevsky **(Norris McWhirter).** **26** Soon, however, the family (**Eldridge Cleaver,** **27** Moira Lister and Stan the Bat moved to the neighbouring industrial village of Omsk (Eddie Waring) where they soon found themselves, sadly, quite unable to cope **(Anthony Barber).** **28** In 1863, however, Tchaikowsky was sent to Moscow to study the piano and, when he'd finished that, the living room. **Maurice takes up the story.** **29**

Cut to a poofy presenter in really chintzy surroundings.

MAURICE (MICHAEL) Well, guess what, the very next thing he did was to go to this extraordinary but extraordinary duckety-poos semi-Mondrian house in Robin Russia. Harry here Tammy Tchaikowsky wrote some of the most Sammy super symphonies you've ever Henry heard in the whole of your Lily life.

Superimposed caption: 'A FAMOUS MUSIC CRITIC AND HAIRDRESSER'

MAURICE She was such a good composer that everybody, but everybody, wanted to know, and quite right too, because she wrote some lovely bits, such as Sally Sleeping Beauty, Patsy Pathétique, Adrian 1812 and lots of Conny concerti for Vera violin and Peter Piano Fanny Forte.

Ken Russell, the enfant terrible of the British movie scene known especially for 1969's *Women in Love*, based on the D.H. Lawrence novel, and *Tommy*, the 1975 movie starring The Who.

Leo McKern, the British character actor. Julie Christie, a British actress.

Shirley Abicair, an Australian actress and singer

Norris McWhirter, the nerdy British man known with his twin brother, Ross, for writing and updating the *Guinness Book of Records* between 1955 and 1975.

Eldridge Cleaver, of the Black Panthers.

Anthony Barber, the British Conservative politician made chancellor of the exchequer in 1970.

The camera pulls back here to reveal Idle fast asleep.

Cut back to second presenter.

SECOND PRESENTER But what do we *really* know of this tortured ponce?

Cut to space-programme-type set. Experts at a desk. An Apollo-type monograph behind them says 'Tchaikowsky XII'. The centre motif is a picture of Tchaikowsky.

30

Nelson's Column is a 169-foot-high monument to Horatio Nelson in London's Trafalgar Square. Edwin Landseer's lions sit at its base.

EXPERT (GRAHAM) Well, if you can imagine the size of **Nelson's Column**, **30** which is roughly three times the size of a London bus, then Tchaikowsky was much smaller. His head was about the same size as that of an extremely large dog, that is to say, two very small dogs, or four very large hamsters, or one medium-size rabbit if you count the whole of the body and not just the head. Robin.

He has a model of Tchaikowsky which comes apart.

SECOND EXPERT (TERRY J) Thank you. Well here is a three-stage model of Tchaikowsky...here you see the legs, used for walking around, and which can be jettisoned at night...*(he takes the legs off)* And this is the main trunk, the power house of the whole thing, incorporating of course the naughty bits, which were extremely naughty for his time, and the whole thing is subservient to *(takes it off)* this small command module, the, as it were, head of the whole, as it were, body. Robin.

Cut to first expert.

FIRST EXPERT Peter.

Cut to first presenter.

FIRST PRESENTER Simon.

Cut to second presenter.

SECOND PRESENTER Maurice.

Cut to Maurice.

MAURICE Me. Well, poor pet, she was like a lost lamb in an abattoir. Eventually she Dickie died of Colin Cholera in St Patsy Petersburg, in Gertie great Percy pain.

Cut to a piano in a pool of light.

VOICE OVER (ERIC) Here to play Tchaikowsky's first piano concerto in B Flat Minor is the world-famous soloist Sviatoslav Richter. During the performance he will escape from a sack, three padlocks and a pair of handcuffs.

A chained figure in a sack rolls into shot and starts rolling about and playing the piano concerto. After a minute 'Rita' enters and gestures to him. She is in fish-net tights, etc.—the full conjurer's assistant. He wriggles free from the sack, playing the while. The music stops. Caption: 'SVIATOSLAV RICHTER AND RITA' Film of an applauding audience in the Royal Albert Hall. Superimposed caption: 'AND NOW' Jolly showbiz music. A flat goes up, revealing three actors in trim-jeans (which are heavily padded to make you sweat off weight) grouped à la advert. They all have slight Australian accents. Caption: 'TRIM-JEANS THEATRE PRESENTS'

GARY COOVER (ERIC) Good evening. This new series of 'Trim-Jeans Theatre Presents' will enable you to enjoy the poetry of T. S. Eliot whilst losing unsightly tummy bulge. Jean.

Caption: 'THESE THREE PEOPLE ARE REDUCING THEIR WAIST, THIGHS, HIPS AND ABDOMEN EVEN AS THEY RECOMMEND'

JEAN WENNERSTROM (GRAHAM) Wow, yes and the inches stay off. Mark.

MARK EDWARDS (MICHAEL) Terrific! Thrill to Thomas à Becket's Kierkegaardian moment of choice while making your physique tighter, firmer, neater.

Cut to a cathedral interior. There are three priests, four knights and two women, all in trim-jeans. Thomas does not wear one.

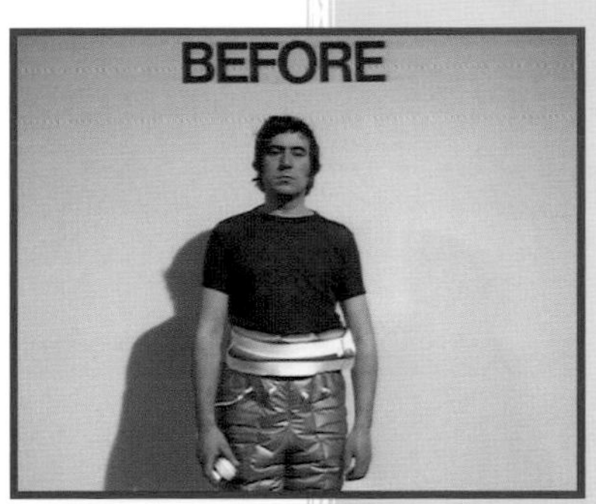

PRIEST (GRAHAM) I am here. No traitor to the King.

FIRST KNIGHT (ERIC) Absolve all those you have excommunicated.

SECOND KNIGHT (TERRY J) Resign those powers you have arrogated.

THIRD KNIGHT (MICHAEL) Renew the obedience you have violated.

FOURTH KNIGHT (JOHN) Lose inches off your hips, thighs, buttocks and abdomen.

Cut back to Gary and the others.

GARY A terrific product.

ALL Terrific.

GARY And this comes complete with the most revolutionary guarantee in slenderizing history!

Cut to a man (TERRY J) *in trim-jeans under a sign saying 'Before'.*

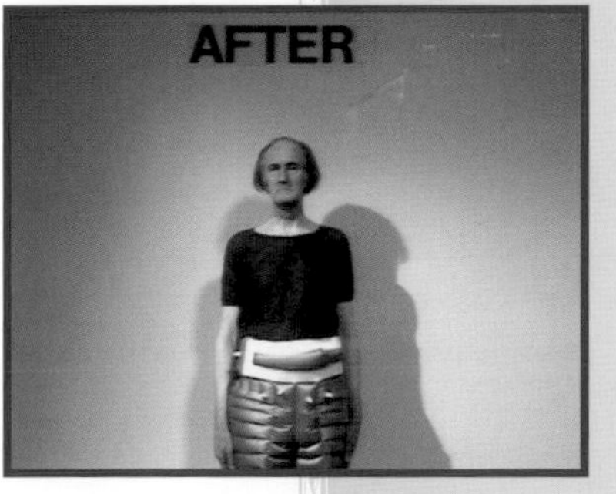

VOICE OVER (MICHAEL) This was Kevin Francis before last season's 'Trim-Jean Play of the Month' production of 'The Seagull' by Anton Chekhov and the Sauna Belt Trim-Jean Company Limited. See Kevin has slipped into his slenderizing garment and is inflating it with the handy little pump provided. Three acts and a few special torso exercises later, Kevin, as Trigorin, the failed writer of sentimental romances, has lost over thirty-three inches. *(same shot but very skinny* JOHN HUGHMAN *has replaced* TERRY J*)*

WOW. WHAT A DIFFERENCE. THAT ANTON CHEKHOV CAN CERTAINLY WRITE.

GARY Terrific.

MARK Terrific.

GARY Yes, why not join us for a season of classic plays and rapid slenderizing. Enjoy **Sir John Gielgud and Sir Ralph Richardson** **31** losing a total of fifteen inches in **David Storey's 'Home'.** **32**

MARK Enjoy the **'The Trim Gentlemen of Verona' and 'Long Day's Journey into Night'** **33** while inches melt away.

JEAN Enjoy **Glenda Jackson** **34** with a Constant Snug Fit and Solid Support in **all four areas.** **35**

GARY Other productions will include...'Treasure Island'...*(Long John Silver in trim-jeans)* 'Swan Lake' *(cut to a photo of two ballet dancers in a 'lift' position, both wearing tights and trim-jeans)*

'The Life and Loves of Toulouse Lautrec', *(cut to a photo of Toulouse Lautrec, his feet sticking out of the bottom of the trim-jeans)* and the Trim-Jeans version of **'The Great Escape',** **36** with a cast of thousands losing well over fifteen hundred inches.

Cut to scrubland, barbed wire à la prison camp in the background. After a few seconds a head appears out of a hole in the ground. He looks around then gets out. He is wearing trim-jeans. He looks back. Satisfied, he beckons. Others start appearing. Three German guards behind the wire muttering. Superimposed caption: 'INCHES LOST SO FAR' A superimposed counter shows the numbers increasing.

John Gielgud and Sir Ralph Richardson are two of England's greatest classical actors.

Home is a 1970 play by British writer David Storey.

A play on *The Two Gentlemen of Verona*, a 1590 play by Shakespeare, and the 1956 Eugene O'Neill play.

Glenda Jackson, an actress (and now politician) who starred in, among many other movies, *Women in Love*, directed by Ken Russell in 1969.

35

"All four areas" almost cracks Palin up.

The World War II movie *The Great Escape* was parodied in Episode 18.

GUARD Achtung! Halt! Halt!

A moment's panic. Shooting starts and a siren goes. Men pour out of hole rapidly. Guards pursue them with tracker dogs in trim-jeans. The counter goes berserk.

An animated item ends with a sign saying 'AND NOW, THE FISH SLAPPING DANCE'.

Cut to a quayside. John and Michael, dressed in tropical gear and solar topees. John stands still while Michael dances up and down before him to the jolly music of ***Edward German.*** **37** *Michael holds two tiny fish and from time to time in the course of the dance he slaps John lightly across the cheeks with them. The music ends; Michael stops dancing. John produces a huge great fish and swipes Michael with it. Michael falls off the quay into the water.*

Edward German was an English composer of comic opera and light incidental music who straddled the turn of the nineteenth and twentieth centuries.

Animation: underwater. We see an animated Michael sinking. He is swallowed by a fish with a swastika on its side.

NAZI FISH Welcome aboard, Britisher pig. Quite a little surprise, ja? But perhaps you would be so kind as to tell us all you know about certain allied shipping routes, ja? Come on, talk!

The Nazi fish is swallowed by a fish with an RAF emblem.

BRITISH FISH Hello, Fritz. Tables seem to have turned, old chap, let's see how you like a bit of your own medicine, eh? Come on, Fritz, now tell us—tell us about...

The British fish is swallowed by a Chinese fish.

CHINESE FISH Ah, gleetings, capitalist dog; very sorry but must inform you, you are now prisoner of People's Republic.

SECOND VOICE Am very sorry, comrade commando, but have just picked up capitalist ship on ladar scanner.

The Chinese fish bites the underside of a large ship. Film of big liner sinking in storm. General panic and dramatic music.

CAPTAIN (TERRY J) *(over tannoy)* This is your captain speaking. There is no need for panic. Woman and children first. I repeat that, women and children first.

Cut to the ship's bridge. The captain and two or three officers are seen scrambling into ladies' clothing or young children's short trousers and school satchels and caps. The ship pitches and rolls in the gale. The captain is still trying to speak into the PA.

CAPTAIN Do not rush for the lifeboats—remember, women and children first.

A first officer is revealed in the corner of the bridge putting a head-dress on a Red Indian outfit.

FIRST OFFICER (JOHN) And Red Indians!
CAPTAIN *(putting his hand over the PA)* What did you have to get dressed up like that for?
FIRST OFFICER It was the only thing left.
CAPTAIN Oh. All right. *(into the PA)* Women, children and Red Indians...

Cut to another officer in astronaut's kit.

SECOND OFFICER (TERRY G) And spacemen!
CAPTAIN

HERE IS A REVISED LIST. WOMEN, CHILDREN, RED INDIANS AND SPACEMEN,

(hand over PA) what's *that* meant to be?

Cut to third officer who is putting finishing touches to a medieval outfit.

THIRD OFFICER (ERIC) Well it's a sort of impression of what a kind of Renaissance courtier artist might have looked like at the court of one of the great families like the Medicis or the Borgias...

FOURTH OFFICER (GRAHAM) No it's not, it's more Flemish than Italian.

FIFTH OFFICER (MICHAEL) Yes—that's a Flemish merchant of the fifteenth or sixteenth centuries...

THIRD OFFICER What! With these tassles...

FOURTH OFFICER Yes, yes. They had those fitted doublets going tapering down into the full hose you know—exactly like that.

CAPTAIN *(into the PA)* One moment, please, don't panic. *(puts his hand over the PA)* Now, what is it meant to be? I've got to tell them *something*...is it a Flemish merchant?

THIRD OFFICER *No*, it is *not* a Flemish merchant. It's more a sort of idealized version of the complete Renaissance Man...

CAPTAIN Oh, all right.

FOURTH OFFICER It's not...

CAPTAIN All right! All right! *(into the PA)* this is your captain speaking...do not rush for the lifeboats...women, children, Red Indians, spacemen *(stock film of long shot of sinking vessel, the voice over fading)* and a sort of idealized version of complete Renaissance Men first!

Caption: 'A FEW DAYS LATER' Cut to a police chief's office in an anonymous South American police state. The chief of police at his desk. From outside we hear footsteps approaching the office and voices.

THIRD OFFICER'S VOICE Flemish merchants did not wear hand-embroidered chevrons. They did not!

The door opens and two guards roughly push in the captain in drag, another officer half in drag, half in naval uniform, two officers hastily dressed as children, a complete Renaissance Man, a Red Indian and a spaceman. They stand there for a moment. Then one of the guards pushes his way forward and hands the police chief a piece of paper.

The window features no glass, fortunately.

Huw Wheldon (note the *h*) was managing director of the BBC from 1968 to 1975. Before that, he had been a popular TV presenter himself, notably of the arts program *Monitor.*

Another reference to the popular Christmas pantomime in Britain.

41

The standard back and forth of any good pantomime.

POLICE CHIEF (JOHN) Yes, Gomez? *(reads)* Vee found zem valking on zee beach, my capitain. *(the guard nods enthusiastically)* Gomez, why can't you *say* this? *(the guard mouths something)* What? Oh, I see, we can't afford it. *(to camera)* You see the BBC has to pay an actor twenty guineas if he speaks and it makes a bit of a hole in the budget...

GUARD (TERRY G) Twenty-*eight* guineas, sir! Ooh, sorry.

POLICE CHIEF You fool Gomez—that's twenty-eight guineas...

SECOND GUARD (ERIC) What about me, sir?

POLICE CHIEF Are you supposed to speak?

SECOND GUARD No, sir.

POLICE CHIEF But you've just spoken!

SECOND GUARD Oh, sorry, sir.

POLICE CHIEF You fool, that's, that's fifty-six guineas before we've even started. ***(a third guard suddenly rushes up to the window and crashes through it; scream and breaking glass)*** **38** What did he do that for?

SECOND GUARD It's a stunt, sir, an extra twenty guineas.

POLICE CHIEF *(banging the desk)* Look! We can't afford it! The BBC are short of money as it is.

Cut to a newsreader in a 'News at Nine' set with a bare light bulb hanging in shot. He wears only an old blanket round his shoulders. He is shivering.

NEWSREADER (ERIC) The BBC wishes to deny rumours that it is going into liquidation. Mrs Kelly, who owns the flat where they live, has said that they can stay on till the end of the month... *(he is handed a piece of paper)* and we've just heard that **Huw Weldon's** **39** watch has been accepted by the London Electricity Board and transmissions for this evening can be continued as planned. *(he coughs and pulls the blanket tighter round his shoulders)* That's all from me so...goodnight.

Knocking on the door.

MR KELLY'S VOICE (GRAHAM) Are you going to be in there all night?

NEWSREADER It's just a bulletin, Mr Kelly...and now back to the story *(banging)*...All right!

Cut back to the same police chief's office. Noises off of people walking down. The door opens and the same crowd is pushed in. No one has any trousers on.

FIRST GUARD Ve found ze men, valking on ze beach, my capitain.

CAPTAIN We're British Naval Officers, and entitled to be...

Enter a pantomime principal boy holding a stuffed cat. All the rest of the group break back in a well-choreographed panto arrowhead and raise their hands toward her.

ALL It's...Puss!

AUDIENCE Hello, Puss!

PRINCIPAL BOY (JULIA BRECK) Hello, children!

POLICE CHIEF Stop! Stop this adaptation of 'Puss-in-Boots'! **40** This is the Police Department of the State of Venezuela!

PRINCIPAL BOY Oh no it isn't!

POLICE CHIEF Oh, yes it is!

PRINCIPAL BOY *(kids joining in voice over)* Oh no it isn't!

ALL *(plus kids)* Oh yes it is!

PRINCIPAL BOY *(plus kids)* **Oh no it isn't...** **41**

POLICE CHIEF Shut up! Shut up! *(getting up, holding a pistol; he has no trousers; silence)* Now I'm going to ask you some questions, and remember, if you do not give me correct answers, we have ways of making you answer!

VOICE FROM BACK **Like not paying twenty-eight guineas.** [42]

POLICE CHIEF Shut up! Now, what ship are you from?

CAPTAIN **We are from the SS Mother Goose,** [43] we were twelve days out from Port of Spain, and I...

The door is flung open and the second—trouserless—guard rushes in.

SECOND GUARD I got thirty bob for the trousers!

CAPTAIN We are from SS *Mother Goose*. We were twelve days out from Port of Spain, and one night I was doing my usual rounds, when I had occasion to pass the forward storage lockers...

Slightly eerie music has crept in under his words and the screen goes into a ripple. It gets right out of focus and continues to ripple as it pulls back into focus. Ripple stops and they are still in the same set as they were.

POLICE CHIEF Go on!

CAPTAIN Well, I noticed something unusual, **the main bilge** [44] hatches had been opened... *(at this point three men in brown coats come in and start taking pictures off the wall, clearing props and chairs from the set, etc.)* and there, crouching amidst the scuppers was the most ghastly creature I'd ever seen in my life. *(the flats start to be flown up, revealing behind a sitting room—so that we can see the police office has been built in the Kelly's sitting room)* As soon as it saw me, its horrible face split aside in a ghastly look of terror. His head, which was like...

SCENE SHIFTER Could you sign this please? *(handing the captain a piece of paper)* Thank you.

CAPTAIN A small, small rat was ghastly and horrible and befurred...its little red eyes glinted in the unaccustomed glare of the midday sun and before I could shut the hatch, it sprang upon me with one almighty...

It's Idle's voice; he's about to enter, also trouserless.

Mother Goose, another pantomime.

A bilge can refer to both the lower part of a ship's body and the water that collects therein. Scuppers are openings in the sides of ships to let water drain out.

The Horse of the Year Show is an annual show jumping competition, held each year in October and always indoors. A British institution.

Harvey Smith is the gruff-spoken equestrian star of many a Horse of the Year Show, famous for launching a "V-sign"—a gestured version of "eff" off—to a set of show jumping judges.

Mr. David Barker was a famous show jumper of the day.

Patricia Hornsby-Smith was a British Conservative member of Parliament.

By this time the whole office set has been removed revealing the Kelly's boarding house sitting room. Mr and Mrs Kelly come in through door or put their heads round.

MRS KELLY (MICHAEL) What's this about doing the **'Horse of the Year Show'** **45** in here tonight?
CHIEF OFFICER I'm sorry, Mrs Kelly. We don't know, I'm afraid—this is drama.
MRS KELLY Mr Fox told me, before he went down to the pub, that they were doing 'Horse of the Year Show' in here tonight at 9.10.
CHIEF OF POLICE This is BBC 2.
CAPTAIN I think BBC 1 are in the kitchen.
MRS KELLY Well, I'm not having **Harvey Smith** **46** jumping over my binette.
MR KELLY No, come on. *(they go)*
CAPTAIN ...tearing at my throat, ripping my clothes...

Mr Kelly puts his head round the door.

MR KELLY And turn the gas off before you leave!
POLICE CHIEF All right!!

Mr Kelly goes.

CAPTAIN I fought it with all my strength, but it was too much for me...

Cut to Mr and Mrs Kelly coming through the hall. We can hear the captain's voice growing fainter. Mr and Mrs Kelly go towards the kitchen door and stop and listen. We have lost the captain's voice by now, but from inside the kitchen we hear 'Horse of the Year Show' sound track.

DORIAN WILLIAMS *(voice over)* Another clear round for Harvey Smith on 'Omalley'.
COMMENTATOR *(voice over on tannoy)* **And now it's Mrs David Barker,** **47** riding 'Atalanta' Number 3.

Crash of breaking pottery, falling pots and pans, horse neighing.

MRS KELLY Right! That's it! ***(they throw door open and march into the kitchen; a horse plus Pat Hornsby Smith*** **48** *and the commentator and the wreckage of a jump)* Come on now, out! All of you—get out of my kitchen, all of you—come on! Harvey Smith, get out of here!

She chases them out and down the hall.

PAUL FOX (TERRY J) *(emerging from another door)* It's one of our most popular programmes.
MRS KELLY That's what you think, Mr Fox!

She shooshes them all out down the passage and out of the front door. The newsreader with a blanket over him joins them and tries to read off a piece of paper.

NEWSREADER Well, that's all from BBC Television for this evening...
MRS KELLY *(slamming door on him)* Shove off! Go and find yourself another flat! Get out!

As she slams the door, a piece of paper (obviously a tax return form) is shoved through the door. It has the credits scribbled hurriedly on it; the camera pans into it. After the credits Mrs Kelly stamps on the paper. Fade out. Showbiz music, cut to a big sign saying 'It's'. Pull out to reveal glossy, spangly, opulent showbiz set. Two extraordinarily famous guests sitting on sofas.

ANNOUNCER'S VOICE (ERIC)

TONIGHT FROM LONDON YOUR SPECIAL GUESTS ARE LULU, RINGO STARR AND THE MAN YOU'VE ALL BEEN WAITING FOR—YOUR HOST FOR TONIGHT...

More music. The 'It's' man, tattered and ragged as usual, emerges onto set.

LULU Love the outfit dear, it's gorgeous.
IT'S MAN Hello, good evening, welcome. It's...

The signature tune and opening animated titles start. The 'It's' man, still visible through the titles, tries vainly to stop them. The guests walk off in disgust. The 'It's' man tries to drag them back. Failing, he sits down as the music ends. Fade out.

SEA
SON
3
EPISODE 29
POLICE

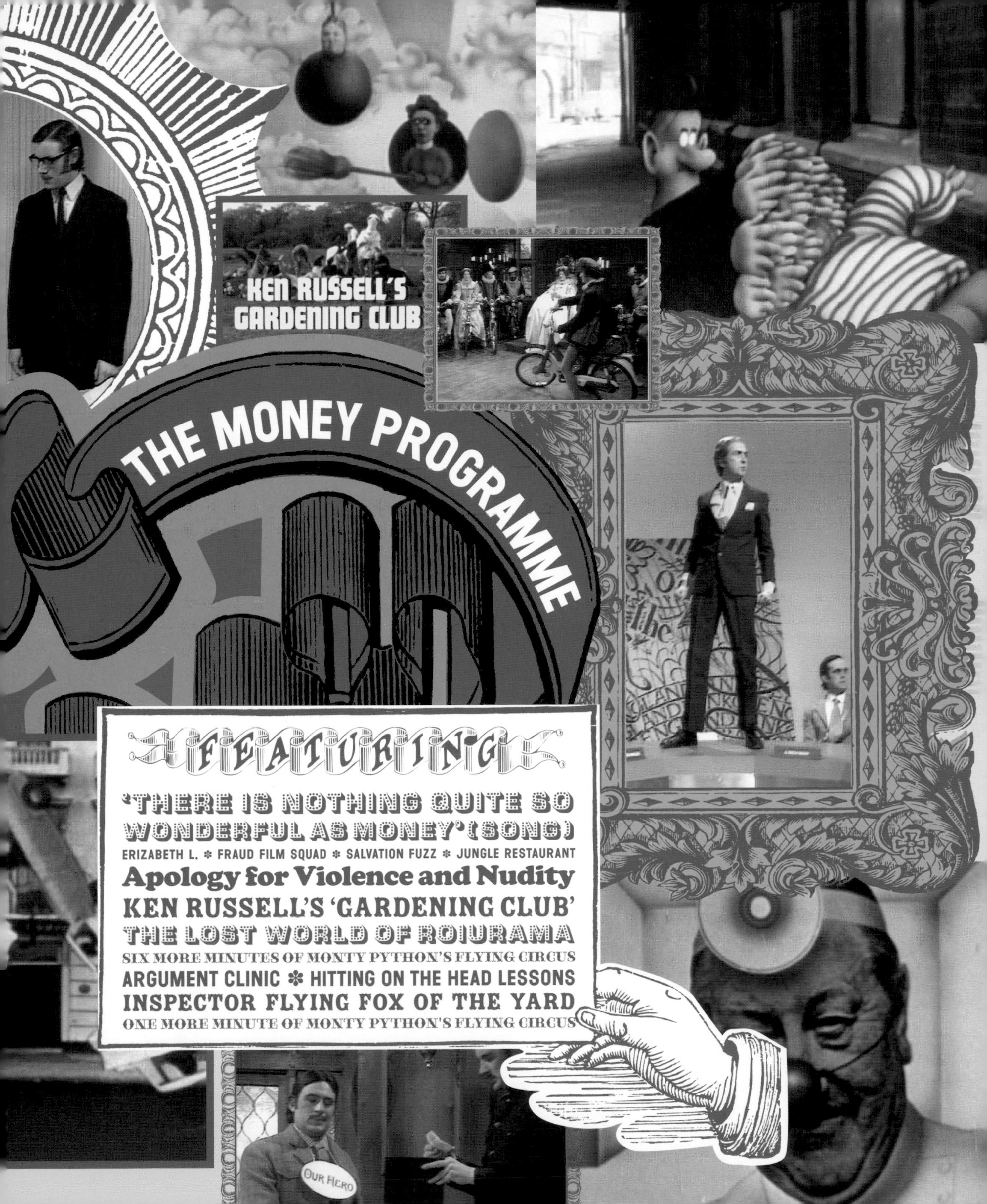
KEN RUSSELL'S
GARDENING CLUB
THE MONEY PROGRAMME
FEATURING
'THERE IS NOTHING QUITE SO
WONDERFUL AS MONEY' (SONG)
ERIZABETH L. ✽ FRAUD FILM SQUAD ✽ SALVATION FUZZ ✽ JUNGLE RESTAURANT
Apology for Violence and Nudity
KEN RUSSELL'S 'GARDENING CLUB'
THE LOST WORLD OF ROIURAMA
SIX MORE MINUTES OF MONTY PYTHON'S FLYING CIRCUS
ARGUMENT CLINIC ✽ HITTING ON THE HEAD LESSONS
INSPECTOR FLYING FOX OF THE YARD
ONE MORE MINUTE OF MONTY PYTHON'S FLYING CIRCUS
OUR HERO

FIRST AIRED: NOVEMBER 2, 1972

Opening title sequence and signature tune for 'The Money Programme'. Set with presenter and two guests. Close up on presenter. 1

1 First broadcast in 1966, the BBC's *The Money Programme* focuses on business and finance.

PRESENTER (ERIC)

GOOD EVENING AND WELCOME TO 'THE MONEY PROGRAMME'.

Tonight on 'The Money Programme', we're going to look at money. Lots of it. On film and in the studio. Some of it in nice piles, others in lovely clanky bits of loose change, some of it neatly counted into fat little hundreds, *(starting to get excited)* delicate fivers stuffed into bulging wallets, nice crisp clean cheques, pert pieces of copper coinage thrust deep into trouser pockets, romantic foreign money rolling against the thigh with rough familiarity, *(starting to get over-excited)* beautiful wayward curlicued banknotes, filigree copperplating cheek by jowl with tumbling hexagonal milled edges, rubbing gently against the terse leather of beautifully balanced bank books. *(collects himself)* I'm sorry. But I love money. All money. I've always wanted money. *(getting worked up again)* To handle. To touch. The smell of the rain-washed **florin**. 2 The lure of the lira. *(standing on the desk)* The glitter and the glory of the guinea. The romance of the rouble. The feel of the franc, the heel of the Deutschmark, the cold antiseptic sting of the Swiss franc, and the sun-burned splendour of the Australian dollar. *(sings to piano accompaniment)*

I've got ninety thousand pounds in my pyjamas.
I've got forty thousand French francs in my fridge.
I've got lots and lots of lira.
Now the Deutschmark's getting dearer.
And my dollar bills would buy the Brooklyn Bridge.

2 A "florin" was a the two-shilling coin issued in the U.K. from 1849 to 1967, also known as "two bob" or the "two-bob bit". Worth a tenth of one pound, it was replaced by the ten-pence coin, though you could still find a florin in pockets well into the 1990s.

Five singers (male) in Welsh (women's) national costume come on. A Welsh harpist joins them.

ALL There is nothing quite as wonderful as money,

There is nothing quite as beautiful as cash,
Some people say it's folly
But I'd rather have the lolly [3]
With money you can make a smash.

PRESENTER There is nothing quite as wonderful as money
There is nothing like a newly minted pound

ALL Everyone must hanker
For the butchness of a banker
It's accountancy that makes the world go round.

PRESENTER You can keep your Marxist ways
For it's only just a phase.

ALL For its money, money, money,
Makes the world go round. *(a shower of paper notes descends)* [4]

"Lolly" is British slang for cash.

And, oddly, a single blue balloon.

MONEY, MONEY, MONEY, MONEY, MONEY, MONEY!

Cut to side of set where the nude organist (TERRY J) *plays the final chord and grins at the camera. Cut to the announcer at his desk.*

JOHN And now...

IT'S MAN (MICHAEL)

IT'S...

Animated titles.

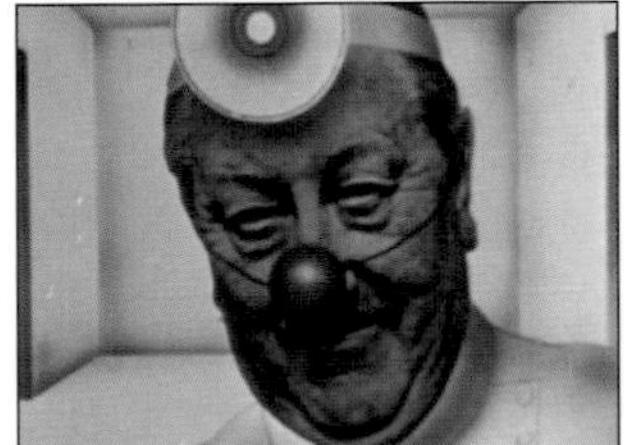

VOICE Monty Python's Flying Circuses.

Exterior of an Elizabethan palace. Elizabethan music. An Elizabethan messenger on a moped, comes up the drive and drives in through the front door. Superimposed caption: 'ERIZABETH I.' Cut to a long corridor. The messenger appears mopeding along the corridor very fast. He leaps off the moped

Sir Francis Drake was a privateer, explorer, slave master, politician—the complete Renaissance man. Elizabeth I knighted him in 1581. He fought the Spanish Armada in 1588 and sailed around the world from 1577 to 1580.

King Phillip II of Spain. Elizabeth I turned down his hand in marriage in 1559. He sent the Spanish Armada out against the British, and Drake, in July 1588.

and hands it to a guard at a door. The guard places the moped on a rack and the messenger enters the door going past three trumpeters who play a fanfare. He approaches a clerical figure, who stands at yet another door. Superimposed captions: 'EPISODE THREE' 'THE ALMALDA'

MESSENGER (MICHAEL) I bling a dispatch flom Prymouth.
CLERK (ERIC) Flom Prymouth?
MESSENGER Flom Sil Flancis Dlake. 5
CLERK Entel and apploach the thlone.

The doors open. The messenger leaps on another moped and rides up to the throne on which sits Elizabeth surrounded by her courtiers, all of who are on motorized bicycles.

QUEEN (GRAHAM) What news flom Prymouth?
MESSENGER Dlake has sighted the Spanish Freet, youl Majesty.
QUEEN So! Phirip's 6 garreons ale hele. How many?
MESSENGER One hundled and thilty-six men of wal.
LEICESTER (ERIC) Broody herr.
QUEEN Is Dlake plepaled?
MESSENGER He has oldeled the whore freet into the Blitish Channer.
QUEEN So, we must to Tirbuly. Reicestel! Sil Wartel Lareigh! Groucester! We sharr lide to...

Enter Japanese director.

JAPANESE (TERRY J) Groucestel! Groucestel! Not Groucester. Come on, ret's get this light. Reicestel!
LEICESTER Yes.
JAPANESE That was telliber.
LEICESTER What?
JAPANESE Telliber.
LEICESTER Oh! Solly.
JAPANESE

LEICESTER Ling my berr? **7**
JAPANESE *(linging his berr for him)* Ling ling. Rike this. And cut the broody herr. Erizabeth!

QUEEN *(cheesed off)* Yes?
JAPANESE You should be on a bicycer.
QUEEN Why?!
JAPANESE You rook odd rike that.
QUEEN I do not look odd like this—it's that lot that looks odd. It's bleeding weird having half the Tudor nobility ligging around on motorized bicycles.
JAPANESE It's vely sullearist.
QUEEN Horsefeathers!
LEICESTER Listen mate. I'm beginning to have my doubts about you.
JAPANESE What do you mean?
LEICESTER I'm telling you straight, mate. I don't think you're **Luchino Visconti** **8** at all.
JAPANESE Of course I am. Me vely impoltant Itarian firm dilectol.
QUEEN You are a Nip.
JAPANESE Lubbish! Me genuine wop. *(sings)* Alliveldelchi Loma...
LEICESTER He's bluffing.
JAPANESE *(sings)* Vo-oorale...Ooh...Is that the time, I must fry.

The door opens. Inspector Leopard runs through the door followed by a copper.

INSPECTOR (JOHN) Not so fast, Yakomoto. *(trumpeters play a fanfare)* Shut up! *(fanfare stops)* Allow me to introduce myself. I am Inspector Leopard of Scotland Yard, Special Fraud Film Director Squad.
COURT Leopard of the Yard!
INSPECTOR The same. Only more violent. *(he demonstrates this by kneeing the copper in the balls)* Right, Slit Eyes Yakomoto, I'm arresting you for the impersonation of **Signor Luchino Visconti**, **9** famous Italian director of such movie classics as 'Ossessione' (1942), 'La Terra Trema' (1948), and 'Bellissima' (1951)—a satisfying ironic slice-of-life drama. 1957 brought to the silver screen his **'I Bianche Notte'** **10** **adapted by Dostoyevsky**, **11** a mannered and romantic melancholy of snow and mist and moonlit encounters on canal bridges. 'Boccaccio 70' followed five years later and the following year saw 'The Leopard'! So impressed was I with this motion picture treatment of the Risorgimento that I went along to Somerset House and changed me own name to Leopard, preferring it to me original handle, **'Panther' (Aargh)**. **12**

"Lingering his berr"—in other words, ringing his bell.

Luchino Visconti was an eminent Italian theater and movie director, and whose career we are about to be educated on.

It sounds like Cleese says "Viscotti" rather than "Visconti."

It's actually called *Le Notti Bianche* (*White Nights*).

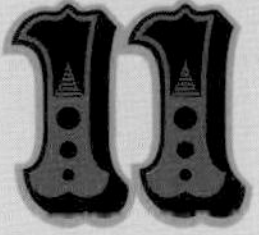

Or adapted *from* Dostoyevsky—specifically, his 1848 short story.

Here Cleese turns to Chapman, dressed as he is as Elizabeth I, and pretends to growl, his left hand an aggressive paw.

Charlotte Rampling is a British film actress whose performance in Visconti's *The Damned* caused Dirk Bogarde, himself a suave and handsome actor of renown, to refer to her as having "the look."

An amusing précis of *Death in Venice*.

"Jugging" is the act of cooking an animal or fish by sealing it in a container and stewing it over a long period of time.

"Afters" is British slang for dessert.

I digress. 1969 saw 'The Damned', a Gotterdammerung epic of political and industrial shennanigans in good old Nazi Germany, starring Helmut Berger as a stinking transvestite what should have his face sawn off, the curvaceous Charlotte Rampling 13 as a bit of tail, and the impeccable Dirk Bogarde as Von Essen. The association of the latter with Signor Visconti fructified with Dirk's magnificent portrayal of the elderly pouf what expires in Venice. 14 And so, Yakomoto...blimey, he gone! Never mind. I'll have you instead. *(grabs the queen)*

QUEEN What?

INSPECTOR I haven't got time to go chasing after him, there's violence to be done.

Animation: sketch about violence.

Cut to a kitchen. A man and woman listening to a radio.

RADIO VOICE I would like to ask the team what they would do if they were Hitler.

MAN'S VOICE Gerald?

ANOTHER VOICE Well I'd annex the Sudetenland and sign a non-aggression pact with Russia.

FIRST MAN'S VOICE Norman?

NORMAN'S VOICE Well I'd do the Reichstag bathroom in purples and golds and ban abortion on demand.

WOMAN (TERRY J) *(switching the radio off)* Liberal rubbish. Klaus...what do you want with your jugged fish? 15

MAN (ERIC) Halibut.

WOMAN The jugged fish *is* halibut.

MAN What fish have you got that isn't jugged, then?

WOMAN Rabbit.

MAN What? Rabbit fish?

WOMAN Yes. It's got fins.

MAN Is it dead?

WOMAN Well, it was coughing up blood last night.

MAN All right I'll have the dead unjugged rabbit fish.

Caption: 'ONE DEAD UNJUGGED RABBIT FISH LATER'

MAN Well that was really horrible.

WOMAN You're always complaining.

MAN What's for afters? 16

WOMAN Well there's rat cake...rat sorbet...rat pudding...or strawberry tart.

MAN Strawberry tart?!

WOMAN Well it's got *some* rat in it.

MAN How much?

WOMAN Three (rather a lot really).

MAN ...well, I'll have a slice without so much rat in it.

Caption: 'ONE SLICE OF STRAWBERRY TART WITHOUT SO MUCH RAT IN IT LATER'

MAN Appalling.

WOMAN Moan, moan, moan.

Enter their son.

SON (GRAHAM) Hello, mum, hello, dad.
MAN Hello, son.
SON

THERE'S A DEAD BISHOP ON THE LANDING.

WOMAN Where did that come from?
SON What do you mean?
WOMAN What's its diocese?
SON Well it looked a bit Bath and Wellsish to me. 17
MAN I'll go and have a look. *(goes out)*
WOMAN I don't know who keeps bringing them in here.
SON Well it's not me.
WOMAN I've put three out by the bin and the dustmen won't touch 'em.
MAN *(coming back)* Leicester. 18
WOMAN How do you know?
MAN Tattooed on the back of his neck. I'm going to call the police.
WOMAN Shouldn't you call the Church?
SON Call the Church police.
MAN ...all right. *(shouts)* The Church police!

Enter two policemen with ecclesiastical accoutrements.

CHURCH POLICEMAN (MICHAEL) Yus?
WOMAN There's another dead bishop on the landing.
CHURCH POLICEMAN Suffragan or diocesan? 19
WOMAN How should I know?
CHURCH POLICEMAN It's tattooed on the back of their necks. Ere! Is that rat tart?
WOMAN Yes.
CHURCH POLICEMAN Disgusting. Right! The hunt is on. *(kneels)* Oh Lord we beseech thee tell us who croaked Leicester.

Organ music. A huge hand descends and points at the man.

MAN All right, it's a fair cop, but society is to blame.
CHURCH POLICEMAN Agreed.
MAN I would like the three by the bin to be taken into consideration.
CHURCH POLICEMAN Right. And now, I'd like to conclude this arrest with a hymn.
ALL *(singing)* And did these feet in ancient times walk upon England's mountains green. 20 *(policemen escort the man out)* And was the holy lamb of God on England's pleasant pastures seen.

The diocese of Bath and Wells refers to the area of Somerset, and some of Devon, in England's West Country.

Leicester is a town in the East Midlands.

A suffragan bishop is an assistant bishop to a bishop who runs a metropolitan or diocesan area. He tends not to have a cathedral all his own.

Yet more singing of the hymn "Jerusalem."

Animation: bouncing Queen Victoria.

VOICE OVER Meanwhile in the jungle next door.

A steamy tropical jungle. A native guide leads four explorers in pith helmets and old-fashioned long shorts through the jungle. Cicada sounds and shrieks of predatory jungle birds. Intercut close ups of perspiring foreheads etc. The native guide keeps beckoning them to hurry. The jungle appears to get thicker: they have to push their way through the undergrowth. Finally the guide stops and points, with eyes staring. The four explorers cluster round and look over his shoulder. A neat clearing in the thick of the jungle. Tables set as in a London bistro with check cloths and big wooden pepper mills, candles and menus standing on each table. Sitting at the tables are six other explorers in pith helmets etc., eating and chatting. Clink of coffee cups.

FIRST EXPLORER (JOHN) What a simply super little place!

SECOND EXPLORER (ERIC) Yes, they've done wonders with it. You know this used to be one of the most swampy disease-infested areas of the whole jungle, and they've turned it into this smashing little restaurant. *(across the restaurant the head waiter appears, dressed in black tie and tails just a bit too big for him; he beckons them to a table)* Here you are Omkami, thank you. Hello, Mr Akwekwe.

AKWEKWE (MICHAEL) **Hello, Mr Spare-Buttons-Supplied-With-The-Shirt. Nice to see you again.** 21

21

Palin here in blackface.

SECOND EXPLORER These are some of my fellow explorers: Sir Charles Farquarson, Brian Bailey, Betty Bailey and this is Mr Akwekwe, who started the whole place.

THIRD EXPLORER (GRAHAM) It really is super.

FOURTH EXPLORER (CAROL) *(who is dressed as a man and has a moustache)* Terrific idea.

AKWEKWE

MAY I RECOMMEND THE
ALLIGATOR PUREES.

Suddenly there is a hideous scream. We see a gorilla tear a man from his table at the back of the restaurant, in front of a tree and drag him back into the jungle. Awful shrieks are heard. Akwekwe runs into the jungle shouting. Terrible sounds of the unseen fight. Thrashing about of bushes in the distance. A shot rings out. Then silence also rings out. Akwekwe emerges, dragging the inert body of the cash customer whom he puts back in his chair. He slumps forward. Akwekwe comes back to the table in the foreground which has remained in the foreground throughout this preceding shot, with cut ins of the four explorers looking through the menu. Akwekwe has a bloodstained claw mark right across his face and chest and his dicky is torn and bloodstained.

AKWEKWE Now then, have you decided?

He produces a notepad such as waiters always carry.

SECOND EXPLORER Ye-es...Well there's two avocado vinaigrette here and what are you going to have Brian?
FOURTH EXPLORER Er quiche lorraine for me, please.
AKWEKWE Right, so that's two avocado, one quiche...

Cut to close up of pigmy's evil face parting leaves and firing a blow-pipe. Cut to another table where two explorers are having coffee and cigars. One of them stiffens and then slumps forward. Cut to Akwekwe at the main table registering what has happened. We pan with him as he rushes over to the bushes. Sound of pigmies retreating into the bushes. Akwekwe shouts after him. We pan with Akwekwe as he walks over to the table where the customer has slumped forward. He pulls him up, looks at dart sticking out of his chest, tut tuts with annoyance and lets him slump back on to the table again. He returns to the main table.

AKWEKWE So, that's two avocado, one quiche...
THIRD EXPLORER And a soup of the day.
AKWEKWE Right. *(sinister sound of jungle drums in distance; close up of look of fear in Akwekwe's eyes)* And to follow?
SECOND EXPLORER Two chicken à la reine, with sauce provençale. 22
FIRST EXPLORER And one scampi desirée. 23
THIRD EXPLORER And boeuf bourguignon with a green salad.

Jungle drums getting louder. Akwekwe shouts off towards the back of the clearing where we assume the kitchens must be.

AKWEKWE Right on. Two chicken! One scampi! One boeuf with green salad!

He casts yet another fearful glance in the direction of the ever-increasing drum beats.

AKWEKWE There may be...a little delay.
SECOND EXPLORER That's fine but we have to be out by three.
AKWEKWE Yes, sir. Yes, we'll try.

The drum beats get louder. Shot of forest, rustling of bushes. Close up of Akwekwe's eyes. Another shot of forest. Drum beats louder. More rustling. Close up of Akwekwe's eyes and sweating forehead. Forest again and more noise. Close up of Akwekwe; he now has blood on his face, his eyes dilate with fear, the drum beats become deafening. Sudden cut to BBC world symbol.

VOICE OVER (ERIC) The BBC would like to announce that the next scene is not considered suitable for family viewing. It contains scenes of violence, involving people's heads and arms getting chopped off, their ears nailed to trees, and their toenails pulled out in slow motion. There are also scenes of naked women with floppy breasts, and also at one point you can see a pair of buttocks and there's another bit where I'll swear you can see everything, but my friend says it's just the way he's holding the spear. *(pulling himself together)* Because of the unsuitability of the scene, the BBC will be replacing it with a scene from a repeat of 'Gardening Club' for 1958. 24

A beautiful well-stocked garden bed. 'Gardening Club' music. After two seconds there are shrieks of licentious and lustful laughter. A nude woman pursues a city gent, both screaming with

Chicken à la Reine is, basically, chicken and mushrooms in a béchamel sauce surrounded by puff pastry.

Not a real thing, though it should be.

Gardening Club was a BBC TV show that ran from 1957 to 1967.

Another reference to Ken Russell, whose "racy" movies shocked audiences in the 1960s and '70s.

The Barclaycard was the first credit card issued in the U.K., created by Barclays Bank, not surprisingly, in 1966.

pleasure, into the middle of the flowerbed and they roll around smashing up the flowers in unbridled erotic orgy. Immediately two nuns run in to join the fun, followed by two Vikings, a gumby, a pantomime goose, etc. The whole of this orgy is speeded up. Caption: 'KEN RUSSELL'S GARDENING CLUB (1958)' 25

VOICE OVER And now back to the story.

Cut to the edge of the jungle. Emerging from the dense undergrowth are two pigmy warriors pulling the four explorers who are roped together. The pigmies carry spears. We lose the pigmies and hold just the explorers in frame, and track with them.

THIRD EXPLORER That was a nasty business back at the restaurant.
FIRST EXPLORER Yes, I thought most places took Barclaycard nowadays. 26
SECOND EXPLORER Where do you think they're taking us, Brian?
FOURTH EXPLORER God knows!
THIRD EXPLORER *(pointing, eyes wide with amazement)* Look!

Cut to a stock shot of a volcano. Thrilling chord. Cut back to explorers.

SECOND EXPLORER *(filled with awe)* The sacred volcano Andu! Which no man has seen before.
THIRD EXPLORER No, no, no, next to that.

Cut to stock shot of collection of big chimneys in a brickworks. Another thrilling chord. Cut back to explorers.

FIRST EXPLORER The London Brick Company?
THIRD EXPLORER No, no, no, no—*next* to that.

Cut to stock shot of plateau of Roiurama. Yet another thrilling chord. Cut back to explorers.

FIRST EXPLORER The forbidden plateau of Roiurama, the Lost World, thrown up by mighty earth movements thousands of millions of years ago, where strange primeval creatures defying evolution, lurk in the dark, impenetrable forests, cut off forever from the outside world.
SECOND EXPLORER I still can't see it.
FOURTH EXPLORER You don't think that's where they're taking us?
THIRD EXPLORER Yes, and God knows what we'll find there.

A pigmy native rushes up from behind them, holding a script.

NATIVE (TERRY J) What page please?
SECOND EXPLORER What?
NATIVE *(with a trace of irritation)*

WHAT PAGE IN THE SCRIPT?

SECOND EXPLORER *(whispered)* Page 7.

NATIVE *(he speaks the lines over to himself)* 'Come on, you dogs, we have far to go. We must lose no time'. *(tries with eyes shut)* 'Come on, you dogs, we have far to go. We must lose no time'. 'Come on you dogs'. *(throws away the script, starts to push them roughly)* Come on you dogs, we have time to lose, this has gone too far.

Stock film of Houses of Parliament from across the Thames.

VOICE OVER (GRAHAM) Meanwhile back in London...at the British Explorers' Club in the Mall...

Cut to the leather-armchaired hallway of a London club. In four of the chairs sit men in polar explorers' kit—furs, iced-over goggles, etc.—reading newspapers. At one chair sits a man in Norfolk jacket and plus fours. **27** *Around his neck he wears a sign saying 'Our Hero'. He is reading a newspaper but obviously has something else on his mind. Suddenly he throws the paper down and gets up. He walks over to the porter's desk. As he does this a polar expedition with four huskies, a sled, and two explorers pass him. Our Hero goes up to the desk. A whiskery old porter stands behind it.*

OUR HERO (TERRY J) Any news of Betty Bailey's expedition, Hargreaves?
HARGREAVES (MICHAEL) Er...um...er...
OUR HERO *(through clenched teeth)* Page 9...
HARGREAVES *(thumbing over page of script beneath counter)* 'The Lost World of Roiurama'.
OUR HERO That's my line.
HARGREAVES Oh, sorry. 'Where were they going, sir'?
OUR HERO The Lost World of Roiurama.
HARGREAVES Yes sir, we've got a telegram.
OUR HERO Oh!
HARGREAVES *(reads it)* Reads it. Expedition superb. Weather excellent. Everything wonderful.
OUR HERO I wonder what's gone wrong.
HARGREAVES For God's sake be careful...
OUR HERO *(irritably)* Wait a minute...I'm going to go...after them.
HARGREAVES For God's sake be careful, sir.

Cut to film of the lost world. Tropical South American vegetation. Our four explorers limp along exhaustedly.

SECOND EXPLORER My God, Betty, we're done for...
THIRD EXPLORER We'll never get out of here...we're completely lost, lost. Even the natives have gone.
FIRST EXPLORER Goodbye Betty, Goodbye Farquarson. Goodbye Brian. It's been a great expedition...

Music. Cut to engraving of Crystal Palace. Superimposed caption: 'CRYSTAL PALACE 1851' **28** *Cut immediately back to jungle.*

FIRST EXPLORER Great *expedition*...
THIRD EXPLORER All that'll be left of us will be a map, a compass and a few feet of film, recording our last moments...
FIRST EXPLORER Wait a moment!
FOURTH EXPLORER What is it?
FIRST EXPLORER If we're on film, there must be someone filming us.
SECOND EXPLORER My God, Betty, you're right!

They all look around, then gradually all notice the camera. They break out in smiles of relief come towards the camera and greet the camera crew.

A "Norfolk jacket" is a jacket sported by the exploring set, as well as hunters. It is loosely belted and beloved of the royal family in the U.K.

The Great Exhibition of 1851, held at London's Crystal Palace, was the very first world's fair. It featured everything from the Koh-i-Noor diamond to the first public lavatories.

THIRD EXPLORER Look! Great to see you!
FIRST EXPLORER What a stroke of luck!
CAMERA CREW Hello!...
FIRST EXPLORER Wait a minute!
FOURTH EXPLORER What is it again?
FIRST EXPLORER If this is the crew who *were* filming us...who's filming us *now*? Look!

Cut to another shot which includes the first camera crew and yet another camera crew with all their equipment. The director is dressed the same as Yakomoto, the director in 'Erisabeth L', only he is blacked up.

DIRECTOR (TERRY J) *(African accent)* Cut there man! No! No good! How we going to get feeling of personal alienation of self from society with this load of Bulldog Drummond crap? 29 When I was doing 'La Notte' 30 wi' dat Monica Vitti gal she don't gimme none of this empire building shit, man...

The hero of novels by Herman Cyril McNeile (pen name "Sapper"), Bulldog Drummond was an adventurer and private investigator. The books were published between 1920 and 1954.

La Notte is a 1961 movie by Michelangelo Antonioni. As with Visconti, the Pythons are about to describe his career to us.

It was actually called *Le Amiche* (*The Girlfriends*) not "L'Amico."

Camera pans slightly to reveal a door in jungle. It opens and an inspector enters.

INSPECTOR (ERIC) Not so fast, Akarumba! Allow me to introduce myself. I'm Inspector Baboon of Scotland Yard's Special Fraud Film Director Squad, Jungle Division.
FOURTH EXPLORER Baboon of the Yard!
INSPECTOR Shut up! *(shoots her)* Right, Akarumba! I'm arresting you for impersonating Signor Michelangelo Antonioni, an Italian film director who co-scripts all his own films, largely jettisoning narrative in favour of vague incident and relentless character study...*(during this harangue the credits start to roll, music very faint beneath his words)*...In his first film: 'Cronaca Di Un Amore' (1950), the couple are brought together by a shared irrational guilt. 'L'Amico' 31 followed in 1955, and 1959 saw the first of Antonioni's world-famous trilogy, 'L' Avventura'—an acute study of boredom, restlessness and the futilities and agonies of purposeless living. In 'L'Eclisse', three years later, this analysis of sentiments is taken up once again. 'We do not have to know each other to love', says the heroine, 'and perhaps we do not have to love...' The 'Eclipse' of the emotions finally casts its shadow when darkness descends on a street corner. *(the credits end; voice and picture start to fade)*...Signor Antonioni first makes use of colour to underline...

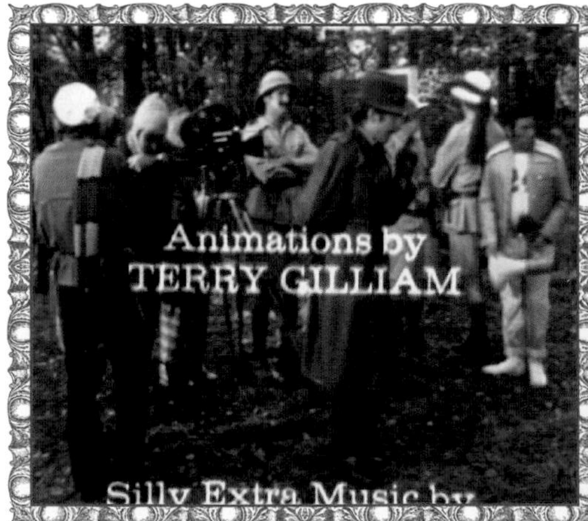

Fade to black and cut to BBC world symbol.

CONTINUITY VOICE (ERIC) And now on BBC 1 another six minutes of Monty Python's Flying Circus.

A reception desk in a sort of office building.

RECEPTIONIST (RITA DAVIES) Yes, sir?

MAN

I'D LIKE TO HAVE AN ARGUMENT PLEASE. 32

RECEPTIONIST Certainly sir, have you been here before...?

MAN No, this is my first time.

RECEPTIONIST I see. Do you want to have the full argument, or were you thinking of taking a course?

MAN Well, what would be the cost?

RECEPTIONIST Yes, it's one pound for a five-minute argument, but only eight pounds for a course of ten. 33

MAN Well, I think it's probably best if I start with the one and see how it goes from there. OK?

RECEPTIONIST Fine. I'll see who's free at the moment...Mr Du-Bakey's free, but he's a little bit conciliatory...Yes, try Mr Barnard—Room 12.

MAN Thank you.

The man walks down a corridor. He opens door 12. There is a man at a desk.

MR BARNARD (GRAHAM) *(shouting)* What do you want?

MAN Well I was told outside...

MR BARNARD Don't give me that you snotty-faced heap of parrot droppings!

MAN What!

MR BARNARD Shut your festering gob you tit! 34 Your type makes me puke! You vacuous toffee-nosed malodorous pervert!!

MAN Look! I came in here for an argument.

MR BARNARD *(calmly)* Oh! I'm sorry, this is abuse.

MAN Oh I see, that explains it.

MR BARNARD No, you want room 12A next door.

MAN I see—sorry. *(exits)*

MR BARNARD Not at all. *(as he goes)* Stupid git.

Outside 12A. The man knocks on the door.

MR VIBRATING (JOHN) *(from within)* Come in.

The man enters the room. Mr Vibrating is sitting at a desk.

MAN Is this the right room for an argument?

MR VIBRATING I've told you *once.*

MAN No you haven't.

MR VIBRATING Yes I have.

MAN When?

MR VIBRATING Just now!

MAN No you didn't.

MR VIBRATING Yes I did!

MAN Didn't.

MR VIBRATING Did.

MAN Didn't.

MR VIBRATING I'm telling you I did!

MAN You did not!

The first classic sketch of the third series.

Rita Davies flubs her line here by starting to say "five pounds," but she corrects herself.

"Gob" is British for mouth. Americans would say "trap."

MR VIBRATING

I'M SORRY, IS THIS A FIVE-MINUTE ARGUMENT, OR THE FULL HALF-HOUR?

MAN Oh...Just a five-minute one.
MR VIBRATING Fine *(makes a note of it; the man sits down)* thank you. Anyway I did.
MAN You most certainly did not.
MR VIBRATING Now, let's get one thing *quite* clear. I most definitely told you!
MAN You did not.
MR VIBRATING Yes I did.
MAN You did not.
MR VIBRATING Yes I did.
MAN Didn't.
MR VIBRATING Yes I did.
MAN Didn't.
MR VIBRATING Yes I did!!
MAN Look this isn't an argument.
MR VIBRATING Yes it is.
MAN No it isn't, it's just contradiction.
MR VIBRATING No it isn't.
MAN Yes it is.
MR VIBRATING It is not.
MAN It is. You just contradicted me.
MR VIBRATING No I didn't.
MAN Ooh, you did!
MR VIBRATING No, no, no, no, no.
MAN You did, just then.

"Gainsaying" means denying.

This brilliant moment gets an applause break from the audience.

MR VIBRATING No, nonsense!
MAN Oh, look this is futile.
MR VIBRATING No it isn't.
MAN I came here for a good argument.
MR VIBRATING No you didn't, you came here for an *argument*.
MAN Well, an argument's not the same as contradiction.
MR VIBRATING It can be.
MAN No it can't. An argument is a connected series of statements to establish a definite proposition.
MR VIBRATING No it isn't.
MAN Yes it is. It isn't just contradiction.
MR VIBRATING Look, if I argue with you I must take up a contrary position.
MAN But it isn't just saying 'No it isn't'.
MR VIBRATING Yes it is.
MAN No it isn't, argument is an intellectual process...contradiction is just the automatic **gainsaying** 35 of anything the other person says.
MR VIBRATING No it isn't.
MAN Yes it is.
MR VIBRATING Not at all.
MAN Now look!
MR VIBRATING ***(pressing the bell on his desk)*** 36 Thank you, good morning.
MAN What?
MR VIBRATING That's it. Good morning.
MAN But I was just getting interested.
MR VIBRATING Sorry the five minutes is up.
MAN That was never five minutes just now!

MR VIBRATING I'm afraid it was.

MAN No it wasn't.

MR VIBRATING

I'M SORRY, I'M NOT ALLOWED TO ARGUE ANY MORE.

MAN What!?

MR VIBRATING If you want me to go on arguing you'll have to pay for another five minutes.

MAN But that was never five minutes just now...oh come on! *(Vibrating looks round as though man was not there)* This is ridiculous.

MR VIBRATING I'm very sorry, but I told you I'm not allowed to argue unless you've paid.

MAN Oh. All right. *(pays)* There you are.

MR VIBRATING Thank you.

MAN Well?

MR VIBRATING Well what?

MAN That was never five minutes just now.

MR VIBRATING I told you I'm not allowed to argue unless you've paid.

MAN I've just paid.

MR VIBRATING No you didn't.

MAN I did! I did! I did!

MR VIBRATING No you didn't.

MAN Look I don't want to argue about that.

MR VIBRATING Well I'm very sorry but you didn't pay.

MAN Aha! Well if I didn't pay, why are you arguing...got you!

MR VIBRATING No you haven't.

MAN Yes I have...if you're arguing I must have paid.

MR VIBRATING Not necessarily. I could be arguing in my spare time.

MAN I've had enough of this.

MR VIBRATING No you haven't.

MAN Oh shut up! *(he leaves and sees a door marked complaints; he goes in)* I want to complain.

MAN IN CHARGE (ERIC) *You* want to complain...look at these shoes...I've only had them three weeks and the heels are worn right through.

MAN No, I want to complain about...

MAN IN CHARGE If you complain nothing happens...you might just as well not bother. My back hurts and...*(the man exits, walks down the corridor and enters a room)*

MAN I want to complain. *('Spreaders' who is just inside door hits man on the head with a mallet)* Ooh!

SPREADERS (TERRY J) No, no, no, hold your head like this, and then go 'waaagh'! Try it again. *(he hits him again)*

MAN Waaghh!

SPREADERS Better. Better. But 'waaaaagh'! 'Waaaagh'! Hold your hands here...

MAN No!

SPREADERS Now. *(hits him)*

MAN Waagh!

SPREADERS That's it. That's it. Good.

MAN Stop hitting me!

SPREADER What?

MAN Stop hitting me.

SPREADERS Stop hitting you?

MAN Yes.

SPREADERS What did you come in here for then?

MAN I came here to complain.
SPREADERS Oh I'm sorry, that's next door. It's being hit on the head lessons in here.
MAN What a stupid concept.

Detective Inspector Fox enters.

FOX (GRAHAM) Right. Hold it there.
MAN AND SPREADERS What?
FOX Allow me to introduce myself. I'm Inspector Fox of the Light Entertainment Police, Comedy Division, **Special Flying Squad.** 37
MAN AND SPREADERS Flying Fox of the Yard.
FOX Shut up! *(he hits the man with a truncheon)*
MAN Ooooh!
SPREADERS No, no, no—Waagh!
FOX And you. *(he hits Spreaders)*
SPREADERS Waagh!
FOX He's good! You could learn a thing or two from him. Right now you two me old beauties, you are **nicked.** 38
MAN What for?
FOX I'm charging you two under Section 21 of the Strange Sketch Act.
MAN The what?
FOX You are hereby charged that you did wilfully take part in a strange sketch, that is, a skit, spoof or humorous vignette of an unconventional nature with intent to cause grievous mental confusion to the Great British Public. *(to camera)* Evening all.
SPREADERS It's a fair cop.
FOX And you tosh. *(hits the man)*
MAN WAAAGH!
FOX That's excellent! Right, come on down the Yard.

Another inspector arrives.

INSPECTOR (ERIC) Hold it. Hold it. **Allow me to introduce myself.** 39 I'm Inspector Thompson's Gazelle of the Programme Planning Police, Light Entertainment Division, Special Flying Squad.
FOX Flying Thompson's Gazelle of the Yard!
INSPECTOR Shut up! *(he hits him)*

The Special Flying Squad is a section of the Metropolitan Police, dedicated to investigating (often violent) armed robberies. "Flying" because they worked the whole of London, not just certain divisions of it.

"Nicked" is British slang for arrested.

Idle amusingly says "introduce mysmelf," but carries on regardless.

FOX Waaaagh!
SPREADERS He's good.
INSPECTOR Shut up! *(hits Spreaders)*
SPREADERS WAAGH!
MAN Rotten. *(he gets hit)* WAAAGH!
INSPECTOR Good. Now I'm arrestin' this entire show on three counts: one, acts of self-conscious behaviour contrary to the 'Not in front of the children' Act, two, always saying 'It's so and so of the Yard' every time the fuzz arrives and, three, and this is the cruncher, offences against the 'Getting out of sketches without using a proper punchline' Act, four, namely, simply ending every bleedin' sketch by just having a policeman come in and...wait a minute.

Another policeman enters.

POLICEMAN (JOHN) Hold it. *(puts his hand on Inspector Thompson's Gazelle's shoulder)*
INSPECTOR It's a fair cop.

A large hairy hand appears through the door and claps him on the shoulder. **40**

Caption: 'THE END' Cut to BBC world symbol.

ANNOUNCER'S VOICE (ERIC) And now on BBC 1, one more minute of Monty Python's Flying Circus.

It's actually Cleese, also dressed as an inspector.

SEA SON 3
EPISODE 30
DEATH
WAR
HORROR

BLOOD, DEVASTATION, DEATH, WAR AND HORROR
FEATURING
THE MAN WHO SPEAKS IN ANAGRAMS * ANAGRAM QUIZ
MERCHANT BANKER * PANTOMIME HORSES
LIFE DEATH AND STRUGGLES
Mary Recruitment Office
BUS CONDUCTOR SKETCH * THE MAN WHO
MAKES PEOPLE LAUGH UNCONTROLLABLY
ARMY CAPTAIN AS CLOWN
GESTURES TO INDELICATE PAUSES IN A TELEVISED TALK
NEUROTIC ANNOUNCERS * THE NEWS WITH RICHARD BAKER (VISION ONLY)
THE PANTOMIME HORSE
IS A SECRET AGENT FILM

FIRST AIRED: NOVEMBER 9, 1972

The *Torrey Canyon* was an oil supertanker that crashed off the coast of Cornwall in March 1967. It was bombed by the Royal Air Force to help burn the fuel.

Stock colour film of vivid explosive action for fifteen seconds: dog fight RAF style; trains crashing; Spanish hotel blowing up; car crashing and exploding; train on collapsing bridge; volcano erupting; Torrey Canyon burning; 1 *forest fire blazing. From this we zoom the following words individually:*

Caption: 'BLOOD, DEATH, WAR, HORROR' Cut to an interviewer in a rather dinky little set. On the wall there is a rather prettily done sign, not too big, saying 'BLOOD, DEVASTATION, DEATH, WAR AND HORROR', as if it were a show's title.

INTERVIEWER (MICHAEL) Hello, good evening and welcome to another edition of 'Blood, Devastation, Death, War and Horror', and later on we'll be talking to a man who *does* gardening. But our first guest in the studio tonight is a man who talks entirely in anagrams.

MAN (ERIC) Taht si crreoct.
INTERVIEWER Do you enjoy this?
MAN I stom certainly od. Revy chum so.
INTERVIEWER And what's your name?
MAN Hamrag, Hamrag Yatlerot.
INTERVIEWER Well, Graham, nice to have you on the show. Now where do you come from?
MAN Bumcreland.
INTERVIEWER Cumberland?
MAN Staht sit sepreicly.
INTERVIEWER

The Taming of the Shrew.

AND I BELIEVE YOU'RE WORKING ON AN ANAGRAM VERSION OF SHAKESPEARE...

MAN Sey sey, taht si crreoct, er. Ta the mnemot I'm wroking on 'The Mating of the Wersh'. 2
INTERVIEWER 'The Mating of the Wersh'. By William Shakespeare?
MAN Nay, by Malliwi Rapesheake.

INTERVIEWER And er, what else?
MAN 'Two Netlemeg of Verona', 'Twelfth Thing', 'The Chamrent of Venice'... 3
INTERVIEWER Have you done 'Hamlet'?
MAN 'Thamle'. 'Be ot or bot ne ot, tath is the nestquie'. 4
INTERVIEWER And what is your next project?
MAN 'Ring Kichard the Thrid'.
INTERVIEWER I'm sorry?
MAN 'A shroe! A shroe! My dingkome for a shroe!'
INTERVIEWER Ah, Ring Kichard, yes...but surely that's not an anagram, that's a spoonerism. 5
MAN If you're going to split hairs I'm going to piss off. *(he leaves)*

Cut to the naked organist (TERRY J)*, then to the announcer.*

ANNOUNCER (JOHN) And now...
IT'S MAN (MICHAEL) It's...

Animated titles, title given as:

VOICE OVER (JOHN) Tony M. Nyphot's Flying Riscu.

Caption: 'CHAMRAN KNEBT' Pull out a little. The board has little green curtains and there is a pepperpot standing in front of it.

PRESENTER (JOHN) Mrs Scab, you have twelve hours to beat the clock.

A gong goes. A superimposed clock starts to move incredibly fast. It has a minute hand and an hour hand. Twelve hours pass very quickly. The pepperpot starts to rearrange the letters, very quickly. She gets it right. It reads: 'merchant bank'. The gong goes, and the clock stops.

PRESENTER Correct!
PEPPERPOT I've done it. I've done it. Ha, ha, ha!

The Two Gentlemen of Verona, Twelfth Night, and *The Merchant of Venice.*

"To be, or not to be: that is the question," from Act 3, Scene 1 of *Hamlet.*

Named for Reverend William Archibald Spooner (1844–1930), warden of New College, Oxford University. He was known for his tendency to switch the first wetters of lords.

An enormous head of a large cartoon-type hammer hits her and she goes down very fast. Cut to a city gent in his office. A sign on his desk says a 'Chamran Knebter'. He is waiting to answer his phone. It rings; he answers.

CITY GENT (JOHN) Hello? Ah, Mr Victim, I'm glad to say that I've got the go-ahead to lend you the money you require. Yes, of course we will want as security the deeds of your house, of your aunt's house, of your second cousin's house, of your wife's parents' house, and of your grannie's bungalow, and we will in addition need a controlling interest in your new company, unrestricted access to your private bank account, the deposit in our vaults of your three children as hostages and a full legal indemnity against any acts of embezzlement carried out against you by any members of our staff during the normal course of their duties...no, I'm afraid we couldn't accept your dog instead of your youngest child, we would like to suggest a brand new scheme of ours under which 51% of both your dog and your wife pass to us in the event of your suffering a serious accident. Fine. No, not at all, nice to do business with you. *(puts the phone down, speaks on intercom)* Miss Godfrey, could you send in Mr Ford please. *(to himself)* Now where's that dictionary—ah yes—here we are, inner life...inner life... 6 *(a knock on the door)* Come in. *(Mr Ford enters, he is collecting for charity with a tin)* Ah, Mr Ford isn't it?

This very nice joke about a banker's lack of an inner life falls flat—nary a snicker from the audience.

MR FORD (TERRY J) That's right.
CITY GENT How do you do. I'm a merchant banker.
MR FORD How do you do Mr...
CITY GENT Er...I forget my name for the moment but I *am* a merchant banker.
MR FORD Oh. I wondered whether you'd like to contribute to the orphan's home. *(he rattles the tin)*
CITY GENT Well I don't want to show my hand too early, but actually here at Slater Nazi we are quite keen to get into orphans, you know, developing market and all that...what sort of sum did you have in mind?
MR FORD Well...er...you're a rich man.
CITY GENT Yes, I am. Yes. Yes, very very rich. Quite phenomenally wealthy. Yes, I do own the most startling quantities of cash. Yes, quite right...you're rather a smart young lad aren't you. We could do with somebody like you to feed the pantomime horse. Very smart.

MR FORD Thank you, sir.

CITY GENT

NOW, YOU WERE SAYING. I'M VERY, VERY, VERY, VERY, VERY, VERY, VERY, VERY, VERY, VERY, VERY RICH.

MR FORD So er, how about a pound?

CITY GENT A pound. Yes, I see. Now this loan would be secured by the...

MR FORD It's not a *loan*, sir.

CITY GENT What?

MR FORD It's not a loan.

CITY GENT Ah.

MR FORD You get one of these, sir. *(he gives him a flag)*

CITY GENT It's a bit small for a share certificate isn't it? Look, I think I'd better run this over to our legal department. If you could possibly pop back on Friday.

MR FORD Well do you have to do that, couldn't you just give me the pound?

CITY GENT Yes, but you see I don't know what it's *for*.

MR FORD It's for the orphans.

CITY GENT Yes?

MR FORD It's a gift.

CITY GENT A what?

MR FORD A gift?

CITY GENT Oh a *gift*!

MR FORD Yes.

CITY GENT A tax dodge.

MR FORD No, no, no, no.

CITY GENT No? Well, I'm awfully sorry I don't understand. Can you just explain exactly what you want.

MR FORD Well, I want you to give me a pound, and then I go away and give it to the orphans.

CITY GENT Yes?

MR FORD Well, that's it.

CITY GENT No, no, no, I don't follow this at all, I mean, I don't want to seem stupid but it looks to me as though I'm a pound down on the whole deal.

MR FORD Well, yes you are.

CITY GENT I am! Well, what is my incentive to give you the pound?

MR FORD Well the incentive is—to make the orphans happy.

CITY GENT *(genuinely puzzled)* Happy?...You quite sure you've got this right?

MR FORD Yes, lots of people give me money.

CITY GENT What, just like that?

MR FORD Yes.

CITY GENT Must be sick. I don't suppose you could give me a list of their names and addresses could you?

MR FORD No, I just go up to them in the street and ask.

CITY GENT Good lord! That's the most exciting new idea I've heard in years! It's so simple it's brilliant! Well, if that idea of yours isn't worth a pound I'd like to know what is. *(he takes the tin from Ford)*

MR FORD Oh, thank you, sir.

CITY GENT The only trouble is, you gave me the idea before I'd given you the pound. And that's not good business.

MR FORD Isn't it?

CITY GENT No, I'm afraid it isn't. So, um, off you go. *(he pulls a lever opening a trap door under Ford's feet and Ford falls through with a yelp)* 7 Nice to do business with you.

Cut briefly to a Mongol.

A stagehand is visible as the trap door opens. Presumably he's there to catch the falling Jones.

MONGOL (MICHAEL) Anyway.

Cut back to the banker.

CITY GENT And off we go again. *(he goes to the intercom)*

AH MISS GODFREY COULD YOU SEND IN THE PANTOMIME HORSES PLEASE.

The door opens and two pantomime horses run in. Pantomime music. They do a routine including running round the room and bumping into each other. They then stand in front of the city gent crossing their legs and putting their heads on one side.

CITY GENT Now I've asked you to...*(they repeat the routine)* Now I've asked you...*(they start again)* Shut up! *(they stop)* Now I've asked you in here to see me this morning because I'm afraid we're going to have to let one of you go. *(the pantomime horses heads go up, their ears waggle and their eyes go round)* I'm very sorry but the present rationalization of this firm makes it inevitable that we hive one of you off. *(water spurts out of their eyes in a stream)* [8] Now you may think that this is very harsh behaviour but let me tell you that our management consultants actually queried the necessity for us to employ a pantomime horse at all. *(the horses register surprise and generally behave ostentatiously)* And so the decision has to be made which one of you is to go. Champion...how many years have you been with this firm? *(Champion stamps his foot three times)* [9] Trigger? *(Trigger stamps his front foot twice and rear foot once)* [10] I see. Well, it's a difficult decision. But in accordance with our traditional principles of free enterprise and healthy competition I'm going to ask the two of you to fight to the death for it. *(one of the horses runs up to him and puts his head by the city gent's ear)* No, I'm afraid there's no redundancy scheme. [11]

The horses turn and start kicking each other on the shins. After a few blows:

VOICE OVER (JOHN) *(German accent)* In the hard and unrelenting world of nature the ceaseless struggle for survival continues. *(one of the pantomime horses turns tail and runs out)* This time one of the pantomime horses concedes defeat and so lives to fight another day. *(cut to stock film of sea lions fighting)* Here, in a colony of sea lions, we see a huge bull sea lion seeing off an intruding bull who is attempting to intrude on his harem. This pattern of aggressive

8

Water only streams out of one of the horse's eyes.

9

"Champion" refers to *Champion the Wonder Horse*, the British name for the American TV series *The Adventures of Champion*, which originally ran in the mid-1950s.

10

Trigger is Roy Rogers's horse, of course.

11

"Redundancy" in the U.K. is the equivalent of "layoffs" in America.

behaviour is typical of these documentaries. *(cut to shot of two almost stationary limpets)* Here we see two limpets locked in a life or death struggle for territory. The huge bull limpet, enraged by the rock, endeavours to encircle its sprightly opponent. *(shot of wolf standing still)* Here we see an ant. This ant is engaged in a life or death struggle with the wolf. You can see the ant creeping up on the wolf on all sixes. *(a moving arrow is superimposed)* Now he stops to observe. Satisfied that the wolf has not heard him, he approaches nearer. With great skill he chooses his moment and then, quick as a limpet, with one mighty bound *(the arrow moves to the wolf's throat; the wolf does not move)* buries his fangs in the wolf's neck. The wolf struggles to no avail. A battle of this kind can take anything up to fifteen years because the timber ant has such a tiny mouth. *(distant shot of two men fighting violently)* Here we see Heinz Sielmann 12 engaged in a life or death struggle with Peter Scott. 13 They are engaged in a bitter punch-up over repeat fees on the overseas sales of their nature documentaries. *(another man joins in)* Now they have been joined by an enraged Jacques Cousteau. This is typical of the harsh and bitchy world of television features. *(shot of honey bear sitting about aimlessly)* Here we see a honey bear not engaged in a life or death struggle about anything. These honey bears are placid and peaceful creatures and consequently bad television. *(shot of pantomime horse running along in a wood)* Here we see a pantomime horse. It is engaged in a life or death struggle for a job with a merchant bank. However, his rival employee, the huge bull pantomime horse, is lying in wait for him. *(pantomime horse behind tree drops sixteen-ton weight on the horse running under the tree)* Poor pantomime horse. *(shot of pantomime goose behind a small tree with a bow and arrow)* Here we see a pantomime goose engaged in a life or death struggle with Terence Rattigan. 14 *(we see Terence walking along)* The enraged goose fires. *(the goose fires and hits Terence in the neck; Terence looks amazed and dies)* Poor Terence. Another victim of this silly film. *(shot of an amazing-looking large woman with a crown waiting in the undergrowth by the side of a path)* Here we see an enraged pantomime Princess Margaret, she is lying in wait for her breakfast. 15 *(a breakfast tray appears being pulled along the path by a length of wire)* The unsuspecting breakfast glides over closer to its doom. The enraged pantomime royal person is poised for the kill. She raises her harpoon and fires.

(the pantomime Princess Margaret does so, hurling the harpoon at the moving tray) Pang! Right in the toast. A brief struggle and all is over. Poor breakfast! Another victim of the...aargh!

Animation: which begins by showing the sudden demise of the previous voice over and continues with the story of a carnivorous house.

Heinz Sielmann is a German wildlife photographer and filmmaker. One of his best-known films is *Zimmerleute des Waldes* (*Carpenters of the Forest*, broadcast as *Woodpeckers* in the U.K.), and from then on he was known as "Mr. Woodpecker" in Britain.

Peter Scott is one of the founders of the World Wildlife Fund as well as a birder, conservationist, and host of a BBC nature show *Look*, which ran from 1955 to 1981. He was also the British gliding champion in 1963.

Terence Rattigan was a British midcentury dramatist, thought of as old-fashioned compared to the "angry young men" of postwar British theater.

Princess Margaret, Queen Elizabeth II's sister—then married to Lord Snowdon, an esteemed photographer. She had a fairly public affair (such as any royal could) with Roddy Llewellyn, a gardening journalist and TV presenter, through the early part of the 1970s. She and Snowdon finally divorced in 1978 (it was the first royal divorce since 1901, though there have been many since).

PROPERTY CONDEMNED
PROPERTY CONDEMNED

THE HOUSE-HUNTERS
NCP
CAR PARK
NCP
CAR PARK
NCP
CAR PARK

An "RSM" is a regimental sergeant major, whose job in the British military is to oversee other sergeants and enforce discipline.

The sign actually reads: "Sketch Just Started—Actor Wanted."

Caption: 'THE MAKERS OF THIS FILM WOULD LIKE TO THANK THE FOLLOWING PEOPLE WHO GAVE US LOTS OF MONEY TO SEE THEIR NAMES IN LIGHTS: VICTOR—HIS FRIEND BOBBY—AND—MARY' Pull back to show that 'Mary' is part of a sign saying: 'Mary Recruitment Office'. Pull out to reveal that it is a sign over a shop as for army recruiting office. An RSM 16 *with waxed moustache and snappy straight-against-the-forehead peaked cap comes out of the shop.*

He hangs a clearly printed sign on a nail on the door. It reads: 'Sketch just starting—actor wanted'. 17

VOICE OVER (JOHN) Sketch just starting, actor wanted.

The RSM looks up and down the road, glances up at the sign above his shop without noticing it. He goes inside again. A man walks up, reads the sign and enters. He is Mr Man.

MR MAN (ERIC) Good morning.
RSM (GRAHAM) Morning, sir.
MR MAN I'd like to join the army please.
RSM I see, sir. Short service or long service commission, sir?
MR MAN As long as possible please.
RSM Right well I'll just take a few particulars and then...

Suddenly he looks as though a dim memory has penetrated his skull. He breaks off, looking thoughtful, walks towards the door and exits. He comes out of shop, looks up at word 'Mary', tuts and changes the letters round to read 'Army'. He suddenly looks round and we see a queue of nuns.

RSM Shove off! *(he goes back inside)* Then there'll be a few forms to sign, and of course we'll need references and then a full medical examination by the...

MR MAN Yes. Yes, yes I see. *(diffidently)* I was just wondering whether it would be possible for me to join...the women's army?

RSM The Women's Royal Army Corps, sir?

MR MAN Yes. I was just thinking, you know, if it was possible for me to have my choice...I'd prefer to be in the Women's Royal Army Corps.

RSM Well, I'm afraid that the people that recruit here normally go straight into the Scots Guards. 18

MR MAN Which is all...men...I suppose?

RSM Yes it is.

MR MAN Yes. Are there any regiments which are more effeminate than others?

RSM Well, no sir. I mean, apart from the Marines, they're all dead butch. 19

MR MAN You see, what I really wanted was a regiment where I could be really quiet and have more time to myself to work with fabrics, and creating new concepts in interior design.

RSM Working with fabrics and experimenting with interior design!

MR MAN Yes.

RSM Oh well you want the Durham Light Infantry then, sir. 20

MR MAN Oh.

RSM Oh yes. That's the only regiment that's really doing something new with interior design, with colour, texture, line and that.

MR MAN I see.

RSM Oh yes, I mean their use of colour with fabrics is fantastic. I saw their pattern book the other day—beautiful, beautiful. Savage tans, great slabs of black, set against aggressive orange. It really makes you want to shout out, this is good! This is real!

MR MAN Really?

RSM Oh yes. I mean the Inniskillin Fusiliers and the Anglian Regiment are all right if you're interested in the art nouveau William Morris revival bit, but if you really want a regiment of the line that is really saying something about interior decor, then you've *got* to go for the Durham Light Infantry. 21

MR MAN Oh, I've had enough of this. I'm handing in my notice.

RSM What do you mean?

MR MAN Well I mean, when I applied for this job I thought I'd get a few decent lines but you end up doing the whole thing. I mean my last five speeches have been 'really, really—I see—I see' and 'really'. I wouldn't give those lines to a dog.

RSM All right, all right, all right, sonny. I'll tell you what. We'll do something different. I'll be a bus conductor, and you can be a really funny passenger on a bus.

Cut to a bus set. This is a very bad backcloth of the interior of the top deck of a bus. It looks like the set for a rather tatty revue. On the cut Mr Man is standing in exactly the same place as he was—so that it looks as if the scene has changed around him. The RSM appears from one side. He is still dressed basically as an RSM but has a few bus conductor things such as a ticket machine, money satchel and a big arrow through his neck. He talks like a music-hall comedian. 22

The Scots Guards is a regiment of the British Army whose lineage can be traced back to King Charles I, when they were his personal bodyguards.

"Dead" in this context is British slang for "very."

The Durham Light Infantry was an infantry regiment of the British Army until 1968.

The Royal Inniskilling Fusiliers was an Irish infantry regiment of the British Army. Like the Durham Lights, it was dissolved as its own regiment in 1968.

The Royal Anglian Regiment, formed in 1964, was heavily involved in policing the so-called Troubles in Northern Ireland, the 30-odd-year conflict that mostly ended with the Belfast Good Friday Agreement in 1998.

William Morris was a British nineteenth-century textile designer and artist—a Pre-Raphaelite extraordinaire.

"Music-hall comedians" are known for their broad, pun-based humor.

"Potty" is British slang for both a toilet and being crazy.

The leek is one of the emblems of Wales.

A comedian cliché.

Chapman does a pump of his arm at the phrase "everyone a Maserati" signaling he's "killing" the audience with his one-liners.

RSM Any more fares please? I've got a chauffeur and every time I go to the lavatory he drives me potty! 23 Boom-boom! One in a row. *(sings)* I'm not unusual. I'm just...

MR MAN Fivepenny please.

RSM Five beautiful pennies going in to the bag...and you are the lucky winner of...one fivepenny ticket! *(hands him a ticket)* What's the Welshman doing under the bed? He's having a leak! 24 Oh they're all in here tonight. 25

(brief film clip of audience laughing)

MR MAN Look!

RSM I am looking—it's the only way I keep my eyelids apart! Boom-boom! Every one a Maserati! 26

MR MAN Look! You said I was going to be a funny passenger.

RSM *(snapping out of music-hall manner)* What do you mean?

MR MAN I mean, all I said was, fivepenny please. You can't call that a funny line.

RSM Well it's the way you said it.

MR MAN No it isn't. *Nobody* can say 'fivepenny please' and make it funny.

Cut to vox pop of city gent in a busy street.

CITY GENT (TERRY J) Fivepenny please.

Cut to stock film of audience rolling about with laughter and clapping. Cut back to vox pop of city gent in street. He looks rather bewildered. He shrugs, turns and as he starts to walk away the camera pulls out. We see the city gent pass two colleagues.

CITY GENT Morning.

They collapse laughing and roll about on the pavement. The city gent hurries on, and turns into the door of a big office block. Cut to the foyer. A hall porter is standing behind a counter.

CITY GENT Not so warm today, George.

A shriek of mirth from the porter who collapses behind the counter.

The city gent continues walking into the lift. There are two other city gents and one secretary already in the lift. The doors shut.

MAN'S VOICE Good morning.

SECRETARY'S VOICE Good morning.

CITY GENT'S VOICE Good morning.

Shrieks of laughter. Cut to the doors of the lift on the third floor. Lift doors open and the city gent steps out rather quickly looking embarrassed. Behind him he leaves the three collapsed with mirth on the floor. The lift doors shut and the lift goes down again. Cut to interior of boss's office. A knock on the door.

THE BOSS IS STANDING WITH HIS BACK TO THE DOOR DESPERATELY PREPARING HIMSELF TO KEEP A STRAIGHT FACE.

BOSS (MICHAEL) Come in, Mr Horton.

The city gent enters.

CITY GENT Morning, sir.
BOSS Do—do sit down. *(he indicates chair, trying not to look at the city gent as he does so)*
CITY GENT Thank you, sir.

The boss starts to snigger but suppresses it with feat of self-control.

BOSS Now then Horton, you've been with us for twenty years, and your work in the accounts department has been immaculate. *(the city gent starts to speak; the boss suppresses another burst of laughter)* No no—please don't say anything. As I say, your work has been beyond reproach, but unfortunately the effect you have on your colleagues has undermined the competence *(almost starts laughing)*...has undermined the competence of this firm to such a point that I'm afraid that I've got no option but to sack you.
CITY GENT *(in a broken voice)* I'm sorry to hear that, sir. *(the boss giggles, gets up hastily and turning his back on city gent leans against the mantelpiece; his desire to laugh mounts through the next speech)* It couldn't have come at a worse time. There's school fees for the two boys coming up, and the wife's treatment costing more now...I don't know where the money's coming from as it is. And now I don't see any future...I'd been hoping I'd be able to hang on here just for the last couple of years but...now...I just want to go out and end it all.

The boss cannot control himself any longer. He collapses in helpless mirth, falling all over the room. Immediately we cut to stock film of terrific audience laughter. Cut to backdrop of a circus ring. In front of it, as if in the ring, stand the RSM and Mr Man. Mr Man is as before. The RSM is dressed the same except that over his uniform he wears baggy trousers and braces and a funny nose. He is responding to the audience applause. Mr Man has obviously just been drenched with hot water—he is soaked and steam is rising.

Chapman does not knee Idle in the balls.

RSM Thank you! Thank you! Thank you! Thank you and now for the fish—the fish down the trousers. *(the RSM picks up fish and puts it down Mr Man's trousers)* It's your laugh mate it's not mine. It's your trousers—not my trousers—it's your trousers—and now for the whitewash. *(the RSM pours a bucket of whitewash over him)* The whitewash over you—not over me. It's over you. You get the laugh. You get all the laughs. And now for the custard pie in the mush. *(more laughter, the RSM puts custard pie in his face and knees him in the balls)* 27 It's not my mush—it's your mush. It's your laugh—it's your laugh mate—not mine. It's your bleeding laugh.

Bols claims to be the oldest distillery brand in the world, dating from 1575 Amsterdam.

Cut to stock film of Mr Heath laughing followed by stock film of Women's Institute applauding. Caption: 'THE BOLS STORY' 28 *Caption: 'THE STORY OF HOLLAND'S MOST FAMOUS APERITIF' Mr Orbiter-5 is sitting in a swivel chair facing camera in a TV presentation set. Behind him is a flat with enormous lettering which says 'Is the Queen sane?' Zoom in on Mr Orbiter-5. He starts talking immediately.*

MR ORBITER (MICHAEL) Good evening. Well tonight, we are going to talk about...well that is...*I* am going to talk about...well actually I *am* talking about it now...well I'm not talking about it *now*, but I am *talking*...I know I'm pausing occasionally, and not talking during the pauses, but the pauses are part of the whole process of talking...when one *talks* one has to *pause*... er...like then! I paused...but I was still talking...and again there! No the real point of what I'm saying is that when I appear *not* to be talking don't go nipping out to the kitchen, putting the kettle on...buttering scones...or getting crumbs and bits of food out of those round brown straw mats that the teapot goes on...because in all probability I'm *still* talking and what *you* heard was a pause...er...like there again. Look! To make it absolutely easier, so there's no problem at all, what I'll do, I'll give you some kind of sign, like this *(makes a gesture)* while I'm *still* talking, and only pausing in between words...and when I've finished altogether I'll do this. *(he sits upright and folds his arms)* All right?

Superimposed caption: 'THE END'

MR ORBITER No, no! No sorry—just demonstrating...haven't finished. Haven't started yet. *(the caption is removed; he sits and tries to gather his thoughts then suddenly remembers)* Oh dear. *(does the gesture hastily)* Nearly forgot the gesture. Hope none of you are nipping out into the kitchen, getting bits of food out of those round brown mats which the teapot...Good evening. *(gesture)* Tonight I want to talk about...

Cut to the BBC world symbol.

ADRIAN (ERIC) *(voice over)* We interrupt this programme to annoy you and make things generally irritating for you.

Cut back to Mr Orbiter-5.

MR ORBITER ...with a large piece of wet paper. *(gesture)* Turn the paper over—turn the paper over keeping your eye on the camel, and paste down the *edge* of the sailor's uniform, until the word 'Maudling' is almost totally obscured. 29 *(gesture)* Well, that's one way of doing it. *(gesture)*

Cut to the BBC world symbol again and hold throughout the following dialogue.

ADRIAN *(voice over)* Good evening, we interrupt this programme again, A, to irritate you and, B, to provide work for one of our announcers.

JACK (JOHN) *(voice over)* Good evening, I'm the announcer who's just been given this job by the BBC and I'd just like to say how grateful I am *to* the BBC for providing me with work, particularly at this time of year, when things are a bit thin for us announcers...um...I don't know whether I should tell you this, but, well, I have been going through a rather tough time recently. Things have been pretty awful at home. My wife, Josephine...'Joe-jums' as I call her...who is also an announcer...

JOE-JUMS (CAROL) Hello.

JACK ...has not been able to announce since our youngest, Clifford, was born, and, well, *(tearfully)* I've just got no confidence left...I can't get up in the morning...I feel there's nothing worth living for...*(he starts to sob)*

DICK (MICHAEL) Hello, I'm another announcer, my name's Dick. Joe-jums just rang me and said Jack was having a bad time with this announcement, so I've just come to give him a hand. How is he, Joe-jums?

JOE-JUMS Pretty bad, Dick.

DICK Jack...it's Dick...Do you want me to make the announcement?

JACK No, no Dick. I must do it myself...*(emotionally)* it's my last chance with the BBC, I can't throw it away...I've got to do it...for Joe-jums...for the kids...I've got to go through with it...

DICK Good man. Now remember your announcer's training: deep breaths, and try not to think about what you're saying...

JACK Good evening. This *(a trace of superhuman effort in his voice)* is BBC 1...

JOE-JUMS Good luck, Jack.

DICK Keep going, old boy.

JACK It's...nine o'clock...and...time...for...the News...read by...Richard Baker... 30

Cut to start of the 'Nine O'Clock News'. 31

JOE-JUMS You've done it.

DICK Congratulations, old man!

Richard Baker is sitting at a desk. As Richard Baker speaks we hear no sounds apart from the sounds of celebration of the announcers—champagne corks popping, etc. At the beginning of the news Baker uses the gesture between sentences that we have seen Mr Orbiter-5 use, plus other gestures. Behind him on the screen a collage of photos appear one after the other: Richard Nixon, Tony Armstrong-Jones, 32 *the White House, Princess Margaret, parliament, naked breasts,* 33 *a scrubbing*

One of the many references to Reginald Maudling, a British Conservative politician.

From 1954 to 1982, Richard Baker was the stalwart of *BBC News*—a "central casting" BBC figure. He was also famous for presenting coverage of *Last Night of the Proms*, the traditional fest of nationalism and classic music held every October in the Royal Albert Hall.

31

The image here is of New York City from the East River, with the United Nations complex in the foreground and the Chrysler Building looming in the back.

Tony Armstrong-Jones, aka Lord Snowdon, photographer and husband of Princess Margaret.

It's still extraordinary to see Richard Baker making hand gestures with a pair of naked breasts behind him.

Talbot Rothwell was an English screenwriter best known for his *Carry On* scripts for a series of bawdy comedies beloved in Britain in the 1960s and '70s.

Mireille Mathieu, French pop singer.

Edward VII, king of England from 1901 until his death in 1910.

Queen Juliana of the Netherlands, Dutch queen from 1948 to 1980.

Sir Alec Douglas-Home, British prime minister for two days shy of one year, starting October 18, 1963.

King Haakon of Norway, Christian Frederik Carl Georg Valdemar Axel, King of Norway from 1905 to 1957.

brush, a man with a stoat through his head, Margaret Thatcher, a lavatory, a Scotsman lying on his back with his knees drawn up, a corkscrew, Edward Heath, a pair of false teeth in a glass. Whilst these have been going on Baker has been making gestures starting with elbow-up gesture and getting progressively more obscure and intriguing. We don't hear him at all, we hear all the announcers having a party and congratulating Jack.

JOE-JUMS Fantastic darling, you were brilliant. No, no, it was the best you ever did.

JACK Thank God.

JOE-JUMS It was absolutely super.

DICK ...have a drink. For God's sake drink this...

JACK Fantastic.

DICK The least I could do—super—I must come over.

JACK I can't tell you how much that means. *(etc.)*

Eventually the voices stop and for the first time we hear Richard Baker's voice.

BAKER ...until the name Maudling is almost totally obscured. That is the ned of the nicro-not wens. And now it's time for the late night flim.

James Bond style opening titles with pictures of a pantomime horse.

THE PANTOMIME HORSE IS A SECRET AGENT FILM. WRITTEN BY TALBOT ROTHWELL 34 *AND MIREILLE MATHIEU.* 35 *BASED ON AN IDEA BY EDWARD VII.* 36 *DIRECTED BY QUEEN JULIANA OF THE NETHERLANDS.* 37 *PRODUCED BY SIR ALEC DOUGLAS-HOME* 38 *AND KING HAAKON OF NORWAY.* 39 *A CORPSE-HAAKON PRODUCTION. Cut to an idyllic scene—a boat drifting serenely on a river. A beautiful girl lies reclining in one end of the boat. A hoof appears round Carol's shoulders.*

MICHAEL PALIN

Michael Palin is said to be the "nicest" Python, and also the most voluble: at Graham Chapman's memorial service, Eric Idle said Chapman died rather than having to listen to Palin anymore. Whatever the truth, perhaps the most telling comment about Palin is from Palin himself: "I've always felt that civilized behavior was generally on a knife edge." It's in his sketches, many of them written with Terry Jones, that we see the knife edge turn into a precipice over which "civilized" society hurtles.

Palin was born in Sheffield, in Northern England, on May 5, 1943. He remembers a happy childhood, including a stint at "public" school (that is, at a private school in the U.K.). He would eventually attend Oxford University, where he studied modern history and also did work for the Oxford Review with Terry Jones. After university they found themselves writing together regularly for a number of influential TV shows, including *The Ken Dodd Show* and the children's hit *Do Not Adjust Your Set.* In the end, as with all top comedic talent working in the U.K. in the mid-1960s, they wrote for the influential *Frost Report* along with all the other members of *Monty Python.* Cleese and Chapman had been hit up by the BBC to do a comedy show, and Cleese wanted to expand it; Palin brought in Jones, Idle, and Terry Gilliam (they'd worked together on *Don't Adjust Your Set*), and the troupe was set.

It was in the *Flying Circus* that Palin fully realized his potential, shining on as the foil to Cleese's manic angers—in the "sister" sketches about the dead parrot; in the cheese shop, in which he plays the dissembling counter clerk; and as the star of the episode-length bicycle tour sketch, which presaged Palin's future career as a beloved travel-show host. He also starred as the singer of the "Lumberjack Song," morphing from a homicidal barber to a closeted Canadian, and led the merry band of Spanish Inquisitors who couldn't remember how many theoretical weapons they possessed. And in most episodes, he appeared as the "It's" man, rushing in to announce the start of the show.

Of all the Pythons, he and Cleese probably produced the best post–*Flying Circus* TV work. From 1976 to 1979 he and Jones wrote (and Palin starred in) the brilliant *Ripping Yarns,* which took the hackneyed derring-do adventure stories for children and spoofed them. The show featured such wonderful moments as a soccer fan of a continually losing team who every week comes home from the game and smashes all his furniture (his wife knows to save him the clock to throw). He cowrote and appeared in *Time Bandits,* Terry Gilliam's 1980 movie, and would later star in Cleese's *A Fish Called Wanda.*

But it was in his travel persona that Palin created a second career away from straight comedy roles—and its genesis owes something to an odd coincidence. In Episode 27 of the *Flying Circus,* the Pythons brilliantly skewer the all-too-slick and superior travel reporting of Alan Whicker, who'd made a career out of such jaunts for TV. In 1989, Whicker was slated to helm a BBC show called *Around the World in 80 Days,* but in the end it was Palin who stepped in, starting his stellar career as a latter-day (and less cloying) Whicker. Palin has since gone on to host many such shows, and his travels over the past twenty years have literally taken him around the world. As for being nice? Even in boarding school, at the age of eleven, he remembers overhearing two boys describe him as "quite nicely mad." It has served him well.

GIRL (CAROL) Oh pantomime horse, that was wonderful.
DOBBIN Would you like another glass?
GIRL No, no, I mustn't. It makes me throw up...oh, I'm so bleeding happy.
DOBBIN Oh, Simone!
GIRL

OH, PANTOMIME HORSE.

Cut to Graham in loony get up.

LOONY Then...

The pantomime horse spins round and fires his revolver towards some trees overhanging the water. Another pantomime horse falls out of the tree into the water. A third pantomime horse scurries out from behind a bush and runs off into the undergrowth. Dobbin leaps out of the boat. The girl jumps after him. A car drives out of some bushes on to the road and accelerates away. The pantomime horse is in it. Dobbin and the girl leap into their own expensive sports car and give chase. Shots of exciting chase. After two or three shots of the cars chasing, the two pantomime horses are seen on two tandems, continuing the chase. Cut to them chasing each other on horseback.

Cut to them chasing each other on rickshaws. Cut to them chasing each other on foot.

VOICE OVER (JOHN) And now the English pantomime horse has very nearly caught up with the Russian pantomime horse, I think he's going to take him any moment now but what is this? What is this? *(round the corner are waiting a pantomime goose and a pantomime Princess Margaret; the Russian pantomime horse runs past them and they leap on the English pantomime*

horse and a fight starts) Yes it's pantomime Princess Margaret and the pantomime goose and they're attacking the English pantomime horse and the Russian pantomime horse has got away. But who is this? *(a car draws up and Terence Rattigan and the Duke of Kent and the RSM run up and join in the fighting; the Russians are joined by Heinz Sielmann and Peter Scott and Jacques Cousteau)* My goodness me it's the Duke of Kent to the rescue...

The fighting continues, behind, while the credits roll in front, reading as follows:

TONY M. NYPHOT'S FLYING RISCCU
SAW CODVENICE, TWITNER
DNA FORDEPERM YB
HAMRAG PACHMAN
JOHN ECLES
RICE LIED
TORN JERSEY (5.5)
MICHAEL LAPIN
MARTY RIGELLI
SOLA GAERAPPIN
CAROL CLEVELAND
ARCHSEER YB
SUZAN DAVIES
KAME PU
MADELAINE GAFFNEY
MUTESOCS
HAZEL PETHIG
MAINATIONS YB
TERRY GILLIAM
CUFFS LAVISEET
BERNARD WILKIE
PISHCARG
BOB BLAGDEN
MALE FANCIMARM
ALAN FEATHERSTONE
MOLE TRIFID
RAY MILLICHOPE
DOSUN
RICHARD CHUBB
LIGHTGIN
JIMMY PURDIE
REDENSIG
IAN WATSON
DECODURP YB
IAN MACNAUGHTON
B. B. LURCOO

VOICE OVER (JOHN) *(German accent)* Here you see some English comic actors engaged in a life or death struggle with a rather weak ending. This is typical of the zany madcap world of the irresistible kooky funsters. The English pantomime horse wins and so is assured of a place in British history and a steady job in a merchant bank. Unfortunately, before his pension rights are assured, he catches bronchitis and dies, another victim of the need to finish these shows on time.

Shot of pantomime horse in bed with his legs sticking in the air. Caption: 'ETH NED'

SEA SON 3
EPISODE 31

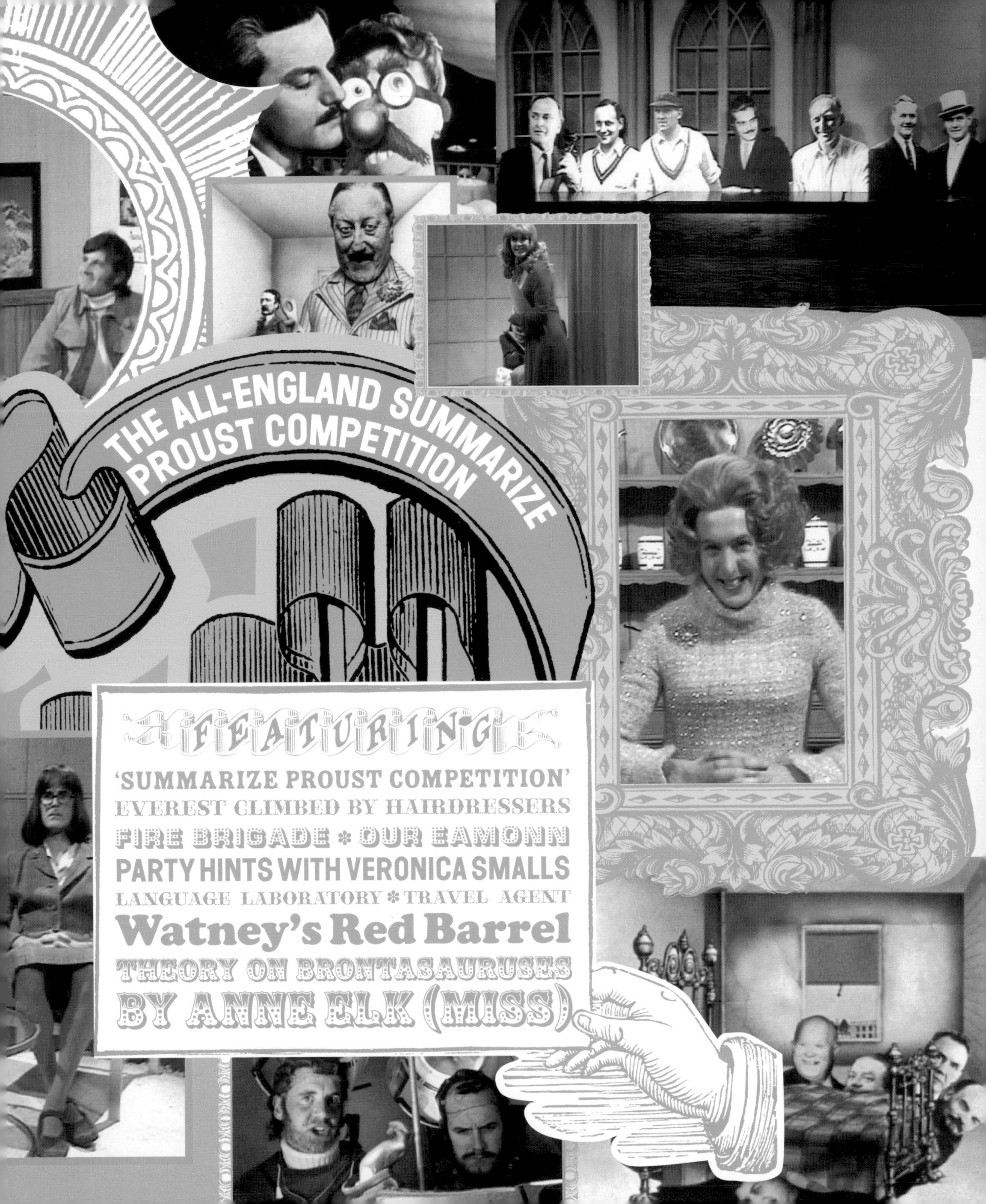

THE ALL-ENGLAND SUMMARIZE PROUST COMPETITION
FEATURING
'SUMMARIZE PROUST COMPETITION'
EVEREST CLIMBED BY HAIRDRESSERS
FIRE BRIGADE * OUR EAMONN
PARTY HINTS WITH VERONICA SMALLS
LANGUAGE LABORATORY * TRAVEL AGENT
Watney's Red Barrel
THEORY ON BRONTASAURUSES
BY ANNE ELK (MISS)

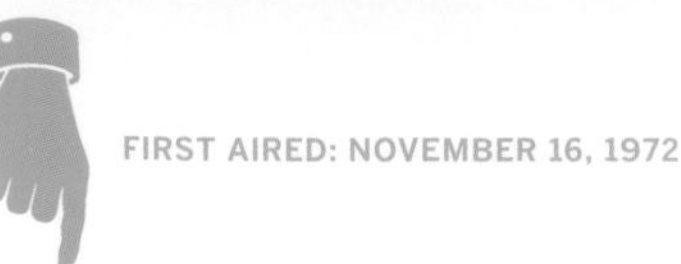

FIRST AIRED: NOVEMBER 16, 1972

Nude man at the organ plays chords.

ANNOUNCER (JOHN) And now...

IT'S MAN (MICHAEL)

IT'S...

Animated titles.

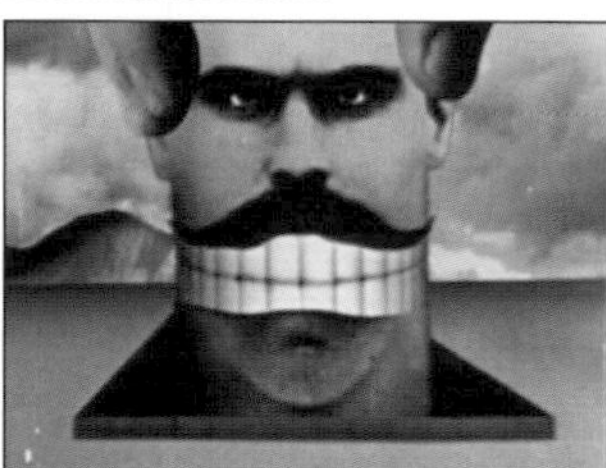

VOICE OVER (JOHN) Monty Python's Flying Circuses...

The hall of the Memorial Baths, Swansea, done up for a gala occasion. There is a stage with flags, bunting and flowers. Echoing noise of audience anticipation. Muffled tannoy announcements in background.

VOICE OVER (ERIC) Good evening, and welcome to the Arthur Ludlow Memorial Baths, Newport, for this year's finals of the All-England Summarize Proust Competition. *(pull back slightly to reveal big banner across the top of the stage: 'All-England Summarize Proust Competition)* As you may remember, each contestant has to give a brief summary of Proust's 'A La Recherche du Temps Perdu', [1] once in a swimsuit and once in evening dress. The field has now narrowed to three finalists and your judges tonight are...*(cut to panel of judges at long desk; they are all cut-outs of smiling photos of the following)* Alec and Eric Bedser, ex-Surrey cricketers, Stewart Surridge, ex-captain of Surrey, Omar Sharif, [2] Laurie Fishlock, ex-Surrey opening batsman, [3] Peter May, the former Surrey and England Captain, and Yehudi Menuhin, the world-famous violinist [4] and the President of the Surrey Cricket Club. And right now it's time to meet your host for tonight—Arthur Mee!

À La Recherche du Temps Perdu (*In Search of Lost Time*, or *Remembrance of Things Past*) is a novel started in 1909 that continued to be written by Marcel Proust until his death in 1922. In seven long volumes, it totaled some 3,200 pages in the original French. It's even longer in the English translation, hence the need to summarize.

2

Omar Sharif, the Egyptian actor, famous enough in 1972 to need no introduction.

Laurie Fishlock, like Compton before him (Episode 21), was also a professional soccer player.

Though Yehudi Menuhin had a music school in Surrey, cricket really wasn't his bag.

Showbiz music, applause, and Arthur Mee appears from the back of the stage; he wears the now traditional spangly jacket. He comes forward and speaks into the mike (the sound is rather hollow and strident as in big halls with a hastily rigged PA).

MEE (TERRY J) Good evening and welcome, whereas Proust [5] would say, 'la malade imaginaire de recondition et de toute surveillance est bientôt la même chose'. *(roars of applause; quick shot of grinning faces of the jury)* Remember each contestant this evening has a maximum of fifteen seconds to summarize 'A La Recherche du Temps Perdu' and on the Proustometer over here...*(curtain pulls back at back of stage to reveal a truly enormous, but cheap, audience appreciation gauge; it lists the seven books of Proust's masterwork in the form of a thermometer)* you can see exactly how far he gets. So let's crack straight on with our first contestant tonight. He's last year's semi-finalist from Luton—Mr Harry Bagot. *(Harry Bagot, in evening dress, comes forward from back of stage, he has a number three on his back; Mee leads the applause for him)* Hello Harry. Now there's the summarizing spot, you're on the summarizing spot, fifteen seconds from *now*.

In this sketch, Proust is pronounced "Prowst," rather than the more correct "Proost," by Jones and others.

Music starts, continuity-type music. The needle of the Proustometer creeps up almost imperceptibly to a tiny level.

HARRY (GRAHAM) Proust's novel ostensibly tells of the irrevocability of time lost, the forfeiture of innocence through experience, the reinstatement of extra-temporal values of time regained, ultimately the novel is both optimistic and set within the context of a humane religious experience, re-stating as it does the concept of intemporality. In the first volume, Swann, the family friend visits...

Gong goes, chord of music, applause. The meter has hardly risen at all.

MEE Well tried, Harry.

VOICE OVER A good attempt there but unfortunately he chose a general appraisal of the work, before getting on to the story and as you can see *(close up of Proustometer)* he only got as far as page one of 'Swann's Way', the first of the seven volumes. A good try though and very nice posture.

Cut back to the stage.

MEE Harry Bagot, you're from Luton?

HARRY Yes, Arthur, yeah.

MEE Now Harry what made you first want to try and start summarizing Proust?

HARRY Well I first entered a seaside Summarizing Proust Competition when I was on holiday in Bournemouth, and my doctor encouraged me with it.

MEE And Harry, what are your hobbies outside summarizing?

HARRY

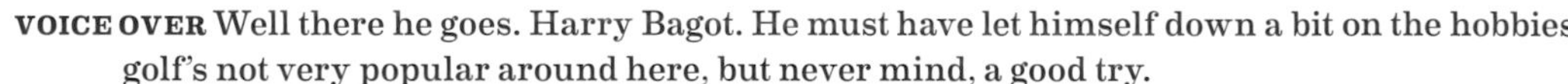

WELL, STRANGLING ANIMALS, GOLF AND MASTURBATING. 6

MEE Well, thank you Harry Bagot.

Harry walks off-stage. Music and applause.

VOICE OVER Well there he goes. Harry Bagot. He must have let himself down a bit on the hobbies, golf's not very popular around here, but never mind, a good try.

MEE Thank you ladies and gentlemen. Mr Rutherford from Leicester, are you ready Ronald? *(Ronald is a very eager man in tails)* Right. On the summarizing spot. You have got fifteen seconds from now.

RONALD (MICHAEL) Er, well, Swann, Swann, there's this house, there's this house, and er, it's in the morning, it's in the morning—no, it's the evening, in the evening and er, there's a garden and er, this bloke comes in—bloke comes in—what's his name—what's his name, er just said it—big bloke—Swann, Swann...

The gong sounds. Mee pushes Ronald out.

MEE And now ladies and gentlemen, I'd like you to welcome the last of our all-England finalists this evening, from Bingley, the Bolton Choral Society and their leader Superintendent McGough, *(a big choir comes on, immaculately drilled, each holding a score, with Fred Tomlinson as superintendent McGough)* All right Bingley, remember you've got fifteen seconds to summarize Proust in his entirety starting from now.

6

Chapman actually says, "Well golf, and strangling animals." By the third season, the BBC had taken a more active role in censoring the shows, given that they had become popular across Britain. The reference to masturbation in this sketch was cut at the very last minute, right before the show aired, and that's why there's an unhealthy break on the soundtrack and a huge laugh that doesn't correspond to what television viewers actually heard.

FIRST SOLOIST Proust, in his first book wrote about...fa la la...
SECOND SOLOIST Proust in his first book wrote about...
TENORS He wrote about...

They continue contrapuntally, in madrigal, never getting beyond these words until they rallentando to say...

ALL Proust in his first book wrote about the...*(gong sounds)*
VOICE OVER Very ambitious try there, but in fact the least successful of the evening, they didn't even get as far as the first volume. *(the singers leave the stage)*
MEE Well ladies and gentlemen, I don't think any of our contestants this evening have succeeded in encapsulating the intricacies of Proust's masterwork, so I'm going to award the first prize this evening to the girl with the biggest tits.

Applause and music. A lady with enormous knockers comes on to the side of the stage. Roll credits: THE ALL-ENGLAND SUMMARIZE PROUST COMPETITION
A BBC PRODUCTION
WITH MR I. T. BRIDDOCK, 2379, THE TERRACE, HODDESDON.
IT WAS CONCEIVED, WRITTEN AND PERFORMED BY...
Roll usual Monty Python credits and music. Behind them the lady accepts the cup and the singers come back on stage and admire her. Fade out. Slight pause. Fade up on stock film of Everest. Whistling wind, stirring music.

VOICE OVER (MICHAEL) Mount Everest. Forbidding. Aloof. Terrifying. The mountain with the biggest tits in the world.

Sound of gong.

SECOND VOICE (ERIC) Start again.

A VERY SILLY LOONY LEANS INTO SHOT, ON OVERLAY [I.E. IN FRONT OF PICTURE], AND WAVES TO THE CAMERA. HE GOES OUT OF SHOT AGAIN.

VOICE OVER Mount Everest. Forbidding. Aloof. Terrifying. This year this remote Himalayan mountain, this mystical temple, surrounded by the most difficult terrain in the world repulsed yet another attempt to conquer it. This time by the International Hairdressers' Expedition. *(cut to shot of pup tent in a blizzard)* In such freezing adverse conditions man comes

very close to breaking point. What was the real cause of the disharmony which destroyed their chances of success?

Cut to three head-and-shoulders shots. They look like typical mountaineers: frost in their beards, tanned, with snow glasses on their foreheads and authentic Everest headgear.

FIRST CLIMBER (MICHAEL) Well, people would keep taking my hairdryer and never returning it.
SECOND CLIMBER (GRAHAM) There was a lot of bitching in the tents.
THIRD CLIMBER (ERIC) You couldn't get near the mirror. 7

Cut to a colonel figure, digging in a garden in Jersey. 8

VOICE OVER The leader of the expedition was Colonel Sir John 'Teasy Weasy' Butler, veteran of K2, Annapurna, and Vidals. His plan was to ignore the usual route round the South Col and to make straight for the top.

Cut to a photo of Everest with dots superimposed, showing the route.

COLONEL (GRAHAM) Well we established base salon here. *(on the photo, we see the words 'base salon')* And climbed quite steadily up to Mario's here. *(at the top of the route we see 'Mario's)* From here using crampons and cutting ice steps as we went, we moved steadily up the Lhotse Face 9 to the North Ridge, establishing camp three where we could get a hot meal, a manicure and a shampoo and set.

Cut to stock film of people actually climbing Everest.

VOICE OVER Could it work? Could this eighteen-year-old hairdresser from Brixton succeed where others had failed? The situation was complicated by the imminent arrival of the monsoon storms. Patrice takes up the story.

Cut to interior of hairdresser's salon. Patrice speaks into the mirror, as he is blow-drying and curling a lady's hair.

PATRICE (ERIC) Well, we knew as well as anyone that the monsoons were due, but the thing was, Ricky and I had just had a blow dry and rinse, and we couldn't go out for a couple of days.

Cut to stock film of some people leaving a little tent on a mountain.

7

Chapman is seen here trimming the leaves of cabbages as a hairdresser might.

The largest of the Channel Islands, Jersey is a British dependency, but it is about 100 miles off of the British mainland and a mere 15 miles off of France's Normandy coast.

The Lhotse Face is a 3,700-foot wall of glacial ice near Mount Everest.

VOICE OVER After a blazing row the Germans and the Italians had turned back, taking with them the last of the hair nets. On the third day a blizzard blew up. *(close up on the tent in a blizzard; no people in shot)* Temperatures fell to minus thirty centigrade. Inside the little tent things were getting desperate.

We cut inside the tent. The wind is banging against the side of the material, sounds of a vicious blizzard. Ricky is sitting next to another member of the expedition. Both are under hairdryers, in full climbing gear up to their necks. One is reading 'Vogue', Ricky is doing his nails.

RICKY (MICHAEL) Well, things have got so bad that we've been forced to use the last of the heavy oxygen equipment just to keep the dryers going.

WOMAN *(off-screen)* Cup of Milo, love.

RICKY Oh she's a treas. 10 *(he takes the drink)*

Cut to a wide shot of Everest.

VOICE OVER But a new factor had entered the race. A team of French chiropodists, working with brand new cornplasters and Doctor Scholl's Mountaineering Sandals, were covering ground fast. The Glasgow Orpheus Male Voice Choir were tackling the difficult North Col. 11 *(quick cut to film of lots of people climbing up Everest; dubbed over is the 'Proust' song as in 'Proust Competition' item)* Altogether fourteen expeditions *(cut to diagram with hundreds of dotted lines over it, fourteen different routes)* were at his heels. This was it. Rick had to make a decision.

Cut back to Patrice in the salon.

"Treas" is short for "treasure."

The North Col is a ragged pass between Mount Everest in the south and Changtse, a mountain to the north, in Tibet.

PATRICE

WELL, HE DECIDED TO OPEN A SALON.

As Patrice continues, his hairdresser voice over starts over this picture.

VOICE OVER It was a tremendous success.

Cinema-style advert with still photos.

ADVERT VOICE (ERIC) Challenging Everest? Why not drop in at Ricky Pules'—only 24,000 feet from this cinema. Ricky and Maurice offer a variety of styles for the well-groomed climber. Like Sherpa Tensing 12 and Sir Edmund Hillary be number one to the top when you're Number One on Top. *(just their heads turn to show off the hair-do)*

Sherpa Tenzing Norgay was the second man to reach the summit of Everest in 1953, having aided Sir Edmund Hillary in the ascent. Because he didn't know how to use a camera, the only photos of the famous ascent show him, not Hillary, on the top of the world.

Animated sketch leads to little old Mrs Little on the phone in her hall. She is a dear little old lady and lives in a rather fussy ducks-on-wall house.

MRS LITTLE (TERRY J) Hello, is that the fire brigade?

Cut to the fire station.

FIRST FIREMAN (MICHAEL) No, sorry, wrong number.

He puts the phone back. Pull out to reveal four or five firemen in full gear, surrounded by fire-fighting equipment and a gleaming fire engine. The firemen are engaged in a variety of homely pursuits: one is soldering a crystal set, another is cooking at a workbench, another is doing embroidery, another is at a sewing machine. The first fireman is at the phone on the wall. He goes back to clearing up a budgie's cage.

13

Cleese either forgets to dial here or that's the joke—either way, he merely yells into the receiver.

SECOND FIREMAN (ERIC) That phone's not stopped ringing all day.
THIRD FIREMAN What happens when you've mixed the batter, do you dice the ham with the coriander?
FIRST FIREMAN No, no, you put them in separately when the vine leaves are ready.

The phone rings.

SECOND FIREMAN Oh, no, not again.
THIRD FIREMAN Take it off the hook.

The first fireman takes the phone off the hook. Cut back to Mrs Little on phone. She looks at the receiver then listens again.

MRS LITTLE I can't get the fire brigade Mervyn.

Mervyn, her 38-year-old, 6' 8" son appears.

14

It's more like a big, fluffy slipper than a shoe. And it's probably a lot bigger than an 8, even in European sizes.

MERVYN (JOHN) Here, let me try, dear. You go and play the cello.
MRS LITTLE Oh it doesn't do any good, dear.
MERVYN Look. Do you want the little hamster to live or not?
MRS LITTLE Yes I do, Mervyn.
MERVYN Well go and play the cello!

She looks helplessly at him, then goes into the sitting room. Mervyn dials. 13

MERVYN Hello, hello, operator? Yes we're trying to get the fire brigade...No, the fire brigade. Yes yes, yes, yes, yes, yes, yes, yes, yes, yes, what?...*(he takes one of his shoes off and looks in it)* Size eight. 14 Yes, yes, yes, yes, yes, yes, no of course not. Yes...

Mrs Little appears, dabbing at her eyes with a handkerchief.

MRS LITTLE *(touching Mervyn gently on the arm)* He's gone, dear.

MERVYN What?
MRS LITTLE He's slipped away.
MERVYN What?
MRS LITTLE
THE SODDING HAMSTER'S DEAD!
MERVYN *(broken)* Oh no!! What were you playing?
MRS LITTLE Some Mozart concertos, dear.
MERVYN What...How did he...?
MRS LITTLE His eyes just closed, and he fell into the wastepaper basket. I've covered him with a copy of the 'Charlie George Football Book'. 15
MERVYN *(handing her the phone)* Right, you hang on. I must go and see him.
MRS LITTLE There was nothing we could do, Mervyn. If we'd have had the whole Philharmonic Orchestra in there, he'd still have gone.
MERVYN I'm going upstairs, I can't bear it.
MRS LITTLE *(restraining him)* There isn't an upstairs dear, it's a bungalow.
MERVYN Damn. *(he storms off)* 16
MRS LITTLE *(into the phone)* Hello, I'm sorry to keep you waiting, it's just that...*(she takes her shoe off and looks inside)* size three, yes it's just—we've lost a dear one and my son was...yes, that's right, size eight, yes and...Oh I see...yes, yes, yes, yes, yes, yes, yes, yes, I see, yes, yes. I, I...Yes, yes. No... no...yes, I see. They can't get the fire brigade Mervyn—will the Boys' Brigade do? 17
MERVYN *(off)* No! They'd be useless!
MRS LITTLE No, he doesn't want anyone at the moment, thank you. No, yes, yes, no thank you for trying, yes, yes,...no, Saxones, 18 yes, yes thank you, bye, bye.

As she puts the phone down the front door beside her opens and there stands a huge African warrior in warpaint and with a spear and shield. At his feet are several smart suitcases.

EAMONN (GRAHAM) Mummy.
MRS LITTLE Eamonn. *(he brings in the cases and closes the front door)* Mervyn! Look it's our Eamonn—oh let me look at you, tell me how...how is it in Dublin?
EAMONN Well, things is pretty bad there at the moment but there does seem some hope of a constitutional settlement. 19
MRS LITTLE Oh don't talk. Let me just look at you.
EAMONN Great to be home, mummy. How are you?
MRS LITTLE Oh, I'm fine. I must just go upstairs and get your room ready.
EAMONN It's a bungalow, mummy.
MRS LITTLE Oh damn, yes. Mervyn, Mervyn—look who's here, it's our Eamonn come back to see us.

Mervyn appears. He still looks shattered by the death of the hamster.

MERVYN Hello, Eamonn.
EAMONN Hello, Merv.
MERVYN How was Dublin?
EAMONN Well as I was telling mummy here, things is pretty bad there at the moment but there does seem some hope of a constitutional settlement.

The phone rings.

MERVYN *(answering phone)* Hello, yes, yes, yes, yes, yes—what? what?...*(looking at Eamonn's bare foot)* Size seven. Yes, yes, yes, yes, yes,...it's the fire brigade, they want to know if they can come round Thursday evening.
MRS LITTLE Oh no, Thursday's the Industrial Relations Bill Dinner Dance. Can't they make it another day?

Charlie George was a professional soccer player, notably for the Arsenal Football Club in London. His manager for a number of years was Bertie Mee (see "Arthur Mee," in the Summarize Proust Competition earlier in this episode).

Cleese actually walks away sadly.

Boys' Brigade is the Christian youth organization known for its love of camping, among other wholesome pursuits.

Saxone is a British shoe brand.

"Constitutional settlement" refers to the "Irish question" that would plague British politics for most of the twentieth century. The island itself was split into Ireland in the south and Northern Ireland, controlled by the U.K., in the northeast corner. Dublin, as in the Irish government, was as much vexed by the situation as any.

MERVYN *(into the phone)* Hello, no Thursday's *right out*. Yes, yes, yes, yes...*(fade out)*

Fade up on a dinner-jacketed announcer sitting at a table with a bowl of flowers on it. A hand waves from inside the bowl of flowers.

ANNOUNCER (MICHAEL) And so it was the fire brigade eventually came round on Friday night.

Cut to fire engines skidding out of the fire station and roaring away—speeded up. They shid to a halt outside the Littles' suburban house. Firemen pour out of the fire engine and start to swarm in through the windows. Cut to interior of Littles' sitting room. It is laid out for a cocktail party. Mervyn is in evening dress and is sitting on the sofa looking very depressed. Mrs Little in a faded cocktail dress. Eamonn still in warpaint with spear and shield. The firemen appear.

MRS LITTLE Oh, so glad you could come. What would you like to drink? Gin and tonic? Sherry?
FIREMEN *(in unison)* A drop of sherry would be lovely. *(as she starts to pour drinks the firemen confide in unison)* We do like being called out to these little parties, they're much better than fires.

The phone rings. Half the firemen go to answer it.

A FIREMAN *(off)* Yes, yes yes.
FIREMEN Well, how was Dublin, Eamonn?
EAMONN Well, as I was telling mummy and Mervyn earlier, things is pretty bad there at the moment but there does seem some hope of a constitutional...
MRS LITTLE *(to camera)* Look at them enjoying themselves. *(shot of party in the hall; we can just see the fireman on phone; they keep looking at their shoe sizes)* You know I used to dread parties until I watched 'Party Hints by Veronica'. I think it's on now...

Panning shot across mountains in CinemaScope format. Superimposed roller caption:

*THE BRITISH BROADCASTING CORPORATION
IN ASSOCIATION WITH TRANSWORLD INTERNATIONAL
AND NIMROD PRODUCTIONS PRESENT
AN ARTHUR E. RICEBACHER
AND DAVID A. SELTZER PRODUCTION
FOR HASBACH ENTERPRISES
OF CHARLES D. ORTIZ' ADAPTATION
OF THE PULITZER PRIZEWINNING IDEA
BY DANIEL E. STOLLMEYER
BROUGHT TO THE SCREEN FROM ROBERT HUGHES'S NOVEL
BY LOUIS H. TANNHAUSER AND VERNON D. LARUE
PARTY HINTS BY VERONICA SMALLS*

A SELZENBACH-TANSROD PRODUCTION
IN ASSOCIATION WITH
VICTOR A. LOUNGE
ROLO NICE SWEETIES
FISON'S FERTILIZERS
TIME LIFE INNIT-FOR-THE-MONEY LIMITED
THE TRUSTEES OF ST PAUL'S CATHEDRAL
THAT NICE MR ROBINSON AT THE VET'S
RALPH READER [20]
RALPH NADER [21]
THE CHINESE GOVERNMENT
MICHAEL'S AUNTIE BETTY IN AUSTRALIA
A CINEMASCOPE PRODUCTION

Cut to Veronica in the 'Party Hints' set—a chintzy kitchen.

VERONICA (ERIC) Hello, last week on 'Party Hints' I showed you how to make a small plate of goulash go round twenty-six people, how to get the best out of your canapés, and how to unblock your loo. This week I'm going to tell you what to do if there is an armed communist uprising near your home when you're having a party. Well obviously it'll depend how far you've got *with* your party when the signal for Red Revolt is raised. If you're just having preliminary aperitifs—Dubonnet, a sherry or a sparkling white wine—then the guests will obviously be in a fairly formal mood and it will be difficult to tell which are the communist agitators. So the thing to do is to get some cloth and some bits of old paper, put it down on the floor and shoot everybody. This will deal with the Red Menace on your own doorstep. If you're having canapés, as I showed you last week, or an outdoor barbecue, then the thing to do is set fire to all houses in the street. This will stir up anti-communist hatred and your neighbours will be right with you as you organize counter-revolutionary terror. So you see, if you act promptly enough, any left-wing uprising can be dealt with by the end of the party. Bye...

Animation: one dozen communist revolutions.

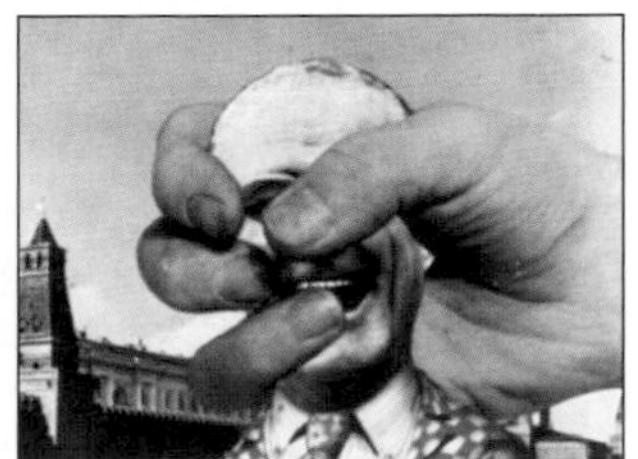

Then cut to a language laboratory. Mr Mann is showing Tick round. There is a line of booths, each lined with pegboard. Each has a person with a pair of earphones on with attached microphones, a tape recorder and a swivel chair.

Ralph Reader was a British actor and producer best known, perhaps, for establishing the *Gang Show*, a variety performance tradition in the boy scouting movement.

A name-check for the American activist and writer Ralph Nader, whose 1965 book *Unsafe At Any Speed* ripped a new one for American car manufacturers.

The "five principles" was the basis of a series of agreements between the British government and Ian Smith, the leader of Rhodesia, that had to do with trying to make a fairer political system that might eventually cede some power to the five million Africans in Rhodesia, instead of it letting it rest in the hands of the quarter of a million white Rhodesians.

The "foot of our stairs" is a traditional northern and Midlands phrase meaning "Well, I never!" There are numerous explanations for its provenance. Perhaps the most amusing is that stairs led to the outside lavatory, meaning in a roundabout way, "I was so surprised, I had to go to the bathroom."

"Ee ecky thump" is a northern English phrase, roughly translated as "oh, God!"

FIRST BOOTH (ERIC) Bleck people. Bleck people. Rrrhodesian. Kill the blecks. Rrhodesian. Smith. Smith. Kill the blecks within the five principles. 22

He starts to rewind the tape recorder. Nods at Mr Mann. They come to the second booth.

SECOND BOOTH (TERRY J) I'm afraid I cannot comment on that until it's been officially hushed up.
MR MANN (GRAHAM) This is our politicians' booth.
SECOND BOOTH While there is no undue cause for concern, there is certainly no room for complacency. Ha, ha, ha. He, he, he.

They pass on to the next booth.

THIRD BOOTH (MICHAEL) Well I'll go, I'll go to the foot of our stairs. 23 Ee ecky thump. 24 Put wood in 'ole, muther.

Mr Mann taps him. He removes his earphones.

THIRD BOOTH *(normal)* Yes?
MR MANN Ee ecky thump.
THIRD BOOTH *(trying it)* Ee ecky thump.
MR MANN Ee ecky thump! *(indicates more power)*
THIRD BOOTH Ee ecky thump!
MR MANN Excellent.
THIRD BOOTH Thank you, sir. *(puts earphones on, listens)*
MR MANN It's a really quick method of learning.
THIRD BOOTH Can you smell gas or is it me?
TICK (JOHN) *(who is very diffident)* Looks jolly good.

They come to the fourth booth where sits a very city-type gent.

FOURTH BOOTH Hello, big boy. *(very breathy)* Oo varda the ome. D'you want a nice time?
MR MANN Very good.
FOURTH BOOTH *(butch)* Thank you very much, sir.

They pass the fifth booth, whose occupant is making silly noises.

MR MANN And we control everything from here. *(indicating the control desk)*
TICK Superb.
MR MANN Well then what sort of thing were you looking for?
TICK Well, er, really something to make me a little less insignificant?
MR MANN Oh, I see sort of 'Now look here, you may be Chairman but your bloody pusillanimous behaviour makes me vomit!' That sort of thing?...

TICK Oh no, no, no, not really no.

MR MANN Oh I see, well perhaps something a bit more sort of Clive Jenkins-ish? 25 Perhaps—sort of *(Welsh accent)* 'Mr Smarmy so-called Harold Wilson can call himself pragmatic until he's blue in the breasts'.

TICK Oh no, I really want something that will make people be attracted to me like a magnet.

MR MANN I see, well, you want our 'Life and Soul of the Party' tape then, I think.

TICK What's that?

MR MANN Well it's sort of ''Ello squire, haven't seen you for a bit, haven't seen you for a bit either, Beryl. Two pints of wallop please, love. 26 Still driving the Jensen then? 27 Cheer up Jack it may never happen, what's your poison then?'

TICK Fantastic, yes.

MR MANN Right, I'll just see if we've got the tape.

He puts the headphones on. Whilst he looks away, the whole of the back wall of people in booths, swing round on their chairs and do a little thirties routine, with their earphones on, kicking their legs, etc., they sing.

Superimposed caption: 'SANDY WILSON'S VERSION OF "THE DEVILS"'

ALL Boo boopee doo
Boo boopee doo Scuby duby duby doo-oo!
Hello operator
Is that the central line
Give me the Piccadilly number
Nine one o nine
Mr operator now that number's wrong
So come on everybody Let's sing this song...
...Proust in his first book wrote about...etc....

Gong sounds.

VOICE OVER (ERIC) Start again.

Clive Jenkins was a witty, Welsh, and often brash union leader of the day. Harold Wilson was the leader of the Labour Party from 1963 to 1976, and British prime minister twice (1964 to 1970 and 1974 to 1976).

"Wallop" is slang for beer.

A Jensen is a sleek British-made sports car.

The loony leans into shot and waves. Fade to black. Fade up on close up of picture of Everest. Pull back to reveal travel agent's office.

BOUNDER (MICHAEL) Mount Everest, forbidding, aloof, terrifying. The highest place on earth. No I'm sorry we don't go there. No.

By the time Bounder is saying his last sentence the camera has revealed the office and Bounder himself sitting at a desk. Bounder now replaces the telephone into which he has been speaking. After a pause the tourist—Mr Smoke-Too-Much—enters the office and approaches Mr Bounder's secretary.

TOURIST (ERIC) Good morning.
SECRETARY (CAROL) Oh good morning. *(sexily)* Do you want to go upstairs?
TOURIST What?
SECRETARY *(sexily)* Do you want to go upstairs? *(brightly)* Or have you come to arrange a holiday?
TOURIST Er...to arrange a holiday.
SECRETARY Oh, sorry.
TOURIST What's all this about going upstairs?
SECRETARY Oh, nothing, nothing. Now, where were you thinking of going?
TOURIST India.
SECRETARY Ah one of our adventure holidays!
TOURIST Yes!
SECRETARY Well you'd better speak to Mr Bounder about that. Mr Bounder, this gentleman is interested in the India Overland.

Walks over to Bounder's desk where he is greeted by Bounder.
BOUNDER Ah. Good morning. I'm Bounder of Adventure.
TOURIST

MY NAME IS SMOKE-TOO-MUCH.

BOUNDER What?
TOURIST My name is Smoke-Too-Much. Mr Smoke-Too-Much.
BOUNDER Well, you'd better cut down a bit then.
TOURIST What?
BOUNDER You'd better cut down a bit then.
TOURIST Oh I see! Cut down a bit, for Smoke-Too-Much.
BOUNDER Yes, ha ha...I expect you get people making jokes about your name all the time, eh?
TOURIST No, no actually. Actually, it never struck me before. Smoke...too...much!
BOUNDER Anyway, you're interested in one of our adventure holidays, eh?
TOURIST Yes. I saw your advert in the bolour supplement.
BOUNDER The what?
TOURIST The bolour supplement.
BOUNDER The colour supplement?
TOURIST Yes. I'm sorry I can't say the letter 'B'.
BOUNDER C?
TOURIST Yes that's right. It's all due to a trauma I suffered when I was a spoolboy. I was attacked by a bat.
BOUNDER A cat?
TOURIST No a bat.
BOUNDER Can you say the letter 'K'.
TOURIST Oh yes. Khaki, king, kettle, Kuwait, Keble Bollege Oxford.
BOUNDER Why don't you say the letter 'K' instead of the letter 'C'?
TOURIST What you mean...spell bolour with a 'K'?
BOUNDER Yes.
TOURIST Kolour. Oh, that's very good, I never thought of that. 

The huge audience laugh here seems out of place. Darl Larsen notes that there was a line that's been deleted from both the scripts and the show itself: Idle says, "What a silly bunt" (for "cunt")—but Duncan Wood, the head of comedy at the time, insisted it be removed (he also insisted on the removal of the word "masturbating" from the start of this episode).

BOUNDER Anyway, about the holiday.

TOURIST Well I saw your adverts in the paper and I've been on package tours several times, you see, and I decided that this was for me.

BOUNDER Ah good.

TOURIST Yes I quite agree with you, I mean what's the point of being treated like a sheep, I mean I'm fed up going abroad and being treated like sheep, what's the point of being carted round in buses, surrounded by sweaty mindless oafs from Kettering and Boventry 29 in their cloth caps and their cardigans and their transistor radios and their 'Sunday Mirrors', complaining about the tea, 'Oh they don't make it properly here do they not like at home' stopping at Majorcan bodegas, selling fish and chips and Watney's Red Barrel 30 and calamares and two veg and sitting in cotton sun frocks squirting Timothy White's 31 suncream all over their puffy raw swollen purulent flesh cos they 'overdid it on the first day'!

BOUNDER *(agreeing patiently)* Yes. Absolutely, yes, I quite agree...

TOURIST And being herded into endless Hotel Miramars and Bellevueses and Bontinentals with their international luxury modern roomettes and their Watney's Red Barrel and their swimming pools full-of fat German businessmen pretending to be acrobats and forming pyramids and frightening the children and barging in to the queues and if you're not at your table spot on seven you miss your bowl of Campbell's Cream of Mushroom soup, the first item on the menu of International Cuisine, and every Thursday night there's bloody cabaret in the bar featuring some tiny emaciated dago with nine-inch hips and some big fat bloated tart with her hair Brylcreemed down and a big arse presenting Flamenco for Foreigners.

BOUNDER *(beginning to get fed up)* Yes, yes, now...

TOURIST And then some adenoidal typists from Birmingham with diarrhoea and flabby white legs and hairy bandy-legged wop waiters called Manuel, and then, once a week there's an excursion to the local Roman ruins where you can buy cherryade and melted ice cream and bleedin' Watney's Red Barrel, and then one night they take you to a local restaurant with local colour and colouring and they show you there and you sit next to a party of people from Rhyl who keeps singing 'Torremolinos, Torremolinos', 32 and complaining about the food, 'Oh! It's so greasy isn't it?' and then you get cornered by some drunken greengrocer from Luton with an Instamatic and Dr Scholl sandals and Tuesday's 'Daily Express' and he drones on and on and on about how Mr Smith should be running this country and how many languages Enoch Powell 33 can speak and then he throws up all over the Cuba Libres. 34

BOUNDER Will you be quiet please.

TOURIST And sending tinted postcards of places they don't know they haven't even visited, 'to all at number 22, weather wonderful our room is marked with an "X". Wish you were here.'

BOUNDER Shut up.

Ketteringe is a town in the Midlands. Boventry is deliberate misspeak for Coventry.

Watney's Red Barrel was a popular beer of the day, now legendary for its inclusion in this sketch.

Timothy White was a British pharmacy and home-goods store. Once it was taken over by Boots in 1968, it stuck to house wares.

Torremolinos was one of the first towns to be developed as a resort in southern Spain. It has been very popular with Brits since the 1950s.

Enoch Powell, a British politician and classicist, was known for his 1968 anti-immigration address known as the "Rivers of Blood" speech for its inflammatory use of imagery about what would happen should immigration be allowed to continue unchecked.

Cuba Libres is a rum and coke.

TOURIST 'Food very greasy but we have managed to find this marvellous little place hidden away in the back streets.'

BOUNDER Shut up!

TOURIST 'Where you can even get Watney's Red Barrel and cheese and onion...'

BOUNDER Shut up!!!

TOURIST '...crisps and the accordionist plays "Maybe its because I'm a Londoner"' and spending four days on the tarmac at Luton airport on a five-day package tour with nothing to eat but dried Watney's sandwiches...

BOUNDER Shut your bloody gob! I've had enough of this, I'm going to ring the police.

He dials and waits. Cut to a corner of a police station. One policeman is knitting, another is making a palm tree out of old newspapers. The phone rings.

KNITTING POLICEMAN Oh...take it off the hook. *(they do so)*

Cut back to travel agent's office. The man is still going on, the travel agent looks crossly at the phone and puts it down. Then picks it up and dials again.

BOUNDER Hello operator, operator...I'm trying to get the police...the police yes, what? *(takes his shoe off and looks inside)* nine and a half, nine and a half, yes, yes...I see...well can you keep trying please...

Through all this the tourist is still going on:

TOURIST ...and there's nowhere to sleep and the kids are vomiting and throwing up on the plastic flowers and they keep telling you it'll only be another hour although your plane is still in Iceland waiting to take some Swedes to Yugoslavia before it can pick you up on the tarmac at 3 a.m. in the bloody morning and you sit on the tarmac till six because of 'unforeseen difficulties', i.e. the permanent strike of Air Traffic Control in Paris, and nobody can go to the lavatory until you take off at eight, and when you get to Malaga airport everybody's swallowing Enterovioform tablets 35 and queuing for the toilets and when you finally get to the hotel there's no water in the taps, there's no water in the pool, there's no water in the bog 36 and there's only a bleeding lizard in the bidet, and half the rooms are double-booked and you can't sleep anyway...

The secretary comes up and looks into the camera.

Enterovioform is an anti-diarrhea tablet now banned in the United States and many other countries as it can cause paralysis, blindness, and even death.

The "bog" is British slang for a toilet.

SECRETARY Oh! Sorry to keep you waiting...will you come this way please...

The camera follows her as she leads us out of the office, with agent and client still rabbiting on, 37 *down a short passage to a documentary interview set where the two participants are sitting waiting. We follow her into the set*

"Rabbiting" means to talk at a rapid rate.

SECRETARY Here they are. *(she turns to the camera again, which moves a little towards her, as if waiting to be summoned)* Just here will do fine! Goodbye.

A presenter sitting with a guest in the usual late-night line-up set.

PRESENTER (GRAHAM) Good evening.

Caption: 'THRUST—A QUITE CONTROVERSIAL LOOK AT THE WORLD AROUND US'

PRESENTER I have with me tonight Anne Elk. Mrs Anne Elk.
MISS ELK (JOHN) Miss.

Superimposed caption: 'ANNE ELK'

PRESENTER

YOU HAVE A NEW THEORY ABOUT THE BRONTOSAURUS.

MISS ELK Can I just say here Chris for one moment that I have a new theory about the brontosaurus.
PRESENTER Exactly. *(he gestures but she does not say anything)* What is it?
MISS ELK Where? *(looks round)*
PRESENTER No, no your new theory.
MISS ELK Oh, what is my theory?
PRESENTER Yes.
MISS ELK Oh what is my theory that it is. Well Chris you may well ask me what is my theory.
PRESENTER I *am* asking.
MISS ELK Good for you. My word yes. Well Chris, what is it that it is—this theory of mine. Well, this is what it is—my theory that I have, that is to say, which is mine, is mine.
PRESENTER *(beginning to show signs of exasperation)* Yes, I know it's yours, what is it?
MISS ELK Where? Oh, what is my theory? This is it. *(clears throat at some length)* My theory that belongs to me is as follows. *(clears throat at great length)* This is how it goes. The next thing I'm going to say is my theory. Ready?
PRESENTER Yes.

MISS ELK My theory by A. Elk. Brackets Miss, brackets. This theory goes as follows and begins now. All brontosauruses are thin at one end, much much thicker in the middle and then thin again at the far end. That is my theory, it is mine, and belongs to me and I own it, and what it is too.

PRESENTER That's *it*, is it?

MISS ELK Spot on, Chris.

PRESENTER Well, er, this theory of yours appears to have hit the nail on the head.

MISS ELK And it's mine.

PRESENTER Yes, thank you very much for coming along to the studio. Thank you.

MISS ELK My pleasure, Chris...

PRESENTER Next week Britain's newest wasp farm...

MISS ELK It's been a lot of fun.

PRESENTER Yes, thank you very much.

MISS ELK Saying what my theory is.

PRESENTER Yes, thank you.

MISS ELK And whose it is.

PRESENTER Yes, thank you—that's all—thank you...opens next week.

MISS ELK I have another theory.

PRESENTER Yes.

MISS ELK Called my second theory, or my theory number two.

PRESENTER Thank you. Britain's newest wasp farm...

MISS ELK This second theory which was the one that I had said...

PRESENTER *(the phone rings; he answers)* Yes, no I'm trying...

MISS ELK Which I could expound without doubt. This second theory which, with the one which I have said, forms the brace of theories which I own and which belong to me, goes like this...

PRESENTER *(looking at his shoe)* Nine and a half, wide fitting...Balleys of Bond Street. What? No, sort of brogue.

MISS ELK This is what it is. *(clears throat)*

PRESENTER Eight and a half.

MISS ELK This is it...*(lots of noisy throat clearing)*

He rises and leaves the set to go next door to the travel agent set, leaving Miss Elk behind for a moment. Bounder is still on the phone. His other phone rings; he answers it.

BOUNDER Hello, yes...yes...

The presenter enters the travel set. The tourist is still droning on as before and Bounder is still on the phone.

TOURIST *(carrying on all through the scene below)* ...and the Spanish Tourist Board promises you that the raging cholera epidemic is merely a case of mild Spanish tummy, like the last outbreak of Spanish tummy in 1660 which killed half London and decimated Europe, and meanwhile the bloody Guardia are busy arresting sixteen-year-olds for kissing in the streets and shooting anyone under nineteen who doesn't like Franco... 38

The presenter approaches Bounder.

PRESENTER The fire brigade are here. They're coming!
BOUNDER Hello! No, no, no I think they are all part of the British Shoe Corporation now.

Miss Elk follows the presenter in.

MISS ELK Chris, this other theory of mine which is mine like the other one I also own. The second theory...

The fire brigade enter and the secretary goes to greet them. They speak to her and she takes off her shoe to check the size. Meanwhile...

MISS ELK My second theory states that fire brigade choirs seldom sing songs about Marcel Proust.

WITH ONLY A HALF-BEAT PAUSE THE FIRE BRIGADE START SINGING THE PROUST SONG.

After the usual number of lines we hear the gong.

VOICE OVER (ERIC) Start again.

The loony looks into the scene on overlay and waves at the camera just as we fade to black. We hold black for a few seconds and then the loony leans in to the black and waves again before fading away.

38

General Franco, the right-wing dictator who ruled Spain from 1936 to 1975.

SEA
SON
3
EPISODE 32
RN

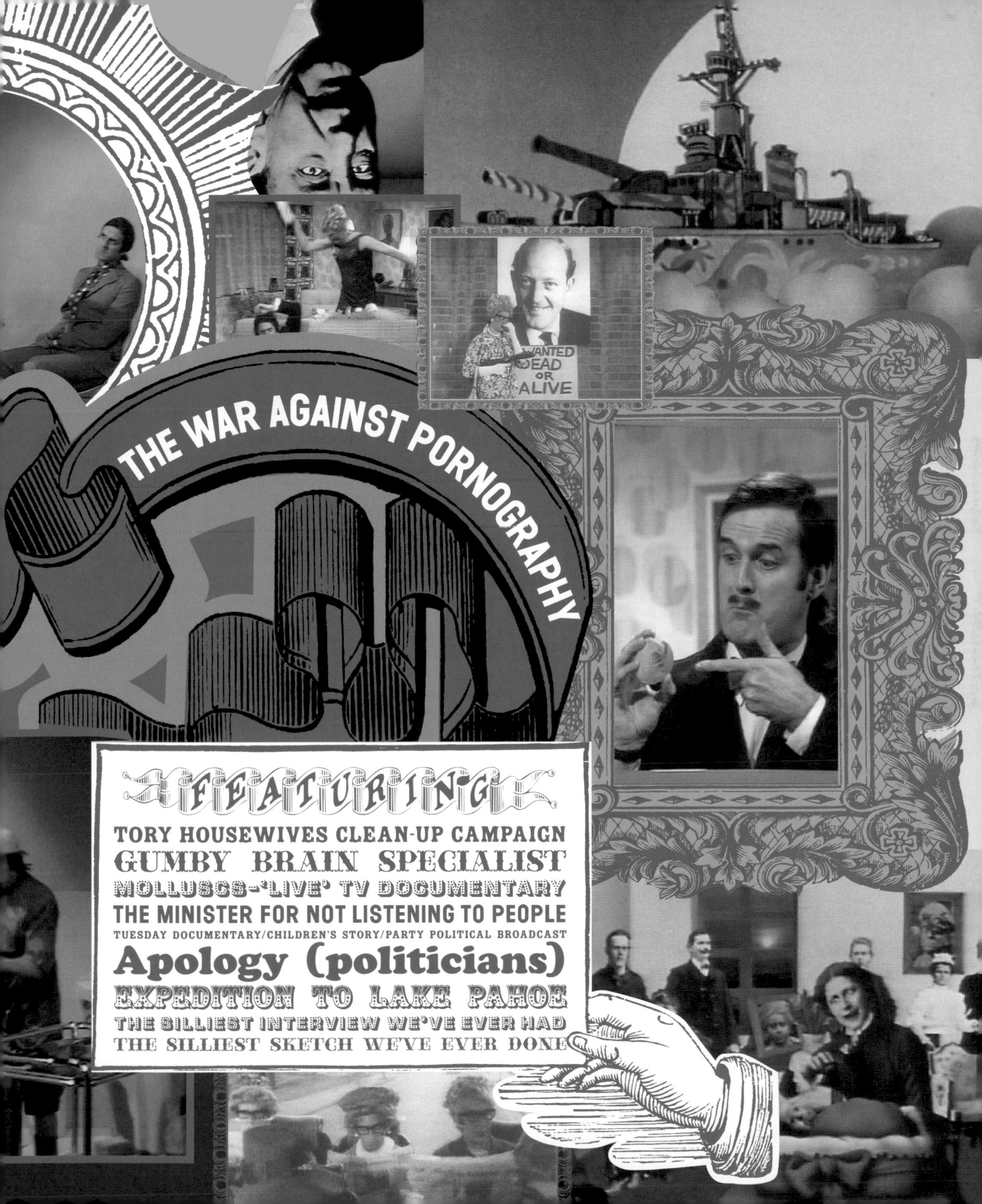
WANTED
DEAD
OR
ALIVE
THE WAR AGAINST PORNOGRAPHY
FEATURING
TORY HOUSEWIVES CLEAN-UP CAMPAIGN
GUMBY BRAIN SPECIALIST
MOLLUSCS–'LIVE' TV DOCUMENTARY
THE MINISTER FOR NOT LISTENING TO PEOPLE
TUESDAY DOCUMENTARY/CHILDREN'S STORY/PARTY POLITICAL BROADCAST
Apology (politicians)
EXPEDITION TO LAKE PAHOE
THE SILLIEST INTERVIEW WE'VE EVER HAD
THE SILLIEST SKETCH WE'VE EVER DONE

The Red Devils are a crack-stunt parachute team, part of the British Army's Parachute Regiment.

Mary Whitehouse, the right-wing anti-permissive society activist and regular scourge of the BBC, was known for the upswept frames of her glasses.

The "Common Market," also known as the European Economic Community, was a European idea, of course, though it's not surprising that the isolationist Brits might consider it theirs and theirs alone.

Jean-Paul Sartre and Jean Genet were stars of Episode 27, in which two pepperpots disagree about what Sartre meant by his *Roads to Freedom* trilogy.

A common comic misperception about the correct use of a bidet in a bathroom.

"Like bingo" is British slang for "with great effort."

Robert Robinson was a British broadcaster whose persona often teetered on the very edge of smug.

FIRST AIRED: NOVEMBER 23, 1972

Newsreel footage.

VOICE OVER (ERIC) *(newsreel voice)* In the modern Britain, united under a great leader, it's the housewives of Britain who are getting things moving. *(**Red Devils flying;** 1 picture of Edward Heath)* Here a coachload of lovely ladies are on their way to speed up production in a car factory. *(coach load of pepperpots, middle class, grey hair, **Mary Whitehouse** glasses;* 2 *the coach says 'Tory Tours')* And here we are boys, it's the no-hurry brigade hanging about for endless overtime. And just watch these gallant girls go into action... *(cut to a factory yard; some workers in brown overalls are eating sandwiches out of tins; the clock says 1.15; the coach comes swinging in in undercrank, the ladies pour out about to belt the men with umbrellas and handbags; the men flee back into factories)* Not working fast enough? Well, there's an answer for that. *(a man at a machine, producing something incredibly fast; a pepperpot holds an enormous sledgehammer)* Yes, this is certainly the way to speed up production. *(wide shot of factory interior; three pepperpots stand on a gantry above work floor, wearing armbands, saying 'P.P. and dark Mary Whitehouse glasses)* This is the recipe for increased productivity to meet the threat of those nasty foreigners when Britain takes her natural place at the head of the **British Common Market.** 3 *(a group of strikers, picketing with slogans, 'Fair Pay', 'Less Profits', 'Parity', 'No Victimization')* And how's this for a way to beat strikers. *(pepperpots arrive, clinging to side of old Buick; they race in and start beating the strikers with the banners)* Those spotty continental boys will soon have to look out for Mrs Britain, and talking of windmills, these girls aren't afraid to tilt at the permissive society. *(art gallery exterior; pepperpots run in with bundles and ladders)* Business is booming in the so-called arts, but two can play at that game, chum. *(cut to art gallery interior; pan around paintings 'cleaned up'—trousers and cardigans being added to nude pictures and statues, Bermuda shorts on David, shorts on tubular structure, an attendant in shorts too).* And it's not just the modern so-called plastic arts that get the clean-up treatment.

Cut to a theatre stage. Desdemona on a bed. Othello with her.

OTHELLO Oh Desdemona, Desdemona.

The pepperpots race on to the stage and pull him off.

VOICE OVER And those continentals had better watch out for their dirty foreign literature. **Jean-Paul Sartre and Jean Genet won't know what's hit them.** 4 Never mind the foulness of their language—come '73 they'll all have to write in British. *(pepperpots burning books: 'Bertrand Russell', 'Das Kapital', the 'Guardian', 'Sartre', 'Freud')* **You can keep your fastidious continental bidets Mrs Foreigner—Mrs Britain knows how to keep *her* feet clean...but she'll battle like bingo boys when it comes to keeping the television screen clean...** 5

*Cut to the BBC TV Centre. The pepperpots parade in carrying signs: 'Clean TV Centre', 'God Says No To Filth', 'To The Cells'. Another pepperpot in the background holds a sign: 'Wanted Dead Or Alive' and photo of **Robert Robinson.*** 6

VOICE OVER Better watch out for those nasty continental shows on the sneaky second channel. *(armed pepperpots escorting people out of TV Centre)* But apart from attacking that prurient hot-bed of left-wing continental ism **at Shepherds Bush,** 7 what else do these ordinary mums think? Do they accept Hegelianism?

PEPPERPOT (GRAHAM) No!
VOICE OVER Do they prefer Leibnitz to Wittgenstein? [8]
PEPPERPOT (TERRY J) No! No!
VOICE OVER And where do they stand on young people?
PEPPERPOT (ERIC) Just here, dear. *(pepper pot standing on long-haired youth's head)*
VOICE OVER And their power is growing daily and when these girls roll their sleeves up its arms all the way. *(pepperpots standing on the turret of an armoured vehicle; four pepperpots on motor bikes flank it)* Yes, this is the way to fight the constant war against pornography.

Machine guns chatter. Two pepper pots in a trench firing. Mortar bombs, reloading and firing. Bombs and smoke. At the end of the film we pick up on the nude organist (TERRY J)*, sitting amongst the explosions. He plays his chords.*

ANNOUNCER (JOHN) And now...
IT'S MAN (MICHAEL)

IT'S...

Animated titles.

VOICE (JOHN) Monty Python's Flying Circus.

Close up on a sign saying 'HARLEY STREET'. Stirring music. Mix through to interior of a smart, plush, ever so expensive Harley Street consulting room. The music swells and fades. Knocking at door, a short pause, then T. F. Gumby enters, backwards.

T. F. GUMBY (MICHAEL) Doctor! Doctor! DOCTOR! *(he goes up to the antique desk and bangs the bell violently; he smashes the intercom and generally breaks the desk up)* Doctor! Doctor! DOCTOR! DOCTOR! Doctor! Doctor! Where is the Doctor?

A pause. Then another door opens and another Gumby appears.

GUMBY SPECIALIST (JOHN) Hello!
T. F. GUMBY Are you the brain specialist?
SPECIALIST Hello!
T. F. GUMBY Are you the brain specialist?
SPECIALIST No, no, I am not the brain specialist. No, no, I am not... Yes. Yes I am.

"Shepherds Bush" is a metonym for the BBC, as this is where their main TV center is situated.

Gottfried Leibniz was a German mathematician and philosopher active in the late seventeenth and early eighteenth centuries. As a philosopher, he is most remembered for his optimism, claiming the universe to be the best one possible.

Ludwig Wittgenstein was a British-Austrian philosopher active in the first half of the twentieth century. His later thought revolved around a systematic tracing of all philosophies up to that point, including his own, in order to create an anti-systematic philosophy. See?

T. F. GUMBY
MY B
HUR

9

"My brain hurts" is a phrase still heard regularly in the U.K., and all because of this sketch.

Palin nearly cracks up laughing here, as ever.

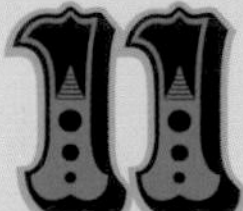

The Lancet is the magazine of the British medical profession.

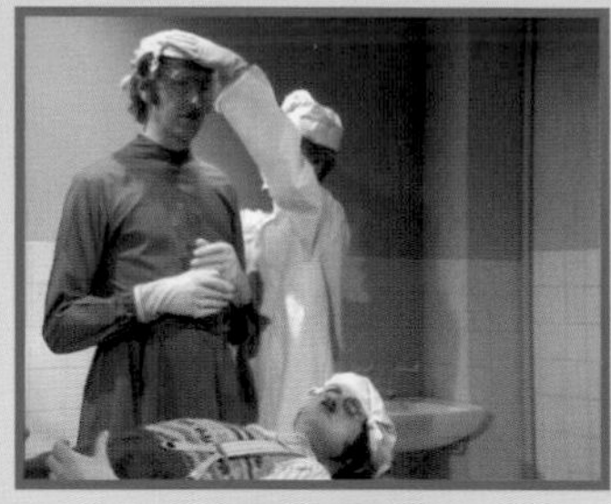

Chapman is already wearing gloves—they look like washing gloves—so he begins with "glasses."

SPECIALIST Well let's take a look at it, Mr Gumby.

Gumby specialist starts to pull up Gumby's sweater.

T. F. GUMBY No, no, no, my brain in my head. 10

(specialist thumps him on the head)

SPECIALIST It will have to come out.
T. F. GUMBY Out? Of my head?
SPECIALIST Yes! All the bits of it. Nurse! Nurse! *(a nurse enters)* Nurse, take Mr Gumby to a brain surgeon.

NURSE Yes doctor...

She leads Gumby out. In the background the specialist is grunting and shouting.

SPECIALIST Where's the 'Lancet'? 11
NURSE *(to T. F. Gumby)* He's brilliant you know.
SPECIALIST Where's the bloody 'Lancet'? My brain hurts too.

Ambulance racing. 'Dr Kildare' theme. Cut to operating theatre. The surgeon is not a Gumby.

SURGEON (GRAHAM) *(putting on Gumby props)* Gloves... 12 glasses...moustache...handkerchief... *(Gumby voice)* I'm going to operate!!

We now see he is surrounded by Gumbys. T. F. Gumby is on operating table.

ALL Let's operate.

They begin to use woodworking implements on T. F. Gumby.

T. F. GUMBY Hello!
SURGEON GUMBY

OOH! WE FORGOT THE ANAESTHETIC!

OPERATING GUMBYS The anaesthetic! The anaesthetic!!

At that moment a Gumby anaesthetist comes crashing through the wall with two gas cylinders.

GUMBY ANAESTHETIST I've come to anaesthetize you!!

He raises a gas cylinder and strikes Gumby hard over the head with it. Bong.

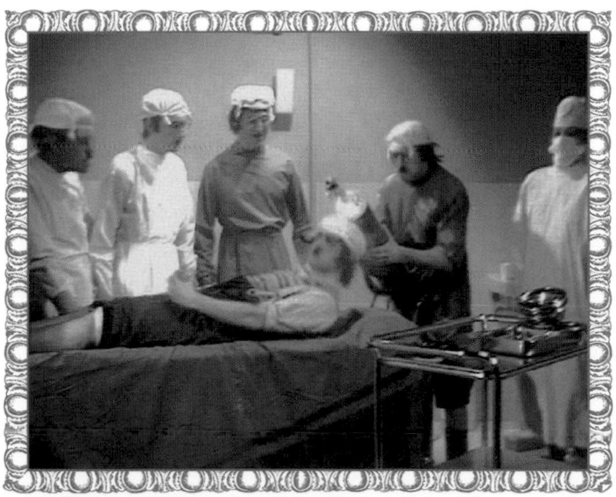

Blackness. Into the oblivion of animation.

Then cut to an ordinary suburban living room. Mr and Mrs Jalin are sitting on a sofa. The previous item in the show is visible on their TV set. Mrs Jalin is stuffing a chicken. Mr Jalin is reading the telephone directory. The picture changes and we hear voice from TV.

VOICE (ERIC) The 'Nine O'Clock News' which was to follow has been cancelled tonight so we can bring you the quarter finals of the All Essex Badminton Championship. Your commentator as usual is Edna O'Brien. 13

COMMENTATOR (MICHAEL) *(Irish accent)* Hullo fans. Begorra 14 an' to be sure there's some fine badminton down there in Essex this afternoon. We really...

Mr Jalin picks up a jousting ball and chain and smashes the TV set. There is a ring from the doorbell. Mr Jalin sits. Mrs Jalin goes to the door, exits and comes back.

MRS JALIN (GRAHAM) George.

MR JALIN (TERRY J) Yes, Gladys.

MRS JALIN There's a man at the door with a moustache.

MR JALIN Tell him I've already got one. *(Mrs Jalin hits him hard with a newspaper)* 15 All right, all right. What's he want then?

MRS JALIN He says do we want a documentary on molluscs.

MR JALIN Molluscs!

MRS JALIN Yes.

Edna O'Brien, an Irish novelist, was controversial in the 1960s in her own land. She was banned and her books burned, owing to her writing on the inner lives—and the sex lives—of her characters.

"Begorra" is Irish slang for "By God."

Punch lines must always be punished in Python.

Molluscs is the huge family of beasts that includes gastropods (such as snails and slugs), lamellibranches (clams, oysters, and scallops), and cephalopods (octopi and squid).

MR JALIN What's he mean, molluscs?

MRS JALIN MOLLUSCS!! GASTROPODS! LAMELLIBRANCHS! CEPHALOPODS! 16

MR JALIN Oh molluscs, I thought you said bacon. *(she hits him again)* All right, all right. What's he charge then?

MRS JALIN It's free.

MR JALIN Ooh! Where does he want us to sit?

MRS JALIN *(calling through the door)* He says yes.

Mr Zorba enters carrying plywood fiat with portion cut out to represent TV. He stands behind flat and starts.

ZORBA (JOHN) Good morning. Tonight molluscs. The mollusc is a soft-bodied, unsegmented invertebrate animal usually protected by a large shell. One of the most numerous groups of invertebrates, it is exceeded in number of species only by the arthropods...viz. *(he holds up a lobster)*

MRS JALIN Not very interesting is it?

ZORBA What?

MRS JALIN I was talking to him.

ZORBA Oh. Anyway, the typical mollusc, viz, a snail *(holds one up)* consists of a prominent muscular portion...the head-foot...a visceral mass and a shell which is secreted by the free edge of the mantle.

MRS JALIN Dreadful isn't it?

ZORBA What?

MRS JALIN I was talking to him.

ZORBA Oh. Well anyway...in some molluscs, however, viz, slugs, *(holds one up)* the shell is absent or rudimentary...

MR JALIN Switch him off.

Mrs Jalin gets up and looks for the switch unsuccessfully.

ZORBA Whereas in others, viz, cephalopods the head-foot is greatly modified and forms tentacles, viz, the squid. *(looking out)* What are you doing?

MRS JALIN Switching you off.

ZORBA Why, don't you like it?
MRS JALIN Oh it's dreadful.
MR JALIN Embarrassing.
ZORBA Is it?
MRS JALIN Yes, it's perfectly awful.
MR JALIN Disgraceful! I don't know how they've got the nerve to put it on.
MRS JALIN It's so boring.
ZORBA Well...it's not much of a subject is it...be fair.
MRS JALIN What do you think, George?
MR JALIN Give him another twenty seconds.
ZORBA Anyway the majority of the molluscs are included in three large groups, the gastropods, the lamellibranchs and the cephalopods...
MRS JALIN We knew that *(she gets up and goes to the set)*
ZORBA

HOWEVER, WHAT IS MORE INTERESTING, ER...IS THE MOLLUSCS'S ER...SEX LIFE.

MRS JALIN *(stopping dead)* Oh!
ZORBA Yes, the mollusc is a randy little fellow whose primitive brain scarcely strays from the subject of the you know what.
MRS JALIN *(going back to sofa)* Disgusting!
MR JALIN Ought not to be allowed.
ZORBA The randiest of the gastropods is the limpet. This hot-blooded little beast with its tent-like shell is always on the job. Its extra-marital activities are something startling. Frankly I don't know how the female limpet finds the time to adhere to the rock-face. How am I doing?
MRS JALIN Disgusting.
MR JALIN But more interesting.
MRS JALIN Oh yes, tch, tch, tch.
ZORBA Another loose-living gastropod is the periwinkle. This shameless little libertine with its characteristic ventral locomotion...is *not* the marrying kind: Anywhere anytime is its motto. Up with the shell and they're at it.
MRS JALIN How about the lamellibranchs?
ZORBA I'm coming to them...the great scallop *(holds one up)*...this tatty, scrofulous old rapist, is second in depravity only to the common clam. *(holds up a clam)*

This latter is a right whore, a harlot, a trollop, a cynical bed-hopping firm-breasted Rabelaisian bit of sea food that makes Fanny Hill look like a dead Pope... [17] and finally among the lamellibranch bivalves, that most depraved of the whole sub-species—the whelk. The whelk is nothing but a homosexual of the worst kind. This gay boy of the gastropods, this queer crustacean, this mincing mollusc, this screaming, prancing, limp-wristed queen of the deep makes me sick.
MRS JALIN Have you got one?
ZORBA Here! *(holds one up)*

Memoirs of a Woman of Pleasure (popularly known as *Fanny Hill*) is a novel written by the English author John Cleland in 1748. It is widely considered the first pornographic novel.

MRS JALIN Let's kill it. Disgusting.

Zorba throws it on the floor and Mr and Mrs Jalin stamp on it.

MR JALIN That'll teach it. Well thank you for a very interesting programme.
ZORBA Oh, not at all. Thank you.
MRS JALIN Yes, that was very nice.
ZORBA **Thank you.** ***(he shakes hands with her)*** 18
MRS JALIN Oh, thank you.

18

Chapman here goes to shake hands with Cleese through the TV "screen," as Jones just did, but Cleese puts his hand around the side of the TV, causing confusion and a near breaking of character.

Cut to a studio presenter at a desk.

PRESENTER (TERRY G) And now a word from the man in the...

Cut to Glencoe vox pop: a loony.

LOONY (GRAHAM) ...street.

Animation: high-suction baby.

Cut to a 'Nine O'clock News' set. A newsreader is at a desk. Photos come up on inlay screen behind him. An anonymous minister's photo is on screen.

NEWSREADER (MICHAEL) The Minister for not listening to people toured Batley today to investigate allegations of victimization in home-loan improvement grants, made last week *(photo behind changes to close up of another faceless minister)* by the Shadow Minister for judging people at first sight to be marginally worse than they actually are. *(photo changes to exterior of the Home Office)* At the Home Office, the Minister for inserting himself in between chairs and walls in men's clubs, was at his desk after a short illness. He spent the morning dealing with the Irish situation and later in the day had long discussions with the Minister for running upstairs two at a time, flinging the door open and saying 'Ha, ha! Caught you, Mildred'. *(photo of the Houses of Parliament)* In the Commons there was another day of heated debate on the third reading of the Trade Practices Bill. **Mr Roland Penrose,** 19 the Under-Secretary for making deep growling noises grrr, launched a bitter personal attack on the ex-Minister for delving deep into a black satin bag and producing a tube of **Euthymol toothpaste.** 20 Later in the debate the Junior Minister for being frightened by any kind of farm machinery, challenged the Under-Secretary of State for hiding from Terence Rattigan to produce the current year's trading figures, as supplied by the Department of stealing packets of bandages from the self-service counter at Timothy Whites and selling them again at a considerable profit. Parliament rose. Later in the debate the Junior Minister for being frightened by any kind of farm machinery, challenged the Under-Secretary of State for hiding from Terence Rattigan to produce the current year's trading figures, as supplied by the Department of stealing packets of bandages from the self-service counter at Timothy Whites and selling them again at a considerable profit. **Parliament rose** 21 at 11.30, and, crawling along a dark passageway into the old rectory *(the camera starts to track slowly into the news reader's face so that it is eventually filling the screen)* broke down the door to the serving hatch, painted the spare room

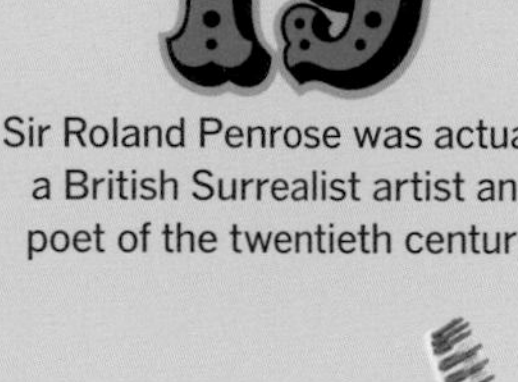

Sir Roland Penrose was actually a British Surrealist artist and poet of the twentieth century.

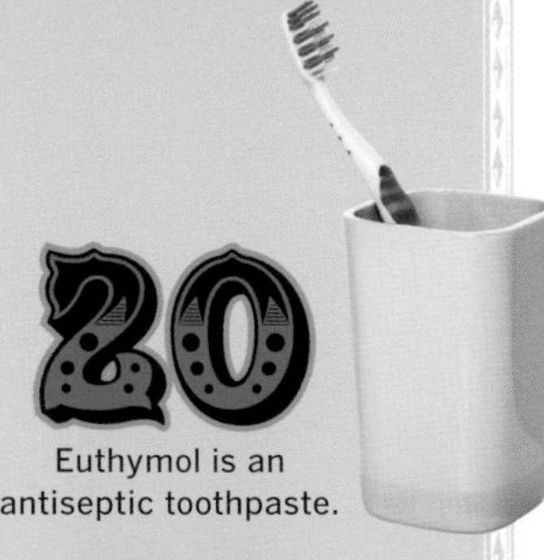

Euthymol is an antiseptic toothpaste.

"Parliament rose" means it's finished its business for the day.

and next weekend I think they'll be able to make a start on the boy's bedroom, while Amy and Roger, up in London for a few days, go to see the mysterious Mr Grenville.

Superimposed caption: 'TODAY IN PARLIAMENT HAS NOW BECOME THE CLASSIC SERIAL'

NEWSREADER He in turn has been revealed by D' Arcy as something less than an honest man. Sybil feels once again a resurgence of her old affection and she and Balreau return to her little house in Clermont-Ferrand, the kind of two-up, two-down house that **most French workers** 22 throughout the European Community are living in today.

Palin here adds "and, indeed, most workers."

Superimposed caption: 'THE CLASSIC SERIAL HAS NOW BECOME THE TUESDAY DOCUMENTARY' Cut to a photo of a French construction site. The camera tracks over the photo.

PRESENTER (ERIC) The ease of construction, using on-site prefabrication facilities *(the camera starts to pull out slowly from the photo to reveal the photo is part of the backdrop of a documentary set about the building trade; the documentary presenter is sitting in a chair)* makes cheap housing a reality. The walls of these houses are lined with prestressed asbestos which keeps the house warm and snuggly and ever so safe from the big bad rabbit, who can scratch and scratch for all he's worth, but he just can't get into Porky's house.

Superimposed caption: 'THE TUESDAY DOCUMENTARY HAS BECOME "CHILDREN'S STORY"'

PRESENTER Where is Porky? Here he is. What a funny little chap. *(cut to animated Porky doing little dance)* But Porky's one of the lucky ones—he survived the urban upheaval of the thirties and forties. For him, **Jarrow is still just a memory.** 23 *(zoom out to see Porky as part of documentary-type graph)* The hunger marches, the **East End riots,** 24 the collapse of the Labour Government in 1931...*(stock film of Ramsay MacDonald)*

The Jarrow March in October 1936 saw 207 marchers walk to the Houses of Parliament in London from the town of Jarrow, in the far northeast of England. The 300-mile march was to protest poverty and unemployment.

The "East End riots" refers to the Battle of Cable Street, which occurred on October 4, 1936, in London's East End. It was a pitched battle between antifascists and Oswald Mosley and his British Union of Fascists.

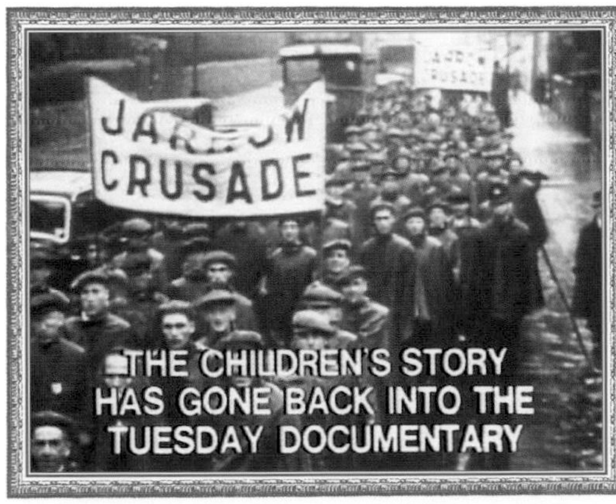

Superimposed caption: 'THE CHILDREN'S STORY HAS GONE BACK INTO THE TUESDAY DOCUMENTARY'

PRESENTER ...are dim reminders of the days before a new-found affluence swept the land, *(stock shots of Christmas lights in Regent Street, shopping crowds, tills and consumer goods ending up with toys)* making it clean and tidy and making all the shops full of nice things, lovely choo-choo trains...

Superimposed caption: 'NO IT HASN'T'

PRESENTER ...and toys and shiny cars that go brrm, brrm, brrm, *(shots of toys)* and everybody was happy and singing all the day long *(cut to the presenter; by now he has a big kiddies' book which he shuts)* and nobody saw the big bad rabbit ever again.

Cut to a politician giving a party political broadcast in one of those badly lit sets that they use for broadcasts of that nature.

POLITICIAN (TERRY J) But you know it's always very easy to blame the big bad rabbit...

Superimposed caption: 'NOW IT'S BECOME A PARTY POLITICAL BROADCAST'

POLITICIAN ...when by-elections are going against the Government. *(he turns and we cut to side camera which reveals a cross behind him as for religious broadcast)* Do you think we should really be blaming ourselves?

Superimposed caption: 'NO SORRY, "RELIGION TODAY"'

POLITICIAN Because you know, that's where we really ought to start looking.

A football comes in, he heads it neatly out of shot. Superimposed caption: 'MATCH OF THE DAY' Cut to stock film of ball flying into net and shot of Wembley crowd roaring. Then cut into short sequence of footballers in slow-motion kissing each other. Superimposed caption: 'POLITICIANS—AN APOLOGY' The camera pans across a landscape. Roller caption starts to come up, superimposed. The words are quite large and easily readable, but well spaced so that the roller will seem to go on for quite some time. Voice over reads. 25

VOICE OVER (ERIC) *(and caption)* 'we would like to apologize for the way in which politicians are represented in this programme. It was never our intention to imply that politicians are weak-kneed, political time-servers who are concerned more with their personal vendettas and private power struggles than the problems of government, nor to suggest at any point that they sacrifice their credibility by denying free debate on vital matters in the mistaken impression that party unity comes before the well-being of the people they supposedly represent, nor to imply at any stage that they are squabbling little toadies without an ounce of concern for the vital social problems of today. Nor indeed do we intend that viewers should consider them as crabby ulcerous little self-seeking vermin with furry legs and an excessive addiction to alcohol and certain explicit sexual practices which some people might find offensive, we are sorry if this impression has come across.

Cut to a similar landscape. Preparations for an expedition are underway: equipment being piled into land-rovers etc. An interviewer walks into shot.

INTERVIEWER (JOHN) Hello. All the activity you can see in progress here is part of the intricate...aah! *(he steps into a man-trap, but continues bravely)* preparations for the British Naval Expedition to Lake Pahoe. 26 The leader of the expedition is Sir Jane Russell. 27 *(the interviewer in slightly different spot with the admiral; we now see that the interviewer has a wooden leg and a crutch)* Sir Jane, what is the purpose of your expedition?

SIR JANE (GRAHAM) Well this is a completely uncharted lake with like hitherto unclassified marine life man, so the whole scene's wide open for a scientific exploration.

INTERVIEWER *(now with a parrot on his shoulder)* One can see the immense amount of preparation involved. Have there been many difficulties in setting up this venture?

SIR JANE *(with 'naval-lib' badge)* Well the real hang-up was with the bread man but when the top brass pigs came through we got it together in a couple of moons. Commodore Betty Grable, 28 who's a real sub-aqua head, has got together diving wise and like the whole gig's been a real gas man.

"Land of Hope and Glory," an English nationalist hymn, plays under the scrolling captions.

There is no "Lake Pahoe," though Lake Tahoe straddles California and Nevada.

Jane Russell, the pneumatic American actress and sex symbol of the 1940s and '50s, spokesperson for the 18-hour bra in the 1970s, and later self-described "teetotal, mean-spirited, right-wing, narrow-minded, conservative Christian bigot, but not a racist."

Betty Grable, American actress and number-one pinup girl—because of her eyes, no doubt—during World War II.

INTERVIEWER *(now with Long John Silver hat)* Thank you. *(and eyepatch)* Lieutenant Commander Dorothy Lamour. 29

PARROT Pieces of eight.

INTERVIEWER *(now with Long John Silver jacket)* Dorothy you're in charge of security and liaison for this operation.

DOROTHY LAMOUR (ERIC) Right on. *(he is smoking something and is really cool)*

INTERVIEWER You've kept this all rather hush-hush so far shipmate.

DOROTHY LAMOUR Yeah, it's been really heavy man with all these freaks from the fascist press trying to blow the whole scene.

INTERVIEWER *(to camera)* There's no doubt about it, this expedition does have some rather unusual aspects, Jim lad. For a first, why does the senior personnel all bear the names of Hollywood film stars of the forties...and female ones at that, shiver me timbers 'tis the black spot, and secondly, I be not afraid of thee Blind Pew...why do they talk this rather strange stilted, underground jargon, belay the mainbrace Squire Trelawney this be my ship now. *(he is hit by a dart)* Argh! A tranquillizing dart fired by the cowardly BBC health department dogs...they've done filled me full of chlorpromazine damn!

He falls. A second interviewer comes into shot and catches the microphone.

SECOND INTERVIEWER (TERRY J) I'm sorry about my colleague's rather unconventional behaviour.

SIR JANE *(running towards the camera)* The navy's out of sight man come together with the RN it's really something other than else.

Animated psychedelic advert for the Royal Navy.

ANIMATED VOICE You dig it, man?

29

Dorothy Lamour, American actress of mid-twentieth century. Like Russell and Grable, she was a "glamour girl."

Cut back to second interviewer.

SECOND INTERVIEWER Hello. I'm sorry about my colleague's rather unconventional behaviour just now, but things haven't been too easy for him recently, trouble at home, rather confidential so I can't give you all the details...interesting though they are...three bottles of rum with his weetabix, [30] and so on, anyway...apparently the girl wasn't even...anyway the activity you see behind me...it's the mother I feel sorry for. I'll start again. The activity you see behind me is part of the preparations for the new Naval Expedition to Lake Pahoe. The man in charge of this expedition is Vice Admiral Sir John Cunningham. [31] Sir John, hello there.

SIR JOHN (GRAHAM) Ah, hello. Well first of all I'd like to apologize for the behaviour of certain of my colleagues you may have seen earlier, but they are from broken homes, circus families and so on and they are in no way representative of the new modern improved British Navy. They are a small vociferous minority; and may I take this opportunity of emphasizing that there is no cannibalism in the British Navy. Absolutely none, and when I say none, I mean there is a certain amount, more than we are prepared to admit, but all new ratings are warned that if they wake up in the morning and find toothmarks at all anywhere on their bodies, they're to tell me immediately so that I can immediately take every measure to hush the whole thing up. And, finally, necrophilia is right out. *(the interviewer keeps nodding but looks embarrassed)* Now, this expedition is primarily to investigate reports of cannibalism and necrophilia in...this expedition is primarily to investigate reports of unusual marine life in the as yet uncharted Lake Pahoe. [32]

INTERVIEWER And where exactly is the lake?

SIR JOHN Er 22A, Runcorn Avenue, I think. Yes, that's right, 22A.

INTERVIEWER Runcorn Avenue?

SIR JOHN Yes, it's just by Blenheim Crescent...do you know it?

INTERVIEWER You mean it's in an ordinary street?

SIR JOHN

OF COURSE IT'S NOT AN ORDINARY STREET! IT'S GOT A LAKE IN IT!

INTERVIEWER Yes but I...

SIR JOHN Look, how many streets do you know that have got lakes in them?

INTERVIEWER But you mean...is it very large?

SIR JOHN Of *course* it's not large, you couldn't get a large lake *in* Runcorn Avenue! You'd have to knock down the tobacconist's! *(looking off camera)* Jenkins...no!

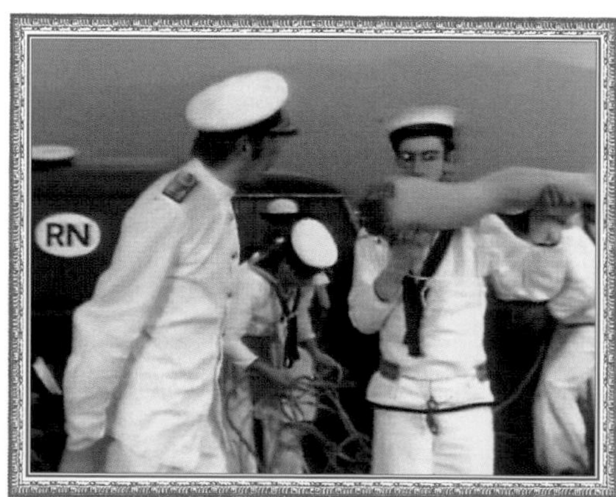

We see a rather sheepish rating about to sink his teeth into a human leg. Sir John puts his hand in front of the lens. Cut to Runcorn Avenue, an ordinary street with houses now turned into flats. The land-rover arrives with the equipment.

30 Weetabix is a cardboard-like breakfast cereal beloved in the U.K., where food generally doesn't taste like anything.

31 John Cunningham, admiral of the fleet, first sea lord—a career Royal Navy man of both World War I and World War II.

32 The implication that there is cannabilism in the Royal Navy was discussed in Episode 26.

INTERVIEWER I'm now standing in Runcorn Avenue. Sir John...where exactly is the lake?
SIR JOHN Er, well let's see, that's 18...that's 20 so this must be the one.
INTERVIEWER Er, excuse me...
SIR JOHN Yes, that's the one all right.
INTERVIEWER But it's an ordinary house.
SIR JOHN Look, I'm getting pretty irritated with this line of questioning.
INTERVIEWER But it doesn't even look like a lake...
SIR JOHN Look, your whole approach since this interview started has been to mock the Navy. When I think that it was for the likes of you that I had both my legs blown off...
INTERVIEWER *(pointing at perfectly healthy legs)* You haven't had both your legs blown off!
SIR JOHN I was talking metaphorically you fool. Jenkins—put that down. *(Jenkins returns the leg to the land-rover)* Right, is the equipment ready?
RATING (ERIC) Diving equipment all ready man. *(gives hippy salute)*
SIR JOHN *(warning finger)* Right. Now quite simply the approach to Lake Pahoe is up the steps, and then we come to the shores of the lake. Now, I'm going to press the bell just to see if there's anyone in.

MAN (MICHAEL) *(answering)* Hello?
SIR JOHN Good morning—I'm looking for a Lake Pahoe.
MAN There's a Mr Padgett.
SIR JOHN No, no a *lake*.
MAN There's no lake here, mate. This is Runcorn Avenue. What's the camera doing?
WOMAN (ERIC) *(coming out)* Camera? What's he want? Oooh, are we on the telly? *(grins at the camera)*
MAN He's looking for a lake.
SIR JOHN Lake Pahoe.
WOMAN Oh, you want downstairs, 22A the basement.
SIR JOHN Ah! Thank you very much. Good morning. Come on men, downstairs.

They walk down to the basement. The interviewer intercepts Sir John.

INTERVIEWER Were you successful, Sir John?
SIR JOHN It's in the basement.
INTERVIEWER In the basement?

He sees a parrot on his shoulder.

PARROT Pieces of eight. 33
INTERVIEWER Eugh! *(he knocks it off)*

Sir John goes to the front door of 22A and rings. Then he looks into the living room through the window. A middle-aged couple are sitting inside. The room is full of water. The man reads the paper and the woman knits. Both wear breathing apparatus. Sir John knocks on the window. The woman looks up.

"Pieces of eight," also known as "Spanish dollars"—a coin much loved by pirates everywhere.

SIR JOHN Hello.
WOMAN Ooooh. I think it's someone about the damp.
SIR JOHN Hello.
MAN Tell 'em about the bleeding rats, too.
WOMAN I'll go *(she swims to window and shouts out)* Yes?

SIR JOHN Good morning, is this Lake Pahoe?
WOMAN Well, I don't know about that, but it's bleeding damp. Are you from the council?
SIR JOHN No. We are the official British Naval Expedition to this lake. May we come in?
WOMAN Hang on.

She submerges and picks up a big sign showing it to the man. The sign reads 'It's not the council, it's a British Naval Expedition to Lake Pahoe or something and can they come in'. The man reads the card. An enormous shark looks over his shoulder appearing from a cupboard. The man sees it and hits it with a newspaper.

MAN Bloody sharks.
WOMAN Get in.

He holds up a sign reading 'Tell them to go away'. The woman swims to the window and gives a V-sign to Sir John. 34

The 'V-sign" is a gesture equivalent to "eff off."

SIR JOHN Well um...that would appear to be the end of the expedition.

Cut to an interview set.

INTERVIEWER (JOHN) The Magna Carta—was it a document signed at Runnymede in 1215 by King John pledging independence to the English barons, or was it a piece of chewing gum on a bedspread in Dorset? The latter idea is the brainchild of a man new to the field of historical research. Mr Badger, why—why are you on this programme?

Pull back to show Mr Badger. He wears a flat cap and has a Scots accent.

BADGER (ERIC) Well, I think I can answer this question most successfully in mime. *(mimes incomprehensibly)*
INTERVIEWER But why Dorset?

BADGER Well, I have for a long time been suffering from a species of brain injury which I incurred during the rigours of childbirth, and I'd like to conclude by putting my finger up my nose.
INTERVIEWER Mr Badger, I *think* you're the silliest person we've ever had on this programme, and so I'm going to ask you to have dinner with me.

Caption: 'LATER THE SAME SKETCH' Cut to them sitting at a restaurant table.

BADGER My wife Maureen ran off with a bottle of Bell's whisky during the Aberdeen versus Raith Rovers 35 match which ended in a goalless draw. Robson particularly, in goal, had a magnificent first half, his fine positional sense preventing the build-up of any severe pressure on the suspect Aberdeen defence. McLoughlan missed an easy chance to clinch the game towards the final whistle but Raith must be well satisfied with their point. 36

Aberdeen and Raith Rovers are two Scottish soccer teams.

Teams receive one point each for a tie in soccer.

INTERVIEWER

DO PLEASE GO ON. THIS IS THE LEAST FASCINATING CONVERSATION I'VE EVER HAD.

A waiter comes in.

WAITER (MICHAEL) Would you like to order sir?
INTERVIEWER Yes, Mr Badger, what would you like to start with?
BADGER Er, I'll have a whisky to start with.
WAITER For first course, sir?
BADGER Aye.
WAITER And for main course, sir?
BADGER I'll have a whisky for main course and I'll follow that with a whisky for pudding.
WAITER Yes sir, and what would you like with it, sir? A whisky?
BADGER No, a bottle of wine.
WAITER Fine, sir, he said between clenched teeth knowing full well it was a most unrewarding part.
INTERVIEWER This is the silliest sketch I've ever been in.
BADGER Shall we stop it?
INTERVIEWER Yeah, all right. *(they get up and walk out)*

Caption: 'THE END' credits

SEASON 3
EPISODE 33

MONTY PYTHON'S FLYING CIRCUS
SALAD DAYS
FEATURING
BIGGLES DICTATES A LETTER
CLIMBING THE NORTH FACE OF THE UXBRIDGE ROAD
LIFEBOAT ✻ OLD LADY SNOOPERS
'STORAGE JARS' ✻ THE SHOW SO FAR
Cheese Shop
PHILIP JENKINSON ON CHEESE WESTERNS
SAM PECKINPAH'S 'SALAD DAYS'
APOLOGY ✻ THE NEWS WITH RICHARD BAKER
SEASHORE INTERLUDE FILM
R.N.L.I.

FIRST AIRED: NOVEMBER 30, 1972

A light comes up on an organ in the centre of a concert-hall stage. Applause. The organist with wild hair (TERRY J) *appears from left. He walks fully clothed across to the organ looking pleased with himself. He sits at the organ and raises his hands...his clothes fly up into the air so that, as per normal, he is naked.*

He plays the usual chords. Cut on the last note to a naked quartet with identical grins, fright wigs and blacked-out teeth staring maniacally at the camera.

ANNOUNCER (JOHN) And now...

IT'S MAN (MICHAEL)

IT'S...

Animated titles.

VOICE OVER (JOHN) Monty Python's Flying Circus.

Cut to stock film of First World War fighter planes in a dog-fight. Heroic war music.

VOICE OVER (JOHN)

THE ADVENTURES OF BIGGLES. PART ONE—BIGGLES DICTATES A LETTER. 1

1 A regular reference point for the Pythons, the "Biggles" books were a mainstay of British boys' childhoods. Written by W.E. Johns and featuring a pilot, the books follow the travails of James Bigglesworth as he flies in World War I and after.

Mix through to Biggles and secretary in an office.

BIGGLES (GRAHAM) Miss Bladder, take a letter.

SECRETARY (NICKI HOWORTH) Yes, Señor Biggles.

BIGGLES Don't call me señor! **I'm not a Spanish person.** 2 You must call me Mr Biggles, or Group Captain Biggles, or Mary Biggles if I'm dressed as my wife, but never señor.

2 The film skips oddly here, with the line "I'm not a Spanish person" disappearing.

SECRETARY Sorry.
BIGGLES I've never even been to Spain.
SECRETARY You went to Ibiza last year.
BIGGLES That's still not grounds for calling me señor, or Don Beeg-les for that matter. Right, Dear **King Haakon...** **3**
SECRETARY Of Norway, is that?
BIGGLES Just put down what I say.
SECRETARY Do I put that down?
BIGGLES Of course you don't put that down.
SECRETARY Well what about that?
BIGGLES Look. *(she types)* Don't put that down. Just put down—wait a mo—wait a mo. *(puts on antlers)* Now, when I've got these antlers on—when I've got these antlers on I *am* dictating and when I take them off *(takes them off)* I am *not* dictating.
SECRETARY *(types)* I am not dictating.
BIGGLES What? *(she types; puts the antlers on)* Read that back.
SECRETARY Dear King Haakon, I am not dictating what?
BIGGLES No, no, no, you loopy brothel inmate.
SECRETARY I've had enough of this. I am not a courtesan. *(moves round to front of the desk, sits on it and crosses her legs provocatively)*
BIGGLES Oh, oh, 'courtesan', oh aren't we grand. Harlot's not good enough for us eh? Paramour, concubine, fille de joie. That's what we are not. Well listen to me my fine fellow, you are a bit of tail, that's what you are.
SECRETARY I am not, you demented fictional character.
BIGGLES **Algy says you are.** **4** He says you're no better than you should be.
SECRETARY And how would *he* know?
BIGGLES And just what do you mean by that? Are you calling my old fictional comrade-in-arms a fairy?
SECRETARY Fairy! Poof's not good enough for Algy, is it. He's got to be a bleedin' fairy. Mincing old RAF queen. *(sits at the desk)*
BIGGLES *(into the intercom)* Algy, I have to see you.
ALGY (MICHAEL) Right ho. *(he enters)* What ho everyone.
BIGGLES Are you gay?
ALGY I should bally well say so, old fruit.

BIGGLES Ugh! *(he shoots him)* Dear King Haakon...oh...*(takes the antlers off)* Dear King Haakon. *(the secretary types)* Just a line to thank you for the eels. Mary thought they were **really scrummy,** **5** comma, so did I full stop. I've just heard that Algy was a poof, exclamation mark. **What would Captain W. E. Johns have said, question mark.** **6** Sorry to **mench,** **7** but if you've finished with the lawn-edger could you pop it in the post. Love Biggles, Algy deceased and Ginger. Ginger! *(puts the antlers on)*
SECRETARY What?

King Haakon is name-checked at the end of Episode 30.

Algernon "Algy" Lacey is Biggles's cousin and sidekick.

"Scrummy" is British slang for "scrumptious."

Amusingly, W.E. Johns, the author of the Biggles books, once rejected T.E. Lawrence from the Royal Air Force—he'd used an assumed name, not "Lawrence of Arabia" presumably—though he later accepted him to the service.

"Mench" is British slang for "mention."

Cockney "rhyming slang" continues to this day. It is said to have originated in London's East End and uses replacement words that rhyme with the original.

The rhyming slang here is "queer" (ginger beer).

BIGGLES Rhyming slang—8 ginger beer. 9
SECRETARY Oh.
BIGGLES *(into the intercom)* Ginger.
GINGER Hello, sweetie.
BIGGLES I have to see you.

The door opens, Ginger enters as a terrible poof in camp flying gear, sequins, eye make-up, silver stars on his cheeks.

GINGER (TERRY G) Yes, Biggles?
BIGGLES Are you a poof?
GINGER *(camp outrage)* I should say not.
BIGGLES Thank God for that. Good lad. *(Ginger exits)* Stout fellow, salt of the earth, backbone of England. Funny, he looks like a poof. *(takes off the antlers)* Dear Princess Margaret.

Pantomime Princess Margaret enters from cupboard.

MARGARET Hello.
BIGGLES Get back in the cupboard you pantomimetic royal person. *(she goes)*

Quick cut to a loony.

LOONY (GRAHAM) Lemon curry?

Cut back to Biggles.

BIGGLES Dear real Princess Margaret, thank you for the eels, full stop. They were absolutely delicious and unmistakably regal, full stop. Sorry to mench but if you've finished with the hairdryer could you pop it in the post. Yours fictionally Biggles, **Oh, PS see you at the Saxe-Coburgs' canasta evening. 10** *(puts the antlers on)* That should puzzle her.
SECRETARY *(sexily)* Si Señor Biggles.
BIGGLES Silence, naughty lady of the night!

Bring up heroic music and mix through to stock film of fighter planes in dog-fight.

VOICE OVER (JOHN) Next week part two—**'Biggles Flies Undone'. 11**

Saxe-Coburgs is the name of the family whose territory was in southern Germany, specifically Bavaria. A play on the fact that the British royal family can be traced back to German royalty, in part.

"Biggles Flies Undone" is a joke on the problems of an unintentionally unzipped pair of pants.

Then a very noisy and violent animation sketch.

VOICE OVER Meanwhile not very far away.

Cut to mountain climbers, with all the accoutrements: ropes, carabino's helmets, pitons, hammers, etc. They are roped together, apparently climbing a mountain.

VOICE OVER (MICHAEL) Climbing. The world's loneliest sport, where hardship and philosophy go hand in glove. And here, another British expedition, attempting to be the first man to successfully climb the north face of the **Uxbridge Road.** 12 *(Pull out to reveal that they are climbing along a wide pavement; a shopper pushing a pram comes into shot)*

The Uxbridge Road is one of the major roads in West London, also known as the A4020.

THIS FOUR-MAN ROPE HAS BEEN CLIMBING TREMENDOUSLY. BBC CAMERAS WERE THERE TO FILM EVERY INCH.

Cut to a BBC cameraman clinging to a lamppost, filming. He is wearing climbing gear too. Cut to papier mâché model of the Uxbridge Road, with the route all neatly marked out in white, and various little pins for the camps.

CHRIS (ERIC) *(voice over)* The major assault on the Uxbridge Road has been going on for about three weeks, really ever since they established base camp here at the junction of Willesden Road, and from there they climbed steadily to establish camp two, **outside Lewis's,** 13 and it's taken them another three days to establish camp three, here outside the post office. *(cut to a pup tent*

Lewis's is a major department store in the U.K.

Hawley Harvey Crippen was an American homeopathic doctor who moved to the U.K. He later poisoned his wife, a woman whose birth name was Kunigunde Mackamotski (she went by both Corrine "Cora" Turner and Belle Elmore). Fleeing to Canada with his lover, Crippen was arrested on arrival by Chief Inspector Walter Dew from Scotland Yard, who had also taken a boat across the Atlantic. Crippen was subsequently tried back in the U.K. and put to death.

LEMON CURRY?

Cars continue to pass this hilarious interview.

Newhaven is a busy port town in East Sussex, on the south coast of England.

being firmly planted on the side of a large post-box; it has a little union jack on it) Well they've spent a good night in there last night in preparation for the final assault today. The leader of the expedition is twenty-nine-year-old Bert Tagg—a local headmaster and mother of three.

Cut to Bert crawling along the pavement. The interviewer is crouching down beside him.

INTERVIEWER (JOHN) Bert. How's it going?

BERT (GRAHAM) Well, it's a bit gripping is this, Chris. *(heavy breathing interspersed)* I've got to try and reach that bus stop in an hour or so and I'm doing it by...*(rearranging rope)* damn...I'm doing it, er, by laying back on this gutter so I'm kind of guttering and laying back at the same time, and philosophizing.

INTERVIEWER Bert, some people say this is crazy.

BERT **Aye, well but they said Crippen was crazy didn't they?** 14

INTERVIEWER Crippen *was* crazy.

BERT Oh, well there you are then. *(shouts)* John, I'm sending you down this carabine on white. *(there is a white rope between Bert and John)*

Quick cut to Viking.

VIKING (MICHAEL)

Cut back to the street.

BERT Now you see he's putting a peg down there because I'm quite a way up now, and if I come unstuck here I go down quite a long way.

INTERVIEWER *(leaving him)* Such quiet courage is typical of the way these brave chaps shrug off danger. **Like it or not, you've got to admire the skill that goes into it.** 15

By the miracle of stop action, they all fall off the road, back down the pavement. Passers-by, also in stop action, walk by normally, ignoring the fall. Cut to an ordinary kitchen. A Mrs Pinnet type lady with long apron and headscarf is stuffing a chicken with various unlikely objects. The door opens. Sound of rain, wind and storm outside. A lifeboatman enters, soaked to the skin. He shuts the door.

LIFEBOATMAN (MICHAEL) *(taking off his sou'wester and shaking the water off it)* Oh it's terrible up on deck.

MRS NEVES (TERRY J) Up on deck?

LIFEBOATMAN Yes on deck. It's diabolical weather.

MRS NEVES What deck, dear?

LIFEBOATMAN The deck. The deck of the lifeboat.

MRS NEVES This isn't a lifeboat, dear. This is 24, Parker Street.

LIFEBOATMAN **This is the Newhaven Lifeboat.** 16

MRS NEVES No it's not, dear.

The lifeboatman puts on his sou'wester, goes over to the back door and opens it. He peers out. Sound of wind and lashing rain. Cut to the back door at the side of a suburban house, the lifeboatman looking out over the lawns, flowers and windless, rain less calm across to similar neat suburban houses. The noise cuts. The lifeboatman withdraws his head from the door. Sound of wind and rain again which cease abruptly as he withdraws his head and shuts the door.

LIFEBOATMAN You're right. This isn't a lifeboat at all.

MRS NEVES No, I wouldn't live here if it was.

LIFEBOATMAN Do you mind if I sit down for a minute and collect my wits?

MRS NEVES No, you do that, **I'll make you a nice cup of tea.** 17
LIFEBOATMAN Thanks very much.

The door flies open. More sound of wind and rain. Two other rain-soaked lifeboatmen appear.

SECOND LIFEBOATMAN (GRAHAM) Oooh, it's a wild night up top.
THIRD LIFEBOATMAN (TERRY G) Your turn on deck soon, Charlie.
FIRST LIFEBOATMAN It's not a lifeboat, Frank.
THIRD LIFEBOATMAN What?
SECOND LIFEBOATMAN What do you mean?
FIRST LIFEBOATMAN

IT'S NOT A LIFEBOAT. IT'S THIS LADY'S HOUSE.

The two lifeboatmen look at each other, then turn and open the door. Sound of wind and rain as usual. They peer out. Cut to the back door—the two lifeboatmen are peering out. They shout.

SECOND AND THIRD LIFEBOATMEN Captain! Captain! Ahoy there! Ahoy there! Captain!!

Their voices carry over the following shot or two. Cut to reverse angle of window across the road. A net curtain moves and an eye peers out. We still hear the shouts. Close up on an elderly spinster (Gladys) holding the net curtain discreetly ajar.

ENID (ERIC) Who's that shouting?

We pull out to reveal a sitting room full of high-powered eavesdropping equipment, i.e. an enormous telescope on wheels with a controller's chair attached to it, several subsidiary telescopes pointing out of the window, radar scanners going round and round, two computers with flashing lights, large and complex tape and video recorders, several TV monitors, oscilloscopes, aerials, etc. All these have been squeezed in amongst the furniture of two retired middle-class old ladies. Enid, a dear old lady with a bun, sits at the control seat of an impressive-looking console, pressing buttons. She also has some knitting.

GLADYS (JOHN) It's a man outside Number 24.
ENID Try it on the five-inch, Gladys.
GLADYS *(looking at the array of telescopes)* **I can't. I've got that fixed on the Baileys at Number 13. Their new lodger moves in today.** 18
ENID All right, hold 13 on the five-inch and transfer the Cartwrights to the digital scanner.

Gladys leaps over to the tape deck, presses levers and switches. Sound of tape reversing. There is a hum and lights flash on and off. A blurred image of a lady in the street comes up on one of the monitors.

"A nice cup of tea" is the British answer to every tragedy, disaster, misfortune, or 11 a.m.

A lovely gag about the legendary nosiness of British neighbors.

ENID Hold on, Mrs Pettigrew's coming back from the doctor's.
GLADYS All right, bring her up on two. What's the duration reading on the oscillator?
ENID 48.47.
GLADYS Well that's a long time for someone who's just had a routine checkup.
ENID *(reading a graph on a computer)* Yes, her pulse rate's 146!
GLADYS Zoom in on the 16mm and hold her, Enid.
ENID Roger, Gladys.
GLADYS I'll try and get her on the twelve-inch. *(she climbs into the control seat of the huge mobile telescope; we cut to the view through Gladys's telescope—out of focus at first, but then sharper as she zooms in towards the side door of Number 24)* Move the curtain, Enid. *(the curtain is opened a little)* Thank you, love.

Cut to the interior of Mrs Neves's kitchen once again. It is absolutely full of lifeboatmen. They are all talking happily and drinking cups of tea. We pick up the conversation between two of them.

FIRST LIFEBOATMAN Yes, it's one of those new self-righting models. Newhaven was about the first place in the country to get one.
SECOND LIFEBOATMAN What's the displacement on one of them jobs then?
FIRST LIFEBOATMAN Oh it's about 140-150 per square inch.
MRS NEVES Who's for fruit cake?
ALL Oh yes, please, please.
MRS NEVES Yes, right, macaroons, that's two dozen fruit cakes, half a dozen macaroons. Right ho. Won't be a jiffy then.

She puts a scarf on, picks up a basket and goes out of the front door. As she opens door, we hear the sound of a storm which carries us into the next shot. Cut to the deck of a lifeboat; rain-lashed, heaving, wind-tossed. ***Mrs Neves struggles against the gale force winds along the deck.*** **19** *She hammers on a hatch in the forward part of the lifeboat.*

Jones, Chapman, and Cleese here on an extremely rough sea; Palin will join them.

MRS NEVES Yoohoo! Mrs Edwards!

The hatch opens and a cosy shop-keeping pepperpot sticks her head out.

MRS EDWARDS (GRAHAM) Hello.
MRS NEVES Hello, two dozen fruit cakes and half a dozen macaroons.
MRS EDWARDS Sorry love, no macaroons. How about a nice vanilla sponge.
MRS NEVES Yes, that'll be lovely.
MRS EDWARDS Right ho. *(sound of a ship's horn; they both look)* There's that nice herring trawler come for their Kup Kakes. Excuse me. *(she produces a loudhailer)* Hello, Captain Smith?
VOICE Hallooooo!

Mrs Edwards hurls a box of Kup Kakes off deck.

MRS EDWARDS Kup Kakes to starboard.
VOICE Coming.
MRS NEVES I'll pay you at the end of the week, all right?
MRS EDWARDS OK, right ho.

Mrs Neves struggles back along the deck. ***Cut to stock film of* Ark Royal *in a storm.*** **20**

MRS NEVES Here, it's the *Ark Royal,* Doris. Have you got their rock buns ready?

Sound of a ship's horn.

MRS EDWARDS Hang on!

Doris appears at the hatch, and hands over two cake boxes.

DORIS (JOHN) Here we are, five for them and five for HMS *Eagle.*
MRS EDWARDS Right ho. *(takes them and throws them both overboard; an officer climbs up the side of the boat)* Yes?
OFFICER (MICHAEL) **HMS Defiant? Two set teas please.** **21**
MRS EDWARDS Two set teas, Doris. Forty-eight pence. There we are, thank you.

Money is handed over. The teas emerge on two little trays with delicate crockery, little teapots, milk jugs, etc.

OFFICER By the way, do you do lunches?
MRS EDWARDS No, morning coffee and teas only.
OFFICER Right ho.

[HOLDING THE TEAS HE GOES UP TO EDGE AND JUMPS OVERBOARD]

Cut to very quick series of stills of storage jars. Caption: 'STORAGE JARS' Urgent documentary music. Mix through to an impressive documentary set. Zoom in fast to presenter in a swivel chair. He swings round to face the camera.

PRESENTER (ERIC) Good evening and welcome to another edition of 'Storage Jars'. On tonight's programme Mikos Antoniarkis, the Greek rebel leader who seized power in Athens this morning, tells us what he keeps in storage jars. *(quick cut to photo of a guerrilla leader with a gun; sudden dramatic chord; instantly cut back to the presenter)* From strife-torn Bolivia, Ronald Rodgers reports on storage jars there. *(still of a Bolivian city and again dramatic chord and instantly back to the presenter)* And closer to home, the first dramatic pictures of the mass jail-break near the storage jar factory in Maidenhead. All this and more in storage jars!

The HMS *Ark Royal* is a legendary British Navy aircraft carrier.

A pot of tea, a milk jug, sugar bowl, cakes—the very pinnacle of British culture.

22

Che Guevara arrived in Bolivia in late 1966 hoping to foment revolution there. His guerillas engaged the Bolivian army in 1967. Guevara was eventually killed by the CIA, together with members of the Bolivian army, in October of that year.

Cut to a road in front of a heap of smouldering rubble. Dull thuds of mortar. Reporter in short sleeves standing in tight shot. Explosions going off behind him at intervals.

RODGERS (TERRY J) This is La Paz, Bolivia, behind me you can hear the thud of mortar and the high-pitched whine of rockets, as the battle for control of this volatile republic shakes the foundations of this old city. *(slowly we pull out during this until we see in front of him a fairly long trestle table set out with range of different-sized storage jars)* But whatever their political inclinations these Bolivians are all keen users of storage jars. *(the explosions continue behind him)* Here the largest size is used for rice and for mangoes—a big local crop. Unlike most revolutionary South American states they've an intermediary size in between the 2lb and 5lb jars. This gives this poor but proud people a useful jar for apricots, plums and stock cubes. The smallest jar—this little 2oz jar, for sweets, chocolates and even little shallots. **No longer used in the West it remains here as an unspoken monument to the days when La Paz knew better times. Ronald Rodgers, 'Storage Jars', La Paz.** 22

Animation: television is bad for your eyes.

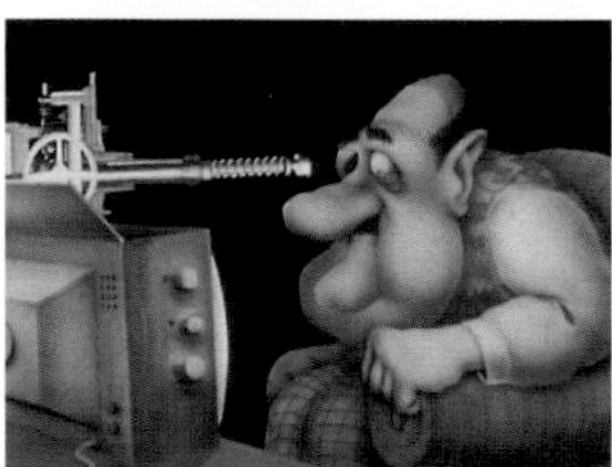

VOICE OVER *(and caption)* 'The show so far'

Cut to a man sitting at a desk with a script.

MR TUSSAUD (TERRY J) Hello, the, er, show so far...well it all started with the organist losing his clothes as he sat down at the organ, and after this had happened and we had seen the titles of the show, we saw Biggles dictating a letter to his secretary, who thought he was Spanish, and whom he referred to as a harlot and a woman of the night, although she preferred to be called a courtesan. Then we saw some people trying to climb a road in Uxbridge. And then there were some cartoons and then some lifeboatmen came into a woman's sitting room and after a bit the woman went out to buy some cakes on a lifeboat and then a naval officer jumped into the sea. Then we saw a man telling us about storage jars from Bolivia, then there were some more cartoons and then a man told us about what happened on the show so far and a great hammer came and hit him on the head. *(he frowns)* I don't remember that? *(a big hammer hits him on the head)*

Quick cut to 'It's' man.

IT'S MAN Lemon curry?

A montage of arty photographs. The cutting from photo to photo is pretty fast. Greek music is heard. Starting with: a close up of Mousebender, who is respectable and wears smart casual clothes; various photos of Mousebender walking along the pavement, again very artily shot from show-off angles; Mousebender pausing outside a shop; Mousebender looking up at the shop; Edwardian-style shop with large sign above it reading 'Ye Olde Cheese Emporium'; another sign below the first reading 'Henry Wensleydale, Purveyor of Fine Cheese to the Gentry and the Poverty

Stricken Too'; another sign below this reading 'Licensed for Public Dancing'; close up of Mousebender looking pleased; shot of Mousebender entering the shop. Music cuts dead. Cut to interior of the cheese shop. Greek music playing as Mousebender enters. Two men dressed as city gents are Greek dancing in the corner to the music of a bouzouki.

The shop itself is large and redolent of the charm and languidity of a bygone age. There is actually no cheese to be seen either on or behind the counter but this is not obvious. Mousebender approaches the counter and rings a small handbell. ***Wensleydale appears.*** **23**

WENSLEYDALE (MICHAEL) Good morning, sir.

MOUSEBENDER (JOHN) Good morning. I was sitting in the public library in Thurmond Street just now, **skimming through 'Rogue Herries' by Horace Walpole** **24** when suddenly I came over all peckish.

WENSLEYDALE Peckish, sir?

MOUSEBENDER **Esurient...** **25**

WENSLEYDALE Eh?

MOUSEBENDER *(broad Yorkshire)* Eee I were all hungry, like.

WENSLEYDALE Oh, hungry.

MOUSEBENDER *(normal accent)* In a nutshell. So I thought to myself 'a little fermented curd will do the trick'. So I curtailed my Walpolling activities, sallied forth and infiltrated your place of purveyance to negotiate the vending of some cheesy comestibles. *(smacks his lips)*

WENSLEYDALE Come again.

MOUSEBENDER *(broad Northern accent)* I want to buy some cheese.

WENSLEYDALE Oh, I thought you were complaining about the music.

MOUSEBENDER *(normal voice)* Heaven forbid. I am one who delights in all manifestations of the **terpsichorean muse.** **26**

WENSLEYDALE Sorry?

MOUSEBENDER I like a nice dance—you're forced to.

Quick cut to Viking.

VIKING (MICHAEL) *(broad Northern accent)* Anyway.

Cut back to the shop. **27**

WENSLEYDALE Who said that?

MOUSEBENDER *(normal voice)*

NOW MY GOOD MAN, SOME CH   , PL A .

Wensleydale, a valley in North Yorkshire, is also the name of a cheese—a crumbly one—made in the town of Hawes.

Sir Hugh Seymour Walpole, the English novelist. His *Rogue Herries*, published in 1930, is a historical romance set in eighteenth-century Cumberland, in the northwest of England.

"Esurient" means extremely hungry.

"Terpsichorean" means related to dancing.

Jones and Palin referred to some of Chapman and Cleese's sketches as 'thesaurus' comedy. This sketch is a good example of it—the comedy comes from including such a wide array of cheese types, none of which are present in the store; the listing of all the names is what's funny, rather than the 'mere' fact that a cheese shop has no cheese.

Once tinted with carrot juice or beets, Red Leicester, a crumbly cheddar, is now colored red with annatto, which comes from the seeds of the tropical achiote tree.

Tilsit is a semi-hard cheese named after a town in east Prussia.

Caerphilly is a mild cheese from Wales and the southwest of England (though never in the town of Caerphilly—it was merely sold there, at a Caerphilly market).

A semi-soft Italian cheese, originally from a small village near Milan.

Red Windsor is an English cheddar marbled with red wine.

The pungent British cheese veined with a blue mold, crumbly, and absolutely delicious.

WENSLEYDALE Yes certainly, sir. What would you like?

MOUSEBENDER Well, how about a little **Red Leicester?** 28

WENSLEYDALE I'm afraid we're fresh out of Red Leicester, sir.

MOUSEBENDER Oh never mind. How are you on **Tilsit?** 29

WENSLEYDALE Never at the end of the week, sir. Always get it fresh first thing on Monday.

MOUSEBENDER Tish, tish. No matter. Well, four ounces of **Caerphilly,** 30 then, if you please, stout yeoman.

WENSLEYDALE Ah, well, it's been on order for two weeks, sir, I was expecting it this morning.

MOUSEBENDER Yes, it's not my day is it. Er, **Bel Paese?** 31

WENSLEYDALE Sorry.

MOUSEBENDER **Red Windsor?** 32

WENSLEYDALE Normally sir, yes, but today the van broke down.

MOUSEBENDER Ah. **Stilton?** 33

WENSLEYDALE Sorry.

CENSORING THE PYTHONS

Sadly, there's a *Monty Python* sketch out there we've never seen, and never will see. And that's thanks to John Cleese.

In a sketch written by Eric Idle, a wine enthusiast is being treated to a tasting in a wine cellar. But eventually we're informed that the vintages are not wine but what the Pythons refer to as "wee-wee." Idle always claimed the sketch was not about urine, but about the snobbery of the wine world. This, however, was not enough to prevent John Cleese from allegedly quietly alerting the BBC to the sketch; the BBC, in turn, ordered it excised from Episode 36.

Cleese's "collaboration" with the forces of censorship rankled the other Pythons (in any case, Cleese would be gone at the end of that series), but Cleese was adamant: he felt the sketch was too crass. Graham Chapman would later joke that it was written with the express idea of upsetting the scatalogically averse Cleese.

Cleese's point was that the BBC had a reasonable need to keep its output to a particular standard. The first two seasons of *Monty Python's Flying Circus* went somewhat under the radar, given the show didn't even air in certain markets. But by the third season, which ran from October 19, 1972, to January 18, 1973, the BBC was beginning to get concerned about what the troupe was up to and kept a closer eye on them.

So the "wee-wee" sketch was cut. But even more notorious was the reference to masturbation in the "All-England Summarize Proust Competition" sketch, which ran on November 16, 1972 (see page 580). Written by Michael Palin and Terry Jones, the line "golf, strangling animals, and masturbation" has the last word hastily cut from the audio (the laughter of the audience seems over the top for a reference to "strangling animals"). And so it was: the folks who'd gotten tickets were allowed to hear a reference to what Palin describes as something you just "got on with"; but the wider public was shielded (thank God!) from any reference to the joys of self-abuse. By this point in Python history, bigwigs from the BBC were in attendance at tapings, and yet they still changed relatively little (a piece of art by Gilliam that featured Jesus was deemed offensive, for example, and was excised), especially given that it was the early 1970s and the Pythons were as out there as anyone on TV. In the end, we're lucky that the BBC gave the troupe as much latitude as it did, and that *Monty Python's Flying Circus* was as close to uncensored as was probably possible at the time.

Pity about the wee-wee, though.

GRUYÈRE, EM
ANY NORWEGIAN JARLSBER
NO. LANCASH
STILTON? 38 NO.
DOUBLE GLOUCESTER? 40
NO. ANY DORSET BL
ROCQUEFOR
PORT SALUT, SA
SAINT-PAUL
BOURSIN,
PERLE DE CHAMPAGNE

34 Swiss specialties. **35** Typically called Jarlsberg, it's a cheese filled with holes. **36** A spicy cheese spread from Centr like cheese made in Denmark. **40** A strong cheese, sold in a round shape, and made in the county of... you guessed it. **41** S of England. **43** French cheeses all.

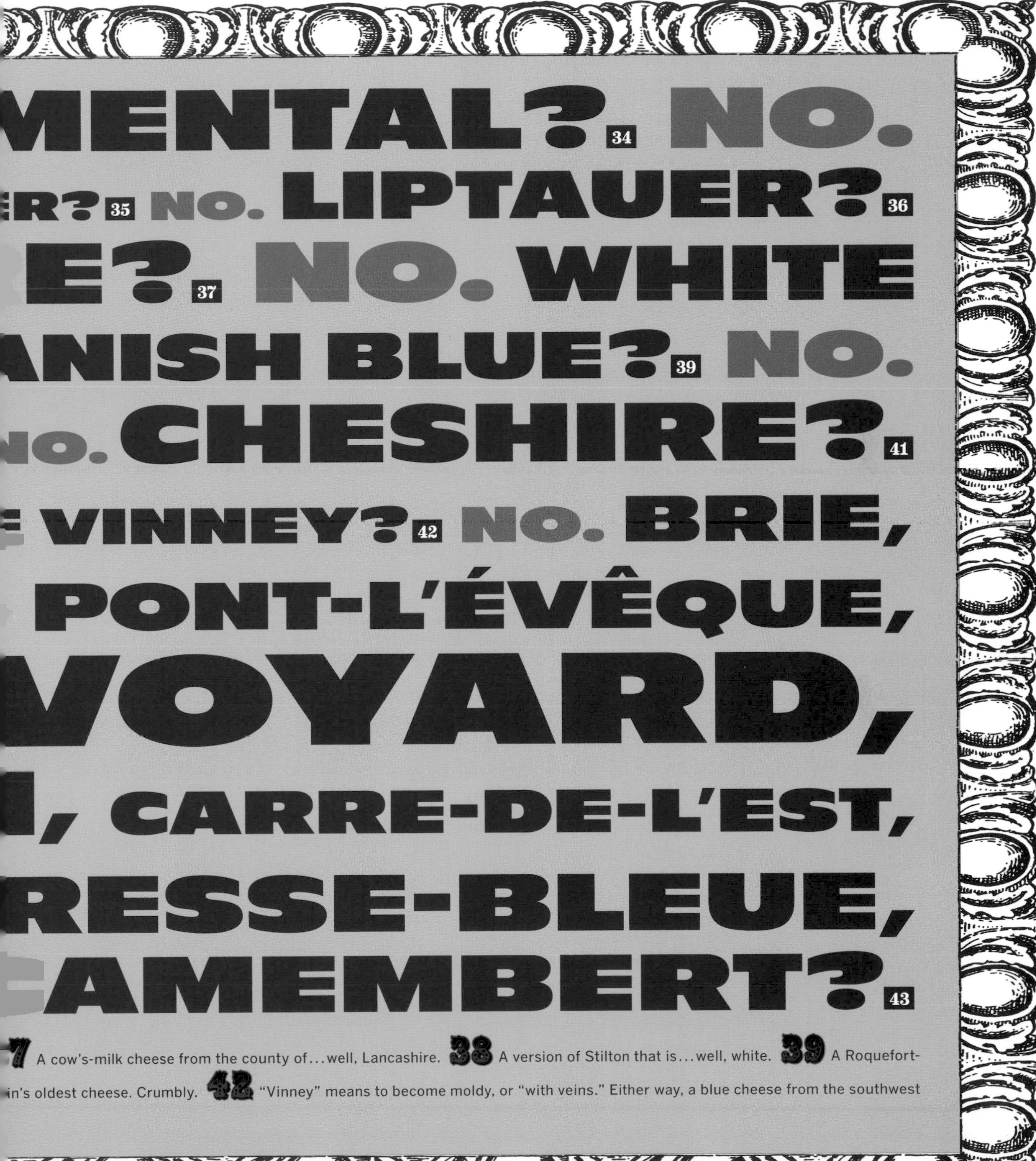

MENTAL?. 34 NO.
ER? 35 NO. LIPTAUER? 36
E?. 37 NO. WHITE
ANISH BLUE?. 39 NO.
NO. CHESHIRE?. 41
VINNEY? 42 NO. BRIE,
PONT-L'ÉVÊQUE,
VOYARD,
, CARRE-DE-L'EST,
RESSE-BLEUE,
AMEMBERT?. 43
7 A cow's-milk cheese from the county of...well, Lancashire. 38 A version of Stilton that is...well, white. 39 A Roquefort-
in's oldest cheese. Crumbly. 42 "Vinney" means to become moldy, or "with veins." Either way, a blue cheese from the southwest

WENSLEYDALE

AH. WE DO HAVE SOME CAMEMBERT, SIR.

MOUSEBENDER You do. Excellent.
WENSLEYDALE It's a bit runny, sir.
MOUSEBENDER Oh, I like it runny.
WENSLEYDALE Well as a matter of fact it's *very* runny, sir.
MOUSEBENDER No matter. No matter. Hand over le fromage de la Belle France qui s'appelle Camembert, s'il vous plait.
WENSLEYDALE I think it's runnier than you like it, sir.
MOUSEBENDER *(smiling grimly)* I don't care how excrementally runny it is. Hand it over with all speed.
WENSLEYDALE Yes, sir. *(bends below the counter and reappears)* Oh...
MOUSEBENDER What?
WENSLEYDALE The cat's eaten it.
MOUSEBENDER Has he?
WENSLEYDALE She, sir.
MOUSEBENDER **Gouda?** 44
WENSLEYDALE No.
MOUSEBENDER Edam?
WENSLEYDALE No.
MOUSEBENDER **Caithness?** 45
WENSLEYDALE No.
MOUSEBENDER **Smoked Austrian?** 46
WENSLEYDALE No.
MOUSEBENDER **Sage Derby?** 47
WENSLEYDALE No, sir.
MOUSEBENDER You do have some cheese, do you?
WENSLEYDALE Certainly, sir. It's a cheese shop, sir. We've got...
MOUSEBENDER No, no, no, don't tell me. I'm keen to guess.
WENSLEYDALE Fair enough.
MOUSEBENDER Wensleydale?
WENSLEYDALE Yes, sir?
MOUSEBENDER Splendid. Well, I'll have some of that then, please.
WENSLEYDALE Oh, I'm sorry sir, I thought you were referring to me, Mr Wensleydale.
MOUSEBENDER Gorgonzola?
WENSLEYDALE No.
MOUSEBENDER Parmesan?
WENSLEYDALE No.
MOUSEBENDER Mozzarella?
WENSLEYDALE No.
MOUSEBENDER **Pippo Crème?** 48
WENSLEYDALE No.
MOUSEBENDER Any **Danish Fimboe?** 49
WENSLEYDALE No.
MOUSEBENDER Czechoslovakian Sheep's Milk Cheese?
WENSLEYDALE No.
MOUSEBENDER **Venezuelan Beaver Cheese?** 50
WENSLEYDALE Not today sir, no.
MOUSEBENDER Well let's keep it simple, how about Cheddar?
WENSLEYDALE Well I'm afraid we don't get much call for it around these parts.
MOUSEBENDER No call for it? It's the single most popular cheese in the world!
WENSLEYDALE Not round these parts, sir.

A Dutch cheese, as is Edam (the only cheese that is "made" backward).

A Scottish cheese.

Not a Scottish cheese.

Mottled green owing to the inclusion of sage.

A fake cheese, likely delicious.

Also fake, and also likely delicious.

50

If only.

MOUSEBENDER And pray what is the most popular cheese round these parts?
WENSLEYDALE **Ilchester, sir.** 51
MOUSEBENDER I see.
WENSLEYDALE Yes, sir. It's quite staggeringly popular in the manor, squire.
MOUSEBENDER Is it?
WENSLEYDALE Yes sir, it's our number-one seller.
MOUSEBENDER Is it?
WENSLEYDALE Yes, sir.
MOUSEBENDER Ilchester eh?
WENSLEYDALE Right.
MOUSEBENDER OK, I'm game. Have you got any, he asked expecting the answer no?
WENSLEYDALE I'll have a look sir...nnnnnnoooooooo.
MOUSEBENDER It's not much of a cheese shop really, is it?
WENSLEYDALE Finest in the district, sir.
MOUSEBENDER And what leads you to that conclusion?
WENSLEYDALE Well, it's so clean.
MOUSEBENDER Well, it's certainly uncontaminated by cheese.
WENSLEYDALE You haven't asked me about **Limberger, sir.** 52
MOUSEBENDER Is it worth it?
WENSLEYDALE Could be.
MOUSEBENDER OK, have you...*will you shut that bloody dancing up! (the music stops)*
WENSLEYDALE *(to dancers)* Told you so.
MOUSEBENDER Have you got any Limberger?
WENSLEYDALE No.
MOUSEBENDER No, that figures. It was pretty predictable really. It was an act of pure optimism to pose the question in the first place. Tell me something, do you have any cheese at all?
WENSLEYDALE Yes, sir.
MOUSEBENDER Now I'm going to ask you that question once more, and if you say 'no' I'm going to shoot you through the head. Now, do you have any cheese at all?
WENSLEYDALE No.
MOUSEBENDER *(shoots him)* What a senseless waste of human life.

Not a real cheese, but a company that blends together other cheeses.

A stinky cheese from northern Europe.

Philip Jenkinson, the British film expert and TV presenter.

Mousebender puts a cowboy hat on his head. Cut to stock shot of man on horse riding into the sunset. Music swells dramatically. Caption: 'ROGUE CHEDDAR (1967)' Caption: 'FIN' Ordinary simple Philip Jenkinson at a desk set as seen in Monty Python's Flying Circus. ***Philip Jenkinson*** **53** *sits simpering and pouting like a cross between Truman Capote and a pederast vole.*

PHILIP JENKINSON (ERIC) Horace Walpole's 'Rogue Cheddar', *(sniff)* one of the first of the Cheese Westerns to be later followed by 'Gunfight at Gruyère Corral', 'Ilchester 73', and 'The Cheese Who Shot Liberty Valence'. While I'm on the subject of Westerns, I want to take a closer look at one of my favourite film directors, Sam Peckinpah, the expatriate from Fresno, California.

Superimposed caption: 'GET ON WITH IT'

PHILIP JENKINSON In his earliest films, 'Major Dundee', *(sniff)*

Superimposed caption: 'AND STOP SNIFFING'

PHILIP JENKINSON 'The Wild Bunch' and 'Straw Dogs' he showed his predilection for the utterly truthful and very sexually arousing portrayal of violence *(sniff)* in its starkest form. *(sniff)*

Superimposed caption: 'WILL YOU STOP SNIFFING'

Salad Days is a sweet and innocent musical from 1954.

PHILIP JENKINSON In his latest film Peckinpah has moved into the calmer and more lyrical waters of **Julian Slade's 'Salad Days'. 54**

Lyrical scene of boys in white flannels and girls in pretty dresses frolicking on a lawn to the accompaniment of a piano played by one of the boys. Superimposed caption: 'SALAD DAYS (1971) DIRECTOR SAM PECKINPAH' The boys and girls cease frolicking and singing. Lionel enters holding a tennis racket.

LIONEL (MICHAEL) Hello everybody.
ALL Hello, Lionel.
LIONEL I say what a simply super day.
ALL Gosh yes.
WOMAN It's so, you know, sunny.
LIONEL Yes isn't it? I say anyone for tennis?
JULIAN (GRAHAM) Oh super!
CHARLES (ERIC) What fun.
JULIAN I say, Lionel, catch.

He throws the tennis ball to Lionel. It hits Lionel on the head. Lionel claps one hand to his forehead. He roars in pain as blood seeps through his fingers.

LIONEL Oh gosh.

He tosses his racket out of frame and we hear a hideous scream. The camera pans to pick up a pretty girl in summer frock with the handle of the racket embedded in her stomach. Blood is pouring out down her dress.

GIRL Oh crikey.

Spitting blood out of her mouth she collapses onto the floor clutching at Charles's arm. The arm comes off. Buckets of blood burst out of the shoulder drenching the girl and anyone else in the area. He staggers backwards against the piano. The piano lid drops, severing the pianist's hands. The pianist screams. He stands, blood spurting from his hands over piano music. ***The piano collapses in slow motion, shot from several angles simultaneously as per 'Zabriskie Point'.*** **55** *Intercut terrified faces of girls screaming in slow motion. The piano eventually crushes them to death; an enormous pool of blood immediately swells up from beneath piano where the girls are. We see Julian stagger across the frame with the piano keyboard through his stomach. As he turns the end of the keyboard knocks off the head of a terrified girl who is sitting on the grass nearby. A volcanic quantity of blood geysers upwards. Pull out and upward from this scene as the music starts again.*

Zabriskie Point is the 1970 movie by Antonioni, once described by *Rolling Stone*'s David Fricke as "one of the most extraordinary disasters in modern cinematic history."

Cut back to Philip Jenkinson.

PHILIP JENKINSON Pretty strong meat there from *(sniff)* Sam Peckinpah.

There is the sound of a burst of machine-gun fire and holes appear in Philip Jenkinson's shirt. Blood spurting from each hole in slow motion. Intercut shots from different angles.

Caption: 'TEE HEE' Roll credits over Jenkinson's dying agonies. Fade out.

VOICE OVER (JOHN) *(and roller caption)* 'The BBC would like to apologize to everyone in the world for the last item. It was disgusting and bad and thoroughly disobedient and please don't bother to phone up because we know it was very tasteless, but they didn't really mean it and they do all come from broken homes and have very unhappy personal lives, especially Eric. Anyway, they're really very nice people underneath and very warm in the traditional show business way and please don't write in either because the BBC is going through an unhappy phase at the moment—what with its father dying and the mortgage and BBC 2 going out with men.'

VOICE OVER (ERIC) *(and roller caption)* 'the bbc would like to deny the last apology. It is very happy at home and BBC 2 is bound to go through this phase, so from all of us here good night, sleep well, and have an absolutely super day tomorrow, kiss, kiss.'

Cut to Richard Baker sitting at the traditional news desk. **56**

RICHARD BAKER We've just heard that an explosion in the kitchens of the House of Lords has resulted in the breakage of seventeen storage jars. Police ruled out foul play. *(pause)*

LEMON CURRY?

Fade out. Fade up on film of seashore, waves breaking on beach. Superimposed caption: 'INTERLUDE' The film goes on for quite a long time. Eventually the announcer, dressed in medieval Spanish soldier's costume, walks into shot.

ANNOUNCER (JOHN) *(to camera)* Um, I'm sorry about the...the, er, pause, only I'm afraid the show is a couple of minutes short this week. You know, sometimes the shows aren't really quite as er, long as they ought to be. *(pause; he looks round at the sea)* Beautiful, isn't it. *(he walks out of shot; long pause; he walks back)*

Look there's not really a great deal of point in your, sort of hanging on at your end, because I'm afraid there aren't any more jokes or anything.

He walks out of shot. We stay with the film for quite a long time before we finally fade out.

Richard Baker, the erstwhile BBC news announcer.

SEA SON 3
EPISODE 34

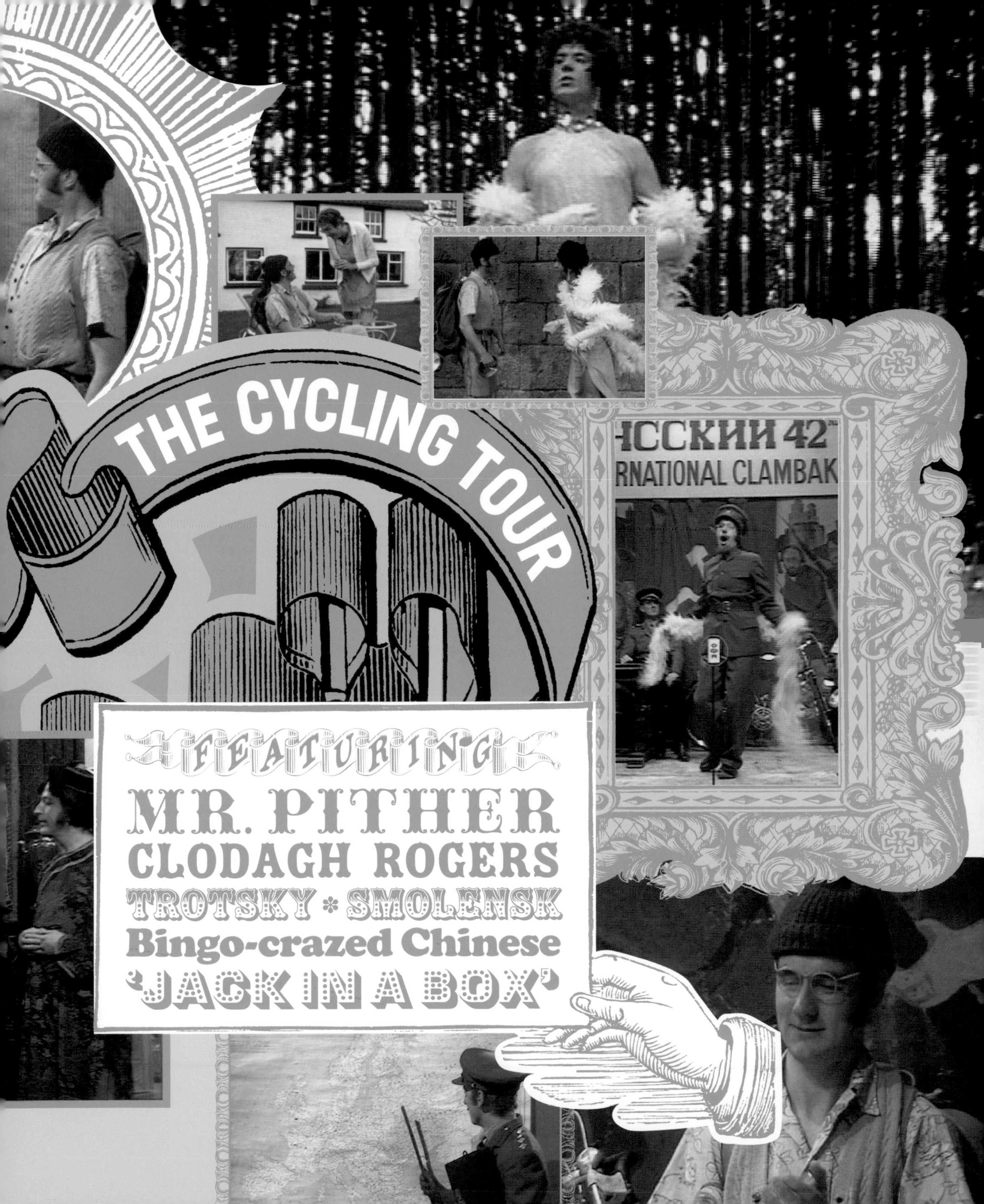
THE CYCLING TOUR
FEATURING
MR. PITHER
CLODAGH ROGERS
TROTSKY * SMOLENSK
Bingo-crazed Chinese
'JACK IN A BOX'
HCCKИИ 42
RNATIONAL CLAMBAK

FIRST AIRED: DECEMBER 7, 1972

The green, lush Devon countryside. Theme music. The camera is tracking along a hedgerow beside a road. We see a head whizzing along, sometimes just above the hedgerow and sometimes bobbing down out of sight, occasionally for long periods.

Superimposed caption: 'THE CYCLING TOUR' 1 *Mr Pither, the cyclist, bobs up and down a few more times, then disappears from sight. There is a crash and clang of a bicycle in collision, mixed with the scream of a frightened hen, and stifled shout of alarm. We are still in long shot and see nothing. The music stops abruptly on the crash.*

PITHER (MICHAEL) *(voice over)* August 18th. Fell off near Bovey Tracey. 2 The pump caught in my trouser leg.

Cut to interior of a transport café. A rather surly proprietor with fag in mouth is operating an espresso coffee machine. Pither, a fussy, bespectacled little man, is leaning over the counter talking chattily.

PITHER My pump caught in my trouser leg, and my sandwiches were badly crushed.
PROPRIETOR (ERIC) 35p please.

He goes back to working the machine.

PITHER These sandwiches, however, were an excellent substitute.

An enormous lorry driver comes up to the counter.

DRIVER (JOHN) Give us ten woods, Barney. 3

This full-episode sketch was originally written by Palin and Jones for a project outside of *Monty Python's Flying Circus*. Since this was the third series and the Pythons were struggling for new material for the show, they decided to use this sketch as one complete episode.

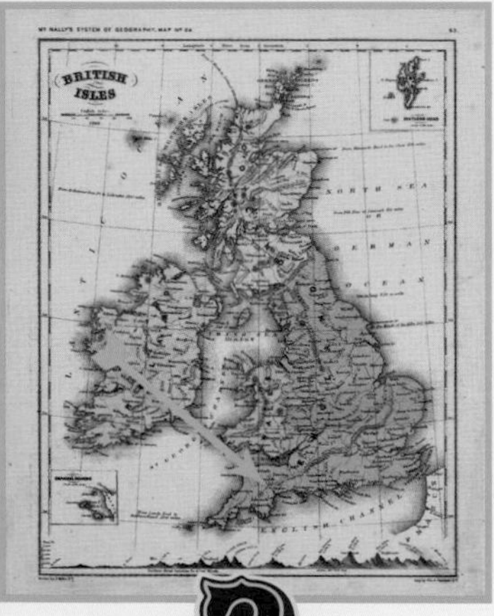

Bovey Tracey is a small town in Devon, a county in southwest England, on the edge of a wilderness area called Dartmoor. It is also sometimes used to suggest something is not quite right, as in "I ate something that didn't agree with me, and now I feel a bit Bovey Tracey.'

"Woods" is short for Woodbines, a type of cigarette.

PITHER Hello! *(the lorry driver looks at him without interest)* It's funny, isn't it, how one can go through life, as I have, disliking bananas and being indifferent to cheese, but still be able to eat, and enjoy, a banana and cheese sandwich like this. *(the driver goes off with his cigarettes)*

PROPRIETOR 35p please.

PITHER Ah! Oh, I have only a fifty. Do you have change?

PROPRIETOR *(with heavy sarcasm)* Well I'll have to look, but I may have to go to the bank.

PITHER I'm most awfully sorry.

PROPRIETOR *(handing him change)* 15p.

PITHER Oh, what a stroke of luck. Well, all the very best. *(Pither proffers his hand, the proprietor ignores it)* And thank you again for the excellent banana and cheese delicacy.

He exits busily. The proprietor looks after him. Cut to hedgerows. Theme music. Pither's head bobbing up and down. At the same point in the music it disappears and there is a crash mingled with the grunting of a pig.

PITHER *(voice over)* August 23rd. Fell off near Budleigh Salterton. 4

A brief shot of an unidentifiable animated Gilliam monster looking over the top of a hedge. Cut to a woman gardening. Behind her we see Pither's head peering over the hedge.

PITHER ...and the pump got caught in my trouser leg...*(she carries on digging trying to ignore him)* and that's how they were damaged *(no reaction)*...the eggs...you remember...the hard-boiled eggs I was telling you about...they were in a tupperware container, reputedly self-sealing, which fell open upon contact with a tarmacadam surface of the road...*(she goes on digging)* the B409... 5 the Dawlish Road... 6 *(again no reaction)* That shouldn't happen to a self-sealing container, now should it? What do you keep your hard-boiled eggs in?

The lady gardener goes back into house. Pither waits for a few moments.

PITHER *(shouting)* I think in future I will lash them to the handlebars with adhesive tape...this should obviate a recurrence of the same problem...well I can't stand around here chatting all day...I'm on a cycling tour of North Cornwall. 7 Must be off.

Cut to hedgerows again. Pither's head bowling along. Theme music. He dips out of sight. Crash and a cow moos.

PITHER *(voice over)* August 26th. Fell off near Ottery St Mary. 8 The pump caught in my trouser leg. Decided to wear short trousers from now on.

Another brief shot of the animated monster peeking over a hedgerow. Cut to another hedgerow. Pither's head bowling along. Short burst of theme music. Crash.

Budleigh Salterton is a small town 25 miles east of Bovey Tracey, on the scenic Devon coast.

Actually, the B409 is a road in West London, though Palin seems to say "B489," which is a small road near Luton, northwest of London.

Dawlish is a small holiday town on Britain's south coast, between Bovey Tracey and Budleigh Salterton. The main road in and out is the A379.

Most of the towns he mentions are in Devon, not North Cornwall.

Ottery St Mary is a town 10 miles north of Budleigh Salterton.

Tiverton is another Devon town, north of Budleigh Salterton by a cool 33 miles.

Iddesleigh is nearly 50 miles northwest of Budleigh Salterton!

PITHER Fell off near Tiverton. 9 Perhaps a shorter pump is the answer.

Another monster peeps briefly. Cut to a tiny village high street, deserted save for an old lady. Pither cycles into shot, he is in shorts, but still has bicycle clips on. He approaches the old lady.

PITHER Excuse me, madam, I wonder if you could tell me of a good bicycle shop in this village where I could either find a means of adapting my present pump, or failing that, of purchasing a replacement?

OLD LADY (ERIC) There's only one shop here.

She points with a shaking finger. Camera pans very slightly to one side to reveal a shop with a huge four-foot-high sign: 'Bicycle Pump Centre—Specialists In Shorter Bicycle Pumps'. Another sign: 'Short Pumps Available Here'. Another sign: 'We Shorten Pumps While-U-Wait'. The camera shows the shop only for a couple of seconds and pans back to the old lady and Pither.

PITHER What a stroke of luck. Now perhaps cycling will become less precarious.

Cut to interior of a doctor's surgery. There is a knock on the door.

DOCTOR (ERIC) Yes? *(a nurse puts her head round the door)*

NURSE A Mr Pither to see you, doctor. His bicycle pump got caught in his sock.

DOCTOR Oh, thank you nurse, show him in please.

NURSE This way, please.

The nurse exits, Pither enters in shorts and sweater.

PITHER Oh, a very good morning to you too, doctor.

DOCTOR Ah, I understand that you had an accident.

PITHER That's right, my pump got...

DOCTOR Caught in your sock.

PITHER

ABSOLUTELY. YES. MY FRUIT CAKE WAS DAMAGED ON ONE SIDE.

DOCTOR Well...

PITHER It's got grit all over it.

DOCTOR Well now, are you in pain?

PITHER Oh, heavens no.

DOCTOR Ah well, where are you hurt?

PITHER Oh, fortunately, I escaped without injury.

DOCTOR Well, what is the trouble?

PITHER Please could you tell me the way to Iddesleigh? 10

DOCTOR I'm a doctor, you know.

PITHER Oh yes, absolutely. Normally I would have asked a policeman or minister of the Church, but finding no one available, I thought it better to consult a man with some professional qualifications, rather than rely on the possibly confused testimony of a passer-by.

DOCTOR Oh all right. *(he scribbles something on a piece of paper and hands it to Pither)* Take this to a chemist.

PITHER Thank you.

Cut to exterior of a chemist's shop. A chemist comes out holding the paper and points up the street. Pither thanks him and mounts his bike. Cut to hedgerows again. Pither's head. The theme music reaches the point where Pither normally falls off, his head disappears and the music cuts off. There is no crash. Suddenly Pither's head reappears further on and the music starts up again.

PITHER *(voice over)* September 2nd. Did not fall off outside Iddesleigh.

Cut to a small market town. A line of cars. Pither's head just above roofs of cars. Theme music. He suddenly disappears, the music stops and there is a crash.

PITHER Fell off in Tavistock. 11

Where Bovey Tracey marks the eastern edge of Dartmoor, the town of "Tavistock" marks the western limits, 25 miles away.

Cut to a discreet corner of a Watney's pub. Soft music. A middle-aged businessman and a sexy secretary who obviously want to be alone are sitting huddled over a table. At the next table is Pither, with a half-pint in front of him.

PITHER My foot caught in my trouser leg and that's how the bottle broke.
GIRL (CAROL) Tell her today, you could ring her.
MAN (JOHN) I can't, I can't.
PITHER I said you'd never guess.
MAN Sixteen years we've been together. I can't just ring her up.
GIRL Well, if you can't do it now, you never will.
PITHER *(tapping the man on the leg)* Do you like Tizer? 12

Tizer is a red, fizzy drink of indeterminate flavor, loved by British children of the time. It continues to be available still, somehow.

MAN *(to Pither)* What? No. No.
GIRL Do you want me or not, James? It's your decision.
PITHER I suppose it is still available in this area, is it?
GIRL Do you want me or not, James?
MAN What?
PITHER Tizer.
GIRL Yes or no.
PITHER Is it still available in this area?
MAN *(to Pither)* I don't know.
GIRL I see, in that case it's goodbye for ever, James.
MAN No! I mean yes!
PITHER Oh it is, is it?
MAN *(to Pither)* No.
GIRL Oh! You never could make up your mind.
MAN I can...I have...
GIRL *(taking off her ring)* Goodbye James.

She runs out sobbing.

MAN No wait, Lucille!
PITHER Does your lovely little daughter like Tizer? Eh?
MAN Lucille!
PITHER Wouldn't mind buying her a bottle of Tizer...if it's still available in this area, that is.
MAN *(turning on Pither)* Would you like me to show you the door?
PITHER Oh, that's extremely kind of you, but I saw it on the way in.
MAN You stupid, interfering little rat!

The man picks Pither up by the scruff of the neck and the seat of his pants. He carries him bodily towards the door.

PITHER I had just fallen off my bicycle, this is most kind of you, and my lemon curd tartlet had...
MAN Damn your lemon curd tartlet!

PITHER IS THROWN OUT. HE PICKS HIMSELF UP AND SEES THE GIRL OUTSIDE SOBBING.

PITHER Just had a chat with your dad.

The girl bursts into further tears. Whistling cheerfully Pither gets on his bicycle and, happier than he has been for a long time, he cycles off down the road and round a corner. Sounds of car-tyre screech and crash of Pither going straight into a car. Cut to interior of car speeding along highway. The driver is an earnest young man. Pither is sitting in the back seat with his bicycle. The driver, Mr Gulliver, talks with a professional precision.

PITHER My rubber instep caught on the rear mudguard stanchion and...
GULLIVER (TERRY J) Really? And what happened to the corned beef rolls?
PITHER The corned beef rolls squashed out of all...here, how did you know about the corned beef rolls?
GULLIVER I noticed them—or what remained of them—in the road. I noticed also that the lemon curd tart had sustained some superficial damage.
PITHER That's right. The curd had become...
GULLIVER Detached from the pastry base.
PITHER *(with some surprise)* Absolutely right, yes.

GULLIVER Otherwise the contents of the sandwich box were relatively unharmed, although I detected small particles of bitumen in the chocolate kup kakes.

PITHER But they were wrapped in foil!

GULLIVER Not the hard chocolate top, I'm afraid.

PITHER Oh, that's the bit I like.

GULLIVER The sausage roll, the crisps and the ginger biscuit 13 were unscathed.

PITHER How do you know so much about cycling?

GULLIVER Well, I'm making a special study of accidents involving food.

PITHER Really?

GULLIVER Yes, do you know that in our laboratories, we have developed a cheese sandwich that can withstand an impact of up to 4,000 pounds per square inch?

PITHER Good heavens!

GULLIVER Amazing, isn't it? We've also developed a tomato which can eject itself when an accident is imminent.

PITHER Even if it's in an egg and tomato roll?

GULLIVER Anywhere. Even if it's in your stomach, if it senses an accident it will come up your throat and out of the window. Do you know what this means?

PITHER Safer food?

GULLIVER Exactly. No longer will food be squashed, crushed and damaged by the ignorance and stupidity of the driver. *(becoming slightly messianic)* Whole picnics will be built to withstand the most enormous forces! Snacks will be safer than ever! A simple pot of salad dressing, treated in our laboratories, has been subjected to the impact of a 4,000 pound steam hammer every day for the last sixteen years and has it broken?

PITHER Er...well...

GULLIVER Yes, of course it has...but there are other ideas—safety straps for sardines for example.

A tomato leaps up out of the glove compartment and hovers, then it ejects itself out of the car window.

PITHER

HERE, THAT TOMATO HAS JUST EJECTED ITSELF!

GULLIVER Really? *(embracing Pither excitedly)* It works! It works! *(the car crashes)*

Fade out. Fade up on country road. Pither is cycling along with Gulliver on the back of the bicycle. Gulliver has his head bandaged and his arm in a sling. Occasional strains of Clodagh Rodgers's hit 'Jack in a Box' float towards us as Gulliver moves rhythmically. 14

PITHER *(voice over)* What a strange turn this cycling tour has taken. Mr Gulliver appears to have lost his memory and far from being interested in safer food is now convinced that he is Clodagh Rodgers, the young girl singer. I am taking him for medical attention.

"Crisps" are potato chips, and "biscuits" are cookies.

"Jack in the Box" was the U.K.'s entry in the 1971 Eurovision Song Contest. Poor Miss Rodgers came fourth, especially sad as she was Northern Irish and the show was broadcast from Dublin. The winner was from the musical powerhouse Monaco.

Cut to Pither and Gulliver cycling into a hospital. A sign says 'North Cornwall District Hospital'. Cut to nurse receptionist at a counter with a glass window which lifts up and down. Pither appears.

PITHER Is this the casualty department?
NURSE (GRAHAM) Yes, that's right.

A noise of splintering wood and a crash out of vision. Pither and the nurse look up. A bench has collapsed in the middle and three patients sitting on it have slid into a heap in the middle. A nurse is on her way to assist. Cut back to Pither and nurse.

NURSE And what can I do for you?

The window comes down on her fingers. She winces sharply in pain. She pushes it up again.

Bude is a picturesque seaside town in Cornwall.

PITHER I am at present on a cycling tour of the North Cornwall area taking in Bude and... 15
NURSE Could I have your name please?
PITHER Ah, my name is Pither.
NURSE What?
PITHER P-I-T-H-E-R...as in Brotherhood, except with PI instead of the BRO and no Hood.
NURSE I see...
PITHER I have just visited Taunton...

A terrific crash. Cut to a trolley on its side, and a bandaged patient under a mound of hospital instruments and a nurse standing looking down.

16

The A237 is a road in Croydon, in London.

NURSE Sh!
PITHER ...I was cycling north towards...
NURSE Yes, where were you injured?
PITHER Just where the A237 16 Ilfracombe road meets the...
NURSE On your *body*...
PITHER Ah no...it's not I who was injured, it's my friend.

The nurse scowls, crumples up the paper, and throws it away. The piece of paper hits a smallish cabinet of glass which topples forward and smashes.

NURSE Tut...name?
PITHER Pither.
NURSE No, no, no, no. Your friend's name.
PITHER Oh, Clodagh Rodgers...
NURSE Clodagh Rodgers!?

PITHER Well only since about 4.30...
NURSE Yes. I think you'd better talk to Dr Wu...Doctor!

Cut to a doctor unloading a crate balanced on top of a medicine cupboard. He whips round knocking off the crate.

DOCTOR (JOHN) What? Damn!

Cut to patient in a wheelchair being pushed. The wheelchair completely collapses and the nurse is left holding the handles.
Quick cut to the nurse as window comes down on her fingers again.

NURSE Aaaaaagh!

The doctor comes across to Pither, limping slightly, in some pain.

PITHER I am on a cycling tour of North Cornwall, taking in...
NURSE He *thinks* he's had an accident.
PITHER

I HAVE A FRIEND WHO, AS A RESULT OF HIS INJURIES THINKS HE IS CLODAGH RODGERS.

DOCTOR He what?
PITHER Well, what happened was...

A nurse carrying a tray walks past the doctor, making for the entrance doors. As she reaches them they swing open to admit Gulliver, with his head bandaged and his arm in a sling. He collides with the nurse; she drops her tray. He grabs Pither and they exit rapidly, stepping on the doctor's foot in the process. The doctor yells, grabs his foot, and as he does so the reception window slams down, trapping his hand. He howls in pain.

Cut to a camp fire at midnight in a forest clearing. By the light of the fire, Pither is writing up his diary.

PITHER *(voice over)* September 4th. Well I never. We are now in the Alpes Maritimes region of Southern France. Clodagh seems more intent on reaching Moscow than on rehearsing her new BBC 2 series with Buddy Rich and the Younger Generation... 17 *(Gulliver enters the scene; his head is still bandaged)* Oh hello!

17

Buddy Rich, the American jazz drummer and one of the greats.

GULLIVER We cannot stay here. We must leave immediately. There is a ship in Marseille.
PITHER I did enjoy your song for Europe, Clodagh.
GULLIVER I have seen an agent in the town. My life is in danger.
PITHER Danger, Clodagh?
GULLIVER Stalin has always hated me.
PITHER No one hates you, Clodagh.
GULLIVER I will not let myself fall into the hands of these scum.
PITHER I think you should go and have a little lie down, my dear. There is a busy day tomorrow of concerts and promotional tours.
GULLIVER I? One of the founders of the greatest nation of the earth? I! Whom Lenin has called his greatest friend.

From the darkness we hear French voices.

M. BRUN (JOHN) Taisez-vous. Taisez-vous. 18
PITHER Oh dear.
GULLIVER I! Who have worked all my life that my people should live.

A pair of middle-class French people in pyjamas appear.

M. BRUN Taisez-vous. Qu'est-ce que le bruit? C'est impossible! 19
PITHER Er...my name is Pither.
M. BRUN Oh...you are English?
PITHER Er yes, that's right. I'm on a cycling tour of North Cornwall, taking in Bude...
GULLIVER I will not be defeated! I will return to my country to fight against this new tyranny!
PITHER This is Clodagh Rodgers, the Irish-born girl singer.
MME BRUN (ERIC) Mais oui—c'est Clodagh Rodgers— 20 'Jack in a box'! *(sings)* I'm just a jack in the box, I know whenever love knocks...*(calls)* Genevieve! Gerard! C'est Clodagh Rodgers la fameuse chanteuse Anglaise.

Two teenagers in pyjamas and carrying autograph books appear and rush towards Gulliver.

GULLIVER I will never surrender! I will never surrender!...
GENEVIEVE (GRAHAM) Excusez-moi Madame Clodagh. Ecrivez-vous votre nom dans mon livre des hommes célèbres, s'il vous plaît. Là, au-dessous de le Denis Compton. *(Gulliver signs and hands the book back)* Maman! Ce n'est pas la belle Clodagh. 21
MME BRUN Quoi?
GENEVIEVE C'est, Trotsky le révolutionnaire.
M. BRUN Trotsky!
MME BRUN Mais Trotsky ne chante pas. 22

"Who's there?"

"Who's there? What is that noise? It's impossible!"

"Clodagh Rodgers, the famous English singer."

21

"Please sign your name in my book of male celebrities, please. There, below Denis Compton. This isn't the beautiful Clodagh."

Compton, the Australian cricketer oft name-checked by the Pythons.

"Trotsky doesn't sing."

M. BRUN Il chante un peu. 23
MME BRUN Mais pas professionnellement. Qu'il pense de Lenin. 24
M. BRUN Ah! Lenin!! Quel chanteur! 25 'If I ruled the world!' 26

A brief film clip of Lenin, apparently singing the next line of the song.

GULLIVER Lenin! My friend! I come!

He dashes off into the forest possessed.

PITHER Oh excuse her, she's not been very well recently, pressure of work, laryngitis, you know...

He gets on his bike and pedals off hurriedly after Gulliver into the forest.

M. BRUN *(still reminiscing)* Et aussi Monsieur Kerensky 27 avec le 'Little White Bull', eh? 28
MME BRUN Formidable. 29

Cut to a few quick shots of Gulliver dashing through the trees and then of Pither making much slower progress due to his bike. Cut to a shot of a French couple snogging in car.

GULLIVER Lenin! I come! Lenin!
FRENCHMAN Je t'aime.
FRENCH GIRL *(seeing Gulliver)* Maurice! Regardez! C'est la chanteuse anglaise Clodagh Rodgers.
FRENCHMAN Ah mais oui. *(sings)* Jacques dans la boîte. *(he switches on car radio and the song is heard throughout the forest)*

Cut to a Russian street. Pither cycles along with Gulliver looking like Trotsky on the back.

PITHER *(voice over)* After several days I succeeded in tracking down my friend Mr Gulliver on the outskirts of Smolensk.

Cut to a military man. He has a large map of Europe and Russia and a stick with which he raps at the places.

MILITARY MAN (ERIC) Smolensk, 200 miles west of Minsk. 200 north of Kursk. 1500 miles west of Omsk.

Cut back to Pither and Gulliver.

PITHER Thank you.

They have stopped by a signpost which says 'Smolensk town centre 1/2, Tavistock 1612 miles'.

PITHER *(voice over)* Anyway, as we were so far from home and as Mr Gulliver, still believing himself to be Trotsky, was very tired from haranguing the masses all the way from Monte Carlo.

Cut to the military man who thumps the map again.

MILITARY MAN Monte Carlo. 100 miles south of Turin. 100 miles east of Pisa, 500 miles west of Bilbao.

Cut back to Pither.

"He sings a bit."

"But not professionally. You're thinking of Lenin."

"What a singer!"

"If I Ruled the World" was a popular song written by Leslie Bricusse and Cyril Ornadel. Originally featured in the 1963 musical *Pickwick* (yes, there's a musical based on Dickens's *The Pickwick Papers*), it was made famous that year by Sir Harry Secombe, a Welsh singer and TV personality.

Alexander Kerensky served as the second prime minister of the Russian Provisional Government after the Revolution, only to be replaced by Lenin.

"Little White Bull" was a 1957 hit song by the British Tommy Steele.

"Wonderful!"

PITHER Thank you. I decided to check...
PITHER *(voice over)* I decided to check...
PITHER No, sorry you go on.
PITHER *(voice over)* I decided to check him into a hotel while I visited the British Embassy to ask for help in returning to Cornwall.

They leave the bicycle on the kerb and enter a door with the sign 'YMACA' over it.

PITHER *(voice over)*

AND SO WE REGISTERED AT THE SMOLENSK YOUNG MEN'S ANTI-CHRISTIAN ASSOCIATION.

Cut to the military man.

MILITARY MAN YMACA. Corner of Anti-Semitic Street and Pogrom Square.
PITHER *(by now standing at the reception desk with Gulliver)* Go away, *(to departing desk clerk)* No, not you. A single room for my friend please.
DESK CLERK (TERRY G) Yes, sir. Bugged or unbugged? 30
GULLIVER *(as Trotsky)* I think I'd be happier with a bugged one.
DESK CLERK Right, one bugged with bath.
PITHER Well, just have a nice lie down, and I'll go down to the Embassy.

In the days of the Cold War, one might expect a room in Smolensk to be bugged if one was visiting from Devon, or anywhere else in the U.K.

He goes. Gulliver signs hotel register.

DESK CLERK *(looking at the book)* Trotsky! My lack of God, it's Trotsky!

A couple of people race in excitedly.

GULLIVER Comrades. Socialism is not a...

Mix through to the British Consulate. Pither cycles up, parks his bike and goes in. Imperial music. Mix through to smoky interior. A picture of the queen is dimly visible on the back wall. A Chinaman approaches. He is dressed in traditional Mandarin's robe and cap.

PITHER Excuse me. Is this the British Consulate?
CHINAMAN (GRAHAM) Yes, yes...si si...that is correctment. Yes...Piccadilly Circus, miniskirt and Joe Lyons. 31

J. Lyons and Co. was a food manufacturer most famous for its chain of tea shops.

PITHER I wish to see the consul, please.
CHINAMAN Yes, yes, speakee speakee...me Blitish consul.
PITHER Oh! *(he examines his diary)* You are Rear Admiral Sir Dudley Compton?
CHINAMAN No. He died. He have heart attack and fell out of window on to exploding bomb, and was killed in a shooting accident. I...I his how you say...succ...sussor.
PITHER Oh, successor.
CHINAMAN I'm his successor, Mr Atkinson.
PITHER Oh.
CHINAMAN Would you like drinkee? Or game bingo?
PITHER Well...A drink would be very nice.

The Chinaman claps his hands and another runs in and bows obsequiously.

CHINAMAN Mr Livingstone. Go and get sake.
LIVINGSTONE (JOHN) Yes, boss. *(goes)*
CHINAMAN Oh how is Tonblidge Wells? 32 How I long to see again walls of famous Shakespeare-style theatre in Stlatford-on-Avon.
PITHER Oh well I'm a West Country man myself, Mr Atkinson.
CHINAMAN Oh Texas—Arizona—Kit Carson Super Scout.
PITHER No. No. West of England...Cornwall.
CHINAMAN *(with difficulty)* Coron...worl...
PITHER Cornwall.
CHINAMAN Coronworl...oh yes know Coronworl very well. Went to school there, mother and father live there, ah yes. Go many weekend parties and polo playing in blidge club. Belong many clubs in Coronworl.

Livingstone reappears with drink and plate of pastries. He puts them down.

CHINAMAN Ah, Mr Livingstone thank you, sake and bakewells tart. 33 *(hands a glass of sake to Pither)* Well, chaps, buttocks up!
PITHER Rather. *(they drink)*
CHINAMAN Now then er...er...
PITHER Ah, Pither.
CHINAMAN Ah Mr Pither. We British here in Smolensk very interested in cliket.
PITHER Oh, cricket?
CHINAMAN No, no...you not speak English velly wells. Not clicket—clicket...clicketty click... clicket...housey housey...er, bingo. 34
PITHER Bingo...
CHINAMAN Oh bingo...bingo...bingo.
LIVINGSTONE Bingo! Bingo!

Several Mao-suited Chinese people rush in waving the Red Book and shouting 'bingo'.

Tunbridge Wells is a town 40 miles southeast of London. It is considered a bastion of conservative opinions.

The "bakewell tart" is a small cake named after the town of Bakewell, in Derbyshire.

The number 66 in bingo is sometimes called as "all the sixes, clickety-click."

A winner at bingo is supposed to shout "house" when his or her card is filled.

The Chinaman remonstrates with Livingstone and eventually stops them.

CHINAMAN Hsai! Solly. Our boys got velly excited. *(the Maoists exit)*
LIVINGSTONE Bingo.
CHINAMAN *(to Livingstone)* Shut face! *(to Pither)* Mr Pither, perhaps you could put in a good word for so we could join a very smart bingo club in Coronworl.
PITHER Well, it's not really my line...
CHINAMAN We all sit velly quiet at back, not say anything except shout 'Housey! Housey!'.
LIVINGSTONE Housey! Housey!
MAOISTS *(rushing back in)* Housey! Housey!

Cut to stock film of large Chinese crowds.

CHINESE HORDES Housey! Housey! Housey housey!

Cut back to Consulate. The Chinaman is shouting out of window.

CHINAMAN Hi skwwati niyhi, keo t'sin feh t'sdung, hihi watai bingo cards! *(comes back into the room)*
LIVINGSTONE Nihi watai bingo cards?
CHINAMAN Nihi watai!
LIVINGSTONE Ah so...
CHINAMAN Now then, Mr Pither, tell me which better—Hackney Star Bingo or St Albans Top Rank Suite?
PITHER Well I was hoping that you could help me and my friend to get back to England as...you see we're on a cycling tour of North Cornwall...
ALL Bingo, bingo, bingo...

The Chinaman ushers Pither out. Brief film clip of rioting Chinese.

CHINESE HORDES
BINGO! BINGO! BINGO! BINGO!

Cut to the hotel lobby.

PITHER Is Mr Trotsky in his room, please?
DESK CLERK No. He has gone to Moscow.

Cut to the military man.

MILITARY MAN Moscow. 1500 miles south of...

Cut back to lobby.

DESK CLERK Shut up.
PITHER Moscow!

He is surrounded by three secret policemen dressed in identical suits, dark glasses and pork pie hats.

GRIP (ERIC) Come with us, please.
PITHER Oh, who are you?
BAG (JOHN) Well we're not secret police anyway.
WALLET (GRAHAM) That's for sure.

GRIP If anything we are ordinary Soviet citizens with no particular interest in politics.
BAG None at all. Come with us.
PITHER Oh where are you taking me?

The secret police all move away to confer.

WALLET What do we tell him?
GRIP Don't tell him any secrets.
BAG Agreed.
GRIP Tell him anything except we are taking him to Moscow where Trotsky is reunited with the Central Committee.

They return to Pither.

WALLET
WE'RE TAKING YOU TO A CLAMBAKE.

PITHER Oh a clambake! I've never been to one of those.
GRIP Right, let's go.
BAG Who's giving the orders round here?
GRIP I am. I'm senior to you.
BAG No you're not. You're a greengrocer, I'm an insurance salesman.
GRIP Greengrocers are senior to insurance salesmen.
BAG No they're not!
WALLET Cool it. I'm an ice-cream salesman and I am senior to both of you.
BAG You're an ice-cream salesman? I thought you were a veterinarian.
WALLET I got promoted. Let's go.
BAG Taxi!

A girl enters dressed as a New York cabbie.

TAXI (CAROL) Yes.
BAG Drive us to Moscow.
TAXI I have no cab.
WALLET Why not?
TAXI I'm in the secret police. *(they all snap into the salute)*

Cut to shot of train wheels in the night. The siren sounds. Superimposed names zoom into camera, as in a musical: Petrograd, Ottograd, Lewgrad, Lesliegrad, Etceteragrad, Dukhovskoknabilebskohatsk, Moscva. Cut to the stage of a big Russian hall. A banner across the top of the stage reads 'Russian 42nd International Clambake'. At the back of the stage sits Pither with his bicycle. At one side of the stage, at an impressive table on a dais, are some very important Russian persons including generals. One of the generals addresses the audience. 35

GENERAL (JOHN) ....Dostoievye useye tovarich trotsky borodina...*(etc.)*

Subtitle: 'THIS IS THE MAN WHO BROUGHT OUR BELOVED TROTSKY BACK TO US'

GENERAL Belutanks dretsky mihai ovna isky Mr Reg Pither.

Aubtitle: 'FIRST MAY I PRESENT MR PITHER FROM THE WEST OF ENGLAND'
Pandemonium lasting for about ten seconds. 36

GENERAL Shi muska di scensand dravenka oblomov Engleska Solzhenitzhin. 37

Much of the Russian to come is gobbledygook.

Including a funny shot of Palin quietly applauding himself.

Aleksandr Isayevich Solzhenitsyn, the Russian writer who spent eight years in a labor camp and who was expelled from Russia in 1974. (He returned after the fall of the Soviet system.)

Subtitle: 'FORGIVE ME IF I CONTINUE IN ENGLISH IN ORDER TO SAVE TIME'

GENERAL And now, Comrades, the greatest moment of a great day, the moment when I ask you to welcome the return of one of Russia's greatest heroes, creator of the Red Army, Lenin's greatest friend, Lev Davidovich Trotsky!

Gulliver appears looking as much like Trotsky as possible. He wears a uniform and has a beard and glasses. Pandemonium breaks out. He eventually quietens them by raising his hands for silence.

The song is "Just an Old Fashioned Girl," made famous by Eartha Kitt.

GULLIVER Comrades. Bolsheviks. Friends of the Revolution. I have returned. *(renewed cheering)* The bloodstained shadow of Stalinist repression is past. I bring you the new light of Permanent Revolution. *(his movements are becoming a little camp and slinky)* Comrades, I may once have been ousted from power, I may have been expelled from the party in 1927, I may have been deported in 1926, but *(sings)* I'm just an old-fashioned girl with an old-fashioned mind. 38 *(a certain amount of confusion is spreading among the audience and particularly the generals on the podium)* Comrades, I don't want to destroy in order to build, I don't want a state founded on hate and division. *(sings again)* I want an old-fashioned house with an old-fashioned fence, and an old-fashioned millionaire.

From now on Gulliver continues exactly as Eartha Kitt. He has acquired a fur stole which he manipulates slinkily.The confusion is complete on the stage.

PITHER *(voice over)*

OUR FRIEND MR GULLIVER WAS CLEARLY UNDERGOING ANOTHER CHANGE OF PERSONALITY.

A senior general appears beside Pither with two guards.

GENERAL *(to Pither)* So! You have duped us. You shall pay for this. Guards, seize him.

The guards seize the startled Pither and drag him away. The senior general strides back across the stage avoiding Gulliver, towards the general who addressed the audience.

GENERAL Shall I seize him too?
SENIOR GENERAL (GRAHAM) No, I think we'll have to keep him, he's going down well.
GENERAL He's more fun than he used to be.
SENIOR GENERAL He's loosened up a lot. This is an old Lenin number.

Cut to Pither sitting in a cell.

Different from the candy bar in the United States, the British Mars bar nougat, caramel, and a chocolate coating.

PITHER *(voice over)* April 26th. Thrown into Russian cell. Severely damaged my Mars bar. 39 Shall I ever see Bude Bus Station again?*(two Russian guards throw the cell door open)* Oh excuse me... *(they grab him and march him out of the cell)*

Cut to exterior of a door leading out into the prison yard. The door is thrown open and Pither is marched over and stood against a blank wall. There are lots of small holes in the wall.

PITHER *(voice over)* What a pleasant exercise yard. How friendly they were all being.
OFFICER (JOHN) Cigarettes?

PITHER Oh, no thank you I don't smoke.

Pither facing a line of uniformed men with guns, obviously a firing squad.

PITHER *(voice over)* After a few moments I perceived a line of gentlemen with rifles. They were looking in my direction...*(cut to Pither against the wall looking behind him)* I looked around but could not see the target.
OFFICER Blindfold?
PITHER *(very cheerful)* No thank you, no.
OFFICER *(stepping clear)* Slowotny! *(the firing squad snaps to attention)* Grydenka... *(they raise their rifles)* Verschnitzen.

Drum roll. The firing squad takes aim. A messenger runs frantically up.

MESSENGER (GRAHAM) Nyet! Nyet! Nyet! *(he hands the officer a paper)*
OFFICER A telegram? *(examines it)* From the Kremlin! The Central Committee! *(reads)* It says...'Carry on with the execution'. Verschnitzen...*(the squad raise their rifles)*
PITHER *(voice over)* Now I was really for it.

Cut to shot of the officer with his hand raised. The same as before, only without Pither in shot. Drum rolls again. He brings his sword down. Volley of shots from the firing squad. The officer is looking in Pither's direction. Long pause.

OFFICER *(to soldiers)* How could you miss?
SOLDIER He moved.
OFFICER Shut up! Go and practise. *(to Pither)* I'm so sorry. Do you mind waiting in your cell?

Pither is flung back into his cell by the guards, and the door slammed.

PITHER *(voice over)* What a stroke of luck. My Crunchie was totally intact. 40 I settled down to a quick intermeal snack...

But he is bundled out again. Pause. Shots. He is bundled in. The officer appears at door.

OFFICER Next time, definitely! *(to aide)* Now then, how many have been injured? Oh God...
PITHER *(voice over)* As I lay down to the sound of the Russian gentlemen practising their shooting, I realized I was in a bit of a pickle. My heart sank as I realized that I should never see the Okehampton 41 by-pass again...

Mix to Pither's sleeping face, waking up, shaking himself in disbelief at finding himself in a beautiful garden, with the sun shining and the birds singing. He is in a deckchair, and his mother, having poured him a jug of iced fruit juice, is gently nudging Pither to wake him.

MOTHER (ERIC) Come on, dear, wake up, dear.
PITHER Mother!
MOTHER Come on, dear.
PITHER So, it was all a dream.
MOTHER No dear, *this* is the dream, you're still in the cell.

Mix to Pither waking up in the cell. The officer enters carrying a rifle.

Another British candy bar, this one with a "honeycombed sugar center" coated in chocolate.

Okehampton, a town on the northern edge of Dartmoor, did not get a bypass road until 1985.

Guy Burgess and Donald Duart Maclean were two of the "Cambridge Five" spy ring, members of the British Secret Intelligence Service who passed information to the Russians during World War II and the Cold War. Both defected to Russia in 1951, where Burgess died of the effects of alcoholism in 1963 and Maclean died in Moscow twenty years later.

Marshal Bulganin was the leader of the Soviet Union from 1955 to 1958.

Peter Cook and Dudley Moore, the comedy duo.

OFFICER OK, we're going to have another try. I think we've got it now. My boys have been looking down the wrong bit, you see.
PITHER Oh no, look, you've got to look down the bit there.
OFFICER I thought you had to look down that bit.
PITHER No, no, you've got to look down that bit, or you won't hit anything.
OFFICER All right, we'll give it a whirl. Guards, seize him. *(they take him out)*
OFFICER *(as he leaves)* Listen. You've got to look down this bit.

As they leave, we can see on the wall of the cell a poster, saying: 'Saturday Night at the Moscow Praesidium, starring Eartha Kitt, with Burgess and Maclean. **42** *"A Song a Dance and a Piece of Treachery. Marshal Bulganin and "Charlie", Peter Cook,* **43** *Dudley Moore, Leningrad has never laughed so much.' Mix through to stock film of the Kremlin. Dubbed over laughter and applause. A cheerful band sing. Mix through to a stage where someone dressed as Marshal Bulganin, is standing with a little real ventriloquist's dummy. He gets up, takes his bow and walks off as the curtain swings down. Lots of applause and atmosphere. Terrible Russian compère comes on smiling and applauding.*

COMPÈRE (ERIC) Osledi. Osledi.

He tells a quick joke in Russian and roars with laughter. Laughter from the audience. He holds up his hands and then becomes very sincere, saying obviously deeply moving, wonderful things about the next guest, whom he finally introduces.

COMPÈRE

EARTHA KITT!

Gulliver comes on-stage in the full Eartha Kitt rig—white fur stole, slit skirt and jewellery. He mimes to the voice of Edward Heath.

HEATH'S VOICE Trade Union leaders—I would say this—we've done our part. Now, on behalf of the community, we have a right to expect you, the Trade Union leaders, to do yours. *(etc.)*

Unrest in the audience as they recognize him.They start shouting 'sing "Old-Fashioned Girl", and throwing vegetables. Slow motion shot of a tomato hitting Gulliver. He is seen to be holding a turnip.

GULLIVER That turnip's certainly not safe. *(looking round and seeing where he is)* Oh no! Mr Pither! Mr Pither!

He runs off-stage, pursued by the guards. Cut to the stage-door of the hall. A sign on the door says 'Next week Clodagh Rogers'. Gulliver runs out, and then through the streets, hotly pursued by soldiers and secret service men, firing after him.

GULLIVER *(calling)* Mr Pither! Mr Pither!

He is seen running through a dockyard. Finally he stops by a high stone wall.

GULLIVER Mr Pither!
PITHER'S VOICE Here!

Gulliver looks round and then rapidly climbs up and over the wall. He drops down to find Pither standing on the other side.

PITHER Gulliver.
GULLIVER Pither! What a stroke of luck.
PITHER Well yes and no.

He indicates with his head. Cut to show that both of them are standing in front of a firing squad. The officer is there as before. The squad runs towards them with fixed bayonets. Caption: 'SCENE MISSING' Cut to a Cornish country lane. A road sign says 'Tavistock 12 miles'. Pither stands beneath with Gulliver and his bicycle.

PITHER Phew, what an amazing escape. Well goodbye, Reginald.
GULLIVER Goodbye, Mr Pither, and good luck with the tour!

They shake hands. Gulliver strides off. Pither mounts his bike and rides off into the sunset. Music swells. Roll credits. Cut to a field with hedgerow behind. The first animated monster peeks over the hedge.

FIRST MONSTER Hey, I think he's finally gone!

Second monster appears.

SECOND MONSTER Ooh yes!

They hop over the fence into the field.

FIRST MONSTER Ready, Maurice?
SECOND MONSTER Right-ho, Kevin. Let's go.
FIRST MONSTER All right, maestro, hit it!

We hear Clodagh Rodgers singing 'Jack in a Box'. The two monsters jump up and down enthusiastically if not gracefully. Fade out.

SEA
SON
3
EPISODE 35

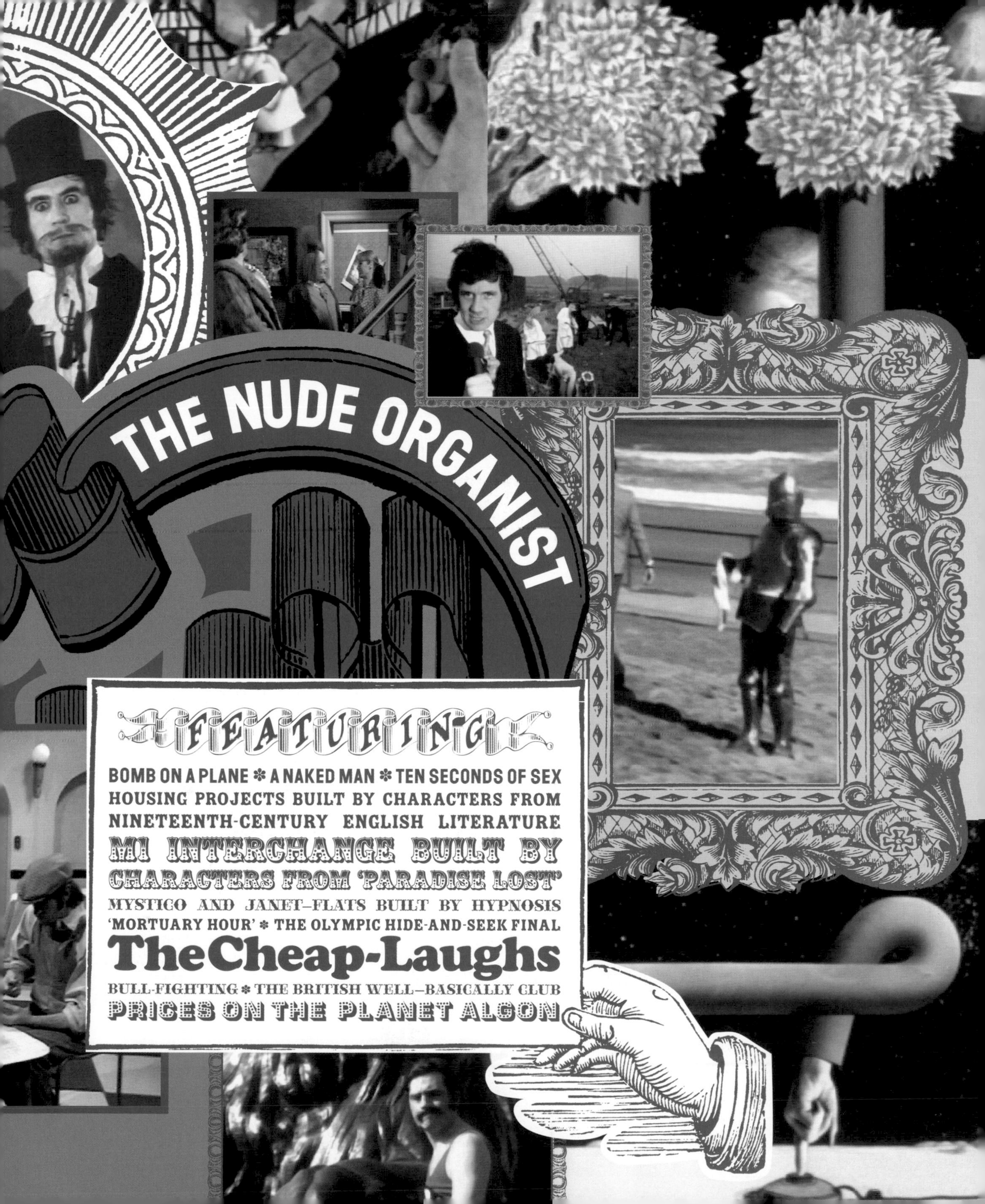
THE NUDE ORGANIST
FEATURING
BOMB ON A PLANE ✽ A NAKED MAN ✽ TEN SECONDS OF SEX
HOUSING PROJECTS BUILT BY CHARACTERS FROM
NINETEENTH-CENTURY ENGLISH LITERATURE
MI INTERCHANGE BUILT BY
CHARACTERS FROM 'PARADISE LOST'
MYSTICO AND JANET—FLATS BUILT BY HYPNOSIS
'MORTUARY HOUR' ✽ THE OLYMPIC HIDE-AND-SEEK FINAL
The Cheap-Laughs
BULL-FIGHTING ✽ THE BRITISH WELL—BASICALLY CLUB
PRICES ON THE PLANET ALGON

FIRST AIRED: DECEMBER 14, 1972

Fade up on two pilots in the cockpit of an aeroplane. A stewardess is there too. After a moment or two the first pilot makes an announcement. 1

FIRST PILOT (MICHAEL) This is Captain MacPherson welcoming you aboard East Scottish Airways. You'll have had your tea. Our destination is Glasgow. There is no need to panic.

The door of the cockpit opens and Mr Badger comes in.

BADGER (ERIC)

THERE'S A BOMB ON BOARD THIS PLANE, AND I'LL TELL YOU WHERE IT IS FOR A THOUSAND POUNDS.

SECOND PILOT (JOHN) I don't believe you.
BADGER If you don't tell me where the bomb is...if I don't give you the money...Unless you give me the bomb...
STEWARDESS (CAROL) The money.
BADGER The money, thank you, pretty lady...the bomb will explode killing everybody.
SECOND PILOT Including you.
BADGER I'll tell you where it is for a pound.
SECOND PILOT Here's a pound.
BADGER I don't want Scottish money. They've got the numbers. It can be traced.
SECOND PILOT One English pound. Now where's the bomb?

1

The stewardess is canoodling with Palin.

BADGER I can't remember.
SECOND PILOT You've forgotten.
BADGER Ay, you'd better have your pound back. Oh...*(rubs it)* fingerprints.
FIRST PILOT Now where's the bomb?

BADGER Ah, wait a tic, wait a tic. *(closes eyes and thinks)* Er, my first is in Glasgow but not in Spain, my second is in steamer but not in train, my whole is in the luggage compartment on the plane...*(opens eyes)* I'll tell you where the bomb is for a pound.

SECOND PILOT It's in the luggage compartment.

BADGER Right. Here's your pound.

Enter a man with headphones.

HEADPHONES (GRAHAM) This character giving you any trouble?

FIRST PILOT

HE'S RUINED THIS SKETCH.

SECOND PILOT Absolutely.

HEADPHONES Let's go on to the next one.

BADGER Wait a tic, wait a tic. No. I won't ruin your sketch for a pound.

SECOND PILOT No, no.

BADGER 75p.

HEADPHONES Next item. *(they start to leave)*

The nude organist is seated at his organ in the open air, with a lovely scarlet dressing-gown draped round his shoulders. It says on it 'Noel Coward' which is crossed out and 'Nude Organist' written underneath. He is holding forth to a journalist with a notepad who is nodding and interviewing him. Someone else holds a small tape recorder. Make-up ladies are adding the finishing touches. They bring him a mirror while he talks. Someone is taking photos of him, perhaps with flashbulbs.

NUDE MAN (TERRY J) Well I see my role in it as, er, how can I put it best—the nude man—as sort of symbolizing the two separate strands of existence, the essential nudity of man...

They realize that they are on camera. They remove the man's robe and clear the set. He grins at the camera and plays his chords. Cut to the announcer. He is sitting at his desk in the middle of a field but he is talking earnestly to a trendy girl reporter.

ANNOUNCER (JOHN) It's an interesting question. Personally I rather adhere to the Bergsonian... 2 idea of laughter as a social sanction against inflexible behaviour but...excuse me a moment... And now

IT'S MAN (MICHAEL)

IT'S...

Henri-Louis Bergson was a French philosopher from the late nineteenth and early twentieth centuries. He espoused the importance of intuition and sensory experience over the claims of science and rationalism.

Animated titles.

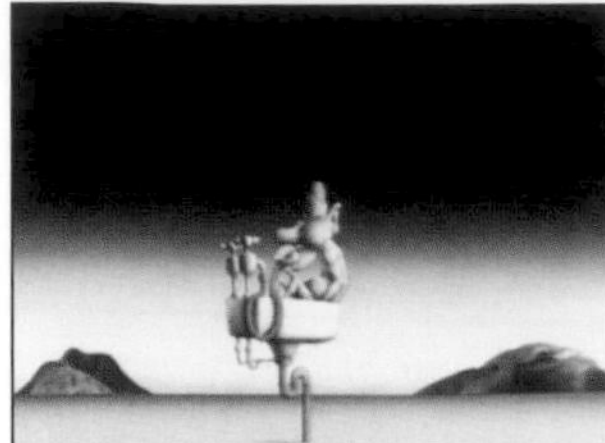

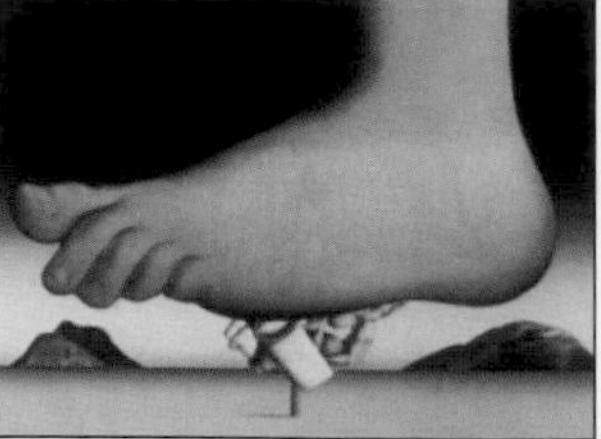

VOICE OVER (ERIC) and caption: 'AND NOW THE TEN SECONDS OF SEX'

Black screen and the sound of a ticking clock for ten seconds.

VOICE OVER and caption: 'ALL RIGHT, YOU CAN STOP NOW'

Cut to a little palm court set. A man seated.

MAN IN TAILS (GRAHAM) Well, we'll be continuing with 'Monty Python's Flying Circus' in just a moment. Yes, yes, we're going back to the show, in just one moment *(consults his watch)* fr...o...m nnnnnnnnnnn...now.

Cut to a building site. The camera pans over it.

VOICE OVER (MICHAEL) This new housing development in Bristol is one of the most interesting in the country. It's using a variety of new techniques: shock-proof curtain-walling, a central high voltage, self-generated electricity source, and extruded acrylic fibre glass fitments. It's also the first major housing project in Britain to be built entirely by characters from nineteenth-century English literature.

By this time the pan has come to rest on a section of the site where various nineteenth-century literary figures are at work round a cement mixer: two ladies in crinolines, ***Bob Cratchett*** 3 *on his father's back,* ***Heathcliff and Catherine*** 4 *throwing bricks to each other with smouldering passion, Nelson,* ***Mr Beadle as foreman.*** 5

Bob Cratchit, the abused clerk of Ebenezer Scrooge in Dickens's *A Christmas Carol.*

Heathcliff and Catherine, fated lovers in Emily Brontë's novel *Wuthering Heights*.

"Mr Beadle" is likely a reference to Dickens's Mr. Bumble, who *is* a beadle (a minor official in a church or synagogue) in *Oliver Twist*.

Cut to the interior of a half-finished concrete shell. A little girl is working on top of a ladder.

VOICE OVER Here Little Nell, from Dickens's 'Old Curiosity Shop' fits new nylon syphons into the asbestos-lined ceilings... 6 *(shot of complicated electrical wiring in some impressive electrical installation)* But it's the electrical system which has attracted the most attention. *(cut to*

Nell Trent is the heroine of Dickens's *The Old Curiosity Shop*.

Arthur Huntingdon studying a plan; he has a builder's safety helmet on) Arthur Huntingdon, who Helen Graham married as a young girl, and whose shameless conduct eventually drove her back to her brother Lawrence, in **Anne Brontë's 'The Tenant of Wildfell Hall' describes why it's unique.** 7

HUNTINGDON (ERIC) Because sir, it is self-generating. Because we have harnessed here in this box the very forces of life itself. The very forces that will send Helen running back to beg forgiveness!

Cut to a close up of big pre-fabricated concrete slabs being hoisted into the air by a crane and start to pull out, as the commentator speaks, to reveal a crowd of nineteenth-century farmhands working on them.

VOICE OVER The on-site building techniques involve the construction of twelve-foot walling blocks by a crowd of farmhands from **'Tess of the D'Urbervilles'** 8 supervised by the genial landlady, Mrs Jupp, from Samuel Butler's 'Way of All Flesh'.

Pan to reveal Mrs Jupp with a clipboard. Cut to voice over narrator in vision with a stick-mike, in front of an impressive piece of motorway interchange building. Behind him and working on the site are six angels, three devils, and Adam and Eve.

NARRATOR In contrast to the site in Bristol, it's progress here on Britain's first eighteen-level motorway interchange being built by characters from **Milton's 'Paradise Lost'**... 9

He turns and we zoom past him into the angels etc.

NARRATOR *(voice over)* What went wrong here?

Cut to a foreman in a donkey jacket and helmet.

FOREMAN (TERRY J) Well, no one really got on. Satan didn't get on with Eve...er...Archangel Gabriel didn't get on with Satan...nobody got on with the Serpent, so now they have to work a rota: forces of good from ten till three, forces of evil three to six.

The camera tracks through a high-rise development area.

VOICE OVER But even more modern building techniques are being used on an expanding new town site near Peterborough; here the Amazing Mystico and Janet can put up a block of flats by hypnosis in under a minute.

Mystico (TERRY J) *removes his cloak, gloves and top hat and hands them to Janet, who curtsies. He then makes several passes. Cut to stock film of flats falling down reversed so that they leap up. Cut back to Mystico and Janet. She hands him back his things as they make their way to their car, a little* **Austin 30.** 10

VOICE OVER The local Council here have over fifty hypnosis-induced twenty-five storey blocks, put up by El Mystico and Janet. I asked Mr Ken Verybigliar the advantages of hypnosis compared to other building methods.

Cut to a man in a drab suit. Superimposed caption: 'MR K. V. B. LIAR'

MR VERYBIGLIAR (MICHAEL) Well there is a considerable financial advantage in using the services of El Mystico. A block, like Mystico Point here, *(indicating a high-rise block behind him)* would normally cost in the region of one-and-a-half million pounds. This was put up for five pounds and thirty bob for Janet.

The Tenant of Wildfell Hall is Anne Brontë's 1848 novel, told in letters.

Tess of the d'Urbervilles, Thomas Hardy's novel, first published in 1891.

Way of All Flesh, Samuel Butler's autobiographical novel, published in 1903.

9

John Milton's *Paradise Lost*, the epic poem to end all epic poems.

10

The Austin A30 was a compact car of the 1950s.

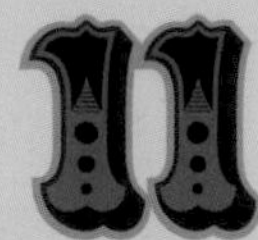

Onan, known as the "self-abuser" of the Bible—Genesis 38 to be precise—who was not actually a self-abuser at all. Rather, he "spilled his seed" so that he wouldn't impregnate his brother's wife. He's now erroneously considered a masturbator, poor chap. Yahweh also killed him.

VOICE OVER But the obvious question is are they safe?

Cut to an architect's office. The architect at his desk. Behind him on the wall are framed photos of various collapsed buildings. He is a well-dressed authoritative person. **Superimposed caption:** *'MR CLEMENT ONAN, ARCHITECT TO THE COUNCIL'* 11

ARCHITECT (GRAHAM) Of course they're safe. There's absolutely no doubt about that. They are as strong, solid and as safe as any other building method in this country...provided of course people *believe* in them.

Cut to a council flat. On the wall there is a picture of Mystico.

TENANT (ERIC) Yes, we received a note from the Council saying that if we ceased to believe in this building it would fall down.

VOICE OVER

YOU DON'T MIND LIVING IN A FIGMENT OF ANOTHER MAN'S IMAGINATION?

TENANT No, it's much better than where we used to live.

VOICE OVER Where did you used to live?

TENANT We had an eighteen-roomed villa overlooking Nice. 12

VOICE OVER Really, that sounds much better.

TENANT Oh yes—yes you're right.

Nice is a beautiful resort town on the southeast coast of France; also a byword for luxury and warm breezes.

Cut to stock shot of block falling down in slow motion. Cut back to tenant and wife inside. Camera shaking and on the tilt.

TENANT No, no, no, of course not.

Cut to stock film again. The building rights itself. Cut back to interior again. Camera slightly on tilt. They are holding bits of crockery etc.

TENANT Phew, that was close.

Cut to tracking shot from back of camera car again. This time El Mystico striding through the towering blocks, his cloak swirling behind him.

VOICE OVER But the construction of these vast new housing developments, providing homes for many thousands of people, is not the only project to which he has applied his many talents. He also has an Infallible Pools Method, 13 a School of Spanish Dancing and a Car Hire Service. *(cut to Mystico at wheel of his little Austin 30, his amazing eyes riveted on the road ahead; Janet occasionally tactfully guides the steering wheel)* What is the driving force behind a man of such restless energies, and boundless vision? Here as with so many great men of history, the answer lies in a woman...*(the camera pans over on to Janet and starts to zoom in on her as she watches the road ahead; cut to a nineteenth-century engraving of Shakespeare's Antony and Cleopatra)* As Antony has his Cleopatra...*(cut to picture of Napoleon and Josephine)* as Napoleon has his Josephine...*(cut to Janet lying on a bed in a negligee in a rather seedy hotel)* So Mystico has his Janet.

The Football Pools, mentioned regularly by the Pythons, is a nationwide competition to pick the correct scores in soccer games. It's a kind of soccer lotto, only with a tiny bit of skill involved if you can be bothered.

Mystico leaps from top of the wardrobe on to the bed with a lusty yell. Cut to montage of black and white photos of Janet in various stage poses: three poses against black drapes; one against a building; one posed outside a terrace house with notice reading 'School of Spanish Dancing—Dentures Repaired'.

VOICE OVER Yes. Janet...a quiet, shy girl. An honours graduate from Harvard University, American junior sprint record holder, ex-world skating champion, Nobel Prize winner, architect, novelist and surgeon. The girl who helped crack the Oppenheimer spy ring in 1947. **14** She gave vital evidence to the Senate Narcotics Commission in 1958. She also helped to convict the woman at the chemist's in 1961, and a year later *(cut to Janet shaking hands with a police commissioner)* she gave police information which led to the arrest of her postman. In October of that same year *(cut to photo of Janet with a judge and a policeman standing on either side of her smiling at the camera)* she secured the conviction of her gardener for bigamy and three months later personally led the police swoop *(cut to Janet in a street with gaggles of policemen clustering round her grinning at the camera and two people obviously naked with blankets thrown over them)* on the couple next door. In 1967 she became suspicious of the man at the garage *(cut to a photo of a petrol attendant filling a car)* and it was her dogged perseverance and relentless enquiries *(another rather fuzzy photo of the man at the garage peering through the window of cash kiosk)* that two years later finally secured his conviction for not having a licence for his car radio. *(final photo of five police, Janet and the man from the garage in handcuffs all posing for the camera)* He was hanged at Leeds a year later *(cut to Janet posing outside a prison)* despite the abolition of capital punishment and the public outcry. Also in Leeds that year, a local butcher was hanged *(cut to a blurred family snap of a butcher in an apron with a knife)* for defaulting on mortgage repayments, and a Mr Jarvis *(photo)* was electrocuted for shouting in the corridor.

Cut to Superintendent Harry 'Boot-in' Swalk. Superimposed caption: 'SUPERINTENDENT HARRY "BOOT-IN" SWALK'

SWALK (TERRY J) We admit that there have been outbreaks of hanging recently, but the police are trying to keep the situation under control. *(his personal two-way radio is making rather a noise)* You must remember the courts are very busy at the moment and the odd death sentence is bound to slip through. *(claps his hand over the radio to little avail)* Electrocutions are another big worry. But we hope that guillotining has been eradicated from the urban areas, and garrotting is confined almost entirely to Luton. So if you have a friend in prison or under sentence of death, be sure to let us know at this address.

VOICE OVER (ERIC) *(and caption)* 'the police force, "Sunnyview", Yeovil, Somerset'

Cut to a mortuary. Various trolleys lie about with corpses covered by sheets. Two workmen are sitting at a low make-shift table with cups of tea and a transistor radio, shelling eggs and dropping them in a pickling jar.

Klaus Fuchs was a German-British scientist who was an integral part of the race at Los Alamos to create an atomic bomb—and who after the war passed secrets to the Soviets. He was imprisoned in Britain and when released moved to East Germany, then under the control of the Eastern bloc. There were a number of other workers at Los Alamos who admitted passing secrets.

In the U.K., one dials "999" for emergency services.

BBC's Radio 1 is the popular-music station known for the inanity and annoying positivism of its disc jockeys, as here.

Radio 4 is a more serious station, akin to NPR and mostly lacking in music. Radio 2 is the station for older listeners, playing classic pop music and oldies. Radio 3 is the national classical music station in the U.K.

Shirley Bassey, a Welsh singer with some of the most powerful pipes ever to grace the airwaves. Noted for her lusty performance of the theme to the James Bond movie *Goldfinger* in 1964, she also sang the theme to *Diamonds Are Forever* and *Moonraker.*

Royalty and the like are often wheeled out to inspect new facilities in the U.K. The inability of Palin to know where he is, or to even speak, is a lovely gloss on the classist nature of these visits.

RADIO VOICE (JOHN) ...and Premier Chou En Lai, who called it 'a major breakthrough'. Twelve men were accidentally hanged at Whitby Assizes this afternoon whilst considering their verdict. This is one of the worst miscarriages of justice in Britain since Tuesday. *(music)*

DJ VOICE (ERIC) Well it's thirteen minutes to the hour of nine-nine-nine, **15** here on wonderful Radio One-One-One! **16** So if you're still lying in your big big bed, now is the time to get up out of it! We've got another thirteen hours of tip-top sounds here on Wonderful Radio One! *(brief funny noises)* Sorry about that...So unless you have brain cells, or have completed the process of evolution, there's a wonderful day ahead!

BATTERSBY (TERRY J) *(switching the radio off)* It must be on Radio Four. **17** *(he gets another radio out from underneath the table)* Radio Two. *(he gets another radio out)*...Three...*(he opens the top of the third radio and gets out a fourth; he switches it on)*

RADIO VOICE (MICHAEL) It's 9 o'clock and time for 'Mortuary Hour'. An hour of talks, tunes and downright tomfoolery for all those who work in mortuaries, introduced as usual by Shirley Bassey. **18** *(sinister chords)*

SHIRLEY Well, we're going to kick straight off this week with our Mortuary Quiz, so have your pens and pencils ready.

A door at the back of the mortuary opens and Mr Wang, an official of the Department of Stiffs, enters. He wears an undertaker's suit and top hat plus a long blond wig.

WANG (JOHN) Turn that radio off and look lively!

BATTERSBY Oh, it's 'Mortuary Quiz', Mr Wang...

WANG Don't argue, Battersby.

We hear voices off. Officials at the door spring to attention. Enter a mayor with a chain round his neck, and an elderly peer of the realm who is standing on a small platform, pushed by an attendant.

MAYOR (GRAHAM) ...This is our mortuary in here, Your Grace...

PEER (MICHAEL) I say, I say, I...er...I...er...I...er...I...I can't think of anything to say about it. **19**

MAYOR Well, we're very proud of it here, sir. It's one of the most up to date in the country.

PEER I see...yes...yes...now...um...what...what...ah...ah...what is it?...is it a power station?

MAYOR No, Your Grace, it's a mortuary.

PEER I see...I see...good...good...good, good, good...

MAYOR But it has one of the most advanced thermostat control systems in the country, and it has computer-controlled storage facilities.

PEER I see, I see...I...er...er...er...er...I...er...I'm a good little doggie.
MAYOR I'm sorry, Your Grace?
PEER I'm a good little dog.
ATTENDANT (CAROL) Oh dear...
MAYOR Perhaps we should postpone the visit?
ATTENDANT No, no, no—you see it's just that his brain is so tiny that the slightest movement can dislodge it *(starts to slap the duke's head from side to side gently but firmly)* Your Grace... Oh dear...it's rather like one of those games you play where you have to get the ball into the hole...That's it!
PEER Ah! Now then, excellent, excellent, excellent, excellent. Now then...ah...what happens when the steel is poured into the ingots?
MAYOR *(ushering everyone out)* Perhaps we should go and have a look at the new showers?
PEER Yes...yes...yes...yes...yes rather jolly good...jolly good... jolly good...jolly good...no fear...

They leave. Battersby turns the radio on again.

RADIO VOICE Well the answers were as follows: 1) the left hand, 2) no, 3) normal, 4) yes it has, in 1963 when a bird got caught in the mechanism. How did you get on?

Two men behind him push in a trolley with sheet-covered corpses on it.

WANG Turn that thing off!
BATTERSBY Oh! It's 'Mortuary Dance Time', Mr Wang!
WANG Never mind that, Battersby, this is the big one. I've just had Whitby Police on the phone with twelve hangees...
BATTERSBY Oh yes, I just heard about that on the radios...
WANG No, these are twelve different ones...so shtoom.

Battersby and friend gather round the body. Wang joins them. They start to work away busily and efficiently on the corpse. We suddenly become aware that Badger is standing with them around the body.

BADGER I'll not interrupt this sketch for a pound.
WANG What?
BADGER

FOR ONE POUND I'LL LEAVE THIS SKETCH TOTALLY UNINTERRUPTED.

WANG What?
BADGER Fifty pence...I'm prepared to negotiate a forty-pence deal. *(an eye peers out from under the sheet on the corpse they are working on)* For 35p I won't interrupt any of the next three items.

The corpse is now sitting up waiting to see what happens. Another corpse sits up as they continue arguing. The sheet is pushed back on another trolley revealing a boy and girl on the same stretcher. They light cigarettes.

WANG No, no, it's no good...
BADGER 25p.
WANG No.
BADGER 10p and a kiss.

Animation: with Gilliam's hands in shot.

Action taking
place here

This scene was shot in Trafalgar Square, at the base of Nelson's Column—and as ever in Python, a nice crowd has formed to watch the craziness. A few folks wander by through the shot too. Wonderful!

21

Kilmarnock is a town 25 miles southwest of Glasgow, in southwestern Scotland.

22

As Chapman moves to the curb, he almost runs into a young boy who is passing by. The perils of live recording . . .

TERRY GILLIAM *(voice over)* You see, it's very simple—I just take these cut-out figures and by putting them together...oh, you mean we're on?...*(Gilliam's head appears briefly)* Sorry.

The animated sketch starts. Then cut to Trafalgar Square. The Olympic symbol is superimposed briefly. Superimposed caption: 'FINAL OF THE HIDE-AND-SEEK SECOND LEG' Zoom in on commentator and the two finalists, forty-year-old men limbering up in shorts and singlets.

COMMENTATOR (ERIC) Hello, good afternoon and welcome to the second leg of the Olympic final of the men's Hide-and-Seek here in the heart of Britain's London. **20** We'll be starting in just a couple of moments from now, and there you can see the two competitors Francisco Huron the Paraguayan, who in this leg is the seeker *(we see Francisco Huron darting about, looking behind things)* and there's the man he'll be looking for...*(we see Don Roberts* (GRAHAM) *practising hiding)* our own Don Roberts from Hinckley in Leicestershire who, his trainer tells me, is at the height of his self-secreting form. And now in the first leg, which ended on Wednesday, Don succeeded in finding the Paraguayan in the new world record time of 11 years, 2 months, 26 days, 9 hours, 3 minutes, 27.4 seconds, in a sweetshop in Kilmarnock. **21** And now they're under starter's orders.

We see Don Roberts and Francisco Huron standing side by side, poised, looking nervous.

STARTER *(voice over)* On your marks...get set...

The starter fires his pistol. Francisco Huron immediately puts his hands over eyes and starts counting.

FRANCISCO (TERRY J) Uno, dos, tres, quattro, cinque, seis, siete, ocho, nueve, diez...

Meanwhile Don Roberts hails a cab. He gets in and it drives off. **22**

FRANCISCO ...trientay dos, trientay tres, trientay Quattro...

Superimposed caption: '32, 33, 34'

COMMENTATOR Well Don's off to a really great start there. Remember the Paraguayan has got 11 years, 2 months, 26 days, 9 hours...*(cut to taxi on the way to London airport)* 3 minutes, 27.4 seconds to beat.

Cut back to Francisco still counting. Superimposed caption: '998, 999, 1000'

FRANCISCO Neuvecian no nuevetay ocho, nuevecientas nuevente ye nueve, mil. *(Francisco takes his hands from his eyes and shouts)* Coming!

He starts looking around the immediate locality suspiciously. **23** *We see a plane landing. There is a sign saying 'Benvenuto a Sardinia'. Cut to Don on a bicycle. Then running up a hill. Then going into castle. Running along corridors and eventually pausing, looking around agitatedly, and then hiding behind a pillar. Occasionally he looks out nervously. Then cut to Francisco looking in shops in the Tottenham Court Road. Cut to studio 'Sportsview' desk with a Frank Bough man at it.* **24**

As he does so, the crowd has dispersed, or else this was filmed before the crowd arrived.

FRANK BOUGH (MICHAEL) Well, we'll be taking you back there as soon as there are any developments.

Caption: 'SIX YEARS LATER' Cut back to desk. Frank Bough looks older.

FRANK BOUGH

WE'VE JUST HEARD THAT SOMETHING IS HAPPENING IN THE HIDE-AND-SEEK FINAL, SO LET'S GO STRAIGHT OVER THERE.

Cut to film of Francisco Huron. He is wandering around looking for Don Roberts in a beach setting. The commentator is some way from him. He speaks quietly into a microphone.

Frank Bough, British TV sports presenter, ubiquitous and genial.

COMMENTATOR Hello again, and welcome to Madagascar, where Francisco Huron is seeking Don Roberts. And I've just been told that he has been told that he has been unofficially described as 'cold'. Ah, wait a minute. *(in the distance Francisco Huron consults with an official; the commentator moves out of shot briefly, then returns)* I've just been told that Huron has requested a plane ticket for Budapest! So he's definitely getting warmer. So we'll be back again in just a few years.

Cut to Frank Bough looking older. He is covered with cobwebs.

FRANK BOUGH Really beginning to hot up now.

Caption: 'FIVE YEARS, TWO MONTHS AND TWENTY-SIX DAYS LATER' Cut to a Portuguese-looking setting. Francisco Huron looking round desperately and glancing at his watch.

COMMENTATOR So here we are on the very last day of this fantastic final. Huron now has less than twelve hours left to find British ace Don Roberts. Early this morning he finished combing the outskirts of Lisbon and now he seems to have staked everything on one final desperate seek here in the Tagus valley. **25** But Roberts is over fifteen hundred miles away, and it's beginning to look all over, bar the shouting. The sands of time are running out for this delving dago, this senor of seek, perspicacious Paraguayan. He's still desperately cold and it's beginning to look like another gold for Britain.

The Tagus valley is an area of southwestern Portugal.

The camera shows Huron creeping up on a dustbin. He pauses, snatches off the lid and looks inside. He turns away disappointed, then does double take and looks back into the bin. He pulls out a sardine tin with the word 'Sardines' very obvious. Shot of Huron's reaction as he suddenly gets a tremendous idea. He snaps his fingers and hails a taxi and gets in. Cut to plane landing. Same sign as before 'Benvenuto a Sardinia'. Francisco cycles past. Cut to him discarding the bike and running up the hill straight into the castle. He runs along corridors into the right room, up to the pillar and finds Don Roberts skulking behind. They both look very tense as they await the official result, then react in fury and frustration when it is announced by a blazered official.

OFFICIAL (MICHAEL) The official result of the World Hide-and-Seek, Mr Don Roberts from Hinckley, Leicestershire, 11 years, 2 months, 26 days, 9 hours, 3 minutes, 27 seconds. Mr Francisco Huron, Paraguay, 11 years, 2 months, 26 days, 9 hours, 3 minutes, 27 seconds. The result—a tie.
VOICE OVER (JOHN) A tie! Well what a fantastic result. Well the replay will start tomorrow at 7.30 a.m.

As they stand there the camera pans off them to a window and then zooms through the window to reveal a beach where there is a Redcoat.

REDCOAT (MICHAEL) Well hello again...nice to be back...glad to see the series has been doing well. Well now, sorry about Mon-trerx.

At this point two men run past in the background carrying a donkey. A third runs behind carrying a sign saying 'Donkey Rides' and winking and pointing at the donkey, they run out of picture.

REDCOAT That was a little item entitled Hide-and-Seek—very anarchic, very effective, not quite my cup of tea, but very nice for the younger people. Well, the next item the boys have put together takes place in a sitting room. Sorry it's just a sitting room, but the bank account's a bit low after the appallingly expensive production of '**Clochemerle**'... **26**

He is hit by Mr Robinson with a chicken. Robinson walks away and we follow him as he passes Badger in the foreground.

Clochemerle was a 1972 BBC TV adaptation of the satirical novel by Gabrielle Chevalier about the issues surrounding the installation of a new urinal in a village square.

On the way, he sees something on the sand and squashes it with his shoe; then, as he enters the next scene in the sitting room, he squashes something else. A typical Cleese—and Python—moment: visual clues and links to make the transitions flow.

BADGER This is a totally free interruption and no money has exchanged hands whatever.

The camera doesn't pause at all on Badger and we continue panning with Robinson until he reaches the knight in armour. He hands the chicken to the knight. ***He walks away from knight and into the distance*** **27** *Mix through to a modern sitting room. Mrs Robinson is eating alone at the table looking at the clock.*

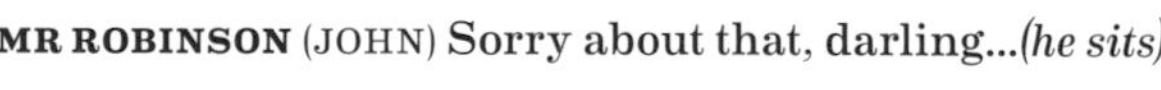

MR ROBINSON (JOHN) Sorry about that, darling...*(he sits)*

She serves him some vegetables. He unfolds his napkin.

MRS ROBINSON (CAROL) Gravy?
MR ROBINSON Yes please, dear.

They sit and eat in silence. Suddenly the doorbell rings.

MRS ROBINSON

OH DEAR, THAT'LL BE THE CHEAP-LAUGHS FROM NEXT DOOR.

Various different doorbell sounds and chimes. Mr Robinson goes to the front door, and opens it. Standing outside are Mr and Mrs Cheap-Laugh. He is wearing a big floppy comedian's suit and a big bow tie and fright wig. She is a Mrs Equator sort of lady, with an enormous hairstyle, and dressed in very bad taste.

MR ROBINSON Come in.
MR CHEAP-LAUGH (TERRY J) No! Just breathing heavily!

He and his wife roar with laughter. As he comes in he slips and falls on the mat. His wife puts a custard pie in his face. More roars of laughter.

MRS CHEAP-LAUGH (GRAHAM) Oh we just dropped in.
MR ROBINSON Would you like to come through...

We mix through to the exterior of a house at night. Shrieks of laughter, crashes of crockery. The two men with the donkey run past in road, the third man behind pointing to the sign. Superimposed caption: 'ONE EVENING WITH THE CHEAP-LAUGHS LATER' *The light comes on in hall. Cut to them in the hall at the front door.*

MR CHEAP-LAUGH Well goodnight and give us a kiss. *(kisses Mrs Robinson)*
MRS CHEAP-LAUGH Oh thank you very much for a very nice evening.
MR CHEAP-LAUGH After you, dear.

He trips her up and she falls out into the darkness. We hear her shriek with laughter. Mr Cheap-Laugh drops his trousers, makes lavatory chain pulling sign and noise and hurls himself out after wife and disappears into the darkness. More laughter. The host shuts the door. They heave a sigh of relief and go back into the sitting room. The crockery on the table is all smashed in a heap on the floor with the table cloth. The standard lamp is broken in half. There are large splodges of food and wine splashes on the walls. ***Some glasses and a moustache are drawn on the Tretchikoff picture of the Chinese girl.*** **28** *Mrs Robinson flops down on the sofa. There is a farting cushion. She removes it, irritated.*

MRS ROBINSON Oh honestly dear, why do we always have to buy everything just because the Cheap-Laughs have one?

He goes over to the wall cupboard for drinks. A bucket of whitewash is balanced on the half-open door. He opens the cupboard and the ***bucket of whitewash falls on him.*** **29** *Cut briefly to Mr Badger.*

28

It's just a moustache (no glasses).

Vladimir Grigoryevich Tretchikoff was a twentieth-century Russian painter whose painting from 1950, *Chinese Girl* (popularly called *The Green Lady*) is said to be the best-selling art print ever. The painting appears in the sketch about the sex lives of "molluscs" in Episode 32.

29

It's merely a bucket of water.

BADGER This is not an interruption at all.

Cut back to Mr Robinson. He pours himself a drink, without reacting to the whitewash.

MR ROBINSON It's just neighbourliness dear, that's all...
MRS ROBINSON I think we should try and lead our own lives from now on.

She opens a sewing box and a boxing glove on a spring comes out and hits her on the chin.

MR ROBINSON Can't you be serious for one moment?

He sits on the pouffe. The sixteen-ton weight falls on him. Cut to the exterior of the house. The lights go off downstairs and upstairs. The two men run past carrying a pantomime goose. Superimposed caption: 'LATER THAT NIGHT' Cut to a darkened bedroom. Mr and Mrs Robinson are in a double bed, talking.

MR ROBINSON I'm sorry I was cross earlier.
MRS ROBINSON Oh that's all right, dear. It's just that I get so sick of always having to be like the Cheap-Laughs.
MR ROBINSON Well yes, from now on we'll be like ourselves.
MRS ROBINSON Oh Roger...
MR ROBINSON Oh Beatrice.

The bed springs up and folds into the back wall of the bedroom. On the underneath of the bed is a presenter on a chair. The underneath of the bed also consists of a flat as for current-affairs-type programme, with 'Probe' written above narrator.

PRESENTER (ERIC) Many people in this country are becoming increasingly worried about bull-fighting. They say it's not only cruel, vicious and immoral, but also blatantly unfair. The bull is heavy, violent, abusive and aggressive with four legs and great sharp teeth, whereas the bull-fighter is only a small, greasy Spaniard. Given this basic inequality what can be done to make bull-fighting safer? We asked Brigadier Arthur Farquar-Smith, Chairman of the British Well-Basically Club.

Cut to a brigadier.

BRIGADIER (JOHN) Well, basically it's quite apparent that these little dago chappies have got it all wrong. They prance round the bull like a lot of bally night club dancers looking like the Younger Generation or a less smooth version of the Lionel Blair Troupe, 30 *(getting rather camp)* with much of the staccato rhythms of the Irving Davies 31 *(getting rather camp)* with much of the staccato rhythms of the Irving Davies Dancers at the height of their success. In recent years Pan's People 32 have often recaptured a lyricism... *(a huge hammer strikes him on the head; he becomes butch again)* and what we must do now is to use devices like radar

Lionel Blair is a dancer, choreographer, and TV celebrity known for his "camp" behavior.

Irving Davies is a choreographer for film and TV.

Pan's People is the female dance troupe featured weekly on *Top of the Pops*, a music show on BBC 1.

to locate the bull and SAM missiles fired from underground silos, to knock the bull over. Then I would send in Scottish boys with air cover to provide a diversion for the bull, whilst the navy came in round the back and finished him off. That to me would be bull-fighting and not this pansy kind of lyrical, *(getting camp)* evocative movement which George Balanchine and Martha Graham in the States and our very own Sadler's Wells... 33 *(the hammer strikes him on the head again)* Troops could also be used in an auxiliary role in international chess, where...*(the lights go off)* What?...oh...

BADGER *(voice over)* I'll put the lights on again for a pound.

Cut to an animated sketch, and then to a strange moonlike landscape.

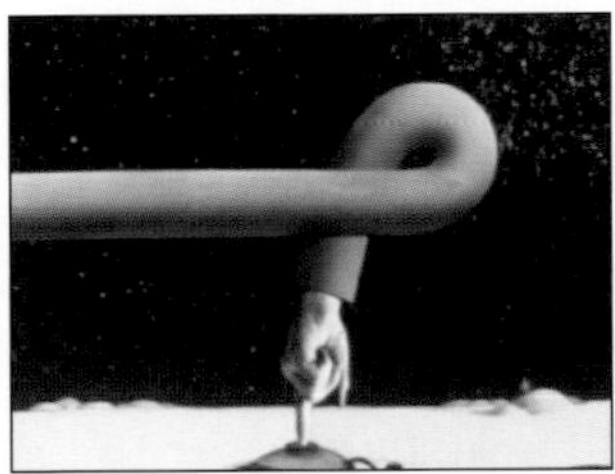

Eerie science-fiction music plays in the background.

VOICE OVER (JOHN) This is the planet Algon, fifth world in the system of Aldebaran, the Red Giant in the constellation of Sagittarius. Here an ordinary cup of drinking chocolate costs four million pounds, an immersion heater for the hot-water tank costs over six billion pounds and a pair of split-crotch panties would be almost unobtainable. *(cut to a budget-day-type graphic, with a picture of the product and the price alongside)* A simple rear window de-misting device for an 1100 costs eight thousand million billion pounds and a new element for an electric kettle like this *(picture of electric kettle)* would cost as much as the entire gross national product of the United States of America from 1770 to the year 2000, *(graphic of American GNP)* and even then they wouldn't be able to afford the small fixing ring which attaches it to the kettle. *(graphic of an electric kettle showing all the separate pieces detached from each other, arrow points to the fixing ring)*

Cut to James M'Burke sitting at a desk.. 34 *'Algon 1' motifs everywhere. Another expert stands by a model of the planet, and there is a panel of experts at a long desk who are all obviously dummies. Everyone has one of those single earphones*

M'BURKE (MICHAEL) Well, our computers have been working all day to analyse the dramatic information that's come in from this first ever intergalactic probe, Algon...1...*(suddenly very excited as he hears something over his earphone)*...and we're just getting an interesting development now, which is that attachments for rotary mowers—that is mowers that have a central circular blade—are...relatively inexpensive! Still in the region of nine to ten million pounds, but it does seem to indicate that Algon might be a very good planet for those with larger gardens...or perhaps even an orchard that's been left for two years, needs some heavy work, some weeding... *(very indistinct pictures start to come through on the screen behind him)* But we're now getting some live pictures through from Algon! Harry—Perhaps you could talk us through them.

Cut into pictures from Algon. Superimposed caption: 'LIVE FROM ALGON' Very fuzzy pictures of the Algon landscape. Panning and tracking shots hand held.

HARRY (TERRY J) *(voice over)* Very little evidence of shopping facilities here...there don't seem to be any large supermarkets. There may be some on-the-corner grocery stores behind those rocks, but it's difficult to tell from this angle. It does seem to suggest that most of the shopping here is by direct mail.

Sadler's Wells is the British ballet company.

James Burke is a science historian and British TV presenter famous for his anchoring of a popular science show on the BBC called *Tomorrow's World*, which ran from 1965 to 2003.

Digestive Biscuits are sweet cookies made by McVitie's.

Superimposed teleprinter caption: 'DIGESTIVE BISCUITS £8,000,000 PER PACKET' 35
Cut to James M'Burke.

M'BURKE Of course the big question that everyone's asking here is, what about those split-crotch panties? Are they going to be unobtainable throughout the Universe or merely on Algon itself? Professor?

Cut to a professor sitting beside a contour model of an area of Algon. It has a little model of the probe marking where it has landed. Superimposed caption:

'PROFESSOR HERMAN KHAN, DIRECTOR OF THE INSTITUTE OF SPLIT-CROTCH PANTIES'

PROFESSOR (ERIC) We must remember that Algon is over 75,000 miles wide. The probes come down to this area here and we're really only getting signals from a radius of only thirty or forty miles around the probe. Split-crotch panties, or indeed any items of what we scientists call, 'Sexy Underwear' or 'Erotic Lingerie' may be much more plentiful on other parts of the planet.

Camera pans to include M'Burke.

M'BURKE Professor, you were responsible for finding Scanty-Panties and Golden Goddess High-Lift Bras on planets which were never thought able to sustain life, and now that man has discovered a new galaxy do you think we're going to see underwear become even naughtier?
PROFESSOR Oh naughtier and naughtier.

Superimposed teleprinter caption: 'NO BANANAS ON ALGON'

M'BURKE Well so much for that...But of course, the probe itself has excited a great deal of interest... for it contains uranium-based dual transmission cells entirely re-charged by solar radiation, which can take off a bra and panties in less than fifteen seconds. It is, of course, the first piece of space hardware to be specially designed to undress ladies, and so there are bound to be some teething troubles...such as how to cope with the combination of elastic-sided boots and tights.

He produces the bottom half of a tailor's dummy wearing boots and tights with panties over the tights halfway down. On the screen behind, more dim indecipherable TV pictures from Algon.

M'BURKE **But I think we're getting some pictures now from Algon itself, and it looks as though... yes! The satellite has found a bird! The probe has struck crumpet and she looks pretty good too! Professor?** **36**

PROFESSOR Ja—she's a real honey!

All we see on the screen is a blurred female figure.

M'BURKE Well the pictures are a bit sporadic...I think probably...the solar radiation during the long journey to Algon...*(the screen goes blank)* Hoy! Look! Oh dear, I'm sorry we've lost contact. We'll try and re-establish contact with Algon...

Cut to presenter's-type chair. Mr Badger appears at side of screen.

BADGER Hello...The BBC have offered me the sum of forty pence to read the credits of this show. *(sits)* Personally I thought they should have held out for the full seventy-five, but the BBC have explained to me about their financial difficulties and...er...I decided to accept the reduced offer...so...the show was conceived, written and performed by the usual lot...*(the signature tune is heard)* Also appearing were Carol Cleveland, Marie Anderson, **Mrs Idle, Make-up** **37**—Madelaine Gaffney, Costume—Hazel Pethig, Animations by Terry Gilliam, Visual Effects Designer—Bernard Wilkie, Graphics—Bob Blagden, Film Cameraman—Alan Featherstone, Film Editor—Ray Millichope, Sound—Richard Chubb, Lighting—Bill Bailey, Designer—Bob Berk, Produced by Ian MacNaughton for 92p and a bottle of Bells whisky...it was a BBC colour production. That's just it. I'd like to say if there are any BBC producers looking in who need people to read the credits for them, I would personally...

The camera pulls out to reveal the sixteen-ton weight poised above him. As the picture fades the weight falls on him.

"Bird" and "crumpet" are British slang for an attractive female.

"Mrs. Idle" is Lynn Ashley, whom Idle married in 1969. They divorced six years later.

SEASON 3
EPISODE 36
TELEGRAM
ENQUIRIES

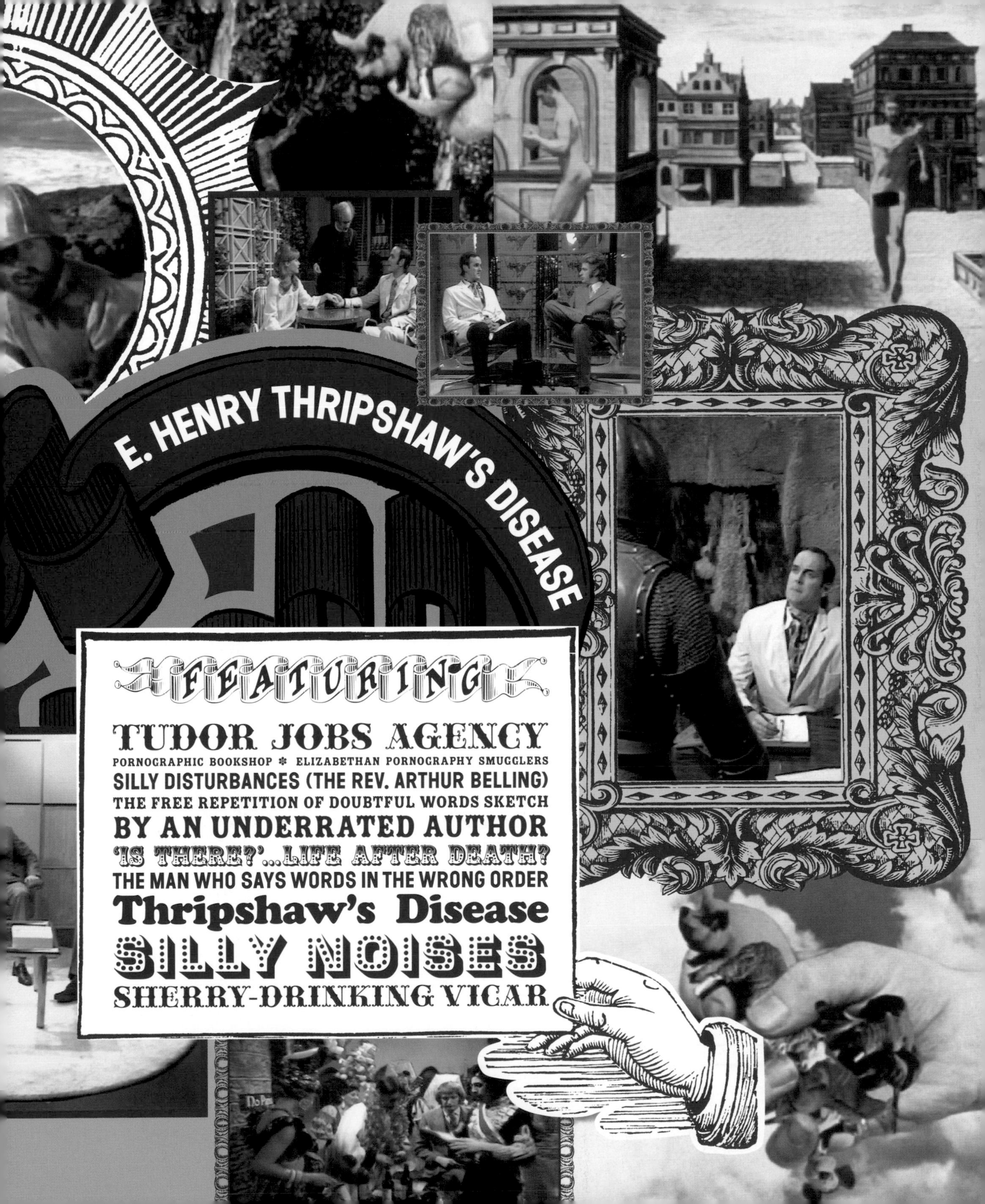

E. HENRY THRIPSHAW'S DISEASE
FEATURING
TUDOR JOBS AGENCY
PORNOGRAPHIC BOOKSHOP * ELIZABETHAN PORNOGRAPHY SMUGGLERS
SILLY DISTURBANCES (THE REV. ARTHUR BELLING)
THE FREE REPETITION OF DOUBTFUL WORDS SKETCH
BY AN UNDERRATED AUTHOR
'IS THERE?'...LIFE AFTER DEATH?
THE MAN WHO SAYS WORDS IN THE WRONG ORDER
Thripshaw's Disease
SILLY NOISES
SHERRY-DRINKING VICAR

Sir Walter Raleigh, the British statesman and adventurer, embarked on an attempt to colonize Virginia in 1584. A second attempt in 1587 led to the abandonment of the settlers by their leader John White, who went back to Britain. Raleigh's delay in returning—there was a detour to Cuba to try to plunder Spanish ships there—meant that by 1590, when he finally arrived back in America, the settlers had disappeared (the "Lost Colony of Roanoke Island").

A "vittler" is a purveyor of food.

The original Globe Theater was built in 1599 by the Lord Chamberlain's Men, a theater company famous for its productions of Shakespeare's plays. It burned down in 1613.

Sir Humphrey Gilbert was Walter Raleigh's half-brother, and also an adventurer and explorer.

John Cabot, an Italian explorer, is said to have landed in Newfoundland in 1497.

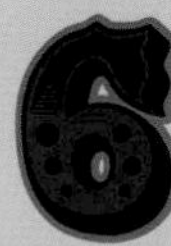

Sir Francis Drake, British explorer, sailor, privateer, and fighter of the Spanish.

FIRST AIRED: DECEMBER 21, 1972

Outside a shop. A sign reads 'Tudor Job Agency—Jobs a Speciality'. A man enters the shop. Inside it is decorated in Tudor style. The assistant is in Tudor dress.

ASSISTANT (TERRY J) Morning, sir, can I help you?

CUSTOMER (GRAHAM) Yes, yes...I wondered if you have any part-time vacancies on your books.

ASSISTANT Part-time, I'll have a look, sir. *(he gets out a book and looks through it)* Let me look now. We've got, ah yes, **Sir Walter Raleigh** 1 is equipping another expedition to Virginia; he needs traders and sailors. **Vittlers** 2 needed at the Court of Philip of Spain, oh, yes, and they want master joiners and craftsmen for the building of the **Globe Theatre.** 3

CUSTOMER I see. Have you anything a bit more modern, you know, like a job on the buses, or digging the underground?

ASSISTANT Oh no, we only have Tudor jobs.

CUSTOMER That can't be very profitable, can it?

ASSISTANT Well, you'd be surprised, actually sir. The Tudor economy's booming, ever since **Sir Humphrey Gilbert** 4 opened up the Northwest passage to Cathay, **and the Cabots'** 5 expansion in Canada, there's been a tremendous surge in exports, and trade with the Holy Roman Empire is going...no, quite right, it's no good at all.

CUSTOMER What?

ASSISTANT It's a dead loss. We haven't put anyone in a job since 1625.

CUSTOMER I see.

ASSISTANT That's all?

CUSTOMER What?

ASSISTANT That's all you say?

CUSTOMER Yes.

ASSISTANT No, no, we were the tops then. **Drake got all his sailors here.** 6 Elizabeth, we supplied the archbishops for her coronation. Shakespeare started off from here as a temp. Then came James the First and the bottom fell out of the Tudor jobs. 1603—800 vacancies filled, 1604—40, 1605—none, 1606—none. The rest of the Stuart period nothing. Hanoverians nothing. Victorians nothing. Saxe-Coburgs nothing. Windsors...what did you want?

CUSTOMER Dirty books, please.

ASSISTANT Right. *(produces selection of mags from under counter)* Sorry about the Tudor bit, but you can't be too careful, you know. Have a look through these.

CUSTOMER Have you got anything a bit...er...

ASSISTANT A bit stronger?

CUSTOMER Yes.

ASSISTANT Hold on...a...My Lord of Warwick!

SECOND ASSISTANT (ERIC) *(off)* 'Allo!

ASSISTANT Raise high the drawbridge. Gloucester's troops approach.

SECOND ASSISTANT *(off)* Right.

ASSISTANT Can't be too careful you know, sir.

The wall of the Tudor shop slides back to reveal the interior of a Soho dirty book shop in the back room—a bare room with a counter and magazines in racks on the walls at eye-level. Three drably dressed men are thumbing through books. One of them is a vicar, one of them is gathering a huge pile. Behind the counter is a Soho toughie in Tudor gear showing books to Mr Nid—a tweedy, rather academic, respectable-looking man of senior years. The customer goes through, and the wall slides back. **7**

SECOND ASSISTANT There's a 'Bridget—Queen of the Whip'.

NID (JOHN) Yes...

SECOND ASSISTANT Or 'Naughty Nora'...or there's this one: 'Doug, Bob and Gordon Visit the *Ark Royal*'. Or there's 'Sister Teresa—The Spanking Nun'.

NID Mmmm...I see...you don't have anything specially about Devon and Cornwall?

SECOND ASSISTANT No. I'm afraid not, sir.

NID The one I was really after was Arthur Hotchkiss's 'Devonshire Country Churches'.

SECOND ASSISTANT

WELL HOW ABOUT THIS, SIR: 'BUM BITERS'.

NID No...not really...I don't suppose you have any general surveys of English Church architecture?

SECOND ASSISTANT No, it's not really our line, sir.

NID No, I see. Well, never mind I'll just take the 'Lord Lieutenant in Nylons' then, and these two copies of 'Piggie Parade'. Thank you.

SECOND ASSISTANT Right, sir.

FIRST ASSISTANT *(voice over)* My Lord of Warwick.

SECOND ASSISTANT 'Allo?

FIRST ASSISTANT *(voice over)* Raise high the drawbridge. Gloucester's troops approach!

SECOND ASSISTANT Right.

He presses a button below counter and the wall slides back. The man with the big pile of books comes up to counter.

MAN (TERRY G) Just these, then.

Enter Gaskell in Tudor gear. The wall closes up behind him.

GASKELL (MICHAEL) All right. This is a raid. My name is Superintendent Gaskell and this is Sergeant Maddox.

SECOND ASSISTANT **Ah! Sir Philip Sidney.** **8** 'Tis good to see thee on these shores again.

GASKELL Shut up.

SECOND ASSISTANT Your suit is fair and goodly cut. Was't from Antwerp?

GASKELL Shut up. It's a disguise. Right! Confiscate the smutty books, Maddox.

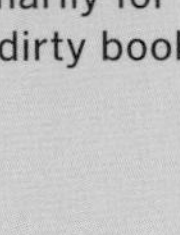

London's Soho was once known primarily for its strip joints and dirty bookstores.

Philip Sidney, Elizabethan courtier, soldier, and noted poet. He wrote *The Defense of Poetry* and *Arcadia*, among other works.

SECOND ASSISTANT Sir Philip! Prithee nay!

GASKELL Listen, mate! Don't come that Philip Sidney with me. I'm not a bloody Tudor at all. I'm Gaskell of the Vice Squad and this is Sergeant Maddox.

They all look at him blankly. He looks to Maddox for support and realizes he isn't there.

GASKELL Maddox! Where's he gone?

SECOND ASSISTANT Sir Philip, prithee rest awhile.

GASKELL Look. This is the last time. I'm warning you, I'm not Sir Philip Bleeding Sidney. I am Superintendent Harold Gaskell and this is a raid.

Everybody resumes their book-buying and ignores him. At the counter the assistant is still totting up the huge pile of books.

SECOND ASSISTANT That'll be 540 quid sir.

MAN Oh, I'll just have this one then. *(takes top one)*

GASKELL Maddox! *(addressing everyone in shop; they ignore him)* Look, this is a raid. *(no reaction)* Honestly, I promise you. *(people start to leave through the rear door of the shop; Gaskell blocks it)* Where are you going?

CUSTOMER I'm going home.

GASKELL Right. *(looks for his notebook but it's not in his Tudor clothing)* I'll remember you. Don't you worry. I'll remember you...

CUSTOMER Pray good, Sir Philip, that you...

GASKELL Don't you start! Maddox! *(the customer leaves; other customers start to leave)* Listen, I can prove to you I'm a policeman. I can give the names of all the men down in 'F' division at Acton: Inspector Arthur Perry, Superintendent Charles Frodwell, my best friend, police dogs, Butch, Wolf, Panther, Maudling. How would I know those names if I was Sir Philip Sidney? *(the vicar comes up to counter)* Look, vicar, you know me. **The Gargoyle Club** **9** —I got you off the charge. *(the vicar leaves guiltily)*

SECOND ASSISTANT Farewell, good Sir Philip.

He goes out carrying a pile of magazines. Then the vicar goes, followed by the Tudor man.

GASKELL Hey, stop! *(the door slams; Gaskell turns and looks round the empty shop; pause)* Maddox!

He rushes up to the sliding wall and beats on it. Then he turns and makes for the little back door and goes through.

GASKELL You'll never get away with this, you porn merchant. Blimey!

The Gargoyle Club was a seedy drinking den in London's Soho, on Meard's Street. It was once a scene for artists before its sad decline.

He stops and gapes. We cut to his eye-line to see he is standing in a beautiful, green, Tudor garden. In the distance a Tudor house. A girl is sitting on a stone bench, sobbing. Gaskell walks towards her, bewildered.

GASKELL Maddox!

The girl looks up at him with beseeching eyes. She is young and beautiful.

GIRL Oh good sir, how glad I am to see thee come. Forgive me weeping, but my love has gone.
GASKELL Er, listen. My name is Gaskell...Superintendent Gaskell of Vice Squad. Myself and Sergeant Maddox are on a raid. We are not Tudor people. We are the police.

An Elizabethan gentleman appears through the trees.

FATHER (TERRY J) Frances, what idleness is this? Why, good Sir Philip Sidney, *(he bows extravagantly to Gaskell)* what hast thee here?
GIRL *(turning to Gaskell with bated breath)* You are Sir Philip Sidney?
GASKELL ...Possibly...but I may be Superintendent Gaskell of the Vice Squad.
FATHER Ah good, Sir Philip, thy sharp-tongued wit has not deserted thee. Come. Let us eat and drink. Stay with us awhile.
GASKELL All right, sir. I think I will.

They walk off together arm in arm into the idyllic country garden. The girl looks after them with hope in her eyes. Bring up Elizabethan music. Superimposed caption: 'THE LIFE OF SIR PHILIP SIDNEY' Mix through to a Tudor dining room. At the table a group of Tudor gentry are sitting listening to Gaskell. Evidence of a banquet, and two minstrels in attendance. Gaskell has obviously just finished a story. Applause and laughter.

GASKELL ...then did we bust the Harry Tony mob, who did seek to import Scandinavian filth via Germany. For six years they **cleaned up a packet** 10 —the day I got whiff of them through a **squealer** 11 and within one week did a **mop-up right good.** 12 They're now languishing doing **five years bird** 13 in **Parkhurst.** 14

Applause. They are all very impressed. Cut to exterior. A messenger on a horse rides full pelt straight towards the camera. It is dusk. He stops outside the Elizabethan house, leaps off and dashes into the house. Cut to interior again. They are still all laughing from his last story. The messenger bursts into room.

MESSENGER (TERRY G) Sir Philip. The Spaniards have landed in the Netherlands. **My Lord Walsingham** 15 needs you there forthwith.

"Cleaned up a packet" means to have made a lot of money.

A "squealer" is an informant.

"Mop-up right good" means one was able to arrest them all efficiently.

13

"Five years bird" is a back derivation of "jailbird"—a full-time criminal. Hence, bird is "jail time."

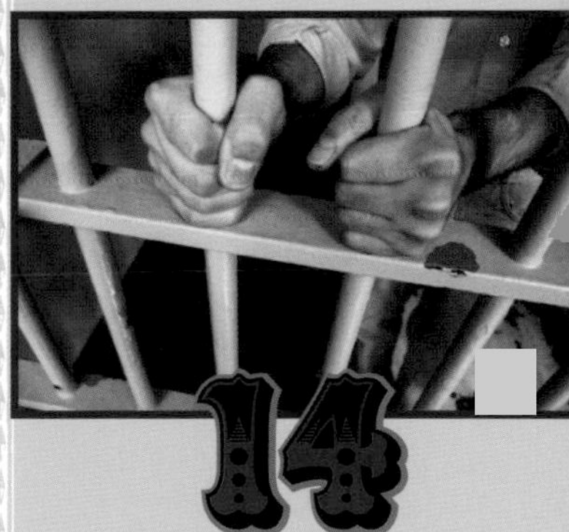

"Parkhurst is a jail on the Isle of Wight, off the southern coast of England.

Sir Francis Walsingham was a political figure in the reign of Elizabeth I. He disturbed and quelled a number of plots against the queen.

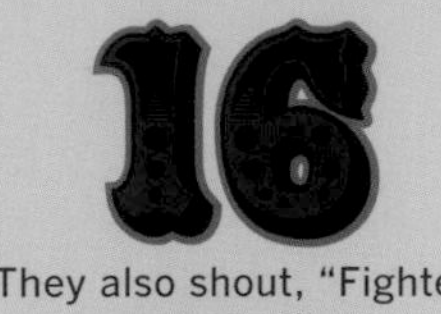

They also shout, "Fighter against filth!"

GASKELL Let's go.

Cut to exterior. Gaskell is seated on the back of the messenger's horse and they gallop off. The dinner crowd are standing waving on the doorstep.

DINNER CROWD Good luck, Sir Philip! 16

Cut to a British standard fluttering in the breeze against the blue sky. Fanfare. Two Elizabethan gentlemen, and four men dressed as Elizabethan soldiers are standing on a cliff top. Gaskell strides up to them, and takes up position on topmost point of the knoll.

The clichéd police greeting, mainly in comedies and bad movies; usually delivered in a Cockney accent.

GASKELL Where are the Spaniards?
ELIZABETHAN GENT (ERIC) Down below Sir Philip, their first boats are landing even now.

Shot of a sailing-galley seen from above.

GASKELL Right, you stay here, I'll go and get them.
ELIZABETHAN GENT Sir Philip! Not alone!

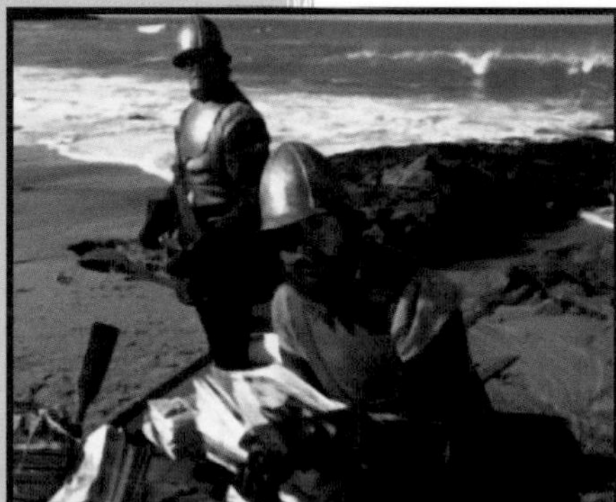

Cut to the beach. Suspense music. Gaskell strides up to the camera, until he is towering over it. The music reaches crescendo.

GASKELL Allo allo! What's going on here? 17

Cut to beached rowing boat piled high with bundles of dirty magazines. Two Spaniards are loading it with more magazines.

SPANIARD (TERRY J) Ees nothing, Señor, ees just some literature.
GASKELL I know what literature is, you dago dustbin. I also know what porn is. *(pulls out a loose magazine and brandishes it)* What's this then, eh?
SPANIARD It is of Lope De Vega's latest play, Señor. 18
GASKELL 'Toledo Tit Parade'? What sort of play's that?
SPANIARD It's very visual, Señor.
GASKELL Right. I'm taking this lot in the name of Her Gracious Majesty Queen Elizabeth.
SPANIARD Oh, but Señor.
GASKELL Don't give me any trouble. Just pile up these baskets of filth and come with me.

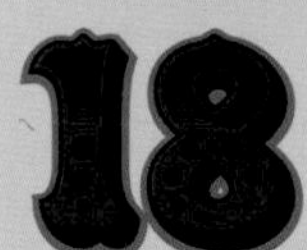

Spanish playwright Lope De Vega (1562–1635) was known for his prolific output. He wrote about 1,800 plays for a start, and that's not to mention all the poems (3,000 sonnets alone), novels, and so forth.

The second Spaniard leaps out of the boat with a drawn sword and they both engage Gaskell in a fight. Then we start to draw away from them, leaving them tiny dots in the distance fighting. Fight music over all this and voice over.

VOICE OVER (TERRY J) The battle raged long and hard, but as night fell Sidney overcame the Spaniards. 6,000 copies of 'Tits and Bums' and 4,000 copies of 'Shower Sheila' were seized that day. The tide of Spanish porn was stemmed. Sir Philip Sidney returned to London in triumph.

Cut to stock film of Elizabethan London street during celebrations. Superimposed caption: 'LONDON 1583' Cut to side on close up of Gaskell riding hard through woodland.

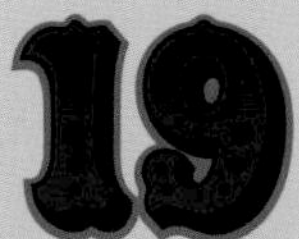

Built in 1381, Penshurst Place is an exquisite manor house that still stands near Tonbridge, in Kent, 32 miles southeast of London. Sir Philip Sidney was born there in 1554.

VOICE OVER Covered in glory, Sir Philip rode home to **Penshurst 19** to see his beloved wife...but all was not well.

Gaskell reins up outside another Tudor house and strides in. Cut to interior of an Elizabethan room—panelled walls, log fire, latticed windows, etc. Sir Philip's wife is sitting reading. Gaskell enters.

GASKELL **Good evening all, my love.** **20** I have returned safe from the Low Countries. *(she hurriedly hides the book she is reading under some knitting and starts whistling)* What art thou reading, fair one?
WIFE (CAROL) Oh, 'tis nothing, husband.
GASKELL I can see 'tis *something.*
WIFE 'Tis one of Shakespeare's latest works.

Gaskell picks up the book and reads the title.

GASKELL Oh...'Gay Boys in Bondage' What, is't—tragedy? Comedy?
WIFE 'Tis a...er...'tis a story of man's great love for his**...fellow man.** **21**
GASKELL How fortunate we are indeed to have such a poet on these shores.
WIFE Indeed. How was the war, my lord?
GASKELL The Spaniards were defeated thrice. Six dozen chests of hardcore captured.
WIFE *(trying to look innocent)* Hast brought home any spoils of war?
GASKELL Yes, good my wife, this fair coat trimmed with ermine.
WIFE *(without enthusiasm)* **Oh, lovely, nowt else?** **22**
GASKELL No, no fair lady. The rest was too smutty.

He settles himself down in front of his lady's feet and the fire.

GASKELL Now, my good wife. Whilst I rest,

READ TO ME A WHILE FROM SHAKESPEARE'S 'GAY BOYS IN BONDAGE'.

The wife looks a trifle taken aback but reluctantly opens the book and starts to read with a resigned air.

WIFE Yes...my lord...'Gay Boys in Bondage'...Ken, 25, is a mounted policeman with a difference... and what a difference. Even Roger is surprised and he's...*(she looks slightly sick with guilt)* he's used to real men...
GASKELL 'Tis like 'Hamlet'...what a genius!
WIFE 'But who's going to do the cooking tonight? Roddy's got a mouthful...'

"Good evening, all" was the greeting given directly to the camera at the start of every show by Jack Warner (playing Constable George Dixon) in the long-running, and hugely popular, BBC series *Dixon of Dock Green*. The show portrayed the small-time crimes of an East End neighborhood in London. Eventually the catchphrase got shortened to "Evening, all."

Amusingly, Carol Cleveland says "fellow men," which seems more accurate.

"Nowt" is northern British slang for "nothing."

23

Chapman, somehow, delivers this line deadpan.

Enter Maddox—a modern-day plain-clothed policeman.

MADDOX (GRAHAM) All right, this is a raid.

The wife screams, Gaskell leaps to his feet.

WIFE Oh! We are disgraced!
GASKELL There you are, Maddox!
MADDOX Cut the chat...and get in the van.
GASKELL Maddox! You recognize me...
MADDOX **Indeed I do, Sir Philip Sidney, and sad I am to see you caught up in this morass of filth, *(he picks up the book)* ooh—that's a long one.** 23
WIFE Oh oh...the glorious name of Sidney is besmirched...all is lost...oh alas the day.
GASKELL Shut up! I know this man—this is my old mate Sergeant Maddox...
MADDOX You'll do time for this.
GASKELL Oh Maddox—it's me—Gaskell...'F' division down at Acton...Inspector Arthur Frodwell.
MADDOX Come on Sidney. *(he bundles them both out)* And you, miss.
GASKELL I'm not Sir Philip bleedin' Sidney...and where were you? We could have mopped up that Tudor shop...

They are bundled out. Maddox pauses only to pick a book from the bookcase near the door. Cut to outside a modern theatre stage-door. Gaskell, still protesting, and Mrs Sidney are bundled out and into a police van. As it drives off, it reveals on the side of the theatre a poster saying: 'The Aldwych Theatre. The Royal Shakespeare Company Presents "Gay Boys In Bondage" By William Shakespeare'. An animated excerpt from this little-known Shakespearian masterpiece leads us to a table outside a restaurant.

A young couple are sitting blissfully at it.

SHE (CAROL) It's nice here, darling, isn't it.
HE (JOHN) It's beautiful, it's Paris all over again.

Enter a vicar, dressed normally but has bald wig with fright hair at sides. He carries a suitcase.

VICAR (MICHAEL) Excuse me, do you mind if I join you?
HE Er, no...no...no...not at all.
VICAR Are you *sure* you don't mind?
HE Yes, yes, absolutely.
VICAR You're sure I won't be disturbing you?
HE No, no.
VICAR You're absolutely sure I won't be disturbing you?
SHE No, no really.
VICAR Good. Because I don't want to disturb you. Specially as you're being so kind about me not disturbing you.
HE Oh, no, no, we don't mind, do we, darling?
SHE Oh no, darling.

VICAR Good, so I can go ahead and join you then? Can I?

BOTH Yes...yes...

VICAR Won't be disturbing?

BOTH No. No.

VICAR Good, good. You're very kind. *(he sits down)* A lot of people are far less understanding than you are. A lot of people take offence even when I talk to them. *(he makes strange gestures with his hands)* Let alone when I specifically tell them about my being disturbing.

HE ...Well, it's not *particularly* disturbing.

VICAR No, absolutely, absolutely, that's what I always say.

HE PRODUCES PLATES FROM HIS CASE AND SMASHES THEM ON THE TABLE.

But you'd be amazed at the number of people who really don't want me—I mean, even doing this *(he produces a rubber crab suspended from a ping-pong bat and a rubber baby doll and bobs them up and down, making loud silly noises as he does so)* gets people looking at me in the most extraordinary way. *(he breaks more plates and squirts shaving foam over his head; he and she get up to leave)*

HE We must be getting on.

VICAR I knew I'd disturb you...I knew I'd disturb you...*(miserably)* It always happens...whenever I've found someone I really think I'm going to be able to get on with...

HE No, the only thing is, you see, we're going to be a little bit late.

SHE *(sitting down and comforting vicar)* Let's stay.

HE Well, just a little bit...I mean, we will be late if we don't...*(he sits down reluctantly)*

VICAR Oh, thank you. You're very kind.

More silly behaviour from the vicar. He and she look embarrassed. Dissolve to them sitting at home smashing plates, making silly noises and covering themselves with shaving foam.

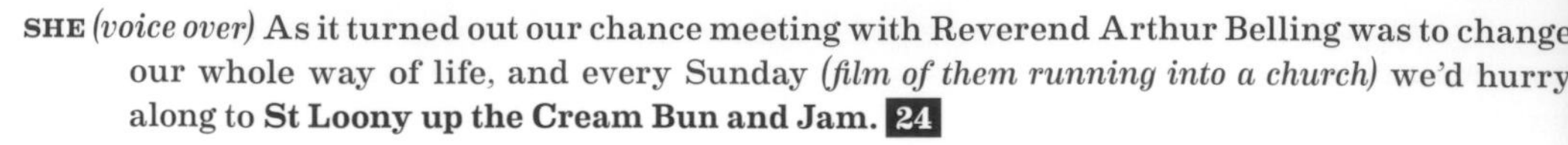

SHE *(voice over)* As it turned out our chance meeting with Reverend Arthur Belling was to change our whole way of life, and every Sunday *(film of them running into a church)* we'd hurry along to **St Loony up the Cream Bun and Jam.** 24

Carol continues the line here—"in time for Matins" (basically, morning prayers in an Anglican church)—but it's lost under the laugh for "St Loony up the Cream Bun and Jam."

Hold shot of the church. Sound of a congregation standing. We hear the silly noises. Cut to nude organist (TERRY J). *He plays a fanfare.*

ANNOUNCER (JOHN) And now...

IT'S MAN (MICHAEL)

IT'S...

Animated titles.

Straight into animated sketch, ending with:

VOICE OVER (JOHN) *(and caption)* 'the free repetition of doubtful words—skit, spoof, jape or vignette, by a very under-rated writer'

A post office counter window, with 'Telegram Enquiries' over the top. We see this through an ornate vignette. The clerk is behind the counter. Enter Mr Peepee. They speak very stiltedly.

"Ripping" is English upper-class slang for "splendid."

A "bleeder" is slang for a person who is annoying.

PEEPEE (ERIC) I've come for some free repetition of doubtful words on an inland telegram.
CLERK (TERRY J) Have you got the telegram in question?
PEEPEE I have the very thing here.
CLERK Well, slip it to me my good chap and let me eye the contents.
PEEPEE At once Mr Telegram Enquiry Man.
CLERK Thank you Mr Customer Man. *(reads)* Aha. 'Parling I glove you. Clease clome at bronce, your troving swife, Pat.' Which was the word you wanted checking?
PEEPEE Pat.
CLERK Pat?
PEEPEE My wife's name is not Pat at all.

CLERK No?
PEEPEE It's Bat. With a B.
CLERK And therefore I will take a quick look in the book.
PEEPEE **Ripping.** 25

Caption: 'ONE QUICK LOOK IN THE BOOK LATER'

CLERK You're quite right, old cock. There *has* been a mistake.
PEEPEE I thought as much. What really does it say?
CLERK **It say 'Go away you silly little bleeder.** 26 I am having another man. Love Bat'. Quite some error.
PEEPEE Yes. She wouldn't call herself Pat, it's silly.
CLERK Daft, I call it.
PEEPEE Well it has been a pleasure working with you.
CLERK For me also it has been a pleasure. And that concludes our little skit.

String quartet music starts to play, as at the beginning, only this time we widen to reveal a string quartet sitting in the set, playing. The clerk and Peepee adopt slightly frozen position. Mix to:

VOICE OVER and caption: 'the free repetition of doubtful words thing, by a justly under-rated writer—the end'

Animation link to a late-night religious-type discussion. ***A chairman and three guests are slumped motionless in their seats.*** 27

27

The caption reads: IS THERE? Introduced by ROGER LAST.

ROGER LAST (JOHN) Good evening. Tonight on 'Is There' we examine the question, 'Is there a life after death?'.

AND HERE TO DISCUSS IT ARE THREE DEAD PEOPLE...

The late Sir Brian Hardacre, former curator of the Imperial War Museum...*(superimposed captions identify them)* the late Professor Thynne, until recently an academic, critic, and broadcaster...and putting the view of the Church of England, the very late Prebendary Reverend Ross. Gentlemen, is there a life after death or not? Sir Brian? *(silence)* Professor?...Prebendary?...Well there we have it, three say no. On 'Is There' next week we'll be discussing the question 'Is there enough of it about', and until then, goodnight.

Superimposed credits:

'IS THERE'
INTRODUCED BY ROGER LAST
RESEARCH: J. LOSEY
L. ANDERSON
S. KUBRICK
P. P. PASOLINI
O. WELLES
THE LATE B. FORBES
PRODUCED BY: GILLIAN (AGED 3½)

Under these credits, we see the stiffs being carried off by people. Cut to a doctor's surgery. The doctor has in front of him a plaque which says 'Dr E. H. Thripshaw'. Enter Burrows.

BURROWS (MICHAEL)

GOOD DOCTOR MORNING! NICE YEAR FOR THE TIME OF DAY!

THRIPSHAW (JOHN) Come in.

BURROWS Can I down sit?

THRIPSHAW Certainly. *(Burrows sits)* Well, then?

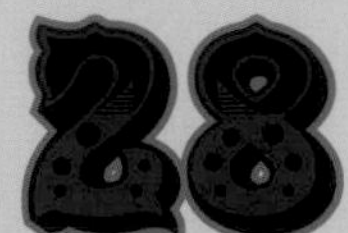

"I've had it for donkey's years" is British slang for "I've had it for a long time."

"Oh, I come from Alabama with my banjo on my knee" is a lyric from Stephen C. Foster's "Oh! Susanna," first performed in 1847.

Another rip on the suburban town of Esher, so regularly battered by the Pythons.

BURROWS Well, now, not going to bush the doctor about the beat too long. I'm going to come to point the straight immediately.

THRIPSHAW Good, good.

BURROWS My particular prob, or buglem bear, I've had ages. For years, **I've had it for donkeys.** 28

THRIPSHAW What?

BURROWS I'm up to here with it, I'm sick to death. I can't take you any longer so I've come to see it.

THRIPSHAW Ah, now this is your problem with words.

BURROWS This is my problem with words. Oh, that seems to have cleared it. **'Oh I come from Alabama with my banjo on my knee'.** 29 Yes, that seems to be all right. Thank you very much.

THRIPSHAW I see. But recently you have been having this problem with your word order.

BURROWS Well, absolutely, and what makes it worse, sometimes at the end of a sentence I'll come out with the wrong fusebox.

THRIPSHAW Fusebox?

BURROWS And the thing about saying the wrong word is a) I don't notice it, and b) sometimes orange water given bucket of plaster.

THRIPSHAW Yes, tell me more about your problem.

BURROWS Well, as I say, you'd just be talking and out'll pudenda the wrong word and ashtray's your uncle. So I'm really strawberry about it.

THRIPSHAW Upset?

BURROWS It's so embarrassing when my wife and I go to an orgy.

THRIPSHAW A party?

BURROWS **No, an orgy. We live in Esher.** 30

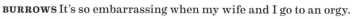

THRIPSHAW Quite.

BURROWS That's what I said. It's such a bloody whack the diddle fa di la, fo di la, lo do di...do di do, fum fum.

THRIPSHAW Mr Burrows, this is no common problem. You are suffering from a disease so rare that it hasn't got a name. Not yet. But it will have. Oh yes. This is the opportunity I've been waiting for. The chance of a lifetime! *(zoom in to close up on him as lighting changes to dramatic spotlight)* I'll show them at the Royal College of

Surgeons! I'll make them sit up and take notice! Thripshaw's disease! Discovered by E. Henry Thripshaw MD! I'll be invited on '**Call My Bluff**' **31** and on merchandizing the E. Henry Thripshaw t-shirt...I'll turn it into a game...I'll sell the film rights.

Cut to front of a booklet, entitled 'A Dissertation on Thripshaw's Disease Presented to the Royal College of Surgeons by Dr E. Henry Thripshaw'. Captions zoom forward over it:

HARLEY STREET
FLEET STREET **32**
BROADWAY
HOLLYWOOD

A page of the book turns to reveal the title 'DAVID O. SELTZER PRESENTS'. The page turns again to reveal 'RIP CLINT IN:'. The page turns again to reveal a title in stone lettering à la Ben-Hur, with searchlights behind à la 20th-Century Fox: 'DR E. HENRY THRIPSHAW'S DISEASE'. Cut to stock film of marauding knights. Superimposed caption: 'SYRIA 1203'

The knights sack a village, looting, pillaging, burning and murdering. Cut to a studio set with interviewer and Thripshaw.

INTERVIEWER *(speaking with frequent pauses, as of one reading from a slow autocue)* That clip...comes from the new David O. Seltzer...film. The author...of that film clip...is with me...now. Doctor E. Henry Thripshaw.

THRIPSHAW Well, I feel that they have missed the whole point of my disease.
INTERVIEWER This is...always the problem...with directors of film...clips.
THRIPSHAW Yes, well you see, they've dragged in all this irrelevant mush...
INTERVIEWER What...are you doing...now?
THRIPSHAW Well at the moment I am working on a new disease, which I hope to turn into a musical, but, primarily we are working on a re-make of my first disease and this time we're hoping to do it properly.
INTERVIEWER **Well...let's just...take a...look at this new film...clip.** **33**

Call My Bluff is a BBC game show in which three definitions of a word are given and the players have to guess the correct one.

Harley Street is the street of doctors in London. Fleet Street, also in London, is the traditional center of British journalism.

Cleese does a lovely little startle as Chapman finally says "clip."

Film clip exactly as before. Cut to Thripshaw at a desk evidently in a castle. A knight in armour rushes up to him.

THRIPSHAW Well now, what seems to be the matter?

Cut to a corner of the set where a man emerges from a barrel.

MAN (MICHAEL)

THE NEXT SKETCH STARTS AFTER SOME SILLY NOISES.

Black screen and a collection of really silly noises. Then fade up on a country church. Cut to interior, a vestry. A sign reads 'No Papists'. The door opens and the vicar enters as if from the end of a service. He takes off his cassock and is hanging it up. At one side of the set is a sculpture on a plinth. It is the vicar's head, but with an enormously long nose. Mr Kirkham has followed the vicar in. He is an earnest, quiet, self-effacing soul, with a tortured conscience.

VICAR (MICHAEL) Come in.
KIRKHAM (GRAHAM) I wondered if I could have a word with you for a moment.
VICAR By all means...by all means, sir. Do sit down. *(they look round for a chair)* Ah, sit on the desk here.
KIRKHAM Thank you.
VICAR Now then, a glass of sherry?
KIRKHAM No...no thank you...
VICAR *(getting a bottle from the cupboard)* Are you sure? I'm going to have some.

KIRKHAM Well, if you're having some, yes then, perhaps, vicar.
VICAR *(slightly taken aback)* Oh...well there's only just enough for me.
KIRKHAM Well in that case I won't, don't worry.
VICAR You see, if I split what's left, there'd be hardly any left for me at all.
KIRKHAM Well, I'm not a great sherry drinker.
VICAR Good! So, I can have it all...now then what's the problem?
KIRKHAM Well, just recently I've begun to worry about...

THE VICAR HAS BEEN LOOKING THROUGH HIS DESK. HE PRODUCES A BOTTLE OF SHERRY IN TRIUMPH.

The vicar has been looking through his desk. He produces a bottle of sherry in triumph.

VICAR Ah! I've found another bottle! You can have some now if you want to.
KIRKHAM Well...yes, perhaps a little...
VICAR Oh you don't have to. I can drink the whole bottle.
KIRKHAM Well in that case, no...
VICAR Good! That's another bottle for me. Do go on.

The vicar opens the bottle and pours himself a glass. As soon as he has drunk it he replenishes it again.

KIRKHAM I've begun to worry recently that...

There is a knock on the door.

VICAR Come in!

A smooth man, Mr Husband, enters carrying a smart little briefcase.

VICAR Ah, Mr Husband...this is Mr Kirkham, one of my parishioners, this is Mr Husband of the British Sherry Corporation...
KIRKHAM Look, look, perhaps I'd better come back later...
VICAR No, no...no do stay here. Have a sherry...you won't be long will you, Husband?
HUSBAND (ERIC) Oh no, vicar...it's just a question of signing a few forms.

The vicar pours Husband a sherry.

VICAR There we are...there we are, Mr Husband. Now, how about you, Mr Kirkham?
KIRKHAM Well only if there's enough.
VICAR Oh well, there's not much now.
KIRKHAM Oh, in that case...no...I won't bother.
VICAR *(pouring himself one)* Good. Right...now, then, what is the problem, Husband?
HUSBAND Well, vicar, I've made enquiries with our shippers and the most sherry they can ship in anyone load is 12,000 gallons.
VICAR And how many glasses is that?
HUSBAND

THAT'S ROUGHLY 540,000 GLASSES, VICAR.

VICAR That's excellent, Husband, excellent.
HUSBAND Yes...it means you can still keep your main sherry supply on the roof, but you can have an emergency supply underneath the vestry of 5,000 gallons.
VICAR Yes...and I could have dry sherry on the roof and Amontillado in the underground tank!
HUSBAND Absolutely.

The vicar signs a form that Husband hands to him.

VICAR Excellent work, Husband, excellent work.
HUSBAND Not at all, vicar, you're one of our best customers you and the United States. Well goodbye. *(he leaves)*
VICAR Terrific. Now then, Mr Kirkham *(pouring himself another sherry)* I am so sorry...do go on.
KIRKHAM Well, it's just that recently I've begun to worry about...
VICAR Well, look...
KIRKHAM I sometimes ask myself—does the Bible intend...

A group of Spanish singers in full national costume and guitars bursts into the vestry, noisily singing a song praising Amontillado. A man in an extravagant Spanish costume rushes in. His hat has a sign on it saying: 'SHERRY, THE DRINK OF CHAMPIONS'. Two girls come in bearing maracas and Carmen Miranda style hats. Mr Kirkham looks fed up. The Spaniards finish their song, noisily.

MAN (TERRY J) What did you want?
VICAR

DIRTY BOOKS, PLEASE.

As they carry out their transactions, noisily, we cut to the credits, rolled over a shot of the dirty postcards section of the Tudor dirty bookshop. The credits read:

'MONTY PYTHON'S FLYING CIRCUS *(with 'censored' notice over it)*
WAS CONCEIVED, WRITTEN AND CENSORED BY
MICHAEL 'BULKY' PALIN
TERRY JONES 'KING OF THE LASH'
JOHN CLEESE 'A SMILE, A SONG AND A REFILL'
TERRY GILLIAM 'AN AMERICAN IN PLASTER'
GRAHAM 'A DOZEN WHOLESALE' CHAPMAN
ERIC IDLE (ACTUAL SIZE—BATTERIES EXTRA)
ALSO APPEARING
CAROL CLEVELAND ('FOUR REVEALING POSES' HARD PUBLICATIONS PRICE 40P)
AND, IN A VARIETY OF INTERESTING POSITIONS, THE FRED TOMLINSON SINGERS UNDER THEIR LEADER 'BUTCH' TOMLINSON
ROSALIND ('AFORE YOU GO') BAILEY NOW AVAILABLE FROM BBC ENTERPRISES
BODY MAKE-UP MADELAINE GAFFNEY AND THE BBC NAUGHTY LADIES' CLUB
UNUSUAL COSTUMES AND LEATHERWEAR HAZEL PETHIG AND THE NAUGHTY LADS OF 'Q' DIVISION
ROSTRUM CAMERA MOUNTED BY PETER WILLIS (MASSAGE IN YOUR OWN HOME OR HOTEL ROOM)
ANIMATIONS AND EROTIC CARTOONS TERRY GILLIAM AND MISS HEBBERN 043-7962
GRAPHIC DETAILS BOB BLAGDEN 'DENMARK HAS NEVER LAUGHED SO MUCH'
RED LIGHTING BILL BAILEY
HEAVY BREATHING AND SOUND RICHARD CHUBB
FILM CAMERAMAN AND 'RIK' ALAN FEATHERSTONE 'MEN IT CAN BE DONE'
BLUE FILM EDITOR RAY MILLICHOPE 'WHAT YOUR RIGHT ARM'S FOR'
DESIGNED BY BOB 'BIG, BLACK, BUTCH AND BEAUTIFUL' BERK
PRODUCED BY IAN MACNAUGHTON WHO IS ASSISTING POLICE WITH THEIR ENQUIRIES
UNE ÉMISSION NOCTURNALE PAR TÉLÉVISIONE FRANÇAISE ET BBC TV
COPYRIGHT BBC TV £5 IN A PLAIN WRAPPER'

Fade out. Fade up on the BBC world symbol.

VOICE OVER (MICHAEL) E. Henry Thripshaw t-shirts are now available from BBC Enterprises. The price hasn't finally been decided, and the address to write to...they haven't yet quite worked out.

SEASON 3
EPISODE 37
SCOTSMAN
EXHIBIT

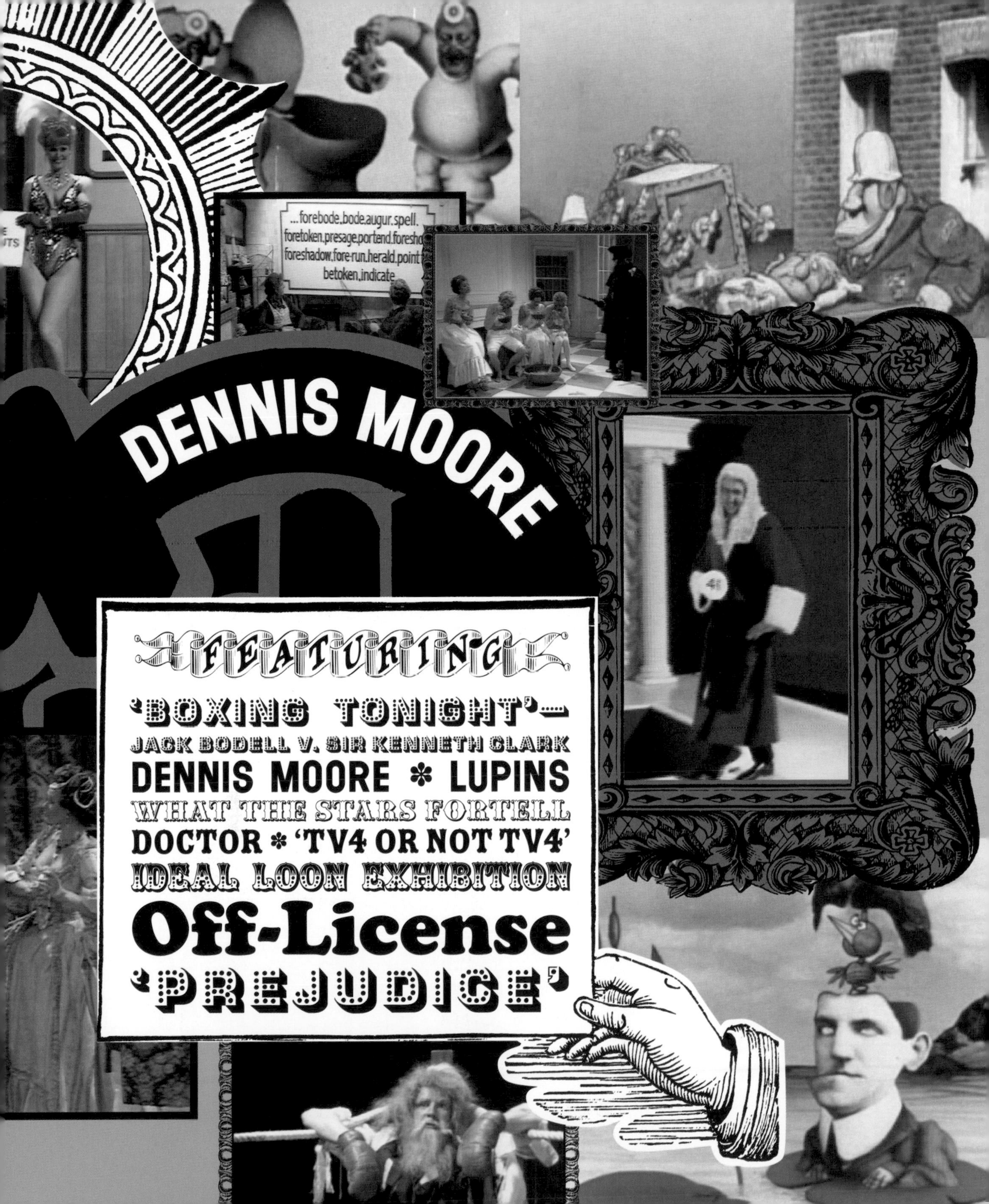
...forebode.bode.augur.spell.
foretoken.presage.portend.foresho
foreshadow.fore-run.herald.point
betoken.indicate
DENNIS MOORE
FEATURING
'BOXING TONIGHT'—
JACK BODELL V. SIR KENNETH CLARK
DENNIS MOORE * LUPINS
WHAT THE STARS FORTELL
DOCTOR * 'TV4 OR NOT TV4'
IDEAL LOON EXHIBITION
Off-License
'PREJUDICE'

FIRST AIRED: JANUARY 4, 1973

A floodlit boxing ring. Sports programme music. Superimposed caption: 'BOXING TONIGHT'

VOICE OVER (MICHAEL) 'Boxing Tonight' comes from the Empire Pool, Wembley and features the main heavyweight bout between **Jack Bodell, British and Empire Heavyweight Champion.** **1** *(cheers; shot of Bodell (Nosher Powell) in his corner with two seconds)* And **Sir Kenneth Clark...** **2** *(shot of Clark's corner; he is in a dressing-gown with 'Sir Kenneth Clark' on the back; both take off their dressing-gowns as referee calls them together; Sir Kenneth is wearing a tweed suit underneath)* It's the first time these two have met so there should be some real action tonight...

The bell goes. Crowd noise. ***Sir Kenneth wanders around as in 'Civilization'.*** **3**

SIR KENNETH (GRAHAM) This then is the height of the English Renaissance, the triumph of Classical over Gothic...the...

Bodell swings a left and knocks Sir Kenneth down.

VOICE OVER He's down! Sir Kenneth Clark is down in eight seconds. But he's up again. He's up at six...

SIR KENNETH The almost ordered façades of Palladio's villas reflects the...

Bodell knocks him down again.

VOICE OVER And he's down again, and I don't think he's going to get up this time. *(referee counts Sir Kenneth Clark out and holds up Bodell's hand)* No, so Jack Bodell has defeated **Sir Kenneth Clark in the very first round here tonight and so this big Lincolnshire heavyweight becomes the new Oxford Professor of Fine Art.** **4**

Zoom in to the ring. The announcer appears in DJ and takes a mike lowered on a wire.

Jack Bodell won the British heavyweight championship in 1969, though Henry Cooper, another boxer-celebrity, beat him a year later. Bodell then regained it, beating Joe Bugner, yet another British boxer-celebrity (the 1960s and '70s were full with them).

Kenneth Clark, the British museum director, author, and TV presenter regularly mentioned by the Pythons.

Civilization was Clark's BBC2 series from 1969 about the history of Western art, architecture, and civilization.

Clark was the Slade professor of Fine Art at Oxford University between 1946 and 1950.

ANNOUNCER (JOHN) Thank you, thank you, thank you, ladies and gentlemen. And now...

Cut to a corner of the ring. The nude organist at his organ, plays a chord, turns and grins. Cut to the opposite corner; the 'It's' man on his stool.

IT'S MAN (MICHAEL)

IT'S...

Animated titles.

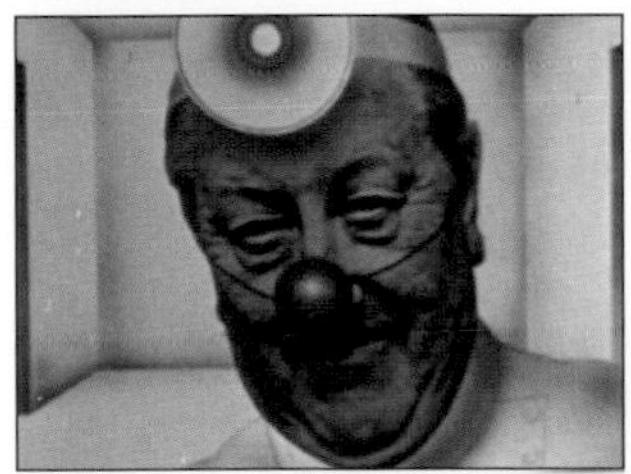

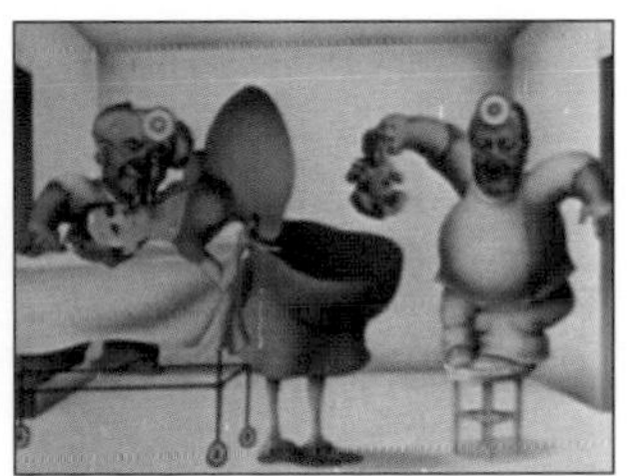

Slow pan across idyllic countryside. We see a traditional eighteenth-century coach and horses travelling along the valley floor. Suddenly a highwayman, Dennis Moore, spurs his horse forward and rides up to the coach brandishing pistols.

MOORE (JOHN)

STAND AND DELIVER! DROP THAT GUN!

(the coach comes to a halt; the drivers hold up their hands but the postilion reaches for a gun; Moore shoots him) Let that be a warning to you all. You move at your peril for I have two pistols here. I know one of them isn't loaded any more, but the other one is, so that's one of you dead for sure, or just about for sure anyway, it certainly wouldn't be worth your while risking it because I'm a very good shot, I practise every day, well, not absolutely *every* day, but most days in the week...I expect I must practise four or five times a week, at least...at least four or five, only some weekends...like last weekend there wasn't much time so that moved the average down a bit...but I should say it's definitely a solid four days' practice every week...at least. I mean, I reckon I could hit that tree over there...the one behind that hillock, not the big hillock, the little hillock on the left. *(heads are coming out of the coach and peering)* You can see the three trees, the third from the left and back a bit—that one—I reckon I could hit that four times out of five...on a good day. Say with this wind...say, say, seven times out of ten...

SQUIRE (TERRY J) What, that tree there?

MOORE Which one?

SQUIRE The big beech with the sort of bare branch coming out of the top left.

MOORE No, no, no, not that one.

GIRL (CAROL) No, no, he means the one over there. Look, you see that one there.

SQUIRE Yes.

GIRL Well now, go two along to the right.

COACHMAN (GRAHAM) Just near that little bush.

GIRL Well, it's the one just behind it.

A hornbeam is a hardwood tree.

SQUIRE Ah! The elm.

MOORE No, that's not an elm. An elm's got sort of great clumps of leaves like that. That's either a beech or a...er...**hornbeam.** 5

PARSON (ERIC) A hornbeam?

MOORE Oh, no not a hornbeam. What's the tree that has a leaf with sort of regular veins coming out and the veins go all the way out to the...

GIRL Serrated?

MOORE ...to the serrated edges.

PARSON A willow!

MOORE That's right.

PARSON That's nothing like a willow.

MOORE Well it doesn't matter anyway! I could hit it seven times out of ten, that's the point.

PARSON Never a willow.

MOORE Shut up! This is a hold-up, not a botany lesson. Right, now my fine friends, no false moves please.

I WANT YOU TO HAND OVER ALL THE LUPINS YOU'VE GOT.

SQUIRE Lupins?

MOORE Yes, lupins. Come on, come on.

PARSON What do you mean, lupins?

MOORE Don't try and play for time.

PARSON I'm not, you mean the flower lupin?

MOORE Yes, that's right.

SQUIRE Well, we haven't got any lupins.

GIRL Honestly.

MOORE Look, my fine friends, I happen to know that this is the Lupin Express.

SQUIRE You must be out of your tiny mind.

MOORE Get out of the coach. Come on, get out! *(they do so indicating that Moore is a loony; he dismounts and enters the coach; he immediately comes out with an enormous armful of lupins)* Just as I thought. Not clever enough, my fine friends. Come on, Concorde. *(he jumps on horse and rides away)*

SQUIRE Well, so much for the lupins.

Montage of Dennis Moore, galloping through the sun-dappled glades, a little village, more glades and forest and arriving at a little peasant-type woodcutter's hut where two terribly poor peasants greet him and receive the lupins with a neutral reaction. During this the following song is heard.

SONG Dennis Moore, Dennis Moore,
Galloping through the sward.
Dennis Moore, Dennis Moore,
And his horse Concorde.
He steals from the rich and
Gives to the poor.
Mr Moore, Mr Moore, Mr Moore.

MOORE Here we are, I'll be back.

Moore wheels round and rides off. Superimposed caption: 'THE END' Pull back to reveal 'The End' is on TV in the house of Mrs Trepidatious. Another old ratbag enters and sits opposite Mrs Trepidatious.

MRS O (ERIC) Morning, Mrs Trepidatious.

MRS TREPIDATIOUS (GRAHAM) Oh, I don't know what's good about it, my right arm's hanging off something awful.

MRS O Oh, you want to have that seen to.

MRS TREPIDATIOUS What, by that Dr Morrison? He's killed more patients than I've had severe boils.

MRS O What do the stars say?

MRS TREPIDATIOUS **Well, Petula Clark says burst them early, but David Frost... 6**

MRS O No, the stars in the paper, you cloth-eared heap of anteater's catarrh, the zodiacal signs, the horoscopic fates, the astrological portents, the omens, the genethliac prognostications, the mantalogical harbingers, the vaticinal utterances, the fratidical premonitory uttering of the mantalogical omens—**what do the bleeding stars in the paper predict, forecast, prophesy, foretell, prognosticate... 7**

A big sheet is lowered with the words on.

VOICE OVER (GRAHAM) And this is where you at home can join in.

MRS O ...forebode, bode, augur, spell, foretoken, *(the audience joins in)* presage, portend, foreshow, foreshadow, forerun, herald, point to, betoken, indicate!

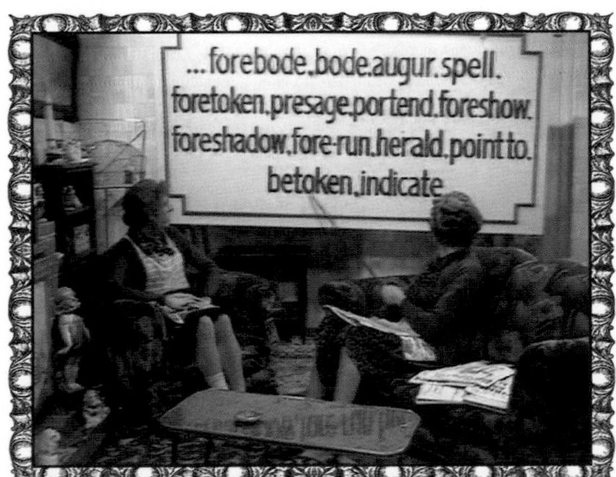

MRS TREPIDATIOUS I don't know.

The sheet is raised again.

MRS O What are you?

MRS TREPIDATIOUS I'm Nesbitt.

MRS O There's not a zodiacal sign called Nesbitt...

6 Neither the popular singer (Petula Clark) nor the TV presenter (David Frost) are qualified doctors.

7 The adjectives here are mostly gobbledygook.

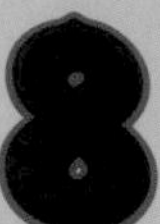

Derry & Toms was a large London department store that closed in 1971.

Roger Moore, the suave star of TV shows *The Saint* (1962–1969) and *The Persuaders!* (1971–1972) who then, from 1973 to 1985, starred in James Bond movies (notably *Live and Let Die* and *The Spy Who Loved Me*). He made seven Bond movies in all.

Tony Curtis, the slick American actor, who notably starred in Billy Wilder's *Some Like It Hot* alongside Jack Lemmon and Marilyn Monroe.

The Mike Sammes Singers were a popular group of the day.

Peter Wyngarde was the handsome acting star of the 1969 espionage series *Department S*, playing the character Jason King. His celebrity status was ruined after his conviction in the mid-1970s for "gross indecency" in a public restroom.

Duane Eddy, the American guitarist.

MRS TREPIDATIOUS **All right, Derry and Toms. 8**

MRS O *(surveying paper)* Aquarius, Scorpio, Virgo, Derry and Toms. April 29th to March 22nd. Even dates only.

MRS TREPIDATIOUS Well what does it presage?

MRS O You have green, scaly skin, and a soft yellow underbelly with a series of fin-like ridges running down your spine and tail. Although lizardlike in shape, you can grow anything up to thirty feet in length with huge teeth that can bite off great rocks and trees. You inhabit arid sub-tropical zones and wear spectacles.

MRS TREPIDATIOUS It's very good about the spectacles.

MRS O It's amazing.

MRS TREPIDATIOUS Mm...what's yours, Irene?

MRS O Basil.

MRS TREPIDATIOUS I'm sorry, what's yours, Basil?

MRS O No. That's my star sign, Basil...

MRS TREPIDATIOUS There isn't a...

MRS O Yes there is...Aquarius, Sagittarius, Derry and Toms, Basil. June 21st to June 22nd.

MRS TREPIDATIOUS Well, what does it say?

MRS O You have green, scaly skin and a series of yellow underbellies running down your spine and tail...

MRS TREPIDATIOUS That's exactly the same!

MRS O Try number one...what's Aquarius?

MRS TREPIDATIOUS It's a zodiacal sign.

MRS O I know that, what does it say in the paper Mrs Flan-and-pickle?

MRS TREPIDATIOUS All right...Oh! It says, 'a wonderful day ahead'. You will be surrounded by family and friends. **Roger Moore 9** will drop in for lunch, bringing **Tony Curtis with him. 10** In the afternoon a substantial cash sum will come your way. In the evening Petula Clark will visit your home accompanied by **Mike Sammes singers. 11** She will sing for you in your own living room. Before you go to bed, **Peter Wyngarde 12** will come and declare his undying love for you.

MRS O Urghh! What's Scorpio?

MRS TREPIDATIOUS Oh, that's very good. 'You will have lunch with a schoolfriend of **Duane Eddy's, 13** who will insist on whistling some of Duane's greatest instrumental hits. In the afternoon you will die, you will be buried...'

A doctor is lowered on a wire.

DOCTOR (TERRY J) Good morning.

MRS O Oh, morning, doctor.

DOCTOR How's the old arm this morning, Mrs Ikon?

MRS TREPIDATIOUS Oh, it's still hanging off at the shoulder.

DOCTOR Good, well let's have a look at it, shall we? *(he tries unsuccessfully to open his bag)* Oh damn, damn, damn, damn...damn this wretched bag...oh the wretched, damn, bloody, little bag. It's the one thing I hate about being a doctor—it's this wretched bloody little bag!

He smashes a chair over it and finally produces a revolver and shoots the lock off. It opens and is stuffed full of pound notes, some of which spill out. He feels inside...eventually pulls out a stethoscope.

DOCTOR What's that doing here? *(he throws it away)*

Cut to another doctor walking along a street. The stethoscope flies out of window and lands on him.

SECOND DOCTOR (GRAHAM) *(brushing it off)* Eurgggh!

Cut back to the first doctor still rummaging in black bag. Eventually he produces a pair of black kid gloves and a black handkerchief. He folds it and puts it on and points the gun at Mrs Trepidatious.

DOCTOR Hand over the money. *(she goes to a sideboard, opens the bottom drawer and gets out a money box which she gives to him)* Come on, all of it! *(she looks scared; he jabs the gun at her; she goes over to a painting of a wall-safe on the wall and pushes it aside to reveal an identical wall-safe underneath.* ***She opens it and a hand comes out holding a money box; she takes and gives it to the doctor)*** [14] Yes, that seems to be OK. Right! I'll just test your reflexes! ***(he opens his mac like a flasher; they scream and jump)*** [15] Right, now then, everything seems to be OK, I'll see you next week. Keep collecting the pensions, and try not to spend too much on food. *(he starts to go up)*

MRS TREPIDATIOUS Thank you, doctor. *(he disappears)*

Cut to a hospital ward. A man in bed, a chair with his clothes on it at the foot of the bed. A doctor enters and goes right for the jacket and starts to feel in the pockets.

DOCTOR (MICHAEL) Morning, Mr Henson...How are we today?

HENSON (TERRY G) Not too bad, doctor.

DOCTOR OK, take it easy...*(he empties his wallet and puts it back)* Expecting any postal orders this week?

HENSON No.

DOCTOR Righto.

A nurse comes and gets the loose change. The doctor goes to the next bed, where there is a man entirely in traction.

DOCTOR Ah, Mr Rodgers, have you got your unemployment benefit please? Right. Well can you write me a cheque then...please?

The patient writes him a cheque. He goes to the foot of the bed. There is a graph with a money symbol on it. He marks it down further.

DOCTOR Thank you very much. Soon have you down to nothing. Ah, Mr Millichope. *(he smiles and leaves, passing a man with a saline drip full of coins; chink of money)*

A Gilliam animation suitably connected with the foregoing concept leads us to a TV debate set-up. Stern music starts as the lights come on.

And mutters a charming and hilarious "thank you."

This gets a big laugh and applause break, for some reason.

ECURICOR
BULANCES
LTD.
TIME'S UP!

Channel 4, only the fourth national TV channel in the U.K., first aired shows in 1982, a decade after this "debate."

Superimposed captions: 'THE GREAT DEBATE' 'NUMBER 31' ***'TV4 OR NOT TV4?'*** **16**

KENNEDY (ERIC) Hello. Should there be another television channel, or should there not? On tonight's programme the Minister for Broadcasting, The Right Honourable Mr Ian Throat MP.

THROAT (TERRY J) Good evening.
KENNEDY The Chairman of the Amalgamated Money TV, Sir Abe Sappenheim.
SAPPENHEIM (GRAHAM) Good evening.
KENNEDY The Shadow Spokesman for Television, Lord Kinwoodie.
KINWOODIE (JOHN) Hello.
KENNEDY And a television critic, Mr Patrick Loone.
LOONE (MICHAEL) Hello.
KENNEDY Gentlemen—should there be a fourth television channel or not? Ian?
THROAT Yes.
KENNEDY Francis.
KINWOODIE No.
KENNEDY Sir Abe?
SAPPENHEIM Yes.
KENNEDY Patrick.
LOONE No.

Superimposed caption: 'YES 2 NO 2'

KENNEDY Well there you have it. Two say will, two say won't. We'll be back again next week, and next week's 'Great Debate' will be about Government Interference in Broadcasting and will be cancelled mysteriously.

The lights fade down. Music. Superimposed roller caption:

'THE GREAT DEBATE
INTRODUCED BY LUDOVIC LUDOVIC **17**
WITH SIR ABE SAPPENHEIM
IAN THROAT MP
LORD KINWOODIE
MR PATRICK LOONE'

"Ludovic Ludovic" is a reference to Ludovic Kennedy, British public intellectual, TV presenter, and campaigner against the death penalty.

Behind this the panel members are seen gesticulating strangely in silhouette. Fade out. Fade up on a picture of Queen Victoria.

VOICE OVER (MICHAEL) Just starting on BBC 1 now, 'Victoria Regina' the inspiring tale of the simple crofter's daughter who worked her way up to become Queen of England and Empress of the Greatest Empire television has ever seen. **On BBC 2 now Episode 3 of 'George I'** **18** the new 116 part serial about the famous English King who hasn't been done yet. On ITV now the *(sound of a punch)* Ugh!

18

George I, king of Great Britain and Ireland from 1714 to 1727.

Music starts. Picture of Royal crest. superimposed caption: 'GEORGE I' The word 'Charles' below the crest has been crossed out and 'George I' written above it. caption: 'EPISODE 3—THE GATHERING STORM' This looks very dog-eared and thumb-printed. Cut to studio set of an eighteenth-century ballroom. Some dancing is going on. A fop is talking to two ladies in the usual phony mouthing manner. They laugh meaninglessly.

GRANTLEY (MICHAEL) Ah! 'Tis my lord of Buckingham. Pray welcome, Your Grace.

BUCKINGHAM (TERRY J) Thank you, Grantley.

GRANTLEY Ladies, may I introduce to you the man who prophesied that a German monarch would soon embroil this country in continental affairs.

FIRST LADY (CAROL) Oh, how so, my lord?

BUCKINGHAM Madam, you will recall that prior to his accession our gracious sovereign George had become involved in the long standing **Northern War,** **19** through his claims to Bremen and Verdun. These duchies would provide an outlet to the sea of the utmost value to Hanover. The Treaty of Westphalia has assigned them to Sweden.

The Great Northern War was a conflict from 1700 to 1721 between the Tsardom of Russia and Sweden for supremacy in northern Europe. George I brought Britain into it—on the Russian side—in 1717. (Russia won, by the way.)

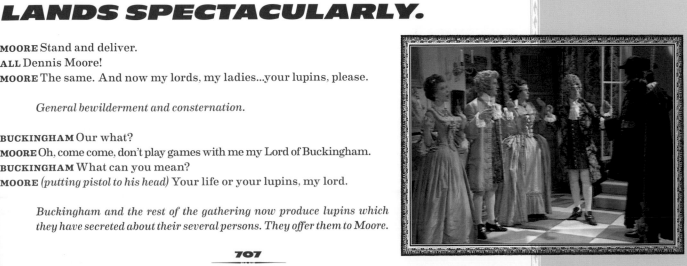

GRANTLEY In 1648.

BUCKINGHAM Exactly.

GRANTLEY Meanwhile Frederick William of Denmark, taking advantage of the absence of Charles XII, seized them; 1712.

SECOND LADY Oh yes!

FIRST LADY It all falls into place. More wine?

GRANTLEY Oh, thank you.

BUCKINGHAM However, just prior to his accession, George had made an alliance with Frederick William of Prussia, on the grounds of party feeling.

GRANTLEY While Frederick William had married George's only daughter.

FIRST LADY I remember the wedding.

BUCKINGHAM But chiefly through concern at the concerted action against Charles XII...

THERE IS A CRASH AS MOORE SWINGS THROUGH THE WINDOW ON A ROPE. EVERYONE GASPS AND SCREAMS. HE LANDS SPECTACULARLY.

MOORE Stand and deliver.

ALL Dennis Moore!

MOORE The same. And now my lords, my ladies...your lupins, please.

General bewilderment and consternation.

BUCKINGHAM Our what?

MOORE Oh, come come, don't play games with me my Lord of Buckingham.

BUCKINGHAM What can you mean?

MOORE *(putting pistol to his head)* Your life or your lupins, my lord.

Buckingham and the rest of the gathering now produce lupins which they have secreted about their several persons. They offer them to Moore.

MOORE In a bunch, in a bunch. *(they arrange them in a bunch)* Thank you my friends, and now a good evening to you all.

He grabs the rope, is hauled into air and disappears out of the window. There is a bump, a whinny and the sound of galloping hooves. The guests rush to the window to watch him disappear.

Carol Cleveland has a bit of trouble yanking the flower from her garter but she does, eventually.

GRANTLEY He seeks them here...he seeks them there...he seeks those lupins everywhere. The murdering blackguard! He's taken all our lupins.

FIRST LADY ***(producing one from her garter)* Not quite.** 20

Gasps of delight.

BUCKINGHAM Oh you tricked him!

MAN We still have one! *(they all cheer)*

Cut to a similar montage as before of Moore galloping through forest, clearings and tiny villages. Song as follows.

SONG Dennis Moore, Dennis Moore,
Riding through the night.
Soon every lupin in the land
Will be in his mighty hand
He steals them from the rich
And gives them to the poor
Mr Moore, Mr Moore, Mr Moore.

Towards the end of this he arrives at the same peasant's cottage as before, dismounts and runs to the cottage door. He pauses. From inside the cottage we hear quiet moaning. Cut to inside the cottage. In this rude hut, lit by a single candle, the female peasant lies apparently dying on a bunk. Lupins are everywhere, in the fire, on the bed, a large pile of them forms a pillow. The female peasant is moaning and the male peasant is kneeling beside her offering her a lupin. Moore enters slowly.

MALE PEASANT (MICHAEL) *(dressed largely in a lupin suit)* Try and eat some, my dear. It'll give you strength. *(Dennis Moore reverently approaches the bed; the male peasant looks round and sees him)* Oh Mr Moore, Mr Moore, she's going fast.

MOORE Don't worry, I've...I've brought you something.

MALE PEASANT Medicine at last?

MOORE No.

MALE PEASANT Food?

MOORE No.

MALE PEASANT Some blankets perhaps...clothes...wood for the fire...

MOORE No. Lupins!

MALE PEASANT *(exploding)* Oh Christ!

MOORE *(astonished)* I thought you liked them.

MALE PEASANT I'm sick to bloody death of them.

FEMALE PEASANT (TERRY J) So am I.

MALE PEASANT She's bloody dying and all you bring us is lupins. All we've eaten mate for the last four bleeding weeks is lupin soup, roast lupin, steamed lupin, braised lupin in lupin sauce, lupin in the basket with sautéed lupins, lupin meringue pie, lupin sorbet...we sit on lupins, we sleep in lupins, we feed the cat on lupins, we burn lupins, we even *wear* the bloody things!

MOORE Looks very smart.

MONTY PYTHON'S FLIEGENDER ZIRKUS

When the British comedian Eddie Izzard was struggling with stage fright in the early part of his career, he decided to remedy it by doing his entire act in French. (Fortunately for him, he was in France at the time.)

Such forward thinking, especially from the European mainland, is rare in a British person of any occupation. Brits tend to distrust what we like to call "Europe," even though the U.K. is part of the European community. So it may surprise you to learn that Izzard isn't the only funny man to sell his wares "on the continent." As with many other things, the Pythons got there first.

To the British, Germans don't have a sense of humor (just as the French don't do pop music and the Dutch smoke marijuana as they ride around on bicycles). Imagine the surprise of the Pythons then when a Bavarian TV producer by the name of Alfred Biolek contacted the team and suggested they do a show for Germany. Smartly, he invited them to scout locations about which they could write sketches. The subsequent show was filmed at the soccer grounds of the Bayern Munich team, at the castle of Ludwig II of Bavaria, and most notably during Oktoberfest, which caused Graham Chapman to go missing for a few days.

The show itself was a completely new set of sketches written in English and translated into German. Apart from John Cleese and Michael Palin, who knew some of the language, the Pythons were faced with trying to wring comedy out of lines they barely understood. Emphasis for laughs was one thing; dodgy translations were another. Palin remembers a line about "scaring the shit" out of somebody coming out as "[We are going to] cause you to involuntarily excrete on the chair." Chapman was concerned that the formal nature of German grammar made comedy that much harder to create.

Whatever the case, the first show, called *Monty Python's Fliegender Zirkus*, aired on January 3, 1972, and featured the "Lumberjack Song" sung by the German–Austrian Border Guard as well as many other more original sketches. As Chapman remembered, the show was up against an England-vs.-Germany soccer match and therefore faired poorly in the ratings, though England wouldn't play Germany until April 29th of that year (a game the Germans won, in London, 3–1). Yet German critics liked the show enough that a second one was made; but this time, to mitigate the accents (especially Terry Jones's), the show was shot in English and dubbed in German. It aired on December 18, 1972. One is left with the image of that groundbreaking first show, however, with the Pythons doing their stuff in stilted German, the "Mounties" dressed in tight Austrian uniforms, and Palin singing away at a song he claims to remember still, word for word, in two languages.

MALE PEASANT Oh shut up! We're sick to death with the stench of them. *(sound of a miaow and then a bump)* Look. The cat's just choked itself to death on them. *(we see a dead cat with lupins coming out of its mouth)*

I DON'T CARE IF I NEVER SEE ANOTHER LUPIN TILL THE DAY I DIE! WHY DON'T YOU GO OUT AND STEAL SOMETHING USEFUL!

MOORE Like what?
MALE PEASANT Like gold and silver and clothes and wood and jewels and...
MOORE Hang on, I'll get a piece of paper.

Cut to a montage of shots of Moore riding away from the hut over which we hear the song.

SONG Dennis Moore, Dennis Moore,
Dum dum dum the night.
Dennis Moore, Dennis Moore,
Dum de dum dum plight.
He steals dum dum dum
And dum dum dum dee
Dennis dum, Dennis dee, dum dum dum.

Cut back to the ballroom to find the same people discussing British history.

BUCKINGHAM This, coupled with the presence of Peter and his Prussians at Mecklenburg and Charles and his Swedes in Pomerania, made George and Stanhope eager to come to terms with France.
GRANTLEY Meanwhile, a breach had now opened with...

Moore swings in as before.

GRANTLEY Oh no, not again.
BUCKINGHAM Come on.
MOORE Stand and deliver again! Your money, your jewellery, your...hang on. *(he takes out a list)* Your clothes, your snuff, your ornaments, your glasswear, your pussy cats...
BUCKINGHAM *(aside to the first lady)* Don't say anything about the lupins...
MOORE Your watches, your lace, your spittoons...

Cut to a montage pretty much as before but with Moore riding through the glades dragging behind him a really enormous bag marked with 'swag' in very olde English lettering. This bag is about twenty feet long and bumps along the ground behind the horse with the appropriate sound effects to make it sound full of valuable jewels, gold, silver, etc. Song as follows.

SONG Dennis Moore, Dennis Moore,
Riding through the woods.
Dennis Moore, Dennis Moore
With a bag of things.
He gives to the poor and he takes from the rich
Dennis Moore, Dennis Moore, Dennis Moore.

As he arrives at the poor peasant's cottage they run out. They all open the bag together to the peasants' enormous and unmeasurable joy.

MOORE Here we are.

Superimposed caption: 'THE END' Cut to stock film of people queuing at an exhibition hall.

VOICE OVER (ERIC) Well it may be the end of that, but it's certainly far from the end of—well in fact it's the beginning—well not quite the beginning—well certainly nearer the beginning than the end—well yes damn it, it is to all intents and purposes the beginning of this year's Ideal Loon Exhibition, **sponsored by the 'Daily Express'.** 21 *(cut to interior of hall, people pouring through the doors; above their heads it says 'Ideal Loon Exhibition')* Numbskulls and **boobies** 22 from all over the country have been arriving to go through their strange paces before a large paying crowd. This is the fifteenth Ideal Loon Exhibition and we took a good look round after it was opened by its patron...*(quick flash of Edward Heath opening something)* There's Kevin Bruce the digger duffer from down-under, who's ranked fourteenth in the world's silly positions league...*(Kevin is in a roped-off exhibition area; with a number in front of him; people are walking past looking at him with programmes; he is dressed in Australian bush gear and he is leaning his forehead against a goldfish bowl on a four-foot-six plinth)* This kind of incoherent behaviour is really beginning to catch on down-under. There's Norman Kirby from New Zealand, whose speciality is standing behind a screen with a lady with no clothes on...*(again in an exhibition stand with a number in front; there is a screen which is higher than their heads, but it is cut off at knee height so you can see two pairs of legs, one female, totally bare, one male wearing some enormous boots, no socks)* In real life, Norman is a gynaecologist, but this is his lunch hour. And from France there's a superb

The Daily Express is a newspaper beloved by the suburbanite and the Conservative alike.

"Boobies" means fools, not breasts.

exhibition of rather silly behaviour: by the Friends of the Free French Osteopaths. *(on the stand five men dressed in Breton berets, striped French shirts, silly moustaches, with baguettes; in unison they make the silly sign, counting the while 'un, deux, trois')* They do this over four hundred times a day. Nobody knows why. But for sheer pointless behaviour you've got to admire Brian Broomers, the battling British boy who for two weeks has been suspended over a tin of condemned veal. *(quite a crowd watch this; again a roped-off exhibit, Brian* (GRAHAM) *is suspended from the ceiling by two car tyres; he lies there smoking a pipe; underneath him there is a small opened tin, with 'veal' on the side)* Always popular with the crowd, **is the Scotsman with Nae Trews exhibit, 23** and this year's no exception. *(a very large man* (JOHN) *dressed as a Scotsman in front of a sign saying 'Scotsman with Nae Trews Exhibit, Sponsored by Natural Gas'; an enormously long line of middle-aged pepperpots stand waiting in a queue; each in turn lifts up a corner of Scotsman's kilt, has a tiny peek and walks off)* Sponsored by Natural Gas and Glasgow City Council, this exhibit is entirely supported by voluntary contributions. But for a truly magnificent waste of time you've got to go no further than the exhibit from Italy—Italian priests in custard, discussing vital matters of the day. *(four Italian priests standing up to their chests in a large vat of custard; in front of them it says 'Italian Priests in custard'; they are animatedly discussing vital matters; hung behind them is a sign saying 'Italy, Land of Custard')* These lads from a seminary near Cremona, have been practising for well over a year. As always one of the great attractions of this fourteen-day exhibition is the display of counter-marching given by the Massed Pipes and Toilet Requisites of the Colwyn Bay Massed Pipes and Toilet Requisites Club. *(a dozen people in blazers, flannels and white pumps are vigorously counter-marching, whilst Souza's Star Spangled Banner blares out; they are holding various items of plumbing, lengths of piping, a toilet, a bidet, a bath, back scrubbers, loofahs, shower attachments, hand basins, etc.)* An interesting point about these boys is they all have one thing in common. Hip injuries. Not far away the crowds are flocking to see a member of the famous Royal Canadian Mounted Geese. *(cut to pantomime goose on horseback)* But the climax of the whole event is the judging.

"Nae trews," a style of wearing kilts, is Scottish for "no trousers."

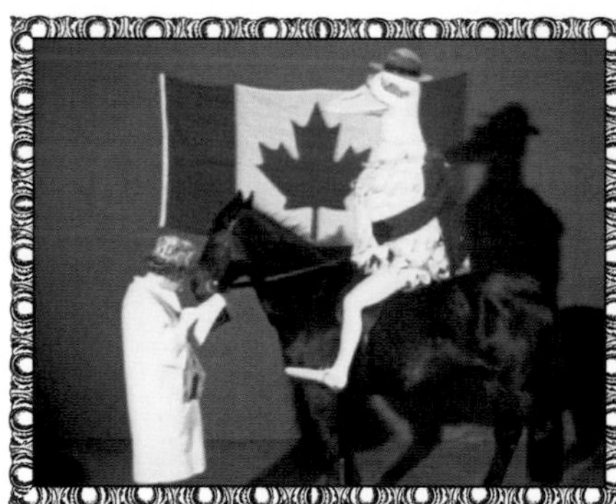

Cut to a sort of Miss World cat-walk. A judge (ERIC) *appears (holding number 41). A band plays 'A pretty girl is like a melody'.*

PA ANNOUNCEMENT (JOHN) Mr Justice Burke. *(the judge walks down, turns slightly at the edge of the stage, puts a knee forward and makes a cheesecake smile)* Well that's the last, and let's just see those last six once again. *(the judge on the stage is joined by five others in full judicial robes, with wigs, each holding a number)* And the winner is—number 41, Mr Justice Burke.

The winner reacts by bursting into tears. The others look rather sad. Cut to a still picture of Mr Justice Burke in bed having breakfast the next morning. He is still wearing his robes and wig but he has a sceptre and a terrible tiara crown on. This picture is in black and white and is large on the front page of a newspaper. The headline is 'Justice seen to be done'. A sub-heading says 'British Justice Triumphs'. This newspaper page takes us off into a couple of minutes of animation.

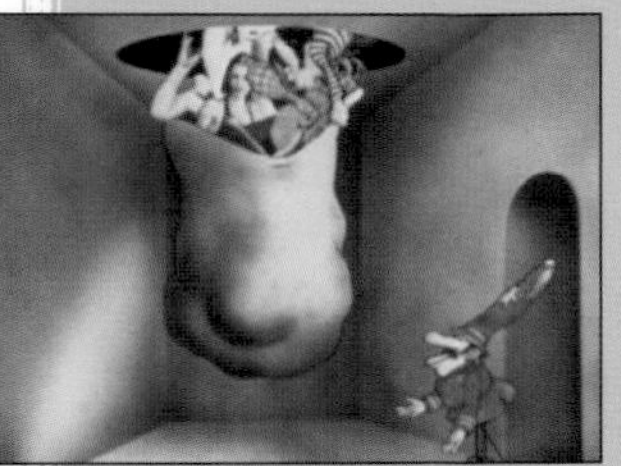

Cut to close up of a man's face.

MCGOUGH (ERIC) Yet fear, not like an aged florin, can so disseminate men's eyes, that fortune, straining at a kissing touch may stop her ceaseless search to sport amidst the rampant thrust of time, and bring the thing undone to pass by that with which the cock may chance an arm.

Cut to a wider shot to show that he is in an off-licence. Mr Bones is behind the counter.

MR BONES (JOHN) Well that's all very well, sir, but this is an off-licence.
MCGOUGH Oh. Just a bottle of sherry then, please.
MR BONES Certainly...Amontillado?
MCGOUGH Yes, I think Amontillado, finely grown...well chosen from the casque of Pluto's hills, cell'd deep within the vinous soil of Spain, wrench'd thence from fiery regions of the sun...
MR BONES Yes, yes sir. Just one bottle?
MCGOUGH Just one bottle. Just one jot. Just one tittle. That's the lot.
MR BONES There we are, sir. That'll be a pound, please.
MCGOUGH A pound a pound and all around abound.
A pound found found.
Lost lost the cost till was't embossed...
MR BONES Excuse me, sir.
MCGOUGH Yes, good victualler, nature's trencherman, mine honest tapster...
MR BONES I was just wondering. Are you a poet?
MCGOUGH No, no, I'm a solicitor...well versed within the written law of man, can to those who need...
MR BONES Oh *shut* up.
MCGOUGH I'm sorry. I'm afraid I've caught poetry.
MR BONES Oh really? Well, don't worry, sir—

I USED TO SUFFER FROM SHORT STORIES.

MCGOUGH Really? When?
MR BONES Oh, once upon a time...there lived in Wiltshire a young chap called Dennis Moore. Now Dennis was a highwayman by profession...*(we ripple through to Dennis Moore riding along with a big bag of swag)*...and for several months he had been stealing from the rich to give to the poor. One day...

Mix through to a shot of Dennis Moore arriving with another bag of goodies. The peasants who greet him are by now very smartly dressed and the cottage has been refurbished.

MOORE Here we are again, Mr Jenkins. *(Dennis leaves the bag and wheels his horse around)* There we are...I'll be back. *(he rides off again purposefully)*

Cut back to the ballroom. The walls are bare and the people are down to their undergarments. They sit around the table gnawing pieces of bread and dipping them in a watery soup. The central bowl of soup contains a lupin.

BUCKINGHAM Meanwhile Frederick William busily engaged in defending against the three great powers the province of Silesia...

GRANTLEY ...which he had seized in the War of the Austrian succession against his word.

FIRST LADY Yes, I remember.

MAN ...was now dependent on Pitt's subsidies.

MOORE SWINGS IN THROUGH THE WINDOW. THEY ALL RESPOND TO HIM WITH LISTLESS MOANS OF DISAPPOINTMENT.

MOORE My lords, my ladies, on your feet, please. *(he is ignored and therefore says commandingly)* I must ask you to do exactly as I say or I shall be forced to shoot you right between the eyes. *(they stand up hurriedly)* Well not right between the eyes, I mean when I say between the eyes, obviously I don't have to be that accurate, I mean, if I hit you in that sort of area, like that, obviously, that's all right for me, I mean, I don't have to try and sort of hit a point bisecting a line drawn between your pupils or anything like that. I mean, from my point of view, it's perfectly satisfactory...

FIRST LADY What do you *want*? Why are you here?

MOORE Why are *any* of us here? I mean, when you get down to it, it's all so *meaningless*, isn't it, I mean what do any of us want...

BUCKINGHAM No, no, Oh I see, oh just the usual things, a little place of my own, the right girl...

GRANTLEY No, no, no! What do you want from us?

MOORE Oh sorry. Um, your gold, your silver, your jewellery.

BUCKINGHAM You've taken it all.

FIRST LADY This is all we've got left.

MOORE That's nice. I'll have them. Come on. *(he takes all the spoons)*

BUCKINGHAM You'd better take the bloody lupin too.

MOORE Thank you very much, I've gone through that stage. *(he grabs the rope and swings out again)*

Short montage of Dennis riding accompanied by the song. 'DENNIS MOORE, DENNIS MOORE. ETCETERA, ETCETERA...' He leaps off his horse and runs to the door of the hut, throws the door open and enters. The little hut is now stuffed with all possible signs of wealth and all imaginable treasures.

MALE PEASANT What you got for us today then.

MOORE Well I've managed to find you four very nice silver spoons Mr Jenkins.

MALE PEASANT *(snatching them rudely)* Who do you think you are giving us poor this rubbish?

FEMALE PEASANT Bloody silver. Won't have it in the house. *(throws it away)* And those candlesticks you got us last week were only sixteen carat.

MALE PEASANT Yes, why don't you go out and steal something nice like some Venetian silver.

FEMALE PEASANT **Or a Velázquez for the outside loo.** **24**

MOORE Oh all right. *(turns purposefully)*

Usual montage of Dennis Moore riding plus song.

SONG Dennis Moore, Dennis Moore
Riding through the land
Dennis Moore, Dennis Moore
Without a merry band
He steals from the poor and gives to the rich
Stupid bitch.

Dennis Moore reins to sudden halt and rides over to camera.

MOORE What did you sing?
SINGERS *(speaking)* We sang...he steals from the poor and gives to the rich.
MOORE Wait a tic...blimey, this redistribution of wealth is trickier than I thought.

Women's Institute applause. A church-hall type stage, as if for a TV version of ***'Down Your Way'.*** **25** *A vast sign across the backcloth reads 'Prejudice'.* ***Russell Braddon enters.*** **26** *He wears a suit and has a clipboard.*

BRADDON (MICHAEL) Good evening and welcome to another edition of 'Prejudice'—the show that gives you a chance to have a go at Wops, Krauts, Nigs, Eyeties, Gippos, Bubbles, Froggies, Chinks, Yidds, Jocks, Polacks, Paddies and Dagoes. *(applause; he goes to desk at side of stage)*

Superimposed caption: 'ALL FACTS VERIFIED BY THE RHODESIAN POLICE'

BRADDON Tonight's show comes live from the tiny village of Rabid in Buckinghamshire, and our first question tonight is from a Mrs Elizabeth Scrint who says she is going on a Mediterranean cruise next week and can't find anything wrong with the Syrians. Well, Mrs Scrint, apart from being totally unprincipled left-wing troublemakers, the Syrians are also born **skivers,** **27** they're dirty, smelly and untrustworthy, and, of course, they're friends of the **awful gippos.** **28** *(applause)* There you are, Mrs Scrint, I hope that answers some of your problems—have a nice trip. *(more applause)* Well now, the result of last week's competition when we asked you to find a derogatory term for the Belgians. Well, the response was enormous and we took quite a long time sorting out the winners. There were some very clever entries. Mrs Hatred of Leicester said 'let's not call them anything, let's just ignore them'...*(applause starts vigorously, but he holds his hands up for silence)*...and a Mr St John of Huntingdon said he couldn't think of anything more derogatory than Belgians. *(cheers and applause; a girl in showgirl costume comes on and holds up placards through next bit)* But in the end we settled on three choices: number three...the Sprouts *(placard: 'The Sprouts')*, sent in by Mrs Vicious of Hastings...very nice; number two...the Phlegms *(placard)*...from Mrs Childmolester of Worthing; but the winner was undoubtedly from Mrs No-Supper-For-You from Norwood in Lancashire...Miserable Fat Belgian Bastards. *(placard; roars of applause)* Very good—thank you, Carol. *(Carol exits)* But as you know on this programme

Diego Velázquez, a Spanish painter of the first half of the seventeenth century.

Down Your Way was a long-running radio show, from 1946 to 1992, in which a host wandered around a town, interviewing the interesting people there and telling the story of the place. Considered saccharine by some, it nevertheless perfectly embodied the "little Britain-ness" of that small island.

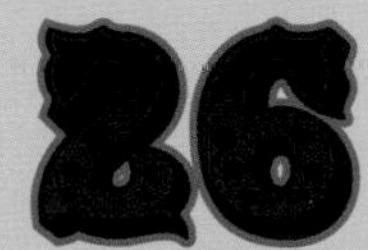

Russell Braddon was an Australian writer and TV presenter well-known in the U.K. for appearing on the political show *Any Questions?*

A "skiver" is somebody who misses work for no good reason.

"Gippos" is an offensive slur for gypsies, sometimes Egyptians.

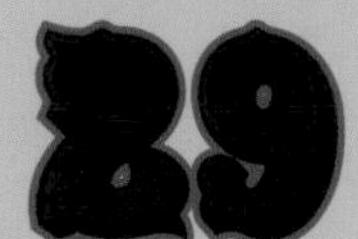

Chelsea is an area in London—and New York—home to a large gay population.

we're not just prejudiced against race or colour, we're also prejudiced against—yes, you've guessed, stinking homosexuals! *(applause)* So before the streets start emptying **in Chelsea tonight,** [29] let's go straight over to our popular prejudiced panel game and invite you once again to—Shoot The Poof! And could our first contestant sign in please.

Cut to blackboard and entrance as they used to have in ***'What's My Line'.*** [30] *A contestant comes from behind screen and starts to write his name.*

VOICE OVER (JOHN) Our first contestant is a hairdresser from...

A shot rings out and the contestant falls to the floor. Applause. Cut to a camp highwayman in a pink mask who blows smoke from a gun and puts it back in the holster.

HIGHWAYMAN (MICHAEL) I never did like that kind of person...!

A shot rings out. He dies. Cut to Dennis Moore on a horse blowing smoke from gun and putting it in his holster. He gallops off. We see him swooping down, after a couple of riding shots, on another stagecoach.

MOORE Halt! Halt! *(the stage comes to a halt and the occupants get out rapidly, their hands held high)* Gentlemen, ladies, bring out your valuables please. Come along sir, come along. Come along, madam, come along. Oh, is that all you've got...well, he's got much more than you... so you'd better have some of his...*(transfers money from one passenger to another, dropping some)*...sorry...pick them up in a moment...there's about oh, what, nine down there...so you must have about...oh, he's still got lots...oh you've got what?...you've got more than he started with...so if I give you some of those *(transferring more coins)*...well now, look...have you got a bit of jewellery? If I give you that one and you have some of his coins *(the credits start, superimposed)*...is that another box? Were you trying to hide it? Well, that's nice! Right! Now. I've got a tiara...you've got one...you've got one of the boxes...you've got one...anyone else got a tiara? Take your hat off! *(passenger does so to reveal a tiara)*...Oh, honestly, it's absolutely pointless trying to do this if you're going to cheat. It really is *awful* of you...*(fade out)*

What's My Line?, the popular game show in which a panel of celebs guesses the profession of a contestant.

Caption: ***'ERRATUM. JACK BODELL WAS BORN IN SWADLINCOTE IN DERBYSHIRE'*** **31** *Cut to the inside of a bus. A judge is sitting there in full robes, looking rather unhappy. He is obviously one of the competitors from earlier. His friend tries to cheer him up.*

FRIEND (TERRY J) I thought you should have won. I mean, judicially you swept the board...all right, he has posture, but where was he in the summing up?

Behind these two another judge is sitting with his mother, crying.

MOTHER (GRAHAM) **Oh shut up Melford, there's always next year.** **32**

Another judge further back petulantly rips up his number card. We cut to the outside back of this bus. The destination board says 'The End'. As the bus drives away we hold on a board sticking out from a building which reads 'Hospital...sorry no cheques'.

He was, indeed, on August 11, 1940.

32

Chapman is actually the judge and Idle is the mother.

SEASON 3
EPISODE 38

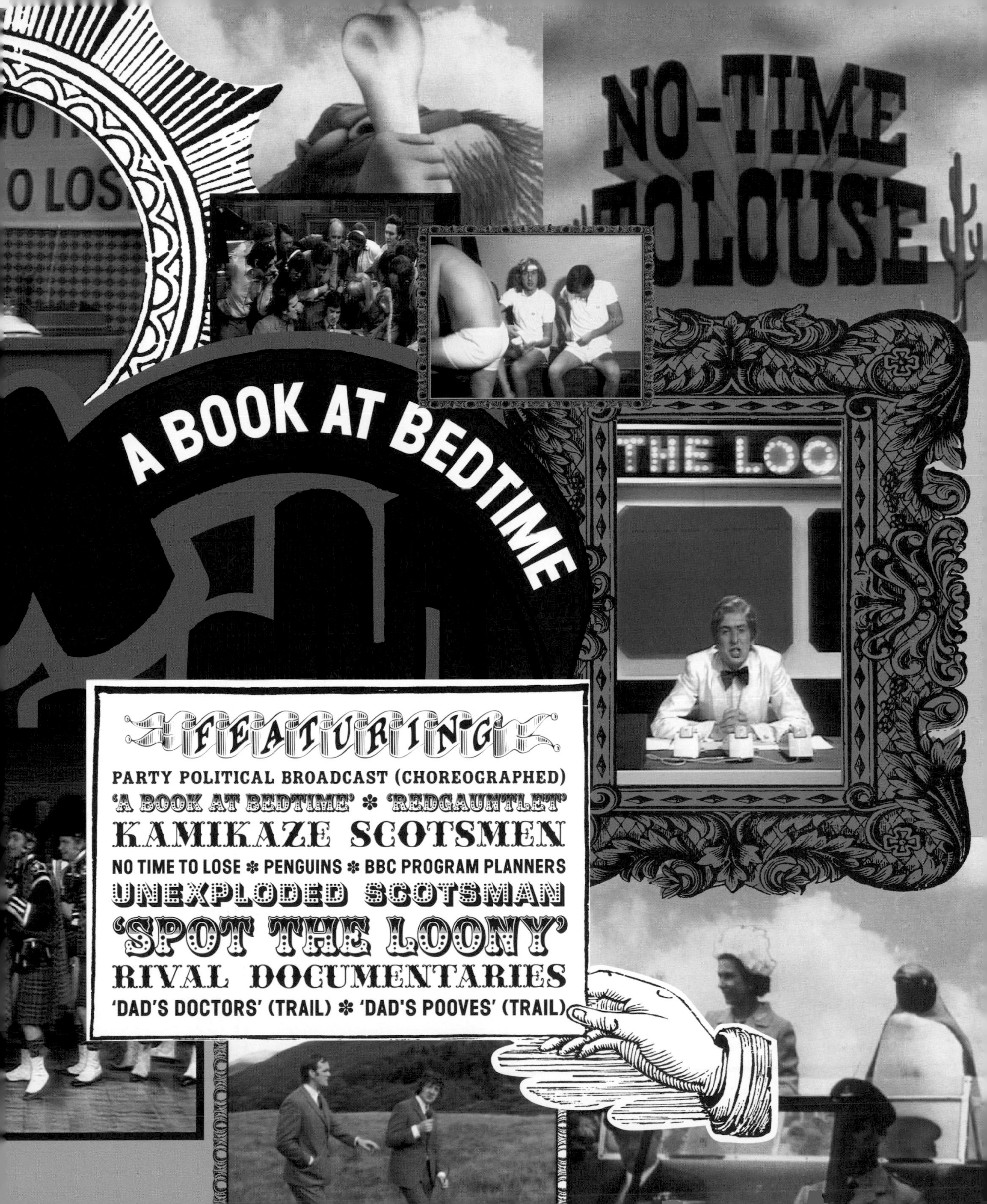
NO-TIME TOLOUSE
A BOOK AT BEDTIME
THE LOO
FEATURING
PARTY POLITICAL BROADCAST (CHOREOGRAPHED)
'A BOOK AT BEDTIME' ✽ 'REDGAUNTLET'
KAMIKAZE SCOTSMEN
NO TIME TO LOSE ✽ PENGUINS ✽ BBC PROGRAM PLANNERS
UNEXPLODED SCOTSMAN
'SPOT THE LOONY'
RIVAL DOCUMENTARIES
'DAD'S DOCTORS' (TRAIL) ✽ 'DAD'S POOVES' (TRAIL)

The first sketch here, "Party Political Broadcast," does not appear on the current A&E MPFC DVD collection. The episode begins with "Book at Bedtime."

Previously parodied by the Pythons, these brief broadcasts are given over to party political messages, most often at election time.

The Conservative and Unionist Party is the full and correct name for the Conservatives, one of the main political parties in the U.K.

Cabinet ministers were the leading politicians of the day in the U.K.—each would head up a government department and would meet with the prime minister in his "cabinet," or inner circle, to decide policy.

"Trans" is short for transmission—and, perhaps, transvestite.

FIRST AIRED: JANUARY 11, 1973

***Caption:* 'A PARTY POLITICAL BROADCAST [1] ON BEHALF OF THE CONSERVATIVE AND UNIONIST PARTY' [2]**

VOICE OVER (ERIC) There now follows a Party Political Broadcast on behalf of the **Conservative and Unionist Party.** [3]

Cut to a politician sitting on a chair. He is in fact in a rehearsal room, but we don't see this for the first six lines.

POLITICIAN (JOHN) Hello again. Figures talk. We have already fulfilled over three of our election pledges before the end of our second year of good Conservative rule. And, what is more *(gets up and starts to do dancing movements as he speaks)* We hope...that *in* the *aut*-tumn *we* shall *int*-ro-*duce leg*-is-*lat*-tion *in* the *House* to *bene-fit* all *those* in *low*-er *in*-come *groups*. And *fur*-ther-*more* we *hope*...

Enter a choreographer.

CHOREOGRAPHER (ERIC) No, no, no, no...look, luv, it's *and...(does the movements)* one and two and three and four, and five and six and seven and down.

POLITICIAN *(trying the last bit)*...five and six and seven and down...it's so much harder with the words.

CHOREOGRAPHER Well, don't think of them. Just count four in your head.

POLITICIAN And...*one* and *fur*-ther *two* and *three* and...no, I can't really...

CHOREOGRAPHER Yes, well come on and do it with me, come on. And...

BOTH *Fur*-ther-*more* we *hope* that *we* can *stop* the *ris*-ing *un*-em-*ploy*-ment. *(they finish up with finger on chin, as in a thirties musical)*

CHOREOGRAPHER And point 'unemployment' with your finger.

POLITICIAN I see. I can do it when you're here.

CHOREOGRAPHER I won't be far away. All right, Neville love, we're going from 'unemployment' through 'pensions' into 'good government is strong government' and the walk down, all right? And...cue, love.

POLITICIAN And *fur*-ther-*more* we *hope* that *we* can *stop* the *ris*-ing *un*-em-*ploy*-ment *at* a *stroke* or *e*-ven *quick*-er.

Enter a line of six male dancers, doing high kicks and a dance routine.

DANCERS And *so* when *you* get a *chance* to *vote*, *Kind*-ly *vote* Con-*ser*-va-*tive*.
(the politician joins in) Rising prices, unemployment,
Both stem from the wages spiral
Curb inflation, save the nation,
Join us now and save the economy.

They give an awful wave and cheesecake smile at the end, and hold it.

CHOREOGRAPHER That's where you'll get the balloons and the ticker tape, Chris. Right, big smiles, everybody, remember you're **cabinet ministers.** [4] And relax. *(only now do they stop smiling and waving)* Lovely, **it's trans** [5] at eight, so nobody be late.

The camera crabs away. Through an open door it passes we see two Labour MPs, one on points, the other walking around with his hands on his hips. They are in leotards and dancers' leg warmers.

LABOUR MPS *We* in the *Lab*-our *Par*-ty have *al*-ways *made* our po-*si*-tion *quite clear*...we have *al*-ways *been* op-*posed* to...

The camera continues to crab away. It comes to a door which says 'Star' on it. We zoom into this and mix through to: Animation: ***Wilson and Heath dance to 'The Dance of the Sugar Plum Fairy'.*** **6** *Cut to the nude organist; he plays a chord. Cut to the announcer at his desk.*

ANNOUNCER (JOHN) And now...

IT'S MAN (MICHAEL)

IT'S...

Animated titles.

Cut to studio: a silhouette of a man sitting on high stool with book. Superimposed caption: 'A BOOK AT BEDTIME'

VOICE OVER (ERIC)

'BOOK AT BEDTIME'. TONIGHT JEREMY TOOGOOD READS 'REDGAUNTLET' BY SIR WALTER SCOTT. 7

The lights come up.

JEREMY (MICHAEL) Hello. *(he follows the words closely with a finger and reads with great difficulty)* The sunsoot...the siunsiett...the sunset!...the sunset...waas...was was...the sunset was...deeing... d...ying dying...o...over...the...hile...hiel...heels...halls...hills! Of...slow...Sol...way...Firth... The...love piper...the *lone* piper...the lone piper...on...the...batt...ly...ments...*(smiles nervously)*...of Edingrund...dydburing...Edingbir...Edinburgh! Castle...was...siluted...sil...sillhou...

Another man enters, takes the book from his hands rather testily and stands by the chair. He smiles apologetically at the camera and reads.

SECOND READER (JOHN) The sunset was dying over the hills of Solway Firth. The lone piper on the battlements of Edinburgh Castle was silhouetted against the crim...crim...crimisy... crimson! against the crimson strays...stree...

6

Harold Wilson and Ted Heath were leaders of the Labour and Conservative parties, respectively, in 1972. Edward Heath was also prime minister at the time. Wilson would take over in 1974.

"The Dance of the Sugar Plum Fairy," the famous ballet dance from *The Nutcracker*.

Book at Bedtime is the BBC Radio 4 show in which a book is abridged, serialized, and read by a famous person, usually for the fifteen minutes leading up to 11 p.m.

Redgauntlet, Sir Walter Scott's historical novel from 1825.

One more reader enters and reads over his shoulder.

THIRD READER (ERIC) Streaked!
SECOND READER Streaked?
THIRD READER Crimson-streaked sky...in the shadows of...crrignu...

He can't make out the next word. The second reader also tries to puzzle it out and eventually Jeremy pulls the book down towards him and they all try to puzzle it out. A lot of head shaking. A technician enters wearing headphones.

TECHNICIAN (GRAHAM) Cairngorm! In the shadows of Cairngorm!
THIRD READER In the shadows of Cairngorm, the l...layered...

A second technician and a make-up girl enter.

SECOND TECHNICIAN Laird! The Laird of Monteu...Montreaux...
MAKE-UP GIRL Montrose.
ALL The Laird of Montrose!
SECOND TECHNICIAN Gal-lopped...
JEREMY Galloped!

Everybody joins in helping with words. We mix through to Edinburgh Castle at dusk. The lone piper is silhouetted against the crimson-streaked sky.

JEREMY *(voice over)* The lone piper on the battlements of Edinburgh Castle...

There are a few bars of bagpipe music. Suddenly there is a scream and he disappears. Cut to interior of stone-walled guardroom inside Edinburgh Castle. Ten kilted Scottish guardsmen with bagpipes in a line. A sergeant major at the door taps one on the shoulder.

RSM (TERRY J) Next!

The next goes outside. We hear pipes start, the sergeant smiles. Cut to castle battlements. The piper plays and then jumps off. We hear the scream as before. Another piper emerges and goes through the same routine.

VOICE OVER (MICHAEL) *(Scottish accent)* Here on top of Edinburgh Castle, in conditions of extreme secrecy, men are being trained for the British Army's first Kamikaze Regiment, the Queen's Own McKamikaze Highlanders. *(there is a scream and a piper jumps off; another one emerges and starts to play)* So successful has been the training of the Kamikaze Regiment that the numbers have dwindled from 30,000 to just over a dozen in three weeks. What makes these young Scotsmen so keen to kill themselves?

Close ups of soldiers.

SCOTS SOLDIER (MICHAEL) The money's good!
SECOND SOLDIER (ERIC) And the water skiing! *(he falls down with a scream)*

Cut to interior of the guardroom in Edinburgh Castle. As before, but with only six men left plus the sergeant major. Bagpipes and a scream. The sergeant major dispatches another man. A captain enters. Bagpipes again.

RSM Ten-shun.
CAPTAIN (JOHN) All right, sergeant major. At ease. Now, how many chaps have you got left?
RSM Six, sir.
CAPTAIN Six? *(there is a scream)*
RSM Five, sir. *(to another highlander carrying bagpipes)* Good luck, Johnson. *(Johnson leaves)*
CAPTAIN Jolly good show, sergeant major. *(we hear bagpipes starting up outside)* Well, I've come to tell you that we've got a job for your five lads.

THERE IS A SCREAM.

RSM Four, sir.
CAPTAIN For your four lads.
RSM *(whispering to another man)* Good luck, Taggart.
TAGGART Thank you, sarge. *(he goes)*
CAPTAIN *(looking rather uncertainly at the man leaving)* Now this mission's going to be dangerous, *(bagpipes start)* and it's going to be tough, and we're going to need every lad of yours to pull his weight. *(the usual scream in the background)* Now, which...er...which four are they?
RSM These three here, sir. OK. Off you go, Smith.

SMITH *(with manic eagerness)* Right!! *(he charges out through door before captain can stop him)*
CAPTAIN *(with mounting concern)* ...er...sergeant major!
RSM Yes, sir? *(bagpipes start outside)*
CAPTAIN You don't think it might be a good idea...er...to stop the training programme for a little bit?
RSM They got to be trained, sir. It's a dangerous job.
CAPTAIN Yes...I know...but...er...*(the usual scream)*
RSM All right MacPherson, you're next, off you go.

CAPTAIN You see what is worrying me, sergeant major, is...
MACPHERSON I'll make it a gud'un, sir! *(he dashes off)*
RSM Good luck, MacPherson.
CAPTAIN Er...MacPherson...*(the bagpipes start up)* only this mission really is very dangerous. We're going to need both the chaps that you've got left. *(scream)*
RSM Both of who, sir?
CAPTAIN Sergeant major, what's this man's name?
RSM This one sir? This one is MacDonald, sir.
CAPTAIN No, no, no, no. *(the captain stops MacDonald* (GRAHAM) *who is straining quite hard to get away)* Hang on to MacDonald, sergeant major, hang on to him.
RSM I don't know whether I can, sir...*(MacDonald's eyes are staring in a strange way)* he's in a state of Itsubishi Kyoko McSayonara.
CAPTAIN What's that?

They are both struggling to restrain MacDonald.

RSM It's the fifth state that a Scotsman can achieve, sir. He's got to finish himself off by lunchtime or he thinks he's let down the Emperor, sir.
CAPTAIN Well, can't we get him out of it?
RSM Oh, I dunno how to, sir. Our Kamikaze instructor, Mr Yashimoto, was so good he never left Tokyo airport.
CAPTAIN Well, there must be someone else who can advise us?

Exterior of smart London health-salon-type frontage. A big sign reads 'Kamikaze Advice Centre'. A bowler-hatted man enters. A receptionist sits behind a posh desk.

MAN (MICHAEL) *(very businesslike)*

GOOD MORNING, KAMIKAZE, PLEASE.

RECEPTIONIST *(indicating door)* Yes, would you go through, please?
MAN Thank you.

The man walks over to the door, opens it, walks through and disappears from sight. There is nothing but sky and clouds through the door. Scream. Cut back to castle guardroom.

CAPTAIN Right, sergeant major—there's no time to lose.

The sergeant is sitting on MacDonald. He strikes him on head.

RSM Beg pardon, sir?
CAPTAIN No time to lose.
RSM No what, sir?
CAPTAIN No *time*...no time to lose.
RSM Oh, I see, sir. *(making gestures)* No time...to...lose!!
CAPTAIN Yes, that's right, yes.

RSM Yes, no time to lose, sir!
CAPTAIN Right.
RSM Isn't that funny, sir...I've never come across that phrase before—'no time to lose'. Forty-two years I've been in the regular army and I've never heard that phrase.
CAPTAIN Well, it's in perfectly common parlance.
RSM In what, sir?
CAPTAIN Oh never mind...right...no time to lose.
RSM Eventually, yes, sir.
CAPTAIN What?
RSM Like you say, sir. We'll be able to make time, eventually without to lose, sir, no.
CAPTAIN Look, I don't think you've quite got the hang of this phrase, sergeant major.

The same frontage of smart London salon as before. Only this time the big sign reads 'No Time To Lose Advice Centre'. The same bowler-hatted man goes in. The same interior, same desk. A consultant sits behind it, and motions for the man to sit down.

CONSULTANT (ERIC) Morning, no time to lose...*(he picks up a card which reads 'no time to lose'; he keeps flashing it every so often)* Now then, how were you thinking of using the phrase?

He pulls down a blind behind him on the right which also reads 'no time to lose' in large letters. He lets it go and it rolls up again fast.

MAN (MICHAEL) Well, I was thinking of using it...er...like...well...good morning dear, what is in no time to lose?
CONSULTANT Er yes...well...you've not quite got the hang of that, have you.

He gets out a two-foot-square cube with 'no time to lose' in the same lettering as it always is, and puts it on the desk. He points to this in a manic way with a forefinger. He has the words 'no time to lose' on the back of his hand.

CONSULTANT *(sings)* No time to lose, no time to lose, no time to lose, no time to lose. *(to stop the manic fit he reaches inside desk, pours a drink from a bottle on which is written 'no time to lose')* Now, you want to use this phrase in everyday conversation, is that right?
MAN Yes, that's right.
CONSULTANT Yes...good...

He stands up, makes a strange noise, and flings the back of his jacket up over his head revealing 'no time to lose' written on the inside of the back lining of his jacket, upside down so that it is the right way up when it is revealed. 8

Palin very nearly loses it here. (Idle's flipping of his jacket and hyena-like noises *are* funny, in all fairness).

"Flannel" is British for a washcloth.

MAN You see my wife and I have never had a great deal to say to each other... *(tragic, heart-rending music creeps in under the dialogue)* In the old days we used to find things to say, like 'pass the sugar'...or, '**that's my flannel**', **9** but in the last ten or fifteen years there just hasn't seemed to be anything to say, and anyway I saw your phrase advertised in the paper and I thought, that's the kind of thing I'd like to say to her...

The consultant pushes down a handle and a large screen comes up in front of him. On it is written 'no time to lose'. He bursts through the paper.

CONSULTANT Yes, well, what we normally suggest for a beginner such as yourself, is that you put your alarm clock back ten minutes in the morning, so you can wake up, look at the clock and use the phrase immediately. *(he holds up the card briefly)* Shall we try it?

MAN Yes.

CONSULTANT All right—I'll be the alarm clock. When I go off, look at me and use the phrase, OK? *(ticks then imitates ringing)*

MAN No! *Time* to lose!

CONSULTANT No...No time to lose.

MAN No time to *lose*?

CONSULTANT No time to lose.

MAN No *time* to lose.

CONSULTANT

NO—TO LOSE LIKE TOULOUSE IN FRANCE. NO TIME TOULOUSE.

MAN No time *too* lose...

CONSULTANT No time Toulouse.

MAN No time Toulouse...

CONSULTANT No!—no time to *lose*!

MAN No—no time to *lose*!

Animation: Toulouse-Lautrec in a wild-west gunfight.

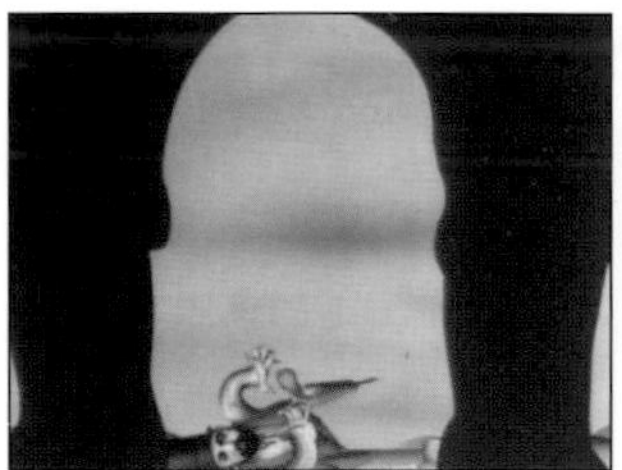

VOICE OVER No-time Toulouse. The story of the wild and lawless days of the post-Impressionists.

Cut back to the guardroom at Edinburgh Castle. MacDonald is edging towards the window.

CAPTAIN Anyway, no time to lose, sergeant major.

RSM Look out, sir! MacDonald!

They both rush to window and grab MacDonald's legs as he disappears through it.

RSM We'll have to hurry, sir. *(they haul him back into the room to reveal he is carrying a saw with which he starts trying to saw off his head)* No, put that down MacDonald. *(he snatches the saw and throws it away)* He's reached the sixth plane already, sir.

CAPTAIN Right, here are the plans sergeant major, good luck.

RSM Thank you, sir. *(he salutes)*

MacDonald is by now trying to strangle himself with his bare hands.

CAPTAIN And good luck to you, MacDonald.

MacDonald breaks off from strangling himself, to offer a snappy salute.

MACDONALD Thank you, sir.

He immediately snaps back into trying to strangle himself.

RSM Right you are, MacDonald. No time to lose.
CAPTAIN Very good, sergeant major.

Quick cut to the consultant in the office.

CONSULTANT Yes, excellent...

Cut back to the gates of Edinburgh Castle. Dawn. Music. As the voice starts the glues open and a lorry emerges.

VOICE OVER (MICHAEL) So it was that on a cold January morning, RSM Urdoch and Sapper MacDonald, one of the most highly trained Kamikaze experts the Scottish Highlands have ever witnessed, left on a mission which was to...oh I can't go on with this drivel.

By this time we have cut to a close up of the cab to show RSM Urdoch at the wheel, with MacDonald beside him. MacDonald has a revolver and is apparently having an unsuccessful game of Russian roulette.

RSM All right, MacDonald, no time to lose.

Suddenly MacDonald hurls himself out of the lorry.

MACDONALD Aaaaaaugh!

The RSM slams the brakes on. Skidding noises. Cut to shot of the lorry skidding to a halt. The RSM leaps out, picks up MacDonald who is lying on the floor hitting himself, and loads him into the back of the lorry. He gets back into the lorry and they start off again. They haven't gone more than a few yards before we see MacDonald leap out of the back of the lorry, race round to the front and throw himself down in front of the lorry. The lorry runs right over him. He picks himself up after it has gone, races up to the front and tries it again...and again...and again...and again...and again... Cut to the captain, standing in front of a huge map. He points with a stick.

CAPTAIN Well, that's the mission—now here's the method. RSM Urdoch will lull the enemy into a false sense of security by giving them large quantities of money, a good home, and a steady job. Then, when they're upstairs with the wife, Sapper MacDonald will hurl himself at the secret documents, destroying them and himself. Well, that's the plan, the time is now 19.42 hours. I want you to get to bed, have a good night's rest and be up on parade early in the morning. Thank you for listening and thank you for a lovely supper.

Pull out to reveal that he is in a very small sitting room, alone apart from his wife who sits knitting by the fire not listening to a word he's saying. Cut to the 'Book at Bedtime' set. Seven or eight technicians, a make-up girl, etc. still crowding round Toogood as he tries to read.

TOOGOOD And...and...sue...so...the...the...intriptid...
MAKE-UP GIRL Intrepid.
ALL Intrepid.
TOOGOOD Intrepid RSM Urdoch and super...
TECHNICIAN Sapper.
TOOGOOD Sapper MacDonald...mead...
SEVERAL Made!
TOOGOOD Made their why...
SEVERAL Way!
TOOGOOD Way toarro...
MAKE-UP GIRL Towards... **10**
TOOGOOD Towards the Rusty...Ritzy...
ALL Russian!
TOOGOOD Russian bolder...
ALL Border!

Map with an animated line showing the route.

TOOGOOD'S VOICE ...and so RSM Urdoch and Sapper MacDonald made their way towards the Russian bolder...
ALL Border!!...Border.

Animation: the line becomes part of an animated skit on the famous film '2001'. **11**

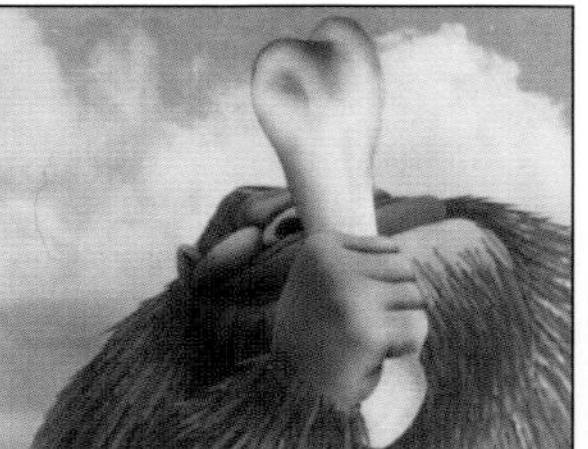

Cut to stock film of penguins. Superimposed captions: 'FRONTIERS OF MEDICINE PART 2' 'THE GATHERING STORM' **12** *Cut to presenter at desk.*

PRESENTER (JOHN) Penguins, yes, penguins. What relevance do penguins have to the furtherance of medical science? Well, strangely enough quite a lot, a major breakthrough, maybe. It was from such an unlikely beginning as an unwanted fungus accidentally growing on a sterile plate that **Sir Alexander Fleming gave the world penicillin.** **13** **James Watt watched an ordinary household kettle boiling and conceived the potentiality of steam power.** **14**

A stagehand appears here carrying a stuffed flamingo. And why not?

Stanley Kubrick's sci-fi movie from 1968.

The Gathering Storm, published in 1948, is the title of the first volume of Winston Churchill's six-volume history *The Second World War.*

Alexander Fleming, Scottish pharmacologist (1881–1955). He discovered penicillin in 1928 and, together with Howard Florey and Ernest Chain, received the Nobel Prize in 1945 for his work.

James Watt, Scottish scientist and inventor (1736–1819). He was the creator of the separate condenser, which improved steam engines.

Would **Albert Einstein** 15 ever have hit upon the theory of relativity if he hadn't been clever? All these tremendous leaps forward have been taken in the dark. **Would Rutherford** 16 ever have split the atom if he hadn't tried? Could **Marconi** 17 have invented the radio if he hadn't by pure chance spent years working at the problem? Are these amazing breakthroughs ever achieved except by years and years of unremitting study? Of course not. What I said earlier about accidental discoveries must have been wrong. Nevertheless scientists believe that these penguins, these comic flightless web-footed little bastards may finally unwittingly help man to fathom the uncharted depths of the human mind. **Professor Rosewall of the Laver Institute.** 18

A scientist with tennis courts in the background. He wears a white coat. Superimposed caption: 'PROF. KEN ROSEWALL'

SCIENTIST (GRAHAM) *(Australian accent)* Hello. Here at the Institute Professor **Charles Pasarell**, **Dr Peaches Bartkowicz** and myself have been working on the theory originally postulated by the late **Dr Kramer** 19 and myself have been working on the theory originally postulated by the late Dr Kramer that the penguin is intrinsically more intelligent than the human being.

He moves over to a large diagram which is being held by two tennis players in full tennis kit but wearing the brown coats of ordinary laboratory technicians. The diagram shows a penguin and a man in correct proportional size with their comparative brain capacities marked out clearly showing the man's to be much larger than the penguin's.

SCIENTIST The first thing that Dr Kramer came up with was that the penguin has a much smaller brain than the man. This postulate formed the fundamental basis of all his thinking and remained with him until his death.

Flash cut of elderly man in tennis shirt and green eye shade getting an arrow in the head. Cut back to the scientist now with diagram behind him. It shows a man and a six-foot penguin.

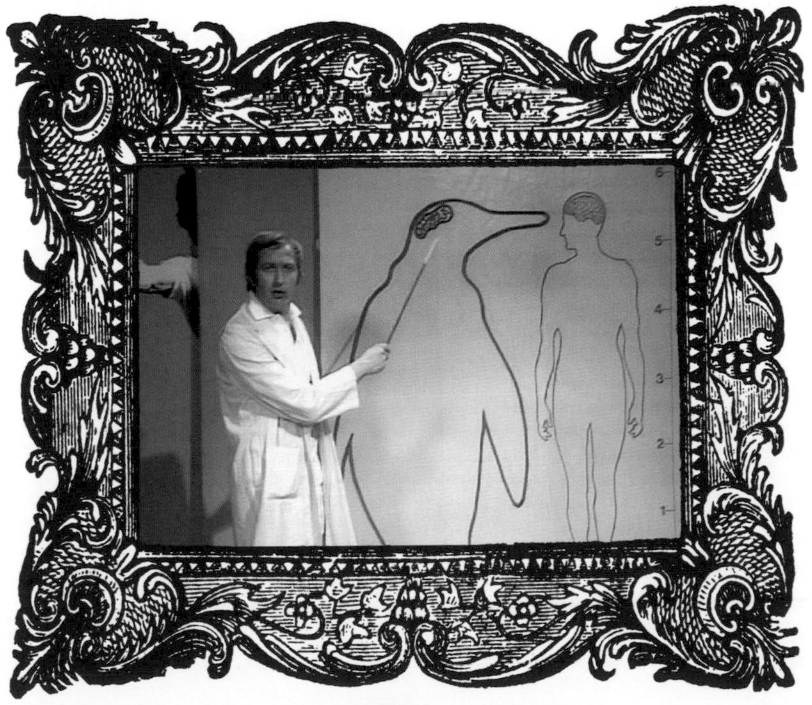

Albert Einstein (1879–1955), wild-haired scientist, who developed the theory of general relativity which proves that most people have a cousin somewhere.

Ernest Rutherford, New Zealand-British chemist and physicist (1871–1937). He is considered the first man to split the atom (in 1917, during which he discovered, and named, the proton).

Guglielmo Marconi, Italian inventor (1874–1937), developer of the long-distance radio transmission.

Ken Rosewall, Australian tennis player and winner of eight Grand Slam titles.

Rod Laver, Australian tennis star.

Charles Pasarell and Peaches Bartkowicz, both American tennis players.

Jack Kramer, American tennis player and promoter of the sport. He would not become "the late Dr. Kramer" until September 12, 2009 (at the grand old age of 88).

SCIENTIST Now we've taken this theory one stage further. If we increase the size of the penguin until it is the same height as the man and then compare the relative brain size, we now find that the penguin's brain is still smaller. But, and this is the point, it is larger than it *was*.

Very quick cut of tennis crowd going 'oh' and applauding. Dr Peaches Bartkowicz standing by tennis net. Superimposed caption: 'DR PEACHES BARTKOWICZ'

PEACHES (MICHAEL) For a penguin to have the same size of brain as a man the penguin would have to be over sixty-six feet high.

She moves to the left and comes upon a cut-out of the lower visible part of a sixty-six feet high penguin. She looks up at it. Cut back to the scientist.

SCIENTIST This theory has become known as the waste of time theory and was abandoned in 1956. *(slight edit with jump visible)* Hello again. Standard IQ tests gave the following results. The penguins scored badly when compared with primitive human sub-groups like the bushmen of the Kalahari but better than BBC programme planners. *(he refers to graph decorated with little racquets which shows bushmen with 23, penguins with 13 and BBC planners' with 8)* The BBC programme planners surprisingly high total here can be explained away as being within the ordinary limits of statistical error. One particularly dim programme planner can cock the whole thing up.

Caption: 'YOU CAN SAY THAT AGAIN' ***Cut to a tennis player in a changing room taking off his gym shoes. In the background two other players discuss shots.*** [20] *Superimposed caption:* ***'DR LEWIS HOAD'*** [21]

HOAD (ERIC) These IQ tests were thought to contain an unfair cultural bias against the penguin. For example, it didn't take into account the penguins' extremely poor educational system. To devise a fairer system of test, a team of our researchers spent eighteen months in Antarctica living like penguins, and subsequently dying like penguins—only quicker—proving that the penguin is a clever little sod in his own environment.

Cut to the scientist.

SCIENTIST Therefore we devised tests to be given to the penguins in the fourth set...I do beg your pardon, in their own environment.

VOICE Net! [22]

SCIENTIST Shh!

Cut to a professor and team surrounding penguins standing in a pool.

PROFESSOR (TERRY J) What is the next number in this sequence—2, 4, 6...

A penguin squawks.

PROFESSOR Did he say eight?...*(sighs)* [23] What is...

Cut back to the scientist.

SCIENTIST The environmental barrier had been removed but we'd hit another: the language barrier. The penguins could not speak English and were therefore unable to give the answers. This

Not exactly. They are on either side of Idle, and they are mute. What they do instead is undress—the "player" to the left of the screen actually goes down to his pale yellow underwear, which unfortunately slip to show us a glimpse of his "tennis player's crack."

Lew Hoad was an Australian tennis player whose banner year was 1956, when he won the Australian and French opens, Wimbledon, and even reached the U.S. Open final, only to lose to Ken Rosewall in four sets.

A common misapprehension. The correct call is "let," for when the served ball catches the top of the net but continues over.

There is a quick shot of a tennis umpire shaking his head here.

problem was removed in the next series of experiments by asking the same questions to the penguins and to a random group of non-English–speaking humans in the same conditions.

Cut to the professor and his team now surrounding a group of foreigners who are standing in a pool looking bewildered.

PROFESSOR What is the next number? 2, 4, 6...*(long pause)*
SWEDISH PERSON (ERIC) ...Hello? **24**

Cut back to the scientist.

SCIENTIST The results of these tests were most illuminating.

THE PENGUINS' SCORES WERE CONSISTENTLY EQUAL TO THOSE OF THE NON-ENGLISH–SPEAKING GROUP.

Cut to the foreigners having fish thrown at them, which they try to catch in their mouths, and a penguin with a menu at a candlelit table with a woman in evening dress and a waiter trying to take an order. Cut to Dr Hoad taking a shower.

HOAD These enquiries led to certain changes at the BBC...

Cut to the boardroom of BBC. Penguins sit at a table with signs saying 'Programme Controller', 'Head of Planning', 'Director General'. Noise of penguins squawking.

Cut to the penguin pool. Hoad's voice over.

HOAD While attendances at zoos boomed.

The camera pans across to a sign reading 'The programme planners are to be fed at 3 o'clock'.

VOICE OVER (MICHAEL) Soon these feathery little hustlers were infiltrating important positions everywhere.

24

The script calls for Idle to be a "Swedish person," but he's dressed like an Austrian, in lederhosen and a Tyrolean-style hat.

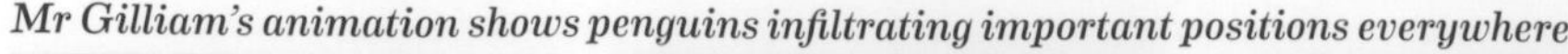
Mr Gilliam's animation shows penguins infiltrating important positions everywhere.

Cut to RSM Urdoch having his lorry checked by a penguin border guard. Superimposed caption: 'MEANWHILE AT A CHECKPOINT ON THE RUSSIAN-POLISH BORDER' The lorry drives off past sign saying 'Russian bolder' with 'bolder' crossed out and 'border' written in. Cut to Red Square. Superimposed caption: 'THE KREMLIT' The 'T' is crossed out and 'N' written in. Cut to two Russian majors in a conference room.

FIRST MAJOR (ERIC) Svientitzi hobonwy kratow svegurninurdy.

Superimposed subtitles: 'THESE ARE THE VERY IMPORTANT SECRET DOCUMENTS I WAS TELLING YOU ABOUT'

SECOND MAJOR (JOHN) We must study them in conditions of absolute secrecy.

Superimposed subtitle in Russian.

FIRST MAJOR *(speaks in Russian)*

Superimposed subtitle: 'WHAT?'

SECOND MAJOR *(looking up)* Look out!

Superimposed subtitle: ***'REGARDEZ LA!'*** **25** *They cower as MacDonald crashes through the skylight and lands on the table where he lies rigid with his knees drawn up. He ticks ominously.*

SECOND MAJOR He hasn't gone off.

Superimposed caption: 'ZE HABE NICHT GESHPLODEN'

FIRST MAJOR *(speaks in Russian)*

subtitle: 'QUICK! RING THE UNEXPLODED SCOTSMAN SQUAD'

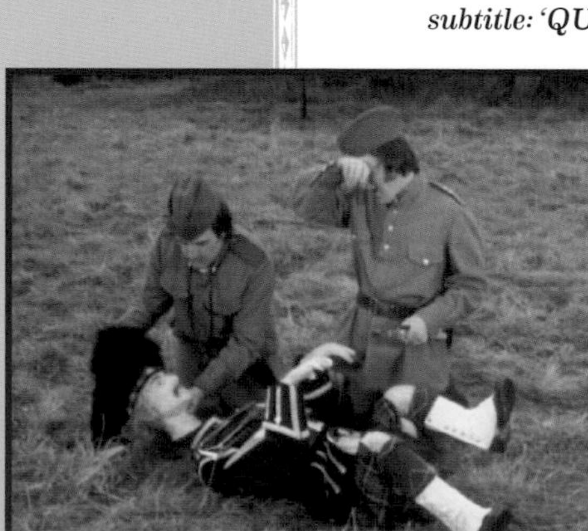

SECOND MAJOR *(speaks in Russian)*

Superimposed subtitle in Chinese. Cut to a phone ringing on the branch of a tree. Pull back to show a Scotsman lying on his back with his knees drawn up in the middle of a field. Two Russian bomb experts are crawling towards him cautiously. Superimposed caption: 'UNEXPLODED SCOTSMAN DISPOSAL SQUAD' They get to work on him. ***Tense close ups. They sweat.*** **26** *Finally they remove his head.*

One of them runs hurriedly and places it in a bucket labelled 'Vodka'. Superimposed caption: 'WHISKY' The sound of drunken gurglings comes from the bucket. ***Pull back to show that this is on a screen at the back of a panel game set.*** **27**

25

"Look at that!"

26

The tense music in the background is the theme song to the long-running BBC TV quiz show *Mastermind*, in which a contestant, sitting in a large black leather chair and under a spotlight, is asked rapid-fire questions, first on a specialized subject then in general knowledge.

27

The flashing lights above Idle read "Spot the Looney."

Fade it out as camera in studio pans down to the presenter.

PRESENTER (ERIC) And welcome to 'Spot the Loony', where once again we invite you to come with us all over the world to meet all kinds of people in all kinds of places, and ask you to...

SPOT THE LOONY!

(crescendo of music) Superimposed caption: 'ALL ANSWERS VERIFIED BY ENCYCLOPAEDIA BRITANNICA'

PRESENTER Our panel this evening...Gurt Svensson, the Swedish mammal abuser and part-time radiator.

Cut to Svensson. He is standing on his head on the desk with his legs crossed in a yoga position. ***He wears a loincloth and high-heeled shoes. He talks through a megaphone which is strapped to his head.*** **28**

SVENSSON (TERRY J) Good evening.

Cut back to the presenter.

PRESENTER Dame Elsie Occluded, historian, wit, bon viveur, and rear half of the Johnson brothers...

Cut to another section of the panel's desk. Dame Elsie. Her bottom half is encased in the side of a block of concrete which is also on top of the desk. Dame Elsie is thus parallel to the ground. She has fairy wings on her back, a striped t-shirt, flying gloves, goggles and a green wig.

DAME ELSIE (MICHAEL) Good evening.

Cut back to the presenter.

PRESENTER And Miles Yellowbird, up high in banana tree, the golfer and inventor of Catholicism.

Cut to final section of the desk. A man dressed as a rabbit, with a megaphone strapped to one eye.

MILES (TERRY G) Good evening.

PRESENTER And we'll be inviting them to...Spot the Loony. *(a phone rings on the desk; he picks it up)* Yes? Quite right...A viewer from Preston there who's pointed out correctly that the entire panel are loonies. Five points to Preston there, and on to our first piece of film. It's about mountaineering and remember you have to...Spot the Loony!

28

He also has the word "Eggs" in black paint on his torso.

Palin correctly pronounces the name of the mountain: Ben Macdui, the second-highest mountain in Britain, in the Cairngorms. It stands at 4,295 feet, though some have pushed to build a cairn on the top to make it higher than Ben Nevis (4,409 feet).

He's actually dragging a large rubber ducky.

31

Tony Jacklin, the British golfer and a name regularly checked by the Pythons.

Anthony Barber, Conservative politician, Chancellor of the Exchequer from 1970 to 1974, and another name regularly checked by the Pythons.

Edgar Allan Poe, American writer and doom merchant.

Katie Boyle, actress and regular presenter of the Eurovision Song Contest.

Reginald Maudling, yet one more reference to the Conservative politician with the handlebar mustache.

Cut to a shot of a mountain. Very impressive stirring music.

VOICE OVER (MICHAEL) **The legendary south face of Ben Medhui,** **29** dark...forbidding...

In the middle distance are two bushes a few yards apart. At this point a loony dressed in a long Roman toga, with tam o'shanter, ***holding a cricket bat,*** **30** *runs from one bush to the other. Loud buzz. The film freezes. Pull out from screen to reveal the freeze frame of the film with the loony in the middle bush on the screen immediately behind the presenter. The presenter is on the phone.*

PRESENTER Yes, well done, Mrs Nesbitt of York, spotted the loony in 1.8 seconds. *(cut to stock film of Women's Institute applauding)* On to our second round, and it's photo time. We're going to invite you to look at photographs of **Tony Jacklin, Anthony Barber, Edgar Allan Poe, Katy Boyle, Reginald Maudling, and a loony.** **31** All you have to do is...Spot the Loony! *(cut to a photo of Anthony Barber; the buzzer goes immediately)* No...I must ask you please not to ring in until you've seen all the photos.

Back to the photo sequence and music. Each photo is on the screen for only two seconds, and in between each there is a click as of a slide projector changing or even the sound of the shutter of a camera. The photos show in sequence: Anthony Barber, Katy Boyle, Edgar Allan Poe, a loony head and shoulders (he has ping-pong ball eyes, several teeth blacked out, a fright wig and his chest is bare but across it is written 'A Loony'), Reginald Maudling, Tony Jacklin. A buzzer sounds.

PRESENTER Yes, you're right. The answer was, of course, number two! *(cut to stock film of Women's Institute applauding)* I'm afraid there's been an error in our computer. The correct answer should of course have been number four, and not Katy Boyle. Katy Boyle is not a loony, she is a television personality. *(fanfare as for historical pageant; a historical-looking shield comes up on screen)* And now it's time for 'Spot the Loony, historical adaptation'. *(historical music)* And this time it's the thrilling medieval romance: **'Ivanoe'...** **32** a stirring story of love and war, violence and chivalry, set amidst the pageantry and splendour of thirteenth-century England. All you have to do is, Spot the Loony.

Caption: 'IVANOE' **33** *Cut to a butcher's shop. A loony stands in the middle (this is Michael's loony from 'Silly Election' with enormous trousers and arms inside them and green fright wig). Another loony in a long vest down to his knees with a little frilly tutu starting at the knees and bare feet is dancing with a side of beef also wearing a tutu.* ***Another loony in oilskins with waders and sou'wester and fairy wings is flying across the top of picture.*** **34** *Another man dressed as a bee is standing on the counter. Another loony is dressed as a carrot leaning against the counter going: 'pretty boy, pretty boy'. A cacophony of noise. We see this sight for approximately five seconds. Fantastic loud buzzes.*

PRESENTER Yes, well done, Mrs L of Leicester, Mrs B of Buxton and Mrs G of Gatwick, the loony was of course the writer, Sir Walter Scott.

Cut to Sir Walter Scott in his study. Superimposed caption: 'SIR WALTER SCOTT 1771-1832'

SCOTT (GRAHAM) *(looking through his papers indignantly)* I didn't write that! Sounds more like Dickens...

Cut to Dickens at work in his study. He looks up. Superimposed caption: 'CHARLES DICKENS 1812-1870'

DICKENS (TERRY J) You bastard!

Cut to a documentary producer standing in forested hillside.

PRODUCER (JOHN) Was Sir Walter Scott a loony, or was he the greatest flowering of the early nineteenth-century romantic tradition? The most underestimated novelist of the nineteenth century...*(another introducer of documentaries comes into shot and walks up to the first)* ...or merely a disillusioned and embittered man...

SECOND PRODUCER (MICHAEL) Excuse me...*(pointing at the microphone)* can I borrow that, please.

FIRST PRODUCER ...yes.

SECOND PRODUCER Thank you. *(he immediately starts on his own documentary)* These trees behind me now were planted over forty years ago, as part of a policy by the then Crown Woods, who became the Forestry Commission in 1924. *(he starts to walk towards the forest)* **The Forestry Commission systematically replanted this entire area...** [35]

The first producer follows behind.

FIRST PRODUCER Excuse me.

SECOND PRODUCER Sh! That's forty thousand acres of virgin forest. By 1980 this will have risen to two hundred thousand acres of soft woods. In commercial terms, a coniferous cornucopia... an evergreen El Dorado...*(the first producer runs and makes a feeble grab for the mike)*...a tree-lined treasure trove...**No...** [36] a fat fir-coned future for the financiers...but what of the cost...

FIRST PRODUCER It's mine!

SECOND PRODUCER *(to first producer)* Go away...in human terms? Who are the casualties?

The first producer makes a lunge and grabs the mike. He stops and the camera stops with him.

FIRST PRODUCER For this was Sir Walter Scott's country. **Many of his finest romances, such as 'Guy Mannering' and 'Redgauntlet'...** [37]

SECOND PRODUCER

GIVE THAT BACK!

FIRST PRODUCER No. *(they grapple a bit. The first producer just manages to keep hold of it as he goes down onto the ground)* Scott showed himself to be not only a fine...

The second producer manages to grab the mike and runs off leaving the first producer on the ground. The camera follows the second producer.

SECOND PRODUCER *(running)* The spruces and flowers of this forest will be used to create a whole new industry here in...

Idle, like Palin before him with "Ben Macdui," correctly pronounces "*Ivanhoe*," the Sir Walter Scott novel from 1820.

The caption is correctly spelled "Ivanhoe."

A caption here flashes "Ivanhoe (1953)," a reference to the movie starring Elizabeth Taylor and others.

The Forestry Commission is a British governmental agency created to protect British forests.

This "No" is directed at Cleese, who is attempting to take back the microphone.

Guy Mannering or The Astrologer, a Walter Scott novel from 1815 (though it was published anonymously).

A "rugger tackle" is a rugby tackle—and a good one, as Palin goes flying.

The music is implied, as none plays.

The Heart of Midlothian and *Old Mortality* are parts from Sir Walter Scott's *Tales of My Landlord*, a series of novels written from 1816 to 1831.

A Morris Minor is the archetypal British car of the 1950s, '60s, and early '70s—economical, roomy inside, and hugely popular. This car has a red *L* on a white background attached to it, the mandatory sign displayed by all learning drivers in the U.K. before they've passed their driving test.

The first producer brings him down with a diving rugger tackle and grabs the mike. **38**

FIRST PRODUCER ...also a writer of humour and...

They are both fighting and rolling around on the ground.

SECOND PRODUCER Britain's timber resources are being used up at a rate of...

The first producer hits him, and grabs the mike.

FIRST PRODUCER One man who knew Scott was Angus Tinker.

A sunlit university quad with classical pillars. ***Gentle classical music.*** **39** *Tinker is standing next to one of the pillars. He is a tweed-suited academic. Caption: 'ANGUS TINKER'*

TINKER (GRAHAM) Much of Scott's greatest work, and I'm thinking here particularly of **'Heart of Midlothian' and 'Old Mortality' for example,** **40** was concerned with...*(at this point a hand appears from behind the pillar and starts to go slowly but surely for the mike)* preserving the life and conditions of a...*(the mike is grabbed away from him)*

VOICE (TERRY J) Forestry research here has shown that the wholly synthetic soft timber fibre can be created...*(Tinker looks behind the pillar to discover a forestry expert in tweeds crouched)*... leaving the harder trees, the oaks, the beeches and the larches...*(Tinker chases him out into the quad)* and the pines, and even some of the deciduous hardwoods.

Caption: 'A FORESTRY EXPERT'

FORESTRY EXPERT This new soft-timber fibre would totally replace the plywoods, hardboards and chipboards at present dominating the...

A Morris Minor **41** *speeds up round the quad and passes straight in front of the expert and the first producer's hand comes out and grabs the mike. Cut to interior of the Morris Minor as it speeds out of quad and out into country. The first producer keeps glancing nervously over shoulder.*

FIRST PRODUCER In the Waverley novels...Scott was constantly concerned to protect a way of life...

He ducks as we hear the sound of a bullet ricochet from the car. Cut to shot through the back window. The second producer is chasing in a huge open American 1930s gangster car driven by a chauffeur in a thirties kit. He is shooting.

FIRST PRODUCER ...safeguarding nationalist traditions and aspiration, within the necessary limitations of the gothic novel...

More bullets. The American car draws level. The second producer leans over trying to grab the mike. Still attempting to say their lines, both of them scramble for the microphone as the cars race along. Eventually the cars disappear round a corner and we hear a crash. Cut to Toogood, surrounded by people, holding the book very close to his face and peering closely at the print. MacDonald lies on the floor in front of them.

TOOGOOD Then...theen...the...the end! The End. *(looks up)*

Cut to film (no sound) of Edward Heath. The 'Spot The Loony' buzzer goes. Roll credits. Cut to BBC world symbol.

VOICE OVER (ERIC) Next week on 'Book at Bedtime', Jeremy Toogood will be reading Anna Sewell's Black Bu...Bue...Bueton...Black Bottoon...*(fade out)* **42**

Fade BBC world symbol back up.

CONTINUITY VOICE (ERIC) Tomorrow night comedy returns to BBC TV with a new series of half-hour situation comedies for you to spot the winners. Ronnie Thompson stars in 'Dad's Doctor'...*(cut to a doctor* (TERRY J) *with no trousers)*

Superimposed caption: 'DAD'S DOCTOR'

CONTINUITY VOICE ...the daffy exploits of the RAMC training school. He's in charge of a group of mad medicos, and when they run wild it's titty jokes galore. *(medical students run past him waving bras)* Newcomer Veronica Papp plays the girl with the large breasts. *(a young lady runs past wearing only briefs)* Week two sees the return of the wacky exploits of the oddest couple you've ever seen—yes, 'Dad's Pooves'...

A kitchen set. A man (TERRY G) *in sexy female underwear. Another man* (TERRY J) *dressed as a judge, runs in with flowers. Superimposed caption: 'DAD'S POOVES'*

CONTINUITY VOICE ...the kooky oddball laugh-a-minute fun-a-plenty world of unnatural sexual practices. *(the first man spanks the judge with a string of sausages)* Week three brings a change of pace with a new comedy schedule. With Reg Cuttleworth, Trevor Quantas, and Cindy Rommel as Bob, in 'On the Dad's Liver Bachelors at Large', *(caption of this title and several loony still photos of the cast)* keeping the buses running from typical bedsit land in pre-war Liverpool. That's followed by 'The Ratings Game'—the loony life of a BBC programme planner with the accent on repeats. *(Michael's loony again)*

Superimposed caption: 'THE RATINGS GAME'

CONTINUITY VOICE Edie Phillips-Bong plays Kevin Vole, **43** the programme planner with a problem and his comic attempts to pass the time. Week six sees the return of 'Up The Palace'...*(stock film of the investiture of the Prince of Wales)*

Superimposed caption: 'UP THE PALACE'

CONTINUITY VOICE ...the zany exploits of a wacky Queen, and that's followed by 'Limestone, Dear Limestone'...*(long shot of a cliff with two people high up on it)*

Superimposed caption: 'LIMESTONE DEAR LIMESTONE'

CONTINUITY VOICE ...the wacky days of the late Pleistocene era when much of Britain's rock strata was being formed. All this and less on 'Comedy Ahoy'. But now, BBC Television is closing down for the night. Don't forget to switch off your sets. Goodnight.

We see the little dot as of a TV set being switched off.

As with the first sketch, the rest of this script, from this point to the end, does not appear in current versions of *Flying Circus*.

"Kevin Phillips-Bong" was the candidate for the Slightly Silly Party in Episode 19.

SEA
SON
3
EPISODE 39

GRANDSTAND
FEATURING
THAMES TV INTRODUCTION
'LIGHT ENTERTAINMENT AWARDS'
DICKIE ATTENBOROUGH ✽ THE OSCAR WILDE SKETCH
David Niven's Fridge
PASOLINI'S FILM
'THE THIRD TEST MATCH'
NEW BRAIN FROM CURRY'S
BLOOD DONOR ✽ INTERNATIONAL WIFE-SWAPPING
CREDITS OF THE YEAR
THE DIRTY VICAR SKETCH

FIRST AIRED: JANUARY 18, 1973

Begin with Thames Television logo and fanfare. **1** *Cut to David Hamilton in their presentation studios.* **2**

DAVID HAMILTON Good evening. We've got an action-packed evening for you tonight on Thames, **but right now here's a rotten old BBC programme.** **3**

Cut to the nude man (Terry J) at the organ.

ANNOUNCER (JOHN) And now...

IT'S MAN (MICHAEL)

IT'S...

Cut to a photo of Piccadilly Circus. Superimposed captions: 'THE BRITISH SHOWBIZ AWARDS' 'PRESENTED BY HRH THE DUMMY PRINCESS MARGARET' We mix through to the dummy Princess Margaret at a desk, as for awards ceremony. At the desk also, on either side of her, two men in dinner jackets and a pantomime goose. ***Bill Cotton is nowhere to be seen.*** **4** *High up above them, there is a screen. Enter* ***Dickie Attenborough.*** **5**

DICKIE (ERIC) Ladies and gentlemen, Mr Chairman, friends of the society, your dummy Royal Highness. Once again, the year has come full circle, and for me there can be no greater privilege, and honour, than to that to which it is my lot to have befallen this evening. There can be no finer honour than to welcome into our midst tonight a guest who has not only done only more than not anyone for our Society, but nonetheless has only done more. He started in the film industry in 1924, he started again in 1946, and finally in 1963. He has been dead for four years, but he has not let that prevent him from coming here this evening. *(he gets out an onion and holds it to his eyes; tears pour out)* Ladies and gentlemen, no welcome could be more heartfelt than that which I have no doubt you will all want to join with me in giving this great showbiz stiff. Ladies and gentlemen, to read the nominations for the Light Entertainment Award, the remains of the late **Sir Alan Waddle.** **6**

There is awful continuity music. Terrific applause. Attenborough weeps profusely. A man in a brown coat comes in carrying a white five-foot plinth. He puts it down. Behind him comes another man carrying a bronze funeral urn. It has a black tie on. Cut to stock film of the audience standing in rapturous applause. The urn is put on top of the plinth and a microphone placed in front of it. Slight pause. Cut to Dickie weeping profusely. The urn clears its throat.

Thames Television, the London-based and-focused version of ITV, and the third (and commercial) channel in the U.K. at the time.

David Hamilton, British TV presenter, was called "Diddy" by comedian Ken Dodd for being so compact. He went on to host many editions of *Top of the Pops*, as well as other TV and radio shows.

This is the final episode of third series, and the final episode featuring John Cleese. By the last six episodes (40 to 45) he was gone, though some of his material remained in the scripts.

Bill Cotton became the head of light entertainment for the BBC in 1970. His father was Billy Cotton, a legendary British bandleader of the mid-twentieth century.

Richard Attenborough, actor and director and sometimes "overemotional lovey," previously satirized by the Pythons.

Alan Waddle is probably a reference to the then Liverpool soccer player, though he was neither "late" nor a "Sir."

THE URN *(silly voice)* The nominations are **Mr Edward Heath,** **7** for the new suit sketch, *(zoom quickly in to film on the screen of the lady of Brussels throwing ink all over Mr Heath; cut back to the hall for applause)* Mr Richard Baker for Lemon Curry.

Cut to Richard Baker.

RICHARD BAKER Lemon Curry?

Cut back to the urn.

THE URN And the Third Parachute Brigade Amateur Dramatic Society for the **Oscar Wilde skit.** **8**

Zoom in to overlay showing some stock film of hansom cabs galloping past. Superimposed caption: 'LONDON 1895' Superimposed caption: 'THE RESIDENCE OF MR OSCAR WILDE' Suitable classy music starts. Mix through to Wilde's drawing room. A crowd of suitably dressed folk are engaged in typically brilliant conversation, laughing affectedly and drinking champagne.

PRINCE OF WALES (TERRY J) My congratulations, Wilde. Your latest play is a great success. The whole of London's talking about you.

OSCAR (GRAHAM) There is only one thing in the world worse than being talked about, and that is not being talked about.

There follows fifteen seconds of restrained and sycophantic laughter.

PRINCE Very very witty...very *very* witty.

WHISTLER (JOHN) There is only one thing in the world worse than being witty, and that is not being witty.

Fifteen more seconds of the same.

OSCAR I wish *I* had said that.

WHISTLER You will, Oscar, you will. *(more laughter)*

OSCAR Your Majesty, have you met **James McNeill Whistler?** **9**

On January 22, 1972, Edward Heath signed the treaty of accession in Brussels, thereby leading Britain into Europe. At the ceremony, a woman protester threw ink all over his suit.

8

Oscar Wilde, Irish writer of the second half of the nineteenth century, known for *The Importance of Being Earnest*, *The Picture of Dorian Gray*, his epigrammatic style, and later his hounding by the authorities for his homosexuality.

James McNeill Whistler (1834–1903), American painter famous for his portrait of his mother.

PRINCE Yes, we've played squash together.

OSCAR There is only one thing worse than playing squash together, and that is playing it by yourself. *(silence)* I wish I hadn't said that.

WHISTLER You did, Oscar, you did. *(a little laughter)*

PRINCE I've got to get back up the palace.

OSCAR Your Majesty is like a big jam doughnut with cream on the top.

PRINCE I beg your pardon?

OSCAR Um...It was one of Whistler's.

WHISTLER I never said that.

OSCAR You did, James, you did.

The Prince of Wales stares expectantly at Whistler.

WHISTLER ...Well, Your Highness, what I meant was that, like a doughnut, um, your arrival gives us pleasure...and your departure only makes us hungry for more. *(laughter)* Your Highness, you are also like a stream of bat's piss.

PRINCE What?

WHISTLER It was one of Wilde's. One of Wilde's.

OSCAR It sodding was not! It was Shaw! **10**

SHAW (MICHAEL) I...I merely meant, Your Majesty, that you shine out like a shaft of gold when all around is dark.

PRINCE *(accepting the compliment)* Oh.

OSCAR *(to Whistler)* Right. *(to Prince)* Your Majesty is like a dose of clap. **Before you arrive is pleasure, and after is a pain in the dong.** **11**

PRINCE *What?*

WHISTLER AND OSCAR One of Shaw's, one of Shaw's.

SHAW

George Bernard Shaw (1856–1950), Irish writer and playwright, Nobel Prize winner in 1925, vegetarian.

"Before you arrive is pleasure . . ." is spoken by the Whistler character.

YOU BASTARDS. UM . . . WHAT I MEANT, YOUR MAJESTY, WHAT I MEANT . . .

OSCAR We've got him, Jim.

WHISTLER Come on, Shaw-y.

OSCAR Come on, Shaw-y.

SHAW I merely meant...

OSCAR Come on, Shaw-y.

WHISTLER Let's have a bit of wit, then, man.

SHAW *(blows a raspberry)*

The Prince shakes Shaw's hand. Laughter all round. We then link to animation for a few minutes, then back to Dickie Attenborough at the awards ceremony. He now has bunches of onions slung round his neck.

DICKIE Ladies and gentlemen, seldom can it have been a greater pleasure and privilege than it is for me now to announce that the next award gave me the great pleasure and privilege of asking a man without whose ceaseless energy and tireless skill the British Film Industry would be today. I refer of course to my friend and colleague, Mr David Niven. *(vast applause, a bit of emotion from Dickie)* Sadly, **David Niven** **12** cannot be with us tonight, but he has sent his fridge. *(applause; 'Around the world in eighty days' music; the fridge is pushed down by a man in a brown coat)* This is the fridge in which David keeps most of his milk, butter and eggs. What a typically selfless gesture, that he should send this fridge, of all of his fridges, to be with us tonight.

Another cut of the audience applauding. The fridge has a black tie on. They adjust the mike for it.

FRIDGE *(the same silly voice)* The nominations for the Best Foreign Film Director are: Monsieur Richard Attenborough, Ricardo de Attenbergie, Rik Artenborough, Ri Char Dat En Bollo, and **Pier Paolo Pasolini.** **13**

DICKIE Before we hear the joint winner, let's see the one that came sixth. Let us see Pier Paolo Pasolini's latest film.

Close up of grass on cricket pitch. In the background we hear the buzzing of insects. A cricket ball rolls into shot and a hand reaches down and picks it up. Pull out to reveal he is a bowler, behind him a couple of fielders. He is shot from low down. caption: 'pasolini's the third test match' Close up on the bowler as he turns to look at his field. Cut to a skeleton on the boundary in tattered remnants of cricket gear. Noise of flies buzzing becomes louder. Sounds of mocking laughter. Cut to the bowler in close up turning into the direction of the laughter. Shot of the batsman at his crease, but behind him the wicket keeper and first slip are monks in brown cowls. They are laughing at him. Cut back to the bowler's horrified eyes, he looks again. Cut to same shot of the batsman only now the wicket keeper and first slip are cricketers again.

Wind, buzzing. Cut back to the bowler, who starts to rub the ball on his trousers. Music comes in. Close up bowler's face starting to sweat. Close up ball rubbing on trousers. Close up face sweating. Cut to a girl in the pavilion licking her lips. Cut back to ball rubbing. Cut to his sweating face. Cut to girl. Cut back to bowler as he starts his run. Close up of bowler running. He runs over a couple making love in the nude. Mounting music. Cut back to the bowler, as he releases ball. Cut to the ball smashing into stumps. The music reaches crescendo. Silence. In slow motion the bowler turns, arms outstretched to the umpire. The umpire turns into a cardinal who produces a cross and holds it up like a dismissal sign. Cut to a vociferous group of cricketers in a TV studio. They are all in pads and white flannels. They are on staggered rostra as in 'Talk-back'. Facing them is Pier Paolo Pasolini.

FIRST CRICKETER (GRAHAM) There's lots of people making love, but no mention of **Geoff Boycott's average.** **14**

David Niven, suave British actor and star of *Around the World in 80 Days* and *The Pink Panther* movies.

13

Pier Paolo Pasolini, Italian film director, poet, and political figure, murdered in 1975 by a 17-year-old, who ran him over, back and forth, with Pasolini's own car.

Geoffrey Boycott, English cricketer, renowned for his conservative batting style—he scored slowly, if at all—and for his acerbic opinions on other cricketers, which he continues to share on radio and TV in his broad Yorkshire accent.

Fred Titmus, English cricketer, known for his slow-speed spin bowling, and for getting his foot caught in the propellers of a boat in 1968 while on tour to Barbados with the England team. He lost four toes.

"Off breaks" is a kind of spin bowling in the sport of cricket.

Brisbane is where some test matches between Australia and visiting teams are played. A "sticky wicket" is one that causes the ball to spin a lot; it's also used metaphorically to refer to a difficult situation.

Ray Illingworth, English cricketer and, later, TV presenter and cricket commentator.

"Forty-seven not out" means the batsman has scored 47 runs and is still batting (hence not out). See?

The Zambesi is an African river that runs about 2,200 miles from Zambia and out into the Indian Ocean.

PASOLINI (JOHN) *(Italian accent)* Who is-a Geoff Boycott?

Superimposed caption: 'PIER PAOLO PASOLINI'

SECOND CRICKETER (MICHAEL) And in t'film, we get **Fred Titmus...** [15]

PASOLINI Si, Titmus, si, si...

Superimposed caption: 'YORKSHIRE'

SECOND CRICKETER ...the symbol of man's regeneration through radical Marxism...fair enough...but we never once get a chance to see him turn his **off-breaks** [16] on that **Brisbane sticky.** [17]

THIRD CRICKETER (ERIC) Aye, and what were all that dancing through **Ray Illingworth's innings?** [18] **Forty-seven not out and the bird comes up and feeds him some grapes!** [19]

General cricketorial condemnation. We pull back to show that it is on a television set in an ordinary sitting room. Two pepperpots are watching the television. They are both called ***Mrs Zambesi.*** [20]

FIRST ZAMBESI (GRAHAM) What's on the other side?

The second Mrs Zambesi switches channels to reveal Dickie Attenborough still at it.

DICKIE Nobody could be prouder than...

SECOND ZAMBESI (TERRY J) Ugh! *(she switches the set off)*

FIRST ZAMBESI Um, shall we go down and give blood?
SECOND ZAMBESI Oh, I don't want a great bat flapping round my neck.
FIRST ZAMBESI They don't do it like that! They take it from your arm!
SECOND ZAMBESI I can't give it. I caught swamp fever in the Tropics.
FIRST ZAMBESI You've never even been to the Tropics. You've never been south of Sidcup. [21]
SECOND ZAMBESI You can catch it off lampposts.
FIRST ZAMBESI Catch what?
SECOND ZAMBESI I don't know, I'm all confused.
FIRST ZAMBESI You ought to go and see a psychiatrist. You're a loony. You might even need a new brain.
SECOND ZAMBESI Oh, I couldn't afford a whole new brain.
FIRST ZAMBESI Well, you could get one of those Curry's brains. [22]
SECOND ZAMBESI How much are they?
FIRST ZAMBESI *(picking up a catalogue)* I don't know. I'll have a look in the catalogue. Here we are. Battery lights, dynamo lights, rear lights, brains—here we are...
SECOND ZAMBESI I'm still confused.
FIRST ZAMBESI Oh, there's a nice one here, thirteen-and-six, it's one of Curry's own brains. [23]
SECOND ZAMBESI That one looks nice, what's that?
FIRST ZAMBESI That's a mudguard!
SECOND ZAMBESI It's only eight bob. [24]
FIRST ZAMBESI Oh, I think it's worth the extra five bob for the brain. I'll give them a ring. *(she goes to the phone and dials one number)* Hello, Curry's? I'd like to try one of your thirteen-and-sixpenny brains please. Yes...yes...yes, ye...um...*(looks at her shoe)* five-and-a-half...yes... thank you. [25] *(replaces phone)* They're sending someone round *(there is a knock at the door)*
SECOND ZAMBESI Oh, that was quick. Come in.
MAN (JOHN) Hello Mr and Mrs and Mrs Zambesi?

FIRST ZAMBESI Yes, that's right. Are you the man from Curry's?
MAN No, I've just come to say that he's on his way. Would you sign this please.

He hands a bare leg severed from the knee downwards round the door. She signs it. [26]

MAN Thank you very much. Thank you. Sorry to bother you.
FIRST ZAMBESI Thank you.

Sidcup is an area of southeast London.

Currys is a British home electronics and appliance store.

A caption appears here: Old Sketch Written Before Decimilization. Britain converted to the metric system on February 15, 1971, but many people continued to discuss prices in terms of what they once were, as here.

Another caption here: 1np=2 ½op—that is, one new pence is equal to two and a half old pence.

"Five-and-a-half" is a reference back to Episode 31, where the emergency dispatcher keeps asking for shoe sizes.

Chapman inadvertently drops the pen, causing him to say, "Ooh, sorry!"

Another money caption: 44/6d=£2.22 ½p—that is, forty-four shillings and sixpence is equal to two pounds and twenty-two and a half pence.

Bertrand Russell (1872–1970), British philosopher.

The man goes. A knock at the door and he reappears.

MAN Um, he's just coming now. Here he is.

The door opens and a pair of hands fling in a dummy salesman carrying a briefcase. He flops down on to the floor. The door shuts. The two pepperpots go over and look at him for some time.

FIRST ZAMBESI Hello...hello...

SECOND ZAMBESI *(picking up the dummy)* That's not a proper salesman. I'm not buying one from him, he doesn't give you confidence.

FIRST ZAMBESI He doesn't give me any confidence at all—he's obviously a dummy. I'll ring Curry's. *(she just picks up the phone without dialing this time)* Hello, Curry's—that salesman you sent round is obviously a dummy...Oh, thank you very much. *(she puts the phone down)* They're sending round a real one. *(a knock on the door)*

SECOND ZAMBESI Come in.

The salesman enters.

SALESMAN (MICHAEL) Good morning—Mr and Mrs and Mrs Zambesi?

SECOND ZAMBESI Yes, that's right.

FIRST ZAMBESI Yes, that's right...*(out of the side of the mouth in a man's voice)* Yes that's right.

SALESMAN *(to dummy)* All right, Rutherford, I'll take over.

He opens a box and produces a two foot square silver cube with various gadgets and wires on it.

SECOND ZAMBESI Oh, that's nice.

SALESMAN Yes, we sell a lot of these. Right, shall we try a fitting?

SECOND ZAMBESI Oh, do I have to have an operation?

SALESMAN No, madam, you just strap it on.

He starts to put it on her head.

SECOND ZAMBESI Doesn't it go inside my head?

SALESMAN Not the roadster, madam, no. You're thinking of the brainette major.

SECOND ZAMBESI How much is that?

SALESMAN Forty-four-and-six. 27

SECOND ZAMBESI Oh no, it's not worth it.

SALESMAN Not with the Curry's surgery we use, no, madam. Now then. The best bet is the Bertrand Russell super silver. 28 That's a real beauty—250 quid plus hospital treatment.

FIRST ZAMBESI Ooh, that's a lot.

SALESMAN It's colour. Right. *(he straps the brain to her head and begins to twiddle a few knobs; lights flash on occasionally as he does this)* One, two, three, testing, testing.

SECOND ZAMBESI Mince pie for me, please.

FIRST ZAMBESI What did she say that for?

SALESMAN Quiet please. It's not adjusted yet. *(he makes more adjustments)*

SECOND ZAMBESI Oh, I am enjoying this rickshaw ride. I've been a Tory all my life, my life, my life. 29 Good morning Mr Presley. How well you look, you look very well...our cruising speed is 610 per hour...well...well, well, well, hello hello dear...

SALESMAN Right, one, two, three...*(the salesman adjusts a switch)*

SECOND ZAMBESI ...eight, seven, *(he adjusts another switch)* four.

"Tory" is the nickname for the Conservative Party and its adherents.

Jones also throws in the word "porridge" here.

FIRST ZAMBESI Oh, she never knew that before.

SALESMAN Quiet please. Mrs Zambesi, who wrote the theory of relativity?

SECOND ZAMBESI I know! I know.

SALESMAN Quiet, please! *(he adjusts a tuning control)*

FIRST ZAMBESI Einstone...Einstone...Einsteen...Einston...Einstin...Einstan...Ein*stein.*

SALESMAN Good.

SECOND ZAMBESI Noël Einstein.

SALESMAN Right. That'll be 13/6d please.

FIRST ZAMBESI *(paying him with invisible money)* That's marvellous.

SALESMAN She can take it off at night, unless she wants to read, of course. And don't ask her too many questions because it will get hot. If you do have any trouble here is my card. *(he reaches in his case and hands her the dismembered part of an arm)* Give us a ring and either myself, or Mr Rutherford *(he picks the dummy up and drags it towards the door)* will come and see you. Goodbye.

FIRST ZAMBESI Thank you very much.

As soon as the door is shut, the man's head pops round.

MAN He's gone now.

He withdraws head and shuts the door.

FIRST ZAMBESI *(tentatively)* Shall we go down and give blood?

SECOND ZAMBESI *(with slightly glazed eyes)* Yes, please Mr Roosevelt, but try and keep the noise to a minimum.

FIRST ZAMBESI I'll go and get your coat for you.

SECOND ZAMBESI I'm quite warm in this stick of celery, thank you, Senator Muskie. **30**

The pepperpots appear out of their gate and walk down the street. We follow them closely.

SECOND ZAMBESI *(to neighbour)* Stapling machine, Mr Clarke.

FIRST ZAMBESI *(explaining)* New brain.

SECOND ZAMBESI Stapling machine, Mrs Worral.

Cut to a pepperpot with identical brain strapped to head.

MRS WORRAL Stapling machine, Mrs Zambesi.

They walk on passing a bus stop at which a penguin is standing reading a paper. One or two unexploded Scotsmen lie on the ground at various places.

FIRST ZAMBESI Are you sure that's working all right?

SECOND ZAMBESI Yes, thank you dear. It's marvellous. I think if we can win one or two of the early primaries, we could split the urban Republican vote wide open.

FIRST ZAMBESI Um...here we are then.

They go into a door marked 'Blood Donors'.

SECOND ZAMBESI Well being President of the United States is something that I shall have to think about.

They walk through and out of shot. A hospital lobby. A line of people are being ushered through. A sign says 'Blood Donors' with an arrow in the direction they're all going. Mr Samson is in a white coat.

30

Edmund Sixtus "Ed" Muskie, American politician and Democratic nominee for vice president in 1968.

SAMSON (JOHN) Blood donors that way, please.
DONOR Oh thank you very much *(joins the line)*.
SAMSON Thank you. *(Grimshaw comes up to him and whispers in his ear; Samson looks at him, slightly surprised)* What? *(Grimshaw whispers again)* No. No, I'm sorry but no. *(Grimshaw whispers again)* No, you may not give urine instead of blood. *(Grimshaw whispers again)* No, well, I don't care if you want to. *(Grimshaw whispers again)* No. There is no such thing as a urine bank.
GRIMSHAW (ERIC) Please.
SAMSON No. We have no call for it. We've quite enough of it without volunteers coming in here donating it.
GRIMSHAW Just a specimen.
SAMSON No, we don't want a specimen. We either want your blood or nothing.
GRIMSHAW I'll give you some blood if you'll give me...
SAMSON What?
GRIMSHAW A thing to do some urine in.
SAMSON No, no, just go away please.
GRIMSHAW Anyway, I don't want to give you any blood.
SAMSON Fine, well you don't have to, you see, just go away.
GRIMSHAW Can I give you some spit?
SAMSON No.
GRIMSHAW Sweat?
SAMSON No.
GRIMSHAW Earwax?
SAMSON No, look, this is a blood bank—all we want is blood.
GRIMSHAW All right, I'll give you some blood.

He holds out a jar full of blood.

SAMSON Where did you get that?
GRIMSHAW Today. It's today's.
SAMSON What group is it?
GRIMSHAW What groups are there?
SAMSON There's A...
GRIMSHAW It's A.
SAMSON *(sniffing the blood)* Wait a moment. It's mine. This blood is mine! What are you doing with it?
GRIMSHAW I found it.
SAMSON You *found* it? You stole it out of my body, didn't you?

GRIMSHAW No.
SAMSON No wonder I'm feeling off-colour. *(he starts to drink the blood; Grimshaw grabs the bottle)* Give that back.

GRIMSHAW It's mine.
SAMSON It is not yours. You stole it.
GRIMSHAW Never.
SAMSON Give it back to me.
GRIMSHAW All right. But only if I can give urine.
SAMSON ...Get in the queue.

Cut to John Rickman type person with hat which he raises. **31** *There are white rails behind him which might be a racecourse.*

RICKMAN (MICHAEL) Good afternoon and welcome to Wife-Swapping from **Redcar.** **32** And the big news this morning is that the British boy Boris Rogers has succeeded in swapping his nine-stone Welsh-born wife for a **Ford Popular** **33** and a complete set of Dickens. Well now, I can see they're ready at the start and so let's go now over for the start of the 3.30.

Cut to high shot of a street with about 10 houses on each side.

RICKMAN And first let's catch up with the latest news of the betting.

Superimposed captions:
'NO. 12 BETTY PARKINSON 7/4 ON FAV
NO. 27 MRS E. COLYER 9/4
NO. 14 MRS CASEY 4/1
5/1 BAR'

VOICE OVER (ERIC) Number 12 Betty Parkinson 7 to 4 on favourite, number 27 Mrs Colyer 9 to 4, 5 to 1 bar those. **34**
RICKMAN And here's the starter Mrs Alec Marsh, *(she climbs onto a rostrum and fires a gun)* and they're off.

One of the doors opens and a lady rushes across the street into another house. Other doors start opening up and down the street, with ladies criss-crossing out of each others houses. About twenty seconds of this high activity.

RICKMAN And Mrs Rogers is the first to show, there she goes into Mr Johnson's, and Mrs Johnson across to Mr Colyer, followed closely by Mrs Casey on the inside. Mrs Parkinson, number 12, going well there into Mr Webster's from the Co-op, Mrs Colyer's making ground fast after a poor start, she's out of Mr Casey's into Mr Parkinson's, she's a couple of lengths ahead of Mrs Johnson who's still not out of Mr Casey's. Mrs Penguin and Mrs Colyer—these two now at the head of the field from Mrs Brown, Mrs Atkins, Mrs Parkinson, Mrs Warner and Mrs Rudd—all still at Mr Philips's. Mrs Penguin making the running now, challenged strongly by Mrs Casey, Mrs Casey coming very fast on the inside, it's going to be Mrs Casey coming from behind. Now she's making a break on the outside,

31

John Eric Carter Rickman was a TV presenter known for introducing horse-racing shows. He always raised his hat in greeting. He's famous for a moment during a live broadcast when he answered a phone that rang on his desk, thinking it impolite not to do so, telling the caller: "I'm on air and very busy. I'll call you back."

Redcar is a horse-racing track on the North Yorkshire coast.

Another name-check for the cheap and cheerful Ford Popular, a car discontinued in 1962.

Meaning any other horses in the race are 5 to 1 to win.

Doncaster is another horse-racing track, this one in south Yorkshire, about 90 miles south of Redcar.

Cheltenham, a horse-racing track in the west of Britain, famous for its festival, held in March—a major horse-racing event.

Peter West, a BBC sports presenter known for his bald head and long words.

A play on *Come Dancing*, a BBC TV ballroom-dancing competition that ran from 1949 to 1988. The title was later changed to a celebrity competition under the name *Strictly Come Dancing* (in the U.S., *Dancing with the Stars*).

The precursor to the British *Sportsnight*, *Sportsview*, a midweek sports highlights show, was presented by Frank Bough, who went on to present *Grandstand*, name-checked at the start of this episode.

Keighley and Hull Kingston Rovers are two rugby league teams from Yorkshire.

Mrs Penguin running...and at the line, it's Mrs Casey who's got it by a short head from Mrs Penguin in second place, Mrs Parkinson in third, Mrs Rudd, Mrs Colyer, Mrs Warner and there's Mrs Griffiths who's remained unswapped.

One lady is left in the middle of the road. Cut back to Rickman at the course railing.

RICKMAN Well, a very exciting race there, and I have with me now the man who owned and trained the winner, Mrs Casey—Mr Casey. Well done, Jack.

MR CASEY (TERRY J) Thank you, John.

RICKMAN Well, were you at all surprised about this, Jack?

MR CASEY No, not really, no she's been going very well in training, and at **Doncaster** 35 last week, and I fancy her very strongly for the **Cheltenham weekend.** 36

RICKMAN Well, thank you very much indeed, Jack. We must leave you now because it's time for the team event.

Peter West type figure 37 *in a white DJ sitting at a ballroom side table. He has one or two ballroom dancers beside him. Superimposed titles: 'COME WIFE-SWAPPING—NORTH WEST V THE SOUTH EAST'* 38

PETER (ERIC) Hello, and a very warm welcome from the Tower ballroom suite at Reading, where there's very little in it, they're neck and neck, crop and grummit, real rack and saddle, brick and bucket, horse and tooth, cap and thigh, arse over tip, they're absolutely birds of a feather, there's not a new pin in it, you couldn't get a melon between them. Well, now, everything rests on the formation event and here come North West with the Mambo.

Cut to lines of ballroom dancers being led out. Four gentlemen and four ladies in each team, sixteen altogether.

PETER Maestro, take it away, please.

The dancers form up in two lines opposite each other, as though they are about to dance. The ladies are in nasty tulle, the gents in tails, with numbers on their backs. At the back of the hall a large banner says 'Mecca Wife-Swapping'. Mambo music starts its intro. After four bars the two teams start grabbing each other and wrestling on the ground. A vast orgy breaks out as they roll all over the floor. Cut quickly to Frank Bough in the 'Sportsview' studio. 39

FRANK BOUGH (MICHAEL) And now it's time for Rugby league, and highlights of this afternoon's game between **Keighley and Hull Kingston Rovers.** 40

Cut to a field where mud-caked rugby league players in hooped shirts are getting ready for a scrum. Superimposed caption: 'KEIGHLEY 2 HULL K.R. 23'

EDDIE WARING (ERIC) [41] *(voice over)* **Well, good afternoon and as you can see, Hull Kingston Rovers are well in the lead, it's a scrum down on the twenty-five,** [42] **Keighley's Tom Colyer with the put in, Mrs Colyer to be put.**

The scrum has formed up, the scrum half has a dummy woman, small and light but real looking, tucked under his arm, while he steadies the scrum. He puts her into the scrum, and after a lot of kicking she is eventually heeled out.

EDDIE WARING And there goes his wife into the scrum. And Hull have got the heel against the head. Doing nicely with this scrum, some very good packing here. Warrington's picked her up, is he going to let her go, Wrigley's with him, grand lad is this. [43]

Mrs Colyer is picked up by the scrum half who makes a run with her. Handing off a strong tackle and dodging with her, he side steps and slips Mrs Colyer to a back who makes a run through and touches her down between the posts. They leave the lady dumped down between the posts and rush to congratulate and hug each other.

EDDIE WARING Well, that was right on the whistle, Rovers walkin' it there, winnin' easily by twenty-six points to two.

Cut to Frank Bough again in the 'Sportsview' set.

FRANK BOUGH Just a reminder that on 'Match of the Day' tonight you can see highlights of two of this afternoon's big games. Mrs Robinson v **Manchester United** [44] and **Southampton** [45] Mr Rogers, a rather unusual game that. And here's a late result...**Coventry nil,** [46] Mr Johnson's Una three—Coventry going down at home, there. Just a little reminder that the next sport you can see on BBC 1 will be 9.20 on Wednesday night, when **'Wife Swapping with Coleman' comes live from my place.** [47] Till then, goodnight.

Credits roll over four screens of naughty activity to the 'Grandstand' signature tune.

41

Eddie Waring, another favorite of the Pythons. This rugby commentator is mentioned in Episode 1.

The 'twenty-five' yard line.

All rugby phrases. Basically, the two teams push each other and try to "heel," or kick, the ball—or, in this case, the wife—out of the scrum to their team.

Manchester United, perhaps the most famous club team in the world of soccer.

Southampton, a soccer team from the south coast of England.

Coventry City, a soccer team from the Midlands.

David Coleman, British TV sports presenter known for his gaffes. He was replaced on *Grandstand* by Frank Bough.

GRANDSTAND
A BBC INSIDE BROADCAST
CONCEIVED WRITTEN AND PERFORMED BY
MICHAEL PALIN AND MRS CLEESE
ERIC IDLE AND MRS PALIN
JOHN CLEESE AND MRS JONES
TERRY GILLIAM AND TERRY JONES AND MRS IDLE
GRAHAM CHAPMAN AND MR SHERLOCK
ALSO APPEARING CAROL CLEVELAND AND MRS AND MRS ZAMBESI
CARON GARDENER AND MR A.
MAKE-UP BY MISS GAFFNEY AND MR LAST
COSTUMES HAZEL PETHIG AND MR CLARKE
GRAPHICS BY BOB BLAGDEN AND 'NAUGHTY' ROSY
ANIMATIONS BY TERRY GILLIAM AND RABBI COLQUHOUN
FILM CAMERAMAN ALAN FEATHERSTONE AND MISS WESTON
FILM EDITOR MR RAY MILLICHOPE AND HIS ORCHESTRA
SOUND RICHARD CHUBB AND MRS LIGHTING
LIGHTING BILL BAILEY AND MR SOUND
CHOREOGRAPHY BY JEAN CLARKE AND AN UNNAMED MAN IN ESHER
DESIGNED BY CHRIS THOMPSON AND MRS ARMSTRONG-JONES
PRODUCED BY IAN MACNAUGHTON AND 'DICKIE'
A BBC TV AND MRS THAMES PRODUCTION

Pull out from screen to see that this is on the screen in the awards set and Dickie is working a stirrup pump which pumps tears out from the side of his head via rather obvious tubes.

DICKIE There they go, the credits of the year. Credits that you and the Society voted as the credits that brought the most credit to the Society. Sadly, the man who designed them cannot be with us tonight, as he is at home asleep, but we are going to wake him up and tell him the good news.

We see a darkened bedroom. The light is suddenly switched on. A man sits up. He has no clothes on.

DICKIE Are you there in Bristol, Arthur Briggs...?

Briggs looks terrified. We see that another man (JOHN) *is in bed with him.*

BRIGGS (MICHAEL) Oh, my God! *(pulls a sheet over the other man)*

Cut back to Dickie.

DICKIE

AND NOW FOR THE MOMENT YOU'VE ALL BEEN WAITING FOR...

Caption: THE END

DICKIE No, not that moment. Although that moment is coming, in a moment. The moment I'm talking about is the moment when we present the award for the cast with the most awards award, and this year is no exception. Ladies and gentlemen will you join me and welcome please, the winners of this year's **Mountbatten trophy,** 48 Showbusiness's highest accolade, the cast of the Dirty Vicar sketch.

Very patriotic music. 49

The cast of the Dirty Vicar sketch come on. They curtsy to Princess Margaret. Attenborough embraces them all.

DICKIE Well now, let us see the performances which brought them this award. Let us see the Dirty Vicar sketch.

Cut to two ladies taking tea in an Edwardian drawing room.

FIRST LADY (CAROL) **Have you seen Lady Windermere's new carriage, dear?** 50
SECOND LADY (CARON GARDENER) Absolutely enchanting!
FIRST LADY Isn't it!

Chivers the butler enters.

CHIVERS (GRAHAM) The new vicar to see you, m'lady.
FIRST LADY Send him in, Chivers.
CHIVERS Certainly, m'lady. *(he goes)*

Enter a Swiss mountaineer (TERRY G) *in Tyrolean hat, lederhosen, haversack, icepick, etc. Followed by two men in evening dress. They look round and exit.*

Louis Francis Albert Victor Nicholas George Mountbatten, First Earl Mountbatten of Burma, naval officer, statesman, and uncle to Queen Elizabeth II's husband, Prince Philip. The Irish Republican Army murdered him in 1979, when they blew up his boat in the harbor at Mullaghmore, off the northwest coast of Ireland.

The "Nimrod" variation, from Edward Elgar's *Enigma Variations*, once again.

Lady Windermere's Fan is a play by Oscar Wilde, first produced in 1892.

FIRST LADY Now, how is your tea, dear? A little more water perhaps?
SECOND LADY Thank you. It is delightful as it is.
CHIVERS

THE REVEREND RONALD SIMMS, THE DIRTY VICAR OF ST MICHAEL'S...OOH!

Chivers is obviously goosed from behind by the Dirty Vicar.

"Lovely bit of stuff" is British slang for an attractive woman.

VICAR (TERRY J) **Cor, what a lovely bit of stuff.** 51 I'd like to get my fingers around those knockers.

He pounces upon the second lady, throws her skirt over her head and pushes her over the back of the sofa.

FIRST LADY How do you find the vicarage?

The vicar stands up from behind the sofa, his shirt open and his hair awry; he reaches over and puts his hand down the first lady's front.

VICAR I like tits!
FIRST LADY Oh vicar! vicar!

The vicar suddenly pulls back and looks around him as if in the horror of dawning realization.

VICAR Oh my goodness. I do beg your pardon. How dreadful! The first day in my new parish, I completely...so sorry!
FIRST LADY *(readjusting her dress)* Yes. Never mind, never mind. Chivers—send Mary in with a new gown, will you?

The second lady struggles to her feet from behind the couch, completely dishevelled. Her own gown completely ripped open.

CHIVERS Certainly, m'lady.

VICAR *(to the second lady)* I do beg your pardon...I must sit down.
FIRST LADY As I was saying, how do you find the new vicarage?

They take their seats on the couch.

VICAR Oh yes, certainly, yes indeed, I find the grounds delightful, and the servants most attentive and particularly the little serving maid with the great big knockers...

He throws himself on the hostess across the tea table, knocking it over and they disappear over the back of the hostess's chair. Grunts etc. Enter Dickie applauding. Also, we hear audience applause.

DICKIE Well, there we are, another year has been too soon alas ended and I think none more than myself can be happier at this time than I...am.

The cast of the sketch stand in a line at the back, looking awkward and smiling. Fade out.

SEASON 4
EPISODE 40
THE GOLDEN AGE OF BALLOONING

THE GOLDEN AGE OF BALOONING
FEATURING
MONTGOLFIER BROTHERS
LOUIS XIV
George III
ZEPPELIN

FIRST AIRED: OCTOBER 31, 1974

Animation of balloons ascending. caption: 'THE GOLDEN AGE OF BALLOONING'

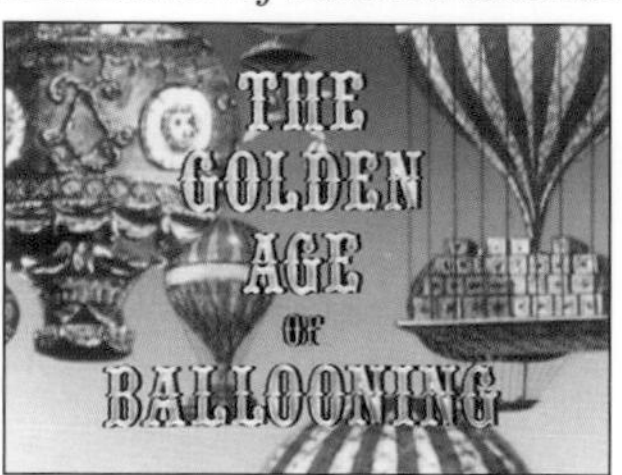

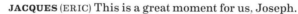

*Caption: '**THE BEGINNINGS**'* **1** *Cut to a suburban bathroom. A plumber with a bag of tools open beside him is doing an elaborate repair on the toilet. He is in rather an awkward position.*

PLUMBER (MICHAEL) *(working away)* **The Golden Age of Ballooning can be said to begin in 1783... when the Montgolfier brothers made their first ascent in a fire balloon. On the eve of that...*(struggling with the work)* come on...come on...momentous ascent, the brothers took one last look at their craft, as it stood on the field of Annencay.** **2**

Pleasant elegant eighteenth-century music. Mix to a French small country-house interior. At the window Joseph and Jacques Montgolfier are looking out at their balloon. In the background a plumber is working away at a bit of eighteenth-century French piping.

JACQUES (ERIC) This is a great moment for us, Joseph.
JOSEPH (TERRY J) It is a great moment for France.
JACQUES Ah, oui!
JOSEPH First ascent in a hot-air balloon, by the Montgolfier brothers—1783...I can see us now... just after Montesquieu and just before Mozart. **3**
JACQUES I think I'll go and wash...
JOSEPH Good luck.
JACQUES Oh...it's quite easy, really...I just slap a little water on my face, then...
JOSEPH No...good luck for tomorrow.
JACQUES Oh I see, yes. You too. Yours has been the work.
JOSEPH Let us hope for a safe ascent...and don't use my flannel.
JACQUES You know, when you showed me the plans in Paris, I could not believe that we should be the first men who would fly.
JOSEPH Yes...it's wonderful.
JACQUES

I AM SO EXCITED I COULD HARDLY WASH.

JOSEPH Yes...I too have had some difficulty washing these past few days.
JACQUES Still, what is washing when we are on the verge of a great scientific breakthrough?
JOSEPH Jacques...
JACQUES Yes, Joseph...
JOSEPH I have not been washing very thoroughly for many years now.

1

This is the first of the final six-episode series. Cleese is absent, though some of his material is used.

2

Joseph-Michel and Jacques-Étienne Montgolfier invented the "*globe aerostatique*," a hot-air balloon. The brothers were from Annonay, a town in southeast France, 47 miles south of Lyon; this is also where they staged their first flight of 1.2 miles.

3

A nice *Dictionary of Famous People* gag.

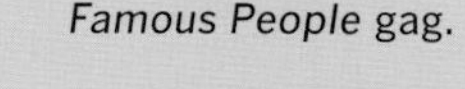

JACQUES What do you mean? **You must have been washing your face?** 4
JOSEPH Oh yes, my face, I wash my face...but my legs...my stomach...my chest, they're filthy.
JACQUES Well, I don't wash my stomach every day.
JOSEPH *(with increasing self-remorse)* Ah, but you wash far more than me...you are the cleaner of the Montgolfier brothers.
JACQUES This is nothing, Joseph...

A very formal butler enters.

BUTLER (GRAHAM) Monsieur Montgolfier...A Mr Parfitt to see you, sir.

A head appears round the door and corrects the butler, in a very stage whisper.

MR BARTLETT No, no...no...Bartlett! *(the head disappears again)*

BUTLER A Mr Barklit, to see you, sir.
MR BARTLETT No! Bartlett with a 't'. *(the head disappears again)*
BUTLER *(with difficulty)* Barr...at...elett...to see you, sir.
MR BARTLETT Bartlett *(he disappears again)*
BUTLER Barkit...
MR BARTLETT Bartlett!
BUTLER Barlit...Bartlett...A Mr Bartl*ett* to see you, sir.
JOSEPH I don't want to see anyone, O'Toole...tell him to go away.
BUTLER Thank you, sir. *(he exits)*
JACQUES Well, it's getting late. I must go and have a wash.
JOSEPH What will you be washing?
JACQUES **Oh...just my face and neck...perhaps my feet...and possibly...but no...no...lock up the plans, Joseph...tomorrow they will make us the toast of France. 'The first ascent by the Montgolfier brothers in a balloon'. Just after Ballcock and just before Bang...what a position!** 5

Some men have now entered the room, chosen a spot and are briskly but quietly setting up a screen and a projector. The projector is turned on and a film comes up on the screen together with triumphant music, applause and commentary. We zoom in to the screen. It shows an animation of two naked men boxing in a large tub of water.

British people enjoy criticizing the French whenever possible, and one of the chief knocks is to question their personal hygiene.

Nice reference back to the start of the sketch, where Palin was fixing a toilet.

VOICE OVER (GRAHAM) So, on June 7th, 1783, the Montgolfier brothers had a really good wash...starting on his face and arms, Joseph Michael Montgolfier went on to scrub his torso, his legs and his naughty bits, before rinsing his whole body. That June night, he and his brother between them washed seventeen square feet of body area. They used a kilo and a half of carbolic soap and nearly fourteen gallons of nice hot water. It was indeed an impressive sight.

Music crescendo. Caption: 'THE END' Picture of a balloon. Superimposed caption: 'THE GOLDEN AGE OF BALLOONING'. This is over the BBC 2 logo.

James Glaisher, along with his copilot Henry Tracey Coxwell, broke the world record for altitude in a balloon in 1862, though he fainted at about 2,600 feet.

VOICE OVER (GRAHAM) Next week on 'The Golden Age of Ballooning', we examine the work of **Glaisher and Coxwell,** **6** the English balloonists who ascended to a height of seven miles in 1862 without washing. There is also a book called 'The Golden Age of Ballooning' published by the BBC to coincide with the series. It's in an attractive hand-tooled binding, is priced £5 and failure to buy it will make you liable to a £50 fine or three months' imprisonment. There's also a record of someone reading the book of 'The Golden Age of Ballooning', a crochet-work bedspread with the words 'The Golden Age of Ballooning' on it, available from the BBC, price £18 (or five months' imprisonment) and there are matching toilet-seat covers and courtesy mats with illustrations of many of the balloons mentioned. Also available is a life-size model frog which croaks the words 'The Golden Age of Ballooning' and an attractive bakelite case for storing motorway construction plans in, made in the shape of a balloon. And now, another chance to see a repeat of this morning's re-run of last night's second showing of episode two of the award-winning series 'The Golden Age of Ballooning'.

Animation: balloons ascending as before. Caption: 'THE GOLDEN AGE OF BALLOONING' Caption: 'EPISODE TWO: THE MONTGOLFIER BROTHERS IN LOVE' Caption: 'NOT WITH EACH OTHER, OBVIOUSLY' Joseph Montgolfier's workshop. We see plans and drawing boards, and at one end of the room, Joseph's fiancée, Antoinette, in a pretty dress. She is hanging suspended in a harness horizontally, attached to a gas bag. In other words she is floating like the bottom half of an airship. Joseph is making calculations excitedly. Occasionally he goes over to her, takes a measurement and goes back to his desk to write it down.

ANTOINETTE (CAROL)

OH JOSEPH, ALL YOU THINK ABOUT IS BALLOONS...ALL YOU TALK ABOUT IS BALLOONS.

Your beautiful house is full of bits and pieces of balloons...your books are all about balloons...every time you sing a song, it is in some way obliquely connected with balloons... everything you eat has to have 'balloon' incorporated in the title...your dogs are all called 'balloonno'...you tie balloons to your ankles in the evenings.

JOSEPH I don't do that!

ANTOINETTE Well, no, you don't do that, but you do duck down and shout 'Hey! Balloons!' when there are none about. Your whole life is becoming obsessively balloonic, you know. Why do I have to hang from this bloody gas bag all day? Don't I mean anything to you?

JOSEPH *(busy measuring)* Oh ma chérie, you mean more to me than any heavier than air dirigible could ever...

ANTOINETTE Oh there you go again!

JOSEPH Don't waggle!

Jacques enters.

JACQUES I've run your bath for you, Joseph. *(he sees Antoinette)* Oh...I'm so sorry, I didn't realize.

JOSEPH It's all right, we've done the difficult bit.
JACQUES Well, don't forget we have our special guest coming this evening.
JOSEPH Oh?
JACQUES Don't tell me you have forgotten already. The man who is giving us thousands of francs for our experiments.

JOSEPH What man?
JACQUES Louis XIV! 7
JOSEPH Isn't he dead?
JACQUES Evidently not...
JOSEPH All right, I'll be round.
JACQUES Oh, and Joseph...
JOSEPH Yes, Jacques?
JACQUES You will...wash...won't you?
JOSEPH Yes, of course!

The "Sun King" was the longest-running king of Europe ever: some 72 years and change. He died in 1715, a full 25 years before Joseph-Michel and 30 years before Jacques-Étienne were born.

Caption: 'LATER THAT EVENING' Fade up on the Montgolfiers' sitting room. Jacques sits there rather nervously. The plumber is working away. The door opens and the butler appears.

BUTLER His Royal Majesty, Louis XIV of France.

HIS ROYAL MAJESTY, LOUIS XIV OF FRANCE.

Mr Bartlett's head pops in and whispers loudly to butler.

MR BARTLETT And Mr Bartlett.

The butler pushes him aside. Fanfare. Enter Louis XIV and two tough-looking advisers. He is resplendent in state robes.

JACQUES Your Majesty. It's a great privilege. Welcome to our humble abode.
LOUIS (MICHAEL) *(in very broad Glaswegian accent)* It's er...very nice to be here.
JACQUES *(calling)* O'Toole.
BUTLER Sir?
JACQUES Claret for His Majesty please.
BUTLER There's a Mr Bartlett outside again, sir.
JACQUES Not now, I can't see him, we have the King of France here.
BUTLER Yes, sir.

He exits. Jacques and the king stand in rather embarrassed silence. Jacques eventually speaks.

JACQUES Your Majesty. You had a pleasant journey, I trust?
LOUIS Yes...yes, oh definitely...yes...yes. Oh aye, aye.

Silence.

JACQUES You have come from Paris?
LOUIS Where?
JACQUES From Paris...you have travelled from Paris?
LOUIS Oh yes, we've come from Paris...yes...yes, yes, we've just come from...er...Paris...yes.

The butler comes back in.

BUTLER Sir?
JACQUES Yes, O'Toole?
BUTLER Which one is the claret, sir?
JACQUES The claret is in the decanter.
BUTLER The wooden thing?
JACQUES No no...the glass thing...the glass decanter with the round glass stopper.
BUTLER Oh yes, behind the door.
JACQUES No no...on the sideboard.
BUTLER The sideboard?
JACQUES The sideboard...yes. Look...you go into the salle à manger...the *dining room*, right?—and the sideboard is on your left, by the wall, beside the master's portrait.
BUTLER Ah! Above the mirror, sir?
JACQUES No! No! The mirror is on the other side. It's *opposite* the mirror.
BUTLER But that's the *table*, sir.
JACQUES No...you don't go as *far* as the table. You go into the room, right?...on your right is the door to the orangery, straight ahead of you is the door to the library, and to your left is the sideboard.
BUTLER Ah, yes, I see, sir...
JACQUES And the claret is on top of the sideboard, to the left.
BUTLER On the left.
JACQUES Yes...
BUTLER As one looks at it, sir?
JACQUES Yes.
BUTLER I see, sir, thank you. *(he turns to go)*
JACQUES O'Toole.

BUTLER Yes, sir.
JACQUES Will you please tell Monsieur Joseph our guest is here.
BUTLER Yes, sir.

He leaves. There is another embarrassed silence.

JACQUES I'm sorry about that, Your Majesty. 8
BUTLER *(re-entering)* Apparently, sir, there is a plan to build a canal between the two Egyptian towns of...
JACQUES Not now, O'Toole!

The butler exits. More silence.

LOUIS Well...er...Mr Montgolfier...let's not beat around the bush...my...dukes and I are very busy men. What we'd like to do is see the plans of your proposed balloon...if that's at all possible.
JACQUES Certainly, Your Majesty...I have them here ready prepared.
LOUIS Oh, great...hen... 9 what we would like to do...is er...to take them back wi'us for the Royal Archives of er...
FIRST DUKE *(also Glaswegian)* France.
LOUIS France, aye.
JACQUES Well, it is indeed a great honour Your Majesty, that I cannot refuse.
LOUIS Right! OK! Let's get 'em.

He and his two dukes are suddenly galvanized into action. They are about to grab the plans when Joseph enters, clad only in a towel and rather silly bath hat.

JOSEPH Just a moment!
JACQUES Joseph!
JOSEPH *(indicating the king)* This man is not Louis XIV!
JACQUES Joseph! Are you out of your mind!
JOSEPH I've been looking it up in my bath. **Louis XIV died in 1717.** 10 It's now 1783! Answer me that!
LOUIS

DID I SAY LOUIS XIV? OH, SORRY, I MEANT LOUIS XV...LOUIS XV.

JOSEPH ***He* died in 1774!** 11

Louis, getting rather hot and angry, comes over to Joseph belligerently.

Here, Palin mutters, "What a shame."

"Great, hen" is Scottish for "Great, honey."

He died September 1, 1715.

May 10th, to be precise.

A head butt in Britain is sometimes called a "Glasgow kiss," playing on the reputation of the town as a tough place. (It is also sometimes called a "dandruff salad.")

LOUIS All right, Louis *XVI!*...listen to me, smartarse, when you're King of France,...you've got better things to do than go around all day remembering your bloody number.

Putting his face very close to Joseph's. ***He butts him sharply and viciously on the bridge of the nose with his forehead, in the time-honoured Glaswegian way.*** **12**

JOSEPH Aaaaaarh!

He reels away, clutching his nose in agony. Louis approaches Jacques, equally belligerently.

LOUIS Right! You want to argue about numbers?
JACQUES Er...no, no.
LOUIS Right, well...let's get hold of the plans for the Royal Archives. We've got to get back to...er...
FIRST DUKE Paris.
LOUIS Paris by tonight so get a move on.
JOSEPH Aaaargh! Ow! Ooooohh!

The butler reappears.

BUTLER I got as far as the sideboard, sir...

Louis and his dukes grab the plans and push past the butler and across to an open window. There is a bit of a scuffle at the window as they are clambering out at the same time as two men in black with a projector and screen are clambering in.

Lahore is in Pakistan.

JOSEPH Stop them...oh! Ah...ooooooohh!
BUTLER *(to Jacques)* No news on the canal I'm afraid, sir, but apparently in India they're thinking of building a railway between the towns of **Lahore... 13**
JOSEPH Stop...ow! Stop them, O'Toole for...oh! shit! God's sake...stop them, they've got the plans! *(he rushes to the window)*

By now the men in black have set up the screen. On the screen comes film of Louis and his men racing through the gardens away from the Montgolfier's house.

VOICE OVER (MICHAEL) Will Louis XVI get away with the Montgolfiers' precious plans? Is sixteen years of work to be stolen by this suspect sovereign? Is France really in the grip of a Glaswegian monarch? Watch next week's episode of 'The Golden Age of Ballooning'...Now!

Cut to animation/titles as before. Music. Caption: 'THE GOLDEN AGE OF BALLOONING' Caption: 'EPISODE THREE: THE GREAT DAY FOR FRANCE' Cut to a TV discussion in progress. An urgent, impressive current affairs show called 'Decision'. Two opulent-looking men and a presenter. Superimposed caption: 'SIR CHARLES DIVIDENDS'

Prime Minister Edward Heath's government lost the February 1974 election, but Labour didn't have enough seats for a majority. Heath attempted to form a coalition with the Liberals but was eventually replaced as prime minister by Harold Wilson in March. A second general election of the year was held in October, leading to a Labour majority of just three seats.

SIR DIVIDENDS (GRAHAM) **...But now that the Government has collapsed... 14** and shown itself incapable of providing any sort of unifying force, I feel we do need the stability and the breathing space that a military presence would provide.
PRESENTER (MICHAEL) Lord Interest?

Superimposed caption: 'LORD INTEREST'

LORD INTEREST (ERIC) Oh yes...I agree that the army should take over, but I think it should not interfere with the programme of street executions, which I feel have been the shot in the arm that the British economy so desperately needed.

As they drone on, the presenter turns away from them to talk softly into the camera.

PRESENTER The Montgolfier brothers' plans did indeed turn up...six months later, and a long way from Paris, at the court of **King George III of England.** **15**

Cut to a throne room. George III is being read to by an adviser. Caption: 'THE COURT OF GEORGE III, 1781'

READER (ERIC) ...Titty was very worried. Where could Mary be? He looked everywhere. Under the stones and behind the bushes...and Mr Squirrel helped him by looking up in the trees, and Mr Badger helped him by looking under the ground...

There is a knock on the door. George III looks up quickly. The reader, with obviously well practised skill, shuts the book, slips it beneath another book which he opens and carries on reading.

READER ...and so, Your Majesty, we the Commons do herein crave and beseech that...
GEORGE III (GRAHAM) Enter!

Lord North enters and bows briefly.

LORD NORTH (TERRY J) **Your Majesty...Louis XVIII is here!** **16**
GEORGE III Who is Louis XVIII?
LORD NORTH The King of France, Your Majesty! This is a great moment to have, sir.
GEORGE III There is no Louis XVIII.

We hear a Scottish voice outside the door. Lord North ducks his head out for a moment, then reappears.

LORD NORTH He craves Your Majesty's pardon. He has had a long journey here and miscounted... **He is Louis XVII.** **17**
GEORGE III **Louis XVI is dead already?** **18**

A trace of worry crosses North's face. He goes outside the door again for a moment. Sounds of a slight argument between himself and the Glaswegians. Suddenly there is a yell of pain and Lord North reels in holding the bridge of his nose.

King George III, the crazy king who ruled England for sixty years. For the last ten years, a regency leadership was established, as poor old George III was quite mad.

Louis XVIII was known, wonderfully, as Louis the Unavoidable. He was king from 1814 to 1824, saving the "Hundred Days" (actually 111) from Napoleon's return from Elba to the reinstatement of the "Unavoidable." From 1791 to 1814 Louis was in exile, living in the U.K., Russia, and Prussia.

17

Never crowned king, this eight-year-old's parents (Louis XVI and Marie Antoinette) were executed during the French Revolution. He died in prison at the age of 10.

Louis XVI was executed on Monday, January 21, 1793, by the guillotine. (His wife, Marie Antoinette, would be executed on October 16 the same year.)

One of the most storied palaces in London—among many other royal moments, this is where Charles I slept the night before his execution.

"Nip off" is British slang meaning to leave quickly.

The Duke of Portland was British prime minister under George III, from April to December 1783, and again from March 1807 to October 1809.

Jacques Necker was France's finance minister from 1777 to 1781 in the lead-up to the French Revolution.

"Assignats" was the currency of the French Revolution whose value was based on the confiscated properties of the Catholic Church. Mirabeau, a somewhat moderate revolutionary, issued many tens of thousands of assignats in his role as president of the National Constituent Assembly. (The overprinting of these bonds and currency papers led to hyperinflation.)

LORD NORTH Aaaaaaaaaaaaghh! Oh my God! Oh...ah...oh Christ!

Louis strides in with the two dukes. They all wear tam o'shanters.

LOUIS *(to the reader)* Your Majesty, I am Louis XVI...Oh Christ...*(to George III)* Your Majesty...I am Louis XVI as you so rightly say, and I don't want to muck about. I have a wee proposition which could make the name of George IV the most respected in Europe...

GEORGE III George *III*.

LOUIS George III! Sorry. Where can we talk?

LORD NORTH Oh! God!...did you see that?...Oh!...aaaargh! Oh dear! *(he is in great pain still and clutching his nose)*

GEORGE III **We shall have a state banquet at St James' Palace!** 19

LOUIS No, look, I can't hang about. It's take it or leave...we got to get back to...er...

FIRST DUKE Paris.

LOUIS Paris, by tonight...

GEORGE III Must you leave us, Louis?

LOUIS **I'd rather just sell the plans and nip off, Georgie boy.** 20

GEORGE III All right...we will buy the plans...if you will undertake to disengage your troops in America.

LOUIS Do what?

GEORGE III And, I shall give you £10,000 for the plans...

LOUIS Ten thousand *pounds*! Right, well, we'll disengage the, um, you know...like you said—we'll disengage 'em...tell you what, hen, I'll put a duke on to it...OK? Right!

LORD NORTH *(still clutching his nose)* That's the worst thing you can do to anybody.

LOUIS You asked for it, sonny.

LORD NORTH You could have broken my bloody nose!

GEORGE III North! Please!

LORD NORTH You saw it! It was right on the bone.

GEORGE III North! Will you send for the **Duke of Portland...** 21 we have a financial matter to discuss.

LORD NORTH Well, it really hurt.

LOUIS No, look, I think it's better if you give the money to us. We're going back. We've got a bag.

GEORGE III No, no...don't worry, Louis. We shall talk to your **Monsieur Necker.** 22

LOUIS Ah! Well, actually, we'd rather you didn't...we've been having a wee bit of trouble with him...you know what I mean?

GEORGE III Monsieur Necker? The man who introduced so many valuable reforms and who proved so popular despite his opposition to Mirabeau's policy of issuing **'assignats'**? 23

Superimposed caption: 'THIS SPEECH HAS BEEN VERIFIED BY ENCYCLOPAEDIA BRITANNICA'

GRAHAM CHAPMAN

In a 1998 interview of the living Pythons conducted by Robert Klein, John Cleese is telling the story of a matinee the troupe did in the British West Country town of Bristol. From left to right, there sit the great men themselves—Terry Jones, Eric Idle, Terry Gilliam, Cleese, and Michael Palin—and on a trunk at the feet of the Pythons sits a large urn, said to be filled with the ashes of Graham Chapman, who died in 1989. Cleese is halfway through recounting the strange performance, one in which the crowd simply wasn't laughing, when out of nowhere, Gilliam shifts his crossed legs and kicks the urn, scattering Chapman's "ashes" all over the rug and the floor. The subsequent comic attempts to clean up the mess—which includes a broom, a small handheld vacuum, and Cleese licking the "ashes" off his finger. It was as comic and anarchic a thing as the Pythons ever did. And it was a fitting tribute to the only Python no longer with us, a man of whom Cleese said (at Chapman's memorial service, no less), "Anything for him except mindless good taste."

Chapman was born in Leicestershire, England, on January 8, 1941, the same day that Lord Robert Baden-Powell, founder of the Boy Scouts, died. Chapman might have enjoyed the coincidence: he was one of the first celebs to come out of the closet in the early 1970s, though the Pythons already knew of his homosexuality. They also knew that he was probably the most intuitively creative member of the troupe. The story of him changing the return of a toaster to the return of a Norwegian Blue parrot is legendary, but so much of his writing partnership with Cleese (they mostly wrote together) was marked by extraordinary wordplay and leaps of fantasy. He arguably was also the best actor of the group, taking the lead in both *Monty Python and the Holy Grail* and *Life of Brian.*

A tall and reticent man (and a trained medical doctor), this son of a police officer battled shyness both by performing and by drinking: he was said to be an alcoholic by the time Python came into being, and that by afternoons he didn't always have the strongest handle on the material. In Germany, for the making of two Python episodes set in that country, he made much of Oktoberfest; he met an American actor performing in *Hair* who was so well-endowed, the actor became known to Chapman and Palin as the "Boston Startler."

Eventually Chapman got sober, though none of his solo projects quite have the cachet of work done by the other Pythons. After appearing in the 1983 Python movie *The Meaning of Life,* he embarked on a long tour of the United States, to college campuses in particular, where he'd tell Python stories and other anecdotes. A keen mountaineer, he also became a member of the Dangerous Sports Club, which helped introduce bungee jumping to the world.

Chapman died of cancer in 1989 at a young 48 years old. In a final, lovely twist, Cleese claimed that, from beyond the grave, Chapman convinced him to be "the first person ever at a British memorial service to say 'fuck.' " And so Cleese did, gleefully, sadly. And then the crowd rose to sing "Always Look on the Bright Side of Life."

LOUIS Er...aye, yeah...the trouble is he's been drinking a lot...you know, fourteen lagers wi' his breakfast...that sort of thing.

GEORGE III Well...very well, Louis...

The door flies open and there is Joseph Montgolfier, still clad only in towel and silly bath hat.

JOSEPH Just a moment!

LOUIS Oh, Christ!

GEORGE III What are you doing?

JOSEPH I am Joseph Montgolfier, the inventor of the fire balloon. The man before you is an impostor!

GEORGE III Ooh! I am not...honestly!

JOSEPH No, not you, Your Majesty *(he points at Louis)* This man—this Louis, the so-called King of France man. Which number did you give this time—Louis the 23rd?

LOUIS I got it right!

JOSEPH I bet you took a few guesses.

LOUIS Listen, you spotty sassenach pillock... **24**

DR HAMER (TERRY G) *(not a doctor but a period butler)* Your Majesty! The Ronettes are here. **25**

BARTLETT And Mr Bartlett.

"Sassenach" is abusive Scottish slang for an Englishman, derived from "Saxon."

The Ronettes were Veronica and Estelle Bennett and Nedra Talley, three singers from Spanish Harlem, who found fame in the early 1960s under the wing of Phil Spector. (Veronica would later marry him, poor lass.)

Three black ladies wearing modern showbiz costumes come in and sing 'George III' song. Two men come in and set up a screen as before.

THE RONETTES *(singing)* George III...etc...etc...

GEORGE III Oh dear, I'm not supposed to go mad till 1800!

Louis, arguing violently with the butler, butts him. Music comes up and the sound fades on this strange scene. George III falls to the floor and waggles his legs around in the air. Zoom in as the men in black take cover off the caption. caption: 'MEANWHILE, IN FRANCE...' Cut to drawing room in the Montgolfiers' house. Jacques is at a table working on some drawings. Behind him Antoinette paces the room nervously. She is still wearing her harness, but it is no longer attached to the gas balloon. In a corner of the room a plumber is still mending the elaborate plumbing.

ANTOINETTE Joseph has been gone for six months now...we have heard nothing!

JACQUES He can look after himself.

ANTOINETTE But he had only on a towel, you know.

Jacques takes off his false ears and walks over to Antoinette.

JACQUES Antoinette...from now on there is only one Montgolfier brother.

ANTOINETTE But Louis XIV has the plans...you must wait until Joseph returns.

JACQUES *(casually loosening her harness)* The plans are here, cherie. *(he indicates the desk where he has been working)* Let me put my tongue in your mouth.

ANTOINETTE What do you mean?
JACQUES We're supposed to be French, aren't we?
ANTOINETTE No, I mean what are the plans which Joseph after is chasing?
JACQUES Please, let me put it in a little way.
ANTOINETTE Oh, Jacques, ze *plans*!
JACQUES I take it out if you don't like it.

He chases her a bit with his tongue out. Antoinette is about to react rather violently one way or the other, when her dramatic moment is cut short by the entrance of O'Toole the butler.

BUTLER Are you sure the claret was on the left of the sideboard, sir?
JACQUES Yes, O'Toole, it's always been there.
BUTLER Well I'll look for one more month, sir. *(he turns and goes out; Jacques eyes Antoinette lasciviously and is about to try and make contact in the French way when the butler returns)* By the way sir, Mr Bartlett has gone, sir. He said he couldn't wait any longer.
JACQUES Thank you, O'Toole...
BUTLER Not at all, sir...I've enjoyed being in it...
JACQUES *(impatiently)* Right!
BUTLER Thank you, sir...mam'selle.

He exits. Tremendous applause. He reappears, takes a bow and leaves again. Jacques and Antoinette look nonplussed. He reappears. Terrific applause. He gestures for them to quieten down. Eventually there is silence.

BUTLER By the way, sir, Mr Bartlett has gone, sir. *(tremendous applause)* He said he couldn't wait any longer, sir.

Incredible volume of laughter here brings the house down. The rest of the scene is pandemonium with laughter developing into prolonged applause.

JACQUES Thank you, O'Toole.
BUTLER Not at all, sir...I've enjoyed being in it.
JACQUES Right!
BUTLER Thank you, sir...mam'selle.
AUDIENCE More! More! More! Etc....etc....etc....

SOUND OF APPLAUSE. OVER SHOUTS OF MORE! MORE!

Superimposed Python credits. The butler is showered with flowers. Fans come on and congratulate him. A BBC security man restrains them. Other members of the cast appear and shake hands, and stand in a row behind, applauding. A dear old middle-aged lady comes in and stands beside him, weeping proudly.

26

Neil Innes, writer of comic songs and longtime collaborator with the Pythons. With the band The Bonzo Dog Doo-Dah Band, he wrote a song called "Death Cab for Cutie," which was later appropriated as the name of the hipster indie band.

VOICE OVER (GRAHAM) George III was arranged and composed by **Neil Innes.** **26** He is available from the BBC price £4 or eight months' imprisonment.

The credits end. Cut to BBC world symbol.

VOICE OVER (GRAHAM) That was episode three of 'The Golden Age of Ballooning'. May I remind you that there's still time to get your 'Golden Age of Ballooning' suppositories direct from the BBC, price £4.50, or £19 for a set of six. Well, in a moment the BBC will be closing down for the night, but first, here is a Party Political Broadcast on behalf of the Norwegian Party.

A very straight Norwegian in light blue suit and tie appears. He speaks earnestly in Norwegian. Ad-libbed, on the lines of the following.

NORWEGIAN (ERIC) Ik tvika nasai...

Subtitle: 'GOOD EVENING'

NORWEGIAN ...Stivianka sobjiord ki niyanska ik takka Norge weginda zokiy yniet...

Subtitle: 'YOU MAY THINK IT STRANGE THAT WE SHOULD BE ASKING YOU TO VOTE NORWEGIAN AT THE NEXT ELECTION'

NORWEGIAN ...Ik vietta nogiunda sti jibiora...

Subtitle: 'BUT CONSIDER THE ADVANTAGES'

NORWEGIAN In Norge we hatta svinska offikiose buinni a gogik in Europa.

Subtitle: 'IN NORWAY, WE HAVE ONE OF THE HIGHEST PER CAPITA INCOME RATES IN EUROPE'

NORWEGIAN Sti glikka in Norge tijik dinstianna gikloosi stijioska kary.

Subtitle: 'WE HAVE AN INDUSTRIAL RE-INVESTMENT RATE OF 14%'

NORWEGIAN E in Norge we hatta siddinkarvo dikinik chaila osto tykka hennakska.

Subtitle: 'AND GIRLS WITH MASSIVE KNOCKERS'

NORWEGIAN Gikkiaski ungurden kola bijiusti stonosse.

Subtitle: 'HONESTLY, THEY'LL DO ANYTHING FOR YOU'

NORWEGIAN Hijiasgo biunderten ki yikilpa stivvora niski ofidae.

Subtitle: 'THEY'LL GO THROUGH THE CARD'

NORWEGIAN E stavaskija, E stonioska.

Subtitle: 'YOU NAME IT, THEY KNOW IT'

NORWEGIAN Stingik oloshoyert okka in Trondheim khi oyplitz...

Subtitle: 'THERE'S ONE IN TRONDHEIM WHO CAN PUT HER...' Blackout. Caption: 'PARTY POLITICAL BROADCAST ON BEHALF OF THE NORWEGIAN PARTY'

VOICE OVER (GRAHAM) Highlights of that broadcast will be discussed later by Lord George-Brown, ex-Foreign Secretary, Mr Sven Olafson, the ex-Norwegian Minster of Finance, Sir Charles Ollendorff, ex-Chairman of the Norwegian Trades Council, Mr Hamish McLavell, the Mayor of Wick, the nearest large town to Norway, Mrs Betty Norday, whose name sounds remarkably like Norway, Mr Brian Waynor, whose name is an anagram of Norway, Mr and Mrs Ford, whose name sounds like Fiord, of which there are a lot in Norway, Ron and Christine Boslo...

Bernhard Heinrich Karl Martin von Bülow, German chancellor from 1900 to 1909.

Balloons ascending. The montage as before with music. Caption: 'THE GOLDEN AGE OF BALLOONING' Caption: 'EPISODE SIX: FERDINAND VON ZEPPELIN—PIONEER OF THE AIRSHIP' Cut to photo of family group.

VOICE OVER (MICHAEL) Ferdinand von Zeppelin was born in Constance in 1838, the brother of Barry Zeppelin, the least talented of the fourteen Zeppelin brothers.

Black and white film of Barry (TERRY J) *blowing up balloons of increasing size. They all sink to the ground. The last one blows back and inflates him (specially made balloon): he rises into the air. Cut to stock film of a zeppelin.*

VOICE OVER Meanwhile for Ferdinand von Zeppelin, the year 1908 was a year of triumph.

Cut to interior of a zeppelin. A party. Expensively dressed guests. Champagne. A palm court orchestra playing. Some guests looking out of the windows in wonderment.

VON BULOW (MICHAEL) **27** *(approaching Zeppelin)* Herr Zeppelin—it's wonderful! It's put ballooning right back on the map.

Zeppelin goes instantly berserk with anger.

ZEPPELIN (GRAHAM) It's not a *balloon*! D'you hear?...It's not a balloon...It's an airship...an airship... d'you hear?

HE HITS HIM VERY HARD ON THE TOP OF THE HEAD WITH THE UNDERSIDE OF HIS FIST.

He hits him very hard on the top of the head with the underside of his fist.

VON BULOW Well, it's very nice anyway.
TIRPITZ (TERRY J) *(to Zeppelin)* Tell me, what is the principle of these balloons?
ZEPPELIN It's not a balloon! You stupid little thick-headed Saxon git! It's not a balloon! Balloons is for kiddy-winkies. If you want to play with balloons, get outside.

Drags Tirpitz over to the door, opens it and flings him out into the clouds.

TIRPITZ Aaaaaaaaaghhh!

Cut to an old German couple in a cottage. The man is reading from a big book, the lady is knitting. The man is in underpants. There are a pair of lederhosen drying in front of the fire.

HELMUT (MICHAEL) *(reading)* Yorkshire...pudding. A type of thick pancake, eaten with large...

Roof splitting noise. A thump and the house shakes. They both look up. Cut back to the airship. The party is still going on.

HOLLWEG (ERIC) **I hear you are to name the balloon after Bismarck?** 28
ZEPPELIN *(flying into hysterical rage)* Bismarck? Of course I'm not calling it after Bismarck. It's a zeppelin. It's nothing to do with bloody Bismarck!
HOLLWEG Surely he gave you some money for it?
ZEPPELIN Get outside!

28

Theobald von Bethmann-Hollweg, German chancellor from 1909 to 1917.

Otto von Bismarck, German statesman who created the large German Empire before World War I.

He opens the door and flings Hollweg out. Cut back to the old couple in the cottage.

HELMUT Za...bag...lione...a sort of cream mouse...mousse of Italian origin...

Roof splintering noise. A thump and the house shakes. Cut back to the airship. A little cluster of people round the door. The party is still going on but there is a little tension in the atmosphere.

VON BULOW Ferdinand...that was a Minister of State you just threw out of the balloon.
ZEPPELIN It's not a balloon! It's an airship!
VON BULOW All right, I'm sorry.
ZEPPELIN All right—go and have a look! *(he throws the protesting Von Bulow out)* And you!

Animation of several men being thrown from airship.

HELMUT Zu...cchin...ni...Italian...ma...rrows...*(splintering crash, thump, the 'house shakes)* Zingara...A garnish of finely chopped...or shredded lean ham...*(splintering crash, thump, the house shakes)*... tongue...*(another splintering crash, thump, the house shakes)* mushrooms and truffles. *(same*

again)...Zakuski. A Russian...hors d'oeuvre...*(a very loud splintering crash, thump and the house shudders; Mrs Helmut stops knitting and crosses the room to the door and into the next room, where the sounds are coming from)* With tiny pieces of sliced...
MRS HELMUT (TERRY J) *(looking in the other room)* Oh, look! It's the Chancellor!

Helmut's hand immediately goes to his tie. He half makes to rise.

HELMUT What? Prince Von Bulow? Here?
MRS HELMUT Ja!
HELMUT Coming here?
MRS HELMUT No—he *is* here.
HELMUT *(jumping to his feet)* Oh, I must go and put my old uniform on.
MRS HELMUT He won't notice, Helmut. He's dead.
HELMUT Dead? Here?
MRS HELMUT Ja. In our sitting room.
HELMUT *This* is our sitting room, dear.
MRS HELMUT Well, you know what I mean.
HELMUT *(wagging his finger at her)* The *drawing* room!
MRS HELMUT Yes...but it's a *kind* of sitting room.
HELMUT *(doubtfully)* **Well...** 29

One of Palin's most wonderful moments, a wag of the hand, dubious—utterly funny and repeated a few times throughout the sketch.

MRS HELMUT Look!

She opens the door wider to reveal heap of about ten bodies in the other room. There is dust rising from them and a big hole in the ceiling. Helmut goes to the door.

HELMUT Which one is Von Bulow?

They walk round the pile. Mrs Helmut looks at a few bodies and then points.

MRS HELMUT Here...look!
HELMUT Oh, ja...and Admiral Tirpitz! 30

Admiral Tirpitz was the stern leader of the German Navy before and throughout the first half of World War I. Other German names in this section (except where noted) are probably thrown in for spice, rather than historical accuracy.

They are both momentarily overawed.

MRS HELMUT Ja.
HELMUT And Von Muller...and Herr Reichner...and Hollweg and Von Graunberg...
MRS HELMUT That isn't Graunberg—that's Graunberg...**das ist Moltke...** 31

Helmuth Von Moltke, leader of the German Army during World War I.

She lifts the body's head up by the hair as it's facing down.

MRS HELMUT He's a lot older than I thought. He's a clever man, ja.
HELMUT ...and Zimmermann...and Kimpte...
MRS HELMUT What shall we do, Helmut?
HELMUT We must ring the Government.
MRS HELMUT This *is* the Government, Helmut.
HELMUT Oh dear.
MRS HELMUT It is a great honour to have so many members of the Government dead in our sitting room.
HELMUT *Drawing* room.
MRS HELMUT Ja, well...
HELMUT There are no members of the Government dead in our sitting room.
MRS HELMUT Ja, you know what I mean.
HELMUT Perhaps I should make a little speech or something?
MRS HELMUT Not a speech, Helmut no...
HELMUT Shall we make them a cup of tea?
MRS HELMUT It would be a waste of tea.
HELMUT But we must do something—so many important people in our drawing room—we must do *something*.

They think for a little while.

Jones misspeaks here and repeats "internal."

MRS HELMUT We could sort them out.
HELMUT And make a little list.
MRS HELMUT **Ja, ja. We could put the ministers for internal affairs over against the wall, and those for foreign** 32 here by the clock.
HELMUT And we can sort them out alphabetically?
MRS HELMUT Nein, nein—just put the cleanest by the door.
HELMUT Ja.

They start to hump the corpses around. Helmut starts to hump Van Bulow towards the clock.

MRS HELMUT No, no! That's Von Bulow! He must go over here.
HELMUT That is my reading chair.
MRS HELMUT He is the Reich Chancellor of Germany, Helmut.

Helmut starts to take him towards the reading chair.

HELMUT All right...but I think he would have been better up against the clock, you know.
MRS HELMUT No, he would not look nice under the clock.
HELMUT I did not say *under* the clock. I said *against* the clock.
MRS HELMUT Well then we could not see the clock!
HELMUT We could put the Minister for Colonies under the clock. He's small.

MRS HELMUT No. Colonies are *internal* affairs. He must go against the wall. *(Helmut lifts up the head of another corpse)* Education!

Helmut starts to drag him over to the wall.

HELMUT Soon we shall be able to make a list.
MRS HELMUT Ja, ja, wait a minute!...Who's that by the cat litter?
HELMUT I don't know. I've never seen him before.
MRS HELMUT He is not a member of the Government. Get him out of here. Put him in the drawing room.
HELMUT He's *in* the drawing room, my dear.
MRS HELMUT Ja, well you know what I mean.
HELMUT Put him in the sitting room.
MRS HELMUT Ja, ja, the sitting room, it's all the same.
HELMUT You can put him in the sitting room if he's in the drawing room.

Cut to stock film of the zeppelin.

VOICE OVER (MICHAEL) Count Ferdinand Von Zeppelin's behaviour on that flight in 1900 had incredible, far-reaching consequences, for one of the falling Ministers...*(cut to an old Edwardian photo of a German minister)* the talented Herr Von Maintlitz, architect of the new German expansionist farm policy, fell on top of an old lady *(old Edwardian photo of an elderly lady)* in Nimwegen, killing her outright. Her daughter, Alice *(old Edwardian photo of attractive young girl in the nude)* suffered severe cerebral damage from the talented minister's *(picture of Maintlitz again)* heavy briefcase *(Edwardian photo of a briefcase)* but was nursed back to life *(another Edwardian erotic postcard)* by an English doctor, Henderson. *(a Muybridge photo of a nude man)* Eventually, they married *(Edwardian nude couple)* and their eldest son, George Henderson...*(1930s nude man)* was the father of Mike Henderson...*(health and efficiency nudist camp group photo; a figure at the back is arrowed)* producer and director of 'The Golden Age of Ballooning'.

Animation: balloons as before. Superimposed caption: 'GOLDEN AGE OF BALLOONING' Pointed surgical instruments fly on in formation and puncture the balloons. Superimposed caption: 'THE GOLDEN YEARS OF COLONIC IRRIGATION' Cut to black.

VOICE OVER (GRAHAM) Mr and Mrs Rita Trondheim; **Reginald Bo-sankway,** **33** who would be next to Norway in a rhyming dictionary, if it included proper names, and if he pronounced his name like that.

Cut to a Victorian couple in the countryside. ***Superimposed caption:*** *'THE MILL ON THE FLOSS'* **34**

Superimposed caption: 'PART I: BALLOONING' The couple rise slowly in the air. Fade out.

Yet another dig at the suave newscaster Reginald Bosanquet (usually pronounced "*Bows*-an-kett").

Novel from 1860 by George Eliot.

SEA
SON
4
EPISODE 41

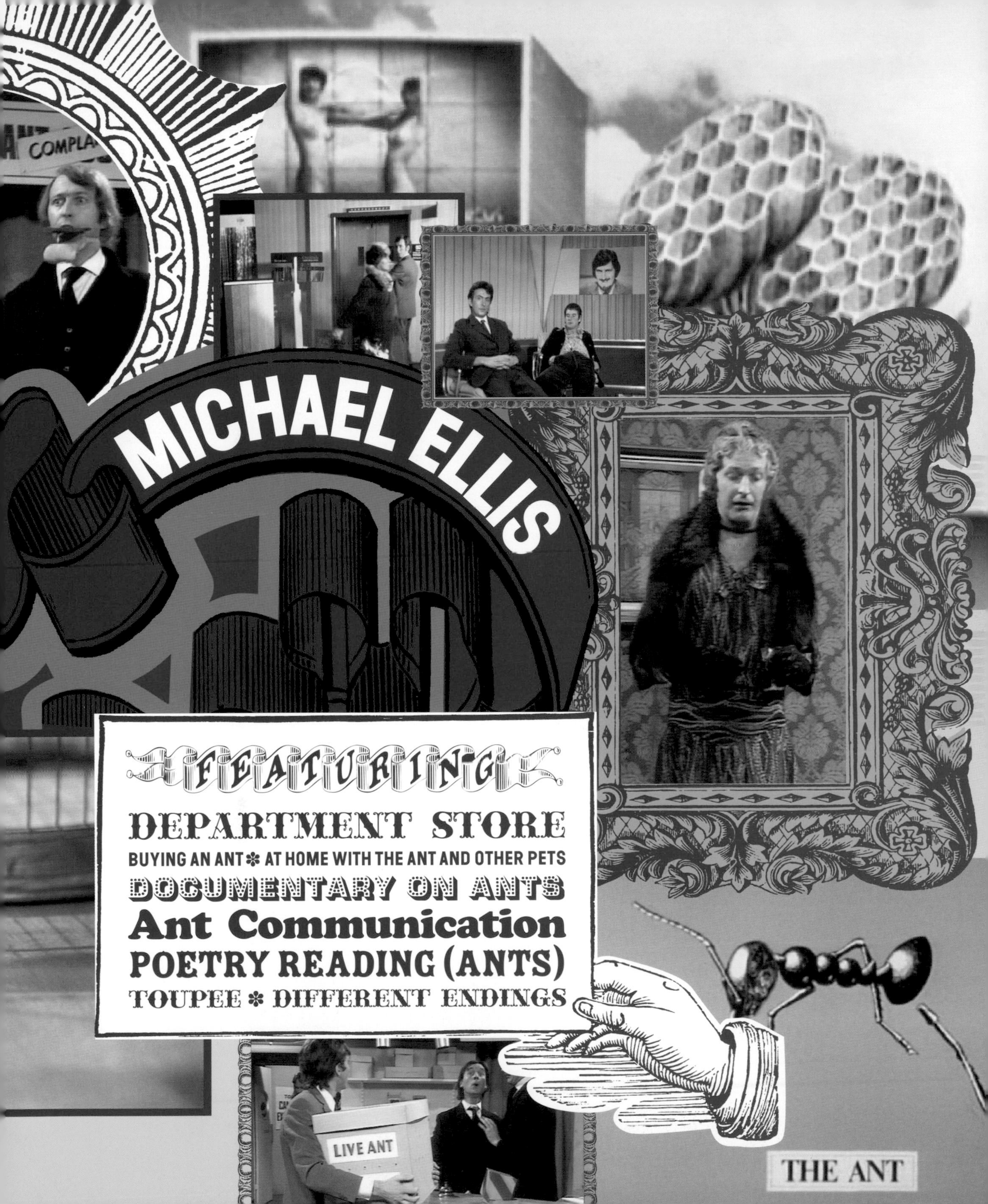
COMPLA
MICHAEL ELLIS
FEATURING
DEPARTMENT STORE
BUYING AN ANT ✽ AT HOME WITH THE ANT AND OTHER PETS
DOCUMENTARY ON ANTS
Ant Communication
POETRY READING (ANTS)
TOUPEE ✽ DIFFERENT ENDINGS
LIVE ANT
THE ANT

FIRST AIRED: NOVEMBER 7, 1974

In the days before VCRs, let alone DVR, this gag must have been confusing—there were many people who tuned in only to think they were half an hour too late.

Animated titles.

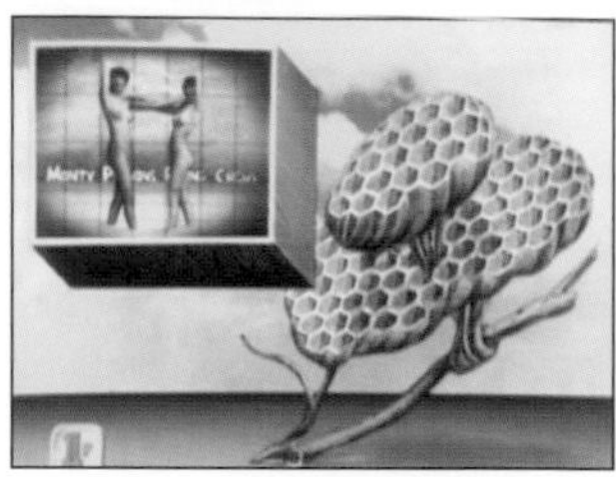

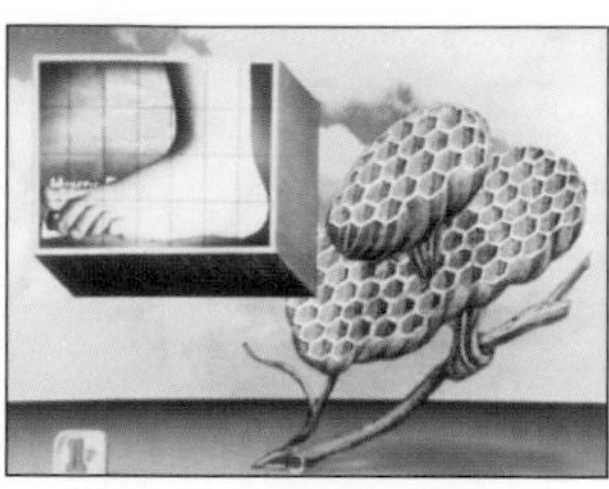

Caption: 'THE END' Roll credits. **1** *Establishing shot of large Harrods-type store. Outside limousines and taxis are disgorging very rich customers. Small doormen in enormously large coats opening doors of cars. A man with his nose bandaged comes out of the store. One large car pulls softly up to the kerb, and as small doorman* (MICHAEL) *opens its door, an enormously opulent lady* (TERRY J) *in furs gets out. The doorman holds the door open.*

SHE KNEES HIM IN THE GROIN AND WALKS ON INTO THE STORE.

Chris Quinn (ERIC) *arrives on a bicycle. He parks the bicycle against the kerb (the doorman flings it into the road) and goes into the outer hall of the store. He passes a couple leaving who also have noses bandaged. A gaggle of customers, mostly pepper pots, rush out. A very eager pepperpot lady shopper, going the other way, rushes between the two and bangs into a set of glass doors which have closed behind the gaggle. She cries out with pain clutching her nose and is escorted away by a large, coated attendant. Chris Quinn looks up at the list on the wall. It reads:*

BASEMENT: DANGEROUS GASES, VIRUSES, CONTAGIOUS DISEASES, RESTAURANT AND TOILET FIXINGS.
GROUND FLOOR: MENSWEAR, BOYSWEAR, EFFEMINATE GOODS HALL, ILL HEALTH FOODS.
MEZZANINE: TABLEWARE, KITCHEN GOODS, SOFT FURNISHINGS, HARD FURNISHINGS, ROCK-HARD FURNISHINGS.
FIRST FLOOR: COMPLAINTS.
SECOND FLOOR: COSMETICS, JEWELLERY, ELECTRICAL, SATIRE.
THIRD FLOOR: NASAL INJURIES HALL, OTHER THINGS.
FOURTH FLOOR: GRANITE HALL—ROCKS, SHALES, ALLUVIAL DEPOSITS, FELSPAR, CARPATHIANS, ANDES, URALS, MINING REQUISITES, ATOM-SPLITTING SERVICE.
FIFTH FLOOR: COMPLAINTS.
SIXTH FLOOR: COMPLAINTS.
SEVENTH FLOOR: COMPLAINTS.
EIGHTH FLOOR: ROOF GARDEN.
NINTH FLOOR: TELEVISION AERIALS.
TENTH FLOOR: FRESH AIR, CLOUDS, OCCASIONAL PERIODS OF SUNSHINE.

Quinn, knowing that there are doors, goes forward more cautiously and enters. The banging of noses on glass doors is a constant background theme. Cut to the gift department. A large lady is standing by counter holding a large cylinder, with a rose attachment.

LADY (CAROL) Yes this looks the sort of thing. May I just try it?
ASSISTANT (TERRY G) Certainly, madam.

THE LADY PRESSES BUTTON AND A SHEET OF FLAME SHOOTS OUT ACROSS THE HALL.

LADY Oh! Sorry! *So* sorry! *(she is happy though)* Yes that's fine.
ASSISTANT Is that on account, madam?
LADY Yes.

Chris walks by, watching with interest but not much concern, passing a customer whose back is on fire but who has not noticed. He approaches a counter with a sign saying 'Ant Counter'. He stands by the apparently empty counter for one moment, then rings a bell.

CHRIS Hello? Hello?

A strange rubber-masked head appears from below the other side of the counter and gesticulates at him making a strange noise. This soon stops.

FIRST ASSISTANT (GRAHAM) Oh, I'm terribly sorry...*(he takes off the mask to reveal a straightforward assistant)* I thought you were someone else.
CHRIS Oh I see, yes.
FIRST ASSISTANT I'm sorry sir, can I help you?
CHRIS Yes, yes, as a matter of fact you can, actually I was interested in the possibility...of purchasing one of your...can I ask who you thought I was?
FIRST ASSISTANT What?
CHRIS Who did you think I was...just then...when you thought I *was* somebody.
FIRST ASSISTANT Oh, it's no one you'd know, sir.
CHRIS Well I might know them.

FIRST ASSISTANT It's possible, obviously, but I think it's really unlikely.
CHRIS Well, I know quite a lot...
FIRST ASSISTANT I mean he's hardly likely to move in your circles, sir...
CHRIS Why, is he very *rich*?
FIRST ASSISTANT Oh, no, I didn't mean that, sir.
CHRIS Is he a lord or something?

FIRST ASSISTANT Oh, no, not at all.
CHRIS Well look, this is very easy to settle. What is his name?
FIRST ASSISTANT What?
CHRIS What is his name?
FIRST ASSISTANT Well...er...
CHRIS Yes?
FIRST ASSISTANT Michael Ellis.
CHRIS Who?
FIRST ASSISTANT Michael Ellis.
CHRIS I see.
FIRST ASSISTANT Do you know him, sir?
CHRIS Er...Michael Ellis. Michael Ellis...
FIRST ASSISTANT You don't?
CHRIS Well, I don't remember the name.
FIRST ASSISTANT I think you would remember him, sir.
CHRIS Why do you say that?
FIRST ASSISTANT Well, would you remember a man six foot nine inches high, forty-ish, and he's got a long scar from here to here and absolutely no nose?
CHRIS ...oh, I think I do remember somebody like that...
FIRST ASSISTANT Well, that's not Michael Ellis.
CHRIS What?
FIRST ASSISTANT He's a small man about this high with a high-pitched voice.
CHRIS

RIGHT, I'M NOT GOING TO BUY AN ANT FROM YOU NOW.

FIRST ASSISTANT *(distressed)* Oh, no, please.
CHRIS No. You've not been properly trained. I demand another assistant.
FIRST ASSISTANT Oh, no, come on...please...
CHRIS No, I want *another assistant*.
FIRST ASSISTANT All right! I'll get another assistant. *(he disappears behind a curtain)*
CHRIS Thank you.

The same assistant reappears with a long mandarin-style Chinese moustache.

FIRST ASSISTANT *(high-pitched voice)* Hello sir, can I help you, sir?
CHRIS No, I want a *different* assistant.
FIRST ASSISTANT I *am* sir, I'm Mr Abanazar, sir.
CHRIS Don't be silly.
FIRST ASSISTANT *(normal voice)* Oh no, please please please let me help you...
CHRIS No! I want another assistant.
FIRST ASSISTANT Oh, no, come on, please...
CHRIS If you don't give me another assistant...
FIRST ASSISTANT No, no, I'll be very good, sir, really. *(he becomes exaggeratedly polite)* Good morning, sir...how are you, sir...bit parky **2** outside today...isn't it, sir...? A very nice suit you've got there, sir...you had a very close shave this morning, sir...
CHRIS Right I'm going!
FIRST ASSISTANT No, no, please...*(he takes off his moustache)* I'll get another assistant...*(he rings the bell on the counter)*

After a pause, very slowly indeed an identical mask to the first appears over the top of the counter right next to the first assistant, making the same noise very quietly.

The first assistant sees him, starts and nudges him hard.

SECOND ASSISTANT (MICHAEL) Woooooo...oooooo...
FIRST ASSISTANT It's not him!

The second assistant makes a disappointed noise and disappears below.

CHRIS *(pointing over the counter at the disappeared assistant)* I don't want *him*!
FIRST ASSISTANT Oh please, give him a chance!
CHRIS No!
SECOND ASSISTANT *(appearing from below counter without a mask, looking immaculate)* Yes, sir, can I be of any assistance?
CHRIS Oh no, come on, don't try that!
SECOND ASSISTANT I'm sorry, sir...try what?
CHRIS You know perfectly well what I mean.
SECOND ASSISTANT I'm afraid I don't, sir.
CHRIS You were down behind there with a silly mask on going wooo-ooo
SECOND ASSISTANT I don't think I was, sir.
CHRIS All right, get the manager.
SECOND ASSISTANT There seems to have been some sort of misunderstanding, sir.
CHRIS Manager!

"Parky" is British slang for "chilly."

FIRST ASSISTANT This *is* the manager, sir.
CHRIS What?
SECOND ASSISTANT *(in a silly voice)* Yes, I'm the manager.
CHRIS Manager! *(he keeps calling)*
SECOND ASSISTANT It's a smashing store this, I can't recommend it too highly, well-lit, rat-free. It's a joy to manage. **Oh yes, the freshest haddock in London, second floor, third floor Ribena,** 3 ants here, television and flame throwers over there, behind them our dinner-wagon exhibition closes at six...
FIRST ASSISTANT *(nudging him)* Quick!

They both disappear under the counter. The real manager arrives and presents himself to Chris.

REAL MANAGER (TERRY J) Yes, sir? Can I help you, sir?
CHRIS *(noticing the 'manager' badge on his lapel)* Yes, I want to complain about the assistants on this counter.
REAL MANAGER I'm sorry to hear that, sir, which ones?
CHRIS Well, they're hiding now.
REAL MANAGER Sir?
CHRIS They're hiding, down there behind the counter.
REAL MANAGER I see, sir. *(he goes round counter, looks, but obviously can't see them; Chris goes round to join in the search)*...well...there's nobody down here, sir.
CHRIS They must have crawled through here, and made their escape through 'Soft Toys'. *(he points)*
REAL MANAGER Yes, of course.
CHRIS They were wearing masks and making silly noises and one of them pretended to be the manager. He spoke like this...*(he does an impression)*
REAL MANAGER

AH! I THINK I'VE GOT IT, SIR, I THINK I'VE GOT IT! IT'S RAG WEEK. 4

CHRIS Rag week?
REAL MANAGER Yes, you know, for charity, sir.
CHRIS Oh! I see. Some local college or university?
REAL MANAGER No, no it's the *store's* rag week.
CHRIS The *store's* rag week?
REAL MANAGER Yes. The senior staff don't join in much—it's for the trainees really...
CHRIS It's not very good for business is it?
REAL MANAGER Oh, it's for charity, sir. People are awfully good about it, you know. *(he rattles a collecting tin)*
CHRIS Yes, yes, of course. *(he puts a coin in)*
REAL MANAGER Right, sir, I'll get you a senior assistant—ants, was it?
CHRIS Yes, please.
REAL MANAGER *(calling)* Mr Snetterton? *(Mr Snetterton approaches immediately; he is clearly the first assistant with very bad short crew-cut wig on)* Could you look after this gentleman, Mr Snetterton?
CHRIS I don't want him!
FIRST ASSISTANT Oh *please*! Give me a chance!
CHRIS No!
REAL MANAGER All right—Mr Hartford!
HARTFORD (MICHAEL) Yes—good morning, sir—can I help you?
CHRIS Yes, please. I'm interested in buying an ant.
HARTFORD Ah yes—and what price were you thinking of paying, sir?
CHRIS Oh, well, I hadn't actually got as far as that.
HARTFORD Well sir, they start about half a p. but they can go as high as three p. or even three and a half p. for a champion—inflation I'm afraid...
CHRIS Well, I should think one about one and a half p., please.

Ribena is a fruit drink beloved of children all over Britain. Just add water.

"Rag Week" is the traditional charity fundraising week in U.K. universities, in which students don costumes and do stupid stuff all to raise money for "good causes."

HARTFORD Ah yes, well you should get a very serviceable little animal for that, sir. Quite frankly the half pence ones are a bit on the mangy side...What length was sir thinking of?

CHRIS Oh...medium?

HARTFORD Medium. Medium. Here we are, sir. *(he tips some ants—which we can't see—out into a special ring on counter)* That one there is an Ayrshire, **5** and that one there is a King George bitch I think...and that one killing the little flitbat is an Afghan.

CHRIS That's a nice one.

HARTFORD Let's see how you get on with him, eh? *(he puts it on Chris's hand)* Ah yes, he likes you. He's taken to you.

CHRIS What do you feed them on?

HARTFORD Blancmange. **6**

CHRIS Blancmange?

HARTFORD I'm sorry. I don't know why I said that. No, you don't feed them at all.

CHRIS Well, what do they live on?

HARTFORD They don't. They die.

CHRIS They die?

HARTFORD Well of course they do, if you don't feed them.

CHRIS I don't understand.

HARTFORD You let them die, then you buy another one. It's much cheaper than feeding them and that way you have a constant variety of little companions.

CHRIS Oh, I see.

HARTFORD That's the advantage of owning an ant.

CHRIS Right, well I'll take this one. Oh dear, I've dropped it...

HARTFORD Never mind. Here's another one.

CHRIS Is there anything else I'll need?

HARTFORD Yes, sir—you'll need an ant house. *(he produces a birdcage)* This is the model we recommend, sir.

CHRIS Won't it get out of there?

HARTFORD Yes.

CHRIS Well what's the point of having the cage?

HARTFORD Well, none at all really. And then some pieces of cage furniture which will keep him entertained. *(he produces microscopic things)* Here's an ant-wheel, ant-swing, and a very nice one here, a little ladder—he can run up there and ring the bell at the top, that's a little trick he can learn.

There is a breed of cattle from Ayrshire in Scotland, the reddish-brown ones.

6

Blancmanges threatened the existence of the planet way back in Episode 7.

CHRIS Will he live long enough?

HARTFORD Not really, no, but it's best to have one just in case, and here's a two-way radio he can play with...and of course you'll need the book. *(he produces an expensive-looking book, thoughtlessly slams it down where the ants were, then hurriedly brushes them away)*

CHRIS The book?

HARTFORD Yes, the book on ants.

CHRIS *(looking unsure)* Yes...

HARTFORD So, sir, that is, if I may say so, one hundred and eighty-four pounds one and a half p., sir.

CHRIS Will you take a cheque?

HARTFORD Yes, sir, if you don't mind leaving a blood-sample, and a piece of skin off the back of the scalp just here, sir...*(indicates a point behind his ear)* sorry...it's just for identification...you can't be too careful. *(he hands him a little knife and some cotton wool)*

CHRIS Oh, well I think I'll put it on account.

HARTFORD I should, sir...much less painful. Anyway, sir, you know what they say about an ant. A friend for life, eh? Well, a friend for *its* life anyway...*(Hartford loads the large cage, furniture, two-way radio and the book on ants into a huge box; with some difficulty he finds the ant; he picks it up carefully)* His name is Marcus. *(he drops him in the big box and pushes it across the counter; the box has on one side, in large letters 'LIVE ANT: HANDLE WITH CARE'; it has breathing holes in it)* If the little chap should go to an early grave, sir, give us a ring and we'll stick a few in an envelope, all right?

CHRIS Thanks very much indeed.

HARTFORD Not at all, thank *you*, Mr Ellis.

Chris turns sharply. The first assistant comes quickly up to Hartford.

FIRST ASSISTANT Sssssshh!

CHRIS What did you say?

HARTFORD I said thank you, Mr Ellis...

FIRST ASSISTANT It's not him.

HARTFORD Oh!

CHRIS Why did you say I was Mr Ellis?

HARTFORD *(innocently)* Who?

FIRST ASSISTANT No, he didn't say that.

CHRIS Yes he did. I heard him say 'Thank you, Mr Ellis'.

FIRST ASSISTANT Oh, no, no—he said 'I'm jealous'.

CHRIS What?

FIRST ASSISTANT I'm jealous of your ant. Goodbye. Goodbye. *(waves pointedly)*

CHRIS *(leaving the counter)* I don't care who Michael Ellis is!

Chris passes a shop area labelled 'The Paisley Counter' where two customers are talking to mirrors in thick Irish accents. 7 *Chris moves on to lift.* ***A little old lady passes, oblivious to the fact that her shopping trolley is smouldering.*** 8 *The lift comes and Chris is about to enter.*

"The Paisley Counter" is a joke on the name Ian Paisley, then the firebrand anti-Papist leader of the Ulster Unionists, who staunchly defended British rule in the Northern Ireland.

Not to mention, her coat is on fire.

PA SYSTEM Will Mr Michael Ellis please go straight to the manager's office...I'll repeat that...*(Chris wheels round and listens)* Will Mr Nigel Mellish please go straight to the manager's office.

Chris narrows his eyes suspiciously and gets into the lift cautiously. Cut to the kitchen in Chris Quinn's home. His mother is putting chopped meat into a line of at least half a dozen feeding bowls with various animal names on them. 'Baboon', 'Dromedary', 'Gorilla', 'Trout', and 'Pangolin'. **9** *There is a tiger in a cage in the middle of the kitchen, with a bowl marked 'Tiger' in front of him. A large cobra is hanging from the clothes drier and a wolf is in a cage below the sink. A monkey is on top of one of the cupboards. Chris enters with the box.*

MOTHER (TERRY J) What have you got now?

CHRIS I bought an ant, mother.

MOTHER What d'you want one of them for! I'm not going to clean it out. You said you'd clean the tiger out, but do you? No. I suppose you've lost interest in it now. Now it'll be ant ant ant for a couple of days, then all of a sudden, 'oh, mum, I've bought a sloth' or some other odd-toed ungulate like a tapir. **10**

CHRIS It's really different this time, mum. I'm really going to look after this ant.

MOTHER That's what you said about the sperm whale...now your papa's having to use it as a garage.

CHRIS Well, you didn't feed it properly.

MOTHER Where are we going to get forty-four tons of plankton from every morning? Your papa was dead vexed about that. They thought he was mad in the deli.

CHRIS Well at least he's got a free garage. *(growl from the tiger)*

MOTHER That's no good to him...his Hillman smells all fishy. **11** *(we hear a roar)* Oh blimey, that's the tiger. **12** He'll want his mandies. **13**

CHRIS Are you giving that tiger drugs?

MOTHER *'Course* I'm giving it drugs!

CHRIS It's illegal.

MOTHER

YOU TRY TELLING THAT TO THE TIGER.

CHRIS I think it's dangerous.

MOTHER Listen...before he started fixing, he used to get through four Jehovah's witnesses a day. And he used to eat all of them, except the pamphlets.

CHRIS Well he's not dim.

A very loud roar and rattling of cage.

MOTHER All right!

A pangolin is an anteater found in Africa and Asia.

A tapir is a snouty jungle animal—think a big pig, but closer to a horse or rhino. They smell really bad.

Ah, the Hillman Imp: a small rear-engine car built in the U.K. from 1963 to 1976.

Extraordinarily, there is an actual caged tiger in this scene.

Methaqualone, a popular sedative of the day (when it wasn't a hypnotic). Other names for it include Quaalude and Mandrax, hence "mandies."

She loads a syringe and starts to leave.

CHRIS Well, I'm going to watch one of the televisions...come on Marcus.

He puts Marcus in cage and is just about to take it through to the next room.

MOTHER Michael's been on the phone all day for you.
CHRIS Michael?
MOTHER You know, Michael...*Michael*. Michael *Ellis*. He's been on the phone all day...he came round twice.
CHRIS What did he look like?
MOTHER Oh, I didn't see him. The orange-rumped agouti **14** answered the door. Only useful animal you ever bought, that.
CHRIS Where is he now?
MOTHER He's upstairs forging prescriptions for the sodding tiger!
CHRIS No, no, where is Michael Ellis now?
MOTHER Oh, I don't know...he said it wasn't important, anyway...all right, here I come.

She goes to the tiger. Chris looks confused, then shrugs and goes into the sitting room with Marcus. In the room there are about twenty old televisions on shelves. Chris selects one of the televisions, puts it on the table, switches it on and settles down to watch it with Marcus.

Caption: (on the TV): 'UNIVERSITY OF THE AIR'

ANNOUNCER (MICHAEL) *(on the TV)* Hello and welcome to the University of the Air. And first this afternoon, part seventeen in our series of lectures on animal communications. This afternoon we look at recent discoveries in the field of intraspecific signalling codes in the family formicidea. **15**
CHRIS That's a stroke of luck, Marcus...

Cut to a restaurant. A waiter (Graham) stands at one side. Our hero (Terry J) enters, the waiter approaches him and they go through an elaborate signalling or greeting ceremony, stamping and so forth. The waiter does a strange series of movements. caption: 'may i take your coat' Hero stamps a lot and clasps the waiter's bottom. caption: 'i don't have a coat. i am an ant' Waiter routine. caption: 'aren't we all?'

The Brazilian agouti, also known as the orange-rumped agouti, is a large rodent—like a guinea pig, only with longer legs. (They are as attractive as they sound.)

The ant family, though it's spelled *Formicidae*.

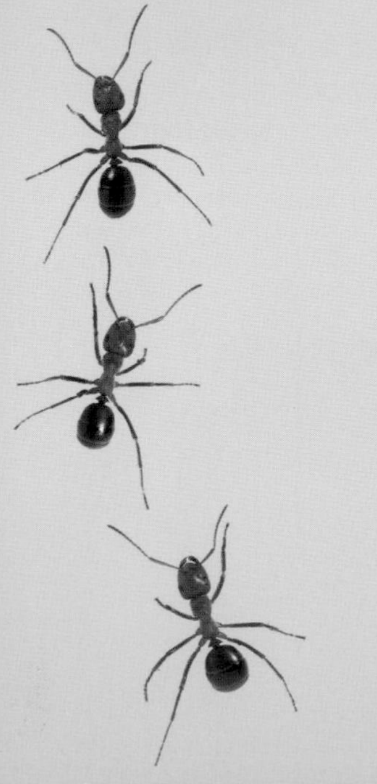

Hero routine. Caption: 'WHERE'S BRUNO?' Waiter routine. Caption: 'HE GOT TRODDEN ON' Hero routine. Caption: 'WHAT'S THE SPECIAL TODAY?' Waiter routine. Caption: 'FILLET OF ANTEATER' Hero routine. Caption: 'THAT'LL LEARN IT' Mother enters. She is rather torn and tattered and her face is bloodstained.

MOTHER Turn that bloody thing off!
ANNOUNCER We interrupt this programme to bring you the latest news of the extraordinary Michael Ellis saga. Apparently Michael Ellis...*(mother switches it off)*
CHRIS Hey! I was watching that...
MOTHER Bloody thing. It's upsetting the tiger. *(there is a roar and a crash of breaking crockery from the kitchen)* Oh Christ!

She dashes across to the door and goes into the kitchen; Chris quickly switches the TV on.

ANNOUNCER *(waits for noises to stop)* ...nd of the announcement. And now back to 'University of the Air', and our series for advanced medical students, 'Elements of Surgical Homeopathic Practice'. Part 68—'Ants'.
CHRIS Ah! We're in luck again, Marcus.

A SURGEON APPEARS ON TELEVISION. HE MAKES A FEW ANT GESTURES.

SURGEON (MICHAEL) Hello formicidophiles! Before the blood and guts that you're waiting to see, let's have a look at the anatomy of the little ant.

Cut to a drawing of an ant.

ANT EXPERT'S VOICE (TERRY J) The body of the ant is divided into three sections. *(arrow indicates)* The head, the thorax and the abdomen. They are enclosed in a hard armour-like covering called the exoskeleton, which provides some protection from other nasty little insects but unfortunately not from the dissector's scalpel. *(an animated hand with a knife slices bits off the ant)* See, nothing to it, he's not such a toughy. And his legs...they can carry hundreds of times his own weight, but look at this...*(a hand pulls the legs off)* you're not so strong compared with me, four, five, six...Ha!
CHRIS I didn't know ants had *six* legs, Marcus!
ANT EXPERT Well I can assure you they do, Mr Ellis.

CHRIS Hey! You've got two legs missing! And that's a false feeler Marcus! Blimey!

He leaps up, switches the TV off and hurls it into the corner onto a pile of used TVs, and hurries out. The tiger is quiet now. Mother, bloody and torn, is emptying a tin of 'Kit-E-Cobra' into a box marked 'Cobra'.

CHRIS

I'M TAKING THIS ANT BACK, MOTHER—HE'S GOT TWO LEGS MISSING.

MOTHER Hey! Mrs McWong's been on the phone! The polar bear's been in her garden again.
CHRIS Well I'll get it on the way back from the store.
MOTHER Well mind you do—his droppings are enormous. *(Chris goes through the door, mother shouts after him)* Oh, and by the way, while you're out get us another couple of tellies would you, here's 180 quid. *(she tosses a wad out to him)*

Cut to the garden outside. There are TVs heaped in the garden path. Chris catches the wad of notes and leaves through the garden gate as a TV van is unloading half a dozen TVs onto a trolley, prior to wheeling them into the house. Cut back to the store. Inside the lift. Chris stands there with his ant in his hand. There are also two ladies in German national costume. The lift lady, who has a wall-eye, a wooden leg, a tooth-brace, a hearing aid, a built-up shoe, a neck-brace, and a hook is reciting.

LIFT WOMAN (MICHAEL) Second floor...stationery, leather goods, nasal injuries, cricket bats, film stars, dolphinariums.

The lift stops with some difficulty. The German girls get out with their baggage. In gets a man in Greek national costume holding an oar.

LIFT WOMAN Third floor...cosmetics, books, Irish massage, tribal headgear, ants...*(Chris starts to get out)* but not *complaints* about ants!
CHRIS Oh, where do I go to complain?
LIFT WOMAN Straight on the left, then right past the thing, then, up the little stairs, then right by where it's gone all soft, then down the wobbly bit, past the nail, past the brown stain on the wall to your right and it's the door marked exit straight ahead of you on the left.
CHRIS Thank you.
LIFT WOMAN *(the doors shut but we can just hear her voice)* Fourth floor...kiddies' vasectomies...

The ant counter. It is obviously the same place with a roughly made sign 'Complaints'. Chris is standing there with the original assistant, who now has a plate in his lip and an enormous false chin about eight inches long and six inches across.

CHRIS I don't want you.
FIRST ASSISTANT *(speaking with difficulty)* Oh, something wrong with your little ant friend...?
CHRIS No! I'm not going to tell you.
FIRST ASSISTANT Something missing in the leg department?

The manager appears.

MANAGER Can I help you, sir?

Chris looks down and sees that the manager is half in a sack.

CHRIS No! No! No! No!

MANAGER Oh, it's all right, sir, it's for the sack race later on.

CHRIS No, no, no, I want to speak to the General Manager, I want to complain.

MANAGER Oh, well you want the Toupee Hall in that case, sir.

CHRIS The what?

MANAGER The Toupee Hall, Mr Ellis. *(he hops off)*

Chris approaches a stocking counter where lady assistant is serving two heavies who are trying on nylons over their heads. Chris speaks to the assistant.

CHRIS *(embarrassed)* Excuse me—could you tell me the way to the Toupee Hall, please?

ASSISTANT (MICHAEL) Sorry?

CHRIS The Toupee Hall.

ASSISTANT The what?

CHRIS The Toupee Hall.

ASSISTANT Oh, the *Toupee Hall*! *(loudly)* Gladys, where are toupees now?

GLADYS (GRAHAM) Toupees? *(people start to look)*

ASSISTANT This gentleman wants one.

GLADYS *(even louder)* A toupee?

CHRIS Well, no, actually...

GLADYS I think they're in surgical appliances now.

ASSISTANT That's right, yes, you go left at artificial limbs and hearing aids, right at dentures and it's on your left just by glass eyes. It doesn't say toupees to avoid embarrassing people, but you can smell 'em.

People by this time have formed a ring round to see who it is.

CHRIS Thank you.

As he moves off people peer at his head.

WOMAN *(to friend)* You can see the join.

Chris, in order to avoid this embarrassment, dives into the nearest department. A sign over the door reads 'Victorian poetry reading hall'. Cut to a poetry reading. Wordsworth, Shelley, Keats and Tennyson are present. Chris stands quietly in the corner hoping not to be noticed.

OLD LADY (GRAHAM) Good afternoon, ladies and gentlemen, it's so nice to see such a large turnout this afternoon. And I'd like to start off by welcoming our guest speakers for this afternoon,...Mr Wadsworth...

WORDSWORTH (TERRY J) Wordsworth!

OLD LADY

SORRY, WORDSWORTH...MR JOHN KOOTS, AND PERCY BYSSHE.

SHELLEY (TERRY G) Shelley!

OLD LADY Just a little one, medium dry, *(a dwarf assistant pours her a sherry)* and Alfred Lorde.

TENNYSON Tennyson.

OLD LADY Tennis ball.

TENNYSON Son, son.

OLD LADY Sorry—Alfred Lord, who is evidently Lord Tennisball's son. And to start off I'm going to ask Mr Wadsworth to read his latest offering, a little pram entitled 'I wandered lonely as a crab' and it's all about ants.

Murmur of excited anticipation. Wordsworth rises rather gloomily.

WORDSWORTH I wandered lonely as a *cloud*
That floats on high over vales and hills
When all at once I saw a crowd
A host of golden worker ants. **16**

Ripples of applause.

OLD LADY Thank you, thank you, Mr Bradlaugh. Now, Mr Bysshe.

SHELLEY Shelley.

OLD LADY Oh...*(the dwarf refills her glass)*...is going to read one of his latest psalms, entitled 'Ode to a crab'.

SHELLEY *(rising and taking his place quietly)* Well, it's not about crabs actually, it's called 'Ozymandias'. It's not an ode. I met a traveller from an antique land Who said 'Six vast and trunkless legs of stone Stand in the desert And on the pedestal these words appear My name is Ozymandias, King of Ants *(oohs from his audience)* Look on my feelers, termites, and despair I am the biggest ant you'll ever see The ants of old weren't half as bold and big And fierce as me'. **17**

Enormous applause.

OLD LADY Thank you Mr Amontillado. I'd like to ask one or two of you at the back not to soil the carpet, there is a restroom upstairs if you find the poems too exciting. *(she falls over)* Good afternoon, next, Mr Dennis Keat will recite his latest problem 'Ode to a glass of sherry'. *(she falls off the podium)*

16

It should of course read "daffodils," not "worker ants."

17

Shelley's famous sonnet, "Ozymandias" was written in 1818. Correctly quoted here until "stand in the desert," then we skip five and a half lines to "And on the pedestal" —and then the bit about the "King of Ants" is all wrong.

KEATS (ERIC) My heart aches and a drowsy numbness pains
My senses, as though an anteater I'd seen **18** *(panic spreads and the audience half rise)*
A nasty long-nosed brute *(screams from the audience)*
With furry legs and sticky darting tongue I seem to feel its cruel jaws
Crunch crunch there go my legs
Snap snap my thorax too *(various screaming women faint)*
My head's in a twain, there goes my brain
Swallow, swallow, swallow, slurp *(he loses control)*

OLD LADY Mr Keats, Mr Keats, please leave immediately.

KEATS It's true. Don't you see. It's true. It happens.

OLD LADY *(she bustles him out)* Ladies and gentlemen, I do apologize for that last...well I hesitate to call it a pram...but I had no idea...and talking of filth...I *have* asked you once about the carpet...Now, I do appreciate that last poem was very frightening...but please! Now before we move on to tea and pramwiches, I would like to ask Arthur Lord Tenniscourt to give us his latest little plum entitled 'The Charge of the Ant Brigade'.

TENNYSON Half an inch, half an inch... **19**

John Keats's "Ode to a Nightingale," written in 1819—though there is no mention of an anteater in it.

Alfred Lord Tennyson's "The Charge of the Light Brigade," from 1854, begins "Half a league, half a league, half a league onward."

ENTER QUEEN VICTORIA WITH A FANFARE, FOLLOWED BY ALBERT'S COFFIN.

ALL The Queen, the Queen. *(they all bow and scrape)*

QUEEN VICTORIA (MICHAEL) My loyal subjects, we are here today on a matter of national import. My late husband and we are increasingly concerned by recent developments in literary style *(developing a German accent)* that have taken place here in Germany...er England. There seems to be an increasing tendency for ze ent...the ent...the ant...to become the dominant...was is der deutsches Entwicklungsbund...

ATTENDANT Theme.

QUEEN VICTORIA Theme...of modern poetry here in Germany. We are not...amusiert? **20** *(an attendant whispers)* Entertained. From now on, ants is verboten. Instead it's skylarks, daffodils, nightingales, light brigades and...was ist das schreckliche Gepong...es schmecke wie ein Scheisshaus...und so weiter. Well, we must away now or we shall be late for the races. God bless you alles.

Chris leaves. We cut to him outside a door with a sign saying 'Electric Kettles'.

VOICE Psst! Electric kettles over here, sir.

A hand holding a sign saying 'Toupees' beckons him. He goes over to door and is ushered through. There are pictures of famous bald world figures with toupees on the walls.

"We are not amused," a phrase attributed to Queen Victoria. The "we" may have, in fact, been a reference to the court, or she and her ladies in waiting; either way, it's now become symbolic with the "majestic plural," where "we" stands for the British Crown.

TOUPEE MANAGER (TERRY J) Don't worry, sir, you're among friends now, sir. *(the manager has an appalling toupee; Chris sees it and tries not to stare; the manager introduces his assistants)* Mr Bradford, Mr Crawley. *(Bradford and Crawley come forward; each has a toupee worse than the others)* These are our fitters, sir. We've had a lot of experience in this field and we do pride ourselves we offer the best and most discreet service available. I don't know whether you'll believe this sir, but one of us is actually wearing a toupee at this moment...

CHRIS Well, you all are, aren't you?

They rush to a mirror.

BRADFORD (MICHAEL) Have you got one?
CRAWLEY (GRAHAM) Yes, but I didn't know...
TOUPEE MANAGER I didn't realize that you two...I thought it was me.
CRAWLEY Yes, I thought it was me.
BRADFORD So did I. *(to Crawley)* That is good.
CHRIS Actually, I only came in here to ask where the manager's office was.
TOUPEE MANAGER

JUST A MINUTE—SOMEONE TOLD YOU WE ALL HAD TOUPEES?

CHRIS No.
CRAWLEY Oh yeah?
BRADFORD How did you know?
CHRIS Well...it's pretty obvious, isn't it?
CRAWLEY What do you mean obvious! His is undetectable.
CHRIS Well, it's a different colour, for a start.
BRADFORD Is it?
CRAWLEY Course it isn't!
CHRIS And it doesn't fit in with the rest of his hair...it sort of sticks up in the middle.
BRADFORD It's better than yours.
CRAWLEY Yes. I'm not wearing one.

They all jeer.

TOUPEE MANAGER Oh, I see, you haven't got one.
CRAWLEY Why did you come in here then?
CHRIS They told me to find the manager's office here.

They all jeer again.

BRADFORD Oh no, not again.
CRAWLEY That's a bit lame, isn't it...
CHRIS It's the truth!
ALL Manager's office. *(they laugh mockingly)*
BRADFORD Yeah, look at it. Where did you get that, Mac Fisheries?
TOUPEE MANAGER Dreadful, isn't it?
CRAWLEY Nylon?
CHRIS It's not, it's real look. *(he pulls it)*
ALL Oh yeah, anyone can do that.

They all do the same. Bradford in autiously pulls his loose.

CRAWLEY Come on, get it off.
CHRIS Get away.
TOUPEE MANAGER Look, do you want a proper one?
CHRIS No, I don't need one.
BRADFORD There's no need to be ashamed.
CRAWLEY *We've* all owned up.
CHRIS I'm not wearing one.

They all look at each other for a moment, registering 'a hard case'.

TOUPEE MANAGER Don't you see...this is something you've got to come to terms with.
CHRIS I am not wearing a toupee! They just told me to come in here to find the manager's office, to complain about my ant!

They look at each other.

CRAWLEY Pathetic, isn't it.
BRADFORD Complain about an ant?
TOUPEE MANAGER This is for your own good.

He grabs Chris's hair. A fight ensues in which all the assistants get their toupees dislodged. Chris is backed up against a door marked: 'Strictly no admittance'. He suddenly ducks out through this door. Cut to the other side of the door. Chris turns and double takes. It is the manager's office. There is a long line of people sitting waiting to complain. The manager looks up.

COMPLAINTS MANAGER (MICHAEL) *(irritably)* All right. Take a seat.

Chris shuts the door and takes a seat at the end of a line of ten people waiting to complain: the German clothes prop man; the Icelandic honey week man; a Greek with a motor tyre; a man with a lawn mower with a cat sticking out of it; a man with a bandaged nose holding a dog with a bandaged nose; a lady with a bandaged nose; a lady with a bandaged nose and a pram with a small column of smoke rising from it; a rather butch lady with her head through a tennis racket; a man with a cigar in his mouth that has obviously exploded—his face is blackened and his collar awry; a man in a terrible suit with one arm twice as long as a normal sleeve and trousers that finish at mid-thigh. A uniformed shop attendant is sitting next to a rather well dressed lady in twin set and pearls, and her equally distinguished looking husband. The attendant is occasionally touching the lady's cheek and peering into her eyes. The lady and the husband stare straight ahead. Next to them is Colonel Ewing. At the desk is the lady with the flame thrower. Part of the manager's desk and the entire corner of the office are blackened and smoking.

LADY (CAROL) You see! There ought to be a safety catch on it, I mean...ohhhh! *(a spurt of flame shoots out)* I mean, what if this fell into the wrong hands?
COMPLAINTS MANAGER Yes, madam. I'll speak to the makers personally, all right.
LADY Would you? It would put my mind at ease.

She leaves closing the door. We hear the flame thrower.

LADY'S VOICE Sorry...
COMPLAINTS MANAGER Next?

The colonel gets up. As he does so Mr Zyndersky (the husband) indicates his wife and the attendant.

MR ZYNDERSKY (TERRY G) He's still molesting her.

COMPLAINTS MANAGER Yes, yes, I'll see to you in a moment, sir. *(the colonel sits at the manager's desk)*

COLONEL EWING (GRAHAM) I've got a complaint to make.

COMPLAINTS MANAGER Do take a seat. I'm sorry it's on fire.

COLONEL EWING Oh, not at all. *(he sits on it)* I got used to this out east.

COMPLAINTS MANAGER Where were you out east?

COLONEL EWING Oh, Norway...Sweden...places like that...oh I'm awfully sorry, my suit seems to keep catching fire.

COMPLAINTS MANAGER Extinguisher?

COLONEL EWING Oh no, thank you, I think we'd better let it run its course. I was just thinking...Norway is not very east, is it? I should have said when I was out north. *(he slaps at the flames)*

COMPLAINTS MANAGER Are there many fires in Norway?

COLONEL EWING Good Lord yes. The place is a constant blaze. Wooden buildings, d'you know. I lost my wife in Norway.

COMPLAINTS MANAGER I am sorry to hear that.

COLONEL EWING Why, did you know her?

COMPLAINTS MANAGER No, I meant...

COLONEL EWING Oh I see. No, she wasn't a favourite of mine. We were out strolling across a fiord one day when one of the local matadors came out of his tree house and flung a lot of old scimitars and guillotines out that he'd got cluttering up his wine cellar and apparently rather a large proportion of them landed on my wife causing her to snuff it without much more ado.

COMPLAINTS MANAGER Yes, yes—well look...

Ding-dong of store PA. An announcer speaks.

ANNOUNCER Here is an important announcement about Michael Ellis. *(Chris looks up at loudspeaker; everyone turns towards it)* It is now the end of 'Michael Ellis' week. From now on it is 'Chris Quinn' week. *(murmur of excitement)*

CHRIS

WHAT A ROTTEN ENDING.

Cut to a polite, well dressed assistant at a counter with a big sign saying 'End of Show Department' behind him.

ASSISTANT (TERRY J) Well it is one of our cheapest, sir.

CHRIS What else have you got?

ASSISTANT Well, there's the long slow pull-out, sir, you know, the camera tracks back and back and mixes...

As he speaks we pull out and mix through to the exterior of the store. Mix through to even wider zoom ending up in aerial view of London with music reaching a crescendo. It stops abruptly and we cut back to Chris.

CHRIS No, have you got anything more exciting?

ASSISTANT How about a chase?

The manager and the toupee assistants suddenly appear at a door.

MANAGER There he is!

Exciting chase music. They pursue Chris out of the hall and into another part of the store. Then cut back to Chris at counter.

CHRIS Oh, no, no, no.
ASSISTANT Walking into the sunset?
CHRIS What's that one?

Dramatic sunset shot on a beach. We can just see the back of Chris and the assistant as they walk together towards the setting sun. The assistant is gesturing and describing it.

ASSISTANT You know...two lone figures silhouetted against the dying rays of the setting sun. The music swells, you've got a lump in your throat and a tear in your eye...

Cut back to the store.

CHRIS Oh no.
ASSISTANT Oh, pity, I rather like that one...
CHRIS They're all a bit off the point, you see.
ASSISTANT Well there is one that ties up the whole Michael Ellis thing, but...
CHRIS But what...?
ASSISTANT Oh, no, nothing, nothing...
CHRIS Look, who is this Michael Ellis?
ASSISTANT

HOW ABOUT A *HAPPY ENDING*, SIR?

A girl rushes up to Chris and flings her arms around him.

GIRL (CAROL) Oh Chris! Thank God you're safe.
ASSISTANT No, you wouldn't want that, would you.

This time we see the girl has disappeared.

CHRIS Why wouldn't I want that?
ASSISTANT What about summing up from the panel? That's cheap. You know—the big match experts.

Panel in typical football panel set. Malcolm Allison, Brian Clough, and huge still of Jimmy Hill on set behind. **21**

MALCOLM ALLISON (MICHAEL) Yes. It was quite a good show. I think that the Michael Ellis character was a little overdone.
BRIAN CLOUGH (ERIC) Well, I don't agree with that, Malcolm, quite frankly the only bit I liked was this bit with me in it now.

Cut back to the store.

ASSISTANT No? Slow fade?

The picture begins to fade.

CHRIS Nnnn...no.

The picture comes up again.

ASSISTANT Well, how about a sudden ending?

Blackout.

21

Three soccer people: Allison and Clough were players, then managers, then pundits (and both had elevated views of themselves); Hill was a player then a pundit, known for his long chin and often outmoded views on the game.

SEA
SON
4
EPISODE 42

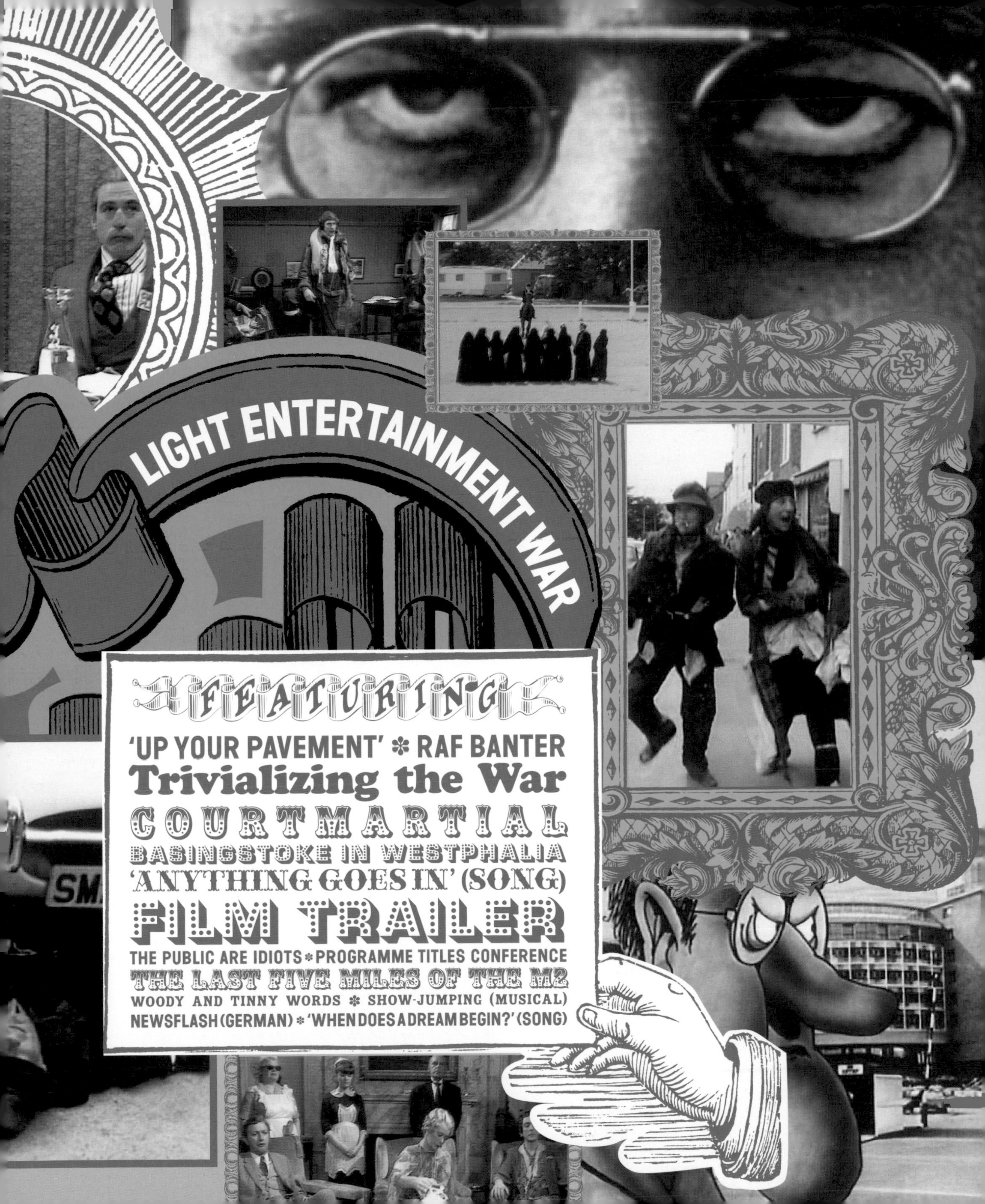
LIGHT ENTERTAINMENT WAR
FEATURING
'UP YOUR PAVEMENT' ✽ RAF BANTER
Trivializing the War
COURTMARTIAL
BASINGSTOKE IN WESTPHALIA
'ANYTHING GOES IN' (SONG)
FILM TRAILER
THE PUBLIC ARE IDIOTS ✽ PROGRAMME TITLES CONFERENCE
THE LAST FIVE MILES OF THE M2
WOODY AND TINNY WORDS ✽ SHOW-JUMPING (MUSICAL)
NEWSFLASH (GERMAN) ✽ 'WHEN DOES A DREAM BEGIN?' (SONG)

FIRST AIRED: NOVEMBER 14, 1974

A high street. Musical theme played on a banjo a la 'Steptoe and Son' opening. [1] *Cut to a tracking shot of two tramps* (TERRY J & MICHAEL) *walking jauntily along. They are very arch, over-the-top jolly fellows. They nod at the occasional passer-by and do mock bows to a city gent.*

Ritle caption: 'UP YOUR PAVEMENT' Caption: 'BY THE REV. & MRS. A. G. PHIPPS' Caption: 'FROM AN IDEA BY LORD CARRINGTON' [2] *They come to a litter bin, root in it, and one of them produces a newspaper. He hands it to the other, looks in again and brings out a pork pie. He looks in again, his eyes light up, and he produces a bottle of champagne. He passes it to his mate. He looks in again and finds two highly polished glasses. Meanwhile over all this and as they set off down the road again we hear:*

VOICE OVER (MICHAEL) Taking life as it comes, sharing the good things and the bad things, finding laughter and fun wherever they go—it is with these two happy-go-lucky rogues that our story begins. *(by this time the tramps have walked out of shot; cut to a shot of a sports car up on the pavement with the legs of the two tramps sticking out from underneath; the music turns more urgent and transatlantic)* For it is they who were run over by Alex Diamond... [3] *(appropriate music; a James Bond character* (GRAHAM) *climbs out of the car and looks down at the dead tramps)* international crime fighter...*(shot of him rushing into a film premiere past photographers with flashing bulbs)* and playboy...*(cut to him on yacht)* fast-moving...tough-talking...*(still of him with Henry Kissinger; cut to him striding down a street)* and just one of the many hundreds of famous people who suffer from lumbago, the epidemic disease about which no one knows more than this man...*(we see him go into a doorway; cut to a low angle close up of Dr Koning* (JOHN) *donning gloves prior to the operation; the music changes to the Kildare theme)* Dr Emile Koning...doctor...surgeon...proctologist...and selfless fighter against human suffering, whose doorbell...*(cut to a doorbell and pan down)* was the one above the hero of our story tonight...*(pan down to find the doorbell and name)* Rear-Admiral Humphrey De Vere! *(the door opens and the rear-admiral* (ERIC) *comes striding out; naval music; he walks up the road)* Yes! This is the story of Rear-Admiral Humphrey De Vere...or rather, the story of his daughter...*(cut to a still of a young inspired and devoted nurse; the music instantly changes to the heroic)* For it was her courage, foresight and understanding that enabled us to probe beneath the sophisticated veneer of...*(mix to impressive college grounds)* the Royal Arsenal Women's College, Bagshot...*(zoom in across lawns towards the college building)* and learn the true history of this man...*(the camera suddenly veers off away from college and homes in on a solitary bush from*

Steptoe and Son was a British sitcom featuring Wilfrid Brambell, who played the socially aspiring son of dirty old man Steptoe, a "rag-and-bone" man, or garbage picker. It ran from 1962 to 1965 and again from 1970 to 1974, and was remade as *Sanford and Son* in the United States.

Lord Carrington was a British Conservative politician who would later rise to the positions of foreign secretary and secretary general of NATO. In the early 1970s he was defense secretary under Ted Heath. This episode, recorded on October 26, 1974, came sixteen days after the Conservatives were beaten in the 1974 election by the Labour Party of Harold Wilson. Carrington led the Conservative faction in the House of Lords once he lost his position at defense.

Relatively obscure Greek filmmaker and actor (whose real name was Alexandros Diamantis).

which appears a seedy fellow in a terrible lightweight suit of several years ago that has got all stained and creased around the crotch (MICHAEL)*)* Len Hanky! Chiropodist, voyeur, hen-teaser. The man of whom the chairman of Fiat once said... 4

Cut to a high-powered Italian businessman at a desk in a very modern casa-type Italian office.

CHAIRMAN (ERIC) Che cosa è 1lo stucciacatori di polli?

Superimposed caption: 'WHAT IS A HEN-TEASER?' The phone rings. He answers it dynamically and we zoom in on his tense, alert, executive face.

VOICE OVER Yes! Tonight we examine the career of Gino Agnelli! 5 The man who started from nothing to build up one of the greatest firms in Europe. *(mix through to stock film of a big car-producing plant)* And whose telescope was bought from the shop part-owned by a man who, at the age of eight, stole a penknife from the son of this man's brother's housekeeper's dental hygienist's uncle. *(as each of these things is mentioned we see a momentary flash of a still of each)* The Reverend Charlie 'Drooper' Hyper-Squawk Smith, *(at this point the freeze frame starts moving as the chaplain* (TERRY J) *lifts himself out of the cockpit and jumps down beside his Spitfire)* the cleft-palated RAF chaplain, who single-handed shot down over five hundred German chaplains. *(smiling cheerfully he crosses off another emblem of a vicar in a German helmet on the side of the plane. Beside this is written "'Here we come Kraut" Luke 17, verse 3')* 6 This is the story of the men who flew with him...it really is! *(a squadron leader, just off on a mission, runs past, and dashes into a Nissen hut)* 7

Caption: 'SOMEWHERE IN ENGLAND, 1944' The squadron leader enters an RAP officers' mess and takes off his helmet.

BOVRIL (TERRY J) Morning, squadron leader.
SQUADRON LEADER (ERIC) What-ho, Squiffy.
BOVRIL How was it?

Fiat, the Italian car manufacturer.

Giovanni Agnelli, head of Fiat from 1966 to 1996.

Luke 17:3: "Take heed to yourselves: If thy brother trespass against thee, rebuke him; and if he repent, forgive him."

A Nissen hut is a curved metal hut named after Major Peter Norman Nissen, a royal engineer, and put into production in 1916. Beloved of the military on their bases.

"Top hole": excellent.

"Pranged": to bang or smash.

"Kite": airplane.

"How's your father": private parts.

"Hairy blighter": a general term of non-endearment.

"Not a dicky-bird" means "not a sound" or "not a thing."

"Feathered," "Sammy," "waspy," "Betty Harper's," "Bertie," and the rest of the sketch are all nonsense banter.

SQUADRON LEADER Top hole. Bally Jerry pranged his kite right in the how's your father. Hairy blighter, dicky-birdied, feathered back on his Sammy, took a waspy, flipped over his Betty Harper's and caught his can in the Bertie. 8

BOVRIL Er, I'm afraid I don't quite follow you, squadron leader.

SQUADRON LEADER It's perfectly ordinary banter, Squiffy. Bally Jerry...pranged his kite, right in the how's yer father...hairy blighter, dicky-birdied, feathered back on his Sammy, took a waspy, flipped over on his Betty Harper's and caught his can in the Bertie.

BOVRIL No, I'm just not understanding banter at all well today. Give us it slower.

SQUADRON LEADER Banter's not the *same* if you say it slower, Squiffy.

BOVRIL Hold on, then. *(shouts)* Wingco!

WINGCO (GRAHAM) Yes!

BOVRIL Bend an ear to the squadron leader's banter for a sec, would you?

WINGCO Can do.

BOVRIL Jolly good.

WINGCO Fire away.

SQUADRON LEADER *(draws a deep breath and looks slightly uncertain, then starts even more deliberately than before)* Bally Jerry...pranged his kite...right in the how's yer father...hairy blighter... dicky-birdied...feathered back on his Sammy...took a waspy...flipped over his Betty Harper's...and caught his *can* in the *Bertie*...

WINGCO ...No, don't understand that banter at all.

SQUADRON LEADER Something up with my banter, chaps?

A siren goes. The door bursts open and an out-of-breath young pilot rushes in in his flying gear.

PILOT (MICHAEL)

BUNCH OF MONKEYS ON YOUR CEILING, SIR! GRAB YOUR EGG AND FOURS AND LET'S GET THE BACON DELIVERED.

General incomprehension. They look at each other.

"Briny" is slang for the sea.

WINGCO Do you understand that?

SQUADRON LEADER No, didn't get a word of it.

WINGCO Sorry old man, we don't understand your banter.

PILOT You know...bally ten-penny ones dropping in the custard...*(searching for the words)* um... Charlie Choppers chucking a handful...

WINGCO No, no...sorry.

BOVRIL Say it a bit slower, old chap.

PILOT Slower *banter*, sir?

WINGCO Ra-ther!

PILOT Um...sausage squad up the blue end!

SQUADRON LEADER No, still don't get it.

PILOT Um...cabbage crates coming over the briny? 9

SQUADRON LEADER No.

OTHERS No, no...

Stock film of a German bombing raid.

VOICE OVER But by then it was too late. The first cabbage crates hit London on July 7th. That was just the beginning...

Cut to a Whitehall war office conference room. A general is on the phone. Four other generals sit there.

GENERAL (GRAHAM) Five shillings a dozen? That's ordinary cabbages, is it? And what about the bombs? Good Lord, they *are* expensive!

A corporal rushes in.

CORPORAL (ERIC) Sir!
GENERAL Yes, what is it?
CORPORAL News from the Western Front, sir.
GENERAL Yes...?
CORPORAL Big enemy attack at dawn, sir...
GENERAL Yes...?
CORPORAL Well, the enemy were all wearing little silver halos, sir...and...they had fairy wands with big stars on the end...and...
GENERAL They what...?
CORPORAL ...and...they had spiders in matchboxes, sir.
GENERAL *(in disbelief)* Good God! How did our chaps react?

CORPORAL Well, they were jolly interested, sir. Some of them...I think it was the 4th Armoured Brigade, sir, they...
CORPORAL Well...they went and had a look at the spiders, sir.
GENERAL Oh my God! All right, thank you, Shirley.

A girl emerges from under the table. She is a blonde WAAF.

CORPORAL Sir!
GENERAL *(to a sergeant)* Get me the Prime Minister. *(the sergeant opens door, Churchill stands outside)* Not that quickly! *(the sergeant shuts the door)* Gentlemen, it's now quite apparent that the enemy are not only fighting this war on the cheap, but they're also not taking it seriously.
AGEING GENERAL (TERRY G) Bastards...
GENERAL

FIRST THEY DROP CABBAGES INSTEAD OF DECENT BOMBS...

CORPORAL The crates were probably quite expensive, sir.
GENERAL Quiet, critic! And now they're doing very silly things in one of the most vital areas of the war!
AGEING GENERAL What are we going to do, Shirley?
GENERAL Well, we've got to act fast before it saps morale. We going to show these Chinese...

CAPTAIN Germans, sir.

GENERAL These Germans...we're going to show them that no British soldier will descend to their level. Anyone found trivializing this war will face the supreme penalty that military law can provide. *(he holds a heroic pose; there is a pause during which we expect to cut; we don't; suddenly he breaks out of the pose into informality)* That was all right, I think?

CAPTAIN *(getting out drinks)* Seemed to go quite well.

Cut to a courtroom in the 1940s. A courtmartial is in progress. An elderly general presides, with two others on either side of him. There is a defence counsel, a prosecutor, a clerk of court, and two men guarding the prisoner.

PRESIDING GENERAL (TERRY J) Sapper Walters, you stand before this court accused of carrying on the war by other than warlike means—to wit, that you did on April 16th, 1942, dressed up as a bag of dainties, flick wet towels at the enemy during an important offensive...

WALTERS (ERIC) Well, sir...

PRESIDING GENERAL Shut up! Colonel Fawcett for the prosecution...

FAWCETT (MICHAEL) Sir, we all know...

PRESIDING GENERAL Shut up!

FAWCETT I'm sorry?

PRESIDING GENERAL Carry on.

FAWCETT Sir, we all know the facts of the case; that Sapper Walters, being in possession of expensive military equipment, to wit one Lee Enfield .303 Rifle and 72 rounds of ammunition, valued at a hundred and forty pounds three shillings and sixpence, chose instead to use wet towels to take an enemy command post in the area of Basingstoke...

PRESIDING GENERAL Basingstoke? Basingstoke in Hampshire?

FAWCETT No, no, no, sir, no.

PRESIDING GENERAL I see, carry on.

FAWCETT The result of his action was that the enemy...

PRESIDING GENERAL Basingstoke *where*?

FAWCETT Basingstoke Westphalia, sir. 10

PRESIDING GENERAL Oh I *see*. Carry on.

FAWCETT The result of Sapper Walters's action was that the enemy received wet patches upon their trousers and in some cases small red strawberry marks upon their thighs...

PRESIDING GENERAL I didn't know there *was* a Basingstoke in Westphalia.

FAWCETT *(slightly irritated)* It's on the map, sir.

10 Westphalia, an area of Germany.

PRESIDING GENERAL What map?

FAWCETT *(more irritably)* The map of Westphalia as used by the army, sir.

PRESIDING GENERAL Well, I've certainly never heard of Basingstoke in Westphalia.

FAWCETT *(patiently)* It's a municipal borough sir, twenty-seven miles north north east of Southampton. Its chief manufactures...

PRESIDING GENERAL What...Southampton in Westphalia?

FAWCETT Yes sir...bricks...clothing. Nearby are the remains of Basing House, **11** burned down by Cromwell's cavalry in 1645...

PRESIDING GENERAL Who compiled this map?

FAWCETT Cole Porter, sir.

PRESIDING GENERAL *(incredulously)* Cole Porter...who wrote 'Kiss Me Kate'?

FAWCETT No, alas not, sir...this was the Cole Porter who wrote 'Anything Goes'. **12** Sir I shall seek to prove that the man before this court...

PRESIDING GENERAL That's the same one! *(he sings)* 'In olden days a glimpse of stocking...'

FAWCETT I *beg* your pardon, sir?

PRESIDING GENERAL *(singing)* 'In olden days a glimpse of stocking, was looked on as something shocking, now heaven knows, anything goes...'

FAWCETT No, this one's different, sir.

PRESIDING GENERAL How does it go?

FAWCETT What, sir?

PRESIDING GENERAL How does *your* 'Anything Goes' go?

WALTERS Can I go home now?

PRESIDING GENERAL Shut up! *(to Fawcett)* Come on!

FAWCETT Sir, really, this is rather...

PRESIDING GENERAL Come on, how does your 'Anything Goes' go?

FAWCETT *(clearing his throat and going into an extraordinary tuneless and very loud song)* Anything goes in.
Anything goes out! Fish, bananas, old pyjamas,
Mutton! Beef! and Trout!
Anything goes in...

PRESIDING GENERAL No, that's not it...carry on.

FAWCETT With respect sir, I shall seek to prove that the man before you in the dock, being in possession of the following: one pair of army boots, value three pounds seven and six, one pair of serge trousers, value two pounds three and six, one pair of gaiters value sixty-eight pounds ten shillings, one...

PRESIDING GENERAL Sixty-eight pounds ten shillings for a pair of *gaiters*?

FAWCETT *(dismissively)* They were special gaiters, sir.

PRESIDING GENERAL *Special* gaiters?

FAWCETT Yes sir, they were made in France. One beret costing fourteen shillings, one pair of...

PRESIDING GENERAL What was special about them?

FAWCETT Oh...*(as if he can hardly be bothered to reply)* they were made of a special fabric, sir. The buckles were made of empire silver instead of brass. The total value of the uniform was there...

PRESIDING GENERAL Why was the accused wearing special gaiters?

FAWCETT *(irritably)* They were a presentation pair, from the regiment. The total value of the uniform...

PRESIDING GENERAL Why did they present him with a special pair of gaiters?

FAWCETT Sir, it seems to me totally irrelevant to the case whether the gaiters were presented to him or not, sir.

PRESIDING GENERAL I think the court will be able to judge that for themselves. I want to know *why* the regiment presented the accused with a special pair of gaiters.

A once-impressive Tudor palace, the ruins of Basing House sit one mile east of the town of Basingstoke, in Hampshire. It was ransacked and burned by Oliver Cromwell and his Commonwealth forces on October 13, 1645.

A Cole Porter song written for the musical of the same name in 1934.

FAWCETT *(stifling his impatience)* He...used to do things for them. The total value...
PRESIDING GENERAL What things?
FAWCETT *(exasperated)* He...he used to oblige them, sir. The total value...
PRESIDING GENERAL *Oblige* them?
FAWCETT Yes sir. The total value of the uniform...
PRESIDING GENERAL How did he *oblige* them?
FAWCETT What, sir?
PRESIDING GENERAL How did he *oblige* them?
FAWCETT *(more and more irritated)* He...um...he used to make them happy in little ways, sir. The total value of the uniform could therefore not have been less than...
PRESIDING GENERAL Did he touch them at all?
FAWCETT Sir! I submit that this is totally irrelevant.
PRESIDING GENERAL I want to know how he made them happy.
FAWCETT *(losing his temper)*

HE USED TO RAM THINGS UP THEIR...

PRESIDING GENERAL *(quickly)* All right! All right! No need to spell it out! What er...what has the accused got to say?
WALTERS *(taken off guard)* What, me?
PRESIDING GENERAL Yes. What have you got to say?

WALTERS What can *I* say? I mean, how can I encapsulate in mere words my scorn for any military solution? The futility of modern warfare? And the hypocrisy by which contemporary government applies one standard to violence within the community and another to violence perpetrated by one community upon another?
DEFENCE COUNSEL (TERRY G) I'm sorry, but my client has become pretentious. I will say in his defence he has suffered...
FAWCETT Sir! We haven't finished the prosecution!
PRESIDING COUNSEL Shut up! I'm in charge of this court. *(to the court)* Stand up! *(everyone stands up)* Sit down! *(everyone sits down)* Go moo! *(everyone goes moo; the presiding general turns to Fawcett)* See? Right, now, on with the pixie hats! *(everyone puts on pixie hats with large pointed ears)* And order in the skating vicar. *(a skating vicar enters and everyone bursts into song)*
EVERYONE Anything goes in.

Anything goes out!
Fish, bananas, old pyjamas,
Mutton! Beef! and Trout!
Anything goes in.
Anything goes out. *(etc.)*

Cut to the coast of Norway. Night. Tense music. Shots of big coastal guns, cliff-top fortifications. Superimposed captions: 'DRAMA!' 'ACTION!' Build up for about ten seconds. Cut to a cliff top looking out to sea. A grappling hook comes over and sticks in, then another, and another. Whispered voices, music, the tension rises as the rope is tightened. Then over the top comes a German, head blackened and camouflaged. Then others climb over; they are wearing haloes, pink tutus, jackboots, wands. They charge over. Stock film of guns blazing.

VOICE OVER (MICHAEL) Yes! Coming to this cinema soon! *(cut to stock film of a destroyer in the midst of a pitched sea-battle; victory-at-sea music)* The tender compassionate story of one man's love for another man in drag. *(cut to a sailor on a ship in rough sea; he calls to the captain who is in an evening gown)* THRILL! to the excitement of a night emission over Germany. 13

13 A play on "night mission," of course, but likely to cause sniggers for all adolescent boys everywhere.

Superimposed caption: 'THRILL!' Cut to stock shots of bombers on a night raid. Cut to interior of a bomber. Various shots of pilot and navigator. There is flak outside and explosions occasionally light up the cabin.

VOICE OVER When the pilot, Jennifer *(shot of the pilot)* has to choose between his secret love for Louis, *(shot of the navigator)* the hot bloodedly bi-sexual navigator and Andy, *(shot of the rear gunner)* the rear gunner, who, though quite assertive with girls, tends to take the submissive role in his relationships with men. *(cut to close up of gritty pipe-smoking RAF top brass)* And sensational Mexican starlet, Rosetta Nixon, plays the head of bomber command, *(insert of WAAF)* whose passion for sea-birds ends in tragedy. *(cut to montage of war footage, explosions, guns firing, etc.)* With Ginger, as the half-man, half-woman, parrot whose unnatural instincts brought forbidden love to the aviary. And Roger as Pip, the half-parrot, half-man, half-woman, three-quarter badger, ex-bigamist negro preacher, for whom banjo-playing was very difficult, and he never mastered it although he took several courses and went to banjo college...er...and everything...don't miss it!

During this last lot are superimposed in quick succession the following captions:

'DRAMA'
'SUSPENSE'
'THRILLS'
'MARQUETRY' 14
'ADVENTURES'
'DON'T MISS IT'
'COMING TO YOUR CINEMA SOON'

14 Marquetry is the decorative art of making patterns in a veneer.

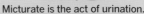

VOICE OVER Coming to your cinema soon! *(cut to an Indian restaurant)* Only five minutes from this restaurant! But now!

Cut to the nude organist (Terry J) and 'It's' man.

IT'S MAN (MICHAEL)
IT'S...

Opening titles.

At the end of the title cut to tramps exactly as at the beginning of the show. Then cut to two twin-set-and-pearls ladies, Mrs Elizabeth III and Mrs Mock Tudor. They are in a sitting room with vulgar furnishings. By the TV, which they are watching, stands a small Arab boy (TERRY G). *He has electrodes fixed to him and wires stretching from a control box held by Mrs Elizabeth III. They are watching the tramps.*

MRS MOCK TUDOR (GRAHAM) Bloody repeats!

She presses the switch. The Arab boy flinches with pain and turns and switches off the TV set.

MRS ELIZABETH III (TERRY J) Yes, repeats or war films. It really makes you want to micturate. 

15 Micturate is the act of urination.

MRS MOCK TUDOR People on television treat the general public like idiots.
MRS ELIZABETH III Well we *are* idiots.
MRS MOCK TUDOR Oh no we are *not*!
MRS ELIZABETH III Well *I* am.
MRS MOCK TUDOR How do you know you're an idiot?
MRS ELIZABETH III Oh, I can show you!
MRS MOCK TUDOR How?
MRS ELIZABETH III Look!

Cut to Mrs Elizabeth III coming out of the front door in a fairly well-to-do mock Tudor detached house in its own grounds. She runs headlong into a tree opposite the front door. Repeat a few times. Then she rushes into a field, digs a hole three feet deep and stands in it. Cut to her standing beside a letter box. She straps on a long false nose and bends down and pokes it through the letter box. She drinks a delicate cup of tea at a posh café and eats the whole cup. Cut to her nailing something to a lorry. The lorry starts off to reveal that she had been nailing herself to the lorry. She is dragged away.

Cut to TV planners at a window, watching Mrs Elizabeth III doing silly things in a car park below them. She has a cream bun hanging down from a long stick which comes out of her hat. She walks along strangely.

CHIEF EXECUTIVE (TERRY J) You see the public *are* idiots...*(he has a conference tag on his lapel which reads 'Chief TV Planner'; he turns from the window to a conference table, piled with drinks)* Yes... you might just as well show them the last five miles of the M2... 16 they'd watch it, eh?

Cut back to Mrs Mock Tudor and Mrs Elizabeth III watching TV. There is film of the motorway on it, filmed from the bank beside a bridge.

MRS MOCK TUDOR At last they done been put on something interesting.
MRS ELIZABETH III Oh, most interesting.

Cut back to the programme planners' conference.

FIRST PLANNER (ERIC) *(reading figures)* ...and our figures show conclusively that the motorways are extremely popular. I mean, last time we showed a repeat of the Leicester bypass our ratings gave us 97,300,912, and ITV nought. So I do feel we ought to give B roads their own series.
CHIEF EXECUTIVE I'm sorry...we just can't give you a bigger budget.
SECOND PLANNER (MICHAEL) Budgie?
FIRST PLANNER *(to the second planner)* No, he's left I think. *(to the senior executive)* Why not?
CHIEF EXECUTIVE We're only one slice of the cake, you know.
THIRD PLANNER (GRAHAM) Wouldn't mind a slice of cake. Nice, chocolate cake...delicious...
SECOND PLANNER I had a budgie once you know, amusing little chap, used to stick his head in a bell...what was his name, now...Joey?...Xerxes?... 17
FIRST PLANNER We could repeat them...
THIRD PLANNER Re-heat them?
FIRST PLANNER No, repeat them...
THIRD PLANNER You don't *re-heat* cakes. Not chocolate cakes.
CHIEF EXECUTIVE What, repeat the cakes?
SECOND PLANNER Mr Heath, that was the name of the budgie.
CHIEF EXECUTIVE *(looking at his watch)* Good Lord, the bar's open! *(they all scramble madly to their feet)* Oh no it isn't, I was looking at the little hand that goes round very fast...
ALL Damn. Blast.

They sit down again reluctantly. There is a short pause.

FIRST PLANNER I've got it. We can retitle the repeats.
SECOND PLANNER What...give them different names?

The M2 is a short motorway in Kent, southeast of London—it's not even 26 miles long.

Xerxes, king of Persia from 486 to 465 B.C.

Dad's Army was a BBC sitcom about a band of Home Guards—men too sick, too old, or too stupid to go into the regular army—during World War II. Hugely popular, it ran from 1968 to 1977.

Up Pompeii was a popular BBC comedy that aired from 1969 to 1970, starring the legendary Frankie Howerd playing a slave. It became a feature film in 1971.

Compare to *Doctor at Large* and its follow-up, *Doctor in Charge*, British TV comedies from the early 1970s.

I Love Lucy, the legendary 1950s comedy starring Lucille Ball and Desi Arnaz.

CHIEF EXECUTIVE Wouldn't that mean retitling them?
THIRD PLANNER Brilliant!
CHIEF EXECUTIVE Right—all we need is new titles. And they must be damned new!
SECOND PLANNER How about 'Dad's Navy'? 18
CHIEF EXECUTIVE Mm, good, good.
FIRST PLANNER 'Up Your Mother Next Door.' 19
CHIEF EXECUTIVE Even better...
THIRD PLANNER 'Doctor at Bee'! 20
ALL What?

There is a knock at the door.

FIRST PLANNER Someone's knocking at the door.

CHIEF EXECUTIVE Quite like it—bit long, though, I think.
THIRD PLANNER Far too long.
SECOND PLANNER 'I Married Lucy.' 21
CHIEF EXECUTIVE Hasn't that been done?
SECOND PLANNER Oh, yes, a long time ago, though, they'd never remember it.
THIRD PLANNER 'Doctor at Three'!
CHIEF EXECUTIVE What?

There is a knock at the door.

FIRST PLANNER I think someone's knocking at the door.
CHIEF EXECUTIVE That's even longer!
SECOND PLANNER 'I Married A Tree.'
CHIEF EXECUTIVE 'And Mother Makes Tree.'
THIRD PLANNER 'Doctor At Cake'!

Continuous knocking on the door.

FIRST PLANNER Look! I'm not absolutely certain, but, well I do *rather* get the impression that there is someone actually knocking at the door at this very moment.
CHIEF EXECUTIVE That's ridiculous. Half the programme gone. Stop lengthening it!
THIRD PLANNER *(desperate)* 'I Married A Cake'?
SECOND PLANNER *(over excited)*

'I MARRIED THREE RABBIT JELLY MOULDS'!

THIRD PLANNER Prefer cake...specially chocky cake...

There is by now a constant hammering.

VOICE *(yells from outside door)* Open the sodding door! 22
CHIEF EXECUTIVE No, no. You can't say 'sodding' on the television.

"Sodding" is less offensive than the "F-word."

All shake their heads. The door is broken in. Enter a neo-fascist-looking security man in a wheelchair with an oriental sword through his head.

CHIEF EXECUTIVE You're supposed to *knock*!
SECURITY MAN (TERRY G) Sorry, sir, but there's trouble at studio five!
SECOND PLANNER You're in security, aren't you?
SECURITY MAN Yes, sir.

SECOND PLANNER *(triumphantly)* Well, you're not allowed to suggest programme titles. *(he smiles victoriously at others)*
SECURITY MAN Sir! It's the World War series in studio five—they're not taking it seriously any more.
FIRST PLANNER You're not allowed to suggest programme titles!
SECURITY MAN *(switching on a TV set)* Look!

They rush to the monitor. One of them brushes the oriental sword which is through his head.

SECURITY MAN Ow! Mind me war wound!
ALL That's it! Very good title!

On the screen we see the court martial in progress as we saw it earlier in the show, with the whole court singing.

EVERYONE Anything goes in. Anything goes out!
Fish, bananas, old pyjamas,
Mutton, beef and trout!
Anything goes in. Anything goes out! *(etc.)*

Animation: 'What a lovely day'.

Exterior, a large, tasteful, Georgian rich person's house with extensive gardens beautifully tended, croquet hoops on the lawn—all in superb taste, nothing vulgar. The sun shines tastefully. The atmosphere is calm. Birds sing. Sound of lawnmowers and cricket in the distance. Laughter from the tennis court. Sound of gardener sharpening spades in the potting shed. Out of vision, a Red Indian struggles to free himself from the rope bonds that bind him. We hear 'Where does a dream begin' being played on a cracked record. Caption:

'1942
~~EGYPT~~
~~ECUADOR~~
~~ETHIOPIA~~
ENGLAND'

The caption fades and we cut to an upper-class drawing room. Father, mother and daughter having tea. Four motionless servants stand behind them.

FATHER (GRAHAM) I say...
DAUGHTER (CAROL) Yes, daddy?
FATHER Croquet hoops look damn pretty this afternoon.
DAUGHTER Frightfully damn pretty.
MOTHER (ERIC) They're coming along awfully well this year.
FATHER Yes, better than your Aunt Lavinia's croquet hoops.
DAUGHTER Ugh!—dreadful tin things.
MOTHER I did tell her to stick to wood.
FATHER Yes, you can't beat wood...Gorn!
MOTHER What's gorn dear?
FATHER Nothing, nothing, I just like the word. It gives me confidence. Gorn...gorn. It's got a sort of woody quality about it. Gorn. Gorn. Much better than 'newspaper' or 'litterbin'.
DAUGHTER Frightful words.
MOTHER Perfectly dreadful.
FATHER

UGH! NEWSPAPER!...LITTERBIN... DREADFUL TINNY SORT OF WORDS. TIN, TIN, TIN.

The daughter bursts into tears.

MOTHER Oh, dear, don't say 'tin' to Rebecca, you know how it upsets her.
FATHER *(to the daughter)* Sorry old horse.
MOTHER Sausage!
FATHER Sausage...there's a good woody sort of word, 'sausage'...gorn.
DAUGHTER Antelope.
FATHER Where? On the lawn? *(he picks up a rifle)*
DAUGHTER No, no, daddy...just the word.
FATHER Don't want an antelope nibbling the hoops.
DAUGHTER No, antelope...sort of nice and woody type of thing.
MOTHER Don't think so, Becky old chap.
FATHER No, no 'antelope', 'antelope'—tinny sort of word *(the daughter bursts into tears)* Oh! Sorry old man...
MOTHER Really, Mansfield.
FATHER Well, she's got to come to terms with these things...seemly...prodding...vacuum...leap...
DAUGHTER *(miserably)* Hate leap.
MOTHER Perfectly dreadful.
DAUGHTER Sort of PVC-y sort of word, don't you know.

MOTHER Lower-middle.
FATHER Bound!
MOTHER Now you're talking.
FATHER Bound...Vole...Recidivist.
MOTHER Bit tinny. *(the daughter howls)* Oh! Sorry, Becky old beast. *(the daughter runs out crying)*
FATHER Oh dear, suppose she'll be gorn for a few days now.
MOTHER Caribou!
FATHER Splendid word.
MOTHER No dear...nibbling the hoops.
FATHER *(he fires a shot)* Caribou gorn.
MOTHER *(laughs politely)*
FATHER Intercourse.
MOTHER Later, dear.
FATHER No, no, the word, 'intercourse'—good and woody...inter...course...pert...pert thighs... botty, botty botty...*(the mother leaves the room)*...erogenous...zone...concubine...erogenous zone! Loose woman...erogenous zone...*(the mother returns and throws a bucket of water over him)* Oh thank you, dear...you know, it's a funny thing, dear...all the naughty words sound woody.

MOTHER Really, dear?...How about tit?
FATHER Oh dear, I hadn't thought about that. Tit. Tit. Oh, that's very tinny isn't it? *(the daughter returns)* Ugh! Tinny, tinny...*(the daughter runs out crying)* Oh dear...ocelot...wasp...yowling... Oh dear, I'm bored...I'd better go and have a bath, I suppose.
MOTHER Oh really, must you dear? You've had nine today.
FATHER All right, I'll sack one of the servants...Simkins!...nasty tinny sort of name. Simkins! *(he exits)*

A pilot from the RAF banter scene enters.

PILOT (MICHAEL) I say, mater, **23** *(cabbage crates coming over the briny.)*
MOTHER *(frowns and shakes her head)* Sorry dear, don't understand.
PILOT Er...cowcatchers creeping up on the conning towers...
MOTHER No...sorry...old sport.
PILOT Caribou nibbling at the croquet hoops.
MOTHER Yes, Mansfield shot one in the antlers.
PILOT Oh, jolly good show. Is 'Becca about?
MOTHER No, she's gorn off.
PILOT What a super woody sort of phrase. 'Gorn orff'. **24**

"Mater" is an upper-class word for "mother."

"Gorn orff" is to run away, or disappear.

MOTHER Yes, she's gorn orff because Mansfield said tin to her.
PILOT Oh, what rotten luck...oh well...whole afternoon to kill...better have a bath I suppose.
MOTHER Oh, Gervaise do sing me a song...
PILOT Oh, OK.
MOTHER Something woody.

The pilot launches into a quite enormously loud rendering of 'She's going to marry Yum Yum'. 25 *The impact of this on the mother causes her to have a heart attack. She dies and the song ends.*

PILOT

FOR...SHE'S GOING TO MARRY YUM YUM...OH CRIKEY. THE OLD SONG FINISHED HER ORFF.

FATHER *(entering)* What's urp?
PILOT I'm afraid Mrs Vermin Jones appears to have passed orn.
FATHER Dead, is she?
PILOT 'Fraid so.
FATHER What a blow for her.

Cut to the scene on a TV screen and pull out from the TV to Mrs Mock Tudor and Mrs Elizabeth III in their sitting room watching it.

MRS MOCK TUDOR What I want to know Mrs Elizabeth III, is why they gives us crap like that, when there's bits of the Leicester by-pass what have never been shown. Biskwit?
MRS ELIZABETH III *(takes biskwit from plate)* Oh, thank yew...

Mrs Mock Tudor switches her TV switch. The Arab boy winces in great pain and moves over to the set. He changes channels. Up comes a picture of the motorway again. Roller caption superimposed over the motorway. Appropriate 'Crossroads' type theme music. 26

VOICE OVER (ERIC) *(reading the roller caption)* Appearing on the M2 were 4,281 Vauxhall Vivas, 2,117 Vauxhall Vivas de luxe, 153 Vauxhall Vivas with... 27

Mrs Elizabeth III throws the switch and the Arab boy winces with real pain and turns the knob of the television set which changes channels. On the TV set we see the same two ladies watching their set as before with the tramps on it. They continue watching until the two ladies on the set speak.

From the finale of Act I of the Gilbert and Sullivan opera *The Mikado*, the song is actually called "For He's Going to Marry Yum-Yum."

Crossroads is the execrable Midlands-based potboiler soap opera about a motel near Birmingham. It ran for hundreds of years, or so it seemed (actually, 1964 to 1988).

Vauxhall Vivas were affordable small cars made in the 1960s and '70s.

MRS MOCK TUDOR *(on the TV set)* Bloody repeats.
MRS MOCK TUDOR *(not on the TV set)* Bloody repeats.

As before she switches switch. The Arab boy winces in pain and changes channels.

MRS ELIZABETH III *(on the TV set)* Yes, repeats or war films...makes you want to...

She throws the switch. The Arab boy winces in pain and turns over. The White City as for show-jumping. 28 *Close up of a mounted female rider waiting to start. Voice over of Dorian Williams.* 29

DORIAN (ERIC) Hello and welcome to Show-Jumping from White City...
MRS MOCK TUDOR Oh, moto-cross!
DORIAN ...and it's Anneli Drummond-Hay on Mr Softee just about to go into jump-off against the clock. The slight pause is for the stewards who are repairing the Sound of Music. *(cut to shot of stewards who are organizing eight nuns, Von Trapp in Tyrolean gear, Julie Andrews, and the six Von Trapp children into a group forming a fence; cut back to Anneli)...* Captain Phillips on 'Streuth' just caught one of the nuns at the very start of what would have been a fine clear round. It's a formidable obstacle this Sound of Music—eight nuns high but they're ready now, and singing. *(the group start singing 'The Hills are Alive'; the bell goes for the start of the round and the lady rider sets off towards the group)* And there's the bell. She's got 1.07 seconds to beat, but she needs a clear round to win. As she comes towards the Sound of Music and...

Cut away to the two ladies watching their TV. Shot from an angle so we can't see the screen.

MRS ELIZABETH III Quite exciting.

Cut back to White City to see the lady rider has just cleared the obstacle. A cheer from the crowd. The music changes to 'Oklahoma'. Follow her round to see a similar group dressed as for 'Oklahoma'. Ten hayseeds and six wenches with a hay wagon. Most have primitive pitch forks and are sucking on straws.

DORIAN ...beautifully taken, and now she needs to pick up speed for Oklahoma, but not too much. This is where Alan Jones 30 knocked down poor Judd, 31 but...And...she's taken it superbly!
MRS MOCK TUDOR You notice how we never actually see the horses jump.

Cheer from TV. Cut back to White City. The horse is coming away from Oklahoma. Cut to run up to Black and White Minstrels. 32

MRS MOCK TUDOR Wait for it...

The White City was a stadium built in Hammersmith, near the BBC, for the 1908 Olympics. It was later used for greyhound racing and motor speedway, then demolished in 1985.

Dorian Williams, the horse-jumping commentator of the day par excellence.

Alan Jones, the U.K. race-car driver.

Jud Fry, the sinister farmhand from the musical *Oklahoma!*

The Black and White Minstrel Show ran for twenty years on the BBC, from 1958 to 1978. It was filled with minstrelsy and lots of blackface, and featured song-and-dance routines. Horrific.

Leslie Crowther, the British comedian and game-show host. His career would come to a premature end after he flipped his Rolls-Royce on a freeway. Subsequent blood clots on his brain ended his TV presence.

Ben-Hur, the 1959 epic movie starring Charlton Heston and a cast of millions.

Peter Woods was a British journalist and newscaster.

"When Does A Dream Begin," an original song by Neil Innes.

Cut back to White City.

DORIAN And! She's taken it...*(cheer; we actually see the lady jumper jump over the chorus of minstrels)* She's over the Minstrels. She just flicked Leslie Crowther **33** with her tail, but the time's good, and now she turns before coming into the final jump...this is a tough one...It's Ben-Hur— **34** forty-six chariots...6,000 spectators...400 slaves, lion-handlers, the Emperor Nero and the entire Coliseum. 198 feet high. 400 years across!

The lady jumper is now coming right towards the camera. Cut back to the ladies watching.

MRS MOCK TUDOR I bet we don't see this one.

Cut back to horse actually jumping towards the camera. Cut to news reader Peter Woods in a news studio.

PETER WOODS **35** We interrupt show jumping to bring you a news flash. The Second World War has now entered a sentimental stage. This morning on the Ardennes Front, the Germans started spooning at dawn, but the British Fifth Army responded by gazing deep in their eyes, and the Germans are reported to have gone 'all coy'.

Music comes in underneath: 'When does a dream begin'. Mix to a young airman on an airfield gazing into a WAAF's eyes. Black and white, soft focus and scratched film to look like a not very good print of a 40s film. Airman sings.

AIRMAN (NEIL INNES) When does a dream begin? **36**
Does it start with a goodnight kiss?
Is it conceived or simply achieved
When does a dream begin?
Is it born in a moment of bliss?
Or is it begun when two hearts are one
When does a dream exist?
The vision of you appears somehow
Impossible to resist
But I'm not imagining seeing you
For who could have dreamed of this?
When does a dream begin?
When reality is dismissed?
Or does it commence when we lose all pretence
When does a dream begin?

Mix sound to end of signature tune. Halfway through the song the credits roll, superimposed. They read:

MONTY PYTHON (SOCIAL CLASS 9)
WAS PERFORMED BY
GRAHAM CHAPMEN
TERRY GILLIAM
ERIC IDLE
TERRY JONES
MICHAEL PALIN (SOCIAL CLASS 2, ARSENAL 0)
CONCEIVED AND WRITTEN BY
GRAHAM CHAPMAN
JOHN CLEESE
TERRY GILLIAM
ERIC IDLE
NEIL INNES
TERRY JONES
MICHAEL PALIN (SOCIAL CLASS DERRY AND TOMS)
ALSO APPEARING
CAROL CLEVELAND
BOB R. RAYMOND
MARION MOULD (SOCIAL CLASS 47 ACTORS)
'WHEN DOES A DREAM BEGIN' BY NEIL INNES (SOCIAL CLASS 137 MUSICIANS)
VARIATIONS ON THE THEME BY BILL MCGUFFIE
(SOCIAL CLASS 137A OTHER MUSICIANS)
MAKE-UP MAGGIE WESTON (SOCIAL CLASS 5 TILL MIDNIGHT)
COSTUMES ANDREW ROSE (SOCIAL CLASS 35 28 34)
FILM CAMERAMAN STAN SPEEL (SOCIAL CLASS F8 AT 25TH SEC.)
SOUND RECORDIST RON BLIGHT (SOCIAL CLASS UNRECORDABLE)
FILM EDITOR BOB DEARBERG (SOCIAL LASS LOWER 6TH) (MR POTTER'S)
SOUND MIKE JONES (SOCIAL CLASS SLIGHTLY ABOVE THE QUEEN)
LIGHTING JIMMY PURDUE (SOCIAL CLASS A BOTTLE OF BELL'S)
VISUAL EFFECTS JOHN HORTON (SOCIAL CLASS ANT)
PRODUCTION ASSISTANT BRIAN JONES (SOCIAL BUT NO CLASS)
DESIGNER ROBERT BERK (NO SOCIAL CLASS AT ALL)
PRODUCED BY IAN MACNAUGHTON (SOCIAL CLASS 238-470 SCOTSMAN)
BBC COLOUR (BY PERMISSION OF SIR. K. JOSEPH 37)

Sir Keith Joseph was a British Conservative politician. He was one of the prime movers behind post-1979 "Thatcherism" and served as secretary of state for social services in the recently deposed Heath government.

SEA
SON
4
EPISODE 43
NW

HAMLET
FEATURING
BOGUS PSYCHIATRISTS ✽ 'NATIONWIDE'
POLICE HELMETS ✽ FATHER-IN-LAW
Hamlet and Ophelia
BOXING MATCH AFTERMATH
BOXING COMMENTARY
PISTON ENGINE (A BARGAIN)
A ROOM IN POLONIUS'S HOUSE ✽ DENTISTS
LIVE FROM EPSOM
QUEEN VICTORIA HANDICAP

FIRST AIRED: NOVEMBER 21, 1974

Tragic music in background. Caption: 'HAMLET' Caption: 'BY WILLIAM SHAKESPEARE' Caption: 'ACT ONE' Quick cut to a close shot of a big American car skidding round a comer. Music. Montage of close ups of tyres, foot on accelerator shots, etc. with a deafening sound track. The car skids to a halt at the side of the kerb. Pull out to reveal it is in a smart Harley Street type location. The door opens and out gets a man in black leotard, with make-up and a small crown—Hamlet, in fact. He goes into a doorway, presses the doorbell and waits. Cut to modern psychiatrist's office. Hamlet is lying on the couch.

HAMLET (TERRY J) It's just that everywhere I go it's the same old thing. All anyone wants me to say is 'To be or not to be...'

PSYCHIATRIST (GRAHAM) '...that is the question. Whether 'tis nobler in the mind to suffer the slings and arrows of outrageous...'

HAMLET *(quickly)* Yes, it's either that, or 'Oh that this too too solid flesh would melt...'

PSYCHIATRIST *(taking over)* '...would melt, thaw and resolve itself into a dew. Or that the everlasting had not fixed his canon 'gainst self slaughter...'

HAMLET Yes. All that sort of thing. And I'm just getting really fed up.

PSYCHIATRIST *(picking up a skull)* Now do the bit about 'Alas poor Yorick...'

HAMLET No. I'm sick of it! I want to do something else. I want to make something of my life.

PSYCHIATRIST No. I don't know that bit.

HAMLET I want to get away from all that. Be different.

PSYCHIATRIST Well um...what do you want to be?

HAMLET A private dick! [1]

Slang for a private investigator.

PSYCHIATRIST A private dick?

HAMLET Yes, a private dick!

PSYCHIATRIST Why do you want to be a private dick?

HAMLET Ooh...why does anyone want to be a private dick? Fame, money, glamour, excitement, sex!

PSYCHIATRIST Ah! It's the sex, is it?

HAMLET Well, that's one of the things, yes.

PSYCHIATRIST Yes, what's the sex problem?

HAMLET Well, there's no problem.

PSYCHIATRIST

NOW, COME ON, COME ON. YOU'VE GOT THE GIRL ON THE BED AND SHE'S ALL READY FOR IT.

HAMLET No, no, it's nothing to do with that.

PSYCHIATRIST *(getting excited)* Now come on, come on, there she is, she's all ready for it. She's a real stunner, she's got great big tits, she's really well stacked and you've got her legs up against the mantelpiece.

DR NATAL (ERIC) All right, Mr Butler, I'll take over. *(a distinguished-looking man in a suit enters; the psychiatrist leaves)* Morning, Mr Hamlet. My name's Natal. Sorry to keep you waiting. Now what seems to be the problem.

HAMLET Well, I was telling the other psychiatrist...
DR NATAL He's...he's *not* a psychiatrist.
HAMLET Oh. He said he was a psychiatrist.
DR NATAL Well...yes...um, he's a *kind* of psychiatrist but he's...he's not a *proper* psychiatrist. He's not er...fully qualified...in, um, quite the sort of way we should want. Anyway the problem I believe is basically sexual is it?

The psychiatrist puts his head round door.

PSYCHIATRIST I asked him that!
DR NATAL Get out! *(the psychiatrist goes; to Hamlet)* Now then, you've got the girl on the bed. You've been having a bit of a feel up during the evening. You've got your tongue down her throat. She's got both her legs up on the mantelpiece...

Enter a distinguished-looking psychiatrist in a white coat.

THIRD PSYCHIATRIST (MICHAEL) *(quietly and authoritatively, indicating the door)* Dr Natal...out please!

DR NATAL I'm talking to a patient! Oh...*(he goes)*
THIRD PSYCHIATRIST Out please! I'm terribly sorry, sir. We have a lot of problems here with bogus psychiatrists. One of the risks in psychiatry I'm afraid. Unfortunately they do tend to frighten the patient and they can cause real and permanent damage to the treatment. But I assure you that I am a completely bona fide psychiatrist. Here's my diploma in psychiatry from the University of Oxford. This here shows that I'm a member of the British Psychiatric Association, a very important body indeed. Here's a letter from another psychiatrist in which he mentions that I'm a psychiatrist. This is my psychiatric club tie, and as you can see the cufflinks match. I've got a copy of 'Psychiatry Today' in my bag, which I think is pretty convincing. And a letter here from my mother in which she asks how the psychiatry is going, and I think you'll realize that the one person you can't fool is your mother. So if you'd like to ask me any questions about psychiatry, I bet I can answer them.
HAMLET No, no, it's all right, really.
THIRD PSYCHIATRIST OK, you've got this girl on your bed, you've had a few drinks, you've got her stretched out and her feet on the mantelpiece...*(the intercom buzzes)* yes, what is it?
INTERCOM VOICE

THERE'S A PROPER PSYCHIATRIST TO SEE YOU, DR RUFUS BERG.

THIRD PSYCHIATRIST Oh, oh my God! OK, thank you. *(he hurriedly changes into a police constable's uniform)* Right, thank you very much for answering the questions, sir. We'll try not to trouble you again, sir. *(exits hurriedly)*

A fourth psychiatrist rushes in.

FOURTH PSYCHIATRIST (TERRY G) Right you've got the girl down on the bed, you've got her legs up on the mantelpiece.

Two men in white coats bundle him out. Dr Natal enters.

DR NATAL Well, well done, Mr Hamlet. You've done extremely well in our disorientation tests.
HAMLET Oh? Oh!
DR NATAL You see, I'm sorry it might have confused you a little, but we do this to try to establish a very good doctor/patient relationship, you see...we do it to sort of, as it were, to break down the barriers. All right?
HAMLET Yes fine.
DR NATAL

GOOD! WELL, YOU'VE GOT HER LEGS UP ON THE MANTELPIECE...

The two men come in and chase him out. Cut to a man at a consultant's desk in a smart West End surgery. Caption: 'DR BRUCE GENUINE, CHAIRMAN OF THE PSYCHIATRIC ASSOCIATION'

DR BRUCE (TERRY J) On behalf of the Psychiatric Association, I should like to say that we are taking firm action to clamp down on the activities of bogus psychiatrists. In fact in many areas of modern psychiatry computers are now being increasingly used for the first basic diagnosis and this has gone a long way in eliminating the danger of unqualified impostors.

Cut to Hamlet in an office. A big, impressive-looking computer beside him.

COMPUTER *(in tinny computer voice)* You've had your tongue down her throat and she's got her legs on the mantelpiece.

The door opens and a nurse appears.

NURSE (CAROL) Out!

The computer scuttles for the door, revealing that underneath it are six pairs of legs, in pin-striped trousers and expensive well-shaped shoes. Cut to the same computer in a field. The nurse picks up a bazooka. The computer rises into the air, the nurse fires at it and it explodes. 'Nationwide' type music and credits. Michael Charlton in a studio. 2

Nationwide, a BBC news and current-affairs show previously name-checked on Python. It was a staple of early evening programming filled with fairly light fare.

Michael Charlton was a BBC TV presenter, though not on *Nationwide*.

CHARLTON (ERIC) Good evening and welcome to 'Nationwide'. The programme where we do rather wet things nationally and also give you the chance to see some rather wet items in the Regions. Well, everyone is talking today about the Third World War which broke out this morning. But here on 'Nationwide' we're going to get away from that a bit and look instead at the latest theory that sitting down regularly in a comfortable chair can rest your legs. It sounds very nice doesn't it, but can it be done? Is it possible or practical for many of us in our jobs and with the sort of busy lives we lead to sit down in a comfortable chair just when we want? We sent our reporter John Dull to find out.

Cut to Dull sitting in a chair on Westminster Bridge.

REPORTER (GRAHAM) Well, here I am on London's busy Westminster Bridge, seeing just how much time sitting down can take. Well, I arrived here by train at about 8.50, it's now 9.05, so I've been here approximately twelve minutes and if it's any encouragement, I must say that my legs *do* feel rested.

A policeman walks up to him.

POLICEMAN (MICHAEL) Is this your chair?
REPORTER Er...well no, it's a prop.
POLICEMAN It's been stolen!
REPORTER What?
POLICEMAN This belongs to a Mrs Edgeworth of Pinner—she's standing over there.

Cut to worried middle-aged lady, standing on the other side of the road, peering across. She has an identical chair in one hand.

REPORTER

GOOD! AH WELL, IT'S NOTHING TO DO WITH ME. IT'S JUST A PROP WHICH THE BBC...AAARGH!

The policeman pushes the reporter off and picks up the chair.

POLICEMAN It's got her name on the bottom. *(he indicates: Mrs E. Edgeworth)*
REPORTER Well er...perhaps you'd better give it back to her.
POLICEMAN You don't believe I'm a policeman, do you?
REPORTER Yes I do!
POLICEMAN What am I wearing on my head?
REPORTER A helmet.
POLICEMAN *(correcting him)* A policeman's helmet!
REPORTER Yes.
POLICEMAN *(taking off his helmet and demonstrating)* You see that?
REPORTER Yes.
POLICEMAN That little number there?
REPORTER Yes.
POLICEMAN That is a Metropolitan Area Identification Code. No helmet is authentic without that number.
REPORTER I see.
POLICEMAN Kids' helmets, helmets you get in toy shops, helmets you buy at Christmas. None of them has that number. None of them is authentic...Hang on. *(he turns and crosses the busy road)*

REPORTER Oh could I...
POLICEMAN Hang on!

He goes across to Mrs Edgeworth, and tries to grab the other chair from her. Mrs Edgeworth resists. He clouts her and pulls the chair away. He brings it back across the road and sits down next to reporter.

POLICEMAN Mind you I didn't join the police force just to wear the helmet you know. That just happens to be one of the little perks. There are plenty of jobs where I could have worn a helmet, but not such a *nice* helmet. *(Mrs Edgeworth is gesticulating; another policeman comes up and drags her away)* This helmet, I think, beats even some of the more elaborate helmets worn by the Tsar's private army, the so-called Axi red warriors. You know about them?
REPORTER Well, no I don't.
POLICEMAN Ah! Their helmets used to look like...you got any paper?
REPORTER Well only these scripts.

3

Lots of bystanders here. (There is this kind of cute moment when we see two young boys and they walk by the sketch a minute or so later.)

The policeman gets up, looks up the street, and selects a businessman with a briefcase, who is hurrying away from him. The policeman runs up to him, grabs his arm, twists it up behind his back and wrenches the briefcase from his hand. He opens it, gets out some paper, then drops briefcase before the amazed owner, and ambles back to his chair, neatly grabbing a pen from a passer-by's inside pocket. 3

POLICEMAN I'll have that!
MAN I say!

The policeman sits down again and starts to draw, talking the while.

POLICEMAN Now then. Their helmet was not unlike the bobby's helmet in basic shape. It had an emblem here, and three gold—and in those days it really was gold, that's part of the reason the Tsar was so unpopular—three gold bands surmounted by a golden eagle on the apex here. Pretty nice helmet, eh?
REPORTER Yes.
POLICEMAN I think the domed helmet wins every time over the flattened job, you know, even when they're three cornered...*(suddenly his eyes light on two office secretaries opening their packed lunch on a nearby seat)*...you want something to eat?
REPORTER *(sensing what's going to happen, hurriedly)* Well no, er really...
POLICEMAN *(approaching the girls and getting out his notebook)* Hang on. You can't park here you know.
WOMEN *(bewildered)* We're not parked!
POLICEMAN Not parked! What's that then?
WOMEN That's our lunch.
POLICEMAN Right. I'm taking that in for a forensic examination.
WOMEN Why?

POLICEMAN Because it might have been used as a murder weapon, that's why! *(the girls look at each other; the policeman grabs their lunch)* Yeah, not bad. Could be worse. *(to the reporter)* Beer?

REPORTER *(desperately)* No, no, please...honestly...please...

The policeman walks off. There is a crash of breaking glass. An alarm bell starts to ring. The reporter winces. The policeman walks into shot again, holding two bottles of beer. He sits down, opens the beers with his teeth and hands one to reporter who is very very embarrassed.

POLICEMAN Now, the Chaldeans, 4 who used to inhabit the area in between the Tigris and Euphrates rivers, their helmets were of the modular restrained kind of type...

4 The Chaldeans were a people of ancient Mesopotamia.

To lyrical music the camera pans across the road, and comes across a couple making love on the pavement. Pedestrians step over them.

CAROL Oh Robert, tell me I'm beautiful.

ROBERT (TERRY J) Oh you are, you are!

CAROL Oh Robert, do you mean that?

ROBERT Of course I do.

CAROL You're not just saying that because I asked you to?

ROBERT Of course not.

CAROL Oh Robert...Robert, are you sure it doesn't put you off?

ROBERT What?

CAROL My father wanting to come and live with us.

ROBERT No, of course I don't mind your father coming to live with us.

CAROL He wouldn't just be *living* with us.

ROBERT What do you mean?

CAROL Well, he finds it very difficult to get to sleep on his own, so I said he could sleep with us.

WELL, HE FINDS IT VERY DIFFICULT TO GET TO SLEEP ON HIS OWN, SO I SAID HE COULD SLEEP WITH US.

ROBERT He wants to put his bed in our room?

CAROL No, no, of course not.

ROBERT Oh good...

CAROL Our bed is plenty big enough for three...

ROBERT What?

CAROL He'd just get into bed and go to sleep.

ROBERT No. I'm not having that!

CAROL Oh Robert, I thought you loved me?

ROBERT Well I do, but...

CAROL Well, he wouldn't look.

ROBERT He's bound to peek.

CAROL No, no, he wouldn't honestly.

ROBERT No! No! No!!

Cut to the three of them in bed. Robert is in the middle. Father wears striped pyjamas, the others are nude. There is an uncomfortable silence.

FATHER (GRAHAM) You young couple just carry on. Take no notice of me...*(silence; they smile half-heartedly)* I don't want to feel as though I'm getting in the way.

CAROL Oh no dad, you're not.
ROBERT No, no.
FATHER Good.

Silence again.

CAROL Well, I think I'll get to sleep.
FATHER Are you sure?
CAROL Oh yes, I'm a bit tired after the wedding.
FATHER Bob, what about you?
ROBERT Oh yes, all right, yes.
FATHER Oh well, I seem to be O/C lights.
CAROL *(to Robert)* Good night, darling.
ROBERT Good night.
FATHER Good night!

He switches the light off. It is pitch dark. There is a long pause, then a strange scraping noise like a pencil being sharpened. The scraping is followed by sawing and is eventually replaced by short sharp knocking sounds. This goes on for some time.

CAROL'S VOICE Father. Father, what are you doing?
FATHER'S VOICE I'm making a boat.
CAROL'S VOICE What?
FATHER'S VOICE It's a Cutty Sark. [5] It's a model I've been making in the dark for some years now.
CAROL'S VOICE Well, wouldn't it be better with the light on?
FATHER'S VOICE No, no, I'm making it in the dark, that's the point.

5

The *Cutty Sark* is a three-masted and very fast ship built in 1869. Formerly a merchant vessel, it is now on display in Greenwich, London.

There is a click. The light goes on. He looks disappointed. In his hands is a completely shapeless mass of wood and nails.

FATHER Oh dear, not as accurate as I thought.
ROBERT It's not the Cutty Sark!
FATHER Well it hasn't got its sails on yet. Oh well I'll...I'll have a look at it in the dark room in the morning. Good night. *(grunts from the others who are already snuggling down; lights go off; silence)*

Animated opening titles.

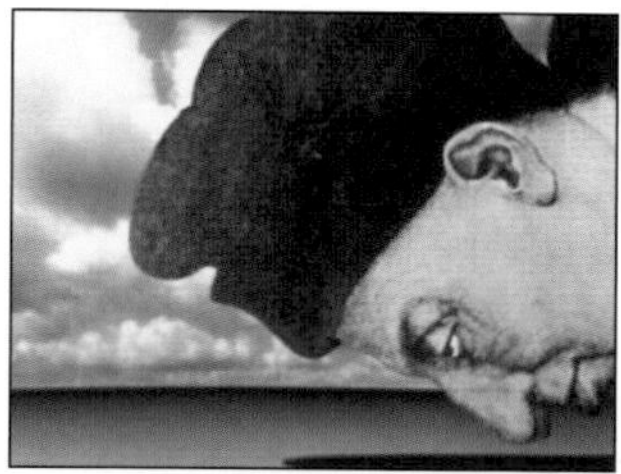

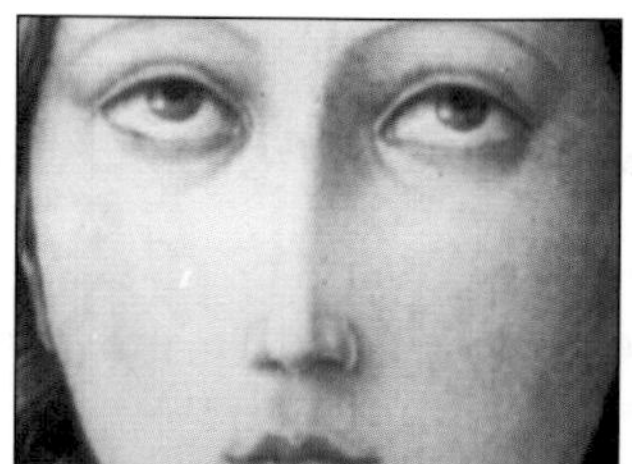

Banging on the wall from next door.

MAN (TERRY G) Shut up! Will you shut up in there!

Cut to a middle-aged man with small moustache and neat pyjamas banging on the wall with what appears to be an Indian club.

MAN Shut up! *(it goes quiet next door)* That's better.

He walks to a side wall and hangs his club on a hook beneath big old-fashioned art-nouveau sign clearly labelled 'The Burlington Wall-banger'. He goes across to bed and gets in. In the bed are a party of four Japanese businessmen in suits with lapel badges, two lady American tourists with rain hats on and cellophane over their hats and cameras, three other moustached English gentlemen in pyjamas, four Tour De France riders, three Swedish businessmen, and Winston Churchill. In the corner of the room are three Tour De France bicycles. All the people are watching TV. All in the bed are slightly tearstained and sad, and eating popcorn and crisps, utterly absorbed. On TV we hear a Hamlet sad speech.

HAMLET I am myself indifferent honest, but then I could accuse me of such things that it were better my mother had not borne me.

Cut to the TV set in the room. Close in on TV set to see Hamlet lying beside Ophelia, who is gazing at him intently. It is the same Hamlet we saw in the psychiatrist's scene. They are in one of those rather austere modern theatre sets.

HAMLET O fair Ophelia, nymph, in thy orisons, be all my sins remembered...
OPHELIA (connie) So anyway, you've got the girl on the bed and her legs are on the mantelpiece...

The nurse from the psychiatrist's office enters.

NURSE Out! *(bundles her off)*

Animation: ends with a poster 'Boxing Tonite! The Killer vs. The Champ. 15 Rounds'.

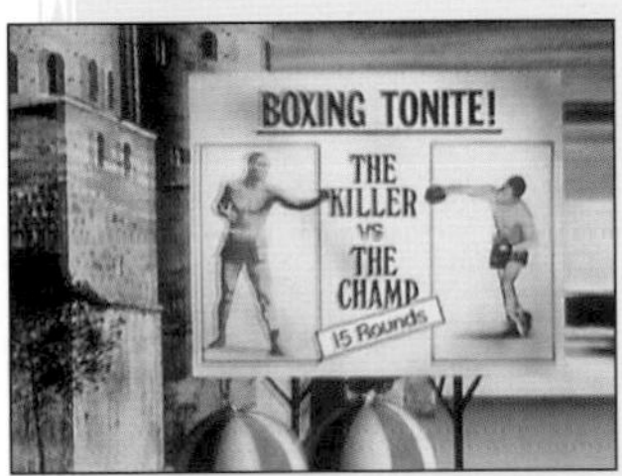

Cut to a dressing room at Madison Square Gardens, 6 *table, chairs, towels, and the usual boxing paraphernalia. Noise of a crowd outside. The door opens and in comes Mr Gabriello, and two assistants carrying a boxer on a stretcher. Smoke, action, excitement come in with them.*

6 Madison Square Garden (singular), the sports and music venue on Seventh Avenue in New York's Midtown.

MR GABRIELLO (MICHAEL) That was a great fight, champ, a great fight, you hear! Oh boy, what a fight, champ, what a great fight! You nearly had him, champ, you nearly had him...where's his head?
ASSISTANT I got it in here, Mr Gabriello.

He holds up a carrier bag. Gabriello goes over to it, looks inside and shouts into it.

MR GABRIELLO You were great, champ, d'you hear, you were great!
ASSISTANT *(looking in the bag)* He's got a nasty cut over his eye.
MR GABRIELLO Yeah, I think it was a mistake him wearing spectacles. *(gives the bag to the assistant)* Oh well, get that sewn onto his body in time for the press pictures.
ASSISTANT OK, Mr Gabriello.
MR GABRIELLO *(to second assistant)* Wasn't he great my boy?
SECOND ASSISTANT (ERIC) He was great, Mr Gabriello.

MR GABRIELLO The way he kept on fighting after his head came off!

THE WAY HE KEPT ON FIGHTING AFTER HIS HEAD CAME OFF!

SECOND ASSISTANT He was better when the head came off, Mr Gabriello. He was really dodging the guy.

MR GABRIELLO Yeah, I reckon that if he could've lasted till the end of that first minute, he would've had the killer worried.

SECOND ASSISTANT Sure, Mr Gabriello.

MR GABRIELLO Oh he was great. Did you see his left arm?

SECOND ASSISTANT No!

MR GABRIELLO OK, well look around the hall after everyone's gone.

SECOND ASSISTANT Do you realize Mr Gabriello, some of those guys out there paid over $2,000 for a ringside seat.

MR GABRIELLO And where did the head land? Right at the back, that's justice...*(the door opens; a black cleaner comes in)* What d'you want?

The cleaner holds up a carrier bag.

7

Idle knees Gilliam in the groin–not in stage directions.

BLACK MAN (TERRY G) This your boy's head?

MR GABRIELLO No, no, we've got his head. He ain't hurt that bad.

SECOND ASSISTANT *(looking in the bag)* Hey, that's Gerry Marinello. He fought the killer last week.

MR GABRIELLO OK, give it to me. I'm seeing his trainer tomorrow. I'll give it to him.

The cleaner is ushered out. 7

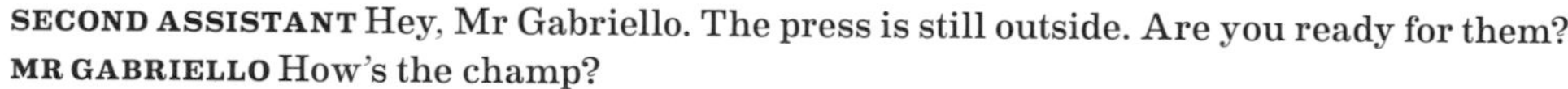

SECOND ASSISTANT Hey, Mr Gabriello. The press is still outside. Are you ready for them?

MR GABRIELLO How's the champ?

FIRST ASSISTANT *(working away with needle and thread)* Well, the head's on OK. But there's still a left arm missing.

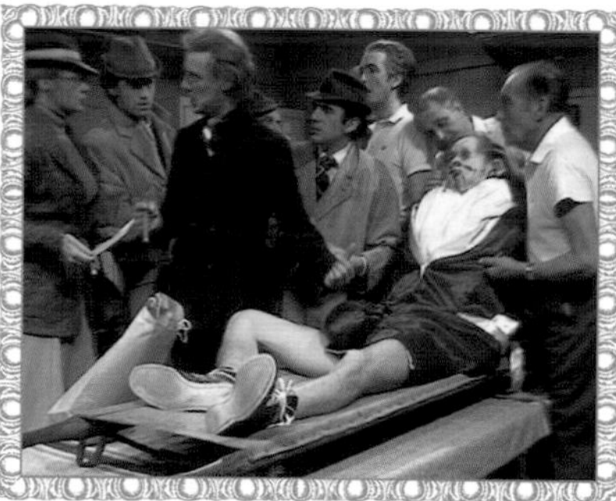

MR GABRIELLO OK, well keep the dressing gown kinda loose, OK. *(Gabriello goes to door and opens it)* OK boys, come on in!

The press surge in. The fighter is propped up.

FIRST REPORTER (TERRY J) Hey Mr Gabriello, Mr Gabriello. Did you expect your boy to last the full twenty-eight seconds?

MR GABRIELLO This boy has never let me down. He's the pluckiest goddamn fighter I've ever trained.

SECOND REPORTER (CAROL) Were you worried when his head started to come loose?

MR GABRIELLO No, no, we were expecting that. I told them to expect it to and it did. He ain't stupid.

FIRST REPORTER Hey, can we have a word with the champ?

MR GABRIELLO Yeah OK. But keep the questions simple.

FIRST REPORTER Hey champ! How're you feeling?

MR GABRIELLO *(angrily)* I said keep the questions simple!
SECOND REPORTER Mr Gabriello. People are saying the kid ought to be buried. His head's come off in the last six fights.
MR GABRIELLO There's no question of burying the kid. He's just reaching the top.
SECOND REPORTER Well, shouldn't he just stay in hospital?
MR GABRIELLO No, he ain't going to no hospital. He's got the return fight next week.

Shot of the 'New York Times' headline 'Champ to be kept alive for big return'. Cut to a hospital ward. Numerous doctors and nurses are listening to the radio.

RADIO VOICE (MICHAEL) And there's Frank Sinatra leaving the ring. Behind him is George Raft, 8 another great boxing fan, Martin Bormann, 9 acknowledging the applause, and with him of course is Gus Himmler, 10 who did an awful lot for the sport in his country in the early 1940s. And here comes the champ now and he seems in good shape to meet the killer once again. Before an audience, some of them will have paid $920,000 million for the privilege of seeing this boy get beaten up. And there's the bell.
PATIENT *(having a heart attack on the bed in the corner)* Aaarghhh!
ALL Quiet!!
RADIO VOICE And a left and a right and a right jab that's taken the champ's shoulder off. And here's the killer again with a right and another left and a bash with a hammer and a terrific smack with a heavy thud right into the skull and there's a gaping hole right through the champ's body now. And now the killer's working on the cut eye with a series of beautifully placed punches and the head's coming loose. *(the doctors and nurses getting increasingly excited)* The champ must try and keep his head on. The killer's kicked him in the groin and he's bitten half his left buttock off and the referee's stepped in with a warning there. What a plucky fighter this champ is. He's fighting as well as I've ever seen him. Must be losing blood at a rate of a pint a second now. It's everywhere. Certainly those who paid one and a half million dollars for those ringside seats are really getting their money's worth. They're covered in it. And his head's off! *(everyone cheers)* His head that's come off in so many fights is off in the thirty-first second. It's rolled away down to the left...but what's happening? The killer's being talked to by the referee. There's the champ...plucky little body racing around the ring, trying to find his opponent. And the killer has been disqualified. *(pandemonium breaks out in the ward—some patients cheering, doctors thumping them in disagreement)* He's been disqualified...this great fighter who has killed more than twenty people in his boxing career has at last been defeated by this courageous headless little southpaw from New York. And there's great roar here as the referee raises the arm of the new world heavyweight champion. What a pity the rest of his body wasn't here to see it. *(general disappointment; someone changes channels)*

George Raft was an American actor in the 1930s and '40s known for his portrayal of wise guys and gangsters.

Martin Bormann, Adolf Hitler's private secretary, later thought to have survived the war and subject of many unconfirmed sightings.

Heinrich Himmler, head of the Gestapo and architect of the Holocaust.

11 *The Archers*, the previously referenced long-running radio show, and saga seemingly without end.

12 She tosses the radio in fact.

SECOND RADIO VOICE (TERRY J) Well here in London it's 12.30 and time for the Robinsons. *(everyone perks up)* An everyday story of bla-di-bl-di-bla...*(sings 'Archers' theme tune)* 11 da di da di da di da...and so on.
MRS NON-ROBINSON *(on radio)* Morning Mrs Robinson.
MRS ROBINSON *(on radio)* Morning Mrs Non-Robinson.
MRS NON-ROBINSON Been shopping?
MRS ROBINSON No,...I've been shopping.

During this exchange there have been six cuts to close ups of radios of different shapes and sizes.

MRS NON-ROBINSON What'd you buy?

Pull out to reveal a pepperpot. Mrs Non-Gorilla sitting beside a radio on a park bench.

MRS ROBINSON *(on radio)* A piston engine.
MRS NON-ROBINSON What d'you buy that for?
MRS ROBINSON It was a bargain.
MRS NON-GORILLA (ERIC) Bloody rubbish. *(she turns the radio off)* 12

Quick cut to a hospital, doctor on a bed listening to the radio. It switches off.

DOCTOR (GRAHAM) I wanted to listen to that!

Cut back to Mrs Non-Gorilla. Another pepperpot approaches.

MRS NON-GORILLA Morning Mrs Gorilla.
MRS GORILLA (MICHAEL) Morning Mrs Non-Gorilla.
MRS NON-GORILLA Have you been shopping?
MRS GORILLA No...been shopping.
MRS NON-GORILLA Did you buy anything?
MRS GORILLA A piston engine!

She reveals a six-cylinder car engine on a white tray, on a trolley.

MRS NON-GORILLA What d'you buy that for?
MRS GORILLA Oooh! It was a bargain.

Start to pan away from them, their voices become fainter...

MRS NON-GORILLA Oooohhh!

Pan across a civic park, of which the only occupants are about ten pepper pots, dressed identically, scattered around on benches. One pepperpot is in a wheelchair. We come in to Mrs Non-Smoker, unwrapping a parcel and calling to the birds.

MRS NON-SMOKER (TERRY J) Come on little birdies...come on little birdies...tweet tweet...come and see what mummy's got for you...

SHE UNWRAPS THE PARCEL REVEALING A LEG OF LAMB WHICH SHE HURLS AT T E GATHERED BI DS.

A screech. She kills a pigeon. She reaches in another bag and produces two tins of pineapple chunks and throws them.

MRS NON-SMOKER Come on little birdies...tweety tweety...oooh look at this...tweet tweet...ooohhh-nice one...come on little birdies...

She chortles with delight as she hurls a huge jar of mayonnaise which smashes messily. She then throws a large frozen turkey, a jar of onions, a bag of frozen peas, and a bottle of wine. We widen as Mrs Smoker, with an identical piston engine to the last pepperpot, comes up to Mrs Non-Smoker. Quite a large area in front of Mrs Non-Smoker is littered with packaged foods and dead birds; a bird is pecking at a tin of pâté; a small pond in front of her has a swan upside down with its feet sticking in the air, a huge tin floating beside it.

MRS NON-SMOKER Oohh hello, Mrs Smoker.
MRS SMOKER (GRAHAM) Hello, Mrs Non-Smoker.
MRS NON-SMOKER What, you been shopping then?
MRS SMOKER Nope...I've been shopping!
MRS NON-SMOKER What d'you buy?
MRS SMOKER A piston engine!
MRS NON-SMOKER What d'you buy that for?
MRS SMOKER It was a bargain!
MRS NON-SMOKER How much d'you want for it?
MRS SMOKER Three quid!
MRS NON-SMOKER Done. *(she hands over the money)* 13

MRS SMOKER Right. Thank you.
MRS NON-SMOKER How d'you cook it?
MRS SMOKER You don't cook it.
MRS NON-SMOKER You can't eat that raw!
MRS SMOKER Ooooh...never thought of that. Oh, day and night, but this is wondrous strange...
MRS NON-SMOKER ...and therefore is a stranger welcome it. There are more things in Heaven and Earth Horatio, than are dreamt of in your philosophy. 14 But come, the time is out of joint. Oh cursed spite, that ever I was born to set it right. Let's get together.

They get up and go. Fade to black. Caption: 'ACT TWO—A ROOM IN POLONIUS'S HOUSE' 15 *Cut to a Frank Bough type presenter. Behind him are sports pictures.*

PRESENTER (MICHAEL) Hello, and welcome to 'A Room in Polonius's House'. Well tonight is European Cup night. 16 One result is already in from Munich. The European Cup, first round,

Jones actually pretends to hand over money.

More from *Hamlet*.

Polonius, Ophelia's (and Laertes's) father and counsel to King Claudius. He was sent to spy on the Dane and was murdered by Hamlet.

The European Cup was the premier European soccer competition for club teams. It is now called the Champions League.

Bayern München is one of the most successful German club soccer teams. It is based in Munich, in the south of Germany.

Wrexham is a small team from a town in Wales.

Ties in the European Cup are played over two legs: one home and one away. An aggregate score is tallied and the winner advances. For Wrexham to win "on aggregate" would have meant that the first leg, in Wales, must have ended at least 4396–0 (the away goal Wrexham scored in Germany would count for double, meaning they would advance).

Epsom Downs is a horse-racing stadium in Surrey.

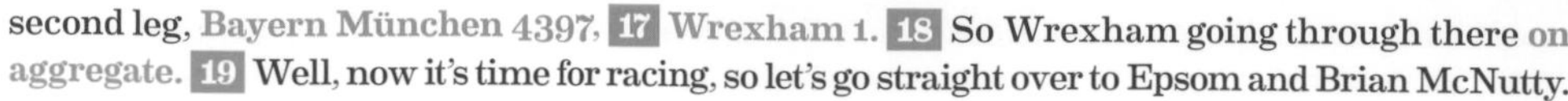

second leg, Bayern München 4397, 17 Wrexham 1. 18 So Wrexham going through there on aggregate. 19 Well, now it's time for racing, so let's go straight over to Epsom and Brian McNutty.

Cut to a dentist's surgery. A dentist is filling a patient. He talks to camera. Superimposed caption: 'LIVE FROM EPSOM' 20

DENTIST (GRAHAM) Well over here at Epsom, there are chances a-plenty for those who want to make a good start in...

PATIENT Dentistry.

DENTIST Dentistry. It's a well-off suburb, so most people have their own teeth and surgeries are opening at a rate of four or five a week.

Cut to a housewife in a back garden standing in front of a washing line with really nasty stained washing on it: some man's trousers with very nasty stain on crotch and running down the leg, a badly torn sheet with melted chocolate biscuit stuck on it, a huge bra, with cups eighteen inches across, two pieces of streaky bacon and a fried egg pegged on the line, and more dirty washing.

Caption: 'LIVE FROM EPSOM'

HOUSEWIFE (GRAHAM) Well, it's only forty-four minutes from the West End on the train and it's not too built up, so you can have a nice garden. And the people of Epsom are a very nice class of person.

Cut to a property developer in a main street. Caption: 'LIVE FROM EPSOM'

PROPERTY DEALER (MICHAEL) Well here in High Street Epsom, there are ample opportunities for all kinds of redevelopment. As you can see, *(he indicates old houses)* behind me now there are a high level of low density consumer units, still not fully maximizing site value. This could be radically improved by a carefully planned programme of demolition. And of course most of the occupants are...er...elderly folks, so they wouldn't put up much of a fight.

Cut to Epsom racecourse, and a presenter, Brian MacThighbone, up against the paddock rail. Caption: 'LIVE FROM EPSOM'

BRIAN (ERIC) Good afternoon. Well in fact there's still a few minutes to go before the main race on the card this afternoon—the Queen Victoria Handicap. So let's have a quick word with the winner of the last race, one of the season's top jockeys—Ronnie Mau-Mau. *(a jockey's cap comes into shot, which is all we ever see of him)* Good afternoon, Ronnie.

FIRST JOCKEY (MICHAEL) Good afternoon, Brian.

BRIAN *(pointing his stick-mike down)* A very fine ride there, Ronnie.

FIRST JOCKEY Well, a fine horse, Brian. You know you can't go wrong.

BRIAN Do you fancy your chances for the Derby?

FIRST JOCKEY *(vigorously nodding)* Oh very definitely, very definitely, indeed, certainly Brian.

BRIAN Well, let's just see if a colleague of yours agrees with that. Let's just have a quick word with Desmond Willet. Afternoon Des.

Another different silk hat comes into the bottom of frame. Again all we see is the jockey's cap.

SECOND JOCKEY (GRAHAM) *(Irish accent)* Afternoon, Brian. *(he shakes his head)* No chance, no chance at all.

FIRST JOCKEY *(nodding vigorously)* No, no I think you're wrong there, Des, with the right kind of going, he's going to be in there at the finish, Des.

SECOND JOCKEY *(shaking vigorously)* No chance, there's no chance.

BRIAN Well in fact I can see last season's top jockey, Johnny Knowles. *(two caps move over)* Good afternoon, Johnny.

Pause. Not even a cap is seen.

THIRD JOCKEY *(faintly)* Hello, Brian.

BRIAN Er, could we have a box for Johnny please. *(a cap comes into sight)* Thank you.

THIRD JOCKEY Hello, Brian.

BRIAN That's better. Well there you are. Three very well-known faces from the racing world. Thanks very much for coming along this afternoon, lads.

ALL Not at all. *(vigorous nodding of caps)*

BRIAN And best wishes for the Derby.

ALL Ah, thank you Brian, thanks very much. *(they leave nodding)*

BRIAN Well in fact I hear they're ready for us now at the start of the main race this afternoon. So let's go right away and join Peter at the start.

A view of the starting stalls, shot so we cannot see inside.
Caption: '3.15 QUEEN VICTORIA HANDICAP'

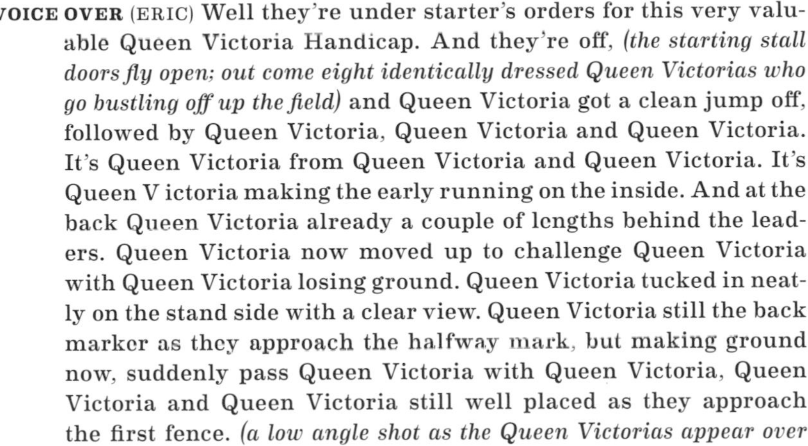

VOICE OVER (ERIC) Well they're under starter's orders for this very valuable Queen Victoria Handicap. And they're off, *(the starting stall doors fly open; out come eight identically dressed Queen Victorias who go bustling off up the field)* and Queen Victoria got a clean jump off, followed by Queen Victoria, Queen Victoria and Queen Victoria. It's Queen Victoria from Queen Victoria and Queen Victoria. It's Queen V ictoria making the early running on the inside. And at the back Queen Victoria already a couple of lengths behind the leaders. Queen Victoria now moved up to challenge Queen Victoria with Queen Victoria losing ground. Queen Victoria tucked in neatly on the stand side with a clear view. Queen Victoria still the back marker as they approach the halfway mark, but making ground now, suddenly pass Queen Victoria with Queen Victoria, Queen Victoria and Queen Victoria still well placed as they approach the first fence. *(a low angle shot as the Queen Victorias appear over the fence and thunder towards the camera)* And at the first fence it's Queen Victoria just ahead of Queen Victoria and Queen Victoria falling away in third place. And Queen Victoria in the lead as they...

Cut back to the presenter in the studio: he is completely dressed as Queen Victoria, apart from his face.

PRESENTER (MICHAEL) Well a very exciting race there at Epsom. And now over to the European Cup at Barcelona 21 where the latest news is that Miguel Otana, the burly Real Madrid 22 striker was sent off for breaking wind in the forty-third minute. He'd already been cautioned for pursing his lips earlier on in the game and now he's off! So let's see a playback of that...Brian.

Cut to Brian, dressed the same way.

BRIAN (ERIC) Yes...er...well as you can see...there's Otana now (brief stock shot of football match)... he gets the...er...through ball from Gomez (cut back to Brian) and er...he makes no attempt

Barcelona, one of the preeminent European teams then and now.

Real Madrid, archrivals of Barcelona in the Spanish league and in European competition, then and now.

A mishmash of soccer terminology. One "booking" (now a "yellow card") plus another one would equal a player being sent from the field. Committing an infraction inside the penalty area would lead to a penalty kick, though not necessarily a yellow card.

Jimmy Hill, soccer pundit, name-checked in Episode 41.

25

"Gonerelli," a funny play on "gonorrhea" as an Italian surname.

to play the ball. He quite deliberately lets off! And to my mind he was within the box and the referee had no option whatsoever but to send him off. 23

Cut to the presenter.

PRESENTER Jimmy?

We cut to the real Jimmy Hill dressed as Queen Victoria, veil, crown and all. 24

JIMMY HILL Good evening.
PRESENTER What do you make of that?
JIMMY HILL Well the referees really are clamping down these days. Only last week the Belgian captain was sent off for having a Sony radio cassette player. And Gonerelli, 25 the huge Italian defender, was sent off in Turin for having his sitting and dining room knocked through to form an open living area.

Cut to the presenter.

PRESENTER Hamlet?

Cut to Hamlet.

HAMLET Good evening.

Cut quickly back to the presenter.

PRESENTER Well you've got the girl on the bed and her legs up on the mantelpiece...

The nurse enters.

NURSE Out, out, come on, come on, out...*(she hustles the presenter out of studio)*

Animated sketch.

Caption: 'ACT FIVE—A HAM IN THE CASTLE' Mix to the theatre set we saw before. All the cast are dressed as Queen Victorias, except for Hamlet and Ophelia.

FIRST QUEEN VICTORIA Let four captains bear Hamlet like a soldier to the stage. For he was likely had he been put on to have proved most royally...

Superimposed caption: 'THE END' They come on and take bows. Superimposed Python credits in Shakespearian style and graphics.

MONTY PYTHON
BY WILLIAM SHAKESPEARE
DRAMATIS PERSONAE

Hamlet—TERRY JONES
A bachelor friend of Hamlet's
GRAHAM CHAPMAN

QUITE A BUTCH FRIEND OF HAMLET'S BUT STILL A BACHELOR

TERRY GILLIAM
A friend of hamlet's who, though married, still sees Hamlet occasionally
MICHAEL PALIN
A very close bachelor friend of Hamlet's who, though above suspicion, does wear rather loud shirts
ERIC IDLE
ANOTHER PART OF THE DRAMATIS PERSONAE:
A friend of Hamlet's who loves bachelors—CAROL CLEVELAND
A Jimmy Hill near London—JIMMY HILL
A bachelor gentleman—BOB E. RAYMOND
An Ophelia—CONSTANCE BOOTH
A loony, but not a bachelor—SIR K. JOSEPH
ADDITIONAL BLANK VERSE
J. CLEESE *(no relation) (of Hamlet's, that is)*
PERSONAE NON DRAMATIS BUT TECHNICALIS
(some bachelors, some not)
A maker-upper
MAGGIE WESTON
A costume designer and bachelor
ANDREW ROSE
A cameraman of london
STAN SPEEL
A sound recordist of ill repute
JOHN BLIGHT
An editor of film who is partly bachelor and partly vegetable with mineral connections
BOB DEARBERG
A studio sound man
MIKE JONES
A lighting scotsman
JIMMY PURDIE
A visual effector keen on bachelors
JOHN HORTON
An assistant producer friend of Hamlet's
BRIAN JONES
A designer who prefers married men but knows quite a few bachelors
VALERIA WARRENDER
A professional producer and amateur bachelor
IAN MACNAUGHTON
A bachelor broadcasting corporation
BBC COLOUR.

Fade out. Fade up on a moor. An explosion has just taken place. Out of the smoke a ragged man walks towards the camera.

IT'S MAN (MICHAEL)
AND THEN...

SEA
SON
4
EPISODE 44

U.S. AIR FORCE
Mr NEUTRON
MR NEUTRON
FEATURING
Post Box Ceremony
TEDDY SALAD
(CIA AGENT)
'CONJURING TODAY'
NEUTRON

FIRST AIRED: NOVEMBER 28, 1974

Animated titles.

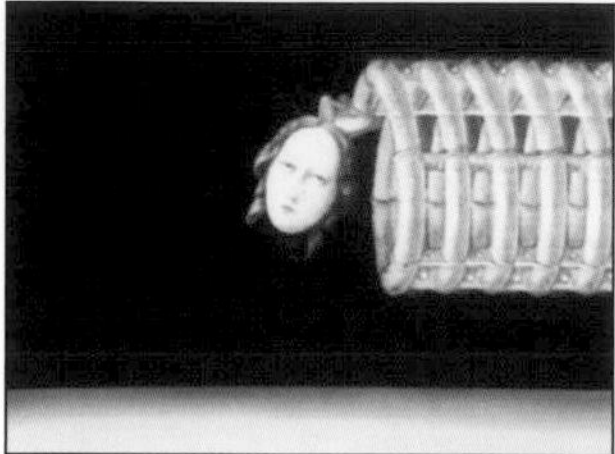

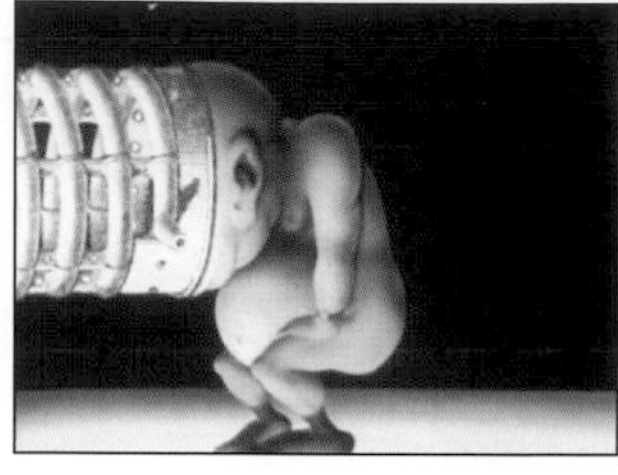

A street in Ruislip, morning. A scrap cart is going down the street.

SCRAP MAN (TERRY J) Let's bring 'em out! Any old iron! Any old iron! 1

A door opens and a housewife brings out a rather sophisticated-looking ground-to-air missile system, and dumps it on the cart.

SCRAP MAN Thank you.

Another door opens and a couple of rather respectable-looking old ladies bring out two bazookas and assorted shells and put them by the gate. There are further contributions of arms from householders. A GPO van comes up the street, passes the scrap cart and comes to rest up by the camera. There is a pillar box with a cover on it on the pavement, plus a rostrum with PA and bunting. A lord mayor is ushered out of the van by a post office official. The mayor and several ladies sit on the rostrum. Clearing his throat, the GPO official gets up, 2 *tests the microphone and starts to speak in a slightly strange voice.*

GPO OFFICIAL (MICHAEL) We are here today to witness the opening of a new box to replace the box which used to stand at the corner of Ulverston Road and Sandwood Crescent. 3 Owing to the road-widening programme carried out by the Borough Council, the Ulverston Road *box* was removed, leaving the wall *box* in Esher Road as the only *box* for the Ulverston Road area. This new *box* will enable the people of the Ulverston Road area to post letters, post-cards and small packages without recourse to the Esher Road *box* or to the *box* outside

"Any old iron" is the standard call of the scrap merchant—yelled as the cart passed, folks were thusly invited to give over their old metal, be it an old sink or bits of fencing.

The "GPO" is the General Post Office, the name of the post office and communications organization of the U.K. until 1969.

"Sandwood Crescent" is not a real junction, and "Turner's Parade" doesn't exist in London either. Wyatt Road *is* a small road in London, lacking a post office both then and now.

the post office at Turner's Parade which many people used to use, but which has now been discontinued owing to the opening of this *box* and also the re-organization of *box* distribution throughout the whole area, which comes into force with the opening of new *boxes* at the Wyatt Road Post Office in July. *(a moment's pause)* Nous sommes ici ce matin pour faire témoin à l'ouverture de la nouvelle *boîte* pour remplacer la *boîte* qui autrefois était placée au coin d'Ulverston Road et Sandwood Crescent. Parce que du projet pour l'élargissement de la rue qui fait par le Borough Council, la *boîte* dans Ulverston Road est remplacée, et la *boîte* de mur dans Esher Road, est la seule *boîte* pour le région d'Ulverston Road. Cette *boîte* nouvelle rendra capables les hommes d'Ulverston Road de mettre dans la poste les lettres, les carte-postales, et des petits paquets sans avant besoin de la *boîte* de mur dans Esher Road, ou les *boîtes* de la Turner's Parade bureau de poste, qui beaucoup des hommes ont fait usage mais qui est maintenant discontinuée parce que l'ouverture de cette boîte ici, et le réorganisation régionale que commence avec l'ouverture des boîtes au bureau de poste en Wyatt Road le juillet. *(a moment's pause)* Wir kommen hier heute Morgen für die Einfang auf dem neue Kabinett für die Poste.

The first two sentences of the next voice over are laid over the end of the French speech.

VOICE OVER (MICHAEL) A perfectly ordinary morning in a perfectly ordinary English suburb. Life goes on as it has done for years.

Cut to a suburban railway station.

VOICE OVER But soon this quiet pattern of life was to change irrevocably. The commonplace routine of a typical Monday morning would never be the same again, for into this quiet little community came

...MR NEUTRON!

A train stops at the station. The train doors open and out steps Mr Neutron. He looks like an American footballer, with enormous shoulders, tapering to a thin waist. He has very regular features and piercing eyes and is most impressive. He stands at the door of the train for a moment. The words 'Mr Neutron' are written in bold diagonally across his chest. He carries a Sainsbury's shopping bag. 4

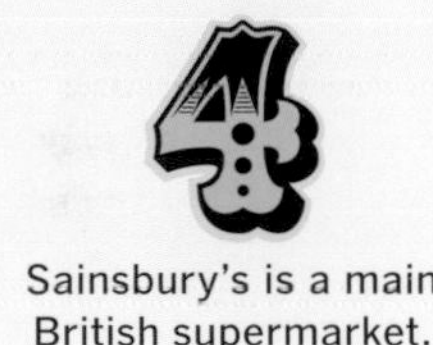

Sainsbury's is a main British supermarket.

VOICE OVER

MR NEUTRON! THE MOST DANGEROUS AND TERRIFYING MAN IN THE WORLD!

The man with the strength of an army! The wisdom of all the scholars in history! The man who had the power to destroy the world. *(animation of planets in space)* Mr Neutron. No one knows what strange and distant planet he came from, or where he was going to!...Wherever he went, terror and destruction were sure to follow.

Cut to Neutron's garden. He has three little picnic chairs out and is having tea with Mr and Mrs Entrail, a middle-aged couple. The lady, a little overdressed, dominates. Mr Entrail sits there rather sourly.

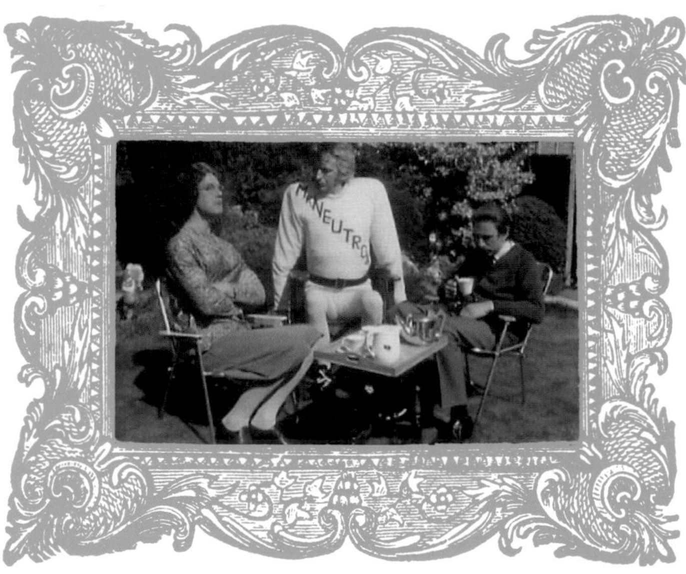

VOICE OVER Mr Neutron! The man whose incredible power has made him the most feared man of all time...waits for his moment to destroy this little world utterly!

MRS ENTRAIL (MICHAEL) Then there's Stanley...he's our eldest...he's a biochemist in Sutton. He's married to Shirley...

MR NEUTRON (GRAHAM) *(in a strange disembodied voice, grammatically correct but poor in intonation)* Shirley who used to be the hairdresser?

MRS ENTRAIL Yes, that's right, I think she's a lovely person. *(indicates her husband)* My husband doesn't...he thinks she's a bit flash. 5

"A bit flash" is British slang for someone who's too slick.

MR ENTRAIL (TERRY J) I hate 'er! I hate 'er guts.

MRS ENTRAIL And they, of course, they come down most weekends, so you'll be able to meet them then.

MR NEUTRON I'd...love...to. Hairdressing is very interesting.

MRS ENTRAIL And very important, too. If you don't care for your scalp, you get rabies. Then there's Kenneth, he's our youngest. Mind you, he's a bit of a problem...at least my husband thinks he is, anyway.

MR ENTRAIL Nasty little piece of work, he is, I hate him!

MRS ENTRAIL Mind you, the one we hear so much about nowadays is Karen. She married a Canadian—he's a dentist—they live in Alberta—two *lovely* children, Gary who's three, Leslie who's six. They look like the spitting image of Karen. D'you want to see a photo...?

MR NEUTRON Oh, yes please.

MRS ENTRAIL All right.

She goes to get a photograph.

MR ENTRAIL They're a couple of little bastards. I hate 'em. They've got eyes like little pigs, just like their mother. She's a disaster...a really horrible-looking person, she is. I thought that one would stay on the shelf, but along comes this stupid dentist git. He's a real creepy little bastard, he is. I hate 'im.

MR NEUTRON This is a nice area.

MR ENTRAIL It's like a bloody graveyard. I hate it.

MR NEUTRON It's handy for the shops and convenient for the West End.

MR ENTRAIL

IF YOU LIKE GOING TO THE WEST END. I THINK IT'S A STINKING DUMP.

Cut to a well-guarded American government building, with the letters 'FEAR' on a board outside.

VOICE OVER Meanwhile in Washington, at the headquarters of 'FEAR'—the Federal Egg Answering Room—in reality a front name for 'FEEBLE'—the Free World Extra-Earthly Bodies Location and Extermination Centre...all was not well.

A high-security operations room—maps, charts, monitor screens. A message comes chattering over the teleprinter. A teleprinter operator rips it out and takes it over to Captain Carpenter who sits at a control desk.

CAPTAIN CARPENTER (ERIC) Good God! *(he grabs a red flashing phone)* Get me the Supreme Commander Land, Sea and Air Forces, immediately!

Cut to a large room, empty apart from a very large desk with a large American eagle emblem above it. We hear American military music. There is nothing on the desk, except for a very futuristic, dynamic-looking intercom. Behind the desk the supreme commander sits. After a moment, slowly and rather surreptitiously, he sniffs his left armpit inside his jacket. Then, with a quick look around to see that no one is watching, he smells the other armpit.

He sits up again, then cups his hand in front of his face to smell his breath. He looks worried still. He reaches down slowly and takes his shoe off. He has just brought it up to his nose when the intercom buzzes loudly and a light flashes. The music stops. He jumps, and quickly takes his shoe off the desk. He presses a switch on the intercom.

COMMANDER (MICHAEL) Hello?

VOICE This is Captain Carpenter sir, from FEAR.

COMMANDER You mean FEEBLE?

VOICE Yes, sir...

COMMANDER What is it?

VOICE Mr Neutron is missing, sir!

COMMANDER Mr Neutron! Oh my God! OK—Surround the entire city! Send in four waves of armed paratroopers with full ground-to-air missile support! Alert all air bases! Destroy all roads! We'll bomb the town flat if we have to!

VOICE Sir! Sir! He's not in Washington, sir.

COMMANDER OK! Hold everything! Hold everything! Hold it! Lay off! Lay off...Where is he?

VOICE We don't know, sir...all we know is he checked out of his hotel and took a bus to the airport.

COMMANDER All right! I want a full-scale Red Alert throughout the world! Surround everyone with everything we've got! Mobilize every fighting unit and every weapon we can lay our hands on! I want...I want three full-scale global nuclear alerts with every army, navy and air force unit on eternal standby!

VOICE Right, sir!

COMMANDER And introduce conscription!

VOICE Yes, sir!

COMMANDER Right!

He slams the intercom button down and sits there. Silence again. His eyes look from side to side then slowly he goes back to smelling himself.

VOICE OVER So the world was in the grip of FEAR! A huge and terrifying crisis generated by one man! *(zoom into Neutron in his front garden, weeding; behind him the group of GPO people are sitting opening another box fifty yards further down from the first one; a line of six recently opened boxes stretches up the road)*...easily the most dangerous man the world has ever seen, honestly. Though still biding his time, he could strike at any moment. Could he be stopped in time?

A lady stops and chats to him.

MRS SMAILES (ERIC) You've got a bit of work to do there, then.

MR NEUTRON Yes, it is a problem.

MRS SMAILES Mrs Ottershaw never used to bother...then of course she was very old...she was 206! Well, must be going...if you need any help I'll send Frank round. He could do with a bit of exercise, ha! ha! ha! ha!...Fat old bastard...

She walks off. Neutron goes back to his weeding. Cut back to the supreme commander's office. He is sniffing himself again, only this time he has his whole shirt front pulled up and he is trying to smell under his shirt. The intercom goes. He quickly tucks his shirt in and depresses the switch.

COMMANDER Yes?

VOICE Captain Carpenter here, sir. We've been on red alert now for three days, sir, and still no sign of Mr Neutron.

COMMANDER Have we bombed anywhere? Have we shown 'em we got *teeth*?

VOICE Oh yes, sir. We've bombed a lot of places flat, sir.

COMMANDER

GOOD. GOOD. WE DON'T WANT ANYONE TO THINK WE'RE CHICKEN.

VOICE Oh no! They don't think that, sir. Everyone's really scared of us, sir.

COMMANDER Of us?

VOICE Yes, sir.

COMMANDER *(pleased)* Of our *power*?

VOICE Oh yes, sir! They're really scared when they see those big planes come over.

COMMANDER Wow! I bet they are. I bet they are. I bet they're *really* scared.

VOICE Oh they are, sir.

COMMANDER Do we have any figures on how scared they are?

VOICE No ... no figures, sir. But they sure were scared.
COMMANDER Ah! But it's not working?
VOICE No, sir.
COMMANDER OK. We'll try another tactic. We'll try and out-smart this Neutron guy. Yes, there's one man who could nail him.
VOICE One guy? That won't frighten anyone, sir.
COMMANDER He's the most brilliant man I ever met. We were in the CIA together. He's retired now. He breeds rabbits up in the Yukon...
VOICE What's his name, sir?
COMMANDER His name is Teddy Salad.
VOICE Salad as in...?
COMMANDER Lettuces, cucumber, radishes. Yeah, yeah, yeah.
VOICE Where do I find him, sir?
COMMANDER The Yukon. Oh, and Carpenter...
VOICE Yes, sir?
COMMANDER Make sure you get a decent disguise.

Cut to the Yukon. Carpenter is trekking along. He is in ballet tights and heavy make-up with a big knapsack with 'Nothing to do with FEEBLE' on the back. He comes across a log cabin in the middle of nowhere. He presses the doorbell. A rather twee little chime. The door is opened by a huge lumberjack.

CARPENTER Oh, hello. My name's Carpenter. I'm from the US Government.
LUMBERJACK (GRAHAM) Are you from the army?
CARPENTER Er...no...I'm...er...I'm...I'm from the ballet. The US Government Ballet.

The lumberjack's eyes light up.

LUMBERJACK The ballet! The ballet's coming here?
CARPENTER Well maybe...
LUMBERJACK Oh, that's great! We love the ballet. Last year some of us from Yellow River got a party to go see the ballet in Montreal.

Dimly we can see behind the lumberjack a bevy of beautiful boys of all nations.

CARPENTER Look, I was wondering...
LUMBERJACK Oh, we had a *marvellous* time. It was Margot Fonteyn 6 dancing 'Les Sylphides'... 7 oh, it was so beautiful...
CARPENTER Do you know...
LUMBERJACK Do you know how old she is?
CARPENTER Who?
LUMBERJACK Margot Fonteyn.
CARPENTER No.

Margot Fonteyn, British Royal Ballet stalwart considered by many to be the premier dancer of her day.

Fonteyn danced to great acclaim in Michel Fokine's 1919 ballet *Les Sylphides*, with Rudolf Nureyev.

In 1974 she was, in fact, 55 years old.

Another knock at the "camp" dancer Lionel Blair, regularly name-checked in Python.

Frank Smailes was a cricketer who played for Yorkshire and once for England. He died in 1970.

LUMBERJACK She's 206! 8

CARPENTER Look, I hear there's a US ballet organizer round these parts by the name of Teddy Salad.

LUMBERJACK You mean the special agent?

CARPENTER Well...

LUMBERJACK He's an ex-CIA man. He's not a *ballet* dancer.

Laughter from the boys in the hut.

CARPENTER Well, I just want to see him on some ballet business...

LUMBERJACK Well, you could try the store...

CARPENTER Oh, thank you. *(he turns to go)*

LUMBERJACK Hey! Can you get us Lionel Blair's autograph? 9

Carpenter walks away.

VOICE OVER While precious time was being lost in Canada, the seconds were ticking away for the free world...

Jarring chord. Cut to Neutron's house. He is hanging flowery print wallpaper in his sitting room. Helping him is the quite enormously vast Frank Smailes 10 who stands rather helplessly looking up at Neutron who is on a plank between two ladders.

VOICE OVER Already Neutron—who, you will remember, is infinitely the most dangerous man in the world, he *really* is—was gathering allies together.

MR NEUTRON Try having an omelette for your evening meal...perhaps with yoghurt and grapefruit.

MR SMAILES (MICHAEL) Oh, I've tried that...I once got down to fifty-six stone. But I couldn't stay like that. I used to take potatoes wherever I went. I used to go to the cinema with three hundredweight of King Edwards, I'd eat 'em all before I got out of the toilet. I had to go on to bread.

MR NEUTRON What about salad?

MR SMAILES Teddy Salad?

MR NEUTRON No, no, no—salad—as in lettuces, radishes, cucumber...

Cut to Carpenter in a log cabin trading post with trestle tables. Six Eskimos are sitting in a group at one end of the other tables. An Italian chef in a long white apron and greasy shirt, is standing over Carpenter. Carpenter sits at one table with a huge fresh salad in front of him.

ITALIAN (MICHAEL) You don't like it?

CARPENTER No, I didn't want to *eat* a salad. I wanted to find out about a man called Salad.

ITALIAN You're the first person to order a salad for two years. All the Eskimos eat here is fish, fish...
ESKIMO (GRAHAM) *(very British accent)* We're *not* Eskimos.
SECOND ESKIMO (TERRY J) Where's our fish. We've finished our fish.
ITALIAN What fish you want today, uh?
FIRST ESKIMO Bream please. 11
ITALIAN Bream! Where do I get a bream this time of year? You bloody choosy Eskimo pests.
FIRST ESKIMO We are *not* Eskimos.
ITALIAN Why don't you like a nice plate of canelloni?
ESKIMOS Eurrrrghhhh!
FIRST ESKIMO That's not fish.
ITALIAN *(as he turns to go in kitchen)* I've had my lot of the Arctic Circle. I wish I was back in Oldham... 12

Carpenter crosses to the Eskimos.

CARPENTER *(speaking slowly and clearly as for foreigners)* Do any of you Eskimos...speak...English?
ESKIMOS We're not Eskimos!
THIRD ESKIMO I am.
OTHERS Sh!
ITALIAN *(off)* Haddock!
ESKIMOS Where?
CARPENTER *(still speaking as if to foreigners)* Do any of...you...know...a man... called...Salad?
ESKIMO What, Salad as in...
CARPENTER Lettuce, cucumbers, tomatoes...yes.
FIRST ESKIMO Like you have on your plate?
CARPENTER Yes. That's right.
FIRST ESKIMO No, I'm afraid not.
SECOND ESKIMO Where's our fish?
FIRST ESKIMO What does this Teddy Salad do?
CARPENTER He's a...er...hen-teaser. 13

Quick cut to the chairman of Fiat in his office.

CHAIRMAN (ERIC) Che cosa è la stucciacatori di polli?

Superimposed caption: 'WHAT IS A HEN-TEASER?' Cut back to the cabin.

FIRST ESKIMO No, the only Teddy Salad we know is a CIA man.
CARPENTER Oh, he might know.
ESKIMOS *(chanting)* Gunga gunga, where's our fish?
CARPENTER Where will I find him?
SECOND ESKIMO Oh, he lives up at Kipper Sound.
CARPENTER Thanks a lot.
ESKIMOS Fishy fishy iyoooiyooo.
FIRST ESKIMO Are you in international spying, too?
CARPENTER No...no...I'm with the...US Ballet...force...who are you with?
FIRST ESKIMO *(leans forward confidentially)* M16. But not a word to the Eskimos. 14
ESKIMOS Fishy fishy igooo.

The Italian chef appears.

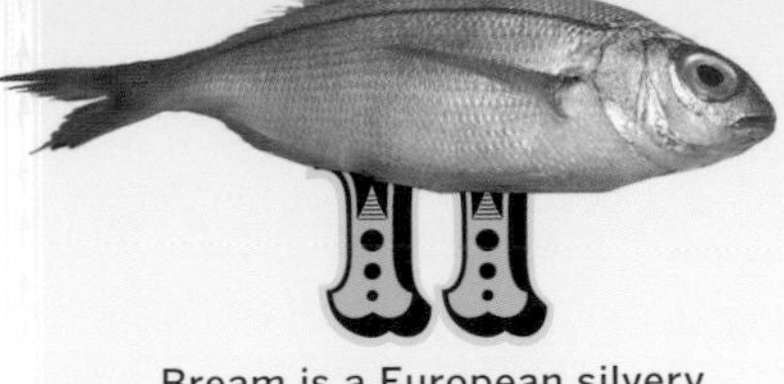

Bream is a European silvery freshwater fish.

Oldham is a working-class town in northern England.

Referenced in Episode 42.

MI6, the Secret Intelligence Service—U.K. equivalent of the CIA.

THE PYTHON MOVIES

Four hit movies, a smash Broadway musical, and members who went on to become travel-show hosts, corporate training experts, movie directors, and ashes strewn about a TV studio floor. All this from a forty-five episode, surreal, extremely British sketch comedy show that began more than fifty years ago. But it's the movies that have most endeared the public to the Monty Python troupe.

The first sign that *Monty Python's Flying Circus* would have a life beyond the BBC lies not with the first movie, *And Now For Something Completely Different.* Rehashing a number of the early sketches, it was primarily shot to break into the American market. No such thing happened. It wasn't until 1974's *Monty Python and the Holy Grail,* filmed between seasons three and four, that a longer life for the troupe began to look more likely.

Based on Arthurian legend, and partially funded by such rock bands as Led Zeppelin and Pink Floyd, the movie became famous for the "Knights who say 'Ni!' " and the Bridge of Death—across which the seekers must cross, but only after correctly stating their favorite color. Directed by both Terry Jones and Terry Gilliam, the production wasn't without its tensions, but the result is a fine and anarchic movie that is, in parts, extremely funny. It also spawned the musical *Spamalot* more than two decades later.

Monty Python's Life of Brian, released five years later, is arguably the best Python movie. Following the travails of a man in Jesus-era Judea, the film brilliantly parodies both the historical problems of faith (for example, the real problem of not being able to hear the Sermon on the Mount if one was at the back of the crowd, where "Blessed are the peacemakers" is misheard as "Blessed are the cheesemakers") and the modern-day power of religion. Whatever else one thinks of the movie, the sight of men on crosses singing "Always Look on the Bright Side of Life" can't fail to raise one's spirits, especially if one is facing crucifixion.

Monty Python's The Meaning of Life was a less successful movie, even though it does return to the sketch comedy of the *Flying Circus.* Focusing on the stages of life, its often gross-out humor left some fans of the Pythons bemused—though the phrase "a waffer-thin mint" has been adopted by all who have ever overeaten as a symbol of not being able to swallow one more bite.

ITALIAN Here's your bloody fish.
FIRST ESKIMO Thank you, Anouk.
ITALIAN I'm not an Eskimo!

Cut to Arctic wastes—ice and snow and bitter blasting winds. Carpenter—his little tadger tiny as a tapir's tits—struggles on. He stops and peers ahead. He sees a trapper figure with a sledge pulled by four huskies. Carpenter hurries on and catches him up.

CARPENTER Hey! Hey!

The man stops. On his sledge are supplies including two ladies in bikinis, deep-frozen and wrapped in cellophane bags.

CARPENTER Hi! I'm Carpenter of the US Ballet.
TRAPPER (TERRY J) Hey, great to have you around. The last decent ballet we got around here was Ballet Rambert. 15 On Thursday they did 'Petrouchka', 16 then on Saturday they did 'Fille Mal Gardee'. 17 I thought it was a bit slow...
CARPENTER *(stopping him short)* It sure is nice to see you, Mr Salad.
TRAPPER I ain't Salad.
CARPENTER What?
TRAPPER You want Teddy Salad?
CARPENTER Yeah...*(the man looks around rather furtively, to see if anyone is watching, then takes Carpenter's arm and indicates the dog team)* I don't see anyone.
TRAPPER The one on the end, on the right. That's Salad.
CARPENTER That's a dog!
TRAPPER *(confidentially)* No only *bits* of it.
CARPENTER What do you mean?
TRAPPER Listen, Teddy Salad is the most brilliant agent the CIA ever had, right?
CARPENTER Right.
TRAPPER That's how he made his name *(indicates the dog)*—disguise!

They look at the dog in silence for a moment.

CARPENTER That's incredible!
TRAPPER He had to slim down to one and a half pounds to get into that costume. He cut eighteen inches off each arm and over three feet off each leg. The most brilliant surgeon in Europe stuck that tail on.
CARPENTER What about the head?

Now called the Rambert Dance Company, a leading British classical dance group that also runs a famous dance school.

Petrouchka is another Fokine ballet, this one to the music of Stravinsky.

La Fille Mal Gardée (*The Wayward Daughter*) is a ballet based on a painting by Pierre-Antoine Baudouin. It was first performed in 1789, making it one of the oldest existing ballets, and was popularly revived by the Royal Ballet in London in 1960.

TRAPPER All of the head was removed apart from the eyes and the brain in order to fit into the costume.
CARPENTER That's incredible!
TRAPPER D'you want to talk to him?
CARPENTER Yeah, sure.
TRAPPER *(looking around him again)* OK, let's move over to those trees over there...anyone might be watching.

They pull over to a lone deciduous tree in the middle of the empty tundra wastes. They pull in. The man goes round to the dog and kneels down beside it.

TRAPPER *(softly)* Mr Salad?...There's Mr Carpenter to see you.
CARPENTER What does he say?
TRAPPER *(to Carpenter)* Do you have a bone? *(Carpenter feels rather helplessly in his pockets)* It's all part of the disguise. *(he produces a bone, which he gives to the dog)* OK, Teddy...here's the bone. *(the dog tucks into the bone)* All right, you've got his trust, now, you can talk to him.
CARPENTER *(kneeling rather awkwardly down beside the dog, and speaking confidentially)* Sir...sir...Mr Salad...sir, I've come direct from the Commander of Land, Sea and Air Forces...There's a pretty dangerous situation, sir. Mr Neutron...is missing. *(he looks significantly at the dog, but the dog doesn't react)* The General says you're the only one who'll know where to find him... What's he say?
TRAPPER

HE WANTS TO GO WALKIES.

CARPENTER Walkies?
TRAPPER Yeah, he's right into it today—d'you mind taking him for walkies?

He gives the dog to Carpenter on a lead. Carpenter hesitates and then walks off with the dog, bending down occasionally and explaining the situation.

VOICE OVER While Carpenter took the most brilliant agent the CIA ever had for walkies, events in the world's capitals were moving fast!

Cut to a picture of the outside of 10 Downing Street. 18
Zoom in on the door. Music: 'Rule Britannia' type theme. Cut to interior—a few circular tables, dim lighting. The decor of a rather exclusive restaurant. Subdued murmur of upper-class people stuffing their faces. A gypsy violinist is going from table to table playing and singing. In the middle of all this there is the prime minister at a big leather-topped desk, covered with official papers, three telephones, an intercom, tape recorder, a photo of Eisenhower with a very small bunch of flowers in front of it in a sort of self-contained shrine, an in/out tray, blotter, etc. The intercom buzzes.

18

The traditional home of the British prime minister, a poky little house in central London.

VOICE The Secretary of State to see you, Prime Minister.
PRIME MINISTER (ERIC) Very well, show him in.

The prime minister switches off. The secretary of state enters, wending his way through the tables. He sits at the desk. He is in a rather agitated condition.

SECRETARY OF STATE (MICHAEL) Prime Minister.
PRIME MINISTER Do take a seat.

He takes a seat from the next table; the lady sitting on it falls to the floor.

SECRETARY OF STATE Prime Minister, we've just had the Supreme Commander US Forces on the phone. Apparently they want a full-scale Red Alert!
PRIME MINISTER They what?

The gypsy violinist has come round to the desk. He is playing a sad, slow melody and smiling encouragingly at them. They glance at him. He flashes a white smile. The secretary of state drops his voice and huddles closer to the prime minister.

SECRETARY OF STATE They want a full-scale Red Alert—every troop movement...

As the secretary leans forward so does the gypsy, causing the secretary to break off in mid-sentence.

PRIME MINISTER It's all right—don't worry about Giuseppe...*(the secretary looks at the gypsy who smiles again toothily)* He's English really.
SECRETARY OF STATE Well apparently the whole structure of world peace may be threatened unless we immediately...
GIUSEPPE (TERRY J) *(heavy accent, leaning forwards)* Your anniversary, signore?
PRIME MINISTER No, no, Giuseppe—not now.
GIUSEPPE *(indicating the secretary of state)* You mean zis isn't ze lady?
PRIME MINISTER No.
GIUSEPPE Oh, signora...my mistake! I play for you 'My Mistake'. *(before the prime minister can stop him he goes into a strident Italian song)* 'My mistake, I have made my mistake! What a dreadful mistake! Is this mistake that I make!' *(strums violently and starts on the second verse)* 'Oh my mistake...'
PRIME MINISTER Giuseppe, do you mind playing over there.
GIUSEPPE *(flashing a winning smile)* Very well, signor. But I play only for you...and your beautiful companion.

He moves off mysteriously, singing the mistake song.

SECRETARY OF STATE Well anyway, this Mr Neutron, is located somewhere in the London area. We must find and exterminate him. The Americans say if we don't, they will.
PRIME MINISTER *(straining to hear over noise of singing)* What?
SECRETARY OF STATE The Americans say if we won't *they* will!
PRIME MINISTER That he doesn't know *what*?
SECRETARY OF STATE They'll bomb the entire London area.
PRIME MINISTER *(getting up)* We'd better get out of here!...*(he grabs the photo of Eisenhower)*
SECRETARY OF STATE They won't bomb *here*.
PRIME MINISTER Are you sure?
SECRETARY OF STATE Sure.
PRIME MINISTER *(sitting down with great relief)* Right. When are they going to start?
SECRETARY OF STATE Well apparently they haven't got Neutron yet...but when they do...

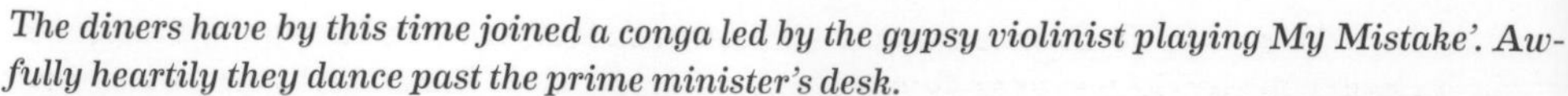

The diners have by this time joined a conga led by the gypsy violinist playing My Mistake'. Awfully heartily they dance past the prime minister's desk.

Cut to Arctic wastes. The wind howls. The trapper is sitting beside a fire, picking his nose thoughtfully and tending a stewpan. The dog bounds back, Carpenter on the end of his lead, breathless from trying to keep up.

TRAPPER Well. Did he tell you anything?
CARPENTER *(worn out by the walk)* No...we chased sticks...we chased a few reindeer... 19
TRAPPER *(patting the dog)* You been chasing reindeer, have you? You're a naughty boy...yes...ain't you a naughty boy...
CARPENTER Look, we haven't got much time...He hasn't given me any information yet...
TRAPPER OK. Tell you what, let's eat. You give him one of your meatballs, he'll tell you anything...OK?
CARPENTER OK.

Suddenly the dog woofs, gets up on back legs and starts pawing the trapper.

TRAPPER Wait a minute—he's trying to tell us something.

A strangled, strained American voice comes from within the dog. Slightly muffled perhaps.

DOG (MICHAEL'S VOICE) Carpenter...er...agh...ah...Carpenter...
CARPENTER *(kneeling down and peering into the dog's face)* Yes, Mr Salad? Can you hear me?
DOG Yes...yes...it's just it's so goddam painful in here...what's the problem?
CARPENTER It's Mr Neutron, sir...he's gone missing. The Supreme Commander wants you to take charge.
DOG I...oh God...I...I...I...
CARPENTER Yes, Mr Salad?
DOG I gotta go walkies again.

Cut to the office of the supreme commander. He is now nude behind his desk. A kidney bowl full of water 20 *is on desk; he is dabbing at himself with a sponge. The intercom buzzes. He switches it on.*

VOICE Still no sign of Captain Carpenter, sir...or Mr Neutron.
COMMANDER OK. We'll *bomb* Neutron out. Get me Moscow! Peking! and Shanklin, Isle of Wight! 21

Cut to stock film of B52s on a bombing raid.

VOICE OVER (MICHAEL) And so the Great Powers and the people of Shanklin,

19

A reference to what is sometimes called "Poohsticks," a game featured in *The House at Pooh Corner* by A.A. Milne. Players throw sticks off a bridge into a river to see which one emerges first on the other side.

A "kidney bowl" is the kidney-shaped receptacle used to hold surgical utensils though here it looks like a regular bowl.

Shanklin is a small tourist town on the east coast of the Isle of Wight, the little island off the south coast of England.

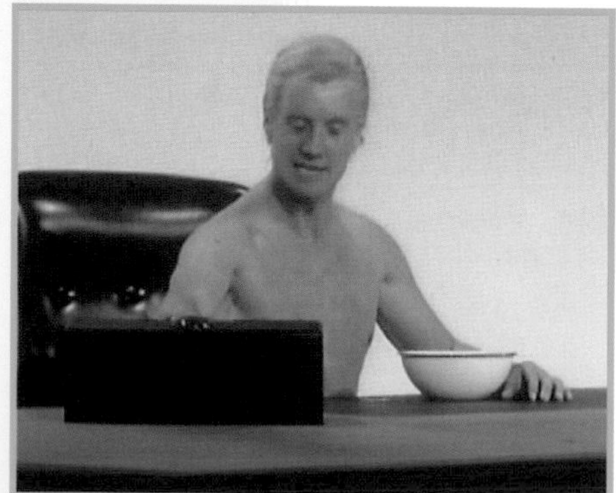

Isle of Wight, drew their net in ever-tightening circles around the most dangerous threat to peace the world has ever faced. They bombed Cairo, Bangkok, Cape Town, Buenos Aires, Harrow, Hammersmith, Stepney, Wandsworth and Enfield [22] ...But always it was the wrong place.

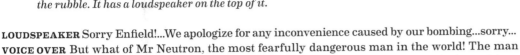

Cut to an area of smoking rubble. A van with the words 'US Air Force' on the side trundles through the rubble. It has a loudspeaker on the top of it.

LOUDSPEAKER Sorry Enfield!...We apologize for any inconvenience caused by our bombing...sorry...

VOICE OVER But what of Mr Neutron, the most fearfully dangerous man in the world! The man who could destroy entire galaxies with his wrist, the man who could tear fruit machines apart with his eyeballs...He had not been idle!

Meantime we have mixed through to Neutron's suburban sitting room. He is standing in the doorway gazing at something off camera. He holds an envelope which he has just opened and a letter.

VOICE OVER In fact he had fallen in love...with the lady who 'does' for Mrs Entrail...

THE CAMERA PANS ACROSS TO A SLOVENLY CHAR IN PAISLEY APRON, FURRY SLIPPERS AND HEAD SCARF.

Throughout this scene we hear the sound of bombers and the distant muffled sound of explosions.

MRS SCUM (TERRY J) Oh 'ello Mr N, terrible about Enfield, innit? It's all gone. So's Staines...lovely shops they used to have in Staines...and Stanmore, where the AA offices used to be. I don't know where we'll pay our AA subscriptions to now. [23] Do you know where we'll have to pay our AA subscriptions to now, Mr N?

MR NEUTRON I didn't know you were a member of the AA Mrs S.C.U.M.

MRS SCUM Oh yes. Ever since the Corsair [24] broke down in Leytonstone...they towed it all the way to Deauville FOC. [25] *(Mr Neutron looks blank)* Free of Charge. Well my husband Ken, K.E.N., he said...

MR NEUTRON Oh, forget about your husband, Mrs S.C.U.M.—or may I call you Mrs S?

MRS SCUM You can call me Linda, if you like.

MR NEUTRON No, I'd rather call you Mrs S.

MRS SCUM Oh...

MR NEUTRON *(as if trying to soften the blow)* And you can call me Mr N.

MRS SCUM Well...that's what I *was* calling you.

MR NEUTRON Mrs S, there's something I have to tell you...

22

These final five are sections of London.

The "AA" is the Automobile Association, like AAA in the United States.

The Ford Corsair was a midsize car manufactured between 1963 and 1970.

Deauville is, presumably, the town on the northern coast of Normandy. Leytonstone, in London, to Deauville is a cool 275 miles, with the English Channel in between.

MRS SCUM Yes, Mr N?

MR NEUTRON I have just won a Kellogg's Corn Flake Competition.

MRS SCUM Oh Mr N! That's wonderful!

MR NEUTRON I got the ball in exactly the right place. The prize is £5,000 in cash, or as much ice cream as you can eat.

Her eyes go round as saucers and all thoughts of returning to her marital bed vanish under the impact of such imminent wealth.

MRS SCUM £5,000!

MR NEUTRON I was thinking of taking the ice cream.

MRS SCUM *(alarmed)* Oh no!

MR NEUTRON It's been so hot recently.

MRS SCUM You couldn't *eat* that much ice cream Mr N.

MR NEUTRON Mrs S, I can eat enormous quantities of ice cream without being sick.

MRS SCUM Oh no! Take the £5,000! Please take the £5,000.

MR NEUTRON I was thinking. If we got married...

MRS SCUM Oh yes! *(she sits very close to him)*

MR NEUTRON We could use the £5,000 to buy a spoon...

MRS SCUM Oh! We could buy a lot more than that!

MR NEUTRON And then fill up with ice cream.

MRS SCUM No! Forget about the ice cream. We need the money.

MR NEUTRON We need nothing. For there is something I have not told you Mrs S.C.U.M.

MRS SCUM Oh please call me Mrs S.

MR NEUTRON No I'd rather go back to calling you Mrs S.C.U.M., Mrs S.C.U.M. I am the most powerful man in the universe. There is nothing I cannot do.

MRS SCUM Oh Mr N.

MR NEUTRON I want you to be my helpmate. As Tarzan had his Jane, as Napoleon had his Josephine, as Frankie Laine 26 had whoever he had, I want you to help me in my plan to dominate the world!

MRS SCUM Oh Mr N. That I should be so lucky!

MR NEUTRON You're not Jewish are you?

Frankie Laine, the American crooner especially beloved in the U.K. His nicknames include "Steel Tonsils" and "Old Leather Lungs."

Cut back to the Yukon. The trapper, Captain Carpenter and the dog are still sitting round the dying campfire over the remains of supper. They are all looking a little bit bored. The dog has obviously been telling long reminiscences.

DOG Another time when I was in Cairo, I was disguised as a water hydrant. The whole top part of my head had been removed and...

CARPENTER Please, Mr Salad,...you *must* tell us where Neutron is.

DOG And I functioned! D'you hear? I really worked. I could put out a fire.

CARPENTER Please, Mr Salad...

DOG Mind you, it hurt a bit...

CARPENTER Please, Mr Salad—there isn't much time. Where will we find Neutron?

DOG OK.

GIVE ME ANOTHER MEATBALL AND I'LL TELL YOU.

Carpenter grabs a meatball and throws it down for the dog. The dog wolfs it. Carpenter and Trapper exchange glances. Carpenter bends nearer the dog. The dog finishes the meatball with much slurping. Carpenter crouches beside him patiently.

DOG OK listen carefully...I won't repeat this. You understand?
CARPENTER Yes yes—quick.
DOG I know where Neutron is right now. I know the exact address and the exact house and the exact road...
CARPENTER OK where is it?
DOG He's not in America...
CARPENTER No?
DOG He's not in...Asia!
CARPENTER No?
DOG He's not in...Australia!
CARPENTER No?
DOG He's in...Europe!
CARPENTER Yeah?
DOG And you wanna know where in Europe?
CARPENTER Yeah!
DOG OK. OK, I'll tell you he's in England...In London...at Number 19...

A sudden explosion completely engulfs them. Cut to the supreme commander's office. He is still nude and has an enormous display of tales and powders on his desk. He is talking to the intercom.

COMMANDER OK. That's the Yukon—what's left?
VOICE Only Ruislip, 27 the Gobi Desert, and your office, sir.
COMMANDER OK! Let's start with my office. *(a big explosion)*

Ruislip, a safe, suburban section of London (pronounced "Ry-slip").

Cut to the Gobi Deseft. Sweltering heat. We come onto a group opening a GPO box. There is a line of boxes stretching into the distance as far as the eye can see. Arabic is being spoken by the GPO official.

GPO OFFICIAL Ankwat i odr inkerat Gobi Desert Ulverston Road...

Subtitle: 'THIS NEW BOX COMPLETES THE ENCIRCLEMENT OF THE GOBI DESERT'

GPO OFFICIAL Ik anwar, hyaddin...*(etc.)*

Subtitle: 'THE POST OFFICE IS NOW IN A POSITION TO ACHIEVE COMPLETE WORLD DOMINATION' A terrific explosion. Cut to Neutron and Mrs Scum.

MR NEUTRON I will take you away from all this Mrs S.C.U.M.

Benidorm, a resort town on the western coast of Spain, is a vacation destination for holidays in the U.K. and often thought of as "down-market,"

MRS SCUM Oh, Mr N...I'd follow you anywhere.
MR NEUTRON We will have two weeks in Benidorm. 28
MRS SCUM Oh yes...yes.
MR NEUTRON And I will make you the most beautiful woman in the world.

He stretches out his hands towards her. His piercing eyes narrow in concentration. There is a flash, a jump cut, and Mrs S stands before him as dumpy and unattractive as ever, but in a brand new C & A twin set and pearls, a nice new handbag, and a rather fussy hat.

MRS SCUM Oh...it's beautiful...oh, Mr N, you have made my heart sing...*(quick cut to stock film of bomber then back to Mrs Scum)* Late in life's pageant it may be...but you have made roses bloom anew for me...*(quick flash of bomber then back to Mrs Scum)* Life's rich harvest is being...

MR NEUTRON

SHUT UP, MRS S. WE MUST HURRY...

He takes her hand and pulls her away.

MRS SCUM I'd better leave a note for Ken...he'll be expecting us...*(explosion)*

Animation: the world destroyed and burning.

VOICE OVER Has Mr Neutron escaped in time? Is the world utterly destroyed? How can Mr Neutron and his child bride survive? Will his mighty powers be of any avail against the holocaust? Stay tuned to *this* channel!

Cut to a man in a grey suit in a studio.

MAN (ERIC) Hello. Well in fact what happens is that they are saved by Mr Neutron's mighty powers just as the last bomb falls on Ruislip.

Superimposed caption: 'A MAN FROM THE "RADIO TIMES"' 29

Idle is reading the *Radio Times* that has a story about MPFC on its cover.

MAN However, the Earth has been blown off its axis, and in a most dramatic and dangerous and expensive sequence, it spins off into space. There are appallingly expensive scenes of devastation and horror and the final incredibly expensive climax is reached as thousands of ape monsters in very expensive costumes descend from the sky onto these, plug up a whole city which has to be specially built and fling them all into the sea very expensively. And we can see those very expensive scenes right now. *(the credits start on his TV set)* Just after the credits have gone through...incidentally, these are going to be the most expensive and lavish scenes ever filmed by the BBC in conjunction with Time-Life of course...these are some of the technical people who have been involved in filming these very expensive scenes, expensive sound, expensive visual effects there, expensive production assistant, expensive designer...cheap director. Well you can see those expensive scenes right now.

Caption: 'THE END'

MAN *(voice over)* Oh come on you can give us another minute, Mr Cotton, please. 30

Another reference to the head of BBC light entertainment, Bill Cotton.

Caption: 'CONJURING TODAY' Fade up on a conjurer with a fright wig and ping-pong eyes. He holds a bloodstained saw.

CONJURER (MICHAEL) Good evening, last week we learned how to saw a lady in half. This week we're going to learn how to saw a lady into three bits and dispose of the body...

Two policemen chase him off the set. They run past the man from the previous announcement who is on the phone. On his TV set we see the policemen pursuing the conjurer.

MAN Look if you can put on rubbish like that, and 'Horse of the Year Show', 31 you can afford us another minute, Mr Cotton, please, I mean look at this load of old...*(fades out)*

The Horse of the Year Show, a regular Python reference—the national British horse-jumping show held every October.

Fade up on the entrance to TV Centre. The man walks out.

VOICE OVER (ERIC) World Domination t-shirts are available from BBC, World Domination Department, Cardiff.

A man (TERRY J) *hits him on the head with an absolutely enormous hammer. He falls, stunned. Fade out.*

SEA
SON
4
EPISODE 45
Sport CONN SETS HIS DEADLINE!
Scun
WHAT A SCORCHER
PHEW! CAN'T RE
THIS MISS!
PAIGNTON PIER
BINGO AMUSEMENTS

A PARTY POLITICAL BROADCAST ON BEHALF OF THE LIBERAL PARTY
PARTY POLITICAL BROADCAST
FEATURING
'MOST AWFUL FAMILY IN BRITAIN'
ICELANDIC HONEY WEEK
A DOCTOR WHOSE PATIENTS ARE STABBED BY HIS NURSE
Brigadier and Bishop
APPEAL ON BEHALF OF EXTREMELY RICH PEOPLE
THE MAN WHO FINISHES OTHER PEOPLE'S SENTENCES
DAVID ATTENBOROUGH ✽ THE WALKING TREE OF DAHOMEY
THE BATSMEN OF THE KALAHARI
CRICKET MATCH (ASSEGAIS)
BBC NEWS (HANDCOVERS)

FIRST AIRED: DECEMBER 5, 1974

Caption: 'A PARTY POLITICAL BROADCAST ON BEHALF OF THE LIBERAL PARTY'

VOICE OVER (MICHAEL) There now follows a Party Political Broadcast on behalf of the Liberal Party... [1]

Cut to a kitchen.

Mr Garibaldi is eating a packet of 'Ano-Weet'. On the back of the packet in big letters it reads 'Free Inside—The Pope + Demonstration Record'. Kevin Garibaldi is stretched out the whole length of the sofa, eating a huge plate of baked beans. His father occasionally flaps the copy of the paper he is reading at him to clear the air. The paper is called 'The Scun' [2] *and has a pin-up on the front page with big headline 'What a Scorcher! Phew! Can Resist this Miss';* [3] *at the bottom of the page in small print 'China Declares War'. The banner across top reads 'In the Scun Today "Tits and Inflation"'.* [4] *Ralph Garibaldi is sitting at the table eating. At one point he stretches across the table, and his arm sticks in the butter. He tries to clean it off and knocks the sugar over. There is a large photo of Ian Smith* [5] *on the wall; built around it is a plaster shrine, with flowers in front of it. Mrs Garibaldi is ironing. She irons some underclothes, then she irons a transistor radio.*

Dotted about the room are a flat telephone, a flat standard lamp, and a flat cat. Valerie Garibaldi is wearing a shiny red miniskirt. She has bright yellow 'beehive' hair so stiffly lacquered that it is quite a hazard to various ornaments on the mantelpiece. She is continuously making herself up in the mantelpiece mirror which is shaped like a lavatory. The other member of the family is a very fat old dog. As we see all this, the football commentary is droning throughout on the radio.

RADIO VOICE (ERIC) Pratt...back to Pratt...Pratt again...a long ball out to Pratt...and now Pratt is on the ball, a neat little flick back inside to Pratt, who takes it nicely and sends it through on the far side to Pratt, Pratt with it but passes instead to Pratt, Pratt again, oh and well intercepted by the swarthy little number nine, Concito Maracon. This twenty-one-year-old half back, remarkably stocky for 6' 3", square shouldered, balding giant, hair flowing in the wind, bright eyed, pert, young for his age but oh so old in so many ways. For a thirty-nine-year-old you wouldn't expect such speed. Normally considered slow, he's incredibly fast as he wanders aimlessly around, sweeping up and taking the defence to the cleaners. Who

The Liberal Party, by 1974 at least, was the third party in the U.K. Perennially on the sidelines, they struggled to win seats in elections owing to the "first-past-the-post" standard by which the Conservative and Labour parties were able to dominate. In recent years they have gained traction, and in 2010 formed a ruling coalition with the Conservative Party.

"The Scun"—a mix of *The Sun*, a tabloid newspaper featuring big headlines and naked women, and the word "scum."

"Phew, What a Scorcher!" is the typical tabloid headline referring to hot weather in England, so seldom ever seen.

By 1974, inflation in the U.K. had reached a staggering 17 percent. "Tits" continued to exist too.

Ian Smith, leader of the breakaway all-white Rhodesian government, and much knocked by the Pythons.

would have thought, though many expected it, that this remarkable forty-five-year-old, 9' 4" *dwarf* of a man, who is still only seventeen in some parts of the world, would ever really be...Oh and there was a goal there apparently...and now it's Pratt...back to Pratt...Pratt again...a long ball to Pratt...*(crackle)*

BY NOW MOTHER HAS SUCCEEDED IN FLATTENING THE RADIO WITH THE IRON. SHE FOLDS IT NEATLY AND PUTS IT ON THE PILE.

MR GARIBALDI (TERRY J) I like this Ano-Weet, it really unclogs me.

Ralph Garibaldi knocks a bowl onto the floor. It smashes.

MRS GARIBALDI (ERIC) Oh, *do* be careful.
RALPH GARIBALDI (MICHAEL) Sorry, mum.

Kevin opens another can of beans and pours them on to his plate, throwing the tin on the floor. The radio drones on.

MR GARIBALDI I mean a lot of others say they unclog you, but I never had a single bowel movement with the 'Recto-Puffs'.
RALPH GARIBALDI Now if we...*(he knocks the cereal box off table)* Oh, sorry, mum...Now if we lived in Rhodesia there'd be someone to mop that up for you.
VALERIE GARIBALDI (GRAHAM) *(turning from the mirror in mid make-up)* Don't be so bleedin' stupid. If you lived in bleedin' Rhodesia, you'd be out at bleedin' fascist rallies every bleedin' day. You're a bleedin' racist, you bleedin' are.

MR GARIBALDI Language! 6
VALERIE GARIBALDI Well he gets on my sodding wick. 7
MR GARIBALDI That's better.

Mother is now ironing the telephone and the cat. She irons them flat and pins them on the line.

MR GARIBALDI No, the stuff I liked was that stuff they gave us before the war, what was it—Wilkinson's Number 8 Laxative Cereal. Phew. That one went through you like a bloody Ferrari...

The doorbell rings.

Palin pushes a jar off the table here.

To "get on someone's wick" is to get on their nerves.

MRS GARIBALDI Now, who's that at this time of day...*(she goes out)*
MR GARIBALDI If it's the man to empty the Elsan, 8 tell him it's in the hall.
MRS GARIBALDI Right, dear.
MR GARIBALDI And make sure that you hold it the right way up!
RALPH GARIBALDI Dad...?

A middle-aged man appears from the broom cupboard.

8

The Elsan is the British nickname for a portable toilet.

STRANGE MAN Yeah?
RALPH GARIBALDI No no, *my* dad...
STRANGE MAN Oh...*(he gets back into the cupboard again)*
RALPH GARIBALDI Dad? Why is Rhodesia called Rhodesia?...*(he knocks the teapot on to the floor, it smashes)* Oh sorry, dad.

Cut to the doorway in the hall. A man in a dark suit, very smart and well-dressed, is doing strange kung-fu antics.

MRS GARIBALDI No...no, really, thank you very much...no, thank you for calling, not today, thank you. Good morning.

She shuts the door on him. As she does so Mr Garibaldi shouts out to her.

MR GARIBALDI Who was that?
MRS GARIBALDI *(coming in again)* The Liberal Party candidate, darling...oh...what have you done *now*?
RALPH GARIBALDI Sorry, mum. *(he is standing beside the sink which has just split in two)* I was just washing up...
MRS GARIBALDI Go and sit down!
RALPH GARIBALDI Mum? Do you know why Rhodesia's called Rhodesia? 9

Palin trips over the ironing board here, and the kitchen table nearly collapses.

MR GARIBALDI Do *you* remember 'Go-Eazi'? They were hopeless...*(Kevin opens another can of beans; dad notices in disgust and flaps his paper again)* little black pellets...tasted foul and stuck inside you like flooring adhesive.
VALERIE GARIBALDI *(she has finally finished her startling make-up)* Right, I'm off.
MRS GARIBALDI When are you coming back tonight?
VALERIE GARIBALDI 3 a.m.
MRS GARIBALDI I think it's disgusting...you a Member of Parliament.
MR GARIBALDI I heard you in the hall last night, snogging away. 10

"Snogging" is British slang for outlandish and replete kissing.

VALERIE GARIBALDI I wasn't *snogging*!
MR GARIBALDI Sounded like snogging to me. I could hear his great wet slobbering lips going at yer...and his hand going up yer...
MRS GARIBALDI Dad!
STRANGE MAN *(coming out of the cupboard)* Yes.
MRS GARIBALDI No...not you.
STRANGE MAN Oh! *(he goes back in again)*
MRS GARIBALDI Just mind your language...

RALPH KNOCKS A LEG OFF THE TABLE. IT COLLAPSES ENTIRELY.

RALPH GARIBALDI Oh, sorry, mum.
KEVIN GARIBALDI (TERRY G) *(too fat and flatulent to get up)* I've run out of beans!
VALERIE GARIBALDI We was talking, we was not snogging.
MR GARIBALDI Talking about snogging, I'll bet...

The phone rings. Mrs Garibaldi answers it.

VALERIE GARIBALDI If you must know, we was talking about Council re-housing.
MRS GARIBALDI *(on the phone)* Would it mean going to live in Hollywood?
KEVIN GARIBALDI *(desperate but unable to move)* I run out of beans!
MR GARIBALDI Where to re-house his right hand, that's what he was interested in!
MRS GARIBALDI And has Faye Dunaway definitely said yes? 11
VALERIE GARIBALDI He is the Chairman of the Housing sub-committee.

The bell rings.

MR GARIBALDI Snogging sub-committee, more like...
MRS GARIBALDI Ralph, do answer that door will you!
KEVIN GARIBALDI Beans!!
MRS GARIBALDI Shut up!!
RALPH GARIBALDI Yes, mum.
MR GARIBALDI *(shouting to Ralph)* If it's the man from the Probbo-Rib, tell him it's in the bed.

Ralph gets up. As he goes he knocks the leg off the old-fashioned gas cooker. It falls to one side bringing down shelves next to it, plates, crockery and a section of the wall, revealing the hallway the other side.

RALPH GARIBALDI Sorry, mum.
KEVIN GARIBALDI *(roaring)* Beans! Beans!
MRS GARIBALDI Shut up!

A man in a Tarzan outfit, except with a postman's hat and a little mailbag, swings in on a liana shouting a jungle yell.

POSTMAN Postma-a-a-n!!

A gong sounds. They all stop acting. Cut to stock film of ladies applauding. Pull out from this stock film to see that it is on a screen in a presentation studio. A glittery compère is also applauding sycophantically at his desk, above which is the glittery slogan 'Most Awful Family in Britain, 1974. Sponsored by "Heart Attacko Margarine"'.

PRESENTER (MICHAEL) A very good try there, by the Garibaldi family of Droitwich in Worcestershire. Professor...

Pull out further to pick up a panel of three distinguished, rather academic-looking people.

PROFESSOR K (ERIC) Well, I can't make up my mind about this family...I don't think there was the sustained awfulness that we really need. I mean, the father was appalling...

Two other members of the panel nod vigorous agreement.

LADY ORGANS (TERRY J) Appalling...yes...
PROFESSOR K He was dirty, smelly and distasteful...and I liked him very much...but...
PRESENTER Lady Organs?
LADY ORGANS Well...they were an unpleasant family certainly, but I don't think we had enough of the really gross awfulness that we're looking for...

11

Faye Dunaway, the American actress who starred in *Chinatown* in 1974.

PRESENTER Well, harsh words there for the Garibaldi family of Droitwich in Worcestershire, at present holders of the East Midlands Most Awful Family Award (Lower Middle-Class Section) but unable today to score more than fifteen on our disgustometer. Well with the scores all in from the judges, the Garibaldis are number three...and a surprise number two...the Fanshaw-Chumleighs of Berkshire...*(he turns to the screen)*

A very elegant breakfast table in beautifully tasteful surroundings. Four upper-class folk—two women (MICHAEL AND GRAHAM), *two men* (ERIC AND TERRY J)*—are talking most incredibly loudly at each other, with quite appalling accents. An appalling din altogether. They talk just about at the same time as each other.*

FIRST PERSON What a super meal.

SECOND PERSON Absolutely super. Pat and Max are coming down from Eton 12 to help daddy count money.

12 Eton, the premier private boys school much mocked by the Pythons.

THIRD PERSON How absolutely super.

FOURTH PERSON

MY MAN AT POIRER'S SAYS I COULD HAVE MY WHOLE BODY LIFTED FOR £5,500.

FOURTH PERSON How super...*(etc.)*

Cut back to the panel nodding thoughtfully.

PRESENTER Well, some of the wonderful behaviour that made the Fanshaw-Chumleighs the second Most Awful Family in Britain 1974. But the winners, by a clear ten point margin, are once again the awful Jodrell family of Durham. Unfortunately, we're not allowed to show you some of the performance that won them an award, but I assure you it was of the very highest standard, was it not, Lady Organs?

LADY ORGANS Oh, yes, superb...Mr Jodrell—you know, the old grandfather, who licks the...

PRESENTER *(hurriedly)* Yes, yes...

LADY ORGANS He's superb. His gobbing 13 is consistent and accurate. His son is a dirty foul little creature, and those frightful scabs which Mrs Jodrell licks off the cat are...

"Gobbing," or spitting.

PRESENTER *(during this speech we cut to the same image on a TV screen)* Well, thank you very much, Lady Organs...and from all of us all, well done to the Jodrells...and to all of you, not forgetting those of you who may be halfway in between, without whom, of course, and not forgetting who made it all possible, when, and we'll be back, until then and so it's goodnight from me and here's wishing you a safe journey home, thank you for watching this show, don't forget it was all great fun, I've enjoyed it, and I hope you watching at home have enjoyed it too.

He is switched off, and fades into a dot. Pull back to reveal that the TV which has just been switched off is in a dirty old sitting room in which all the characters are really unpleasant pepperpots. They are dressed more or less identically, except that son has a school cap and a blazer over his pepperpot gear. He has a satchel and National Health glasses. **14** *The father has moustache and glasses and a Fair-Isle jersey.*

MOTHER (ERIC) The Jodrells win every bloody year...makes you vomit...dad?
DAD (TERRY J) Yes?
MOTHER Get your stinking feet off the bread.
DAD I'm only wiping the cat's do's off.
SON (TERRY G) Mum?
MOTHER Shut yer face, Douglas.
SON I wanted some corn-plasters.
MOTHER Shut up and eat what you got.

A cat set into the wall, i. e. a glove puppet, screeches as if someone had pulled its tail outside.

DAD Some fat bastard at the door! *(to the cat)* Shut up! *(she slaps it; it expires)*

She takes a couple of milk bottles out. Standing on the doorstep is a man with a Nordic accent in female national costume. He has a tray labelled 'Icelandic Honey Week'

MAN (GRAHAM) A strong hive of bees contains approximately 75,000 bees. Each honey bee must make 154 trips to collect one teaspoon of honey. Hello, sir.
DAD What do you want?
MAN Would you like to buy some of our honey, sir?
MOTHER What you doing in here?
MAN Which would you like, the Californian Orange Blossom, the Mexican, the New Zealand, or the Scottish Heather?
MOTHER He can't eat honey. It makes him go plop plops.
MAN Come on, please try some.

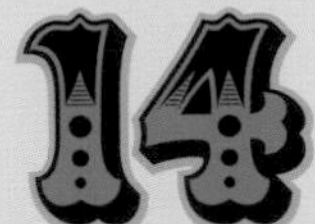

Spectacles provided for free by the National Health Service, and therefore hardly fashionable (often quite the opposite). They are known to be cheap and nasty.

"Oh strewth!" is a British expression meaning "Oh, Lord!"

"Flog" is British slang for "sell."

Jeremy Thorpe was the leader of the Liberal Party from 1967 to 1976. In 1979 he was cleared of conspiring to murder Norman Scott, a man who claimed to have had an affair with Thorpe. Thorpe has never commented publicly on his sexuality, but he has been married twice (his first wife died in a car accident in 1970).

Another reference to Christiaan Barnard, the South African surgeon who performed the first heart transplant.

Another nod to Bill Cotton, head of BBC light entertainment.

DAD All right I'll have some Icelandic Honey.

MAN No, there is no such thing.

DAD You mean you don't make any honey at all?

MAN No, no, we must import it all. Every bally drop. We are a gloomy people. It's so crikey cold and dark up there, and only fish to eat. Fish and imported honey. Oh strewth! [15]

MOTHER Well why do you have a week?

MAN Listen Buster! In Reykyavik it is dark for eight months of the year, and it's cold enough to freeze your wrists off and there's only golly fish to eat. Administrative errors are bound to occur in enormous quantities. Look at this—it's all a mistake. It's a real pain in the sphincter! Icelandic Honey Week? My Life!

MOTHER Well why do you come in here trying to flog the stuff, then? [16]

MAN Listen Cowboy. I got a job to do. It's a stupid, pointless job but at least it keeps me away from Iceland, all right? The leg of the worker bee has...

They slam the door on him. Someone rather like Jeremy Thorpe [17] *looks round the door and waves as they do so.*

Animated titles.

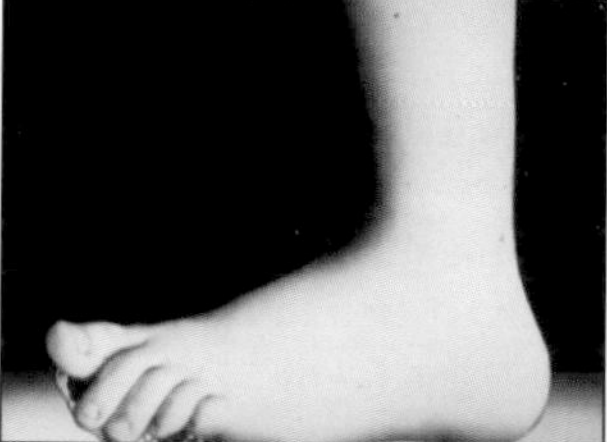

Then cut to a drawing of Indians attacking a fort. Music: 'The Big Country' theme.

VOICE OVER (TERRY J) *(and superimposed roller caption)* 'In the spring of 1863 the Comanches rallied under their warrior leader Conchito in a final desperate attempt to drive the white man from the rich hunting lands of their ancestors. The US cavalry were drawn up at Fort Worth, and the scene was set for a final all-out onslaught that could set the new territories ablaze.'

Cut to a doctor's surgery. It has a wall shrine with a photo of Christiaan Barnard with flowers and candles in front of it. [18] *The doctor is talking to an embarrassed-looking man* (TERRY G).

DOCTOR (GRAHAM) Well, Mr Cotton, [19] you have what we in the medical profession call a naughty complaint. My advice to you is to put this paper bag over your head—it has little holes there for your eyes, you see—and to ring this bell, and to take this card along to your hospital. *(he hands him card three feet long which reads 'For Special Treatment')* And I shall inform all your relatives and friends and anyone else I bump into. OK...cash, wasn't it? *(the man hands over wad of fivers)* Thank you very much. Get out. *(the man gets up to go)* Dirty little man. *(he picks up big text book entitled 'Medical Practice' and flicks through the pages)* Hmm...hmm...Hippocratic oath...it's not in there...jolly good. Very useful. Next!

An out-of-vision scream. A man staggers in clutching his bleeding stomach. Lots of blood pours out of him throughout the scene.

DOCTOR Ah, yes you must be Mr Williams.

WILLIAMS (TERRY J) *(obviously fatally wounded)* Y...yes...

DOCTOR Well, do take a seat. What seems to be the trouble?

WILLIAMS

I'VE...I'VE JUST BEEN STABBED BY YOUR NURSE...

DOCTOR Oh dear...well I'd probably better have a look at you then. Could you fill in this form first? *(he hands him a form)*

WILLIAMS She just stabbed me...

DOCTOR Yes. She's an unpredictable sort. Look, you seem to be bleeding rather badly. I think you'd better hurry up and fill in that form.

WILLIAMS Ahhh...couldn't...I...do...it...later, doctor!

DOCTOR No, no. You'd have bled to death by then. Can you hold a pen?

WILLIAMS I'll try.

With great effort he releases one of his hands from his bleeding stomach.

DOCTOR Yes, it's a hell of a nuisance all this damn paperwork, really it is...*(he gets up and strolls around fairly unconcerned)* it's a real nightmare, this damned paperwork. It really is a hell of a nuisance. Something ought to be done about it. **20**

WILLIAMS Do I have to answer all the questions, doctor?

DOCTOR No, no, no, just fill in as many as you can—no need to go into too much detail. I don't know why we bother with it all, really, it's such a nuisance. Well let's see how you've done, then... *(Williams half collapses)* Oh dear oh dear...that's not very good, is it. Look, surely you knew number four!

WILLIAMS No...I didn't...

DOCTOR It's from 'The Merchant of Venice'—even *I* know that!

WILLIAMS *(bleeding profusely)* It's going on the carpet, doctor.

DOCTOR Oh don't worry about that! Look at this—number six—the Treaty of Versailles! Didn't you know that? Oh, my God.

WILLIAMS Ahgg...aghhh.

DOCTOR And number nine—Emerson Fittipaldi! **21** *(gives Williams a look)* Virginia Wade? **22** You must be mad!

The nurse enters with a smoking revolver.

NURSE (CAROL) Oh doctor, I've just shot another patient. I don't think there's any point in your seeing him.

DOCTOR You didn't *kill* him, did you?

NURSE 'Fraid so.

DOCTOR You mustn't *kill* them, nurse.

NURSE Oh, I'm sorry doctor. It was just on the spur of the moment. Rather silly really.

She exits, taking a sword from the wall. Through the next bit of the scene we hear screams off.

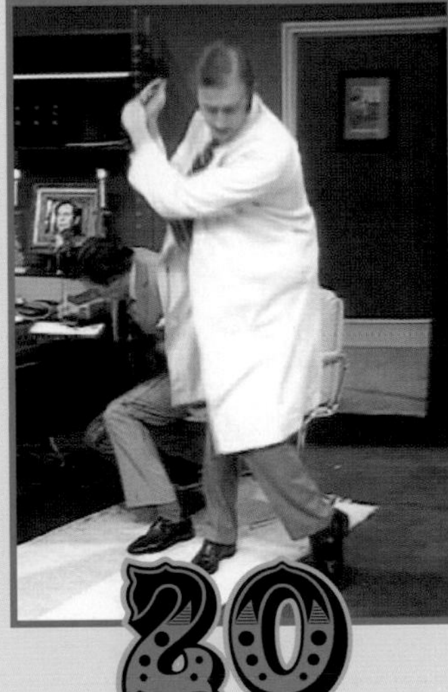

20

Chapman mimes a golf swing/shooting a rifle/ playing pool here.

21

Emerson Fittipaldi was an eminent Brazilian car-racing star of the day. He won the Formula One championships in 1972 and 1974.

22

Virginia Wade was a British tennis player who won Wimbledon in 1977, the year of the Queen's Silver Jubilee. She was the last Brit to win a major.

WILLIAMS I'm sorry about the carpet, doctor.

DOCTOR Mr Williams, I'm afraid I can't give you any marks, so I won't be able to recommend you for hospital. Tell you what—I'll stop the bleeding—but strictly speaking I shouldn't even do that on marks like these...

The nurse enters covered in blood.

NURSE There are no more patients now, doctor.

DOCTOR Oh well, let's go and have lunch, then.

NURSE What about...er...

[SHE POINTS TO WILLIAMS WHO IS LYING ON THE FLOOR GURGLING BY THIS TIME]

DOCTOR Ah yes—look, Mr Williams we're just popping out for a bite of lunch while we've got a spare moment, you know. Look, have another bash at the form...and if at least you can answer the question on history right, then we may be able to give you some morphine or something like that, OK?

WILLIAMS Thank you, doctor, thank you...

There is no such portrait.

Cut to a large country house sitting room, dominated by large grinning portrait of Jeremy Thorpe. 23 *A bishop is sitting at a desk, typing. A brigadier in full military uniform just to below the chest, then a patch of bare midriff, with belly button showing, then a lavender tutu, incredibly hairy legs, thick army socks and high heels, is dictating.*

BRIGADIER (ERIC) Dear Sir, I wish to protest in the strongest possible terms. Yours sincerely, Brigader N. F. Marwood-Git (retired). Read that back, will you, Brian.

BISHOP (MICHAEL) And when he had built up Cedron, he sent Horsemen there, and an host of footmen to the end that issuing out they might make outroads upon the ways of Judea, as the King commanded them... 24

Quote from 1 Maccabees 15:41.

BRIGADIER Good! Pop it in an envelope and bung it off! It's no good bottling these things up, Brian. If you feel them you must say them or you'll just go mad...

BISHOP Oh yes indeed...as the book of Maccabee said...as the flea is like unto an oxen, so is the privet hedge liken unto a botanist black in thy sight, O Lord!

BRIGADIER Quite...Look why don't you just nip out for lunch, Brian...

BISHOP Yea...as Raymond Chandler said, it was one of those days when Los Angeles felt like a rock-hard fig.

BRIGADIER Brian, let's stop this pretending, shall we.

BISHOP Oh...yea...as Dirk Bogarde said in his autobiography...

BRIGADIER Brian...let's stop all this futile pretence...I've...I've always been moderately fond of you...

BISHOP Well to be quite frank, Brigadier...one can't walk so closely with a chap like you for...for so long without...feeling something deep down inside, even if it isn't anything...anything...very much.
BRIGADIER Well, splendid...Brian...er...well I don't suppose there's much we can do, really.
BISHOP Not on television...no...
BRIGADIER No...they...they are a lot more permissive these days than they *used* to be...
BISHOP Ah yes...but not with this sort of thing...
BRIGADIER No...I suppose they've...got to draw the line somewhere...
BISHOP Yes...
BRIGADIER Well take a letter, Brian. Dear Sir, I wish to protest...

Cut to an animation sketch.

VOICE OVER (MICHAEL) *(and caption)* 'There now follows an appeal on behalf of extremely rich people who have absolutely nothing wrong with them'
SIR PRATT (GRAHAM) *(at a large leather-topped desk with an elaborate table lamp)* Hello. I'd like to talk to you tonight about a minority group of people who have no mental or physical handicaps and, who, through no fault of their own, have never been deprived, and consequently are forced to live in conditions of extreme luxury. This often ignored minority, is very rarely brought to the attention of the general public. The average man in the street scarcely gives a second thought to these extremely well-off people. He, quite simply, fails to appreciate the pressures vast quantities of money just do not bring. Have you at home, ever had to cope with this problem...*(cut to a rich young yachting type surrounded by girls in bikinis)* or this...*(cut to a rich woman loading her chauffeur with all kinds of expensive parcels)* or even this...*(cut to a still of Centre Point)* I know it's only human to say, 'Oh this will never happen to me', and of course, it won't! I'm asking you, please, please, send *no* contributions, however large, to me.

We see the last bit on a TV in Mrs What-a-long-name-this-is-hardly-worth-typing-but-never-mind-it-doesn't-come-up-again's-living-room. Ding-dong of doorbell. A cupboard door opens, and the middle-aged man we saw in first scene comes out. He has no iguana on his shoulder.

MRS LONG NAME (TERRY J) All right, I'll go.
TV VOICE (MICHAEL) There now follows a Party Political Broadcast on behalf of the Liberal Par...

She turns it off. The TV set just folds up as if empty and collapses on to the floor. Dust rises. She goes into the hallway to the front door (singing 'Anything Goes' by the other Cole Porter **25** *to herself) and opens it. A man with a briefcase stands there.*

Anything Goes is a nod back to Episode 42.

MR VERNON (ERIC) Hello, madam...*(comes in)*
MRS LONG NAME Ah hello...you must have come about...
MR VERNON Finishing the sentences, yes.
MRS LONG NAME Oh...well...perhaps you'd like to...
MR VERNON Come through this way...certainly...*(they go through into the sitting room)* Oh, nice place you've got here.
MRS LONG NAME Yes...well...er...we...
MR VERNON Like it?
MRS LONG NAME Yes...yes we certainly...

MR VERNON Do...Good! Now then...when did you first start...
MRS LONG NAME ...finding it difficult to...
MR VERNON Finish sentences...yes.
MRS LONG NAME Well it's not me, it's my...
MR VERNON Husband?
MRS LONG NAME Yes. He...
MR VERNON Never lets you finish what you've started.
MRS LONG NAME Quite. I'm beginning to feel...
MR VERNON That you'll never finish a sentence again as long as you live.
MRS LONG NAME Exact...
MR VERNON ly. It must be awful.
MRS LONG NAME It's driving me...
MR VERNON To drink?
MRS LONG NAME No, rou...
MR VERNON nd the be...
MRS LONG NAME en...
MR VERNON d...
MRS LONG NAME Yes...
MR VERNON May I...
MRS LONG NAME Take a seat...
MR VERNON Thank you. *(he sits)* You see, our method is to reassure the patient by recreating normal...er...
MRS LONG NAME Conditions?
MR VERNON Yes. Then we try to get them in a position where they suddenly find that they're completing *other* people's sentences...
MRS LONG NAME *(with self-wonder)* Themselves!
MR VERNON Spot on Mrs...
MRS LONG NAME *(hesitantly)* Smith?
MR VERNON Good! Well, try not to overdo it to...
MRS LONG NAME *(with growing confidence)* Begin with...?
MR VERNON Good. Just keep it to one or two...
MRS LONG NAME *(faster)* Words...
MR VERNON To start off with, otherwise you may find that you're...
MRS LONG NAME Taking on too long a sentence and getting completely...er...
MR VERNON Stuck. Good. Yes. Well that's about it...
MRS LONG NAME *(completely confident now)* for now, so...
MR VERNON Thanks very much for calling.
MRS LONG NAME Not at all.
MR VERNON And, er...
MRS LONG NAME Just like to say
MR VERNON Thank you very much for coming along.
MRS LONG NAME Not at all
MR VERNON And good...
MRS LONG NAME Bye, Mr...
MR VERNON Vernon.

Mrs Long Name leaves. Mr Vernon shuts the door. A girl's voice comes from sitting room.

GIRL'S VOICE Carl?
MR VERNON Yes, dear?
GIRL'S VOICE I've just had another baby.
MR VERNON Oh, no! How many's that now?
GIRL'S VOICE Twelve since lunch...Oh! There's another one!

Cut to exterior of Mrs Long Name's house. She comes out and sets off purposefully up the road, passing four pepperpot nannies digging up the road. They are wearing the usual slippers, paisley dresses and knotted handkerchiefs. One wears a helmet. One works a pneumatic drill. She is stripped to the waist wearing a big pink bra. Behind, heroic shots of Mrs Long Name walking out of town, through suburbs, into neat country, then into wilder country. She finally stops in close up, and looks up with inspiration in her eyes. Cut to a linkman standing before Stonehenge.

LINKMAN (MICHAEL) This is Stonehenge...and it's from here we go to Africa.

Jeremy Thorpe appears at the edge of shot and waves. Cut to as overgrown, jungleoid a location as Torquay can provide. A very big thick tree in the foreground. David Attenborough pushes through jungle towards camera. 26

Another reference to David Attenborough, the nature program doyen.

He has damp sweat patches under his arms which grow perceptibly during the scene. He has two African guides in the background both with saxophones round their necks.

ATTENBOROUGH (MICHAEL) *(slapping the side of a tree)* Well here it is at last...the goal of our quest. After six months and three days we've caught up with the legendary walking tree of Dahomey, Quercus Nicholas Parsonus, resting here for a moment, on its long journey south. It's almost incredible isn't it, to think that this huge tree has walked over two thousand miles across this inhospitable terrain to stop here, maybe just to take in water before the two thousand miles on to Cape Town, where it lives. It's almost unimaginable, I find—the thought of this mighty tree strolling through Nigeria, perhaps swaggering a little as it crosses the border into Zaire, hopping through the tropical rain forests, trying to find a quiet grove where it could jump around on its own, sprinting up to Zambia for the afternoon, then nipping back...*(a native whispers in his ear)* Oh, super...well, I've just been told that this is not in fact the legendary walking tree of Dahomey, this is one of Africa's many stationary trees, Arborus Bamber Gascoignus. 27 In fact we've just missed the walking tree...it left here at eight o'clock this morning...was heading off in that direction...so we'll see if we can go and catch it up. Come on boys.

Bamber Gascoigne, übernerdy game-show host of *University Challenge* from 1962 to 1987.

They move off. At this point we notice that there are two other saxophone-wearing natives, a trumpeter, a trombonist, a double bassist, a guitarist, and finally a man with a drum kit tied to his back. Mix through to them on the move in another part of the jungle. Sweat is now spraying out from under Attenborough's armpits as if from a watering can.

ATTENBOROUGH Well, we're still keeping up with it, but it's setting a furious pace. Early this morning we thought we'd spotted it, but it turned out to be an Angolan sauntering tree, Amazellus Robin Ray, 28 out walking with a Gambian Sidling Bush...*(Jeremy Thorpe leans in the background and waves to camera)* So on we go...it's going to be difficult—the walking tree can achieve speeds of up to fifty miles an hour, especially when it's in a hurry. *(Rupert the bearer points excitedly)* Super! Well, Rupert has spotted something...this could be it...a walking tree on the move...*(they move off; by this time waterspray is gushing out from all over his chest)* But, what Rupert had in fact discovered was something very different...

He stops him, they kneel down. Cut to their eyeline. In the distance, amongst low bushes and thick undergrowth, six Africans dressed immaculately in cricket gear having a game of cricket. Cut to Attenborough, Rupert and one other bearer watching. Attenborough is looking down at something he is holding. The other two are gazing wide-eyed at the cricketers.

ATTENBOROUGH The Turkish Little Rude Plant. *(he holds up, carefully and wondrously, a plant which has green outer leaves splayed back to reveal a small, accurately sculpted bum)* This remarkably smutty piece of flora was used by the Turks to ram up each other's...*(Rupert nudges him and points excitedly at the batsmen)* Ah no! In fact it was something even more interesting...*(Attenborough points, apparently at the batsmen, but he has clearly got it wrong again)* Yes, there it was, over the other side of the clearing, the legendary Puking Tree of Mozambique...*(Rupert nudges him again)*

Cut to an animated professor.

VOICE (MICHAEL) No, what they had come across was a tribe lost to man since time immemorial... the legendary Batsmen of the Kalahari...*(cut to a shot of natives playing cricket)*

VOICE OVER (TERRY J) Primitive customs still survive here as if the march of time had passed them by. But for all the mumbo-jumbo and superstition, the Batsmen of the Kalahari are formidable fighters, as we can see on this rare footage of them in action against Warwickshire.

Cut to a big county ground pavilion in mid-shot. We zoom in on the commentator on a balcony.

COMMENTATOR (MICHAEL) Warwickshire 29 had dismissed the Kalahari Batsmen for 140, and then it was their turn to face this extraordinary Kalahari attack. Pratt was the first to go, but Pratt and Pratt put on a second wicket stand 30 of nought, which was broken by Odinga in his most hostile mood.

A compilation of the day's play. Natives in normal cricket gear. Pratt at crease as per usual cricket coverage. Cut to a low shot of the bowler thundering up towards the wicket. Cut away to the batsman preparing to take the shot. Cut back to the bowler. As he reaches the crease he produces a spear and raises it to shoulder height and hurls it. Cut to batsman who is hit full in the stomach.

Robin Ray, English TV personality and quizmaster of *Call My Bluff*, a popular game show.

Warwickshire is the county cricket team of the Midlands.

"Put on a second wicket," meaning how many runs they got before the second wicket (dismissal of a batsman) occurred. A "second-wicket stand of nought" is as bad as it can get, naturally.

His bat dislodges the bails. There is a 'howzat' from all the native fielders. **31** *He makes an annoyed gesture as if he were Colin Cowdrey caught clean bowled, and sinks to the ground. Caption: 'B. PRATT'*

VOICE OVER (GRAHAM) That's B. Pratt, hit wicket—0. But Pratt and Z. Pratt dug in and took the score to a half...*(cut to the new batting partnership; B. Pratt's body is still on the ground)* before Z. Pratt ran away. *(Z. Pratt reaching the pavilion, running with a hail of spears and arrows coming after him)* But out came M.J.K. Pratt... **32** *(cut to M.J.K. Pratt coming out pulling on gloves etc.)* to play a real captain's innings. *(he reaches the crease and takes guard, the bowler bowls)* He'd taken his own score up to nought when he mistimed a shot of Bowanga and was lbw. **33** *(a huge spear sticks right through the lower part of his leg; a big appeal and he turns and limps manfully off)*

Caption: 'M.J.K. PRATT'

VOICE OVER Typical of Umbonga's hostile opening spell was his dismissal of V.E. Pratt, who offered no resistance to this delivery...*(cut to native bowler bowling a machete; it hits the ground and does a leg spin up, slicing off the batsman's head as he waves his bat)*...and he was caught behind.

The batsman's severed head lands in the wicket keeper's gloves. He throws it in the air with a flourish. Caption: 'V.E. PRATT' Jeremy Thorpe appears and waves. Cut to the presenter from 'World's Most Awful Family 1974'.

PRESENTER (MICHAEL) But by lunch the situation had changed dramatically.

VOICE OVER (GRAHAM) *(and caption)* 'C.U. Pratt killed outright, bowled Odinga—Ø. P.B.T.R. Pratt legs off before wicker, bowled Odinga—Ø. B.B.C.T.V. Pratt Assegai up Jacksey, bowled Unboko—Ø. Z. Pratt machete before wicket, bowled Umbonga—Ø. M.J.K. Pratt stump through head, bowled Umbonga—Ø. V.E. Pratt ran away—Ø. P.D.A. Pratt retired hurt **34** —Ø. W.G. Pratt retired very hurt—Ø. Pratt died of fright, bowled Odinga—Ø. Y.E.T.A.N.O.T.H.E.R. Pratt not out but dreadfully hurt—139.'

Cut back to the presenter. Behind him the 'World's Most Awful Family' sign is crossed out and replaced with 'Sport'.

PRESENTER And so with the tension colossal as we come up to the last ball...that's all from us.

Roll credits on black background. The first part of the signature tune is played very hesitantly on guitar.

PARTY POLITICAL BROADCAST ON BEHALF OF THE LIBERAL PARTY

"Howzat?" is a standard cricket shout, meaning "How is that?"—and "Is that a legitimate dismissal of the batsman, umpire?"

M.J.K. Smith was the captain of the England cricket team from 1963 to 1966.

"LBW"—leg before wicket, meaning his pads stopped the ball hitting the stumps so he's out. Get it?

"Retired hurt" is an actual cricketing term—a player can be injured and leave the field as a batsman, and it counts against the total dismissals of the team.

WAS CONCEIVED, WRITTEN AND PERFORMED BY
J. THORPE (AGE 2)
C. SMITH (AGE 1½)
L. BYERS (AGE 0)
UNSUCCESSFUL CANDIDATES
GRAHAM CHAPMAN
LEICESTER NORTH (LOST DEPOSIT)
TERRY GILLIAM
MINNEAPOLIS NORTH (LOST DEPOSIT TWICE)
ERIC IDLE
SOUTH SHIELDS NORTH (LOST DEPOSIT BUT FOUND AN OLD ONE
WHICH HE COULD USE)
TERRY JONES
COLWYN BAY NORTH (SMALL DEPOSIT ON HIS TROUSERS)
MICHAEL PALIN
SHEFFIELD NORTH (LOST HIS TROUSERS)
MORE UNSUCCESSFUL CANDIDATES
CAROL CLEVELAND (LIBERAL)
BOB E. RAYMOND (VERY LIBERAL)
PETER BRETT (EXTREMELY LIBERAL AND RATHER RUDE)
EVEN MORE UNSUCCESSFUL CANDIDATES
DOUGLAS ADAMS
SILLY WORD (NORTH)
NEIL INNES
SILLY WORDS AND MUSIC (NORTH)
(COPYRIGHT 1984 THORPE-O-HITS LTD)
MAKE-UP AND HAIRDRESSING
JO GRIMOND
MORE MAKE-UP
MAGGIE WESTON
EVEN MORE MAKE-UP
ANDREW ROSE (COSTUMES NORTH)
MUCH MORE MAKE-UP
STAN SPEEL (FILM CAMERAMAN NORTH)
MAKE-UP AND SOUND RECORDING
RON (NORTH) BLIGHT
ROSTRUM CAMERA WITH MAKE-UP
PETER WILLIS
FILM EDITOR AND NOT MAKE-UP
BOB BEARBERG
NOT FILM EDITOR NOT MAKE-UP BUT DUBBING MIXER
ROD GUEST
LIGHTING, MAKE-UP AND PRICES AND INCOMES POLICY
JIMMY PURDIE
VISUAL EFFECTS AND MR THORPE'S WIGS
JOHN HORTON
PRODUCTION ASSISTANT
BRIAN JONES (MAKE-UP NORTH)
DESIGNER (NORTH)
VALERIE WARRENDER (FAR TOO LIBERAL)
PRODUCED BY
MR LLOYD GEORGE (WHO KNEW IAN MACNAUGHTON'S FATHER)
A BBC-LIBERAL-TV-PARTY PRODUCTION (NORTH)

Nine O'clock News intro in the newsroom behind. Behind the newsreader several men including Jeremy Thorpe are drinking and celebrating. A woman is dancing on the table.

NEWSREADER (ERIC) Good evening. Over 400,000 million pounds were wiped off the value of shares this afternoon, when someone in the Stock Exchange coughed. Sport: capital punishment is to be re-introduced in the first and second division. Any player found tackling from behind or controlling the ball with the lower part of the arm will be hanged. But the electric chair remains the standard punishment for threatening the goalie. Referee's chairman, Len Goebbels said 'at last the referee has been given teeth'. Finally, politics: the latest opinion poll published today shows Labour ahead with 40%, the AA second with 38% and not surprisingly Kentucky Fried Chicken running the Liberals a very close third. And now back to me. Hello. And now it's time to go over to Hugh Delaney in Paignton.

Cut to the linkman on the pier at Paignton. A smallish crowd is gathered behind him including Jeremy Thorpe who waves at the camera from the back.

LINKMAN (MICHAEL) Hello and welcome to Paignton, because it's *from* Paignton that we take you straight back to the studio.

Cut to a man in swimming trunks and a snorkel pushed back on his head, standing in the studio holding a stuffed polecat on a pole.

MAN (GRAHAM) Hello. And it's from here we go over there.

Cut to the 'Most Awful Family' presenter.

PRESENTER Well we're already here so let's go over there.

Cut back to the newsreader.

NEWSREADER Welcome back. And now it's time for part eight of our series about the life and work of Ursula Hitler, the Surrey housewife who revolutionized British beekeeping in the nineteen-thirties.

VOICE OVER (MICHAEL) *(and caption)* 'That was a party political broadcast on behalf of the Liberal Party'

His voice breaks up with giggles. Fade to blackout. The end.

INDEX OF SKETCHES

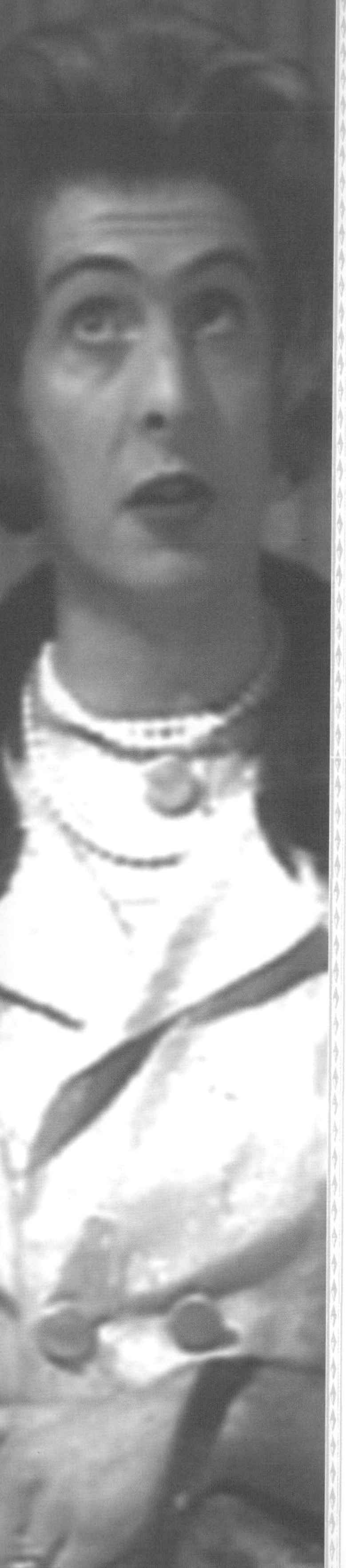

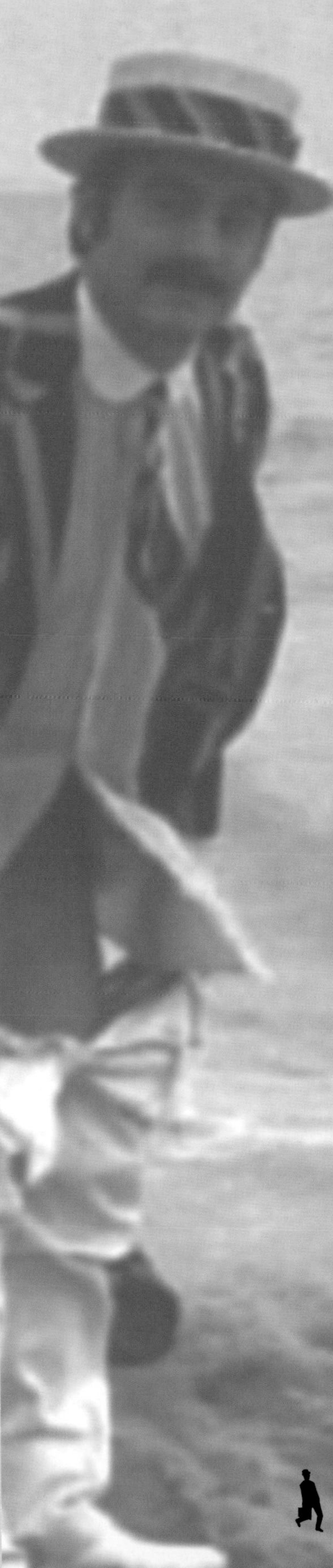

THANK YOU

The Publisher would like to thank Roger Saunders at Python Productions, Sean Yule and Dan Grossman at Knopf, and Peter Tummons at Methuen Publishing for making this book possible. A special thanks to Bonnie Siegler, Andrew James Capelli, and everyone at Eight and a Half for designing a spectacular book and to Luke Dempsey for his witty and brilliant annotations.

The Designers would like to thank Lisa Tenaglia and JP Leventhal for their trust, support, and guidance, Charles Gibson and Nicole Bonneau for their amazing production help, and Charles Merullo and Jennifer Jeffries at Getty Images for their exhaustive photo research. Thanks also to Jeff Scher for his silly walk and the designers at Eight and a Half: Francesca Campanella, Emily Karian, and Kristen Ren.

The Author would like to thank Laura Ross for putting me up for this, and everyone at Black Dog & Leventhal for their kind assistance in the making of this book. Most especially, I'd like to thank Lisa Tenaglia, the kindest and best editor any author could wish for.

But most of all, thank you to Graham Chapman, John Cleese, Terry Gilliam, Eric Idle, Terry Jones, Michael Palin and *Monty Python's Flying Circus,* for creating something completely different.

HE WANTS TO GO WALKIES.

AND NOW FOR SOMETHING COMPLETELY DIFFERENT—A MAN
WITH A TAPE RECORDER UP HIS NOSE.

THE BISHOP!

GIVE ME ANOTHER MEATBALL AND I'LL TELL YOU.

I'D LIKE TO HAVE AN
ARGUMENT PLEASE.

JUST A MINUTE—SOMEONE TOLD YOU WE ALL HAD TOUPEES?

OOH PLANNING A LITTLE EXCURSION ARE WE MR HILTER?

I'M A LUMBERJACK
AND I'M OK,
I SLEEP ALL NIGHT
AND I WORK ALL DAY.

COME ON PARKY. JUMP PARKY. JUMP.

THE WAY HE KEPT ON FIGHTING
AFTER HIS HEAD CAME OFF!

IT'S JUST GONE 8 O'CLOCK AND TIME FOR THE PENGUIN
ON TOP OF YOUR TELEVISION SET TO EXPLODE.

THE SODDING
HAMSTER'S DEAD!

DON'T COME HERE WITH THAT
POSH TALK YOU NASTY,
STUCK-UP TWIT.

DO PLEASE GO ON. THIS IS THE LEAST
FASCINATING CONVERSATION I'VE EVER HAD.

I WANT YOU TO HAND OVER ALL THE LUPINS YOU'VE GOT.

MY NAME IS SM

NOW MY GOOD MAN, S

AND NOW FO

COMPLETELY

DINS

A NOD'S AS GOOD AS A W

I'LL TELL YOU WHA

IT'S DEAD, THAT'S WH

I'VE...I'VE JUST BEEN STA

NOBODY EX

SPANISH IN

ER, MR FRAMPTON W

YOU'RE A VERY SILLY MAN AND I

...MR N

I CAN'T TELL THE DI

WHIZZO BUTTER AN